AMERICAN
JEWISH

DESK REFERENCE

American Jewish Historical Society

PRODUCED BY THE PHILIP LIEF GROUP, INC.

Random House, Inc.
New York

American Jewish Desk Reference:
The Ultimate One-Volume Reference to the Jewish Experience in America

Copyright © 1999 by The Philip Lief Group, Inc.

This book is available for special purchases in bulk by organizations and institutions, not for resale, at special discounts. Please direct your inquiries to the Random House Special Sales Department, toll-free 888-591-1200 or fax 212-572-4961.

Please address inquiries about electronic licensing of reference products, for use on a network or in software or on CD-ROM, to the Subsidiary Rights Department, Random House Reference & Information Publishing, fax 212-940-7370.

Visit the Random House Web site at www.randomhouse.com

Typeset and printed in the United States of America.

Book design by G&H Soho

Library of Congress Cataloging-in-Publication Data

American Jewish desk reference : the ultimate one-volume reference to
    the Jewish experience in America / the American Jewish Historical
    Society. — 1st ed.
        p.   cm.
    Includes bibliographical references and index.
      ISBN 0-375-40243-8
      1. Jews—United States Encyclopedias.   2. Judaism—United States
Encyclopedias.   3. United States—Civilization—Jewish influences
Encyclopedias.   I. American Jewish Historical Society.
    E184.35.A44   1999
    973'.04924'003—dc21   99-37154
                                                        CIP

First edition

0 9 8 7 6 5 4 3 2 1

October 1999

ISBN 0-375-40243-8

New York Toronto London Sydney Auckland

Staff

Editorial Director   Ralph Carlson

Executive Editor   Maryanne Wagner

Managing Editor   Andrew Ambraziejus

Developmental Editor   Linda Perrin

Contributing Writers   John Berman, Felicia Herman, Paula E. Hyman, Hilary Mac Austin, Deborah Dash Moore, Rafael Medoff, Susan Osborn, George Robinson, Faith Rogow, Moshe D. Sherman, Holly Snyder, Kathleen Thompson

Production Editor   Marybeth Fedele

Copy editor   Geraldine Albert

Photo Researcher   Hilary Mac Austin

Administrative Assistant   Brenda Garcia

Editorial Review Board   Michael Feldberg
Jeffrey Gurock
Rafael Medoff
Deborah Dash Moore
Geoffrey Wigoder

Acknowledgments

The publisher wishes to offer special thanks to the following distinguished authors and reviewers for their contributions to the *American Jewish Desk Reference*:

Michael Feldberg, Executive Director of the American Jewish Historical Society. He is the author, co-author, or editor of five books in history and criminal justice, including *The Philadelphia Riots of 1844* and *The Turbulent Era: Riot and Disorder in Jacksonian America*.

Jeffrey Gurock, Libby M. Klaperman Professor of Jewish History at Yeshiva University and chair of the Academic Council of the American Jewish Historical Society. His many publications include *When Harlem Was Jewish: 1870–1930* and *A Modern Heretic and a Traditional Community: Mordecai M. Kaplan, Orthodoxy, and Modern Judaism*. He is the editor of *American Jewish History*, an eight-volume series of articles.

Felicia Herman, Ph.D. candidate in Near Eastern and Judaic studies at Brandeis University and research assistant at the American Jewish Historical Society.

Paula E. Hyman, the Lucy Moses Professor of Modern Jewish History at Yale University, co-editor of the award-winning *Jewish Women in America: An Historical Encyclopedia*, and author of numerous other books, including *Gender and Assimilation: The Roles and Representation of Women*.

Rafael Medoff, Visiting Scholar at SUNY Purchase, member of the Academic Council of the American Jewish Historical Society and member of the editorial board of *American Jewish History*, co-author of the *Historical Dictionary of Zionism*, author of *Zionism and the Arabs: An American Jewish Dilemma, 1898–1948*, and author of numerous scholarly essays.

Deborah Dash Moore, Professor of Religion at Vassar College, co-editor of the award-winning *Jewish Women in America: An Historical Encyclopedia*, and author of numerous other books, including *At Home in America: Second Generation New York Jews* and *To the Golden Cities: Pursuing the American Jewish Dream in Miami and L.A.*, published in paperback by Harvard University Press.

Faith Rogow, author of *Gone to Another Meeting: The National Council of Jewish Women, 1893–1993*, as well as producer, composer, and performing artist for the cassette of original Jewish feminist music, *The Courage to Dare*.

Moshe D. Sherman, Associate Professor, Graduate School of Jewish Studies, Touro College, whose publications include *Orthodox Judaism in America: A Biographical Dictionary and Sourcebook*.

Geoffrey Wigoder, at his death in 1999, was the foremost editor of reference books on Jewish history and culture. Beginning with the monumental *Encyclopedia Judaica* in the late 1960s, he edited scores of publications, culminating in the CD-ROM edition of *Encyclopedia Judaica* in 1997.

Contents in Brief

Contents

Part 11 : Radio, Television, and Film

Part 14 : Science, Medicine, and Social Science 571

Preface

The American Jewish Historical Society is proud to sponsor the *American Jewish Desk Reference*, the first comprehensive, single-volume guide to the history, religious observances, culture, and achievements of the Jewish people in the United States.

Since 1892, the Society has published a variety of authoritative works documenting and recording the Jewish experience in America. The first volume of its journal, now titled *American Jewish History*, appeared in 1893. Since that time the Society has produced or sponsored a myriad of projects that tell the story of America's Jews. In 1992, to mark its centennial, the Society joined with Johns Hopkins University Press to publish a monumental five-volume, five-author work, *The Jewish People in America* and in 1997 partnered with Routledge to create the pathbreaking two-volume reference work, *Jewish Women in America: An Historical Encyclopedia*.

American Jewish Desk Reference now joins the Society's other distinguished publications. We hope that you, the reader, find the *Desk Reference* enlightening, enjoyable and useful. If you would like more information on any of the topics you find in this reference work or wish to become a member of the American Jewish Historical Society, please feel free to contact the Society at either of its two locations, New York City or Waltham, Massachusetts, or via the Internet at ajhs@ajhs.org. As the nation's oldest ethno-religious historical organization, we are delighted to be of service and happy to further your interest in the proud achievements of the Jewish people in the United States.

The Society owes a number of individuals its gratitude for their support of, or participation in, this project: Charles Levine and Saul Steinmetz of Random House; Ralph Carlson, Linda Perrin, Maryanne Wagner, and Philip Lief of the Philip Lief Group; and the numerous expert contributors who penned (or word processed) each entry deserve thanks for creating the work itself. In reviewing the manuscript, the late Geoffrey Wigoder and Rafael Medoff provided valuable insights and made the book far better for their efforts. Professor Jeffrey Gurock of Yeshiva University, chair of the Society's Academic Council, and Professor Deborah Dash Moore of Vassar College, co-editor of *Jewish Women in America* and a member of the Council, provided overall guidance for this project, for which the Society is very grateful.

Finally, the American Jewish Historical Society wishes to acknowledge the thousands of trustees, officers, staff, members, and supporters who, for 107 years, have sustained the Society and allowed it to serve as the documenter of American Jewry's remarkable participation in the great democratic experiment known as the United States of America.

Michael Feldberg, Ph.D., Director
American Jewish Historical Society
New York City

A Guide to Using this Book

The *American Jewish Desk Reference* contains nearly 900 entries on all aspects of American Jewish history and culture. To allow the reader to browse the volume more easily, the entries are arranged in thematic chapters. If you want to know about Jewish Americans in government, turn to the part entitled "Law, Government, and Politics." Within each part, the entries are arranged alphabetically and begin with a complete list of the contents of that part.

The book opens with a chronology of the American Jewish experience and concludes with appendices providing information about additional resources.

The entries include biographies of individuals and essays on topics, organizations, and movements. The quickest way to find any specific entry is to consult the comprehensive index at the end of the book. All page citations in bold in this index refer to entries.

Bold Names in the Text

A name in bold in the text of an entry means that this name has its own entry elsewhere in the book. Thus the sentence "**Mordecai Kaplan** was the founder of the **Reconstructionist Movement**" indicates that there are entries on both Kaplan and on the Reconstructionist Movement. The quickest way to find these entries is to look them up in the index. To minimize the amount of boldface type in the book, an entry appears in bold only the first time it appears in an entry. The one exception to this rule is in Part 1, "The History of Jews in America," where entries always appear in bold.

Part 1

History of Jews in America

Strangers in a Strange Land, 1585–1775
Taking a Place in a New Country, 1775–1829
The Country Prepares for War, 1830–1860
War and Its Aftermath, 1861–1879
A New Community, 1880–1920
Americanization, Anti-Semitism, and Isolationism, 1920–1930
The Holocaust, 1930–1940
War and Beyond, 1941–1949
The Transformation of American Jews and American Judaism, 1950–1999

STRANGERS IN A STRANGE LAND, 1585–1775

1585

First Known Jew

The first known Jew to step on American soil, Joachim Gaunse (Ganz), lands on Roanoke Island.

1649

Solomon Franco makes an unsuccessful attempt to settle in Boston. After a brief period he is "warned out."

1654–1664

First Settlers

European Jews make their way to the American colonies in small numbers and by circuitous routes.

The first group to come to North America is Dutch, but comes from Brazil. In 1654 twenty-three Jewish refugees landed in what would one day be New York City. Although several Jewish merchants preceded them by several months, these twenty-three created the first permanent Jewish settlement, and it is their arrival that began American Jewish history. Portuguese, Spanish, and Ashkenazi Jews, they had fled from Recife in Brazil after the Portuguese took the colony from the Dutch. One of sixteen Jewish vessels heading back to Holland, they were sidetracked by Spanish pirates and seized by Spanish officials of the Inquisition near Jamaica. They managed to get to Cuba and from there set sail to New Amsterdam.

They met considerable hostility in New Amsterdam despite being Dutch subjects. Peter Stuyvesant and his fellow colonists made their legal position, and therefore their social and economic position, extremely difficult. Eventually, under pressure from Amsterdam Jewry, Stuyvesant ceded limited rights to members of the small Jewish community that began to form around the first refugee group. Enlightened self-interest played a role in Stuyvesant's decision as well, since Jewish merchants were a valuable contribution to the colony.

1656

First Cemetery

Congregation Shearith Israel, although not yet allowed to worship in a synagogue, buys a cemetery site near what is now Chatham Square in New York City. It is believed to be the oldest Jewish cemetery in the country, and 5 of the 107 graves have bronze tablets dedicated in 1932 by the Daughters of the American Revolution. The Congregation was the first and is now the oldest continuous Jewish community in North America. They held their first public services around 1686 and officially adopted the name Congregation Shearith Israel in 1728.

1657

First Citizens

Four Jews petitioned in the spring of 1657 to be granted burgher rights. The petition was granted and Jews were granted the same freedoms enjoyed by the other inhabitants of New Amsterdam.

Asser Levy pressured Stuyvestant for more extensive civil rights, becoming the first Jew in New Amsterdam and North America to have the right to serve in the militia, engage in retail trade, to be licensed as a butcher, and own a house. He went into fur trading and real estate and became one of six licensed butchers in the colony. He was, for religious reasons, excused from slaughtering hogs. He became one of the richest men in New Amsterdam.

1664

English Takeover

The English take over New Amsterdam from the Dutch and name it New York.

1665

Trading Restrictions

With trading restriction against Jews in force, Abraham de Lucena is arrested for selling at retail and fined 600 guilders, a huge sum at the time. Jacob Cohen Henriques is ordered to stop baking bread for sale. Within a few years Jews in the colony win the right to trade.

1671

Philanthropy

Asser Levy advances a Lutheran congregation the funds to build their first church in New York.

1678

Newport Cemetery

Jews in Newport, Rhode Island, buy a cemetery, even though there is no permanent community.

1700s

Growth of New Communities

In New York most trading and property restrictions against Jews were lifted by 1700. Jews were still forced by law to support the established church of the colony, and their status was that of second-class citizens. In other colonies the situation was much the same. There were only about two or three hundred Jews in North America. Although they were allowed to vote in some places, they were not allowed to hold any offices except those considered burdensome by the Christian colonists, such as that of constable. The British Plantation Act (1740) made it possible for a colonial Jew to become a naturalized citizen, with rights of trade within the empire. Political rights were still withheld.

Six synagogue communities were established in Montreal, Philadelphia, New York, Newport, Savannah, and Charleston, South Carolina. All but Montreal were tidewater cities. Until 1720, most American Jews were Sephardim, with a Spanish-Portuguese background. After that date, most came from Central and

Eastern Europe, by way of England. While in England, they often adopted English names and learned the language. By the middle of the 1700s, most Jews in the colonies were English-speaking immigrants who were originally from Germany.

Most Jewish families were supported either by a small shop or by a trade such as soapmaking, distilling, or tailoring. A few became wealthy through provisioning the British armies in North America or through involvement in exporting. A few participated in the slave trade. Francis Salvador was one of the few large planters, growing indigo on his South Carolina plantation. At one point, the Salvador family owned 100,000 acres. In Georgia, the Sheftalls were cattle ranchers as well as merchants. **Myer Myers** was a renowned silversmith who began his business in New York and branched out to Philadelphia. During the late seventeen and early eighteenth centuries, the Jewish population of North America grew slowly but steadily.

Religious Observance

Most Jews in the colonies were devout and tied closely to the synagogue community, in part because they had no other options. While there were no rabbis until 1840, each congregation had a *hazzan*, a *shohet*, and a *shammash*. Sometimes the same person held more than one position. These congregations performed considerable social service work for their members, providing medical help to the sick and dying, educational aid for the children of the poor, and continuing help to arriving immigrants. The newer immigrants from Germany were Ashkenazim, but they accepted the already established Sephardic worship services.

Anti-Semitism

Their position as citizens without full rights was the primary oppression early Jewish Americans experienced. Overt anti-Jewish acts were few and far between. There were no compulsory ghettos and virtually no anti-Jewish violence. There was less persecution for religious beliefs than was experienced by, for example, the Baptists in Virginia. There were laws against blasphemy in most of the colonies but only

one instance of a Jew being prosecuted for denying the divinity of Jesus. That man, Jacob Lumbrozo, was not punished.

Men of wealth found considerable acceptance within the Christian community and exercised no little political power. There was a great deal of acculturation and intermarriage, as well as identification with the welfare of the larger community. Many Jews participated, for example, in charities designed to serve both Jewish and Christian poor. In 1711, some of the most notable Jewish businessmen in New York, including the *hazzan*, lent their financial resources to the building of Trinity Church.

1730

Shearith Israel Synagogue

After being in existence for the better part of a century Congregation Shearith Israel builds a synagogue on Mill Street in what had become New York City. It was the first synagogue on the mainland of North America. This building is no longer standing. The present synagogue is on Central Park West, and the congregation still observes the **Orthodox** Sephardic ritual.

1740s

Philadelphia Cemetery

Philadelphia Jewry has a cemetery and conducts services.

1745

Discontinuation of Portuguese

The Portuguese language is used for the last time in the official records of Shearith Israel Congregation, New York.

1763

Oldest Synagogue

Touro Synagogue is consecrated in Newport, Rhode Island. It is the oldest extant synagogue building in the United States. The Jews of Newport fled the city when the British occupied it in 1776. The Newport Jewish community was revitalized with the arrival of Jews from Europe, and in 1783 the synagogue was reopened and reconsecrated.

TAKING A PLACE IN A NEW COUNTRY, 1775–1829

REVOLUTIONARY WAR

By the time of the American Revolution there were upwards of 2,500 Jews in the colonies in a total population of 2,500,000 people. They were largely middle-class shopkeepers with modest lives who shared the values of their neighbors. Like most of their neighbors, they did not quickly take sides in the conflict between the motherland and the revolutionary forces abroad in the colonies. When they did—again like most of their neighbors—they became Whigs, supporting the American patriot cause.

An enormous number of books and articles have been written about these early Jewish Americans, leading to the often-repeated jest that they are the "most written about Jews in the history of the Diaspora."

The war for independence was not an easy or popular war. Many colonists, of whatever national or ethnic background, hoped that the differences with England could be settled without open rebellion. At the same time, most of them felt keenly that there were serious problems, the most significant of which was taxation without representation. Jews in America in the middle eighteen century thought of themselves as Americans. They did not mind British control as long as it was relatively minimal, but they were ready to fight what they saw as exploitation. Their weapons of choice were economic—refusal to import or export and boycotts. Their hope was that these weapons would prevail, but they did not.

On July 20, 1775, the Continental Congress asked all church congregations to gather to pray for a peaceful settlement with the British. They made the request to Jewish synagogues as well and, like their neighbors, Jews sent up prayers that the colonies might be spared war. When war was declared Christians and Jews alike supported it. Those who remained loyal to Britain were in the minority.

Those who actively participated in the American Revolution were businesspeople as well as soldiers. **Hayam Salomon**, for example, was known as "the financier of the Revolution." According to legend, he was a member of the radical Sons of Liberty, and it is certainly true that he committed his resources as well as his own time and courage to the cause of liberty. Israel Moses donated a great deal of his personal fortune to feeding Revolutionary soldiers. Aaron Lopez lost most of his great wealth when his fleet of merchant ships, serving the cause of the Revolution, was confiscated by the British.

Some Jewish merchants were blockade runners, using armed merchant ships to commandeer needed supplies from enemy ships. Among these was Jonas Phillips, who wrote the list of supplies he was seeking in Yiddish, hoping that it would be overlooked by the British if he were caught. His plan backfired. When the British seized one of his ships and saw his list, they declared that it was in code and impounded his ship.

Among the Jewish soldiers who fought in the Continental Army were the three Yale-educated sons of Jacob Pinto and Elias Pollock. Mordecai Sheftall attained the rank of colonel, and both David S. Franks and Solomon Bush were lieutenant colonels. One South Carolina outfit was known as "Jews Company" because approximately thirty of its members were Jewish. The company fought with distinction at the Battle of Beaufort. Among those who died for the Revolution was a prominent South Carolina planter, Francis Salvador. David Emanuel, later governor of Georgia, fought bravely, as did Captain Jacob Cohen of Virginia and Captains Jacob De Leon and Jacob De Lamotta, who served under General DeKalb in New Jersey. Dr. Phillip Moses Russel took care of the sick and wounded at Valley Forge during the terrible winter of 1777–1778.

1777

Rights in New York

New York grants full political rights to Jews.

The First Jew to Die for American Independence

Francis Salvador, the first Jew to hold an elective post in the New World, became a member of the South Carolina Provincial Congress on January 11, 1775. On July 31, 1776 he was killed in a skirmish, becoming the first Jew to die for American independence.

1780s

Richmond Congregation

An organized Jewish community is established in Richmond.

1783

Immigrant Aid Society

Philadelphia Jewry establishes the first immigrant aid society in the United States. Two members of Philadelphia's Mikveh Israel Congregation also sign a petition to the Council of Censors asking that the oath of office be changed to include non-Christians.

1784

In Charleston, South Carolina, Jews establish their first social welfare organization.

1787

The Northwest Territory Act offers Jews equality in all future territories and states.

Rights Protest

Jonas Phillips writes to the Constitutional Convention saying to ". . . swear and believe that the New Testament was given by divine inspiration is absolutely against the religious principle of a Jew." Six years later, in 1793, he is fined ten pounds in Philadelphia for refusing to testify on the Jewish Sabbath.

1788

The United States Constitution is adopted by a majority of the states. Under federal laws—not state laws— Jews are given full rights. Not until 1877 do Jews have full political rights in every state.

1796

First State Legislator

Dr. Levi Myers of Georgetown, South Carolina, is the first Jew to serve in a state legislature.

1801

First Orphan Care Society

The first American Jewish orphan care society is established in Charleston, South Carolina.

1802

First Ashkenazi Synagogue

The first American Ashkenazi synagogue, Rodeph Shalom, is established in Philadelphia.

1818

Rights in Connecticut

Connecticut grants full political rights to Jews.

1819

Female Hebrew Benevolent Society

Rebecca Gratz helps organize the Female Hebrew Benevolent Society to help Jewish women and children because Christian charities too often proselytize those they help. This is the first Jewish charity not ad-

---

Jean Laffite, Pirate

Jean Laffite, the buccaneer who helped Andrew Jackson turn the tide at the Battle of New Orleans in 1814, was a descendant of the Sephardic Jews who were forced to convert to Christianity. Like many of these so-called *marranos*, Laffite's family maintained a covert loyalty to their Jewish faith. Indeed, it was in no small part his knowledge of the Spanish persecution of his people that made Laffite a terror to Spanish shipping in the Gulf of Mexico and the southern Atlantic.

ministered by a synagogue. It remained active and independent for almost 100 years.

1820s

German Immigration

A mass migration of German Jews to America starts. At the beginning of the influx in 1820 there were fewer than 3,000 Jewish Americans. Sixty years later, in 1880, there were more than 250,000. In 1820, there were eight Jewish American congregations. Twenty years later, there were nineteen. By 1877 there were almost 300. The vast majority of the immigrants were young women and men with little education or resources. Because of repressive laws in what would become modern-day Germany, life in their European homes held little possibility of prosperity or happiness for them. Fortunately, they arrived in the United States at a time of huge economic growth and a great many of them flourished. Their success ranged from respectable livings made in small retail stores in the Midwest to huge fortunes made in investment banking.

1821

Rights in Massachusetts

Massachusetts grants full political rights to Jews.

Awakening of a Reform Movement

In Charleston, South Carolina, the first attempt is made to organize a **Reform Movement** in American Judaism. After a proposal for reforming the Sabbath service is rejected by the congregation as a whole (1824), a splinter group of about fifty young Jews in Congregation Beth Elohim organizes the Reformed Society of Israelites (1825). The society lasts until 1833, during which time the members install an organ, stop wearing yarmulkes, and stop praying for the arrival of the Messiah. Its stated policy was that its members were "their own teachers, drawing their knowledge from the Bible and following only the laws of Moses, and those only as far as they can be adapted to the institutions of the society in which they live and enjoy the blessings of liberty."

1826

Rights in Maryland

Maryland, after a difficult ten-year fight, grants its Jewish population the same political rights as its other citizens.

1829

Isaac Leeser, the father of American modern Orthodoxy, becomes the *hazzan*-minister-rabbi of Congregation Mikveh Israel in Philadelphia. An immigrant from Westphalia, he speaks for Jewish Americans who want a traditional form of Judaism that reflects the American culture.

THE COUNTRY PREPARES FOR WAR, 1830–1860

1836

Monticello

Uriah Phillips Levy purchases Monticello, the home of Thomas Jefferson, and restores and repairs it. Without his intervention, it is doubtful the home would have been saved for the American people.

1837

Passover Haggadah

The first Passover *Haggadah* is printed in America and published by S. H. Jackson.

1838

First Jewish Sunday School

Rebecca Gratz establishes the first Jewish Sunday school in the United States in Philadelphia. It is Orthodox and gives Jewish women in this country a role in determining Jewish educational curriculum for the first time.

1840

First Diplomate Rabbi

Abraham Rice, the first diplomate rabbi to officiate in America, takes office in Baltimore. From Germany,

Rice was one of the few fully ordained resident rabbis in Orthodox Jewry in this country until the 1880s.

Damascus Protest

American Jews protest the persecution of Jews in Damascus.

1840s–50s

German Rabbis

Leo Merzbacher, Max Lilienthal, **Isaac Mayer Wise**, Bernhard Felsenthal, David Einhorn, Samuel Adler, and other German rabbis come to America to serve the new German congregations. They are active in promoting reforms in Judaism.

1841

First Permanent Reform Synagogue

Charleston's Beth Elohim becomes the first permanent Reform Jewish synagogue in the United States, after a prolonged struggle between Reform and Orthodox factions in the congregation. The Reformed Society of Israelites split off from this congregation in 1825. A group under the leadership of young attorney Abraham Moise, with the support of *hazan* Gustavus Poznanski, won custody of the synagogue building in a legal battle. The defeated Orthodox group withdrew and formed Shearith Israel.

First Congressman

David Levy Yulee is the first Jew to serve in Congress, representing the state of Florida as a Senator. He was the son of Moses Elias Levy, a Moroccan Jew who made his fortune in timber in the Caribbean, then bought 50,000 acres of land near Jacksonville, hoping to create a New Jerusalem for Jewish settlers. Levy County and the city of Yulee are named after this family.

1843

Leeser's Occident

Isaac Leeser, *hazzan* of the Sephardic synagogue of Philadelphia, publishes *The Occident and American Jewish Advocate* a strong voice for Orthodoxy. It is the

---

A Man with Two Synagogues of His Own

It sometimes seems to a student of American Judaism that every synagogue was founded by a group of dissidents who split off from their former congregation, either over a matter of ritual, theology, or a disagreement with their Rabbi. These contentious "breaks" as a part of tradition are perhaps nowhere better encapsulated than in the following joke. It is taken from the wonderful recent compilation *A Treasury of American-Jewish Folklore*, by Steve Koppman and Lion Koppman.

> A Jewish adventurer is shipwrecked on a previously uninhabited island for five years. When finally discovered, he proudly shows his rescuers around the island, pointing out his large house, the orchards and pastures, the irrigation system he's built, everything done completely by himself. And those, he says, pointing in the direction of two structures on the far corner of the island are the synagogues.
>
> *Two* of them! his guests laugh. But you're all alone by yourself here!
>
> Well, explains the modern-day Crusoe, *this* one, pointing to the closer, is the one I pray in. And the *other one*, he says with a look of profound disgust coming to his face, I wouldn't go in if you *paid* me!

Koppman, Steve, and Lion Kappman. *A Treasury of American-Jewish Folklore*. Northvale, N.J.: Jason Aronson, 1996.

---

first successful Jewish newspaper in this country and remained in publication for twenty-five years. As its editor, Leeser became the most famous Jewish religious leader in pre-Civil War America.

B'nai B'rith Founded

B'nai B'rith, a mutual aid and fraternal order, is established in New York City. Its purposes include social service projects such as orphanages, hospitals, homes for the aged, and help for new immigrants. Among its early undertakings was giving aid to victims of the Great Chicago Fire.

1845

Temple Emanu-El

The foremost Reform congregation in the United States, Temple Emanu-El in New York City, is formed by thirty-three members of a cultural society on the Lower East Side. They first consulted with the Charleston, South Carolina, Reform congregation and with leaders of the Reform movement in Baltimore. In 1854 the congregation moved to Twelfth Street, taking over a former Baptist Church and in 1868 built its own building.

1846

Isaac Mayer Wise

Isaac Mayer Wise, the organizer of the American Jewish **Reform Movement**, comes to the United States from Bohemia. He later becomes rabbi of Congregation B'nai Yeshurun in Cincinnati (1854), where he remained until his death. He published the *Israelite*, later the *American Israelite*.

1853

Leeser Translation

Isaac Leeser publishes an English translation of the Bible. His *Twenty-Four Books of the Holy Scripture* was the standard Jewish translation of the Bible in the United States for more than sixty years.

Fremont Expedition Photographs

Solomon Nunes Carvalho accompanies John C. Fremont on his Western expedition. While Fremont assessed the viability of a transcontinental railway, Carvalho documented the trip taking daguerreotypes with heavy and unwieldy equipment under difficult and dangerous conditions. Carvalho later helped organize the Hebrew Benevolent Society of Los Angeles.

1855

Organization Attempt

Rabbi **Isaac Mayer Wise** calls a meeting in Cleveland, Ohio, to unite American Jewry religiously, hoping to establish a common prayer book (*Minhag America*), a college, and generally a single religious form for American Judaism. Although the conference was successful in many ways, it did not lead to unity or even harmony. David Einhorn insisted that Wise had compromised too much with the Orthodox rabbis, ceding

them the absolute authority of the Talmud. **Isaac Leeser**, who reluctantly participated, later dissociated himself from the positions adopted by the conference.

1859

Kidnapping Protest

Jews meet in several towns to protest the action of papal authorities who seized Edgar Mortara, a Jewish child, to rear him as a Catholic. The child's nurse had secretly had him christened during an illness and the Roman Catholic Church insisted that he must be brought up as a Christian. The case helps to unify Jewish Americans and gained considerable sympathy from Christian Americans for the persecution of Jews around the world. In its wake, Rabbi Samuel Isaacs formed the Board of Delegates of American Israelites. It was the first national meeting of American Jewish religious leaders and included among its members both traditionalist **Isaac Leeser** and Reform leader **Isaac Mayer Wise**.

1860

Congressional Prayer

Morris Raphall becomes the first rabbi to open a session of the United States Congress with prayer. He was rabbi of New York's Orthodox Congregation B'nai Jeshurun at the time. On the day he was to appear, tensions in Congress concerning slavery were so high that it appeared the assembly would be unable to elect a Speaker of the House. Raphall, wearing skull cap and prayer shawl, prayed, ". . . thou who makest peace in the high heavens, direct their minds this day that with one consent they may agree to choose the man who, without fear, and without favor, is to preside over this assembly." The prayer was credited with breaking the tension in the room and allowing the election to take place.

WAR AND ITS AFTERMATH, 1861–1879

CIVIL WAR

To the chagrin of the abolitionist movement, American Jews generally shared the sentiments of their

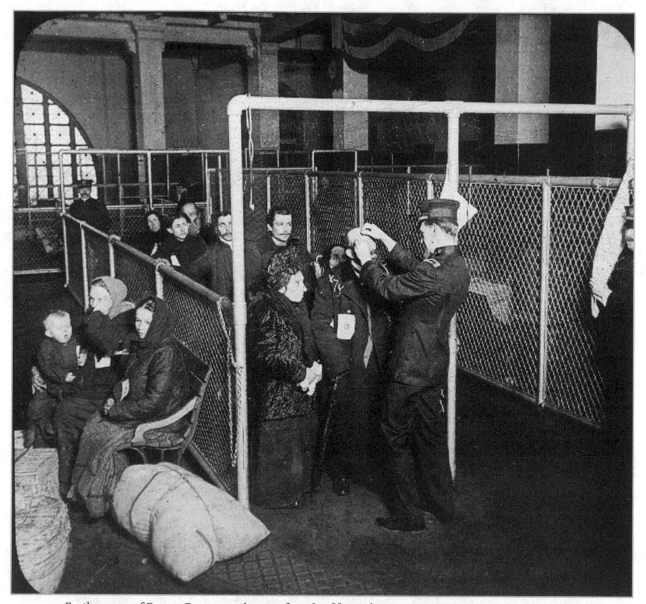

For the masses of Eastern Europeans who came from the 1880s to the 1920s immigration was not a pleasant experience. At Ellis Island, which opened on January 1, 1892, inspectors "in uniforms like soldiers . . ." are shown here checking the eyes of immigrants. Those found to have diseases could be retained or returned to Europe. (Private collection)

neighbors concerning slavery. They were also split regionally over the other economic and political causes of the Civil War. There were prominent Jewish participants on both sides of the bloody conflict.

Historians estimate that there may have been as many as 7,000 Jewish soldiers in the Union Army, while about 3,000 fought for the Confederacy. There were more Jewish residents of the Northern states, accounting for the numerical inequality. The total number of Jews in the general population at the time—

150,000—would have justified considerably smaller numbers. Many of these soldiers fought with "Jewish" companies. Although there were no entirely Jewish companies in either the Union Army or that of the Confederacy, there were many with a Jewish majority. They came from cities as widely separated as Macon and West Point, Georgia, in the South to Syracuse and Chicago in the North. The Texas Legion had two Jewish companies. For the most part, it seems to have been the Jewish soldiers themselves who chose to serve together.

Colonel Edward S. Salomon led the Eighty-second Illinois Volunteer Infantry, a "Jewish" regiment, in the Battle of Gettysburg, covering himself and his men with glory. They were in the middle of the successful effort to repulse Pickett's Charge. At least three Union officers of Jewish origin were brevetted generals during the Civil War.

Southern Supporters

In the Confederate government the most important Jewish figure was **Judah P. Benjamin**. One of the most outstanding legal figures in the South, he was elected to the United States Senate in 1853 when he was forty-two years old. An ardent states' rights advocate who wanted to preserve slavery, he was an early secessionist. Benjamin was appointed Attorney General at the inception of the Confederacy and later, Acting Secretary of War. He later became Secretary of State, responsible for enlisting the aid of other countries, a thankless task. "The brains of the Confederacy," as he was called, fled the country after the surrender.

A number of Jewish businessmen and companies provided significant support for the Southern cause, including Benjamin Mordecai, the L. Heyman & Brother foundry, and John Mayer. Phoebe Yates Levy Pember, daughter of Southern patriot Jacob Clavius Levy, ran the largest military hospital in the country in Richmond. Her sister, Eugenia Levy Phillips, was arrested for sedition twice and was once put in a Union prison for three weeks on charges of spying for the Confederacy.

Northern Supporters

In the North, one of President Lincoln's most influential informal advisors was the Jewish chiropodist Dr. Isachar Zacharie. Zacharie's profession led to his acquaintance with the president and to considerable ridicule. He was Lincoln's close friend and unofficial diplomat, making several trips to the South on the chief executive's behalf.

Supporting the war in material ways were Jewish clothing manufacturers such as the Mack, Stadler & Glazer consortium and Joseph Seligman and his brothers. The Seligmans sold millions of dollars worth of Union bonds in Germany and Holland. August Belmont was a powerful advocate for the North among European statesmen and financiers. He played a huge role in preventing other countries from weighing in on the side of the Confederacy, with which many of them had strong economic ties.

General Orders No. 11

In spite of the Jewish presence in the upper echelons of the war effort, an infamous piece of anti-Semitism was perpetrated in the name of the Union. On December 17, 1862, U. S. Grant issued General Orders No. 11. Its effect was to expel all Jews from the "Tennessee Department," which included portions of Tennessee, Kentucky, and northern Mississippi. The motivation for this action was the desire to rid the area of traders who were buying cotton that would otherwise have been conscripted by the army. Since a number of traders and peddlers were Jewish, Grant generalized the entire population. The order was in effect for two months before Abraham Lincoln rescinded it, under pressure from Jewish activists. During that time, Jewish merchants, craftspeople, and farmers, as well as traders, were driven from their homes.

Grant later acknowledged and apologized for his actions, but G.O. No. 11 remained with him for the rest of his life. Even the minister who delivered his eulogy mentioned and tried to excuse him for it. In no other area of his life, however, did Grant reveal an anti-Semitic strain. Indeed, he appointed General Salomon to the governorship of the Washington Territory after the war.

Jewish Chaplains

Another front on which Jewish rights had to be defended was the chaplaincy. The Chaplaincy Law declared that only a "regularly ordained minister of some Christian denomination" might serve as chaplain to a Union Army company. When the "Jewish" Fifth Cavalry elected one of their number, Michael Mitchell Allen, to lead prayers and conduct services there was no immediate objection. However, a YMCA worker felt compelled to report the breach and Allen was forced to vacate his post. It took almost a year for outraged Jews around the country to get the law changed, but after 1862 chaplains in the U.S. Armed Forces would never again be solely Christian.

Decline of the Southern Jewish Aristocracy

With the end of the Civil War, Southern culture underwent a sea change. The culture of the Southern Jewish aristocracy virtually disappeared. There remained, however, a significant Jewish population in the South.

Rise of Industrial Fortunes in the North

There was a new prosperity in the North after the War. Many of the great American fortunes were based on Civil War profits. Jewish merchants and manufacturers were among those who emerged from the war financially and socially ahead. In addition, the struggle for Jewish rights that began with opposition to G.O. No. 11 and the Chaplaincy Law now grew stronger. An increased feeling of being a part of the American culture gradually led to the expansion of **Reform Judaism.**

1867

First Rabbinical School

Isaac Leeser establishes Maimonides College, the first rabbinical school in the United States. Leeser died not long after and the school closed. Only four students graduated during its short life.

1869

First Reform Statement

A group of Reform rabbis under the leadership of Samuel Hirsch and David Einhorn meet in Philadelphia to publish the first statement on the Jewish Reform posi-

tion in America. The group rejects both the concept of the Jewish restoration of Palestine and the belief in physical resurrection held by Orthodox Jews. The rabbis also make an attempt to increase the role of Jewish women in a number of life-cycle commemorations.

1871

First Hebrew Weekly

Hazofeh B'eretz Hahadashah, the first Hebrew weekly in America, is published by Zvi Hirsch Bernstein. Its intended audience is the immigrant community from Eastern Europe, particularly the intellectuals called *maskilim.* It remained in publication for about two years. The next Hebrew weekly, *Heikhal ha-'ivriyah* (1877–1879?), came out as a supplement to Chicago's Yiddish *Izraelitishe prese* (1877–1884).

1873

Association of Congregations

The Union of American Hebrew Congregations (now the central congregational body of **Reform Judaism** in the Western Hemisphere) is established in Cincinnati after a conference of Jewish congregations from the South and the West, inspired by the vision of **Isaac Mayer Wise** of a single organization representing the entire American Jewish community. Its founders (mostly laymen from Wise's own synagogue) hoped that it would embrace all American synagogues, although its stated "primary object" was to establish a Hebrew theological institute. In 1879, the major Eastern congregations joined the Union. In the same year, the Board of Delegates of American Israelites became a part of the Union and by the end of the decade 118 congregations had joined. This number represented over half of the congregations in the country.

1875

Hebrew Union College

The **Hebrew Union College** (now the primary seminary of the **Reform Movement**) is established in Cincinnati, Ohio, by the Union of American Hebrew Congregations to prepare rabbis for all types of American Jewish synagogues. The goal of **Isaac Mayer Wise**, its founding president, was to create an institution that did not offend the traditionalists, but at the same time provided education for Americanized rabbis. It is now the oldest center of Jewish higher education in the United States.

1876

Ethical Culture Movement

Felix Adler, son of a Reform rabbi, creates the Ethical Culture movement with help from the president of Temple Emanu El, Joseph Seligman. The movement stresses the importance of ethical behavior independent of religious beliefs. Adler's goal was to universalize the religious liberalism of **Reform Judaism**, transforming it into public action. He gave Sunday lectures open to both Jews and Christians and, with his wife, Helen Goldmark Adler, founded schools, a free kindergarten, and a newspaper called *The Standard*. They inspired the building of model apartment houses for Russian immigrants and called attention to the substandard working and living conditions of workers in New York City. The Ethical Culture School produced a great many influential Jewish Americans.

1877

Rights in New Hampshire

New Hampshire is the last state to offer Jews political equality.

A NEW COMMUNITY, 1880–1920

1880

First Census

The Union of American Hebrew Congregations publishes the first census of American Jewry, which it estimates to be 250,000.

1880–1924

Eastern European Immigration

More than two million Jews immigrate to the United States from Eastern Europe. The majority of these immigrants are from the Russian empire. They flee virulent anti-Semitism stirred up by governments anxious to get rid of Jews, as well as official government policies that make it difficult to earn a living. They are also immigrating to a "land of opportunity." This mass migration ends when the United States adopts immigration laws in (1921 and 1924) severely limiting the number of Eastern and Southern Europeans who can be admitted into the country.

1882

First Yiddish Play

The first Yiddish play in this country is produced by Jewish American saloon owner Frank Wolf in New York City. The cast is a troupe of Yiddish performers from London, some local people, and a young man named **Boris Thomashefsky** who becomes one of the most famous actors of the Yiddish theater. The first performance was not particularly successful, but by the end of the year Yiddish shows are being presented regularly in a beer hall called the Old Bowery Garden.

1883

Treyf *Banquet*

The infamous *Treyf* Banquet is held at **Hebrew Union College** to celebrate its first graduating class. It is attended by representatives of more than one hundred Union of American Hebrew Congregations. Shellfish (prohibited by Jewish law) is inadvertently served. Many of those present are so offended that, for this reason among others, they begin to work toward the establishment of an alternative school. This new school is the **Jewish Theological Seminary of America**.

1885

Pittsburgh Platform

Seeking to find a middle ground between Judaic traditionalists and **Felix Adler**'s Ethical Culture movement, which rejected theism, **Kaufmann Kohler** calls a conference of Reform Rabbis in Pittsburgh. They create a "Declaration of Independence," also called the Pittsburgh Platform. It states, among other things, that "Judaism presents the highest conception of the God-idea" and that the Bible reflects "primitive ideas of its own age." Another plank describes the Jews as a "religious people" and explicitly states they were not a nation.

First Yiddish Daily Newspaper

Kasriel H. Sarasohn launches the *Tageblatt*, the first Yiddish daily paper, in New York City.

1886

The **Jewish Theological Seminary** Association is established, with Rabbi **Sabato Morais** as president. Its founders believe in a more open approach to theology and scholarship than the American **Orthodox** movement offered, but they feel that the **Reform** movement has become too radical. The Seminary becomes the focus and impetus for the **Conservative** movement.

1888

The Jewish Publication Society of America is founded in New York by Rabbi Joseph Krauskopf and Solomon da Silva Solis-Cohen. Dedicated to publishing works of Jewish history, religion, and literature, it published over 820 books and distributed over eight million volumes by 1988.

United Hebrew Trades

The United Hebrew Trades is established by socialists in New York City to encourage and direct the development of unions. They fight an uphill battle to organize Jewish workers, especially in the garment industry. The tide does not turn for more than two decades.

1889

Central Conference of American Rabbis

The Central Conference of American Rabbis is established under the leadership of **Isaac Mayer Wise** in Cincinnati. Originally intended to be a regional organization, it quickly spread throughout the country. Today it is the official organization of Reform rabbis in the United States.

Union of Orthodox Jewish Congregations of America

The Union of Orthodox Jewish Congregations of America is established by Orthodox Jews from Western Europe in an attempt to provide organization unity to American Orthodoxy. However, Eastern European congregations did not join the organization until well into the twentieth century. Today the Union is considered the dominant voice of American Orthodox Judaism.

1891

Philanthropy

Baron Maurice de Hirsch, a European philanthropist, establishes the Baron de Hirsch Fund to benefit American Jewry. The fund's focus was aid to East European émigrés.

1892

American Jewish Historical Society Founded

The American Jewish Historical Society is founded on June 7 in New York City, where it is housed in two crowded rooms in the **Jewish Theological Seminary**. Now the oldest continuously functioning ethnic historical society in the United States, its activities comprise a wide variety of research, archival, and publication projects, including this book. In 1999 it joined with other institutions dedicated to preserving and disseminating Jewish history in the Center for Jewish History (see below).

1893

The National Council of Jewish Women

The **National Council of Jewish Women** is founded, coming out of the World Parliament of Religions, which was convened as part of the Chicago World Exposition. It is the first national organization created by Jewish women to promote the Jewish religion.

Jewish Chautauqua Society

The Jewish Chautauqua Society is organized. Like its Christian counterpart, it provides lectures on edifying subjects, often supplemented by musicians or slide shows, all in a tent.

The Educational Alliance

A group of German Jewish philanthropists, including **Jacob Schiff** and Myer S. Isaacs, opens a settlement house on New York City's Lower East Side. It would be enormously influential in the Jewish community. Their goal is to help newly arrived East European immigrants adapt to their new homeland, and, they stated, "the scope of the work shall be of an Americanizing, educational, social and humanizing character." Classes were taught in Yiddish and included all the necessary education for naturalization and more. For young people, the classes ranged from art to Greek to typing. In 1895, the Breadwinners' College lecture series began. Later there were summer camps, a Legal Aid Bureau, and a hall of fame. Among the famous alumni are sculptor Sir Jacob Epstein, composer **George Gershwin**, comedian **Alan King**, and sculptor **Louise Nevelson**.

1895

Rejection of Halakah

The Central Conference of American Jewish Rabbis, the rabbinical association of the **Reform** Movement, officially rejects the authority of *halakah*, Jewish traditional oral law, a position many of its members had held for some time.

1897

First European-Style Yeshiva

Rabbi Isaac Elchanan Theological Seminary, the first European-type yeshiva, is founded in New York City. It later becomes Yeshiva College and eventually **Yeshiva University**. It was originally designed as a place of study for European rabbinical scholars who had come to the United States.

Denunciation of Zionism

Rabbi **Isaac Mayer Wise** denounces the new Zionism of Theodor Herzl at a meeting of the Central Conference of American Rabbis. The Conference adopts a resolution stating, "we totally disapprove of any attempt for the establishment of a Jewish state." The statement is made in anticipation of the first Zionist congress, which was to be held in Basel, Switzerland.

Jewish Daily Forward

The **Jewish Daily Forward**, a socialist newspaper concerned with the problems of workers, publishes its first issue in New York City in Yiddish. It is probably the single most influential publication of its time, reaching almost a quarter of a million readers at the height of its circulation.

1898

Federation of American Zionists

The first nationwide body of Zionist organizations, the Federation of American Zionists, is established in New York City. Professor Richard Gottheil of Columbia was president, Joseph Bluestone and Herman Rosenthal were vice presidents, and Rabbi **Stephen S. Wise** was secretary.

1899

National Conference of Jewish Charities is organized. Forerunner of the Conference of Jewish Communal Services, it arose after federations of Jewish charities were organized in major cities. In 1900, there were three local federations. In 1989, there were 204.

American Jewish Yearbook

American Jewish Yearbook begins publication, under the auspices of the Jewish Publication Society of America, with the purpose of providing demographic information and information about major cultural and sociological developments in the Jewish community. In 1909, it becomes a joint publication of the American Jewish Committee. It is still being published.

1900

Workmen's Circle

A Jewish fraternal order with cultural concerns and a socialist orientation, Workmen's Circle is organized to serve its members' educational, social, and recreational purposes. Its forerunner, the Workingmen's Circle, or *Arbeter Ring*, came into existence in 1892 and organized programs providing medical care and death benefits. It also fought against child labor and sweatshops. In 1933, the Workmen's Circle is the first organization to hold a public demonstration against the rise of Hitler. It continues its work today (on a smaller scale than earlier in the century) with its continuing commitment to human freedom and dignity in the spirit of its motto: "All for One, One for All."

Rabbinical Assembly

The official organization of Conservative rabbis, the Rabbinical Assembly is established in New York as an association for rabbinical graduates of the **Jewish Theological Seminary** of America. It soon opened its membership to graduates of other rabbinical schools.

International Ladies' Garment Workers Union

The International Ladies' Garment Workers Union (ILGWU) is organized by East European labor groups. Eventually to become one of the nation's most powerful unions, it began with eleven Jewish men who represented seven local unions. With the exception of one skirt maker, they were all cloak makers. They excluded women who worked in cap making, "white goods," and men's garments on the grounds that they were not "skilled workers." Not until the shirtwaist was popularized by Charles Dana Gibson's illustrations would women move out of piece work in the household and into the factory. At that point, they began to join the ILGWU and, in the 1909 Uprising, transformed it.

1901

Jewish American Play

Jewish playwright and producer **David Belasco** presents one of the few plays dealing with the Jewish experience. *The Auctioneer*, which he wrote with Charles Klein and Lee Arthur, told the story of a Lower East Side peddler.

Jewish Encyclopedia

Isidore Singer and the publishing company Funk and Wagnalls put together a board of eminent Jewish scholars to create the *Jewish Encyclopedia*, a reference work that would help to combat anti-Semitism by educating the public about the achievements of Jews. The first volume appeared in 1901.

Publication continued only after several Jewish businessmen, including **Jacob Schiff** and Cyrus Sulzberger, guaranteed the increasingly expensive project financially. Hundreds of scholars from around the world cooperated with the project, which was the first compilation of all historical, literary, philosophical, and religious information about the Jewish people. The twelve-volume set was completed in 1906. It signaled the emergence of Jewish scholarship in America and remained the standard reference until the *Encyclopedia Judaica* was published in 1971.

1902

Union of Orthodox Rabbis

The Union of Orthodox Rabbis of the United States and Canada is founded by Eastern European rabbis. The group set standards for the rabbinate and played a leadership role in Orthodox Jewry, remaining the most important Orthodox organization until the 1950s.

Solomon Schechter

Solomon Schechter is appointed president of the **Jewish Theological Seminary** of America. He furthered Conservatism as a separate Jewish denomination.

1903

Kishinev Pogrom

On Easter weekend a pogrom in Kishinev, Russia, leaves 49 Jews dead and more than 500 injured, 700 houses looted and destroyed, 600 businesses looted, and 2,000 families left homeless. In reaction to this tragedy, American Jewry moves to become a more tightly knit community.

Kaufmann Kohler

Kaufmann Kohler is elected president of **Hebrew Union College**, which became the most important institution in American Reform Judaism. Kohler was a leader of the Reform movement and served as rabbi of Temple Beth-El in New York.

1906

Immigration

During this year 153,748 Jewish immigrants arrive in the United States. Most are from Eastern Europe.

American Jewish Committee

American Jewish Committee, a secular defense organization, is established by the American Jewish elite. It advocates that the United States make a response to Russian pogroms and pushed for more open immigration.

First Cabinet Member

Oscar Solomon Straus is named by President Theodore Roosevelt to head the newly created Department of Commerce and Labor. He is the first Jew to head a cabinet department.

Menorah Society

A cultural organization, the Menorah Society, is founded by Jewish students at Harvard. Inspired by the humanist studies of William James and George Santayana, Henry Hurwitz founds the society to pursue the humanist values of Judaism. Several chapters were established at other schools and, in 1913, the Menorah Association was founded. It was the first intercollegiate Jewish body, prospering well into the twentieth century and laying the groundwork for such groups as **Hillel**.

1907

Free Synagogue

Free Synagogue is established as a platform for Rabbi **Stephen S. Wise**. It meets on Sunday mornings at Carnegie Hall and differs from traditional synagogues, including absolute freedom of the pulpit, no fixed dues for pews, and open criticism of social problems. The Free Synagogue also advocated looking for specifically religious approaches to those problems.

First American Jew Wins Nobel Prize

Albert Michelson is the first American Jew to win a Nobel Prize, which was established a few years earlier. Michelson was a physicist with a continuing interest in the issue of light and its properties, especially velocity. In 1887, he performed one of the most important experiments to that date in the history of science. He was able to determine that light travels at a constant speed, no matter what its direction, thereby disproving the ether theory. His discoveries provided a basis for **Albert Einstein**'s special theory of relativity. Michelson was also the first person to measure the dimensions of a star.

Graduate School

Dropsie College for Hebrew and Cognate Learning is chartered in Philadelphia as a graduate school awarding the Ph.D. degree.

1909

Teachers' Training

Gifts from **Jacob H. Schiff** lead to the establishment of Jewish teachers' training programs at the **Jewish Theological Seminary** and **Hebrew Union College**.

Kehillah

The Kehillah (Jewish community) of New York City is established in an attempt to organize New York City's East European Jews. With **Judah L. Magnes** at its head, it was sponsored by the **American Jewish Committee**. Through the Kehillah, representatives of traditional organizations address problems ranging from crime on the Lower East Side to the lack of good Jewish edu-

---

The Jew at the Alamo

Among the many men and women who fell defending the Alamo from the Mexican Army in 1836 was a young Englishman named Antony Wolfe, who was serving as a private in the Army of the Republic of Texas. Wolfe, almost certainly the only Jew in the battle, is reputed to have been one of the last defenders to be killed.

cation. The organization did not survive for long, coming to an end in 1922.

Hebrew Sheltering and Immigrant Aid Society

Hebrew Sheltering and Immigrant Aid Society (HIAS) is formed from a merger of two older organizations—the Hebrew Sheltering House Association (1884) and the Hebrew Immigrant Aid Society (1902). In its first decade HIAS helps half a million immigrants make legal entry into the country, find basic subsistence and work, get citizenship instruction, and locate their relatives.

Uprising of 1909

The Triangle Shirtwaist factory workers, mostly young Jewish women, had been on strike for two months. An overflow crowd of International Ladies Garment Worker members were in the Great Hall at New York's Cooper Union waiting to be addressed by **Samuel Gompers**, president of the American Federation of Labor, and other prominent men. A teenage factory worker named Clara Lemlich spoke up, "I want to say a few words." The crowd around her called for her to get onto the platform and the chairman agreed that she should. After what a press report called ". . . a philippic in Yiddish," Lemlich called for a general strike. The chairman asked all those present to ". . . take the old Jewish oath. If I turn traitor to the cause I now pledge, may this hand wither from the arm I now raise." The resultant strike, often referred to as the "Uprising of the 20,000," revolutionized the Jewish labor movement.

1911

Passport Protest

American Jewry succeeds in inducing Congress to abrogate the 1832 treaty with Russia because the czarist regime would not honor an American passport carried by an American Jew.

Triangle Shirtwaist Factory Fire

On March 25, fire breaks out in the Triangle Shirtwaist Company, which occupies the eighth, ninth, and tenth floors of the Asch Building in New York City. Workers from the ninth floor are trapped because doors to fire

This undated photograph of Clara Lemlich was probably taken around the time she burst on the national scene with her 1909 speech that led to the "Uprising of the 20,000." (From the Keele Center, Cornell University)

escapes are locked by the Jewish owners of the factory to prevent "stealing time," theft, union organizing, and spontaneous walkouts. Of the 500 mostly Jewish workers present on the day of the fire, 146 were killed and many more injured. In court, the proprietors were acquitted. They collected insurance on the fire and reopened their factory at a different location. They offered one week's wages to the family of each victim. The fire and its aftermath radicalized the Jewish working community.

1912

Hadassah

The first meeting of the women's Zionist organization takes place in the vestry rooms of Temple Emanu-El in New York City. More than thirty women, including **Henrietta Szold**, Mathilde Schechter, Emma Leon Gottheil, **Rosalie Solomons Phillips**, and Lotta Levesohn commit themselves to action on behalf of Zionism.

The fire at the Triangle Shirtwaist Company in 1911 was one of the worst industrial disasters in the history of New York City. In less than twenty minutes, 146 workers lost their lives. Most of those who died were young Jewish women, many of whom leapt to their deaths from the ninth floor rather than face the unbearable flames. The tragedy generated great public sympathy for the demands of the union movement. (Private collection)

Actively involved in Palestine in health care and educational services since the early 1920s, **Hadassah** continues to be an active presence in Israel and the United States. They have over 300,000 members and are the largest women's organization in the United States.

Louis Marshall, one of America's most distinguished Jewish layman, becomes president of the **American Jewish Committee**.

1913

United Synagogue of Conservative Judaism

United Synagogue of Conservative Judaism, the international organization of **Conservative** congregations, is organized. It now has 800 congregations as members.

The Promised Land by Mary Antin is published. It is an immigrant's evaluation of the United States.

Potash and Perlmutter, a stereotypical comedy about life in the Lower East Side, opens on Broadway. It is so

One of the most widely publicized anti-Semitic incidents in American history was the murder conviction in 1913 (and subsequent lynching) of Leo Frank. A group of men is shown here presenting a petition for his release. (Courtesy of the American Jewish Historical Society, Waltham, Massachusetts, and New York, New York)

successful that it later becomes a continuing series on the stage and in motion pictures.

B'nai B'rith Anti-Defamation League

With anti-Semitic feelings and activity growing in the United States, **B'nai B'rith** establishes the **Anti-Defamation League** (ADL) to combat discrimination against Jews and others. The ADL was active in the 1920s against the Ku Klux Klan and in the 1930s and 1940s against fascist groups. After World War II, its focus shifted to the battle for civil rights. Throughout its history, the ADL has fought specific instances of anti-Semitism, such as the march of American Nazis in Skokie, Illinois, in 1977.

People's Art Guild

Responding to the revolutionary Armory Show of Eu-

ropean modernists, John Weichsel founds the People's Art Guild, which exhibits many important Jewish artists. The Guild publishes its brochures in Yiddish as well as English, holds special meetings on Friday evenings, and emphasizes the cultural aspects of Jewish life.

1913–1915

Leo Frank Case

In one of America's great anti-Semitic tragedies, Leo M. Frank was lynched for a murder there is virtually no evidence he committed. In 1913 thirteen-year-old Mary Phagan, a worker at an Atlanta, Georgia, pencil factory, was killed in the empty factory. The company's janitor, Jim Conley, accused Frank of the crime, possibly in order to turn attention from himself. The editor of an anti-Semitic newspaper, Tom Watson, worked hard to arouse feeling against the Jewish Frank, who was convicted in an atmosphere of fear and hatred. In 1915, Georgia governor John M. Slaton ordered a retrial for Frank. The governor's mansion was, as a result, attacked by a mob of angry Christians, while another mob managed to kidnap Frank from prison and lynch him. The Frank case was chronicled in the book *Night Fell on Georgia*, by Charles and Louise Samuels in 1956, and became the subject of a novel by **David Mamet** in 1997, and of a dramatic musical by playwright Alfred Uhry in 1998.

1915

Jewish Governor of Idaho

Moses Alexander, a German Jewish immigrant, is elected governor of Idaho.

The **American Jewish Joint Distribution Committee** unites various American Jewish ethnic groups to save East European Jewry.

Rabbi Isaac Elchanan Theological Seminary and Yeshiva Etz Chaim (an Orthodox elementary school) unite under **Bernard Revel**, using the name of the former institution. The school combines Talmudic and secular studies. It would later become Yeshiva College and then **Yeshiva University**.

1916

First Supreme Court Justice

Louis D. Brandeis is nominated to the United States Supreme Court by President Woodrow Wilson. The four-month confirmation battle in the Senate is seen by many, including Brandeis himself, as motivated primarily by anti-Semitism. When the Senate approves his nomination (by a vote of 47 to 22), he becomes the first Jew to serve on the highest court in the land. With the appointment of **Stephen Breyer** in 1994, a total of seven American Jews have served on the Supreme Court.

1917

English Translation of Hebrew Bible

An English translation of the Hebrew Bible is published by the Jewish Publication Society of America. This huge undertaking is one of the greatest accomplishments of the Society and would be followed up with a second translation, in three volumes, later in the century (1962, 1978, 1981).

Jewish Telegraphic Agency

Serving the Jewish and general press, the Jewish Telegraphic Agency is established. It was the Jewish equivalent of Associated Press or United Press International.

Balfour Declaration

The British government issues the Balfour Declaration, promising support for the establishment of a Jewish national home in Palestine, which would soon be under British control.

World War I

The United States enters World War I. About 250,000 Jews served in the armed forces, 40,000 of whom were volunteers. About 3,500 Jews were killed and 12,000 were wounded. Among the almost 11,000 officers were Major General Julius Ochs Adler, Brigadier Generals Milton J. Foreman, Abel Davis, and Charles H. Laucheimer, and Rear Admirals Joseph Strauss and Joseph K. Taussig. The Seventy-seventh Infantry Division, which fought bravely in the Meuse-Argonne Battle, was 40 percent Jewish. Six Jewish American soldiers were awarded the Congressional Medal of Honor, and more than 1,100 citations for bravery were awarded to Jewish American soldiers by Allied commands. The National Jewish Welfare Board was created to serve the religious needs of American Jews in the army and navy.

1918

Women's League for Conservative Judaism

The Women's League for Conservative Judaism is formed and becomes the largest women's synagogue

---

American Nobel Prize Winners, 1901–1995

During the first ninety-six years of Nobel Prize Awards, a total of 243 Americans received this coveted honor. Of these, seventy-one were Jewish.

group in the world with 700 affiliates. The mission of the group is to "perpetuate traditional Judaism in modern society." It helps to support the **Jewish Theological Seminary** and publishes the national quarterly magazine *Outlook*.

Yiddish Art Theater

There are seven Yiddish theaters in New York City alone and many others around the country. The theater was so powerful a force in Jewish culture that disagreements about the nature of the art alienated neighbors and came close to breaking up families. Producer, director, actor **Maurice Schwartz** took over the Irving Place Theater and put together an ensemble of some of the finest actors in the American Yiddish theater. The group presented the play *Forsaken Nook*, by Peretz Hirshbein, in a simple, realistic style that contrasted sharply with the broad, declamatory playing of the Yiddish theater. The highly successful production crystallized a distinction in the community that was more than artistic. It reached into the political and philosophical arena.

First American Jewish Congress

The Balfour Declaration is an important item on the agenda at the Paris Peace Conference, and representatives of the **American Jewish Congress** attend the Conference to represent the views of American Jews. This new organization came out of the dissatisfaction of East European American Jews with the primarily German membership of the **American Jewish Committee**, which expected to represent American Jews at the Peace Conference.

Rabbi **Stephen Wise** led a vigorous opposition from his Free Synagogue, and in 1917 an election was held in which 130,000 American Jews voted. They elected representatives of an American Jewish Con-

gress, with which the Committee agreed to cooperate. In Paris, the Congress attempted to induce the great powers to establish a Jewish homeland in Palestine and to protect East European Jewry through the granting of minority rights. The Congress eventually became a permanent organization, committed to Zionism.

AMERICANIZATION, ANTI-SEMITISM, AND ISOLATIONISM, 1920–1930

1920S

Immigration Acts

The Immigrant Acts of 1921 and 1924 attempt to close America entirely to East European Jews and others. The 1921 Act limited each country's quota to three percent of the number of its countrypeople living in the United States in 1910. The quotas were smallest for the countries with most recent immigrants—Italy and Eastern Europe. The 1924 act reduced the percentage to two percent. This legislation was motivated, in part, by pseudo-scientific racial concepts and is strongly opposed by organizations within the Jewish American community.

Henry Ford and Anti-Semitism

The 1920s were a time of much anti-Jewish sentiment in the United States. The first World War and then the Bolshevik victory in Russia seemed to infect this country with a severe case of xenophobia. Most notable was the anti-Jewish activity of Henry Ford, who used the pages of his *Dearborn Independent* for anti-Semitic propaganda. He accused Jewish Americans of corrupting American culture, particularly baseball and music. He declared that New York was secretly ruled by Jews. Finally, he published the virulently anti-Semitic *Protocols of the Elders of Zion* (1920), a collection of apocrypha that was created by czarist police in Russia to foment anti-Jewish feeling. As the result of a lawsuit and the threat of a boycott of his automobiles, Ford wrote a retraction and an apology and ceased publishing his hate-mongering literature.

1920

American Academy for Jewish Research

American Academy for Jewish Research is founded. It incorporates in 1929. The Academy, an organization of scholars, rabbis, and interested laymen, makes it their goal to propagate scholarship concerning Jewish culture and religion through public meetings for learned discussion, publication of scholarly works, and joint scholarly projects. The group has financed the publications of critical editions of classical Jewish texts, such as *Midrash Leviticus Rabbah*.

1921

Hadoar

The periodical of Histadruth Ivrith, the Hebrew Language and Cultural Association, *Hadoar,* begins publication, emphasizing the primacy of Hebrew in Jewish culture. Beginning as a daily newspaper, it reorganizes as a weekly in 1922. *Hadoar* has published prominent Hebrew writers such as Moshe Feinstein, Reuven Grossman, and Abraham Regelson. It has maintained a devoted, though small, readership over the decades.

American Jewish Congress, organized to represent the Zionist-minded East European element at the Paris Peace Conference, becomes a permanent organization.

First Reconstructionist Organization

Mordecai Kaplan founds the Society for the Advancement of Judaism (SAJ), a synagogue in New York City. This act marks the beginning of the **Reconstructionist Movement**. Kaplan worked with other synagogue members to develop a new approach to Judaism that was intended to be more relevant to twentieth-century America. The congregation engaged in a number of experiments, among which was the inclusion of women in more ritual observances. The *SAJ Review* was published to disseminate these ideas.

1922

Hebrew Theological College

The Hebrew Theological College, an Orthodox rab-

binical school, opens in Chicago. It grew out of the Hebrew high school Yeshiva Etz Chaim, which was established in 1899. It is the first Orthodox rabbinical institution in this country to supplement its Talmud and Codes studies with mandatory courses in Bible, Jewish philosophy, and history. Its first president was Rabbi Saul Silber.

Jewish Institute of Religion

The Jewish Institute of Religion is founded by **Stephen S. Wise** to train rabbis (mostly for the Reform group) with a more national orientation than **Hebrew Union College**. It produced for the most part pro-Zionist rabbis. It merges with Hebrew Union College in 1948.

Bat mitzvah

The **bat mitzvah** ceremony is introduced by **Mordecai Kaplan** and the Society for the Advancement of Judaism. Originally created for Kaplan's own daughter, Judith, it was accepted by about one-third of all Conservative synagogues by 1948. The ceremony took a number of different forms, but by the 1980s it was very similar to the **bar mitzvah** ceremony for boys. Girls are called to read from the Torah and chant a *haftarah*. The bat mitzvah has become an incentive to keep girls involved in supplementary religious education and is regarded by many as an important symbolic recognition of the equality of women.

1923

First Hillel Foundation

First **Hillel** Foundation is established at the University of Illinois at Champaign-Urbana by Rabbi Ben Frankel. He remains its director until his death four years later. His successor, Abram Leon Sachar, built Hillel into a national organization under the sponsorship of **B'nai B'rith** beginning in 1925. For many years, Hillel was the sole Jewish center on most college campuses. It still functions as an umbrella organization for the various denominational and political Jewish campus groups.

First World Congress of Jewish Women meets in Vienna. Nineteen countries were represented by the 200 women in attendance. An ongoing organization is formed, headed by Rebekah Kohut, an American woman active in Jewish activities and in public service.

1925

First Pulitzer Prize

Edna Ferber becomes the first Jew to win the Pulitzer Prize for her best-selling novel *So Big*. Her work celebrates the variety and strength of the American people.

New York City Jewish Population

As a result of heavy immigration in the late nineteenth and early twentieth centuries, one of every three New Yorkers is a Jew. Jewish culture has a profound effect on the city's atmosphere and identity.

1926

World Union for Progressive Judaism

The World Union for Progressive Judaism is founded in London to promote and sustain the ideas and practice of liberal Judaism. A large part of its mission is to take Judaism back in a meaningful way to countries where totalitarian governments had tried to eradicate it. By the end of the twentieth century, 1.5 million Reform, Liberal, Progressive, and Reconstructionist congregations were affiliated with the movement in more than 35 countries. The central office is in Jerusalem.

Synagogue Council of America

At the June 1925 gathering of the Union of American Hebrew Congregations, Rabbi Abram Simon calls for a meeting of congregational and rabbinical groups to discuss shared issues. Out of that meeting the Synagogue Council of America is organized with a constitution adopted in 1926. Members of the council comprised three rabbinical groups—the Central Conference of American Rabbis, the Rabbinical Assembly, and the Rabbinical Council—and three congregational groups—the Union of American Hebrew Congregations, the United Synagogue of America, and the Union of Orthodox Jewish Congregations.

1927

Population Distribution

A survey shows that there were Jews in 9,712 towns and rural districts in the United States. There are 4,228,000 Jews, 17,500 Jewish organizations, and 3,118 congregations in the United States.

1928

Yeshiva College

Yeshiva College, which grew out of the Rabbi Isaac Elchanan Yeshiva, becomes the first general institution of higher education under Jewish auspices in this country. It includes the various schools that went into its establishment, including the Rabbi Isaac Elhanan Theological Seminary and the Teachers Institute, as well as high school and college departments.

National Conference of Christians and Jews

The 1928 presidential election is plagued by religious prejudice, with Roman Catholic Alfred W. Smith running against Quaker Herbert Hoover. In its wake, a group of prominent men of various faiths calls a conference to found an organization that would promote "the advancement of amity, justice, and peace" among Jews and Christians. It was first called the National Council of Catholics, Protestants, and Jews. The name was changed because the Roman Catholic Church did not allow its members to participate in interfaith organizations until after the Ecumenical Council in the 1960s.

1929

Union of Sephardic Congregations

Rabbi David de Sola Pool organizes the Union of Sephardic Congregations with the participation of leaders from Shearith Israel in New York, Mikvch Israel in Philadelphia, and Shearith Israel in Montreal. With the cooperation of Sephardic congregations around the country, the organization published Sephardic prayer books, translated and edited by Rabbi de Sola Pool, that have been used throughout the English-speaking world.

Jewish Agency

In August, the Jewish Agency is established. Its aims are to assist and encourage Jews throughout the world to help in the development and settlement of Erez Israel. Until the establishment of the State of Israel, the Agency is the principal liaison between the League of Nations Mandate and world Jewry and the National Home. In 1948, the new government of Israel takes over many, but not all, of the Agency's functions.

THE HOLOCAUST, 1930–1940

1932

Council of Jewish Federations

Council of Jewish Federations is established. Jewish Federations in fifteen American cities come together to form a council to take over the work of the Bureau of Jewish Social Research (1919) and the National Appeals Information Service (1927). Both organizations did studies of local Jewish communities, providing information to individual Jewish Federations. When they merged, they expanded their scope, doing community planning, providing aid in fundraising, and publishing annual reports on developments in social services and other fields. When the Council was founded, there were fewer than seventy Jewish Federations. Welfare funds in this country raised about ten million dollars a year. A few decades later, the member groups numbered in the hundreds and the funds raised were in the hundreds of millions.

Benjamin Nathan Cardozo

Benjamin Nathan Cardozo is appointed to the United States Supreme Court. His nomination was opposed by some on the grounds that he was a liberal and a Jew. (There was already one Jew, **Louis Brandeis**, on the Court). Cardozo was the second Jewish American to serve on the Court.

1933

Hitler Elected

Adolf Hitler becomes the chancellor of Germany, after an election in which his Nazi party received one-third of the votes. Anti-Semitic groups begin to make public appearances in the United States.

1934

Jewish Labor Committee

In New York City, leaders of several trade unions, as well as other Jewish labor organizations, meet to form the Jewish Labor Committee. Its goals are to support Jewish labor groups in Europe, aid the anti-Hitler underground, help victims of Nazism, work with other American labor groups to fight anti-democratic forces, and battle anti-Semitism.

Reconstructionism

Judaism as a Civilization, by **Mordecai Kaplan**, is published. Kaplan makes the Jewish people the defining characteristic of Judaism rather than the doctrine of monotheism. Kaplan states that it is the civilization of the Jews that sets them apart from other peoples or religions, not any notion of having been "chosen" by God. To Kaplan, the teachings of Jewish Law represented the insights of the Jews into the nature and meaning of life, not any pre-ordained "rules" that were immutable. The doctrines propounded by Kaplan would ultimately lead to the creation of a "fourth branch" of Judaism, **Reconstructionism**.

1935

Rabbinical Council of America

An organization of English-speaking Orthodox rabbis, the Rabbinical Council of America, is formed by a merger of the Rabbinical Council of the Union of Orthodox Jewish Congregations and the Rabbinical Association of the Rabbi Isaac Elchanan Theological Seminary. It is the rabbinical authority of the Union of Orthodox Jewish Congregations, and most of its members are graduates of either **Yeshiva University** or the Hebrew Theological College in Chicago. One of the functions of the RCA is to keep a *bet din* on family problems, specifically divorce, in order to aid individual rabbis with difficult cases.

Clifford Odets

Playwright **Clifford Odets**' *Awake and Sing!* opens in New York City, presenting a poor and badly troubled Jewish family, realistically and without stereotypes. It represents a crucial development in the portrayal of Jewish Americans in the theater.

Zionism in the Reform Movement

In response to the growth of Nazism in Germany, the Central Conference of American Rabbis agrees to reevaluate the anti-nationalist stand it has held since the Pittsburgh Platform was adopted in 1885. Led by **Abba Hillel Silver**, the Zionist faction proposes a new set of Guiding Principles of Reform Judaism, which were written by Samel S. Cohon, a professor of Jewish theology. The Columbus Platform, as it was called, did not end opposition to Zionism in the Reform movement. That was accomplished by the news from Europe.

1937

Growing Population

A survey shows 4,771,000 Jews in the United States and 3,728 congregations.

Refugees

In the late 1930s German Jewish refugees fleeing Nazi persecution start arriving in the United States. Approximately 150,000 Jews entered the United States from German-speaking Europe. Unlike most earlier immigrants, they did not come to America willingly, looking for a new life. They came to save their lives. The refugees were largely middle class, with a strong identification as Germans as well as Jews. Their entry into American life was difficult. Professional men and women often had to take jobs below their qualifications and sometimes had to work as menials.

1938

Anti-Semitic Radio

Father Charles E. Coughlin, a Catholic priest in Detroit, makes a series of radio broadcasts that rival Henry Ford's newspaper articles for virulent anti-Semitism. Millions of American listen to the broadcasts, and Coughlin's fan mail numbered up to 80,000 letters per week.

Evian Conference

From July 6 to July 15 delegates from thirty-two countries meet in Evian, Francc, to discuss the rapidly increasing problem of Jewish refugees caused by Germany's annexation of Austria in March. Unfortunately, very little is accomplished. The United States will not change its restrictive policy on accepting refugees, and neither would any of the other nations present. This lack of action dooms most of the refugees to death in the Holocaust.

Kristallnacht *Outrages Roosevelt*

On November 9 and 10 a pogrom described as *Kristallnacht* (Night of the Broken Glass) is conducted throughout Germany and Austria. Under the explicit orders of the German government, mobs destroy thousands of synagogues and Jewish-owned stores and physically attack Jews. Over 30,000 Jews are arrested and sent to concentration camps. President Roosevelt recalls the United States ambassador to Germany as a protest and publicly expresses his outrage.

1939

White Paper on Palestine

The British White Paper on Palestine is issued, limiting immigration to that country to 75,000 over a five-year period, followed by a complete cessation. The Paper also bans additional purchase of land in Palestine by Jews. This and others in a series of White Papers make it clear that the British are treating

Palestine, not as a mandated territory held in trust, but as a colonial possession.

World War II Begins in Europe

On September 1 Germany invades Poland and on September 3 France and Great Britain declare war on Germany.

Illegal Immigration

Illegal immigration to Palestine is approved by the Jewish Agency at the twenty-first Zionist Congress in Vienna.

Supreme Court Justice

Felix Frankfurter becomes an associate justice of the United States Supreme Court, replacing **Benjamin Nathan Cardozo**. He is the third Jewish American to serve on the court.

United Jewish Appeal

Founded by the merger of three important Jewish humanitarian organizations, the United Jewish Appeal serves Jews in America and around the world. The three groups were the **Joint Distribution Committee**, the United Palestine Appeal, and the United Service for new Americans. The merger is a response to Hitler's Kristallnacht of 1938.

Manhattan Project

Albert Einstein writes to President Roosevelt warning that the Germans could be developing a program to build an atomic bomb and urges the President to begin a U.S. program. Roosevelt begins a program immediately and the "Manhattan Project," as it became known, is led by **J. Robert Oppenheimer**.

S.S. St. Louis

Carrying 936 refugees from persecution, the S.S. *St. Louis* is turned away from all ports in the United States. It is forced to return its passengers to Europe and a dangerously uncertain fate.

Agudath Israel of America

The American branch of Agudath Israel was a long time in coming. Founded in 1912 in Kattowitz, Upper Silesia, the international organization was originally intended to oppose the Tenth Zionist Congress. Orthodox rabbis from Germany, Hungary, Poland, and Lithuania declared that religious Judaism could not coexist with a secular Jewish culture. A 1922 attempt to establish an American branch failed, although a youth group, Zeiri Agudath Israel, was founded.

Over the years, the focus of the organization changed and, after the Holocaust, the anti-Zionist position was dropped. Today Agudath Israel is a primary representative of ultra-Orthodox Judaism in this country. It operates the Jewish Education Program, in which Jewish public school children are taken to synagogues and yeshivot by yeshiva students and given religious instruction. It also set up the Orthodox Jewish Archives (1978) to document world Judaism. The organization's influence is limited by its unwillingness to participate in any larger group that includes non-Orthodox Jews.

1940

YIVO Institute for Jewish Research

The YIVO Institute for Jewish Research moves from Vilna, Lithuania, to New York City. Founded in 1925, it is dedicated to preserving and transmitting the heritage of Eastern European Ashkenazi Jewry, with particular emphasis on Yiddish language and culture. Its collections include substantial printed material as well as massive archive collections. Its photographic collection is especially comprehensive. In 1999 it joined with other institutions dedicated to preserving and disseminating Jewish history and culture in the Center for Jewish History (see below).

Jewish Reconstructionist Foundation

Jewish Reconstructionist Foundation is formed by **Mordecai Kaplan** to support the efforts of the Reconstructionist program.

WAR AND BEYOND, 1941–1949

1941–45

World War II

At least 550,000 Jews served in the American armed

forces during World War II, the equivalent of thirty-seven divisions. More than 10,000 died and another 25,000 were wounded, captured, or missing. About 26,000 Jewish soldiers were awarded the Medal of Honor or the Purple Heart. There were six major generals, thirteen brigadier generals, one admiral, two rear admirals, and one commodore among Jewish officers. Of all Jewish physicians under the age of 45, 60 percent were in uniform. Brilliant engineer Admiral Ben Morel created the Seabees. Commander Edward Ellsberg was described by the navy as "the foremost expert in the world on deep-sea rescue work." Admiral **Hyman G. Rickover** was largely responsible for the Navy's switch from conventional to nuclear power. Not liable to the draft, 311 American rabbis enlisted in the army and navy, serving as chaplains.

1942

News of the Killing

Jews in the United States become aware of the massacre of Jews in Eastern Europe by the invading Germans. The **American Jewish Congress** releases the information to journalists that Hitler was planning to exterminate the entire Jewish population of Europe.

Anti-Zionist Organization

Some anti-Zionist Reform rabbis and anti-Zionist laymen organize the American Council for Judaism. It held the position that the Jews were only a religious group and in no way a nationalist group.

Biltmore Program

In May, representatives of Zionist organizations meet at the Biltmore Hotel in New York. By unanimous agreement those present affirm their belief that Jews could no longer rely on the British government to help establish a Jewish National Home. Jewish authority, they stated, must be established over Palestine.

1943

Zionism and Reform Judaism

The Central Conference of American Rabbis adopts a resolution agreeing that both the Zionist and anti-Zionist positions are compatible with **Reform Judaism**.

American Government and the Holocaust

American government officials do little to try to persuade President Roosevelt to admit European Jewish refugees in substantial numbers. Secretary of the Treasury **Henry Morgenthau, Jr.** is an exception.

1944

National Society for Hebrew Day Schools

National Society for Hebrew Day Schools (Torah Umesorah) is founded by Rabbi Feivel Mendlowitz to work with the several hundred Orthodox day schools in the United States and Canada. The organization publishes three magazines: *Olomeinu*, for children; *The Jewish Parent*, for parents; and *Hamenahel*, for principals. It also sponsors teacher training programs and, in more recent decades, helps to administer U.S. anti-poverty projects.

War Refugee Board

Henry Morgenthau, Jr., secretary of the treasury, delivers a report to Franklin D. Roosevelt indicting the State Department for failing to help rescue victims of Nazism and, worse, of having actually obstructed rescue efforts. The report went on to say that the State Department, under the leadership of anti-Semitic Assistant Secretary of State Breckenridge Long, failed to cooperate with organizations working to help Hitler's victims and that it also failed in intelligence concerning Hitler's destruction of the Jewish population.

Roosevelt's response to these charges was to create the War Refugee Board. Representatives of the board were posted in key cities in and around Europe. From its inception, the WRB did everything in its power to aid refugees from the horrors of Hitler's Europe. It sponsored Swedish businessman Raoul Wallenberg, who developed a scheme using Swedish passports to save at least 20,000 Hungarian Jews.

1945

Atomic Bomb

The United States drops the atom bomb on the Japanese, which hastens the of end of World War II in the Pacific. It is the beginning of a controversy that still rages about the use of nuclear weapons. Jews were among the nuclear scientists who perfected the atom, hydrogen, and neutron bombs.

Jewish Miss America

Bess Myerson becomes the first and (so far) only Jewish Miss America. She enters the pageant using her own (Jewish) name, against all advice. In spite of threatening phone calls to judges, Myerson wins. Three of the five sponsors of the pageant, for unspecified reasons, declined to exercise their right to have that year's Miss America advertise their products.

Myerson began speaking for the **Anti-Defamation League** against all forms of racial hatred. She continues to work for Jewish causes. In 1997 she donated $1 million to New York's new Museum of Jewish Heritage to establish an archive of Holocaust films.

In 1945 Bess Myerson became the first Jewish Miss America. She transformed her fame into a successful career. During her year as the reigning Miss America, Myerson encountered anti-Semitism frequently and experienced the humiliation of being turned away by a country club that did not admit Jews. (Private collection)

Yeshiva University

Samuel Belkin, a talmudic authority and Semitic scholar, took over the presidency of Yeshiva College in 1943 and immediately began expanding the school. Within two years, the institution becomes a full-fledged university and is called **Yeshiva University**. In little more than a decade, the university adds the Albert Einstein College of Medicine (1955) and the Wurzweiler School of Jewish Social Work (1957). **Stern College** (1954), an undergraduate women's school, and the James Striar School of Jewish Studies (1955) are also added. Stern offers a program of secular and Judaic studies for women and is the first school of this kind in the world.

1945–52

Displaced Persons

Under directives from President Harry S. Truman, hundreds of thousand of displaced persons were admitted to the United States. In 1948, Congress passed the Displaced Persons Act, allowing the entry of a limited number of Europeans who had been displaced by World War II and the takeover of Eastern Europe by Communist regimes. Insisting that national quotas be maintained in some fashion, Congress devised an elaborate system that allowed European displaced persons to enter the country by a kind of "borrowing" against future national quotas. Approximately 400,000 European refugees were admitted under the Displaced Persons Act between 1948 and 1952.

1947

Jewish Museum

The Museum of Ceremonial Objects is started as an addition to the library of the **Jewish Theological Seminary** in 1929. A bequest from Frieda Warburg (the wife of **Felix Warburg**) made it possible to move the museum into the former Warburg mansion on Fifth Avenue in 1947, where it became The Jewish Museum. Over the years, paintings were added to the collection and special exhibitions presented.

Palestine Divided

On November 29 the United Nations General Assembly votes to end the British mandate and divide Palestine into two sovereign states, one Jewish and one Arab.

American Jewish Archives

The American Jewish Archives is established by Jacob Rader Marcus on the campus of **Hebrew Union College** in Cincinnati, the oldest rabbinical seminary in the United States. As of 1998, the American Jewish Archives contained almost 5,000 linear feet of archives, manuscripts, photographs, audio and video tapes, microfilm, and genealogical materials.

1948

Brandeis University

Brandeis University is established in Waltham, Massachusetts, as the first secular university in the United States under Jewish auspices. Named after U.S. Supreme Court Justice **Louis D. Brandeis**, it is an accredited, private, co-educational school founded by a group of community leaders. Near Boston, the university began its life with 107 students and 14 faculty members. By 1998, there were 3,020 undergraduates, 1,199 graduate students, and over 350 full-time faculty.

Israeli Independence

On May 14 the British mandate over Palestine ends and Israel declares its independence. President Truman recognizes the new state eleven minutes after it came into existence.

First Arab-Israeli War

On May 15 the British leave Palestine. Arab forces from Egypt, Syria, Tranjordan (Jordan), Lebanon, and Iraq invade Israel. Fierce fighting raged for months. The last armistice agreement (with Syria) was not signed until July 17, 1949. American Jewry raised more than $150 million to help Israel defend itself.

1949

United Nations recognizes Israel

On May 11—almost a year to the day after Israel declared its independence—the United Nations votes to accept Israel as a member.

THE TRANSFORMATION OF AMERICAN JEWS AND AMERICAN JUDAISM, 1950–1999

1950

School Merger

Hebrew Union College merges with the Jewish Institute of Religion. A third branch of the school opens in Los Angeles in 1954 because of the growing Jewish population of the city. A fourth branch is established in Jerusalem in 1963. The institution adds a variety of programs over the years including a School of Graduate Studies, a School of Biblical Archaeology, and Schools of Education, Jewish Communal Service, and Sacred Music.

Lubavitch Hasidim

Rabbi **Menachem Mendel Schneersohn** succeeds his father-in-law as rebbe of the Lubavitch **Hasidim** after a struggle with his brother-in-law Rabbi Samarius Gourary. He is formally installed in 1951 and quickly begins a far-reaching program to disseminate **Orthodox Judaism**, particularly Chabad Hasidism, setting up day schools in a number of American and Canadian cities. He also establishes "Chabad houses" around the country. They function as a combination of synagogue, school, drop-in center, and counseling center. By 1990, there were more than 250 Chabad houses in the United States. Schneersohn also led the Lubavitch movement to publish textbooks and periodicals and broadcast speeches on radio and cable television.

Rosenberg Case

One of the most controversial court cases in American history involved Julius and Ethel Rosenberg. Charged with conspiracy to convey U.S. nuclear secrets to the Soviet Union, they were tried in a New York court and convicted. The judge, the principal witnesses, the chief prosecutor, and the defense lawyers in the case were all Jewish. When the Rosenbergs were sentenced to death, there was outrage around the country and around the world. No civilian had ever been executed as a spy in the United States before, and the Rosenbergs' offense occurred in peacetime. The Rosenberg's were executed on June 19, 1953. The case continues to arouse strong emotions, and it has been the subject of a number of books and articles and a rallying point for political causes.

1951

UAHC Move

The major Reform organization, the Union of American Hebrew Congregations, moves from Cincinnati to New York City. The action is symbolic as well as practical, indicating a determination to expand its leadership role in **Reform Judaism** and in American Judaism generally.

Conference on Material Claims against Germany

The Conference on Material Claims against Germany is established by Nahum Goldmann, founder of the World Jewish Congress. The Conference, representing twenty-three Jewish organizations in the U.S., France, Britain, Canada, Germany, Australia, South Africa, and Israel becomes an ombudsman to secure financial reparations for Jewish Holocaust survivors.

1952

Holocaust Reparations

On January 7, while the Israeli parliament debates the acceptance of reparations from Germany, riots erupt outside the Knesset. Menachem Begin and others strongly oppose reparations as blood money. However, in September, Chancellor Konrad Adenauer signs an agreement that the Federal Republic of Germany will provide $715 million in goods and services to the State of Israel as compensation for taking in survivors; $110 million to the Claims Conference for programs to finance the relief, rehabilitation, and resettlement of Jewish Holocaust survivors; and direct reparations to selected individuals over a twelve-year period. Germany was once compensating 275,000 survivors. Today the number is approximately 120,000.

1953

Lieberman Clause

A difficult issue for women in Judaism arose from the fact that a woman whose husband left her without issuing a Jewish divorce was unable to remarry. The first step toward resolving this problem came when the Law Committee of the Conservative movement adopted the "Lieberman clause," which made the Jewish marriage contract a binding agreement in civil law, requiring both parties to abide by the recommendations of a Jewish court of law if their marriage ended.

1954

Women's College

Stern College for Women, the first liberal arts women's college under Jewish auspices, opens in New York City as a counterpart of Yeshiva College, **Yeshiva University's** college of arts and sciences for men.

1955

Women and Aliyah

The Committee on Jewish Law and Standards of the **Conservative Movement** decides to permit women to be called up for *aliyahs*, if the local rabbi approves. The option was at first implemented only in a few synagogues in Minneapolis.

Leo Baeck Institute

The Leo Baeck Institute is established in New York City as a research institution dedicated to the study of the history of German-speaking Jewry. In 1999 it joined with other institutions dedicated to preserving and disseminating Jewish history and culture in the Center for Jewish History (see below).

Conference of Presidents of Major American Jewish Organizations

The Conference of Presidents of Major American Jewish Organizations, one of American Jewry's most powerful organizations, is formed to promote unified action among major American Jewish organizations with regard to issues in the Middle East. In 1966, the group became a conference of organizations rather than of presidents.

Albert Einstein College of Medicine

Albert Einstein College of Medicine opens. A division of **Yeshiva University**, it is the first medical school ever established under Jewish auspices in the United States

1956

Increase in Synagogue Membership

Statistics in the *American Jewish Year Book* show a great increase in Jewish synagogue membership in the previous fifteen years, particularly in the Reform and Conservative groups, and a great increase in Jewish religious school attendance.

Arab-Israeli War

From 1949 to 1956, an armed truce existed between Israel and the Arab countries. Although enforced in part by United Nations forces, it was interrupted by outbreaks of violence, which resulted in over 1,300 Israel civilian casualties. Beginning in August of 1956 Egypt began preparations for a military assault. In a preemptive strike on October 29, 1956, Israeli forces, under the leadership of Moshe Dayan, attacked Egypt's Sinai peninsula from the air and on the ground. An Anglo-French invasion along the Suez Canal bolstered Israeli successes. Israel captured several significant pieces of territory before the November 6 ceasefire. It withdrew from these areas in 1957 and turned them over to a United Nations emergency force.

1964

Civil Rights Act

Congress passes the Civil Rights Act, which prohibits discrimination in public facilities, guarantees voting rights for all races, and establishes the Equal Opportunity Commission. The act had far-reaching consequences in the areas of education, sports, business, and government.

Student Struggle for Soviet Jewry

Student Struggle for Soviet Jewry is founded at Columbia University on April 27. Its first public activity is a thousand-student protest outside the Soviet United Nations mission against the USSR's treatment of its Jewish citizens. For the next three years the organization works (often through demonstrations or vigils) to educate the American public about the plight of Soviet Jewry.

1965

Immigration and Nationality Act

The Immigration and Nationality Act did away with quotas based on nation of origin, substituting limits on total immigration. It also instituted a system of occupational and family preferences to determine who would be allowed in under these limits. The Act is a rejection of the attempt to freeze the ethnic makeup of the United States.

1967

Six-Day War

During the early sixties, border incidents between Israel and its Arab neighbors increase. In May of 1967, Egypt's President Nasser mobilizes units in the Sinai and closes the Gulf of Aqaba to Israel. On June 5, Israel launches a massive air strike, followed by an invasion of ground forces, that results in military control of the Sinai peninsula within three days. After another three days, the war was over, and Israel also controlled Jerusalem's Old City and the strategically important Golan Heights. American Jewry raises more than $317.5 million to support the war.

1968

Reconstructionist Rabbinical College

The Reconstructionist Rabbinical College is established. It is the final step in creating the **Reconstructionist** Movement. The college, located in Wyncote, Pennsylvania, has a working connection with Gratz College.

1969

Association for Jewish Studies

Association for Jewish Studies formed as a learned society and professional organization to promote teaching and research in Jewish Studies in institutions of higher learning. Regular publications of the Association include the *AJS Newsletter*; the *AJS Review*, a scholarly journal, and *Positions in Jewish Studies: Information Bulletin*.

1971

Touro College

Touro College is founded in New York City by Dr. Bernard Lander as a Jewish-sponsored independent institution of higher and professional education. Named after brothers who were leaders in colonial America, the college opened with a class of thirty-five students. A Women's Division is later added to the College of Liberal Arts and Sciences, as are schools of General Studies, Law, and Health Sciences. About 8,000 students are currently enrolled in the various schools and divisions of Touro. There are sister institutions in Israel and Russia.

1972

First Woman Rabbi

Hebrew Union College ordains the first woman rabbi, **Sally Priesand**.

Ezrat Nashim

Ezrat Nashim, a group of young women who were largely brought up in the camps and schools of the **Conservative Movement**, calls for the affirmation of the equality of women from the Conservative Rabbinical Assembly (CRA). They demand that women be granted the following rights: membership in synagogues, participation in a *minyan*, full participation in religious observances, recognition as witnesses in Jewish law, ability to initiate divorce, admission to rabbinical and cantorial schools, service as rabbis and cantors in synagogues, positions of leadership in the community, and responsibility to fulfill all the *mitzvahs* equally with men.

Gay and Lesbian Synagogue

Beth Chayim, the first Gay and Lesbian Synagogue, is established in Los Angeles. About ninety percent of its members are gay. In addition to all the traditional synagogue programs, it offers support for HIV and AIDS victims.

1973

Yom Kippur War

The Yom Kippur War begins when Egypt and Syria attack Israel. Israel is again victorious. In November the Council of Jewish Federations creates a fund of $3 million to be used to mobilize American Jews and the American government to support Israel.

Women in Minyan

The Committee on Jewish Law and Standards of the Conservative Movement passes a *takkanah* (enactment) allowing women to count in a *minyan* equally with men. The United Synagogue of America, the Conservative Movement's congregational association (now called the United Synagogue of Conservative Judaism), decides to allow women to participate in synagogue rituals and to promote equal opportunity for women for positions of leadership, authority, and responsibility in congregational life.

Nobel Peace Prize

Henry Kissinger of the United States and Le Duc Tho of North Vietnam receive the Nobel Peace Prize in recognition of their efforts to end the war in Vietnam.

Aliyot

From 1972 to 1976, the number of Conservative congregations giving *aliyot* (the honor of being called to the Torah) to women increases from seven percent to fifty percent.

1974

Women Equal in Ritual

The Conservative Movement adopts a series of proposals that equalize men and women in all areas of ritual, including serving as prayer leaders.

1975

Zionism Denounced

The United Nations General Assembly declares Zionism "a form of racism and racial discrimination." The American Ambassador, Daniel P. Moynihan, declares that the United States "will never acquiesce in this infamous act," and an enormous rally protesting the resolution is held in New York City.

1976

Yeshiva University opens the **Benjamin N. Cardozo School of Law**, the only law school in the country founded under Jewish auspices. It now ranks among the seventy most selective law schools in the nation and has 2,000 students every year competing for the 250 spots in its entering class.

1978

Drisha Institute

Drisha Institute for Jewish Education is started by Rabbi David Silbert to give women an education in Judaism equal to that of men. Although Drisha allows women to study the Talmud, it has not taken a position on controversial issues such as the legality of women's prayer groups, women serving as *poskot*, counting women in a *minyan*, or ordaining women as rabbis.

Denver Experiment

Rabbis from Reform, Conservative, and Traditional synagogues in Denver form a joint *Beit Din* to oversee conversions. There was no Reconstructionist rabbi in Denver, and Orthodox rabbis declined participation. The program was intended to prevent a situation in which rabbis did not recognize each other's converts to Judaism. Each rabbi still retained the authority to perform his own conversions. About 750 people underwent conversion through the communal rabbinic court before its dissolution in 1983. The dissolution was the result of a resolution on patrilineality adopted that year by the Central Conference of American Rabbis, which persuaded Conservative and traditional rabbis that they could no longer be part of the court.

Shifting Affiliations Among American Jews		
	1970	1990
Reform	33%	39%
Conservative	42%	40%
Orthodox	11%	7%
No affiliation or "other"	14%	14%

The Chronicle of Higher Education

1979

Camp David Accords

At the instigation of and with the personal intervention of American President Jimmy Carter, Israel and Egypt sign a peace treaty on the lawn of the White House. President Carter met with Egyptian President Anwar el-Sadat and Israeli Prime Minister Menachem Begin at his retreat at Camp David, Maryland, for more than ten days to hammer out the agreement.

1980

The National Yiddish Book Center

The National Yiddish Book Center is founded by Aaron Lansky to save and collect Yiddish books when their readers and owners die and leave no Yiddish-speaking heirs. Under Lansky's leadership, the center has collected more than 1.3 million volumes. It has helped to create core collections of Yiddish books at 225 universities and research libraries. Originally operating out of an unheated factory loft, in 1996 the Center opened an $8 million, ten-acre "campus" in Amherst, Massachusetts. It now offers a summer camp in Yiddish culture for both children and adults.

1983

Women in Rabbinical School

The **Jewish Theological Seminary** faculty votes 34 to 8, with one abstention and more than half a dozen absent in protest, to admit women to their Rabbinical School to pursue a course of study leading to ordination. The basis in Jewish law for their decision was the *responsum* of Rabbi Joel Roth, which argues that individual women could become rabbis and prayer leaders if they assume the same degree of religious obligations as men. Those opposed to the decision formed the Union for Traditional Conservative Judaism, which became a separate group in 1990, changing its name to the Union for Traditional Judaism.

Patrilineal Descent

The Central Conference of American Rabbis declares that a child would be considered Jewish if either parent, mother or father, were Jewish and if the child publicly and formally identified with the Jewish faith and people, receiving a Jewish education and upbringing. The decision is motivated by fears concerning the survival of the Jewish people in the face of increasing intermarriage. A 1991 survey of American rabbis by sociologist Samuel Heilman showed that more than half of all Reform spiritual leaders viewed the decision as one of the most divisive acts in contemporary Jewish life.

1985–90

U.S.S.R. Dissolution

The U.S.S.R. disbanded. Over 300,000 Russian Jews emigrate, with almost 85,000 coming to the United States, and many more settling in Israel. In the first three years of the 1990s, almost 400,000 Russian Jews emigrate from the former Soviet Union to Israel.

1985

First Conservative Woman Rabbi

Amy Eilberg graduates from the Rabbinical School of the **Jewish Theological Seminary** and is ordained as a Rabbi in Conservative Judaism. She was the first, but by the middle 1990s, there were seventy-two woman members of the Central Conference of American Rabbis.

Who Is a Jew?

Orthodox groups in Israel attempt to amend the Law of Return to deny citizenship to new immigrants who were converted to Judaism by non-Orthodox rabbis. United States Jews, where about ninety percent of whom are affiliated, if at all, as Reform or Conservative, were outraged. They charge that the amendment would not only deny their Jewishness, but would also undermine their movements.

1986

Nobel Peace Prize

Elie Wiesel is awarded the Nobel Peace Prize. He has dedicated his life to making certain that the world knows about the atrocities committed during the Holocaust and to working to create a world in which such actions can never happen again.

1990

Intermarriage

The National Jewish Population Survey documents that the rate of interfaith marriages among Jews has risen to fifty-two percent. This sets off a firestorm of debate about the future of Judaism in the United States. Many argue that Jews will become so assimi-

---

Same Sex Marriage for Jews?

Only the Reform Movement in American Judaism has raised the question of sanctioning same-sex marriage, and they have yet to take any official position. There was a high-profile marriage in Philadelphia in June of 1998 between two women who were consciously making a statement about the issue. The women were Reform Rabbi Sue Levi Elwell, the assistant director of the Union of American Hebrew Congregations' Pennsylvania region, and Nurit Shein, the executive director of the Philadelphia AIDS Task Force and a retired lieutenant colonel in the Israeli army. "It is unabashedly a *kiddushin* (sanctified marriage)," Rabbi Elwell told *The Jewish Week*. "It is a marriage. The state hasn't recognized it yet, but we have." Four people officiated at the wedding—Rabbi Leonard Gordon, a Conservative rabbi; Rabbi Rebecca Alpert, a Reconstructionist rabbi; Phyllis Berman, a leader of the Jewish Renewal movement; and Rabbi Richard Address, a Reform rabbi.

lated that the uniqueness of Jewish culture and people would soon disappear.

Woman Cantors

Women were eligible to study in the Cantors Institute from its beginning in 1952, but when seminary chancellor **Ismar Schorsch** announces in 1987 that the **Jewish Theological Seminary** is going to confer the diploma of *hazan* on two women, the Cantors Assembly strongly objects. Resolutions to admit women to the Assembly were defeated in 1988, 1989, and 1990. Women were admitted in December of 1990 by a decision of the executive council of the Assembly. Within a few years, fifty percent of the student body in the Cantors Institute were women. However, in 1996, only 38 of the 476 of the Cantors Assembly members were women.

1993

United States Holocaust Memorial Museum

In April the United States Holocaust Memorial Museum opens in Washington. Located next to the mall, the Museum is erected on land donated by the federal government, but built with private funds. The permanent exhibit has proved to be one of the most visited sites in the nation's capital, with over four million visitors during the first two years alone. Crowds are often required to stand in line for hours for tickets.

In 1997 the Museum became the principal center for Holocaust studies in the United States, with the establishment of the Center for Advanced Holocaust Studies. The archives of the Museum includes over eight million pages of documents and microfilm. The **Steven Spielberg** Film and Video Archive includes over 200 hours of historical film.

Steven Spielberg

Schindler's List, by **Steven Spielberg**, is released. It is based on the true story of a German businessman who saved more than 1,100 Jews from extermination. It wins Academy Awards for best picture and best director.

Move toward Reconciliation

The Israelis and Palestinian Arabs seek to reconcile their political differences. Prime Minister Yitzhak Rabin shook hands with PLO Chairman Yasser Arafat on the White House lawn.

1995

Pluralism

At the American Zionist Movement's January convention, a resolution is passed demanding religious pluralism in Israel. The three Orthodox constituents immediately withdraw from the coalition.

Estimates of Jewish Population in the United States, 1654–1996	
1654	25
1700	200–300
1776	1,000–2,500
1790	1,243–3,000
1800	2,000–2,500
1820	2,650–5,000
1826	6,000
1830	4,000–6,000
1840	15,000
1848	50,000
1850	50,000–150,000
1860	150,000–200,000
1870	200,000
1880	230,000–280,000
1890	400,000–475,000
1900	937,800–1,058,135
1910	1,508,000–2,349,754
1920	3,300,000–3,604,580
1927	4,228,029
1937	4,641,000–4,831,180
1940	4,770,000–4,975,000
1950	4,500,000–5,000,000
1960	5,367,000–5,531,500
1970	5,370,000–6,000,000
1980	5,500,000–5,920,890
1992	5,828,000
1996	5,900,000

Sources: Marcus, Jacob Rader *The American Jew, 1585–1990: A History.* Brooklyn, N.Y. Carlson Publishing, Inc., 1995; and *American Jewish Yearbook.* Philadelphia: American Jewish Committee, 1997.

First Woman Senior Rabbi

Debra Newman Kamin is the first woman to serve as senior rabbi of a major Conservative congregation, Am Yisrael, in Northfield, Illinois.

1999

The Center for Jewish History

The Center for Jewish History opens in New York City on Sixteenth Street between Fifth and Sixth Avenues. It brings under one roof four major Jewish research institutions: The American Jewish Historical Society, The Leo Baeck Institute, Yeshiva University Museum, and the YIVO Institute for Jewish Research. The American Sephardi Federation is headquartered at the Center. The 125,000-square-foot facility houses 100 million archival documents and tens of thousands of photographs, posters, paintings, and artifacts. The library includes over one-half million volumes. The Center is the largest repository of Jewish cultural history outside Israel.

Part 2

Judaism and Community in America

OVERVIEW

Two strong forces contended in the development of American Judaism. On one side was the appeal of tradition, ritual, and religious law—the need to be true to a religious heritage that went back thousands of years. On the other was the desire to live in the world one was born into, to respond to American culture in both its positive and its negative aspects. Complicating and reinforcing this tension was immigration. Time and time again, as American Jews began to accommodate the culture of the United States, a new wave of immigrants from Europe arrived and insisted on the old ways and the old loyalties. Out of this flux came four distinct movements in American Judaism—**Orthodox**, **Reform**, **Conservative**, and **Reconstructionist**.

The first, and the one to which all the others have been in a sense a reaction, is the Orthodox movement. The earliest Jews in America established Orthodox congregations that followed a Dutch Sephardic version of ritual and custom. After the arrival of large numbers of Jews from the German states and Central Europe during the first half of the 1800s, most Orthodox synagogues in America reflected Ashkenazi practice.

In the 1840s, the arrival of Central European immigrants began to turn the Reform impulse into a legitimate movement. **Issac Mayer Wise** from Bohemia, a moderate Reformer, and David Einhorn from Bavaria, a militant, became influential and sometimes antagonistic pioneers in building and determining the direction of the Reform Movement in its formative years from 1850 to 1870.

In response to the Reform movement, Orthodox clergy struggled to maintain tradition. However, most Orthodox congregations were headed, not by rabbis, but by American-born, American-educated, English-speaking "ministers." The massive immigration of the 1880s from Eastern Europe brought in an entirely different leadership. Rabbis and Talmud scholars trained in the great yeshivas of Eastern Europe were among the immigrants. Hundreds of small synagogues, mikvahs, butcher shops, and Jewish bookstores began to spring up in the Lower East Side of New York City and then in Brooklyn, Newark, New Brunswick, and Trenton, New Jersey. In 1887, representatives from several Lower East Side congregations established the *Agudath Kehillot Yisrael Ortodoksit b'America* (Association of American Orthodox Hebrew Congregations). Shortly thereafter, they chose Rabbi **Jacob Joseph** of Vilna, Lithuania to become "Chief Rabbi of New York."

Loyalty to European tradition manifested itself fifteen years later when fifty-nine rabbis convened in New York City to establish a rabbinic union known as the *Agudath ha-Rabbonim* (the United Orthodox Rabbis of America, later changed to the Union of Orthodox Rabbis of the United States and Canada). Only rabbis who had been trained at the great yeshivas of Europe and ordained by well-known European Talmud scholars were eligible for membership. No "American" rabbis need apply.

In the meantime, some Jewish Americans tired of the struggle between Orthodox and Reform. They laid the groundwork for the Conservative Movement in 1886 by founding the **Jewish Theological Seminary of America** in opposition to what they saw as the increasing radicalization of the Reform Movement as expressed in its 1885 Pittsburgh Platform. The Conservatives saw themselves as combining traditionalism with a more moderate approach to adapting to American culture. The movement grew steadily into the twentieth century.

Coming up on another flank were **Mordecai Kaplan** and the Reconstructionists, although this movement has never had more than a small percentage of Jews as adherents. Beginning in 1922, Kaplan gathered Jews who were disaffected with other congregations and committed to "reconstructing" American Judaism so that it spoke meaningfully to the twentieth-century world. Synagogue members were encouraged to interpret Jewish tradition freely and to create a more democratic Jewish institutional life.

The stage was now set. The actors were in place. The rest of the twentieth century would see the drama enacted. In the Orthodox movement, it took more than three decades for rebellion to ferment. In 1935, graduates of the Rabbi Isaac Elchanan Theological Seminary and some other American yeshivas formed their own rabbinic organization, the Rabbinical Council of America. In the years following World War II, the Orthodox movement found itself once more challenged from the other side by an influx of European Jewish leaders demanding more adherence to law and tradition. At the same time, the Conservative Movement began to rival the Reform Movement in terms of numbers of members. The Reconstructionist Movement moved toward becoming official—a synagogue association, a rabbinical council, and a theological seminary. By the 1960s, the moderate Rabbinical Council became the predominant Orthodox rabbinic body and an important institution in the politics of American Jewish life. In the 1970s through 1990s Reform, Conservative, and Reconstructionist Judaism responded to the exigencies of democracy and expanded the role of women.

The tension between the forces of tradition and acculturation, which has continued and will continue into the twenty-first century, has produced conflict and faction among American Jews. It has prevented the achievement of unity in American Judaism. At the same time, it has served to make Judaism a living force in the religious life of this country.

AMERICAN JEWISH COMMITTEE

Founded November 11, 1906, the American Jewish Committee was the first organization established by American Jews to address the need to defend Jewish civil rights in the United States and throughout the world. Sparked by the large wave of anti-Jewish pogroms in czarist Russia, particularly the two massacres of Jews in Kishinev in 1903 and 1905, three American Jewish leaders—Oscar S. Straus, **Jacob H. Schiff**, and Cyrus L. Sulzberger—undertook to raise funds for relief of the victims and thereby put in place the machinery for significant fundraising within the Jewish community, the first of its kind in the United States.

In early 1907, joined by **Cyrus Adler**, **Louis Marshall**, **Judah L. Magnes**, Simon Wolf, and other important American Jewish jurists and industrialists of the established German-Jewish elite, they formed a Committee of Fifty to establish a permanent organization that aimed "... to prevent the infraction of the civil and religious rights of Jews, in any part of the world" and "... to render all lawful assistance" to those Jews whose rights were threatened. In its early years the American Jewish Committee acted to keep the doors of the United States open to Jewish immigrants and lobbied for the defense of the rights of American Jews traveling in Russia.

The latter project, following a key speech by Louis Marshall, resulted in the American government's abrogation of the 1832 Russo-American Treaty of Commerce in 1911 because of Russia's refusal to comply with an American demand for equal treatment of Jews. In arguing for the inviolability of American citizenship, Marshall invoked universal themes when he stated, "We can never suffer any question here concerning individual rights but such as relates to the entire American people."

Under Marshall's leadership The American Jewish Committee expanded its mission to the defense of the rights of all Americans, regardless of race, creed, or religion. In 1913 the Committee was one of a number of groups that lobbied the United States government to press for human rights guarantees following the end of the Balkan Wars and supported the New York State Civil Rights Law, which prohibited the advertisement of discriminatory restrictions in hotels and other public places. During World War I the Committee was instrumental in the founding of the **American Jewish Joint Distribution Committee**, a relief organization, and the National Jewish Welfare Board, a social welfare organization devoted to the needs of American servicemen, both Jewish and non-Jewish.

In the post-war world the Committee's agenda increasingly reflected American domestic concerns. In the 1920s the Committee, through an *amicus curiae* (friend of the court) brief, supported the right of Catholics to send their children to private parochial schools rather than to public school. Between 1933 and 1940 the Committee sponsored an educational campaign in the United States to counter Nazi and other anti-Semitic propaganda. It also worked with the press, civic organizations, businesses, labor unions, veterans organizations, and church groups to promote its message of tolerance. In 1948 the Committee filed a brief with the United States Supreme Court opposing racially restrictive covenants and, in 1952, successfully advocated before the Court the position that damages were not applicable should such a covenant be broken.

Beginning in 1956 the Committee began to sponsor conferences and studies by distinguished social scientists concerning Jewish continuity in the Diaspora, relations with Israel, and the present and projected role of religious and ethnic minorities in American life. As part of its mission to break down barriers separating groups from one another, the Committee invited Pope Pius XII to confer with them on issues regarding racial and religious persecution and the status of refugees in 1957. Activities such as these, which remain ongoing today, led President Eisenhower to praise the Committee on the occasion of its fiftieth anniversary in 1957. Saluting the Committee and its membership as "champions of liberty," Eisenhower wrote: ". . . they have helped to protect and strengthen the institutions of American democracy, they have helped to secure equal opportunities for all our citizens. By adding substance to our principles, deeds to our words, they help us make effective witness in the cause of world peace."

AMERICAN JEWISH CONGRESS

The American Jewish Congress was founded in March 1916 as a temporary body, after many months of agitation by radical Russian and East European Jews, as a more democratic alternative to the **American Jewish Committee**, which was widely perceived among Eastern European immigrants as elitist and anti-democratic. Many of those who pushed for the founding of the Congress were important figures in the Zionist movement, coming primarily from the Federation of American Zionists (founded in 1898), who felt that the American Jewish Committee did not adequately endorse the establishment of a Jewish state.

Among the important early leaders of the Congress movement were **Louis D. Brandeis**, **Louis Lipsky**, **Horace Kallen**, and **Stephen S. Wise**. Initially formed with the purpose of working on a relief fund to aid the suffering Jews of Eastern Europe, the Congress came to play a significant role in the Paris Peace Conference in 1919. At the end of World War I, the principal goal of the Congress was not the establishment of a Jewish state but the rebuilding of Eastern European Jewry and securing elementary human rights for these Jews.

The Congress, in its initial incarnation as a temporary organization, disbanded in 1920. It was re-established as a permanent body in 1922, with the support of the **Zionist Organization of America**. Upon its rebirth, the Congress took as its primary goal the achievement of political and social justice, making

laws serve the needs of Jews and other minorities in the United States and of Jews throughout the world. Since 1945, the Congress has continued to press for civil equality for all Americans through its Commission on Law and Social Action. The American Jewish Congress was among the first organizations to support the struggle of African Americans for civil rights, inviting Dr. Martin Luther King, Jr. to speak at its Annual Convention in 1958. The Congress has continued to advocate for social justice as the moral conscience of American Jewry.

AMERICAN JEWISH JOINT DISTRIBUTION COMMITTEE

On November 27, 1914, two existing relief committees, the American Jewish Relief Committee (sponsored by the **American Jewish Committee**) and the Central Committee for the Relief of Jews (sponsored by the Union of Orthodox Congregations), came together to establish the Joint Distribution Committee for the Relief of Jewish War Sufferers. This action represented the culmination of various efforts to prepare for the impact on European Jewry of the outbreak of World War I. It arose out of a recognition that a single agency would be needed to ensure the efficient distribution in Europe of the relief funds being raised from American Jews. Later, the People's Relief Committee, representing Jewish labor groups, became a third sponsor of the Joint Distribution Committee.

The founding of the JDC, as it soon came to be known, reflected the resolve of American Jewish leaders not to be idle while the Jews of Europe and Palestine were caught in the crossfire of contesting European powers. As a non-political, humanitarian agency for the distribution of relief and assistance to Jews in need throughout the world, the JDC's philosophy encompassed the firm belief ". . . that Jews have a right to live in countries of their birth or in countries of their adoption" and that Jews ". . . have a right, as human beings, to reside there with full rights, including among them the right to emigrate." Though originally intended as a temporary means of providing assistance, the JDC continued its activities after the end of World War I in response to the continuing needs of its clientele in post-war Europe.

The JDC worked to provide the basic necessities (food, clothing, and medical assistance) to Jews deported from their homes or trapped in war zones. Acting in conjunction with existing relief organizations in the local areas it served, the JDC was successful in funneling aid monies to needy Jews wherever they could be found. By the end of World War I, the JDC, working through Jewish agencies in the Netherlands, Germany, Russia, and Austria, had reached out to thousands of European Jews. In Palestine, the JDC granted loans, extended cash relief to scholars and rabbis, aided religious institutions, distributed food to school children, and addressed critical medical and sanitation problems.

Following the end of the war, the JDC increased its demands on the American Jewish community in order to assist the displaced Jews of Europe in rebuilding their communities. Working with American aid agencies such as the YMCA, the American Relief Administration, and the American Red Cross, the JDC also expanded the scope of its activities, sending abroad its own field workers and experts to work with Jews in local communities. By 1939, when the JDC was called upon to intercede on behalf of the victims of Nazism, its activities fell into three main categories: direct action by its American emissaries in local activity; the action of local JDC groups to aid and rescue, and intervene in relevant political matters; and the funding of local relief activities.

The JDC efforts reached a large number of Jews, providing critical resources to a vast and desperate population throughout Europe and Asia. Following the end of the war, the JDC (in conjunction with a host of other relief agencies) continued to supply funds for the relief of Displaced Persons and helped to further immigration to Palestine. Following the establishment of the State of Israel in 1948, the JDC, in partnership with the Israeli government, airlifted nearly 50,000 Yemenite Jews from Aden to Israel in "Operation Magic Carpet." In 1950, Iraqi and Kurdish Jews were airlifted in "Operation Ezra." By 1951, over 450,000 Jews had been brought to Israel with the help of the JDC, including 270,000 from Europe. During the Cold War, the JDC also extended aid to Jews trapped behind the Iron Curtain. The JDC today continues its mission to provide assistance to needy Jews wherever they may be found. Through 1994 the organization has spent over $2 billion in its efforts.

ANTI-DEFAMATION LEAGUE

The Anti-Defamation League (ADL) was established by **B'nai B'rith** in 1913 at the urging of Chicago attorney Sigmund Livingston in response to the rampant anti-Semitism, crude stereotyping, and discrimination against Jews of that time. Its charter stated the League's mission was "to stop, by appeals to reason and conscience, and if necessary, by appeals to law, the defamation of the Jewish people . . . to secure justice and fair treatment to all citizens alike . . . to put an end forever to unjust and unfair discrimination against, and ridicule of, any sect or body of citizens."

Over the course of the twentieth century ADL has played a major role in fighting anti-Semitism, racism, and other forms of bigotry and discrimination in the United States and throughout the world. In its early years, ADL took steps to eradicate negative images of Jews in print and their stereotyping on stage and cinema. It persuaded **Adolph Ochs**, publisher of *The New York Times*, to write to newspaper editors discouraging objectionable references to Jews in the media. ADL got President Wilson to recall a U. S. Army manual portraying Jews as cowards and slackers. In the 1920s, ADL began using the weapon of exposure to warn Americans about the newly re-energized Ku Klux Klan, to denounce automobile pioneer Henry Ford's anti-Semitism, and to influence public opinion against discrimination in employment and higher education.

With the advent of fascism and the increase of anti-Semitism in Europe, ADL expanded its operations and launched a fact-finding operation to monitor and investigate Nazi front organizations in the United States. It also began its continuing relationship with law enforcement agencies at all levels of government that continues today. After World War II, ADL fought for civil rights laws against discrimination in housing, employment, and education; waged a "crack the quota" campaign against anti-Jewish discrimination in university admissions; launched a massive educational campaign using film, radio, billboards, car cards, and (later) television to confront racial and religious bigotry. Exploring new frontiers in social and judicial reform, ADL filed its first *amicus* brief in 1948 and has filed briefs in virtually every church-state and civil rights case ever since.

In the 1950s and 1960s ADL escalated its educational efforts by developing and publishing tools to teach democracy. ADL was an active player in the Civil Rights Movement, advocating for equal rights for African Americans, filing an *amicus* brief in Brown v. Board of Education, and, through its network of regional offices, working with local communities to defuse tensions arising from the implementation of desegregation. The League's major research study with the University of California set the standard for how to document anti-Semitism and prejudice in America. Committed to the security and well-being of the State of Israel, ADL worked to enhance US-Israel relations, oppose the Arab boycott and Arab propaganda, and interpret events in Israel to the American public.

In the 1970s and 1980s ADL was in the forefront of the advocacy movement on behalf of Soviet Jewry. The ADL Annual Audit of anti-Semitic Incidents, first published in 1979, became a model for other minority groups. ADL's award-winning *A World of Difference* anti-bias programs, introduced in 1985, are in schools, colleges, corporations, and communities throughout the United States and Europe.

In recent years the League has put considerable energy into exposing extremists, neo-Nazi skinheads, Holocaust deniers and armed anti-government groups, such as the militias, and fighting hate crimes. ADL's model penalty-enhancement hate crimes statute has been adopted or adapted into law by nearly all states, and its constitutionality upheld by the United States Supreme Court. It has led the struggle against the anti-Semitic and racist pronouncements and activities of Louis Farrakhan and the Nation of Islam.

The Anti-Defamation League continues to be one

For over eighty-five years the Anti-Defamation League has been in the forefront of the fight to "stop the defamation of the Jewish people . . . to secure justice and fair treatment to all citizens alike." Shown here is the long-time National Director of the League, Abraham H. Foxman, with Pope John Paul II. (Courtesy of the Anti-Defamation League.)

of the most powerful and influential voices of Jewish leadership in the United States and abroad, and its opinions and positions are taken seriously by Jews and non-Jews alike. Its leadership and influence have rendered it one of the great success stories in building a Jewish institutional presence in twentieth-century America.

B'NAI B'RITH

B'nai B'rith (Sons of the Covenant) is the oldest and most influential Jewish fraternal organization in the United States. Founded in 1843 by twelve German Jews living in New York City to provide social services for the then Jewish American population of 15,000, B'nai B'rith has grown to become the single largest Jewish institution in the world, with a membership that has reached half a million.

Modeled on the Freemasons, B'nai B'rith evolved

out of a network of similar charitable and benevolent associations created specifically to serve the German Jewish community. Of the eleven lodges that were established by 1851, nine conducted their transactions entirely in German. German Jews viewed B'nai B'rith as an organization that could serve as a unifying presence at a time of serious divisions in American Judaism between religious traditionalists and reformers. The nineteenth-century B'nai B'rith provided programs and services for German Jews within an inclusive framework, and the organization helped promote solidarity by creating hospitals, orphanages, homes for the elderly, and by sponsoring cultural events through its social clubs. The association assisted the process by which German Jews became integrated into American society while at the same time ameliorated the forces of assimilation through its unique fusing of Jewish symbolism and transplanted German values.

B'nai B'rith began its rapid growth as a massive and well-endowed international Jewish organization in the early twentieth century, creating new chapters and developing a more formalized lodge system of governance. The organization broadened its scope in 1913 to include the fight against anti-Semitism and discrimination with the establishment of the **Anti-Defamation League**. In 1923 it began to focus attention on Jewish youth with the establishment of the **Hillel** Foundation, which was dedicated to providing Jewish college students with an alternative to the fraternity and sorority system. Chapters provided students with a religious, moral, and social outlet where they could both learn the principles of Judaism and develop themselves as individuals. The first Hillel was established in 1923 by Rabbi Ben Frankel at the University of Illinois. There are now 400 local chapters on campuses in thirty-one countries. In 1925 the B'nai B'rith Youth Organization for teenagers was created to serve the same needs among this younger group.

B'nai B'rith Women (BBW) created their first permanent chapter in 1909 in San Francisco, with the aim of "... promote[ing] sociability among B'nai B'rith lodge members and their families," but the organization's auxiliaries soon proved to have far broader goals.

Before the onset of World War I, over a dozen women's auxiliaries had been created from New Jersey to California. The BBW auxiliaries served as an important part of the Progressive-era movement by American women to enter the public sphere through the creation of their own voluntary social and charitable associations. Jewish women paralleled the work of their Christian sisters by developing their own groups, which developed cultural activities and promoted philanthropy and community service projects. In 1927 the BBW created B'nai B'rith Girls and then B'nai B'rith Young Women, with long-time BBW youth activist Miriam Albert serving as its first national president.

By 1935 BBW membership increased to 12,000 women in 103 auxiliaries. By the beginning of World War II these numbers had nearly tripled as B'nai B'rith Women took on an increasing role in exercising political influence through voluntary organizations. By the end of 1944 BBW had over 100,000 members who raised over $1 million plus food, clothing, and equipment to assist the fledgling State of Israel in 1948.

B'nai B'rith International continued its massive expansion after World War II as burgeoning Jewish communities such as Miami Beach and Los Angeles established new lodges and new organizational chapters. Philip Klutznick became the international president during this time and the organization continued to take on new charitable concerns throughout the United States and the world. Klutznick also presided over the Conference of Presidents of Major American Jewish Organizations—created to express American Jewry's united support for the State of Israel. Even though the B'nai B'rith began the twentieth century with no formal connection to the American Zionist movement, its benevolent activities increasingly included fundraising for material aid projects to Israel, including the B'nai B'rith Women Children's Home in Jerusalem. In addition, the Israel Commission, which organizes tours and volunteer programs in the region, became a major department within the B'nai B'rith International.

In the 1960s B'nai B'rith took an active role in the War on Poverty's fight against illiteracy and in anti-poverty programs and B'nai B'rith Women campaigned for issues such as free choice in abortion, equal social security benefits for women, assistance for displaced homemakers, women and infant's health care, and programs to meet the needs of career women and older women.

After several years of internal and sometimes acrimonious debate, B'nai B'rith Women and B'nai B'rith International reached an agreement whereby B'nai B'rith Women would be a completely independent, self-governing organization, affiliated with B'nai B'rith International. (In 1995 BBW changed its name to Jewish Women International.)

Today B'nai B'rith retains its position as the largest international institution in the Jewish world, with affiliates in fifty-five countries. It ". . . offers programs designed to ensure the preservation of Jewry and Judaism—Jewish education, community volunteer service, expansion of human rights, assistance to Israel, housing for the elderly, leadership training, [and fights for the] rights of Jews in all countries to study their heritage." Unquestionably, the creation and evolution of this small fraternal order to its current level of prestige and stature represents one of the great success stories in American Jewish history.

BELKIN, SAMUEL (1911–1976)

Rabbi, educator

Samuel Belkin was both a renowned intellectual and Talmudic scholar and a visionary leader of Yeshiva College for over thirty years (the institution became **Yeshiva University** under his leadership). Born in Poland in 1911, Belkin immigrated to the United States in 1929 and served as Talmud instructor in New Haven, Connecticut, before joining the faculty of Yeshiva in 1936. There he taught Talmud and established himself as an authority on ancient Greek literature with the publication of *Philo and Oral Law* (1940). With the death of **Bernard Revel**, Belkin was appointed the college's new president in 1943.

Belkin's tenure as Yeshiva's president came at a time when **Conservative Judaism** began making sig-

nificant inroads into a new generation that viewed Orthodoxy as increasingly irrelevant to the contemporary age. He fought to advance modern Orthodoxy by promoting an anti-assimilationist ideology and by training a cadre of scholars who could work in a variety of Jewish community-based institutions and bring religious values to non-Orthodox Jews. To this end, he initiated a formal Jewish studies program in 1956 that provided students lacking formal background in Jewish learning to attend Yeshiva College and study subjects connected to Judaism without being required to complete the full Yeshiva program.

A believer in the positive role of women in Orthodox Jewish life, Belkin established **Stern College**, the undergraduate women's school of the university. He also established a medical school that would later become Albert Einstein School of Medicine, which gave Jewish students an opportunity to take part in a medical program that would also allow them to maintain their Orthodox religious commitment.

One year after resigning from the presidency of Yeshiva, Belkin died in 1976.

CANTORS

In contemporary Judaism, the cantor (*hazzan*) is the religious official who conducts the liturgical portion of the service, sings or chants the prayers, and leads the congregation in the songs associated with holidays and festival worship. Historically, the position of the cantor has varied among Jewish traditions. In Ashkenazic synagogues, cantors usually received training for their musical talents and understanding of the liturgy with a special focus, especially in the Eastern European tradition, on vocal ability. By contrast, cantors in the Sephardic tradition followed traditional charts and melodies and vocal prowess was always a lower priority. In recent years, Conservative and Reform congregations have tended to de-emphasize the role of the cantor and to simplify cantorial music in the synagogue. At the same time, cantors remain key participants in Jewish synagogue life and culture.

Cantors originally served as congregational functionaries and were responsible for supervising children's studies and prayer meetings. In talmudic times, cantorial duties included only occasional leading of the prayer service. Several subsequent changes including a desire to add beauty and formality to the service, a decline in the general public's knowledge of Hebrew, and the addition of the liturgical poems (*piyyutim*) that benefited from musical accompaniment led to an upgrading of the cantor's position as an institutional leader within the congregation. Even with formalization of the post and the increasing desire for vocal ability, rabbinic requirements still favored someone with a weak voice who understood the prayers over one who had a strong voice but lacked a solid liturgical foundation.

Because the first American Jewish communities did not have rabbis, cantors often took on leadership roles in congregations. The Spanish-Portuguese Synagogue in New York began with only its *hazzan* to represent it to the general community. In the late eighteenth century, Isaac Touro became the cantor of the Jeshuat Israel Congregation of Newport, Rhode Island, where he conducted all services, read from the Torah Scroll, and supervised the education of Jewish youth. **Gershom Mendes Seixas** (1746–1816), the cantor at Congregation Shearith Israel in New York City, preached in the vernacular on a number of public occasions in New York and pioneered Jewish participation in special state and city celebrations. By the early nineteenth century, the status of cantor had been elevated to the pastoral equivalent of a minister and *hazzanim* had earned the title of "Reverend." Increasingly, many congregations offered their cantors long-term contracts, and some went so far as to offer them pensions in the event of disability.

With the increase in immigration of Ashkenazi German Jews in the mid-nineteenth century, the situation changed dramatically. Most of the new religious leaders believed that a rabbi was superior to the *hazzan* and only those ordained by the rabbinate should be permitted to lead services or to decide matters of Jewish laws. This dispute over the roles of the rabbi and the cantor raged fiercely for a number of years. Overall, the status of the cantor declined as the Jewish population became larger and more institutionalized.

The German-Jewish leadership, anxious to modernize the practice of Judaism, sought to maintain clear hierarchies between the rabbinate and the rest of the congregation.

The massive influx of immigrants from Eastern Europe in the last two decades of the nineteenth century brought the cantor back to the center of American Jewish worship. The era became known as the "Golden Age of *Hazzans*" because of the emergence of several well-known cantors. For these new immigrants, the *hazzan* retained a central position as the highest official in charge of the services. For many of them, the status and position of a synagogue and its economic solvency depended on the vocal talents of the *hazzan*. The cantorial tradition most familiar to Americans derives from the East European tradition of giving prominence to the solo voice, vocal improvisation, singable melodies, and relatively simple arrangements. Because East European Jewry had its roots in a ghettoized religious community, the cantor emerged as the community's leading musical personality as well as a synagogue leader. The most popular cantors often combined religious practice in several villages with concerts for the general public—a tradition that continued in the United States.

American congregations began to compete with each together for the services of "star" *hazzanim* and new immigrants flocked to cantorial concerts, which provided them with a connection to *shtetl* culture and the old world they had left behind. Well-known cantors of this era such as Gershon Sirota, Mordecai Herschman, and Zavel Kwartin gained considerable recognition. The "King of the Cantors" during this period was **Yossele Rosenblatt** (1882–1933). Often called "The Jewish Caruso," Rosenblatt made over 120 recordings.

By World War I cantorial music, in decline in Europe, had re-emerged in America. An increasing number of *hazzanim* immigrated to the United States and many congregations employed them on a full-time basis. In addition, guest cantors were also hired for *shabbat* services or concerts in densely populated Jewish neighborhoods such as the New York City's Lower East Side. Between the two world wars, cantors such as the Koussevitzky brothers, Berle Chagy, Leib Glanz, and Pierre Pinchik drew large audiences to their concerts. In addition, the new amalgam of the cantor-opera singer became even more popular, led by such luminaries as **Richard Tucker** and **Jan Peerce**. To Eastern European Jews, the cantor attained extraordinary importance.

The importance of cantors in the early part of the twentieth century was also partly economic. Large synagogues often carried substantial mortgages, and popular cantors could attract large audiences for special fee-for-admission concerts on holidays and special occasions. Congregations considered cantors' salaries, unlike those of rabbis, to be profitable investments.

The star *hazzan* began to decline by the 1930s as did the overall role of the cantor in American Jewish life. After World War II, the rise in the economic level of the Jewish community meant that the idea of bringing in a well-known cantor to support a congregation diminished in importance. Affluence also generally resulted in the elevation of the importance of the rabbi above that of the cantor. In the 1940s and 1950s, the challenge that confronted American Jewry equally confronted the *hazzan*—how to make the role and image relevant to modern Jewish life.

To this end, Jewish leaders created cantorial schools designed to invigorate the tradition of the *hazzan*. **Yeshiva University** initiated a music education program and a musical department in 1946, which included activities for prospective cantors, teachers, and group leaders. In 1951, the program began a Cantorial Workshop, which by 1954 had developed into the Cantorial Training Institute. At the same time, the Reform **Hebrew Union College** developed the School of Sacred Music and the Conservative **Jewish Theological Seminary** established the College of Jewish Music. The aim of these programs was to provide intensive training for cantors and, along with three professional cantorial membership groups, these new institutional supports pumped new energy and brought new blood into the profession.

Until the 1970s the cantorate was an exclusively male domain. Following the ordination of **Sally Priesand** in 1972 as the first female rabbi in the United States, the **Reform Movement** of Judaism began to accept female music students for formal cantorial studies. In 1975, Barbara Ostfeld-Horowitz was ordained by Hebrew Union College as the first female cantor, receiving immediate pulpit placement in addition to formal induction into the American Conference of Cantors. By 1995, ninety-four other women cantors had graduated from HUC. In 1984, the Jewish Theological Seminary admitted its first two women, Erica Lipsitz and Marla Rosenfeld Barugel, for ordination as *hazzans* in the Conservative branch of Judaism.

Until recently the Conservative professional organization, the Cantors Assembly of America, has refused to grant admission to female cantorial graduates, reflecting the unwillingness of many of its members to accept women functioning in cantorial pulpits. The Orthodox cantorial training at Yeshiva University continues to be closed to women. The Women's Cantor Network, founded by Cantor Deborah Katchko-Zimmerman in 1981, began with twelve members and had grown to nearly a hundred by 1996.

Although the era of the star *hazzan* has largely vanished, there are still congregations that feature cantors in *shabbat* and in concert and people who come out on a regular basis to hear them. For the most part, the cantor has a limited but important role and continues to serve an integral role in the Jewish community. Most cantors participate in a variety of educational and musical programs of the congregation and are especially involved in reaching out to Jewish youth and engaging them in the life of the synagogue. They also retain a vital role in co-leading High Holy Day services, especially Yom Kippur. The cantorate has been an important institution in American Jewish life and, despite various social changes, it continues to have a central role in the modern congregation.

CONSERVATIVE JUDAISM

Conservative Judaism is the largest of the four major religious classifications of Jews and the branch that perceives itself as most rooted in the philosophy of the Talmudic rabbis. Tracing its origins back to nineteenth-century Europe and the "positive-historical" school of Zachariah Frankel, Conservative Judaism supported the Westernization of Jews while at the same time affirming the value and importance of maintaining Jewish traditions in the modern world. Initially a relatively small presence in the United States compared to the **Reform Movement**, Conservative Judaism became the fastest growing Jewish religious philosophy in the mid-twentieth century. In the contemporary era, its leaders have taken on a new assertiveness and openness in formulating a theological vision and have become more prominent in executive positions within Jewish communal agencies. Jewish feminism has also had a strong influence on creating an egalitarian movement within established Conservatism.

As a religious philosophy, Conservative ideology views Judaism as an amalgam of religion and ethnic nationhood evolving from biblical times to the present that embraces all human conduct and governs all human relationships and the relationship between an individual and God. The Conservative Movement differs from its Reform counterpart in its belief that changes in the practice of traditional Judaism can only be made within Jewish law and that ritual must be an important component of Jewish worship. In contrast to **Orthodoxy**, however, Conservatism maintains that the content of Jewish law must evolve to meet modern circumstances and that Jewish law is flexible enough to meet the needs of modern life. In addition, Conservative Judaism has been committed to pluralism and change within its ranks.

The groundwork was laid for the Conservative Movement in the United States with the establishment of the **Jewish Theological Seminary of America** in New York City. In 1886 a group of rabbinical leaders opposed to what they saw as the increasing radicalization of the Reform Movement as expressed in its 1885 Pittsburgh Platform established the Seminary. The charter clearly stated that the Seminary's purpose was ". . . the preservation in America of the knowledge and practice of historical Judaism." The Seminary began the slow process of building a movement that offered a viable alternative to both the Orthodox and Reform Movements in the United States.

The traditionalists organized themselves around the principle of ". . . observing the law as well as studying it." The academic grounding of the Conservative Judaism under the umbrella of the Seminary continued throughout the century. For **Solomon Schechter**, the president of the Seminary from 1902 to 1915, the intellectual basis for the Conservative Movement came from the scholarly, historical understanding of Judaism as an organic entity capable of absorbing modern knowledge without radically altering its fundamental nature. By inviting outstanding Conservative scholars from a variety of countries to come to the Seminary, Schechter turned the institution into one of the leading centers of Jewish scholarship in the Western world.

Concerned about creating institutions that would address the needs of a rapidly growing Jewish immigrant community, Schechter established the United Synagogue of America in 1913 as a lay organization to help bring the Seminary into a larger national coalition. The Rabbinical Assembly was established several years afterward to complete the institutional triad that became the public face of the Conservative Movement in America. Schechter's great hope was that what he called "historical Judaism" would eventually gain the allegiance of major segments of observant Jewry, including the moderate wing of the Orthodox movement. Although this vision never took shape, it created a range and diversity of opinion within Conservative Judaism that rendered it less rigidly ideological than other groups. In spite of Schechter's towering presence and leadership, the Conservative Movement remained relatively small in the first two decades of the twentieth century.

After World War I Conservative Judaism began to gain strength as many of its leaders, most notably Israel Friedlander, **Louis Finkelstein**, and **Mordecai Kaplan**, took up the mantle of spiritual Zionism as closely connected to their desire to reframe Jewish traditionalism in a modern context. For these Conservative stalwarts, fulfilling Zionism worked in tandem with stimulating a religious revival anchored in historic Judaism. As children of immigrants came of age, many of them found in the Conservative Movement the perfect synthesis of their new American identity with the traditional Judaism of their childhood. By looking both forward and back, Conservative Judaism hit on the right formula for a transitional generation that saw itself becoming modern American citizens while at the same time feeling anxiety and fear at the prospect of total assimilation. What mattered to most of these new adherents to the movement was less its intellectual base than its authenticity, its warmth, and its aesthetic improvements and moderate approach to religious practice, which allowed them to feel a sense of belonging in a Conservative synagogue regardless of the degree of their personal observance.

Finkelstein became president of the Seminary in 1940 and presided over the greatest period of growth in American Conservative Judaism in the post-World War II era. An innovative administrator as well as a prolific scholar, he strengthened the institution's influence on the Jewish community at large and created a center where scholars and clergy from a variety of faiths examined moral and social issues that had special resonance with the destruction of European Jewry in the Holocaust. He also initiated pioneering efforts to improve lines of communication among the leadership of the Jewish, Roman Catholic, Protestant, and other religious communities and among academicians in the sciences and the humanities.

Although he remained a strong supporter and leader in the American Zionist movement in the years immediately preceding the establishment of Israel, Finkelstein and many members of the Conservative rabbinate began to express fears that the struggle for statehood would bring war and destruction to the region. They also felt that the secularized state and the single-minded pursuit of political sovereignty would compromise the moral and spiritual values that they held as vital to Judaism.

By the 1950s there was an international dimension to the movement, with Conservative rabbis serving congregations on two continents. In the early 1960s, Rabbi Marshall Meyer, a Seminary graduate, established a rabbinical school in Argentina that provided a strong foundation to the movement's South American branch. Conservative Judaism as an institution also created new educational and cultural initiatives including a camping organization, the Eternal Light and Commitment radio and television series, the Solomon Schechter Day Schools, and New York's Jewish Museum.

As the Conservative Movement grew, it began to encompass a range of ideological trends and points of view, ranging from an almost neo-orthodoxy to radical views that were close to Reform. The Rabbinical Assembly's Committee on Jewish Law continued to debate the interpretation of Jewish law but ultimately left considerable autonomy to individual congregations. Gerson Cohen succeeded Finkelstein as president of JTS and under his administration the more liberal elements within the movement gained strength and far-reaching changes were introduced.

Among the most important of these changes concerned the role of women. As early as 1955, women had gained the right within Conservatism to be called for an *aliyah* (going up) to the Torah. But the late 1960s and 1970s witnessed the beginnings of a dynamic feminist movement (see **Jewish Feminism**). In 1972, the members of Ezrat Nashim, a women's organization that had formed within the Conservative Movement the previous year, attacked the sexism in *halakah* (Jewish law) during the annual convention of the Rabbinical Assembly. A year later, the Committee on Jewish Law and Standards (CJLS) decided to count women in the prayer quorum (*minyan*), and shortly afterward the organization adopted a series of proposals that equalized the roles of men and woman in all areas of Jewish ritual. As a result of these changes, a Conservative rabbi could allow a woman to serve as a prayer leader, count in the quorum for Grace, and function as a witness in religious ceremonies. The National Women's League played a vital role in this movement through its organizing of congregational sisterhoods that formed a core component of the educational mission of the Conservative synagogue.

Conservative synagogues throughout the United States spent the remainder of the next decade grappling with further ritual change involving gender roles. By 1983, after a decade-long fight, women won the right to study for the rabbinate and, in 1985, the

Jewish Theological Seminary ordained its first female rabbi, **Amy Eilberg**. Unlike the earlier changes, which were adopted relatively smoothly, this issue threatened to split the movement. It led to the mobilization of a minority right-wing group of rabbis and layman that became established as the Union for Traditional Conservative Judaism. (It subsequently dropped the "conservative" from its name to appeal to modern Orthodox Jews.) In 1987, Chancellor **Ismar Schorsch** announced that the Seminary would confer the diploma of cantors on two women, Marla Barugel and Erica Lipitz, although it took three more years for the Cantors Assembly to admit women.

By 1985 the Rabbinical Assembly had 1,200 members, three times as many as it had thirty years earlier. In an effort to decentralize the synagogues, subgroups of Jews began practicing informal religious fellowship (*havurah*) as an alternative to formal institutional affiliation. Conservative leadership also began issuing new daily, Sabbath, and festival prayer books, and a *Haggadah*, and 830 congregations (with a total membership of more than a million) became affiliated with the United Synagogue of America. To complement the Rabbinical Assembly, Conservative Judaism has established new professional organizations including the Cantors Assembly, the Jewish Educators Assembly, the Jewish Youth Directors Association, and the National Association of Synagogue Administrators.

Since the mid-1980s the movement has lost members, with both Orthodox and Reform congregations gaining former Conservative adherents. The percentage of Conservative Jews in the organized synagogue community declined from forty-two percent in 1970 to forty percent in 1990. Modern Conservatism has devoted considerable energy and achieved considerable success in creating new creative expressions to attract the younger generation. Conservative synagogues and organizations have also made significant efforts in recent years to narrow the gap between the Jewish practices of the rabbinate and those of the laity. United Synagogue Youth instituted a Shabbat Enhancement Program directed toward teenagers, and many synagogues have instituted family education programs to teach young families how to observe the Sabbath and other Jewish festivals. Women have continued to make inroads within the Conservative Movement with Debra Newman Kamin becoming the first woman to serve as senior rabbi of a major Conservative congregation—Am Yisrael Conservative Congregation of the North Shore in Northfield, Illinois. Avis D. Miller is Associate Rabbi at Adas Israel Congregation in Washington, D.C., the largest and oldest Conservative congregation in the Washington metropolitan area.

A movement that began as the twentieth century was opening, Conservative Judaism has sought to reconcile change and tradition for over 100 years. This atmosphere of open inquiry combined with a commitment to Jewish law and community insure that it will be a central part of American Jewish life in the twenty-first century.

EDUCATION IN JUDAISM

In the United States education in the traditions of Judaism has had a complex history, which has been dominated by numerous shifts in its orientation and goals. From the colonial period when the small Sephardic community established its first private school, to the congregational schools established by the German-Jewish community in the mid-nineteenth century, to the community-based Talmud Torah schools that served the Eastern European immigrants of the early twentieth century, Jewish education has attempted to parallel and complement the American educational system and to create lasting institutions that preserve and sustain Jewish life as a vital force for the next generation.

Jewish education has been used both for Americanization and for preserving European Jewish culture and tradition. It has been the source of controversy and debate over the relationship between religious and secular education. During the past half century, the movement to create Jewish day schools has grown, fueled largely by the Orthodox preference for educating their children in programs shielded from Gentile life, but also by the **Conservative Movement**'s Solomon Schecter Day Schools, and even by new Reform Jewish institutions.

The earliest Sephardic Jewish settlers in North America either educated their children privately in their own homes or paid for them to be taught in private schools. In the colonial era and throughout the early nineteenth century, education was not considered to be a Jewish communal responsibility. The first official school under Jewish auspices was established at Shearith Israel (the Spanish and Portuguese Synagogue) in 1731 in New York City. Focusing on Hebrew studies, the school (although attached to the synagogue) operated as a separate entity with its own fees. In 1755, Shearith Israel expanded to include secular subjects, such as English composition. After closing during the Revolutionary War, the school reopened and functioned as a day school until 1821, receiving state funds as part of New York's newly created common school system that enabled poor Jewish children to receive an education. Overall, few eighteenth-century congregations established lasting institutions. There was a general belief that Jewish education was part time and secondary. Secular and religious studies were seen as separate activities.

In the mid-nineteenth century, the new German Jewish immigrants, dissatisfied with the content and quality of Jewish studies, began to establish congregational day schools that combined secular and religious education. B'nai Jeshurun, New York City's first Ashkenazi synagogue, became the first to organize a day school in 1842. A few years later, **Issac Mayer Wise** founded the Talmud Yeladim in Cincinnati and, in 1851, the Hebrew Educational Society was established in Philadelphia. Despite tremendous initial enthusiasm, these schools did not last beyond the Civil War era. By the 1870s, the Jewish congregation day school movement had collapsed in disarray for a variety of reasons, including the lack of national coordination and the transient nature of the Jewish population. Also, state education systems began to satisfy the needs of many Jewish parents.

By the late nineteenth century a growing number of German Jews began to believe that Jewish day schools would create an unhealthy division between Jewish and gentile communities at a time when Central European immigrants and their children were themselves becoming part of the American mainstream. American culture and integrated schooling were embraced as a tool of socialization.

At the same time as Jews became more integrated into general, public education, synagogues began developing supplementary Jewish schooling for religious instruction. **Rebecca Gratz** established the first Sunday school in Philadelphia, and other synagogues began full-day Sabbath and afternoon programs. The influence of **Reform Judaism**, focusing on the universalism rather than the particularism of Judaism, meant that many of these synagogue programs eschewed Hebrew and the study of classical texts in favor of monotheism and English translations of the Bible. The first Hebrew free schools also emerged, in the post-Civil War era, as a means of providing Jewish education for the children of less affluent parents and to counteract the influence of the Christian mission schools in Jewish neighborhoods.

The late nineteenth and early twentieth century witnessed the arrival of hundreds of thousands of Eastern European immigrants who felt little or no connection to most of the Jewish education options available. They generally rejected the free schools and the universalism of the Reform supplementary programs, with some in New York City gravitating instead to the community-based Talmud Torah schools, which used their native Yiddish as the language of instruction and emphasized traditional learning of Torah and Talmud. Not surprisingly, the established German Jewish community viewed the Talmud Torah schools negatively because of their belief that sustaining the East European shtetl traditions and religious practices represented a step backward from becoming full-fledged and culturally refined Americans.

Although settled "American Jews" created educational institutions such as the Educational Alliance to transform immigrants and clashed with the newcomers over their desire to preserve old world ways, it did not take long for East European Jewish immigrants to accept the public schools for the education of their sons and daughters. The community cohesion necessary to create Jewish day schools that both offered religious studies and also satisfied new state education requirements proved daunting. Despite the reverence for tradition on the part of new immigrant families, most parents wanted their children to learn the language and values of their new home. Although Eastern European Jewish men created *heders* (religious elementary schools) to replicate educational institutions similar to those in the old country, American-influenced sons did not necessarily share the enthusiasm of their fathers for the *heder rav* (leader) and the world he represented. By the beginning of World War I only one-quarter of school-aged children received any Jewish education in New York City.

In significant decline, Jewish education required an infusion of modernization and new blood, and it came in the person of Samson Benderly. Benderly became professionally committed to Jewish education while studying medicine in Baltimore. In the second decade of the twentieth century he came to New York to develop and lead the new Bureau of Jewish Education, which had been established as part of **Judah Magnes**'s Kehillah of New York. The Kehillah itself had been formed to bring New York Jewish organizations together to combat problems plaguing its immigrant community. As its main goal, the Bureau sought to unite the city's Jewish population by connecting traditional Jewish forms to contemporary American ideals. Benderly encouraged Jewish educators to view the process of Americanization as compatible with building a viable Jewish culture in the United States. At the same time as **Louis Brandeis** began to frame **Zionism** as fundamentally aligned with American values, the founders of modern Jewish education used much of the same rhetoric to promote Jewish education as blending the best of American and traditional Jewish thought and practice.

Benderly and others such as **Mordecai Kaplan** began to identify and recruit college graduates to the field and to promote Jewish education as transformative and vital to living and participating in a bicultural world. The list of notable educators that he brought into the field include Alexander Dushkin, Isaac Berkson, Emmanuel Gamoran, and Rebecca Aronson Brickner. New Jewish educators attempted to embrace religious instruction and elevate Hebrew into a living language. More importantly, they portrayed Judaism as a modern civilization with a rich tradition that young people needed to learn to become Jewish American citizens. The Bureau of Jewish Education became the institutional arm of the new Jewish education, with Benderly attempting both to raise the relevance and quality of instruction and increase community responsibility.

Although the Bureau sought to build a Jewish "common" school, its limited financial resources shifted its focus to working with New York City's Talmud Torahs to improve and invigorate their curricula. It especially focused on the new "Direct Method" of teaching Hebrew that had succeeded in smaller cities such as Baltimore and Detroit. The Bureau also sought to include teaching materials dealing with modern Jewish history, contemporary Jewish events, and Jewish art and culture.

The Bureau's aim was greatly curtailed by the decline of the New York Kehillah in 1917. But the new proliferation of Jewish educators precipitated the establishment of Bureaus of Jewish Education in a variety of other cities between 1915 and 1938, including Minneapolis, Pittsburgh, Detroit, Buffalo, and Baltimore, and led to the founding of new Hebrew teachers colleges.

Eastern European Jewish tradition tended to favor education for boys far more than for girls, with a focus on **bar mitzvah** preparation and prayer recital taught by private tutors or in the exclusively male *heder* setting. By 1920, the Jewish education of girls became more accepted and the seminaries for training teachers for the Hebrew schools enrolled an increasing number of female students. In addition, in the Yiddish secular schools that developed during the 1920s from socialist and labor Zionist foundations, girls studied equally with boys. Most Jewish private day schools continued to be exclusively for boys. In the 1930s, Shulamith, the first day school for girls, opened with a curriculum virtually identical to that of the day schools for boys.

As Jews increasingly began to move out of densely settled, homogeneous urban neighborhoods, and as the urban-rooted immigrant culture became a synagogue-based American-born culture, the synagogue took on a greater prominence as the center of Jewish life. The community-based Talmud Torahs lost out in favor of a return to the congregational school as the setting for Jewish education. Beginning in the late 1930s and accelerating during and especially after World War II, the development of new Jewish congregational schools led to a focus primarily on religious rather than cultural education. Congregational schools of different Jewish denominations were able to develop in new urban and especially suburban settings, but the Yiddish schools and the more radical and nationalist educational programs fared less well because of increasing economic mobility and the acculturation of the children of immigrants. With the establishment of the State of Israel, the nationalist message became institutionalized within all but the most traditional Orthodox Jewish congregational schools.

In the contemporary era, congregational schools providing supplementary education continue to be important in Jewish life. Enrollment in Jewish education peaked in the mid-1960s at 550,000; the number decreased slowly since then and is now approximately 350,000. Enrollments are highest for children ages ten to thirteen as they prepare for **bar** and **bat mitzvahs**. In recent years the relatively small number of secondary school age youth attending Congregational programs has increased.

One of the most astounding changes in modern Jewish education has been the growth of private Jewish day schools, a phenomenon that harkens back to the colonial era and the mid-nineteenth century. This movement evolved because of the immigration of ultra-Orthodox Hasidic refugees arriving from Europe before and after World War II. With no desire to integrate themselves into the American mainstream or to separate general from religious instruction, these Hasidim developed separate schools for boys and girls to prepare them to become observant, ultra-Orthodox Jews.

In recent years other Orthodox groups developed days schools, generally more focused on secular education than the Hasidim, with **Yeshiva University** and

its day schools for boys and girls serving as important models. More surprising perhaps has been the development by the Conservative Movement of its own Solomon Schecter Day Schools, which have been established in more than sixty communities. The Reform Movement has begun to develop day schools, although they represent only two percent of the overall total of these programs. The proliferation of these schools can be traced to the belief among many Jewish families born and educated in America that it is no longer necessary to send their children to public school to acculturate them as Americans. These parents want a Jewish educational system for their children because they want to imbue them with Jewish thought and values.

Jewish education in the United States continues to evolve based on the changing needs of its different population groups and the realities of the political and economic climate of the country. The growing number of college undergraduate and graduate students enrolling in Jewish studies classes and majoring in the field points to a strong hunger on the part of many young adults to learn Jewish history, religion, and culture. Formal education in Judaism is thriving in America as it never has before.

EILBERG, AMY (1954–)

Rabbi

In 1985, Amy Eilberg became the first female rabbi ordained by the **Conservative Movement**. Eilberg's ordination was the culmination of a decade of struggle among Conservative Jewish leaders and the faculty of the **Jewish Theological Seminary** that resulted in admittance of women to the rabbinical school only two years earlier. She has been hailed as a pioneer for her dedication to fulfilling her dream of becoming a rabbi and for helping to elevate a new generation of women to leadership positions in Conservative Judaism. Between 1985 and 1996, the Jewish Theological Seminary had ordained fifty-one women, thanks in large part to Eilberg's perseverance.

Born in Philadelphia in 1954 and raised in a moder-

Is Hebrew School Part of an Astronaut's Education?

"Judy was the best student I have ever had in Hebrew School," says Rabbi Philip Salzman (Temple Beth El, Akron, Ohio) of Judith Resnick, the first Jewish astronaut. She also excelled in secular school, as well, scoring a perfect 800 on her math SAT tests. Her bat mitzvah was in 1962, twenty-two years before her flight in space on the shuttle *Discovery*.

ately observant Jewish family, Eilberg earned a M.S.W. at Smith College in the early 1980s before entering the rabbinical program at the Jewish Theological Seminary in 1984. Since her ordination she has served as a Jewish chaplain at the Methodist Hospital of Indiana, a rabbi of Har Zion congregation in Penn Valley, Pennsylvania, and as director of Yad L'Chaim, the Jewish Hospice Care Program in Philadelphia.

Eilberg has frequently asserted that her spirituality is rooted in her commitment to feminist and human empowerment.

EISENSTEIN, IRA (1906–)

Rabbi, Reconstructionist leader

Reconstructionist leader Ira Eisenstein was born in New York City in 1906. In 1931, at the age of twenty-five, he headed the Society for the Advancement of Judaism, the synagogue that was a forerunner of the Reconstructionist movement. A son-in-law of Reconstructionist founder **Mordecai Kaplan**, he was ordained a rabbi at the **Jewish Theological Seminary** in 1939. (His wife was Judith Kaplan, a renowned Jewish musicologist, who made history when she had the first **bat mitzvah** in the United States.) He remained at the Society until 1954. That year, he became rabbi of the Anshe Emet synagogue in Chicago. He returned to New York in 1959 to became president of the Reconstructionist Foundation and editor of the magazine *Reconstructionist*. In 1968, the Reconstructionist Rabbinical College was founded in Wyncote, Pennsylvania, and Eisenstein was appointed its first president.

Eisenstein did much to spread the views of his mentor Kaplan. His books include *Creative Judaism* (1936), *What We Mean by Religion* (1938), and *Judaism under Freedom* (1956). He also coedited a number of Reconstructionist prayer books.

FEINSTEIN, MOSHE (1895–1986)

Rabbi

Moshe Feinstein gained a reputation as one of the leading Talmudic scholars and *halakhic* authorities in America after World War II. Born in Minsk in 1895, Feinstein came from a family of prominent Jewish theologians and intellectuals. He was ordained in Russia at the age of twenty-one and served as leader of a small congregation in Luban until he immigrated to the United States in 1936.

As director of Mesivtia Tiferet Jerusalem yeshiva in New York for almost five decades, Feinstein served as mentor to thousands of students who came in droves to study under his supervision and to seek rabbinical ordination under his instruction. By the 1950s, he established himself as a leader in applying *halakha* to important contemporary opinions dealing with science, technology, and medicine. He wrote extensively on these themes in addition to publishing a series of Talmudic commentaries. Feinstein was known for the range of his knowledge and for his ability and willingness to embrace controversial matters in modern Judaism in a thoughtful, learned manner. Orthodox Jewish organizations sought his opinion on a variety of concerns related to Jewish communal life, and he served as chairman of Agudath Israel of America and the president of the Union of American Orthodox Rabbis of the United States and Canada.

GOLDSTEIN, HERBERT (1890–1970)

Rabbi

Herbert Goldstein was one of the first graduates of the **Jewish Theological Seminary** and one of the few American-born and educated Orthodox rabbis of the

Education in the Hebrew language can begin at a young age. This photograph from the 1950s is of a class at Temple Emanuel (in Massachusetts). (Courtesy of American Jewish Historical Society, Waltham, Massachusetts and New York, New York)

early twentieth century. Despite his roots in Orthodoxy, Goldstein was also a colleague of **Mordecai Kaplan**'s and like Kaplan he believed that an English-speaking, university-trained rabbinate was necessary if Orthodoxy was to reach a new generation of American Jews—the children of the Eastern European immigrants.

Goldstein became best known for his championing of the synagogue as a full-service Jewish center. As rabbi of the Institutional Synagogue on Manhattan's upper west side, he became known as a "Jewish Billy Sunday" because of his forceful preaching style

and for bringing formerly non-observant people to Judaism through a variety of community-based initiatives.

For several decades Goldstein served in a variety of leadership roles in the community. He conducted lectures for both the Harlem Young Men's Hebrew Orthodox League, a social and recreational organization, and the Harlem Hebrew League, a group that developed courses in Jewish themes and organized regular modern Orthodox prayer services. He also participated in government projects at the local, state, and federal levels.

Despite his ties with the Jewish Theological Seminary, Goldstein became far more involved with the Rabbi Isaac Elchanan Theological Seminary for many years. He died in 1970 at the age of 79.

GOLDSTEIN, ISRAEL (1896–1986)

Rabbi

Born in 1896, Israel Goldstein is considered the rabbi most responsible for revitalizing the congregation at B'nai Jeshurun, the oldest Conservative synagogue in New York City as well as an indefatigable national Jewish leader in the **Conservative Movement**. Goldstein expanded the scope of the modern synagogue by creating educational programs including weekday Hebrew classes, a high school department, and junior congregation—a concept that was emulated by congregations throughout the country. In 1921, he helped establish the B'nai Jeshurun Community Center.

An ardent Zionist and charismatic orator, Goldstein was president of the Jewish National Fund in the pivotal years from 1934 to 1943. He then served as a leader of the **Zionist Organization of America**, where he helped enlist the support of political and Jewish leaders for the establishment of a Jewish commonwealth in Palestine.

In 1946 he helped develop the National Confederation of General Zionists, an organization that sought to bring together the right and left wings of the Zionist movement; he served as the organization's president until 1961. As world chairman of the Keren Hayesod-United Israel Appeal, Goldstein traveled around the globe to raise funds to support immigration and settlement programs.

Goldstein's accomplishments also include founding the National Conference of Christians and Jews and helping to establish **Brandeis University**. A political liberal, he served as president of the **American Jewish Congress** in the 1950s, where he helped steer the organization to support civil rights and school desegregation and to oppose McCarthyism.

Goldstein retired from B'nai Jeshurun in 1960 and moved to Israel in 1961. He headed the Keren Hayesol-Israel United Appeal until 1971 and died in Jerusalem in 1986.

GRATZ, REBECCA (1781–1869)

Educator, community leader

Noted community leader Rebecca Gratz was born into a wealthy family in Philadelphia on March 4, 1781. Well educated at home and in various women's academies, Gratz became active at an early age in Philadelphia's literary community. She corresponded with such prominent women as British novelist Maria Edgeworth, actress Fanny Kemble, and Jewish British theologian and educator Grace Aguilar.

Gratz showed an early interest in Jewish culture and thought and devoted considerable time and effort to the welfare of the community. In about 1801, she cofounded, with her mother, sister, other Jewish and gentile women, the Female Association for the Relief of Women and Children in Reduced Circumstances. Gratz served as secretary of the organization for many years. She was also involved in the founding of the Philadelphia Orphan Asylum (1815), serving as its secretary for forty years.

Because Christian charities tended to evangelize while providing services, Gratz formed the Female Hebrew Benevolent Society to minister to Jewish women and children. The organization was the first Jewish charity not administered by a synagogue, and it remained active and independent for many years. Gratz also founded the Hebrew Sunday School in Philadelphia—the first of its kind—which gave Jewish women a role in determining Jewish educational curriculum for the first time. In the 1850s, she was instrumental in the founding of the Jewish Foster Home, which later merged with several other institutions to form Philadelphia's Association for Jewish Children.

GREENBERG, IRVING (1933–)

Rabbi, educator

Prominent Orthodox rabbi Irving Greenberg was born in Brooklyn, New York, where he grew up and attended

Brooklyn College. In 1953, he graduated from college and was ordained a rabbi at Beth Joseph Rabbinical Seminary, also in Brooklyn. He then left the borough to attend Harvard University, receiving a doctorate in American history in 1960. In the meantime, he served as **Hillel** director at **Brandeis University** for one year and began a thirteen-year professorship at **Yeshiva University**. He has been rabbi of the Riverdale Jewish Center since 1965.

In 1974, he co-founded, with **Elie Wiesel**, the National Jewish Center for Learning and Leadership (CLAL), to provide Jewish education to the lay leadership of the American Jewish community.

As a writer, Greenberg has attempted to reconcile Orthodox Jewish beliefs and customs with a more modern perspective, and his stands are often controversial. He believes, for example, that the Jewish law can be separated from its custom-bound trappings, especially with regard to the participation of women in Jewish life and ritual. In this he is supported by his wife, Blu, whom he married in 1957. In addition, he has insisted that forms of Jewish spirituality other than Orthodoxy have validity and has even suggested that Christianity is a true religion.

He shocked his Orthodox constituents by declaring that the covenantal relationship between God and his Chosen People ended with the Holocaust and that Jews voluntarily renewed the covenant when they founded the State of Israel. Greenberg's books include *Guide to Shabbat* (1981) and *The Jewish Way* (1985). Since 1985 Greenberg has been working with the CLAL toward Jewish unity.

HASIDISM

The Hasidic movement has been an important component of efforts to establish and promote Orthodox Judaism to the United States. Less a new philosophy of Judaism than a renewed emphasis on specific ideas from the Torah and the Talmud, Hasidism gained a significant number of devoted followers in twentieth-century America through its two largest and most well-known groups—the Satmar and the Lubavitcher Hasidism.

Founded by Israel ben Eliezer (Ba'al Shem Tov), Hasidism began in Poland in the eighteenth century and referred to the ideal of *hasidut* (saintliness): an astute sensitivity to the demands of religious life. From Ba'al Shem's lifetime to the modern era, Hasidism became equated with the notion of the holy man who acts as a spiritual guide to his followers and who prays to God on their behalf. Hasidism at its core is founded on two specific ideas: *Tsaddik*—the channel through which divine grace flows, and *Devekut*—having God in mind at all times.

The literature of the Hasidic movement provides evidence of a tension throughout its history between populism and elitism. Although Hasidism began as a revolt against dry intellectualism and succeeded at bringing prayerful joy and religious enthusiasm to ordinary Jews, the philosophy of its belief system has also been used to proclaim that demands of a saintly life can only be acquired by a select worthy few.

The development of a specific American Hasidic movement began just prior to World War I, when thousands of mostly *Lubavitch* Hasidim arrived from Eastern Europe. Although the majority of these immigrants did not pass along their traditions to their children and grandchildren, the leadership of the sixth Lubavitcher Rebbe, Joseph Schneerson, and his year-long visit to America in 1929, rekindled enthusiasm for Hasidism among Orthodox youth who were attracted by its intense spiritual dimension. As conditions in Europe worsened in the 1930s, new Hasidic leaders and their followers immigrated to the United States in large numbers, making way for the increasing influence of Hasidic Jews in New York City, especially in the post-World War II era when these communities began to flourish.

Hasidic immigrants were divided when it came to the extent to which they chose to adapt their culture to the social mores of modern American life. The Satmar Rebbe **Joel Teitelbaum**, a Hungarian refugee who settled in Williamsburg, Brooklyn, after World War II believed in the importance of re-establishing his community in the exact form as it had existed in Europe, preserving the clothing, the Yiddish language, and the old European manners and customs. Teitelbaum achieved considerable success in creating a Hasidic world that completely rejected American modernism and established its own schools, synagogues, and self-contained neighborhoods. His followers constitute the largest Hasidic group in the United States. Other Hasidic leaders who developed communities modeled after Teitelbaum included Rabbis Solomon Halberstam, Joseph Grunwald, Y. Y. Halberstam, and Jacob Twersky.

At the same time the Satmar Hasidim created strong and insular communities in the United States, Schneerson (who had moved to Brooklyn in 1940) and his Lubavitcher disciples began a campaign to bring Orthodox Judaism to the Jewish masses in the years following World War II. Upon the elder Schneerson's death in 1950, his son-in-law **Menachem Schneerson** became the seventh Lubavitcher Rebbe. He expanded and refined the Hasidic outreach program with the assistance of hundreds of Soviet refugees who joined with him.

The *Baal Teshuvah* (Repentance) Movement gained its greatest influence during the 1960s, when thousands of Jews from non-Orthodox backgrounds adopted Orthodoxy, largely as a result of the efforts of the Lubavitcher Hasidic rabbis whose successes encouraged other Orthodox groups to take on similar outreach work. In the early 1970s, Schneerson's followers began establishing Chabad houses in the United States that operated as synagogues, schools, and drop-in and counseling centers. Although a number of non-Orthodox Jews resented what they considered the heavy-handed tactics of the *Baal Teshuvah* movement, others were attracted to the strong sense of community and religious and scholarly discipline of the Lubavitcher Hasidim. It is estimated that there are 200,000 Lubavitchers worldwide.

Despite these successes, American Orthodoxy became more divided by the late 1960s between Modern Orthodoxy and Yeshiva World Orthodoxy. Hasidic groups, particularly the Satmars, generally aligned themselves with the Yeshiva World or "right wing" Orthodox tendencies. The Satmars opposed any type of secular studies and continued to believe in the retention of the Eastern European as opposed to the American way of life. They also stood resolutely opposed to cooperation with non-Orthodox Jewish religious institutions and believed that women's sole role was in the context of the Jewish family. Satmars opposed the creation of Israel, believing that a Jewish state could only be created with the coming of the Messiah. Teitelbaum even went so far as to refer to the Zionist movement as the devil incarnate and organized his fellow Hungarian refugee anti-Zionist rabbis into a united body, the Central Rabbinical Congress. He expressed his most virulent criticism for the Orthodox and Hasidic groups who supported Israel and developed a weekly Yiddish newspaper that promoted his anti-Israel views.

In contrast, the Lubavitchers, despite maintaining the social conservatism of other Hasidic groups, both actively supported the state of Israel and attempted to influence its policies. Menachem Schneerson, the most influential Hasidic leader in the contemporary era, argued that the Torah and Jewish law precluded Israel from turning over any land to the Arabs.

With the deaths of Teitelbaum and, more recently, Schneerson, the Hasidic movement lost its two most charismatic leaders and has struggled to find new visionaries to carry on the tradition. Although Hasidism has little influence in towns with small Jewish populations, it continues to maintain a small but powerful presence in metropolitan areas, including Baltimore, Los Angeles, Miami Beach and, especially, in New

---

A "Royal" Hasidic Wedding in Brooklyn

At the beginning of September 1998, Chaim Halberstam and Raiza Meisels were married in the Williamsburg section of Brooklyn. It was no ordinary wedding, and they are no ordinary couple. The ceremony united two of the leading international Hasidic dynasties. The groom is the grandson of the Bobover Hasidic dynasty Grand Rabbi, Shlomo Halberstam, and the bride is the granddaughter of the Satmar Grand Rabbi, Moses Teitelbaum. The two grand rabbis are the descendants of the first Hasidic leaders in Europe. *The New York Times* estimated the number of guests at 8,000. Both grandfathers were joyfully present.

York City. The Hasidic traditions and beliefs have and continue to exert a powerful pull for many American Jews.

HESCHEL, ABRAHAM JOSHUA (1907–1972)

Philosopher, religious leader

One of the most prominent religious intellectuals in the twentieth-century American Jewish community, rabbinical scholar and philosopher Abraham Joshua Heschel was born in Poland in 1907 to a family of prestigious Hasidic lineage. After completing traditional yeshiva studies, Heschel earned a doctorate at the University of Berlin. He also studied and taught Talmud at the Hochschule für die Wissenschaft des Judentums.

In 1937 Heschel was named successor to Martin Buber as director of the Jüdisches Lehrhaus at Frankfort am Main but was deported to Poland by the Nazis in October 1938. An invitation to join the faculty of the Reform movement's **Hebrew Union College** in Cincinnati qualified Heschel for one of the scarce entry visas to the United States in 1940. He taught at HUC for five years before joining the faculty of the **Jewish Theological Seminary**, the rabbinical school of **Conservative Judaism**, with which he more closely identified.

A powerful orator and prolific writer, Heschel soon attracted a broad following, both of lay people who attended his public lectures in increasingly large numbers, and of intellectuals who were impressed by his numerous articles and books on Jewish philosophical topics. Two of his best known works, *Man Is Not Alone* (1951) and *God in Search of Man* (1955), emphasized the need for traditional rituals to guide a person's daily life as well as personal discourse with the Divine to achieve heightened spirituality.

An outspoken opponent of American involvement in the Vietnam war, Heschel was prominent in the antiwar group Clergy and Laity Concerned. He was also an active supporter of the African-American civil rights movement, personally participating in marches led by the Reverend Martin Luther King, Jr.

INTERMARRIAGE

Perhaps the most controversial issue in contemporary American Jewish life is the subject of intermarriage—the marriage between a Jew and a gentile. Although some Jews have always married outside the faith, it is only over the last three decades that the percentage has increased dramatically. Accompanying that increase has been the discussion and debate within the Jewish community about the significance of intermarriage. Many Jews, especially religious Jews, have warned that intermarriage poses a threat to the Jewish community and, ultimately, to the existence of Jews as a people; there is also evidence that a number of Jewish-born spouses continue to maintain a Jewish identity. Nevertheless, although both Conservative and Reform rabbis perform conversion ceremonies, only Reform rabbis, as a rule, are willing to perform interfaith weddings.

Because there were only a small number of Jews in America during the eighteenth and early nineteenth centuries and there were many more Jewish men than women among these early settlers, intermarriage was common. Generally, these Jews did not formally convert to Christianity but their children were raised as Christians. Thus, the population of Jews, small to begin with, continued to shrink in the early nineteenth century.

Intermarriage declined with the growth of the American Jewish community, beginning with the German Jewish immigration in the mid-nineteenth century and especially after the Eastern European influx beginning in the 1880s. At the same time, nativism and anti-Semitism increased among Protestant Americans after the Civil War and Jews, who had generally been embraced in mixed unions, were viewed as unacceptable partners by many Christian families. Between 1900 and 1920, only two percent of Jews chose to marry gentiles, and the rate of intermarriage remained relatively stable over the next two decades—at three percent through the 1920s and 1930s.

This percentage increased only slightly in the 1940s and 1950s, but by the 1960s the intermarriage rate spiraled. Diminishing anti-Semitism on the part of the Christian majority led to the belief that Jews were both acceptable and even desirable marriage partners. Greater social mobility by a more American-ized and more affluent Jewish population resulted in increased interaction with gentiles and greater oppor-tunities for intermarriage. The social changes of the era also led many young Jews to view love as more im-portant than religion in choosing a marriage partner. According to first *National Jewish Population Survey* (conducted in 1971), the rate of intermarriages be-tween 1956 and 1960 increased to 17.4 percent and then rose to 31.7 percent between 1960 and 1965.

Although there were those who questioned the ac-curacy of these figures, many Jewish community lead-ers voiced alarm and viewed this as a crisis, especially given the destruction of one-third of world Jewry dur-ing the Holocaust. These individuals cited evidence that intermarriage lead to *syncretism* or religious neu-trality in the home which, they argued, ultimately turned into cultural Christianity. Many Orthodox and some Conservative rabbis rallied against the extent of Jewish assimilation in modern America, claiming that the overall success and prosperity of Jews had led to a loss of Jewish identity. In addition, Jewish spokespeo-ple cited a reduction in synagogue attendance and the decreasing involvement in Jewish life as evidence that the American Jewish community was imperiled. They blamed intermarriage.

Jewish scholars in the 1970s explored the causes of intermarriage and determined that demographic, so-cial, economic, and cultural factors all had an influ-ence. Not surprisingly, those living in smaller Jewish communities were more likely to marry outside the faith. More revealing, however, was that intermarriage became more likely as the age of marriage increased. Higher educational and occupational levels also seemed to correlate to increased mixed-faith mar-riages. Research also showed that the increasing social acceptance of Jews marrying outside the faith and the decline in the centrality of religion, religious obser-vance, and Jewish communal organizations all con-tributed to the growth in the rate of intermarriage. These explanations provided evidence that inter-faith unions may have been more a result than a cause of the lessening of formal Jewish institutional involve-ment.

In a study commissioned by the **American Jewish Committee** in 1979, Egon Mayer painted a slightly more complicated picture. While acknowledging that intermarriage did indeed constitute a threat to Jewish life, he also found that the marriage union by itself was not the determining factor as much as the commit-ment or lack thereof by the Jewish-born spouse to maintain and affirm his or her Jewish identity. In ad-dition, Mayer noted that if the non-Jewish partner chose to convert to Judaism, the union and family tended to be strongly Jewish-identified.

The question of conversion has greatly complicated the analysis of intermarriage. Some have argued that because more than three-quarters of the ten thousand non-Jews who convert each year are female, intermar-riage would have minimal effect on the overall num-bers of Jews in America, since Jewish identification is determined by the Jewish lineage of the mother. At the same time, the role of conversion in Jewish life contin-ues to raise significant questions and uncertainties. Although most denominations embrace converts, many religious leaders have been reluctant to encour-age the process itself. Adding more fuel to the fire was the **Reform Movement**'s 1983 ruling that children would be considered Jewish if either parent was Jew-ish and if the child identified with the Jewish faith and people.

There continues to be considerable division in the Jewish community over how much energy and atten-tion to devote to outreach to intermarried couples who are not religiously affiliated, especially those who have children. Many Reform and some Conservative rabbis willing to perform interfaith marriages believe that by embracing the union within the Jewish faith it will en-courage the family to maintain a Jewish identity. Or-thodox rabbis will not perform interfaith weddings under any circumstances, nor do they accept the Jew-ish identities of converts unless they have been through an Orthodox ceremony.

Because of the resurgence of religious and cultural identification among many young Jews (including some who are either in or the products of interfaith unions), it appears as though the dire warnings of the end of Jewish life have begun to subside. Nonetheless, the issue of intermarriage and its impact on Jewish life and culture is not likely to go away any time soon. It will undoubtedly continue to a be a major theme addressed by the American Jewish community as it moves into the next millennium.

JEWISH FEMINISM

by Paula E. Hyman

Challenging all varieties of American Judaism, feminism has been a powerful force for popular Jewish religious revival. Of America's four Jewish denominations, all but the Orthodox have accepted women as rabbis and cantors. In contrast to the past, girls are now welcomed into the Jewish community with impressive ceremonies that celebrate their birth, and they are being educated in Judaism at virtually the same rate as boys. Feminist scholarship has begun to recover the previously ignored experience of Jewish women and offers new perspectives for the interpretation of classical Jewish texts. Although men still predominate in positions of power within the organized Jewish community, the presence of Jewish feminists in communal institutions ensures that issues of gender equality are discussed rather than suppressed.

The movement toward gender equality in the American Jewish community in the past generation was spurred on by a grassroots movement of Jewish feminism. Well-educated and liberal in their political and cultural orientation, many Jewish women participated in what has been called the second wave of American feminism that began in the 1960s. Most did not link their feminism to their religious or ethnic identification. Some women, whose Jewishness was central to their self-definition, naturally applied their newly acquired feminist insights to their condition as American Jews. Looking at the all-male *bimah* (stage) in the synagogue, they experienced the feminist "click"—the epiphany that things could be different—in a Jewish context.

Femimism and Conservative Judaism. In the early 1970s, Jewish feminism moved beyond the small, private consciousness-raising discussion groups that characterized the American women's movement to become a public phenomenon. Calling themselves Ezrat Nashim, a small study group of young feminists associated with the New York *Havurah*, a countercultural fellowship designed to create an intimate community for study, prayer, and social action, took the issue of equality of women to the 1972 convention of the Conservative Rabbinical Assembly. The founding members of Ezrat Nashim represented the highly educated elite of, primarily, Conservative Jewish youth.

In separate meetings with rabbis and their wives, the women of Ezrat Nashim issued a "Call for Change" that put forward the early agenda of Jewish feminism. That agenda stressed the "equal access" of women and men to public roles of status and honor within the Jewish community. It focused on eliminating the subordination of women in Judaism by equalizing their rights in marriage and divorce laws, counting them in the *minyan* (the quorum necessary for communal prayer), and enabling them to assume positions of leadership in the synagogue as rabbis and cantors. In recognition of the fact that the secondary status of women in Jewish law rested on their exemption from certain *mitzvot* (commandments), the statement called for women to be obligated to perform all *mitzvot*, as were men. Ezrat Nashim caught the eye of the New York press, which widely disseminated the demands of Jewish feminism.

Feminists used a number of strategies to bring the issue of gender equality before the Jewish community. Feminist speakers presented their arguments from the pulpit in countless synagogues and participated in lively debates in Jewish community centers and local and national meetings of Jewish women's organizations. Jewish feminists also brought their message to a wider public through the written word. Activists from Ezrat Nashim and the North American Jewish Students' Network published a special issue of *Response* magazine, devoted to Jewish feminism in 1973. That year, *Lilith*, a Jewish feminist magazine, was established.

Through their publications and speaking engagements, Jewish feminists gained support. Their innovations—such as baby-naming ceremonies, feminist Passover seders, and ritual celebrations of *rosh hodesh* (the new month, traditionally deemed a woman's holiday)—were introduced into communal settings, whether through informal gatherings in a home or in the synagogue. Participants in the celebration of new rituals spread them through word of mouth. Aimed at the community rather than the individual, new feminist celebrations designed to enhance women's religious roles were legitimized in settings that became egalitarian through the repeated performance of these new rituals. Indeed, one of the major accomplishments of Jewish feminism was the creation of communities that modeled egalitarianism for children and youth.

Feminism and the Reform and Reconstructivist Movements. The concept of egalitarianism resonated with American Jews, who recognized that their own acceptance as citizens was rooted in Enlightenment views of the fundamental equality of all human beings. With growing acceptance of women in all the professions, the **Reform Movement**, which rejected the authority of *halakah* (Jewish law), acted on earlier resolutions that found no obstacles to women serving as rabbis. **Hebrew Union College**, the seminary of the Reform Movement, ordained the first female rabbi in America, **Sally Priesand**, in 1972, and graduated its first female cantor in 1975. The **Reconstructionist Movement** followed suit, ordaining Sandy Eisenberg Sasso as rabbi in 1974.

Feminism and the Conservative Movement. The issue of women's ordination was fraught with conflict for the **Conservative Movement**, but it, too, responded to some feminist demands. In 1973, the Committee on Jewish Law and Standards of the Conservative Rabbinical Assembly ruled that women could be counted in a *minyan* as long as the local rabbi consented. The 1955 recommednation on *aliyot* for women by a minority of the Committee was widely disseminated, leading to a rapid increase in the number of congregations willing to call women to the Torah.

The most striking achievement of Jewish feminism is the acceptance of women as rabbis and can-

tors in the Conservative Movement. Because the Conservative Movement considers *halakah* binding, but also acknowledges that Jewish law is responsive to changing social conditions and concepts, the decision to ordain women as rabbis and invest them as cantors had to be justified in *halakic* terms. After a contentious national debate, which lasted from 1977 to 1983, the faculty of the **Jewish Theological Seminary** (the educational institution of the movement) voted to accept women into the rabbinical school as candidates for ordination. **Amy Eilberg**, who completed most of the requirements for ordination as a student in the seminary's graduate school, became the first female Conservative rabbi in 1985. Women were welcomed into the Conservative cantorate in 1987. As of 1996, there were almost four hundred women rabbis, including seventy-eight female members of the Conservative Rabbinical Assembly, seventy-three female graduates of the Reconstructionist Rabbinical College (which has accepted women since its founding), and between 250 and 300 women in the Reform Central Conference of American Rabbis. The Academy for Judaism, a nonsectarian seminary located in New York City, has also ordained women rabbis.

Orthodox Feminism. Although the Conservative Movement was the center of Jewish feminist activism in the 1970s and 1980s, Jewish feminism has always been diverse in its constituency and its concerns. The case for Orthodox feminism was made most eloquently by Blu Greenberg in her 1981 book *On Being a Jewish Feminist.* Small groups of courageous Orthodox women established women's *tefilla* (prayer) groups that respected all the *halakic* constraints on women's public prayers and persisted in their activity in the face of rabbinic opposition. Despite the fact that most Orthodox spokesmen deny feminist claims of the secondary status of women within traditional Judaism and disavow feminist influence, Jewish feminism has had an impact on American Orthodoxy, however unacknowledged. Girls are now provided with a more comprehensive Jewish education in Orthodox schools than ever before. In altered forms that conform to Jewish law, feminist rituals such as celebrations of the birth of a daughter and **bat mitzvah** rites have found their place within modern Orthodox communities.

Secular Jews as Feminists. Judaism as a religious tradition has animated Jewish feminism. But secular or "cultural" Jews have also contributed to Jewish feminist ranks. Some feminist Jews rediscovered their Jewishness as they encountered anti-Semitism within the women's movement. Jewish women who participated in the 1975 United Nations Conference on Women were stunned by the prevalence of anti-Semitic statements. They were angered in the 1980s that some feminists articulated anti-Zionist statements that incorporated anti-Semitic assumptions and stereotypes.

Feminism and the Jewish Liturgy and Culture. Beginning in the 1980s, Jewish feminists raised issues that went beyond the acceptance of women into male-defined positions of visibility and power. The emergence of women as religious leaders and as equal participants in the non-Orthodox synagogue allowed women to see themselves in public Jewish ritual. However, feminists were increasingly concerned that women's sensibility and experience be reflected in Jewish life. They hoped that women would be allowed to reshape the rabbinate and the cantorate, rather than simply follow traditional male models. Most importantly, they sought to incorporate women's voices and insights into Jewish liturgy and into the interpretation of classical Jewish texts. Arguing that Jewish liturgy and culture should reflect the understanding of women as well as men, Jewish feminists called for a revision of the *siddur*, the prayer book, and the Passover *Haggadah* and for the creation of feminist *midrash*, interpretation of biblical and Talmudic texts. Scholar-activists such as Judith Plaskow and Ellen Umansky challenged the male-dominated concepts of Jewish theology and God-language that drew primarily upon masculine imagery. The poet and Hebrew scholar **Marcia Falk** created blessings that supplant traditional liturgy with innovative forms that introduce feminist concepts: a sub-

version of hierarchy and naturalistic images of God gendered in Hebrew in the female.

The issue of God-language raised by feminists has, to one extent or another, influenced the prayer books and other ritual texts, particularly in the Reform and Reconstructionist movements, but also in the Conservative movement. All denominations have refrained from altering the Hebrew liturgy, and reconceptualizing images of God in light of feminist critiques has made only modest inroads.

Feminism's Goals. Despite having greatly influenced the American Jewish community, Jewish feminism has not achieved all its goals. Women who remain under the jurisdiction of Jewish law are still victimized in divorce proceedings. Some Orthodox men use their privilege in Jewish divorce law to extort large sums from their wives or leave them *agunah* (deserted wives), unable to remarry according to Jewish law.

Although women are more visible and wield more power in the institutions of the Jewish community than a generation ago, they have not yet attained parity. Only a handful of the women ordained as rabbis have secured positions as senior rabbis in large, prestigious congregations. Many prosperous congregations refrain from considering female candidates when they search for a rabbi.

The failure is even more blatant in the secular organized Jewish community than in its religious denominations, perhaps because more power and money are at stake in this sphere. Although there are more women board members of Jewish communal institutions than ever before, and some women have advanced into executive positions, men predominate in the top positions, especially in the largest communities.

Jewish feminism faces particular challenges in the contemporary American Jewish community. Many communal leaders consider feminist issues secondary to more pressing concerns, such as assimilation or communal unity. Often they present feminism as a danger to "Jewish continuity," the current buzzword for Jewish survival. Yet Jewish feminists persist in their activism, animated by the vision of a diverse and inclusive Jewish community, created and sustained by women and men sharing responsibility and power.

JOSEPH, JACOB (1848–1902)

Rabbi

An important Talmudic scholar and preacher, Jacob Joseph, was known as the "Chief Rabbi" of New York City and is generally considered to be the first rabbinic figure of international status to settle in the United States. Born in the Kovno district of Lithuania in 1848, Joseph studied under the mentorship of Rabbi Hirsch Berlin. He later became so well respected that he was elected as *magid* (communal preacher) and rabbinic judge in Vilna. In 1888, several Orthodox congregations in New York selected him to immigrate to New York and act as their Chief Rabbi.

Despite this lofty title, Joseph's actual jurisdiction was limited to the several dozen Lower East Side synagogues that had united and asked him to take on this leadership role. He had to endure internecine rivalries between rabbis and lay leaders that weakened his position. At the same time, Joseph's moral authority was substantial and transcended neighborhood boundaries. He and his lay assistants worked to establish the conditions for a traditional European-style Orthodox community in New York. Thus they created a rabbinic authority with a rabbinic court that consisted of several other Orthodox rabbis who entered the United States on Joseph's request.

Joseph ran into trouble, however, when he tried to impose a tax on Kosher meat in an attempt to bring order to the industry. Not only were working-class immigrant Jews in New York enraged, but other powerful quarters of the Jewish community opposed the tax. His efforts to license the ritual slaughterers and ban those whom he deemed incompetent created a groundswell of opposition to Joseph's authority. Other rabbis, many of whom were slaughters themselves, believed that the Chief Rabbi was trying to monopolize *kashrut* supervision in New York City and thereby destroy their chief source of livelihood. His effort was an almost complete failure.

Joseph was immobilized by a stroke in 1895 and was an invalid for the rest of his life.

KAPLAN, MORDECAI (1881–1983)

Rabbi, founder of Reconstructionist Movement

Mordecai Menahem Kaplan was born in Lithuania in 1881 and came to the United States with his family at the age of eight or nine. He studied at the College of the City of New York and Columbia University, then at the **Jewish Theological Seminary**, where he was ordained in 1902. In 1909 he became principal of the Teachers' Institute at the Seminary and, a few months later, began teaching homiletics in the rabbinical school and, later, *Midrash* and philosophies of religion.

Always active in the religious community, he was one of the founders of the New York Kehillah and organized the first synagogue-center (the Jewish Center, an Orthodox congregation) in 1916. The Center put into practice Kaplan's belief that a synagogue should serve all aspects of Jewish life. It included both athletic and social facilities. After five years as rabbi of the Jewish Center, he left to found the Society for the Advancement of Judaism, a synagogue not far from the Center on Manhattan's Upper West Side. The members of this new organization followed him into the increasingly liberal area he was staking out for himself in modern Judaism.

Kaplan published his landmark book *Judaism as a Civilization* in 1934, causing a tremendous upheaval in American Jewish religious thought. The book advanced his belief that Judaism was an "evolving religious civilization." In it, he denied the orthodox concept of revelation and of the "chosen people." He affirmed a theology that is a Jewish version of the "social gospel." He argued that, for Judaism as a "religio-national" civilization, a homeland was necessary. In spite of this Zionist stance, however, he believed that

Jewish people in the Diaspora can and will survive. He called his new approach "Reconstructionist."

In 1935, Kaplan founded the Jewish Reconstructionist Foundation and began publishing *The Reconstructionist* magazine. He continued to teach at the **Jewish Theological Seminary**, influencing five decades of Conservative rabbis.

KELMAN, WOLFE (1923–1990)

Born in Vienna in 1923, Wolfe Kelman served as chief executive and executive secretary of the Rabbinical Assembly, the international association of Conservative rabbis, from 1951 until 1989. Under Kelman's leadership, the Assembly grew rapidly and gained significant stature both within the **Conservative Movement** and among American Jewry at large. When Kelman first took office, the membership was 300 rabbis serving primarily metropolitan congregations. Thirty-five years later it numbered more than 1,200 members in more than a dozen countries.

Kelman was known both for his optimism and for the flexibility necessary to steer the Assembly through a number of important new developments within Conservative Judaism. These included the increasing number of rabbis trained at rabbinical schools other than the Jewish Theological Seminary, the secession of the **Reconstructionists** to form their own denomination, and the continuing struggle around whether to admit women as rabbis. He maintained a strong commitment to the autonomy and freedom of the rabbinate to speak its conscience and adamantly believed that both the right and left wings within the Rabbinical Assembly deserved an opportunity to speak and be heard.

Kelman supervised a number of Assembly publications including the *Weekday Prayer Book*, the journal *Conservative Judaism*, and the *Proceedings* of its annual conventions and closely participated in the affairs of the Committee on Jewish Law and Standards. He helped transform the Assembly's social justice program with a new activist phase that encouraged Conservative rabbis to champion civil rights both from picket lines as well as from their pulpits.

Kelman retired from his position at the Rabbinical Assembly after almost forty years in 1989 and he died in June 1990.

KOHLER, KAUFMAN (1843–1926)

Rabbi, President of Hebrew Union College

An eminent Reform rabbi, Kaufman Kohler was born in Fürth, Bavaria, in 1843. Descended from rabbis, he began his rabbinical studies when he was very young. When he was a teenager, he went to Frankfurt to attend the gymnasium and there met Samson Raphael Hirsch, who strongly influenced his thinking. After receiving his doctorate in 1867, he found that his radical views, as expressed in his dissertation, had closed virtually all rabbinical doors to him. Finally, he was offered the position of rabbi of Congregation Beth El in Detroit. He accepted the position in 1869 and then, in 1871, moved to Sinai Congregation in Chicago. In 1874, he succeeded David Einhorn, his father-in-law, at Temple Beth El in New York.

Kohler first came to national prominence in 1885 when he defended **Reform Judaism** against the attacks of Alexander Kohut with a series of sermons entitled *Backward or Forward* (1885). He assembled a conference of Reform rabbis in Pittsburgh, which adopted a controversial platform that Kohler had written. The Pittsburgh Platform described the bible as "reflecting the primitive ideas of its own age." In 1903, he took over the presidency of **Hebrew Union College**, rejuvenating it with a distinguished faculty, an improved curriculum, and a new campus. When he retired in 1921 he was given the title of president emeritus. He then returned to New York.

Among Kohler's many publications was the book *Jewish Theology* (1918), which was highly influential, and hundreds of scholarly articles. He served as editor of the department of philosophy and theology of the *Jewish Encyclopedia* (1901–1906). He also contributed 300 articles to that encyclopedia. When the Jewish Publication Society decided to sponsor a new English translation of the Bible, he served on the board of editors. He had a profound effect on Reform Judaism through his thinking and writing and through his activities in the Central Conference of American Rabbis.

KUSHNER, HAROLD (1935–)

Rabbi, author

Rabbi Harold Kushner was born on April 3, 1935, into in a Conservative Jewish household in Brooklyn, New York. He attended Columbia University, receiving his B.A. in 1955 and his M.A. in 1960. He obtained his rabbinical training from the **Jewish Theological Seminary**, where he was ordained in 1960. He earned his Ph.D. from the Seminary in 1972. He also studied at the Hebrew University in Jerusalem and at the Harvard Divinity School. In 1966, he became the rabbi for Temple Israel in Natick, Massachusetts. He served as that congregation's leader for twenty-four years. Upon his retirement, he became the Temple's rabbi laureate.

Kushner became nationally known when he published his first bestseller in 1981, *When Bad Things Happen to Good People*. The book has since been translated into twelve languages and was named one of the ten most influential recent books by Book of the Month Club members. His other books include *When Children Ask about God* (1972) and *To Life!* (1993). In 1995, he won the Christopher Medal for his book *When All You've Ever Wanted Isn't Enough*. His most recent book, also a bestseller, is *How Good Do We Have To Be?* (1996).

LEESER, ISAAC (1806–1868)

Rabbi, editor, Bible translator

The prominent American rabbi and scholar Isaac Leeser was born in Westphalia, Germany, in 1806. In 1824, at the age of eighteen, he came to the United States. Five years later he became *hazzan* at the Mikveh Israel congregation in Philadelphia. While serving there, he became editor of a monthly newspaper entitled *The Occident*, one of the early Jewish journals. He also founded the Jewish Publication Society of America, which was the first Jewish publishing company in the United States. Leeser published the first American translation of the Bible and edited a number of prayerbooks. He has been claimed by both Conservatism and modern Orthodoxy as a forerunner of their respective movements. An energetic and involved participant in American Jewish life for almost forty-five years, Leeser played a major role in the perpetuation of Judaism in the United States.

LEVINTHAL, ISRAEL (1888–1982)

Rabbi

Israel Levinthal was one of the most important leaders in Brooklyn Jewry and in the national **Conservative Movement** of the twentieth century. As the founding rabbi of the Brooklyn Jewish Center, Levinthal built the synagogue into a model of the synagogue-center advocated by **Mordecai Kaplan**. An especially gifted orator, he was considered one of the masters at delivering a Jewish sermon, calling his preaching the most important work of his ministry.

The descendant of twelve generations of rabbis, Israel Levinthal was born in Vilna in 1888, came to America in 1891, and spent his formative years in Philadelphia, where his father founded the Union of Orthodox Rabbis in 1902. Ordained in 1910, Levinthal briefly left his rabbinical career to study law but returned to the pulpit in 1915. He began to lay the foundations for a new Conservative synagogue at Brooklyn's Petach Tikvah, introducing late Friday night services, directing youth clubs, and administering a daily Hebrew school. After encountering resistance, Levinthal left Petach Tikvah and began his long and extraordinary career as rabbi at the Brooklyn Jewish Center.

By 1925 Levinthal succeeded in making his dream of having a synagogue function as a true community institution—with a pool, a gymnasium, an auditorium, a two story synagogue, and a membership of one thousand families. The Center also housed a school, a variety of community-based organizations, and an adult education program.

Levinthal served as president of the Rabbinical Assembly from 1930 to 1932 and was founder and first president of Brooklyn Board of Rabbis, the Brooklyn Zionist Region, and Brooklyn Jewish Community Council. He also published numerous volumes of sermons highlighting significant themes in traditional Judaism and their connections to contemporary Jewish life. Levinthal was known for his superb ability to bring new messages from traditional rabbinic texts to radically different generations of American Jews.

LOOKSTEIN, JOSEPH (1902–1979)

Rabbi

Born in Russia in 1902, Joseph Lookstein immigrated to the United States as a young boy. He later established himself as one of the leading modern Orthodox rabbinical leaders of his generation. At a time when many children of Eastern European immigrants had begun to acculturate into American society, Lookstein stressed the need for Orthodox clergy to offer charismatic and relevant sermons and for Orthodoxy as a belief system to be cosmopolitan, contemporary, and well educated in the mores of American society.

As senior rabbi of New York City's Kehilath Jeshurun for several decades, Lookstein encouraged the implementation of synagogue sisterhoods, men's clubs, Friday night lectures, and youth groups, all in the hope that an expanded notion of an Orthodox synagogue would be appealing to young American Jews. A superb preacher, Lookstein's sermons frequently captivated his audiences.

He believed in building modern Orthodox institutions and developed the now-famous Ramaz School, which served as a new model for Hebrew day school education in the United States. It was co-educational and worked on the schedule of a regular school calendar rather than the Hebrew calendar. Lookstein strongly supported Torah education for Orthodox Jewish women and served as an important initiator of the Shulamith School and, later, the founding of **Yeshiva University**'s **Stern College for Women**.

Lookstein also contributed to the development of the Rabbinical Council of America in the 1930s, which served as home of sorts for rabbinic alumni of Yeshiva who felt unaccepted by the Agudath ha-Rabbonim, a rabbinic union under the exclusive leadership of Eastern European rabbis. Lookstein was also an ardent Zionist and served as an important member of the Mizrachi Organization of America.

Considered to be among the most articulate representatives for Orthodoxy to the non-Orthodox Jewish community, Lookstein participated in a number of intradenominational rabbinic organizations, especially the New York Board of Rabbis and the Synagogue Council of America.

MENDES, HENRY PEREIRA (1852–1937)

British-born Henry Pereira Mendes was an important spokesman for a modern Americanized **Orthodox Judaism**. He believed in conducting services in English rather than Yiddish and favored short, easy to comprehend sermons, rather than complex Torah discussions. He was a staunch Zionist at a time when few Orthodox leaders embraced the cause and served as a close confidant to Theodor Herzl.

Mendes studied both medicine and rabbinics. He choose the latter as a career and succeeded Jacques Judah Lyons at New York's Congregation Shearith Israel in 1877, where he remained for forty-three years. In addition to his distinguished tenure as synagogue rabbi, he was an important member of the group of rabbis that helped establish the **Jewish Theological Seminary** in 1886 as a response to the forming of the reform-oriented **Hebrew Union College**. Later Mendes abandoned the Jewish Theological Seminary for the more traditional Rabbi Isaac Elchanan Theological Seminary, where he served as the first instructor of pedagogy and homiletics in 1917.

In addition to his staunch advocacy for Jewish higher education and synagogue cooperation, Mendes worked with non-Orthodox rabbis to improve overall Jewish welfare in New York and nationwide. He was active in support of a number of charities and organized colleagues to protest the American government's restrictive post-World War I immigration laws.

A prolific writer, Mendes began publishing a weekly periodical, *The American Hebrew*, in 1879. Among his books were *Jewish History Ethically Presented* (1895), *The Jewish Religion Ethically Presented* (1895), and *Jewish Life Ethically Presented* (1917).

MORAIS, SABATO (1823–1897)

Rabbi, founder of the Jewish Theological Seminary

Founder of the **Jewish Theological Seminary**, Sabato Morais was born in Italy in 1823. When he was twenty-two, he became assistant *hazzan* at the Spanish and Portuguese (Bevis Marks) congregation in London He continued to work with that group for five years before moving to the United States to take a position as *hazzan* of Mikveh Israel congregation in Philadelphia. He remained at Mikveh Israel until his death forty-seven years later.

While carrying out his rabbinical duties, Morais made a number of translations into English of the writings of Jewish Italian scholars and encouraged the use of Hebrew by writing prose and poetry in that language. These and other scholarly pursuits won him an honorary LL.D. from the University of Pennsylvania. He was the first Jew to be so honored. In his own congregation, he worked for the unity of Sephardic and Ashkenazi elements. A leader of Conservative forces in American Judaism, he came to believe that the **Hebrew Union College** did not offer the training needed for Conservative rabbis. As a result, he helped found the Jewish Theological Seminary and served as its president until his death in 1897.

NATIONAL COUNCIL OF JEWISH WOMEN

by Faith Rogow

Founded in 1893, the National Council of Jewish Women (NCJW) was the first national organization to unite Jewish women to promote the Jewish religion. From its inception, the NCJW adopted a pluralistic approach to Judaism, insisting on active involvement in the religion but not on adherence to particular practices. This approach of Americanizing without giving up Jewish identity was quite popular. In its first five years, more than five thousand American Jewish women, mostly of German descent, joined the fledgling organization.

The excitement generated in the council's early years masked significant internal divisions. The organization's mission to "save Judaism" from the internal threat of assimilation as well as the external threat of anti-Semitism attracted a variety of women with very different approaches to furthering ". . . the best and highest interests of Judaism and humanity."

The dominant group among the NCJW membership were the "clubwomen"—usually well-to-do women who spent their free time serving in civic and philanthropic organizations. They were the greatest influence in the NCJW's early years, with some groups transforming themselves from literary or sewing circles into NCJW sections. However, also among the founders was a second group that formed an influential minority. These women were somewhat younger than their clubwomen counterparts and usually single. Many were professional social workers. Where clubwomen raised money for settlement houses and occasionally conducted programs there, these women staffed settlement houses. The two factions came together in their commitment to social justice, the preservation of Judaism and the Jewish community in the United States, and a vision of religion that combined the two. Together they made a formidable team—one group with the capacity to raise funds and the other with the experience and energy to design and implement the programs for immigrants that would come to be the core of the organization's identity.

At first much of America's Jewish leadership applauded the council's efforts. Where rabbis were seemingly fighting a losing battle against assimilation, the NCJW brought a new and powerful weapon to the fray—motherhood. The NCJW declared that motherhood was the primary religious responsibility of every Jewish woman. That traditional stance was tempered by domestic feminism. If mothers were now to be the "saviors" of Judaism in America, as some rabbis declared, then mothers needed a voice in Jewish communal institutions as well as in the home. Members of the NCJW pressed for, and often won, positions on the boards of synagogues and other Jewish agencies. By 1920, the organization had initiated Council Sabbaths, a once-a-year recognition of the NCJW's work in which women led services at their home congregations, often for the first time.

The NCJW's commitment to pluralism nearly resulted in the organization's demise. The NCJW's founding leadership overwhelmingly identified with **Reform Judaism**. Some observed the Sabbath on Sunday rather than the traditional Saturday. These leaders understood that their Jewish practices would not be accepted by everyone, but they did not understand that for some members issues like adherence to the traditional Sabbath were nonnegotiable. To cross that line was not merely to Americanize Judaism but to abandon the faith. That the leaders of an influential Jewish organization, especially an organization that often represented the Jewish community to non-Jews, would be perceived as abandoning central Jewish practices was unacceptable. The issue came to a climax at the 1913 convention. Those advocating adherence to a more traditional interpretation of Judaism lost, and many left the organization. In the aftermath of this schism the organization increasingly focused on social service, especially immigrant aid work. That shift was so powerful that many people still (incorrectly) consider the NCJW a nonreligious, or even antireligious, organization.

The NCJW was actually the first Jewish organization to develop a vision that social work and political action constituted important religious expression. The NCJW adopted the philosophy that social work was God's work. This social justice-based religion would significantly influence institutions such as Jewish federations and synagogue social action committees.

The NCJW's actual practice of Jewish social justice reflected turn-of-the-century Progressive politics, a reaction to the deplorable conditions of America's urban poor. The council's broad-ranging work centered around programs to help immigrant Jewish girls. The NCJW replaced the model of benevolent charity common in the Jewish community with preventive philanthropy. Rather than asking individuals to give on an as-needed basis, the NCJW stressed efficiency in services designed to help clients become self-sufficient.

The NCJW provided services to more than twenty thousand immigrant Jewish girls who arrived on American shores without guardians. They met girls at ports of entry, built settlement houses, provided vocational training and Americanization classes, shared tips on etiquette, and provided cultural programs. They visited girls in their homes to see how they were doing and acted as advocates for those in legal trouble.

Many NCJW members were ambivalent about training girls to enter the workforce, doing so because they recognized the economic necessity but regretful that women who worked could not pay "proper" attention to care of children and home. Resulting policies included support of protective legislation for working women and corollary opposition to the Equal Rights Amendment.

The NCJW differed from other (largely Christian) organizations that saw poor immigrant girls as "fallen" and in need of saving. The council believed that their clients were generally good people who merely needed to overcome unfortunate circumstances. The help they provided was therefore material, not spiritual. The NCJW's model of immigrant aid was highly successful. No organization wielded more influence over immigrant Jewish girls than the NCJW.

Though internationally renowned for its immigrant aid work, the NCJW was not as clearly committed to other Progressive ideas. For example, the organization never took an official stand on woman suffrage. However, the NCJW was a leader on other women's issues. Margaret Sanger credited the council with being the first organization in the United States publicly to demand the legalization of birth control. For the NCJW, support for birth control was not so much an issue of sexuality, or even of women's rights, as it was a natural part of their concern for Jewish immigrants and a belief that family planning was necessary to conquer poverty.

The NCJW, like the rest of the world's Jewish community, was transformed by World War II. Though the group did not change its emphasis on motherhood or social welfare work, it did reflect transformations occurring throughout the American Jewish community. Most noticeable was the organization's growth. Spurred by postwar public proclamations of ideal womanhood that promoted voluntarism and supported the council's glorification of motherhood, membership in the NCJW nearly doubled between 1945 and 1970, going from 60,000 to 110,000 members in nearly 200 sections.

Another postwar change was the adoption of **Zionism**. Previously unwilling to take an official stand for fear of divisiveness, the horrors of the Holocaust overrode members' ambivalence about the need for a Jewish state. Predictably, the NCJW's support of Israel came in the form of sharing expertise in immigrant aid, social work, education, and child care. Early council efforts centered around assistance to Hebrew University. In the arena of child care, the council introduced the Home Activities for Toddlers and Their Families program in 1972. The council also pioneered the Home Instruction Program for Preschool Youngsters (HIPPY), which was implemented nationally by the Israeli government in 1975 and has become one of the most acclaimed parenting programs for at-risk families in the world.

Council programs have always been open to non-Jews, and it was always NCJW's policy to invest resources in starting new programs until others (like government agencies) recognized their importance and took them over. In the Progressive Era, such was the outcome of projects like school lunch programs, installation of public water fountains and sanitation systems, and the creation of juvenile courts. In the 1960s, inspired by the civil rights movement, the council actively fostered the transfer of long-standing programs to other hands. In many cities, council sections turned over settlement houses to civil rights leaders.

Because the NCJW's approach to social welfare work was preventive, the organization always pressed for political change, even as it provided programs. The council's political approach is most easily labeled as liberal. Where it has sought change, it has called for reform rather than revolution. It has shared a belief with most other Jewish organizations that American democracy is good for Jews, and members' own economic success has provided few reasons to question the basic structure of the American economy. Even in terms of gender roles, the NCJW's consistent emphasis on motherhood has kept it from being a radical organization, leading women back into traditional home structures even as it provided opportunities to act outside family service.

Yet, the council's liberal politics have led others to label the organization as threatening. In the early years, the criticism came from traditional Jews who questioned the council's expansion of women's roles or apparent acceptance of Reform Judaism. In more recent times, the NCJW's opposition to nuclear weapons, McCarthyism, and the Vietnam War, as well as its advocacy of civil rights, earned the organization an FBI file and the (unwarranted) suspicion that it was a communist front.

The specifics of the council's political policies continue to be shaped by the organization's emphasis on motherhood and social welfare. To provide an informed foundation for its political positions, the NCJW created the Center for the Child, which conducts research on the effectiveness of programs that serve families. Other motherhood-inspired policies have included advocacy for government support of quality child care and the strengthening of women's economic clout. The latter concern, as well as a shift in feminist thinking influenced by the civil rights movement of the 1960s, led the NCJW to reverse its original opposition to the Equal Rights Amendment. By the mid-1970s, the council became one of the strongest Jewish voices in favor of the ERA. Equally strong has been the NCJW's support for reproductive choice, including the right to abortion. This position is an extension of the council's belief in individual liberty and its efforts to combat poverty.

As with all women's voluntary organizations, membership in the council declined from its heyday in the 1950s and 1960s as more women have entered the workforce. It has survived, in part, because its structure allows individual sections the flexibility to concentrate their efforts on meeting local needs. That flexibility, however, has produced a diversity of activity

Although concentrated in large urban areas, National Council of Jewish Women members throughout the country provided services to their communities. This photo is of an NCJW bookmobile (probably from the 1930s), which spread the habit of reading throughout the Greensboro, North Carolina, area. (Courtesy of the National Council of Jewish Women)

that has made it difficult for the council to establish a clear national identity. Despite this challenge, the NCJW continues to act as a bridge between traditional motherhood and political activity, the Jewish community and other women's organizations, Judaism and politics, and between diverse segments of the Jewish community itself.

ORTHODOX JUDAISM

by Moshe D. Sherman

The earliest communities of Jews who settled in America during the colonial period established Orthodox congregations according to a Dutch Sephardic ver-

sion of ritual and custom. The synagogues they formed, including Congregation Shearith Israel, New York (1686), Congregation Nephuse Israel, Newport, Rhode Island (1754, changed to Yeshuat Israel in 1764), and Congregation Mikveh Israel, Philadelphia, (1771), were responsible for the early institutions of Orthodox Jewish life in America. These congregations founded America's first mikvahs, kosher slaughtering facilities, Hebrew schools, and charities.

Following the arrival of large numbers of Jews from the German states and Central Europe during the first half of the 1800s, most Orthodox synagogues in America reflected Ashkenazi practice. By the middle of the nineteenth century, with the arrival of Rabbis Abraham Rice (1802–1862) and Bernard Illowy

(1814–1871), an Orthodox rabbinic leadership emerged. Together with several talented ministers, including **Isaac Leeser**, (1806–1868), Samuel Isaacs (1804–1878), and Morris Raphall (1798–1868), Orthodox clergy led the struggle to protect the integrity of tradition in the face of the growing influence of the **Reform Movement.**

By the early 1880s most Orthodox congregations were headed by non-ordained "ministers." Moreover, the leading Orthodox clergy at the time were Western or American-born, English-speaking, and university educated. Among the prominent Orthodox religious leaders was American-born, Bernard Drachman (1861–1945), English-born and educated **Henry Pereira Mendes** (1852–1937), Italian-born **Sabato Morais** (1823–1897), and American-born Henry Schneeburger (1848–1916). The institutions they founded, including the **Jewish Theological Seminary of America** (1886) and the Union of Orthodox Jewish Congregations of America (1898), had a profound influence on the development of Conservative and Modern Orthodox Judaism.

Following the czarist-inspired pogroms in the early 1880s, almost one million Jews arrived from Eastern Europe, many of whom were Orthodox. Numerous rabbis and Talmud scholars trained in the great yeshivas of Eastern Europe joined the throngs of immigrants to America. By the turn of the century, hundreds of small synagogues, *mikvahs*, butcher shops, and Jewish bookstores dotted the Lower East Side of New York City, soon spreading to Brooklyn and across the Hudson to Newark, New Brunswick, and Trenton, New Jersey. Prompted by the passing of Rabbi Avraham Yoseph Ash on May 6, 1887, one of New York's most eminent Talmud scholars, a small group of Lower East Side synagogues organized to invite an outstanding European Talmud scholar to become "Chief Rabbi." At a meeting, held at the Beth Hamidrash Hagadol synagogue, on May 23, 1887, representatives from several Lower East Side congregations established the *Agudath Kehillot Yisrael Ortodoksit b'America* (Association of American Orthodox Hebrew Congregations). Shortly thereafter, they chose Rabbi **Jacob Joseph** of Vilna, Lithuania, to become "Chief Rabbi of New York."

These Eastern European immigrants were responsible for developing America's first yeshiva institutions. Until the 1880s, Orthodox children attended public school in the morning and Talmud Torah Hebrew school in the afternoon. In 1886, an elementary yeshiva day school, Etz Chaim, was established on the Lower East Side. In 1897, a higher-level yeshiva for older students was established on the Lower East Side named for the revered Chief Rabbi of Kovno, Rabbi Isaac Elchanan Spektor, (1817–1896), who had died the previous year. Several years later, under the direction of **Bernard Revel**, the Rabbi Isaac Elchanan yeshiva established a high school (1916), Yeshiva College, 1928, and numerous graduate and professional school programs. Since 1945, the school has been known as **Yeshiva University**.

With the growing number of Jews immigrating to America, Orthodox Jewish life was becoming increasingly varied and divisive. Some rabbis and ministers felt that an inclusive, broad-based effort was required to bring together Ashkenazi and Sephardic synagogues, Eastern and Western European Jews, to form an Orthodox congregational union. On June 8–9, 1898, delegates from uptown Manhattan synagogues, Eastern European *shuls* on the Lower East Side, and from congregations outside New York City met at Congregation Shearith Israel, New York, and the Eldridge Street Synagogue on the Lower East Side, to establish the Orthodox Jewish Congregational Union of America (later known as the Union of Orthodox Jewish Congregations of America).

The growth of Orthodox Jewish life in America brought about division among various communities of Orthodox Jews. American Orthodox Jews were ethnically and culturally diverse. Congregations and religious institutions were formed along lines of national and cultural background. Sephardic, German, Lithuanian, Polish, Hungarian, and Galician congregations were only some of the distinct communities represented in New York, Philadelphia, Baltimore, and other cities throughout the United States. They also differed in such matters as the modernization of synagogue services.

Tension between the Western-educated modern

Orthodox clergy and the Eastern European yeshiva-trained rabbis was aggravated when an assembly of fifty-nine rabbis representing communities throughout the United States and Canada convened in New York City in July 1902 to establish a rabbinic union known as the Agudath ha-Rabbonim (the United Orthodox Rabbis of America, later changed to the Union of Orthodox Rabbis of the United States and Canada). The organization emphasized the importance of encouraging Sabbath observance, improving *kashruth* standards, developing religious education, supporting charitable activity, assuring that marriages and divorces were performed by qualified rabbis, and providing political and financial support for colleagues throughout the country. However, only rabbis who had been trained at the great yeshivas of Europe and ordained by well-known European Talmud scholars were eligible for membership. The exclusion of English-speaking, Western-educated rabbis from membership in the Agudath ha-Rabbonim was part of a growing tension between the modern Orthodox rabbis who had emigrated from Central and Western Europe prior to the 1880s, and the Eastern European, yeshiva-trained rabbis who arrived in America from 1881 to 1914.

Orthodoxy in general, and the Eastern European immigrants in particular, faced the challenge of how to successfully pass on traditional law and custom to the younger generation. By the second decade of the 1900s a growing community of American-raised, modern-educated Orthodox youth were becoming alienated from the Yiddish-oriented, Orthodox synagogues. Objecting to what they considered to be poor decorum, with the auctioning of Torah honors, and the lack of congregational singing, groups of young people negotiated with established synagogues to permit them to organize their own *minyans* and lead their own services.

In time, new congregations of young adults, called Young Israel, were established in the Lower East Side and elsewhere throughout New York. These synagogues employed no rabbis or cantors, services included English sermons, congregational singing, and limited pledging, if any, during Torah reading. They also sponsored lectures and social events for young adults, and arranged for kosher dining facilities on college campuses. Most Eastern European rabbis viewed these developments as problematic accommodations to American society.

The founding of the Rabbinical Council of America in 1935 aggravated the strain between modern Orthodox clergy and the Eastern European rabbis of the Agudath ha-Rabbonim. Discouraged by their exclusion from the Agudath ha-Rabbonim, and alienated from the attitudes and priorities of the Eastern European-born, Lithuanian-educated scholars, graduates of the Rabbi Isaac Elchanan Theological Seminary and some other American yeshivas met in Belmar, New Jersey, on July 2, 1935, to form their own rabbinic organization, the Rabbinical Council of America. By the 1960s, the Rabbinical Council became the predominant Orthodox rabbinic body, and an important institution in the politics of American Jewish life.

Differences between Eastern European-trained rabbis and modern Orthodox Eastern European immigrants were also evident in the direction of the Rabbi Isaac Elchanan Theological Seminary (RIETS). While the Agudath ha-Rabbonim placed their official support behind the school, there was disagreement about its direction. In 1915 the elementary school, Etz Chaim, merged with the upper-level yeshiva, Rabbi Isaac Elchanan, forming one large institution. That same year, the yeshiva hired Rabbi Dov (Bernard) Revel as administrative director of RIETS. Under Revel's leadership, the school was transformed from a small yeshiva into a large educational institution. Revel established a yeshiva high school in 1916, developed a program of rabbinic ordination, attracted high-level *rosh yeshivas* to teach Talmud, including the eminent Rabbi Shlomo Polachek and Rabbi Moshe Soloveitchik. In 1928 he established Yeshiva College, a four-year liberal arts school. This alienated some members of the Agudath ha-Rabbonim who were opposed to the formal integration of secular studies at a yeshiva.

The Rabbi Isaac Elchanan Theological Seminary was not the only yeshiva producing modern Orthodox graduates. Following World War I, several other yeshivas were established in America, including Torah Vodaath, founded in 1918 as an elementary school to serve the growing community of Orthodox Jews in Brooklyn. Torah Vodaath, at that time, taught religious subjects in Hebrew and emphasized the importance of modern educational techniques. Following financial and administrative problems, Rabbi Shraga Feivel Mendlowitz was hired in 1921. A charismatic man with enormous talent and charm, Mendlowitz restructured the educational program by substituting Yiddish for Hebrew as the language of Talmud instruction. In 1926, Mendlowitz established a yeshiva high school, and four years later, when Torah Vodaath graduated its first class of high school students, a post-high school yeshiva. While university studies were not formally integrated into the curriculum of Torah Vodaath, it was not uncommon for Torah Vodaath students to earn a college degree by attending evening school at the City University of New York.

Others yeshivas formed in the 1920s included the Hebrew Theological College (1922) in Chicago, supplementing a yeshiva high school that had been founded two decades earlier. The Hebrew Theological College, like RIETS, included secular subjects in its course of study and trained young men for the rabbinate. In New Haven, Rabbi Yehuda Heschel Levenberg and Rabbi Moshe D. Sheinkop formed the New Haven College of Talmud (later called the Orthodox Rabbinical Seminary) in 1923, one of the first yeshivas located outside New York City.

Levenberg left New Haven in 1929 for a rabbinic position in Cleveland. One of his first tasks was to reestablish the New Haven yeshiva in Cleveland, which he hoped to accomplish with the assistance of Rabbi Sheftel Kramer, who agreed to join him in the midwest. The yeshiva faculty was immediately enhanced when Kramer's son-in-law, Rabbi Yaakov Yitzchak Ruderman, joined it in 1930. Despite Ruderman's departure from the yeshiva in 1933, the school successfully graduated dozens of students before closing in 1938 following the death of Levenberg. Among the yeshivas founded during the 1930s were Mesivta Tipheret Jerusalem (MTJ), whose *rosh yeshiva* was Rabbi Yoseph Adler. Rabbi **Moshe Feinstein** came to MTJ in 1938

after serving for a short while as a Talmud instructor at the Cleveland yeshiva in 1937. The Ner Israel yeshiva in Baltimore was formed in 1933 under the direction of Rabbi Yaakov Ruderman. Yeshiva Rabbi Chaim Berlin, which had opened as an elementary school in Brownsville in 1906, formed a post-high school yeshiva in 1939 under the leadership of Rabbi Yitzchak Hutner.

American Orthodox Judaism in general and yeshiva education in particular, were transformed following World War II, when several distinguished rabbis, *rosh yeshivas*, and Hasidic rebbes fled Europe and relocated their institutions in America. Rabbi Eliyahu Meir Bloch and Rabbi Chaim Mordechai Katz established a Telshe yeshiva in Cleveland in 1941. Initially comprised of a small number of European students who had escaped war-torn Europe, by the 1960s the Telshe yeshiva had developed a boys high school, a post-high school yeshiva, a *kollel*, and a girls seminary. In 1944, Rabbi Aharon Kotler established the Beth Midrash Gevoha in Lakewood, New Jersey. After developing some outstanding students of Talmud, the Lakewood yeshiva came to have an enormous influence on American Orthodoxy as its graduates established new yeshiva schools and *kollels* throughout North America.

These transplanted European yeshivas were different from the American institutions established prior to World War II. The American yeshivas established prior to World War II encouraged secular study and promoted programs in rabbinical ordination, while the Telshe yeshiva in Cleveland, Beth Midrash Gevoha in Lakewood, and other postwar yeshivas were founded by eminent European *rosh yeshivas*, encouraged Torah study exclusively, and eschewed accommodation with American mores.

Not all distinguished *rosh yeshivas* agreed with this approach. A new era of authority and leadership for modern Orthodoxy began when Rabbi **Yoseph Dov Soloveitchik**, the eminent Talmud scholar, was appointed Talmud instructor at RIETS in 1941. Inspired by Rabbis Soloveitchik's brilliance in both secular and religious knowledge, modern Orthodox Jews in particular looked to him for direction not only in matters of *halakha*, but also regarding religious and political issues confronting Jewish life in general. Rabbi Soloveitchik's leadership was crucial as modern Orthodoxy continued to grow in America alongside a growing community of *haredim*.

In addition to new yeshivas headed by prominent Talmud scholars, American Orthodoxy, following World War II, was also influenced by the arrival of Hasidic refugees. With few exceptions, notably Pinchas David Horowitz, the Bostoner Rebbe, and Rabbi Mordechai Shlomo Friedman, the Boyaner Rebbe, there were no Hasidic leaders in America until the arrival of Rabbi Joseph Isaac Shneersohn, the Lubavitcher Rebbe, in 1940, and Rabbi **Joel Teitelbaum**, the Satmar Rebbe, in 1947. While individual Hasidim had emigrated to America as early as the 1880s, many had abandoned their attachment to Hasidic ways. With no Hasidic leader or community of fellow pietists, immigrant Hasidim tended to assimilate into the mainstream of Orthodoxy. Since World War II, several Hasidic courts, including Lubavitch, Satmar, Bobov, Skver, and others, have developed sizable communities in Borough Park, Crown Heights, Williamsburg, Monroe, Monsey, New Square, and Toronto. With great resourcefulness, they have built yeshivas, synagogues, charities, and other institutions of Orthodox Jewish life.

While Hasidim in America formally eschewed accommodation with the modern world, and their distinct custom, dress, external appearance, and exclusive neighborhoods set them apart from other Orthodox Jews, they have adapted aspects of American society into their community. Modern technology, business and public relations skills, and diverse occupations are some of the ways in which Hasidim have been affected by American life.

The transplanting of Eastern European yeshivas and the development of Hasidic courts were not the only features of American Orthodoxy's development since World War II. The explosion of day schools and yeshivas in cities with relatively small populations of Orthodox Jews, the formation of *kollels*, the emergence of religious returnees or *baalei teshuva*, are additional examples of an American Orthodoxy that has trans-

formed itself during the past few decades. Aided by an increasingly tolerant, multicultural America, these achievements, together with a relatively high birthrate, has brought about a growing self-confidence among America's Orthodox community.

PRIESAND, SALLY (1946–)

Rabbi

Sally Jane Priesand was born in Cleveland, Ohio, on June 27, 1946. She attended the University of Cincinnati and began her rabbinic studies as part of the university's joint undergraduate program with **Hebrew Union College–Jewish Institute of Religion (HUC-JIR)**. In 1968, upon graduation from the University of Cincinnati, she entered HUC-JIR full time. In 1972, she became the first woman in Judaism to earn a seminary ordination. From 1972 through 1979, she was assistant, then associate rabbi at the Stephen Wise Free Synagogue in New York City. She then moved on to a part-time position at Temple Beth El in Elizabeth, New Jersey, while at the same time serving as chaplain for the Lenox Hill Hospital in Manhattan. In 1981, she finally found a congregation ready and willing to have a woman as their senior rabbi, the Monmouth Reform Temple in Tinton Falls, New Jersey. She still holds that position today. Among her writings, her most famous work is her rabbinic thesis, "Judaism and the New Woman" (1975).

RABBINATE

When the Jewish community began to grow in the United States in the mid-nineteenth century, the role of the rabbi as institutional leader took on a new and significant importance. Pioneering rabbis such as the Orthodox **Isaac Leeser** and the Reform **Issac Mayer Wise** became important and influential forces in the effort to build a modern American Judaism out of the foundation of the German-Jewish experience. In the twentieth century, the members of the American rabbinate took on new levels of local and national political leadership while also devoting significant energy to building their own congregations and expanding the parameters of synagogue life. In the modern era, each major Jewish denomination has engaged in serious debate and discussion concerning a variety of social issues involving the role and purpose of rabbinical leadership. After years of struggle, both **Reform** and **Conservative Judaism** accept women for ordination as rabbis. While a number of rabbis have exerted considerable intellectual, philosophical, and theological influence among all denominations of American Judaism, many have also sometimes found themselves torn between their responsibilities to synagogue boards and their own teaching and scholarly ambitions.

Originally an expression of respect, in the first century of the Christian Era, the word rabbi ("my master") became an official title conferred on ordained members of the *Sandhedrin* who established their reputations as experts in Jewish law. Although ordination as it was practiced in ancient times ended in the fourth century, the term continued to be used and permission to teach had to be conferred by one or more recognized scholars. Because Jews in the European and African Diaspora remained a community united by adherence to the laws and teachings of the Talmud, gentile rulers granted them the status of an autonomous corporate entity, and the rabbinate became a paid position. The primary task of the rabbi was to expound on Jewish law and judge according to Jewish law both in religious matters and civic litigation. In large cities, rabbis received training in the Torah and then headed yeshivahs and supervised ritual slaughters and ritual baths. At the same time, the rabbinical role as preachers was limited to conducting sermons twice a year—on the Sabbaths preceding Passover and the Day of Atonement.

With the advent of the Enlightenment in Europe, rabbis lost their judicial role and were increasingly required to gain a certain degree of secular knowledge to augment their Jewish learning. As Jews were granted citizenship rights throughout Europe, the heretofore insular communities began to participate in the world of the host society, and the narrow training provided by the *yeshivoth* was deemed largely irrelevant. Beginning in the nineteenth century, rabbinical seminaries were founded for the training of rabbis in both religious and secular subjects.

The American rabbinate is often referred to as "a new profession with an old name" because, despite the existence of Jewish congregations extending to the colonial era, the first seminary-trained rabbis did not take on synagogue leadership until the 1850s. (The very first was rabbi Abraham Rice, who arrived in Baltimore in 1840.) Because there was no autonomous corporate entity as had existed in the "old world," many community matters had ceased to be the function of the rabbi. As synagogues multiplied throughout the nineteenth century, the role of the modern rabbi as we know it began to take shape. The American denominations (**Orthodox**, **Conservative**, **Reform**, and **Reconstructionist**) developed their own seminaries, congregational unions, and rabbinical associations, each with a unique standard of rabbinical practice. Generally speaking, the American rabbinate that developed, except among the ultra-Orthodox, focused on pastoral, social, educational, and interfaith activities.

In the United States, arguments began to be made for an English-speaking, locally-trained rabbinate during the period of heavy immigration from Central Europe in the early to mid-nineteenth century. In 1867, Isaac Leeser established the first seminary, Maimonides College in Philadelphia, but it fell apart immediately after his death the following year. Issac Mayer Wise argued for the need to create such an institution from the time of his arrival in the United States in 1846. His dream was realized when **Hebrew Union College** (HUC) opened in 1875 in Cincinnati. Wise was one of the founders and the first president of HUC, now the oldest Jewish institution of higher education in the country. Although the college had as its stated goal the training of students for service to all denominations, it rapidly became a standard bearer for radical reform.

Orthodox leadership responded to the Reform focus of HUC by establishing the **Jewish Theological Seminary** of America in New York in 1886, which was re-organized under the leadership of **Solomon Schechter** and the new Conservative Movement in 1902. Despite significant differences in ideology, the curriculum of both of these seminaries emphasized the new responsibilities of rabbis, placing less emphasis on the Talmud and more attention on subjects that would enable the rabbi to lead services and teach in congregations whose members had themselves received a secular education. In the late nineteenth and into the early twentieth century, some rabbis even called themselves "ministers" and were referred to as "reverend" in same manner as cantors had been in earlier years.

The early twentieth century witnessed the evolution of the modern synagogue as a center of Jewish life and culture. Young American-born rabbis such as Jacob Kohn of the venerable B'nai Jeshurun in New York replaced older European-born leaders, as congregations sought to bring the children of Eastern European immigrants into their synagogues. Kohn took over his post in 1910 and immediately inspired a new awakening, popularizing the study of Hebrew by both children and adults. Similar transformations occurred in neighboring congregations, as rabbis such as Benjamin Tintner, Bernard Drachman, and Phillip Klein all attracted a youthful following. In general, both German and Eastern European congregations employed similar policies in attempting to reach a Jewish population that was increasingly Americanized. Seminary-trained rabbis became accepted in a variety of synagogues, giving credence to the argument that forward-looking representatives of all Jewish denominations should recognize the need to readjust Judaism to the impact of American culture.

The attempts to use dynamic rabbis to build stronger congregations was not limited to the Reform and Conservative Movements. Orthodox Judaism, which appeared left behind by the Reform Judaism of the German Jews, the *landsmanshaftn* synagogue embraced by Eastern European immigrants, and the new Conservative Movement began a process of re-evaluation in the mid- to late 1920s that resulted in the creation of a formal rabbinic program at Rabbi Isaac Elhanan Theological Seminary (RIETS) in New York (later a part of **Yeshiva University**) to produce American-trained, English-speaking Modern Orthodox rabbis. By the end of the decade, a small cadre of these

Orthodox rabbis established themselves in a number of prominent synagogues. A similar institution, the Hebrew Theological College, was founded in Chicago in 1922 with Rabbi Saul Silver as its president. Several smaller Modern Orthodox rabbinical schools also emerged in Brooklyn and Manhattan's Lower East Side at this time. Graduates of these schools and several other English-speaking Orthodox rabbis founded the Rabbinical Council of America in 1935.

As Modern Orthodoxy emerged in the United States, there was also a parallel development of a new, American-style traditional Orthodoxy largely centered in the Williamsburg section of Brooklyn around the *Mesifta Torah V'daath,* directed by Rabbi Shraga Feivel Mendelowitz. Under Mendelowitz's leadership, the school came to include a rabbinical program with several prominent scholars on the faculty. What differentiated *Torah V'daath* from RIETS as a rabbinical training program was a more critical attitude toward Western culture and a stricter interpretation of Jewish law.

Mordecai M. Kaplan gained a significant following in the early and mid-twentieth century. Initially rabbi at the Orthodox Kehillah Jeshurun Congregation in New York City, Kaplan drew from the secular writings of Durkheim, Marx, Freud, Darwin, Welhausen, and James to break both from Orthodoxy and then, later, the normative Conservative thinking of the time. In 1922, Kaplan founded a congregation called the Society for the Advancement of Judaism, which evolved into the Reconstructionist Movement.

If the changes in the style and substance of the rabbinate in America seem to have changed dramatically in the first three decades of the new century, Fascism in Europe, along with economic depression and increasing anti-Semitism at home, made the 1930s a crucial decade in American Judaism. At the 1937 conference of Reform rabbis, a commission proposed sweeping changes in guiding principles that both injected the concept of Jewish peoplehood into Reform ideology and embraced the more traditional rituals the movement had earlier rejected, such as lighting candles at Shabbat, sanctifying the wine, and reciting new prayers for special occasions. Reform rabbis became both more observant, more ritually inclined, and began embracing a pro-Zionist position.

The move toward **Zionism** was embraced by many American rabbis in the 1930s and 1940s, and all denominations sought to frame the ideology within the foundation of their belief systems. Reform rabbis such as Louis Newman of New York, Felix Levy of Chicago, and Bernard Nussbaum all shared a vision of Zionism that would have been unthinkable among the Reform rabbinate just a decade earlier. Writing before evidence of Hitler's "final solution" became public knowledge, Levy claimed that Jewish nationalism (Zionism) and the demands of a prophetic universalism were not only compatible but interdependent. Perhaps no Reform rabbi was more associated with Zionism than **Stephen Wise**. Wise, who had established the Free Synagogue in New York City in 1907, became president of the **Zionist Organization of America** in 1936, and was co-chairman of the American Zionist Emergency Committee from 1939 to 1945.

Even a number of prominent Modern Orthodox rabbis began to embrace Zionism, although their insistence on the role of *halakah* (Jewish law) in the enterprise distinguished them from their more liberal colleagues. Rabbi Morris Max, executive vice president of the Rabbinical Council of America, made the claim that Jewish national life was contingent upon its peoples' acceptance of Torah. **Joseph Lookstein**, a leader of the Mizrachi movement and rabbi of Kehilath Jeshurun in New York, maintained the belief that ". . . a return to Zion must be preceded by a return to Judaism."

Solomon Schechter, the highly influential president of the Jewish Theological Seminary and a leader of the Conservative Movement, was an early and ardent Zionist. It is not surprising that the Conservative rabbinate played the most prominent role in the transmission of Zionism to a majority of Americans. Baruch Treiger of the Agudath Achim Congregation in New Jersey consistently wove Biblical liturgy into his sermons preaching on behalf of a Jewish state in Palestine. Louis Levitsky, president of the Rabbinical Assembly and spiritual leader of Congregation Oheb Shalom, uttered similar sentiments in declaring both that ". . . no Jew who calls himself religious can fail to be a Zionist and no Jew who claims to be a Zionist can understand his cause without understanding the religious element involved in the belief system."

The Second World War and the events that led up to it played a significant role in the development of Jewish theology in the United States. Among Jewish intellectuals, it created a strong dissatisfaction with established forms of American Jewish thought and was responsible for an influx of refugee scholars and theologians who represented new ways of thinking about religion. Rabbis such as **Joseph Soloveitchik** and **Abraham Joshua Heschel** and Jewish scholars such as Emil Fackenheim and Will Herberg became known as leaders of a new Jewish theology and mentors of a post-war generation of Conservative, Reform, and Orthodox rabbis. Challenging the strong anti-theological bias prevalent in the established Jewish community, these men sought to win legitimacy for their discipline, to create original theologies on their own, and to delineate the basic principles for writing Jewish theology that their peers could follow.

Abraham Joshua Heschel immigrated to the United States from Poland and Germany in 1940. After teaching at Hebrew Union College for five years, he moved to the Jewish Theological Seminary, where he taught until his death in 1972. Always a theological iconoclast, he believed that American Jews were handicapped by reductionistic conceptions of God and of the Jewish tradition. He argued that the living God could not be cut down to mere symbols or to *halakah*. He blamed secular civilization for its "distorted" values and went so far as to claim that Nazism represented, in part, an extreme perversion of the callousness of modern civilization. Heschel also railed against what he called "vicarious" Judaism and demanded that American Jews emulate the God who cares passionately about truth, holiness, and justice. In his book *Not Man Alone*, he emphasized that God was the source of Jewish energy and not big synagogues, community centers, money, or responsibility toward Israel. Heschel justified his political activism in the Civil Rights and anti-Vietnam war movements as based on traditional Jewish religion.

Joseph Soloveitchik, an immigrant from a leading

Lithuanian rabbinic family, became the most important spiritual influence on post-war Modern Orthodox Judaism. A Talmudic scholar, teacher, philosopher, and theologian, Soloveitchik educated hundreds of Orthodox American rabbis at Yeshiva University and acted as both religious and *halakic* advisor to his students. In articles and lectures, he attacked liberal Judaism. In his most famous writings, "The Man of Halacha" and "The Lonely Man of Faith," Soloveitchik sought to revive biblical models of thinking together with their traditional interpretations and to establish a dialectical relationship between the pre-modern and modern as a "third way." Soloveitchik became a role model for a Modern Orthodox Movement that was seeking to acculturate. He wore American clothes, always spoke English in public, and used academic terminology in his writing and lectures. At the same time, he viewed the Talmud as pre-eminent and retained Yiddish as his mode of expression in private life.

On an opposite plane in the Orthodox movement, the Lubavitcher Rebbe **Menachem Schneerson** built a loyal following through the publication of textbooks and periodicals, along with lectures, and radio speeches, all designed to encourage American Jews to join his movement, which urged strict interpretation of *halakah* in conjunction with building political power and influence in the United States and Israel. In contrast, anti-Zionist Satmar leader **Joel Teitelbaum** rejected all attempts to join the modern world, seeking instead to re-establish his community exactly as it was in Europe and preserve the Yiddish language and customs associated with the old world.

Perhaps because it offers the greatest parameters for a theoretical framework, Conservative Judaism witnessed significant discussion and debate among rabbinical leaders with respect to ideology and law. After Mordecai Kaplan set the stage, the movement published an extraordinary amount of creative and competing theology from people such as Jacob Agus, Ben Zion Bokser, Robert Gordis, Simon Greenberg, Louis Jacobs, Jacob Kohn, David Novak, Richard Rubenstein, Harold Schulweis, and **Milton Steinberg**. Perhaps the movement's most well-known popularizer, **Harold Kushner**, wrote a book of healing and comfort

using his interpretation of Conservative Judaism as a foundation. Entitled *When Bad Things Happen to Good People* (1981), it became a national best-seller.

Within Reform Judaism, Rabbis Maurice Eisendrath, Nelson Glueck, Jacob Rader Marcus, and Joseph Glaser were greatly responsible for helping reshape the movement in the years after World War II. The dynamic Eisendrath was determined to reinvigorate the movement. He became the executive director of the Union of American Hebrew Congregations in 1943 and the president in 1946. Serving until 1973, he transformed the organization into an activist body both in the Jewish community and in American national politics. Glueck became president of Hebrew Union College in 1947 and set upon an energetic expansion campaign. In 1950 the College merged with Stephen Wise's Jewish Institute of Religion in New York. In 1954 he established a branch in Los Angeles, and in 1963 a campus in Jerusalem was begun.

As teacher to more than a generation of Reform rabbis, Jacob Marcus may have done more than any rabbinical leader to establish American Jewish history as a recognized academic discipline. His books and articles would fill a small library. In 1971, Joseph Glaser became the executive vice-president of the Central Conference of American Rabbis and immediately launched a campaign to revise the entire liturgy of the Reform Movement to reflect its growing diversity. His efforts culminated in the publication of the *Gates of Prayer*, an anthology of services and readings ranging from traditional to non-theistic.

The most radical change in the American rabbinate came in 1972 when **Sally Priesand** became the first female graduate of Hebrew Union College and the first woman ordained as a rabbi. By 1997, there were 274 Reform women rabbis in the United States. Following closely behind, Sandy Sasso was ordained as the first Reconstructionist woman rabbi in 1974. It would not be until 1985, however, that the Conservative Movement, after years of discussion, ordained its first female graduate, **Amy Eilberg**. But by 1997 there were already seventy- eight Conservative women rabbis.

Women's participation in the rabbinate over the last two decades has contributed to a number of challenges and changes. Gender-inclusive liturgical reform has competed with desires to preserve the language of Jewish tradition, and the two tendencies have struggled to find common ground. In 1993, the Reform Movement published a "gender-sensitive" liturgy designed to supplement *Gates of Prayer*, which was initially published in 1975. The new edition does not employ male pronouns to refer to God, and it offers gender-neutral English prayers and translations. Changes in the Hebrew text itself are limited to including the names of the matriarchs alongside liturgical references to the patriarchs.

Although it took longer for women rabbis to have an impact on the Conservative Movement, there has been considerable change over a decade. Women have begun to occupy a number of pulpits throughout the country. Although egalitarianism has not been universally embraced by the Conservative Movement, it has become the dominant position largely because of the leadership of women among the rabbinate. Here, too, changes in the liturgy are being formulated, discussed, and debated.

Susannah Heschel (Abraham Joshua Heschel's daughter) and Judith Plaskow have emerged as the two best-known Jewish feminist theologians. Both have attempted to locate the causes for the exclusion of women from Jewish thought and practice. They have developed new interpretations of Judaism that will support women's dignity and humanity and allow their full religious expression.

In the contemporary era, the rabbinate continues to reevaluate its role in American Jewish life and society. For synagogue rabbis, considerable pressure is often exerted by congregational boards of directors to use their positions to bring in new members. At the same

What is history to one generation is commonplace to another. Here is Sally Priesand (front row center), the first woman to be an ordained rabbi, on her visit to Hebrew Union College-Jewish Institute of Religion on the twenty-fifth anniversary of her graduation. Everyone else in the photograph is a rabbinical student, except for Karla Goldman, second from right, who is a faculty member. (Photograph courtesy of Karla Goldman)

time, rabbis have faced the difficult task of navigating between the official theological foundation established by the national leadership of their denomination and staking out a claim for themselves as independent scholars and thinkers. Meanwhile an increasing number of ordained rabbis are choosing to work in non-synagogue posts or take on leadership roles within secular Jewish organizations.

Debate and dialogue within the rabbinate about philosophical, political, and theological issues have shaped the face of contemporary Judaism. Although the rabbinical foundation that emerged and evolved in the United States during the nineteenth and twentieth century is rooted in old world traditions, it has taken on a life of its own through its intersection with American culture and society and now has its own distinct historical legacy upon which to build.

RECONSTRUCTIONISM

The smallest of the four branches of American Judaism, Reconstructionism, originated in the philosophy of one individual—**Mordecai Kaplan**. Kaplan

---

Is Your Rabbi Really a Rabbi?

For much of the history of Jews in America, the spiritual leader of a congregation was not an ordained rabbi. The first fully ordained resident rabbi in the United States was Rabbi Abraham Rice, who arrived in 1840, almost 200 years after the first congregation was organized.

believed that Judaism was a "religious civilization" emerging from the history and culture of the Jewish people. As a "civilization" it was constantly evolving, and it was the goal of Jewish thinkers at any given time to interpret Judaism in the light of contemporary life and thought without abandoning its traditional values. It is like **Reform Judaism** in its call for re-examination of religious beliefs, and kin to **Orthodox** Jewry in its desire to preserve the forms and symbols of religious practice. Reconstructionism is committed to Jewish nationhood, and it stresses the ties between the State of Israel and Jewish communities in the Diaspora.

The beginning of Reconstructionism can be dated to 1922, when Kaplan founded the Society for the Advancement of Judaism, a synagogue in New York City. Kaplan gathered Jews who were disaffected with other congregations and committed to "reconstructing" American Judaism so that it spoke meaningfully to the twentieth-century world. Synagogue members were encouraged to interpret Jewish tradition freely and to creating a more democratic Jewish institutional life. Kaplan rejected the notion that the Torah and the Talmud had literally been revealed by God at Sinai or that *halakah* (Jewish law) served as an absolutely binding set of commandments. Instead, he argued that the development of Jewish belief and practice had always adapted to ever-changing social conditions, political challenges, and cultural influences.

In essence, Kaplan's goal was to build a civil religion for the United States with American culture rather than biblical tradition as the primary transmitter of Jewish religious values. He believed that Jewish Americans lived in two civilizations. His reconstructionism sought to promote a blending of American and Jewish values. In this respect, he can be equated to the American **Zionists** of this period, most notably **Louis Brandeis**, who believed that an organized Zionist movement needed to be filtered through the prism of American constitutionalism.

Kaplan believed in the urgency of "re-constructing" Judaism precisely because of the radical dislocations in Jewish life as a result of the Enlightenment, the political emancipation of the Jewish people, and the modern technological revolution. Although he be-

lieved the modern West had much to offer Jews with respect to reconstructing Jewish civilization in accord with American democratic values, he viewed the Roman Catholic Church rather than American Protestantism as a model of group cohesion for Jews.

In 1934 Kaplan published his highly influential book *Judaism as a Civilization*, considered by many to be one of the major twentieth-century works of Jewish thought. The positive reception of the book led to the establishment in 1935 of *The Reconstructionist* magazine, edited by Kaplan and then subsequently by his preeminent disciple and exponent, son-in-law Rabbi **Ira Eisenstein**. More controversial have been Reconstructionist liturgical texts *The New Haggadah* (published in 1941) and especially *The Sabbath Prayer Book* (published in 1945), which altered the wording of the traditional Hebrew text, substituting alternate wording for phrases referring to the chosenness of Israel, the resurrection of the dead, and the Messiah.

The Reconstructionist Movement had at its core the stated belief that God could not literally choose one people over another and that the idea of privileged access to God promoted dangerous feelings of superiority. Kaplan instead argued that all peoples and civilizations had equal access to the Divine, and he was willing to embrace the belief that non-Jews could also operate as transmitters of religious ideals.

By defining Judaism as a "civilization," Kaplan made it into an all-embracing way of life that includes languages, literature, customs, civil and criminal law, art, music, food—all the elements of any civilization, but elements usually considered secular. This definition encouraged Jews alienated from traditional theology and practice, but still with strong cultural ties to their heritage, to become part of the movement.

As a result of their belief that American Jews lived in two civilizations, Kaplan and his followers believed they had a collective responsibility to speak out against social and economic injustice in contemporary society. The pages of *Reconstructionist* magazine have historically taken strong positions criticizing American militarism, unfair labor practices, and institutionalized racism.

At the same time as the Reconstructionist Movement embraced a universalistic vision, Kaplan also deeply believed in developing both Jewish unity and a Jewish civilization and was a strong supporter of Zionism. Although critical of both the secular/religious dichotomy in Israeli society and of Israel's foreign policy, he made *aliyah* late in his life and lived in Jerusalem.

Kaplan saw no need to start a separate movement to achieve his goals. His goal was to create a unified American Judaism without denominational factionalism. However, it became clear to his followers that, if Kaplan's visions were to be realized, a separate movement was needed. In 1940, the Jewish Reconstructionist Foundation (JRF) was established to support works that promoted the Reconstructionist program. In 1954, the SAJ joined with three other synagogues to form the Reconstructionist Federation of Congregations as the synagogue arm of the foundation. The organization grew at a gradual pace throughout the 1960s and 1970s under the leadership of Ira Eisenstein and Rabbi Ludwig Nadelmann. It then doubled in size in the 1980s under the direction of Rabbi David Teutsch.

In 1968, the Reconstructionist Rabbinical College was founded in Wyncote, Pennsylvania, with Eisenstein as its first president. The decision to found the college can clearly be seen as a move by Eisenstein and other Reconstructionist leaders to officially "found" a fourth alternative in American Jewish life.

The movement has been in the leadership on Jewish identity issues. It pioneered the adoption of patrilineal descent and warmly welcomes intermarried couples. The College officially announced in 1984 that it would admit qualified students who are open about their gay or lesbian sexual orientation, and this position was subsequently adopted by the Reconstructionist Federation of Congregations and the Reconstructionist Rabbinical Association, which was founded in 1974.

The movement has always been in the forefront of the movement for the equality of women in Judaism. Kaplan's daughter Judith had the first **bat mitzvah** in American (in 1922), and Kaplan firmly believed that: "The Jewish woman must demand the equality due her as a right to which she is fully entitled." One of the

The founders of Reconstructionist Judaism are shown here in the early 1930s embarking on a trip with their families. The two men in the back are Ira Eisenstein (left) and Mordecai Kaplan (right). The woman between them is Judith Kaplan Eisenstein (the daughter of Mordecai and the wife of Ira). In 1922, she had the first bat mitzvah in the United States. The other women (from left to right) are her sister Naomi, her mother, Lena, and her other two sisters, Selma and Hadassah. (Courtesy of Reconstructionist Rabbinical College)

first graduates of the Reconstructionist Rabbinical College was Sandy Eisenberg Sasso, who achieved rabbinic ordination there in 1974.

Although the Reconstructionist movement in the United States has never been large, it has had a vital importance in American Jewish life. In its attempt to reinvigorate and transform Judaism for a new generation, reconstructionism has provided a new awareness of the importance of Jewish renewal and understanding.

REFORM JUDAISM

Reform Judaism is the largest and oldest liberal religious movement in world history. Although it developed in Germany in the early and middle decades of the nineteenth century, the Reform Movement enjoyed its greatest success in the United States, where its ability to link Jewish religious values and practices with American political liberalism had a strong resonance.

The Golden Age of Liberal Judaism began in the post-Civil War era, when the movement witnessed such consistent growth that by the 1880s most of the

Rabbi Isaac Mayer Wise led the movement for Reform Judaism in the United States from his base in Cincinnati, Ohio. One achievement he was especially proud of was the creation of Hebrew Union College, now the oldest institution for Jewish higher education in the country. (Courtesy of American Jewish Historical Society, Waltham, Massachusetts, and New York, New York)

older synagogues had become Reform institutions and Reform Judaism had developed into the public face of American Judaism. By adapting to changing circumstances, the predominantly German Jewish Reform Movement, initially slow to take hold among the Eastern European Yiddish-speaking immigrants in the early twentieth century, brought a greater number of these newcomers into its orbit by the 1920s. Likewise, Reform Judaism, which began as strongly anti-Zionist softened its hard-line position in the 1930s and 1940s.

Reform Judaism rejects the belief in the unchanging nature of the written law in favor of adapting Jewish thought and practice in accord with contemporary outlooks and requirements. Stimulated by the early teachings of Moses Mendelssohn, the reform idea that

the doctrines of Judaism originated from universal reason made Judaism compatible with European Enlightenment concepts and allowed Jews to go beyond the traditional religious framework and value education outside the narrow rabbinical system. Reform Judaism also became the first religious movement of American Jews to configure itself on a non-denominational basis.

Although the earliest attempt to organize a Reform synagogue in the United States took place in a society of Americanized Jews of Sephardic descent in Charleston, South Carolina, in the 1820s, it was the arrival of Central European immigrants twenty years later that began to turn the Reform impulse into a legitimate movement. **Issac Mayer Wise** from Bohemia, a moderate Reformer, and David Einhorn, from Bavaria, a militant, became influential and sometimes antagonistic pioneers in building and determining the direction of the Reform Movement in its formative years from 1850 to 1870.

Wise, a strong believer in Americanizing Judaism, fought for a number of religious reforms including a single prayer book (*Minhag America*) that would replace the divergent European rituals that he believed had no place in the New World. He organized Congregation Anshe Emeth in New York, the first synagogue in the United States to allow men and women to sit together during services. He became best known as the leader of Bene Jeshurun in Cincinnati, where he founded the monthly newspaper the *Israelite*. Hoping to unite American Jewry under one banner, Wise established the Union of American Hebrew Congregations and then **Hebrew Union College**, which he hoped would ordain rabbis for all sectors of the Jewish community.

Einhorn published his own prayer book, *Olat Tamid*, an original German work, and a monthly German-language journal, the *Sinai*. Einhorn's progressive political ideology had a tremendous influence on the Reform Movement in the post-Civil War era, and he emerged as the leading theologian of his day.

The first unified statement of American Reform Judaism was drafted at a conference of Reform rabbis in Pittsburgh in 1885. Initiated by Einhorn's son-in-law,

Kaufmann Kohler, the Pittsburgh Platform preserved the Reform Movement's emotional ties to historical Judaism but rejected all Jewish customs ". . . not adapted to the views and habits of modern civilization" and asserted that Jews were a "religious community" and no longer a "nation." The Pittsburgh Platform aimed to stake out a middle ground between the pure universalism and atheism of future Ethical Culture leader **Felix Adler** and the positive-historical (**Conservative**) stance of Hungarian immigrant Rabbi Alexander Kohut.

Although the Platform had its critics from all sides of the religious spectrum, it was remarkably successful at articulating a workable foundation within which Reform Judaism would enter the next century. In 1889, Wise formed the Central Conference of American Rabbis, which served as the third branch of Reform's national apparatus and set out to create a uniform liturgy and strengthen the religious authority and professional autonomy of the individual synagogue rabbi. By 1900, what became known as "American Judaism" or "Classical Reform" had been institutionalized by the German Jewish establishment. With Wise's death, Kohler became president of Hebrew Union College.

The massive influx of Eastern European Jewish immigrants entering the United States around the turn of the century forced the classical reformers to rethink their agenda. The poor and working-class newcomers had little affinity for the middle-class American mores of the reform synagogue and created their own institutions to respond to their very different cultural histories. The new immigrants who made their way into the Seminary also had far more affinity for traditional Jewish practice and none of the ideological opposition to traditional Judaism that defined many of the German reformers. The Reform Movement acted quickly to respond to these new challenges. By 1909 it began to abandon its earlier efforts to reframe Judaism in the context of American Protestantism. Increasing anti-Semitism in Europe and throughout the world, the advent of World War I, and the Zionist initiative all combined to shift the universalistic, evolutionary classical Reform of the late nineteenth century out of favor.

Politically, Reform Jewish leadership was slow to address issues raised by the uprisings of what became known as the Jewish labor movement—a struggle that these German Jewish institutions had trouble relating to because of the immense class and cultural gaps involved. At the same time, the Reform Movement responded relatively early, if not unequivocally, in support of universal suffrage and women's rights within the synagogue.

In 1913, a group of women organized in independent, local synagogues united to form the National Federation of Temple Sisterhoods (NFTS) with Carrie Simon as its first president. The primary goal of the NFTS was to broaden women's sphere of responsibility within Judaism and the synagogue to enhance the religious spirit of Jewish life. The NFTS balanced a commitment to Reform Judaism with an interest in general philanthropic work and political issues. In its formative years its leaders were especially active in supporting the separation of church and state in the public schools, in promoting the prevention of war, and encouraging international peace efforts.

Jane Evans, who became the NFTS's first full-time executive director in 1933, pushed the organization beyond its mandate of providing service to the congregation and community by demanding that Reform Jewish women be given more of a voice both on issues directly related to the Reform Movement and other political challenges of the day. Under her forty years of leadership, the NFTS endorsed resolutions supporting access to birth control information, civil rights, fair housing, and child labor legislation. In the years following World War I, both the faculty of Hebrew Union College and the Central Conference of American Rabbis voted to support ordaining women as rabbis, but the College's board of directors overruled the decision. It would not be until 1971 that the Reform Movement finally endorsed allowing women to lead congregations with the ordination of **Sally Priesand**.

During the Depression years, when overall synagogue membership declined and the advent of fascism in Europe occupied the minds of American Jews, Reform leaders began to rethink the theology and anti-nationalism of the fifty-year-old Pittsburgh Platform.

In 1937, the Central Conference adopted a pro-Zionist position in its platform—a significant turning point in the history of the movement that paved the way for a major shift in the ideology of Reform Judaism. Leading the pro-Zionist charge were **Stephen Wise**, **Abba Hillel Silver**, and Samuel Cohen, who as professor of Jewish theology at HUC drafted a new set of Guiding Principles of Reform Judaism that spoke of ". . . the obligation of all Jewry to aid in [the] upbuilding [of Palestine] as a Jewish homeland."

Nevertheless, the anti-Zionists within the Reform Movement created splits within the institutional community during the early years of World War II, when issues such as raising a Jewish army in Palestine and demanding immediate statehood were hotly debated. With the news of the destruction of European Jewry, however, the opponents of Zionism lost much of their influence. After the establishment of the State of Israel in 1948, Reform Judaism as an institution became unequivocally Zionist in its orientation.

The membership of Reform Judaism exploded in the post-war years, with affiliate congregations in the UAHC soaring from 265 with 59,000 members in 1940 to 520 congregations with 255,000 members by 1955. Jews who had become more suburbanized and prosperous, including many from secular backgrounds, looked to the Reform synagogue for a sense of Jewish culture and community in their lives. Two rabbis, Maurice Eisendrath and Nelson Glueck, played especially important leadership roles in Reform Judaism throughout the 1950s and 1960s. Eisendrath became the new director of the Union of American Hebrew Congregations, moving its headquarters from Cincinnati to New York and broadening its focus, which had been criticized for being excessively confined. The Reform Movement became more actively involved in social justice issues outside the religious community, including civil liberties, civil rights, and the American peace movement. Eisendrath was particularly vocal in his opposition to the American involvement in the war in Vietnam. He encouraged the UAHC to develop a lobby in Washington and succeeded in opening a Religious Action Center that supported the increasingly progressive Reform agenda.

Glueck succeeded Julian Morganstern as president of HUC in 1947, presided over the college's merger with Stephen Wise's Jewish Institute of Religion, and established new branches of the HUC/JIR in Los Angeles in 1954 and Jerusalem in 1963.

By the mid-1960s the post-World War II momentum of the Reform Movement began to wane. The Six Day War and Israel's overwhelming military victory in 1967 challenged the generally anti-war and anti-military sentiments of many Reform Jews. The anti-Zionist positions of much of the American political left created anger and alienation among a significant percentage of the liberal Jewish community. The Civil Rights Movement's overall shift from integration to black power also had a similar deleterious effect.

Religious tensions among Reform leadership also developed during the late 1960s and early 1970s, with the most bitter centering around the question of rabbinic officiation at mixed marriages. Although a divided Central Conference reaffirmed its overall opposition to the practice in 1973, the number of Reform rabbis who performed such marriages continued to rise.

Women's participation fueled the resurgence of Reform Judaism in the 1970s. Female HUC graduates gained the right to become rabbis, and women comprised the large majority of converts to Reform Judaism during this era, often taking active roles in their congregations. Despite a general commitment to gender equity on the part of Reform institutions, women continue to push both for the hiring of more female rabbis in large congregations and for greater gender diversity in faculty positions at HUC-JIR campuses. In the 1980s and 1990s, a core group of women pushed for gender-neutral language in Reform prayer books.

During the 1970s and 1980s, the Central Conference of American Rabbis (CCAR) conducted a major campaign to revise the entire liturgy of the Reform Movement to reflect its religious diversity, culminating in a new prayer book anthology of services and readings and a parallel volume for the High Holy Days. Important national leaders in this era included **Alfred Gottschalk**, Alexander Schindler, and Joseph Glaser. The Reform Movement also developed new institutions including the Association of Reform Zionists of America, which promoted Jewish religious pluralism in Israel and provided American Reform Jews with a modicum of influence in the World Zionist Organization. Similarly, the Reform Movement's Outreach program led to the CCAR's decision to adopt a resolution in 1983 that supported patrilineal descent as a means of determining the divisive question of who is a Jew. This period also saw a dramatic increase in membership, with 39 percent of all American Jews in 1990 identifying themselves as Reform as opposed to 33 percent in 1970.

The current state of American Reform Judaism is the subject of much debate. Although some leaders argue that the movement has lost its identity, new representatives and fresh ideas continue to inspire a new generation attracted to the flexibility and accessibility of Reform institutions. The Reform Movement continues to occupy a primary role in American Jewish life—a situation that does not seem to be in danger of changing any time soon.

RUBENOVITZ, HERMAN (1883–1966)

Rabbi

The Lithuanian-born Herman Rubenovitz was one of the early pioneers of **Conservative Judaism**. It was Rubenovitz, the rabbi at Miskan Tefila in Boston for almost forty years, who first presented a plan for a union of conservative forces in America to the Seminary Alumni Association, which resulted in the founding of the United Synagogue of America in 1913. In 1914, he also helped establish the first northeast branch of the **Jewish Theological Seminary**.

Six years later Rubenovitz found himself frustrated by the United Synagogue's unwillingness to revise the prayer book to make Jewish law more in sync with the modern world. He joined **Mordecai Kaplan** to organize the Society for Jewish Renaissance, the pre-cursor of **Reconstructionism**.

A strong Zionist from early in his life, Rubenovitz headed the Zionist Council of Greater Boston from 1912 to 1915, and the New England Board of the Jewish National Fund from 1935 to 1938. He also initiated and

led the Rabbinical Association of Greater Boston from 1935 to 1950.

SCHNEERSON, MENACHEM MENDEL (1902–1994)

Perhaps the most controversial and charismatic contemporary Orthodox Jewish leader, Menachem Mendel Schneerson, the seventh Lubavitcher Rebbe, inspired both a legion of devoted followers and band of critics who denounced his leadership as a cult of personality.

Born in the Ukraine in 1902, Schneerson was the third rebbe of the Chabad dynasty and a child prodigy in the study of the Talmud and kabbalah. After studying in Germany and then in France, he immigrated to the United States in 1941 and settled in the Crown Heights section of Brooklyn, where his father-in-law, Rabbi Joseph I. Schneersohn (1880–1950), the sixth Lubavitcher Rebbe, had begun a headquarters for the Lubavitch Hasidim. Upon the elder Schneerson's death, his son-in-law took on the new leadership role and expanded and refined the Hasidic outreach program with the assistance of several hundred Soviet refugees who worked with him.

Unlike other Hasidic sects in the United States, which maintained insular communities, the Lubavitch movement was committed to expanding its membership and bringing all Jews into its circle. Schneerson established Lubavitch centers, Chabad houses, and modern technological innovations such as toll-free numbers, satellite hookups, *mikvah* tanks, and *sukah* mobiles. Through these campaigns and extensive educational campaigns on college campuses, the Lubavitch movement attracted followers from non-Hasidic and non-Orthodox families.

Schneerson also differed from many of his fellow Hasidim in his strong support for the State of Israel and his desire to influence internal Israeli politics. Believing that the Bible and Jewish law prohibited negotiating with Arab countries regarding the boundaries of Israeli territory, he vehemently opposed the Camp David Accords. Schneerson also sought to change Israel's Law of Return so that conversions performed by non-Orthodox rabbis would be invalidated.

During the 1970s and 1980s, Schneerson's empire grew and many of his followers created a cult of personality around him, with many Lubavitch claiming that Schneerson himself might be the Messiah. These messianic claims created a major rift between Lubavitch Hasidim and other Orthodox Jews. After a long illness and crippling stroke, Schneerson died in 1994. With no heirs to take on his leadership, his death left a significant void in the Chabad community.

SEIXAS, GERSHOM (1746–1816)

First Native-Born Rabbi

Gershom Mendes Seixas was born in New York City on January 15, 1746, to Rachel and Isaac Seixas. After studying with Rabbi Joseph Pinto, Seixas became rabbi of Congregation Shearith Israel (he was actually the cantor, but he assumed all the responsibilities carried out in Europe by a rabbi), a synagogue for the Spanish and Portuguese population of New York. When the British threatened to attack the city in 1776, Seixas left, as did most of his congregation. After a time in Connecticut, he went to Philadelphia, where he helped to found Mikveh Israel. Back in New York in 1784, he involved himself in a number of Jewish community activities. The first rabbi in America to give sermons in English, Seixas maintained close ties with the European Jewish community. He was a leader in raising money to build synagogues around the country and a trustee of Columbia College.

SILVER, ELIEZER (1882–1968)

Rabbi

Born in Kovno Province, Lithuania, in 1882 and educated in Talmudic scholarship by his father and the great East European Torah luminaries, Meir Simcha and Joseph Rosen, Silver became one of the most important and influential leaders in American Orthodox Jewish life.

After immigrating to the United States in 1907, Silver made his mark as a synagogue rabbi, first in Harrisburg, Pennsylvania, then in Springfield Massachusetts, and finally in Cincinnati, Ohio. At the same time as he built strong community-based congregations, Silver also established himself as a national Orthodox leader in the Agudath ha-Rabbonim and, with Israel Rosenberg, as a co-founder of Ezrat Torah.

During World War II, Silver especially distinguished himself in providing a rescue agency for European Jewry—the *Vaad Hatzalah*—and assisting in the creation of a safe haven for hundreds of Torah scholars. After the war, Silver founded *Keren Aliya*, a fund to help Holocaust survivors immigrate to Palestine.

A regular contributor to a number of Torah journals and periodicals, Silver published *Anfei Erez*, a volume of commentary focusing on core components of the Talmud.

SISTERHOODS

by Felicia Herman

For over a century, American Jewish women have banded together in their synagogues and temples to form sisterhoods. Over the years, these sisterhoods have labored in several different fields, serving as a vehicle for the expansion of the American synagogue into new areas of activity. American Jewish leaders, inspired by the notion that women were uniquely suited to saving Judaism, the synagogue, or a particular movement from internal and external crises, have looked to Jewish women for salvation. In response, sisterhoods have served as philanthropic organizations, pursuing a communally-oriented vision of uplift to the poor; they have provided innumerable services to their own congregations, raised much-needed funds, maintained religious schools, fostered congregational unity, and sponsored educational programs for adult women and men. They have engaged in national endeavors, offered succor to soldiers during times of war, taken sides in national political debates, and promoted better relations among Americans of all faiths and ethnicities. Not least, sisterhoods offered Jewish women a place to gather together as women and as Jews, to socialize with each other, and to strengthen the bonds that connect them. Even the word "sisterhood" indicates a certain type of relationship that members have always striven for among themselves: a closeness, a sisterliness, a familiar, familial feeling.

Precursors. Sisterhoods were not the first type of women's organization in American synagogues. During the nineteenth century—though less formal groups existed even during the colonial period—female benevolent societies, modeled after the European *chevrot nashim* (women's societies), performed the traditional duties of caring for sick and dying women and preparing female bodies for burial. These groups also often served as local charitable organizations, collecting small amounts of money to give to the local poor, particularly to women and children affiliated with their congregations; occasionally, these societies would raise funds for their congregations as well.

In 1820 in New York, the women of the United States' oldest congregation, Shearith Israel, joined together to form the Female Hebrew Benevolent Society (a year after **Rebecca Gratz** founded her extra-synagogal Female Hebrew Benevolent Society in Philadelphia) to offer financial assistance to "indigent females *particularly*" (emphasis in original) but also to entire families. In the 1850s, the society's purposes expanded to include "afford[ing] the aged and indigent female members of [Shearith Israel] a comfortable residence, support, employment, medical and other necessary care." The Central European Jews who immigrated to the United States throughout the nineteenth century continued to operate this type of women's organization. The *Tugendhafte Frauen*—the Society of Righteous Women—founded in 1850 at New York's Ahawath Chesed Congregation, was typical: its members visited the sick, relieved the poor, and prepared deceased members' bodies for burial. These women were inspired by what they described as a "solid foundation of sisterly affection and a broad idea of mutual assistance to each other, to the Widow, the Orphan and the Suffering."

Social Service: The Sisterhoods of Personal Service. Traditional benevolent societies could not meet the enormous challenge confronting American Jews in the 1880s: caring for the mass influx of Jews fleeing the severe economic conditions and oppressive anti-Jewish legislation that plagued Eastern Europe. These Jews often arrived in the United States penniless and with few skills suitable to finding employment in a modern, industrializing nation. They needed assistance in learning English, finding jobs, conducting their way through the maze of the citizenship process, and coping with the social, cultural, and religious problems of new immigrants to America.

The sense of crisis provoked by this mass immigration came on top of other, earlier worries that had troubled American Jewish leaders since the 1870s. American Judaism was under siege, they asserted, from the twin evils of apathy and neglect. The American-born children of an earlier generation of immigrants from Central Europe seemed alienated from Judaism, disenchanted both with an **Orthodox Judaism** that seemed too antiquated and European and with a **Reform Judaism** that discouraged congregational participation and appeared increasingly formalistic and dry.

For aid in resolving both of these crises—the plight of needy immigrants and the decline of Jewish observance—several important American Jewish leaders, especially in New York, the center of greatest immigrant concentration, turned to women. In the late 1880s and early 1890s, the rabbis and layleaders of ten of New York's most important synagogues, representing an ideological spectrum ranging from staunchest Orthodox to the most radical Reform, founded "sisterhoods of personal service." The middle- and upper-class members of these first sisterhoods assumed a multitude of responsibilities, guided by the ideals of the late-nineteenth-century scientific charity movement. Instead of haphazardly disbursing sums of money to people forced to seek their help, sisterhood women maintained a diverse catalogue of communal activities focused on preventing the onset of poverty rather than on dealing with it after the fact. Among the sisterhoods' many programs were settlement houses, religious schools, kindergartens, day nurseries, mothers' meetings, sewing classes for girls and unemployed women, employment bureaus, services for juvenile delinquents (especially girls), and clubs and outings for children. When necessary, they also dispensed material relief to women, children, and even entire families.

After joining together to form a Federation of Sisterhoods in 1896, the members of the sisterhoods of personal service acted as "friendly visitors" for New York's United Hebrew Charities, visiting immigrant families in their homes and offering advice on and access to medical care, nutritional information, employment, and American housekeeping techniques. This aid was not always offered without a sprinkling, or even a heavy dose, of condescension and *noblesse oblige*, and not all immigrants welcomed sisterhood women's involvement in their lives. Many sisterhood women realized the potential pitfalls of their work, and they often attempted to inject a feeling of equality—of sisterliness—between sisterhood members and the people they aided. With or without condescension, however, countless immigrants and their children were aided in some way by the women of the sisterhoods of personal service.

To justify this appeal to women as saviors, American Jewish leaders drew on nineteenth-century American Protestant notions of women's inherently pious and charitable nature. They maintained that these ideas had always been present in Judaism as well, as evidenced by the images of pious and kind women in the Hebrew Bible and Jewish folklore. Nonetheless, the sisterhoods of personal service were something entirely new in American Jewish history. Unlike the earlier women's synagogal organizations, these new societies required the *personal service* of their members: no longer could charitable society members remain isolated from the "needy and distressed," fulfilling their duties simply by making financial contributions. Instead, members were expected to devote their time to actually working with the needy themselves. And this work drew women far from their usual domain—their homes. For the first time, American Jewish women could participate in communally-sanctioned public activities on behalf of the Jewish community; rabbis and sisterhood leaders promoted a vision of women as civic mothers and social housekeepers responsible for a very broad interpretation of "home" and "family."

Synagogue leaders also hoped that the sisterhoods of personal service would help to revitalize Judaism. By expanding the activities of the temple or synagogue and by offering opportunities to perform social welfare work under religious auspices, Jewish leaders believed they could attract younger, American-born Jews to the synagogue—people for whom the synagogue's worship services seemed to hold little appeal. This idea would become more popular in the interwar period, promoted by **Mordecai Kaplan**. The late nineteenth-century sisterhoods offer evidence that such ideas were being tested in a period before Kaplan and his "synagogue-center" ideas. Though the sisterhoods did not succeed in enticing large numbers of unaffiliated Jews to perform synagogue work or to attend religious services, there is no doubt that a few women found in sisterhood work a mode of being Jewish that was congenial to them and a way of being active in reform movements that did not require them to ignore or deny their Jewishness.

Whatever they accomplished for immigrants or for Judaism, the sisterhoods of personal service were short lived: in 1936, the last active sisterhood of personal service closed the doors to its settlement house. Most had discontinued their social welfare activities in the 1920s. The reasons for the demise of the sisterhoods of personal service are numerous and complex. Perhaps most important was the fact that social work had become a profession, thus obviating the need for groups of largely untrained female volunteers. Jewish charity also became more centralized, and New York's Federation for the Support of Jewish Philanthropies assumed many of the fund-raising responsibilities sisterhood women had previously undertaken. The immigration crisis was also gradually receding from the forefront of the American Jewish consciousness: Jewish immigration slowed during World War I and ended almost entirely with the immigration restriction laws of 1921 and 1924. Another crisis soon loomed, however, a more dangerous challenge to American Jewish survival, and one that would require an entirely new type of women's organization in the synagogue.

Service to Judaism: Synagogue and Temple Sisterhoods. Though American Jewish leaders decried the presence of apathy among American Jews as early as the 1870s, in the period between the two world wars this crisis intensified. With the ebb and eventual cessation of Jewish immigration in the 1920s, American Jews could no longer rely on waves of religious immigrants to sustain Jewish life and to keep it vibrant. The new task was to "Judaize" the Americans: to prevent Jews' complete assimilation into American culture and to preserve a Jewish identity that could exist in harmony with American ideals. Urban America in the 1920s held many distractions for American Jews, especially for the American-born children of Eastern European immigrants. The period F. Scott Fitzgerald termed the "Jazz Age" was a time when new forms of entertainment and new ideas about the world proliferated. Automobiles, music clubs, films, and a prevailing modernist, anti-religious, and anti-Victorian spirit mitigated against the development and maintenance of a religious identity, especially one that appeared to many young Jews as formalistic, dry, and outdated.

Again, synagogue leaders turned to women for help. The new sisterhoods that rabbis founded in the 1910s and beyond, in all parts of the country and across the ideological spectrum of American Judaism, were primarily devoted to three goals: service to the synagogue, to Judaism, and to their respective movements. The roster of activities the sisterhoods established in this period have continued on to this day, though the perception of crisis has waxed and waned.

Sisterhoods were dedicated primarily to serving their congregations. By making the synagogue or temple a more welcoming, comfortable, friendly, and even home-like place, they hoped to encourage synagogue attendance and membership. In conjunction with congregational brotherhoods, which were founded in the 1920s, 1930s, and 1940s, they promoted "sociability" among members, making special efforts to welcome visitors and new members, providing flowers and other decorations for synagogue services and holidays, offering refreshments for social hours after services, and sponsoring events like congregational Seders, Hanukkah parties, and Purim carnivals. Sisterhood members also often undertook the responsibility of maintaining or at least enlivening religious education for the children of the synagogue. Whether they served as teachers, administrators, or fundraisers, or simply provided special gifts at holidays and graduations, sisterhood women—as the "mothers" of their congregations—endeavored to improve the education of the congregation's children and to intensify their connection to Judaism.

Sisterhoods as organizations also helped to strengthen the synagogue by serving as vehicles for attracting non-affiliated or inactive women to synagogue activities. In the interwar period, auxiliaries such as sisterhoods and brotherhoods were founded explicitly as key components in the creation of "synagogue-centers"— synagogues intended as more than places of worship, as places for educational, social, and even athletic activities. As they had done in a previous era, sisterhoods provided women who might not be interested in attending religious services with other ways of expressing their Jewish identities—though the underlying hope was that these women would eventually seek out the synagogue's religious activities as well.

In the financial realm, sisterhoods proved indispensable to American synagogues and temples. Though women had been contributing financially to their synagogues since colonial times, the sisterhoods of the interwar and postwar periods served as particularly useful venues for raising the funds needed to support new congregational buildings, special congregational projects, and even to cover shortfalls in annual budgets. Fundraising became an especially important element of sisterhood work during the Depression years and has continued to this day as an essential element of most sisterhoods' activities.

Beyond supporting their individual synagogues, sisterhoods have always endeavored to strengthen Judaism as a whole. In the interwar period, sisterhoods struggled to counteract the apathy and "hedonism" of the times by presenting Judaism as a beautiful, meaningful, and moral way of life that could exist in complete harmony with modern American values. To this end, they attempted to create interesting and relevant educational programs and reading materials for adults—especially sisterhood members—and for children. In these efforts, the sisterhoods were led by their three national coordinating agencies: the National Federation of Temple Sisterhoods (NFTS), founded in 1913 (now Women of Reform Judaism); the National Women's League of the United Synagogue, founded in 1918 (now Women's League for Conservative Judaism); and the Women's Branch of the Orthodox Union of Jewish Congregations of America, founded in 1923. Through their publications, their activities in the Jewish community, and the educational materials and programs offered to their constituents, these national organizations have consistently promoted religious knowledge and observance. All three organizations have emphasized the special role of the mother in preserving and transmitting Judaism: mothers can foster warm, Jewish atmospheres in their homes, can encourage their families—husbands and children alike—to attend synagogue services and become involved in synagogue activities, and can teach their children about Jewish life and encourage them to attend religious school.

Local sisterhoods and their national organizations have also worked to strengthen their respective movements. Aside from promoting a movement-specific agenda in their publications and educational programs, the national organizations also raised funds for the institutions connected to their movements. Women's League and the NFTS have raised millions of dollars for the support of their respective rabbinical seminaries, the **Jewish Theological Seminary of America** and **Hebrew Union College**. They provided general institutional support, sponsored numerous scholarships, built dormitories, and, in the case of Women's League, annually sponsored and decorated an elaborate Sukkah for faculty and students. The national organizations have also cooperated with the rabbinical and other lay organizations of their movements (such as the national brotherhood and youth organizations) to promote knowledge about and loyalty to their particular interpretation of Judaism.

Synagogue and temple sisterhoods have also endeavored to meet many of the other challenges confronting American and world Jewry over the years. As early as the 1920s, sisterhoods sent financial support to the Jews of Ethiopia. In the 1970s and 1980s they supported efforts to aid Jews in the Soviet Union and then assisted many of the Russian Jews who immigrated to the United States. To combat the anti-Semitism rife in American society and in Europe in the 1930s and again in later periods, sisterhoods became active in interfaith activities, with the national sisterhood organizations often joining national interfaith groups, and local sisterhoods promoting interfaith services, pulpit exchanges, and joint social service activities in their own communities.

Before the founding of the state of Israel, sisterhoods' national organizations promoted **Zionism** to varying extents, depending on the positions adopted by their movements. Women's League, for example, vigorously disseminated knowledge about Palestine and assisted in the creation of synagogues, schools, and educational programs for Palestinian Jewish women, often in cooperation with **Hadassah**, the Women's Zionist Organization of America. Once Israel was founded, all of the national sisterhood organizations offered educational programs about Israel and its people and sometimes sponsored trips to Israel for sisterhood members and their families. Most sisterhood gift shops—now an almost ubiquitous presence in American synagogues—carried products made in Israel as a way of supporting Israeli craftspeople, educating American Jews about Israel, and promoting a modern, Jewish aesthetic for home decoration.

Sisterhoods have also consistently endeavored to participate in and contribute to American society. During times of war, sisterhoods engaged in a range of activities to support the American war effort. In both world wars, local sisterhoods sewed bandages and assembled packages for the Red Cross, provided entertainment for soldiers on leave, turned their offices and synagogue vestry rooms into makeshift hospitals, sold War Bonds, and trained for national defense and for wartime jobs. Before World War II, sisterhoods cared for refugees from Nazi Europe; after the war, they sponsored war orphans, assisted Holocaust survivors who immigrated to the United States, and supported Jewish reconstruction work in Europe. Outside their war activities, sisterhoods have been involved in many of the other important issues confronting Americans: national sisterhood organizations and many local sisterhoods supported the civil rights movement. The national organizations have engaged in national child care and welfare debates and encouraged efforts to aid the elderly and the disabled.

The women's movement of the 1970s and 1980s brought a new challenge to synagogue and temple sisterhoods. Whether sisterhoods are or have historically been feminist is a question still subject to considerable debate. With the feminist challenges to Judaism that appeared in the 1970s and 1980s, Women's League and the NFTS promoted an expanded role for women in Jewish religious life, supporting women's desire to assume larger roles in synagogue worship and, ultimately, to become rabbis.

Women's Branch, though it would hardly label itself feminist, has always promoted better religious education for girls and women. It has been working for decades to ameliorate the condition of the *agunah*, the wife whose husband has disappeared or who refuses to divorce her. Women's Branch sisterhoods have also struggled with the issues of all-women *tefillah* (prayer) groups and the form—if any—a girl's **bat mitzvah** should take.

Conclusion. Whatever their ideological position—feminist or non-feminist, Conservative, Reform, Orthodox or even Reconstructionist—synagogue and temple sisterhoods have offered countless American Jewish women a public and active way of expressing their identities as Jews and as women. As an institution, the sisterhood has served as an instrument for the expansion of the synagogue into more diverse spheres of activity in the Jewish community and in American society as a whole. By raising money for their synagogues, teaching English classes to new immigrants, supporting religious schools, decorating temple altars, or leading religious services at national conventions and even in their own synagogues, for over a hundred years, the sisterhoods have provided Jewish women with an outlet for their religious expression and have helped synagogues, American Jewish movements, and even American Judaism itself to survive.

SOLOVEITCHIK, JOSEPH (1903–1993)

Rabbi, Talmud Scholar

Joseph Soloveitchik is generally considered to be one of the pre-eminent Talmudic scholars in twentieth-century America. Born in Pruzahn, Poland, in 1903 to an intellectual and religious family, Soloveitchik was tutored in religion by his father, a rabbi, and in secular subjects by his mother. These influences led him to Berlin, where he studied philosophy and economics, and engaged in Talmudic studies under the tutelage of the renowned scholar Rabbi Chaim Heller.

In the 1930s, Soloveitchik immigrated to America, where he became rabbi of Congregation Chevra Shas in Boston and established an elementary day school and high school. A Zionist member first of Agudath and then the Mizrachi movement, Soloveitchik was a passionate advocate for the State of Israel after World War II.

Perhaps most important, however, in assessing Soloveitchik's influence were the forty years he spent as the leading Talmudic instructor at the Rabbi Isaac Elchanan Theological Seminary in New York, where he established a reputation as an outstanding teacher and stirring orator. Soloveitchik also served as head of the Halakha Commission of the Rabbinical Council of America, where he mentored many Orthodox Jews regarding issues of Jewish law and its relationship to contemporary life.

STEINBERG, MILTON (1903–1950)

Despite a short life, rabbi and author Milton Steinberg played an influential role in the left wing of the Rabbinical Assembly (the international association of Conservative rabbis) and as a compatriot of **Mordecai Kaplan** in developing a Jewish ideology compatible with the modern world.

Born in 1903 and raised in Rochester, New York, Steinberg began his rabbinical career at Temple Beth-El Zedeck in Indianapolis but became best known for his pioneering leadership of the Park Avenue Synagogue in New York City from 1933 until his death in 1950. As the congregation's rabbi, he attracted new members through initiating study circles and by his stimulating sermons focusing on resolving contemporary social problems through Jewish tradition. In a decade, he expanded the membership of the synagogue from 120 to 425 families.

On a national level, Steinberg joined Kaplan on the editorial board of the biweekly *Reconstructionist* in 1934 while remaining a critical participant in the Rabbinic Assembly, chairing its Committee on Social Justice, and issuing an official protest against the lynchings of African Americans. In the 1940s, he broke from the Assembly over what he perceived as its unwillingness to engage in serious liturgical modification of its Sabbath and Festival prayer book. He worked with Kaplan on the Reconstructionist Sabbath prayer book.

Steinberg also wrote a number of important books and essays, probably the most important being *The Making of the Modern Jew*, which analyzed Jewish survival in the Middle Ages and the factors that had made that survival more difficult since Jewish emancipation. His other works included *A Partisan Guide to the Jewish Problem*, which presented a Reconstructionist view on solutions to post-war Jewish identity and survival, *Basic Judaism* (1947), and a novel, *As a Driven Leaf* (1939).

TEITELBAUM, JOEL (1886–1979)

Staunch anti-Zionist rebbe Joel Teitelbaum gained recognition as the world leader of the ultra-Orthodox Satmar Hasidic community. Born in Hungary in 1886, Teitelbaum followed in his father's footsteps as chief rabbi of the Sighet Hasidic dynasty and by 1934 was considered one of the leading rabbis in Hungary and Romania. He narrowly escaped deportation and eventual death in Auschwitz when he was included in the Kaszmer train that transported 1,600 Jews from Hungary to neutral Switzerland. He immigrated to the United States in 1947 and settled in the Williamsburg section of Brooklyn, which became home to the American Satmar community.

In his writings and speeches in the 1950s and 1960s, Teitelbaum stressed his belief that Jews were forbidden to create their own state prior to the coming of the Messiah. Unlike many religious Zionists, he was opposed not only to a Jewish secular state but also to a Jewish state run according to Orthodox Jewish principles. Teitelbaum's most intense criticism was directed against his Orthodox and Hasidic opponents who supported Israel, especially Aguduth Israel and the Lubavitch, Klausenberg, and Vishnitz Hasidic groups, all of whom he accused of cooperating with the State of Israel.

In 1956, Teitelbaum organized Hungarian refugee anti-Zionist rabbis into the Central Rabbinical Congress and he initiated a weekly Yiddish newspaper, *DEDYID*, as the voice of his community. Although best known for his anti-Zionism, Teitelbaum also believed in the importance of re-creating East European Jewish *shtetl* life in America. He strongly rejected all aspects of American modernity, whether in language, clothing, or prayer. He viewed all Eastern European manners and customs as sacrosanct and to be adhered to without reservation.

In 1977, Teitelbaum established the town of Kiryat-Joel in Monroe, New York, as a new and independent Satmar community. He lived there until his death two years later.

WISE, ISAAC MAYER (1819–1900)

Rabbi, Editor, Leader of American Reform Judaism

The founder of **Reform Judaism** in the United States, Rabbi Isaac Mayer Wise was born on March 29, 1819, in Steingrub, Bohemia. When he was twenty-seven years old, he came to the United States, becoming rabbi at synagogue Beth El in Albany, New York. He used his position there to fashion a distinctly "American Judaism," with the hope of uniting the chaotic American Jewish community under its banner.

In 1850 Wise was forced to leave Beth El. Many synagogue members rebelled against his "radical" reforms, and they especially did not appreciate his refusal to follow the orders of the temple lay leadership. His supporters began a new congregation, Anshe Emeth, with Wise as rabbi. It was the first synagogue in the United States to allow mixed seating.

In 1854 Wise moved to Cincinnati to serve as rabbi of Congregation B'nai Jeshurun. He remained there for the rest of his life. While serving as rabbi, he also edited two weekly newspapers, one in English and one in German. In addition to the two papers, the *American Israelite* and *Die Deborah*, respectively, Wise wrote and edited books of history and theology, as well as novels and plays. His books include *History of the Israelitish Nation from Abraham to the Present Time* (1854), the *Cosmic God* (1867), and *Pronaos to Holy Writ* (1891).

Ever an advocate of "reform" judaism, Wise organized his first successful rabbinic conference in 1855. But many of those present felt that he had conceded too much to Orthodoxy. Undeterred, Wise issued his own prayer book, *Minhag America*, a year later and continued to lobby for a "union" of American congregations. His fondest dream was for a college to train rabbis in the United States.

After much contentious jockeying for ideological and practical leadership in American Judaism following Wise's conference (there were "national" conferences in Philadelphia, Cleveland, Cincinnati, and New York during the period), a group of layman, largely from Wise's own congregation, organized the Union of American Hebrew Congregations (UAHC) in 1873. Thirty-four congregations joined initially. In the following two years an additional thirty-eight affiliated and, by 1890, 118 congregations (more than half of the congregations in the country) had joined the Union. Reform Judaism was born.

In 1875 another of Wise's dreams was realized when the Union created **Hebrew Union College**, with Wise as its first president. He built it into a major center of Jewish education and scholarship.

In 1899, a year before Wise's death, he and a group of like-minded rabbis founded the Central Conference of American Rabbis. Originally intended to be a regional organization, it quickly spread throughout the country. Today it is the official organization of Reform rabbis in the United States.

Wise married Therese Bloch in 1844, and they had ten children. She died in 1874. Two years later, he married Selma Bondi, with whom he had four children. He died in Cincinnati, Ohio, on March 26, 1900, having forever changed the face of American Judaism.

WISE, STEPHEN SAMUEL (1874–1949)

Rabbi, Zionist leader

Stephen Wise was born in Budapest, Hungary, on March 17, 1874. His family moved to the United States while he was still an infant. Brought up in New York City, Wise followed in his father's footsteps (Aaron Wise, originally Weiss) and became a rabbi. He received both his B.A. (1892) and his doctorate (1901) from Columbia University. He obtained his rabbinical training from his father, Alexander Kohut, and Gustav Gottheil. In 1893 he was ordained by Rabbi Adolph Jellinek of Vienna.

From his ordination to 1900, Wise served as assistant rabbi, then rabbi, to the congregation of the Madison Avenue Synagogue in New York City. In 1900, he became rabbi at Temple Beth Israel in Portland, Oregon. While in Oregon he promoted interfaith cooperation and social service programs and served as Oregon's child labor commissioner. In 1906 he was asked to return to New York to become the rabbi of Temple Emanu-El. A dispute arose with the Temple's

---

Where Were Your Relatives?

Rabbi Stephen S. Wise was renowned for his one-liners. It is reported, perhaps apocryphally, that when a self-important questioner in a public discussion established her credentials by stating that her relatives were present at the signing of the Declaration of Independence, Wise interrupted that *his* relatives were present when Moses brought the Ten Commandments down from Mount Sinai.

An ardent Zionist and committed theological liberal, the highly articulate Stephen Wise was a frequent public speaker, not only before Jewish groups, but also to Christian congregations and the general public. (Courtesy of American Jewish Historical Society, Waltham, Massachusetts, and New York, New York)

One of the first people to recognize the dangers of Nazism, Wise warned and educated not only the American public, but also President Franklin D. Roosevelt and the State Department. His commitment to humanity was not limited to Jews and Judaism. From his pulpit and on the street, he supported the rights of workers to unionize and fought for shorter work weeks for factory women. He was a vocal champion of the workers striking against U.S. Steel in 1919. Ten years earlier, he co-founded the National Association for the Advancement of Colored People. In 1920, he co-founded the American Civil Liberties Union. Among his published works are *The Improvement of Moral Qualities* (1902), *How to Face Life* (1917), *Child versus Parent* (1922), *Challenging Years* (his autobiography, 1949), and the ten-volume series of his sermons, *The Free Synagogue Pulpit.* He died on April 19, 1949, having lived a life devoted to bettering humanity's lot on earth.

For Further Reading

See Appendix 2 (Organizations and Resources) for a bibliography of general reference books about Jews and the Jewish experience in America. All of the volumes listed there include information about the history of Jews and Judaism in America.

Antler, Joyce. *The Journey Home: Jewish Women and the American Century.* New York: Free Press, 1997.

Baum, Charlotte, Paula Hyman, and Sonya Michel. *The Jewish Woman in America.* New York: Dial Press, 1976.

Birmingham, Stephen. *"Our Crowd": The Great Jewish Families of New York.* New York: Harper & Row, 1967.

Cohen, Naomi W. *Encounter with Emancipation: The German Jews in the United States, 1830–1914.* Philadelphia: Jewish Publication Society, 1984.

Dawidowicz, Lucy. *On Equal Terms: Jews in America, 1881–1981.* New York: Holt, Rinehart & Winston, 1982.

Eichhorn, David Max. *Jewish Folklore in America.* Middle Village, N.Y.: Jonathan David Publishers, 1996.

Eisen, Arnold. *The Chosen People in America.* Bloomington, Ind.: Indiana University Press, 1983.

Feingold, Henry L., gen. ed. *The Jewish People in America.* Five volumes. Baltimore, Md.: Johns Hopkins University Press, 1992. This magisterial set, sponsored by the American Jewish Historical Society, includes *A Time for*

board of trustees over the issue of Wise's freedom of speech from the pulpit, and as a result Wise founded the Free Synagogue of New York, where he was rabbi until his death.

In addition to his rabbinical duties, Rabbi Wise helped found, and served as president of, the Federation of American Zionists (1898), the **American Jewish Congress**, the World Jewish Congress, and New York City's Jewish Institute of Religion (which merged with **Hebrew Union College** in 1950). Wise worked tirelessly to promote Zionism, bringing it to the attention of, among others, President Woodrow Wilson. He served as chairman of the United Palestine Appeal on several occasions and spoke on the issue of Zionism at the Versailles Peace Conference in 1918–19.

Planting: The First Migration, 1654–1820, by Eli Faber; *A Time for Gathering: The Second Migration, 1820–1880*, by Hasia R. Diner; *A Time for Building: The Third Migration, 1880–1920*, by Gerald Sorin; *A Time for Searching: Entering the Mainstream, 1920–1945*, by Henry L. Feingold; and *A Time for Healing: American Jewry since World War II*, by Edward S. Shapiro.

Gay, Ruth. *Unfinished People: Eastern European Jews Encounter America*. New York: W. W. Norton, 1996.

Glazer, Nathan. *American Judaism*. Second revised edition. Chicago: University of Chicago Press, 1989.

Gurock, Jeffrey S. *When Harlem Was Jewish*. New York: Columbia University Press, 1979.

Hertzberg, Arthur. *The Jews in America: Four Centuries of an Uneasy Encounter*. New York: Columbia University Press, 1989.

Howe, Irving. *World of Our Fathers: The Journey of the East European Jews to America and the Life They Found and Made*. New York: 1976.

Howe, Irving, and Kenneth Libo. *How We Lived: A Documentary History of Immigrant Jews in America, 1880–1930*. New York: Richard Marek, 1979.

Jick, Leon A. *The Americanization of the Synagogue, 1820–1870*. Hanover, N.H.: Brandeis University Press, 1976.

Joselit, Jenna Weisman. *New York's Jewish Jews: The Orthodox Community in the Interwar Years*. Bloomington, Ind.: Indiana University Press, 1990.

———. *The Wonders of America: Reinventing Jewish Culture, 1880–1950*. New York: Hill and Wang, 1994.

Karp, Abraham. *Haven and Home: A History of the Jews in America*. New York: Jason Aronson, 1985.

Koppman, Steve, and Lion Koppman. *A Treasury of American-Jewish Folklore*. Northvale, N.J.: Jason Aronson, 1996.

Levitan, Tina. *First Facts in American Jewish History*. Northvale, N.J.: Jason Aronson, 1996.

Marcus, Jacob Rader. *The American Jew, 1585–1990: A History*. Brooklyn, N.Y., 1995. Carlson Publishing, Inc.

———. *The Colonial American Jew, 1492–1776*. Three volumes. Detroit, Mich.: Wayne State University Press, 1970.

———. *Early American Jewry*. Two volumes. Philadelphia: Jewish Publication Society of America, 1951–1953.

———. *Memoirs of American Jews, 1775–1865*. Three volumes. Philadelphia: Jewish Publication Society of America, 1955–56.

———. *United States Jewry, 1776–1985*. Four volumes. Detroit: Wayne State University Press, 1989–93.

———, and Abraham J. Peck, eds. *The American Rabbinate: A Century of Continuity and Change, 1883–1983*. Hoboken, N.J.: Ktav Publishing, 1985.

Meyer, Michael A. *Response to Modernity: A History of the Reform Movement in Judaism*. Detroit: Wayne State University Press, 1995.

Moore, Deborah Dash. *At Home in America: Second Generation New York Jews*. New York: Columbia University Press, 1981.

Nadell, Pamela S. *Conservative Judaism in America: A Biographical Dictionary and Sourcebook*. Westport, Conn.: Greenwood Press, 1988.

Olitzky, Kerry M. *The American Synagogue: A Historical Dictionary and Sourcebook*. Westport, Conn.: Greenwood Press, 1996.

———, Lance J. Sussman, and Malcolm H. Stern, eds. *Reform Judaism in America: A Biographical Dictionary and Sourcebook*. Westport, Conn.: Greenwood Press, 1993.

Raphael, Marc Lee. *Profiles in American Judaism: The Reform, Conservative, Orthodox, and Reconstructionist Traditions in Historical Perspective*. San Francisco: Harper & Row, 1984.

Rischin, Moses. *The Promised City: New York's Jews, 1870–1914*. Cambridge, Mass.: Harvard University Press, 1962.

Sachar, Howard M. *A History of the Jews in America*. New York: Knopf, 1992.

Sarna, Jonathan D., ed. *The American Jewish Experience*. New York: Holmes & Meier Publ., Inc., 1986.

Schloff, Linda Mack. *And Prairie Dogs Weren't Kosher: Jewish Women in the Upper Midwest since 1855*. St. Paul, Minn.: Minnesota Historical Society, 1996.

Schoener, Allon. *The American Jewish Album, 1654 to the Present*. New York: Rizzoli, 1983.

———. *Portal to America: The Lower East Side, 1870–1925*. New York: Holt, Rinehart & Winston, 1967.

Seltzer, Robert M., and Norman J. Cohen, eds. *The Americanization of the Jews*. New York: New York University Press, 1995.

Sherman, Moshe D. *Orthodox Judaism in America: A Biographical Dictionary and Sourcebook*. Westport, Conn.: Greenwood Press, 1996.

Wertheimer, Jack, ed. *The American Synagogue: A Sanctuary Transformed*. New York, 1987.

Part 3

Rituals, Celebrations, Holidays, and Family Life

OVERVIEW

Judaism is not only a system of beliefs. It is a way of life that involves ritual practices and ceremonial observances. These serve to remind the Jewish people of God's place in their lives. They are also a way of reliving the experiences of Jewish ancestors. In the past, observance has had survival value in terrible situations, strengthening the individual's loyalty to the community and thereby strengthening the whole.

There are four categories within the traditional practice of Judaism. First, Jews are required to pray, traditionally three times each day. Praying at the synagogue helps to form and maintain the community. Second, Jews are required to observe dietary laws. Third, there are festivals and holy days commemorating events of great importance in the history of the Jews and having specific spiritual meanings. The most important of these are the weekly Sabbath, the major holidays of **Rosh Hashanah**, **Yom Kippur**, **Sukkot**, **Simchat Torah**, **Passover**, and **Shavuot**, and the minor holidays of **Hanukkah**, **Purim**, and **Tisha B'Av**. Finally, there are lifecycle rites, marking the events of personal and family life. These include *bris*, or male circumcision, **bar mitzvah** and **bat mitzvah**, **marriage**, and funeral rituals.

In the past two centuries, Jews have questioned the wisdom of strict observance of traditional Jewish practices. **Orthodox** Jews uphold their necessity. **Reform** Jews perform only those rituals they believe are directly related to leading a God-oriented life. **Conservative** Jews hold a middle position, making fewer changes in tradition and always justifying their decisions with reference to Jewish law (*halakhah*). In the United States, various aspects of observance have had gains and losses in popularity. For example, the bar mitzvah ceremony was rare in nineteenth century Reform synagogues, but it is virtually universal today.

There are other important currents in modern Jewish life. In the late 1960s young American Jews influenced by counterculture ideas began to gather in groups in living rooms to pray and study the Torah. They felt that most synagogues were too materialist and that they put the rabbi between the worshiper and the deity. The movement acquired the name "Jewish Renewal." Its influence grew as it focused on the deep spiritual significance of Jewish ritual and the need for it to serve all Jews. It gave many groups within Judaism the possibility of making their voices heard and has strongly influenced more mainstream groups. It has especially been a conduit for women to make known their need for equality within modern American Judaism.

Today, women are having a powerful effect on Jewish practice. In addition to gaining the right in the Reform, Conservative, and Reconstructionist movements to be ordained as rabbis, they are being accepted in **minyans** and having their right to *daven* recognized. They are influencing synagogues to use "gender-inclusive" prayers, in which masculine forms are not used. Poet **Marcia Falk** has written a prayer book in which there is no anthropomorphizing at all.

At times when the pressure to assimilate has been great, Jewish Americans have often devalued the importance of Jewish practices. Today, when all ethnic groups in the United States are seeing the virtue of recovering and maintaining cultural heritage, Jews are looking anew at the question of observance. However, their re-evaluation is informed by a new perspective on the rights of each individual.

BAR MITZVAH

Popularly translated as "son of commandment," the bar mitzvah is the attainment by a Jewish boy of his religious maturity and adulthood on reaching the age of thirteen. The bar mitzvah ceremony includes wearing **tefillin**, reciting the Torah blessings, chanting a portion of the Law (*Maftir*), and reading from the Prophetic portion of the *Haftarah*. In both Sephardic and Ashkenazi communities, modern bar mitzvahs have incorporated a discourse by the thirteen-year-old showing his understanding of the rabbinic explications and expanding on points in Talmudic law. Generally, the young man's Hebrew teacher writes this address for the bar mitzvah honoree to memorize and present to the congregation. After the ritual, he is included in the prayer quorum (*minyan*).

The bar mitzvah concept traces its origins to the Talmud where it was originally written that at age thirteen the male child becomes liable for his own transgressions and the father no longer has this responsibility. It was after the late Middle Ages, however, when the ceremony itself became formalized. In the earliest East European Askenazi tradition, young men were called to the Torah to recite the benediction and to chant several verses from the week's Pentateuchal reading on the first Monday or Thursday after they turned thirteen. The custom of having the reading take place at Saturday morning Sabbath services began in Western Europe and spread throughout the Diaspora.

Other practices that have become associated with the contemporary bar mitzvah ceremony developed over the course of the years. Some Western Ashkenazi and Sephardic communities instituted the recitation of a special prayer by the bar mitzvah boy as he stood before the rabbi or the Holy Ark. Generally, it has become customary in the modern ceremony for the rabbi to address the young man after the Reading of the Law and for the rabbi to then read the *Mi-she-Berakah* prayer on the candidate's behalf. Among most Sephardim, the thirteen-year-old also recites the *Sheheyanu* blessing.

In the nineteenth century the burgeoning **Reform Judaism** movement viewed the bar mitzvah as archaic and instead substituted the group confirmation ritual for both boys and girls in their late teens. By the mid-twentieth century, most Reform congregations began to moderate their views and re-incorporated the traditional celebration in their religious practices. In contemporary America, the bar mitzvah has become especially important as an occasion for the young man to assert his Jewish identity and for congregations to persuade the bar mitzvah family to join their

Sometimes criticized as nothing more than an excuse to have an elaborate teenage party, the bar mitzvah ceremony has, if anything, become more "grown-up" in late-twentieth-century America. The "bar mitzvah boy" is often required to give a sermon, in addition to reading from the Torah. The bar mitzvah class pictured above dates from the 1920s in Malden, Massachusetts. (Courtesy of the American Jewish Historical Society, Waltham, Massachusetts and New York, New York)

synagogue. Often, the bar mitzvah celebrant is expected to give a "sermon" based on the weekly Torah reading.

The festivities following the bar mitzvah have become a major social event for the teenager and his family. It is an occasion for him to receive gifts from parents, friends, and relatives. Although originally intended as a third meal eaten after the Sabbath Afternoon Service, the bar mitzvah reception has moved from a *kiddush* at the Morning Service and a family dinner to its current incarnation as an all-day and all-evening affair.

The bar mitzvah is an integral part of contemporary Jewish religious life and is a significant moment in the life of the teenager who completes its rites. The ritual continues to have such resonance that it has been embraced by many Jewish adults who never had the opportunity to celebrate a bar mitzvah at age thirteen. It serves a meaningful purpose in affirming Jewish heritage and culture.

BAT MITZVAH

by Paula E. Hyman

"The Friday night before the service my father decided what I was to do. I was to recite the blessings, read a portion of the Torah *sidra* . . . in Hebrew and in English and conclude with the blessing—and that was it. . . . And that was enough to shock a lot of people, including my own grandparents and aunts and uncles."

So reminisced Judith Kaplan Eisenstein, the daughter of Rabbi **Mordecai Kaplan**, about her 1922 bat mitzvah ceremony, widely considered the first to have occurred in America. The bat mitzvah is the female equivalent of a boy's **bar mitzvah**, the ritual that signifies his entrance into religious majority at age thirteen. To mark the occasion, in the synagogue the boy is called to the Torah for the first time and, if the Sabbath is the chosen day, chants the *haftarah*, the prophetic portion of that week.

The bat mitzvah ritual was introduced into American Judaism as both an ethical and a pragmatic response to gender divisions in traditional Judaism. For boys, reaching religious majority occasioned a ritual ceremony in the synagogue, but for girls, attaining the status of adult received no communal attention. Jewish tradition declared a girl's majority to begin at age twelve, but her transition from child to adult was not reflected in the synagogue. Women had no part in the public reading of the Torah except as listeners, segregated in the women's gallery. On the ethical plane, the new rite was designed to demonstrate that, in the modern age, women were considered equal with men. On the practical level, it provided a stimulus for educating women in Judaism as preparation for their presumed role as transmitters of Jewish culture and religious sensibility.

The bat mitzvah ceremony has its roots in developments in nineteenth-century Judaism of Western Europe and America. As Jews became exposed to Western culture in the nineteenth century, acquired a measure of political rights, and began the process of social integration, they adapted aspects of their religious tradition to the values of the larger society. Concerned that the limited roles of women within traditional Judaism might suggest that Jews were "Orientals" rather than Westerners, Jewish leaders included girls in the new ceremony of group confirmation that they instituted. The ceremony generally took place as a ritual conclusion to one's Jewish education. Confirmation was a regular feature of the American **Reform Movement** by the second half of the nineteenth century. Its growing popularity displaced the individual bar mitzvah rite.

The Reform Movement diminished the importance of the bar mitzvah, and **Orthodox** Jews accepted the gender segregation of the traditional synagogue as a divine mandate, so it fell to the **Conservative Movement** to struggle with the issue of the bat mitzvah ceremony. Committed to both tradition and modernity, Conservative Judaism became the most popular denomination among American Jews in the interwar years, when the children of Eastern European immigrants became the predominant group in the Jewish community. Even within the Conservative Movement, however, Kaplan's 1922 innovation had few immediate followers. A decade later, only a handful of synagogues had adopted the rite. By 1948, some form of

---

Ann Rezak—A Bat Mitzvah Girl Surrounded by Her Grandchildren and Great-Grandchildren

Ann Rezak had her bat mitzvah at the age of 86. She was among sixty women from across the country who participated in a group bat mitzvah at the eighty-fourth Hadassah National Convention in 1988 in New York City. Born the same year Henrietta Szold started Hadassah (1912), Rezak is the mother of three, grandmother of eleven, and great-grandmother of "lots."

Barbara Spack, Hadassah's national education chair, served as the cantor for the packed service. She explains: "Growing up, most of these women did not have the opportunity to study Torah or to observe a bat mitzvah ceremony. They looked on enviously as their fathers and brothers participated. This program enables women to feel like equal partners in Jewish spiritual life."

bat mitzvah ceremony was held in about one-third of Conservative congregations. By the 1960s it had become a regular feature within the movement.

Until the past decade or so, the ritual was not a precise parallel of the bar mitzvah. It was often held at Friday night services, when the Torah is not read. Even Judith Kaplan, whose bat mitzvah took place on Sabbath morning, read a passage in Hebrew and English from the printed *Humash* (first five books of the Bible), rather than from the Torah scroll, after the completion of the regular Torah service.

Although designed simply to offer public recognition of a girl's coming of age religiously, the bat mitzvah rite raised questions about the status of women within the synagogue. How could a girl be called to the Torah as a bat mitzvah and then never have such an honor again? In 1955, the Conservative Rabbinical Assembly's Committee on Jewish Law and Standards discussed the issue of extending *aliyot* (the honor of being called to the Torah) to women. A favorable minority opinion fostered the dissemination of this practice and paved the way for the full equality of women within the Conservative synagogue that gradually prevailed in the 1970s and 1980s.

Equality for women in the Reform Movement had sources other than the bat mitzvah, although there were some bat mitzvah ceremonies in Reform temples from 1931. The rehabilitation of ritual within Reform Judaism in recent decades has led to a greater attention to both the bat and bar mitzvah ceremonies as an important component of public worship. While in 1953 only 35 percent of Reform temples offered the bat mitzvah to their members, the ritual has since become close to universal.

With the emergence of Jewish feminism in the 1970s, the need to acknowledge the equality of women as Jews has led to the adoption of some type of bat mitzvah ceremony by every American Jewish denomination from Reform to modern Orthodoxy. Even within Reform, Reconstructionist, and Conservative Judaism, women have generally enjoyed ritual equality for less than a generation. Some adult women have also turned to the bat mitzvah ceremony as a way to expand their Jewish knowledge and skills and to signify

"No thunder sounded. No lightning struck," recalled Judith Kaplan Eisenstein of her history-making 1922 bat mitzvah ceremony, the first in America. She is pictured here at her second bat mitzvah ceremony, where she was honored by a number of prominent Jewish women. (Courtesy of Reconstructionist Rabbinical College)

their assumption of the rights and responsibilities of Jewish adulthood in the past fifteen years. Unlike younger celebrants, they often perform the ritual as members of a group.

The form of the bat mitzvah rite varies according to the custom of the particular denomination. In non-Orthodox synagogues the bat mitzvah, like her male counterpart, may simply be called to the Torah and recite the *haftarah* or may also chant the Torah portion and deliver a *devar Torah*, a talk based on the weekly reading. In Orthodox synagogues, the constraints of Jewish law prevent a girl from being called to the

Torah, but some synagogues allow a bat mitzvah to give a *devar Torah* after the conclusion of the service or at a festive meal. In a few Orthodox communities a women's *tefilla* (prayer) group enables the celebrant to perform all the roles of a non-Orthodox bat mitzvah, with the exception of reciting the blessings. The once-radical innovation of the bat mitzvah has become widely accepted in American Judaism and symbolizes the changing roles of women in the American Jewish religious community.

BRIS AND CIRCUMCISION

The act of circumcision, the removal of part or all of the foreskin covering the penis, is a nearly universally practiced Jewish ritual. Circumcision is considered a symbol of the covenant between God and the descendants of Abraham as stated in Genesis 17. Most Jews in the United States and throughout the world view circumcision of the male infant as both sacrosanct and pre-ordained. The circumcision is traditionally performed on the eighth day of a male child's life as part of a ceremony known as a *bris*. The Jewish laws detailing the various aspects of ritual circumcision can be found in a number of biblical sources, oral tradition, and rabbinical enactments.

Besides the covenant with the children of Abraham, circumcision also appears in the Bible in several additional stories that have become the foundation for differing theories regarding the origins of the ritual. In one from Genesis, Jacob's sons object to the impending marriage of their sister to Schechem the Hivite who is uncircumcised. In another story from Exodus, Zipporah, the wife of Moses is said to have taken a flint to ". . . cut off her son's foreskin" when "God encountered him and sought to kill him." A third, less overt reference to circumcision can also be found in Joshua.

Traditionalists generally view circumcision as a divine commandment and have historically believed that the practice was done for both hygienic (cleanliness) and moral (the symbolic control of one's sexual desires) reasons. Others have emphasized that many ancient peoples before the time of Abraham practiced circumcision as a tribal initiation ceremony, a male

fertility ritual, or a magical rite designed to appease angry gods and protect human males from their rage. While God provides land to the Jews as an "everlasting holding" as part of the circumcision covenant in Genesis, the more spiritual and symbolic "circumcision of the heart" described in Deuteronomy and Jeremiah is also evoked as a metaphor to explain the importance of the ritual.

Circumcision is also viewed as many embodying notions of Jewish resistance and survival. At the time of the Macabees, the Greek king, Antiochus, outlawed the practice and created shame on the part of some Jews who tried to disguise that they had been circumcised. When the Macabees revolted they saw it as their responsibility to circumcise fellow Jews as a sign of pride and power. Several centuries later, the Jews of Rome rebelled when the emperor condemned circumcision.

Unlike other Jewish traditions deeply rooted in liturgical texts, circumcision of infant males continues to be practiced among most contemporary Jews in the United States, whether or not the parents are otherwise religiously observant. It is also considered an essential element in the conversion to Judaism for adult males. Even if the convert is already circumcised, a ritual drawing of a drop of blood must be performed as part of Jewish law.

The basic circumcision ritual has been augmented by new customs that have developed over time. A traditional bris takes place in the presence of a quorum of ten adult Jewish males. On the morning of the eighth day, the godmother takes the child from the mother and hands him to the godfather, who carries the infant into the room of the circumcision. There the child is given to the person who will place him in the "Chair of Elijah." In some countries the Chair of Elijah is where the godfather sits during the ceremony, but in the United States it is generally a separate chair in which the child is placed briefly prior to the circumcision itself. The prophet Elijah is invited to every circumcision as a "witness" who testifies to God that the children of Israel have maintained their covenant.

The infant boy is then taken from the chair and passed to his father, who puts him back on the lap of his Godfather to hold during the ceremony. In a bris

Circumcision of male infants continues to be practiced among most contemporary Jews in the United States, whether or not the parents are otherwise religiously observant. The instruments used in the ceremony could sometimes be part of an ornate "set." Pictured above is the Seixas family circumcision set. (Courtesy of American Jewish Historical Society, Waltham, Massachusetts and New York, New York)

the circumcision is performed by a *mohel* (circumcisor), although some Reform and other less observant Jews accept a medical doctor as a substitute and sometimes forego the bris altogether in favor of a private circumcision.

In earlier generations, the *mohel* drew blood from the circumcision orally, but in contemporary America and throughout most of the world, a knife, shield, or probe is now used. After the circumcision, the *mohel* gives the child back to the person who will hold him during the naming ceremony, where a special blessing is recited over a cup of wine and the boy receives his Jewish name. The *bris* is followed by a festive meal. Although the ceremony is sometimes performed in a synagogue, it has increasingly become a ritual conducted in the family's home.

Under Jewish law, ritual circumcision *must* be performed on the eighth day of life and takes precedence over the observance of Shabbat, other festivals, and even Yom Kippur. Postponement of the circumcision is allowed only in cases where there may be a danger to the infant's health. If two male children in a family have died following circumcision, it is not necessary for further infant boys to be circumcised.

Given the great diversity of the American Jewish community and their wide variety of religious beliefs, it is remarkable that circumcision remains sacrosanct to such an overwhelming majority of the population. Other ethnic groups also believe in the value and importance of circumcision, but it is the Jewish people who have universally embraced the practice as essential to their identity. The act of circumcising Jewish male babies and the ceremony that frequently accompanies it look to be enduring rituals which will continue into the next millennium and beyond.

CEMETERIES

The cemetery comprises a specific set of Jewish traditions and customs connected to the burial of the dead. Known in Hebrew as *bet kevarot*, "place of the graves," and *bet olam*, "house of eternity," the land of the cemetery is usually considered holy and a special consecration ceremony reserved for Jews takes place on its inauguration. At the same time, the cemetery is also a source of ritual impurity—those of priestly descent are not permitted to enter except to attend the burial of near relatives, and many people observe the ritual of washing the hands upon leaving cemetery grounds as a sign of purification.

Establishing a cemetery is one of the first and highest priorities for a new Jewish community, and a Jewish cemetery is generally purchased and supported with communal funds. Congregations and Jewish burial societies have acquired their own cemeteries, and private Jewish cemeteries that sell grave sites to the general Jewish public also have developed in the contemporary era.

Many older traditions associated with cemeteries have been maintained over the years. Graves are arranged in rows with a distance of six "handbreaths" between each one. It is considered inappropriate to drink, read, or study in a Jewish cemetery. It is considered a mocking of the dead to wear *tefillin* or carry a Scroll of the Law within four cubits of a grave. In addition, a number of leading rabbis have spoken out against using expensive or elaborate tombstones to mark the graves and voiced their preference for serving the memory of the dead through contributions to charity while keeping the gravestones simple and inexpensive. There is generally a building erected at the cemetery for use as a chapel and sometimes as a site to prepare the body for burial.

Other aspects of Jewish cemeteries are more open to variations, including having separate rows for men and women, dividing Sephardim from Ashkenazim, burying in chronological order of death, and having family plots. Traditionally, specific rows were reserved for rabbis and communal leaders deemed as particularly pious or upstanding. Conversely, there were also designated rows for suicides, apostates, and transgressors, usually near the cemetery wall. Although these customs are no longer the rule in most cemeteries, it is still considered important that a pious person should be buried near another pious person and that enemies should not be buried next to each other.

The most common occasions for visiting grave sites include: at the end of seven days of mourning; thirty days after burial; and annually on the date of death. In some communities, it is also traditional to visit the cemetery during the month of *Elul*, prior to the New Year. Some people also pay their respects on the ninth of *Av* and the eve of **Yom Kippur**.

In traditional Jewish custom, those entering a cemetery after an absence of over thirty days recite a blessing affirming that God is the master of life and death who will lead us to new life hereafter. The prayer concludes with "Blessed are You, who revives the dead."

CONFIRMATION

Confirmation is the public ceremony primarily found in non-Orthodox congregations in the English-speaking world in which young adolescents profess their commitment to Judaism and the Jewish community. Unlike the Christian confirmation on which it was

The confirmation ceremony has served different purposes at different times in American Jewish history. It has always symbolized a rite of passage or graduation to a new and more mature stage of Jewish education. The above confirmation class photograph is from 1902 in Philadelphia, Pennsylvania, and includes both young women and young men. (Courtesy of American Jewish Historical Society, Waltham, Massachusetts and New York, New York)

loosely based, Jewish confirmation does not require a formal declaration. In contemporary form, confirmation is a group ceremony for boys and girls who master a course of Torah study in a congregational religious school program within the foundation of a synagogue *Shavuot* service. Confirmants take an active and creative role in developing and carrying out the service that symbolizes a rite of passage or graduation to a new and more mature stage of Jewish education.

The practice of Jewish confirmation traces its roots to the German Jewish **Reform Movement** of the nineteenth century. The earliest reformers, tracing their origins to the Kingdom of Westphalia, viewed confirmation as complementary to the **bar mitzvah**. They saw the older ritual as implying a technical change of status while the newer one reflected knowledge, motivation, and personal commitment.

This attitude shifted among the leading reformers who entered the United States in mid-century. For them, group confirmation ceremonies represented a process of acculturation and adaptation of Jewish religious tradition to the values of American democracy and supplanted the individual bar mitzvah. Confirmation also provided an opportunity to include girls in a "coming of age ritual" reinforcing the Reform Movement's identification with contemporary and western mores.

In contemporary America confirmation has increasingly served to supplement rather than replace the individual bar mitzvah ceremony. The growing popularity of the **bat mitzvah** ritual for girls has strengthened the belief of many in all denominations of Jewish life that individual and group rites both deserve attention. This has been especially true for **Conservative** Jews who use the phrase *ben* or *bat Torah* to refer to Confirmants. Nevertheless, the role of confirmation and its relationship to the bar or bat mitzvah continues to be a source of dialogue and debate within Jewish circles.

Ideological differences have also surfaced around other issues related to confirmation such as whether girls and boys should be confirmed together or separately; whether the ritual should be held in a public hall or school, or a synagogue; and, if in a synagogue, as part of the regular service or at a special convocation. There are those who believe in the idea of individual rather than group confirmation activities. In addition, age has also emerged as a point of discussion. Although the reformers who initiated confirmation as a replacement for the bar mitzvah chose the same age, thirteen, for the new ritual, it is now more likely to occur at age fifteen as a means of ensuring that children will continue their Jewish education for several years after their bar or bat mitzvahs. Most Orthodox Jews continue to reject the notion of Jewish confirmation ceremonies since they are not biblically sanctioned.

Although confirmation is a relatively modern concept, it has served an important role in forging the identities of Jews in America and throughout the English-speaking Diaspora. It appears to have a secure future among Conservative and especially Reform Jews.

FAMILY LIFE

Jewish immigrants brought traditions of family life with them while also establishing customs and practices rooted in their new lives in the United States. With successive generations born in America, Jewish families increasingly became more assimilated and mirrored the norms of the society in which they lived. Thus, as societal values have changed in the United States so have those of Jewish families. Nonetheless, many Jews have maintained familial relations at least partly rooted in a legacy that goes back for centuries. Family life for Jews in the United States represents a broad amalgam of old and new, secular and religious, constancy and change.

Home and family have been the backbone of Jewish life from time immemorial. The sages viewed it as continuing many of the traditions of the ancient temple. The Jewish home is said to be permeated with sanctity when the Jewish family lives according to Jewish values and traditions. Domestic harmony was an ideal that Jewish families held to and this harmony was achieved not only through the give and take of interpersonal relationships but also through the experience of ritual and holy events. The celebrations and commemorative events in the Jewish year and lifecycle served to unify the family and elevate the mundane to the level of the holy. The pattern of Jewish family life set down in the Talmud was the model and practice until modern times.

In the United States, Jews throughout successive stages of immigration developed strong extended family and kin networks. Despite numerous stresses and difficulties, the family, broadly defined, remained the major element of stability for immigrants in a strange and often hostile and unpredictable new world. This was especially the case for the masses of mostly poor Eastern European Jews who arrived in the United States with few resources other than their families.

The vast majority of first-generation Jews lived in family units, often with grandparents and aunts and uncles. With all the problems of adjustment that most of them faced, the extended clan network stood at the heart of immigrant life and was crucial to the survival of its members. The focus of religious practice (which in Europe was centered in the synagogue) also began to shift for American Jews from the house of worship to the home. Rabbis, who were strong authority figures in the old country, often had little influence in the United States.

Jewish families increasingly became the source of continuity for holiday celebration and other forms of ritual. While the responsibility for assuring conformity with Jewish tradition was frequently shared for many immigrants among an extended family network, in twentieth-century America the nuclear family began to assume a greater measure of centrality in the expression and maintenance of Jewish identity. At the same time, the rapid acculturation process of first-generation Jews sometimes created rifts and division within the family as the values of parents clashed with those of their children, especially with respect to the maintenance of Jewish religious and communal traditions.

During the first two decades of the twentieth century, intergenerational rifts among immigrant families were so strong that the Yiddish-language **Jewish Daily Forward**'s popular "*Bintel* Briefs" (literally, "bundle of letters") column was flooded with letters from both parents and children chronicling the conflicts that each had with the other over values and expectations. This was a particular difficulty for Jewish daughters, who often faced restrictions on their mobility and frequently were deprived of the educational opportunities their brothers enjoyed.

Although the majority of Jewish parents have been American-born, struggles between the generations fueled by societal changes have had and continue to have an impact on the Jewish family as a whole. As in past generations, these conflicts are often focused on parental expectations for their children regarding home, family, and religious commitment versus the children's desire for increased freedom and autonomy.

Despite massive changes in the Jewish family and the American family as a whole, Judaism remains a religion centered around familial life. Almost all Jews who join synagogues do so as family units. The most frequently practiced observances—the **Passover Seder**, the lighting of the **Hanukkah** candles, and the **Rosh Hashanah** holiday meal—are primarily family events. Overall, affiliation rates with Jewish institutions increase dramatically with the birth of children and then rise even more rapidly as children attain school age. Although performance of traditional ritual practices, such as frequent worship, dietary law observances, and Sabbath candle lighting declines significantly with each generation, Jews who raise families are far more likely to observe Jewish holidays and ceremonies and to take part in Jewish institutional life than those who are childless. Evidence shows that the Jewish family continues to play a central role in the transmission and expression of "Jewishness."

In addition to the holiday and *Shabbat* celebrations and rituals connected to them, Jewish families maintain a continuity with their traditions through birth, wedding, **bar** and **bat mitzvahs**, anniversary celebrations, and, at the end of life, through Jewish funeral rites and the process of mourning, which includes the *shiva* period. Even parents who do not consider themselves otherwise religiously observant perform circumcision rites for their male children on the eighth day after birth, join synagogues to enable their sons or daughters to receive bar and bat mitzvahs, and plan weddings that incorporate at least some elements of Jewish tradition.

More religiously observant Jews continue to view the home as a "minor sanctuary," as was written in the ancient texts, and they embrace a number of ritual symbols of sanctity and tradition. These include a *mezuzah* on each doorpost containing the opening paragraph of the basic Jewish confession of faith written on parchment paper, the Sabbath candles, the cup for *kiddush*, the spicebox for *havdalah* at the end of the Sabbath, and the eight-branched menorah for Hanukkah. Families that maintain kosher traditions separate meat and milk utensils and prepare food according to ancient Jewish dietary laws.

Most importantly, Jews have always viewed the home and the family as the place where Jewish values were communicated by parents to children through formal education and instruction. A steady number of parents send their children to Hebrew school programs. For many **Orthodox** and even some **Conservative** Jews, the all-day Jewish school has become an important avenue for transmitting the texts and belief systems of Judaism from generation to generation. Secular Jewish parents, while eschewing formal religious study for their children, often believe that there are deeper moral and ethical values rooted in the Jewish heritage that must be passed down to their families.

With the acculturation of Jews to American society, many customs that characterized the traditional Jewish home and family have been abandoned except among the strictly Orthodox. Nevertheless, the rituals that continue to endure tend to be child-centered, rooted in family life, and more easily interpreted in humanistic, universal terms.

Over the past several decades, the American family has undergone sweeping changes and transitions that have deeply effected Jews. The contemporary feminist movement has raised significant questions about women's role within the Jewish family and has challenged many of the patriarchal conventions associated with traditional Judaism. Historically, Jewish women have been expected to take responsibility for the maintenance of religious Judaism within the home and to assume the traditional domestic roles that contributed to maintaining a proper Jewish home. The women's movement has attempted to expand the role of Jewish women in the home beyond that of mother and housewife while also demanding a leadership role and "place at the table" in public Jewish life.

At the same time, the increasing prevalence of divorce and the proliferation of single-parent families has raised new questions about how the Jewish home and family are to be defined. Controversial issues such as intermarriage and homosexuality have exploded in Jewish life and often created a firestorm of emotional upheaval within the family. American Jewish leaders have spoken out on these topics and have consistently framed their positions from the point of view of the impact on the Jewish family. There have been an increasing number of institutions established by "alternative" household members outside existing institutions including gay synagogues and *chauvarot*—worship and study communities—composed primarily of single and childless young people. Synagogues and community centers have also increasingly developed programs especially designed for singles, divorcees, or intermarried couples.

The impulse to accommodate growing numbers of nontraditional families continues to be resisted by many within the broader Jewish community on both cultural and religious grounds. Jewish law traditionally rejects homosexuality largely because the sexual act cannot result in procreation—one of the most important functions of sex according to the Jewish sages. Orthodox Jews oppose the modern tendency to legitimize homosexual behavior and adhere to the strict *Halakic* interpretation of the practice (although not the individuals involved) as an "abomination." Conversely, American Jews have been and continue to be active leaders in the gay and lesbian movements, with many demanding to be considered both "queer" and Jewish. Homosexual Jews with children have fought to be considered and treated as legitimate Jewish "families."

Until recent times, marrying outside the faith was also condemned in the Jewish community and parents sometimes observed mourning rites for a child who had intermarried. The rise of non-Orthodox movements in Judaism over the last century loosened rabbinic control over most of the Jewish community and introduced a larger element of personal choice into the process of choosing a marriage partner. While intermarriage continues to be condemned by a sizable minority who believe it will lead to the destruction of the Jewish family, the practice is also accepted by many Jews who believe it is important to embrace the children of interfaith unions as full-fledged members of the Jewish community rather than to alienate them from that community. There is also evidence showing that a significant number of Jewish parents in interfaith unions have made put much effort into ensuring that their children grow up with a sense of their Jewish identity.

A Mitzvah in Memory of My Father

When Meyer Michael Greenberg died in June 1995, his obituary was prominently featured in *The New York Times*, not for his professional accomplishments (he earned his living as a print coordinator in an advertising agency), but for a three-decade dedication to a simple "good deed."

When his father died in 1963, Mr. Greenberg (remembering how cold he had often been growing up poor in New York City) vowed to honor his father's memory by providing warmth for those who most needed it—the homeless on the Bowery's Skid Row. He decided that gloves would be the most useful article of clothing he could provide and he spent his spare time every winter for the next thirty years distributing them to the homeless.

"Who was that guy?" asked one recipient. The simple answer from his neighbor on the sidewalk, "Gloves." When asked what he charged for the gloves, Mr. Greenberg responded, "a handshake." Meyer Michael Greenberg spent thirty years of his life performing a *mitzvah*. It gained him a famous obituary and the gratitude of thousands of people who knew him only as "Gloves." His father's memory was well served.

Other changes have also greatly affected the American Jewish family. Suburbanization and geographic and social mobility have meant a decline in the role of the extended family and the broad kinship network in Jewish life. Likewise, the family's role in caring for elderly parents, relatives, and family members has shifted from the home to senior residences and nursing homes—many under the auspices of Jewish institutions and Jewish leadership. Increasingly, Jews in the social work field have specialized in Jewish family services with a particular focus on gerontology and the needs of the Jewish elderly.

The Jewish family in contemporary America has witnessed a sea of transformations and dislocations over the last century. At the same time, Jewish home and family life continues to be the foundation and cornerstone of Jewish cultural continuity. As the overall Jewish community has become more affluent and prosperous, Jewish social welfare organizations have proliferated with a goal of providing community supports to Jewish families and services to the newest groups of immigrant Jews.

It is somewhat ironic that at the same time as traditional familial authority has eroded and diminished within the Jewish population and American society at large, the home and nuclear family has, in many respects, become stronger and more important as the repository for Jewish values and education, especially with the loosening of broader communal ties. Jewish families continue to have a significant influence on American Jewish life and culture.

FOOD AND COOKING

Jewish immigrants arriving in America brought with them a rich culinary tradition that evolved through many years in the Diaspora. In their lives in the United States, Jews have maintained a distinct cuisine and style of cooking and baking that has been altered and changed by modern American living but has persevered over generations. Jewish foods such as bagels, blintzes, borscht, and chicken soup with noodles have become widely popular in numerous urban and suburban communities and now are considered part of an international culinary culture. Food has also served as a powerful vehicle by which Jews have expressed a religious, cultural, and ethnic identity in the old world and the new.

Certain foods have long histories among Jews. Fish may be the oldest traditional Jewish dish, since it is mentioned prominently in the Torah. When the Israelites were in the wilderness, they complained about their monotonous diet, saying, "we remember the fish that we used to eat freely in Egypt." The attractiveness of fish came from the fact that it did not call for ritual slaughter and could be eaten with dairy or meat meals under Jewish dietary laws. In the United States, cold fish in particular such as smoked salmon, lox, whitefish, herring, and sable have been among the foods most associated with Jewish cuisine. The popularity of fish salads and chopped liver among the general population can also be traced to Jewish influence.

The observances associated with the Sabbath and holidays contributed to making Jewish cuisine different from that of other peoples. A typical Ashkenazi Friday evening *shabbat* menu includes chopped herring or gefilte fish (fishballs), chicken soup with noodles, roasted chicken or meat, *tsimmes* (a side dish of carrots and prunes), and a fruit compote. The highlight of the Sabbath midday meal has historically been a steaming hot *tcholent* consisting of potatoes, beans, barley, groats, and meat placed in a heated oven and allowed to stew and thicken. Chopped eggs and onions or chopped chicken liver serve as side dishes, often with a noodle or potato *kugel* (pudding). Although many of these traditions have softened among American Jews, grains such as kasha and barley and root vegetables such as carrots, yams, and potatoes continue to be popular in various incarnations in Jewish soups, salads, and main dishes.

Breads and other baked goods made from flour are enormously important in Jewish cuisine. In ancient Eretz Yisrael, bread was considered the "staff of life"— the basic food—and in biblical times it was used extensively as an accompaniment to various types of sacrifices and offerings. In Talmudic times, the practice began of reciting the *Ha-Motsi* benediction prior to eating bread. Hallah, the festival bread made from one of five grains—wheat, barley, spelt, oats, or rye— may be the most important symbolic representation of Jewish cuisine in America. On **Shabbat** the blessing is always recited over two hallah loaves and on **Rosh Hashanah**, the Jewish New Year, the hallah loaves are usually baked round or in different shapes, each with a symbolic meaning. The hallah for the pre-**Yom Kippur** fast meal is traditionally round and braided. Even nonobservant Jews frequently purchase hallah for festive occasions and regular meals.

Baked desserts also play an essential role in Jewish culinary culture. Chocolate and cinnamon pastry known as *rugalach*, chocolate-laced *mandel* bread, and *hamantashen*—three-cornered pastry filled with prune, raspberry, or apricot—are all staples of Jewish bakeries. On **Passover**, when food containing leavened flour is forbidden, Jewish families eat cakes made of matzah meal or potato flour; almond and coconut macaroons; and matzah puddings. On **Shavuot**, special desserts include fruit strudels, cheese cakes, cheese *kreplach*, and baklava.

A number of famous Jewish dishes are associated with holidays. Besides blintzes, which were originally traditional only for Shavuot but are now eaten throughout the year, latkes, pancakes made of grated potatoes and fried in oil, are a symbol for **Hanukkah**. *Teyglakh*, a confection made with honey, is a typical **Sukkot** delicacy.

Most of the foods that Americans associate with Jewish cuisine are generally of Ashkenazi origin. However, Sephardim who came from North Africa and the Middle East brought with them to the United States recipes for different dishes, which included herbs, spices, olive oil, vegetables, and lamb. The names of most Sephardi dishes tend to be of Judeo-Spanish, Arabic, or Persian origin while Ashkenazi dishes usually have Yiddish names.

Because Jewish dietary laws forbid eating meat and dairy products together, Jewish **kosher** restaurants generally specialize in one or the other. Dairy restaurants serve hearty vegetable and potato soups, fish salads, blintzes, and kasha and barley dishes. Jewish delicatessens, both kosher and non-kosher, have become renowned in the United States for their pastrami and corned beef sandwiches and hot dishes such as stuffed cabbage and brisket. Both types of restaurants generally provide a variety of fresh bread and rolls including bagels, onion rolls, bialys, and pumpernickel, black, and Jewish rye breads. Jewish dairy restaurants and, especially, Jewish delicatessens have become popular with many non-Jews in a number of American cities and a source for numerous imitations. Some of the most famous Jewish delicatessens in New York have been enshrined into popular culture, most especially the Carnegie, where **Woody Allen**'s Protestant girl friend in the movie *Annie Hall* orders corned beef on white bread with mayonnaise, much to the chagrin of Allen and the Jewish waiters.

Despite the popularity of Jewish restaurants, Jewish food and cooking is intimately tied to family gatherings in the home and special occasions, holidays, and other rituals. For Jews, both in the New World and the old, food is associated with welcoming and warmth. Food has served as a means by which Jewish immigrants both adapted their culture to that of the United States and attempted to hold on to time-honored culinary traditions. Not all the Jewish communities entering the United States drew from the same array of dishes, since what became Jewish American cooking was also determined by the regions in which Jews lived and what resources were available.

Many of the German Jewish women who started settlement houses during the turn of the century years attempted to teach Eastern European girls how to build a fire, cook, and bake. Lizzie Black Kander, who established the Milwaukee Jewish Mission, sponsored cooking classes every Sunday for new immigrants and taught them how to prepare dishes such as German *kuchen*, cranberry jelly, and waffles. She also published (in 1901) a book of American recipes called *The Settlement Cook Book: The Way to a Man's Heart*, which sought to use the culinary arts as a tool for successful assimilation. The proceeds were donated to institutions providing help to new immigrants. The cookbook contained one hundred non-kosher German Jewish and turn of the century American recipes. It turned out to be enormously popular and had sold nearly two million copies by 1984.

The first national Jewish women's' organization, the **National Council of Jewish Women** (founded in 1893) also put out cookbooks with a decidedly German slant—featuring shellfish (not permitted under kosher laws), many goose recipes, and American hybrid dishes such as chicken chow mein made from leftover chicken soup!

Although Eastern European Jews hoped for a new life, many also wanted to retain their Orthodoxy, which included keeping kosher dietary laws. (Other Eastern European immigrants did rebel against these ancient traditions.) At one time, there were almost four thousand kosher butcher shops in New York City alone and, by 1917, it was estimated that one million Jews ate as much as 156 million pounds of kosher meat a year. Demonstrations against rising prices of kosher meat and bread took place in New York City in 1902 and were nicknamed the "war of the women against the butchers."

At the same time, the burgeoning food business provided economic opportunities for these immigrants. Many of the newcomers who began their working lives in New York's Lower East Side, Chicago's west side, Boston's north end, and south Philadelphia as butchers, bakers, and pushcart peddlers of herring and pickles were able to forge new careers for themselves as independent grocers, wine merchants, and wholesale meat, produce, and food providers. The sexual segregation of Jewish practice almost always meant that women bought and cooked the food, while the jobs outside the home were predominantly taken by men.

The transformations in food processing technology had, by the second decade of the twentieth century, transformed Jewish cooking. Jewish women who had made their own yeast, corned their own beef, and prepared their own pickles and condiments increasingly took advantage of new food processing and packaging. The invention of vegetable shortening also significantly changed Jewish cooking to the extent that Procter and Gamble advertised Crisco as a product for which the "Hebrew Race had been waiting 4,000 years!" Other inventions such as cream cheese, gelatin, pasteurized milk, phyllo dough, and frozen foods all affected Jewish cooking in the United States.

Jews entered the packaged food business themselves and several entrepreneurs built lucrative careers. A Chicago baker named Charley Lubin decided that in the new age of frozen foods he could sell his cheese cakes in bulk and build a new industry. Lubin's strategy succeeded beyond his wildest dreams and he named his new company Sara Lee, after his daughter.

Meanwhile, a dual process emerged in which mainstream America was becoming aware of Jewish cooking while Jewish cuisine became more influenced by American-derived foods. Just as the popular radio and television program, *The Goldbergs*, introduced non-Jews to Molly Goldberg's kitchen and her Jewish recipes, so too did Jewish cookbooks began to include recipes for Creole dishes, chicken fricassee using canned tomatoes, and *kuchen* using baking powder. Large food companies (Crisco and Manishewitz were among the most prominent) also began to produce Yiddish-English cookbooks to advertise their products. Maxwell House Coffee produced its own **Passover *Haggadah***, which it gave away with purchases of

---

The Kashering of Coca-Cola

Thanks to Rabbi Tobias Geffen (an Orthodox rabbi who served Atlanta's Congregation Shearith Israel from 1910 until his death in 1970), Coca-Cola became kosher in 1935, forty-nine years after it went on the market. After having been asked by several Orthodox rabbinic colleagues around the country about the status of the beverage (Coke's headquarters are in Atlanta), Geffen approached the company and asked if he could have access to the highly secret formula for the drink—perhaps one of the best-kept trade secrets in the country. After swearing him to absolute secrecy, the company provided him with a list of ingredients. They were not all kosher. Working with the rabbi, the company substituted other products which were, and now even the most observant Jews can feel comfortable that "things go better with Coke."

---

its products. In the post–World War II era, Edith Green became host of a popular television program, *Your Home Kitchen*, that emphasized teaching its viewers American "gourmet" cooking and the use of new mechanical implements such as electric mixers and electric can openers.

By the 1960s, Jewish cuisine had become increasingly Americanized while non-Jews became familiar and comfortable with many previously unheard-of Jewish foods. In addition, just as European regional cuisines influenced the Jewish culinary styles that emerged in the United States, Jewish foods took different shapes in various regions of America depending on regional traditions and the availability of ingredients. Gefilte fish might be made with whitefish in the midwest, salmon in the west, and haddock in the northeast. Jews in Vermont eat latkes with maple syrup while Californians frequently eat them with goat cheese, and New Yorkers prefer their latkes with sour cream or apple sauce. Despite the modernization and Americanization of Jewish foods, the kosher foods movement has also expanded by leaps and bounds and has become a major industry unto itself.

Jewish food and cooking have exerted a significant influence on American culture and society. Jewish culinary traditions have been intimately linked with the overall Jewish experience in the United States and reflect both the changes and continuities associated with that experience. Meanwhile, bagels, no matter how altered they are now from their original form, will continued to be consumed by millions of Americans—Jews and non-Jews alike.

FUNERALS

Jewish burial rituals have their roots in religious and philosophical practices that date back three thousand years. Although many Jewish Americans do not follow all the customs and conventions of traditional Jewish funeral ceremonies, a large percentage do observe core aspects of religious rites in services for their loved ones. The Jewish burial service has a long history within both Ashkenazi and Sephardic communities and it has evolved slightly differently in each. Overall, however, there are many threads common to funeral rites of observant Jews that cut across both national and denominational lines.

In ancient Jewish practice, when a death occurred the family immediately contacted the *Chevra Kadisha*, a holy society or holy group of friends that prepared the body for burial—a tradition that continues among many Jewish families today. One of the most meaningful tasks performed by the *Chevra Kadisha* has been the religious ritual bath of *Taharah* (purification) done on the morning of the funeral with men conducting the rites for men and women for women. Following the recitation of the prayers for *taharah*, Jews perform a 2,000-year-old custom of burial in *Takhrikhin* (shrouds), preceding the placement of the deceased in the casket. This tradition originated in the first century when Rabbi Gamaliel asked that he be buried in a very simple garment since he came into the world like everyone else and should return to God in the same way.

In the funeral procession, rabbis perform *keri'ah*—the rending of the garments on all those in attendance, then chant verses and psalms from biblical liturgy as they lead the mourners into the cemetery. Often, the group makes three stops along the route to the grave site to permit mourners to express their grief. The rabbi then performs a eulogy either in the funeral chapel or as the coffin is lowered into the grave.

Historically, adult males led by the mourners then cast three shovelfuls of earth until the mortal remains are covered. In recent years and in non-Orthodox congregations, this practice has increasingly become one that is shared between men and women who are part of the *Chevra Kadisha*. At either the grave site or the chapel, the mourners then read an extended version of the *Kaddish* that alludes to God's revival of the dead and the prayer for Jerusalem's restoration followed sometimes by an *azkarah* memorial prayer. The funeral service concludes with those present forming two rows between which the mourners walk and are offered traditional words of consolation. Before leaving the cemetery it is also traditional for Jews to pick a few blades of grass and recite either Psalm 72 or Psalm 103 and then wash their hands.

Although some Ashkenazi communities have adopted various Sephardic funeral rituals, especially in Israel, the traditional Sephardic funeral service has its own unique rituals. Sephardim generally begin the funeral service in synagogue rather than in the chapel of the cemetery and women often do not attend the actual interment. After *Kaddish* is recited at the synagogue prior to the burial, Syrian Jews blow a ram's horn (*shofar*). Western Sephardim (Spanish and Portuguese Jews) usually begin and conclude their services in the burial ground's chapel where the rending of garments occurs prior to the cortege leaving for the grave site. Unlike Christian funerals, Jewish tradition does not permit open caskets in burial services and the body of the deceased remains covered in shrouds or in a closed casket at all times.

JEWISH HOLIDAYS

Rosh Hashanah

Rosh Hashanah, observed for two days, marks the beginning of the Jewish New Year and the commencement of the ten days of awe (also known as the ten days of repentance and return), which reach their culmination on Yom Kippur, the day of atonement. Rosh Hashanah begins a time of reflection, renewal, and contemplation. Because it is observed on what is the seventh month of the Hebrew calendar, *Tishri*, it echoes the contemplative spirit of the Sabbath.

The phrase "Rosh Hashanah" does not appear in the Bible. By the time the organizing principles of the Jewish people were written in the law code of the *mishnah*, the rabbis determined that if the new moon of *Tishri* is when God is crowned king then it is also when the king passes judgment on the world by either renewing life or passing the sentence of death on human beings. It also speaks of all mankind passing before God on the New Year like a flock of sheep. Although it is celebrated in the seventh month, this day of judgment came to be known as the New Year—Rosh Hashanah. In the *Talmud*, written three hundred years later, the sages added another dimension to the holiday, that of redress of human beings toward one another as well as to God. Righteousness in giving, prayer, good conduct toward others, and self-examination in the light of Judaism's highest ideals are all mentioned in the Rosh Hashanah liturgy and have become key to understanding the holiday itself.

One of the high points of both days of Rosh Hashanah (unless the first day coincides with the Sabbath) is the blowing of the *shofar* (ram's horn). This symbol serves as a biblical injunction and a rousing call for individuals to repent as is written: "Awake you sleepers, and ponder your deeds; remember your Creator, forsake your evil ways, and return to God!" Rosh Hashanah liturgy includes the liturgical poems (*piyyutim*) and *Avinu Malekenu*. In the Ashkenazi prayer, the *U-Netanneh Tokef*, the Judgment Day theme is amplified in a hopeful manner with worshippers proclaiming: "Repentance, Prayer, and Good Deeds can avert the evil decree."

Many Jews observe the ritual of *Tashlich*, the symbolic casting of one's sins into a body of water, on the afternoon of the first day of Rosh Hashanah. This marks the beginning of ten days of reflecting on the past year, making amends, and cleansing oneself of vices and transgressive behaviors.

The traditional Rosh Hashanah dinner includes a piece of hallah and apples dipped in honey. Hallah loaves baked specially for the festival are usually round with a crust in the shape of a ladder to signify hopes to direct one's life upward to God.

Yom Kippur

Yom Kippur, the day of atonement, is considered the holiest and most solemn day in the Jewish religious calendar. It also represents the culmination of the ten days of awe that begin with Rosh Hashanah. Yom Kippur has also historically been the time when the Jewish people most affirm their spiritual connection. Many Jews mark the day by fasting—regarded as the final phase of the reflection and cleansing of the soul that has taken place over the previous nine days. More American Jews attend synagogue on the evening of Yom Kippur, the *Kol Nidre* service, than any other day in the year.

The book of Leviticus and the commandments "to make atonement before the Lord" and "afflict your soul" serve as the biblical foundation for Yom Kippur. The sages interpreted afflicting the soul as abstaining from food and drink. They viewed atonement as consisting of three related acts that would relieve the individual from the burden of sin: acknowledging transgressions, declaring repentance through a process of confession, and praying before God to receive forgiveness. The fast, the readings, and the formulas of confession all focus on these themes.

Although one can be absolved of one's sins against God through reflection, prayer, and spiritual cleansing, the philosophy of Yom Kippur dictates that individuals can atone for their sins against other people only through their actions. It has become traditional on the Day of Atonement for pious Jews to seek reconciliation with those whom they may have hurt or offended over the course of the previous year. This act of apology enables the individual to begin the Yom Kippur religious ceremony with a clear conscience.

Yom Kippur consists of five services each having its own special features and unique liturgy. The common thread that binds them is the confession of sins, which is repeated from the beginning of *Kol Nidre* to the concluding *Neilah* service the following night. All the confessionals are recited in the first person plural to remind participants of their collective responsibility for the actions of each individual and the individual's responsibility for the broader community. In most American Jewish communities, the doors of the Ark remain open throughout the day as a symbol that the Book of Life continues to allow for new opportunities to seek sincere repentance. *Neilah* is recited as twilight beckons and it ends with the chanting of *Avinu Malkenu*, followed by the *Shema* proclamation of God's unity. The *shofar* is then blown to symbolize the end of the fast and the call to the new day.

Traditional clothing for Yom Kippur includes the wearing of white as a symbol of purity and forgiveness. In Ashkenazi congregations, the rabbi and cantor both wear white *kitels* or gowns, although Sephardim do not observe this ritual. In addition, many Jews replace leather shoes with non-leather shoes and slippers before worshippers leave for the synagogue.

Sukkot

Sukkot, the Festival of Tabernacles, is celebrated during the fall harvest full moon after the High Holy Days of **Rosh Hashanah** and **Yom Kippur**. It is considered both the fulfillment of the moon of *Tishri* and the yearly cycle of the sun. Sukkot celebrates the glory of the earth fulfilled and its bounty. It is observed as a festival of thanksgiving for the riches of nature granted during the past year. In addition, like **Passover** and **Shavuot**, it is a Pilgrim Festival symbolizing the ancient pilgrimages made by Jews to the Temple in Jerusalem. Many modern congregations construct a *sukkah* and share at least one meal within its walls.

The most visual celebration of the holiday is the construction of the *sukkah*, an edifice built from cut vegetation such as tree branches or bamboo poles to remind Jews of the booths in which the Israelites lived in the wilderness after they left Egypt. Rabbis have suggested that the insubstantial nature of the *sukkah* symbolizes the human reliance on Divine protection. The top of the *sukkah* is covered with detached foliage or other natural growth so that stars can be seen through it at night. *Halakah* states that the *sukkah* must be large enough to hold the body of at least one person together with a table at which to eat.

In the older books of the Bible, Sukkot receives more attention than any other holiday. Its centrality diminished when the Hebrew people lost their connection with agriculture after the destruction of the Second Temple. An essential component of the festival are the four species, plants (one being a fruit) that are held together and waved at different points in the festival service to "rejoice before God:" the *lulav* (palm branch), the *etrog* (citron), the *haddassim* (three myrtle twigs), and the *aravot* (two willow branches).

On the first seven days of the festival, other than the Sabbath, the *lulav* is shaken during the *Hallel* (a chant of praise consisting of Psalms 113 through 118) in the four compass directions, in addition to up and down to affirm God's omnipotence and sovereignty over the entire universe. The reading for Sukkot is the book of Ecclesiastes.

In ancient times, the celebration of Sukkot was enhanced by the water-drawing festival when congregants poured water libations over the altar to highlight the petitions for rain that had been offered on Sukkot. The eighth and final day of Sukkot is marked today by prayers for rain to fall in Israel, a blessing considered central to a fruitful year.

Simchat Torah

Simchat Torah is a joyous festival celebrated when the yearly cycle of the Pentateuch (first five books of the Bible) reading in the synagogue is completed and a new one begins. In North America and other parts of the Diaspora, Simchat Torah is observed on the day after *Shemini Atseret*, the last day of **Sukkot**, making that holiday an extended nine-day celebration.

Although no specific biblical or Talmudic source exists for the separate festival of Simchat Torah, the holiday celebrates the process of Torah reading. In the Evening Service after *Attah Hreta La-Da'at*, congregants remove all the scrolls from the Ark and display them around the *bimah* (reader's platform) and the synagogue in a seven-part procession while chanting "Anna Adonai hoshi'ah na" (O God, save, we beseech you!), followed by an alphabetical doxology. Each procession is generally separated from the next one by a singing and dancing interlude in which other members of the congregation join those carrying the Torah scrolls in a spirit of jubilant religious fervor. Children are an integral part of the promenade, carrying Simchat Torah flags or miniature scrolls. In some synagogues, a reading of part of the next to the last chapter of the Pentateuch concludes the evening ritual.

In the next day's Morning Service, the congregation reads the final chapters of the Pentateuch (Deuteronomy 33–34) and individual members are called up to the *bimah* for the Reading of the Law. In some Jewish religious communities, several Torah readings occur simultaneously while in others entire groups ascend to the bimah and recite the benedictions together. Many **Orthodox** synagogues still only call men for the Reading of the Law, but in the vast majority of synagogues women and men are both invited to the platform. In addition, children under age thirteen also take part in a special reading while being covered by a large woolen prayer shawl. A blessing is pronounced over the youngsters quoting the words of Jacob's blessing to his grandchildren.

The last section of Deuteronomy is traditionally read by one of the *Hatan Torah* (Bridegrooms of the Law), a particularly honored congregant. Immediately after this reading, a second scroll is taken and the continuum of annual reading from the Pentateuch begins again. The congregation reads the first section of the Bible, and the Prophetical reading for the day is the first chapter of the book of Joshua.

Hanukkah

Although relatively minor compared to other Jewish holidays, Hanukkah ("Dedication") is a festival celebrated for eight days on 25 *Kislev* (the ninth month) that commemorates the victory of the traditionalist Maccabees over the Hellenistic Syrians. The main events connected to Hanukkah occurred between 165 and 163 B.C.E., making it a post-Biblical holiday and not a full festival. In contrast to other Jewish days of worship, there is no significant synagogue service. The event is expressed in the liturgy, especially in the introduction of the *al ha-nissim prayer* in the *Amidah* and Grace after Meals.

One of the central tenets of the story of Hanukkah

is the desecration of the Temple in Jerusalem by the Greek Syrians and its rededication by the Macabees. After a three-year struggle, the Macabees led by Judah Macabee rebuilt the defiled altar and produced new vessels for the Temple service including a candelabrum (menorah), an altar for incense, a table, and curtains. In Talmudic tradition, the miracle of Hanukkah is that only enough consecrated oil was in the Temple to burn for one day. The oil lasted eight days, and thus, the festival was established with the ceremony of lighting the menorah for eight nights. This ritual gave the holiday the additional name of *Hag ha-Urim*, "the festival of lights."

The Talmud interprets the candle lighting as publicizing the miracle and in ancient times Jews put the menorah in the doorway or in the street for this purpose. The lighting takes place after dark except on Friday evening when the ritual is conducted thirty minutes before sunset. The candles should burn for at least a half an hour and are traditionally placed in a conspicuous place such as in front of a window. The recognized process for kindling the Hanukkah lights is to light one candle (or oil lamp) on the first night and one additional candle each night until the last night when eight candles are lighted. The middle candle known as the *shammas* ("serving light") is used to kindle the other lights.

It has become a tradition to hold Hanukkah parties, with songs and games, especially for children. The most famous of the toys used is the dreidl, a spinning top with Hebrew letters on all four sides. Because of the association of the holiday with oil, *latkes* (potato pancakes) and *sufganiyot* (doughnuts) have become traditional holiday foods. In the United States, the giving of gifts has become an important part of the celebration.

Tu Bi-Shevat

A minor festival in the Jewish calendar, Tu Bi-Shevat (New Year for Trees), is a Jewish arbor day celebrated in the middle of *Shevat* (late winter). This special day, not mentioned in the Bible, arose in the late Second Temple (circa 500 B.C.E. to 70 C.E.) period as the time when a fixed cut-off day for assessing the tithe levied on the produce of fruit trees occurred. Fruits grown before

the New Year for Trees were included in the grower's calculations for the old year, and everything produced after that date was taxed for the following year.

With the destruction of the Second Temple in 70 C.E., the laws of tithing lost their relevance but the festival lived on. It began to symbolically mark the connection of Jews with *Eretz Yisrael*. Even as they were surrounded by winter snows, Tu Bi-Shevat reminded them of the warm, sunny climate of their ancient homeland. By the fifteenth century, the mystic of Safed initiated new rituals marking the New Year for Trees, especially that of eating fruits and reciting scriptural passages in praise of the Holy Land and its produce. Special significance has been given to the carob and almond trees, both of which grew extensively throughout *Eretz Yisrael*. A wonderful Shephardic folktale has the trees stretching out their branches at midnight and embracing each other, wishing each other a good New Year. In modern Israel, school children plant hundreds of thousands of new seedlings on Tu Bi-Shevat.

Purim

Purim, the most playful of Jewish festivals, celebrated on 14 *Adar* (late February or March) commemorates the deliverance of Persian Jewry led by Queen Esther from its destruction at the hands of Haman, the chief minister of King Ahasuerus, as described in the Book of Esther.

Purim comes from the Akkadian word *pur* meaning "dice" and alludes to Haman's casting of lots in order to select a date for his planned massacre of the Jews. The main religious observance for Purim is the reading of the scroll of Esther (the *Megillah*) at both evening and morning synagogue services. The Scroll of Esther reflects the spirit of the holiday, which uses humor to alleviate fear and to destroy the pretensions of all tyranny.

In most congregations, Purim is marked by an exuberant carnival-like atmosphere. Adults and children are encouraged to attend the Torah reading in fancy dress and to stomp their feet and sound noisemakers whenever Haman's name is mentioned. A mood of wild excess and frivolity characterizes the celebration, and the Megillah states that Purim is the one day of the year when rabbis sanction intoxication. Parties and traditional celebrations are a major part of the occasion. Rabbinic law states that these festivities should include the exchange of food gifts among relatives, friends, and neighbors; donations to charity; and a festive meal in every home during the afternoon. Traditional dishes for Purim include tri-cornered, filled pastries known as *hamentashen.*

Masquerades, parodies, and satirical plays are a major part of the Purim festival. In *Yeshivots* (Talmudic academies), students are often chosen to act as the "Purim rabbi" and from this pulpit they mimic and poke fun at their teachers.

Holocaust Memorial Day

Holocaust Memorial Day (*Yom Ha-Shoah*) is observed in Israel on 27 *Nissan* and in Diaspora communities on April 19 to honor the memory of the six million Jews murdered by the Nazis. The Israeli date of commemoration was established in 1951 by the Knesset (Parliament) most likely because it falls during the *omer* period (the days between Passover and Shavuot). In the Diaspora, April 19 has been the focus of observance, especially by Holocaust survivors, because in the Western calendar, it marks the beginning of the Ghetto resistance. Others have recommended that the Nazi Holocaust be included among the disasters reflected upon on **Tisha B'Av**, the Memorial Day for the Destruction of the Temple (see Tisha B'Av below).

Observance of Holocaust Memorial Day varies. It has become a custom for congregations and individuals to light six *yahrzeit* candles in memory of the six million Jews killed in the Holocaust. Ritual commemorative activities also include recitation of the Mourners' *Kaddish* and *Eyl Maleh Rachamim*, components of the traditional service for mourning the dead. Some congregations and Hillel houses on college and university campuses have recently begun to conduct group readings of *Nightwords: A Midrash on the Holocaust*, a drama by David Roskies that combines poetry in Yiddish, Hebrew, and English with passages that recite the nightmare of the Holocaust with accompanying prayer. Parts in the book can be assigned to

thirty-six people because of the tradition that only the continuing existence of thirty-six decent people makes possible the survival of the world.

Other forms of secular public gatherings in observance of *Yom Ha-Shoah* include the reciting of Yiddish poetry and the playing of Jewish music from Eastern Europe as a way of asserting that the Nazi effort to destroy Yiddishkeit culture failed and that this Diaspora culture continues to enrich and nourish new generations of Jews throughout the world.

Israel Independence Day

The birth of modern Israel was officially proclaimed on May 14, 1948. The date itself is a public holiday in Israel and the Sunday before or after has become a day of rallies and celebrations throughout the Diaspora and especially in the United States.

In Hebrew the day is known as *Yom Ha-Atzma-ut*, which translates to "affirmation" or "self-affirmation" meaning that it celebrates not only a past event but continued yearning in the present and future to affirm one's identity. In Israel, the joyous *Yom Ha-Atzma-ut* begins after the mournful day of *Haizikkaron* or Remembrance, in honor of those who died fighting for Israeli independence. As night falls and the holiday starts, people begin to dance in the street and explode fireworks. The next day is marked by parades, public rallies, hikes to historic sites, and family picnics. The speaker of the Knesset lights a torch near the grave of Theodor Herzl, the founder of modern-day Zionism, and there is a gun salute with the number of rounds corresponding to the number of years of independence.

In the Diaspora, *Yom Ha-Atzma-ut* has become a day of public rallies in support of and solidarity with Israel, which include speeches by political leaders, parades with floats, high school bands, and contingents from many organizations that choose to honor Israeli independence. Jewish music and folk arts are also a major component of the festivities.

In Israel, rabbinical authorities have introduced new liturgical patterns into their services in honor of the day, but few congregations have adopted this practice in Diaspora communities. Some congregations read alternate Torah portions from Deuteronomy, either the more foreboding passage in which Moses addresses the people about their impending entry into Canaan and warns of its dangers or the gentler section in which the Hebrew people re-enter the land of Israel much later in the future and move from an exile of punishment into a land of delight and well-being.

Passover

Passover, celebrated for eight days commencing on 15 *Nisan* (late March or April), is one of the three Pilgrim Festivals (with **Shavuot** and **Sukkot**) and one of the most important holidays in the Jewish calendar. Like the other two Pilgrim Festivals, Passover has both an historical and agricultural dimension. Its historical focus is the most well known. Passover commemorates the exodus of the Children of Israel from Egyptian slavery and Jews throughout the world honor this story through a ritual known as a Seder conducted on the first two nights (Reform Jews often have a seder only the first night) of the holiday. But Passover's agricultural component as a spring festival (*Hag ha-Aviv*), which celebrates the beginning of the barley harvest, is also significant and is incorporated in the *Haggadah* (narration) used for the Passover Seder.

In addition to being known as the Festival of Freedom and the Festival of Spring, Passover has three other names. One of them, *Hag ha-Matsot*, the Festival of Unleavened Bread (Exodus 12:15), refers to the commandment to eat only unleavened bread, matzah, to remember the escape of the Jews from Egypt when they had time to prepare only unleavened bread. Observant Jews empty their houses of *hamets* or leavened food prior to the first night of Passover and follow Jewish law by not eating this prohibited food for the eight-day duration of the holiday. In Talmudic law, *hamets* applies to any grain that has been subjected to a leavening process including wheat, barley, spelt, rye, and oats. Sephardim allow rice and legumes while Ashkenazim do not.

Passover is also referred to as "*Pesach*" (literally Passover) because of its relation to the biblical narration in which the angel of death "passed over" the homes of the Children of Israel when God slew the first-born of the Egyptians (Exodus 12:27). *Pesach* is also used to apply to the paschal lamb which, as recorded in the Bible, was given to each family a few days prior to the Exodus. The lamb was to be slaughtered and some of its blood sprinkled on the doorposts of the homes of Israelites as a sign for the angel of death to pass over these houses on the way to slay the first-born children of the Egyptians. As part of the Seder, a plate is prominently displayed on the table where the paschal lamb is presented along with *maror* (the bitter herb), symbolizing the bitterness of slavery; the *karpas* (greens), representing spring; the *charoset* (a mixture of apples, nuts, cinnamon, and wine), as a sign of both the mortar of the bricks that the Children were forced to make for the Egyptian pharaohs and the sweetness of freedom; salt water for tears; and an egg, which stands for fertility and new life.

In addition to the ritual of the Seder plate and the telling of the story of the Exodus, the Passover Seder also includes the asking of the four questions by the youngest person in attendance. These questions focus on differentiating Passover from all other days of the year and the symbolic invitation for Elijah the prophet to witness the Seder by placing a special ceremonial cup on the outside of the door. Elijah is traditionally viewed as the representation of the Messiah and the visionary hope for a future time of freedom and peace for all. Children also search for the *afikomen*, a piece of matzah hidden by one of the adults. It is ransomed off by the children when it is found. It is an obligation at the Seder to drink four cups of wine or kosher grape juice, read the Haggadah, dip various vegetables in salt water, and partake of the *afikomen*.

There is no prohibition against having additional seders during the eight-day holiday, and seders with different celebrants are frequently created, including interfaith seders with Christians, gay and lesbian seders, and vegetarian seders. Perhaps the most written-about "new" seders are the feminist celebrations, the most famous of which is sponsored by Ma'ayan, the Jewish Women's Project, in New York City. It attracts hundreds of participants.

Because it is a Pilgrim Festival, congregants read one of the five scrolls on Passover—the Song of Songs because of its connection to the spring season. Passover liturgy includes readings from Exodus 12 on the first day and Exodus 13–15 on the seventh day, which contains the story of the crossing of the Red Sea. The *Yizkor* (Memorial) service is read in Ashkenazi synagogues on the last day.

Lag B'Omer

This minor festival is observed during the counting of the *omer* ("thirty-third [day] of the *omer*") between **Passover** and **Shavuot**. Although its origin is uncertain, it is generally thought to commemorate the end of a plague that killed the students of Akiva during Bar Kokhba's war against Rome. Others claim that it celebrates the day Akiva resisted Roman authorities by bringing his students into the wilderness to study Torah and disguised his motives by taking bows and arrows so that it would look like they were hunting game. It is for this reason that Jews have often observed the day with archery contests in the woods.

For most Jews who recognize *Lag B'Omer*, it is looked upon as a day for relaxation and release from the mourning that comprises much of *omer* season. In contemporary practice among American Jews, it is a day for hikes in the woods and for picnics, especially among children and youth. For **Conservative** and **Orthodox** Jews it has become a day for weddings and public concerts of Jewish music that are otherwise prohibited during most of the *omer* season. It has also gained significance in the history of Jewish nationalism as a day to remind future generations of the Jewish struggle for freedom.

Shavuot

The second of the three Pilgrim Festivals, referred to in English as the Feast of Weeks, *Shavuot* is celebrated on the 6–7 *Sivan* at the end of the spring. In the Temple period, *Shavuot* was celebrated when the farmer set out with his neighbors in joyous procession to Jerusalem to offer a selection of the first fruit harvest of the year. In post-Temple times, the main focus of the festival shifted to the anniversary of the giving of the Torah at Sinai when God proclaimed the Ten Commandments to the assembled Children of Israel.

The name itself derives from the biblical command to count seven weeks from the time of the **Passover** harvest festival at the end of which a second harvest festival would be observed. *Shavuot* marks both the end of the grain harvest that began at Passover time and the culmination of the process of freedom that started with the exodus at Passover.

Although there are fewer special laws and customs governing *Shavuot* than the other Pilgrim festivals, a number of traditions exist. The prescribed readings include the Ten Commandments, the liturgical poem *Akdamut Millin* on the first day, and *Yetsiv Pitgam* prior to the *Haftarah* on the second day. In addition, the Book of Ruth is a central text for the festival because of the non-Jew Ruth's commitment to the people. The faith of Naomi is considered a lesson for *Shavuot*, a festival commemorating the acceptance of the Torah by the children of *Eretz Yisrael*.

Because of the Sinaitic (coming from the Sinai) aspect of Shavuot, it has also been considered traditional since the Middle Ages to begin the formal Jewish education of young children at this time of year. In contemporary America it is common for synagogues to have confirmation ceremonies for teenagers who have finished two years of post-bar or bat mitzvah Jewish education and consecration ceremonies for children beginning their religious studies. Shavuot is also a holiday to honor the converts to Judaism, some of whom go to the *mikvah* (ritual bath) to commemorate their conversion.

Synagogues are adorned with flowers or plants during Shavuot partly because the floral decoration symbolizes the main summer harvest and partly because Mount Sinai, the land of the Divine Revelation, was covered with vegetation in honor of the historic event.

Tisha B'Av

Unlike the other major fast day on the Hebrew calendar, **Yom Kippur**, which is a joyful fast, *Tisha B'Av* is a day of deep mourning—synonymous with oppression and exile. *Tisha B'Av* (ninth of *Av*) mourns the destruction of the First Temple by the Babylonians in 586 B.C.E. and the Second Temple by the Roman legions of Titus in 70 C.E. Observed in late July or August in the civil calendar, the ninth of *Av* is also associated with numerous other painful chapters in Jewish history that all occurred close to this date—from the fall of Bar Kokhba's fortress to Hadrian's legion in 135 C.E. to the banishing of all Jews from England by Edward I in 1290 C.E.

Beginning at sundown, congregants observe traditional mourning customs. Besides not eating or drinking, other prohibitions include shaving, bathing, sexual relations, wearing leather, engaging in work, and even conducting normal Torah reading. When night begins, the curtain is removed from the Holy Ark, the cloth is taken away from the reading desk, and the lights dimmed. Congregants sit on low stools or on the floor without talking to one another and study only the saddest and darkest parts of the Bible and the Talmud—the Book of Lamentations, Job, and Jeremiah's prophecies. *Tisha B'Av* also includes the reading of the *kinot* (elegies), a collection of religious poems that express the Jewish people's constant yearning for Zion, and the service concludes with *Eli Tsiyyon*, sung to a more upbeat tune.

Tallit (prayer shawls) and *tefillin* are not worn at the Morning Service because they are considered religious ornaments inappropriate for the occasion of deep mourning. Congregants read the portion of Deuteronomy that prophesies the destruction, and they conduct an additional reading from the prophetic section of Jeremiah.

When the congregation gathers for the late afternoon *mincha* service, the atmosphere shifts to the hope for Israel's redemption and the belief that the Messiah will soon be born and bring great joy and celebration. Congregants break the fast together after sundown, wash their faces, and go out outside to do the celebratory *kiddush levana*—hallowing the moon.

Although **Reform** Jews formerly abandoned the observance of *Tisha B'Av* as anachronistic, many have recently begun to commemorate the day's relevance, even if they do not keep it as a fast. In contemporary Israel, *Tisha B'Av* is a day of public mourning with tens of thousands praying and attending services at the Western Wall.

Tu B'Av

Tu B'Av (fifteenth of *Av*) derives its origins from a folk festival during the Second Temple era when young bachelors would choose their wives from among the unmarried young women. The Jerusalem and Babylonian Talmuds provide other reasons for this minor festival, including: it was the day when the tribes that had previously been forbidden to intermarry were allowed to do so; it was when the Benjaminites were permitted to intermarry with other tribes; and it was the time when those killed at Betar in the Bar Kokhaba rebellion could finally be buried.

It is probable that *Tu B'Av* originated from the sacrificial service of the Temple since 15 *Av* was marked as the day when the trees ceased to be chopped down for the fire that burned on the altar. In the *Megillah*, 15 *Av* is called "the time of the priests wood" because the Israelites could not find any wood in the stockpile upon returning from Babylonia, causing the prophets of the time to proclaim that people must donate wood on this day even if the stockpiles were full.

In the contemporary era, *Tu B'Av* is perhaps the most minor holiday on the Hebrew calendar, marked only by a ban on eulogies or fasting and the elimination of the *Tahanun* (supplication) prayer after the Amidah.

KOSHER

The word kosher is the term designating foods Jews are permitted to eat under *kashrut*, the system of Jewish dietary laws set forth in the Talmud and subsequent law codes. These laws set forth which foods are allowed and which are prohibited, foods that may not be eaten together, how animals should be slaughtered, and how food should be prepared and served. There are three categories of kosher food: dairy *(milchig)*, meat *(flayshig)*,

What's Kosher?

1. All fresh fruits and vegetables, grains, and cereals.
2. Milk and dairy products. (Cheeses made with enzymes or other nonmilk animal products are kosher by some standards, not kosher by others.)
3. Fish with fins and scales (no shellfish).
4. Eggs from kosher fish and fowl.
5. An animal that has split hooves and that chews its cud. (It must be slaughtered in a kosher slaughtering house.) Cows and sheep are kosher; horses and pigs are not.

Milk and meat are eaten separately. Some people wait three hours—others wait six hours—after consuming meat before consuming a milk product. Foods that are *parve*—neither milk nor meat—can be eaten with either milk or meat products. Fowl falls under the category of meat.

From *Jewish Family and Life: Traditions, Holidays, and Values for Today's Parents and Children*, by Yosef I. Abramowitz and Rabbi Susan Silverman. New York: Golden Books, 1997.

and *pareve*, those foods that are neither a meat nor a milk product. Dairy and meat may not be eaten together. *Pareve* foods can be eaten with either dairy or meat products and include all fruits, vegetables, and many fish and eggs. Seafood that does not have fins and scales such as lobster, oysters, shrimp, and clams is not kosher, nor is any land animal that does not have cloven hooves and chew its cud. Thus, the camel, rabbit, and pig are not acceptable for consumption. Food that is not kosher is referred to as *treyf*. (See sidebar for general rules about what is kosher and what isn't.)

In kosher food preparation and serving, all utensils used for dairy foods must be used only for dairy and all utensils used for meat must be used only for meat. Although the majority of American Jews do not maintain kosher homes, a significant number do, especially those of Orthodox backgrounds.

Although the word kosher does not literally appear in the Torah, there are a number of references made to the animals acceptable for consumption in accordance with Jewish (Talmudic) law. Those who keep kosher frequently cite Biblical commands as their rationale. The reference most frequently cited by Jews maintaining *kashrut* is Deuteronomy, which states that "the mammals and birds that may be eaten must be in accordance with Jewish law."

The separation of meat and dairy is mentioned implicitly on three separate occasions when the Torah states that one should not "boil a kid in its mother's milk." *Kashrut* law requires that one must wait from three to six hours between eating meat and dairy. Animal fat is considered meat for purposes of *kashrut*. The Torah also prohibits the consumption of blood and blood must be removed from the flesh of all animals before they can be considered kosher.

Kosher status can be transmitted from food to utensil only in the presence of heat. The condition of the plates is not an issue if one is eating cold food in a non-kosher establishment. Likewise, it is permitted to use the same knife to slice cold cuts and cheese as long as the knife is cleaned in between. Stove tops and sinks become non-kosher utensils because they consistently come into contact with both meat and dairy in the presence of heat. Those keeping kosher must use dishpans when cleaning dishes (and not soak them directly in the sink) and use separate spoon rests and trivets when putting things down on stove tops. Separate towels and potholders for meat and dairy are also necessary.

Jewish dietary laws are based more on religious rather than health reasons. Based on modern scientific knowledge, there is no evidence that camel or rabbit meat is any less healthy than cow or goat meat. Most Jews who follow *kashrut* believe that whether or not the texts provide a reason for following these laws, the fact that they are inscribed means that they should be honored. Some rabbis suggest that

OU Kashrut Supervision and Certification Service

The familiar symbol of a circle with a *u* in the middle on a food product indicates that it has received *Kashrut* certification by the Union of Orthodox Jewish Congregations. The first product with the OU logo was Heinz ketchup. Today, the Orthodox Union is in 2,300 plants, watching over 220,000 products.

A Kosher Marriott Comes to Brooklyn

In July of 1998 the Brooklyn Marriott had its grand opening. It claims to be the first hotel of its kind to have a pre-designed kosher kitchen, available to all kosher caterers. The hotel is also described as "Sabbath-Ready," with such amenities as special elevators for Shabbot that stop on every floor, allowing guests to ride without breaking Jewish laws. It even provides metal keys and locks, so observant guests are not dependent on the now almost ubiquitous electric door locks.

Jewish dietary laws are designed as a call to holiness. Others view *kashrut* as symbolic of the ability to distinguish between right and wrong, good and evil, and the sacred and profane—all concepts that are extremely important in Judaism. In addition, the process of keeping kosher ritualizes the everyday act of eating and marks it with a religious foundation. In rabbinic literature, the Jewish dinner table is often compared to the Temple altar.

In recent years, terms such as "halak" (smooth) and "glatt" have begun to accompany the term "kosher," denoting meat products in which the highest degree of *kashrut* is maintained. These procedures require that certain internal organs of the animal be examined and the entire carcass rejected if they appear to have any defect.

A certificate guaranteeing rabbinical supervision, which is now found on mass-produced foods in the United States, has made the task of keeping kosher considerably easier. Almost three-quarters of all packaged foods have some type of kosher certification, generally taking the form of an easily recognized symbol and sometimes with the name of the rabbi, authority, or organization providing the supervision. Increasingly, airlines, hotels, restaurants, and catering firms all over the world distribute kosher food on a regular basis. Some ultra-Orthodox groups refuse to accept the *kashrut* of the chief rabbinate and provide their own "attestation" of approved foods. "Kosher for Passover" refers to food that in addition to being kosher under normal rules is certified to contain no leavened flour.

"Kosher" has also become a term used to describe ethnic dishes such as "kosher dill pickles," knishes, bagels, blintzes, matzoh ball soup, and other European Jewish foods. The expression "kosher style" indicates a specific kind of cuisine, not the ritual fitness of a dish from the standpoint of Jewish law. When a restaurant calls itself "kosher style," it means that it serves traditional Jewish foods and it usually indicates that the food is not actually kosher. Chinese food and Italian specialties such as pizza can be kosher if they are prepared in accordance with Jewish law, and there are an increasing number of kosher pizzerias and kosher Chinese restaurants in cities with major Jewish populations.

The preparation and sale of kosher food in the United States is now a major industry, with total sales estimated at $3.25 billion and total consumers at 7.5 million. There are over 41,000 commercial products certified to be kosher and over 8,400 companies producing these products.

MARRIAGE

The act of marriage is a divine commandment and a natural and desirable situation for every adult. In religious terms, marriage represents a sacrament between a man and a woman and is often called *Kiddushin* (sanctification). Judaism elevates the marriage vow from the realm of private contract to that of moral union. One of the duties of the father stated in the Talmud is to find his son a wife. Additionally, the High Priest was not permitted to perform the Day of Atonement rituals unless he was married. Despite social changes within Judaism, this basic philosophical foundation continues today.

The primary purpose of marriage, according to the Torah, is to create a home and family, and thereby perpetuate society. One of the most important developments in the Talmudic age was the transformation of marriage from a personal civil procedure to a public religious ceremony. The act of marrying had three distinct stages, beginning with the betrothal, where the couple formally made the commitment to marry. This was followed by the ceremony establishing a nuptial the wedding recites the blessing over the wine, the bride and groom drink from the glass, and the groom recites the traditional consecration vow. It is then that he places the unadorned ring on the bride's finger, which over the centuries has become the official means by which Jews establish the marriage contract. The couple reads their *ketubabbah* (wedding vows) and the rabbi recites the seven wedding blessings over a second glass of wine. The ceremony ends with the breaking of a glass (done to remind those present of the destruction of the Temple and of Jerusalem), after which the bride and groom enter a private room for *yihud* (seclusion) that signifies the culmination of their marriage.

Conservative and **Reform** weddings follow this traditional pattern with several nuances. Neither of these denominations practice the groom's fast, the covering of the face of the bride before the ceremony, or the *yihud*. Conservative and Reform wedding rituals have introduced the double ring ceremony, in which the bride also puts a ring on the groom's finger. The Reform ceremony also adds poetry, prose, and song that the rabbi or the couple selects. Jewish communities throughout North America and around the world have adapted many traditional Jewish wedding rituals and combined them with their own values and customs to create weddings that fit their needs.

MOURNING

The process of grieving over the death of a loved one has tremendous resonance in Jewish religion and history. Jewish law provides a foundation to guide mourners through their grief that applies to males over the age of thirteen and to females over the age of twelve who have lost family members. Biblical and rabbinic literature also contains many references to mourning and Judaism, overall, has a strong element of the acceptance of death. References to death occur throughout the Torah as the natural end of life and not something to fear. The *Midrash* states that death is a positive feature incorporated by God in the creation of the universe.

The Jewish laws of mourning attempt to strike a

What marriage ceremony would be complete without the obligatory photographs of the bride and groom? (Courtesy of American Jewish Historical Society, Waltham, Massachusetts and New York, New York)

relationship, considered the first piece of the actual marriage process itself. The final stage was the *nissu'in* when the marriage was officially consecrated and the bride moved out of her parent's home and into the house of the groom.

Contemporary Jewish weddings vary according to denominational customs, yet share certain core components. In the most traditional ceremonies, practiced by many in **Orthodox** communities, the groom fasts during the day of the wedding and recites the Day of Atonement confession. He is then led to the bride whose face he covers with a veil. The couple proceeds to the *huppah* (marriage canopy) with the father accompanying the groom and the mother the bride. When they are under the *huppah* the rabbi conducting

Saying Kaddish Is Not for Girls!—Who Says?

"Bella Abzug's father died in 1933 and she emerged as an outspoken thirteen-year-old girl-child willing to break the rules. Prohibited by tradition from saying *kaddish* for her father in synagogue, Bella did so anyway. Every morning before school for a year, she attended synagogue and davened. The congregants looked askance and never did approve, but nobody ever stopped her. She just did what she needed to do for her father, who had no son—and learned a lesson for life: Be bold, be brazen, be true to your heart."

From Blanche Cook's article on Bella Abzug in *Jewish Women in America: An Historical Encyclopedia*, edited by Paula E. Hyman and Deborah Dash Moore. New York: Routlege, 1997.

balance between emotionalism and wisdom. Mourners are encouraged to cry, tear their garments, and fully participate in the burial ceremony. At the same time, the stages of mourning also emphasize a limited time period and the importance of recovering from the loss and renewing a focus on living.

Traditional Judaism delineates stages of mourning. The first, *aninum* or *aninut* (deep sorrow), occurs from the moment of death until the burial, which usually takes place within twenty-four hours after death. During this period of deep grieving the *onen* (person in *aninut*) is freed from any responsibility of performing any positive *mitzvot*, including reciting the *Shema*, putting on **tefillin**, or reciting grace after meals. Even close friends are instructed not to express condolence "when the dead lies before him." During this period, the only responsibility of the *onen* is to arrange the funeral. It is only after the family leaves the funeral ceremony that the community of mourners is permitted by tradition to utter the traditional words of comfort—"May God comfort you among all the other mourners of Zion and Jerusalem." In Jewish custom, a mourner must rend a garment, an action that can take place after receiving the news of the death, just before the funeral, or immediately after the funeral.

The second stage of mourning, *shiva*, encompasses the seven days after the day of burial. Shiva begins immediately after the burial, in the home of the deceased. In particularly observant homes, the mourners eat a meal of bread and a hard boiled egg prepared by friends or extended family members as a symbol of compassion and concern.

During the shiva, it is customary for friends and acquaintances to visit the home of the mourners and offer them support and consolation. In many communities, people bring or prepare food, so that the mourners do not have to entertain guests. Mourners sit on the floor or on low cushions or benches during the shiva period. Upon entering the house, a member of the family generally lights a shiva candle, which is almost always provided by the funeral home and which burns for seven days. The shiva candle serves as a mark of respect to the memory of the deceased.

Shiva is considered a transitional period in which expressions of sorrow are encouraged. At the same time a process is set into motion that leads the bereaved gently back to life and the world of the living. The shiva is terminated if the festivals of **Rosh Hashanah**, **Yom Kippur**, **Sukkot**, **Passover**, or **Shavuot** fall on any of the seven days. If a burial takes place during the middle days of Sukkot or Passover, the observance of shiva begins after the festival ends. In addition, public display of mourning is generally not permitted on Shabbat, although the mourning laws continue to be observed privately. In some communities, mourners sit somewhere other than their regular seats in synagogue on the Sabbath. In some Sephardic communities, other members of the congregation leave their own seats to sit beside the mourners for at least part of the service as a sign of respect and empathy.

After the shiva concludes, the third stage of mourning, *sheloshim*, continues for thirty days or more. It is a time when mourning of a lesser intensity takes place. Mourners may return to work during *sheloshim*, but they continue to recite *Kaddish* in the presence of a *minyan* three times a day and do not attend parties or other festive occasions, nor do they attend movies, sporting events, or purely social gatherings. Especially observant Jews will not have their hair cut, shave, or wear new clothes during *sheloshim*. After *sheloshim*, most mourners may return to a full business and social life. Mourning for parents lasts for one full year during which mourners continue to recite *Kaddish* at a daily *minyan* or regularly at Shabbat services. Mourners who have lost parents are free to choose whether or not to restrict their social activities over the first year after the parent's death.

The final stage of mourning is called *Yahrzeit* (anniversary), observed on the yearly anniversary of the death of a parent or close relative. Many mourners recite *Kaddish*, chant a *haftarah*, and kindle memorial lights in the home that burn for twenty-four hours. Some Orthodox Jews also choose to fast on *Yahrzeit*. In addition, the *Yizkor* service on Yom Kippur is used to mourn the death of parents during the first year after their death.

The laws of mourning do not apply if the deceased had a reputation as a notorious transgressor of Torah law. In the case of a suicide, the laws of mourning are also not generally observed unless there is evidence of insanity.

As with virtually all Jewish rituals, the ones associated with mourning are followed to a greater or lesser extent by individuals depending on their religious backgrounds, their denominations, and their cultural experiences. Although many Jews do not observe all the mourning rites of Jewish law, many embrace at least some aspect of observance, whether it be reciting the *Kaddish*, sitting *Shiva*, or lighting a Yahrzeit candle.

RITUALS

The practice of Judaism has a variety of rituals connected to different parts of religious worship. Although not all are used by Jews of every denomination, the following represent some of the most common.

Covering the Head

Among many Ashkenazi and some Sephardic Jews, the wearing of a skullcap known as a *Kippah* (or *Yarmulke* in Yiddish) during synagogue services is viewed as a badge of loyalty to Jewish tradition. Although this practice was originally restricted to adult males, head coverings for Jewish females (other than among the ultra-Orthodox) have also become common. **Orthodox** Jewish men cover their heads in public at all times.

Although biblical law does not require any form of headgear, the practice began with rabbis in the Middle Ages who began associating the wearing of headgear with piety and bareheadedness with frivolity. In addition, Jews in Europe began to think of worship without one's head covered as a gentile custom. While the covering of a man's head has generally been regarded as a pious act, the covering of a married woman's hair was considered in biblical times to be a defense of her modesty and the use of a wig for women became fashionable in the eighteenth century. Today women are more likely to wear a hat, headscarf, or Yarmulke in synagogue. Orthodox women will cover their heads when going outdoors or attending social functions.

Kiddush

The *kiddush* (sanctification) is the prayer recited on Sabbaths and festivals, usually over a cup of wine to sanctify the day. The sages of the Talmud interpreted the biblical injunction to remember the holy day as meaning to remember it over wine. The practice of *kiddush* originated in ancient times, although it is unclear whether it was originally recited before or after the meal.

In contemporary Judaism the *kiddush* comprises both the blessing over wine and the benediction of the day. On Sabbath eve, the biblical phrases in Genesis 1:31 and 2:1–3 precede the *kiddush*. The blessing focuses on the idea that Israel was made holy by God's commandments and that it was favored by having been given the Sabbath as an inheritance to remember the Creation. *Kiddush* for Jewish festivals follows a similar pattern with the special day being sanctified. The *She-heheyanu* (who has kept us alive) prayer follows. This prayer reads: "Blessed are You, God, who has kept us alive, sustained us, and brought us to this season."

The main *kiddush* is recited in the evening prior to the beginning of the Sabbath or the festival. It is traditional for congregants to stand for either the entire evening *kiddush* or for the introductory prayers from Genesis. It is common practice for participants in the meal *kiddush* to wash their hands following the *kiddush* in preparation for the blessing over the bread.

The rabbis also instituted a morning *kiddush* before the first meal of the day during the Sabbath and festivals, known as "*Kiddusha rabba.*" Many congregations recite a public *kiddush* in synagogue after Sabbath services followed by other refreshments and an opportunity for social interaction. Some observant Jews keep personal goblets, often made of silver, that are reserved for the wine blessing.

Lighting the Candles

Although oil lamps were used for rituals in ancient times, once candles became common they became sanctioned for Jewish festivals and Shabbat. The ceremony of candle lighting, performed just before sundown, is seen as a symbol of the light and joy shed by God's holy day and is considered an essential component of Jewish worship.

In sanctifying the Sabbath and Jewish festivals, lighting at least two candles in honor of the dual commandment to "remember" and "observe" is essential. The Havdalah ceremony at the conclusion of the Sabbath day includes the lighting of a candle made of at least two intertwined wicks because the liturgy of the blessing recited over them ("who creates the light of fire") refers to a plural fire.

In addition to the regular holiday blessings, candles are also used in the search for *hamets* (leavened flour) on **Passover** eve. They are also sometimes kindled in the darkened synagogue during the reading of the Book of Lamentations and elegies on the eve of *Tisha B'Av.* Candles are also kindled in rituals for mourning the dead with the lights symbolizing the person's soul as reflected in the verse "The spirit of man is the lamp of God." It is also traditional for a Memorial Light to be kept burning throughout the Day of Atonement (**Yom Kippur**). In the wedding cer-

emonies of some **Orthodox** Jews, the fathers of the bride and the groom accompany the groom down the aisle holding lighted candles.

Mezuzah

The *mezuzah* (literally, doorpost) is a casing that contains handwritten biblical verses from the Shema prayer. It is affixed to the doorposts of Jewish homes. The first passage of the Torah on the *mezuzah* contains the opening paragraph of the Shema, including the commandments to love God; study the Torah; read the Shema prayer, expressing the unity of God, twice daily; wear *tefillin*; and attach a *mezuzah*. The second passage connects prosperity and well-being with regular observance of the commandments. When the *mezuzot* are affixed, a resident of the home recites a short benediction. In the Diaspora, the placement of the *mezuzah* can be delayed for thirty days after entering a rented dwelling.

The *mezuzah* must be written by a qualified scribe on parchment created from the skin of a clean animal. It is always attached to the upper part of the doorpost at the entrance of each room in a slanting position. The scroll is rolled and placed into a case with a tiny opening that shows the letter *shin*, from one of the Hebrew names for God (Shaddai) written on the back of the parchment or it may be written on the outside of the casing. Sometimes the name itself is written.

It has become traditional among many Jews to touch and kiss the *mezuzah* on leaving or entering the house to express awareness of the fulfillment of the commandment and to show faith in God's protection. Although synagogues and public residences are exempt from the commandment, it is now customary to attach *mezuzot* to their entrances as well.

Mikvah

The *mikvah* (gathering of water) is a Jewish ritual purification bath that traces its roots back to ancient times. Its first mention comes in the Pentateuch, where it is written that "only a spring, cistern, or collection of waters shall be cleansing." Among the causes of impurity were contact with a corpse, child-birth, menstruation, and venereal disease. Jews in the time of the First Temple could not participate in any religious ceremony for which they had to be ritually pure without resort to the mikvah.

Both men and women have used the mikvah for ritual purification, but it has always held special significance for Jewish women. Jewish law prescribes that women immerse themselves in the waters of the mikvah following their menstrual periods or after childbirth in order to become ritually pure and be permitted to resume sexual activity.

The source of the mikvah must be either underground water, such as a spring, or rainwater or melted snow or ice. The water itself cannot be tapped by human agency through collection in a container and instead it must fall into a built-in or carved-out pool or bath. The pipes through which the water passes cannot be made of any materials that are considered unclean according to biblical standards and must be made of earthenware, stone, concrete, cement, or plastic.

In the contemporary Diaspora, the mikvah is now almost exclusively the province of **Orthodox** communities, although **Conservative** Judaism does insist on *tevilah* (immersion) for those undergoing the conversion process. **Reform** Judaism in the United States considers the mikvah unnecessary. Jewish feminists have taken two opposing views on the mikvah. Some have embraced the ritual as a vehicle for women's spiritual renewal, and others have urged women to cast off the restrictions imposed by Jewish law with its emphasis on women's biological functions.

Minyan

The *minyan* is a traditional prayer quorum of at least ten males above the age of thirteen who assemble for public worship and religious observances. Throughout the ages, rabbis have stressed the importance of maintaining a *minyan* for religious decision making, perhaps because of Judaism's stress on the building of community. According to the Talmud, when the Holy One enters a synagogue and does not find ten worshippers there, His wrath is immediately kindled.

Reform Judaism has adopted the practice of allowing women to count as part of a *minyan* and, beginning in 1974, the **Conservative Movement** has also. A *minyan* is required for a variety of activities including the recitation of the Barekhu invocation and the Shema in public worship; the repetition of the Amidah with Kedushah prayer; the chanting of the Priestly Blessing; the congregational Reading of the Law; recitation of the *Kaddish* in public worship; and the Seven Benedictions recited at weddings.

Tallit

The *tallit* (prayer shawl) is the four-cornered, fringed garment worn while specific prayers are recited, in fulfillment of the commandment of the fringes. After the blessing, which honors the commandment to wrap oneself in tallit, the individual proceeds to use the tallit to cover the head and remain that way for the "time it takes to walk four cubits" after which the tallit is arranged around the shoulders.

Although all males are required to wear the tallit in Sephardic and German communities, this practice is limited to married men for many Ashkenazi Jews. In all denominations, it is traditional for only married men to cover their heads. In recent years, the feminist movement has encouraged Conservative, Reform, and Reconstructionist women to don prayer shawls. Women in the Conservative movement's rabbinic program pledge to maintain all the commandments required of the male, including the wearing of the tallit during prayers.

Generally, congregants wear the tallit for every Morning Service and each Additional Service except on **Tisha B'Av** when it becomes part of the Afternoon Service. On **Yom Kippur**, the tallit is worn for all five prayers and, at the times when **tefillin** are used, the tallit is always put on first. Readers wear tallit at the Afternoon Service and, in some congregations, at the Evening Service too. A tallit must be worn by those called to the reading of the law before reciting the Torah blessings. When the rabbis bless the people, they traditionally place the tallit over their head and hands as a symbol that God's Divine Presence rests on their hands when they pronounce the Priestly Blessing.

Tefillin

Tefillin (phylacteries) are two black leather straps each holding a small box that a religious Jewish male from the age of thirteen wears on his left arm and head during the weekday morning Service. The tefillin are made from parchments taken from the outermost hide of a **kosher** animal inscribed with permanent black ink. The Hebrew letter *shin* is inscribed on the front of the box.

The rabbinical decree to wear tefillin is based on four biblical paragraphs from Exodus and Deuteronomy which are written by a scribe on one piece of parchment and placed on the tefillin itself. These Torah sections define the foundations of Judaism in terms of God's unity, acceptance of Divine rule, acceptance of God's providence, and faith in the world's redemption. Thus, the act of binding oneself with tefillin, although not explicitly mentioned in the Bible, has become a regular reminder to observant Jews to be bound up in service to God.

Tefillin are worn regularly during the Morning Service and removed on the new Moon at the beginning of the Additional Service. They are removed for the Sabbath and on major festivals, since the holidays are considered sufficient reminders of the responsibilities of the Jewish people to God. It is also inappropriate to wear tefillin on the first day of mourning, by a groom on his wedding day, or by anyone who has been excommunicated. On **Tisha B'Av**, they are worn for the Afternoon rather than the Morning Service.

The arm tefillin is placed on the muscle of the inner side of the left forearm. The strap is tightened and wound several times around the arm between the elbow and the wrist and three times around the middle finger. The head tefillin is placed on the head so that the front edge of the case lies slightly above the spot where the hair begins and directly above the space between the eyes. While the strap is fastened at the nape of the neck, the congregant recites the benedic-

---

Elvis the Shabbos Goy

Still don't believe Elvis is everywhere? Get this: Shortly before he became the King of Rock and Roll, a teenaged Elvis Presley was the Shabbos goy for his upstairs neighbor, the local rabbi in the Jewish section of Memphis, Tennessee. Rabbi Alfred Fruchter and his wife Jeannette were particularly fond of the boy, who would turn on the electricity or light the gas for them on the Sabbath. "Elvis refused to take money," Mrs. Fruchter was quoted as saying. "He said it was his pleasure to help us keep our Sabbath." Another neighbor reported that, after Elvis began to make money, he donated a whole room to the Jewish Community Center then under construction. When Presley's mother died, he put her name, address, and a Star of David on her footstone "because," relates the neighbor, "he loved the Jewish people."

The Jewish Week, August 22, 1997.

---

tion for the binding of the tefillin followed by the words "Blessed be the name of His glorious kingdom forever." When the tefillin are removed at the end of the Morning service, the head tefillin is always removed before the hand tefillin.

Shabbat

One of the central tenants of Judaism is the sanctification of the seventh day of the week, *Shabbat* (Sabbath), as the day of rest. For Jews that day begins on Friday at sunset and continues until dusk on Saturday.

The Biblical injunction to observe the Sabbath comes from the story of the Creation in Genesis where God finished the work of creating the world on the seventh day, rested from His work, and declared the day as holy. Similar commands to observe Shabbat can be found in Deuteronomy and Exodus with the common feature being to refrain from work of all kinds. More than twenty chapters in the *Mishnah* (oral law) describe the kinds of labor prohibited on the Sabbath. The forbidden work is based on the thirty-nine different categories of labor performed in the building of the sanctuary. The subject is later expounded upon in the Talmud. The first tractate of *Order Mo'ed* in the *Mishnah* also includes laws regarding the kindling of the Sabbath candles and other miscellaneous laws pertaining to observing Shabbat.

All denominations in contemporary Judaism acknowledge the importance of Shabbat. Although the **Reform Movement** has been historically more distant from traditional observances and practices, today both Conservative and Reform congregations hold their main weekly synagogue service on Friday night and/or Saturday morning. Additional private Shabbat rituals include lighting candles in the home and reciting the kiddush. Jews are encouraged to refrain from commercial activities and gainful employment and to dedicate the Sabbath day to spiritual and reflective activities. Festive meals, the hosting of guests, and conjugal relations are all considered part of Shabbat observances. While the Sabbath is set aside as a day of joy, relaxation, and a change of pace from workdays, the specific form of expression given to these values is considered a matter of individual interpretation.

Observant Jews will often refuse to answer the telephone, use an automobile or other source of motorized transportation, ride an elevator, or carry money or writing utensils on Shabbat. Although the vast majority of Jews in the contemporary Diaspora do not follow all of these Sabbath rituals, a significant number do obey the precept to refrain from conducting business and to attend synagogue services.

The Sabbath begins with the lighting of the candles approximately twenty minutes before sunset accompanied by the invocation "Blessed are You our God, who has hallowed us by Your commandments to kindle the Sabbath light." The sages viewed the kindling of the Sabbath lights to be of such importance that they believed if a person had to choose between buying wine for the *kiddush* or candles for Shabbat, the candles should be the priority.

Shabbat begins with the *Kabbalat* or welcoming service at twilight. Sephardic synagogues recite Psalm 29, while Ashkenazi congregations read Psalms 95–99 and Psalms 92–93. The Reconstructionist *Kabbalat* service opens with biblical passages from Deuteronomy and Isaiah.

Lighting Shabbat *candles is an important ritual in Judaism. This splendid photograph of an older women performing the ceremony is especially poignant. (Courtesy of American Jewish Historical Society, Waltham, Massachusetts and New York, New York)*

During the Evening Service, congregants recite a special *Amidah* followed by a reading from Genesis. After blessing God, the reader recites the paragraph *Magen avot* ("shield to our forefathers") and the service is concluded. Reform synagogues offer ten alternative Sabbath evening services, none of which include *Magen avot*. When a festival coincides with Shabbat, the festival *Amidah* is read. Shabbat in the home consists of the reciting of the Priestly blessing, the singing of *Shalom Alkeikhem* welcoming the Sabbath angels, recitation of the kiddush, and the blessing over the bread.

Sabbath morning follows the basic Morning Service text, followed by a Reading of the Law sidrah of the week, a selection from the *Haftarah*, and the Additional Service. The Morning Service on Shabbat differs from the rest of the week in the introductory prayers read prior to the *Shema*. In many congregations, it also traditional for the rabbi to deliver a sermon to honor the importance of the Sabbath as a day of learning. Many communities also follow the morning services by a congregational Kiddush.

In the Afternoon Shabbat Service, the Torah is read prior to the Amidah with three congregants chanting the Reading of the Law in front of the congregation. The Evening Service takes place considerably after sunset after the recitation of Psalms 16, 144, and 67 by Sephardim and the latter two by Ashkenazim. Most people recite the *Havdalah* service, the ritual which ends the Sabbath, at home, although an increasing number of congregations read the service together in the synagogue.

Rabbinical law states that there must be three meals on the Sabbath day. The third and final meal, known as the *Se'udah Shelishit*, is the only one that expressly does not include kiddush and it is customarily accompanied by the singing of *Zemirot* (table hymns sung during and after Shabbat). This meal is served late enough to conclude just in time for the Evening Service.

In addition to special candles inscribed with the Shabbat blessing and specially designed Kiddush cups, some Jewish homes also maintain bread knives with relevant phrases affixed to them for Sabbath use only. Because food cannot be warmed over an open fire on the Sabbath, many **Orthodox** Jews place a piece of tin or copper over a burning fire or gas stove.

Contemporary innovations to Shabbat services in some American congregations include having the Friday evening service after dinner because of the difficulty of reaching the synagogue at the traditional hour and the addition of instrumental accompaniment to the service, especially in Reform synagogues. A number of communities also have begun a tradition of having different congregants deliver short "sermons" at the Saturday Morning Service. Additionally, a growing number of informal networks of prayer fellowships (*Havurah*) have emerged in response to the frustration of some with the large, impersonal synagogues. These groups frequently conduct Shabbat rituals and services together either in addition to or instead of the formal synagogue programs.

For Further Reading and Reference

Abramowitz, Yosef I., and Rabbi Susan Silverman. *Jewish Family and Life: Traditions, Holidays, and Values for Today's Parents and Children*. New York: Golden Books, 1997.

Brener, Anne. *Mourning and Mitzvah: A Guided Journal for Walking the Mourner's Path through Grief to Healing*. Woodstock, Vt.: Jewish Lights, 1993.

Cowan, Paul, and Rachel Cowan. *Mixed Blessings: Overcoming the Stumbling Blocks in an Interfaith Marriage*. New York: Penguin USA, 1989.

Diamont, Anita. *The New Jewish Wedding*. New York: Summit, 1986.

—— and Howard Cooper. *Living a Jewish Life: A Guide for Starting, Learning, Celebrating, and Parenting*. New York, 1991.

Donin, Hayim Halevy. *To Be a Jew: A Guide to Jewish Observance in Contemporary Life*. New York: Basic Books, 1991.

Falk, Marcia. *The Book of Blessings*. New York: Harper San Francisco, 1996.

Goldin, Barbara Diamond. *Bat Mitzvah: A Jewish Girl's Coming of Age*. New York: Viking Children's Books, 1995.

Greenberg, Blu. *How to Run a Traditional Jewish Household*. Northvale, N.J.: Jason Aronson Inc., 1989.

Greenberg, Irving. *The Jewish Way: Living the Holidays*. New York: Touchstone Books, 1993.

Holtz, Barry W. *The Schocken Guide to Jewish Books: Where to Start Reading about Jewish History, Literature, Culture and Religion*. New York: Schocken Books, 1992.

Nathan, Joan. *Jewish Cooking in America*. New York: Random House, 1994.

——. *The Jewish Holiday Kitchen*. New York: Schocken Books, 1979.

Ross, Lesli Koppelman. *Celebrate! The Complete Jewish Holidays Handbook*. Northvale, N.J.: Jason Aronson Inc., 1994.

Strassfeld, Michael. *The Jewish Holidays, a Guide and Commentary*. New York: Harper Collins, 1993.

Umansky, Ellen M., and Dianne Ashton, eds. *Four Centuries of Jewish Women's Spirituality*. Boston: Beacon Press, 1995.

Waskow, Arthur I. *Seasons of Our Joy: A Modern Guide to the Jewish Holidays*. Boston: Beacon Press, 1991.

Children's Books

Brownstone, David M. *The Jewish-American Heritage*. New York: Facts on File, 1988.

Goldin, Barbara Dimond. *A Child's Book of Midrash*. Northvale, N. J.: Jason Aronson Inc., 1990.

Hoobler, Dorothy, and Thomas Hoobler. *The Jewish American Family Album*. New York: Oxford University Press, 1995.

Muggamin, Howard. *The Jewish Americans*. New York: Chelsea House Pub., 1988.

Sussman, Susan. *There's No Such Thing as a Chanukah Bush, Sandy Goldstein*. Morton Grove, Ill.: Albert Whitman & Co., 1993.

The Internet

There are an enormous number of Web sites that provide information about all aspects of Jewish ritual, celebrations, and culture (our favorite name is Chickensoup.org, a site about health issues). For a list of URLs, please consult the appendix in Abramowitz's *Jewish Family and Life* (above) or the following books: Lerner, Michael. *The Guide to the Jewish Internet*. San Francisco, Calif.: No Starch Press, 1996; and Romm, Diane. *The Jewish Guide to the Internet*. Northvale, N.J.: Jason Aronson Inc., 1997.

Part 4

Law, Government, and Politics

OVERVIEW

Along with African Americans, Hispanic Americans, Asian Americans, and women of every stripe, no Jew has ever been elected, nominated, or even seriously considered by the pundits as a candidate for president of the United States. Only a few have been state governors, and Jews in federal electoral positions have usually been in the House rather than the Senate. Nonetheless, Jewish Americans have served in positions of responsibility and respect in American government, have made a strong impact as political activists, and have risen to the highest ranks in the American legal and judicial system.

Even before the first large wave of Jewish immigrants in the 1840s, when there were probably no more than 15,000 Jewish Americans, Mordecai Noah was appointed consul general in Tunis, and Emanuel Hart was a congressman. Jewish political activists were active in the campaign to abolish religious qualifications for voting and holding office and later organized around two issues of international import. They opposed U. S. negotiation of a commercial treaty with Switzerland that permitted the nation to expel American Jews and denounced the failure of U.S. political leaders to intervene after Papal authorities kidnapped a Jewish boy in Italy.

During the Civil War era, the new German Jewish population flexed their political muscle by working for the formation of the new Republican Party. When the Eastern European immigration of the 1880s vastly increased the Jewish population of America, the Jewish presence in electoral politics increased as well. Jewish congressmen were elected in Maryland, Louisiana, and New York, and Cincinnati elected a Jewish mayor, Julius Fleischmann. The first Jewish justice was seated on the Supreme Court (after a difficult confirmation battle in the Senate), when President Woodrow Wilson appointed **Louis D. Brandeis** in 1916. **Benjamin Cardozo** faced similar anti-Semitism when he was appointed to the bench by President Herbert Hoover in 1932.

Not all Eastern European immigrants felt comfortable in politics as usual. Many were attracted to and became mainstays of the Socialist Party. Socialist Jews established the Workman's Circle, an important fraternal and educational organization. **Meyer London**, protégé of socialist presidential candidate Eugene Debs, ran unsuccessfully for Congress from New York's Lower East Side in 1910 and 1912 before becoming, in 1914, the second socialist ever to sit in the House of Representatives. The first was Austrian Jew Victor Berger who was elected from Milwaukee for six terms beginning in 1910.

The Jewish labor movement had both a political and an economic agenda, and Jewish women were involved in the suffrage struggle. Anarchists **Emma Goldman** and Alexander Berkman advocated more radical means to achieve social and economic justice. During the pre-war years, militant social movements, often with Jewish leadership, pushed to organize industrial workers.

In the 1920s and 1930s Jewish participation in government increased, with increasing numbers of Jewish Americans in Congress, most of them Democrats. The candidacy of Franklin Delano Roosevelt unified Jewish voters in a new way. In each of his four elections Roosevelt received 90 percent of the Jewish vote, in part because a number of Jewish Americans served as his close friends and advisors, including **Henry Morgenthau, Jr.**, an important member of the New Deal cabinet.

The political situation changed drastically with the revelation of the Holocaust and the ensuing pressure to establish a Jewish state. **Zionism** became the primary focus of Jewish American politics. National Jewish organizations such as the **American Jewish Committee** and the **American Jewish Congress** increasingly put their attention into gaining American support for the state of Israel. The other overweening issue of the time, the anti-Communist crusade, found Jews on both sides, as in the trial of Julius and Ethel Rosenberg. They were accused of passing atomic spy secrets to the Soviet Union and were prosecuted, tried, and sentenced to death by other Jews. Blacklisting sometimes occurred with no more "evidence" of communist activity than a Jewish surname.

The Civil Rights movement was another strong focus of Jewish political activity. From the early decades of the twentieth century, Jewish attorneys had worked through the NAACP and the **Anti-Defamation League** to expand equal protection under the law, and for many years Jewish men headed the NAACP itself. In the 1960s, American Jews made up two-thirds of the white Freedom Riders who traveled to the south in the campaign to desegregate public facilities. While working in the voter registration drive in Mississippi, Jewish civil rights activists Andrew Goodman and Michael Schwerner were murdered along with black organizer James Chaney.

Jews entering government continued the trend begun under Roosevelt and remained solidly in the Democratic Party camp. These liberal political figures included Abraham Ribicoff, Secretary of Health, Education, and Welfare in the administration of John F. Kennedy and later a powerful voice in the Senate against the war in Vietnam, as well as Jewish feminists **Bella Abzug** and Elizabeth Holtzman in the House of

Representatives. Among New Left activists, there were Abbie Hoffman and Jerry Rubin, co-founders of the Yippies, and many other young Jewish Americans in such groups as Students for a Democratic Society. The second wave of feminism was inspired by **Betty Friedan** and led by Friedan, **Gloria Steinem**, and a number of other Jewish women. The most famous Jewish American in government in the late 1960s and early 1970s was **Henry Kissinger**, National Security Advisor and later Secretary of State under Presidents Nixon and Ford.

In recent decades, New York City and San Francisco voters have elected Jewish majors and Vermont a Jewish woman governor. The United States Senate has welcomed Jewish American members, including two women, **Dianne Feinstein** and **Barbara Boxer**, from California. President Clinton broke with tradition to appoint two Jewish Supreme Court justices, **Ruth Bader Ginsburg** and **Stephen Breyer**. Many of the barriers to full participation in the democratic process for Jewish Americans have been broken down.

ABZUG, BELLA (1920–1998)

Congresswoman, political activist

Famous for her hats and her *chutzpah*, Bella Savitzky Abzug was born in the Bronx on July 24, 1920 one month before American women were granted the right to vote. By the time she was eight, she was an outstanding student in the Talmud Torah school she attended and her Hebrew school teacher, Levi Soshuk, recruited her to a left-wing labor Zionist group, *Hashomer Hatzair* (the young guard). When her father, Emanuel, died, she proved willing to break the rules of Judaism. Although she was prohibited by tradition from saying *Kaddish* in synagogue for her father, who had no son, the thirteen-year-old appeared and davened every morning before school for a year. No one ever stopped her. She went to Florence Marshall Hebrew High School after classes at Walton High School and to the Hebrew Teachers Institute at the **Jewish Theological Seminary** after classes at Hunter College. A political science major,

she was active in the American Student Union and was an early and ardent champion of civil rights and civil liberties.

Abzug went to Columbia University Law School on a scholarship. She married Martin Abzug in 1944 and, after law school, joined a labor law firm that represented union locals. During the 1950s, she opened her own office, defending teachers and entertainment personalities attacked by the McCarthy witch-hunt. She also defended Willie McGee, a black Mississippian she believed to be falsely accused of raping a white woman with whom he had had a long-term consensual relationship. Despite worldwide publicity, protest marches, and Abzug's passionate plea to prevent another legal lynching, McGee went to the electric chair.

In 1961, Abzug co-founded Women Strike for Peace. During the next decade, she became a prominent national speaker against the war and against poverty, racism, and violence. In 1970, she was the first woman elected to Congress on a women's rights/peace platform. As chair of the Subcommittee on Government Information and Individual Rights, she co-authored three important pieces of legislation: the Freedom of Information Act, the Government in the Sunshine Act, and the Right to Privacy Act. She was also the first member of Congress to call for President Nixon's impeachment. She initiated the congressional caucus on women's issues, helped organize the National Women's Political Caucus, and served as chief strategist for the Democratic Women's Committee, which achieved equal representation for women in all elective and appointive posts, including presidential conventions. She wrote the first law banning discrimination against women in obtaining credit, credit cards, loans, and mortgages. She introduced pioneering bills on comprehensive child care, Social Security for homemakers, family planning, and abortion rights. In 1975, she introduced an amendment to the Civil Rights Act to include gay and lesbian rights. Reelected for three terms, Abzug served from 1971 to 1977 and was acknowledged by a *U.S. News and World Report* survey of House members as the "third most influential"

This woman's place is in the House...
the House of Representatives!

Bella Abzug
for Congress.

The first woman elected to Congress on a women's rights/peace platform, Bella Abzug cast her first vote for the Equal Rights Amendment. (Library of Congress)

House member. In a 1977 Gallup poll, she was named one of the twenty most influential women of the world.

After Abzug was defeated in a four-way primary race for the Senate in 1976 by less than one percent, President Carter appointed her chair of the National Commission on the Observance of International Women's Year, and later co-chair of the National Advisory Commission for Women. Active in the United Nations Decade of Women conferences in Mexico City (1975), Copenhagen (1980), and Nairobi (1985), Abzug became an esteemed leader of the international women's movement. She also led the fight against the Zionism Is Racism resolution passed in 1975, at the 1985 Women's Conference in Nairobi. She remained active into her seventies and died in 1998 following heart surgery.

ANARCHISM

Anarchism had a relatively brief but important history among Jews in the United States. The anarchist movement, organized around the principle that government was inherently authoritarian and coercive and should be replaced by a society of autonomous communities and associations, gained its greatest strength from the mid-1880s until World War I.

The two leading spokespeople for anarchism in the United States, **Emma Goldman** and Alexander Berkman, were both Russian Jewish immigrants who arrived in New York City in the 1880s. Berkman and Goldman helped establish a community of like-minded comrades with the goals of supporting revolutionary movements in Europe and the struggles of labor and working people in the United States through anarchist tactics of disruption and collective resistance. Unlike the Socialist Party, Jewish immigrant anarchists had no interest in or patience for working within the American political system and believed that the act of voting re-enforced the legitimacy of the state.

Anarchism gained new strength and energy in the radical climate of the first two decades of the twentieth century. Goldman traveled around the country conducting speaking tours, addressing strike support rallies, and writing essays in the pages of *Mother Earth*, an anarchist magazine she and Berkman founded. In her passionate speeches and writing, Goldman addressed a litany of issues, especially the emancipation of women and guaranteed access to birth control. Anarchists embraced a cultural as well as a political radicalism, and the pages of *Mother Earth* were filled with fiction, poetry, and Goldman's own essays on the significance of modern drama. In 1919, after serving prison time for opposing the draft, Berkman and Goldman were deported back to Russia as part of Attorney General A. Mitchell Palmer's anti-immigrant, anti-radical purges.

Although the public face of anarchism diminished after World War I, Jewish anarchist activity continued in the United States. The *Frie Arbiter Stimme* (Free Voice of Labor), the Yiddish anarchist newspaper, began in 1890 and continued well into the 1970s. Although the subscription list was never large, it had a loyal and devoted following.

Anarchism will best be remembered for its role in American immigrant Jewish radicalism during the Progressive Era. Along with the socialist movement (see **Socialism**) and the **Labor Movement**, anarchists were an a component of Jewish radical culture in the early years of the twentieth century.

BENJAMIN, JUDAH (1811–1884)

Lawyer, statesman

One of the most important figures in early Jewish American history, Judah Benjamin was born in St. Thomas, the Virgin Islands, in 1811 to an English Jewish father and a Portuguese Jewish mother. After his parents moved to the United States, Benjamin attended Fayetteville Academy and Yale University. He was admitted to the Louisiana bar in 1832 and quickly prospered. Active in business and politics as well, he was elected to the state senate in 1842 and by 1852 he was serving in the United States Senate.

When the Civil War broke out, Benjamin became attorney general of the Confederacy. He was briefly Secretary of War and later Secretary of State under Jefferson Davis. He became hugely unpopular for advocating that enslaved Americans be enlisted in the army and given their freedom in exchange for service. After Davis's capture in 1865, Benjamin fled to England where he became a Queen's Counsel. There he wrote the legal classic, *The Sale of Personal Property* (1868). He argued major cases before the House of Lords.

BOXER, BARBARA (1940–)

United States Senator

Politician Barbara Boxer was born in Brooklyn, New York, on November 11, 1940, the child of Jewish immigrants. She graduated from Brooklyn College in 1962 with a degree in economics. After working as a stockbroker and a journalist, Boxer became involved in politics. In 1977, after several years of organizing at the grassroots level, she was elected to her first political position as a member of the Marin County (California) Board of Supervisors. A member of the Board from 1977 through 1981, she became its first female president during her last year. In 1982 she was elected to the U.S. House of Representatives and in 1992, during the "Year of the Woman" election sweep, she joined her California colleague **Dianne Feinstein** in the Senate.

Barbara Boxer's politics are unabashedly liberal. She is well known for her commitment to domestic and feminist issues. She has worked to control defense spending, to safeguard abortion rights, to maintain environmental protections, and to increase awareness of sexual harassment. Though not known as an activist on Jewish issues, she has won both the Hannah G. Solomon Award from the **National Council of Jewish Women** and the Woman of Achievement Award from the **Anti-Defamation League**.

BRANDEIS, LOUIS D. (1856–1941)

Lawyer, Associate Justice of the Supreme Court

Distinguished jurist Louis Dembitz Brandeis was born in Louisville, Kentucky, on November 13, 1856, the son of German Jewish parents. After graduating from Harvard Law School, he opened a law practice with Samuel Warren, and their firm was soon hugely successful. By 1897 Brandeis was also active in the era's reform movements. In 1907 he presented a Supreme Court brief, in an Oregon case to limit women's working hours, that contained months worth of research and supporting data. It was a revolutionary legal document, recognizing the need to go beyond legal precedents to deal with social conditions in the community.

Brandeis firmly believed in the regulation of big business. In 1912 he began working with Woodrow Wilson to establish legal restraints, such as the Federal Reserve Act, the Clayton Antitrust Act, and the Federal Trade Commission Act.

During World War I, Brandeis took a position of leadership in the American Zionist movement, raising millions of dollars for the cause and for war relief. However, in 1921 he resigned from the Zionist Organization of America in protest against certain European Zionist attitudes.

In 1916 Brandeis was appointed to the Supreme Court and, in spite of anti-Semitic protest, was confirmed. He served on the court for twenty-three years, staunchly defending individual liberties. Even his dissenting opinions had a profound effect on future rulings. He retired from the Court in 1939 and died in 1941.

BREYER, STEPHEN (1938–)

Associate Justice of the Supreme Court

Supreme Court Associate Justice Stephen Breyer was born in San Francisco on August 15, 1938. He attended Stanford University, graduating with great distinction and an A.B. degree in 1959. He then moved on to Oxford University as a Marshall Scholar, receiving his B.A. and First Class Honors in 1961. After Oxford, he attended law school at Harvard where he was the articles editor for the *Harvard Law Review* and graduated magna cum laude in 1964.

For the year following his graduation from law school, Breyer served as a clerk for Supreme Court Justice **Arthur Goldberg**. In 1967 he joined the faculty at Harvard Law School. Later, he taught at the Kennedy School of Government. He was also a visiting professor at the College of Law in Sydney, Australia, and the University of Rome.

From 1965 through 1967, Breyer was an assistant in the Justice Department. In 1973 he became an Assistant Special Prosecutor for the Watergate Special Prosecution Force. He was also Special Counsel (1974–1975) and Chief Counsel (1979–1980) for the Senate Judiciary Committee. In 1980, he became a judge for the First Circuit Court of Appeals in Boston. Ten years later, he became that court's Chief Judge. A front-runner for the 1993 Supreme Court position that eventually went to **Ruth Bader Ginsburg**, he became an

Associate Justice—nominated by President Clinton—in 1994. A centrist politically, Breyer has written several books on administrative law and economic regulation.

CARDOZO, BENJAMIN NATHAN (1870–1938)

Lawyer, Supreme Court Justice

The seventy-fifth justice to sit on the Supreme Court, Benjamin Nathan Cardozo was born in New York City on May 24, 1870, into a family of Sephardic Jews who had lived in New York since before the American Revolution. He graduated from Columbia College when he was nineteen and received his master's degree a year later while he was attending Columbia Law School. After passing the bar, the brilliant young lawyer entered private practice and, for twenty-two years, quietly earned an outstanding reputation among other lawyers.

At the age of forty-three Cardozo was elected to a judgeship. Within a few years, he was chief judge of the New York State Court of Appeals. His extraordinary wisdom, knowledge, and literary ability were such that he had an influence on law of far greater magnitude than his position seemed to justify. He became a legal legend and the obvious choice for a seat on the nation's highest court. When Oliver Wendell Holmes, Jr. retired in 1932, President Herbert Hoover nominated Cardozo to replace him, virtually by popular demand. Cardozo served on the court for just over five years, but he made a lasting mark with his judicial contributions and with his personal writing, including *The Nature of the Judicial Process*, *The Growth of the Law*, and *Paradoxes of Legal Science*.

COMMUNIST PARTY

The Communist Party occupies an important and controversial role in the history of Jews in the United States—a role that continues to be hotly debated and contested today. During the McCarthy era anti-Communist crusade many of the people attacked were Jews, and it is clear now that many of them had nothing to do with the Communist Party. However, the emotions aroused by McCarthyism make it is difficult to assess the true impact of the Communist Party on American Jews or to discuss the subject among those who were close to it.

Given its roots in the Russian Bolshevik Revolution, it is not surprising that Jewish immigrants fleeing Czarist terror would be attracted to the organization most directly associated with the resistance movement. When the Communist Party first emerged in the early 1920s to challenge the Socialist Party's dominance in radical circles, Jews comprised 15 percent of its members. By the 1930s, when the Communist Party of the United States of America gained its greatest strength, its membership was more than 40 percent Jewish.

Jews began joining the Communist Party in serious numbers during the depths of the American Depression. Many Jewish immigrants from Eastern Europe already had well-developed radical politics and, when the stock market crashed in 1929, it appeared to many of them that American capitalism was collapsing. For many left-wing Jews of this era, the Socialist Party had ceased to be sufficiently militant. While some Jewish workers, educators, and artists who affiliated with the Communist Party in the 1930s looked to the Soviet Union for inspiration, what drew most Jews to the Party was the dynamic ability of many of its members to organize in the labor movement and its hard-line stand against racism at home and fascism abroad.

The Party's strength in Jewish population centers, especially New York, led to the publication of the *Freiheit*, a Yiddish communist daily, in 1922. Initiated by a group of young poets commonly referred to as *di Yunge*, these writers rebelled against the older Jewish socialist establishment and sought to create their own proletarian literature and drama in their native language—Yiddish. Although the *Freiheit* never remotely approached the ***Jewish Daily Forward*** in its circulation, it acquired a devoted following and elevated the writer Moshe Nadir to prominence within the left. The poets, dramatists, pedagogues, and fraternal activists who supported the *Freiheit* helped establish the Jewish Folk Chorus under the leadership of Jacob Shaffer; Camp Kinderland, a largely Yiddish Communist summer camp; and the Jewish People's Fraternal Organization, designed to compete with the Workman's Circle.

Although the Party gained ground among Jews and Americans at large in the early 1930s, it was still perceived as a fringe sectarian organization by the overwhelming majority of Americans. In 1934 the Communist Party International shifted its organizing strategy toward a left-liberal alliance with New Deal Democrats and their supporters. During this era (which became known as the Popular Front), Party leadership embraced American folklore and American culture, even supporting President Roosevelt's re-election in 1936, while attempting to push his administration to the left. In the late 1930s membership in the Communist Party USA reached its peak of 65,000 members. Many formerly reluctant Jews became active Party members or worked openly with Communists on a variety of social causes, including defending the Scottsboro Boys case, building the Congress of Industrial Organization (CIO), and supporting the Spanish Republicans against Franco's fascist incursions. Jews represented 40 percent of the 3,000 Americans who fought in Spain in the Communist-supported Abraham Lincoln Brigade.

Communists also established a large following among students in universities with large Jewish populations, especially City College of New York where, during the 1930s, political debates were far more likely to be between Communist Party stalwarts and their Trotskyist opponents than between Democrats and Republicans. Notable Jewish communists or close supporters included labor leaders such as Fur and Leather Workers Union president Ben Gold; crusading attorneys **Carol Weiss King** and Joseph Brodsky; playwright **Lillian Hellman**; and former Party general secretary Benjamin Gitlow.

During the heady days of the Depression and New Deal, the Communist Party and its adherents also generated vociferous opposition among other Jewish radicals—most notably the intellectual circle loyal to deposed Soviet leader Leon Trotsky. The New York Intellectuals, as they came to be known, were as critical of what they considered the low-brow aesthetics and pro-Americana kitsch of Communist Party members as they were of Stalin's authoritarian and autocratic regime. Other Jewish liberals were equally critical of what they perceived as the members' slavish devotion to Soviet policy.

The liberals' accusations gained credibility when Stalin signed a non-aggression pact with Nazi Germany in 1939. The Pact signaled the end of the Popular Front as the Communist Party USA's anti-fascist slogans were replaced by anti-imperialist and anti-war sloganeering. A number of Jews left the Party.

After Hitler invaded the Soviet Union in 1941, the Communist Party USA regrouped and re-united with American liberals in an all-out war against fascism. The Party took an ultra-patriotic position during World War II and the American government did its best to position the U.S.S.R. and Stalin as a loyal friend and ally. This new united front came to a grinding halt in the late 1940s with the beginning of the Cold War. For Jews, what became known as the McCarthy era was particularly wrenching as they found themselves on every conceivable side of the issue.

Because the climate of paranoia and intimidation in the nation had particular resonance for them, Jewish liberals especially feared that being linked to an unpopular political movement would unleash a new wave of anti-Semitism; thus, some were especially emphatic about denouncing communism. At the same time, a significant number of Jewish communists, former communists, and even those who might have only attended one or two Party meetings, lost their jobs and had their lives destroyed in this era. McCarthyism hit Jews in entertainment, education, and government particularly hard. Perhaps the most controversial case of the Cold War era, the trial and subsequent conviction of Communist Party members Julius and Ethel Rosenberg was symbolic of the multiple sides on which Jews found themselves during this period. With Jewish attorneys serving both the defense and the prosecution teams, Jewish Judge Irving Kaufman sentenced the couple to death for the crime of passing atomic spy secrets to a Soviet agent. Many

Jewish critics of the decision have argued for years that Kaufman's decision to invoke the maximum penalty possible stemmed from his own obsession with distancing himself as much as possible from the politics of his fellow Jews.

By the late 1950s, the anti-Communist purge, Khrushchev's revelations about Stalin's anti-Semitism, and the Soviet invasion of Hungary had turned the Communist Party USA into a shell of itself. Jewish members remained and continue to remain to this day, although the substantial Jewish presence in American communism has come and gone. Nevertheless, what became known as the Old Left didn't completely disappear. Many children of communist parents (known as "Red Diaper Babies") gravitated to the **New Left** in the 1960s, even though a large percentage rejected what they viewed as the authoritarian, bureaucratic, and dogmatic tendencies of their parents' generation.

Although many scholars and thinkers now look disdainfully at Jewish involvement in American communism and view its adherents as at best naive and at worst Party dupes, such a view fails to appreciate the enormous appeal of a movement representing ideals that were firmly rooted in American and not Soviet realities. In the 1920s and especially in the 1930s, many Jews viewed the Communist Party as the political organization that would help realize the socialist dream they brought with them from Europe.

DERSHOWITZ, ALAN (1938–)

Lawyer

Alan Dershowitz is probably the most famous defense lawyer currently practicing in the United States. He is certainly the only American Jew with the *chutzpah* to call his book reflecting on what it means to be a Jew in today's world *Chutzpah*. The 1991 book was number one on *The New York Times* best seller list for a number of weeks. In it, Dershowitz examines anti-Semitism, the Holocaust, assimilation, Zionism, civil rights, changes in eastern Europe, and the conflicts in the Middle East, all in his own inimitable style.

Alan M. Dershowitz was born on September 1, 1938 in Brooklyn, New York. He attended Yeshiva University high school and then moved on to Brooklyn College where he received his B.A. in 1959. In 1962, he graduated first in his class from Yale Law School, where he was editor-in-chief of the *Yale Law Review*.

After he left Yale, Dershowitz served as a clerk to U.S. Court of Appeals Chief Judge David L. Bazelon. He then obtained a clerkship with Supreme Court Justice **Arthur J. Goldberg**. In 1964 he joined the faculty at Harvard Law School and was promoted to full professor three years later, the youngest (twenty-eight years old) full professor in the school's history. He remains on the faculty today.

Dershowitz rose to prominence in the popular culture because of his defense of famous clients including Claus von Bulow, Patricia Hearst, Anatoly Shcharansky, F. Lee Bailey, Leona Helmsley, Michael Milken, and O.J. Simpson. He has also written many books about his cases. Among the most popular are *The Best Defense* (1982), *Reasonable Doubts: The O. J. Simpson Case*, and *The Criminal Justice System* (1996), and *Reversal of Fortune* (1986), which was made into a film in 1990. In addition to his books, Dershowitz has written a weekly newspaper column since 1984.

In 1997 he published *The Vanishing American Jew. In Search of Jewish Identity for the Next Century*, which is an analysis of Jewish life at the end of the 1990s and a call for action. Dershowitz is married to Carolyn A. Cohen, who holds a Ph. D. in psychology, and he has three children and two grandchildren. His latest book is *Just Revenge*, a novel about the Holocaust, and he is working on a nonfiction work entitled *The Genesis of Justice*.

FEINSTEIN, DIANNE (1933–)

United States Senator

Senator Dianne Feinstein (née Goldman) was born on June 22, 1933 in San Francisco. As a child, she attended a Jewish religious school before transferring to the Convent of the Sacred Heart, a prestigous private Catholic high school. She later went to Stanford University, graduating in 1955. Her first job in government came in 1960 when she was appointed by (then) Governor Pat Brown to the California Women's Board of Terms and Parole. In 1968, she became a member of the San Francisco mayor's committee on crime and committee on adult detention. She was elected as the president of the Board of Supervisors (the first woman to hold that position) the following year. She served as mayor of the city for two terms, from 1979 through 1987. In 1992, she was elected to fill Pete Wilson's Senate seat for the remainder of his term. (He left to become governor of California.) In 1994, she won a reelection bid for a full six-year term.

Known best for her long-standing commitment to anti-crime legislation, Feinstein is active on many issues including health care, medical reform, and immigration. She is a member of the Senate Judiciary Subcommittee on Immigration and the Centrist Coalition. She has received many awards for her public service, including France's Légion d'Honneur and a public service award from the **American Jewish Congress**.

FIEDLER, BOBBI (1937–)

Congresswoman

The child of an observant Jewish family, Bobbi Fiedler (née Roberta Horowitz) was born in Santa Monica, California on April 22, 1937. She entered the political arena in 1976 in response to one issue—the court-ordered busing of school children in Los Angeles County. Within a year, Fiedler had organized a grassroots group called BUSTOP and was elected to a seat on the Los Angeles Board of Education, where she succeeded in halting busing. In 1980, she was elected to the House of Representatives and served for three terms. She ran for a Senate seat in 1987 but lost.

A good friend of Ronald Reagan, Fiedler was an independent Republican who supported traditional Republican platforms such as tax cuts and defense spending as well as traditional liberal legislation such as the Equal Rights Amendment and abortion rights. Many of her political positions, especially the busing issue that got her into politics, were formed by her experience as a Jew. The idea of treating people differently because of their race or ethnicity, as would happen in busing children, reminded her of the historic example of the rise of Nazism. This also explains her deep opposition to any powerful central government and her entry into traditional Republican politics.

FORTAS, ABE (1910–1982)

Associate Justice of the Supreme Court

Supreme Court Associate Justice Abe Fortas was born into an orthodox family on June 19, 1910 in Memphis, Tennessee. He attended Yale University Law School, graduating first in his class in 1933. He then became an assistant professor there. From 1937 through 1946, he worked in various capacities in the federal government. In 1946, he entered private practice, building his firm into one of the most powerful in Washington, D.C.

In 1963 Fortas argued his most famous case before the Supreme Court, *Gideon v. Wainwright*. The story of this case, which established the right of the accused to counsel regardless of economic considerations, is immortalized in the book, *Gideon's Trumpet*. Two years after this groundbreaking success, Fortas was nominated by President Johnson and accepted by the Senate to serve on the Supreme Court.

In 1968 President Johnson nominated the traditionally liberal Fortas for the position of Chief Justice. However, there was strong resistance from conservatives in the Senate and Fortas asked that his name be withdrawn. He was the first nominee for Chief Justice since 1795 to fail to secure the position. One year later, Fortas resigned from the Supreme Court. He had been involved years earlier with a financier who was eventually jailed for securities violations. Because of this, Congress appeared to be preparing impeachment proceedings. Fortas was the first Supreme Court Justice to resign under such a threat. He returned to private practice and died on April 6, 1982, in Washington, D.C.

FRANK, BARNEY (1940–)

Congressman

Barney Frank has a well-earned reputation as one of the most gifted speakers and debaters in the House of Representatives. The New Jersey–born Frank became involved in Massachusetts politics while a student at Harvard in the 1960s, working for Boston Mayor Kevin White. In 1972 he was elected to the state legislature and eight years later he won election to a Congressional seat from Brookline, previously held by anti-war activist Father Robert Drinan. He has held the seat ever since, despite redistricting in 1982 that forced him into a race against another incumbent, Margaret Heckler.

Frank's popularity in a liberal area like Brookline should come as no surprise; he is among the most outspokenly liberal members of Congress. In 1987 he did something that might have shaken his working-class constituents in more conservative Fall River: in answer to a reporter's question, the congressman said he was gay. His district remained solidly behind him, even after a scandal broke two years later in which it was revealed that a former aide had been involved in male prostitution. Having shrugged off that seeming setback, Frank became a highly visible figure in the Democratic minority. As point man for the party in the 1994 debates on the so-called Contract With America, he acquitted himself brilliantly on the floor and on television. In the 1996 Congressional elections, he won his seat again, by a margin of three to one.

FRANKFURTER, FELIX (1882–1965)

Legal educator, Supreme Court Justice

Civil liberties advocate Felix Frankfurter was born in Vienna, Austria in 1882 and immigrated to the United States twelve years later. After graduating from Harvard Law School, he became an Assistant U. S. Attorney in New York before moving on to a legal position in the War Department in Washington. From 1914 until 1939 he was professor of law at Harvard. He took a leave of absence from 1917 to 1919, during which time he served as chairman of the War Labor Policies Board, represented Chaim Weizmann at the Paris Peace Conference, and negotiated an important Zionist-Arab agreement.

In 1920, Frankfurter was a founder of the American Civil Liberties Union. This is just one example of his continuing interest in issues of civil liberties. In his writings, he protested powerfully against the injustices of the Sacco-Vanzetti case and wrote extensively on labor rights.

After repeatedly refusing appointments to public legal positions, in 1939 Frankfurter accepted Franklin Roosevelt's offer of a Supreme Court appointment. He was, until his retirement in 1962, an influence for individual rights, tempered by a respect for the division between the judicial branch, on the one hand, and the legislative and executive branches, on the other.

GINSBURG, RUTH BADER (1933–)

Supreme Court Justice

Supreme Court Justice Ruth Bader Ginsburg was born in Brooklyn, New York on March 15, 1933. Her father was a Russian Jewish immigrant and her mother's parents were Polish Jewish immigrants. She attended Cornell University, graduating in 1954. Later that year she married David Ginsburg. In 1956, she entered Harvard University Law School. Two years later, she transferred to Columbia Law School. When

she graduated, she was tied for first in the class. At both schools, she was on the *Law Review*.

Though highly recommended, Ginsburg was turned down for a clerkship with Supreme Court Justice **Felix Frankfurter** because she was a woman. Instead, she became a law clerk for Judge Edmund L. Palmieri. In 1963, she became a law professor at Rutgers University, and in the late 1960s, she began working for the ACLU on sex discrimination cases. When the ACLU established the Women's Rights Project in 1972, she became its co-director. That same year she left Rutgers and be-

The first Jewish woman appointed to the Supreme Court, Ruth Bader Ginsburg was a passionate advocate of women's rights in her years as a lawyer. In a speech after her appointment she said, "I am a judge born, raised, and proud of being a Jew. The demand for justice runs through the entirety of the Jewish tradition. I hope . . . I will have the strength and the courage to remain constant in the service of that demand." (Photograph by Richard Strauss, Smithsonian Institution. Courtesy of the Supreme Court)

"No Dogs or Jews Allowed"

"I am alert to discrimination. I have memories as a child . . . of being in a car with my parents and passing a place in Pennsylvania, a resort with a sign out in front that read: 'No Dogs or Jews allowed.' "

Ruth Bader Ginsburg in her testimony at her confirmation hearing to be an Associate Justice of the Supreme Court.

came the first female tenured professor at Columbia Law School. In 1980, President Carter appointed her to the influential District of Columbia Circuit Court of Appeals and in June of 1993, President Clinton nominated her to the Supreme Court. She is the first Jewish woman and the second woman to sit on the Court. Though not a religiously observant Jew, Ruth Bader Ginsburg credits the concept of justice in the Jewish tradition with helping to determine her choice of career.

GOLDBERG, ARTHUR J. (1908–1990)

Associate Justice of the Supreme Court, diplomat

The son of Russian Jewish immigrants, Arthur J. Goldberg was born in Chicago, Illinois on August 8, 1908. When he was only twenty he passed the Illinois bar and then began to practice law in Chicago. In 1938, he represented the Chicago Newspaper Guild during its strike. In 1948, he left his law practice to become the general counsel for both the United Steelworkers of America and the Congress for Industrial Organizations (CIO). He was an important force in the 1958 merging of the CIO with the American Federation of Labor (AFL). Around this time, he was also involved in purging the labor movement of unions that were considered unduly influenced by communists or the mob.

From 1961 through 1962, Goldberg served as Secretary of Labor. In 1962, he was appointed Associate Justice of the Supreme Court. However, he stayed with the Court for only three years. In 1965, Lyndon B. Johnson appointed him to serve as the U.S. Ambassador to the United Nations. He stayed in that position until his frustration over the Vietnam War forced him to resign in 1968. After losing a bid to become governor of New York, Goldberg returned to Washington, D.C., and resumed his private legal practice. In the final two decades of his life, he continued to work as a labor lawyer, oversaw international arbitration cases, and became involved in several human rights projects. On two occasions, he also acted as an ambassador-at-large for Jimmy Carter. He died in Washington, D.C., on January 19, 1990.

GOVERNMENT

Despite considerable institutional constraints and resistance, American Jews played important roles in the government of the United States. Because the Jewish population is largely concentrated among a few large cities, particularly New York, Jews in federal electoral positions have tended to be in the decentralized House of Representatives, which consists of many small, localized districts rather than in the Senate with its two members who must each be elected by an entire state. No Jews have been elected, nominated, or even seriously considered as presidential candidates. Only a few Jews have been elected state governors. Interestingly, four of these state leaders all served in the early 1930s (see sidebar on page 147). Jews have, however, made their mark in state legislatures, as party leaders, as Supreme Court Justices, as federal Cabinet appointees, and in numerous positions in city and local government.

Jews in the colonial era embraced the early Democratic Party of Thomas Jefferson, which they perceived as more dedicated to separation of church and state and more supportive of freedom of religion than the Federalists. Although the Jewish population probably totaled no more than 15,000 in the entire country prior to the 1840s, several Jews made a name for themselves in official government capacities. The most prominent were Mordecai Noah, who served as consul general in Tunis during the administration of James Madison, and Emanuel Hart, who established an early Jewish presence as a leader in New York City's Tammany Hall in the 1820s and later served as a Congressman.

During the Civil War era the new German Jewish population, dismayed by the negotiation of an anti-Semitic commercial treaty with Switzerland by the Democratic administration of James Buchanan, became active participants in the formation of the new Republican Party and supporters of Abraham Lincoln.

With the massive influx of Jews from Eastern Europe beginning in the 1880s, the Jewish presence in the electoral arena increased markedly. Jewish Congressmen were elected in Maryland, Louisiana, and New York in the late 1800s. Cincinnati elected a Jewish mayor, Julius Fleischmann, in 1900. In the second decade of the twentieth century, Jews achieved particular success in New York, running successfully for several Congressional seats with a few such as Henry Schimmel emerging victorious in state assembly races as well.

Although new Jewish immigrants joined both of the major political parties, the more affluent German Jews increasingly supported the Republican Party. In California, a state with a fairly small number of Jews, Republican Julius Kahn was elected to a Congressional seat in 1916. When he died in 1924 his wife, **Florence Prag Kahn**, won a special election to replace him and went on to win reelection five times in her own right (1925–1937).

For many of the more radical Eastern European newcomers, neither mainstream party fit their brand of politics. These Jewish immigrants became important players in the burgeoning Socialist Party. **Meyer London**, a Russian Jewish immigrant himself and protégé of Socialist presidential candidate Eugene Debs, ran unsuccessfully for Congress from New York's heavily Jewish Lower East Side in 1910 and 1912. In 1914 he became only the second Socialist to ever sit in the House, the first being the more strait-laced Austrian Jew Victor Berger, who was elected as Congressman from Milwaukee for six terms beginning in 1910. In addition, **Morris Hillquit**, a Russian Jew from Latvia narrowly missed being elected on the Socialist ticket for Congress and then made a respectable showing on two occasions in his campaign for mayor of New York.

London's defeat in 1918 mirrored the shrinking fortunes of the Socialist Party as its position opposing World War I rendered it politically vulnerable during a time of inflamed tensions and anti-radical hysteria. One Jew in particular, **Bernard Baruch**, stood closer to the political establishment, chairing the War Industries Board under President Woodrow Wilson and later serving on the Supreme Economic Council of the Versailles Conference.

It was the overwhelming support of New York Jews for an Irish Catholic candidate for governor, Alfred E. Smith, in 1924 that precipitated a lower than expected Jewish vote for Socialist Party candidate Norman Thomas. Although Jewish women had been shut out of formal elective office, it was the daughter of an East European Jew, Belle Moskowitz, who became among the most powerful of Smith's advisors. Politicians and reporters frequently learned that they had to go through Moskowitz in order to reach Smith. The 1920s also saw the rise of **Robert Moses**, a German Jew who became Parks Commissioner in New York City and would go on to wield enormous power over city planning decisions for the next half-century although he was never elected to any office.

The second decade of the twentieth century witnessed the first Jewish justice seated on the Supreme Court when President Woodrow Wilson appointed **Louis Brandeis** in 1916 in the face of a contentious confirmation battle. **Benjamin Cardozo**, appointed to the Bench by President Herbert Hoover after a long and distinguished judicial career, also faced anti-Semitic resistance prior his confirmation in 1932.

Despite the more conservative climate in the 1920s, Jewish participation in government increased during this decade with thirteen Jews elected to Congress, the most famous being Emanuel Celler, a liberal Democrat from Brooklyn who went on to serve in the House for nearly half a century. Although three of the thirteen Jews who gained admission to Congress were Republicans and one was a Socialist, it was clear by the end of the decade that the allegiance of Jewish candidates was increasingly with the Democratic party. In 1930, six of the eight Jews elected to Congress were Democrats.

The election of Franklin Roosevelt as president marked the beginning of the overwhelming allegiance of Jewish voters for the Democratic Party. FDR was revered by Jews who gave him upward of 90 percent of the vote in each of his four election bids. **Henry Morgenthau, Jr.**, previously chair of the New York Agricultural Advisory Commission during Roosevelt's governorship, became an important member of the New Deal cabinet and one of the President's closest advisors. Morgenthau first headed the Federal Farm Board and the Farm Credit Administration. In 1934 FDR appointed him Secretary of the Treasury, the highest cabinet position attained by a Jew up to that time. Roosevelt appointed several other Jews to New Deal agencies including Louis Bean, who served on the Agricultural Adjustment Administration from 1933 to 1939. The president also recognized the talents of American Clothing Workers president **Sidney Hillman** who became FDR's main conduit to organized labor and a reliable source of getting out the union vote to support his presidency, especially during the tumultuous years of World War II when Hillman directed the CIO's Political Action Campaign (CIO-PAC). Roosevelt appointed **Felix Frankfurter**, an Austrian Jewish immigrant, to the Supreme Court to fill the seat vacated by Cardozo's death in 1939.

At this same time, Hillman, along with **David Dubinsky** and Max Zaritsky, initiated the American Labor Party as a way for New Yorkers with a socialist orientation to support the New Deal without endorsing the Tammany Democratic machine. Known primarily for its crucial role in electing pro-labor Italian-Americans Vito Marcantonio to Congress and Fiorello La Guardia to City Hall, the American Labor Party also endorsed a Jewish candidate, Leo Isaacson, who won election to Congress from the South Bronx in 1948.

The postwar years brought an increase of Jewish representation in government at the same time the economic status of most Jews improved markedly. As ethnic politics began to wane, many Jews sought to play down their immigrant roots in favor of an American universalism. The security of the State of Israel became a major focus both for Jewish office seekers as well as the overall Jewish electorate. Jews entering government continued the trend begun under Roosevelt and remained solidly in the Democratic Party camp usually with strong liberal leanings. One example of such a figure is Abraham Ribicoff, Secretary of Health, Education, and Welfare in the administration

Barbara Boxer and Dianne Feinstein were both elected to the Senate in 1992, the "Year of the Woman" in American politics. This group photograph depicts the "Senate Women" in early 1993, with Hillary Rodham Clinton. From left to right are: Carol Moseley-Braun, Patty Murray, Barbara Mikulski, Hillary Rodham Clinton, Boxer, Feinstein, and Nancy Kassenbaum. (White House Photograph)

The First Jew in the Cabinet

Oscar S. Straus of New York City was appointed Secretary of Commerce and Labor by President Theodore Roosevelt on December 12, 1906. He was the first Jew to receive a Cabinet appointment.

---

of John F. Kennedy, who became better known in later years as a Senator from Connecticut who fervently opposed the war in Vietnam. Jewish feminists **Bella Abzug** and Elizabeth Holtzman from New York were each elected to the House of Representatives in the early 1970s in part because of their equally strong condemnation of the war in addition to their militant advocacy of women's rights.

It is ironic that the most famous Jewish face in government in the tumultuous late 1960s and early 1970s was their adversary—**Henry Kissinger**, a German Jewish immigrant of the Holocaust generation who served as National Security Advisor and later Secretary of State under Presidents Nixon and Ford. He oversaw the progress of the war in Vietnam as well as the ancillary conflicts in Laos and Cambodia. At the same time, one of the most popular members of Congress was also a Jewish Republican, albeit a liberal one. **Jacob Javits**, a member of the House of Representatives from 1946 to 1954, became best known as a Senator from New York, winning election in 1956 and serving for an extraordinary twenty-four years.

In the 1960s, Democratic presidents Kennedy and Johnson appointed two more Jews as Supreme Court justices although neither stayed on the bench for very long. Kennedy appointed **Arthur Goldberg**, his Secretary of Labor, to fill what had become known as the "Jewish seat" on the High Court in 1962 after Frankfurter's retirement. In 1965 Johnson lured Goldberg away from the bench to become his ambassador to the United Nations, a decision that Goldberg soon regretted as his disillusionment with the war in Vietnam increased. Johnson filled Goldberg's seat by appointing his personal friend, **Abe Fortas**. Ethical improprieties prevented Fortas from advancing to Chief Justice in 1968 and several months later he resigned from the Court.

The 1970s and 1980s brought the elections of the first Jewish mayors in a number of cities. Despite being the epicenter of American Jewish life, New York City had never elected a Jewish mayor until Abraham Beame in 1974. Presiding over the worst fiscal crisis in the city's history, Beame was defeated for re-election by another Jew, former Congressman **Edward Koch**, who served as mayor for twelve years. In San Francisco, **Dianne Feinstein** became mayor in 1978 after the death of her predecessor, and was later elected for two additional terms before becoming Senator from California where she was later joined by another Jewish woman Senator from her state, **Barbara Boxer**.

In the conservative 1980s, Jews in governmental positions generally remained aligned with the Democratic Party but there were signs of change. President Ronald Reagan's Under-Secretary of State, Elliot Abrams spoke for a new breed of Jews in the political arena, the **"neoconservatives"**—former liberals who had increasingly moved to the right and become Cold War hawks. Although Jewish Democrats such as Senators Howard Metzenbaum of Ohio adhered to more old-line liberal values, the issues of military aid to Is-

---

8% of All State Governors Were Jews

When Franklin Roosevelt was serving his first term as President, four of forty-eight states had Jewish Governors. The Governors were Herbert H. Lehman in New York, Henry Horner in Illinois, Julius Meyer in Oregon, and Arthur Selligman in New Mexico.

Senator Abraham Ribicoff (1910–1998)

Abraham Ribicoff was one of the best vote getters in Connecticut history and a close personal friend and political ally of John F. Kennedy. He and Kennedy were both young Congressmen in 1948; Ribicoff nominated Kennedy for Vice President in 1956; was the convention floor manager for Kennedy in 1960. He was the first person Kennedy named to his Cabinet—as Secretary of Health, Education, and Welfare.

The child of Polish Jewish immigrants, Ribicoff capped his campaign for Connecticut Governor by telling an Italian-American audience that "nowhere except in the Democratic Party could a boy named Abe Ribicoff be nominated for governor of this state." He became the first Jewish governor of Connecticut in 1954, only 111 years after the state constitution was amended to allow Jews to worship openly. He subsequently served three terms in the United States Senate.

For a generation of Americans, the image they remember of Abraham Ribicoff is at the podium of the 1968 Democratic convention. With television coverage of Chicago police beating anti-war demonstrators outside the convention hall being beamed around the world, Ribicoff pounded his fist on the podium, looked Chicago Mayor Richard J. Daley in the eye, and denounced the "Gestapo tactics" taking place outside. It was his finest public hour!

---

rael and advocacy for Soviet Jewry sometimes united Jewish politicians of otherwise opposed ideologies and contributed to a growing conservatism among the Jewish electorate in this era. In the economic arena, **Milton Friedman** and **Arthur Burns** served as advisors to Presidents Reagan and Bush and became leading advocates for deregulation, open markets, and "trickle down" economics. During the 1980s, another conservative Jewish economist, **Alan Greenspan**, was named to head the Federal Reserve. Jewish Republicans, Rudy Boschowitz of Minnesota and Warren Rudman of New Hampshire, won elections to the Senate. At the same time, Jewish Democrats Carl Levin of Michigan, Edward Zorinsky of Nebraska, and Frank Lautenberg of New Jersey also won election to the Senate.

The late 1980s and 1990s brought important breakthroughs in the electoral arena that directly involved Jews. In Vermont, Madeleine Kunin was elected only the second female Governor, and the first

Joseph Lieberman is the only observant Orthodox Jew serving in the United States Senate. First elected in 1988, Senator Lieberman often speaks out on religious and moral issues and participates in ecumenical gatherings on Capitol Hill. His one concession to the political life is that he has been known to stay late on Friday night in the Senate when votes are being taken. When the Senate then adjourns he walks the four-and-a-half miles home to Georgetown. (Office of Senator Lieberman)

Jewish woman Governor, in American history. A few years later Vermont elected the first self-proclaimed socialist in decades when Bernie Sanders, the former mayor of Burlington, won a seat in Congress as an independent. **Barney Frank** became the first openly gay member of Congress when he was elected to the House of Representatives from Massachusetts. In a surprise victory, Paul Wellstone, a strong progressive, bucked the conservative trend to become the second Jewish Senator from Minnesota in 1988. In the early 1990s, President Clinton appointed the first Jewish woman to the Supreme Court, **Ruth Bader Ginsburg**, as well as a Jewish man, **Stephen Breyer**.

Over the course of American history, Jews have gained an increasing presence as political officeholders on both a local and a national level. Barriers to Jewish advancement in the electoral arena still exist, especially when it comes to attaining the highest office in the land—the presidency.

HARMAN, JANE (1945–)

Politician

Jane Harman was born in New York City on June 28, 1945 the daughter—on her father's side—of refugees from Nazi Germany. She attended Smith College, graduating in 1966, then moved on to Harvard Law School. After graduating from law school in 1969, Harman went to work for the federal government. During this period, she served as Senator John Tunney's legislative assistant and as the deputy secretary to the Cabinet during Jimmy Carter's administration. During the 1980s she worked for the Democratic National Committee.

In 1992 Harman won the House of Representatives seat for the thirty-sixth Congressional District representing the Los Angeles neighborhood of South Bay. She held the seat in two close elections in 1994 and 1996. Considered progressive politically, Harman is pro-Israeli, pro-choice, and anti-school prayer. She has been effective in maintaining government support for the defense industries (many of which are located in her district) and has supported the rights of homosexuals in the military. She is a member of the House National Security Committee, the House Intelligence Committee, the Congressional Caucus on Anti-Semitism, and the Congressional Caucus On Women's Issues.

HAYS, ARTHUR GARFIELD (1881–1954)

Lawyer

Attorney and civil liberties advocate Arthur Garfield Hays was born in Rochester, New York in 1881. After practicing law for two decades, he became general counsel of the American Civil Liberties Union in 1925. In the years that followed, Hays was a crucial part of the defense in some of America's famous civil liberties trials. He was co-counsel with Clarence Darrow in the notorious Scopes "monkey trial," testing the right to teach evolution in the public schools. He was instrumental in the defense of Sacco and Vanzetti. He was also involved in the Scottsboro trial, in which a group of young African American men was falsely accused of raping a young white woman. Their conviction was, as a result, reversed in the U.S. Supreme Court. In defense of the Bill of Rights, Hays also represented some whose beliefs were abhorrent to him, including the Friends of New Germany, a Nazi organization that had been deprived of access to meeting places in New Jersey. Among Hays's publications were *Trial by Prejudice* (1933) and his autobiography, *City Lawyer* (1942).

JAVITS, JACOB (1904–1986)

United States Senator

Jacob Javits was born on May 18, 1904. His parents were Jewish immigrants living on the Lower East Side of Manhattan. Javits attended the public schools and worked his way through both Columbia University and New York University School of Law.

A liberal Republican in a traditionally Democratic city, in 1946 Javits stunned his own party and his opponents when he won a seat in the House of Representatives. In that election, and for the rest of his political career, he swayed liberal and Jewish voters who were frequently Democrats. He served three terms in the House before being elected as New York Attorney General, a post he held for two years. In 1958 he was elected to the United States Senate, where he remained for the next twenty-four years.

A long-time member of the Senate Foreign Relations Committee, Javits supported aid to Israel and was instrumental in gaining passage of the 1973 War Powers Act. He was also influential in civil rights and urban redevelopment legislation. In recognition of his service to the nation, he was awarded the Medal of Freedom and the Charles Evans Hughes Gold Medal. He died on March 7, 1986.

KAHN, FLORENCE PRAG (1866–1948)

Congresswoman

Congresswoman Florence Prag Kahn was born in Salt Lake City, Utah on November 9, 1866. She grew up in San Francisco and her parents were influential members of San Francisco's Jewish community. Brought up in a religious household that stressed education, Florence Prag attended the University of California. After she graduated in 1887, she became a teacher. In 1899, she married Republican Congressman Julius Kahn.

Throughout her husband's career, Florence Prag Kahn served as his secretary. In 1919 and 1920 she also wrote columns for the *San Francisco Chronicle*. When Julius Kahn died in 1924, Florence took over his seat in the House of Representatives, becoming the first Jewish woman in Congress. She went on to serve five full terms and developed her own reputation as a savvy strategist.

Conservative, both religiously and politically, Kahn, like her husband, was deeply committed to military preparedness. In 1930, she became the first woman to serve on the House Military Affairs Committee. Prior to 1911, when California adopted women's suffrage, Kahn had been opposed to the vote for women. Later, however, she took a more liberal stance in opposing Prohibition and censorship of the film industry. She died on November 16, 1948.

KAYE, JUDITH S. (1938–)

Chief Judge, State of New York

Judith Kaye (née Smith) was born in Monticello, New York on August 4 1938. She attended Barnard College, graduating with a B.A. in 1958. She then attended New York University Law School where she earned her law degree in 1962. From 1969 through 1983, she worked with the law firm Olwine, Connelly, Chase, O'Donnell and Weyher. Starting out as a litigation assistant, she became the firm's first woman partner.

Judith S. Kaye, the first woman to serve as chief judge of the State of New York, is a member of Congregation Shearith Israel in New York City, the oldest Jewish congregation in North America. One of her idols, Benjamin Cardozo, was also a member of the Congregation. (Office of Judge Kaye)

In 1983 she was appointed by Governor Mario Cuomo to the New York State Court of Appeals, the first woman to serve in this position. She started out as an associate judge and later became the Court of Appeals' Chief Justice. Ten years after she was appointed to the Court of Appeals, Governor Cuomo appointed Kaye Chief Judge for the State of New York. Again, she was the first woman to hold that position. Especially committed to gender issues as they relate to the law, Kaye has spent much of her life championing causes for women and children. She has given special attention to domestic violence.

Judge Kaye is the mother of three children. She and her husband, Stephen Rackow Kaye, are members of Congregation Shearith Israel, the oldest Jewish congregation in North America.

KING, CAROL WEISS (1895–1952)

Lawyer

Carol Weiss King was born on August 24, 1895. She attended Barnard College, graduating in 1916. She then went to New York University Law School where she earned her law degree in 1920. While still in school, she became involved in the labor movement and began working for Local 25 of the International Ladies Garment Workers Union.

After graduation, Weiss became involved with a group of radical lawyers including Joseph Brodsky, Swinburne Hale, Walter Nelles, and Isaac Shorr. She became best known for her work in immigration law. Throughout her career, she represented hundreds of radical immigrants who were threatened with deportation, sometimes taking the cases as far as the Supreme Court. Among her most famous clients were **Communist Party** leaders and organizers William Schneiderman and Angelo Herndon and labor leader Harry Bridges. She also represented the Scottsboro Boys and served as general counsel for the American Committee for the Foreign Born.

Among her most important victories was *Sung v. McGrath*. In that case, the Supreme Court ruled that the Immigration and Naturalization Service was bound by the same rules as other federal departments. This had a powerful effect on stemming the deportation of radical immigrants. In addition to her work as a trial lawyer, Weiss edited the ACLU's *Law and Freedom Bulletin* (1924–1931) and helped found both the International Juridical Guild and the National Lawyer Guild. She died on January 22, 1952.

KISSINGER, HENRY (1923–)

Foreign policy expert

Former Secretary of State Henry Kissinger was born in Frankfurt, Germany on May 27, 1923. Fleeing from

Henry Kissinger and his family were members of an Orthodox synagogue in Germany before they immigrated to New York City in 1938. He is shown here being sworn in as Secretary of State in 1973. President Richard Nixon looks on, Kissinger's mother Paula stands at his side, and Chief Justice Warren Burger administers the oath of office. (Courtesy of American Jewish Historical Society, Waltham, Massachusetts and New York, New York)

Nazi persecution, the Kissinger family arrived in the United States in 1938. After serving in the U. S. army during World War II, Kissinger earned his B.A. and Ph.D. from Harvard. He took a position as professor of government at the university in 1962.

His book, *Nuclear Weapons and Foreign Policy*, published in 1957, brought Kissinger national attention. He became a security advisor to three consecutive American presidents—Dwight Eisenhower, John Kennedy, and Lyndon Johnson. In 1969, he became special assistant to President Nixon for national security affairs and executive secretary of the National Security Council. In 1973, he accepted the position of Secretary of State.

Kissinger believed that world peace would come as a result of a balance of power in the world. He worked toward detente with the Soviet Union by urging the United States to maintain military strength while seeking contacts and connections in other areas, such as culture, economy, and science. The approach led to the first Strategic Arms Limitation Treaty (SALT I). He also negotiated a ceasefire in Vietnam, for which he and chief North Vietnamese negotiator Le Duc Tho were awarded the 1973 Nobel Peace Prize. During the October 1973 Arab-Israeli War, he was able to avoid Soviet intervention and to negotiate ceasefires.

Some of Kissinger's tactics were sharply criticized, especially after it was revealed that he supported covert bombings in Cambodia in 1970 and secret CIA operations designed to disrupt the Allende government in

How Does Henry Kissinger Differ from Abba Eban?

During a visit to the United States, Israeli Prime Minister Golda Meir was received officially at the White House by President Nixon and Secretary of State Kissinger.

During their conversation, President Nixon commented to Mrs. Meir, "Madame Prime Minister, it must be a source of great satisfaction to you to observe that in the United States Jews are so well regarded and are given the political equality that they so well deserve that in my administration a Jew serves as my Secretary of State, or, to use the nomenclature employed in your country, my Foreign Minister."

Golda Meir smiled and said, "This certainly is one of the many indications that the United States is truly a genuine democracy." Then she added facetiously, "I am sure that you will be delighted to know, Mr. President, that our Foreign Minister is also a Jew who differs in one respect from your Foreign Minister. Our Foreign Minister (Abba Eban) speaks English without an accent."

From *Jewish Folklore in America*, by David Max Eichhorn.

Chile, as well as American support for anti-government forces in Angola. In 1975, President Gerald Ford replaced him as national security advisor. He left the office of Secretary of State in 1976.

KOCH, EDWARD IRVING (1924–)

Politician

One of the most visible Jewish politicians in the United States, Ed Koch, the son of Polish immigrants, began his professional life as an attorney. He was involved with the Democratic Party in New York City in the early 1960s and was first elected to the City Council in 1966. In 1968 he was elected to the United States House of Representatives where he served for nine years.

Koch was elected mayor of New York City in 1977, only the second Jew to hold that office. His brash demeanor proved popular among New York's voters. He and only two other mayors, Fiorello La Guardia and Robert F. Wagner, were elected to three consecutive

terms. In 1989, however, he was defeated in the New York Democratic mayoral primary by David Dinkins. Since leaving office Koch has remained in the public eye as a newspaper columnist, a radio talk show host, and the judge in a "people's court" television program.

KUNSTLER, WILLIAM (1919–1995)

Lawyer, civil rights advocate

Controversial attorney William Kunstler was born in New York City on July 7, 1919. After receiving his LL.B. degree from Columbia University School of Law in 1948, he became a law partner with his brother. During the 1950s, he began working on occasion for the American Civil Liberties Union (ACLU).

Kunstler's legal destiny was changed in 1961 when he went to Mississippi for the ACLU to defend freedom riders for the Congress of Racial Equality (CORE). From that point on, he worked with extraordinary dedication for clients who were part of the struggle for greater freedom and equality in the United States. He was special counsel for Martin Luther King Jr. and the Southern Christian Leadership Conference (SCLC), general counsel for the Mississippi Freedom Democratic Party (MFDP), and counsel for the Student Nonviolent Coordinating Committee (SNCC). Individual clients included Adam Clayton Powell, Stokely Carmichael, and the Berrigan brothers.

In 1969, Kunstler came to national attention when he represented the Chicago Seven, who were charged with conspiracy to incite violence at the 1968 Democratic National Convention. He managed to obtain an acquittal for all the defendants. For the next twenty-five years, Kunstler was popularly known as the "people's lawyer." He died in New York in 1995.

LAW AND THE JUDICIAL SYSTEM

In no area of American life have Jews had a greater impact than in the field of law. The practice of law and the judicial system provided Jewish immigrants with a path for upward mobility as well as a way to gain prestige and political influence in their new country. Jews

Louis D. Brandeis was the first Jew appointed to the Supreme Court. A champion of the cause of free speech during his tenure on the Court, Brandeis was also one of the leading figures in American Zionism. (Courtesy of American Jewish Historical Society, Waltham, Massachusetts and New York, New York)

arrived in the United States with a deeply rooted sacred-law tradition derived from the legal codes in the Torah. Judaism as a religion has always had significant legalistic components. Despite centuries of exile, rabbinical courts continued to ensure the enforcement of the core principles of Jewish law within the Diaspora. Jewish immigrants to America brought with them a strong legal orientation.

In the industrial America of the late nineteenth century, Jews found the legal system and its vision of freedom and equality appealing and the profession itself created opportunities for advancement. By the turn of the century, as the commercial climate expanded in urban America, several German Jewish lawyers became prominent. Among the best known were Mayer

Sulzberger of Philadelphia, who was one of the first Jewish judges in the country and Lewis Dembitz, an important legal scholar based in Louisville. In New York, German Jews gained a particular foothold, establishing law firms to represent the Jewish corporate elite.

It was Dembitz's nephew, **Louis Brandeis**, who became the most well-known and highly regarded legal authority in the first three decades of the twentieth century. After establishing a thriving corporate law practice in Boston, Brandeis became notable in the Progressive Era for taking on cases that challenged metropolitan corruption and corporate monopolies, and for representing indigent defendants.

Brandeis's Jewish identity was late in arriving. Raised in a non-observant household, it was not until the age of fifty-four, when he was called to negotiate a settlement in a strike among the garment workers in New York's Jewish East Side, that Brandeis developed a kinship with fellow Jews. After years of "reforming" American corruption, Brandeis undertook on a new cause. Beginning in 1914 he led the American Zionist movement with deal of skill and essential political savvy. (See **Zionism**.)

The other person in this era who had complete success blending his Jewish identity with his status in the world of law was **Louis Marshall**. Just as Brandeis, a liberal Democrat, redefined Zionism to make it more compatible with American patriotism, so Marshall, a conservative Republican, sought to frame Judaism as a perfect fit with the American constitutional tradition. Marshall argued that the respect for the law rooted in ancient Jewish traditions gave Jews a special understanding of their modern responsibilities as American

---

So, You Want to Be a Lawyer?

When she graduated first in her class from Columbia Law School in 1959, "Not a single law firm in the entire city of New York" offered Supreme Court Justice Ruth Bader Ginsburg a job. She explains: "In the fifties, the traditional law firms were just beginning to turn around on hiring Jews. . . . But to be a woman, a Jew, and a mother to boot, that combination was a bit much."

Confirmation Battle

When Woodrow Wilson nominated Louis Brandeis to be Associate Justice of the Supreme Court in January of 1916, Brandeis was already a major figure in American law. But the nomination triggered a contentious, four-month confirmation battle. A. Lawrence Lowell, the president of Harvard (where Brandeis had graduated first in his class from law school), circulated a petition against Brandeis. The first Jew to be nominated for the Court, Brandeis knew all too well why his opponents hated him—"[I am] considered a radical and [am] a Jew."

Felix Frankfurter was the third Jewish Justice on the Supreme Court. Many scholars of the Court consider him to be among the finest Justices ever to have served. Raised in an observant Jewish family, he did not participate in organized religion as an adult. (Courtesy of American Jewish Historical Society, Waltham, Massachusetts and New York, New York)

citizens. He alternately interpreted sacred Jewish laws as applicable to secular American legal matters and referred to the American Constitution as "holy."

Both Brandeis and Marshall recruited like-minded cohorts to articulate the Americanization of what they viewed as key Jewish legal tenets such as the rule of law and the importance of social justice. Marshall became president of the **American Jewish Committee** in 1906, where he worked with both Sulzberger and Julian Mack, while Brandeis served as mentor to future Supreme Court Justice **Felix Frankfurter** in building a legal case for Zionism to American audiences. Brandeis became the first Jew to be appointed to the Court, taking his seat in 1916, but only after a highly contentious, four-month-long confirmation battle in the Senate, which many (including Brandeis himself) felt had an underlying motif of anti-Semitism.

Although these German Jews had all gained tremendous power and recognition, anti-Semitism and xenophobia combined to restrict many Jews, especially the newer immigrants from Eastern Europe, from gaining access to the legal profession. The prohibitive cost of law school made entry difficult for those lacking financial means and those who did gain entry to the Bar found elite law firms resistant to hiring Jewish attorneys. Members of the Protestant hierarchy used negative ethnic stereotypes to demean Jewish immigrants for their supposed "character deficiencies." Overall, East European Jews had great difficulties gaining access to influential sectors in the world of law until after World War II.

Jewish women entering the legal profession also experienced barriers in the early twentieth century. In 1918, Mary Belle Grossman became one of the first of two women admitted to the American Bar Association. She later gained a strong reputation in her home state of Ohio for her staunch advocacy of woman suffrage and other causes of concern to women. Emile Bullowa began a law practice with her brother and became known for her skills as a trial lawyer, her advocacy on behalf of low income clients, and her tenure as president first of the Women's Lawyer's Association of New York City and then of the National Association of Women Lawyers. During the same time, Rosalie Loew Whitney became Acting Attorney-in-Chief of the New York Legal Aid Society. Equally typical were the cases of Clarice Baright and Alice Petluck. Baright, an outstanding Progressive Era advocate for New York City's poor children and families, was passed over for three separate judicial appointments on both state and city levels. Petluck, the first woman lawyer to argue a case in New York's intermediate court of appeals, was refused admittance to the Bronx Bar Association as late as 1928 simply because she was a woman.

President Herbert Hoover nominated **Benjamin Cardozo** to the Supreme Court in 1932, but there were reservations on the part of some Senators who felt that "one Jew on the Court was enough." Cardozo's distinguished career as Chief Judge of the State of New York overcame any latent anti-Semitism that may have been present in the Senate.

The 1930s proved to be both the best of times and the worst of times for Jews seeking to enter the legal profession. As the economy deteriorated, private sector opportunities for Jewish law school graduates, always limited, declined even further. At the same time, President Franklin Roosevelt's New Deal initiatives increased the possibilities of public law work in the expanding world of government regulatory agencies. The New Deal provided an impetus for a new group of Jewish lawyers to gain prominence in Washington circles. **Felix Frankfurter** became the most well known and successful of those who came of age in this era. Frankfurter had gained a name for himself as chairman of the War Labor Policies Board during World War I. He was also known for his virulent opposition to the conviction of Italian anarchists, Sacco and Vanzetti, while a Harvard law professor. Frankfurter became a key member of FDR's brain trust. Roosevelt nominated him to the Supreme Court in 1939.

Many other Jewish lawyers and legal minds had their careers jump-started by their involvement in the New Deal, including Jerome Frank, Charles Wyzinski, Jr., **Abe Fortas**, Simon Rifkind, and Samuel Rosenman. The 1930s also witnessed the ascension of labor law as an important specialty within the field, attracting a number of Jewish lawyers with liberal political leanings, including **Arthur Goldberg**, who preceded Fortas to the Supreme Court bench in the 1960s. Other more radical Jewish voices also emerged in the labor law field, including **Carol Weiss King** whose first

Benjamin Cardozo was the second Jewish Justice on the Supreme Court. He always tried to defend the rights of "ordinary citizens" against special interests and attributed this dedication to the lessons he drew from the history of the oppression of Jews throughout Western history. (Courtesy of American Jewish Historical Society, Waltham, Massachusetts and New York, New York)

legal work had been defending foreign-born workers who had been victims of the raids conducted by Attorney General A. Mitchell Palmer after World War I. Ida Klaus also worked on labor law issues in New Deal agencies and later became Solicitor of the National Labor Relations Board in the Truman administration.

Jewish attorneys also became involved in a variety of racial and economic justice causes in the 1930s. Just as Frankfurter rallied the public to the defense of Sacco and Vanzetti, renowned criminal lawyer Samuel Leibowitz served as an early chief litigator defending the Scottsboro Boys, nine young African Americans accused of raping two white women in Alabama. Carol

The Jewish James Madison

Law professor Albert Blaustein had an unusual specialty—he wrote constitutions for countries. In a long and distinguished career, he was involved in drafting the constitutions for post-Soviet Russia, Romania, Nicaragua, Zimbabwe, Bangladesh, Peru, Liberia, Fiji, and scores of other countries.

His obituary in *The New York Times* quoted him as saying: "A constitution is more than a structure and framework for government. It is in many senses a nation's frontispiece. It should be used as a rallying point for the people's ideals and aspirations, as well as a message to the outside world as to what the country stands for."

In helping countries establish themselves, Albert Blaustein was participating in a tradition of the "rule of law" that is a part of the definition of Jewish civilization.

Weiss King and her law partner Joseph Brodsky also defended the Scottsboro Boys in a number of their ongoing appeals in conjunction with the Communist Party–affiliated International Labor Defense. Louis Marshall became a board member of the National Association for the Advancement of Colored People in the 1920s. He argued against restrictive covenants and wrote the brief that eventually led to the Supreme Court ruling that the state of Texas could not exclude African Americans from voting in party primary elections—elections that had previously been all white.

Although Jewish lawyers frequently felt an altruistic desire to support African American citizens, it is also likely that the lynching of Jewish manufacturer Leo Frank in 1915, a case that Marshall took all the way to the Supreme Court, brought an immediate connection for many Jews with the racist violence directed at African Americans. German Jews, fearful of being perceived negatively by their peers if they spoke out too loudly against anti-Semitism, may have also believed that if African Americans gained greater equality, the positions of Jews would also improve. In addition, **Reform Judaism's** decree that no minority could live safely unless the rights of all minorities could be ensured proved highly influential for Jewish attorneys who embraced the cause of civil rights.

The coming to prominence of Jewish lawyers in the New Deal administration proved, however, to have its contradictory elements. Because these attorneys were enmeshed in the ideals and policies of the Roosevelt administration, they generally did little to prevent the restriction of Jewish refugees from Europe and paid minimal attention to the Holocaust. Likewise, the complete identification of Joseph Proskauer, leader of the American Jewish Committee, with the American government led to his unwillingness to tolerate an independent Jewish position at odds with the White House.

World War II was a turning point in opening up new opportunities for Jews in the legal profession. Jews were increasingly able to gain middle class professional status through both private corporate law firms and public advocacy work in the areas of civil rights and civil liberties. Jewish attorneys took on an increasingly public role as authorities in constitutional law in national organizations such as the American Civil Liberties Union. During the McCarthy era, the National Lawyers Guild, founded in the New Deal era with significant Jewish participation to create a progressive and racially integrated alternative to the American Bar Association, became one of the few organizations that defended blacklisted citizens and those accused of crimes connected to their affiliation with the **Communist Party**. Sympathetic Jewish lawyers, such as future Congresswoman **Bella Abzug**, defended Party members whom they believed could not receive fair trials.

Jewish representatives in the legal profession found themselves on both sides of the many criminal and constitutional cases involving American communism in the late 1940s and 1950s. It was the trial and subsequent conviction of Julius and Ethel Rosenberg that became the most debated criminal case of the Cold War era. With Jewish prosecutor Irving Saypool directing the government's case against the Rosenbergs and Jewish defense lawyer Emmanuel Bloch defending them, Jewish Judge Irving Kaufman found the couple guilty of passing atomic spy secrets to the Soviet Union and sentenced them to death in the electric chair—a decision so momentous and controversial

Jewish Supreme Court Justices

Supreme Court Justice	Years of Service
Louis Brandeis (1856–1941)	1916–1939
Benjamin Cardozo (1870–1938)	1932–1938
Felix Frankfurter (1882–1965)	1939–1962
Arthur J. Goldberg (1908–1990)	1962–1965
Abe Fortas (1910–1982)	1965–1969
Ruth Bader Ginsburg (b. 1933)	1993–
Stephen Breyer (b. 1938)	1994–

that it overshadowed the remainder of Kaufman's judicial career. Roy Cohn, also a Jew, who served as co-counsel for the prosecution in the Rosenberg case, was the attorney and closest confidant of anti-Communist crusader Senator Joseph McCarthy.

The 1950s and 1960s brought major openings in the legal field to Jews of Eastern European descent and to Jewish women. In 1957, Birdie Amsterdam became the first woman elected to the New York State Supreme Court and Jennie Barron capped a long, distinguished career when she became the first woman appointed justice of the Massachusetts Superior Court. Justine Wise Polier, a pioneer in promoting the rights of children in the legal system, litigated a ground-breaking case proving that segregation existed in the New York City schools. Polier later established the Citizens Committee for Children and helped organize lawyers in support of welfare reform in addition to serving as vice-president of the **American Jewish Congress**.

Many prominent Jewish lawyers were involved in the Southern Civil Rights Movement. By 1960, the American Jewish Congress had more civil rights attorneys than the United States Justice Department and many of them conducted campaigns throughout the nation to demand adequate educational opportunities, fair employment, voting rights, and an end to residential segregation. One of the most influential and important of these legal activists was Morris Abram, a southern Jew of modest means, who as John F. Kennedy's Georgia campaign manager, urged the presidential candidate to intervene when Martin Luther King Jr. was jailed in Atlanta and then helped negotiate King's release. Abram later served as the United States representative to the United Nations Commission on Human Rights where he co-authored an international treaty outlawing racial discrimination. In the case of *Aelony v. Pace*, he defended voter registration organizers in Americus, Georgia, who had been jailed for sedition.

Although a number of Jewish lawyers became associated with the social movements of the 1960s, probably the most well-known is **William Kunstler**, who defended the radical activists known as the "Chicago Seven" who were prosecuted for their anti-war civil disobedience during the Democratic National Convention of 1968. Flamboyant and controversial, Kunstler took on the cases of marginalized population groups and spoke out frequently against what he perceived as systemic inequities in the administration of justice in the United States.

A number of attorneys, influenced by the feminist movement, took on litigation involving a variety of "women's" causes, including employment discrimination, access to birth control, and reproductive freedom. In collaboration with Margaret Sanger's attorney Morris Ernst, Harriet Pilpel served as chief litigator on five different birth control cases over a twenty-five-year period, all of which were decided by the Supreme Court. The most famous of her cases, *Griswold v. Connecticut*, established that the practice of birth control was protected under the right to privacy. Pilpel also served as general counsel to both Planned Parenthood

---

Upstairs to the Women's Gallery, Please

Judith S. Kaye, Chief Judge of the State of New York, is a member of Congregation Shearith Israel in New York City (it was the first synagogue built in the city in 1730), which continues its tradition of separate seating for men and women. Thus, the State's Chief Judge may not pray in the main sanctuary, but must sit upstairs in the women's gallery. Ironically, it was another Chief Judge of the State of New York—Benjamin N. Cardozo—who argued eloquently for retaining separate seating when the synagogue moved to its present quarters.

In his position as the seventh Jewish Justice on the Supreme Court, Stephen Breyer has a remarkable legacy to maintain. In his early years on the Court, he gives every indication that he is equal to the challenge. (Photograph by Richard Strauss, Smithsonian Institution. Courtesy of the Supreme Court)

Federation of America and the American Civil Liberties Union and co-authored an amicus brief in the case that would later become renowned as *Roe v. Wade*.

The 1960s brought the nominations of Arthur Goldberg and Abe Fortas to the Supreme Court by President Lyndon Johnson. Neither tenure lasted long. Goldberg was convinced by Johnson to leave the bench to become Ambassador to the United Nations and Fortas was forced to resign when it was discovered that he accepted consulting fees while serving on the high court. There would be no Jewish representatives on the Supreme Court until President Bill Clinton appointed **Stephen Breyer** and **Ruth Bader Ginsburg** in the 1990s.

A number of Jewish attorneys have also become known for their defense of constitutional rights. **Alan Dershowitz** has combined a post as a Harvard law professor with a high-profile career as litigator and media critic speaking out on issues where he believes questions of due process have been violated. Ira Glaser and Norman Siegal both served in leadership positions with the ACLU, an organization that generated controversy and dissent among American Jews in the 1970s when it protected the right of the American Nazi Party to march through Skokie, Illinois, a town whose population included several thousand Holocaust survivors.

The 1980s and 1990s continue to have large numbers of Jews earning a livelihood and gaining a voice as lawyers, judges, and justices. While many Jewish attorneys have become both successful and wealthy as partners in prestigious private firms, a number continue to work in the lower-paying areas of public defense and legal aid. Jews are also represented as law professors and constitutional scholars, as well as in the fields of tax, real estate, and divorce law.

It seems highly unlikely, given the non-Talmudic background of most Jewish American lawyers, that their success is related to their Judaism. What is clear is that after a beginning filled with quotas and outright anti-Semitism, in the twentieth century American Jews have changed the face of American jurisprudence. From the stern, somewhat prim face of Ruth Bader Ginsburg, who strikes terror into the hearts of Supreme Court litigants, to the audacity of Harvard Law School's Alan Dershowitz (who had the *chutzpah* to write a book called *Chutzpah*), American Jews have made themselves an integral part of the American legal profession. It would be a different profession without them.

LEHMAN, HERBERT (1878–1963)

Lawyer, statesman

Liberal governor of New York during the 1930s, Herbert Lehman was born in New York City on March 28, 1878. After graduating from Williams College and working for a time with a textile firm, he joined the Lehman Brothers banking house. During World War I, he was an officer in the army, working in the office

In additional to his highly successful political career (he continues to hold the record for the most state-wide elections won in New York), Herbert Lehman was active in numerous philanthropic activities including the Joint Distribution Committee and the United Jewish Appeal. He is shown here with his wife Edith, who was herself actively involved in philanthropy. (Library of Congress)

of the Secretary of War to procure and transport supplies. He also served as vice-chairman of the Jewish **Joint Distribution Committee.**

Lehman became active in politics in 1926 when he managed the reelection campaign of New York's Governor Alfred E. Smith. When Franklin Roosevelt ran for governor two years later, he chose Lehman as his lieutenant governor. In 1932, when Roosevelt went on to the presidency, Lehman was elected governor. He was reelected three times, becoming known as the champion of the people. The liberal legislation passed during his tenure in office gained his administration the tag Little New Deal.

In 1942, Lehman decided not to run for a fourth term. He became the first director of the United Na-

tions Relief and Rehabilitation Administration. Although he was defeated in a bid for the United States Senate in 1946, he was elected in 1949 to fill out Robert F. Wagner's unexpired term and then was reelected in 1950. In the Senate he strongly opposed McCarthy and the House Un-American Activities Committee. After he retired, he remained a force in New York politics until his death in 1963.

LEVY, URIAH P. (1792–1862)

Naval officer

Uriah Levy was a lightning rod for controversy, the highest-ranking Jewish officer in the United States Navy prior to the Civil War, the man who eliminated flogging in that service, and the man who saved Monticello. He was also court-martialed on six separate occasions and cashiered from the Navy twice, each time the victim of anti-Semitism among his fellow officers.

Levy's love of the sea began early. The son of a prominent Sephardic family, he ran away to serve as a cabin boy when only ten, returning home at thirteen for his **bar mitzvah**. After attending a naval apprentice school in his home town, he returned to sea again. By the age of twenty, Levy was the sailing master and part owner of his own ship. When the War of 1812 broke out, he joined the United States Navy and was captured with his crew by a British warship, the result of a valiant but overmatched sea battle. He spent the better part of the war in Dartmoor Prison.

Despite that unpleasant experience, Levy had found a professional home. By 1817 he was made a lieutenant and shortly thereafter he rose to a full captaincy. His rapid rise from within the ranks, combined with his Judaism, made him a favorite target of detractors in the officer corps—his numerous battles with military law were the result. His competence was undeniable and he was eventually made a commodore, then the highest rank the Navy could bestow, and placed in command of the Mediterranean squadron. Levy retired shortly before the outbreak of the Civil War. When that conflict began he contacted President Lincoln, offering the Commander-in-Chief the use of his considerable personal fortune (he had been a successful businessman and Democratic Party activist when ashore).

Levy also made good use of his money elsewhere. A great admirer of Thomas Jefferson, particularly for his pioneering support of religious tolerance, Levy purchased Jefferson's Monticello home when it was facing imminent demolition. He intended to present it to the nation as a shrine to the third President, as his will specified. However, due to the vagaries of probate and family legal battles Monticello remained in the Levy family until 1923, when the Commodore's wishes were finally fulfilled.

LONDON, MEYER (1871–1926)

Lawyer, socialist leader

Prominent American socialist Meyer London was born in Poland in 1871. The Russian Jewish young man came to the United States when he was twenty years old and became an attorney in New York City. He soon was active in politics, developing a reputation as a friend of workers and unions. In 1914, London was elected to the U. S. House of Representatives on the socialist ticket from the immigrant district of the Lower East Side. While war raged in Europe, he headed the Peoples Relief Committee, an organization sponsored by labor and political leftist groups for aid to Jews in Eastern Europe. The organization joined with others to become the Jewish **Joint Distribution Committee**.

In 1917, London voted against entering World War I and, during the conservative years following the war, he failed to be reelected.

LOWEY, NITA M. (1937–)

Congresswoman

Democratic Congresswoman Nita Lowey (née Melnikoff) was born on July 5, 1937 in New York City. She attended Mount Holyoke College, graduating with a B.A. in 1959. Prior to her career in Congress, she

worked for many years in New York's Department of State. From 1985 through 1987 she served as New York's Assistant Secretary of State. In 1988, she won the seat for New York's Eighteenth Congressional District.

A member of a Conservative synagogue, Lowey is a strong supporter of Israel and has authored or co-authored several pro-Israeli amendments, including the 1995 Lowey Amendment, which makes it illegal for any U.S. official to meet with Palestinian officials in the city of Jerusalem. She is a member of the House Appropriations Subcommittee on Foreign Operations, the Appropriations Committee, the Bipartisan Congressional Caucus for Women's Issues, and the House Pro-Choice Task Force. She is also a strong supporter of the United Jewish Appeal.

MARCUS, DAVID "MICKEY" (1902–1948)

Military leader

Mickey Marcus went from tough street kid to tough prosecutor to tough soldier. In an era in which Jews were not known for their physical courage, he embodied a very masculine set of virtues and became one of the first martyrs of the Israeli War of Independence.

David Marcus was born to Jewish immigrant parents in the Brownsville section of Brooklyn, a ghetto where kids from several ethnic groups battled over turf regularly. Marcus decided early on that he would not be a victim of any of them; he took boxing lessons at a local Y and handled himself on the street with ease. An outstanding athlete and student, he accepted an appointment to the United States Military Academy at West Point in 1920. There he excelled, too, graduating with high scores. He served his mandatory hitch as an officer in the Army, then went to law school. For most of the 1930s, Marcus was a federal prosecutor, part of the team whose work led to the deportation of Mafia chieftain Lucky Luciano. In recognition of his achievements as a crime fighter, Mayor Fiorello LaGuardia appointed Marcus Commissioner of Corrections.

Marcus realized before many other Americans that

David "Mickey" Marcus went from the child of Jewish immigrant parents in Brooklyn to a general in the Israeli army. He is shown here receiving the distinguished service medal of the United States in May of 1945 from Major General John Hilldring. (Courtesy of American Jewish Historical Society, Waltham, Massachusetts and New York, New York)

war in Europe was inevitable. He re-enlisted in the Army in 1940. In 1942 he was put in charge of the new Ranger school, training top troops for jungle warfare. He was in the vanguard of paratroopers who were dropped into France on the eve of D-Day. As an Army officer who was also an attorney, Marcus helped draw up the surrender terms for the Germans. Marcus was a rising star in the Army.

History had other plans for Mickey Marcus. One of his duties in planning for a post-war Europe was overseeing the fate of the Nazi death camps and those few Jews who had survived them. Marcus saw the piles of Jewish corpses firsthand, met the survivors of the nightmare that was the Holocaust, and was named chief of the War Crimes Division for the Army. For the first time since his childhood days on the streets of Brownsville, Mickey Marcus encountered anti-Semitism, but in a more pernicious form than he could have imagined possible. He had not been a Zionist before. He became one.

Marcus returned to civilian life in 1947. David Ben-Gurion contacted him and asked him to find an American officer who could advise the nascent Israeli army. Marcus decided, after getting permission from the War Department, to take on the assignment himself. In January 1948, he arrived in Tel Aviv under the name Michael Stone. Marcus redesigned the command structure of the Israeli forces, wrote new training manuals, and designed new defensive strategies for the protection of the Negev and the new quarter of Jerusalem. His hit-and-run tactics enabled the Israelis to pin down the larger Egyptian army. Ben-Gurion named him Lieutenant General, the first Jewish general of an Israeli army in 2,000 years.

Unfortunately, Marcus didn't live to savor the honor for very long. Six hours before the cease-fire that brought peace to the newly formed Israel, Marcus was killed by one of his own sentries in a tragic accident. He is buried in the cemetery at West Point, where his is one of the most visited graves at the Academy.

MARSHALL, LOUIS (1856–1929)

Lawyer, community leader

A prominent leader of the German Jewish elite in New York City, Louis Marshall was born in Syracuse, New York in 1856 to working-class German Jewish immigrants. In 1876, he entered Columbia Law School, where he completed the two-year program in a single year. After passing the bar, he joined a firm in Syracuse and quickly developed a remarkable reputation. When he was thirty-eight, he joined a prestigious New York firm. At the same time, he worked for civil rights for African Americans, Japanese Americans, and Catholics as well as Jews.

In the early 1900s Marshall became active in the affairs of the Jewish community, especially the congregation of Temple Emanu-El. He became chairman of the board of the **Jewish Theological Seminary** and, later, president of the **American Jewish Committee**. During World War I, he served as president of the American Jewish Relief Committee. Although not enthusiastic about **Zionism**, he supported the resolutions of the **American Jewish Congress**, a group formed by Eastern European Jews to settle Palestine as a Jewish homeland. In 1929, when the Jewish Agency was formed, he again supported Zionists in their yearning for Palestine.

Marshall dedicated his own wealth to the cause of American Judaism in many ways. He paid one-quarter of the cost of the Jewish Publication Society when it was established to reprint Jewish classics, and when he died, a tenth of his fortune went to philanthropic concerns.

MEYER, ANNIE NATHAN (1867–1951)

Activist, Barnard College founder, writer

Annie Nathan Meyer was born on February 19, 1867 into a family that descended from colonial rabbi **Gershom Mendes Seixas**. Kept at home by her mother, she schooled herself in her parents' library. She married at the age of twenty but had ambitions of a writing career and was determined to attend college. There was no liberal arts college that admitted women in the city of New York, so Meyer set out to create her own. In 1888, at the age of twenty-one, she began the campaign that would result in the founding of Barnard College in 1889. Annie Meyer became a member of the board of trustees and took responsibility for much of its fundraising.

During her career as a writer, Meyer focused on women's issues in plays and stories, as well as one short novel, *Helen Brent, M.D.*, which describes a woman's choice of a career in medicine over marriage. In 1891 she edited *Woman's Work in America*, documenting the progress women had made in some of the professions. She took an anti-suffrage stand for many years, insisting that no woman should vote and only childless women should enter the professions. Meyer was active in the struggle for minority rights, working with the NAACP and becoming a close friend and supporter of Zora Neale Hurston, who dedicated her book *Mules and Men* (1935) to Meyer. She also wrote a powerful anti-lynching play, *Black Souls* (1932). At about the same time, she began to draw attention in her writing to Nazi anti-Semitism. Her autobiography, *It's Been Fun*, was published in 1951, shortly after her death.

MILK, HARVEY (1930–1978)

Gay rights activist, politician

Harvey Milk was the first openly gay elected official in America, a vocal champion of gay rights and other politically progressive causes, and a role model for thousands of gay men and women who followed him into electoral politics.

Milk was born in the prosperous and largely Jewish suburban town of Woodmere, New York. His grandfather was a Lithuanian Jew who had immigrated to Louisiana, where he worked himself up from store clerk to the owner of a major department store. Milk's parents, both Navy veterans, inherited the family business.

Harvey went to college in upstate New York before following his parents into the Navy. He made the rank of lieutenant, received an honorable discharge in 1955, and then went back to Woodmere to teach. He went through a series of white collar jobs and discovered a talent for predicting business trends, but eventually abandoned his successful career in business and moved to San Francisco. There he became involved in politics, beginning with his opposition to the war in Vietnam. On his third try, in 1977 he was elected to the Board of Supervisors. Once there, he worked actively on gay rights issues. He was in the forefront of the successful statewide campaign against an anti-gay ballot initiative.

Milk had made many enemies with his politics and lifestyle. One of them was a former firefighter and fellow Supervisor, Dan White. White resigned his seat on the Board in protest against the defeat of the anti-gay initiative, then changed his mind. When Mayor George Moscone, a political ally of Milk's, refused to reinstate him, White decided to kill the mayor. On November 27, 1978, he went to City Hall with a gun and murdered both Moscone and his enemy Harvey Milk. White's lawyers put forth an almost laughable "Twinkie defense," claiming that his judgment had been impaired through overindulging in junk food. The judge sentenced him to only seven years, eight months for voluntary manslaughter.

The short political career of Harvey Milk was a milestone in American politics. The first of what are now many openly gay elected officials (including Congressman **Barney Frank**), it is a tragedy that he is often remembered solely because of the circumstances of his death. His fellow Supervisor, **Dianne Feinstein**, decided to run for Moscone's open position as mayor. She now serves as the senior Senator from California.

MORGENTHAU, HENRY, JR. (1891–1967)

Secretary of the Treasury

Franklin Roosevelt's most trusted fiscal advisor was born in New York City on May 11, 1891, the son of Henry Morgenthau, who would later be the American ambassador to Turkey. After graduating from Cornell University, he bought a farm in Dutchess County, New York to test his theories about agriculture. During World War I, he went to France as an agricultural expert and, when Franklin Roosevelt became governor of New York, Morgenthau became chairman of the Agricultural Advisory Commission.

Morgenthau followed Roosevelt to Washington in 1932 to become, first, governor of the Federal Farm Board and, later, Secretary of the Treasury. In this position he vocally opposed the incarceration of Japanese Americans in early 1942. In 1943 and 1944 he played a major role in publicizing the Nazi Holocaust and the lack of any response by the American State Department to the plight of Jewish refugees. He asked his staff to look into the situation and with their report in hand (entitled "Report to the Secretary on the Acquiescence of This Government in the Murder of the Jews") he went straight to President Roosevelt. The result was the creation of the War Refugee Board, which has been estimated to have played a crucial role in saving the lives of 200,000 Jews.

Throughout his tenure in office, Morgenthau conceived and carried out innovative and humanitarian fiscal reforms. He was largely responsible for the creation of the World Bank and the International Monetary Fund. After the war Morgenthau and President Harry Truman disagreed about the best way to deal with Germany and Morgenthau resigned in July of 1945. His term as Secretary of the Treasury had lasted for eleven years and resulted in profound changes to the American economy. He retired to his farm and led an uneventful life there until his death in 1967.

NEOCONSERVATIVES

Neoconservatism was a term coined to describe a group of predominantly Jewish former Marxist intellectuals who moved to the center of the Democratic party in the 1940s and 1950s, then shifted right after the radical cultural ferment of the 1960s, with many becoming supporters of Ronald Reagan in the 1980s. Some of the best known of voices of neconservatism have included: **Irving Kristol**, **Norman Podhoretz**, Gertrude Himmelfarb, Nathan Glazer, and Seymour Martin Lipset.

Beginning as anti-Stalinist Marxists in the 1930s, future neoconservatives began to embrace the Cold War state in the 1950s as the necessary bulwark against what they perceived as the far greater evil of Soviet Communism. In addition, a number of the "New York Intellectuals" who had spent the 1930s as consummate outsiders were elevated to new positions of influence in post-war America. These pundits and writers who had grown up in poor, immigrant families gained affluence and middle class status in this era—another factor that helped them increasingly identify with a country that had once felt alien and oppressive. Finally and importantly, the establishment of the State of Israel became a focus by which they became tied to the American political and military establishment.

Although these thinkers usually still identified themselves as liberal Democrats in the 1960s, neoconservative stalwarts Podhoretz and Kristol found themselves dismayed by what they perceived as the anti-Americanism that evolved from the anti-war movement. They were especially alienated from the Democratic Party when it nominated George McGovern for president in 1972. They considered him a dangerous leftist. Besides supporting a strong national defense, neoconservatives resented the growing radical politics of African Americans and women, and tended to voice criticism of anything they perceived as "preferential treatment." Glazer voiced the feelings of many of his colleagues when he argued that affirmative action was "un-American" because it violated the notion of equal treatment for all.

The neoconservative movement largely supported Democrat Jimmy Carter for president in 1976 as a rebuff to the more liberal wing of the party. After his election he was castigated by the very same people, especially in the pages of *Commentary* magazine where Podhoretz dismissed him as both weak and naive and unable to lead the nation in its efforts to resist the Communist enemy. When Ronald Reagan defeated Carter in 1980, the neoconservative movement had swung all the way to the right and Kristol and Podhoretz were among the new President's most enthusiastic backers. Other Jewish neoconservatives including Max Kampelman and the younger generation represented by Kristol's son William and Podhoretz's son-in-law, Elliot Abrams, all gained important positions in the Reagan administration.

Neoconservatism differed from traditional conservatism as well as the new social conservatism in several important respects. Most neoconservatives still supported many welfare state reforms, including Social Security, unemployment insurance, family assistance, and other forms of social legislation that provided, in Kristol's words, needed security and comfort to the individual with a minimum of bureaucratic intrusion. Neoconservatives also believed that government had a role to play in regulating the economy and they rejected the "supply side" theories of Jewish economist **Milton Friedman** that informed Reagan-era politics.

Since the fall of the Soviet Union the neoconservative movement has exercised less power in both Jewish life and American politics. As the Democratic Party has embraced an agenda more comfortable to many of these thinkers, a number of them including Glazer, Lipset, and sociologist Daniel Bell have returned to the party. Podhoretz and both Irving and William Kristol have, however, became staunch supporters of the Republicans, even going so far as to court the fellowship of the Christian fundamentalists.

Predominantly a movement of intellectuals, neoconservatism represents the important journey of a set of thinkers who came of age at a particular time in the nation's history. As such, it reflects an experience that is both distinctly Jewish and quintessentially American.

NEW LEFT

"New Left" is the term used to describe the radical political agenda advanced by student activists in the civil rights and anti-war movements of the 1960s. Many of these activists were Jewish. Jews comprised nearly half of the national membership of Students for a Democratic Society (SDS). Likewise, young Jewish organizers constituted a significant percentage of the radical civil rights organization, the Student Non-violent Coordinating Committee (SNCC) and Jewish women became instrumental in the growth of the second wave of the feminist movement. Jews were also well-represented in the intellectual and cultural orbit of the New Left as writers, scholars, lawyers, musicians, and film makers.

Unlike earlier generations of immigrant and working class Jewish radicals, the mostly middle class and American-born Jews who participated in the explosive movements of the 1960s rarely identified their activism as rooted in their Jewish heritage. Although many could trace their family connections to an earlier brand of political struggle, frequently through socialism, **Zionism**, communism, or trade union involvement. At the same time, the "New" Left also developed in opposition to what many activists felt was the rigid, bureaucratic, and hierarchical nature of the "old" left represented especially by the **Communist Party**.

Many Jewish radicals had grown up in homes where social justice was taught as an important value, even though it may have been tempered by affluence and conformity. Some young Jewish New Leftists cited the long shadow of the Holocaust as informing their deep belief in the necessity of speaking out and taking action against all immoral acts of violence, including those they believed were committed by their own government in Vietnam.

Although the New Left movement often frowned on the notion of formal leadership, two of the best-known and most colorful agitators of the era were the two Jewish founders of the Yippies (Youth International Party), Abbie Hoffman and Jerry Rubin, who became known for their political militancy, their outrageous mocking of the corporate elite, and their advocacy of recreational drug use—an important component of the culture of the time. Many of the pioneering members of SDS, including Al Haber, Todd Gitlin, and Dickie Magdoff, were also Jewish, as were the older intellectual influences on the movement, such as German émigré sociologist Herbert Marcuse and linguist **Noam Chomsky**.

Folk and rock-and-roll music became the soundtrack of resistance from the younger generation. There was no more prominent emblem of the New Left than the Jewish singer/songwriter from Minnesota who took the name **Bob Dylan** and wrote many anthems of the times including the idealistic "Blowin' in the Wind," the prophetic "The Times They Are a Changin'," and the angry "Masters of War." Of those topical songwriters who followed in Dylan's footsteps, the most radical was Phil Ochs, whose biting satires of American life and politics captured the rebellious spirit of the times. In addition, Jewish poets and writers, most notably **Alan Ginsberg**, known for inspiring the Beat Movement in the 1950s, and Paul Krassner, editor of the *Realist*, served as important cultural figures in the New Left.

PHILLIPS, ROSALIE SOLOMONS (1867?–1946)

Philanthropist, political and community worker

Rosalie Solomons Phillips was born in Washington, D.C. sometime around 1867. A descendant of the Revolutionary War financier **Haym Salomon**, and the daughter of philanthropist Adolphus S. Solomons, Rosalie Solomons continued the family tradition of political work and community service.

In the political arena, Solomons served as a member of the Democratic County Committee for the Fifth Assembly District. In 1918, she became the co-leader of the Seventh District of New York. Between 1920 and 1936, she served as an official New York delegate and participated in six conventions. From 1928 through 1943, she was the vice-chair of the Women's Division of the State Democratic Committee.

On the community front, Solomon's is best known as one of the founders of **Hadassah**, along with **Henrietta Szold**. Solomons was the organization's first chair. She also served as president of the Columbia Religious and Industrial School for Jewish Girls and as vice-president of the **National Council of Jewish Women**, New York Section. She was involved with many other organizations as well, including the Union of Orthodox Jewish Congregations of America, the Daughters of the American Revolution, and the National Society of Patriotic Women of America. She died at her home in New York City on February 5, 1946.

POLITICS

Jews have had a major impact on American politics. From their embrace of the religious freedom laid out in the United States Constitution to their contemporary participation in civil rights, social welfare, economics, and law, Jewish Americans have put tremendous energy into both local and national public affairs. Jews have also been important intellectual figures in the analysis and critiquing of world and national events.

The small Jewish American population of approximately 2,500 in the eighteenth century adamantly supported the colonists in the war for independence. Jewish merchants such as Joseph Simon and Andrew Levy furnished ammunition to assist the war effort and wealthy Jewish financiers Haym Salomon and Aaron Lopez were important economic supporters of the Revolution.

Although the small, mostly Sephardic Jewish community in the new nation grew to no more than 15,000 through the early nineteenth century, it made its presence felt. Jewish political activists were instrumental in the state by state campaign to abolish religious qualifications for voting and holding office. In Connecticut all religious qualifications for full citizenship were granted in 1818, in Massachusetts in 1821, and in Maryland (after a hard-fought eight-year struggle) in 1826. In Rhode Island, New Hampshire, and North Carolina, full inclusion did not occur until later in the century.

For the most part, the early Jews were middle class business people—merchants and traders—whose main concern was being able to exercise full citizenship rights, to participate equally and freely in the decision-making apparatus of the state, to make a comfortable living, and to practice their religion without coercion. These Jews were relatively conservative compared to their successors and their power base, originally in Charleston, shifted to New York City in the 1830s as Jewish influence in the Democratic Party increased with the evolution of Tammany Hall under the leadership of Emmanuel Hart.

The 100,000 German Jews who immigrated to the United States between 1848 and the beginning of the Civil War shifted the orientation of Jewish politics toward a European liberalism that rejected the pro-slavery Democratic Party along with the nativist Whigs. Jewish political activism in the 1850s coalesced in opposition to two international issues: the United States negotiation of a commercial treaty with Switzerland permitting the nation to expel American Jews and the failure of U.S. political leaders to intervene after Papal authorities kidnapped a Jewish boy in Italy. In New York, Chicago, and Philadelphia, Jews were disproportionately represented in organizing mass meetings to mobilize the fledgling Republican Party. Although a majority of the small southern Jewish community supported slavery, most Jews in the east and midwest vehemently opposed it and became strong champions of Abraham Lincoln's humanitarian vision.

During the last half of the century, German Jews established a network of institutions that had profound political implications for Jewish history in the United States, with the **B'nai B'rith** having the most important and far-reaching influence. They also developed the first *Landsmanshaftn* (Jewish fraternal organization). In the 1880s, the first major socialist party in the United States, the Socialist Labor Party led by Daniel DeLeon, a Sephardic Jew, helped organize the United Hebrew Trades. In 1906, German Jews organized the **American Jewish Committee**, which fought attempts to deny Jews their rights anywhere in the world.

It was the mass immigration of hundreds of thousands of Jews from Eastern Europe between 1880 and 1920, along with the reform movements of the Progressive Era, that catapulted Jewish political participation into the limelight. Unlike the earlier generations of Jewish settlers in America, these new immigrants were primarily poor or working-class and more willing to use their Jewish ethnicity to inform their politics. *Yiddishkeit*, a culture deriving from the language of the Diaspora, became a means of establishing group solidarity for many East European newcomers.

While many members of this generation worked within the political mainstream, a significant number brought with them a more radical brand of politics. Some of the most prominent names in the first two decades of the twentieth century included Socialist Party leaders **Morris Hillquit**, Victor Berger, and **Meyer London**, who favored a calculated electoral strategy to achieve their ends. Anarchists **Emma Goldman** and Alexander Berkman favored more insurrectionary means to achieve social and economic justice. Jewish neighborhoods like the Lower East Side of New York became homes of radical intellectual thought, labor activism, and reform movements. Socialist Jews established the Workman's Circle, an influential fraternal and educational organization, in 1900. The *Jewish Daily Forward* published by **Abraham Cahan** became the most influential and widely read Yiddish socialist newspaper in the nation. The mainstream political parties also cultivated the votes of the growing Jewish immigrant population. By the turn of the century the community was deeply divided among the Democrats, Republicans, and socialist alternatives. While

the *Forward* was the best known of the Yiddish newspapers, the conservative *Tageblatt* also had a substantial readership.

Organized labor as a political force had its roots in the predominately Jewish needle trades. Future immigrant institutional leaders in the union movement, **Sidney Hillman** and **David Dubinsky**, began to gain influence in the second decade of the new century. Women such as Clara Lemlich, **Fannia Cohn**, and **Pauline Newman**—pioneers in the fledgling International Ladies Garment Workers Union—and **Bessie Abramowitz**, later Hillman's wife—were major players in the creation of the Amalgamated Clothing Workers of America. **Rose Schneiderman** established the Women's Trade Union League as a vehicle for middle class women to support the rights of labor. The Jewish labor movement had both a political and an economic agenda as organizers attempted to push for structural changes on the local and national levels to improve conditions for working people. Jewish women were also involved in the suffrage struggle, although the Protestant, middle-class orientation of that movement sometimes mitigated against their full participation.

The Progressive Era was a time of major social reform and the establishment of the Settlement House Movement had a significant influence in the lives of Jews living in tightly packed tenements in poor urban ghettos. In New York City, the Henry Street Settlement under the direction of **Lillian Wald**, a registered nurse who established the Visiting Nurses Association, emerged as one of the most famous of these organizations. Wald, a German Jewish socialist, agitated for improved housing, sanitation, and education programs and against child labor. She created a center at

Henry Street for citizenship classes, recreational programs, and cultural events aimed at improving the lives of immigrants, especially the young.

As World War I and the crisis in Czarist Russia came to a head, Jews in America increasingly turned their political energies overseas. Attempts to assist Jews victimized by *pogroms* took on a new urgency. Jewish immigrants found themselves on both sides of the war issue with socialists and other radicals taking strong anti-war positions while other Jews strongly supported President Wilson's brand of internationalism.

Although Jewish political activity reached new heights during the first decade of the twentieth century, it hit its peak during the Depression years of the 1930s. American Jews overwhelmingly supported Franklin Roosevelt, and his New Deal administration provided considerable opportunity for Jewish political leadership. There was a proliferation of militant social movements designed to organize new groups of industrial workers as well as the unemployed. Jewish participation, especially from Hillman and Dubinsky, was essential to the creation of the Congress of Industrial Organization and to the wave of strike activity that took place in that era.

The **Communist Party**, shifting its organizing strategy in the mid 1930s to form coalitions with American liberals, gained a strong following among many Jews through its effective organizing skills and its strong support of racial equality—an issue that Jewish Americans embraced earlier than much of the general population. A number of Jewish attorneys, most prominently criminal lawyer Samuel Leibowitz, worked with the Communist Party-influenced International Legal Defense on behalf of the Scottsboro Boys, and others lobbied for anti-lynching legislation. Several Jews, including Benjamin Gitlow, took on important leadership positions in the Party.

The politicization of Jews in the 1930s included intellectuals, writers, academics, and the literati. "New York Intellectuals" became a term used to describe a group of mostly Jewish immigrants including Max Schactman, Phillip Rahv, **Sidney Hook**, and **Lionel Trilling**, who gravitated to the literary magazine *The Partisan Review*. These writers and scholars shared a

---

Let's Elect a Jew

The 1934 election for Governor of New York pitted two Jews against each other, which may be the only time in American history that two Jews vied for a state's highest office. Herbert Lehman, the candidate of the Democratic party, was the incumbent and his Republican opponent was the now-legendary Robert Moses. Lehman won in a landslide. It should be noted that all his life Moses tried to distance himself from his Jewish heritage (his mother was Jewish), once threatening to sue the editors of the *Jewish Encyclopedia* for libel when he learned that they were planning to include his biography.

---

devotion to Marxism and staunch opposition to Stalinism and to the Communist Party, which these writers viewed as bureaucratic, authoritarian, and insufficiently radical. Many of those associated with the "New York Intellectuals" supported exiled Soviet revolutionary leader Leon Trotsky. Schactman in particular was instrumental to the development of the Trotskyist Socialist Workers Party. Ironically, many of these anti-Stalinist intellectuals shifted dramatically to the right after World War II and became supporters of Cold War anti-communism and American military expansionism. Others such as **Irving Howe** rejected this orientation and attempted instead to fuse a Democratic Left alternative to Communism.

By the late 1930s the attention of most Jewish Americans had shifted overseas to the rise of the Nazi movement in Germany. Jewish organizations, especially the American Jewish **Joint Distribution Committee**, focused their political energies on providing aid and support to Jews fleeing Europe and on agitating, mostly unsuccessfully, to push the American government to take action on behalf of these refugees. American Jews fought isolationist sentiment and entrenched anti-Semitism until the United States entered the war in 1941. Meanwhile, some of the Holocaust refugees who did enter the country became important political players, especially those in psychology, sociology, and atomic science. German Jews were pivotal in the development of both the atomic and the hydrogen bombs. Many of these same immigrants, most notably **Albert Einstein**, later became vociferous advocates for international controls over atomic energy.

After World War II, **Zionism** and the creation of the State of Israel became a core focus of Jewish politics. National Jewish organizations such as the American Jewish Committee and the **American Jewish Congress** focused increased energy on garnering support for the State of Israel within the United States. Prominent Jewish clerical leaders often had different opinions on the issue. Reform Rabbi **Stephen Wise**, who had earlier served as president of the **Zionist Organization of America**, became co-chairman of the American Zionist Emergency Committee and favored compromise on creating a Jewish state in exchange for non-Zionist endorsement of unrestricted Jewish immigration into Palestine. Rabbi **Abba Hillel Silver** took a more militant position, arguing for the necessity of a Jewish state in the Middle East.

During the Cold War era, Jews also found themselves on both sides of the anti-Communist crusade—most symbolically represented by the trial of Julius and Ethel Rosenberg. The two Jews accused of passing atomic spy secrets to the Soviet Union were sentenced to death by a liberal Jewish judge, Irving Kaufman. Jewish actors and screenwriters were victimized by the Hollywood blacklist and by the purging of the left wing from colleges and universities. **J. Robert Oppenheimer**, the director of the Manhattan Project, had his security clearance taken away in the 1950s. Conversely, Roy Cohn and David Schine, both Jews, served as close confidants to anti-Communist zealot, Wisconsin Senator Joseph McCarthy.

Jews had been active participants in the campaign for African American civil rights from the early decades of the twentieth century, with Jewish attorneys working through the NAACP and the **Anti-Defamation League** to expand equal protection under the law. In the 1960s, as the Civil Rights Movement intensified, American Jews again played an important role as activists and supporters composing two-thirds of the white Freedom Riders who traveled to the south in the campaign to desegregate public facilities. Jewish civil rights activists Andrew Goodman and Michael Schwerner were murdered along with black organizer James Chaney, while attempting to register new voters in Mississippi.

There was significant Jewish involvement in the student-based **New Left** and the anti-war movement, with two of the best-known and most flamboyant activists, Abbie Hoffman and Jerry Rubin, establishing the Youth International Party, better known as the Yippies. Throughout the mid- and late 1960s, many young Jews were drawn to the Students for a Democratic Society (SDS). Jewish radical lawyer **William Kuntsler** became well known for his championing of the rights of anti-war protesters and marginalized population groups. Other attorneys such as Ira Glaser of the American Civil Liberties Union sought to continue a legacy of Jewish legal activism by expanding the rights of the disenfranchised.

Jews were active in the second wave of the feminist movement with women such as **Gloria Steinem**, **Betty Friedan**, and **Bella Abzug** playing important roles in challenging the institutional ceiling for American women. Others such as Shulamith Firestone and Ellen Willis presented a more radical institutionalized critique of gender inequalities in the United States.

In the 1970s and 1980s, much of Jewish institutional political energy centered on the campaign

---

Barry's Yiddishkeit

This headline on Barry Goldwater's obituary in *The Jewish Week* (6/5/98) sums up the "bluntness, lack of artifice, and . . . honesty" of the man who was ". . . the closest thing [America] ever had to a Jewish presidential nominee from a major party."

His grandfather, "Big Mike" Goldwasser, immigrated from a Polish *shtetl* in the 1820s, but Barry was baptized and raised as an Episcopalian. "I was told I was an Episcopalian before I ever learned that my father was Jewish," Goldwater was quoted as saying, "but I am proud of my Jewish ancestors."

In many ways, they would have been proud of him. To quote Paul Wellstone, a Democratic Senator from Minnesota and a Jew, in his memorial speech on the Senate floor: "[Barry Goldwater] set a standard, especially when it comes to personal integrity and intellectual integrity and political integrity . . . today I think people in our country really yearn for that."

for Soviet Jewry and the development of organizations supporting this immigrant population. Although Jews have always had more liberal voting patterns than the general public, the Jewish community as a whole began to become more conservative in this era. The increasing repression of dissidents in the Soviet Union contributed to a more hard-line position against detente on the part of many American Jews. At the same time, Israel's growing role as a militarized nation that supported U.S. foreign policy goals also influenced large numbers of Jews into supporting a more conservative American state. A backlash to the Civil Rights Movement, a division with African Americans over the question of Palestine, and the evolving role of Jews as comfortable middle class members of the American political establishment all played a role in shifting the Jewish political landscape to the right. Intellectuals aligned with *Commentary* magazine—**Irving Kristol**, **Norman Podhoretz**, and Midge Decter—and economists such as **Milton Friedman** and **Alan Greenspan** all are modern voices of Jewish conservatism.

Nevertheless many Jewish scholars, activists, and leaders continued to maintain liberal and radical critiques of American policy. American Jews remain overwhelmingly represented in the Democratic Party.

The role of Jewish religious leaders has influenced American politics, both on the local and the national levels. **Abraham Joshua Heschel**, rabbinic scholar and writer, viewed his social and political activism in the Civil Rights, anti-war, and Soviet refugees support movements as rooted in his religious theology. Lubavitcher Rebbe **Menachem Mendel Schneerson** used his deep-seated belief that the Bible and Jewish law prohibited negotiating with Arab countries regarding the boundaries of Israeli territory to agitate against the Camp David Accords in the United States and to persuade the Israel Knesset's Orthodox members to reject coalition with the Labor government that supported a peace conference with the Palestinians.

As the twentieth century comes to an end, Jewish participation in the United States political landscape continues to be important. In civil liberties, international diplomacy, the academy, organized labor, and **Zionism**, as leaders in both Jewish and multi-religious and multi-ethnic institutions, Jews have shown their commitment to public affairs. They have expressed a desire to be involved in all public policy decisions affecting their lives and the lives of everyone in the country they now call home.

RIFKIND, SIMON (1901–1995)

Jurist

Simon Rifkind was born in Meretz, Russia on June 5, 1901. He immigrated to the United States in 1910. He attended City College of New York where he graduated with a B.S. degree in 1922. He next attended Columbia University where he received his law degree in 1925. From 1927 through 1933 he was Senator Robert F. Wagner's legislative secretary. In 1930, he also became a partner in Wagner's law firm.

In 1941, he left the firm to serve as a federal district court judge for southern New York. Nine years later, he left that position to join the law firm that would later be known as Paul, Weiss, Rifkind, Wharton and Garrison. In 1956, the Supreme Court asked him to arbitrate the dispute of the western states over the Colorado River water rights. In the early 1960s, President Kennedy chose him to examine labor disputes in the railroad industry. Among his many high-profile cases, Rifkind represented the Municipal Assistance Corporation, which helped save New York City from bankruptcy. He also represented Jacqueline Kennedy Onassis in two lawsuits.

In the late 1940s Rifkind served as General Dwight D. Eisenhower's advisor on Europe's Jewish affairs. For his work in this area, he was awarded the Medal of Freedom. He also served on New York City's Board of Higher Education and held positions at the **American Jewish Committee** and the **Jewish Theological Seminary**. He died in New York City on November 15, 1995.

ROSE, ERNESTINE (1810–1892)

Suffragist, women's rights activist

"I was a rebel at the age of five," said Ernestine Rose. She was born in the Jewish quarter of the town of Piotrkow, central Poland, on January 13, 1810, to a scholarly rabbi who was supported by his wife's dowry. It was her own life experience in a community in which women were little more than chattel that gave her the impetus to spend her life fighting for equality for women. After her mother's death when she was sixteen, she inherited a substantial estate. Her father decided that her inheritance would serve as a dowry to be given to a groom he selected. Ernestine decided to contest her father's decision in the Polish courts and, speaking with great eloquence, won her case. She immediately left Poland for Germany, where she set herself up successfully as a businesswoman and manufacturer. From there she moved once again, this time to London, where she became involved in Robert Owen's socialist circles and met and married William Rose, a silversmith who was a follower of Owen's ideas about cooperatives.

In 1836 the newlyweds set sail for the United States, determined to spread Owen's ideas. Over the next two decades, Ernestine and William Rose would be at the forefront of feminist, abolitionist, and free speech and press struggles. Ernestine helped found the utopian community at Skaneateles in upstate New York. From 1840 through 1848 she labored alongside other prominent women's rights advocates like Elizabeth Cady Stanton to win passage of a bill that would allow married women in New York State to control property they owned at the time of their marriage.

Rose was a tireless lecturer, writer, and an ardent spokeswoman for unpopular causes of the time like divorce, birth control, and temperance. As the women's rights movement itself became more intolerant of foreign-born influences, she and her husband retired to England and it was there that she died in 1892.

ROSENBERG, ANNA M. (1902–1983)

Public official

Anna Marie Rosenberg was born in Budapest, Hungary in 1902. She immigrated to the United States when she was ten and was naturalized as an American citizen in 1919. In 1934, she joined the National Recovery Administration. Later, she became its New York State Director. In 1936, she became the first female Regional Representative for the Social Security Administration. In 1942, she became the Regional Director of the War Manpower Commission. From 1944 through 1945, she was a special envoy to Europe, overseeing military personnel issues for both President Roosevelt and President Truman. She held the position of Assistant Secretary of Defense from 1950 through 1953. She died in 1983 at the age of eighty-one.

SALOMON, HYAM (1740–1785)

American patriot

Hero and patriot Hyam Salomon was born in Poland in 1740 and fought with Pulaski for the liberation of that country. Fleeing Poland to save his life, he came to the United States, became a successful broker, and married Rachel Franks. He joined the Sons of Liberty and, when the Revolutionary war broke out, he was arrested by the British as a spy. After some time, he was released from prison and returned to his revolutionary activities. He was arrested again, tortured, and condemned to death. He was able to escape and spent the rest of the war in Philadelphia, raising money for the war effort. Salomon was also active in furthering the rights of Jews in America, arguing against a New Testament oath used in swearing in officeholders in Philadelphia.

SOCIALISM

Socialism is intimately entwined with the experience of Eastern European Jewish immigrants in the United States. During the first two decades of this century, socialism permeated the streets of the cities where Jews settled. Jewish socialists built trade unions in the garment industry and organized strikes demanding decent working conditions and fair labor practices. They developed benevolent institutions such as the Workman's Circle and influential Yiddish socialist newspapers such as the ***Jewish Daily Forward.*** On New York City's Lower East Side, Yiddish-speaking socialists gave "soapbox" speeches on street corners and engaged in passionate debates and discussions about how to create a model society built on economic and social justice.

The revolutionary socialism that blossomed in the United States had its roots in the *shetl* society in the Pale of Settlement where Russian Jews were forced to live. By the 1880s and 1890s, this political ferment had reached its zenith in the Jewish tradition of *Haskalah* (a movement begun in eighteenth-century Germany, which urged Jews to become a part of the modern world), while *pogrom* activity and persecution of Jews at the hands of the Czarist government increased. Socialism for Jews in the region was closely tied to their culture (*Yiddishkeit*), which they also brought with them to America.

Although many Jews arrived in the United States with already developed socialist beliefs, it was in their new homeland that Jewish socialism became a political movement. Up until the massive immigrant influx of the late nineteenth century, the most influential Jewish socialist had been Daniel DeLeon, a Sephardi from Curacao, who became an important leader in the Socialist Labor Party (SLP). The SLP had lost most of its influence by the time Socialist Jews entered America en masse and by 1901 had been replaced by the Socialist Party of America (SP). Eastern European Jewish immigrants immediately became vital players in building the organization and expanding its influence.

Jewish leaders in the Progressive Era Socialist Party included **Meyer London**, a Russian immigrant who ran unsuccessfully for Congress from New York's Lower East Side in 1910 and 1912. In 1914 he became only the second Socialist ever elected to the House of Representatives. Austrian Jew Victor Berger was elected to Congress from Milwaukee for six terms beginning in 1910. **Morris Hillquit**, a Russian Jew from Latvia, lost very close elections for Congress on the Socialist ticket and then narrowly missed becoming the mayor of New York City on two separate occasions. Jewish voters in New York City became major strongholds in the national development of the Socialist Party, providing its congressional candidates with large percentages of their vote and contributing to the strong showing of charismatic Socialist Party candidate Eugene V. Debs in his 1908 and 1912 campaigns for president.

Jewish socialism was always about more than electoral politics. In the New York City of the early twentieth century, the socialist movement had deep roots in Jewish Yiddish immigrant life. Socialism became the catalyst for activists in the needle trades, who helped build the International Ladies Garment Workers Union and the Amalgamated Clothing Workers Union. These activists included its male leaders, **Sidney Hillman** and **David Dubinsky** and the grassroots female organizers **Fannia Cohn**, Theresa Malkiel, and **Pauline Newman**. At the same time the Workman's Circle evolved from Yiddish socialist culture and established itself as the most important Jewish fraternal organization in America, with a membership reaching more than 80,000 by 1920. The Yiddish-language *Jewish Daily Forward* published by **Abraham Cahan** not only had the largest circulation of any socialist newspaper in the United States, it also had an influence that ranged far beyond the 200,000 people who read it.

Socialist Zionism also played a role in American Jewish radicalism of the time. Ber Borokhov, the founder of the Zionist Socialist Workers Union, argued that Jewish laborers should strive to control their own economic system in a Jewish state. Nachman Syrkin believed that a mass settlement of the Jewish working class in Palestine, with cooperative enterprises and trade unionism, would lay the foundations for a new free Jewish socialist society.

World War I and the anti-radical, anti-immigrant backlash that followed the war badly impeded the socialist movement in the United States. Jews continued to comprise up to 40 percent of the Socialist Party's national vote, the Jewish labor movement grew, and the Workman's Circle gained an increasing number of members. With the onset of the Depression, the Socialist Party had a resurgence with Norman Thomas gaining a respectable percentage of the vote and substantial Jewish support in the 1932 presidential election. As the New Deal took shape, however, more and more former Socialists (and Jewish Socialists in particular) flocked to the Democratic Party, especially as it moved left in 1936. The **Communist Party** also made significant inroads in the Socialist Party's base of support in the 1920s and the 1930s.

Changes in the international climate necessitated changes in the socialist movement during the 1930s. As Stalin consolidated power in the Soviet Union, a new group of Jewish Socialists, most notably Max Schactman, broke with the Socialist Party and attempted to build a new organization that supported the political agenda of exiled Bolshevik leader Leon Trotsky. The Socialist Workers Party (the Trotskyists) staked out a position at odds with the Communist Party and the New Deal. A group of Jewish socialists who became known as the New York Intellectuals gravitated to the Trotskyist orbit with a variety of writers and scholars (including **Sidney Hook**, **Irving Howe**, Phillip Raav, and **Lionel Trilling**) filling the pages of the *Partisan Review* with essays critical of both American capitalism and Stalinism.

Jewish Socialists as well as Communists generally united around the need to defeat fascism in World War II. In the post-war era the left as a whole lost ground that it would not regain until the 1960s. As Jews prospered and became a part of the American mainstream, the ideal of socialism appeared to fade more and more into the realm of history. While the Communist Party was crushed in the McCarthy era, many anti-Stalinist Socialists moved to the right and became liberal defenders of American Cold War policies in pages of magazines such as **Commentary**. As the old Jewish labor movement dissipated, the socialism of the needle trade unions became nothing more than a defense of the liberal New Deal welfare state and a nostalgic reflection of the "old days" among its leadership. In addition, many former Jewish Socialists began to focus their energies on defending the state of Israel and became increasingly reliant on the American government for support.

Irving Howe attempted to breathe life back into the Jewish socialist tradition by founding the magazine *Dissent* in the late 1950s, which gained significant influence in left intellectual circles. With the birth of the **New Left** in the 1960s, the old Socialist Party shifted to the right and seemed to have little relevance to a new generation of student activists who sought to rid themselves of what they perceived as the dogmas of the older generation of radicals. It is equally clear that the student movement as represented by documents such as the *Port Huron Statement* of the Students for a Democratic Society could trace its roots back to the early vision of the socialist movement that included Jewish immigrant radicals.

Despite the major decline of socialism in the modern era, there have been a few stirrings and successes. The best notable example is Bernie Sanders, a Brooklyn-born, self-proclaimed Jewish Socialist, who became mayor of Burlington, Vermont in the 1980s. He then used this position to catapult himself into a Congressional seat as an independent in the 1990s.

SOLOMON, EDWARD S. (1836–1913)

Civil War general, governor of Washington Territory, California legislator

Edward Selig Solomon (Salomon) was born in Schleswig-Holstein in 1836 and came to the United States as a teenager. He studied law in Chicago before entering the military at the outbreak of the Civil War. He helped to form the Eighty-second Illinois Infantry Regiment, which included more than a hundred Jewish soldiers, and served as an officer. His brilliance and courage were notable, and he became commander of the regiment, leading his men onto the field at the Battle of Gettysburg. For his cool effectiveness in this battle, he was promoted to brigadier general.

Returning to Chicago, Solomon became Cook County Clerk. Five years later, Ulysses S. Grant appointed him governor of the Territory of Washington. After two years in the post, he resigned and moved to San Francisco. There, he was elected to the state legislature and later became district attorney.

SPELLMAN, GLADYS NOON (1918-1988)

Congresswoman

Congresswoman Gladys Noon Spellman was born in New York City on March 1, 1918. She grew up in New

York and in Washington, D.C. where she attended George Washington University and the graduate school of the Department of Agriculture. On finishing school, she became a teacher in Prince Georges County, Maryland, a suburb of Washington.

Spellman became involved in local politics in the 1960s, serving on the Prince Georges County board of commissioners from 1962 through 1970. She was the board chair in 1966. At the same time she was chair of the board of trustees for Prince Georges General Hospital. In 1967, she became a member of Lyndon Johnson's Advisory Commission on Intergovernmental Relations and from 1971 through 1974 was the Prince Georges County councilwoman-at-large. In 1972 she became president of the National Association of Counties. In 1975 she won her first run for Congress. She served three terms, and in late 1980, won a fourth. Unfortunately, a few days prior to the election she was incapacitated by a heart attack. Because she was unable to resume her duties by February 1984, the House was forced to declare her seat vacant. She died on June 19, 1988.

SPINGARN, ARTHUR (1878–1971)

President of the NAACP

Arthur Barnett Spingarn was born into a wealthy New York family on March 28, 1878. After graduating from Columbia Law School and being admitted to the New York bar, Spingarn began practicing law. Early in his career, he tried a civil rights case and was outraged by the injustice of the situation. In 1909, when the National Association for the Advancement of Colored People was founded, Spingarn immediately became active in the organization. Without charge, he served as the NAACP's counsel and won a string of important victories in civil rights cases. From 1911 until 1940, he was a vice president of the group. In 1940, he became president, succeeding his brother Joel and served until 1965.

Arthur Spingarn was the author of a number of books and articles of significance on legal and race-related subjects. He was also a book collector and, in 1948, he donated his collection of more than 5,000 books and artifacts relating to African Americans to Howard University Library.

STRAUS, OSCAR (1850–1926)

U.S. Cabinet member and Ambassador

Oscar Straus was born in Otterberg, Bavaria—now Germany—on December 23, 1850. He immigrated to America when he was four. His brothers, Nathan and Isidor Straus, were the owners of R.H. Macy & Co., the famed New York department store, as well as Abraham & Straus, a Brooklyn department store.

Oscar Straus attended Columbia University, then Columbia Law School. In 1887, he had his first overseas posting for the U.S. government when he was sent as emissary to Constantinople—now Istanbul—Turkey. Later, he would serve in Turkey two more times, again as emissary (1898–1900), and as its first U.S. Ambassador (1909–1910).

In addition to his ambassadorial service, Straus was a member of the Permanent Court of Arbitration at The Hague, first appointed in 1902 and reappointed in 1908, 1912, and 1920. He also served as a delegate of the League to Enforce Peace to the Versailles Peace Conference (1919), and was a vocal advocate for the protection of Jewish people in Europe. His greatest claim to fame is as the first Jewish cabinet member in American history. He served under Theodore Roosevelt as Secretary of Commerce and Labor from 1906 through 1909. In 1922, he published his autobiography, *Under Four Administrations: From Cleveland to Taft*. He died in New York City on May 3, 1926.

For Further Reading

See Appendix 2 for a bibliography of general reference books about Jews and the Jewish experience in America. All of these volumes include information about American Jews in law, government, and politics.

Auerbach, Jerold S. "From Rags to Robes: The Legal Profession, Social Mobility and the American Jewish Experience," *American Jewish Historical Quarterly*, December 1976.

Baker, Leonard. *Brandeis and Frankfurter: A Dual Biography.* New York: Harper & Row, 1984.

Burt, Robert. *Two Jewish Justices: Outcasts in the Promised Land.* Berkeley, Calif.: University of California Press, 1988.

Berlin, William S. *On the Edge of Politics: The Roots of Jewish Political Thought in America.* Westport, Conn.: Greeenwood Publishing Group, 1978.

Isaacs, Stephen D. *Jews and American Politics.* Garden City, N.Y.: Doubleday, 1974.

Levin, Nora. *While the Messiah Tarried: Jewish Socialist Movements, 1871–1917.* New York: Schocken Books, 1977.

Morris, Jeffrey B. "American Jewish Judges," *Jewish Social Studies,* Summer–Fall 1976.

Weyl, Nathaniel. *The Jew in American Politics.* New Rochelle, N.Y.: Arlington House, 1968.

Part 5

American Zionism and United States Relations with Israel

OVERVIEW

As the nineteenth century gave way to the twentieth, a very old dream became new again in the hearts of the world's Jews. The yearning for a national home in the ancient homeland of Palestine acquired a name— **Zionism**. In the United States, however, emotions were mixed. Many German Jews had lived for three or four generations in the New World. They wanted to be seen as Americans, with the rights and loyalties of Americans. They did not experience, in this country, the deep and abiding hatred that Jews of the Diaspora lived with in Europe. In fact, they often thought of the United States as a new Zion. Even many Orthodox and Conservative Jews rejected the idea that redemption lay in regaining Eretz Yisrael, and members of the Reform movement were adamant in their opposition to Zionism. For most Jews of the time, being a Zionist and being an American were fundamentally incompatible. The Federation of American Zionists, the largest Zionist coalition in the United States, had a membership of only 12,000 out of a Jewish population of two and one-half million in the years leading up to World War I.

This situation began to change when **Louis Brandeis** assumed leadership of the American Zionist movement during the war. A coalition of groups formed the Provisional Executive Committee for General Zionist Affairs, otherwise known as the PEC, with Brandeis as chair. He proceeded to declare that a Jew could be loyal to both America and Zionism and that, indeed, the two were simply different expressions of the same basic values. He also propounded a new view of America in which the goal of assimilation was replaced by one of maintaining cultural heritage within a larger unity. Brandeis's influence went far in persuading Woodrow Wilson to support a Jewish homeland and pressure the British government into making the Balfour Declaration of 1917.

By making Zionism acceptable to Americans,

Brandeis had made it too bland for European Jews who fiercely opposed his secular vision. To them, the national home was not to be simply a refuge for persecuted people, but a distinctly Jewish homeland. In 1921, the European view won the day at the World Zionist organization convention under the leadership of Chaim Weizmann and the American **Louis Lipsky**, head of the **Zionist Organization of America**. American Zionism became divided. In addition to Weizmann-Lipsky followers and Brandeis followers, there was **Hadassah**, which went its own, thoroughly independent way. Hadassah's president from 1926 to 1928, Irma Levy Lindheim, utterly refused to coordinate the organization's actions with those of Lipsky and the ZOA, which she considered a poorly run organization. Lipsky attacked Hadassah for its independence and Lindheim for her "unwomanly" behavior when she refused to cosign a bank loan for the United Palestine Appeal of the ZOA

As Hitler ascended to power, the stakes rose and cooperation among these disharmonious groups became crucial. Unable to influence American foreign policy to the extent of providing refuge for those fleeing the Holocaust, American Zionists nevertheless greatly increased their constituency. In the face of Hitler's atrocities, the Jewish community in the United States came to see a national home as a necessity. Even those who had most opposed Zionism became supporters. The Biltmore Program, adopted in May of 1942, made Jewish control of Palestine and the establishment of the State of Israel official Zionist policy.

In the years that followed the establishment of Israel in 1948, Zionist organizations became less necessary and, therefore, less powerful. With official recognition of the State of Israel by President Truman, American foreign policy was committed to the existence of the Jewish homeland. There was, however, still a place for American Jews in supporting their newly created nation. American Jews contributed large amounts of financial aid to help Israel defend itself against its Arab neighbors and against the assaults of Palestinian terrorists—more than $150 million during the War of Independence in 1948 and more than $317.5 million during the Six-Day War in 1967.

In the 1970s and 1980s support for Israel became less fervent and more qualified. Idealists were disillusioned by what they perceived as Israel's aggressive behavior toward Palestinians. Other American Zionists were angered by Israel's refusal to accept Diaspora Jews as equals within Judaism. Still, American Zionism has been a crucial element in the creation and continuation of the Jewish state. The horrors of the Holocaust notwithstanding, the post–World War II commitment to Israel would have failed without the American Zionist movement. Support for Israel has remained strong ever since, both among the American Jewish community and as the official policy of the United States government.

AMERICAN ISRAEL PUBLIC AFFAIRS COMMITTEE (AIPAC)

In a very short time AIPAC has arguably become one of the most powerful lobbying groups in the United States and one of the leading forces shaping Washington's Middle East policy. Founded in 1951, AIPAC (originally the American Zionist Council) began as an amalgam of fourteen leading American Zionist groups with the goal of providing a unified public relations arm for the new Jewish state. AIPAC's growth and influence began shortly after the Six-Day War in the early 1970s, when Israel became a major player in American foreign and military policy. It was not until the Reagan administration of the 1980s that AIPAC acquired the power and status that it holds today.

In its first two decades AIPAC was a relatively modest, virtual one-man operation under the helm of its founding director, I. L. Kenen, who used a friendly and collegial lobbying style to promote support for Israel as a humanitarian cause. AIPAC's governing board, consisting of the major organizations that rallied in defense of Israel in the 1950s, provided Kenen with the names of key lawmakers who required extra lobbying efforts and the director in turn elicited the assistance of Jewish community leaders who called and wrote letters to these representatives.

By the early 1970s, however, American Middle East policy had become a high-stakes game as President

Nixon made Israel the largest single recipient of American foreign assistance and a key player in Cold War politics. AIPAC's individual membership rose dramatically and its budget grew from $400,000 to $1.2 million. Its key contact list went from a few hundred names to 11,000. Under its new director, Morris Amitay, AIPAC became known for highly effective lobbying strategies.

It was not until the 1980s, when Thomas Dine began his tenure as staff director, that AIPAC rose to the prominence it enjoys today. The organization's membership grew five-fold to more than 50,000 and its budget rose ten-fold to $15 million. AIPAC redefined the business of lobbying, working directly with officials in the executive branch to shape policy at the State and Defense departments. It was in the 1980s that it became politically dangerous to challenge AIPAC in Congress. Politicians who questioned American policy toward Israel, such as former Illinois Senator Charles Percy, were targeted by AIPAC for defeat. AIPAC has also placed considerable time, energy, and money into defeating all resolutions that call for Israeli compromises with the Palestinians.

AIPAC's success can be traced to its ability to court both Republicans and Democrats and gain non-partisan support with a simple, coherent message and commitment to a cause. The organization has become proficient at rapidly turning out policy statements to the President, State Department, and Congress, and circulating the *Near East Report*. AIPAC organizes conferences focusing on a variety of issues important to Israel and it encourages and organizes expeditions to the region. At the century's end, AIPAC's influence appears to be undiminished. It will doubtless continue to be a significant player in American politics for the foreseeable future.

GREENBERG, HAYIM (1889–1953)

Writer, editor, Zionist leader

Writer, editor, and Zionist leader Hayim Greenberg was born in Bessarabia, Russia in 1889. While still a teenager, he moved to Odessa to become a speaker and writer on Jewish political and philosophical issues. At the beginning of World War I, he moved to Moscow and became editor of the Russian Jewish newspaper *Rasvet*. Following the Russian Revolution, Greenberg's continued Zionist activities brought him into conflict with Communist officials, and he moved to Berlin to edit the official weekly of the World Zionist Organization, *Haolam*.

In 1924 Greenberg moved to the United States to edit *Farn Folk*, a Yiddish Zionist publication and in 1934 became editor of *The Jewish Frontier*, the Labor Zionist monthly. He became increasingly active in Zionist activities and has been credited with persuading a number of Latin American delegates to the United Nations to vote in favor of the establishment of a Jewish State. He was also instrumental in helping the new country of Israel to form strong connections with other nations. Greenberg's many publications include *The Inner Eye* (a collection of his essays) and the *Hayim Greenberg Anthology*, which was published in 1968.

HADASSAH

by Deborah Dash Moore

Formative Years, 1912–1933. When seven women concluded on February 14, 1912 " . . . that the time is ripe for a large organization of women Zionists" and issued an invitation to interested friends "to attend a meeting for the purpose of discussing the feasibility of forming an organization" to promote Jewish institutions in Palestine and foster Jewish ideals, they scarcely anticipated that their resolve would lead to the creation of American Jews' largest mass-member-

This 1913 photograph includes the first two American nurses sent by Hadassah to Jerusalem, Rose Kaplan (on the left) and Rachel Landy (on the right), with a visitor in between. They are posing outside the original Hadassah welfare station, which provided maternity care and treatment of trachoma. (Courtesy of Hadassah, The Women's Zionist Organization of America, Inc.)

ship organization. Hadassah, the Women's Zionist Organization of America, became the most popular American Jewish organization within a short span of years, maintaining that preeminence to this day. It also is the most successful American women's volunteer organization, enrolling more women and raising more funds than any other national women's volunteer organization.

The first meeting drew over thirty female Zionists to the vestry rooms of New York City's Temple Emanu-El on February 24, 1912. At the meeting's conclusion, almost two-thirds of those in attendance were elected officers or directors, suggesting the leadership opportunities Hadassah would offer women. **Henrietta Szold**, at age fifty-two, was the senior leader, deeply committed to Zionism as a political and moral movement of Jewish renewal.

Hadassah recruited a leadership cadre from women of Eastern European, German, and Sephardic backgrounds. Many were native-born college-educated American Jews, both young and middle-aged. Their level of formal learning was unusual for women in this period and signified their cultural aspirations. Hadassah enrolled members from varied socioeconomic and ethnic backgrounds, but many were working women—teachers, stenographers, shopgirls, and garment workers.

Hadassah focused on women's health issues, reflecting the social feminism of settlement house work. In January 1913, with 122 members and $542 in dues collected, Hadassah agreed to support a nurse in Palestine for two years. Emma Gottheil's sister, Eva Leon, who had worked with Jerusalem midwives, raised $5,000 from wealthy Chicago non-Zionists for a second nurse. Two weeks later, Rose Kaplan and Rachel [Rae] Landy sailed for Jerusalem, where they established Hadassah's Nurses Settlement, a first step to "bring order to that land of chaos."

The decision signaled organization growth. After Leon reported that the nurses needed guidance, Hadassah created a Palestine Advisory Committee in New York City to supervise them, setting an important precedent that policy decisions were to be made in America. By July 1913 Hadassah had chapters in Philadelphia, Boston, Baltimore, and New York. In the fall of 1914 the Hadassah School of Zionism opened to provide "intellectual substance," to counteract Christian missionaries, and to prepare Hadassah women to speak in public. On June 19, 1914 Hadassah held its first national convention in Rochester, New York, where it officially adopted the name Hadassah and its purpose: " . . . to promote Jewish institutions and enterprises in Palestine and to foster Zionist ideals in America." Hadassah had already chosen a motto, suggested by Israel Friedlaender, from Jer. 8: 19–23, *Aruchat Bat Ami*, translated as "The Healing of the Daughter of My

People," and a seal, designed by Victor Brenner, of myrtle (*hadas*) branches around a Jewish star. It affiliated with the Federation of American Zionists (FAZ).

Hadassah introduced many innovations to Zionist organization and ideology. Male leaders of FAZ criticized Hadassah for not engaging in Zionist work designed to change Jews into a self-conscious political entity. Hadassah, they claimed, merely did work meant to improve Jewish living conditions. Hadassah's decision to establish an urban nurses' settlement ran counter to Zionist emphasis on cooperative rural settlements and European methods of colonization. Hadassah stressed women-to-women work on humanitarian and religious grounds, as well as American social feminism. Hadassah's Zionism was distinctly nonideological, a form of practical idealism that Szold considered characteristically Jewish.

World War I challenged Hadassah, which had thirty-four chapters and 2,100 members when the United States entered the war. Turkish repression of Zionist activities in Palestine forced Hadassah to close its Nurses Settlement in 1915. At home, domestic politics strained Hadassah's unity. Many leaders identified themselves as progressives and advocated socialism, racial equality, and, most important, pacifism. Others ardently supported the Allies.

Despite the internal conflicts all the "factions" of Hadassah worked together to raise thousands of dollars to fund the American Zionist Medical Unit (AZMU), consisting of forty-five physicians, dentists, and nurses, as well as tons of supplies. The Unit arrived in Palestine in 1918 and established hospitals in six cities. The hospitals followed Hadassah's policy of providing services to all regardless of race, color, or creed. As soon as municipal authorities were prepared to run the hospitals, Hadassah turned them over. Hadassah rejected Zionist policy of creating institutions only for Jews in Palestine.

In 1918, Hadassah joined the restructured **Zionist Organization of America** (ZOA), despite doubts about its district plan of organization. Hadassah soon discovered it had lost its autonomy. Nevertheless, its membership grew—by 1922 Hadassah enrolled over twelve thousand—while the membership of ZOA declined. In 1920 it started the *Hadassah Newsletter* and the Central Committee also authorized the creation of Junior Hadassah, for girls eighteen and older, despite competition with Young Judaea, the Zionist youth movement.

By 1921 Hadassah began its steady rise to prominence. By mid-1926 Hadassah had achieved virtual autonomy in its program. Growth registered in numbers—by 1928 membership reached a peak of over thirty-seven thousand—while activities demonstrated a commitment for practical work in Palestine, infused with Zionist idealism. Each project's specificity enabled members to identify with the individual undertakings. These included the Hadassah School of Nursing (1919), an urban recreation program (1928), a school lunch program (1923), as well as health and day care centers and a children's village.

Patterns established during the formative years were subsequently strengthened. Hadassah maintained its social feminism, progressive political commitments, and understanding of Zionism as a movement to renew Jewish practical idealism. It also remained staunchly protective of its autonomy, its focus on specific projects helping women and children, and its openness to women of all backgrounds. Its leaders continued to include an elite of educated women who drew young women into their ranks. Hadassah fostered close personal ties with the land of Israel and many early leaders spent years living in Palestine, while a significant number of Hadassah's presidents settled there.

Consolidation and Growth, 1933–1953. Only in 1933 did Hadassah achieve complete independence from the ZOA, although it remained affiliated with the World Zionist Organization (WZO). Hadassah's organizational, political, and ideological autonomy allowed it to chart its own distinctive course as a women's organization, to consolidate its achievements, to initiate new projects, and to expand its membership.

From 1935 to 1945, Hadassah's membership increased from over 38,000 to over 142,000, and in 1952 Hadassah reached a new peak of almost 275,000 members. Critical to its broad appeal was the increase in the numbers of native-born American Jews who found its

The "Drop of Milk" (Tipat Halav) station was set up by Hadassah nurse Bertha Landsmann in 1921 in Palestine to provide pasteurized milk to parents. The program was such a success that she established the Donkey Milk Express to deliver bottles, each labeled with a baby's name and packaged in ice. Notice that the sign on the container is in both Hebrew and English. (Courtesy of Hadassah, The Women's Zionist Organization of America, Inc.)

brand of American Zionism compelling, as well as Hadassah's decision to adopt Youth Aliyah in 1934.

Szold agreed to direct this program of rescuing young people from Germany and bringing them to Palestine to settle on *kibbutzim* and in youth villages. Taking young people from their parents, who it was hoped would follow them to Palestine, Hadassah became their foster parents, nurturing and educating them. Szold dedicated the last twelve years of her life to Youth Aliyah and definitively shaped it into an educational movement and national organization of rescue. Hadassah's practical idealism put it in the forefront of American Jewish organizations. It began

to rescue Jews from Nazism before any other Zionist group by choosing a project that expressed its social feminist orientation as a women's organization. By 1967, every tenth Israeli under fifty was a Youth Aliyah graduate.

Hadassah also created institutions in Palestine. In 1938, Hadassah and the Hebrew University, located on Mount Scopus, established a joint graduate school of medicine. In 1939 the Rothshild-Hadassah Hospital on Mount Scopus opened. World War II transformed the new hospital into a medical center for the entire region. In 1942, Hadassah opened its vocational school for girls.

Despite its focus on Palestine projects, Hadassah also experimented with new ways to foster Zionist ideals in America. In 1934 it continued its early work in adult education by sponsoring the School for the Jewish Woman under the direction of Trude Weiss-Rosmarin. It also helped establish the American Zionist Youth Commission in 1940, directed by Shlomo Bardin. The Speaker's Bureau became well established and helped spread Hadassah's message throughout the country. In America, Hadassah leaders often cooperated with individuals associated with the newly established **Reconstructionist Movement**. Both shared a common attachment to American democratic progressive traditions as well as a deep dedication to Zionism as an international Jewish movement of renewal.

Hadassah forged an independent political path in the Zionist movement. In 1937, it ran its own slate of eighteen delegates to the WZO Congress. It supported the Biltmore Platform of 1942 calling for a Jewish state, even though it had abstained from the prewar debate on the partition of Palestine. Hadassah worked actively on the American political scene to support the establishment of a Jewish state. Women spread the word in their local communities in favor of partition. The personal cost of founding the State of Israel hit Hadassah on April 13, 1948. That night, Arabs ambushed and murdered seventy-five nurses, physicians, and technicians, including Dr. Hayim Yassky, head of the Hadassah Medical Organization, in a convoy on its way to Mount Scopus. Faced with the inability to protect its staff, Hadassah evacuated the medical center it had worked so hard to build, leaving it under Israeli army guard. In 1952 Hadassah broke ground at Ein Kerem to build for the second time a medical center in Jerusalem.

Hadassah's recruitment drives after the establishment of Israel on May 14, 1948 emphasized the relationship of Zionist ideals and American democratic values. New chapters organized that year reflected the suburbanization of American Jews. Hadassah appeared on Long Island from Levittown to Hollis Hills, in New Jersey from Princeton to Deal, and in Maryland from Silver Spring to Chevy Chase.

Hadassah effectively negotiated the transition from a "small, compact organization" to a large, national one during years of world war and the destruction of European Jews. It adapted its Zionist practical idealism to the political reality of the State of Israel by becoming one of the founding constituents of the World Confederation of General Zionists. Hadassah has a seat on the executive of the Jewish Agency for Israel and the Zionist General Council. It is also accredited with the United Nations as a nongovernmental organization. Hadassah integrated its democratic American commitments into its social feminism.

Mass-Membership Organization, 1953–1976. "Those were the days when if you sat next to a woman, your first question was, 'Are you a member of Hadassah?' If the answer was 'no,' you signed her up on the spot," Rose Dorfman recalled of the 1950s. Hadassah membership drives reached all sections of the country, all states in the union. Young women, mostly married with children and barred from working outside the home by strong social conventions, joined Hadassah for its sociability, its idealism, and the opportunities it offered to learn and to acquire new skills, including those of leadership. The constant recruitment offset normal attrition. Only after the Six-Day War of 1967 did membership increase steadily to a new high of 360,000 by 1977.

A successful mass-membership organization, Hadassah's presence registered forcefully on the American scene. When the Conference of Presidents of Major American Organizations was organized in 1956, Hadassah became a constituent member. In 1970, Hadassah was a founding member of the reorganized American Zionist Federation. In 1967, when the ZOA withdrew financial support from Young Judaea, Hadassah merged Junior Hadassah with Young Judaea into Ha-Shahar (the dawn) and restructured the summer camp activities, leadership training, and study scholarships in Israel that it had sponsored since 1940. Hadassah then assumed financial responsibility for all youth programs.

Although Hadassah continued to turn over many of its health centers and programs to municipalities or the Israeli government, it also initiated such new projects as a model family and community health program in a poor Jerusalem neighborhood, Kiryat ha-Yovel, in 1953 and the Rural Vocational Guidance Center at K'far Vitkin in 1952. The latter offered education and training for Arab as well as Jewish youth, maintaining Hadassah's well-established policy of providing equal treatment.

Perhaps Hadassah's biggest postwar achievement was the rapid construction of the Hadassah Medical Center in Ein Kerem. In cooperation with the Hebrew University, Hadassah established a teaching and research hospital with over fifteen medical departments, as well as a school of dentistry and pharmacy. President Miriam Freund-Rosenthal dedicated the new buildings in 1960. She had convinced the famous Jewish artist, Marc Chagall, to design twelve stained-glass windows for the hospital's chapel. In 1967, when Israel's stunning victory in the Six Day War reunited the divided city of Jerusalem, Hadassah discovered itself once more in possession of its hospital on Mount Scopus. In 1975 Hadassah rededicated its restored and rebuilt hospital there.

In 1968 Hadassah subscribed to the Jerusalem Platform of the World Zionist Congress, including the unity of the Jewish people and centrality of Israel, the ingathering of Jews in their historic homeland, strengthening the State of Israel, preserving Jewish identity through education, and protection of Jewish rights everywhere. Hadassah previously had joined the struggle to free Soviet Jewry, and many of its presidents had made *aliyah* to Israel. In 1969, it sent the first group *aliyah*, graduates of Young Judaea, to settle in Neve Ilan near Jerusalem.

Hadassah continued to draw women from diverse backgrounds into its top ranks of leadership. Lola Kramarsky, president from 1960 to 1964, left Holland with her husband and three children just before the Nazis invaded. Faye Schenk, president from 1968 to 1972, was the daughter of an Orthodox rabbi. She married a rabbi and spent ten years in Australia before returning to the United States. Rose Matzkin, president from 1972 to 1976, was born on Ellis Island, the day her mother arrived in the United States. She joined Hadassah immediately after she married. Like many

Hadassah leaders, she also joined other organizations, like the League of Women Voters and the Red Cross. The tradition of leadership, social feminism, and Zionism, passed on from mothers to daughters, carried Hadassah to new heights during the 1970s, making it the preeminent American Jewish women's organization.

The Challenge of Contemporary Feminism, 1976–Present. In 1980, Hadassah commissioned a survey that revealed the gradual graying of Hadassah members, a decline in the percent of younger members who considered themselves Zionists, a wide diversity of religious affiliation, and increasing levels of education among younger members. Hadassah remained predominantly an organization of married women. Feminist feelings were widespread among all women surveyed, while Zionist sentiment was not.

The survey did not document that, along with its success, Hadassah had acquired negative stereotypes. "Hadassah ladies" appeared to young feminists to be the antithesis of the new Jewish woman they hoped to create through the feminist movement and Jewish feminism. Hadassah responded to criticism by increasing its identification with Israel, becoming active in international women's conferences, and initiating a new series of educational programs.

In 1989, Hadassah published *Jewish Marital Status* to reach unaffiliated families. Over sixty seminars on Jewish family issues followed. In 1991, Hadassah held a three-day symposium devoted to "Israeli and American Jews: Understanding and Misunderstanding." The event, and subsequent one-day symposia on university campuses, involved collaboration with scholars and activists, including feminist women who previously had rejected Hadassah.

Such initiatives did not stop the aging of Hadassah's membership, but they did reflect creative engagement with issues important to Jewish women at the close of the twentieth century, as well as continuity with Hadassah's own history. Innovations accompanied regular Hadassah programs of medical research and care, Youth Aliyah, education, and reclamation of the land through cooperation with the Jewish National

Fund. Hadassah, with close to 300,000 members, remains one of the largest, most active, and most socially committed women's organizations in the world. The seven signers of that first invitation eighty years earlier would be pleased. With a dedication to practical idealism, they laid the foundation for a large organization of women Zionists that continues to thrive.

ISRAEL–UNITED STATES RELATIONS

Since its establishment in 1948, the State of Israel has looked to the United States government for economic, military, and political support. Washington provided minimal aid during the new nation's first and most vulnerable decade, but America's ties with Israel began to grow slowly during the 1960s. They escalated dramatically after the Six-Day War of 1967, before reaching an unprecedented level when Richard Nixon became president and declared the Jewish state to be a vital strategic asset in the Cold War. For the next three decades, American support for Israel increased dramatically, with multibillion dollar aid packages and major arms sales.

The American government, despite some disputes, has resolutely stood by Israel and, as part of an implicit agreement, both Israel and the increasingly large Israeli lobby in the United States have unconditionally supported American foreign and military policy. Although American politics shifted with the demise of the Soviet Union, Washington's relationship with Israel became institutionalized to the point that it continues to be politically dangerous for candidates, elected officials, or cabinet members to challenge this alliance.

The origins of this coalition occurred in a significantly different political climate. The Truman administration played an important role in Israel's formal independence (Truman was the first major leader to recognize Israel). However, the State Department convinced the White House that sending American arms to Israel would stand in the way of developing ties to the Arab world and enable the Soviet Union to strengthen its influence there. Ironically, it was Soviet client state Czechoslovakia that sold Israel the weapons

it used as leverage to sign armistice agreements with its Arab neighbors in 1949. That same year, Israeli foreign minister Moshe Sharrett visited the United States and declared that the Israeli government would allow no interference by Jews outside its borders and that the American Zionist leadership should not mettle in the internal affairs of Israel. Although Congress passed statements of support for Israel, American financial aid for the Jewish state never amounted to more than a tiny fraction of the total foreign aid budget in these years.

Although Truman provided the first material aid package to Israel in 1952, the arms embargo remained in effect throughout most of the Truman and Eisenhower administrations. In 1953, Eisenhower's Secretary of State, John Foster Dulles, held up a $26 million loan earmarked for Israel and threatened to cancel the tax exemption on charitable donations by the United Jewish Appeal in protest of Israel's irrigation plan to remove water from the upper Jordan to the Negev dessert. Three years later, the administration aligned itself with Egypt during the Suez crisis. Despite declarations of friendship, the United States and Israel were not allies in the late 1940s and throughout most of the 1950s. Washington aligned itself with Iraq, Turkey, and Iran in the Baghdad Pact. Israel was kept out for fear of offending Muslim allies.

By the late 1950s, American policy began to slowly shift and the political and military ingredients were put in place that led President John F. Kennedy to provide the first anti-aircraft weapons to the Jewish state in 1961. He then approved a transfer of Hawk missiles that was formally consummated after his assas-

---

From the Desk of the President

"This government has been informed that a Jewish state has been proclaimed in Palestine, and recognition has been requested by the provisional government thereof. The United States recognizes the provisional government as the de facto authority of the state of Israel."

Text of President Harry Truman's memo recognizing the State of Israel, dated May 14, 1948, 6:11 P.M., eleven minutes after Israel declared its independence.

sination in 1964. Both Kennedy and his successor Lyndon B. Johnson continued to cultivate relations with Israel partly because of the Jewish involvement in both of these administrations and partly because the two presidents increasingly viewed many of the Arab states surrounding Israel, especially Egypt, as American antagonists. Johnson was the first American president to receive an Israeli prime minister on a state visit when he welcomed Levi Eshkol in 1964. In 1966, he approved the first sale of American warplanes to Israel.

Both Kennedy and (especially) Johnson recognized that Jews were a significant voting block in the United States and that support for Israel could go a long way in securing their allegiance to the Democratic Party. Thus, American Jews who "only" provided Democratic candidate Adlai Stevenson with 60 percent of the vote in 1956 gave Kennedy an overwhelming 82 percent in 1960 and Johnson a staggering 90 percent in 1964. In addition, as American Jews gained power and prestige, their influence began to hold more sway with respect to American policy toward Israel.

The Six-Day War of 1967, in which Israel routed the threatening Arab armies and occupied the west bank of Jordan, the Golan Heights, and the Sinai Peninsula, expanded the American-Israeli military relationship by leaps and bounds. When Israel's chief weapons supplier up to that point, France, decided to embargo its former clients, Washington stepped in to fill the void and has never looked back. The annual aid package grew from $13.1 million in 1967 to $76.8 million in 1968 to $600 million in 1971.

The war was an enormous turning point for relations between the American government and Israel. It also greatly strengthened and emboldened the so-called "Jewish" or "Pro-Israeli" lobby in the United States and throughout the West. After the war, Israel developed an image in the press and in the annals of popular opinion as "David" fighting (and winning) against a sea of Arab "Goliaths," an image that played a significant role in lobbying for greater military aid for a number of years. The **American Israel Public Affairs Committee** (AIPAC), which began its ascension into one of the most powerful lobbying groups in the

United States, urged Congress to support arms sales as vital to Israel's defense.

From a geopolitical angle, the war also marked a turning point. The Soviet Union and the entire Communist world, with the exception of Romania and Cuba, suspended all diplomatic ties with Israel in protest. The Jewish state became a solid part of the American and Western camp, while Arab nations increasingly purchased Soviet weapons. The U.S.S.R. also began arming and training Palestinian and Arab terrorists. From a global perspective, Israel had suddenly emerged as an important player in the Cold War. It became both expedient and symbolic for the United States to side with Israel.

The increasing pressure for massively expanding military support also had its economic rationale. Defense companies recognized that they could significantly increase their profits with lucrative arms sales and they began to cultivate a new degree of mutual cooperation between the American and the Israeli air forces.

When Richard Nixon was elected president in 1968, he recognized this tendency and expanded political and military support for Israel far beyond previous levels, despite receiving virtually no Jewish support in his successful campaign against Hubert Humphrey. Nixon made Israel both the largest single recipient of American foreign aid and began to guarantee substantial American weapons sales to the Jewish nation.

Although Jews remained solidly in the Democratic camp, the Republican president's embrace of Israel did win him significant praise and support from many in the American Jewish community. The majority, however, continued to oppose Nixon for his anti-liberal Cold War bombast. His reputation was further sullied when the Watergate tapes that eventually forced him to resign from office exposed his anti-Semitism. Nevertheless, the increasing exposure of the Soviet oppression of Jews and the Soviet government's animosity toward Israel, the Third World's animosity toward Israel, and Zionism created a subtle but substantive shift to the right among many traditionally liberal Jews. This shift would gain influence in the 1970s and 1980s with the ascent of **Neoconservatism**.

For the American government, Israel increasingly served as an important Cold War asset. Just as President Johnson attempted to equate support for Israel with "saving" Vietnam from communism, Nixon encouraged Prime Minister **Golda Meir** to speak out publicly in support of the Vietnam War and to appeal privately to Jewish leaders to endorse his policies of communist containment.

By the 1970s, the face of Jewish leadership became far more militant in its defense of Israel and its belief that the world was a hostile place, divided between Jewish friends and enemies. Increasingly, loyalty to the Jewish people became defined as loyalty to Israel. In addition, after the Yom Kippur War in 1973, virtually all of the major Jewish organizations vocally opposed the formation of "Breira" (alternative), a group which sought to promote its views of Israeli-Palestinian "mutual recognition" to the Jews in the United States. By mid-1976, the Conference of Presidents of Major American Jewish Organizations, the Synagogue Council of America, and the **American Jewish Committee** working closely with Israeli ambassador Simcha Dintz came to three conclusions: Israelis were the only ones entitled to decide Israeli policy, American Jews were obligated to stand publicly united with Israel, and Israel could at no point negotiate with Palestinian terrorists, since to do so would grant them legitimacy.

While the Jewish establishment sought to limit public dissent among Jews with respect to Israeli policy, influential non-Jewish politicians such as Senator Henry Jackson began to gain clout as Israel's strongest defenders in Washington. With the help of the so-called Jewish Big Three (the **Anti-Defamation League**, the American Jewish Committee, and the **American Jewish Congress**), Jackson began the process that resulted in outlawing American business compliance with the Arab economic boycott of Israel.

Jimmy Carter was elected President of the United States in 1977 at the same time as the right wing Likud party under Menachem Begin ended fifty years of labor party rule in Israel. Because Carter viewed ending the Middle East conflict as a personal mission, he instantly found himself in a head-on collision with

Strong, proud, defiant are three words that are often used to describe Golda Meir. She also had a sense of humor. A probably apocryphal but nonetheless typical story has President Nixon telling her that he would trade any three American generals for General Moshe Dayan. "Okay," she says, "I'll take General Motors, General Electric, and General Dynamics." (From the Archives of the YIVO Institute of Jewish Research.)

the hawkish Begin. The power struggle between the two men might have continued were it not for the commitment of Egyptian president Anwar Sadat to sign a peace treaty with Israel. After one and a half years of torturous and sometimes acrimonious negotiations, Egypt and Israel signed what became known as the Camp David accords in March 1979. In an otherwise unpopular presidential administration, the agreement stood out as Carter's crowning achievement, although it left the question of Palestinian recognition unanswered.

While Carter and Sadat emerged from the Camp

Henry Kissinger and Golda Meir

Soon after Henry Kissinger was appointed Secretary of State, he wrote to Golda Meir, Prime Minister of Israel: "As you know, I have been appointed Secretary of State. I very much hope that we shall be able to work well together for the benefit of our countries. In order that there may be complete understanding between us, I trust that you will always be aware of my priorities, which are in this order: I am an American citizen, Secretary of State, and a Jew."

To which Golda Meir replied: "Your letter makes me very happy. Now I am sure that we shall at all times be in complete accord.

P.S. I am sure that you are aware that in Israel we read from right to left."

From *Jewish Folklore in America*, by David Max Eichhorn.

David negotiations as conciliatory and committed to peace, Begin's position sparked a national protest movement within Israel and created significant division and unease within the American Jewish community. Although the Israeli Prime Minister appeared to pay attention to these concerns, his government increasingly began to ignore established agencies that raised questions about Israeli policy (such as the National Jewish Community Relations Advisory Council) and concentrated all his attention on promoting his position to the AIPAC and the Conference of Presidents of Major Jewish Organizations.

Ronald Reagan's administration recognized the possibility of creating a partnership with AIPAC. It used the lobbying organization to sell administration policies to Democrats and to American Jews that the Republican administration would have been unable to promote on their own. Throughout the 1980s, AIPAC lobbyists assisted Reagan in lining up Democratic Congressional support for his foreign policy agenda, ranging from aiding the Nicaraguan contras to training security forces in Zaire to secretly arming Iran. AIPAC made the argument to liberals that Israel required that its friends compromise on other issues in order to maintain strong American support for Israel. Lobbyists also argued that a strong American defense

was good for Israel, since a weakened America would not be able to defend its small allies.

In exchange, the Reagan administration became the most pro-Israel in United States history. In 1981, the Jewish nation was allowed for the first time to sign a military pact with Washington, making it a full partner in American policy. The two countries cooperated in weapons development and the sharing of technology and military intelligence. They finalized formal Free Trade Area agreements removing all impediments to trade between them—the broadest trade liberalization agreement the United States has developed with any nation, including Canada. Reagan invited Israel to participate in his Strategic Defense Initiative and in return Israel agreed to have the Voice of America build two massive radio transmitters in the Negev. American aid to Israel skyrocketed and the major legacy of the eight-year Republican administration was an institutionalization of the American-Israeli military connection. Reagan also appointed a large number of Jewish neoconservatives to administration posts.

Even though many established Jewish voices embraced both Reagan and Israeli government policy, the majority remained liberal Democrats who opposed the president's policies on abortion, school prayer, and civil rights. In addition, although most Jews continued to endorse unequivocally Begin's policies, these policies did create a divide between hawks and doves in the American Jewish community. While Begin dismissed his critics as anti-Semites, some moderate voices in American Judaism indicated that they were disturbed by his government's policies.

The election of George Bush as president in 1988 paralleled the escalation of the Palestinian "Intifada" (uprising) and the mounting violence in the West Bank and the Gaza Strip. Bush's Secretary of State, James Baker, realized that the growing instability in the region threatened American interests. He attempted to strike a balance between continuing Washington's commitment to Israel while attempting to negotiate a freeze on the contentious issue of Israeli settlements on the West Bank and the Gaza Strip.

After the Gulf War of 1991 and the attacks by Iraq on Tel Aviv, which exposed Israel's vulnerability, Bush attempted to secure a place for himself in diplomatic history by attempting to negotiate a "land for peace" agreement in which the United States would both broker a peace treaty with neighboring Arab states and help pay the exorbitant costs involved in settling the masses of Soviet émigrés who were overwhelming Israel in exchange for Israel's agreement to give up territory. The plan failed miserably and Bush became the pariah of the American Jewish establishment, contributing to his defeat in the 1992 elections.

Meanwhile, a weary and divided Israeli population voted Yitzak Shamir's Likud government out of power and turned to the more moderate Labor alternative of elder statesman Yitzak Rabin. Nevertheless, neither Shamir nor Rabin seemed willing to recognize the Palestinian Liberation Organization (PLO) as a legitimate representative of the Palestinian people, given the organization's founding statement that declared its intention to destroy the State of Israel and its violent history of trying to do so.

In a shock to virtually everyone, Rabin did an aboutface in 1993 and negotiated a peace agreement with PLO president Yasser Arafat that provided limited Palestinian autonomy in two towns with a continued commitment to further negotiations. The beneficiary of this shift in Israeli attitude was the new American President Bill Clinton, who helped finalize what came to be known as the Oslo Accords.

Although the Accords began with great promise, they rapidly steered off course into a sea of violence and mistrust, with Palestinian terrorist attacks killing numerous Israeli civilians. While a number of Palestinians viewed the agreement as not going nearly far enough toward their goal of statehood, many Israelis were enraged that their government had negotiated a peace treaty with Arafat, a man they considered a terrorist.

The Clinton administration attempted to use its authority to keep the terms of the agreement in sight, but there was little it could do to halt the bloodshed in the region that reached its zenith when Rabin was assassinated by an Orthodox Israeli law student in 1995. The assassin saw the Prime Minister as a traitor and his death as a religious imperative. Rabin's successor, Shimon Peres, was in many ways more liberal than Rabin, but despite Clinton's partisan support, Peres was unable to keep an increasingly fractured Labor Party coalition together. His shaky government fell to Likud under the leadership of Benjamin Netanyahu.

Despite these twists and turns in Israel and the Middle East, the United States government remained steadfastly loyal. Although the relationship has had its tense moments, Israel has become far too much of a partner with the United States and a strategic asset in the region to risk major damage. Israel and the United States continue to be involved in collaborative military maneuvers, medical evacuation exercises, and strategic planning operations. The Jewish state has become a major military asset for the United States in the region, capable of assembling a massive army using American-made weaponry. Thus, increasingly, the United States government seems to need Israel almost as much as Israel needs the United States.

The relationship between the United States and Israel is about more than global politics. Israel has growing and powerful support in and around Washington. Not only has AIPAC become one of the most powerful lobbying groups in America. Israel also enjoys a powerful and influential circle of friends both inside and outside the beltway, many of whom are not Jewish and have different reasons for supporting the Jewish nation—most having little to do with any great love for Israel or the Jewish people.

Although it is without question that Israel enjoys enormous clout in the United States, this power has sometimes been taken to anti-Semitic extremes and been viewed as analogous to Jewish power or a so-called Jewish conspiracy. Such a perspective makes the assumption that the Jewish lobby somehow subverts United States policy against its own best interests in favor of Israel. The reality is that American policy toward Israel is both rational and pragmatic. It is just as easy to argue that the United States–Israeli alliance created contemporary American Jewish political power as it is to argue the reverse. The United States government began to actively support Israel only when its own military and political interest benefited from such an alliance. Domestic Jewish influence was, at best, a secondary incentive. It has only been recently that this has begun to change.

During the 1980s, the Israeli economy was in shambles and substantial American aid was provided to help stabilize the country. Netanyahu's commitment to economic independence for Israel and the nation's overall recovery raises the possibility that American material aid may be reduced in the new century.

There is still an insistence from AIPAC and other Israel advocates in the United States that the Jewish state will continue to need military assistance. Although the Israel government will not necessarily do whatever Washington wants it to do, as witness the Bush catastrophe, it is clear that every Israeli leader must consider the United States position with great care and not risk a long-term rift with the White House or Congress. Given that reality, few signs exist that the strong coalition that exists between the two nations is likely to change dramatically any time in the near future.

LIPSKY, LOUIS (1876-1963)

Zionist leader, writer

One of America's most influential Zionists, Louis Lipsky was born in Rochester, New York in 1876. As a young man, he edited the weekly newspaper *Shofar* and was an ardent Zionist. At the age of twenty-five, he founded the magazine *The Maccabean*, the first Zionist periodical in English to be published in the United States. He also edited *The American Hebrew*. His commitment to the cause of Zionism went beyond his journalistic activities.

Lipsky was secretary and later chairman of the executive committee of the Federation of American Zionists, an organization that was later superseded by the **Zionist Organization of America** (ZOA). He was president of ZOA from 1922 to 1930. In 1915, he spoke out in favor of an American Jewish Congress dedicated to the creation of a Jewish national home. When the first **American Jewish Congress** was elected in 1918, Lipsky

became absorbed in its activities. He was vice president of the organization and chairman of its governing council. In the years before and during World War II, he worked ceaselessly with the AJC to publicize the persecution of European Jews and to effect the rescue of as many as could be saved.

From 1930 to 1959, Lipsky was president of the Eastern Life Insurance Company. He wrote a number of books, including *Thirty Years of American Zionism*, *Stories of Jewish Life*, and *Shields of Honor*, the last of which was a collection of plays and short stories. These three books were published in a three-volume set in 1927 as Lipsky's *Selected Works*.

MAGNES, JUDAH L. (1877–1948)

Rabbi, Zionist, president of Hebrew University

Chancellor and first president of the Hebrew University of Jerusalem, Judah L. Magnes was born in San Francisco in 1877. His parents were immigrants from Poland and Germany. He attended **Hebrew Union College**, was ordained a rabbi, and studied in Germany. There, his exposure to Jewish life led him to a lifelong commitment to Zionism.

Back in New York, Magnes became occupied with rabbinical duties and Zionist activism until, in 1912, he left congregational work to devote all his energies to public service in the Jewish sphere. However, his pacifism during World War I put him in disfavor with a community that was concerned with proving its loyalty. In 1922 Magnes and his family emigrated to Palestine where he helped to establish the Hebrew University. He was the university's chancellor from 1925 to 1935 and, in 1935, became its first president.

With the rise of Nazi Germany, Magnes abandoned his pacifism and called for war. He was extremely active in wartime activities, including work with **Henrietta Szold**'s Youth Aliyah and the Emergency Council of **Hadassah** in Palestine. He was also chairman of the Middle East Advisory Council of the **American Joint Distribution Committee** and worked tirelessly with Jews who managed to escape from Hitler's German into the Middle East. Magnes was a firm believer that

Judah L. Magnes was active with both the American Jewish Committee and the American Civil Liberties Union before he immigrated with his family to Palestine, where he helped to establish the Hebrew University. He was the university's chancellor from 1925 to 1935 and in 1935 he became its first president. (American Jewish Archives)

Jews and Arabs should reach an accord in Palestine and build a binational state. He was in New York promoting his fervently held beliefs when he died on October 27, 1948.

MEIR, GOLDA (1898–1978)

Zionist, politician, Prime Minister of Israel

Israeli leader Golda Meir was born Golda Mabovitch in Kiev, Ukraine (then part of the Russian Empire) on May 3, 1898. Her early life, which greatly influenced her later passion for Jewish security, was filled with both poverty and pogroms. In 1906, her family immigrated to the United States and settled in Milwaukee. As a teenager, she lived with her sister in Denver for a short period where she was introduced to her future husband, Morris Meyerson, and to the politics of Zionism, which would become her passion. After she returned to Milwaukee, she attended a teacher's training college, taught at the Jewish Center, and took to the streets to promote Labor Zionism. In late 1917, she married Meyerson and in 1921 they moved to the Merhavia kibbutz in Palestine.

Meir was happy, active, and successful on the kibbutz. Meyerson wasn't. Never as passionate about Zionism as his wife and uncomfortable with her success, he forced a move to Jerusalem where the couple's two children were born. After four years of attempting to be a traditional wife and mother, and living in poverty, Meir took a position as secretary of the Histadrut (General Federation of Labor). She left her husband, took the children, and moved to Tel Aviv. Though they never legally divorced, the marriage had ended.

Free to pursue her interests, by 1934 Meir was a member of Histadrut's Executive Committee. In 1936, she became head of its political department. During World War II, she was a member of the Jewish Agency (the de facto government of the Jewish settlement). She served as the Agency's spokesperson with the British authority and as its acting head when the men were arrested.

In 1948, after the State of Israel was established, Meir traveled to the United States where she raised fifty million dollars from the American Jewish community. The same year, she was appointed ambassador to the Soviet Union. In 1949 she was elected to the Knesset and became the minister of labor. In 1956, she was named foreign minister and changed her name to the more Hebrew-sounding Meir. She became the secretary of the unified Labor Party in 1967 and in early 1969 was named Israel's Prime Minister.

She held the position for four years. Meir and the Labor Party were held accountable for the heavy Israeli losses in the 1973 Yom Kippur War and lost popular-

Including a prime minister of Israel in an American Jewish book might be questioned. But seen here playing the Statue of Liberty in the Poale Zion pageant in Milwaukee, you know that Golda Mabovitch was a Wisconsin girl in her roots. (American Jewish Archives)

ity. Unable to form a government, she resigned in 1974. Toward the end of her life, she became the country's elder statesman. She died on December 8, 1978, having been one of the most important and respected political leaders of the twentieth century.

SILVER, ABBA HILLEL (1893–1963)

Rabbi, Zionist leader

Born in Lithuania in 1893, Abba Hillel Silver was brought to the United States as a child and grew up on New York City's Lower East Side. Deeply impressed by the influential Zionist preacher Zvi Hirsch Masliansky, Silver developed a reputation of his own as a mes-

merizing orator, equally eloquent in Yiddish, Hebrew, and English. After graduating from the Reform Movement's **Hebrew Union College**, Silver became spiritual leader of Cleveland's The Temple, one of the country's most prominent Reform congregations, in 1917. Assuming the leadership of Cleveland's Zionist community—one of the largest districts of the **Zionist Organization of America**—Silver spearheaded protests against British restrictions on Jewish immigration to Palestine and organized boycotts of products from Nazi Germany.

The escalating Nazi persecution of Jews, the apathetic response of the Roosevelt administration to news of Hitler's atrocities, and England's refusal to open Palestine to refugees from Hitler stimulated a mood of growing militancy in the American Jewish community during the late 1930s and early 1940s. Silver gave voice to American Jewish militancy and helped encourage its spread. In August 1943, Silver was appointed co-chair of the American Zionist Emergency Council (AZEC), a coalition of the leading U.S. Zionist groups, alongside Rabbi **Stephen Wise**, whom he quickly supplanted.

Under Silver's leadership, American Zionism assumed a vocal new role in Washington. Mobilized by the AZEC in 1943–1944, grassroots Zionists deluged Capitol Hill with calls and letters urging Congressional support for creation of a Jewish national home in Palestine. In the summer of 1944 Silver also campaigned successfully for the inclusion of pro-Zionist planks in the election platforms of the Republican and Democratic parties.

During the post-war period, Silver and the AZEC stepped up their pressure on the Truman Administration with protest rallies, newspaper advertisements, and educational campaigns urging the creation of a Jewish state. The AZEC also sponsored the American Christian Palestine Committee, which activated grassroots Christian Zionists nationwide, and the Christian Council on Palestine, which spoke for nearly 3,000 pro-Zionist Christian clergymen.

A torrent of protest activity spearheaded by Silver and the AZEC helped convince the President to recognize the new State of Israel just minutes after its creation. Silver's protests against the U.S. arms embargo on the Middle East, however, were rebuffed by the administration.

In the aftermath of Israel's birth, Silver resumed full-time rabbinical duties at The Temple, turning his attention to religious scholarship, reading voraciously and publishing several well-received books on Judaism. He died suddenly in 1963.

Silver's reign marked a political coming of age for American Jewry. His lobbying victories infused the Jewish community with confidence and a sense that their agenda was a legitimate part of American political culture. The Silver years left their mark on the American political scene as well. After the inclusion of Palestine in the 1944 party platforms, Zionist concerns assumed a permanent place in American electoral politics, and the swift U.S. recognition of Israel in 1948 was a major first step in cementing the America-Israel friendship that has endured ever since.

SYRKIN, MARIE (1899–1989)

Writer, journalist, educator

Marie Syrkin was born in Bern, Switzerland on March 23, 1899, the daughter of a Socialist-Zionist theoretician and a feminist revolutionary activist. She immigrated to the United States with her family when she was nine years old. She attended Cornell University. After receiving her M.A., she became an English teacher at Manhattan's Textile High School, a position she held for over twenty years. At the same time, she became one of the first people to translate Yiddish poetry into English.

In 1934, after her first trip to Palestine, Syrkin began to work for the Labor-Zionist publication *Jewish Frontier* and began her career as an influential journalist and political commentator. She wrote the first exposé in English of the Moscow Trials (1937) and the first editorial in the American press reporting that the systematic extermination of the Jews was already under way (1942). After the war, she spent time in displaced persons camps in both Germany and in Israel.

In 1950 Syrkin became an English professor at the newly founded **Brandeis University**, teaching the first university level course in the literature of the Holocaust, as well as teaching a popular course on American Jewish fiction. While at Brandeis, she served as editor for *Jewish Frontier* and the Herzl Press, on the editorial board of *Midstream*, and as a member of the World Zionist Executive. Among her most famous appearances was a debate sponsored by *Dissent* where she vehemently attacked **Hannah Arendt**'s book, *Eichmann in Jerusalem*. She retired from Brandeis in 1966 but remained active as a writer and lecturer. Among her many books are *Your School, Your Children* (1944), *Blessed is the Match* (1947), *Golda Meir: Israel's Leader* (1970), and *The State of the Jews* (1980). She died on February 2, 1989.

SZOLD, HENRIETTA (1860–1945)

Zionist, Hadassah founder, humanitarian

The remarkable Henrietta Szold was born in 1860 in Baltimore, Maryland, the child of Rabbi Benjamin Szold and his wife Sophie. A political liberal and a religious traditionalist, Rabbi Szold taught his daughter German, Hebrew, and the Jewish sacred texts to supplement her public school education. In her teens she began to work with him as translator and editor. She later become a teacher and wrote for a number of Jewish journals.

Henrietta Szold's first trip to Palestine was in 1909 when she was forty-nine years old. She had found her life's vocation—the recreation of the Jewish homeland. She is shown here in 1921, clearly dressed for the job. (Courtesy of Hadassah, The Women's Zionist Organization of America, Inc.)

In 1888 she was chosen to be one of the nine members of the publication committee of the Jewish Publication Society (JPS). The only woman on the committee, she collaborated with **Cyrus Adler** on a contribution to JPS's first publication, *Outlines of Jewish History*. She also helped to edit Heinrich Gratz's classic *History of the Jews*. In 1893 she became executive secretary of the publications committee and, for over two decades, was instrumental in the editing, translating, and publication of some of the most important works in American Judaism.

One of the first proponents of Zionism, she gave a speech in 1896 outlining her philosophy—Jews should be allowed to return to their ancient homeland *and* Jews should work to revive Jewish culture. In 1898 she became a member of the Federation of American Zionists (FAZ) executive committee, the only woman in the group.

In 1909 Szold visited Palestine and became intensely involved in the work to reconstruct the Jewish homeland. At the age of forty-nine she had discovered her vocation. She devoted the rest of her life to Palestine—the promised land. Back in America, she founded **Hadassah**, the Zionist organization for women. This group was by no means a "ladies auxiliary" to male Zionist organizations. Under Szold's leadership, in fact, it became larger and more powerful than any other Zionist group in the country. Among its projects was providing medical care and education to the Jewish community in Palestine. During the 1930s, Hadassah expanded its work to include the Youth Aliyah programs for settling and educating young refugees from Nazi Europe.

In 1920 Szold arrived in Palestine to personally take charge of Hadassah's medical unit. She settled there and devoted the remaining twenty-five years of her life to humanitarian work with the Jews of her adopted land. Her work, both in providing health and educational services to residents of Palestine and in rescuing children from the Holocaust, earned her the title "mother of the *yishuv*" (the Jewish community in Palestine). The Youth Aliyah program could not have succeeded to the extent that it did without her mastery of the administrative complications involved in "liber-

In 1920 Henrietta Szold arrived in Palestine to take charge of the American Zionist Medical Unit. She is pictured here with the first graduating class (1921) of the Hadassah Training School for Nurses, in Jerusalem. (Courtesy of Hadassah, The Women's Zionist Organization of America, Inc.)

ating" children from Europe, transporting them to a new country, and ensuring that their physical and emotional needs were met in this strange, new land.

Although her cultural roots were clearly in the United states (at her last Passover seder in 1944 she sang African American spirituals), Szold had clearly become a "resident" of her adopted homeland. She died in 1945, three years before the creation of the State of Israel, which she had done so much to make possible.

ZIONISM

Zionism and the belief in a Jewish state have proved to be among the most politically potent and controversial ideas confronting Jews in America. Tracing its earliest origins back to when Jews persecuted over many generations in Europe prayed to Zion for redemption, the modern Zionist movement began in Europe in 1896 when Theodor Herzl published *The Jewish State*. At a time of escalating violence and pogrom activity, Herzl argued that only the creation of a Jewish homeland would resolve the perpetual problem of institutionalized anti-Semitism and Jewish oppression in the European Diaspora. His writings dealt little with Judaism as a religion and his voice was that of a generation besieged by anti-Semitism within the Pale of Settlement.

The late-nineteenth-century ideas about Zionism brought to the United States were substantially different in approach. "Practical Zionists" believed that the groundwork for the new Jewish state had to be laid slowly and in stages over a number of years. "Political Zionists" believed that a state must be created immediately and dramatically through international action. "Labor Zionists" viewed the return to Zion as deeply rooted in a socialist mission. "Territorialists" were willing to consider territories other than Palestine as a shelter for Jews, while "Zionists of Zion" adamantly rejected any substitute to the ancestral homeland. Herzl himself was initially indifferent as to where the Jewish state might be located, until he realized that Palestine had a historical resonance with the Jewish people lacking in any other geographic region. Thus, European Zionism, although primarily a secular, political response to the persecution of Jews, had the spiritual dimension of evoking a biblical homeland.

Although there was initial enthusiasm for Zionism in America, the country's earliest Zionist societies faced far more difficulties than those in Europe. German Jews who had been in the United States since the 1840s had little interest in looking overseas for a homeland. Their primary concern was full recognition as Americans. Many German Jews were also concerned that the Christian majority might perceive them as somehow disloyal and thus less deserving of equal rights if it appeared their allegiance was to a new nation rather than to the United States.

Jews had not faced the kind of entrenched, systematic oppression in America that they had confronted in Europe. Although anti-Semitism had increased in the years following the Civil War, it was more connected

Israel 1948–1998

Over fifty years of nationhood, the Jews of Israel have fought among themselves over innumerable issues. But all would agree that it is indeed a miracle that (to quote *The New York Times*) ". . . a people dispersed for 2,000 years in 140 countries, speaking 100 tongues, managed to return to their ancient homeland and to start speaking its ancient language."

to increasing xenophobia and to general tensions involving immigrant groups in the United States than to the intense hatred of Jews found in the old world. One reason many Jews in the United States as well as some number of prominent organizations such as the **American Jewish Committee** were initially lukewarm to Zionism was that they perceived America as a new Zion.

Reform congregations were especially adamant in their rejection of a desire to return to Eretz Yisrael and many Orthodox and Conservative Jews believed that they would find their redemption on American soil rather than in the land of their ancestors. Likewise, the new and far less affluent immigrants arriving *en masse* from Eastern Europe were initially far too busy struggling to make a living to be moved by the Zionist pull. For most Jewish immigrants at the turn of the century, becoming a Zionist and becoming an American were viewed as fundamentally incompatible. The Federation of American Zionists (FAZ), the largest Zionist coalition in the United States, had a membership of only 12,000 out of a Jewish population of two and one-half million in the years leading up to World War I. The FAZ also faced the initial problem of having to negotiate among its many local societies, which had very different political agendas with respect to Zionism, from socialist to conservative.

Social and economic changes in the United States and worldwide in the years immediately prior to and during World War I combined, however, to dramatically increase enthusiasm for Zionism, especially among the newer Jewish immigrants. No person did more to cultivate a reformulation of Zionist philosophy to make it more compatible to an American as well as a Jewish vision than **Louis Brandeis**. When the war began in Europe in 1914, a coalition of pro-Zionist groups, recognizing the need to seek emergency assistance for the economically ravaged Zionist settlements, held meetings and established Brandeis as chairman of the Provisional Executive Committee (PEC) for General Zionist Affairs. Brandeis not only galvanized American Jews to support their brethren in Palestine but also turned the PEC and American Zionism into an important political force.

Brandeis took on the leadership position at a historical moment in which United States social reform philosophy had begun shifting from an "all or nothing" melting pot concept to more of a cultural pluralist ideology. Under this formulation, which Brandeis frequently articulated, one did not have to choose between being a Zionist and being an American. One could have dual loyalties if the two philosophies supported each other, which he argued they most certainly did. Zionism and Americanism shared identical values for him and for many of the new spokespeople for the movement. In the rhetoric of the moment, Zionist settlements in Palestine would be developed with the same ideals that guided the American founding fathers. Conversely, the notion of Jewish assimilation, formerly seen as a necessary good, began to be viewed as dangerous and even "suicidal."

In addition, the Eastern European immigrants who had never had the same desire to discard their Jewish and *Yiddishkeit* identity (as did the more established and affluent German Jews) began to be captivated by the promise of Zionism. Many Jewish immigrant radicals viewed the kibbutz as the quintessential socialist institution. They held out the hope that, if their vision of the model society was not possible in the United States, it could be built through "Labor Zionism" in Palestine.

Zionist organizers had a broader political agenda during the war years, however, than simply winning the hearts and minds of Jews in America. Brandeis gained considerable influence with President Woodrow Wilson and convinced him to have the United States government endorse a Jewish homeland in Palestine. This provided the impetus for the British "Balfour Declaration" of November 1917, which called for a Jewish homeland to be established after the war.

The war years saw the re-organization of the Zionist movement under the umbrella of the **Zionist Organization of America** (ZOA) in 1918. In its founding statement (referred to as the Pittsburgh Platform), the ZOA staked out what it considered the tenets of American Zionist policy, including the political and civil equality of all residents of Palestine regardless of race, sex, or faith; equality of opportunity, with public own-

Pioneer Women, the Labor Zionist women's organization in the United States, was founded in 1925 and had among its members Golda Meir. Members of the organization are shown here in 1945 protesting British policies in Palestine. (Courtesy of American Jewish Historical Society, Waltham, Massachusetts and New York, New York)

ership of land, natural resources, and utilities; free public education; and Hebrew as the national language. The older European conception of Zionism had been transformed. The spiritual and religious identification of Jews with their ancestral homeland was left unmentioned as was the linking of the "Return to Zion" with the transformation of the Jew into a "new man." In successfully gaining the support of assimilated Jews and non-Jews in America, Brandeis and his supporters created deep divisions in the international Zionist movement.

The schism between American and European Zionism as well as between other interpretations of

Zionism deepened during the post-war years. Chaim Weizmann and other European Zionist leaders rejected what they considered the watered down "Jewishness" of American Zionism, arguing that Brandeis and his coterie had turned a visionary ideal for Jewish redemption into nothing more than a philanthropic activity. European Zionists viewed their own futures as tied to making *"Aliyah"* (returning to the homeland). They saw themselves as personally involved with farming the land, rebuilding the soil, and creating a distinctly Jewish homeland. Zionism for them was a way of life rather than simply a political strategy. Although a number of American Zionists chose to make *Aliyah* and committed themselves to becoming pioneers in Palestine, this percentage was always extremely small and was never a central tenet for any United States-based Zionist organization the way that it was for groups in Europe.

At the 1921 World Zionist Organization convention, Weizmann took control of the organization by finding an American ally, **Louis Lipsky**, who also viewed the Pittsburgh Platform as deficient in articulating a core Jewish vision. Weizmann and Lipsky used their support for maintaining the independence of the new Zionist fund, the *Keren Hayesod*, as the issue that catapulted them into power. Brandeis had wanted tight control of the fund as well as of the overall accounting of the World Zionist Organization. He sought to hire American experts to administer projects in Palestine, an idea strenuously opposed by the Europeans. For the next two decades, the American Zionist movement would be split into the Weizmann-Lipsky group that controlled the ZOA; the Brandeisians (Brandeis had gone on to be appointed Supreme Court Justice) who established the new Palestine Economic Committee (PEC); and **Hadassah**, the Women's Zionist Organization, which followed an independent course.

The split led to a halt in momentum of the Zionist movement with membership in the ZOA dropping from 180,000 in 1919 to 18,000 in 1929. Lipsky's ineffective leadership, the end of the wartime emergency, the conformist political climate of the 1920s, and the belief among many American Zionists that the battle had been won with the endorsement of the Balfour Declaration contributed to a decline of energy for organizational Zionism in the United States.

Hadassah and American women's participation in the Zionist movement proved to be a notable exception. Jewish women built on their own distinct experiences in American and Jewish life to inform their own brand of Zionism. Poet **Emma Lazarus** became one of the earliest proponents of a proto-Zionism in the United States and her writings from the early 1880s foreshadowed the themes advanced in Theodor Herzl's treatise a little more than a decade later. **Rosa Sonneschein**, publisher and editor of the *American Jewess,* became an important early supporter of Herzl dur-

ing the first years of the twentieth century and she attended the First Zionist Congress in Basel as the magazine's representative. Because the mainstream organizations were mostly male enclaves, **Henrietta Szold**, Emma Leon Gottheil, and other prominent women involved in study groups established Hadassah in 1912. It became an important force, although not the only one, for women to assert their leadership in the evolution and development of American Zionism.

Hadassah came to the forefront immediately by sending nurses to Palestine to provide emergency health care, then followed up by raising thousands of dollars for the creation of an American Zionist Medical Unit, which consisted of forty-five physicians, dentists, and nurses. It also sent tons of medical supplies. The Unit arrived in Palestine in 1918 and established hospitals in six cities. While the rest of the movement was floundering in the 1920s Hadassah successfully organized Jewish religious schools to contribute desperately needed hot lunch money for "sister" schools in Jerusalem and developed an effective grassroots cadre of women activists to speak out on behalf of the needs of Zionist settlers. Hadassah's president from 1926 to 1928, Irma Levy Lindheim, refused to follow the dictates of Lipsky and the ZOA, which she considered a poorly run organization. Lipsky in turn attacked Hadassah for its independence and Lindheim for her "unwomanly" behavior when she refused to cosign a bank loan for the United Palestine Appeal of the ZOA.

Catapulted by Hadassah and other similar smaller organizations, women also began to make more of a dent in national Zionist leadership. Minette Baum was elected president of the Zionist District in Fort Wayne, Indiana in 1919 and served until 1936. During the 1920s Hannah Hoffman became the first American-born female pioneer to make *Aliyah* and commit herself to living in Palestine. Poet Jesse Sampter used the pages of the *New Palestine* to rally for additional groups of American men and women to make a similar commitment to creating a new society in Zion built on justice, equality, and cooperation. Eastern European immigrant **Golda Meir**, captivated by the vision of Labor Zionism, left the United States in the 1920s to join a *kibbutz*. Little could she or anyone else have anticipated that more than forty years later she would be elected Prime Minister in the new state of Israel.

Although these women and many other Americans were energized by the hope and promise of Zionism as a pioneering enterprise, the national organizational structure had fallen on hard times. Weizmann and **Louis Marshall** established what became known as "the Jewish Agency" in 1929 as a method of getting non-Zionists who might be uncomfortable about a Zionist political agenda to contribute economic, social, and cultural aid for the rebuilding of Palestine. The overall movement was badly splintered by the end of the decade. The beginnings of the Depression caused most American Jews to focus on basic survival issues. It was only the rise of Nazism in Germany that brought the issue of Zionism back to center stage with a new and immediate set of crises and controversies.

The ascension of Hitler to power paralleled increased Arab resistance to Jewish settlement in Palestine and the abandonment of the Balfour policy by the British. **Stephen Wise** and Robert Szold, two Brandeis protégés, took on leadership roles in the ZOA in the early 1930s, condemned the British action, attempted to prevent a cutoff of Jewish immigration, and focused their energies on helping tens of thousands of Jews fleeing Europe to settle in Palestine.

The American Zionist movement received heavy criticism at the time and in retrospect from other Jews for failing to develop national coalitions that might have pressured the government to take in German Jewish refugees who ended up perishing in the Holocaust. Peter Bergson and Ben Hecht became the leading voices decrying the insufficient response by the established Jewish institutions, attacking the Roosevelt administration, and calling for the establishment of a Jewish Army. Bergson argued that his renegade group, the Emergency Committee to Save the Jewish People of Europe (ECSJPE), and not the American Zionists were the true saviors of European Jewry.

The issue is complex. American Zionism was weaker and less influential than it had been during World War I and the mood of the country and the government during the Depression era was both mili-

tantly isolationist and economically insecure. The government was extremely resistant to supporting expanded immigration. While there is considerable evidence to suggest that the government could have done more to rescue European Jews, it is debatable whether the American Zionist movement could have had a greater impact on public policy if it had used a different set of strategies.

Despite their relative powerlessness in the face of overwhelming obstacles, the public protests organized by American Zionists in the 1930s and 1940s brought thousands of new members into the ZOA, Hadassah, and other smaller groups. The Jewish refugee crisis transformed American Zionism by convincing many Jews that some form of nationalism was a necessity for the survival of their people in the Diaspora. As World War II intensified and the destruction of European Jewry came to light, the Jewish community in the United States increasingly viewed a safe heaven for Jews as a priority. The Holocaust fundamentally determined the evolution of American Zionism.

The most important meeting for Zionists during the war years was the Biltmore Conference of 1942, which included not only all the American Zionist leaders, but also Weizmann, David Ben-Gurion, and other World Zionist Organization leaders. The platform adopted called for an independent Jewish state in Palestine with full autonomy and the right to determine its own immigration patterns. For the next six years, this program became the focal point for the leaders of American Zionism, who established the American Zionist Emergency Council (AZEC) to further their goal.

Despite general agreement when it came to a vision, the AZEC's directors, Wise and **Abba Hillel Silver** clashed over strategies and tactics. Wise, a close ally of President Roosevelt's, favored a moderate, low-profile organizing approach that would not risk alienating non-Jews and he expressed faith in the President's good will. He was also willing to compromise on the creation of a Jewish state if non-Zionist support for unlimited migration into Palestine could be assured. Silver tolerated no such middle ground. Far less enamored with Roosevelt than Wise, Silver favored pressuring the administration to take immediate action on behalf of a Zionist state through political activity. He argued that the absence of a Jewish home led to persecution and murder.

The war years also saw an intense power struggle between American Zionist leadership and mainstream non-Zionist organizations. Representatives of the powerful and non-Zionist American Jewish Committee walked out of the 1943 American Jewish Conference arguing that it was dominated by the AZEC and other pro-Zionist factions. By the end of the war with the horrors of the Holocaust coming to light, the American Zionist movement's charismatic calls to end Jewish "homelessness" succeeded in winning over the allegiance of most American Jews. By 1946, even the American Jewish Committee had chosen to cooperate with the Zionist agenda.

Although Wise's more moderate leadership of the AZEC had won out at the beginning of the war, the Biltmore Conference marked the turning point in shifting power of the organization. The accusation that Wise had withheld evidence of the extermination of the Jews in Germany for three months in 1942 at the request of Roosevelt's state department also hurt his standing. By 1946, the American Zionist position had become unequivocally committed to challenging British rule over Palestine in order to establish a Jewish state. To further this mission, Silver and his supporters began secretly arming the Palestinian settlers and helping thousands of new immigrants enter the Holy land. American Zionist leaders also effectively rallied the non-Jewish population to support their position and convinced President Harry S. Truman to force the British to allow 100,000 Holocaust survivors to enter Palestine.

It is important to note that even though support for Zionism reached its peak during and immediately after World War II, not all Jews in America supported the movement. Many Orthodox Jews continued to believe that a Jewish state could be created only after the coming of the Messiah and could not be brought about through political means alone. Some liberal Jews, and especially German Jews who had a long history of anti-Zionism, continued to believe that a Jewish nation state represented a backward step toward a tribal or ghetto impulse. They argued for cultural pluralism and assimilation within modern multi-ethnic societies. Others rejected the core Zionist assertion that the rescue and salvation of European Jewry was dependent on Jewish statehood.

Most significantly, a number of prominent liberals, including journalist I. F. Stone, cautioned against the potential dangers of a state where Jews had more rights than others. After a trip to Palestine toward the end of the war, Stone argued that Zionist ideology had neglected to concern itself with the concerns of Palestinian Arabs who feared being dominated and subjugated in a new Jewish state. Because they viewed the war against fascism as a fight against the excesses of nationalism, many liberal anti-Zionists supported the position espoused by Reform Rabbi **Judah L. Magnes** (who would become the first president of the Hebrew University of Jerusalem), which called for a binational state where Jews and Arabs shared power equally. Magnes argued that any attempt to turn Palestine into either an Arab or a Jewish state would inevitably lead to war and bloodshed. He proposed that an additional half-million Jews be allowed to settle in Palestine, creating a numerical parity with the nation's one million Arabs. This would ensure that neither group could achieve a majority in the state.

At the end of the war the vast majority of influential liberals, including many Christians, had become firm Zionist supporters. Reinhold Niebuhr, one of the most respected Christian theologians in the United States, wrote and spoke out frequently and forcefully in support of the Zionist idea. He asserted that because the war had left millions of Jews "homeless" and "disinherited" the world had an obligation to provide the Jews with a post-war home. Other important Christian pro-Zionists included Protestant clergymen and intellectuals such as Henry Atkinson and Paul Tillich, who became active in the Christian Council on Palestine, and politicians such as Senator Robert Wagner, who served on the American Palestine Committee. These Christian support groups proved to be extremely important to the Zionist public relations campaign, which grew by leaps and bounds in the mid-1940s.

By 1947 the American Zionist movement had nearly one million members, an extraordinary increase from the previous decade. It controlled the American Jewish community at large and Silver and his allies used the huge, foreboding shadow of the Holocaust to rally support for the Jewish State. Zionist leaders cast the British, previously viewed as a benevolent benefactor, as an accessory in the slaughter of six million Jews.

The American delegation at the United Nations pushed for the resolution calling for a partition of Palestine into Jewish and Arab states. It was adopted in November of 1947, six months before the British mandate over Palestine ended. On May 14, 1948 a provisional Jewish government declared Israeli independence. President Truman recognized the new State only eleven minutes after British rule came to an end.

Just as it had in the Brandeis era, the American Zionist movement gained increased support and influence through educating the American public and by eliciting financial and political support for the Jewish settlers—not by calling for *Aliyah*. Again, Zionist leaders used American rhetoric and American political devices to mobilize around what they considered an American campaign. They used non-religious appeals to convince non-Jews that the only adequate response to the victimization of the Jews in the Holocaust was to support a Jewish state in Palestine.

Israel's establishment as an independent nation forced American Zionism to completely rethink its role and mission. The always inadequate financial support that Zionist organizations had provided to the settlers was no longer an issue because of the millions of dollars in aid to Israel provided by the American government. Zionism became institutionalized within the United States after 1948 with most Jews supporting Israel's existence. Aside from Hadassah, which continued to have active programs, the older Zionist organizations seemed to lose focus after the war and their membership declined drastically.

In the 1950s and through most of the 1960s, American Jews, as well as many non-Jews, put massive resources into support for Israel. They funneled their financial support to large Jewish organizations such as the United Jewish Appeal rather than the older and smaller, specifically Zionist, groups. In addition, while the American government's endorsement of a Zionist state had never been purely altruistic, its support for Israel in the 1950s and 1960s became a core component of its own foreign and military policy agenda. Going further than Brandeis could ever have imagined, a narrowly defined Zionism took on a new dimension as a mainstream American foreign policy rather than a fringe Jewish concern. Despite dissenting voices, Israel's security and survival became intertwined with American business and government in the post-war years. Conversely, the **American-Israel Public Affairs Committee** (AIPAC), lobbying on behalf of the Jewish state, argued that support for Israel was crucial precisely because its interests were so intimately connected to those of the United States.

As was the case during the Brandeis years but on a far broader scale, American Zionism benefited throughout most of the next three decades from its extraordinarily close association with the goals and values of the government. Most Americans saw Israel as an underdog fighting against hostile Arab countries bent upon destroying the new nation and its people. They perceived Israel's victory in the 1967 Six-Day War as especially heroic. By the same token, Zionism equaled nothing more than support for the Jewish state in the eyes of most Americans and even most American Jews. Any association of Zionism with a broader notion of cultural or spiritual transformation had faded.

The late 1970s saw attitudes toward Israel begin to shift subtly as the Western press accused the Israeli government of imposing unnecessarily harsh conditions on Palestinians living under their control. Israel was viewed by some Americans as unnecessarily aggressive. Because the Zionist movement was tied to Israel's acting in the image of how Americans perceived their own country in its early years, manifestations of violence created increased criticism of Israel and of Zionism and its meaning and role in the modern world. Among some more liberal and radical groups, Zionism became negatively associated with a perception of Israel's policies toward its Arab population as belligerent. Nevertheless, Israel receives more military and economic aid from the United States than any other nation—a policy that is supported by the majority of Americans, Jews and non-Jews alike.

While American Jews continued to rally to the defense of Israel, the relationship between American Zionists and the Jewish state experienced considerable friction in these years. Israelis adamantly held to the idea that true Zionism meant *Aliyah*. Israel leaders also angered many American Zionists by rejecting the notion that Jewish groups in the Diaspora had parity with those in Israel.

Just as earlier in the century, Zionist societies continued to evolve and send new groups of willing pioneers to live in the Holy Land, with the movement reaching its peak in 1969, when five thousand American Jews made *Aliyah*. By the late 1970s and early 1980s even that movement had changed. As Israel became more established and more militarily powerful, the nature of settlement into the region shifted. While the move to Zion still attracted idealists, the older utopian, collective, and socialist dreams of the *Kibbutzim* began to be countered by a new breed of settlers who saw their pilgrimage to the Holy Land as primarily concerned with contributing to the defense of greater Israel against its enemies.

The Israeli government's policies in the 1980s encouraging settlement of new Jewish families in the West Bank contributed to enormous tensions between these newcomers and the Palestinians who viewed the land as belonging to them. The majority of settlers in the West Bank viewed themselves as Zionists carrying out a mission and viewed their Palestinian Arab neighbors with suspicion and fear. Conversely, Palestinians saw these Zionist settlers as symbolic of their subjugation at the hands of the Israel government and considered them appropriate targets for threats and attacks. Tensions reached a head during the Palestinian Intifada (uprising) of the late 1980s and continues to be a major source of division among American Jews as well as among Israeli citizens and the Zionist nation's two political parties.

Most Zionists making *Aliyah* in the modern era choose, however, to settle within Israel's pre-1967 borders and they represent all spectrums of the political compass. For many American Jews, the spiritual pull toward the land, and the country, and a desire to connect more deeply with their religious and cultural history continues to inform their commitment to creating a new life for themselves in Zion. The vast majority of American Jews sympathetic to the Zionist idea still choose to stay in the United States and live as Americans. Thus the official American Zionist position has changed very little since the Brandeis era.

As a political movement, American Zionism has been enormously effective, considering its modest beginnings. Pivotal leaders such as Brandeis, Weizmann, Wise, Silver, and the women of Hadassah transformed a little-known ideology into an essential part of the thinking of American Jews. Despite the horrors of the Holocaust, the post–World War II commitment to establishing the Jewish state would not have occurred without the enormous groundswell of political activism generated by the American Zionist movement. Since 1948 support for the Zionist state has been a strong unifying point for the vast majority of American Jews, despite any other differences they might have. With the success of Israel, the ideals of cultural and spiritual regeneration that animated the American Zionist movement before World War II have lost some of their strength. The success of American Zionism ultimately contributed to leaving behind some of what it made it unique.

ZIONIST ORGANIZATION OF AMERICA

The Zionist Organization of America began in 1898 as the Federation of American Zionists (FAZ), the first national Zionist movement in the United States. It published a monthly magazine, *The Maccabean* (later *The New Palestine* and, after Israel's creation, *The American Zionist*). The FAZ's youth movement, Young Judea, was organized in 1909. It later evolved into the Intercollegiate Zionist Association, then Avukah, and, today, Masada. The ZOA's women's division, **Hadassah**, was established in 1912 (it later became an independent organization).

The acceptance by the prominent attorney **Louis D.**

Brandeis of the leadership of American Zionism in 1914 proved to be a turning point in the movement's history. Brandeis's stature, especially after he was named to the Supreme Court in 1918, made the movement acceptable to many Jews who previously feared Zionism could compromise their status as American citizens. This, combined with the enthusiasm surrounding the issuance of the Balfour Declaration and the conquest of Palestine by the British, swelled the FAZ's membership ranks.

After visiting Palestine in 1919 Brandeis became convinced that the FAZ—now renamed the Zionist Organization of America—should focus on raising funds for specific development projects in Eretz Yisrael, igniting a clash with World Zionist Organization president Chaim Weizmann. Many in the ZOA favored continuing traditional Zionist political and cultural activities in the Diaspora and supported Weizmann, resulting in the ouster of Brandeis and his supporters in 1921.

The Palestinian Arab riots of 1929 and England's shift away from Zionism sparked the return of the Brandeis faction to the ZOA. The ZOA's membership swelled as the rise of Nazism in Germany aroused increased sympathy for Zionism in the American Jewish community during the 1930s. After the outbreak of World War II, the ZOA leadership was initially reluctant to criticize Britain during wartime and fearful of accusations that they were trying to drag America into overseas conflicts. In the face of escalating Nazi persecutions the ZOA leadership organized the 1942 Biltmore conference, which adopted more forceful language in its articulation of Zionist demands and contributed to the emerging militant mood in the American Zionist community. ZOA leaders who still favored a more cautious and less anti-British approach were voted out in favor of an activist faction headed by Rabbi **Abba Hillel Silver**.

Silver led a nationwide political action effort that mobilized a large segment of the American Jewish community as well as many American Christians on behalf of the demand for Jewish statehood. By the late 1940s, the ZOA's membership had reached an all-time high of some 250,000. Silver's lobbying efforts won widespread support for Zionism in the U.S. Congress, increased the pressure on England to leave Palestine, and helped win U.S. support for the 1947 United Nations plan to partition Palestine into Jewish and Arab states. Although unsuccessful in its bid to end the U.S. arms embargo on the Middle East, the ZOA's pressure campaign did play a role in President Truman's decision to recognize the new State of Israel just minutes after its creation.

In common with other American Zionist organizations, the ZOA began to decline, in both membership and political influence, after the creation of Israel. With the movement's primary goal achieved, many American Jews lost interest in Zionist activities. The emergence of the **American Israel Public Affairs Committee** (AIPAC) in 1954 and the Conference of Presidents of Major American Jewish Organizations in 1955 usurped the ZOA's previous position as the Jewish community's voice in Washington. The ZOA devoted an increasing share of its attention to its philanthropic projects in Israel—ZOA House, a cultural center in Tel Aviv (established in 1953), and *Kfar* Silver, a vocational training campus near Ashkelon (established in 1955).

The ZOA experienced a revival in the mid-1990s after adopting activist tactics and focusing on the issue of Palestinian Arab violations of the Israel-PLO accords. This approach attracted many new members and gained the organization growing influence in Washington.

For Further Reading

See Appendix 2 for a bibliography of general reference books about Jews and the Jewish experience in America. All of the volumes listed there include information about Zionism in America and the relations between Israel and the United States.

Cohen, Naomi W. *American Jews and the Zionist Idea.* New York: KTAV Publishing, 1975.

Cohen, Steven M. *The Attitude of American Jews toward Israel and Israelis.* New York, 1983.

Feingold, Henry. *The Politics of Rescue: The Roosevelt Administration and the Holocaust, 1938–1945.* New Brunswick, N.J.: Rutgers University Press, 1970.

Feinstein, Marnin. *American Zionism, 1884–1904*. New York: Herzl Press, 1965.

Ganin, Zvi. *Truman, American Jewry, and Israel, 1945–1948*. New York: Holmes and Meir, 1979.

Grose, Peter. *Israel in the Mind of America*. New York: Alfred A. Knopf, 1983.

Halperin, Samuel. *The Political World of American Zionism*. Detroit, Mich.: Wayne State University Press, 1961.

Meyer, Isadore, Ed. *Early History of Zionism in America*. New York: Theodor Herzl Foundation, 1958.

Postal, Bernard, and Henry W. Levy. *And the Hills Shouted for Joy: The Day Israel Was Born*. Philadelphia: David McKay Company, Inc., 1975.

Sachar, Howard M. *A History of Israel from the Rise of Zionism to Our Time*. New York: Alfred A. Knopf, 1976.

Shapiro, Yonathan. *Leadership of the American Zionist Organization, 1897–1930*. Urbana, Ill.: University of Illinois Press, 1971.

Urofsky, Melvin. *American Zionism from Herzl to the Holocaust*. Garden City, N.Y.: Anchor Press, 1975.

_____. *We are One! American Jewry and Israel*. New York: Anchor Press, 1978.

Wyman, David. *The Abandonment of the Jews: America and the Holocaust, 1941–1945*. New York: Pantheon Books, 1985.

Part 6

Business, Labor, and Finance

OVERVIEW

It is not difficult to make generalizations about Jewish Americans in business. It is only difficult to make true generalizations. There is no doubt that, from the early days of the colonies, Jews were limited in their participation in the American economy. They had to carve out niches for themselves in a world that was dominated by Gentiles who did not welcome them. When they were successful, they were often accepted as suppliers and customers by people who rejected them as dinner companions or fellow club members. Nonetheless, Jewish Americans have made a tremendous contribution as merchants, financiers, and leaders of America's labor movement.

The earliest Jewish contribution to business in America was mercantile. The largely Sephardic immigrants usually had resources and connections that the young country could benefit by. Later immigrants, usually from Germany, came without resources and built their stores and fortunes on the foundations of a peddler's pack or a pushcart. Finally, the Eastern European immigrants of the latter part of the nineteenth century came in such numbers and with so few material belongings that tens of thousands of them had to take jobs in the factories created by their forerunners, as well as Gentile industrialists. These immigrants not only flooded into the garment industry and other manufacturing plants, they took the lead in organizing unions.

Most of these union organizers were socialists. Their convictions were so strong and far-reaching that they created an alternative to traditional religious beliefs and customs for many Jewish Americans. Many worked in strictly Jewish unions, but cultivated a sense among their members that they should yearn for and work toward, not the Messiah, but the millennium when the proletariat would rule. Others worked in the larger labor movement, turning away from traditional Jewish beliefs in favor of a socialist ideal.

Countering these workers were the entrepreneurs who created department stores, investment firms, and motion picture studios. They made their way into businesses not already dominated entirely by Christians and made their mark on American society. Their names—Gimbel, **Straus**, **Schiff**, **Goldwyn**, **Spielberg**— are part of America's legend. Although the board rooms of the largest Fortune 500 corporations continue to be dominated by a Christian elite, American Jews have become extraordinarily successful in the world of business and finance. As entrepreneurs, merchants, investment bankers, and media managers, Jews have become middle class, affluent, and influential in the United States.

During the many different historical eras of the United States, Jewish Americans have proved their skills and proficiency in developing flourishing small businesses that grew into classic examples of achievement and enterprise. At the same time, Jewish involvement in the financial world has sometimes been the object of anti-Semitic derision by critics of all ideological stripes, who have railed against supposed conspiracies to undermine the country by Jewish bankers and financiers, especially during times of economic depression. Despite these obstacles, Jews have had a deep and profound impact on American culture and society through their participation in the business world.

ABRAMOWITZ, BESSIE (1889–1970)

Labor Union Leader

"I was Bessie Abramowitz before he was Sidney Hillman." She was indeed. As a fifteen-year-old immigrant button sewer in Chicago, Bessie Abramowitz organized a shop committee to protest conditions in the garment factory where she worked. This began her lifelong career as an activist in the labor movement that has sometimes been overshadowed by the fame of her husband **Sidney Hillman**.

Abramowitz led an initial walkout in 1910 of sixteen women at the Hart, Schaffner, and Marx factory that eventually turned into a successful mass strike of 8,000 shop workers. The strike led to both union recognition and increased wages. She helped lead the campaign for garment workers in Chicago, New York, and other cities to break away from the conservative United Garment Workers to form the Amalgamated Clothing Workers of America, in which she served on the executive board while her future husband became the new union's president.

Bessie Hillman later did extensive volunteer work for the Women's Trade Union League; served as education director of the Laundry Workers Joint Board, an affiliate of the Amalgamated; and continued to organize workers in Pennsylvania, Ohio, New York, and Connecticut. During World War II, while her husband solidified tight political bonds between labor and the Roosevelt administration, she helped lead the union's war efforts and was appointed by Governor **Herbert Lehman** of New York to the advisory board of the New York Office of Price Administration.

After her husband's death in 1946, the Amalgamated hired Bessie as a paid vice president in charge of the union's education program. In this position she spoke at conferences; organized summer schools for rank-and-file leaders; and pushed the union to work for stronger efforts on behalf of civil rights, world peace, and economic justice. She remained active in union and civic affairs until her death in 1970.

AGRICULTURE

Although most people think of American Jewish history as the story of an urban-dwelling population, Jews have important roots as farmers and agrarian workers in the United States. Unlike the vast majority of farm families in the United States, however, the Jewish agricultural legacy is more tied to group than to individual settlement. From the early nineteenth century, with the creation of Ararat in upstate New York, Jewish colonization in rural America became intimately connected to a visionary and sometimes utopian vision of building self-sustaining agricultural communities. With the *Am Olam* movement of Eastern European immigrants during the turn of the century years, Jewish experiments in group farming peaked and achieved their greatest successes in southern New Jersey, financed by philanthropic organizations that exercised considerable control over the day-to-day operations of the settlements. The most notable twentieth-century agrarian success story, the Toms River Community of Jewish farmers, encompassed as many as 360 families in Depression-era America.

The Jewish connection to the land goes back to biblical times, and Jews remained an agricultural people even after they left the Holy Land in the medieval period. Talmudic law and Jewish religious practices are filled with agrarian references, and the cycle of the holidays is largely based on the ancient agricultural calendar. Jews have also historically turned to farming both as a means of survival and as a mechanism to normalize their role in the greater society. In Czarist Russia, thousands of Jewish families subsisted as farmers despite government repression and marginalization.

The earliest Jewish immigrants in the United States embraced the rural frontier ideals of Jeffersonian America and explored the possibilities of group farming. In 1825, influential playwright and politician Mordecai Noah established Ararat in upstate New York as a Jewish farming collective where his brethren could "till the soil, reap the harvest, and raise flocks." Although this experiment was short lived, German Jewish members of New York City's Anshe Chesed congregation established the Sholem farm colony near Ellenville, New York, which lasted until the depression of the mid-1840s.

In the 1880s, a group of Russian Jews struggling with the racism and bigotry of the European Diaspora organized themselves as the *Am Olam* (eternal or world people) movement with the goal of promoting group agricultural settlement on farm land in the United States. Adopting the slogan "Work on the land [for] the spiritual and physical revival of our people," several new Russian Jewish immigrant communities sprung up in various parts of rural America financed by established groups such as the Franco-Jewish Alliance, the American Hebrew Emigrant Aid Society, and the Baron de Hirsch Fund.

The idea of rural colonization swept through the Jewish world of the late nineteenth and early twentieth centuries for a variety of reasons. In one respect, western agrarian settlement represented a nostalgia for the biblical idea of Israel, but without the denominational controversy aroused by Palestine settlements of the same era. At the same time, because farming was traditionally viewed as an honorable endeavor by Americans, rural settlement also took the form of a strategic attempt to curtail anti-Jewish and anti-immigrant sentiment. German Jewish philanthropists embraced these settlements as a model of self-help and as a tool for enabling poor immigrants to "stand on their own two feet."

At Catahoula Parish, Louisiana, four hundred miles north of New Orleans, the "First Agricultural Colony of Russian Israelites in America" was incorporated in 1881. Despite their idealism and lofty ambitions, none of the original forty-two settlers had any farming experience and all their hard labor proved insufficient to surmount the flooding that destroyed their cotton and corn crops. The project was abandoned and its members left for either urban employment or other Jewish farm ventures.

Other *Am Olam* groups in rural Kansas, Michigan, Oregon, Utah, South Dakota, and South Carolina had

The Baron de Hirsch Fund was one of several philanthropic organizations that provided money to allow Jews in the United States to purchase land and equipment in order to become farmers. This portrait is from their archives. (Courtesy of the American Jewish Historical Society, Waltham, Massachusetts and New York, New York)

both more tools and greater means of moral as well as practical support. Renowned Reform rabbi, **Isaac Mayer Wise**, who pleaded in his journal *The American Israelite* to "Let us make as many Jewish free farmers as can be" directly assisted the Beersheba colony in Kansas. Nevertheless, *Am Olam* settlers faced obstacles such as poor soil, lack of water, wood, and other materials, prairie fires, and distance from transportation and markets. They also struggled with ideological and religious differences among themselves, which contributed to communal disintegration.

In rural southern New Jersey, and particularly Salem, Cumberland, and Cape May counties, Jewish farming communities achieved far more success and

longevity. Although these South Jersey colonies had their share of nationalists, socialists, agrarians, and radicals of all stripes, the majority of the settlers were driven more by a desire for economic opportunity than by any ideological agenda. Unlike the Palestinian colonies, the major goals of the New Jersey settlements tended to be social and economic integration rather than national or cultural revival. Generally, the organizational sponsors, rather than the immigrant intellectuals or radicals, controlled the development of the colonies. Policy decisions usually came from above by those whose priorities of Americanizing the immigrant required lessons in private enterprise rather than socialism. At the same time, the new arrivals found in the New Jersey colonies a genuine training ground and an opportunity to work with others toward both collective and individual goals.

The earliest settlement, known as the Alliance, began in the spring of 1882 when nearly four hundred Eastern European Jewish immigrants cleared fifteen acres of land for family farms in a desolate, overgrown region of Vineland, New Jersey. These pioneers faced severe obstacles in their early years, including the difficulty in getting sufficient farm implements, draft animals, drinking water, and cooking supplies. Because they could not support themselves on the income generated from the crops alone, these immigrants, including mothers and children, trekked long distances to seek out jobs picking cranberries, strawberries, and blackberries. Geographically isolated, these farm communities lacked access to medical care and often had to result to home remedies for severe medical problems.

Despite these struggles, the community persevered and new ones emerged in rural southern New Jersey with names like Carmel, Rosenhayn, Norma, Mizpah, Hebron, and Zion. One of the greatest success stories was Woodbine, founded in Cape May County in 1891 and later incorporated as a township. Billed by the Educational Alliance, a key financial backer, as the "first self-governed Jewish community since the fall of Jerusalem." Woodbine was planned to provide a balance of both farms and factories to enable immigrants to augment their income during difficult times. In addition to fifty homesteads built on thirty-acre farm plots, Woodbine included a three-story shirt factory. In 1894, Woodbine established its Baron de Hirsch Agricultural School, which provided an education in the agricultural sciences and experience in the school's model dairy farm, orchards, and nurseries to a new generation of Jewish immigrant children.

The Norma community also achieved recognition for its corn, fruit, and sweet potatoes. It became self-sufficient in agricultural production by cultivating grapes and forming a marketing cooperative that helped promote their grape juice and wine in stores throughout Philadelphia and New York. Rosenhayn achieved similar success paying their mortgage by selling chickens, eggs, and, especially, strawberries. They became so proficient at cultivating the berries that production reached record annual shipments by the turn of the century.

Jewish agrarianism in twentieth-century America required adaptation to a new set of changes. Urbanization and technological changes made it even more crucial for those living on the land to find new ways to support themselves, and poultry farming and egg production became increasingly popular. Although Jewish farmers continued to attempt to balance self-help with community, a greater number embraced individual homesteads rather than group settlements. In some locations, such as the Catskills, agrarian communities supplemented their incomes through the creation of country inns for vacationers.

The most well known of the twentieth-century Jewish agricultural settlements, the Toms River Community of Jewish Farmers, was organized in the 1920s by sixty families through the guidance of the Jewish Agricultural Society. Although some of the settlers financed their purchases through loans from the Society, many drew exclusively from their own savings. They became a collective to lower costs through cooperative purchasing. During the height of the Depression of the 1930s, the community expanded sixfold and even absorbed European refugees. Community residents also collected funds for the **Joint Distribution Committee** and organized protests against Nazi terror in Germany and anti-Jewish boycotts in Poland. Just as the German Jews of the Educational Alliance provided financial assistance for the earlier settlements of Eastern European immigrant farmers, so, too, did the descendants of the next generation of settlers assist the new refugee population.

After World War II the number of American farmers precipitously declined and most of the earlier settlers moved to towns and cities. Although the Jewish agrarian population never topped 100,000, its frequently neglected history represents a heritage of immigrant idealism and a pioneering vision of rural self-sufficiency that is rooted in both American and Jewish historical traditions.

ALINSKY, SAUL (1909–1972)

Labor organizer, community activist

Saul Alinsky was born in Chicago, Illinois, on January 30, 1909. His initial training was in archeology and criminology. When he was twenty-nine years old he became involved in community organizing, creating the groundbreaking Back of the Yards Council for the working-class Chicago neighborhood of the same name. Two years later, in 1940, he created the Industrial Areas Foundation, which trained future activists in organizing techniques.

In addition to his work training community and labor organizations throughout the country, Alinsky created an important model for African American inner city community activists when he founded The Woodlawn Organization of Chicago. He also wrote several books including *Reveille for Radicals (1946)*, *The Professional Radical* (1970), *Rules for Radicals* (1971), and a biography of John L. Lewis (1949). He was a tireless organizer until his death on June 12, 1972 in Carmel, California.

ANNENBERG, WALTER H. (1908–)

Publisher, diplomat, philanthropist

The publisher of some of America's most popular magazines, Walter H. Annenberg was born on March 13, 1908 in Milwaukee, Wisconsin. He took his father's Triangle Publications, which was based on the *Daily Racing Form*, and built it into a publishing empire that includes *Seventeen* magazine, *TV Guide*, and *The Inquirer*. He was also a major shareholder in the Pennsylvania Railroad and the Campbell Soup Company. In 1988, he sold Triangle to Australian media mogul Rupert Murdoch.

From 1969 to 1975 Annenberg served as ambassador to the United Kingdom. His wife, Leonore, was chief of protocol under President Ronald Reagan. Annenberg's philanthropic activities are especially impressive.

In 1991 he willed his large collection of Impressionist and Post-Impressionist paintings to New York City's Metropolitan Museum of Art and made a $10 million pledge to the Los Angeles County Museum of Art. He currently focuses his philanthropy on education, dedicating large sums to making good schools available to those most in need of help, particularly the urban poor. In 1993, he announced a $500 million contribution to public education reform. He has also contributed $50 million to the United Negro College Fund; $150 million to the Corporation for Public Broadcasting; and $1.7 million to the rebuilding of black churches that were torched by arsonists in 1996. Walter Annenberg's charitable contributions to date total more than $1 billion. He is considered by some to be the most important philanthropist in America since the days of Andrew Carnegie and John D. Rockefeller.

BAMBERGER, LOUIS (1855–1944)

Merchant, philanthropist

Prominent businessman Louis Bamberger was born in Baltimore, Maryland in 1855. As a young man, he moved to New York and, in 1892, founded a small department store with his brother-in-law, Felix Fuld. Guided by Bamberger's advanced techniques of marketing and publicity, L. Bamberger and Company grew quickly. In 1929, the store was sold to R. H. Macy, but Bamberger remained president and was well known for his unusually generous policies toward employees.

Louis Bamberger also owned a radio station in Newark, New Jersey and was particularly active in philanthropic activities in that city. In 1930, he and his sister, Caroline Bamberger Fuld, founded the Institute for Advanced Study at Princeton University, an enterprise dedicated to the support of research and scholarship in a wide variety of fields. The Institute became the scholarly home to some of the most significant thinkers of the twentieth century, including more than a dozen Nobel Laureates who have been either faculty members or residents, including scientist **Albert Einstein**.

BARUCH, BERNARD MANNES
(1870–1965)

Financier, philanthropist, presidential advisor

Powerful, influential Bernard Baruch was born in 1870 in Camden, South Carolina into a Jewish Portuguese-Spanish family. When he was ten years old, the family moved to New York City. Baruch graduated from the College of the City of New York in 1889. Before he was thirty, he had made a fortune speculating on the New York Stock Exchange. During World War I, President Woodrow Wilson appointed Baruch a gov-

A self-made millionaire, Bernard M. Baruch served as an advisor to seven American Presidents. He is shown here in 1926 presenting the Williamsburg Settlement Award to Sadie Annenberg, who was active in many of the same philanthropic causes he was. (Private Collection)

ernment advisor and, later, chairman of the War Industries Board. That position gave Baruch tremendous power over American industrial production. At the war's end, he participated in the peace conference that resulted in the Treaty of Versailles.

Baruch continued to be an advisor to presidents through the administrations of Warren Harding, Calvin Coolidge, and Herbert Hoover. When World War II began, he consulted with President Franklin Roosevelt about mobilizing American resources. After the war, President Harry Truman made him the first United States representative on the United Nations Atomic Energy Commission.

Having broken with Truman for policy reasons, Baruch supported Dwight Eisenhower's presidency in 1952, but was again advising a Democratic president when John F. Kennedy took office. He wrote a number of books, including two parts of his autobiography, before he died in 1965.

BELLANCA, DOROTHY JACOBS
(1894–1946)

Labor leader

Labor leader Dorothy Jacobs Bellanca was born in Latvia on August 10, 1894 and immigrated to Baltimore, Maryland when she was six. She began working in a Baltimore sweatshop when she was thirteen and started organizing her fellow workers when she was fifteen. At first affiliated with the United Garment Workers of America, in 1914 Bellanca took her local union over to the newly formed Amalgamated Clothing Workers of America. She participated in the founding convention of the ACWA, became secretary of the Joint Board, and founded the union's Education Department. In 1916, she became the only woman on the General Executive Board and, later the same year, was elected vice president. In 1917, she was named the ACWA's women's organizer.

Throughout the 1920s Bellanca continued to be a powerful influence in trade unionism. In the 1930s she helped to found the American Labor Party (1936) and served on Franklin Roosevelt's Maternal and

Child Welfare Committee (1938). During World War II she worked with many organizations and committees, including the Women's Policy Committee of the War Manpower Commission. Dorothy Bellanca spent her career ensuring that employers and union leadership met the needs of female workers. She was also active in promoting racial harmony and equal treatment of minorities. She died on August 16, 1946.

BLAUSTEIN, LOUIS (1869–1937)

Entrepreneur

Louis Blaustein, the founder of Amoco Oil, was born in Lithuania (then Prussia) on January 20, 1869. He immigrated with his family to the United States in 1888, when he was nineteen. He began to support his family by selling kerosene door-to-door. Four years later he became a manager of the Standard Oil Company of New Jersey. In 1910, Blaustein left Standard Oil, and, with his son Jacob, founded the American Oil Company (later called Amoco) in Baltimore, Maryland. The company incorporated in 1922, the same year Blaustein incorporated the Lord Baltimore Filling Stations. In 1933, the American Oil Company merged with Pan Am Petroleum & Transport Company and its subsidiaries.

Blaustein served as the chairman of the board of the American Oil Company, the Mexican Petroleum Corporation, and the Lord Baltimore Filling Stations, Inc. and as president for several of their subsidiaries. He also developed the first high-test gasoline and invented the precursor to the railroad tank car. He died in Baltimore, Maryland on July 27, 1937. Today, Amoco Oil is worth $1.3 billion. The Louis and Henrietta Blaustein Foundation continues to give money to various Jewish causes in addition to funding higher education and science programs.

BRONFMAN, EDGAR M. (1929–)

Businessman, president of the World Jewish Congress

Edgar M. Bronfman, chairman of The Seagram Company Ltd., was born into a wealthy family in a suburb of Montreal in 1929. His father had immigrated to Canada from Russia as a child and, with his brother, built a thriving distillery. The Bronfmans practiced their religion at home, but young Edgar was sent to Protestant schools. After attending Williams College and McGill University, he moved to New York and became a United States citizen. In the early 1970s, he began his involvement with the World Jewish Congress (WJC). He soon became chairman of the North American section. He was elected president in 1981.

Under Bronfman's leadership, the WJC worked to gain freedom for Jews in the Soviet Union and exposed Kurt Waldheim's Nazi past. Most recently, he has been at the forefront of the effort to recover the assets Jews had on deposit in German banks when the Nazi Party took power. His constant communication with devout Jews finally awakened his interest in the Jewish religion. In 1996, he published his autobiography, *The Making of a Jew*, which is dedicated "to the memory of my grandparents, who yearned to be free and braved the harsh realities of western Canada to bring up their children in the New World, and to the memory of my parents, whose lives were an inspiration." In 1998 he published another memoir, *Good Spirits: The Making of a Businessman*.

BURNS, ARTHUR FRANK (1904–1987)

Economist

Arthur Burns was a key economic advisor to American Presidents from Eisenhower to Jimmy Carter. Austrian-born, Burns earned his Ph.D. in economics at Columbia University in 1934, while teaching at Rutgers. He served as director of research for the National Bureau of Economic Research from 1945 to 1953, and returned to the Bureau four years later as its president, a position he held for a decade.

In 1953, Burns was appointed chair of the Council of Economic Advisors, a position he held for three years. He was called back to Washington repeatedly by Presidents Nixon, Ford, and Carter, serving as chair of the Federal Reserve Board from 1970 to 1978. Burns was a pragmatic Keynsian, manipulating the money supply to combat inflation and recession alternately. The former was a particular bugbear of his, and he was one of the founders of the Committee to Fight Inflation in 1980. It is likely that his Keynsianism was the reason that the Reagan Administration, dominated by supply-siders, chose to give him an ambassadorial appointment (West Germany, 1981–1985), rather than utilize his experience and knowledge in the economic sphere.

BUSINESS AND FINANCE

The issue of Jews in American business is a thorny one. Throughout the history of the Diaspora, in virtually all European countries and colonies, Jews have been restricted to business as a way of keeping body and soul together. Denied the right to own land in a fundamentally agrarian world, Jews became artisans and merchants when they could and moneylenders when they had to. Then, having done the best they could within the limitations imposed by Christians, they found themselves accused by Christians of being mercenary, greedy, and concerned only with the material things in life.

When Jews immigrated to the United States, they came with the skills they had developed over centuries of business activity and the stereotypes connected with those skills. In the colonial era, Jews were sometimes welcomed because they were people of business. The welcome was not unalloyed with prejudice, and the colonies benefited from Jewish savvy and generosity. A small number of relatively well-to-do Sephardic Jews were active participants in trade and commerce, helping to set up New York Board of Stockholders, which later became the New York Stock Exchange. Haym Solomon, known as the leading bond broker of the American Revolution, extended personal loans to many eminent individuals and members of the Continental Congress and sold bonds that established America's credit in European markets. At the same time, Abigail Minis, one of the first Jewish businesswomen and landowners, operated a well-known tavern in Savannah and helped supply provisions for the Continental line, Georgia militia, and French forces in the area.

The German Jews who began arriving in the United States in the 1830s had a somewhat different background and orientation. Fewer were already prosperous before they reached American shores. Most began with little in the way of material resources but, again, they had skills, experience, and a long business heritage. In the words of Leon Harris in *Merchant Princes*, "The Kaiser and the czar made more merchants than the Harvard School of Business or Pennsylvania's Wharton School—men who preferred peddling in the coldest county in New England or the hottest humid parish of Louisiana, preferred even the risk of being scalped in Arizona, to serving as a private in the Prussian army or as a victim of Cossack amusements." The traditional success story for these Jewish Americans began with a peddler's pack or even a tray to carry door to door. Success came when the pack became a storefront, and the success was more than financial. In smaller towns, the proprietor of the dry goods store was also likely to fulfill other roles, among them postmaster, telegraph operator, and bookseller. The family of the storekeeper had a certain visibility and, often, even prominence.

A few went far beyond that storefront, building some of the great retail stores in this country. William Filene went from peddler to owner of Filene's Department Stores in Boston. His son Edward, or E. A., created the automatic markdown system that made Filene's Basement famous around the world, introduced the credit union to the United States and fought for its legal acceptance. He founded the Chamber of Commerce in Boston and then nationally and internationally. Another peddler, Lazarus Straus, leased space in the basement of a store owned by a man named Macy. Thirteen years later, he bought the business and Macy's Department Stores went on to become one of New York's legendary rivals, Macy's and Gimbel's. (A few decades later, Hattie Carnegie rose from her position as a teenage messenger girl at Macy's with a wardrobe of three blouses and one skirt to preside over an $8 million fashion empire that included her own retail store for dresses in New York.)

The Gimbel's half of the rivalry was founded by Adam Gimbel, who began as a peddler like the others,

Bronx Boys in a Bottle Battle

This headline from the August 21, 1998 issue of the *Forward* sounds like the story to follow will be about fighting in the streets, but, in fact, it is about two "nice Jewish boys" who are among the most successful fashion trend-setters of the late twentieth century. Calvin Klein is claiming in a suit in Federal Court that Ralph Lauren's new perfume, Romance, copies not only the fragrance but also the bottle design of his scent Eternity. Jews clearly have reached the pinnacle of success in the American cosmetics business!

but then went to a trading post. He established such a reputation for integrity that one of his customers once dropped a bag of gold coins on his counter without counting them and told Gimbel to credit him with the amount inside, saying, "Why should I bother to count money given to Adam Gimbel?" After Gimbel conquered the Milwaukee department store market, his sons went on to found branches in Philadelphia and New York.

A comprehensive list of Jewish retail giants would be too long for this space, but mention must be made of the Kaufmanns in Philadelphia, the Riches in Atlanta, and the Goldsmiths in Memphis. Further west there were the Texas Marcuses, the Arizona Goldwaters, the Oregon Meiers and Franks, and California's Magnins. Of course, there was also **Levi Strauss** who went to San Francisco in 1850 at the age of twenty and began selling prospectors a tough overall made from blue canvas with a heavily stitched pocket. It was the precursor to the blue jean or "Levi" that eventually made Strauss wealthy and famous. These and hundreds of other Jewish Americans found in selling cotton, ribbons, and hats the path to participation in the American Dream.

Not all successful German Jewish businesspeople were in retail, of course. Mayer Lehman established a large cotton and banking firm. Meyer Guggenheim was a mining magnate. Adolph Lewisohn owned a copper mine. Henry Morgenthau was a financier and diplomat. By the mid-nineteenth century, investment banking was growing as a force in an increasingly

urban America and many former German Jewish merchants began their own firms. The families involved in this new enterprise included the Seligmans, the Lehman brothers, Abraham Kuhn and Solomon Loeb, Philip Heidelbach, and Marcus Goldman. Kuhn and Loeb operated general stores in Indianapolis and Cincinnati before entering the banking business. In 1867, they opened a private banking office in New York that grew rapidly over the next two decades and eventually rose to be second in prestige only to the Gentile firm of J. P. Morgan. Marcus Goldman left peddling in 1869 to become a dealer in commercial paper and in 1882 formed a partnership with his son-in-law, Samuel Sachs. By the early 1900s, the firm had begun specializing in the underwriting of retail store securities, becoming the leader in the field after World War I. In the Progressive Era, these former peddlers composed the core of America's German Jewish elite.

No one individual epitomized this small group of wealthy Jewish immigrants better than Frankfurt-born **Jacob Schiff**, who became one of the nation's most influential financiers in the late nineteenth century. Schiff was a key figure in the re-organization of the Union Pacific Railroad and also floated a $200 million bond to help Japan defeat Russia in their 1905 war. The second generation of German Jewish success in the world of high finance is well-represented by **Bernard Baruch**. Born in South Carolina, Baruch reaped tremendous profits from his investments in railroads and other industries at the turn of the century and quickly became a millionaire financier without starting his own investment bank. In World War I, President Woodrow Wilson appointed Baruch chairman of the War Industries Board where the self-made entrepreneur coordinated the nation's entire industrial establishment.

German Jews also developed manufacturing businesses in several American cities. Increasingly, their employees, especially in the garment industry, were their Jewish brethren from Eastern Europe whom they sometimes viewed with disdain for being too tied to old-world Jewish traditions. In addition, German Jews also ventured into the real estate business and sometimes owned the very tenements that the new generation of Jews was forced to live in, exacerbating the tensions between the two groups.

The twentieth century has seen the growth of great business empires founded and maintained by Jewish Americans. No longer tied to either retail or finance, Jewish family fortunes have been built on diverse foundations and show imagination and flexibility.

The Newhouse family owns and operates a communications empire that began in 1922 when teenaged Samuel I. Newhouse (born Solomon Neuhaus) got a job with Hyman Lazarus' *Bayonne Times* in New Jersey. Within a few years, Newhouse was a partner and the company was expanding. In 1932, after gaining financial control, Newhouse began accumulating a chain of papers that eventually became the largest privately owned chain in the country. In the late 1950s, he acquired Condé Nast, with its prestigious *Vanity Fair* and *Vogue*. By the 1990s, the Newhouses owned twenty-nine newspapers, fifteen magazines, the publishing companies Alfred Knopf and Random House (which they sold in 1998), and a number of cable television companies.

The Pritzker family business began in Chicago in 1902 when Nicholas Pritzker, who came to the city from Kiev, finished night school and opened a law practice. His son Abraham followed him into the legal profession, as did Abraham's sons Jay and A. N. (Abram). Eventually, Pritzker and Pritzker was solely concerned with the family business, which had grown to include manufacturing and hotels. In 1957, Jay Pritzker founded the Hyatt chain of hotels and Robert Pritzker acquired Royal Caribbean cruise ships. Other family assets include airlines, magazines, Ticketmaster, and Coast-to-Coast Savings and Loan.

The Lauder family business derived from the talents of **Estée Lauder**, who began selling cosmetics in her father's hardware store in Queens. With her husband Joseph Lauter—they changed the spelling of the name—she built Estée Lauder, Inc. By the 1950s, the company was thriving and, in the 1960s, the family began making significant philanthropical contributions. Another cosmetics giant was **Helena Rubenstein** who established a multi-million-dollar business, with international holdings in fourteen countries.

Rose Blumkin—The Queen of Retail

Warren Buffett, the legendary investor, was quoted on the success of Rose Blumkin, the founder of the Nebraska Furniture Mart, in her *New York Times* obituary (August 13, 1998) as follows: "Put her up against the top graduates of the top business schools or chief executives of the Fortune 500 and, assuming an even start with the same resources, she'd run rings around them." The daughter of a rabbi from Russia, Blumkin (1893–1998) founded the Mart in 1937 and built it into the nation's largest home furnishings store. She continued selling carpet in the store well past her one-hundredth birthday.

Later, Adrien Arpel, at age eighteen, began a business devoted to women's skin care from $400 that she had earned from baby-sitting, eventually owning 500 salons.

The capital that seeded the **Tisch** family fortune came from Al Tisch's garment business and two New Jersey summer camps. In 1946, Al's son **Laurence** used money from his father and a family friend to buy a resort hotel, the first of a chain. Eventually, the Tisch family acquired the CNA financial insurance company, Bulova watches, the Lorillard tobacco company, and CBS television (they would sell CBS in 1995 to Westinghouse).

Although the founder of the **Annenberg** publishing empire, Moses Annenberg, was convicted of bribery and tax evasion, it was his firm, Triangle Publications, that son **Walter** turned into a media giant. With *Seventeen* magazine and *TV Guide*, Triangle became a property worth $3.2 billion to tycoon Rupert Murdoch in 1988. Annenberg invested as well in real estate, the Pennsylvania Railroad, and the Campbell Soup Company.

Michael Rothstein started out as a linoleum salesman in Boston. His later business as a liquor wholesaler paid his son's way through Harvard. That son, who changed his name to **Sumner Redstone**, joined his father's business and expanded his father's movie chain from 12 theaters to 855. When he was in his seventies, he leveraged the buyout of Viacom, Inc. and thereby acquired Blockbuster Video, Simon & Schus-

William J. Levitt—the Creator of Suburbia

In 1947 William J. Levitt created Levittown in Long Island, the first mass-produced single-family tract home development. The project has recently been attacked for excluding African Americans (the first leases had "Caucasian only" clauses), but Levitt staunchly denied any racial prejudice on his part. However, Levitt, the grandson of a rabbi, also built housing on Long Island that excluded Jews.

ter, and Paramount Studios. Another publishing fortune began with a humor magazine called *Ziff's*, later *American Humor*, founded by William Ziff. His son, Bill Jr., expanded the business to include such periodicals as *Popular Photography* and *Car & Driver*. Later, he was responsible for the publication of some of the earliest and most popular computer periodicals, such as *PC Magazine* and *PC Weekly*. In the 1990s, Ziff's sons sold their father's businesses for $1.4 billion and established Ziff Brother Investments.

Grounded in distilling, the Bronfman fortune today includes huge entertainment and communications industry holdings, including about 80 percent of MCA, Inc. and 15 percent of Time Warner. The Crown family fortune began with a gravel firm in 1919 and has since grown to include real estate, construction, aerospace, and even a stake in a number of sports teams. In 1888, **Louis Blaustein** came to the United States from Russian and began selling kerosene. In 1910, he and his son Jacob founded the American Oil Company, which is now known as Amoco. Over the years, Louis invented the first high-test gasoline and Jacob the metered gas pump. The Wexner family began with a women's clothing store in Columbus, Ohio. The second generation of Wexner business began in 1965 when Leslie Wexner opened The Limited, a chain of sportswear stores that was phenomenally successful. Wexner now owns Henri Bendel, Abercrombie & Fitch, Lane Bryant, and Victoria's Secret.

In 1958, Alexander Grass founded Rite Aid Corporation with a single discount drug store in Harrisburg, Pennsylvania. Three decades later, the company had grown to include nearly a thousand stores nationwide, becoming the third largest chain in the United States with over $1 billion in sales each year. At the same time, Julia Waldbaum expanded the business that her husband had begun several decades earlier, eventually earning more than $1 billion a year from 140 stores in New York, Connecticut, and Massachusetts.

A number of Jewish families became prominent as real estate developers, builders, and contractors. Frederick Rose entered the construction business that his father had begun in the 1920s and 1930s, and expanded it significantly, building a number of hotels and apartment buildings in New York City, the Keystone Building in Boston, and Pentagon City, a 116-acre tract in Virginia across from Washington, D.C. Other Jewish giants of the construction and real estate fields have included Webb and Knapp, the Uris Brothers, Tishman, Levitt, Rudin and Wolfson Enterprises, Helmsley-Spear, and Zeckendorf.

Charles Bendheim, a metallurgical engineer by training, bought Phillip Brothers Chemical in 1945 and achieved great success while maintaining a strong connection to the Orthodox tradition in which he was raised. After fleeing Germany when the Nazis took control, Max Stern, an Orthodox Jew, began Hartz Mountain pet-supplies stores, and his son Leonard massively expanded the business in the 1950s and 1960s to achieve a hundred-million-dollar fortune by age forty. Jacob Kaplan, son of a Russian Orthodox rabbi, bought the Welch grape juice company, modernized seven plants in seven different states and initiated the cooperative as a method of employing his grape farmers.

Judith Kessler took advantage of the increasing globalization of American technology by starting her own company, Kessler International, which began in 1946 by selling automotive parts to foreign governments at prices well below those offered by the car manufacturers themselves. Over the next three decades, she expanded the business into road and dam building equipment, electronics and communications components, and military support supplies.

Ironically, one of the great symbols of blonde, non-Semitic femininity, the Barbie Doll, was created by a

Jewish woman, Ruth Mosko Handler, who formed the Mattel Toy Company with her husband and put the doll, named after her daughter Barbara, on the market in 1959. Thirty years later, sales of Barbie and the Ken doll, which the Handlers named after their teenage son, had exceeded one billion dollars. Another successful entrepreneur, Beatrice Alexander, turned her business, the Alexander Doll Company, into one of the largest doll manufacturing companies in the United States.

One of the great innovators and path breakers in the post–World War II generation was Edwin Herbert Land, who developed a plastic material he called Polaroid. It cut glare without distorting the light passing through it. With this material, Land pioneered the development of the instant camera and started the Polaroid Corporation, where he served as president and CEO until 1980, amassing stock worth around $100 million.

The modern era signaled some major changes in the national arena, including the evolution of the service business. Leon Greenbaum founded the Hertz Rent-All Corporation in 1960 and within a decade Hertz became the largest rental car company in the United States, and thousands of other American companies embraced Greenbaum's original concept. In a similar vein, Elmer Winter, a self-made businessman from Milwaukee, founded Manpower, Inc.—the forerunner in the world of corporate temporary staffing agencies.

Probably no individual epitomizes the late-twentieth-century artist/designer/corporate businessman better than fashion guru Calvin Klein. Born in the Bronx to a poor family, Klein began his career with the help of a $10,000 loan that he used to open his own coat business in the mid 1960s. In less than two decades, he constructed a multi-million-dollar empire selling merchandise ranging from ready-to-wear men's and women's fashions to eyewear and fragrances.

Jewish names continue to proliferate in contemporary American finance, with Ira Harris, Stephen Friedman, and Bruce Wasserstein some of the biggest. Jerome Kohlberg and his partner Henry Kravis be-

> ### Does She . . . or Doesn't She?
>
> This is one of the many now classic advertising headlines written by one of the most successful advertising copywriters ever—Shirley Polykoff (1908–1998). While she is most famous for the ads she wrote for Clairol products when she worked for Foote, Cone & Belding ("The closer he gets, the better you look."), one of our favorites is from early in her career selling a Brooklyn fashion store—"Look like you're going to the races when you're only racing to the grocers."

came well-known in the merger mania of the late 1970s with Kravis making a number of leveraged buyouts including the largest up to that time, $25 billion for RJR Nabisco. Carl Icahn, chairman of TWA and the largest shareholder in Texaco, became one of the most infamous and feared corporate raiders in the United States.

The two men who best epitomized the unsavory world of 1980s high finance were Michael Milken and Ivan Boesky, both of whose names became synonymous with the world of insider training and junk bonds. They made hundreds of millions of dollars, but they each were indicted and convicted of felony charges as a result of their unethical business practices. Most Jews who have become successful in the business arena have, however, built their reputations within the confines of the law.

In recent years, **Michael Eisner**, president and CEO of Walt Disney Corporation, has gained recognition as one of the most successful corporate executives in the nation, an ironic evolution given the corporation's reputation for being a Protestant enclave during its founder's lifetime. In fact, all three of the top executives at Disney, as of this writing, were Jewish Americans. The Disney executives are not, of course, alone among Jewish Americans in finding success in **Hollywood**. Indeed, the Jewish influence in the motion picture business is so profound, from **Samuel Goldwyn** and the **Warner** Brothers to **Steven Spielberg**, that it is covered in a separate entry in this book.

The history of Jewish Americans in business has been, until recently, a story of entrepreneurs, largely

JACOB HENRY SCHIFF

Abraham Kuhn invited Jacob Schiff (above), a young member of a prosperous Frankfurt, Germany, banking family to join his New York firm, Kuhn, Loeb & Co. Under Schiff's guidance the firm became the largest underwriter of railroad stock in the world and raised capital for some of America's most successful corporations. Schiff used his wealth to support numerous Jewish institutions, including the Young Men's Hebrew Association, the Educational Alliance, and the Jewish Theological Seminary of America. (Courtesy of the American Jewish Historical Society, Waltham, Massachusetts and New York, New York)

because the old boys' network was closed to non-Christians. Although Jews have done extraordinarily well in the corporate world, they still faced obstacles to their upward mobility. Of the largest 1,200 American corporations, only a few have any top Jewish executives. There has never been a top Jewish executive in the automobile industry and, even in New York City, only a few Jews serve as senior management officials. It remains difficult for a qualified Jew to head a major corporation that is not already controlled by Jewish

owners. It is for this reason, perhaps, that Jews have embraced the entrepreneurial path of creating and cultivating their own businesses and enterprises.

All this has changed somewhat, in part because of the growth of Jewish businesses in which there is opportunity for advancement and because of a change in the atmosphere of American business. Three prominent Jews in the financial arena came of age in the 1950s and 1960s. Felix Rohatyn, Sanford Weill, and John Guterfrund all rose from Eastern European, lower-middle-class families without connections to the Wall Street establishment or major corporations. Rohatyn, working for the investment firm of Lazard Freres, gained recognition for reshaping American business for three decades by developing and arranging corporate mergers and combinations and for orchestrating the plan that bailed New York City out of its mid-1970s fiscal crisis. Weill developed a brokerage empire on route to becoming president of American Express and then president of Primerica. As chairman and CEO of Salomon Inc., Gutfreund transformed the bond trading house into one of the most important securities firms in North America.

Frank Lautenberg, who became a Democratic Senator from New Jersey, first gained recognition as chairman and chief executive officer of Automatic Data Processing. Founded by Henry Taub, son of a Polish immigrant, in 1949 to handle payroll for different companies thus lowering the cost to each, ADP's revenues by the 1980s had exceeded $550 million with over 100,000 clients. Maynard Wishner, another Jewish entrepreneur who also had a career in public affairs, as the president of the **American Jewish Committee**, built his fortune as the CEO of Walter E. Heller and Company of Chicago, the principal commercial financing and factoring operating subsidiary of Walter E. Heller International Corporation.

Brooklyn-born Shirley Polykoff began her career as a low-paid copywriter for a woman's specialty shop, rose to fame by dreaming up the monumentally successful advertising slogan "Does She . . . or Doesn't She?"—the line that made hair coloring respectable and raised Clairol's advertising budget from $400,000 to $33 million a year. Estelle Joan Sommers pioneered a different kind of fashion by introducing a new fabric, Antron-Lycra Spandex, into her designs for Capezio's bodywear.

A number of businesswomen have established themselves in the expansion of department store retailing. Helen Galland, born in Brooklyn to immigrant Jewish parents, joined Bonwit Teller as a buyer of millinery in 1950 and rose through the ranks to serve as senior vice president before becoming president and CEO of the specialty chain store in 1980. G. G. (Gertrude Geraldine) Michaelson started as a management trainee at Macy's in 1948, rose to assistant to the labor relations manager, became vice president for employee personnel in 1963, and was senior vice president for external affairs from 1980 to 1992. As chair of the trustees of Columbia University from 1989 to 1992, she was the first woman to lead the board of an Ivy League institution. She was also the first female member of the New York State Financial Control Board.

In the foreseeable future, Jewish Americans, like other minorities, will probably find that their greatest successes in business will continue to be those they forge for themselves.

CLAIBORNE, LIZ (1929–)

Fashion designer

Liz Claiborne was born to American parents in Brussels, Belgium on March 31, 1929. Her family moved constantly. By the time she was a teenager she had lived all over the United States. Never finishing high school, in her late teens she moved to Paris to study painting. At age twenty she won a design contest sponsored by *Harper's Bazaar*. A year later, she returned to New York City and initially found work as a sketch artist and model. In the mid-fifties she became a junior designer with a women's sportswear company. (Here she met her second husband and future business partner, Arthur Ortenberg.) Later, she became the chief designer for Youth Guild, the junior dress division of the apparel giant, Joshua Logan, Inc.

In late 1975 Claiborne left her job at Joshua Logan. In 1976, with Ortenberg and two other partners, she founded Liz Claiborne, Inc. The company created comfortable, fashionable clothing for successful businesswomen—filling a need in the market at the time. After being in business only a year and a half the company was grossing $7 million. In 1978, Liz Claiborne, Inc. grossed $23 million. In 1981, the company went public. In 1986 it entered the Fortune 500 list, one of the youngest companies to ever have achieved this. After its initial huge success with women's sportswear, the company diversified and began to develop additional lines of men's and children's clothing, cosmetics, and accessories. Liz Claiborne products are currently sold in department stores in over sixty countries as well as through the company's own retail stores. Claiborne, a true revolutionary in the fashion industry, retired in 1989.

COHN, FANNIA (1885–1962)

Labor union activist

In the first half of the twentieth century, Fannia M. Cohn was one of the leading Jewish women trade union activists in the United States. When the political center of gravity of the unions shifted to the right, she remained a staunch believer in radical social change. Even within a community of outsiders, Cohn was herself an outsider.

Cohn was privately educated, a product of the middle class, when she came to the United States from Russia in 1904. Her ambition was to be a pharmacist, but after observing social conditions among Jewish immigrants, she decided that her place was alongside working people. She took a factory job in the garment industry and by 1909 was a member of her local union's executive board. Eventually she became an organizer for the burgeoning International Ladies Garment Workers Union (ILGWU) and in 1916 was elected the ILGWU's first woman vice president. Two years later she was named head of the union's education department, a position she held until she was bypassed by the more conservative leadership of union president **David Dubinsky**. She continued to be active in the union, retaining the primarily honorary title of executive secretary until her retirement in September of 1962. She died three months later, on December 24.

DUBINSKY, DAVID (1892–1982)

Labor leader

American labor leader David Dubinsky was born in Belorussia and raised in Lodz, Poland where he gained his first union experience as secretary of the Lodz Bakers Union, a militant group organized by the Jewish Socialist Bund. Jailed at age sixteen for organizing strikes against his own father's bakery, Dubinsky was arrested in 1909 for making radical speeches and punished by exile to Siberia.

Escaping before his train reached its final destination, Dubinsky made his way out of Russia and reached the United States in 1910. There he joined with his older brother, found work as a clothing cutter, and became active in the International Ladies' Garment Workers' Union. Dubinsky rose to the presidency of the Cutters' Union in 1921, to the general executive board of the ILGWU in 1923, and finally became president of the ILGWU in 1932, remaining its leader until 1966.

Dubinsky was also active in American politics. He was an early and enthusiastic supporter of Franklin Roosevelt for president, and helped establish the American Labor Party in 1936. When Communists gradually came to dominate the ALP, Dubinsky, a staunch anti-Communist, broke away to found the Liberal Party.

Dubinsky served on the executive committee of the Jewish Labor Committee, and took part in its efforts to protest Nazism and assist refugees fleeing Hitler. He was also a supporter of Labor Zionism and, after 1948, of the State of Israel.

EISNER, MICHAEL (1942–)

Television and film executive

Michael Eisner was born in 1942 in Mt. Kisco, New York and was brought up on Park Avenue in New York City. He attended Denison University where he first studied pre-med and later shifted to a focus on literature and theater. In 1966, he went to work for ABC television. After working his way up the corporate ladder, he was named senior vice president of prime-time production and development. Under his leadership, ABC's prime-time schedule went from last to first place among the networks.

In 1976 Eisner left ABC to take the position of president and chief operating officer for Paramount Pictures. His success at ABC was repeated at Paramount: The studio went from last place to first among Hollywood's top six studios. In 1984 Eisner moved again, this time to Walt Disney Productions, becoming chairman and chief executive. (In 1986, the company was renamed the Walt Disney Company.)

The Walt Disney Company has been revitalized under Eisner's leadership. It again leads the industry in making classic feature-length animated films. Disney's Touchstone Films are also successful and well respected as is the company's cable television station. In 1996 Eisner became one of the most powerful media executives the world when the Disney Company acquired Capitol Cities/ABC, Inc.

FRIEDMAN, MILTON (1912–)

Economist, educator

The recipient of the Nobel Prize in Economics in 1976, Milton Friedman has been a leader in economic and political thought in the United States for over fifty years. He was born in Brooklyn, New York on July 31, 1912. After receiving his Ph.D. from Columbia University in 1946, he began his teaching career at the University of Chicago and quickly established what continues to be known as the "Chicago School" of economic thought, a system of analysis that calls for an end to government intervention in all aspects of the economy. Friedman and the "Chicago school" also believe that the quantity of money in circulation is of central importance to the country's economic health. In *A Monetary History of the United States, 1867–1960*, co-written with Anna J. Schwartz, Friedman traces the history of the nation's money supply and uses this history to argue for his position.

A proponent of minimal government control over the lives of individuals, Friedman has been a lifelong Republican, serving as economic advisor to both Richard Nixon and Ronald Reagan. His book *Capitalism and Freedom*, co-written with his wife, Rose D. Friedman, also an economist, was published in 1962 and has as its major theme (to quote the authors): "the role of competitive capitalism—the organization of the bulk of economic activity through private enterprise operating in a free market—as a system of economic freedom and a necessary condition for political freedom." The book has sold over 400,000 copies to date. In 1978 Friedman received the nation's highest civilian honor, the Presidential Medal of Freedom. He retired from the University of Chicago in 1982. He had been a senior research fellow at the Hoover Institution in Stanford, California, since 1977 and he continues in that position.

In 1980 he hosted a ten-part television series entitled "Free to Choose" and co-wrote a book of the same name with his wife. In 1984 they teamed up again for a TV series and a book entitled *Tyranny of the Status Quo*. In 1998 they published a joint autobiography, *Two Lucky People*.

The Nobel citation mentions *Capitalism and Freedom* and goes on to point out that it is "very rare for an economist to wield such influence, directly or indirectly, not only on the direction of scientific research but also on actual practice."

GOLDMAN, EMMA (1869–1940)

Political activist

Great revolutionary Emma Goldman was born in Lithuania to Abraham and Taube Goldman. The family moved from place to place to escape the anti-Semitic persecution of czarist Russia and Goldman immigrated to New York when she was sixteen years old. At first she chose marriage and a job in the garment industry in Rochester but soon became disillusioned with both. Inspired by the courage as well as the ideals of the anarchist organizers who were arrested, tried, and unjustly hanged for Chicago's Haymarket bombing in 1887, she left her husband to find political activity on New York's Lower East Side. In the cafes and other meeting places, she proved herself a powerful speaker, advocating the rights of workers, sexual and reproductive freedom, and the right to self-expression. She was bold, charismatic, and a woman; the combination began to attract attention, even though she spoke primarily Yiddish and German.

Goldman soon broke through the language barrier into English, reaching out to workers of all ethnic backgrounds and became increasingly threatening to the establishment. After being sentenced to a year in prison in 1893, she came out more determined than ever to be heard. In 1892, Goldman's close friend Alexander Berkman attempted to assassinate steel magnate Henry Clay Frick, and in 1901, President William McKinley was shot by anarchist Leon Czolgosz. These acts and others, real and imagined, created an association between anarchism and terrorism, which Goldman suffered from. But her eloquence, courage, and integrity were magnetic. She became one of the most important political figures of her time and one of the most intriguing political activists this country has produced.

When the United States entered World War I, Goldman spoke out against conscription. Labeled a threat to national security, she was sent to federal prison for eighteen months and then deported. She returned to Russia for a time, and then took up exile in Europe and Canada. In all of these places she encountered anti-Semitism and fear of her anarchist political stand. As totalitarianism began to triumph in Stalinist Russia, Nazi Germany, and Franco's Spain, she began to speak more and more about the thread that tied these disparate regimes together—the thread that was strangling freedom.

Never a religious Jew, she identified with the Jewish culture and spoke out against the historical and political oppression associated with Christianity. She also spoke and acted against what she thought of as religious superstition within the Jewish culture. She initially reacted negatively to the Zionist movement, believing that the ideal world could not be ruled by nationalism. Ultimately, however, she reluctantly came to believe that a Jewish refuge was necessary. She insisted, however, that the rights of the people of the host country must be scrupulously respected. In 1940, as war tore through Europe and the atrocities of the Holocaust came to light, Emma Goldman died, in Toronto.

GOMPERS, SAMUEL (1850–1924)

Labor leader

The man who would serve as president of the American Federation of Labor (AFL) for thirty-seven years was born in London on January 27, 1850 to Dutch Jewish parents. He came to the United States with his family when he was thirteen years old and soon became a journeyman cigar maker on New York City's Lower East Side. Over the next decade, Samuel Gompers talked with his fellow workers, attended classes at Cooper Union Institute, read, and gradually developed a strong worker's consciousness. Throughout his life, he refused to identify himself along ethnic lines, and had minimal interest in Jewish concerns.

In 1875 Gompers became president of the Cigarmakers' Local 144. His subsequent rise in the labor movement was rapid. In 1881 he became a leader in the Federation of Organized Trades and Labor Unions of the United States and Canada. When the federation failed and was succeeded by the AFL, Gompers was elected its first president and, with the exception of 1895, served in that capacity until his death in 1924. During his time in office, he guided the organization through the Homestead and Pullman strikes, World War I, and other tests of its solidarity, and the membership of the organization rose from 150,000 to almost three million. His books include *Labor in Europe and America* (1910) and *American Labor and the War* (1919). His autobiography, *Seventy Years of Life and Labor*, was published in 1925, the year after his death.

Born in London to Dutch Jewish parents, Samuel Gompers became involved in American labor movement at an early age and was elected the first president of the American Federation of Labor in 1886. He remained president (except for one year) of this increasingly important labor union until his death in 1924. (Courtesy of the American Jewish Historical Society, Waltham, Massachusetts and New York, New York)

GREENSPAN, ALAN (1926–)

Economist

Alan Greenspan was born in New York City on March 6, 1926. After he graduated from New York University, he became a private economic consultant. In 1974, President Gerald Ford appointed him to chair the Council of Economic Advisors. He stayed at the Council until 1977, when he returned to the private sector. From 1981 through 1983, he served as chairman of the bipartisan National Commission on Social Security Reform. The commission worked toward remedying the crisis in America's social security system.

In 1987 President Ronald Reagan appointed

Greenspan to the position he still holds today, chairman of the Federal Reserve Board. In an almost unprecedented move, both succeeding presidents have reappointed him to this position, President Bush in 1992 and President Clinton in 1996. An early follower of **Ayn Rand**, Greenspan supports free-market economics and is against government intervention in economic affairs. Throughout his tenure at the Federal Reserve he has concentrated on fighting inflation.

GROSSINGER, JENNIE (1892–1972)

Hotelier

Jennie Grossinger was born on June 16, 1892 in Baligrod, a small village in Galicia, at that time a district of the Austro-Hungarian Empire. She came to New York when she was eight years old. Her family lived on the Lower East Side, which was in its Yiddish heyday. Jennie enrolled in a Hebrew school as well as P.S. 174.

In spite of years of effort, Jennie's father found himself unable to support the family in New York City and in 1914 he decided to buy a farm in the Catskills. He would return to his farming roots and prosper.

Jennie moved with him to help and her new husband, Harry Grossinger (a cousin) stayed in the city during the week and became a farm hand on weekends. As they struggled to make the farm a success, they had no inkling that they were soon to change the history of the New York hotel industry, the entertainment industry, and the New York Jewish community.

They were unable to make the farm a going concern, so Jennie devised a plan to convert it into a small hotel. She ran the kitchen and hired the staff while Harry recruited potential guests in New York City. Grossingers' was a nearly instant success, in no small part thanks to Jennie's graciousness as a hostess. In 1919 she engineered the purchase of adjoining land and another, larger building, and the "Borscht Belt" was on the way to becoming a reality (and eventually a legend). At its peak, Grossingers' would serve 1,200 guests a day, offering them sumptuous kosher meals, recreation and sports (often with world-class athletes like **Benny Leonard** on the premises as ballyhooed guests), and entertainment.

HILLMAN, SIDNEY (1887–1946)

Labor leader

No Jewish labor leader had a greater impact on American politics than Sidney Hillman. Born in Lithuania in 1887, Hillman was educated at the Slobadka Rabbinical Seminary in Lithuania. His formative years were influenced by the social democratic and Jewish Bund movements in Russia.

Immigrating to the United States in 1907, Hillman launched his career as a labor organizer while an apprentice garment cutter in Chicago, where he vigorously fought to establish a union shop at Hart, Schaffner, and Marx. This leadership catapulted him to the presidency of the fledgling Amalgamated Clothing Workers of America and began his campaign to bring the Jewish labor movement into the political mainstream and to provide the fruits of American democracy to working people.

During the Depression, Hillman gained increasing influence as one of the pioneer founders of the Con-

Sydney Hillman is shown here in 1914 (front row, center) with the executive board of the Amalgamated Clothing Workers. His future wife, Bessie Abramowitz, is seated next to him. On her right is the up-and-coming lawyer Fiorello La Guardia. (Photograph courtesy of Philoine Fried)

gress of Industrial Organizations and as an advocate of efforts to organize unskilled workers. Hillman viewed Franklin Roosevelt's New Deal as a fulfillment of his own vision of industrial democracy. He developed a strong personal relationship with the President and other members of the administration—connections that he used to lobby for an agenda that championed the rights of organized labor.

Hillman's increasingly close affiliation with the Roosevelt administration won him respect and prestige as well as scorn and envy, especially as the President increasingly capitulated to business interests at the onset of World War II. While some rank-and-file activists viewed Hillman's unconditional support for FDR as making the union movement hostage to the dictates of Washington, labor's enemies vilified him for being Roosevelt's "right-hand man" in setting industrial policy.

One of Hillman's last acts was developing the CIO-PAC, which attempted to turn the power of the union movement into a political force to support candidates who promoted a progressive and pro-labor agenda. The PAC's success in the 1944 election gave Hillman cause for hope and he embarked on a new campaign to build an international labor federation. His death in 1946 came before the Cold War and the beginning of the decline of union militancy. Hillman was mourned as one of twentieth-century labor's greatest representatives.

HILLQUIT, MORRIS (1869–1933)

Labor leader

Born Moses Hillkowitz in Riga, Latvia in 1869, Morris Hillquit played a leading role in the American Socialist Party from its formation until his death and became a major proponent of adapting European-style social democracy to Jewish American life.

Immigrating to the United States in 1885, Hillquit worked in the garment trades of New York City's Lower East Side, joined the Socialist Labor Party (SLP), and helped to organize the United Hebrew Trades. After the demise of the SLP, he became one of the most visible New York City organizers in the new Socialist Party under the national leadership of Eugene V. Debs.

Hillquit believed in building a socialist base within established American institutions, especially the American Federation of Labor (AFL), rather than creating new labor organizations, putting him at odds with the Industrial Workers of the World. At the same time, he fought hard against AFL attempts to restrict immigration during the second decade of the new century and took a firm stand against American involvement in World War I.

Although unsuccessful in his two runs for Congress in 1906 and 1908, Hillquit's campaigns garnered significant public interest and helped lay the foundation for fellow socialist **Meyer London**'s victory a few years later. He earned a hefty 20 percent of the vote in his New York City mayoral campaign of 1918, which enabled other Socialist candidates to gain elections to city and state offices that year.

Hillquit also established a reputation as one of the leading popularizers of socialist theory, writing *The History of Socialism in the United States* and *Socialism in Theory and Practice*. Although initially hopeful about the Russian revolution, he ultimately became a vocal opponent of the Communist regime.

Despite being stricken by tuberculosis by 1920, Hillquit continued to serve as a senior figure in the weakened Socialist Party, even running one last time for mayor in 1933 and winning a quarter of a million votes. He died a few months later, just few weeks after the publication of his autobiography, *Loose Leaves from a Busy Life*.

KAHN, OTTO (1867-1934)

Businessman, philanthropist

Otto Kahn was born on February 21, 1867 in Germany. In 1893, after working in London for Berlin's Deutsche Bank, he joined the New York banking firm of Speyer & Co. Four years later, he joined the firm of Kuhn, Loeb & Co., where he remained for the next thirty-seven years. In the business world, Kahn is best known for his role in Edward Harriman's reorganization of the American railway systems.

As a philanthropist, Kahn gave to many causes, the most famous being the Metropolitan Opera Company of New York. In 1903, he became a stockholder and helped pay off its debts. More importantly, he was responsible for bringing Giulio Gatti-Casazza and Arturo Toscanini to the Met in 1908. In 1918—a year after he became an American citizen—he became president of the company, a position he held until 1931. At the time of his death, on March 29, 1934, he owned 84 percent of its stock.

In addition to his work with the Met, Kahn funded various museums as well as the building of the New Theater and the restoration of the Parthenon in Athens and he endowed prizes for African American artists. He lectured widely on subjects as varied as art (he was an important collector) and politics and his addresses were frequently published in pamphlet form.

KARAN, DONNA (1948–)

Fashion designer

Fashion designer Donna Karan (née Faske) was born in Forest Hills, New York on October 2, 1948. Both her parents were in the clothing business and she soon followed in their footsteps. At age fourteen, she began selling clothes in a New York boutique. She enrolled at Parson's School of Design, but dropped out in 1968. After leaving school, Karan began working for Anne Klein, one of New York's top designers. After nine months with the company, she was fired. After a short time away, she was rehired.

Anne Klein died of cancer in 1974 and Karan became the company's chief designer. A year later, Karan convinced designer Louis Dell'Olio to join her at Anne Klein. Together, the two designers flourished. They won the Coty American Fashion Critics Award twice (1977 and 1983) and were admitted into its Hall of Fame. In 1983, Karan secured the fortunes of the Anne Klein Co. by introducing "Anne Klein II," a less expensive, "bridge" line of designer clothes.

A year later, Karan left Anne Klein to create her own company, Donna Karan Co. In 1988, she introduced her own bridge line, DKNY. Since the bridge line's debut, the company has diversified and now sells everything from blue jeans to hosiery. Today, Donna Karan and DKNY are among the most recognizable and successful names in fashion.

KLEIN, CALVIN (1942–)

Fashion designer

Calvin Klein is one of the most well-known clothing designers in the world today. Born in the Bronx, New York on November 19, 1942, he attended New York's famed Fashion Institute of Technology, graduating in 1962. The same year he got his first job as a designer, working for a garment district coat-and-suit manufacturer. In 1968 he opened his own company. At that time, the fashion industry was producing clothing inspired by the hippie movement. Klein went in another direction. He created clean understated lines, initially gaining attention for his suits and coats, but rapidly influencing the world of sportswear separates. From 1973 through 1975, he was awarded three consecutive Coty Awards for women's wear, the first designer to earn this distinction. He was inducted into the Coty

Hall of Fame in 1976, the youngest ready-to-wear designer to earn such an honor. Known today for his controversial advertising as well as his wide range of products—everything from underwear to perfume, Calvin Klein made the American fashion industry a presence throughout the world.

KRAVIS, HENRY (1944–)

Financier, investment banker

Henry Kravis was born on January 6, 1944 in Tulsa, Oklahoma. His father was in the oil business, a partner for a time with Joseph P. Kennedy. Kravis attended Claremont College before moving on to Columbia University where he graduated with an M.B.A. in 1969. He then joined the firm of Bear Stearns working under Jerome Kohlberg, the firm's corporate finance manager. In 1976, Kohlberg, Kravis, and Kravis' cousin George Roberts left Bear Stearns and founded their own investment banking firm, Kohlberg Kravis Roberts & Co. (KKR).

Kravis and KKR pioneered the leveraged buyout. They were also among the most successful investment bankers on Wall Street. Frequently, though certainly not always, KKR was the "white knight," saving companies from hostile takeovers. Kravis was responsible for some of the largest corporate takeovers in history. Among the companies KKR bought and sold over the years are Safeway, Beatrice, Playtex, Samsonite, and Texaco. Perhaps the company's most famous buyout was the 1988 deal for RJR Nabisco, which sold for $24.88 billion, at the time the highest price ever paid for a commercial enterprise. The buyout process was dramatized in the book and film, *Barbarians at the Gates*.

In 1987 Jerome Kohlberg retired from KKR and Kravis became senior partner. Kravis sits on the boards of Duracell, Safeway, Borden, and UnionTexas Petroleum among many others. He has also given enormous sums to charity, specifically Mount Sinai Hospital and the Metropolitan Museum of Art, and is the chairman of the Board of Trustees of New York City's public television station.

LABOR MOVEMENT

Jews have been in the forefront of the American labor movement since the late nineteenth century. Inheritors of a tradition of workers' struggles in Eastern Europe, Jewish immigrants played important roles in the fights for trade union representation, fair wages, and improved working conditions in the factories and workplaces of the United States between 1890 and 1930. Jews took on leadership roles in the development and formation of the Amalgamated Clothing and Textile Workers and the International Ladies Garment Workers Union, two unions that began with a predominately Jewish labor force. They also were prominent in political organizations advocating labor rights, as well as in unions that were not perceived as part of what became known as "the Jewish labor movement," such as the fur, cap, and millinery trades.

Because many Jewish immigrants during the early twentieth century came from socialist and anarchist traditions, Jews frequently were catalysts in pushing organized labor toward an increased radicalism and militancy. These Jewish labor activists viewed the transformation of the wage/class system as the cornerstone to building a new society freed from coercive and exploitative relationships between labor and capital.

The Jewish labor movement served as a subculture that attempted to fuse Jewish heritage with socialism using Yiddish literature and the press, especially the *Jewish Daily Forward,* and fraternal organizations such as the Workmen's Circle as a foundation. Jewish labor activists, the great majority of whom were secularists, perceived their movement as an organizational and ideological alternative to the traditional Jewish religious community.

Jews who became active in the labor movement differed in their own relationship to their Jewish identity. **Samuel Gompers**, a cigar maker from a Dutch and English background, became the first president of the American Federation of Labor in 1886, refused to identify himself along ethnic lines and had minimal interest in Jewish concerns. Gompers believed that labor should stay out of politics and concentrate on wage and hour issues. New York Socialist Party representative **Morris Hillquit** argued that Jewish workers should unite as a class and work within the A. F. of L. rather than organize into ethnic labor movements.

But Gompers and Hillquit represented an older generation of labor leaders who arrived in the United States prior to the great wave of Eastern European Jewish immigration. These newcomers, who came to America both to seek economic opportunity and to escape anti-Semitic violence in Europe, did not separate their identity as Jews (and in particular their *Yiddishkeit* heritage) from their politics or the struggle to improve their working conditions. In addition, the socialism of those who began immigrating in the first decade of the twentieth century (as the political situation in Russia worsened) drew on a specific cultural identity of the Jewish worker that differed dramatically from the universalism of Hillquit's organizing model.

Jewish immigrant workers entered the garment trades in massive numbers, but early attempts to organize them through the United Hebrew Trades and the United Garment Workers had minimal success. In the 1890s, Jewish **anarchist** and **socialist** movements struggled internally as they attempted to create garment locals. The early years of the International Ladies Garment Workers Union, founded in 1900, were marked by political infighting. The largely skilled male tailors and cloakmaker founders did little to organize or involve young immigrant women shirtwaist workers in the organization. Influenced by increasing political radicalism as the first decade of the century ended and spurred on by the commitment of the *Forward*

Agitate! Agitate! Agitate!

"I move that we go on a general strike." With those words Clara Lemlich (Shavelson) concluded her stirring 1909 speech to a strike meeting in New York City that lead to the "Uprising of the 20,000," by far the largest strike to date in American women's history. A union activist all her life, she spent her last years at the Jewish Home for the Aged in Los Angeles, where she helped the orderlies organize a union and persuaded the administrators to honor the grape and lettuce boycott then being promoted by the United Farm Workers.

In 1915, the predominantly Jewish Amalgamated Clothing Workers Union went out on strike. Their objective was the abolition of the sweatshop and home work, and a reduction of the twelve-hour workday. (Courtesy of American Jewish Archives)

and its unqualified support for the ILGWU union campaign, the situation changed dramatically in 1909 with the Uprising of the 20,000.

This massive strike of female shirtwaist makers in New York City began when a small number of workers from the tiny but radical Local 25 called an industry-wide meeting. With thousands of women workers in attendance, Clara Lemlich addressed the crowd in Yiddish from the audience declaring that the time had come to call for a general strike. This agitation set the stage for a two-month shirtwaist workers strike followed by a strike of 50,000 cloakmakers in 1910. These acts of labor resistance initiated by Jewish

women workers called for increases in wages, shorter hours, better working conditions, and full union recognition for female garment workers. In addition, women workers garnered public support for the strikes of 1909–1910 by emphasizing the immoral and unjust nature of their day-to-day treatment in the garment factories.

Besides Lemlich, Jewish immigrant women such as **Fannia Cohn**, **Pauline Newman**, and Theresa Serber Malkiel emerged as leaders of the shirtwaist strikers. Cohn spoke of the need for a broader vision of unionism that spoke to the human spirit as well as the bread and butter issues of pay, hours, and working conditions. She later convinced the ILGWU to create the first education department in an international union. Newman organized women workers for the ILGWU in New England and the Midwest and played an important role in strikes in Cleveland and Philadelphia before serving as New York State organizer for the Socialist Party in 1915 and founding the ILGWU's health center in 1924. Malkiel, a militant socialist and organizer of the earlier Infant Cloak Makers Union strike, wrote a novel called *The Diary of a Shirtwaist Worker* in which the young Jewish heroine becomes liberated from industrial exploitation. Overall, Jewish women workers, largely shut out from the male-dominated institutional leadership of trade unions, took on essential roles as grassroots shop floor activists and created their own organizations such as the Women's Trade Union League led by **Rose Schneiderman**. Schneiderman later took on an important leadership position in the ILGWU's Local 25.

Workers in the men's clothing industry also began organizing more effectively in this era with a massive strike in Chicago at the Hart, Shaffner, and Marx factory. Again, this strike was initiated by a group of Jewish women led by **Bessie Abramowitz** (Hillman). In New York, labor agitation among clothing workers came to a head in the division between the old guard ILGWU and the new and more militant immigrant Jewish socialists led by **SidneyHillman** (Abramowitz's future husband) who walked out of the ILGWU and established the Amalgamated Clothing Workers of America. Hillman kept the ACWA independent of the American Federation of Labor until 1933 and during this time he arguably became the most influential Jewish labor leader in the country, along with the new president of the ILGWU, **David Dubinsky**.

Although the strikes in the clothing industry were not total successes, they went a long way toward shifting public opinion more strongly in favor of labor reform. Nevertheless, the continuing dangers of unsafe working conditions at garment factories resulted in the tragic fire at the Triangle Shirtwaist Factory in New York in 1911 that killed 146 mostly Jewish women workers. Although this incident was the catalyst for greatly strengthened fire and safety regulations in

Rose Pesotta, a leader in the International Ladies Garment Workers Union, is shown here speaking to a national convention. A fervent anarchist, she saw her politics as a natural outgrowth of her Jewish background. (Courtesy of Keele Center, Cornell University)

New York State, these gains were limited to the garment industry and they had limited influence on the country at large.

Jewish labor activists in the garment unions found themselves outside the orbit of the more conservative craft-dominated American Federation of Labor. The advent of World War I created further friction in the labor movement, with most Jewish socialist labor activists standing beside the more radical wings of the labor movement (such as the Industrial Workers of the World) in opposing American involvement, while the A. F. of L. supported the war effort. In addition, Jewish immigrants who worked outside of the garment industry often faced anti-Semitism and xenophobia, especially in the more conservative craft organizations such as the bookbinders and carpenters unions. But they did sometimes make inroads by organizing their own sections within these unions and even going so far, as in the case of the United Hatters of North America, to threaten to become strikebreakers to pressure the established union to accept Jewish members.

World War I, the Bolshevik Revolution, and the increasingly anti-radical, anti-immigrant stance of the American government wreaked havoc on the labor movement in 1920s. For Jewish workers in the garment industry, this era marked the beginning of what became a long-standing and divisive conflict between Jewish socialists who left the Socialist Party to became members of the newly formed **Communist Party** and those who became increasingly anti-Communist as the decade progressed. This division became especially pronounced in the Fur Workers Union and in the ILGWU where Communists, arguing that the union leaders had taken control from the rank and file, gained increasing strength in New York City locals. In 1926 Communists initiated and directed a six-month general strike of the New York City garment trade. The strike ended in defeat and resulted in the suspension of many left-wing locals. The old guard socialist leaders reasserted their control of the union and blamed the Communist Party for continuing the strike long after it could have been settled, thus severely depleting the ILGWU's financial resources.

Communists were considerably more successful at gaining power in the Fur and Leather Workers Union through effective and militant grassroots organizing on behalf of the New York City rank and file. Ben Gold, one of the chief organizers of the progressive faction of the union (and openly a Communist Party member) became the union's president in the late 1920s. He served in that position for the next four decades, gaining an impressive array of benefits for workers, initially in the fur industry, and then, later, in the harder-to-organize leather industry as well.

After the setbacks of the 1920s and following the collapse of the American economy that closed the decade, the American labor movement revived dramatically in the 1930s under President Franklin Roosevelt's New Deal. Dubinsky, Hillman, and Max Zaritsky were vital players in the creation of the Committee for Industrial Organization (CIO), an attempt to organized unskilled and semi-skilled workers within the A.F. of L. It later became a separate federation, the Congress for Industrial Organization. Gold's Fur and Leather Workers Union, which had organized its entire industry, became a pioneer member of the CIO.

Dubinsky, along with Alex Rose, also founded the American Labor Party (ALP), which provided Socialist Party trade unions and fraternal organizations with an electoral vehicle to support FDR and his New Deal without endorsing the Democratic Party machine. In addition, the ALP also sought to push Roosevelt to take a more pro-labor position and to recruit and endorse other candidates who had strong roots in the labor movement.

Most importantly, Jews in the labor movement in the 1930s helped push through Congress the most far-reaching legislative reforms for working people in the twentieth century, including the National Labor Relations (Wagner) Act, and bills that provided for social security, unemployment insurance, and workers compensation. Labor gained its greatest victories through massive rank-and-file organizing campaigns that helped spark a dramatic upturn in union membership throughout the country. Jewish labor activists were helped by a sympathetic national administration, and a cultural milieu that elevated the concerns of working people in an era of massive unemployment. Perhaps the high water mark of labor reaching out to a broader audience came when the ILGWU produced an immensely successful Broadway musical revue *Pins and Needles* with the entire cast composed of union members from Local 22 in New York. It ran for more than 1,000 performances in 1937.

Although the New Deal paid little attention to the concerns of women workers and the CIO from its inception functioned as a male enclave, Jewish women such as Lilian Hernstein and Rebecca Coolman Simonson took on important roles as union organizers. Rose Pesotta became the vice president of the ILGWU at this time. Women united behind the goal of extending New Deal legislation beyond traditionally male manufacturing jobs to the predominately female ranks of domestic workers, public sector employees, retail clerks, and part-time laborers who had previously been ignored by government reforms. The Jewish-led State County and Municipal Workers of America (later the United Public Workers), the Distributive Workers, and the United Office and Professional Workers of America, are all examples of efforts to expand the parameters of organized labor beyond blue-collar, male industrial workers.

Jewish involvement in the labor movement took

Albert Shanker was the long-time president of the national teachers' union, the American Federation of Teachers, and, at the same time, the New York local, the United Federation of Teachers. He is shown here with Sandra Feldman, who succeeded him as president of the AFT (and for a time, the UFT) and Ann Kessler, legislative liaison for the UFT. (Courtesy of United Federation of Teachers)

place in a very different context and with a different generation of Jewish activists than in the Progressive Era. The number of Jews working in the garment industry continued to decline rapidly. The bonds that tied an earlier generation of Jewish labor activists together began to dissolve as a new generation found their identity with the United States and the New Deal rather than with the older Yiddish and *shtetl* traditions in a workforce that had fewer Jewish laborers. In addition, the rise of fascism in Europe increased the concerns of Jewish labor leaders for specifically Jewish causes, leading to the creation of the Jewish Labor Committee, which mobilized labor in defense of international Jewry.

As the 1930s came to a close, tensions among Jewish labor leaders came to the fore. Dubinsky increasingly began to distance himself from the CIO, which he denounced as Communist-led, and from Hillman. He opposed his former mentor's willingness to work with Communists within the CIO and resented Hillman's close relationship to Roosevelt. In 1939 Dubinsky led the ILGWU back into the A.F. of L. and formed the vociferously anti-Communist Liberal Party.

Jews loyal to the labor movement found themselves

at both ends of the spectrum. The effectiveness of rank-and-file Communists as organizers and the relatively non-sectarian, pragmatic strategy of the Communist Party during the 1930s brought many prominent Jews into the Party's orbit, although the signing of the Hitler-Stalin Pact in 1939 decreased these numbers sharply. At the same time, many Jewish labor allies who identified themselves as socialist (Dubinsky being the best example) or as former Communists (Jay Lovestone and his followers who were known as Lovestonites) became rabid anti-Communists. They opposed Stalin's tyranny but were also increasingly willing, especially in the McCarthy era, to support repressive and non-democratic means to rid unions of Communist influence.

By the onset of World War II, the socialism of the ACWA had blurred into little more than an expansion of the welfare state, with Hillman serving as Roosevelt's advisor while Dubinsky's ILGWU socialist principles increasingly became a nostalgic remembrance of the union's earlier days. In the post-war era, the ranks of the garment industry became increasingly filled by African Americans and Puerto Ricans, and later by Asians.

Jewish participation in the labor movement since 1945 became increasingly concentrated among paid union leaders rather than the rank-and-file and from the ranks of professional unions, such as teachers or government workers. Jews served as key leaders in the organizing of teachers in urban public schools both through the United Federation of Teachers, whose long-time head was **Albert Shanker**, as well as through its adversary, the left-wing New York City Teacher's Union, which was destroyed in the 1950s during the height of the McCarthy scare.

In certain respects Shanker and Victor Gotbaum, president of the State and Local Government Employees from the late 1960s to the early 1980s, traced a lineage back to Samuel Gompers. Both these contemporary labor leaders, like Gompers, had less concern with the ethnic character of the workforce than had their Jewish labor ancestors of the first part of the century. Jewish leadership in the labor movement had come, in some respects, full circle.

The labor movement fundamentally changed the relationship between employers and employees in the United States. Jewish participation in mobilizing male and female workers to fight for their political and economic rights transformed the American landscape and challenged the country to live up to its highest values and ideals.

LAUDER, ESTÉE (1908–)

One of the great Jewish cosmetic queens, Estée Lauder was born Josephine Esther Mentzer in Queens, New York to Max and Rose (Schotz Rosenthal) Mentzer. Her family lived above her father's hardware store where she learned her first lessons in merchandising. One of her uncles taught her to make a face cream that would be the basis of her cosmetics company. It was during the Depression, when she was in her thirties, that Lauder founded her company, modifying her uncle's recipe and creating other products of her own. In 1937 she gave the company her married name, Lauter, changing the spelling. She and her husband, Joseph, were divorced two years later, but they remarried in 1942. He became her business partner and the two continued to build Estée Lauder together.

Lauder marketed her products in fine department stores and focused her advertising on "the Estée Lauder kind of woman," emphasizing luxury and taste. She chose the models for her print ads with great care and had them photographed by brilliant Chicago photographer Victor Skrebneski, who published a book of photographs of the Lauder models. In the 1960s she came out with a men's line of cologne and skin care products, marketing them with great success. Another of her innovations was the Clinique line of fragrance-free cosmetics, appealing to a new generation of women who did not respond readily to the elegant and costly main brand. In recent years the company has added several other lines, including Prescriptives, Bobbi Brown Essentials, M. A. C., and Origins. Lauder has also been extremely successful overseas, with approximately half of her sales made in seventy-five foreign countries.

Although she describes her religion as "ecumeni-cal," Lauder makes very large contributions to Jewish charities and causes. In recent years her son Leonard has taken over the operations of the company, continuing to sell, with great vision, the possibility of beauty to women around the world.

LUBIN, DAVID (1849–1919)

Agricultural organizer, businessman

An early leader in organizing farmers, David Lubin came to the United States when he was around four years old. He was born in Klodowa in Russian Poland on June 10, 1849, but the conditions in the area forced his family to flee, first to England, then to New York City, where Lubin grew up and attended school. In 1874 he opened a dry-goods business in Sacramento, California and soon expanded it into a mail-order business that became the largest on the West Coast.

A successful businessman only ten years after his arrival in California, Lubin made a trip to Palestine that changed his life. Moved by his experience in the Holy Land, he shifted his focus from business to social improvement and became as successful at agricultural reform as he had been in business. He created the California Fruit Growers Association and with the organization lobbied to create safeguards and subsidies for farmers. In 1896, he moved on to developing plans for an International Institute of Agriculture. The Institute would provide centralized information on world agricultural conditions and issues. By 1905 Lubin had gotten the attention of Italy's King Victor Emmanuel. In Rome, five years later, forty-six nations ratified a treaty that formally created the Institute. For the remainder of his life, Lubin was on the permanent board of the Institute as the United States representative. He died in Rome on January 1, 1919.

NEWHOUSE FAMILY

Publishers

Newhouse, S.I., Sr. (1895–1979)
Samuel Irving Newhouse Sr. (née Solomon Neuhaus)

was born in New York City on May 24, 1895. In 1922 he bought the *Staten Island Advance*. Two years later he incorporated the company. He then used the profits to buy other small, failing newspapers in the New York and New Jersey area. He had an uncanny ability to turn these failing publications into profitable enterprises.

In 1949, he changed his company's name to Advance Publications. A year later he bought the *Portland Oregonian*. In 1955 he purchased the St. Louis *Globe-Democrat* and in 1959, Condé Nast publications, which owned *Vogue*, *Glamour*, and *House & Garden* among other magazines. In the 1960s and 1970s, Newhouse purchased the Times-Picayune Publishing Company, the Cleveland *Plain Dealer*, and Booth Newspapers Inc., which published eight Michigan dailies and *Parade* magazine.

Newhouse, Sr. was known for his "hands-off" attitude toward editorial content. Unlike many other newspaper magnates, he never tried to alter a newspaper or magazine's editorial perspective—he just made sure the publication showed a profit. At the time of Newhouse Sr.'s death on August 29, 1979, the family owned the third-largest newspaper chain in the United States—a total of thirty-one newspapers. It also owned seven magazines, five radio stations, six television stations, and fifteen cable television systems. The print-media companies in the Newhouse empire are gathered under Advance Publications, Inc. The electronic media holdings are part of the Newhouse Broadcasting Corporation. Both companies are owned privately by the Newhouse family, making the family members among the richest people in the world.

Newhouse, S.I., Jr. (1928–)
Newhouse, Donald E. (1930–)

After Newhouse Sr. died, S.I. Newhouse, Jr. and his brother Donald took over management of the company. Donald became responsible for the newspaper and broadcast holdings and S.I., Jr. (called "Si") took over the magazine, and later, book publishing holdings. The brothers are reportedly very close and rarely disagree about how to run their empire. Donald is the less well known of the two. In building and maintaining the newspaper and broadcast sides of the family holdings, Donald has garnered far less attention than his more notorious brother. By the 1990s, Donald's domain included the newspapers his father had purchased as well as a burgeoning cable television business. In 1994, the Newhouse Broadcasting Corp.'s cable company—with 1.4 million subscribers—joined with Time Warner, Inc., making the joint venture the second-largest cable television conglomerate in the country. In addition to the Newhouse Broadcasting Corp.'s cable television subscribers, the company also owns the Discovery Channel and the Learning Channel.

Si Newhouse is far more famous than his brother Donald. He has become infamous in the publishing world for his sometimes abrupt changes in the editorial staff of his magazines, but he has been extremely successful. Soon after his father's death, Si began to expand his side of the family business. In 1980 he purchased Random House for a reported $60 million. The firm's several imprints included Knopf, Crown, Pantheon, and Times Books. Five years later he purchased *The New Yorker* and a year after that he purchased Citibank's magazine, *Signature*, which was turned into Condé Nast's *Traveler*. He added many more magazine titles to Advance Publications' holdings including resurrecting a dormant *Vanity Fair*, creating *Self*, and buying *Gentleman's Quarterly* and *Details*. In March 1998 Advance Publications agreed to sell Random House to Bertelsmann AG, a German firm, for an estimated $1.4 billion.

NEWMAN, PAULINE (1890?–1986)

Labor organizer

Pauline Newman was born in Kovno, Lithuania around 1890. She came from a deeply religious family. In 1901, after her father died, she immigrated to the United States with her mother and sisters. Once in New York, she began to work in the sweatshops of the Lower East Side. For seven years she worked at the Triangle Shirtwaist Factory. At the same time she began to educate herself by reading the socialist Yiddish and English press.

In the winter of 1907–1908, radicalized by the living and working conditions of poor New Yorkers, Newman organized the largest rent strike the city had ever seen. The next year she ran as the Socialist Party nominee for Secretary of State for New York. At the same time, Newman began to organize women garment workers. In 1909 she helped organize and maintain the largest women's strike up until that point, New York's Uprising of the 20,000. She then became the first woman general organizer for the International Ladies Garment Workers Union, while still working for the Socialist Party and campaigning for suffrage with the Woman's Trade Union League. In 1913, during the aftermath of the tragic 1911 Triangle Shirtwaist Fire—in which she lost many friends—she went to work for New York's Joint Board of Sanitary Control. In 1923, she was appointed educational director for the ILGWU health center.

During the 1920s and 1930s, Newman and her lover, Frieda Miller, became increasingly involved in government. Both women were great friends of—and consultants to—Eleanor Roosevelt. Newman served on the U.S. Women's Bureau Labor Advisory Board, the United Nations Subcommittee on the Status of Women, and the International Labor Organization's Subcommittee on the Status of Domestic Laborers.

Ultimately, Newman worked for the ILGWU for seventy years and for the New York and National Women's Trade Union League for almost as long. She was a pivotal figure in the twentieth-century labor, socialist, and women's suffrage movements. Throughout her career, she wrote about the conditions she struggled to change. Her writing provided an important and rare record of life in the sweatshops.

REDSTONE, SUMNER (1923–)

Entrepreneur

Born Sumner Murray Rothstein in May 1923, Sumner Redstone grew up and still lives in the Boston area. After graduating from Harvard with a degree in languages, he spent World War II deciphering Japanese codes. After the war, he attended Harvard University Law School but practiced law for only six years. He then went into the family business, drive-in movie theaters. Today, he is the owner of Viacom, Inc., which owns Blockbuster Video; the MTV and Nickelodeon cable networks; Paramount Studios; and the two Paramount sports franchises, the New York Knicks and the New York Rangers. Well-known for his philanthropy, Redstone has given millions to both Jewish and non-Jewish causes, from the Massachusetts General Hospital burn center (which treated him after he was badly burned in a hotel fire) to the Combined Jewish Philanthropies of Greater Boston.

ROSENWALD, JULIUS (1862–1932)

Mail order entrepreneur, philanthropist

Retail innovator Julius Rosenwald was born in 1862 in Springfield, Illinois into a family of German Jewish immigrants. He entered the clothing business at the age of seventeen as an apprentice to his uncles in New York City. After operating his own successful business for more than a decade, he bought into the mail-order firm of Sears, Roebuck and Company. Instituting a money-back guarantee and other procedures for quality control, Rosenwald helped to turn the company into a major force in American retailing. A little more than a decade later, he was president of the company and, by 1925, chairman of the board.

Inspired by noted Reform Rabbi Emil G. Hirsch, Rosenwald came to believe that, as a Jew, social justice was his personal responsibility. At the height of his business success he undertook the mission of educating African Americans, especially in the south where the effects of segregation and discrimination were most pronounced. Rosenwald was never a person to undertake a task halfway. Between 1913 and 1932 he helped establish 5,357 public schools. He required each local community to contribute matching funds for their school and to provide some of the labor themselves. By 1932, 90 percent of the population in the

South had Rosenwald schools in their counties. Rosenwald also became a trustee and one of the strongest supporters of the Tuskegee Institute at a time when it needed help the most. The Hampton Institute also received substantial bequests from him. His Rosenwald fund provided fellowships for African American teachers and African American hospitals and funded efforts to improve race relations. Rosenwald made an incalculable contribution to the education, and therefore the advancement, of African Americans.

He also contributed substantially to institutions designed to help the large numbers of impoverished Jewish immigrants from Eastern Europe who settled in Chicago at the turn of the century. He supported the Associated Jewish Charities of Chicago and served as president of the organization in 1907. The Chicago Hebrew Institute was another philanthropic activity he helped maintain. He died in Chicago on January 6, 1932.

RUBINSTEIN, HELENA (1870–1965)

Beauty industry pioneer

Helena Rubinstein was born on December 25, 1870 in Cracow, Poland. As a teenager, she was introduced to the world of business by serving as her father's bookkeeper and to the world of beauty products by her mother's friend, the actress Helena Modjeska. The actress introduced Rubenstein's mother to the chemist who made skin cream for her. The "beauty cream" was compounded from a formula of herbs, essence of almonds, and extract from the bark of the Carpathian fir tree. After refusing to marry her parent's choice of a husband, Rubinstein left Poland and went to stay with relatives in Australia. Many Australian women suffered from sun-damaged skin and it wasn't long before Rubenstein had given away almost all of the "Modjeska" cream she had brought with her. Her mother sent more and, around 1890, Rubenstein opened her first shop. Eight years later, the shop was wildly successful and she began to expand the business, adding products and opening additional salons, first in London, then in Paris.

In 1915, she moved to New York City and opened a

When she left her home in Poland to live with relatives in Australia, Helena Rubinstein took with her twelve pots of face cream her mother had gotten from a Cracow chemist. She offered them for sale, and the rest is history. (Courtesy of American Jewish Archives)

salon there. A year later she expanded to San Francisco and Philadelphia. By 1917 she had salons in most major North American cities including Boston, Los Angeles, and Toronto. In addition to selling her products, Rubinstein stressed exercise, good nutrition, and mental health as important parts of any beauty regimen. She was years before her time when she also recommended not smoking and drinking only in moderation. When she died on April 1, 1965, she left behind a multi-million-dollar cosmetics business, with laboratories, factories, and salons in fourteen countries. She established the Helena Rubinstein Foundation to provide money for the arts and to charitable institutions and donated $500,000 to the Tel Aviv Museum.

Her autobiography, *My Life in Beauty,* was published in 1966, a year after her death.

SACHS, SAMUEL (1851–1935)

Financier, philanthropist

Samuel Sachs was born in Baltimore, Maryland on July 28, 1851. Initially in the mercantile business, in 1882 he became a banker. That was the year he founded the banking house M. Goldman & Sachs with his father-in-law, Marcus Goldman. Three years later, when other partners joined the business, they renamed the firm Goldman, Sachs & Company. In 1904, Goldman died and Sachs became senior partner. As head of the company, Sachs built it into one of the most important banking firms of its day. In addition to branch offices in cities such as Chicago, St. Louis, Boston, and Philadelphia, the company also developed close ties with many of Europe's most influential banking houses.

Under Sachs, Goldman, Sachs & Company increased its specialization in industrial securities and served as the investment banking house for many of America's leading companies, including Sears, Roebuck & Co., Woolworth's, Macy's, and B. F. Goodrich. He retired as senior partner in 1928, but continued as a special partner until his death. An active philanthropist as well as financier, Sachs served on the advisory committee for the Columbia University school of business and endowed Harvard University's Sachs Research Fellowship. He died in New York City on March 2, 1935.

SCHIFF, JACOB HENRY (1847–1920)

Financier, philanthropist

Jacob Henry Schiff was born on January 10, 1847 in Frankfurt, Germany into a well-known rabbinical family. He immigrated to the United States when he was eighteen. He joined the powerful banking firm Kuhn, Loeb & Co. and later headed that firm. With the backing of the firm, Schiff was instrumental in the expansion of the American railway system and floated loans to governments both here and abroad. Throughout his career, he sat on the boards of or was advisor to a number of growing corporations.

A pious Reform Jew from an Orthodox background, Schiff gave to a large variety of causes, both Jewish and non-Jewish. He opposed Czarist Russia because of its treatment of Jews and refused to have business dealings with that country. He gave generously to Barnard College and Montefiore Hospital. He helped establish the **Jewish Theological Seminary**, **Hebrew Union College**, and the Jewish Divisions of both the New York Public Library and the Library of Congress. Committed to protecting Jewish rights around the world, he was a founder of the **American Jewish Committee** and the Jewish Welfare Board. He died on September 25, 1920, leaving behind a legacy of leadership and generosity.

SCHNEIDERMAN, ROSE (1882–1972)

Union organizer, Roosevelt advisor

Originator of the famous phrase "bread and roses," Rose Schneiderman was an advocate for the rights of American working women. Born on April 16, 1882 to a Jewish family in Saven, Poland, Schneiderman received an education at her parents' insistence, in spite of tradition. Her family moved to the city of Chelm when she was six years old so that she could attend a Russian public school. A year later, the Schneidermans moved to New York. For financial reasons, Rose was forced to leave school at the age of thirteen and take a job. She began her union work at age twenty-one when she organized her shop for the United Cloth Hat and Cap Makers' Union (UCHCMU), which had been founded and was run by socialist Jews. By 1906, she was vice president of the New York Women's Trade Union League (NYWTUL) and also became deeply involved in the International Ladies' Garment Workers' Union (ILGWU).

In the course of her long career, Schneiderman worked for better wages and working conditions, as well as for schools, recreational facilities, and other aids to a better quality of life. She was also an ardent suffragist. In the 1920s, she became close friends with Eleanor and, later, Franklin Roosevelt. During the Roosevelt administration she was the only woman on the National Labor Advisory Board. When she left Washington, she became secretary of labor for New York State. Before retiring from public life in 1949, she spent many years helping European Jews resettle in Palestine.

SOROS, GEORGE (1930–)

Financier, philanthropist

George Soros was born on August 12, 1930 in Budapest, Hungary. In 1947—after eluding the Nazis during World War II—he moved with his family to London, where he attended the London School of Economics and studied under philosopher Karl Popper. He then began to work for the London bank Singer & Friedlander. In 1956 Soros moved to New York City and soon became a well-known analyst of European securities. In 1969, he founded the Quantum Fund.

Ten years later, Soros was successful enough to create the Soros Foundations, a network of philanthropic organizations focused largely on giving in Eastern Europe, especially Hungary. As the iron curtain fell and the Soviet Union collapsed, Soros expanded his giving into Poland, Czechoslovakia, Yugoslavia, and Russia.

Soros's reputation as a genius of the markets was firmly established in late 1992 when he correctly predicted the devaluation of the British pound and made approximately $1 billion from his prediction. Two years later, he had less success when he incorrectly predicted a drop in the Japanese yen. Instead, the yen rose and Soros lost between $600 million and $1 billion.

STRAUSS, LEVI (1829–1902)

Entrepreneur, philanthropist

No one really knows the story of how Levi Strauss created his first pair of "blue jeans." The records of his company were destroyed in a fire following the 1906 San Francisco earthquake. What is known is that Levi Strauss was born in Bavaria in 1829, immigrated to the United States in 1847 to join the dry-goods business of his two brothers in New York City, and left for California soon after gold was discovered in 1849. A material salesman, Strauss came up with the idea of canvas pants when he arrived in San Francisco and hired tailors to sew them. It wasn't until a few years later that Strauss started using the tough and durable new material, denim. He was the first to use this material in pants and the first to dye it blue. A local tailor, Jacob Davis (who later became his partner), came up with and patented the idea of the rivets on the pockets. Levi Strauss never married. When he died, on September 26, 1902, he left millions of dollars to both Jewish and non-Jewish groups and charities.

TISCH, LAURENCE (1923–)

Entrepreneur

Legendary businessman Laurence Tisch was born in the Bensonhurst section of Brooklyn, New York in 1923. His father, Al Tisch, a former All-American basketball player at the City College of New York, owned a garment-manufacturing company and then bought two summer camps in New Jersey, which his wife, Sadye (Brenner) Tisch, helped him operate.

Tisch finished both high school and college in five years, graduating from New York University cum laude in 1942. The next year he earned a master's degree from the Wharton School at the University of Pennsylvania. For the next three years he was in the Army's Office of Strategic Services (the OSS—forerunner of the CIA), with a specialty in writing secret codes.

In 1946, Tisch followed his father into the hotel business with the purchase of Laurel-in-the-Pines, a resort in Lakewood, New Jersey, financed with money from his father and a family friend. In 1948 Tisch's younger brother Bob joined him. Always a close-knit family, the two brothers and their families were virtually inseparable—they socialized together, played tennis together, and went to Temple together.

This first hotel was an immediate financial success and Tisch begin to buy additional property, usually using his patented formula for turning a business around—cut costs and improve service. Nine years later he owned a chain of twelve hotels. In 1959 Tisch gained control of the Loews Corporation, a movie theater chain. Today, among the many assets owned by the Loews Corporation are hotels, a tobacco company (Lorillard), an insurance company (CNA Financial), as well as Bulova watches and Diamond Offshore Drilling.

In the mid-eighties, at the request of the company, Tisch began to purchase stock of CBS and, in September 1986, he became acting chief executive. **William Paley**, the company's founder, became acting chairman. In January 1987 the board of directors unanimously elected Tisch president and chief executive officer. In 1995, CBS was sold to Westinghouse. Tisch and his brother remain co-chief executive officers of the Loews Corporation.

Proud of his Jewish heritage, Tisch has served as president of the United Jewish Appeal of New York and as a trustee of the Federation of Jewish Philanthropies. He is chairman of the board of trustees of New York University. He and his brother donated $2 million to the school for Tisch Hall, named in honor of their father and in 1982 they gave $7.5 million to the university for the division now called the Tisch School of the Arts.

TOURO, JUDAH (1775–1854)

Businessman, philanthropist

The first large-scale Jewish philanthropist in America, Judah Touro was born in 1775 in Newport, Rhode Island. His father, Isaac Touro, was the *hazzan* (cantor) of the Newport Yeshuat Israel Synagogue. After his father's death in 1783 he was raised by his uncle, who trained him to be a merchant. When he was twenty-one Touro moved to New Orleans to start his own business. A smart and conservative businessman, Touro's success grew alongside the city of New Orleans. He made money investing in real estate and

shipping (steamships). He fought under Andrew Jackson in the final battle of the War of 1812, the Battle of New Orleans, as a civilian volunteer. While recovering from a wound, Touro met Virginia merchant Rezin Shepard, who became his lifelong friend and the executor of his will.

In 1839 or 1840 Touro met another man who would change his life, Gershom Kursheedt. There are some who credit Kursheedt both with reawakening Touro's sense of Judaism and with prompting his generous philanthropy. Upon his death, in 1854, Touro left an estimated half-million dollars to both Jewish and non-Jewish charities and causes. His money built almshouses in Israel, established a synagogue and hospital in New Orleans, endowed every traditional synagogue in the United States, enclosed a cemetery in Newport, and helped erect the Bunker Hill Monument. His will left more money to charitable causes than had ever been given before in the United States. Judah Touro's generosity helped establish the tradition of Jewish philanthropy in the United States.

WARBURG, FELIX (1871–1937)

Financier, philanthropist

Felix Moritz Warburg was born on January 14, 1871 in Hamburg, Germany. He immigrated to the United States in 1894 and joined the famed banking firm of Kuhn, Loeb & Co. In 1897 he became a partner in the firm. At the time of his death, he was the company's senior partner. Though he was certainly involved in the rise of Kuhn, Loeb & Co. into one of the leading international banks in the world, Warburg is remembered primarily for his humanitarianism and philanthropy.

He served a wide variety of institutions but was especially interested in education, art, and Jewish causes. In 1901 he became a director of the **Jewish Theological Seminary of America** and helped found its museum and its library. He also gave generously to **Hebrew Union College**. In 1902 he helped pass the first legislation to provide juvenile offenders with a system of probation and in 1907 he became the first state commissioner of probation. From 1902 through 1906, he was a member of the New York City Board of Education. During the early years of the century, he also served as secretary of the Immigrant Educational Institution. Warburg became the director of the Henry Street Settlement House in 1919, a position he held until his death. He served as the president of its board of directors from 1927 through 1933.

Among the many Jewish causes Warburg supported was the **American Jewish Committee**. In 1912 he became a member, and in 1929, he rose to its executive committee. In 1914 he helped establish both the American Jewish Relief Committee and the **Joint Distribution Committee**. The latter became one of the most active relief agencies in World War I and post-war Europe and Russia. In 1917 he helped create the Federation for the Support of Jewish Philanthropic Societies.

Consistently active in the arts, Warburg was a trustee and director of the Juilliard School of Music as well as a director of the New York Philharmonic Symphony Society. He purchased the instruments that created the Stradivarius Quartet and from 1927 through 1932 was a member of New York City's Art Commission. Due to his support and generosity, the hall of Harvard's Fogg Museum was named after him.

Amazingly enough, all of the activities listed above are only a few of the causes Warburg supported. He died in New York City on October 20, 1937, still active in trying to make the world a better place.

For Further Reading

See Appendix 2 for a bibliography of general reference books about Jews and the Jewish experience in America. All of these volumes include information about the American Jews in business, labor, and finance.

Ehrlich, Judith Ramsey, and Barry J. Rehfeld. *The New Crowd: The Changing of the Jewish Guard on Wall Street.* Boston: Little Brown & Company, 1989.

Epstein, Melech. *Jewish Labor in the United States, 1882–1914.* New York: KTAV Publishing House, 1950.

———. *Jewish Labor in United States, 1914–1952: An Industrial, Political, and Cultural History of the Jewish Labor Movement.* New York: KTAV Publishing House, 1953.

Harris, Leon. *Merchant Princes: An Intimate History of Jewish Families Who Built Great Department Stores.* New York: Harper & Row, 1979.

Herberg, Will. "The Jewish Labor Movement in the United States." In *American Jewish Yearbook,* New York: American Jewish Committee, 1952.

Hower, Ralph M. *A History of Macy's of New York, 1858–1919.* Cambridge, Mass.: Harvard University Press, 1969.

Mendelsohn, Ezra, Ed. "Essays on the American Jewish Labor Movement," *YIVO Annual,* New York: YIVO Institute, 1976.

Tcherikower, Elias, Ed. *The Early Jewish Labor Movement in the United States.* New York: YIVO Institute, 1961.

Wechsberg, Joseph. *The Merchant Bankers.* Boston: Pocket Books, 1966.

Part 7

Education and Intellectual Life

OVERVIEW

The story of Jews in American education is fundamentally the story of how religion and religious teaching relate to secular education. In the beginning, the religion at issue was Christianity. As late as the early nineteenth century, most American schools and colleges saw the inculcation of Christian values as part of their educational mission. Many required prospective faculty to pass tests on Christian texts before teaching mathematics or science, much less the more evaluative subjects. Given this Christian orientation, it is not surprising that there were many Jewish immigrants who felt uncomfortable about the education their children would receive in these institutions and created an alternative for younger students, the day school, which combined religious and secular studies. Most day schools were associated with synagogues, including B'nai Jeshurun, Ansche Chesed, Rodeph Shalom, and Shaarey Hashamayim. However, several independent Jewish schools also developed in the 1840s and 1850s.

It was not until the Civil War that American education began to focus more on secular scholarly achievement, with the result that Jewish academics began to gain greater acceptance as teachers. Also, many Jewish Americans began to see two very powerful uses for secular education in their attempts to become successful in the larger society. First, getting a good education in the American sense and in American institutions might be a way to deflect anti-Semitism. Second, a college education could be a way to move up the economic and social ladder. In this new atmosphere, the Jewish day school waned and more and more Jewish young people attended public schools. From the 1890s to World War I, young Jewish students began to flood into American colleges and universities—young Jewish *male* students, that is. Few Jewish families sent their daughters to college until after World War I.

In the second half of the nineteenth century the Jewish community addressed a form of education that no one else could provide for them. In 1875 Rabbi **Isaac Mayer Wise** founded **Hebrew Union College** to train American rabbis for American **Reform** congregations. A little over a decade later, in 1886, Jewish Americans who favored a more traditional form of Judaism founded the **Jewish Theological Seminary of America**, which spawned the **Conservative** Movement.

By the beginning of the twentieth century, most American universities had Jewish faculty members, virtually all of whom were from assimilated and established German Jewish families. Their presence was due in part to the growing prosperity and influence of German Jewish communities and congregations. Temple Sinai, for example, supported the University of Chicago financially and in return received a seat on the Board of Trustees and the appointment of its rabbi, Emil Hirsch, to the faculty. The president of the university then continued to appoint Jewish faculty, including Nobel Prize-winning physicist **Albert Michelson** and economist Isaac Hourwich. However, there were still significant barriers for all women and especially for those who, like Jewish women, bore the second burden of anti-Semitism. Hunter College in New York City was one of the few institutions to welcome Jewish women academics.

Progress in education for Jewish Americans faced a terrible setback in the 1920s and 1930s. Fear engendered by the Great Depression created an atmosphere in which racial and ethnic prejudices intensified. Discriminatory practices and policies at American institutions of higher learning became increasingly common. Yale provides a striking example. The university refused to grant any Jew a tenure-track position on their faculty until the late 1940s. Harvard University's president tried to institute an actual Jewish quota on student admissions. To escape this sort of discrimination, Jewish students fled to public universities and colleges where restrictions of this kind were illegal. Many went to the Midwest and Southwest, while others attended New York City's Hunter College and City College. At this time, the Jewish community also created their own alternative, Yeshiva College (later **Yeshiva University**) in New York City, the first undergraduate degree-granting Jewish institution in the United States. In 1948, the first Jewish-sponsored, nonsectarian liberal arts university or college in the United States, **Brandeis University**, was founded.

Discrimination against Jewish faculty abated during and after World War II with the influx of prestigious refugee scholars and also the teacher shortage occasioned by the Baby Boom. In addition, several states passed anti-discrimination laws and, finally, in 1964, Title VI of the Civil Rights Act legally outlawed discrimination on the basis of ethnic background as well as of race and sex. By the end of that decade, 12 percent of college teaching positions in the United States and more than 20 percent of those at elite private universities were filled by Jewish Americans. Title VI and subsequent developments had another, more surprising outcome. By the early 1970s, Jewish women outnumbered Jewish men on many campuses.

At this point, something interesting happened. The Jewish day school, abandoned a century before, began to return. The immigration of an ultra-Orthodox European refugee population created a demand that was met by separate day schools for boys and girls, providing both secular and religious education under strict religious control. After these Hasidic groups revived the Jewish day school, it began to draw attention from less conservative Jews who had been drawn back to their Jewish roots.

Jewish Americans have had an enormous impact

on American education and American intellectual life in general. **Albert Einstein** and **Robert Oppenheimer** helped to move America into the nuclear age and then became crucial voices in the debate about the use of nuclear power. **Hannah Arendt**, the first woman to become a full professor at Princeton University and one of America's most outspoken thinkers, stunned the world in 1963 when her book *Eichmann in Jerusalem* introduced the concept of "the banality of evil." **Clement Greenberg**, the theoretical voice of Abstract Expressionism, dominated art criticism in this country for three decades, and **Lionel Trilling** had almost as great an impact on literary criticism. **Noam Chomsky** has been called the creator of modern linguistics and is a highly influential, if controversial, figure in political activism. These are only a few of the important Jewish figures in American intellectual life. Without the voices of American Jews, intellectual debate and discussion in this country would have been immeasurably diminished.

ACADEMIA

Jews have played a significant role in the world of American higher education. Despite the deep-seated institutional anti-Semitism in many of the elite colleges and universities, Jewish intellectuals across numerous disciplines have gravitated to the academy and have exercised major influence on its development as teachers, scholars, and administrators. At some institutions, the percentage of Jewish professors now approaches almost half the total faculty. College and graduate education has been an important avenue for Jewish students to gain professional recognition, leadership, and a secure middle-class identity in the United States. In addition, the evolution of the Jewish university and the increasing importance of Jewish studies as an academic discipline have had a major impact on American higher education.

In the early nineteenth century most colleges saw their mission as inculcating Christian discipline and many went so far as to require prospective faculty to undergo rigorous religious tests to determine their fitness for the position. Ironically, one of the few Jews who did secure a university teaching position, mathematics scholar Joseph Sylvester, was an Englishman who accepted a post at the University of Virginia because his Jewishness created an even greater barrier to his teaching in England. After the Civil War, as the American philosophy of higher education shifted away from the Christian orientation toward a focus on secular scholarly achievement, Jewish academics began to play a more important role as college professors. This was especially true in institutions where college presidents exhibited particularly strong pro-Jewish sympathies such as Johns Hopkins University and the University of Chicago.

Initially, many Jewish immigrants to the United States hesitated to expose their children to Protestant-sponsored institutions, but as the academy opened its doors to Jewish students and faculty in the late nineteenth century, an increasing number of Jews began to view participation in American secular higher education as a vehicle to help alleviate anti-Semitism. In addition, Jewish families soon realized that a college education could provide significant upward mobility and considerable social and economic advancement. From the 1890s to World War I, the Jewish college student population grew dramatically and Jewish undergraduates gained a high degree of visibility.

This opening was, however, largely a male phenomenon and Jewish parents generally exhibited a preference for sending their sons to college while keeping their daughters home. Although the number of Jewish women enrolled in college programs increased over the course of these years, they still remained a small fraction of the undergraduate student population up through World War I. Jewish women represented approximately 5 percent of the enrolled students at the all-female colleges of the northeast.

The beginning of university willingness to appoint Jewish academics to teaching posts in this era reflected in part the growing prosperity and influence of German Jewish communities and congregations. Temple Sinai provided important financial support to the University of Chicago and in return received a seat on the Board of Trustees and the appointment of its rabbi, Emil Hirsch, to the faculty. College presi-

American's First Hebrew Teacher— A Convert to Christianity

Judah Monis, America's first full-time instructor of Hebrew, taught students at Harvard College from 1722 to 1760. Born into a family of formerly Portuguese *conversos* and educated at Jewish academies in Italy and Holland, Monis immigrated to New York City around 1715. Although he had studied with and taught Christians for a number of years, he did not convert to Christianity until a month before he was appointed Harvard's first full-time Hebrew instructor. The university required all of its faculty to be professed Christians.

dent William Rainey Harper continued to appoint a number of Jews as professors, including physicist **Albert Michaelson** and economist Isaac Hourwich. Likewise, New York City's German Jewish community became a source of contributions and endowments for Columbia University. Although its elitist Board of Trustees refused to allow Jews to become members for another thirty years, its president during the turn of the century years, Seth Low, believed that the university, known as a finishing school for young (Christian) gentlemen, had a public obligation to open up its teaching ranks. During his tenure, Low appointed several prominent Jewish faculty including Romance language professor Adolph Cohen, Semitics and rabbinics professor Richard Gottheil, economist E.R.A. Seligman, and literature professor Joel Spingarn.

By the first decade of the twentieth century, most universities had hired a small but increasing number of Jews for their faculty, virtually all of whom were from assimilated and established second-generation German Jewish families. The majority of these Jewish appointments came in Semitics departments and the sciences, but fields that interpreted past and present Western Christian culture such as history, religion, English literature, and art remained difficult for Jews to penetrate. The distinguished Jewish anthropologist **Franz Boas** paved the way for Jewish scholars to gain entry to university anthropology departments.

Jewish women faced greater obstacles to advancing in academia. One of the very few hired in this era, economist Jessica Peixotto joined the faculty of the University of California at Berkeley in 1904 and, in 1918, became the first woman to earn the rank of full professor in the college. She later served as head of the economics department before retiring in 1935. Hunter College in New York City proved to be one of the more hospitable institutions for Jewish women academics, with several gaining teaching positions in the first two decades of the century, including Elizabeth Vera Loeb, Anna Jacobson, Dora Askwith, and Adele Bildersee. In 1924, Florence Bamberger became the first woman elected to the school of philosophy as full professor at Johns Hopkins University. Bessie Bloom Wessel secured a teaching position at Connecticut College, while Theresa Wolfson was appointed to the Brooklyn College faculty. Overall, Jewish women continued to be severely under-represented among all college and university professors.

By the end of World War I, it appeared as if upward mobility was continuing to bring new Jewish immigrants into the American mainstream. Children of Eastern European immigrants who had grown up in poverty entered undergraduate programs and increasingly looked to graduate school for careers in higher education. With the growth of colleges and universities in the United States and the increasing rate of Jewish economic success and visibility, the future appeared bright. Instead, the 1920s and 1930s witnessed an anti-Semitic backlash against Jews in the academy, especially at the more prestigious private institutions. Increasing xenophobia, paranoia, and the desire on the part of students, alumni, and administrators to preserve the so-called Anglo-Saxon superiority of their colleges took a toll. College admissions officers used new popular scientific theories of racial hierarchy to justify discriminatory policies. Although these restrictions were not aimed at Jews alone, Jews were often affected more than other ethnic and religious minorities because, unlike Catholics or African Americans, they developed few colleges specifically for their own students.

During this period, Harvard, Yale, Princeton, and Columbia all established practices for manipulating

Harvard's Jewish Problem

In 1922 Harvard's president, A. Lawrence Lowell, proposed that the university establish a quota on the number of Jews admitted—they should represent no more than 15 percent of the student body. His recommendation was not made in a vacuum. Traditionally a "people of the book," Jews had been flocking to American institutions of higher education since the early years of the twentieth century. In 1919 almost 80 percent of the students in New York City's Hunter and City colleges were Jewish; the figure at Columbia was 40 percent; and Jews had increased at Harvard from 7 percent in 1900 to 21 percent in 1922. After an extended and contentious public debate, Lowell retracted his recommendation.

admissions to reduce or prevent the entry of Jewish students. College admissions personnel attempted to get around anti-discrimination laws by interviewing students one by one and evaluating them on the basis of "character" and "background," which enabled them to reject students by terming them "undesirable" or "unrefined," all code words that frequently were implicit references to their ethnic identities. These selective admissions, first devised at Columbia, were especially designed to exclude New York City's new Eastern European Jewish immigrants. Harvard president Abbot Lawrence Lowell went even further when he publicly advocated a strict quota on the number of Jewish students enrolled in the university. Indeed, he had some ground for concern. The Jewish enrollment had gone from 6 percent in 1909 to nearly 22 percent by 1922. He was roundly attacked for such an open advocacy of what was tacitly happening in many institutions and the policy never went into effect.

Not surprisingly, Jewish students who did end up attending high-profile private colleges often struggled to blend into the culture of institutions that were suspicious of, and hostile to, their presence. In general, they received little support or assistance from college administrators when confronted with hostility or ostracism. Jewish students frequently dealt with their ostracism by focusing extra attention on their academic

pursuits, often earning a reputation for their scholarly diligence.

Jewish undergraduates also established a number of Jewish academic and social organizations designed to ease their transition into college life. At Harvard, Jewish undergraduates organized the first of what became known as Menorah Societies, which resembled nineteenth-century collegiate literary communities. They had as their purpose the promotion in American colleges and universities the study of Jewish history, culture, and problems, and the advancement of Jewish ideals. Self-defined Jewish sororities and fraternities also sought to alleviate the isolation that many Jewish students faced in the university environment through helping them assimilate into the dominant American college milieu. Their membership restrictions and defensive posture about countering stereotypical "Jewish" behavior, however, created negative feelings among some Jewish students.

The development of **Hillel** societies, first begun in the 1920s at the University of Illinois, attempted to provide Jewish students with a religious and social community that provided education in Judaism in a pluralist and inclusive environment. Although it began slowly, Hillel soon spread to other universities including Illinois, Wisconsin, Ohio State, Michigan, California, Cornell, West Virginia, and the University of Texas.

Jewish faculty experienced similar struggles with discrimination during this era. Yale, in particular, was notorious for its outright hostility to Jewish faculty, refusing to grant any Jew a tenure track position as professor until the late 1940s. At Yale and elsewhere Jews who did manage to achieve teaching positions such as sociologist Lewis Feurer and chemist Lafayette Mende needed to have sponsors who would testify that the candidate did not "push" his Jewish traits and was "courteous and quiet in disposition." The ingrained anti-Semitism within many academic departments at the undergraduate level was, thus, implicitly, communicated to Jewish students as well.

One of the few examples of Jewish faculty confronting this prejudice came in 1939 when the faculty committee of Harvard University led by Arthur Schlesinger, Sr. and future Supreme Court Justice

Felix Frankfurter publicly exposed the issue and issued the statement that the institutionalized anti-Semitism at the university constituted a betrayal of Harvard's and the nation's best traditions. They also argued that the barriers to Jewish faculty appointment and advancement had deprived the school of the opportunity to recruit the best intellects, to achieve academic diversity, and to be a shining beacon for its sister institutions. The faculty committee expressed special concern that "Jews are gradually being eliminated from the educational field and will ultimately be charged with making no contribution to it."

It is somewhat ironic that some of the best and most well-known Jewish intellectual voices such as **Sidney Hook**, **Irving Howe**, **Lionel Trilling**, and Daniel Bell were nurtured in this restrictive environment. With the impediments to Jewish participation in the elite private Eastern institutions, Jewish students flocked to urban public universities and colleges in the Midwest and South where restrictions were less of a problem. Because of the Constitution's Fourteenth Amendment prohibiting discrimination in public institutions, these colleges could only limit the number of Jewish students by restricting out-of-state matriculations. In the epicenter of Jewish culture, New York City, City College became the avenue of choice for many young Jewish men who would go on to join the ranks of academia when the climate shifted in the post–World War II era. Hunter College served a similar role for Jewish women in this era.

The late 1920s also saw the development of Yeshiva College (later **Yeshiva University**) in New York City, the first undergraduate degree-granting Jewish institution in the United States. Although it experienced initial growing pains, Yeshiva achieved success within two decades and spawned several satellite programs including **Stern College for Women**, the Wurzweiler School of Social Work, the **Benjamin Cardozo School of Law**, and the Einstein College of Medicine. It eventually expanded to include campuses in Los Angeles and Jerusalem.

Depression at home and the rise of fascism abroad gave rise to an increase in student activism at a number of colleges in the 1930s. Many Jewish students

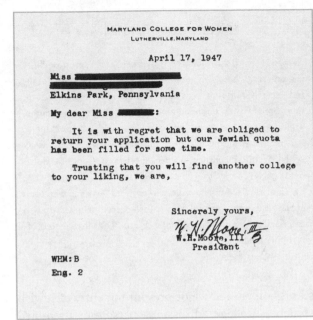

Anti-Semitism and "Jewish Quotas" were a fact of American college life from the beginnings of higher education in this country. But, it does seem surprising that as late as 1947 a school would admit that quotas were a part of its admission policy. (Courtesy of the American Jewish Historical Society, Waltham, Massachusetts and New York, New York)

joined the largest national campus organization, the American Student Union, and they spoke out on a variety of economic justice and peace issues. In some college towns, the association of Jewish students with socialist or communist leanings reinforced and escalated the anti-Semitism of certain residents. Jewish campus protesters were charged with being anti-American when the students demanded that the United States do more to save European Jewry, but this anger died down after the country entered World War II in 1941 and Jewish student politics and American foreign policy merged.

During and after World War II, significant numbers of German Jewish refugee scholars gained appointments to prestigious university posts and an overwhelming number of them became leaders in the physical and biological sciences and sociology and psychology. The war created a need for additional college faculty to replace those men serving overseas, and Jewish intellectuals and teachers capitalized on these opportunities. The new realities of American foreign and military policy also created openings in which intellectual considerations replaced social ones as priorities in faculty appointments. Yale, perhaps the most exclusive of the Ivy League colleges, hired Japanese expert Bernard Bloch and Malayan language scholar Isidore Dyen to teaching positions and each went on to long-term academic careers.

The horrifying reality of the Holocaust and European anti-Semitism also quelled objections to Jewish faculty appointments. Once a sizable number of Jewish professors established themselves within university departments, they had to be taken into consideration when new hiring and promotion decisions were made. Other developments such as rapidly rising undergraduate enrollments because of the rising birth rate and the G.I. Bill created a faculty shortage in the post-war era making it that much less advantageous for colleges to discriminate. In addition, while many colleges maintained their selective admissions policies, they were increasingly confronted with litigation and regulatory legislation designed to curtail discrimination on the grounds of race, creed, color, or national origin. Several states passed additional anti-discrimination laws and, finally, in 1964, Title VI of the Civil Rights Act, while designed to ensure equal protection for African Americans and Hispanics, also ensured equal treatment for Jews.

Although colleges and universities continued to impose quotas on Jewish enrollment, Jewish men and women entered the world of higher education in droves during the 1950s. By 1960, nearly two-thirds of Jews aged eighteen through twenty-four attended college. Post–World War II Jewish college students slowly became accepted as part of the undergraduate mainstream while an increasing number pursued masters and doctoral degrees.

Although anti-Semitism abetted considerably, the concept of academic freedom was challenged in the Cold War 1950s by the McCarthy anti-Communist crusade. Many Jewish professors who were either dismissed or denied appointments on the basis of their politics found that, despite its lofty rhetoric, the university offered them little protection from the pervasive political climate of the day.

The decline of fraternities and sororities helped Jews feel increasingly at home within the university in the 1960s, while the rise of ethnic celebrations led to an increasing number of Jewish-identified organizations on campus. Jewish students took on significant leadership roles in the civil rights and anti-war movements of the era and they also composed a substantial percentage of the membership in campus organizations. Jewish women took on particularly active roles in the burgeoning feminist movement and, by the early 1970s, their numbers began to surpass those of their male counterparts at many college campuses.

For Jewish professors, the 1960s was a time of both security and confusion. Many struggled to balance their Jewish identities with the norms and expectations of the profession. Numerous scholarly articles claimed that Jewish professors had become boxed into a secular intellectual subculture that left them out of touch with their non-academic Jewish brethren. It is likely, however, that this perception oversimplified the reality. Many Jewish academics had secured their positions precisely because they were viewed as more assimilated. As a result, many had adopted a cautious attitude with respect to overt expressions of their Jew-

The "Dean" of American Jewish Historians

Jacob Rader Marcus (1896–1995) almost single-handedly created the field of American Jewish history. He published over forty books and hundreds of articles. He was the guiding force behind the creation of the American Jewish Archives on the campus of Hebrew Union College, now a major center devoted to the documentation of the history of the Jewish people in America. At a dinner meeting of scholars of American Jewish history, Professor Jonathan Sarna, the organizer of the conference, patted himself on the back by saying that "Never before has so much knowledge about the American Jewish experience been in the same room." But then he qualified it by adding "except perhaps when Jacob Rader Marcus dined alone."

American Jewish Nobel Prize Winners, 1901–1995

Those with asterisks received their awards before immigrating to the United States.

World Peace
1973—Henry Kissinger (b. 1923)
1986—Elie Wiesel (b. 1928)

Literature
1976—Saul Bellow (b. 1915)
1978—Isaac Bashevis Singer (1904–1991)
1987—Joseph Brodsky (1940–1996)

Physiology and Medicine
1922—Otto Meyerhof* (1884–1951)
1930—Karl Landsteiner (1868–1943)
1936—Otto Loewi* (1873–1961)
1944—Joseph Erlanger (1974–1965)
1944—Herber Spencer Gasser (1888–1963)
1946—Hermann Joseph Muller (1890–1967)
1952—Selman Abraham Waksman (1888–1973)
1953—Fritz Albert Lipmann (1899–1986)
1958—Joshua Lederberg (b. 1925)
1959—Arthur Kornberg (b. 1918)
1964—Konrad Bloch (b. 1912)
1967—George Wald (b. 1906)
1968—Marshall W. Nirenberg (b. 1927)
1969—Salvador Luria (1912–1991)
1970—Julius Axelrod (b. 1912)
1972—Gerald Maurice Edelman (b. 1929)
1975—David Baltimore (b. 1938)
1975—Howard Martin Temin (b. 1934)
1976—Baruch S. Blumberg (b. 1925)
1977—Rosalyn Sussman Yalow (b. 1921)
1978—Daniel Nathans (b. 1928)
1980—Baruj Benacerraf (b. 1920)
1985—Michael Stuart Brown (b. 1914)
1985—Joseph L. Goldstein (b. 1940)
1986—Stanley Cohen (b. 1922)
1986—Rita Levi-Montalcini (b. 1909)
1988—Gertrude Bell Elion (b. 1918)
1989—Harold Eliot Varmus (b. 1939)

Chemistry
1961—Melvin Calvin (b. 1912)
1972—William Howard Stein (1911–1980)
1979—Herbert Charles Brown (b. 1912)
1980—Paul Berg (b. 1926)
1980—Walter Gilbert (b. 1932)
1981—Roald Hoffmann (b. 1937)
1989—Sidney Altman (b. 1949)
1992—Rudolph Arthur Marcus (b. 1923)

Physics
1907—Albert Abraham Michelson (1852–1931)
1921—Albert Einstein* (1879–1955)
1943—Otto Stern (1888–1969)
1944—Isidor Isaac Rabi (1898–1988)
1952—Felix Bloch (1905–1983)
1959—Emilio Segré (b. 1905)
1960—Donald A. Glaser (b. 1926)
1961—Robert Hofstadter (1915–1990)
1965—Richard Phillips Feynman (1918–1988)
1965—Julian Schwinger (b. 1918)
1967—Hans A. Bethe (b. 1906)
1969—Murray Gell-Mann (b. 1929)
1975—Benjamin R. Mottelson (b. 1926)
1976—Burton Richter (b. 1931)
1978—Arno Allan Penzias (b. 1933)
1979—Steven Weinberg (b. 1933)
1979—Sheldon L. Glashow (b. 1932)
1988—Leon M. Lederman (b. 1922)
1988—Melvin Schwartz (b. 1932)
1988—Jack Steinberger (b. 1921)
1990—Jerome I. Friedman (b. 1930)
1995—Martin L. Perl (b. 1927)
1995—Frederick Reines (1918–1998)

Economics
1970—Paul A. Samuelson (b. 1915)
1971—Simon Kuznets (b. 1901)
1972—Kenneth J. Arrow (b. 1921)
1976—Milton Friedman (b. 1912)
1978—Herbert A. Simon (b. 1916)
1980—Lawrence R. Klein (b. 1920)
1985—Franco Modigliani (b. 1918)
1987—Robert M. Solow (b. 1924)
1990—Harry Markowitz (b. 1927)
1992—Gary Stanley Becker (b. 1930)

ish identity that was difficult to change over a relatively short time span. There is also evidence that the extraordinary scholarly achievements of Jewish professors had minimal influence on their individual levels of religious observance.

By the end of the 1960s, Jews composed 12 percent of college teaching positions in the United States and more than 20 percent of the faculty at elite private universities—a remarkable turnaround in the course of only three decades. On average, Jewish academics earned higher salaries than their gentile colleagues, acquired higher ranks, and published a greater number of articles.

This period also witnessed the increasing presence of Jewish studies as a field of study on the graduate and undergraduate levels. Although originally focused on Jewish philosophy, religion, and studies of the Hebrew language, Jewish studies expanded into the more secular social history of Jews in the European and American Diaspora. The Holocaust and the creation of Israel also have greatly influenced the content of contemporary Jewish studies. The field has spread to hundreds of campuses throughout the country and it has become a discipline in which new faculty have continued to specialize.

Although anti-Semitic incidents still occur on campuses and in the field of higher education at large, Jewish students are universally accepted and embraced in virtually all colleges and universities across the United States. By 1990, surveys showed that Jewish males and females had earned higher levels of education than their gentile white counterparts. Jewish women in particular had achieved considerably greater levels of educational achievement than their non-Jewish white female contemporaries and by the late 1990s, they had achieved virtual parity with Jewish men.

In the contemporary era, even institutions with histories of discrimination against Jews such as Columbia and Princeton have hired Jewish presidents. At the same time, Jewish faculty continue to compose a larger percentage of faculty appointments in colleges throughout the country and Jews have continued to

gain increased entry on university boards of trustees, as academic deans, and in other high-level administrative positions.

More than any other ethnic minority, Jews have used higher education as a steppingstone to professional success and upward mobility. The Jewish historical legacy of embracing scholarship and intellectual life has carried over to its peoples' contemporary experience in the United States. Jews will undoubtedly continue to participate as key players in the American academic world.

ADLER, CYRUS (1863–1940)

Educator, community leader

A pivotal member of the Jewish community remembered for both his scholarship and his public service, Cyrus Adler was born in Van Buren, Arkansas on September 13, 1863. He was raised in Philadelphia and graduated from the University of Pennsylvania. He received his doctorate in Semitics from Johns Hopkins University, the first person to receive one from an American university. He went on to teach Semitics there from 1884 to 1893.

After leaving Johns Hopkins, Adler went to work at the Smithsonian Institution, first as curator of Semitics, later as librarian and assistant secretary. He also served as president of Dropsie College and, after 1915, concurrently as the president of the **Jewish Theological Seminary**. He was a founder of the Jewish Publication Society. He was also instrumental in founding and, at various periods, was president of the American Jewish Historical Society, the **American Jewish Committee** and the United Synagogue of America. He was an editor of the *American Jewish Yearbook*, the *Jewish Encyclopedia* (1905), and the *Jewish Quarterly Review*. He spoke up against anti-Semitic pogroms in Eastern Europe and, using his position as president of the American Jewish Committee, led the effort to rescue Jewish scholars from Nazi Germany. Throughout Cyrus Adler's many years of public service he built bridges between Jews and non-Jews in government

Cyrus Adler played an absolutely unique role in American Jewish life. He was a founder of the American Jewish Historical Society and its president for more than twenty years. He helped organize the American Jewish Committee, was a founder of the Jewish Publication Society, and was president of Dropsie College in Philadelphia for thirty-two years, while for many of those years he was also president of the Jewish Theological Seminary in New York. And, he still found time to edit and write. (Courtesy of the American Jewish Historical Society, Waltham, Massachusetts and New York, New York)

and scholarship and created dialogues within the Jewish community between strictly observant and more secular Jews.

ADLER, FELIX (1851–1933)

Educator, ethicist

Founder of the Society for Ethical Culture, Felix Adler was born on August 13, 1851 in Germany. The son of a rabbi, he immigrated to the United States when he was five. He attended Columbia University, graduated in 1870, and went on to study at the universities of Berlin and Heidelberg. In 1874 he became a professor of Hebrew and Oriental literature at Cornell University. In 1876, back in New York City, he founded the Society for Ethical Culture. This was the beginning of the Ethical Movement, which proposed that an ethical reality existed independently of religion or belief in a supreme being. Active in the social reform movement of the day, Adler lobbied for proper housing for the poor, for the creation of child labor laws, and for progressive education in the public schools. In 1902 he became a professor of political and social ethics at Columbia University. His published work includes *Creed and Deed* (1877), *The Moral Instruction of Children* (1892), *The World Crisis and Its Meaning* (1915), *An Ethical Philosophy of Life* (1918), and *The Reconstruction of the Spiritual Ideal* (1923). He died on April 24, 1933 in New York City.

ADLER, MORTIMER (1902–)

Professor, editor, philosopher

Mortimer Adler was born in New York City on December 28, 1902. In 1922, he obtained his Ph.D. from Columbia University. For much of his career he was on the faculty at the University of Chicago teaching philosophy of law. He served as the director of the Institute for Philosophical Research, chairman of the Board of Editors of *Encyclopedia Britannica*, and senior associate of the Aspen Institute for Humanistic Studies. He also co-founded—with Max Weisman—the Center for the Study of the Great Ideas and was editor-in-chief of *Philosophy Is Everybody's Business*.

Adler's best-known work was as the editor—with Robert Hutchins—of the fifty-four-volume series *Great Books of the Western World* (1952) and its two-volume index, the *Synopticon* (1952). Later, he and Hutchins edited the ten-volume *Gateway to the Great Books* and the twenty-volume *Annals of America*, both published by *Encyclopedia Britannica*. Adler was the director of planning for the publication of the fifteenth edition of the *Encyclopedia* itself. In addition to his editing projects, he wrote over fifty books, including

How to Read a Book (1940), *Philosopher at Large: An Intellectual Autobiography* (1977), and *A Guidebook to Learning* (1986).

ARENDT, HANNAH (1906–1975)

Political philosopher

One of the most influential political thinkers of the 1950s and 1960s, Hannah Arendt was born on October 14, 1906 in Hanover, Germany to Russian Jewish parents. Raised and educated in Königsburg, she later studied at the University of Marburg with Rudolf Bultmann and Martin Heidegger and at the University of Heidelberg under Karl Jaspers. She had a brief, but passionate, affair with Heidegger (who was married and a father) while she was studying with him. She remained a friend of Heidegger all his life and has been criticized for not attacking him for his cooperation with the Nazi regime.

In the 1930s, as the National Socialists rose to power, Arendt began working with the German Zionist Organization. Arrested by the Gestapo, she was able to escape to Paris where she worked with Youth Alivah to rescue Jewish children. In 1941 Arendt and her second husband, Heinrich Blücher, came to the United States and settled in New York. Ten years later she published *The Origins of Totalitarianism*, which traces developments in Europe that led to the horrors of Nazi Germany and the Holocaust and to the tyranny of Joseph Stalin.

Arendt's first book was followed by three others on political philosophy: *The Human Condition* (1958), *Between Past and Future* (1961), and *On Revolution* (1968). In 1963 her most controversial book, *Eichmann in Jerusalem*, which was based on her journalistic coverage of the trial of the S.S. officer who had been captured by Israeli agents and tried in Israel, was published. Arendt's terrifying vision of "the banality of evil" captured the intellectual imagination of political thinkers around the world, making clear for the first time that atrocities could be committed by people who were "just following orders" rather than anti-Semitic monsters. Hannah Arendt was the first woman to become a full professor at Princeton University and also taught at the University of Chicago, Wesleyan University, and the New School for Social Research. She died in 1975 after a quarter-century as one of America's most important and outspoken intellectuals.

BARON, SALO (1895–1989)

Historian

Jewish historian Salo Wittmayer Baron was born in Galicia in 1895. He graduated from the University of Vienna with doctorates in political science, law, and philosophy and taught at the Judisches Paedagogim from 1919 to 1925. Baron settled in the United States in 1926 and took a teaching position at Columbia University in New York City, occupying the first chair in Jewish history at an American college.

Baron is best known for his eighteen-volume work, *A Social and Religious History of the Jews* (Columbia University Press, 1952–1983), which emphasizes the place of Jewish history within the context of general history, as well as the interaction between Jewry and the non-Jewish world. Dismissing what he called "the lachrymose conception of Jewish history," which he felt placed too much emphasis on anti-Jewish persecution, Baron instead stressed Jewish creativity and endurance.

Baron's *The Russian Jew under Tsars and Soviets* was the first major study of contemporary Russian Jewry.

Original, controversial, and daring, the philosophical works of Hannah Arendt divided Jewish thinkers but left their indelible mark on sociopolitical theory in the twentieth century. She is pictured here at a Hillel symposium at the University of Maryland in 1965. (Courtesy of the American Jewish Historical Society, Waltham, Massachusetts and New York, New York)

His *Steeled by Adversity: Essays and Addresses on American Jewish Life* and *The Jews of the United States, 1790–1940: A Documentary History* are must reading for students of American Jewish history.

A prominent figure in Jewish scholarly organizations, Baron served, at various times, as president of the American Jewish Historical Society, the American Academy of Jewish Research, and the Conference on Jewish Social Studies. He edited the scholarly journal *Jewish Social Studies* from 1939 until his death in 1989.

BRANDEIS UNIVERSITY

The first Jewish-sponsored, nonsectarian liberal arts university or college in the United States, Brandeis University was founded in 1948. Named for Supreme Court Justice **Louis Dembitz Brandeis**, the school took over the premises of Middlesex University, a medical school in Waltham, Massachusetts. It was established by a group of Jewish community leaders from New York and its first freshman class included 107 students. The goal of the founders was to create a school with the highest possible standards and absolutely no discrimination on the basis of race, religion, or national origin. A sign of this determination not to discriminate was the construction on the campus of three chapels—Jewish, Protestant, and Catholic.

The first president, Abram L. Sachar, set out immediately to build a faculty of national stature. With an often strained budget, he hired first-rate scholars and the result was full academic accreditation in 1954. The Graduate School of Arts and Sciences soon opened and the Florence Heller Graduate School for Advanced Studies in Social Welfare was added in 1959. It was the first of several professional schools established at Brandeis over the years. The university is a major research institution, attracting some of the top scholars in the country. It has an outstanding reputation for undergraduate education. In 1998 it had 3,020 undergraduates and 1,199 graduate students. That same year the famous *U.S. News and World Report* ranking of American universities put Brandeis at number thirty-one. An incredible accomplishment for a school celebrating its fiftieth anniversary!

Distinguished historian Jehuda Reinharz is the seventh president of Brandeis University. Under his leadership (he was inaugurated in 1995) the school continues to build on the international reputation for excellence in education and research established by his predecessors. He is shown here at the 1999 commencement, where one of the honorary degree recipients was Senator John Glenn. The first American to orbit the Earth, Glenn was born in 1921, twenty-seven years before Brandeis was founded. (Photo courtesy of Brandeis University)

BENJAMIN N. CARDOZO SCHOOL OF LAW

A branch of **Yeshiva University** in New York City, Benjamin N. Cardozo School of Law was founded in 1976 in Greenwich Village. Named for the highly respected Jewish Supreme Court Justice, it has built a remarkably solid reputation. After only two decades in existence, it ranks among the seventy most selective law schools in the nation and has eight students every year competing for each of the 250 spots in its entering class. The faculty of the school is particularly eminent in the fields of criminal law, intellectual property and entertainment law, constitutional law and First Amendment rights, European jurisprudence, public interest law, and law and literature. There are four publications of the law school: *Cardozo Law Review, Cardozo Arts & Entertainment Law Journal, Cardozo Journal of International and Comparative Law,* and *Cardozo Women's Law Journal.* Among the special programs of the school is the Innocence Project, founded in 1993, which has made possible through DNA evidence the release of nine men wrongly imprisoned for capital crimes.

COHEN, MORRIS RAPHAEL (1880–1947)

Philosopher, college teacher

Philosopher Morris Raphael Cohen was born in Russia and immigrated to the United States at age twelve with his family, in 1892. After earning his undergraduate degree at City College, Cohen went on to earn his doctorate in philosophy at Harvard under the tutelage of two of the leading scholars in the field, William James and Josiah Royce. He began his teaching career in 1912 at City College and remained there for the rest of his life, except from 1938 to 1942, when he was a visiting professor at the University of Chicago. A legendary teacher devoted to the Socratic method, he was once asked by a frustrated student why he answered all questions in class with a question. You can guess his answer: "Why not?"

In major works such as *Reason and Nature: An Essay on the Meaning of Scientific Method* (1931) and *An Introduction to Logic and Scientific Method* (1934), coauthored by Ernest Nagel, Cohen postulated that while the universe possesses a logical order independent of any human mind, the irrational aspect of the universe makes man's knowledge of facts only probable rather than certain.

After the rise of Nazism, Cohen took a more active interest in Jewish affairs. In 1933 he founded the Conference on Jewish Relations to encourage scientific research on Jewish issues. Six years later he founded the journal *Jewish Social Studies.* In his autobiography, *A Dreamer's Journey* (published in 1949, after his death), Cohen attributed his early interest in legal philosophy to his upbringing. His parents were active in the Jew-ish labor movement, which was often arrayed against the anti-labor attitudes of American judges who, in Cohen's view, derived their views from conservative eighteenth-century concepts of natural law. His critique of such concepts was detailed in his 1933 study, "Law and the Social Order."

DAY SCHOOLS AND YESHIVAS

Throughout most of American history the majority of Jews have viewed Jewish education as supplementary to the education provided by public schools. Jewish day schools did serve an important function in the education of Jewish youth at two crucial periods in American history—in the middle of the nineteenth century (before the advent of universal public education) and in the beginning of the twentieth century. At the end of the twentieth century they are enjoying a remarkable renaissance.

The first Jewish day schools in the 1840s were developed by the new German Jewish immigrants who had begun entering the United States twenty years earlier. Although the public school movement had already gained ground in other states, there was essentially no public education in New York City, already the nation's largest Jewish community. In addition, these Ashkenazi Jews voiced frustration at the limited quality of Jewish studies and discomfort with Sephardic synagogue rituals. In an effort to improve these deficiencies in the education of their children, German Jewish immigrants established the first day schools that combined religious and secular studies. The majority were associated with synagogues, including B'nai Jeshurun, Ansche Chesed, Rodeph Shalom, and Shaarey Hashamayim, but several private Jewish schools unattached to congregations also developed in the 1840s and 1850s.

By the beginning of the Civil War era the changes in public education laws away from any explicit Christian religious influence and the overall improvement in the public school system, combined with the growing assimilation of the German Jewish community, signaled the demise of the Jewish day school. In addition, the increasing influence of **Reform Judaism** created a

Jewish women in America became professional teachers to an unprecedented extent. In terms of percentages, most of them taught in New York City, but they were spread out through the country as well. This 1909 photograph shows Belle Zimmerman with her grade school class in a small Wisconsin town. (Courtesy of the Jewish Historical Society of the Upper Midwest)

climate that encouraged separation between secular and religious studies and pointed to the development of the supplementary Jewish Sunday School to augment secular public education.

Throughout the remainder of the nineteenth century and into the twentieth century, Jewish families continued to rely overwhelmingly on the American public school system to educate their sons and daughters. In the early twentieth century, newly established Bureaus of Jewish Education developed several short-lived modern day school programs. Labor Zionists formed several Yiddish secular Jewish day schools—the largest founded by the Workmen's Circle in 1918 for the purpose of promoting socialism and Jewish nationalism.

The first three decades of the twentieth century witnessed the development of the Yeshiva or Yeshivot—the Orthodox Jewish day school dedicated to the study of core Jewish texts. The Yeshivot movement has as its foundation the belief that secular and religious education cannot be separated and that it is a moral obligation for all Jewish young adults to become conversant and knowledgeable in Talmudic scholarship.

The creation of the most famous Orthodox institution of higher learning, **Yeshiva University**, evolved from several elementary and secondary schools that developed on the Lower East Side of New York City in the late nineteenth century. The Yeshiva Etz Chayim, established in 1886, became one of the first day schools in the city to focus on teaching religious studies and a secular academic program under the same roof. In 1915 the school merged with the Rabbi Isaac Elhanan Theological Seminary (RIETS), which had been established eighteen years earlier as the first Orthodox seminary to draw from the curriculum of the East European Yeshivas. **Bernard Revel** took on the leadership of this new expanded institution and established a high school using a more advanced model of talmudic and secular integrative studies. The combined elementary school, high school, and seminary paved the way for the establishment of Yeshiva College (later Yeshiva University) in 1928.

Between 1917 and 1939 the number of Yeshivas in the country grew steadily, with twenty-eight new schools established in several cities with densely populated Jewish neighborhoods, including Baltimore, Chicago, and Boston (Dorchester). The center of the Yeshivot continued to be in New York City and the most famous school established during this era was the Hebrew Institute of Borough Park in Brooklyn, the first Yeshiva to introduce Hebrew as the sole language of instruction in the religious studies department.

It was only after World War II that the day school movement began to grow in serious numbers. Aided by the in-migration of an ultra-Orthodox European refugee population, these Yeshivot have grown in popularity. Establishing separate day schools for boys and girls, the ultra-Orthodox provided both secular and religious education under strict religious control. Al-

though these Hasidic groups were the initial catalysts for reviving the Jewish day school, others with more modern Orthodox affiliations have continued the trend.

Not surprisingly, with the growth of the Yeshivot have come disagreements among its different adherents in the Orthodox community over the proper role of a Jewish day school. Modern Orthodox leaders have continued to stress the essential role of Torah and talmudic study, but they are also committed to western culture and values and the importance of secular education in their Yeshivas. The ultra-Orthodox find little of value in secular education or contemporary culture and view the Yeshiva as a shield against the modern world.

More recently, the Conservative Movement has established its own Solomon Schechter Schools to promote a very different brand of Judaism. In contrast to the Orthodox desire to use their day schools to separate themselves from secular American culture, Conservative and even Reform Jews no longer believe they have to send their sons and daughters to public schools to ensure that they become instilled with a national identity as Americans. The movement appears to be partially in response to a belief that Jewish ethical, religious, and moral values will strengthen the ability of children to become successful American citizens. One of the first and most successful of the Solomon Schechter Schools was established in Silver Spring, Maryland in the mid-1960s. Under the leadership of headmaster, Shulamith Reich Elster, the school grew into a model institution with over a thousand students.

The Jewish day school and Yeshivot movement has come full circle. It is enjoying a newfound renaissance at the end of the twentieth century, with 11 percent of total Jewish school-age children attending these programs. In contrast to earlier eras, girls are now almost as likely as boys to attend day schools. New schools continue to open all around the country, with one of the most recent in Atlanta, Georgia. In its new incarnation, the Jewish day school has become, once again, an important part of American Jewish life.

FELDMAN, SANDRA (1939–)

Educator, labor leader

Labor leader Sandra Feldman was born on October 14, 1939 and grew up in the Coney Island section of New York City. The granddaughter of Jewish immigrants from Hungary and Romania, she was educated in the city's public schools. In 1966, after teaching (and helping organize other teachers) on the Lower East Side, Feldman became a field representative for New York City's United Federation of Teachers. She became the first president of the union in 1986. When **Albert Shanker** died in 1997, she was elected to serve concurrently as the president of the national union, the American Federation of Teachers. Unlike Shanker, who held both positions for decades, she resigned her UFT position in January of 1998 in order to focus all of her energies on the national union. Throughout her career, Sandra Feldman has never lost her commitment to public education or the teachers who foster it.

FINKELSTEIN, LOUIS (1895–1991)

Rabbi, President of Jewish Theological Seminary

Rabbi Louis Finkelstein was born in Cincinnati, Ohio in 1895. He attended the College of the City of New York, graduating in 1915. He then moved on to postgraduate work at Columbia University, where he earned his Ph.D. in 1918. The following year he received his rabbinic ordination at the **Jewish Theological Seminary of America** (JTS). He served for over twenty years (1919–1930) as the rabbi of New York City's Congregation Kehallath Israel.

Finkelstein's most influential work was with JTS. He became a member of the faculty a year after his ordination, and ultimately became the Solomon Schechter Professor of Theology. In 1940 he was appointed president of the seminary. He held this position until 1951, when he became chancellor. Upon his retirement in 1972, he was named chancellor emeritus.

Not only did Finkelstein help make JTS a major

university, during his years as chancellor he was the acknowledged leader of **Conservative Judaism**. During his tenure, he created the "Eternal Light" radio and television programs and edited over one hundred works including *The Jews: Their History, Culture and Religion* (two volumes, 1949, 1960). In addition to his editorial work, he authored of a number of scholarly works of his own, mostly dealing with late biblical and early rabbinic Judaism including *The Pharisees: The Sociological Background of Their Faith* (two volumes, 1938) and *Akibah: Scholar, Saint and Martyr* (1939). He died in 1991, in New York City at the age of 96.

FLEXNER, ABRAHAM (1866–1959)

Educator, educational critic

Prominent educator Abraham Flexner was born in Louisville, Kentucky in 1866 to Bohemian immigrants. He was educated at Johns Hopkins University and in 1890 founded an innovative college preparatory school that dispensed with most traditional structure. Returning to Harvard for further studies in 1905, he then went on to the University of Berlin and worked with historian, philosopher, and educator Friedrich Paulsen.

Flexner first came to the attention of the educational establishment with his book *The American College*, published in 1908. His report on American medical schools, *Medical Education in the United States and Canada* (1910), was highly critical of the profit-driven system and its deplorable lack of standards. It occasioned vast reforms in all areas of medical education. Flexner carried on a number of important investigations in both the U. S. and Europe over the next two decades, and his publications included *A Modern College* (1923), which propounded revolutionary and highly influential pedagogical ideas, and *Universities: American, English, German* (1930), which deplored the vocational approach of American higher education.

In 1930, Flexner founded the Institute for Advanced Study in Princeton, funded by the **Louis Bamberger** and Caroline Bamberger Fund. Conceived as a nurturing setting for the scholarly and scientific work, the Institute served as a base for **Albert Einstein** and many other important intellectual workers. Abraham Flexner died in 1959, having had an immeasurable impact on American education.

GOTTSCHALK, ALFRED (1930–)

Rabbi, educator

Alfred Gottschalk was born in Oberwesel, Germany on March 7, 1930. He fled the Nazis with his family in 1939 and immigrated to New York. He received his B.A. from Brooklyn College in 1952. He then moved on to post-graduate study at **Hebrew Union College-Jewish Institute of Religion (HUC-JIR)**, earning a Bachelor of Hebrew Literature degree from the New York campus in 1954 and an M.A. from the Cincinnati campus in 1956. In 1957, he was ordained by HUC-JIR, Cincinnati.

Alfred Gottschalk has spent most of his adult life building Hebrew Union College-Jewish Institute of Religion into one of the major educational institutions in the Jewish world. He has published widely and been a leading spokesman for Reform Judaism. What he may be most remembered for in the public mind is the ordination of the first female rabbi in America, Sally Priesand. The two of them are pictured here. (Courtesy of American Jewish Archives)

Immediately upon his ordination, Gottschalk moved to California to direct the newly established HUC-JIR campus there. He served first as its acting dean (1958–1959) and then as its dean (1959–1971). In 1971, he became president of HUC-JIR. During his tenure, he ordained the first female rabbi in history (**Sally Priesand**) and oversaw the first ordinations of Reform rabbis in Israel. For many years he was among one of **Reform Judaism**'s foremost spokesmen and helped the denomination grow and prosper. Among his many published works on the subjects of Jewish history and Jewish service are *Your Future as a Rabbi: A Calling that Counts* (1967), *The Future of Human Community* (1968), and *Building Unity in Diversity* (1989). He was an original member of the United States Holocaust Memorial Council. He retired from his position as president of HUC-JIR in 1996.

HANDLIN, OSCAR (1915–)

Historian

Historian Oscar Handlin was born in Brooklyn, New York on September 29, 1915. The son of Russian Jewish immigrants, he began attending Brooklyn College when he was fifteen. He then moved on to Harvard, receiving an M.A. in 1937 and a Ph.D. in 1940. He also taught at both Brooklyn College and Harvard. He ran the Center for the Study of Liberty in America (1958–1967) and the Charles Warren Center for Studies in American History (1965–1973), and was the director of the Harvard University Library (1979–1985).

His first published work was *Boston's Immigrants, 1790–1865* (1941). He won the Pulitzer Prize in History for his second book, *The Uprooted* (1951). His other books on American social and immigrant history include *Race and Nationality in American Life* (1956), *Fire-Bell in the Night* (1964), and *Truth in History* (1979). He also wrote on Jewish themes including *Adventure in Freedom: Three Hundred Years of Jewish Life in America* (1954). Mary Frug, his first wife, often assisted him with his research and writing. She received co-author credit on the book *Facing Life* (1971).

Liberty in America, 1600 to the Present (1986) was co-written with his second wife, Lilian Handlin.

HEBREW UNION COLLEGE/JEWISH INSTITUTE OF RELIGION

In 1875 Hebrew Union College (HUC) was established by Rabbi **Isaac Mayer Wise**. Located in Cincinnati, Ohio Hebrew Union was the first Jewish school of higher education in America. It was founded specifically to train rabbis for Rabbi Wise's new **Reform Movement**. In 1913 the college's museum was established. In the 1930s—recognizing the danger of the rise of fascism—the college became home to many refugee Jewish scholars. This program of rescue earned the college the nickname "the Jewish College in Exile."

In 1906 Rabbi **Stephen S. Wise** (no relation) formed the Free Synagogue after he ran into conflict at the famous Reform Temple Emanu-El over the issue of freedom of speech in his sermons. Wise created the Jewish Institute of Religion in New York City to train rabbis in his more liberal, egalitarian Judaism in 1922. Despite Wise's dispute with the Reform Emanu-El, his Institute and Hebrew Union College shared similar religious and philosophical outlooks. In 1950, a year after Stephen Wise died, the two schools merged, keeping both their Cincinnati and New York campuses. Four years later, a third campus was opened in Los Angeles, California. In 1963 the school's fourth branch was established in Jerusalem.

Today, each HUC-JIR campus includes a rabbinical school and a school of graduate studies. The New York branch also has a school of sacred music. The Los Angeles branch houses the Hirsch School of Education, the Daniels School of Jewish Communal Service, and the Louchheim School of Judaic Studies, which provides undergraduate classes to students at the University of Southern California as well as a sacred music program. The Jerusalem branch of the college has several rabbinic schools as well as the postdoctoral Glueck School of Biblical Archeology.

The Cincinnati campus includes the Hebrew Union College–University of Cincinnati Center for the Study of Ethics and Contemporary Moral Problems, the Starkoff Institute of Ethics, the American Jewish Archives, and the Klau Library. The American Jewish Archives is a major center for historical information on American Jewish history. The Klau Library contains one of America's most comprehensive collections of Hebraica and Judaica. The college's publications include the *Hebrew Union College Annual, Studies in Bibliography and Booklore, Bibliographia Judaica*, as well as the Sacred Music Press.

Throughout its history, HUC-JIR has been the academic and rabbinical center of the Reform Movement in America. The first female rabbi ordained in America, **Sally Priesand**, was educated and ordained through the college as were Israel's first Reform rabbis. The school is also known for its work in the area of ecumenism and for its Interfaith Fellowship Program for Christian Scholars.

HILLEL

In 1923 Rabbi Ben Frankel founded Hillel at the University of Illinois to serve the religious and social needs of the Jewish students there. It was America's first Jewish campus organization. Two years later, the organization was made a part of **B'nai B'rith**. Frankel served as Hillel's director until his death, four years after he established the organization.

Hillel's second director was Abram Leon Sachar, who lead the organization through its early period of rapid growth. He became the group's national director as the organization began to be established on college campuses across America. Eventually, he became chairman of Hillel's governing body, the B'nai B'rith Hillel Commission.

For the first half of the twentieth century, Hillel remained virtually the only official Jewish campus organization. For the past forty years the number of Jewish campus organizations has been steadily increasing. Today, Hillel Foundations not only maintain their own programs of religious, social, and cultural services, but also often serve as a national umbrella organization for a variety of Jewish campus groups. Among the organization's many cooperative ventures is the Association of Hillel and Campus Workers, which was created to involve unaffiliated campus staff in Hillel's activities. Hillel has also established a National Student Secretariat and a National Jewish Law Student Association.

Over the years Hillel's funding sources have become more diverse. They now include not just B'nai B'rith, but also various Jewish federations and welfare funds as well as individual donations from students, parents, and faculty. This increased funding has made it possible for Hillel to expand its activities and sponsorships and to become more socially and politically active, especially on the subjects of Israel and Soviet Jewry. In 1987 Hillel sponsored four thousand students at a rally in support of Soviet Jewry in Washington, D.C. The organization regularly sends students and faculty to Israel for seminars and volunteer service. It also hosts annual leadership training seminars on Jewish rights.

Currently, Hillel has campus groups at over four hundred colleges and universities throughout the world. Countries where Hillel now has offices include the United States, Australia, Great Britain, Brazil, South Africa, Israel, the Netherlands, Switzerland, Argentina, and Venezuela. Its headquarters, the Hillel International Center, is at the B'nai B'rith offices in Washington, D.C. The organization also has regional centers, affiliates, foundations and a number of campus facilities.

HOOK, SIDNEY (1902–1989)

Philosopher, educator

Sidney Hook was born in New York City on December 20, 1902. He received his post-graduate education at Columbia University, earning his doctorate in 1927. While at Columbia, he was profoundly influenced by John Dewey. For most of his career—1927 through 1969—he taught at New York University. From 1973 until his death he was a senior research fellow at Stanford University's Hoover Institution on War, Revolution, and Peace.

One of the first American scholars to study Marx-

ism, Hook was a firmly committed liberal democrat. In that tradition, he was also a secularist and rationalist, vocally opposed to totalitarianism in all its forms. Either as author or as editor, he published over thirty-five works. Among the most important are *Towards the Understanding of Karl Marx: A Revolutionary Interpretation* (1933), *The Hero in History* (1943), *Education for Modern Man* (1946), *In Defense of Academic Freedom* (1971), and *Revolution, Reform, and Social Justice* (1975). He also wrote an autobiography, *Out of Step: An Unquiet Life in the 20th Century* (1987). He died in Stanford, California on July 12, 1989.

HOWE, IRVING (1920–1993)

Literary critic, historian, activist

Although Irving Howe was one of our most astute literary critics and a leading force in America's small but ardent democratic socialist movement, he will probably be best remembered as a chronicler of the lives of Jewish immigrants in his native New York City. His best-known book on that subject, *The World of Our Fathers* (1976), probably sold more copies than all of his political and literary offerings combined. As a self-described secular Jew and Yiddishist, Howe undoubtedly would not have minded much.

Howe grew up in a Jewish neighborhood much like the ones he wrote about in *The World of Our Fathers*, a Bronx neighborhood in which one could go all day without having to speak anything but Yiddish. His parents were immigrants from the Ukraine who, although they had coincidentally come over on the same boat, didn't meet until they were both living on the Lower East Side. After Irving's birth, they moved to the Bronx, where his father ran a small grocery store until the Depression wiped him out. His parents ended up working together in a garment factory and joining the International Ladies Garment Workers Union. When the union struck in 1933, Irving got his first taste of political activity, seeing his parents on the picket line. He began reading Marx in high school and became a member of the Young People's Socialist League, the youth wing of the Socialist Party. By the time he entered City College of New York (CCNY) in 1936, he was a committed Trotskyist, a vehement opponent of Stalinism.

Howe graduated from CCNY in 1940 and began working in a factory and editing a labor weekly. In 1942 he was drafted into the Army and ended up in an outpost in Alaska. It was a blessing in disguise; with little else to do, Howe read voraciously, developing a new interest in literature. When he left the Army at the end of the war, he came back a literary critic as much as a political activist.

Howe began writing book reviews on a freelance basis, most prominently for *Partisan Review*. Gradually he established himself as an incisive and witty analyst of literature and, although he had no doctorate, Howe began to find himself considered for teaching positions. He accepted a professorship in English at **Brandeis University** in 1953, later teaching at Stanford, and finally in the City University system that had given him his start.

In 1954 Howe and a group of friends and colleagues founded *Dissent*, a quarterly journal of democratic socialist thought; he would remain an editor until his death. *Dissent* became an important platform for anti-Stalinist socialist thought from a wide range of progressive writers. Around the same time as *Dissent* began publication, Howe was also establishing himself as a translator, anthologist, and critic of Yiddish literature; Yiddish was, after all, his first language. Perhaps it was a logical path from there to *The World of Our Fathers*. No other book has given a more vivid or complete picture of the life of Jewish immigrants in New York in the years of the great wave of Jewish immigration from 1880 to 1920. A documentary on Howe's life (along with the lives of three of his CCNY school mates—Daniel Bell, Nathan Glazer, and **Irving Kristol**), *Arguing the World*, was released in 1998.

JEWISH THEOLOGICAL SEMINARY OF AMERICA

The Jewish Theological Seminary of America (JTS) was established in 1886 with Rabbi **Sabato Morais** as its first president. Initially called the Jewish Theologi-

cal Seminary Association, JTS was created to be an alternative to the increasingly radicalized American **Reform Movement** of Judaism. The Seminary's purpose, to quote its charter was "the preservation in America of the knowledge and practice of historical Judaism." In its first year of operation, the seminary was made up of ten rabbinical students and housed in the vestry of New York's oldest synagogue, the Spanish Portuguese Shearith Israel. Among the most important scholars Morais mentored was **Cyrus Adler**, who later became president of the Seminary.

In 1902 Cambridge University scholar **Solomon Schechter** became the second president of the Seminary. Schechter was responsible for dropping the word "Association" from the Seminary's name and for broadening its charter. More importantly, he defined the Seminary as the founding institute of a new religious movement, **Conservative Judaism** in America. Schechter is frequently referred to as "the father of Conservative Judaism." He was also one of the foremost Judaic scholars of his day and helped establish JTS's academic reputation by recruiting many of Judaism's most distinguished scholars to serve on the Seminary's faculty. In 1904 he helped the Seminary create the Jewish Museum, which is currently housed in New York City's Warburg mansion.

When Schechter died in 1915 his close friend and early advocate, Cyrus Adler, became the "temporary" president of JTS while concurrently holding the same position at Dropsie College. In 1924 Adler was made the Seminary's permanent president. He held that position until his death in 1940. During Adler's tenure as president JTS built its "new" buildings in Manhattan at Broadway and 122 Street, which were opened in 1930.

The Seminary's fourth president (1940–1951), **Louis Finkelstein**, was also its first chancellor (1951–1972). Finkelstein inaugurated JTS's Camp Ramah program in 1947, a network of Hebrew-speaking, educational sleep-away and day camps across North America. The same year, the Seminary's Los Angeles affiliate, the **University of Judaism** was founded. The Seminary's second chancellor was noted historian Gerson D. Cohen (1972–1986). In 1983, during his tenure as chancellor, the Seminary opened the Rabbinical School to women. JTS's current chancellor, **Ismar Schorsch**, opened the Cantors Institute to women in 1987.

The Jewish Theological Seminary of America remains the center of Conservative Judaism in the United States both academically and spiritually. The New York campus houses five separate schools including the Rabbinical School, the H. L. Miller Cantorial School, and College of Jewish Music. JTS's undergraduate school, List College, grants its own undergraduate degrees and has joint study programs with Barnard College and Columbia University. The Graduate School grants M.A., M.Phil., D.H.L., and Ph.D. degrees in Judaic Studies and is the largest program for advanced Judaic studies in the United States. The Seminary's library contains one of the best collections of Hebraica in the world. The school's most recent addition is the William Davidson Graduate School of Jewish Education, which opened in 1996. JTS also runs Jerusalem's Shocken Institute for Jewish Research.

KALLEN, HORACE MEYER (1882–1974)

Social philosopher

Social philosopher Horace Kallen was born in Germany but raised in Boston. As an undergraduate student at Harvard, Kallen was profoundly influenced by the famed philosopher William James and literature professor Barrett Wendell, who emphasized the Hebraic roots of Puritan culture. Wendell kindled within Kallen a positive view of the Jewish ethnicity he had abandoned as a teen. James's emphasis on America's pluralistic qualities helped Kallen form his own vision of the United States as a collection of separate ethnic groups, in contrast to the "melting pot" metaphor popular in the late 1800s and early 1900s.

During his Harvard years Kallen joined with Henry Hurwitz and **Harry Wolfson** to establish the Menorah Society, one of the earliest Jewish university campus groups. After completing his Ph.D. at Harvard, Kallen briefly joined its faculty, before taking up a post in the

philosophy department at the University of Wisconsin, where he remained for eight years. In 1918 Kallen accepted a position at the New School for Social Research, where he remained for the rest of his academic career.

Kallen's landmark essay, "Democracy versus the Melting Pot," which was published in *The Nation* in 1915, pictured American society as an orchestra, in which individual ethnic and religious groups, like musical instruments, maintain their distinctive identities while contributing to the harmonious sound of the collective society. Kallen's argument was taken up with vigor by Jewish intellectuals opposed to assimilation, and particularly by American Zionists, who regarded it as a means of proving that adherence to Zionist ideology did not necessarily conflict with loyalty to America. Kallen's philosophy of "cultural pluralism" was crucial to convincing **Louis Brandeis** to become leader of the American Zionist movement. Kallen himself was an active Zionist, particularly during the years of Brandeis's leadership.

LAMM, NORMAN (1927–)

Rabbi and educator

Norman Lamm was born on December 19, 1927 in Brooklyn, New York. He attended Yeshiva and Mesivta Torah Vodaath for elementary and high school. He then moved on to Yeshiva College, graduating in 1949. He pursued post-graduate studies at both Yeshiva and the Polytechnic Institute of Brooklyn. In 1951 he was ordained as a rabbi by Yeshiva's Rabbi Isaac Elchanan Theological Seminary. In 1966 he received his Ph.D. in Jewish philosophy from the Bernard Revel Graduate School of Yeshiva—no longer a college, now a university. The same year he was appointed the university's Erna and Jakob Michael professor of Jewish Philosophy. In 1976 he was elected the first native-born president of Yeshiva, a position he still holds.

In addition to his teaching and administrative work, Lamm has served as the rabbi for the Congregation Kodimoh in Springfield, Massachusetts and the assistant rabbi for the Congregation Kehilath Jeshurun in New York City. He is also a member of the Ethics Commission for the State of New York. His books include *Faith and Doubt* (1971), *Torah Lishmah* (1972), and *Torah Umadda* (1990). He was the founding editor of *Tradition: A Journal of Orthodox Jewish Thought*.

MYERHOFF, BARBARA (1935–1985)

Anthropologist, filmmaker

Groundbreaking anthropologist Barbara Myerhoff was born on February 16, 1935. She studied at UCLA and the University of Chicago and began work in the field of ritual and symbolic studies. Her first book, *Peyote Hunt: The Sacred Journey of the Huichol Indians* (1974), was nominated for a National Book Award. She then turned her attention to the study of elderly Jewish Americans, a project she carried out while teaching at the University of Southern California.

Choosing this group as her subject was a bold step at the time, but her work quickly gained respect and attention. Her insights into the rituals and practices that helped to ensure emotional survival were startlingly new, particularly as she discussed the superior abilities of women to establish a sense of self-worth through nurturing. Myerhoff worked with filmmaker Lynn Littman to make a documentary about the Jewish senior center where she carried out much of her research. The film, *Number Our Days*, won an Academy Award for best short documentary film in 1977. It was followed by a prize-winning book of the same name, which was later adapted as a play. When Myerhoff became seriously ill in the early 1980s, she worked again with Lynn Littman to make a documentary, *In Her Own Time*, about her illness and the final weeks of her life. She died on January 7, 1985.

REVEL, BERNARD (1885–1940)

Educator, Orthodox leader

The founder of Yeshiva College, Bernard Revel was born in Kovno, Lithuania in 1885. When he was twenty-one he immigrated to the United States. After studying at New York University and Dropsie College in Philadelphia, he moved to Oklahoma, where he owned an oil refinery. Back in New York, he was co-editor of the Hebrew encyclopedia *Ozar Israel* (1913). In 1915 he took over the job of reorganizing the Isaac Elchanan Theological Seminary. First, he opened it to teachers and laymen as well as rabbinical students. In 1916 he founded Talmudical Academy, the first institution in the United States to combine an academic high school and a yeshiva. In 1928 he founded Yeshiva College, which was the first liberal arts college under Jewish auspices. He was opposed in this expansion of the seminary by Jewish scholars and leaders who believed that the introduction of conventional liberal arts courses would dilute the study of the Torah. While serving as president of Yeshiva College, he took his expansion one step further when he created the graduate school of Jewish studies in 1937. The school, which was named after him, was a crucial step in the development of **Yeshiva University**.

The first institutional head in the United States to give *semikah* to Orthodox rabbis, Revel was honorary president of the Union of Orthodox Rabbis of the United States and Canada. He was also vice president of the Jewish Academy of Arts and Sciences.

RICHMAN, JULIA (1855–1912)

Educator, administrator

Julia Richman was known as much for her compassion as for her skills as an educator and administrator. Born in New York, she attended the Female Normal School, now Hunter College, and New York University. Her first appointment was as a teacher and shortly thereafter she became vice principal at PS 77. Within a few years, she became the principal of its girls' school. In 1903, as a result of her remarkable dedication and talents, she became district superintendent of schools. She was the first woman in New York to serve in that capacity and remained in the position until her death nine years later.

Richman's work was marked by her absolute determination to ameliorate the condition of immigrant children as they tried to adjust to life in America. Beyond educational efforts that might have been expected from one in her position, she waged a battle against truancy and juvenile crime, even creating an employment agency for young people who left school early. She also found ways to provide medical and social services to her students. Another of her causes was education for mentally retarded children. As part of her determination to work with the parents of her students, she was one of the earliest organizers of the Parent-Teacher Association. Richman was also strongly involved in community activities, serving as director of the Hebrew Free School Association and as the first president of the Young Women's Hebrew Association. She also chaired the committee on religious school work of the Council of Jewish Women. Among her publications were the books *Good Citizenship* (1908) with Isabel Richman Wallach and *Methods of Teaching Jewish Ethics* (1914). A high school in Manhattan now bears her name.

SCHECHTER, SOLOMON (1847–1915)

Scholar, educator

Solomon Schechter was born into a religious household in 1847 in Foscani, Rumania. Initially taught rabbinical studies by his father, a Habad Hasid. He continued his education in Vienna, where he attended the *bet ha-midrash* from 1875 to 1879. He then attended the Berlin *Hochschule fuer die Wissenschaft des Judentums* and the University of Berlin. When a fellow student at the *Hochschule*, Claude Goldsmid Montefiore, invited him to be his tutor in London, Schechter accepted.

In England he became a well-known Judaic scholar. He was appointed lecturer in Talmudics in 1890 at Cambridge University and in 1892 became reader in rabbinics there. In 1899 he also became professor of Hebrew at University College, London. His most famous scholarly achievement was his recovery in Egypt of the Cairo *Genizah*, over one hundred thousand ancient Hebrew manuscripts and manuscript fragments. This material was presented to Cambridge

Solomon Schechter built the Jewish Theological Seminary of America into a major educational institution and was instrumental in the emergence of Conservative Judaism as one of the two leading denominations in American Judaism. (Courtesy of the American Jewish Historical Society, Waltham, Massachusetts and New York, New York)

University by Schechter and Charles Taylor, the master of St. John's College, who had made Schechter's trip possible.

In 1902 Schechter resigned his positions in England and came to the United States to become president of the **Jewish Theological Seminary of America**. After finding himself unable to unite with **Reform Judaism**, he began to develop a distinct movement of his own, coining the phrase "**Conservative Judaism**." In 1913, he helped found the United Synagogue of America as a network of synagogues that would promote these beliefs. Schechter was considered both the father of Conservative Judaism in America and a leading scholar in Judaic studies and thought worldwide. He built the Jewish Theological Seminary into one of the foremost centers of education and scholarship in the world, attracting such scholars to the faculty as

Louis Ginzberg, Israel Friedlaender, Alexander Marx, Israel Davidson, and **Mordecai M. Kaplan**. Schechter's publications were widely distributed and played an essential part in the acceptance of Conservative Judaism. They include *Studies in Judaism* (three volumes, 1896–1924), *Some Aspects of Rabbinic Theology* (1909), and *Seminary Addresses and Other Papers* (1915). He died in New York City in November of 1915, while still president of the Seminary.

SCHORSCH, ISMAR (1935–)

Rabbi, educator

Ismar Schorsch was born in Hanover, Germany on November 3, 1935. He graduated with a B.A. degree from Ursinus College in 1957. He then moved on to Columbia University where he earned an M.A. in 1961 and a Ph.D. in 1969. He received his rabbinical training from the **Jewish Theological Seminary of America** (JTS) and was ordained in 1962. In 1964 he became a member of the seminary's faculty. In 1975 he became a dean of the Graduate School and in 1980 became the university's provost. He was named the Jewish Theological Seminary's sixth chancellor in 1986, a position he still holds today, while concurrently serving as its Rabbi Herman Abramovitz Professor of Jewish History.

Under Schorsch's leadership, JTS opened its Cantors Institute to women and established the William Davidson Graduate School of Jewish Education, the first of its kind in the United States. In 1994 he served on President Clinton's official delegation to the signing of the Israeli-Jordanian peace treaty. He is the author of many articles and essays as well as the book, *From Text to Context: The Turn to History in Modern Judaism* (1994).

SHANKER, ALBERT (1928–1997)

Labor leader

Albert Shanker forever changed the nature of the teaching profession in the United States in his dual positions as the longtime president of New York City's United Federation of Teachers and its national parent organization, the American Federation of Teachers. Before Shanker's appearance on the scene, teachers in public schools were, by and large, dutiful employees who had little say in how decisions were made in their school systems. With his leadership, they became a profession with influence on their employers, albeit an influence that was sometimes criticized.

Born in New York City, Shanker worked first as a public school teacher (1952–1959) and then as a union organizer. In 1964 he became president of the local teacher's union—the United Federation of Teachers (UFT), an organization with 55,000 members. As the UFT's representative in contract negotiations, he won many gains for teachers, including improvements in teaching practices in inner city schools.

In 1968 Shanker led his union in three city-wide teachers' strikes. The strikes were precipitated by the decentralization of some of New York City's schools, under a proposed plan that would have transferred power to thirty elected school boards. In a test case district, a local administrator tried to replace all of the union teachers. The union, and Shanker, fought back. Unfortunately, the district was African American and Puerto Rican and many of the teachers for that district were Jewish (as were the majority of teachers throughout the system). The fight became ugly as charges were made of racism and anti-Semitism. Despite these problems, Shanker won a settlement that achieved the union's main goals.

As president of the AFT, Shanker was a national spokesman for educational reform on a wide variety of issues. He fervently lobbied for the rights he believed teachers deserved; at the same time, he was an articulate advocate for a better educational environment for students throughout the country. At his death in 1997 the AFT had 900,000 members and the New York City local, the UFT, had grown to 85,000. In 1998 President Clinton awarded him the country's top civilian honor, the Presidential Medal of Freedom, posthumously.

STERN COLLEGE

In September 1954 an inaugural class of thirty-two students enrolled at Stern College for Women, a division of **Yeshiva University** and the first liberal arts college in America for women under Jewish auspices. Named in honor of the parents of Max Stern, one of the university's major benefactors, and located in the Murray Hill section of Manhattan, Stern College offered baccalaureate programs in the arts and sciences and religious education with a heavy emphasis on Judaic studies. Its dual curriculum was modeled on that of Yeshiva College, the university's men's undergraduate school. During the school's first two decades, Stern enrollment rose to five hundred students as the school accommodated the diversified educational needs of a student body that hailed from Conservative as well as from Orthodox Jewish homes. In September 1977, Karen Bacon was appointed dean of Stern College, becoming the first woman to occupy that post.

Increasingly, the women drawn to Stern are graduates of Orthodox day schools. Those from non-metropolitan areas who choose Stern have significantly

In September 1954 an inaugural class of thirty-two students enrolled at Stern College for Women, as Yeshiva University opened the first Jewish liberal arts college for women in America. Note that this early photograph of students includes manual typewriters. (Courtesy of Yeshiva University)

better Jewish educations than their sisters of a generation ago since they have been the beneficiaries of the proliferation of secondary Jewish schools in every area of the United States. Most students at Stern College spend a year of study in a women's yeshiva in Israel.

Responding to a more learned student body's desire for advanced training in Judaica, in 1980 Stern College reorganized its multi-tiered Jewish studies department to provide its students with greater facility in analyzing classical Jewish texts. The study of Talmud and allied rabbinic literature, the bedrock of learning in the traditional yeshiva and a discipline that some Orthodox Jews withhold from women, was intensified. Finally, Stern College students of this most recent generation are training for a variety of careers, since teaching has become but one of several professional pursuits attractive to Orthodox young women who seek still to combine professions with traditional Jewish family lives. In 1996 psychology was the most popular major at Stern College and biological sciences second One hundred twenty-two of the students majored in business and accounting at the university's Sy Syms School of Business, an undergraduate school that has offered a business alternative to Stern College's own liberal arts and sciences curriculum since 1987.

SUMMER CAMPS

Summer camps served an integral function in American Jewish life and culture. In the years after World War I, when summer camping first became an institution in the United States, Jews created their own institutions providing a variety of religious and ideological orientations. From the Zionist Hadassah Camps to the Conservative and Hebrew camps Massad and Ramah to the Socialist Kinder Ring and the Communist influenced Kinderland, self-consciously defined Jewish day and overnight camps have evolved throughout the twentieth century to create programs for millions of Jewish children.

From the onset Jewish institutions viewed the summer camp as striking a balance between promoting assimilation and strengthening the ethnic identity of its campers to create the essence of cultural synthesis. Because of this dual emphasis on both Americanization and Jewish tradition, staff members at many of these camps frequently combined activities that promoted patriotism, such as the Pledge of Allegiance, with the singing of Hebrew songs. At Camp Council and Camp Woodmere, fundamentals of good citizenship and democracy were stressed along with Shabbat services, the lighting of candles, and Jewish tales designed to convey moral values to campers.

The work of organizations such as the Federations of Jewish Philanthropy were part of an effort to offset the missionary attempts by some Christian camping organizations, in addition to their belief that poor urban children would benefit from a structured summer program in the country. Cejwin Camps established by the Central Jewish Institute in 1919 in Port Jervis, New York as one of the first of the Jewish summer camps advertised its camp for boys, Aviv, and their girls camp, Aviva, as both "educational enterprises" and as recreational programs providing "fresh air" for its campers and a pluralistic system of "Jewish living and thinking." Seven years later the New York City Bureau of Jewish Education created the first camp that emphasized the teaching of Hebrew. The Massad camps, also established in the late 1920s, became known for modernizing the Hebrew language through its use in everyday recreational athletics.

Between the 1920s and the 1950s, hundreds of Jewish camps were established. In addition to the camps founded on Hebrew and religious principles, immigrant radicals also established their own summer programs to nurture a set of different values. Perhaps the earliest was Camp Nigadegit, founded by unionists affiliated with the International Ladies Garment Workers Union in 1923 who rented land in upstate New York and established the camp as a cooperative with a socialist orientation. In the same year Jewish progressives active in the non-partisan *shuls* (synagogues) founded Camp Kinderland, which became part of the Jewish section of the International Workers Order, an organization closely connected to the **Communist Party**. Kinderland focused its children's programs on working-class Jewish history and values, eschewing most Jewish religious rituals and operating in tandem with an adult extension, Camp Lakeland, which occupied adjoining property.

Whatever the political and religious tendencies of the Jewish summer camp, the predominant focus still required creating programs that parents believed would be in the best interests of their children. Camp directors in the 1920s and the 1930s reassured many immigrant families, unfamiliar with the notion of a summer camp, by comparing themselves to parents and their camps to Jewish homes.

Jewish summer camps used the rural environment as a major selling point, promoting their programs as being wholesome alternatives to the city. Several camps went as far as to use exalted religious language, in extolling the virtues of nature and the great outdoors, hailing the bucolic setting of their program as "God's own tonic." Despite the hyperbole, it is clear that parents cared deeply about freeing their children from the problems of the city. Urban Jewish families in the first three decades in the century sent their children to summer camp in part to shield them from the poverty and disease of the ghetto. Author **Chaim Potok** notes that his family initially sent him to camp in the hope that it would prevent him from contracting polio at a time when that disease was ravaging New York City.

By the end of World War II, millions of Jewish children attended summer camp in the northeast alone. Camp Ramah, first established in Wisconsin by the **Jewish Theological Seminary** became the most well-known of **Conservative Judaism**'s summer camps, with the goal of bridging the gap between "what the school was teaching and what the Jewish child was experiencing in the home," according to their literature and by "providing a new milieu which could act as a surrogate home." The Ramah movement led to the creation of a number of camps throughout the northeast all of which combined sports and recreation with formal class studies, prayer services, and songs.

Jewish summer camps generally consisted of separate girls and boys programs on segregated campuses with regular (though limited) opportunities for social intermingling between the two sexes. Camp activities were frequently gender-typed according to prevailing social norms, with boys receiving considerably more sports and hiking and girls being engaged in more crafts and performing arts programs, although this differed among the specific camps and has changed considerably in the contemporary era.

Although overnight Jewish summer camps continue to receive the most publicity, day camps began to evolve in the post–World War II years as Jews increasingly became a more affluent and suburban population. The most popular and well-attended day camps included more than a thousand programs sponsored by YM and YWHA's and a variety of other programs sponsored by synagogues, Jewish day schools, and national Jewish organizations.

At the end of the twentieth century Jewish camps are thriving. They continue to provide a Jewish cultural milieu for thousands of campers and their role and importance appears to be secure into the twenty-first century.

TEACHING

As much as law or medicine, Jews in twentieth-century America have gravitated to the field of education. Although a number of Jewish men entered the teaching profession, especially on the high school level, it has been primarily Jewish women who have become teachers in huge numbers. They still make up a large percentage of educators in an American public school system that remains dominated by women.

Almost as soon as the common school movement began in the United States, public school teaching began to be perceived as a women's field, as educational reformers touted women's nurturing qualities and moral superiority in addition to their "willingness" to accept lower wages. Teaching was perceived as a "proper" role for women and women's participation in the field a necessity to fill the void left as men took on higher-paid and more prestigious jobs. As early as 1870 as many as 61 percent of the country's public school teachers were women and from 1890 to 1920 this proportion expanded to nearly 80 percent.

Although the Irish represented the first group of immigrant women to take up the teaching mantle en masse, several Jewish women became prominent in the field. Margarethe Meyer Schurz set up the first English speaking kindergarten in Boston, Judith Peixotto served as principal of an all-girls public school in New York, and Hannah Marks Solomon became the youngest (and only) woman principal in San Francisco. By the first decade of the twentieth century Jews had begun to emerge as the predominant ethnic group entering the education profession.

The more assimilated German Jews made up the bulk of the first wave of Jewish teachers. Perhaps the most well-known and successful of this cadre, **Julia Richman**, taught for two decades in the New York City school system before becoming the first Jewish elementary school principal in 1884 and then a district superintendent in 1903. In this position, Richman lobbied for the public schools to take an increased responsibility for the welfare of the children, advocating the adoption of all-day kindergarten classes, nutritious meals, improved playgrounds, and regular health examinations. The role of the school, as Richman and other German Jewish teachers saw it, was also to immerse immigrant children in the English language and to wean them away from the language and customs of their homelands. To that end, New York City "uptown" German Jews created organizations such as the Educational Alliance to "Americanize" their downtown Eastern European brethren with English classes and instruction in sports, cooking, and other activities that its founders believed promoted assimilation and citizenship. In the Progressive Era German Jewish educators in New York and other cities taught the massive population of poor Jewish immigrants with both a concerned paternalism and an air of superiority.

In a matter of a few decades, however, the demographics of Jewish teachers began to change substantially. Unlike the medical or legal fields, which remained dominated by German Jews until World War II, the "second-generation" daughters of Eastern European Jews became teachers in massive numbers. For Eastern European immigrant parents, just as "my son the doctor" evoked feelings of great pride and prestige, so too did "my daughter the teacher" become a revered boast. Over a twenty-year stretch from 1920 to 1940, Jewish women, most of them from Eastern European stock, went from comprising 26 percent of the new teachers in the New York City School system to 56 percent.

Jewish immigrants had always embraced the public school system and used it both as a source of education for "Americanization" and a means of upward economic mobility. For the first generation of poor and working-class Eastern European Jews, girls frequently were denied the opportunity that boys received to complete their education. They were often expected to drop out of school to supplement the family wage. It was these women who encouraged their own daughters to receive an education and to become teachers. Although the low salaries for this predominantly female field generally meant that teaching could not be a vehicle for total independence for these Jewish women, the decision to educate a daughter for the teaching profession became a part of long-term planning for the family's future. Women could work as teachers until they could afford to devote full-time effort to being wives and mothers.

The 1920s were an important decade for this new generation of Jewish women making a name for themselves in the education field. Child psychology and child development had gained increasing importance in the philosophy of teaching. In New York, Miriam Finn Scott, who began her career doing part-time work at the University Settlement as a teenager, founded a clinic in her home to promote parent education as a force for improving their children's achievement in school. Dorothy Walter Baruch organized and directed the Gramercy Cooperative Nursery School and conducted experimental work in children's language development in Los Angeles. In addition, several Jewish women took on new educational leadership positions in a number of cities. Mary Goldsmith Prag became the first Jewish member of the San Francisco Board of Education after serving as vice principal of the city's Girls High School and Florence Bamberger served as the first female school supervisor in Baltimore.

Between 1920 and 1940 the number of Jewish students at new public teacher training schools increased throughout the United States (especially in New York City), as did the number receiving education degrees from four-year colleges. Although men also entered these institutions in the early years of the Depression, students in these schools were overwhelmingly female. The 1930s represented both the best and the worst of worlds for Jewish teachers in urban public school systems, as influential educational reform ideas led to the adoption of more student-centered teaching methods, while the economic crisis caused by the Depression led to major budget cutbacks in materials and equipment. Teachers faced more crowded classrooms and endured freezes on their salaries and sometimes pay cuts.

With the rise of the trade union movement in the United States, the collective organizing of teachers gained ground, with Jewish educators central to these efforts. The Teachers Union (TU), originally an American Federation of Labor union founded by New York City school teachers in 1916, experienced rapid growth during the Depression. There were strong locals in Philadelphia, Chicago, Boston, and Atlanta, especially among substitute teachers who had been hired in large numbers in this era.

It was at the union's epicenter in New York City that the union gained its greatest strength. The Teachers Union's major issues included relief from overcrowded classrooms, provision for child welfare, solutions to teacher unemployment, democratization of the schools, and federal and state aid to schools. Some of the best known TU militants including Celia Zitron, Abraham Lederman, Rebecca Simonson, and Isodore Rubin had liberal and frequently socialist leanings, with many of its leaders coming from union families. As the **Communist Party** developed a larger following in the 1930s, some of the union's members began moving in the Party's orbit, creating major division and bitterness and resulting in the secession of some of the old leadership, including Simonson, who formed the fledgling Teachers Guild.

Although both New York City-based unions continued to grow throughout the decade, its members struggled with vindictive responses to their activism among some school principals, who used this participation as an excuse to transfer them or give them negative performance ratings. The late 1930s also witnessed union leaders receiving angry anonymous letters tinged with anti-Semitism. This backlash was mild compared to the attacks on alleged communists among New York City teachers launched by the Rapp-Coudert Committee of the New York State Legislature in the early 1940s and then the massive purge of TU-affiliated teachers during the McCarthy era. The McCarthy era anti-Communist crusade resulted in the firing of hundreds of Jewish educators, including many with long and distinguished reputations. Celia Zitron, a teacher in the school system for twenty-seven years, who had pioneered the study of Hebrew in New York City schools and had been an activist in the Teachers Union since its inception, is one of the best known of the group who had their careers terminated in the 1940s and 1950s for supposed un-American sympathies. The anti-Communist campaigns, which deeply affected New York City teachers, also permeated other school districts throughout the country.

As a result of the purges, the Teachers Union lost considerable ground to the Teachers Guild, which was renamed the American Federation of Teachers (AFT) in the post-war era. Although it disdained the radicalism of the Teachers Union, the AFT championed the rights of teachers in the 1950s and 1960s as it gained significant institutional power and bargained for better salaries and working conditions for its members and greater job security. The decline in anti-Semitism and the newfound strength of the AFT gave Jewish teachers a firmer foundation than they had ever had before. Jewish women continued to join the ranks of public school educators in record numbers throughout the country. Jewish men also entered the system during this era, mostly as high school teachers. In addition, Jews increasingly began to seek teaching positions in private schools.

Jewish teachers found themselves in a period of transition. Although many had gained considerable economic ground and often viewed themselves as middle-class "professionals," teaching salaries re-

mained relatively low and working conditions difficult. In the 1950s and 1960s, teachers were forced to resort to job actions, strike threats, or actual walk-outs in school systems throughout the nation in order to challenge what they perceived to be continuing unfair and unjust treatment at the hands of principals, superintendents, and school boards. Jewish educators took an active role in the Civil Rights Movement, with many traveling to southern states to teach during the summer while the AFT stood firmly in support of integration and equal opportunity for minority students.

At the same time, as the quality of northern urban public schools continued to deteriorate, some minority parents and community organizations accused the Jewish-led AFT, despite its long socialist roots, of reinforcing an unresponsive and discriminatory educational system. In a highly contentious case that had national repercussions, **Albert Shanker**, president of New York City's local AFT, the United Federation of Teachers (UFT), led his union on strike in opposition to the attempts on the part of African American parents in one community to gain control of teacher hiring and selection, school finances, and administration from the UFT and the Board of Education. Although Shanker and the UFT eventually won the battle, a number of Jewish teachers sided with the African American community-control advocates and crossed the picket lines, resulting in a bitter divide that resonated for years after the strike concluded.

Shanker became the national president of the AFT in the 1970s and continued as a highly controversial figure, winning praise for his ability to lobby effectively for teachers at the national level, though he was criticized for his educational conservatism and his attempts to discourage dissent within the union. After Shanker's death in 1996 his protégé, **Sandra Feldman**, who had also served for a number of years as head of the United Federation of Teachers, became AFT president.

Americans Jews continue to contribute greatly to the field of education as classroom teachers, principals, superintendents, scholars, and writers. Jewish educators have taken on major educational leadership positions at the local and national levels. They have been at the forefront of a host of efforts to reform and reshape teaching and improve the overall functioning of schooling in the United States. Their activism and involvement in the numerous debates and discussions concerning the world of education shows no sign of diminishing.

TOURO COLLEGE

Founded in 1970 in New York City by Bernard Lander, Touro College opened in 1971 with thirty-five students. Lander's purpose in establishing the school was to enrich the Jewish heritage in this country and to reach out to the larger community. Touro College was named for Judah and Isaac Touro, leaders in the American colonies who founded Touro Synagogue and were inspired by the democratic tenets of George Washington. The family endowed the first free library on the North American continent, a number of universities, community health facilities, and, later, pioneering settlements in Israel.

Since its founding, the college has grown significantly. The College of Liberal Arts and Sciences now has the Women's Division. Schools of General Studies, Law, and Health Sciences have been added. There are also sister schools in Israel and Russia. In 1989 Touro added the School for Lifelong Education, which offers a nontraditional, mentor-based program.

TRILLING, LIONEL (1905–1975)

Literary critic, writer

A literary critic, Lionel Trilling, was born on July 4, 1905 in New York City, where he lived his entire life. He attended Columbia University (getting his B.A. in 1925) and for most of his career taught literature there.

His first book, *Matthew Arnold*, published in 1938, was based on his doctoral dissertation. His second book, *E. M. Forster* (1943), developed the approach to criticism that would mark the remainder of his career. His criticism was based on the concept that novels, poems, and words themselves reflect larger moral, cultural, and psychological changes in society. His other works include *The Liberal Imagination* (1950), *The Op-*

> ### On Being a Jew
>
> "Being a Jew is like walking in the wind or swimming: you are touched at all points and conscious everywhere."
>
> Lionel Trilling 1928 notebook entry, published in the *Partisan Review* 50th Anniversary Edition edited by William Phillips, 1985.

posing Self (1955), *A Gathering of Fugitives* (1956), *Beyond Culture* (1965), and *Sincerity and Authenticity* (1972). Throughout his life, Trilling explored man's conception of himself through the written word. His own fiction includes the novel *The Middle of the Journey* (1947) and stories such as "Impediments" (1925) and "Of This Time, Of That Place" (1943). Trilling wrote about Judaism in some of his stories and in two later essays, one on Isaac Babel (1955) and another entitled "Wordsworth and the Rabbis" (1955). He died in New York on November 5, 1975.

TUCHMAN, BARBARA (1912–1989)

Historian

Popular historian Barbara Tuchman (née Wertheim) was born on January 30, 1912 in New York City. Her parents were both prominent members of New York's Jewish elite. She attended Radcliffe College, graduating in 1933. After college she began writing for her father's journal *The Nation* as well as contributing to *Foreign Affairs*. Her first book, *The Lost British Policy: Britain and Spain Since 1700* (1938), came out of her experience as foreign correspondent for *The Nation*, which sent her to cover the Spanish Civil War. Her other books include *Bible and Sword: England and Palestine from the Bronze Age to Balfour* (1956), *The Zimmerman Telegram* (1956), *The Proud Tower: A Portrait of the World before the War 1890–1914* (1966), *Notes from China* (1972), *A Distant Mirror* (1978), and *The March of Folly: From Troy to Vietnam* (1984). She won two Pulitzer Prizes for her writing. The first was for *The Guns of August* (1962), the second was for *Stilwell and the American Experience in China, 1911–1945*

(1971). Her last book *The First Salute* (1988) was still on the *New York Times* best-seller list when she died on February 6, 1989.

UNIVERSITY OF JUDAISM

The University of Judaism (UJ) is a liberal arts research university in Los Angeles, California. It was founded in 1947 as an affiliate of the New York based **Jewish Theological Seminary of America** (JTS). Initially, the chancellor of JTS was also the chancellor of UJ. When longtime UJ president David Lieber retired in 1992, the two institutions had signed an agreement that redefined their relationship. Since Lieber's retirement, Robert Wexler has been president of the university and under his leadership, UJ has become increasingly independent from JTS.

Today, the University of Judaism offers undergraduate degrees through Lee College, which was founded in 1982. The college offers degrees in Bioethics (premedical education), Business, English and Literature, Jewish Studies, Journalism, Liberal Studies, Literature and Politics, Political Science, Psychology, and U.S. Public Policy. The University also has a number of graduate programs including the Fingerhut School of Education, the School of Management, the David Lieber Graduate School, the Graduate School of Judaica, the University College of Jewish Studies, and the Ziegler School of Rabbinic Studies. In addition to graduate degrees in education, in 1996 Fingerhut began one of America's few M.A. programs in behavioral psychology. The School of Management offers one of America's few M.B.A. programs with a focus on not-for-profit management.

The Ziegler School of Rabbinics is probably the University of Judaism's most famous program. In 1996 it became the first independent religious seminary west of the Mississippi to offer complete rabbinical training. Founded in 1971, the Ziegler School was initially a two-year preparatory program for Conservative rabbis. To be ordained, candidates had to complete their education at JTS in New York. In 1995 UJ received an anonymous donation of $22 million to expand the Ziegler School. When the announcement was made, JTS officials and many East Coast Conservative rabbis expressed concern, if not outright criticism, over the plan. The critics were afraid that a second Conservative seminary—and one with a different focus—would split the Conservative movement.

One difference between the two schools is that the expanded Ziegler School offers courses year-round, enabling students to complete their studies in four years, rather than the six years required at JTS. Another difference is that the Ziegler School requires only a semester in Israel, as opposed to JTS's requirement of a year. Most importantly, perhaps, and of greatest concern to the Conservative establishment on the East Coast, is the Ziegler School's emphasis on community outreach in its rabbinical training, as opposed to JTS's focus on scholarship.

Despite the controversy surrounding the University, it continues to grow and attract scholars from around the United States from all Jewish denominations. It remains an important influence in the spiritual and intellectual life of West Coast Jewry.

WOLFSON, HARRY AUSTRYN (1887–1974)

Historian, Philosopher

The prominent historian of philosophy Harry Austryn Wolfson was born in Russia and given a traditional yeshiva education as a youngster. Emigrating to the United States at the age of 16 with his family in 1903, Wolfson went on to study at Harvard. In 1912 he was awarded a traveling fellowship from Harvard that enabled him to return to Europe for research.

As a rising young star in the discipline of philosophy, Wolfson was invited to join the Harvard faculty as professor of Hebrew literature and philosophy in 1925. He also taught for several years at the Jewish Institute of Religion (later **Hebrew Union College**) in New York City. At various times, Wolfson served as president of the Academy for Jewish Research and the American Oriental Society. A Harry Austryn Wolfson Jubilee Volume was published, in English and Hebrew, in his honor. Wolfson's first book, an analysis of the work of the philosopher Crescas, spelled out his "hypothetico-deductive method of textual study," as he called it. This method, which some have compared to the Talmudic study technique known as *pilpul*, involves attempting to understand the intention and implications of an author's words, not merely their plain meaning. He utilized the same innovative approach in his two-volume study of Spinoza (1934) as well as his two-volume study of Philo (1947). Wolfson contended that Philo's philosophic writings were far more significant to the development of religious philosophy in Judaism, Christianity, and Islam than is usually acknowledged.

YESHIVA UNIVERSITY

Yeshiva University was initially a Lower East Side elementary school: the Yeshiva Eitz Chaim founded in 1886. The other half of what ultimately became Yeshiva University was the Rabbi Isaac Elchanan Theological Seminary (RIETS) founded in 1896. In 1915 the two institutions merged. The school's first president was **Bernard Revel**. Under his leadership, Yeshiva began its historic commitment to both Talmudic and secular study, despite resistance, at times, from segments of the Orthodox community.

One of Revel's first acts was to open a high school, adding secondary education to the existing primary and seminary programs. In 1928 New York State gave Yeshiva College its official charter. The school then began offering its first B.A. degrees in liberal arts and sciences. A year later the college moved to a new building in the Washington Heights neighborhood of Manhattan. By 1935 the college was offering graduate courses.

Yeshiva's second president, **Samuel Belkin**, served from 1943 through 1975. Two years after he ascended to the post, Yeshiva College became Yeshiva University and was authorized to grant graduate degrees. During Belkin's tenure as president, Yeshiva University grew to incorporate an increasing number of graduate and undergraduate programs. In 1954, the **Stern College for Women** was opened. A year later the college established the Albert Einstein College of Medicine. In 1957 the University founded the Wurzweiler School of Jewish Social Work.

In 1976, after Samuel Belkin died, **Norman Lamm** became president of the University. That same year the **Benjamin N. Cardozo School of Law** opened. Lamm's tenure as president—he still holds the position today—has been marked by an expansion of both the school's graduate and undergraduate programs, including a new undergraduate school of business.

In addition to these programs, Yeshiva's undergraduate schools now include the Breuer College of Hebraic Studies, the Striar School of General Judaic Studies, the Syms School of Business, and the Yeshiva Program/Mazer School of Talmudic Studies. The graduate program has added the Azrieli Graduate Institute of Jewish Education and Administration, the Revel Graduate School, and the Ferkauf Graduate School of Psychology among others. The Albert Einstein College of Medicine houses several important national research institutions, including the Irwin S. and Sylvia Chanin Institute for Cancer Research and the Rose Fitzgerald Kennedy Center for Research in Mental Retardation and Human Development. The University's S. Daniel Abraham Joint Israel Program enables students to study at a variety of Israeli institutions as well as at the University's Jerusalem center, the Caroline and Joseph S. Gruss Institute.

Throughout its history Yeshiva has maintained RIETS as an independent division of the University. It is currently America's leading training ground for Orthodox rabbis. The University still maintains a girl's and a boy's high school. The University's other affiliates include the Philip and Sarah Belz School of Jewish Music and the Yeshiva University Museum.

Over the years Yeshiva University has grown to become one of America's largest and most diverse Jewish institutes of higher learning. It has six undergraduate schools and seven graduate and professional schools. Yeshiva's three New York City campuses are the Joel Jablonski Campus in Washington Heights, the Midtown Center in Murray Hill, and the Jack and Pearl Resnick Campus in the Bronx. In addition to its center in Jerusalem, the University also has a center in Los Angeles. Classes are taught in either English or Hebrew and the current enrollment is around 7,000. The famous *U.S. News and World Report* survey of

"America's Best Colleges" ranked Yeshiva University number forty-two in 1998.

For Further Reading

See Appendix 2 for a bibliography of general reference books about Jews and the Jewish experience in America. All of these volumes include information about American Jews in education and intellectual life.

Brumberg, Stephan F. *Going to America, Going to School: The Jewish Immigrant Public School Encounter in Turn-of-the-Century New York City.* New York: Praeger, 1986.

Coser, Lewis. *Refugee Scholars in America: Their Impact and Their Experiences.* New Haven, Conn.: Yale University Press, 1984.

Fermi, Laura. *Illustrious Immigrants: The Intellectual Migration from Europe, 1930–41.* Chicago, Il.: University of Chicago Press, 1968.

Kessner, Carole S., ed. *The "Other" New York Jewish Intellectuals.* New York: New York University Press, 1994.

Klingenstein, Susanne. *Jews in the American Academy, 1900–1940: The Dynamics of Intellectual Assimilation.* New Haven, Conn.: Yale University Press, 1991.

Markowitz, Ruth Jacknow. *My Daughter, the Teacher: Jewish Teachers in the New York City Schools.* New Brunswick, N.J.: Rutgers University Press, 1993.

Murphy, Marjorie. *Blackboard Unions: The AFT and the NEA, 1900–1980.* Ithaca, N.Y.: Cornell University Press, 1990.

Oren, Dan A. *Joining the Club: A History of Jews and Yale.* New Haven, Conn.: Yale University Press, 1985.

Rubin-Dorsky, Jeffrey and Shelley Fisher Fishkin. *People of the Book: Thirty Scholars Reflect on Their Jewish Identity.* Madison, Wis.: University of Wisconsin Press, 1996.

Synott, Marcia Graham, "Anti-Semitism and American Universities: Did Quotas Follow the Jews?" In *Anti-Semitism in American History,* pp. 233–271. Edited by David A. Gerber, Urbana, Ill.: University of Illinois Press, 1986.

———. *The Half-Opened Door: Discrimination at Harvard, Yale, and Princeton, 1900–1970.* Westport, Conn.: Greenwood Press, 1979.

Steinberg, Stephen. *The Academic Melting Pot: Catholics and Jews in American Higher Education.* New York: McGraw-Hill, 1974.

Part 8

Sports and Games

OVERVIEW

Although few people in the contemporary era equate Jews with the world of sports, Jewish Americans have a long and rich history in amateur and professional athletics. Sports provided Jewish immigrants with an opportunity to feel "Americanized" and express their ethnic pride. Because of the broad popularity of athletics among diverse sectors of the American public, success in the field gave Jews a measure of social status and respect. Through their involvement in a common American experience, Jews helped allay notions that they were alien and undesirable without sacrificing their Jewish identity or their importance to the Jewish community at large.

Modern sports evolved in the United States in the nineteenth century and the religiously liberal, upwardly mobile German Jews viewed involvement in organized athletics as a means of gaining stature and recognition. The wealthiest of this group such as August Belmont bought race horses, while others purchased teams in the new and evolving sport of baseball. This generation of immigrants established the Young Men's Hebrew Association (YMHA) in 1874, aimed at emulating the Christian YMCA in using sports and recreational activities to improve the moral, social, and educational life of young German Jews.

The late nineteenth and early twentieth centuries witnessed both a flood of new Jewish immigrants into

American Jewish Olympic Medal Winners

1896—none

1900
Prinstein, Myer
  Triple jump—Gold
  Long jump—Silver

1904
Berger, Samuel
  Heavyweight boxing—Gold
Frank, Daniel
  Long jump—Silver
Hess, Philip
  Lacrosse—Silver
Lehman, Albert
  Lacrosse—Silver
Prinstein, Myer
  Long jump—Gold
  Triple jump—Gold

1908
Jacobs, Charles "Clair" S.
  Pole vault—Bronze
Simon, Harry
  Free rifle—Silver

1912
Kiviat, Abel
  1,500-meter run—Silver
Meyer, Alvah T.
  100-meter dash—Silver

1920
Gerson, Samuel
  Freestyle featherweight wrestling—Silver
Meyer, Frederick
  Freestyle heavyweight wrestling—Bronze
Mosberg, Samuel
  Lightweight boxing—Gold

1924
Clark, Louis A.
  400-meter relay—Gold
Fields, John "Jackie"
  Featherweight boxing—Gold
Jelinek, Sydney
  Rowing, coxed-fours—Bronze

1928
Copeland, Lillian
  Discus throw—Silver
Devine, Harold "Harry"
  Featherweight boxing—Bronze

1932
Bor, Nathan
  Lightweight boxing—Bronze
Copeland, Lillian
  Discus throw—Gold
Erenberg, Philip
  Gymnastics, club swinging—Silver
Gulack, George
  Gymnastics, rings—Gold
Jaffee, Irving
  5,000-meter speed skating—Gold
  10,000-meter speed skating—Gold
Schwartz, Albert
  100-meeter freestyle swimming—Bronze

1936
Balter, Samuel
  Basketball—Gold

1948
Fuchs, James
  Shot put—Bronze
Seymour, Steve
  Javelin throw—Silver
Spellman, Frank
  Middleweight weightlifting—Gold
Wittenberg, Henry
  Freestyle light-heavyweight wrestling—Gold
Worth, George
  Fencing, team saber—Bronze

1952
Fuchs, James
  Shot put—Bronze

Wittenberg, Henry
  Light-heavyweight freestyle wrestling—Silver

1956
Berger, Isaac
  Featherweight weightlifting—Gold

1960
Axelrod, Albert
  Fencing, individual foil—Bronze
Berger, Isaac
  Featherweight weightlifting—Silver
Halperin, Robert
  Star-class yachting—Bronze

1964
Ashworth, Gerald
  400-meter relay—Gold
Berger, Isaac
  Featherweight weightlifting—Silver
Bregman, James
  Middleweight judo—Bronze
Brown, Lawrence
  Basketball—Bronze
Joseph, Ronald
  Figure skating—Bronze
Joseph, Vivian
  Figure skating—Bronze
Ramenofsky, Marilyn
  400-meter freestyle swimming—Silver

1968
Spitz, Mark
  400-meter freestyle swimming relay—Gold
  800-meter freestyle swimming relay—Gold
  100-meter butterfly swimming—Silver
  100-meter freestyle swimming—Bronze

1972
Asch, Peter
  Water polo—Bronze

American Jewish Olympic Medal Winners

Cohen, Donald
  Dragon-class yachting—Bronze
Shapiro, Neal
  Equestrian team jumping—Silver
  Equestrian individual jumping—
  Bronze
Spitz, Mark
  100-meter butterfly swimming—Gold
  200-meter butterfly swimming—Gold
  100-meter freestyle swimming—Gold
  200-meter freestyle swimming—Gold
  400-meter freestyle swimming relay—
  Gold
  400-meter medley swimming relay—
  Gold
  800-meter freestyle swimming relay—
  Gold
Weitzenberg, Barry
  Water polo—Bronze

1976
Grunfeld, Ernest
  Basketball—Gold
Lieberman, Nancy

  Basketball—Silver
Master, Edith
  Equestrian team dressage—Bronze
Weinberg, Wendy
  800-meter freestyle swimming—
  Bronze

1980—none

1984
Berland, Robert
  Middleweight judo—Silver
Gaylord, Mitch
  Team gymnastics—Gold
  Gymnastics, vaulting—Silver
  Gymnastics, parallel bars—Bronze
  Gymnastics, rings—Bronze
Torres, Dara
  400-meter freestyle swimming relay—
  Gold

1988
Bauer, Seth
  Eight-oared shell with coxswain
  rowing—Bronze

Gilbert, Brad
  Singles tennis—Bronze
Torres, Dara
  400-meter freestyle swimming relay—
  Bronze

1992
Greenbaum, Dan
  Volleyball—Bronze
Jacobi, Joseph
  Canadian slalom pairs canoeing—
  Gold
Strug, Kerri
  Gymnastics, team combined
  exercises—Bronze
Torres, Dara
  400-meter freestyle swimming relay—
  Gold

1996
Strug, Kerri
  Gymnastics, team combined
  exercises—Gold

American cities and an increasing symbolic attachment to encouraging athletic prowess for the nation as a whole and especially for young American males. At a time when massive urbanization and immigration drastically altered the composition and demographic of the country, many Protestant reformers expressed anxiety about the decline of the virtuous values associated with the rural frontier. They bemoaned the "softness" and "complacency" associated with the development of modern society. The Jewish voice urging involvement in sports was loudest among the most assimilated and successful sectors of the German Jewish community who viewed it as a core component of acculturation.

Although the YMHA as an institution continued to serve German Jews, its programs increasingly sought to teach Eastern European newcomers what it considered to be the necessary components of Americanization. For its leaders, athletics and morality went hand in hand. Jewish institutions such as the YMHA and the Educational Alliance embraced the belief that participation in sports was an important method of easing the transition from immigrant to American. Both Jewish and non-Jewish reformers sought to develop organized sports clubs and athletic associations as a means of developing "teamwork" and "cooperation" skills among these new immigrants. Progressive Era reformers viewed team sports as a tool to prevent vice and delinquency among youth by moving them out of the streets and into supervised spaces such as gymnasiums, play grounds, and ball fields. In 1911 **Julia Richman** recommended to the Committee on Education of the Educational Alliance that the gym be opened on certain afternoons for "girls between the ages of eleven and fifteen, who are wandering aimlessly about the streets and who might be attracted to amusement halls and other places of dubious influence."

German Jews, already defensive about the possibility of increased anti-Semitism brought on by the arrival of their poor and working class immigrant brethren, hoped that promoting athletic achievement would refute the arguments that the Jews were a weak and alien race whose people historically eschewed physical endeavors in favor of religious and intellectual study.

In New York City, the center of immigrant Jewish culture, the YMHA established the Atlas Athletic Club in 1898 with the stated goal of cultivating elite Jewish athletes and helping them gain recognition at a time when other similar clubs were closed to them. William Mitchell, the YMHA superintendent, stressed that Atlas members should strive for the highest goals in sports and he declared that he hoped "some day to see some of our own boys take a prominent part in athletic competition and thus disprove that our own people do not give proper attention to physical development."

Even more than the settlement houses or Jewish community centers, the YMHA, which moved to Ninety-second Street and became known as the Ninety-second Street Y in 1901, was successful in attracting young Jewish men from the Lower East Side to its gymnasium programs. In its first year in the larger building, more people participated in the Y's sports programs than any other single endeavor. In 1904, the Y added a varsity basketball squad to its burgeoning intramural sports programs, which competed against settlement house teams and against other YMHAs and YMCAs throughout the east coast and, after 1912, within what became known as the Metropolitan YMHA league. A similar proliferation of sports activity took place in other cities with significant but smaller Jewish communities, including Pittsburgh, Philadelphia, Boston, Providence, Detroit, Los Angeles, and, especially, Chicago.

Although athletic pursuit was frequently framed as a male activity, settlement house workers also sought to promote physical exercise, recreation, and participation in sports for working-class Jewish immigrants in their girls clubs. Likewise, the establishment of the Young Women's Hebrew Association (YWHA) created athletic opportunities for Jewish girls. They held classes in gymnastics, swimming, basketball, and dancing.

The ideology of sports and physical fitness for female immigrants served to reinforce gender divisions in American society. Many Progressive Era reformers explicitly stated that these poor and working-class women needed physical exercise to fulfill domestic roles and to offset the negative influence of unsanitary urban conditions. At the Educational Alliance female gender–appropriate physical fitness emphasized "health-building" sports rather than competition. At the same time, Jewish organizations promoted women's basketball in intramural and club leagues, with the YWHA's touting the sport as the greatest of indoor games while at Chicago's Jewish Peoples' Institute, girls basketball teams won three championships.

During these pivotal early years of the twentieth century, the Jewish press catering to an Eastern European immigrant population, stressed the importance of developing Jewish athletes. In 1909 the Chicago-based Yiddish language *Jewish Messenger* wrote that the Jew "has left behind . . . lands of oppression" and in the "free country" of America "desires to improve his physical equipment to meet adequately the demands of the strenuous life." In the following decades, Jewish athletes would respond to this call by carving out an important place for themselves in the American scene.

ALCOTT, AMY (1956–)

Golfer

Amy Alcott has established herself as one of the finest women golfers of all time. Born in 1956 in Kansas City and raised in California, Alcott began cultivating her talents in the sport as a teenager. At age nineteen she had reached such a high level of proficiency that she joined the Ladies Professional Golf Association (LPGA) rather than attending college. From that time until 1986, she achieved the remarkable feat of at least one tour victory every year. Alcott has won four major championships, including the U.S. Women's Open in 1980. In 1983 she became only the sixth golfer to win $1 million on the LPGA tour.

Alcott is known for her sense of humor and colorful presence within women's golf, telling the public that she would donate the winnings of her victory in a Archdiocese-sponsored event to the United Jewish Appeal. She played the last hole of the 1995 Big Apple Classic wearing a hat with fake dreadlocks. She has also been recognized for her altruism, earning the LPGA's Founders Cup in 1986 for her contributions to the betterment of society.

In 1988 Alcott enjoyed her best year with fifteen top-ten finishes. That same year she became only the third member of the LPGA to pass the $2 million mark in career earnings. She continues to perform and excel in women's golf on route to the LPGA Hall of Fame.

AUERBACH, ARNOLD "RED" (1917–)

Basketball coach

Generally acknowledged as the most successful professional basketball coach of all time, Arnold "Red" Auerbach coached the Boston Celtics to an extraordinary nine NBA championships in a sixteen-year career. Born in Brooklyn to Eastern European immigrant parents, Auerbach grew up with a passion for basketball even in the face of his father's fierce opposition. Despite earning a basketball scholarship at George Washington University, Auerbach recognized that his playing talents were limited and his vision always involved becoming a coach. Beginning with the Basketball Association of America's Washington Capitals from 1946 to 1949, where he won two division titles, Auerbach made a mark for himself as a master strategist and motivator on the court. The year after the NBA and BAA merged, he took over the coaching helm of the Celtics, where he stayed until 1966 winning an astounding 1,037 games while losing only 548. After leaving coaching, Auerbach became Gen-

Brooklyn-born Arnold "Red" Auerbach is the son of a Russian immigrant. He learned to play basketball at P.S. 122 in Williamsburg. He went on to become the most successful coach in basketball history. (Courtesy of Naismith Memorial Basketball Hall of Fame)

eral Manager and helped direct his team to five more championships. He was named NBA Executive of the Year in 1981.

Auerbach was inducted into the Basketball Hall of Fame in 1968. In 1971 he was named the "Silver Anniversary Coach," symbolizing the league's honor as the best coach of the NBA's first quarter century.

BAER, MAX (1909–1959)

Boxer

Jewish on only one side of his father's family, heavyweight boxing champion Max "Maxie" Baer was an important symbol of power and strength for American Jews when he defeated the Hitler-supported German title holder Max Schmeling in 1933. Although he was knocked out by James Braddock only one year later, Baer continues to be remembered for challenging anti-Semitic stereotypes about Jewish weakness at a time of rising fascism in Europe.

Born in 1909, Baer grew up in Omaha, Nebraska with no formal connection to his partial Jewish heritage. He rose rapidly through the heavyweight ranks in the 1920s becoming as well known for his colorful "playboy" lifestyle as for his prowess in the ring. Despite his status as a hero to many Jews, Baer was accused of being a shameless self-promoter who used his Jewish identity as a ploy to increase his box-office value (he traditionally wore a Jewish Star of David on his boxing trunks). His historical legacy has also been sullied by his willingness to be promoted in racist terms as a "Great White Hope" in his later years prior to an unsuccessful bout with African American champion Joe Louis. Nevertheless, Baer was touted by the Jewish press and most Jewish institutions as a source of pride and prowess throughout his career.

Baer followed his victory over Schmeling with a knockout of Italian contender Primo Carnera, another symbolic achievement to American Jews because of Italy's own fascist politics. After his defeat by Braddock, Baer's boxing career faded and he never regained his crown. He was a moderately successful actor in the post–World War II era, but his significance will always be his knockout of Schmeling.

BARRON, HERMAN (1909–1976)

Golfer

Herman Barron was one of the top professional golfers of the 1930s and 1940s and the first Jewish profession to excel in the sport. Born in 1909, Barron won his first major tournament, the Philadelphia Open, in 1934. Twelve years later in 1946 he reached his peak of success, winning the Philadelphia Inquirer Open and the All America Championship in Chicago, while finishing only one stroke behind Ben Hogan in the U.S. Open.

The Port Chester, New York native also earned a spot on America's Ryder Cup Team that defeated England in 1947, but health problems forced him into retirement the next year. Barron became an accomplished teaching pro over the next fifteen years before returning in the early 1960s to play in the PGA Senior Circuit, winning the 1963 championship. In 1964, at the age of fifty-five, he registered the eleventh hole-in-one of his career.

In the 1970s Barron helped develop Israel's first golf course at Caesarea. He continued to work as a teaching pro until his death in 1976.

BASEBALL

From the founding of the National Association in 1871 to the present, Jews have had some level of participation in the world of professional baseball. In contrast to the poor and working-class backgrounds of most Jewish boxers, Jewish baseball players have been more likely to come from middle class and assimilated families. As the national pastime, baseball frequently transformed Jewish players into symbols of both Americanization and ethnic pride to fellow Jews. For many children of Jewish immigrants, baseball defined their American identities as no other sport or aspect of American life and culture could.

The first Jewish American to participate in organized baseball was Lipman "Lip" Pike, who played in the first season for the National Association's Troy Haymakers in 1871 and then played and managed for twenty years with eight different teams in six leagues. Pike, who was known for his great speed in the outfield and his slugging ability, had a career batting average of over .300.

During the Progressive Era, German Jewish immigrant Barney Dreyfuss became owner of the National League's Pittsburgh Pirates and three Jews (all from the Midwest or the South) established themselves as successful baseball players. Pitcher Barney Pelty, nicknamed the "Yiddish Curver," won ninety-one games in a ten-year career. In 1906, outfielder George Stone had the highest batting average in the American League and went on to an outstanding seven-year career. Erskine Mayer, a right-handed pitcher, won more than twenty games in both 1914 and 1915. Also enjoying a distinguished career was Johnny Kling, born in Kansas City, who had an eleven-year tenure as a catcher for the Chicago Cubs and helped them win four pennants and two World Series.

Because these players all grew up in towns removed geographically and culturally from Jewish immigrant constituencies, neither the Jewish press nor the majority of Jewish families in these communities paid much attention to them. In addition, a number of less successful Jewish baseball players hid their Jewish backgrounds for a variety of reasons.

The public persona of Jews in baseball changed dramatically after the Black Sox Scandal of 1919. The role of the Jewish gambler Arnold Rothstein in "fixing" the World Series reinforced anti-Semitic stereotypes of conspiratorial un-American Jews and was followed by the public pronouncements of Henry Ford who viewed the scandal as evidence of an international Jewish conspiracy to corrupt Anglo-Saxon institutions. In the 1920s both Jews and non-Jews became more aware of the ethnic background of baseball players and the identity of Jews achieving success at the major league level increased dramatically in its importance.

Recognizing the symbolic significance of Jewish baseball players to the second generation of immigrants and believing that it would help his team's attendance and popularity, John McGraw, manager of the New York Giants, actively sought to find an identifiable Jewish star to promote on his team. Andy Cohen, who began with the Giants in the 1928 season, looked like that player and his initial success turned him into baseball's first Jewish folk hero. Both the mainstream and the Jewish press extolled Cohen's prowess and Jewish fans flocked to the Polo Grounds to cheer him on. His popularity grew to such an extent that the Giants hired a secretary to handle his fan mail and in the off-season in 1928 and 1929 he was offered his own vaudeville show.

Although Cohen's career quickly went downhill in his third year, his short stay in the major leagues encouraged other Jews to believe in the possibility of participating in the national pastime. A number of pundits went so far as to claim that Cohen's brief moment as a celebrity presence served as a middle ground between Jews and the gentile majority and helped dispel fears that an alien immigrant population could not be absorbed into the American mainstream. Despite these optimistic pronouncements, Jews continued to face considerable barriers in the institutional sports world and in the nation at large during the 1920s and 1930s.

The number of Jewish players reaching major league baseball increased considerably in the interwar period. Most of them enjoyed only minimal success, including Moe Berg, Morrie Arnovich, Harry Danning, Phil Weintraub, Jimmy Reese, and Goody Rosen. Buddy Myer began a solid seventeen-year career in which he recorded a career batting average of .303.

But it was New York City native **Hank Greenberg** who rose to become one of the greatest power hitters in baseball history and the first Jew elected to the Baseball Hall of Fame. Greenberg's illustrious career as first baseman–outfielder for the Detroit Tigers included leading the American league in home runs for four years and runs batted in for five years, earning the major league single season record of most games with two home runs or more, and winning the American League's Most Valuable Player award in 1935 and 1940. Although never particularly religious, Greenberg won accolades from concerned Jews when he refused to play baseball on Yom Kippur in 1934 with his team in the heat of a pennant race.

Despite being taunted by anti-Semitic abuse from opposing players and fans throughout his career, Greenberg inspired great pride and love among Jews throughout the country and won the respect of thousands of gentiles both for his tremendous talent and his grace and courage. He stood as the most significant Jewish American athlete at a time when the second generation of American Jews struggled to resolve the tension between their American and Jewish identities and saw in Greenberg a way of embracing both. He provided comfort and hope for a population threatened by economic depression at home and fascism abroad and did so in ways that asserted a physical and defiant Judaism that countered stereotypes about Jewish weakness.

The post–World War II world witnessed new openings for Jewish athletes, and baseball produced a number of notable Jewish stars in this era. They included outfielder–third baseman Sid Gordon, who hit twenty-five or more home runs five years in a row from 1948 to 1952; pitcher Saul Rogovin, whose earned run average led the major leagues in 1952; and third baseman Al Rosen, who won the American League's Most Valuable Player Award in 1953 and was a four-time all-star prior to becoming a major league executive. Relief pitcher Larry Sherry played an important role in the Los Angeles Dodgers World Series victory in 1959. In addition, **Thelma "Tiby" Eisen** starred in the short-lived All-American Girls Professional Baseball League, the only professional women's league in the game's history in the 1940s and the 1950s.

It was the enormous success of Brooklyn-born left-handed pitcher **Sanford "Sandy" Koufax** that defined Jewish involvement in post-war American baseball. Koufax, shy and introspective, let his arm do his talking for him, leading the National League in victories three times, earned-run average five times, and strike-outs four times. He also pitched four no-hitters and won the Cy Young Award three times before injuries forced him into an early retirement in 1966. Although the increased tolerance of the era allowed Koufax to escape the pressures and dilemmas that Greenberg faced as an ethnic standard bearer, he was still criticized for not pitching the first game of the 1965 World Series, which fell on Yom Kippur.

Jewish baseball players in the contemporary era represent a tiny minority of the major league roster. While several including Mike Epstein and Kenny Holtzman enjoyed successful careers and Art Shamsky, Steve Stone, and Ron Blomberg had productive years, Jewish ballplayers in the major leagues are now few and far between.

BASKETBALL

As the quintessential urban sport, basketball had tremendous appeal for the children of Jewish immigrants and in the years between the 1920s and 1950s many rose to prominence as professional and collegiate play-

---

The "Jewish Basketball Team" at St. John's

St. John's University is a New York–based Catholic college renowned for an excellent basketball program. Its alumni in the NBA include Chris Mullin, Bill Wennington, and Jayson Williams. The first of the great St. John's teams emerged in the 1920s, the "Wonder Five." Four of those wonderful ones—Max Posnack, Max Kinsbrunner, Allie Shuckman, and Jack "Rip" Gerson—were Jewish. The team went 68–4 between 1928 and 1931, including a 21–1 record in the boys' senior year. The entire starting five went immediately into the fledgling American Basketball League as the New York Jewels.

---

ers. Because of its limited space and equipment requirements, working-class Jewish immigrant youth found basketball both accessible and appealing. In New York City, settlement houses produced championship teams dominated by Jewish players. By the second decade of the century, professional basketball, still in its infancy, began attracting young Jewish men from New York, Philadelphia, and other eastern cities.

The two most well-known early Jewish professional stars, Max Friedman and Barney Sedran, played for a variety of different teams scattered throughout the northeast and won two championships as teammates in the New York State and Interstate Leagues in the 1920s. At the same time, Lower East Side-born **Nat Holman** began his long and illustrious career as head basketball coach at the City College of New York. He also established himself as an outstanding player, both for the New York Whirlwinds and for the original Celtics, where he became known for his shooting ability, defense, and passing skills. Jewish scholars and journalists embraced Holman for his ability to balance intellectual pursuits traditionally associated with Jews with athletic excellence. One article in *The American Hebrew* identified Holman's success with his ability to fuse ethnic and family values with distinctly American traits. Another, in the *National Jewish Monthly* viewed him as a role model capable of breaking down anti-Semitic stereotypes that characterized Jews as unfit for American life because of their perceived physical weakness.

Nat Holman first learned to play basketball on New York's Lower East Side. In 1949 he traveled to Israel to teach basketball, the first American coach to do so. (Courtesy of Naismith Memorial Basketball Hall of Fame)

In the 1930s as basketball grew in popularity Jews made their mark on the sport. Perhaps the most notable Jewish success story in the basketball arena was the South Philadelphia Hebrew Association, which became the dominant team in the professional American Basketball League from 1933 to 1946. Coached by Eddie Gottlieb, the SPHAs (so named because the South Philadelphia Hebrew Association bought the players' uniforms) began as an amateur team before becoming Gottlieb's ABL franchise entry in 1933. Featuring many of the top college players from the northeast, including Harry Litwack, Cy Kasselman, Davey Banks, Moe Goldman, Shikey Gotthoffer, and Irv Torgoff, the SPHAs won seven league champi-

onships in thirteen seasons until the league folded after the war.

Jewish basketball players who established themselves at the collegiate and professional levels in the 1930s and 1940s were overwhelmingly New York City–born children of poor Eastern European immigrants who began playing basketball in the playgrounds of public schools, settlement houses, and community centers. Moe Spahn, Jammy Moskowitz, and Sammy Kaplan are just a few of the many who went from the streets of the Lower East Side, the Bronx, and Staten Island to great success at Brooklyn College, New York University, Long Island University, and, especially, City College. For these second-generation children, basketball became part of their coming of age and established their American identities.

The post-war years led to more Jews making their mark on the basketball court. Sid Tannenbaum, Ralph Koplowitz, Leo Gottlieb, Sonny Hertzberg, Nathan Militz, Leonard Rosenbluth, Barry Leibowitz, Rick Weitzman, Art Heyman, Barry Kramer, Neal Walk, and Max Zaslofsky were outstanding college players before going on to varying degrees of success in professional basketball. Bronx-born **Adolph "Dolph" Schayes**, one of the tallest forwards of his era at 6 feet, 8 inches, gained recognition first at New York University and then as the greatest Jewish player in the professional ranks with the Syracuse Nationals between 1948 and 1964. By the time he retired as an active player, Schayes owned five NBA records—most consecutive games played, most field goals, most free throws made, and most points scored. He became player-coach of the Philadelphia 76ers during his last year and then coached the team to the NBA championship the following year.

The 1950s also represented the end of an era for New York City College basketball prowess. In 1951 several players on the City College team, including a number of Jewish athletes, were involved in a point-shaving scandal. Although Coach Holman was cleared of wrongdoing, the basketball team never completely recovered. As increasingly affluent Jewish families enrolled their children in more elite private colleges, Jewish participation in the sport decreased dramatically in the 1960s and the

1970s. By the 1980s only two Jews, Grunfeld and Dolph's son Danny Schayes, remained on NBA rosters.

As Jewish participation on the court diminished, many former Jewish players gained reputations as coaches and general managers and played critical roles in the boom of the National Basketball Association as club presidents and league commissioners. **Arnold "Red" Auerbach** won nine championship as coach of the Boston Celtics during their glory years in the 1950s and 1960s before going on to become the team's general manager. **William "Red" Holzman** coached the New York Knicks to two NBA titles in 1970 and 1973. More recently, Larry Brown, a former successful player in the old American Basketball Association, was recognized as one of the top coaches in the game at the college level, leading the University of Kansas to the Championship of the NCAA. He went on to coach the San Antonio Spurs, Los Angeles Clippers, Indiana Pacers, and Philadelphia 76ers. Maurice Podoloff, a Russian immigrant became the first commissioner of the NBA from 1949 to 1963 and David Stern has led the league into its heyday in the 1990s.

Several Jewish women made a mark for themselves in basketball. **Senda Berenson**, an immigrant from Lithuania, became known as the "Mother of Women's Basketball" for her pioneering work as director of physical education at Smith College in Massachusetts early in the twentieth century. She also wrote women's basketball rule books to promote skill among potential female athletes and contributed to the sport's popularity in YWCAs and YWHAs. More recently, **Nancy Lieberman-Cline** dominated the women's collegiate basketball in the 1970s at Old Dominion University and made the 1980 Olympic team.

BOXING

In the years between the two World Wars, Jews were an important force in boxing, a sport identified with poor urban dwellers. The first prominent Jewish boxer, Joe Choynski, won bouts against future heavyweight champions James J. Jeffries, Jack Johnson, and Gentleman Jim Corbett in the 1890s despite giving away between thirty and seventy pounds. Other Jews who attained prominence in the pre–World War I era included world champion middleweight Al McCoy (Louis Wallach), bantamweight Harry Harris, featherweight Abe Attell (Albert Knoehr), and heavyweight Battling Levinsky (Barney Lebrowitz), Joe Bernstein, and Leach Cross (Louis Wallach).

As important as these men were, during the twenty years after the end of the war Jews produced more champions and top contenders in all major boxing divisions than any other ethnic group. Jewish boxers came from working-class, immigrant, inner-city backgrounds. Their prowess in the ring, often with considerable parental opposition, symbolized for many of them a toughness and grit gained from learning to fight on the streets of cities such as New York and Philadelphia. Frequently donning the Star of David on their trunks, successful Jewish boxers celebrated their ethnicity as a challenge to the anti-Semitic taunts about Jewish weakness. The boxers and their fans viewed victories in the ring against gentiles as making a statement affirming Jewish identity and strength. The list of Jewish champion boxers in this era is extensive. It includes Louis "Kid" Kaplan, Benny Bass, Ruby Goldstein, Al Singer, Lew Tendler, Joe Benjamin, Joe Leopold, Phil Bloom, Charlie White, Jackie Fields, Abe Simon, and Solly Krieger.

Four Jewish boxers gained special recognition for their achievements in these years: light heavyweight **Maxie Rosenbloom**, lightweights **Benny Leonard** and **Barney Ross**, and heavyweight **Max Baer**. Born as Barnet David Rosofsky to Orthodox parents on the Lower East Side of New York and raised in Chicago, Ross was the first fighter to hold three divisional titles simultaneously and was considered the inspiration for the 1948 film *Body and Soul*. Leonard held the lightweight championship from 1917 to 1925 and became an almost mythic hero in the Jewish community for his supposed defense of Jewish neighborhoods and synagogues from anti-Semitic acts of vandalism. One reporter wrote that during his championship tenure, Leonard was "the most famous Jew in America beloved by thin-faced little Jewish boys who, in their poverty, dreamed of themselves as champions of the world." Rosenbloom, known as "Slapsie Maxie," was

When Boxing Was a Jewish Sport

There were ten world championship fights between 1905 and 1934 in which both contenders were Jewish.

light heavyweight champion from 1930 to 1934 and fought a record 106 times during that four and a half years before losing the crown to fellow Jewish fighter Bob Olin. Baer was of Jewish ancestry on only one side of his grandparents' family, but he always wore the Star of David on his trunks when he fought.

At the same time, Jewish promoters such as Mike Jacobs, Jack Begun, Irv Schoenwald, and Maurice Feldman made a name for themselves in the boxing world, as did referees Davey Miller and Ruby Goldstein. Many of the most successful managers of individual fighters were also Jewish, including Al Weill, Sam Pian, Frank Bachman, and Max Waxman.

After 1939 the number of Jews in boxing decreased dramatically almost in tandem with the beginnings of Jewish upward mobility and flight to the suburbs. As the children of the next generation of Jews increasingly gained middle-class status, boxing became an anachronism and a relic of the past. Just as Jews followed the Irish as the dominant ethnic group achieving success in boxing, Italian Americans and then African Americans replaced Jews in the ring during World War II and the post-war years. Mike Rossman, the half-Jewish and half-Italian light-heavyweight champion of 1978, has been the only boxer of Jewish identity to compete for any title since the halcyon days of the 1930s.

BERENSON, SENDA (1868–1954)

Sports educator

Nicknamed the "Mother of Women's Basketball," Senda Berenson did more to establish the sport among female college students than any other individual. Born in Vilna, Lithuania in 1868, Berenson's family immigrated to the United States when she was seven. In an effort to improve the frail youngster's strength and endurance, Senda's family sent her to the Boston Normal School of Gymnastics where she received training in anatomy, physiology, and hygiene and began her career teaching physical education.

Shortly after securing a teaching position at Smith College, Berenson met the inventor of basketball, James Naismith, who encouraged her to adapt the sport as a team exercise for her female students. On March 22, 1893 Berenson conducted the first official game of women's basketball with Smith sophomores competing against the freshmen. By 1895 the game's popularity led to the formation of hundreds of collegiate women's basketball programs throughout the country and to the development of other team sports for women.

Berenson went on to develop the official rules book for women's college basketball and to write numerous articles on the sport. Many of the rules she developed became the standard ones that were used for seventy years. In 1905 Berenson was appointed chair of the basketball rules committee of the American Association for the Advent of Physical Education.

After her marriage in 1911, Berenson became director of physical education at Burnham School, a position she held for a number of years. She died in 1954 and, in 1984, was posthumously inducted as the first woman in the Basketball Hall of Fame.

COPELAND, LILLIAN (1904–1964)

Track and field athlete

Frequently regarded as the greatest female Jewish athlete of all time, Lillian Copeland crowned her brilliant track and field career by winning a gold medal in the 1932 Olympic Games in the discus throw. She was also National Amateur Athletic Union Champion in the shot put and javelin throw in 1926 and ran the lead-off leg on the United States 400-meter relay team that set a new world record at the 1928 Olympic trials.

Born in New York City in 1904 to an Eastern European immigrant family, Copeland grew up in Los Angeles. She entered the University of Southern California in the late 1920s where she won every track event that she entered. After curtailing her athletic activities briefly to attend USC law school, she returned to competition in 1931 and won national championships in both the shot put and the javelin. Switching to the discus throw for the 1932 Olympics in Los Angeles, Copeland made what the *Los Angeles Times* called a "perfect throw" and set new Olympic and world's records.

Copeland participated in the 1935 World Maccabiah Games in Tel Aviv where she won the triple championship in the discus throw, javelin throw, and shot put. She participated in the boycott of the 1936 Olympic games in Berlin. She later served twenty-four years as a juvenile officer for the Los Angeles County Sheriff's Office until her retirement in 1960.

Lillian Copeland was so anxious to compete in the 1935 Maccabiah Games in Palestine that she paid her own way. She is shown here throwing the shot put, one of her three events. She held the world record in both the javelin and the discus. (Library of Congress)

One of the greatest woman athletes in the history of track and field, Lillian Copeland refused to compete in the 1936 Olympics in Berlin to protest the blatant anti-Semitism of the Nazi regime. (Courtesy of Amateur Athletic Foundation Library)

EISEN, THELMA "TIBY" (1922–)

Baseball player

Born in Los Angeles in 1922 Tiby Eisen starred for nine years in the All-American Girls Professional Baseball League (AAGPBL), the only professional women's league in the game's history. In her best season, 1946, she led the league in triples, stole 128 bases, and made the All Star team.

Eisen began playing competitive sports at age fourteen on southern California softball teams and in 1944 was one of six Los Angeles athletes to try out for the new women's baseball league, earning a spot on the Milwaukee team that relocated to Grand Rapids, Michigan the next year. In addition to her outstanding years in the league, she also played on the AAGPBL All-Star team that toured Latin America in 1949.

After ending her career with AAGPL in 1952, Eisen returned to the Los Angeles area where she continued to play softball for many years. Although the short-lived women's baseball league faded into obscurity after it folded in 1954, the film *A League of Their Own* inspired renewed interest in its historical legacy. In 1993, Eisen was elected to the board of directors of the

In 1995, center-fielder "Tiby" Eisen was voted one of the top twenty greatest players in the All-American Girls Professional Baseball League, where she played from 1944 till 1952. The league had largely been forgotten until the 1992 hit movie A League of Their Own *made it famous to a new generation of American sports fans. (Courtesy of Thelma Eisen)*

AAGPBL's Players Association, where she helped established an exhibit at the Baseball Hall of Fame, raised funds for reunions, and recorded oral histories of women baseball players.

EPSTEIN, CHARLOTTE "EPPY" (1884–1938)

Swimming coach

Charlotte Epstein pioneered women's swimming as a recognized sport in the United States and it was her tireless advocacy that led to its inclusion at the 1920 Antwerp Olympic Games. Given the opportunity to compete, the United States women's swim team excelled at the games. Epstein's forceful leadership not only elevated the sport to a new level, it also contributed to women's track and field events and other sports being included in the 1928 Olympics.

Born in New York in 1885 Epstein learned to swim at a young age at the YWHA and city settlement houses. As a young woman she founded, organized, and managed the Women's Swimming Association (originally the National Women's Life Saving League) to promote the health benefits of swimming. During her leadership of the WSA, Epstein attracted young swimmers who sought to participate and compete in the sport and for whom she became a mentor. With "Eppy" serving as mentor, WSA produced future Olympic champions Gertrude Ederle, Aileen Riggin, and Eleanor Holm. Epstein's swimmers held fifty-one world records and won thirty national champion team relays during her twenty-one years with the organization. The organization also provided her with a vehicle to persuade the U.S. Amateur Athletic Union to allow women swimmers to register as athletes for the first time.

A court stenographer by trade and never a competitive swimmer herself, Epstein managed the American women swim team in the 1920, 1924, and 1932 Olympiads. Although she died at a young age in 1938, the "Mother of Women's Swimming in America" transformed and shaped the history of female amateur athletics.

FOOTBALL

In comparison with baseball, boxing, and basketball, a relatively small number of Jews have achieved a high level of success in either professional or college football. Because of football's roots in elite universities that practiced ethnic discrimination, Jewish participation was institutionally limited in the sport's early years. Several Jewish football players made a name for themselves despite these barriers including Joe Alexander, a three-time All American lineman at Syracuse University in 1917 and 1918; Arthur "Bluey" Bluethenthal, an outstanding center at Princeton in

1911 and 1912; and Sigmund "Sig" Harris, a quarterback on two undefeated teams at the University of Minnesota in 1903 and 1904.

The 1920s and 1930s witnessed the ascension of college football throughout the country and Jewish gridiron stars included Ukranian-born Charles "Buckets" Goldenberg, an All-Midwest running back for the University of Wisconsin from 1930 to 1933 before going on to a solid thirteen-year NFL career with the Green Bay Packers. There was also Benny Lom, a multi-talented halfback with the University of California in the late 1920s and quarterback Harry Newman, who received the Douglas Fairbanks Trophy as the outstanding college player of the year for Michigan from 1930 to 1932 and led the New York Giants to the NFL title game in his rookie year.

Jewish football players, although far smaller in numbers, received the most attention of all Jewish collegiate athletes in this era. In the first three decades of the century college football became, like no other sport, symbolically equated with American and Christian masculinity. It was imbued with the task of creating men who were strong willed, moral, and physically fit. The Jewish press and Jewish institutions viewed football prowess as challenging anti-Semitic claims of Jewish debility and weakness while celebrating their inclusion in the American mainstream.

The three most famous Jewish players in the modern era, were unquestionably **Benny Friedman**, Marshall "Biggie" Goldberg, and **Sid Luckman**. The Cleveland-born Friedman, generally considered football's first great passer, starred as quarterback and halfback with the University of Michigan from 1924 to 1926 before going on to a distinguished seven-year professional career. Luckman, an All-American tailback at Columbia University, won four NFL championships as the first T-formation quarterback with the Chicago Bears, was voted the league's most valuable player in 1943, and set numerous passing records before being elected to the Football Hall of Fame. Goldberg, a West Virginia high school legend as fullback and halfback, led the

University of Pittsburgh to a Rose Bowl victory in 1936 and the national collegiate championship in 1937 and, in an era when football players played both offense and defense, was named All-Pro Defensive Back with the Chicago Cardinals in 1946, 1947, and 1948.

Very few Jews played football in the 1960s and 1970s. Ron Mix, an outstanding offensive lineman for the San Diego Chargers and Randy Grossman, an All-American offensive end at Temple University and a member of the Super Bowl-winning Pittsburgh Steelers, gained prominence at their positions. Jews have continued to be well represented among coaches, with Allie Sherman, Sid Gillman, and Marv Levy achieving varying degrees of success on the bench while Caroll Rosenbloom, Sonny Werblin, and Al Davis became well known as owners of football franchises.

FRIEDMAN, BENNY (1905–1982)

Football player

Generally considered football's first great passer, Benny Friedman also made a name for himself as an outstanding runner and place-kicker in both college and professional ranks. Friedman starred as quarterback and halfback for the University of Michigan, earning All-American honors in 1925 and 1926 before embarking on a successful seven-year career in the National Football League where he was selected as an All-Pro every year from 1927 to 1931.

Born in Cleveland in 1905, Friedman, the child of Russian Jewish immigrants, became an instant hero to thousands of American Jews because of his great prowess on the football field. When he was named captain of the 1926 Wolverine squad, the *American Hebrew* published a profile on the multi-talented senior praising him as a Jewish prodigy in America's greatest sport.

Friedman's "triple threat" ability set an example that transformed football from a straightforward running contest to a modern pass-and-run game. After his playing career, he served as head football coach at City College of New York from 1934 to 1951 and at **Brandeis**

University from 1949 to 1963. Friedman was among the first players to be elected to the College Football Hall of Fame.

GLICKMAN, MARTY (1917–)

Track and field athlete, sports broadcaster

Marty Glickman had two successful sports careers, first as an outstanding collegiate sprinter and then as a premier sports broadcaster for several decades. Born in the East Bronx in 1917 and raised in Brooklyn, Glickman starred on his high school track and football teams before receiving an athletic scholarship to attend Syracuse University.

Establishing a reputation in the 100-meter race and 400-meter relay team, he participated in Olympic tryouts in the summer of 1935 and his successful showing in the relay gained him a spot on the team headed for Berlin the following year. At the last minute, U.S. Olympic track coach Dean Cromwell removed Glickman and Sam Stoller from the relay team and replaced them with Ralph Metcalfe and Jesse Owens, who had both already won medals in other events. Although the official explanation for their removal was that the American team needed more experienced runners to counter evidence of Germany's "super sprinters," Glickman remained convinced throughout his life that anti-Semitism and the desire of U.S. officials to appease Hitler were the real reasons for the decision. Just months afterward, he did have an opportunity to run with Owens and Metcalfe in the four-person relay in international competition when the team set a world 4x100 record in a London meet, topping the mark posted by the U.S. Olympic team in Berlin.

After ending his track career, Glickman entered broadcasting and was the radio voice of the National Football League's New York Giants from 1948 to 1971, the New York Jets from 1972 to 1979, and the National Basketball Association's New York Knicks from 1946 to 1970. He also served as commentator for major track and field meets and a broad variety of collegiate sporting events in addition to major league baseball, horse racing, sports highlights, and interview shows.

GOLF AND TENNIS

Prior to World War II, golf and tennis were the purview of upper-class white Protestants who played at exclusive country clubs that generally excluded Jews, African Americans, and Catholics. After the war, upwardly mobile Jews created their own private clubs and began embracing these sports. Although Jews embraced both these sports as forms of recreation, only a few achieved stardom.

Herman Barron was the first and most successful Jewish golfer, winning two major tournaments in 1946 and garnering more prize money in that year than any player on the PGA circuit other than Ben Hogan. Barron's career stretched for thirty years and he paved the way for other Jews to play and gain recognition on the professional golf circuit, including Arnold Blum and Roger Ginsburg, in addition to women such as Andrea Cohn and Gail Denenberg. Most recently, **Amy Alcott** has excelled on the LPGA tour, winning four tournaments in three separate seasons in the 1970s and 1980s. She continues to be a contender in women's golf and is known for her sense of humor—once announcing that she would donate the winnings from an Archdiocese-sponsored event to the United Jewish Appeal.

In tennis, **Richard "Dick" Savitt** became a hero to many Jews after his victory at the 1951 Wimbledon Open and the subsequent cover story on him in *Time* magazine. Savitt went on to win the Australian Open the same year and the National Indoor Singles Championship in three successive years. During the same era, **Victor Seixas** won Wimbledon's men's singles and the French and Australian doubles with Tony Trabert. Unlike most other sports that have witnessed a decline in Jewish participation, Jews are an increasing presence in the ranks of professional tennis. Recently, Harold Solomon, Brian Teacher, Eliot Teltscher, Brad Gilbert, Aaron Krickstein, Jay Berger, and Andrea Leand have become recognized among the elite of the tennis world, although they generally have fallen short of achieving the championship stature of Savitt and Seixas.

Besides Leand, many other Jewish women have

been recognized for their talents in the sport including Helen Bernard, Barbara Bright, Julie Heldman, Ena Marcus, Nadine Metter, Stacy Margolin, and Renee Richards. In addition, Natalie Cohen is generally recognized as an important force in popularizing tennis in the United States first as a successful player, then as president of the Southern Tennis Association, and finally as an umpire. **Gladys Heldman** (Julie's mother) had a short but solid career on the court but established her legacy as a pioneer for equal purse money and equal recognition for women's tennis players and for creating, editing, and publishing *World Tennis Magazine* for more than twenty years.

GREEN, MILTON (1913–)

Track and field athlete

One of the premier collegiate track stars of the 1930s, Milton Green equaled the world record in the 45-yard high hurdles four times in 1935 and accomplished the same feat in the 60-meter high hurdles the following year. Although at the peak of his ability, Green refused to be considered for the 1936 Olympics in support of the U.S. movement to boycott the games. He went on to set a number of records in the high and low hurdles and the long jump.

Born in Massachusetts in 1913, Green starred on Harvard University's outstanding track and field teams of the early 1930s. His first record-equaling performance came in the 1935 triangular meet against Yale and Princeton when he ran the 45-yard high hurdles in 5.8 seconds. Only two weeks later in a Knights of Columbus meet at the Boston Garden he matched the record twice in the same event—first in a qualifying heat and then in winning the race. He tied the world record in the 60 meters in a qualifying heat at the 1936 Millrose Games.

Although Green's decision not to compete in the Berlin Games deprived him of his only opportunity to earn an Olympic medal, he never regretted having made the decision. He was elected to the Harvard Athletic Hall of Fame in 1961.

GREENBERG, HENRY "HANK" (1911–1986)

Baseball player

Hank Greenberg was one of the most important Jewish athletes of all time. In thirteen seasons as one of major league baseball greatest power hitters, Greenberg compiled a lifetime batting average of .313, led the American League in home runs and runs batted in on four different occasions, and was voted the League's Most Valuable Player in 1935 and 1940. More importantly, Greenberg's presence and power inspired American Jews during the Depression years of increasing anti-Semitism at home and the threat of fascism abroad.

Born on the Lower East Side and raised in the Bronx, the six-foot, four-inch Greenberg was signed by the Detroit Tigers at age nineteen and within four years he had led the team to the 1934 American League pennant with a .339 average and 139 runs batted in. Though he was not a religious man, Greenberg's decision not to play on Yom Kippur that season was a source of great pride to American Jews and many in the Detroit press praised him loudly for making this choice. Although Jews revered Greenberg as a role model and he earned the respect and admiration of many non-Jews as well, he was subject to considerable anti-Semitic abuse throughout his career, especially from opposing fans and players. This baiting and taunting did nothing to diminish Greenberg's performance on the field.

Greenberg lost four years of his playing career because of World War II military service and he retired two years later. He was elected to the Baseball Hall of

---

Signed in Hebrew

Hank Greenberg is a legend among American Jews for not playing on Yom Kippur during the 1934 pennant race and the 1935 World Series. What is less well known is that he used to sign autographs for fans outside Yankee Stadium in Hebrew. In the 1930s in the Bronx, Hebrew was indeed a second language—well, maybe third after Yiddish.

Henry "Hank" Greenberg was many Americans' first exposure to a Jewish athlete. The son of Orthodox parents from Romania, Greenberg didn't make a big deal of his Jewishness, but he didn't hide it either. When it looked like he had a chance to break Babe Ruth's 1927 record of sixty home runs in a season, his mother promised to make him sixty-one baseball-shaped gefilte fish portions if he succeeded. (He didn't.) (Courtesy of National Baseball Hall of Fame Library Cooperstown, N.Y.)

Fame in 1956 and during the same year served as general manager and part-owner of the Cleveland Indians.

HELDMAN, GLADYS (1922–)

Tennis player, magazine publisher

Gladys Heldman was a pioneer in the development and promotion of women's tennis in the United States. Heldman enjoyed a successful although brief career in competitive tennis, winning a number-one ranking in Texas in the early 1950s and gaining a berth at Wimbledon in 1954. But it was as the creator, editor, and publisher of *World Tennis Magazine* that she established her long-term influence in giving women in the sport increased recognition, stature, and financial support.

Born in New York in 1922 to scholarly Jewish parents, Heldman lived in Texas most of her adult life. From the late 1950s to the present, she has fought to end the disparity in earnings between men's and women's tennis through sponsorship of her own tours and the initiation of a successful lawsuit against the United States Lawn Tennis Association. In 1969 Heldman staged three tournaments for women and the following year she organized a separate women's tournament just prior to the U.S. Open as a direct protest against the Open's unequal purses for women performers. The lawsuit that she and Billie Jean King won against the U.S.L.T.A. in 1973 resulted in women's and men's playing at the same events for the same pay. In the 1970s, Heldman's daughter Julie went on to become an excellent tennis player in her own right, but her high prize money would not have been possible without her mother's perseverance and dedication.

HOLMAN, NAT (1896–1995)

Basketball player

No one bettered symbolized New York City basketball at its peak than Nat Holman. As a star player in the 1920s when the professional leagues were in their infancy and as coach at City College for an extraordinary thirty-six years, Holman earned the nickname "Mr. Basketball" for his unparalleled knowledge and understanding of the game.

Born in 1896 and raised on New York's Lower East Side, Holman honed his basketball skills in the streets, school yards, and settlement houses of his youth. After playing with distinction for City College in the second decade of the century, he took over as the team coach in 1919 at the age of only twenty-three. At the same time as he began a coaching career that would last until 1960, Holman starred in the fledgling professional leagues, which in these early years were really more of a semi-pro association that only scheduled games on weekends and required minimal amounts of traveling. Beginning with the New York Whirlwinds in 1920 and 1921, he earned his greatest fame with the Original Celtics (who also played in New York), where he remained until the team disbanded in 1929. Known for his extraordinary ball-handling, play-making, and prowess with the two-hand set

shot, Holman turned Celtic games into virtual basketball clinics. He also pioneered concepts that revolutionized basketball such as the "give-and-go" and the "center pivot" play.

As a coach, Holman's CCNY teams compiled a stunning record of 422 victories against 188 loses. His 1949–50 team was the first and last team to win both the NCAA and National Invitational League Championship in the same year. Although deeply hurt by the point shaving scandal of the following year, Holman was cleared of any wrongdoing and continued coaching for another nine seasons. In 1949, he was the first American to coach in Israel and in 1973, he became the president of the United States Committee on Sports for Israel, sponsors of the U.S. Maccabiah Games Team. One year shy of his one hundredth birthday, Holman died in 1995.

HOLZMAN, WILLIAM "RED" (1920–1998)

Basketball coach

With the second highest winning percentage in National Basketball Association history, Red Holzman earned distinction as one of the finest basketball coaches in history. Best known for leading the New York Knicks to championships in 1970 and 1973, Holzman also coached teams in Milwaukee and St. Louis after completing a successful playing career.

Born in 1920 in New York City, Holzman achieved status as All-American at City College in 1942. He starred professionally for the Rochester Royals, one of the eight original franchises in the Basketball Association of America, the forerunner of the National Basketball Association. He made the All-league team as a rookie and then earned All-Star status on the Royals' 1950–51 Championship Team in the NBA's first season.

As the coach of the Knicks in late 1960s and into the 1970s, Holzman's teams earned a reputation for being smart and unselfish. Holzman believed in stressing fundamentals such as passing, rebounding, and defense. Even if his squads sometimes lacked speed and size, they made few mistakes and were

Basketball legend William "Red" Holzman coached, among many other famous athletes, Bill Bradley, who went on to become a United States Senator from New Jersey. Bradley was one of Holzman's greatest fans. (Courtesy of Naismith Memorial Basketball Hall of Fame)

known for being physically and mentally tough. Holzman retired as coach after the 1981–82 season with 696 victories, making him second in the NBA to **Red Auerbach** of the Boston Celtics who, at retirement, had 938 wins. He died on November 13, 1998.

KARFF, MONA (N.) MAY (1914–1998)

Chess player

Known as the "queen of American chess," Mona May Karff was one of the dominant forces in the game for over forty years. Born in the Russian province of Bessarabia, she moved to Palestine when she was a teenager and came to the United States in the 1930s. According the Karff, she was nine when she learned

chess from her father, Aviv Ratner, a Zionist who was something of a real estate mogul in Tel Aviv and became one of the richest men in Israel. She made a name for herself with a victory in the United States Women's Championship in 1938 at age twenty-four. She went on to capture the tournament a total of seven times, the last in 1974. She was one of the first four Americans to attain the rank of international woman master. She represented Palestine in the 1937 women's world championships in Stockholm and placed sixth. In the 1939 championships in Buenos Aires, she played for the United States and came in fifth.

Mona May Karff (the N. appeared and disappeared at her whim) was recognized on numerous occasions as a pioneer in women's chess and as an important figure in elevating the women's game to a broader popularity. She was a fixture at the Marshall Chess Club on West Tenth Street in New York City in her later years. She died in New York City on January 10, 1998.

KOUFAX, SANFORD "SANDY" (1935–)

Baseball player

One of the most dominant pitchers to ever play in major league baseball, Sanford "Sandy" Koufax established a number of unprecedented records despite begin forced to end his career early because of arm problems. Koufax led the major leagues in strikeouts four times, won the Cy Young Award as best pitcher on three different occasions, and the earned run average title a remarkable five consecutive years. He was also the first pitcher in major league history to throw four no-hitters, including a perfect game in 1965.

Born in Brooklyn in 1935 Koufax played on both the baseball (as a first baseman) and the basketball teams of Lafayette High school. When he joined the Brooklyn Dodgers in 1955, Koufax was touted as a home grown hero, especially among the borough's large Jewish community. Wild and erratic in his first few years, he achieved his fame and prominence the year after the team moved west to Los Angeles.

It was a source of considerable pride to the Jewish public at large when Koufax, not an especially reli-

Sandy Koufax was one of the greatest pitchers of all time. In order to make certain that he pitched as frequently as he could, the Brooklyn Dodger management paid especially close attention to the pitcher rotation during the High Holy Days. Koufax never had to choose between his faith and his pitching. (Courtesy of National Baseball Hall of Fame Library Cooperstown, N. Y.)

gious man, refused to pitch the first game of the 1965 World Series because it fell on Yom Kippur. Because he gained stardom in a more accepting and tolerant era, the quiet and reflective Koufax did not encounter anywhere near the struggles faced by **Hank Greenberg**, the renowned Jewish baseball star of the 1930s and 1940s. In 1972, Koufax became the youngest player ever to be elected to the Hall of Fame.

LEONARD, BENNY (1896–1947)

Boxer

In an era in which Jews dominated boxing, no one was more dominant than Benny Leonard. Born Benjamin

Leiner, Benny began fighting under his ring name in 1911, wanting to shield himself from the inevitable disapproval of his religiously observant family. Within six years, Leonard won the world's lightweight championship, defeating Freddy Welsh convincingly for the title. In the ring, Leonard was a brilliant tactician and a potent puncher. Out of the ring, he was quiet, intelligent, and gentle. In 1925 he retired from boxing at his mother's request, still the lightweight champion of the world.

The stock market crash of 1929 wiped out most of Leonard's savings and he reluctantly returned to the ring in 1931 as a thirty-five-year-old welterweight. It was a mistake. The following year, Jimmy McLernin became the first man to knock Leonard out. Leonard retired again, completing his pugilistic career with a sterling 209–5 record, including sixty-eight knockouts. (Of the five losses, three came at the beginning of his career and another was awarded on a foul.)

Leonard served in the Armed Forces in both World Wars, particularly impressive when one realizes that by the time World War II broke out he was nearing fifty. He died of a heart attack while refereeing a prizefight in 1947.

LIEBERMAN-CLINE, NANCY (1958–)

Nancy Lieberman is generally acknowledged as the greatest women's basketball player in the history of the game. Leading Old Dominion University to two national championships in the 1970s, Lieberman was a three-time Kodak All-American and Street and Smith's All-American, winning the Wade Trophy as the outstanding women's collegiate basketball athlete in 1979 and 1980 and setting a number of scoring records in the process.

Born in 1958 in Far Rockaway, New York, Lieberman developed her basketball skills and love for the game from a young age. Her prowess on the court in her freshman year at Old Dominion brought Lieberman immediate recognition and a place on the 1976 Olympic team where she became the youngest basketball player in history to win a medal. Although there were no professional leagues for women when Lieber-

Nancy Lieberman-Cline is one of the greatest women's basketball players in the history of the game. She is sometimes not included in "Jewish" reference books because she converted to Christianity. We have included her here because of her Jewish birth and because we really wanted to write about her. (Courtesy of Naismith Memorial Basketball Hall of Fame)

LUCKMAN, SYDNEY "SID" (1916–1998)

Football player

Known as "The Master of the T-Formation," Sidney "Sid" Luckman was recognized as the premier quarterback of his generation and one of the greatest Jewish players in the history of professional football. In nine seasons as signal caller for the Chicago Bears, his teams won four NFL championships and five Western Conference titles. Luckman captured the league's Most Valuable Player award in 1943, the year he threw a record seven touchdowns against the New York Giants.

Born in Brooklyn in 1916, Luckman gained initial fame as an All-American tailback at Columbia University in 1937 and 1938. It was in the professional game, at a time when football was shifting from a "single wing" to a "T" formation, that he made his greatest mark on the sport. In the T-formation, the quarterback took on an elevated role as the offensive leader and football's passing game grew in importance. Luckman mastered the new system flawlessly, helping to open up and popularize professional football and bring it into the modern era after World War II. A passer of pinpoint accuracy and precision, Luckman finished his career passing for 139 touchdowns and setting numerous records along the way. He retired in 1950 and was elected to the professional football Hall of Fame in 1965. He died in Aventura, Florida on July 5, 1998.

ROSENBLOOM, MAXIE (1904–1976)

Boxer

In an era when Jews dominated the sport of boxing, Maxie "Slapsy" Rosenbloom held the light-heavyweight championship from 1930 to 1934. With his colorful personality and unusual open glove style of fighting, Rosenbloom was a crowd favorite who went on to a successful movie career after his years in the ring.

Born in Leonard's Bridge, Connecticut in 1904, Rosenbloom learned to box at Harlem's Union Settlement in New York. After defeating Jimmy Slattery to

man graduated, by 1986 the fledgling United States Basketball League gave her a new opportunity to continue a career as a basketball player for the next three years with the Long Island Knights and the Springfield Flames.

The USBL folded after the 1988 season but the success of the new Women's National Basketball Association in the 1990s encouraged Lieberman (now Lieberman-Cline following her marriage) to make a comeback at age thirty-nine in 1998. Clearly, the newfound popularity of women's basketball and women's athletics in general owes a debt to Lieberman's talents and dedication. She was inducted into the Naismith Memorial Basketball Hall of Fame in 1996.

capture the light-heavyweight crown, Rosenbloom fought an extraordinary 106 times defending his title before losing to Bob Olin by decision in 1934.

At a time of increasing anti-Semitism in America, Rosenbloom was frequently demeaned in the press, with a number of reporters ridiculing the champion's clownish personality to perpetuate negative Jewish stereotypes. Nevertheless, Rosenbloom achieved great stardom, winning 232 out of the 299 bouts he fought and being elected to the Boxing Hall of Fame in 1972.

ROSS, BARNEY (1909–1967)

Boxer, war hero

Barney Ross's life story is one of tragedies overcome by sheer force of will. When Ross (born Barnet Rosofsky) was fourteen, his father was killed in a hold-up of the family grocery store in Chicago. His younger siblings sent to an orphanage, Ross's response was a rebellion against his Orthodox upbringing that included his running with Chicago underworld figures. But boxing kept him off the streets and gave him a direction for his life.

Ross had a brilliant amateur career and turned pro in 1929. Within four years he made enough money as a fighter to reunite the family. That same year he won a title fight against Tony Canzoneri to become the lightweight champion of the world. He successfully defended the title against Canzoneri six months later. Like many young fighters, Ross found that as he grew it became harder to make weight, and he moved up in weight class to the welterweight division. There he met the champ, Jimmy McLarnin (who had ended the career of another great Jewish fighter, **Benny Leonard** in 1931) in three ferocious battles in 1934–5. Ross won the first and third of these matches. His 1934 victory made him the first fighter to hold the lightweight and welter titles simultaneously. Ross's boxing career ended in 1938 with a ferocious beating at the hands of Henry Armstrong (although Ross stayed on his feet for fifteen brutal rounds). His career record was 78–4, with twenty-four knockouts. He was never knocked out, all four of his losses coming on decisions.

In 1942, Ross created another kind of history. At age thirty-three he was a marine, fighting against the Japanese on Guadalcanal. Trapped behind enemy lines with a squadron of fellow marines, he held off a Japanese attack with rifle fire and grenades, killing twenty-two of the enemy and earning the Silver Star. But the price of that valor was severe shrapnel wounds and a case of malaria. In the military hospital, he was given heavy doses of morphine as a painkiller and by the time he was discharged from the hospital and the service in 1944 he was an addict. Ross struggled with his addiction for two years, finally surrendering to Federal authorities in 1946, undergoing successful rehab at a federal hospital. In later years he was an eloquent spokesman about the problems of drug addiction.

SAVITT, RICHARD "DICK" (1927–)

Tennis player

During the 1950s, Dick Savitt was one of the top players in men's tennis. His upset victory over Ken McGregor at Wimbledon in 1951 gained him a cover profile in *Time* magazine and number three ranking in the world. That same year Savitt became the first non-Aussie to win the Australian Singles title in thirteen years and he was selected as the number one player on the United States Davis Cup team.

The Bayonne, New Jersey, native, born in 1927, developed his early skills at the predominately Jewish Berkeley Tennis Club in Orange, New Jersey. But it was during his high school years in El Paso, Texas that Savitt's game flourished. At Cornell University, he moved up the ranks of top players and reached the finals of the U.S. Open at Forest Hills shortly after his graduation.

Following his victories in the Australian and Wimbledon Opens, Savitt continued his prominence in the tennis world by winning the 1952 National Indoors Singles Championship. Savitt retired from tennis briefly after what he perceived was a snub by the Davis

Cup Coaches who would not allow him to compete in the championships against the Australian team after he had led the American squad to the title round. Although there were rumors that anti-Semitism may have played a role, Savitt himself never pressed the point. He returned to competitive tennis part-time in 1956 and repeated his National Indoors Singles victory in 1958 and 1961, making him the first to accomplish this feat three times. In 1961, he won both the Singles and the Doubles Championships at the World Maccabiah Games in Israel.

SCHAYES, ADOLPH (1928–)

Basketball player

Dolph Schayes was the premier Jewish basketball player in the post–World War II era and one of the most prolific scorers and rebounders ever to participate in the sport. Schayes won the Rookie of the Year award in 1949, earned twelve consecutive All Star nominations, and set five National Basketball Association records by the time he retired in 1964. At 6 feet, 8 inches, he also became known for pioneering the concept of the "power forward."

Born in the Bronx in 1928 to Rumanian Jewish immigrants who had been in the country only eight years, Schayes developed his basketball skills and his love for the sport through a Jewish sports club he formed with a group of friends in junior high school. After starring for the DeWitt Clinton High School team, the heavily recruited Schayes attended New York University on an athletic scholarship and became a unanimous All-American choice and collegiate star.

Schayes played most of his professional career with the Syracuse Nationals, leading them to the NBA championship in 1955 and becoming the highest scorer in NBA history in 1958. He spent his last year as player-coach for the Philadelphia 76ers and then led them to the title the following year as full-time coach. Schayes served as supervisor of officials from 1966 to 1970, returning to coaching with the Buffalo Braves from 1970 to 1972. In 1977, he was head coach of the gold-medal winning United States Maccabiah Games

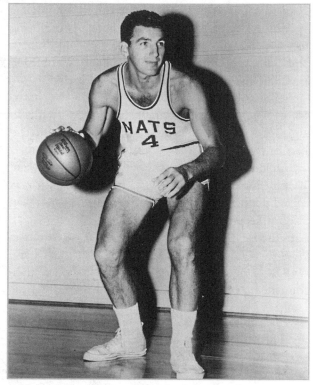

Adolph "Dolph" Schayes got both his love of sports and his height (6 feet, 8 inches) from his father, a Romanian Jew. When he retired from playing basketball in 1963, he had scored more points than any other player in the game. (Courtesy of Naismith Memorial Basketball Hall of Fame)

basketball team, largely because of the exploits of his son, Danny, who also went on to a distinguished NBA career. Dolph Schayes was elected to the Naismith Memorial Basketball Hall of Fame in 1972.

SEIXAS, VICTOR (1923–)

Tennis player

At roughly the same time **Dick Savitt** made a name for himself as the first prominent Jewish presence in the tennis world, Vic Seixas achieved notable success among the sport's pro ranks. Born in Philadelphia in 1923, Seixas's first major victory was for the University of North Carolina, where he won the Southern Conference Men's Tennis championship in 1948. In 1953, he began his four-year championship run by winning the Wimbledon men's singles championship, capturing the French and Australian doubles with Tony Trabert, and both the United States Open and Wimbledon mixed doubles championships with Doris Hart.

Seixas continued this string by winning the United States Open singles championship at Forest Hills in 1954, French Open and Australian doubles with Trabert in 1955 and 1956, and four more mixed doubles championships with Hart at both the U.S. Open and Wimbledon in 1954 and 1955. In 1956, with a new mixed doubles partner, Shirley Fry, Seixas again won at Wimbledon.

Although Seixas won no more major tournaments after 1956, his record of achievement in singles and doubles competition over a short time period is undiminished. He was inducted in the National Tennis Hall of Fame in 1971.

SPITZ, MARK (1950–)

Swimmer

In one of the most extraordinary performances in Olympic history, Mark Spitz won a remarkable seven gold medals and set four individual records in swimming at the 1972 Games in Munich. Although overshadowed by the tragic murder of eleven Israeli athletes in the Olympic village, Spitz's exploits in Munich elevated him to the rank of the greatest competitive swimmer of all time.

The 1972 Olympics was the culmination of nearly a decade of competitive swimming for the native of Modesto, California. Beginning his career by participating in the Maccabiah games in 1965 where he won ten medals, Spitz went on to capture thirty-one National Amateur Athletic Union (AAU) titles, eight NCAA Championships, and five Pan-American golds, setting thirty-three world records in the process. He won two gold medals in relay events at the 1968 Games in Mexico City and captured a silver in the 100-meter butterfly along with a bronze in the 100-meter freestyle.

Spitz was voted "Swimmer of the Year" in 1967, 1971, and 1972. In 1971 he became the first Jewish recipient of the James E. Sullivan Award given to the outstanding amateur athlete of the year. In addition to earning a successful post-Olympic living in real estate and business, Spitz has helped raise money to support the very same U.S. Maccabiah Games that launched his career.

STRUG, KERRI (1978–)

Gymnast

Eighteen-year-old Kerri Strug's vault on a badly injured ankle to give the 1996 U.S. women's gymnastics team the gold medal was one of the most memorable and dramatic moments in Olympic history. Despite her young age, Strug has established herself as an outstanding gymnast, winning a silver medal in the 1992 games and finishing in the top ten in a number of international competitions.

The great-grandchild of Eastern European Jewish immigrants, Strug grew up in a secular, middle-class family in Tucson, Arizona. The diminutive youngster established her gymnastics talents from early childhood and gained immediate recognition that resulted in her inclusion on the Barcelona Olympic team, where she missed winning the all-around finals by a fraction of a point. After four years of intensive training, including several erratic performances, Strug reached the pinnacle of success at the 1996 Atlanta games under the tutelage of controversial coach Bela Karolyi. Although Strug's gold medal performance was a source of great pride for the American gymnastic team, her injury raised questions about Karolyi's win-at-all costs training methods.

Since her Olympic victory, Strug has traveled to Israel to help light the torch at the 1997 Maccabiah Games, and has written a children's book and an autobiography. She also began college at UCLA and toured with the Ice Capades.

TRACK AND FIELD

An American Jewish presence in track and field can be traced back to the nineteenth century when Lon Myers became the first person to run the quarter-mile in less than 50 seconds. In the 1879 National (U.S.) Amateur Athletic Union Championships, Myers won a triple victory winning the 220-, 440-, and 880-yard runs. From 1880 to 1888 he held world records for both the 440-yard and 880-yard events and the 100 yard dash.

In the early twentieth century Russian immigrant Myer Prinstein became a five-time Olympic track and field medalist in the long jump and triple jump, winning gold medals in both the 1900 games in Paris and the 1904 Olympiad in St. Louis. Abe Kiviat established himself as an outstanding distance runner in 1911 when he won both the United States Amateur Athletic Union 600-yard and 1,000-yard Indoor Championship. He also won a silver medal at the 1912 Stockholm Olympic Games in the 1,500-meter run.

The decade of the 1930s proved to be an important one for Jewish track and field competitors. One of the greatest female athletes of all time, **Lillian Copeland** won an Olympic gold medal for discus throwing in the 1932 games in Los Angeles, establishing a world record in the process. Copeland also set world records in the javelin, discus, and shot-put while a student at the University of Southern California. Running for Harvard University in 1935 and 1936, **Milton Green** set or equaled a number of collegiate records in the high and low hurdles. **Marty Glickman** and San Stoller went to the Berlin Olympic Games in 1936 expecting to compete in the 4x100 meter relay, but were replaced at the last minute in a decision tinged with anti-Semitic overtones.

In the post-war era, shot puter James Fuchs and javelin thrower Steve Seymour each won medals at the 1948 Olympic Games in London. German Jewish refugee Henry Laskau dominated American race-walking, winning forty-two National Amateur Athletic Union championships between 1947 and 1956. In 1964 Gerald Ashworth won an Olympic Gold Medal in the 400-meter relay. In the last three decades Jewish athletes have been omnipresent in American track and field, but none have achieved the greatness of their predecessors.

For Further Reading

See Appendix 2 for a bibliography of general reference books about Jews and the Jewish experience in America. All of the volumes listed there include information about American Jews in sports.

Levine, Peter. *Ellis Island to Ebbets Field: Sports and the American Jewish Experience.* New York: Oxford University Press, 1992.

Ribalow, Harold, and Meir Ribalow. *The Jew in American Sports,* 4th ed. New York: Hippocrene Books, 1981.

Seigman, Joseph. *Jewish Sports Legends,* 2d ed. International Jewish Sports Hall of Fame, Virginia: Brassey's Inc., 1997.

Slater, Robert. *Great Jews in Sports* (Introduction by Red Auerbach). Middle Village, N.Y.: Jonathon David Publishers, Inc., 1983.

Part 9

Art, Architecture, and Photography

OVERVIEW

Jewish Americans were latecomers in their influence on art, but they hit the ground running. Beginning at the end of the nineteenth century, the world of Ameri-can art began to resound with Jewish names and feel the effect of ideas brought to this country by European Jewish immigrants. The Realist school of painting and sculpture included such names as **Ben Shahn**, **Theresa Bernstein**, and the **Soyer** brothers. Modernists were inspired and encouraged by **Alfred Stieglitz** and Edward Steichen and their 291 Gallery and found an honored ancestor in **Max Weber**. Art photography was introduced to American audiences by Steichen and Stieglitz and found some of its most extraordinary practitioners in Jewish photographers such as **Paul Strand** and **Man Ray** (born Emanuel Rabinovitch). **Alfred Eisenstaedt**, a well-respected German photographer who fled the Nazis in 1935, became *Life* magazine's foremost photographer, combining the artistic and the documentary styles in a way that few others have ever approached.

The most profound influence of Jewish artists, however, was the Abstract Expressionist movement in painting and sculpture. After World War II, because of the devastation of Europe, the center of the international art world moved to New York. Great figures of European art, many of whom fled their native countries to escape persecution as Jews, now lived and worked in New York neighborhoods. This influx of great artists included Jews such as Marc Chagall, **Jacques Lipchitz**, and Naum Gabo. The introduction of their highly modern approach had enormous repercussions for the American art scene. For the first time, American artists were introduced to the idea that art might be a fundamentally intellectual undertaking. Soon, a school of artists that included **Philip Guston**, **Lee Krasner**, Adolph Gottlieb, **Franz Kline**, **Barnett Newman**, **Ad Reinhardt**, and **Mark Rothko** created the style of painting known as "action painting," "American-type painting," or "Abstract Expressionism."

Abstract Expressionism dominated American art for more than two decades. When it at last loosened its grip, Jewish Americans were among those who experimented with new styles and feelings. Among "Pop Artists" were **Larry Rivers**, **Roy Lichtenstein**, and **Jim Dine**. Feminist artists included **Judy Chicago** and **Barbara Kruger**. However, it may have been the photographers who made the most powerful statements about life in America in the decades of the fifties, sixties, and seventies. Jewish Americans such as **Robert Frank**, Bruce Davidson, **Richard Avedon**, **Irving Penn**, and **Diane Arbus** startled the world with the quality and the content of their photographs. They recorded fash-

ions, protests, and poverty. Their film, whether it was moving or still, began to represent the conscience of America.

Paralleling the development of painting and sculpture were the great movements in architecture. Here again Jewish Americans were in the forefront, from **Dankmar Adler** in the early years of the twentieth century to Modernists Rudolph M. Schindler and **Richard Neutra**, the only American in the 1932 landmark exhibition "The International Style: Architecture since 1922" at the Museum of Modern Art. When Modernism began to wear out its welcome, Jewish American **Louis Kahn** led the respectful opposition and **Robert A. M. Stern** the less respectful Post-Modernist movement.

In art, as in other areas of American life, Jewish Americans have had an impact greater than their proportion in the population, reflecting the importance of art in Jewish American culture.

ADLER, DANKMAR (1844–1900)

Architect

The engineering genius behind the success of architect Louis Sullivan, Dankmar Alder was born in Stadtlengsfeld, Germany, but grew up in the United States and was educated in this country. He served as an engineer during the Civil War and then went into practice as an architect in Chicago. In 1879 he took Louis Sullivan into his firm as chief draftsman, and two years later the two became partners. The firm of Adler and Sullivan revolutionized urban architecture in America. Rejecting the dependence on historical styles and heavy ornamentation, they created buildings in which structure was expressed in the design. They used ornamentation in a way that did not disguise the steel frame of their new style of skyscraper.

Adler's brilliance as an acoustical engineer led to one of the firm's most important commissions. The two men had designed a temporary structure in the Interstate Exposition building. It was an auditorium with acoustics that were so nearly perfect that one of the exposition's sponsors hired Adler and Sullivan to design a building on the corner of Congress and Michigan in Chicago that would contain, in addition to hotel and business offices, a magnificent auditorium theater. The result was the Auditorium Building, one of the landmarks of Chicago architecture. The acoustics in its beautiful theater established Adler in the front ranks of the world's acoustical engineers.

The Columbian Exposition of 1893 set off a demand for neo-classical architecture that effectively destroyed the firm of Adler and Sullivan. Adler left the partnership in 1895 because there was insufficient work. He died five years later at the age of fifty-six. Sullivan continued to work for another two decades, designing small bank buildings in towns around the Midwest.

ARBUS, DIANE (1923–1971)

Photographer

Renowned for her voyeuristic photos of freaks, transvestites, and other odd characters, Diane Arbus was a deeply troubled person who took her own life at the peak of her career. Born Diane Nemerov (her brother was poet **Howard Nemerov**), she was raised in the luxury of a wealthy family. Educated at elite New York private schools—the Ethical Culture School and Fieldston—and the Cummington School of the Arts, she married Allan Arbus at eighteen after meeting him in her father's department store, where he worked. When Arbus was drafted into the Army and assigned to the Signal Corps, she tagged along, picking up from him the rudiments of photography. Subsequently she studied with the legendary photographer Bernice Abbott.

After the war Diane and Allan opened their own studio together, specializing in fashion photography. But Diane had begun studying with Lisette Model, another brilliant Jewish photographer, who was fascinated by the grotesque and outrageous, a taste that Diane was rapidly acquiring herself. When *Harper's Bazaar* published a portfolio of Arbus's work in 1961 under the title "Portraits of Eccentrics," she was launched on a new career path. She received two

Guggenheim Fellowships (in 1963 and 1966), freelanced extensively, taught photography at prestigious art schools like the Rhode Island School of Design and Cooper Union, and received several major museum exhibits.

All this time Arbus was struggling with severe depression. Finally, in 1971, declaring to friends that her work "doesn't do it for me anymore," she committed suicide.

ARCHITECTURE

Jewish Americans entered architecture in the United States earlier than they did most of the other arts. While important Jewish painters and sculptors in this country did not appear until almost the twentieth century, the first architect of note began his career before the Civil War. Leopold Eidlitz (1823–1908) was a prominent figure in the Gothic revival movement that shaped the appearance of public buildings and, especially, churches in the middle of the nineteenth century. Eidlitz himself built many churches, including Christ Church Cathedral in St. Louis, sometimes called "the most churchly church" in the country. He also built the former Temple Emanu-El. Not long after Eidlitz began to make his name, a far more important figure in American architectural history came to the fore.

Dankmar Adler, the man who worked with Louis Sullivan in developing the American skyscraper, was born in Germany but came to the United States when he was very young. He trained as an architect and served as an engineer during the Civil War. After the war, he opened his own company in Chicago and hired Louis Sullivan as chief draftsman. Two years later, the two became partners. From the first, the firm of Adler and Sullivan began to reshape the face of urban architecture in America. They threw out the historical styles and heavy ornamentation that were then so popular and created buildings in which structure was expressed in the design. Their ornamentation did not disguise the steel frame of their new style of skyscraper but emphasized it. Sullivan was the design genius behind their remarkable buildings, but Adler was an engineer of extraordinary brilliance. His acoustics in such buildings as the Auditorium Building in Chicago are virtually unsurpassed.

The Columbian Exposition of 1893 set off a demand for neo-classical architecture that effectively destroyed the firm of Adler and Sullivan. For almost two decades, American building design backtracked. Jewish architect Arnold Brunner (1857–1925) worked well in the historical styles. He designed mostly public buildings, including a number of synagogues, which were all in the Romanesque style with a touch of Islamic and Byzantine until after the Exposition. Then they were neo-classical. Brunner, however, insisted that his shift to the Greco-Roman was not a matter of fashion but a result of investigation into the design of synagogues in ancient Galilee. Ely Jacques Kahn believed in the Adler-Sullivan-Wright emphasis on proportion, function, and materials rather than ornamentation and built a number of skyscrapers using those principles. He also yielded to the demands of his customers and built "historical" buildings, including homes and country clubs.

After World War I, American architecture began to change drastically as an influx of European immigrants brought with them the ideas of the Bauhaus. Among the most influential of these new Americans were Rudolph M. Schindler (1887–1953) and **Richard Neutra**, both of whom emigrated from Vienna, Austria. Neutra joined Schindler in Los Angeles after having worked and studied in New York and Chicago and, most significantly, in Wisconsin with Frank Lloyd Wright. In 1927, he designed the Jardin Apartments in Los Angeles. The reinforced concrete building was chosen for the landmark exhibition "The International Style: Architecture since 1922" at the Museum of Modern Art, as was his steel-framed Lovell House (1927–29). The latter building, a rambling ranch-style house, established Neutra as an internationally important architect and proponent of Modernism. He was the only American included in the MOMA exhibit. The houses that Neutra and Schindler designed in the next decade-and-a-half made Los Angeles a showcase for modern domestic architecture. They were luxurious, with an extensive use of open spaces, glass, and often reflecting pools.

Also important in introducing America to the International Style was **Albert Kahn**, possibly the most influential industrial architect of the first half of the twentieth century. Having immigrated to this country from Germany when he was eleven, Kahn received his training here but was very receptive to European ideas. In 1902 he opened his own practice and, a year later, designed his first automobile plant. For the next four decades, he built virtually every important industrial installation in the automobile industry. Although his buildings were remarkably consistent in their dedication to the practicalities of the workplace, they varied in style, reflecting the important design trends of their time. Other important Jewish American architects in period between the wars and just after World War II included Morris Lapidus, who specialized in luxury hotels; Bertrand Goldberg, who worked largely in reinforced concrete and had a liking for circular forms; Victor Gruen, who virtually created the suburban shopping center; and Albert Mayer, city planner and architect.

The International Style, which stressed function in architecture above all else, gradually became the dominant force in architecture in the United States. In the years after World War II, it preempted all other movements, particularly in the design of corporate office buildings. Among the large architectural firms that perpetuated the style were Harrison and Abramovitz and Skidmore, Owings, and Merrill. In addition to his work as a partner in the former firm, Max Abramovitz was deputy of the Planning Office of the United Nations, and his company built the United Nations Secretariat, incorporating design ideas from an international panel of architects. The firm also built such monuments to the International Style as the Alcoa Building (1953) in Pittsburgh and the Socony Mobil Building (1956) in New York. Abramowitz also designed the new Philharmonic Hall in New York. For Skidmore, Owings, and Merrill, **Gordon Bunshaft** designed the landmark Lever House, the first skyscraper to have a glass curtain wall covering three of its sides.

One Jewish American architect marked out a different path for himself. **Percival Goodman**, who worked as a city planner and architect before the war, was profoundly affected by the Holocaust and its aftermath.

He made the decision to turn away from commercial building and dedicate himself entirely to designing synagogues. His buildings were intimate, often small, built to a human scale, and filled with warmth and light. They were also filled with fine art. Goodman regularly commissioned modern artists to create works of painting, textile, and sculpture for his synagogues. Before Goodman and one or two other modernist architects, synagogues had reflected the architectural styles of their time and country or region. In the years after World War II, however, American architects developed a modern style with a strong emphasis on the expression of religious values and tradition through fine art.

In the early 1960s a reaction against the decades of rigid Modernist dominance set in. It was led by Jewish American **Louis Kahn**. Kahn was born on the island of Osel in Estonia and came to the United States with his family when he was four years old. He grew up in Philadelphia and graduated from the University of Pennsylvania in 1924 with a degree in architecture. For the next quarter of a century, he worked as an architect in Philadelphia, developing a strictly local reputation. Then, in 1949, Kahn took a position teaching at Yale University, and a new phase of his life began. In the academic atmosphere, he was able to develop the theoretical basis of his architectural vision. He and his students became increasingly bold and imaginative in their approach to the problems and tasks of modern building. His first important building was the Yale University Art Gallery (1952–54), which he designed with Douglas I. Orr. For the gallery, he created a tetrahedral concrete ceiling that allowed an enormously flexible approach to exhibit planning and lighting. This sort of practical creativity was characteristic of his designs.

From his post at Yale, Kahn led the reaction against the often sterile minimalism of the International Style in the United States. His work was clean and functional but marked by a beauty of form and richness of materials that sometimes approached visual poetry. He freed American architecture from its servitude to the "less is more" philosophy. He also fostered a new tradition of working with the client to discover specific needs and preferences. This was a marked change from the Bauhaus arrogance in which the architect's vision was absolute and the client's sole responsibility was to pay the bills.

Kahn did not abandon the basic tenets of Modernism. He and other American architects of the time simply interpreted that philosophy in a new way, one that turned out to have international appeal. **Richard Meier**, for example, built major buildings in eight of the twelve nations in the European Community, including the Museum of Contemporary Art in Barcelona and the city hall and the central library in the Hague. For his work, Meier received the Pritzker Prize, architecture's equivalent of the Nobel.

Also at this time, an interest developed in the possibilities of prefabricated construction and other practical approaches to beautiful housing for the masses of people. One of the two great designers of this movement, along with R. Buckminster Fuller, was **Moshe Safdie**. Born in Israel, Safdie moved to Canada in the 1960s. In 1967 he designed the revolutionary Habitat apartment complex for the Montreal World Fair, thus establishing himself as one of the most innovative architects of his time.

While Kahn, Meier, and Safdie maintained many of the Modernist principles, architects of the 1970s were inspired by their rebellion to turn further and further away from the Bauhaus. As the high-rise housing project, symbolic of the Modernist ideal, was revealed as an architectural fiasco and a human tragedy, young architects looked again to the past. At the forefront of the new movement were Jewish American **Denise Scott Brown** and her gentile husband Robert Venturi. His book *Complexity and Contradiction in Architecture* (1966) and their collaboration *Learning from Las Vegas* (1972), which was co-authored with Steven Izenour, set out the principles of a new approach. The convenient label for the widely varied styles of the new generation of architects was Post-Modernism. Its salient characteristic was a re-interpretation of historical styles in a way that is often described as "ironic."

One reason for the success of this new approach was its emphasis on creating buildings that "fit." A library built by the firm of Venturi Scott Brown would, by duplication of material and ironic homage to historical styles, "fit" into a university setting of nineteenth-century buildings. A New England summer home would "fit" the shore and the fisherman's shacks that surrounded it. After the stark and uncompromising buildings of the Modernist period, this quality was warmly welcomed by the community.

Another of the important Post-Modernist architects was **Robert A. M. Stern**. He began with a series of vernacular-style houses in the Hamptons on Long Island in the early 1970s. These new houses had shingles, gables, and pitched roofs. They were, quite simply, "gracious homes," and people responded to them on an emotional level that had been absent in domestic architecture for some time. They were the first of many Stern designs that would respect the environment in which they were built. An office tower in Boston would reflect that city's stately past. A building complex at the University of Virginia would have a Jeffersonian flavor. A museum devoted to Norman Rockwell would be as simple clapboard structure, while the Disney animation building in Burbank, California, would feature a towering version of Mickey Mouse's hat from *The Sorcerer's Apprentice*.

Others leaders of the Post-Modernist movement included **Peter Eisenman**, whose oddly asymmetrical designs have been constructed in Spain, Germany, and Japan, as well as the United States, and the often controversial **Frank Gehry**. Eisenman and Gehry both made architecture comment on itself and on society. They moved beyond Stern's emphasis on history and memory into an acknowledgment of the discordance of the modern world. Gehry often used raw materials that could be seen as "confrontational": corrugated metal, chain-link fencing, even cardboard. He designed furniture made of leftover pieces of lumber and glass combined with industrial lights and old car seats. Eisenman went even further, putting intentional gaps in a bedroom floor. In 1988 Gehry and Eisenman were among seven architects featured at another seminal MOMA show, "Deconstructivist Architecture." Gehry has won the Pritzker.

In the 1990s Jewish Americans figure among the world's most acclaimed architects. The firm of Venturi Scott Brown recently designed an addition to London's National Gallery of Art. Frank Gehry's firm built the American Center in Paris and part of the Villa Olimpica in Barcelona. Both firms were among the five finalists when the archdiocese of Los Angeles, the largest in the United States, chose an architect for a new cathedral in the center of the city. Richard Meier recently won a commission from the Vatican to design a church for the year 2000.

AVEDON, RICHARD (1923–)

Photographer

Richard Avedon was born in New York City on May 15, 1923. A photographer from the age of ten, he received his formal training while in the Merchant Marines and later at the New School for Social Research. He began working with *Harper's Bazaar* in 1945 and was a regular contributor to the magazine until 1965. He was one of *Vogue*'s main photographers from 1966 to 1990.

One of the leading photographers in America, Avedon is known for his austere yet elegant images and for his stark portraits, especially of celebrities. In 1974 he completed a series of photographs of his father, Jacob Israel Avedon, shortly before the latter's death. In 1975 a retrospective of his work was held at New York's Marlborough Gallery, and in 1978 the Metropolitan Museum of Art presented a major exhibition of his fashion work.

Avedon's work is published in several books including *Observations* (1959, text by Truman Capote), *Nothing Personal* (1974, text by James Baldwin), *Portraits* (1976), *Avedon: Photographs, 1947–1977* (1978), *In the American West* (1985), *An Autobiography* (1993), and *Glitter Slave* (1995). The movie *Funny Face* (1957) was based on his life. Since 1992 he has been working regularly with *The New Yorker* magazine.

BERENSON, BERNARD (1865–1959)

Art historian, connoisseur

The first great American art historian, Bernard Berenson was born in 1865 in Butrimonys, Lithuania, a Jewish ghetto village. His family immigrated to Boston when he was nine years old, and his father worked as a peddler. Nonetheless, the young Bernard was able to attend Harvard University, where he worked to erase his working-poor background. He became this country's foremost expert on the painting of the Italian Renaissance and was able to build on his reputation in that field to establish himself as a world-famous "art expert." For three full generations, he judged the authenticity of thousands of paintings, helped to create collections for multi-millionaires, and wrote authoritative monographs on Western art.

Berenson became rich through his association with dealer Joseph Duveen in ways that were not entirely consistent with his reputation for integrity, although he later came to regret the association. He was aided in his work by his wife, Mary Costello, who acted as ghost writer on her famous husband's most famous book, *The Venetian Painters of the Italian Renaissance* (1894), and who sometimes made his attributions for him in his absence. The Berensons lived most of their life in a villa in Florence, and Berenson converted to Roman Catholicism. His achievements were tremendous, especially when viewed against the anti-Semitism of the time, and his life demands the same consideration.

BERNSTEIN, THERESA (1890–)

Painter

Realist painter Theresa Bernstein was born in Philadelphia in the last decade of the nineteenth century, daughter of European immigrants Isidore and Anne (Ferber) Bernstein. She received her training in art from the Philadelphia School of Design for Women and the Art Students League in New York. She was married in 1919 to fellow artist William Meyerowitz. Bernstein was influenced by the Ashcan School of Realism and was inspired by the popular culture of the city. Painting trolleys, Coney Island, and elevated trains, she was highly respected during the 1920s. As Realism was replaced in critical esteem by more abstract forms of painting, however, her reputation suffered. She continued to paint, exhibit, and sell her work. The women's

movement of the early 1970s brought her work again to the fore. Although she did not specialize in Jewish subject matter, her love for the city embraced Jewish community life, and she painted moving images of weddings and other religious services. She was a committed Zionist and visited Israel a number of times. Her works are included in important private collections and in many major museums, including the National Museum of Women in the Arts, the Jewish Museum, and the Museum of the City of New York.

BLUME, PETER (1906–)

Painter

The extraordinary "magic realist" painter Peter Blume was born in Smorgon, Russia, between Vilna and Minsk. He came to the United States with his family when he was five years old. He grew up on the Lower East Side and started going to art school at the age of twelve. For the next five years, he supported himself as a jewelry designer and letterer while he studied at the Art Students League and the Beaux-Arts Institute of Design, becoming enormously proficient in the technical aspects of painting. Beginning his career in a precisionist style similar to that of Charles Sheeler, he soon revealed a strong vein of irony. He has been mining that vein in his meticulously planned and painted works ever since. He first made his mark with the painting *Parade* (1930), in which a workman carries a suit of armor past a row of factories. In 1934 he caused considerable controversy when his *South of Scranton* won the Carnegie International Award. Homer Saint-Gaudens, the exhibition director, suggest that the picture was "insane" and added that "what garlic is to salad, insanity is to art."

Controversy struck again in 1939 when *The Eternal City* was rejected by the Corcoran Gallery Biennial as too inflammatory. It depicted Mussolini as a jack-in-the-box with a green head glowering at a surrealistic landscape of a ruined Italy while a group of American tourists look on. Each of Blume's paintings takes a number of years, and therefore, in spite of a long career, his output has not been large. Two of his most important works are *Light of the World* (1932), which is at the Whitney Museum, and *The Rock* (1945–1948), which is at the Art Institute of Chicago.

BUNSHAFT, GORDON (1909–1990)

Architect

The designer of the architecturally influential Lever Building in New York City, Gordon Bunshaft was born in Buffalo, New York. In 1946, at the age of thirty-seven, he became a partner in the prestigious architectural firm of Skidmore, Owings, and Merrill. A few years later, he designed one of the most important buildings in modern American architecture. The Lever Building (1952) was clean, stark, and modern—the first skyscraper to be covered on three sides by a glass curtain wall. Soaring above the New York skyline, it was soon imitated by architects around the country. Bunshaft went on to design many other office and industrial buildings. He also designed the Albright-Knox Art Gallery in Buffalo, New York, the Library for Manuscripts and Rare Books at Yale University, and the Hirshhorn Museum in Washington, D. C. Under Bunshaft's artistic direction, Skidmore, Owings, and Merrill kept American urban architecture faithful to the tenets of Modernism for decades.

CAPA, ROBERT (1913–1954)

Photojournalist

Robert Capa was the ideal of the photojournalist and war correspondent: utterly fearless to the point of recklessness, handsome and sexy, committed to his work above all else, and a brilliant practitioner of his art. Born Endre Erno Friedmann, he was expelled from his native Hungary for leftist agitation when he was only seventeen. He ended up in Berlin, where he took a darkroom job for Ullstein Verlag, publishers of a prestigious photo weekly. He quickly branched out to making pictures himself, scoring his first journalistic coup with a candid shot of the exiled Leon Trotsky at a meeting in Copenhagen from which other photographers had been barred. With the rise to power of the Nazis in 1933, Friedmann found himself exiled again, this time to Paris. It was there that he changed his name, partly to avoid confusion with another famous photographer, George Friedmann, partly to sidestep a Nazi ban on the use of Jewish photographers by German syndicates and publications.

In Paris, Capa shared digs with another talented Jewish photojournalist, David "Chim" Seymour, and the two became closely allied with Henri Cartier-Bresson. Out of that friendship and collegial relationship grew the most famous of photo agencies, Magnum, which the trio founded in order to maintain the rights to the photos they made. They were joined in 1935 by Robert's brother, Cornell, who like his older sibling graduated from darkroom work to a photojournalism career. Given his political bent, it was only natural that Capa should go to Spain to cover the Civil War. There he made one of his most famous images, of a Republican soldier being hurled backward at the exact moment that he is struck by an enemy bullet.

By now Capa's work was known all over the world and, not surprisingly, when it became increasingly difficult for a leftist and Jew to work in Europe, he became a favorite photographer of *Life* magazine. For them, he covered the Sino-Japanese War and, most memorably, World War II. In order to cover airborne troops, Capa trained to become a parachutist. He landed at Omaha Beach with American soldiers on D-Day. Finally, it was precisely such swashbuckling adventurousness that killed him. While covering the war of independence in French Indochina, Capa stepped on a land mine and was killed almost instantly.

CHICAGO, JUDY (1939–)

Artist

Installation artist Judy Chicago (originally Cohen) was born in Chicago, Illinois, on July 20, 1939. She came from a non-practicing Jewish family, but her father was descended from a long line of rabbis. She attended the Art Institute of Chicago and then the University of California, Los Angeles, where she received her M.F.A. in 1964. In 1970 she opened the Fresno Feminist Art Program at California State University, which moved the next year to the California Institute of the Arts in Valencia.

One of the first modern artists to bring blatantly feminist issues and imagery into her work, Chicago uses many media in her installations, including sculpture, painting, embroidery, writing, and ceramic work. Her most famous and controversial work, *The Dinner Party* (1974–1979), commemorates the missing women of history. Her other work includes *The Second Decade 1973–1983* and *The Birth Project* (1980–1985). In 1985 she began to explore her Jewish identity. This resulted in the mixed media installation *The Holocaust Project: From Darkness into Light* (1985–1993).

DAVIDSON, JO (1883–1952)

Sculptor

Premier portrait sculptor Jo Davidson was born in New York City and received little formal training in art. He did, however, make the obligatory visit to Paris when he was in his early twenties. When he returned, he began his lifelong specialty in portrait busts. During World War I, he did a series of busts of Allied leaders, including General Pershing and Marshal Foch. After the war he went on to do portraits of the great world leaders who gathered at Versailles for the Peace Conference. As the years passed, he sculpted busts of such other prominent people as Mahatma Gandhi, **Gertrude Stein**, Franklin D. Roosevelt, and James Joyce. Among his full-length portraits are those of Will Rogers and Walt Whitman. Although he worked during a time that Abstraction was becoming increasingly dominant in American art, Davidson kept to his bold, naturalistic style throughout his career.

DINE, JIM (1935–)

Painter, sculptor

One of the first and most popular Pop artists, Jim Dine was born in Cincinnati, Ohio, and studied at the University of Ohio. He moved to New York City in his early twenties and began presenting "performances" in which he combined the visual arts with theater, music, and dance. At the time, performance art was one of the new forms being tried by artists who were in rebellion against the dominance of Abstract Expressionism. Among the other avenues being explored were assemblage, collage, and construction painting. Jim Dine did them all. In 1961 he had his first one-man show, which comprised paintings of articles of clothing, often with an actual article pasted on the canvas. In this first show, he used a variety of painting styles, from *trompe l'oeil* to Expressionist. Soon he was painting huge, realistic-looking ties and being discussed as part of the Pop Art movement with Jasper Johns and **Roy Lichtenstein**.

For a number of years after his show, Dine painted theatrical backdrops for ordinary objects. He also did actual theater designs, including costumes and sets for the San Francisco Actor's Workshop production of *A Midsummer Night's Dream* (1966). In the late 1960s he turned to more traditional sculpture and published a volume of poems. In 1970 he had his first retrospective exhibit at the Whitney Museum. He has exhibited regularly and widely ever since.

In 1996 a short film about the artist, *Jim Dine: A Self-Portrait on the Walls*, was nominated for an Academy Award for Best Documentary (Short Subject). The film documents the making of an exhibition at Kunstverein Ludwigsburg in Germany, where Dine spent six days producing large charcoal drawings on the walls of the museum. The drawings were painted over at the end of the six week exhibition.

EISENMAN, PETER (1931–)

Architect

The strikingly original architect Peter Eisenman was born in Newark, New Jersey, and educated at Cornell, Columbia, and Cambridge Universities. He began to make a major impact on the world of architecture when, from 1967 to 1982, he served as Director of the Institute for Architecture and Urban Studies in New

York City. In that position, he worked to find and encourage architects whose reaction against Modernism went beyond references to history and memory. In his own work, he strove to reflect societal dislocations and to question the nature of structure itself. He attempted to present his theoretical basis in the book *House of Cards* (1987), explaining why he might build a stairway going into a wall instead of up to another level or a hole in a bedroom floor. He also makes design allusions to the previous history of a site or environment. His design for San Francisco's Jewish Museum is an example. The museum is housed in an old power plant and features an "electronic facade" in the form of a screen at the rear of the building.

Currently Irwin S. Chanin Professor of Architecture at Cooper Union in New York City, Eisenman has also taught at Princeton and Cambridge. Among his important buildings are the University Art Museum of the California State University at Long Beach (1986); the Greater Columbus Convention Center (1989–93) in Columbus, Ohio; the Zoizumi Sangyo Office Building in Tokyo; and the Wexner Center for the Visual Arts (1982–89) at Ohio State University.

EISENSTAEDT, ALFRED (1898–1995)

Photographer

When his parents gave him a camera for his **bar mitzvah**, they could never have guessed that they had sealed Alfred Eisenstaedt's fate and chosen his career path for him. Eisenstaedt served with distinction in World War I, receiving wounds in both legs. When the war was over he found it necessary to work as a button and belt salesman to support the family, but his love of photography never diminished. With a friend, he constructed a primitive enlarger for his home darkroom, and he continued taking photos. When he made a sale to the prestigious *Berliner Tageblatt*, he quit his job to pursue photography full time. Eisenstaedt's eye for detail gave him a unique vision, one that quickly became prized by the most important of German photo agencies, Associated Press (not affiliated with the American news bureau of the same name).

When the Nazis came to power he realized that his time in Germany was running out and left for the United States in 1935. There he became one of the mainstays of *Life* magazine. His photograph of a young officer from West Point was published on the cover of the second issue of the magazine. By 1972 he had taken more than seventy of the magazines cover photographs. Eisenstaedt photographed some of the most important figures of his time, and his work has a strength and stark beauty that made him one of the most famous photographers of his generation. He published five collections of photographs, including *Witness of our Time* (1966) and *Eisenstaedt's Album: 50 Years of Friends and Acquaintances* (1976). He died on August 23, 1995.

EVERGOOD, PHILIP (1901–1973)

Painter

Realist painter Philip Evergood was born in New York City but educated in England. He studied at Cambridge University and the Slade School before returning to New York in 1923. He worked under George Luks at the Art Students League, then spent some time at the Académie Julien in Paris. His first show in New York in 1927 focused on biblical subjects. The Depression, however, turned him from biblical and literary themes to questions of social, political, and racial oppression. He became active in the American Artists Congress and the Artists Union, both of which were committed to promoting civil rights in the artistic world.

During the 1930s, Evergood was supervisor of the Easel Painting Division of the Works Projects Administration (WPA) Federal Art Project in New York. He also painted major murals in the Richmond Hill, New York, Public Library and the post office in Jackson, Georgia, and at Kalamazoo College in Michigan. His painting *American Tragedy* (1937) was a landmark of Social Realism, portraying a police attack on striking workers at a steel plant in Chicago. Another important painting was *Don't Cry, Mother* (1938–44), which showed a mother and her children in a tenement.

Evergood was not limited to Social Realism. Many of his works fall more readily into the category of magical realism, mining a vein of fantasy with an American flavor. His greatest painting in this style is the glorious *American Shrimp Girl* (1954), inspired by Hogarth's eighteenth-century *Shrimp Girl*. It is a tremendously vital expression of bounteous life and feminine strength. It has been said that Evergood disguises his tremendous technical facility behind a deliberately colloquial, even clumsy style, but if so, the disguise is faulty. His work is as extraordinary for its draftsmanship and control as for its imaginative power.

FRANK, ROBERT (1924–)

Photographer

Robert Frank was born in Zurich, Switzerland, on November 9, 1924. He became a professional photographer at age twenty-two and soon achieved success as a fashion photographer for *Harper's Bazaar*. Shortly after the end of World War II—around 1948—he left fashion photography because he found it too artistically limiting.

What **Allen Ginsberg** and Jack Kerouac were to 1950s literature, Robert Frank was to mid-century photography. Perhaps the only "Beat" photographer, Frank photographed Europe in 1950 and 1953. In 1955 and 1956, he traveled across America. He was funded for these trips by the first Guggenheim grant ever awarded to a photographer. During the post-war glow of the 1950s, Frank's work stood out because he dared to show the bitter, disaffected side of American life. The photographs of this period were published as a monograph entitled *The Americans* (1959). Jack Kerouac wrote the book's introduction. At the time of the book's publication, Frank's work was looked down on by many in the artistic establishment. It was thought to be too bleak in its outlook and subject matter. Nonetheless, Frank's style was one of the most powerful influences on the rise of 1960s socially conscious photojournalism.

After *The Americans*, Frank became more and more interested in cinematography. His first film *Pull My Daisy* (1959) was a critical success, but he never achieved the fame or influence with film as he had with photography.

FRANKENTHALER, HELEN (1928–)

Painter

Maintaining her significance in American art through five decades, Helen Frankenthaler overcame the masculine bias of the Abstract Expressionist movement to make her mark on history. Born in New York City to a prominent Jewish family, she grew up on the Upper East Side. Her father was a judge of the New York State Supreme Court and she was educated at Bennington College. She also studied in Provincetown, Massachusetts, with Hans Hofmann. During a relationship with critic **Clement Greenberg** that lasted for several years, she traveled extensively through Europe to study the old masters. Later, she married and subsequently divorced painter Robert Motherwell.

Frankenthaler made her mark quite early with a series of paintings in which she used a revolutionary style of paint application, thinning her oils so that they would stain the canvas rather than accumulate on its surface. The technique had an immediate impact on other artists and, by the time she was twenty-four, she had laid the basis for an entirely new movement—color field painting. Her first solo exhibit had taken place a year earlier. Since then, she has remained at the forefront of American art.

GEHRY, FRANK O. (1929–)

Architect

Frank Gehry is generally acknowledged to be one of the most creative of the so-called Post-Modern architects (a label he doesn't like), an innovative designer noted for his use of unconventional building materials and stylishly witty designs that utilize inexpensive techniques. Or, as Gehry himself calls it—"cheapskate" architecture. Hallmarks of Gehry's work include a particular concern that people exist comfortably within the spaces that he creates, and an insistence that his buildings address the context and culture of their sites.

Born Frank Goldberg, he moved with his family from Canada to Los Angeles in 1947. Gehry (who changed his name in the 1950s) studied architecture at UCLA as an undergraduate. He did his graduate work in urban planning at Harvard, then served as a project designer for firms in Los Angeles and Paris. After his Parisian stint, he returned once again to Los Angeles, starting his own firm.

Gehry has done innovative work in the design of single-unit homes, an area that had been virtually ignored by creative architects for much of the post-World War II era. A good example is his own home in Los Angeles, a converted 1920s building; he recreated it with a profusion of found materials ranging from chain-link fence to rusted corrugated steel. His work often has an "unfinished" look that draws attention to the idea of architecture as a process rather than a product.

Although Gehry was typed early in his career as a regional architect (most of his major assignments being situated in Southern California), he began to break out into the international scene in the late 1980s, most prominently with a series of museum designs that included the Vita Design Museum in Basel, Switzerland, the American Center in Paris, and, most recently and with the greatest fanfare, the new Guggenheim Museum in Bilbao, Spain. In 1989 Gehry was awarded the Pritzker Prize, the highest honor that can be bestowed on an architect by his colleagues.

GOLDIN, NAN (1953–)

Photographer

Photographer Nan Goldin was born in 1953 and grew up in a Maryland suburb of Washington, D.C. She was eleven when her eldest sister committed suicide, a pivotal experience in her life. Three years later, Goldin ran away from home. After traveling around the United States, she ended up at the Satya Free School in Boston. There she met David Armstrong, who introduced her to photography.

Through the late 1960s and the 1970s, Goldin photographed her life and friends. This ever-changing personal visual diary became her most successful and well-known work. A series of over 800 slides, *The Ballad of Sexual Dependency*, portrays Goldin and her friends during her days as a junkie in New York City. First shown in New York clubs in 1979, it was published in book form in 1986.

In 1988 Goldin checked herself into a drug rehab clinic. Her "post-drug" work includes *The Other Side* (1993), *A Double Life* (1994), and *Tokyo Love* (1995). In 1996 the Whitney Museum mounted a twenty-five-year retrospective of Goldin's work entitled "I'll Be Your Mirror." Though she rarely does commercial work, she has photographed advertising campaigns for Matsuda and designer Helmut Lang.

Goldin has been credited with—or accused of—starting the trend of "heroin chic" in fashion photography. She denies this. Citing photographer Larry Clark as a major influence, her work is considered unique not only because of her subject matter, but also because she shoots in color. Her success in that medium, both artistically and critically, is a rarity in art photography.

GOLUB, LEON (1922–)

Artist

Graphic, disturbing, confrontational artist Leon Golub was part of the generation that served in the military in World War II. When he returned to civilian life, he studied at the Art Institute of Chicago and then embarked on a career that would continually challenge complacency, especially with regard to violence and oppression. He spent the years from 1959 to 1964 in Paris but returned to participate in the revolutionary atmosphere of the 1960s and early 1970s. He did not, however, still his protest as so many artists did as the years passed. He has continued to speak out on canvas and in many other media against the terror and ugliness of the world. In so doing, he creates art that is itself terrifying. Often painted on large, unstretched canvasses nailed to the walls of galleries, his paintings graphically depict torture, war, and violence. Golub's artistic philosophy is straightforward. "In its most significant aspects," he says, "contemporary art is ugly and chaotic, a threat to the ordering of society and man's conventional concept of himself." Golub frequently exhibits jointly with his wife, Nancy Spero, who shares his political outrage and artistic vision, though not his particular style of expression. They have been artistic partners for forty years, excoriating a world that they see as far too brutal and full of hate. Together and separately, they have exhibited in major galleries and museums around the world.

GOODMAN, PERCIVAL (1904–)

Architect

The man who committed his life to building synagogues, Percival Goodman was born in New York, brother of writer and psychotherapist Paul Goodman. He studied in this country and in France before becoming an architect, city planner, and professor of architecture at Columbia University. After World War II, however, he changed his focus. Feeling profoundly altered by the Holocaust and its implications, he felt unable to go back to ordinary commercial work. From that time on, he dedicated himself to the creation of synagogues.

Goodman's synagogues were constructed of warm materials such as wood and filled with light. Often small, they focused on humanity and a human scale. Also, feeling that fine art had been undervalued in the Jewish religious community, Goodman commissioned modern artists to work with him, providing works of painting, textiles, and sculpture to his synagogues. His first such collaboration was at the B'nai Israel synagogue (1951) in Millburn, New Jersey, which included the work of artists Herbert Ferber, Robert Motherwell, and **Adolph Gottlieb**. This building was so successful that Goodman continued the practice. At Temple Beth El (1953) in Springfield,

Massachusetts, he worked with Motherwell and Gottlieb again and commissioned a sculpture by Ibram Lassaw. Largely as a result of Goodman's efforts, synagogal art has become a tradition in the United States.

GREENBERG, CLEMENT (1909–1994)

Art critic

America's most influential post-war art critic, Clement Greenberg was born in 1909 in the Bronx to a family of Lithuanian Jews. The household he grew in up was Yiddish-speaking and socialist. He began his career as a social critic and his political consciousness never deserted him. However, he came to be an advocate for formalism in art. In essays in *Partisan Review*, **Commentary**, and the *Nation* he helped to define Abstract Expressionism and perpetuate it as the dominant movement in American art from 1945 until the 1960s.

In the early years of the sixties his influence on artists began to wane. Confused and frustrated by the newer movements that followed on Andy Warhol's pop art, he stopped writing in 1968, when he was not yet sixty. Greenberg was acutely aware of the effect of his Jewishness on his thinking about art and the paradoxes contained therein, but he was less aware of the effect of his political training. According to critic and philosopher Arthur C. Danto, the eminent art historian chose the one strain of Modernism that most suited him temperamentally, and that was the interest in manifestos. Combining that with a fervent belief in progress in history and in art, he saw the movement away from traditional figurative art toward abstraction and conceptualism as forward movement, as, indeed, improvement. Because of his brilliance and personal persuasiveness, he was able to stamp this view on a generation.

GROPPER, WILLIAM (1897–1977)

Artist, activist

Because of the dire poverty of his youth in New York City, William Gropper was always conscious of the exploitation of the working class. He was forced to leave school as a child in order to help support his family but was able to save enough money to study art with the Realist painters Robert Henri and George Bellows at the Ferrer School. Later he attended the National Academy of Design and the New York School of Fine and Applied Art. He began his career in art as a political cartoonist for the Sunday New York *Tribune* and throughout his career he specialized in illustrations, cartoons, and murals dealing with political and social injustice. Although he was published in *Vanity Fair*, most of his political work appeared in leftist publications because, in his words, "no other newspaper has enough courage to allow an artist his freedom of expression." In the 1920s, he began painting and did several mural commissions during the 1930s.

In 1953 Gropper was attacked by Senator Joseph McCarthy and the House Un-American Activities Committee for his *Pictorial Map*, which contained references from folklore—including, for example, the Salem witchhunt—and brought before the committee. Because he was not allowed to make a statement concerning his commitment to freedom, he invoked the Fifth Amendment. He was effectively blacklisted as a result. He fought back with a brilliant set of lithographs that included a viciously effective caricature of McCarthy as a witchlike figure. During the 1960s, his work was less satirical. One series portrayed older Jews in a somewhat biblical spirit.

GROSS, CHAIM (1904–1989)

Sculptor

Powerful wood sculptor Chaim Gross was born in the Carpathian Mountains in Austria, and his early life was marked by the turmoil of World War I. He immigrated to New York City in 1921 and studied at the Educational Alliance Art School and the Beaux-Arts Institute while working as a delivery boy. He also studied briefly at the Art Students League before beginning his long and successful career as a sculptor. His first important sculpture was *Mother and Child at Play*, which exploited the grain and bulk of the wood to stunning effect. He also created, as he would later, a textured surface that resulted from distinctive use of the wood chisel. Often less than life size, his work was not marked by any sense of miniature preciousness, in large part because he eliminated details in his sculpture and emphasized large forms.

Gross's work was often playful, as when he took for his subjects circus acrobats. Among these were *Handlebar Riders* (1935) and *Girl on a Wheel* (1940). He increased the size of his sculpture for *Alaskan Snowshoe Mail Carrier* (1935), which was cast in aluminum for the Post Office Building in Washington, D.C. In the early 1950s, he began to create plaster, full-scale maquettes for bronze castings, which allowed him to work in larger forms with more open space. From 1927 until 1989 he was a teacher at the Educational Alliance and, from 1942 to 1959, at the school of the Brooklyn Art Museum. He also taught for a number of years at the New School for Social Research and wrote a memoir, *A Sculptor's Progress* (1938), and the book *The Technique of Wood Carving* (1957).

GUGGENHEIM, PEGGY (1898–1979)

Art collector, patron

The influential collector Peggy Guggenheim was born in New York, the daughter of a wealthy family. Her uncle Solomon Guggenheim was founder of the Guggenheim Museum. In her early twenties, she traveled in Europe, living for a number of years in Paris. There she became acquainted with the rising generation of artists and writers. In 1938 in London she opened her first gallery, Guggenheim Jeune, and organized important showings of abstract and surrealist artists such as Calder, Kandinsky, and Max Ernst. It was her habit to buy one work from each exhibit. With the outbreak of World War II, she returned to Paris and turned her focus to collecting, quickly acquired works by Picasso, Brancusi, Klee, and other leaders of the new school of art developing in Paris. Indeed, she declared that she would buy "a picture a day." Because so many artists were raising funds to leave the country, she was able to buy most of her tremendous collection of modern art for about $40,000.

When Germany occupied France in 1941, Guggenheim fled back to the United States and opened another gallery, Art of This Century. She filled its walls with the works of important European Modernists, many of whom were then immigrating to the United States from war-torn Europe. Soon, she added the American Abstract Expressionists, including Jackson Pollock, **Mark Rothko**, Robert Motherwell, and Adolph Gottlieb. While it lasted, the gallery was of enormous importance in the establishment of modern art in America. In 1946 Guggenheim closed the gallery and returned to Europe. In Venice, she opened her third and last gallery. She willed that gallery and her personal collection to the Solomon R. Guggenheim Foundation.

GUSTON, PHILIP (1913–1980)

Painter

The continually surprising and exciting artist Philip Guston was born Philip Goldstein in Montreal, Canada, in 1913 to immigrant parents from Odessa. He was torn between an observant mother and an agnostic father. Although he never concealed his Jewish identity, he changed his name when he was twenty-two. In later years, he refused to talk about this change and even his daughter was unaware of it. When he was six years old, his family moved to Los Angeles. Faced with extreme poverty, his father committed suicide. Young Philip found him hanging from a rafter.

In high school Guston met and became fast friends with future artist Jackson Pollock. The two were even expelled together. Guston dropped out of school at fifteen and had his first one-man show at eighteen, at a gallery in Los Angeles. In 1935 he moved to New York, where he worked on murals for the WPA. In the early 1950s, he changed styles and emerged as one of the most important of the Abstract Expressionists. His work was lyrical, delicately colored, and highly successful.

In 1970 Guston outraged his compatriots by making another radical change in style. After a four-year absence from the New York gallery scene, he mounted an exhibit at the Marlborough Gallery of crude, garish paintings filled with cartoon images. The response was fierce enough to end long-standing friendships, but Guston was undeterred. He had found new ground to explore and he was determined to do so. After his death in 1980, these works gained considerable popularity.

HESSE, EVA (1936–1970)

Sculptor

Innovative sculptor Eva Hesse was born in Hamburg, Germany, on January 11, 1936, to Ruth Marcus House and Wilhelm Hesse. Her family fled Nazi persecution and she grew up in New York City. She received her education at the High School of Industrial Arts, Pratt Institute of Design, Cooper Union, and the Yale School of Art and Architecture. She married sculptor Tom Doyle, whom she later divorced in 1961. She began working in two dimensions, painting and drawing in an abstract style that foreshadowed her move to sculpture. At Doyle's suggestion, she made the transition in 1964 by working in plaster and string. She later incorporated a number of unconventional materials into her work, including net bags and rubber tubing. By the late 1960s she was creating haunting grids and circles, shape repetitions, and careful jumbles in fiberglass and latex. She died of a brain tumor in 1970.

KAHN, ALBERT (1869–1942)

Architect

The father of American industrial architecture in this century, Albert Kahn was born in Rhaunen, Germany. He came to the United States when he was eleven and received his training in an architectural firm in Detroit. After a year of study in Europe on a traveling scholarship, he returned to Detroit to work. In 1902 he opened his own practice and a year later designed his first automobile plant. For the next forty years he designed virtually every important industrial installation in the automobile industry. His genius was for creating eminently practical factory buildings, without the ornamentation that would have been out of place and even ridiculous in the context, but that reflected the important design trends of their time. His most important buildings include the General Motors Building (1901) and the Fisher Building (1927), both in Detroit, and the Ohio Steel Foundry Company Building (1940). He was commissioned by the Soviet government in 1930 to design a series of factories in the Volga. Perhaps his most photographed building is the Dodge Half-Ton Truck Plant (1938) in Warren, Michigan. His later industrial buildings are often credited with helping to introduce the International Style to this country.

KAHN, LOUIS I. (1901–1974)

Architect, educator

At a time when American architecture was dominated by the chilly impersonality of the International Style, Louis Kahn was training a generation of architects in the principle of keeping the spiritual and human in sight when they designed. Kahn was not only a powerful teacher, as an architect of grace and creativity, but practiced what he taught.

Kahn was born on the Estonian island of Osel (now Saaremaa), his family moved to the United States before he was five, and he grew up in the city in which he would spend most of his career, Philadelphia. A precocious youngster with both musical and visual gifts, Kahn helped his impoverished family by playing piano at a local movie theater while still a boy.

He was a superb student, educated at the Philadelphia Academy of Fine Arts and the University of Pennsylvania. Once he had completed his architecture degree at Penn, Kahn went to work for the city architect's office. He rose quickly by dint of his exceptional talent and, at twenty-four, was appointed the designer of the city's Sesquicentennial Exposition, a heady commission for such a young man. After the exposition was finished, Kahn went to Europe for two years of travel and study. There he acquired a taste for classical architecture and the aesthetic principles that would guide him for the rest of his life.

By 1934, once more in Philadelphia, the young architect opened his own office. At the same time, he became involved with a group of other young designers, organizing the Architectural Research Group. This was a budding think tank of Philadelphia-based architects and urban planners, giving work to those young men in the field who had been hit by the Depression and creating a center for new thinking on city planning issues. Over the next fifteen years, Kahn also served on the city's planning commission and its housing authority, trying to bring his progressive, humanist ideas into practice. In 1947 he found another way to extend his influence, becoming a professor of architecture at Yale; he would return to Penn in 1957, teaching at his alma mater for the rest of his life.

After 1950 Kahn, whose reputation as an architect had been primarily local (although he was nationally known as a teacher), began to enjoy some major national and international commissions. He was responsible for the Yale University Art Galley; designed Dacca, the capital city of Bangladesh; the Salk Institute; and Philips Exeter Academy. At the same time, he evinced a tremendous interest in applying his spiritual ideas to his own heritage. Kahn designed several major synagogues in the 1950s and 1960s: Ahavath Israel in Philadelphia, the Jewish Community Center in Trenton, New Jersey, and Temple Beth-El of Chappaqua, New York, were among his most prominent commissions in this field.

Kahn received one of the highest honors available in his field in 1970 when the American Institute of Architects conferred on him its gold medal. Two years later, the Royal Institute of British Architects gave him its Royal Gold Medal in recognition of his career achievements.

KLINE, FRANZ (1910–1961)

Painter

One of the most influential painters of the second half of the twentieth century, Franz Kline was born in

Wilkes-Barre, Pennsylvania, and went to school at the Art Students League in Boston. He then studied for a time in London, intent on becoming an illustrator. He always had an affinity for cartoons, political and otherwise, and the stylish black and white illustrations of John Held, Jr. He began his painting career as a Realist, painting the hills of Pennsylvania, black with coal, and the trains that ran through them. After World War II, however, he had a passing involvement with Cubism, then began to feel the influence of Willem de Kooning and the other early Abstract Expressionists. His particular interpretation of that impulse in art was striking and immediately successful. Limiting himself to black and white for most of his career, he created large, slashing works, often with a big brush. They are usually dynamic pieces, with a suggestion of clashing forces, but they can sometimes be stark, solid, and filled with authority. Unlike most Abstract Expressionist work, Kline's paintings are often semi-representational, alluding chiefly to the same environment he pictured in his earlier years.

Kline has been enormously influential. His style, usually with color added, was adopted by countless art students and inspired several important artists, including Richard Serra and Cy Twombly. However, he was the only one of the New York School who was uninterested in talking about the conceptual basis of his work. The result is that, while his paintings are collected by museums and sold for millions, his legacy is sometimes underrated.

KRASNER, LEE (1908–1984)

Abstract Expressionist painter

One of America's most significant Abstract painters, Lee Krasner was born in New York City nine months after her mother Anna arrived from Russia to rejoin her husband Joseph Krassner. She was reared in a traditionally observant Jewish home in Brooklyn and attended Hebrew school as well as public school. The most highly trained of the New York School of artists, she studied art at the Washington Irving High School in Manhattan, the Women's Art School of Cooper Union, and the National Academy of Design. After graduation from the National Academy in 1932, she worked in several jobs before being accepted by the Works Projects Administration's Federal Art Project.

In 1937, while still employed by the WPA, she began studying with German Expressionist Hans Hofmann, who encouraged her move toward abstraction. During the 1940s Krasner participated in a number of group exhibitions with the American Abstract Artists group and met artist Jackson Pollock. They were married in 1945, and Krasner devoted a great deal of her time, energy, and resources for the next fourteen years to the task of keeping Pollock afloat, emotionally, artistically, and financially. In 1956 she became fed up with his drinking and his adultery and decided to spend a summer away from him in Europe. Without her supervision, he wrecked his car in the front yard of their farm while drunk and killed himself.

Krasner was able to commit to her own work again and began producing abstractions that combined a variety of media and were notable for their color and feeling. She had her first retrospective at the Whitechapel Gallery in London in 1965. Her first New York retrospective was at the Museum of Modern Art in December 1984, six months after her death.

KRUGER, BARBARA (1945–)

Artist

The strikingly original artist Barbara Kruger was born in Newark, New Jersey, on January 26, 1945. She studied at Syracuse University, the School of Visual Arts, and the Parsons School of Design, with **Diane Arbus** and Marvin Israel. Through Israel she began a successful career with Condé Nast Publications and, at the age of twenty-two, was chief designer at *Mademoiselle*. Her time spent in the world of advertising and popular journalism strongly affected her and her artistic sensitivity. In the late 1960s, influenced by John Heartfield and Hannah Hoch—two German artists of the 1920s—and Magdalena Abakanowicz, Kruger began to produce poster-like work that drew on collage, photo-montage, and other graphic arts methods. She exhibited at the

Whitney Biennial and in group and solo shows. In the mid-1970s, Kruger began to develop the political content of her work and to branch out into television and film criticism. She also began displaying her pieces in public places, such as the subway. One of her most famous depicted, in the style of a 1950s advertisement, a girl looking with admiration at a boy making a muscle. The "poster" was captioned, "We don't need another hero."

LEIBOVITZ, ANNIE (1949–)

Photographer

Annie Leibovitz was born in Westbury, Connecticut, on October 2, 1949. She attended the San Francisco Art Institute, where she initially studied painting before gravitating to photography. She graduated with a B.F.A. in 1971. While still in college, she spent five months in Israel living at the Kibbutz Amir, working on the archaeological site of King Solomon's Temple and taking pictures.

Leibovitz's photographs of Israel (as well as a photograph of **Allan Ginsberg**) were good enough to secure her a position with *Rolling Stone* magazine, which she joined shortly after graduation. Two years later she became the magazine's chief photographer. Throughout the 1970s she built her reputation as one of the finest celebrity photographers of her generation. *Rolling Stone* magazine covers became virtually synonymous with Annie Leibovitz portraits. One of her most famous photographs from this period is the 1980 portrait of John Lennon curled around Yoko Ono. It was taken just hours before Lennon was murdered.

In 1983 Leibovitz left *Rolling Stone* and went to work for *Vanity Fair*. While still shooting magazine portraits, she began doing advertising photography as well. Her ad campaign for American Express is especially well known. The recipient of numerous awards, Leibovitz is only the second living photographer to have a one-person show at the National Portrait Gallery. Her work has been published in several books including *Annie Leibovitz: Photographs* (1983), *Annie Leibovitz: Photographs, 1970–1990* (1991), and *Olympic Portraits* (1996).

LEVINE, JACK (1916–)

Painter

The great American Social Realist Jack Levine was born in 1916 in a working-poor neighborhood in Boston. He was the eighth child of an immigrant Lithuanian shoemaker and began studying art in an after-school program at a settlement house after his family moved to Roxbury. In his teen years, he was mentored by artist and scholar Denman Ross from Harvard University. In addition to providing tutoring and an introduction to the old masters, Ross arranged an exhibition of Levine's drawings at Harvard's Fogg Art Museum when Levine was only seventeen years old.

During the Depression, Levine received support for his painting from the WPA and used his profoundly satiric style to portray the poverty and despair he saw in the streets around him. "I thought I might get fired because of the subject matter," he said many years later. "Strangely, I never was, because wiser heads determined this was not propaganda. This was genuine social concern." After serving in the military during World War II, he returned to paint some of the most startlingly satiric and deeply disturbing paintings America has ever seen. Oddly, they are also quite beautiful.

Often, Levine's Jewish heritage is a visible element in his work. Although not a religious Jew, he has been to Israel more than a dozen times. He never adopted the methods of Abstract Expressionism, which came to dominate the art scene after the war. Instead, he fulfilled what he saw was the artist's function, "to bring the great tradition, and whatever is great about it, up-to-date."

LICHTENSTEIN, ROY (1923–1997)

Pop artist

The man who made comic strip romance into high art, Roy Lichtenstein was born on the Upper West

Side of New York. After a traditional education and training in art, he began a teaching career at Ohio State University. Failing to get tenure at that institution, he became a house husband, taking care of his children while his wife worked as a decorator. After taking another teaching job at Douglass College in New Jersey, he found his métier when he adapted the techniques of comic book artists to the service of what came to be known as Pop Art. At a time when the creation of an Abstract Expressionist masterpiece seemed to require at least as much conceptual hot air as paint, his blown-up comic book panels were shocking, refreshing, and more fun than art had been for decades. They were seen by some as incisive commentary on American culture and by others as a huge artistic put-on that would be unmasked by time. Within a few years, the major museums of the world were in competition for his work and his posters adorned hip young homes around the United States. Lichtenstein was able to use benday dots, heavy outlining, and cross-hatching to comment on everything from Picasso to modern advertising and, until his death in 1997, was still making it work. His paintings are in collections all around the world, and the five-story-high *Mural with Blue Brushstrokes* adorns the lobby of New York's Equitable Center.

LIPCHITZ, JACQUES (1891–1973)

Sculptor

Legendary sculptor Jacques Lipchitz was born in Druskininkai, Lithuania, and moved to Paris when he was eighteen years old, attending the Académie Ranson and becoming part of the *Esprit Nouveau* group. He began to work in a Cubist style during World War I, then used a lost-wax technique to create "transparent" sculptures. He began to work in a more naturalistic style in the 1930s. Two of his first sculptures in this style were *Mother and Child* (1930) and *Return of the Prodigal Son* (1931). In the years leading up to World War II, he expressed his horror and anger through the use of biblical and mythological subjects such as *Jacob Wrestling with the Angel* (1932) and *The Rape of Europa*

II (1938). By this time many of his works were monumental in scale.

In 1941 Lipchitz fled the Nazis as they invaded France. Established in New York, he began to create passionate and often painful sculptures related to the tragic destruction of Jews in Europe at the time. Commissioned to do a baptismal font for the Church of Assy in France after the war, he produced a representation of the Virgin Mary under the canopy of heaven that is considered one of the most important religious sculptures of the twentieth century. His early models and drawings for the piece were destroyed by a fire in his New York studio in 1952, but he re-created them. He continued to work until his death in 1973, publishing an autobiography, *My Life in Sculpture*, the year before.

MEIER, RICHARD (1934–)

Architect

Modernist architect Richard Meier was born in Newark, New Jersey, and received his architectural training at Cornell University. He then went on to work with a number of important architectural firms including Skidmore, Owings, and Merrill and Marcel Breuer. He opened his own office in 1963. Since then he has created a number of important buildings, always in a Modernist style. He works largely in white, Neo-Corbusian forms, accented by enameled panels, glass, ramps, and handrails. A major figure in the "New York Five," a group of Modernist architects, he has resisted all recent trends, remaining with the design philosophy of his youth. Among his most famous buildings are the High Museum of Art (1983) in Atlanta, Georgia, and the Museum of Decorative Arts (1981–84) in Frankfurt, Germany. Meier was awarded architecture's highest honor, the Pritzker Prize, in 1984. In addition to the Getty Center, which was completed after twelve years at the end of 1997, he is currently at work on United States Federal Courthouses in Islip, New York, and Phoenix, Arizona, and the Euregio Bank building in Basel, Switzerland.

MYERS, MYER (1723–1795)

Silversmith, Revolutionary War patriot

Silversmith Myer Myers was born in New York of Jewish parents who had emigrated from Holland. When he was twenty-three, he opened his own shop in New York. Nine years later his trade had expanded to include Philadelphia. Myers was active in the Jewish community, serving two terms as president of the Congregation Shearith Israel in New York, in 1759 and in 1770. He was also a respected member of the larger community and, during the American Revolution, an avid patriot. He aided the cause in any way he could, using his skills to melt down metal household goods to make bullets. Having spent most of the war in Philadelphia, Myers returned to New York in 1783 and was one of many to sign a petition addressed to Governor George Clinton from the "congregation of Israelites lately returned from exile." Highly skilled and talented in his craft, Myers was the first silversmith to create Jewish ceremonial objects in America. His work is included in many museum collections, and some of his pieces are still in use in American synagogues.

NEUTRA, RICHARD J. (1892–1970)

Architect

The founders of what came to be called the International Style included only one American architect—Richard Neutra. Neutra was born and educated in Austria and began his career there. He moved to the United States when he was thirty-one. He worked in New York, Chicago, and in Wisconsin with Frank Lloyd Wright. Later, he joined another Austrian American Jew, Rudolph Schindler, in Los Angeles. In 1927 he designed the Jardin Apartments in that city. The reinforced concrete building was chosen for the exhibition "The International Style: Architecture since 1922" at the Museum of Modern Art, as was his steel-framed Lovell House (1927–29). The latter building, a rambling ranch-style house, established Neutra as an international ly important architect and proponent of Modernism.

The homes that Neutra and Schindler designed in the next decade-and-a-half made Los Angeles a showcase for modern domestic architecture. These houses were luxurious, with an extensive use of open spaces, glass, and, often, reflecting pools. Neutra also expanded into school design. After World War II he increasingly worked on large public buildings. He also wrote a number of influential books, including *Survival through Design* (1954) and *Building with Nature* (1971).

NEVELSON, LOUISE (1899–1988)

Sculptor

Louise Nevelson created a sculptural style that was a unique synthesis of African and pre-Columbian sculpture, contemporary architecture, found objects, and sleekly modern materials. She was comfortable—and effective—in a profusion of media, but her most memorable works were done in wood, often painted or lacquered. By the end of her long career, she was acknowledged not only as the progenitor of environmental sculpture, but also as one of the key figures in twentieth-century American art.

She was born Louise Berliawsky, the daughter of Russian Jews who immigrated to the United States when she was six. They ended up in the small town of Rockland, Maine, an unlikely destination at a time when most immigrant families were destined for the Lower East Side of New York, but one that had a lasting effect on the young girl. Nevelson maintained that her childhood experience of the rugged New England seacoast had a singular influence on her art.

In 1920 Nevelson met and married businessman Charles Nevelson, and the couple moved to New York City, where she studied dance and theater, as well as painting and sculpture. Eventually she began to concentrate on the latter two fields, studying at the Art Students League. Nevelson spent a highly formative year in Germany in 1932, studying with Hans Hoffman. She later said of that experience that it was while working with Hoffman that she "recognized the cube," the geometric form that became an integral part of her work. Returning to New York, she worked under Diego Rivera on his commission to paint the murals in the new Rockefeller Center. No doubt inspired by his example, she spent much of the remainder of the decade traveling in Latin America, where she developed an interest in Mayan and other pre-Columbian art.

It was also in the 1930s that Nevelson began exhibiting her sculpture in New York galleries. Reflecting the influence of the pre-Columbian art she was so enthralled by, her early works were often terra-cotta figures. She was also experimenting with constructions using found objects, and it was in that direction that her work gradually evolved. She had her first one-woman show in 1941, but none of the pieces sold, so she hauled them back to her loft and destroyed every one of them. It was another eighteen years before Nevelson made her first sale.

Throughout the 1940s, the period that Nevelson called the "unfolding" of her style, she continued to work increasingly with found objects, searching through the rubble of abandoned buildings for architectural decorations, doorknobs, pieces of discarded furniture, to integrate into her sculptures. In the following decade her years of hard work began to bear fruit. Throughout the 1950s she mounted a series of one-woman shows that brought her increasing attention in the art world.

By now she was working in the style for which she would become famous, creating "environments," sculptural pieces of a single color arranged in such a way that a viewer is almost literally immersed in them. Her work became larger and more complex, and by the 1960s she was receiving commissions for major installations, often with Jewish themes. Major works by Nevelson can be found in Temple Beth-El in Great Neck, New York, and in Temple Israel in Boston; her fifty-foot-high memorial to the victims of the Holocaust stands in the lobby of the federal courthouse in Philadelphia.

In the 1960s Nevelson began to incorporate modern materials into her work—plexiglass, aluminum, formica. Her work continued to grow in size, reaching its greatest breadth with the mammoth *Sky Gate-New York*, a 1978 piece that stands outside the World Trade Center at a plaza that now bears her name. To the end, Nevelson remained a flamboyant, independent figure, known as much for her wildly colored scarves, wide-brimmed hats, and her trademark cigars as for her work. She once observed that if Michelangelo were to come back to earth he might not recognize what she did as sculpture.

NEWMAN, BARNETT (1905–1970)

Painter

A man of great integrity and compassion, Barnett Newman was also a figure of considerable importance in American art. Born in 1905 in New York and educated at Cornell University, he began his career by trying a variety of European styles. He even ran for mayor of New York in a Duchampian gesture. In 1940 he stopped working entirely. More than twenty years later, he gave this explanation: ". . . we felt the moral crisis of a world in shambles, a world devastated by a great Depression and a fierce world war, and it was impossible at that time to paint the kind of paintings that we were doing—flowers, reclining nudes, and people playing the cello." When he began working again in 1944, he destroyed all of his old work, his flowers and cellos, so to speak, and started from scratch. His organic shapes floated on colored backgrounds. His lines slid, crept, and skidded across the page. His icons and totems, gathered equally from the Brooklyn Botanic Gardens and the Northwest Coast Indians he had studied at Cornell, mark a striving for some sort of mythic community.

In the years that followed, Newman moved increasingly away from the figurative and toward his own forms of abstraction. His best-known work is probably the *Stations of the Cross* series that he began in 1958. Though they were painted more than a decade after World War II, they represent his response to the Holocaust, to Hiroshima, and to the suffering and death that haunted his generation as well as the hope for redemption and resurrection.

PAINTING AND SCULPTURE

The Jewish influence in American art really began in the twentieth century, although there were both artists and collectors in the Jewish community long before that. During the colonial period silversmith **Myer Myers** created exquisite pieces that included a number of Jewish ceremonial items. At the same time, a number of wealthy Jewish families commissioned portraits, which were the primary form of artistic expression at the time in this country. During the ante-bellum period, when landscape painting was burgeoning with the exploration of the West, there are a few names to remember. Solomon Nunes Carvalho (1815–1897), a Sephardic Jew, accompanied John Charles Frémont on his Western expedition. Carvalho was a painter and one of the first Jewish American photographers. Joshua (1767–1826) and John (1782–1823) Cantor were directors of the Charleston Academy of Fine Arts. Theodore Moise (1808–1885) was a Charleston portraitist who later moved to New Orleans. Jacob Hart Lazarus (1822–1891), a New York portraitist, painted mostly Jewish commissions. During the Civil War, Henry Mosler (1841–1920) illustrated Civil War battles for *Harper's Weekly*.

In the years after the Civil War Jewish artists were outside the two major American movements, Romanticism and Realism, which included the Hudson River School and the Native Realists. Sculptor Moses Jacob Ezekial (1844–1917) became an expatriate in Rome, doing primarily portrait busts of Victorian heroes, although he received a commission from B'nai B'rith for the monument *Religious Liberty* in Philadelphia's Fairmount Park. In the late nineteenth century, a few more Jewish artists began to emerge, including landscapist Max Weyl, and other minor figures such as Herman N. Hyneman (1849–1907), Frank Moss (1837–1924), Katherine M. Cohen (1859–1914), and Max Rosenthal (1833–1918). The first figure of importance in American art is probably Robert F. Blum (1857–1903), who painted in the tradition of English classicism. His significance pales, however, as we move into the twentieth century and Jewish artists become a major force.

In the years between 1880 and 1920 the huge influx of Eastern European Jews into the United States transformed the American Jewish community. Among the immigrants were trained and established artists in all fields, from music and theater to painting, sculpture, and architecture. Soon there was a cadre of Jewish artists that included both immigrants and native-born artists who had received their training from these immigrants.

The first of these immigrants to become truly prominent in the art world was not a painter or a sculptor but a scholar. **Bernard Berenson** arrived in the United States in 1874, when he was nine years old. He grew up in Boston and attended Harvard University. By the turn of the century he was well on his way to becoming America's final authority on all matters of art. By working with multi-millionaire collectors, he developed tremendous power and a large personal fortune.

In the late 1890s, the Educational Alliance, the leading Jewish settlement house in New York City, began offering art classes and, in 1917, the organization established an art school. Both Abraham Walkowitz (1878–1965) and Jacob Epstein (1880–1959) studied at the Educational Alliance. Epstein moved to England in 1903 and became known primarily as an British artist, but Walkowitz remained in the United States and developed a reputation as one of the country's finest graphic artists. His early work evinced a striving to capture motion, and he gained considerable attention for a series of drawings of dancer Isadora Duncan in motion. He was also known for his portrayals of Lower East Side life. In the 1920s he turned his attention to oils but was forced to quit painting in the 1930s by trouble with his eyes. Others who studied or taught at the Educational Alliance included Leonard Baskin (1922–), **Peter Blume, Jo Davidson, Philip Evergood, Mark Rothko**, Adolph Gottlieb (1903–1973), **Louise Nevelson, Barnett Newman**, and the **Soyer brothers**, Isaac, Raphael, and Moses.

The artistic atmosphere in the early years of the twentieth century was one of exploration. The restrained realism of Thomas Eakins and Winslow Homer had dominated the late nineteenth century.

Now, there were painters and sculptors who were impatient with the polish and perfection of that earlier generation, and several of them broke away to form a movement of their own. The Ashcan School insisted upon looking directly at life, especially modern urban life, and attempting to portray its vitality, even at the expense of technique and elegance. None of the five primary members of this school was Jewish, but their major protégé, Alexander Kruse (1888–1979), was. Unlike his mentors, Kruse was actually born and raised in the slums of New York City, and his work bears no imprint of romanticizing or sentimentality. On the other hand, it is often marked by a humor that enriches his vision of the Lower East Side. Sharing a sensibility with the Ashcan school was painter **Theresa Bernstein**, who vigorously painted urban landscapes and the beaches of Coney Island in bright, Fauvist colors.

Other artists looked toward Europe for new inspiration. Among these were the painters, photographers, and sculptors who gathered around **Alfred Stieglitz**'s 291 Gallery. Here, in a tiny space run by one of America's foremost photographers, progressive artists were able to exhibit their work—often influenced by European trends and movements—at a time when modernism had not become a dominant element in American art. **Max Weber**, a native of Bialystock, Poland, who grew up in New York, was one of the most influential. He studied art in New York City and later in Paris. When he returned to the United States, he became a teacher at the Art Students League. A close friend of Stieglitz's, Weber shaped his gentle, sophisticated work from a Cubist perspective. William Zorach (1887–1966), later an important abstract sculptor, was at this time a painter who began exploring abstract forms. Born in Lithuania and reared in Cleveland, Ohio, he studied at the Cleveland School of Art and the National Academy of Design. Two years of further study in France inclined him toward the progressive styles that were shown at the 291 Gallery. Among the many younger painters and sculptors who exhibited there were some who would become the core of the Abstract Expressionist movement, including Mark Rothko, then known as Marcus Rothkowitz.

A number of Jewish artists were involved in the pivotal artistic event of this period, the Armory Show in 1913, including Walkowitz, Zorach, and Leon Kroll. This exhibition brought European Modernism to America for the first time and shocked a public accustomed to French Impressionism and American Native Realism. As part of the Jewish artistic community's response to the stunning Armory Show, John Weichsel established the People's Art Guild, exhibiting Walkowitz, Kroll, and Jo Davidson, as well as, younger artists such as Theresa Bernstein. The Guild published its brochures in Yiddish as well as English, held special meetings on Friday evening, and generally stressed the cultural, rather than the religious aspects of Jewish life.

The Armory Show included a range of artistic styles and in its wake American painting and sculpture went in two quite disparate directions. One group of artists continued to explore the possibilities of Realism, taking it in new directions. The other looked to abstraction. Realism had its innings first. Its proponents included prominent non-Jewish artists such as Charles Burchfield, Reginald Marsh, George Bellows, Rockwell Kent, and Edward Hopper, as well as a large number of Jewish artists. This was not the Native Realism of a few decades before, focused largely on countryside and hearth and it was not directly descended from the Ashcan School, either. Indeed, it was not homogeneous at all.

Leon Kroll, a native New Yorker who studied at the Art Students League and the National Academy of Design, developed a smooth, highly deliberate style with a strong graphic element. Early paintings featured many urban and industrial landscapes, but he later focused on still life and the human figure. **Philip Evergood**, educated at Cambridge, the Slade School, and Paris's Académie Julien, concealed his extensive academic training behind a deliberately clumsy style that powerfully expressed moral outrage. At other times he turned to a looser, more sensual style, depending on his subject. **Ben Shahn** focused his almost abstract compositions with a deep sadness and profound anger. He served an early apprenticeship as a lithographer and his powerful protests against suffering, and injustice were informed by a strong graphic sense. The Soyer brothers—Isaac, Moses, and Raphael—were also among these Realists. It might also be possible to include Lucille Corcos (1908–1973), whose modern primitive paintings were regularly exhibited at the Museum of Modern Art, the Whitney, and other important venues.

There was another group, however, who followed in the footsteps of Salvador Dali, creating a kind of "magic realism." In this camp were Jewish artists **Peter Blume** and Morris Graves. Russian-born Blume began his career in the precisionist style of Charles Sheeler, but his sense of the ironic soon overcame him. He employed a smooth, hard, Dali-like line in his strange and imaginative paintings, full of intellectual symbol and meaning. In 1939 he caused considerable controversy when his painting *The Eternal City* was rejected by the Corcoran Gallery Biennial for being too inflammatory. It depicted Mussolini as a green-headed jack-in-the-box reigning over a surrealist interpretation of Italian life with American tourists observing the scene. Much less political, Graves found his inspiration in the Pacific Northwest, becoming part of what has sometimes been called the "Northwest School" with painters Kenneth Callahan and Mark Tobey. He concentrated on fine, almost delicate, drawing and looked for inspiration toward the Buddha.

Interestingly, given developments still in the future, the leading proponents of the movement toward non-objective art were non-Jewish artists such as Joseph Stella and Charles Demuth. Rothko and Gottlieb had also begun their move in this direction. With Ilya Bolotowsky, Ben-Zion (1897–1987), and others, Rothko was a founder of The Ten, a group of artists who were influenced by Expressionism. However, his early work was more Surrealist than abstract. By 1941, Gottlieb had begun the development of his "pictographs," which would lead to a rich strain of Abstract Expressionism, but they were still in their early stages and contained largely representational elements.

The Jewish artists who most clearly embraced the abstract in the years before World War II were sculptors. William Zorach and Theodore Roszak (1907–1981) were already involved in exploring the possibilities of form and space. Their work was still figurative, but it was no longer strictly representational. Influenced by Cubism, Surrealism, and Constructivism, they found individual ways to express their personal and social concerns. Roszak, for example, was making geometric constructions of wood and plastic during the years from 1936 to 1945. Zorach had been carving wood in a simplified, cubic style since the teens of the century.

Jewish Americans were far more prominent among the Social Realists. Especially during the years just before and during the Depression, Realism reigned. Very American and largely rural expressions of the Realist spirit could be seen in the work of non-Jewish artists Thomas Hart Benton and Grant Wood. A more urban, as well as more socially and politically conscious form was being developed by an amazing number of Jewish artists, including those mentioned above as well as younger painters such as **Jack Levine**, Ruth Gikow (1915–1982), and Hyman Bloom.

Social Realism was a powerful movement, fueled by the need to use art to criticize and satirize American society, and the work of these artists is powerful as well. Philip Evergood's moral power came into its own during the Depression, as he left behind biblical and literary themes to focus on racism, poverty, and political oppression. He produced three important murals dealing with labor and a number of major social protest paintings, including *American Tragedy* (1937), which showed a police attack on striking steel workers in Chicago. He was supervisor for Easel Painting for the WPA in New York, one reason that social protest painting was tolerated by that agency. Ben Shahn did government-sponsored work during the Depression as well. In addition to photographs for the Farm Security Administration, he designed some of the very few posters he ever did for that agency. *Years of Dust*, which shows the despair of a Dust Bowl farmer, was his first. Today, it seems ironic that some of the greatest social protest painters did their work at the behest of and under the sponsorship of the government.

Jack Levine, eighth child of Lithuanian immigrants, acquired his social consciousness in the poor Boston neighborhood where he grew up. During the

Depression he received a subsidy from the WPA and used his profoundly satiric style to portray the poverty and despair he saw in the streets around him. "I thought I might get fired because of the subject matter," he said many years later. "Strangely, I never was, because wiser heads determined this was not propaganda. This was genuine social concern." He often took as his subject the corruption of the higher echelons of social and political life, treating it with a corpulent, cartoon-like drawing style that seems blurred by a haze of drink and indulgence. Levine had been mentored during his teens by Harvard professor Denman Ross, and the combination of social consciousness and extraordinary grounding in the history of art made his work remarkable and unique. Hyman Bloom brought a flamboyant style and high color to subjects such as raw meat hanging in a butcher shop, creating a shocking beauty. Ruth Gikow painted in a more psychologically intense style, focusing on the pain and isolation of individuals in society.

There were other Jewish artists who defied categorization. Foremost among these was **Florine Stettheimer**, sometimes called the Grandma Moses of the Upper West Side, a catchy misnomer. She was far more sophisticated than the American primitive. Born into New York City's Jewish elite in 1871, she studied extensively in the United States and Europe and did not abandon a traditional academic style until she was in her forties. Then she developed an absolutely unique way of painting that was too decorative to be taken seriously by the art establishment and too colorful, playful, and idiosyncratic to be fashionable. Far from naive, she drew on influences as diverse as Persian miniatures, Brueghel, Freudianism, Bergson, and Surrealism.

One evidence of the increasing prominence of Jewish artists is that, in the Museum of Modern Art's "Painting and Sculpture by Living Americans" exhibition (1930–1931), five of the thirty-two artists were Jewish. In MOMA's exhibition the following year of "American Painting and Sculpture (1862–1932)," twelve Jewish artists were represented.

After World War II the focal point of innovation in art moved from Paris to New York, as Europe tried to recover from devastation and European émigrés began to influence the American art scene. Suddenly, the streets of New York were dotted with the great figures of European art, many of whom fled their native countries to escape persecution as Jews. This influx of great artists included non-Jews such as André Breton, Marcel Duchamp, and Max Ernst, as well as Jews such as Marc Chagall, **Jacques Lipchitz**, and Naum Gabo. Their sophisticated, highly modern approach had a tremendous impact on the American art scene.

The onslaught of Surrealism and its advocates introduced the New York art world to an utterly different way of looking at art. Surrealism was at its base a philosophical and psychological ideology, and the art was merely an expression of that ideology. American artists were introduced to the idea that art might be a fundamentally intellectual undertaking. The idea fell on fertile ground, but the Americans shaped it to their own needs and temperaments. Under the influence of the Europeans, a school of artists that included such Jewish figures as **Philip Guston**, **Lee Krasner**, Adolph Gottlieb, **Franz Kline**, **Barnett Newman**, **Ad Reinhardt**, and Mark Rothko created the style of painting known variously as "action painting," "American-type painting," and "Abstract Expressionism." It was the last name that finally stuck to this "New York School," which included sculptors as well as painters. Also of importance in the movement were critics and writers such as **Clement Greenberg** and Harold Rosenberg, who helped to express and shape its theoretical underpinnings, and dealers such as **Peggy Guggenheim**, who brought the work to the attention of art patrons.

Peggy Guggenheim's gallery Art of This Century was at first the physical center of the movement. Opened during World War II, it was defined in its first press release as "a research laboratory for new ideas." This definition would have puzzled the great masters, but it forecast the future of American art, even to the present day. This new group of artists rejected the Social Realism that dominated the 1930s. They also rejected the geometric abstraction that had been the only real alternative to Realism in this country. Instead, they found their inspiration in Europe, especially in Cubism and Surrealism. They believed, as Rothko put it, that "art was not about an experience, but was itself the experience." Or, as Clement Greenberg declared somewhat more dogmatically, "the illusionist methods of art must . . . be renounced."

The popularity of Abstract Expressionism reached its zenith in the years after Peggy Guggenheim closed her gallery in 1947. New dealers took over her mission and many of her artists. They included, among others, Samuel Kootz and Sidney Janis. A number of little magazines also offered support by publishing articles, illustrations, and artistic statements. In 1948 Rothko joined Robert Motherwell, William Baziotes, and sculptor David Hare to establish the short-lived Subjects of the Artist school. It was a forerunner of Studio 35, where Gottlieb, Newman, Reinhardt, Rothko, and critic Harold Rosenberg all lectured. Great talkers, the Abstract Expressionists also founded, in 1949, the Club, which met in a rented loft. Kline and Reinhardt were founding members, later joined by Guston, Rosenberg and others. The Club presented discussions on the visual arts and readings by poets. In May 1950 eighteen of the artists in this cohesive group signed a letter protesting the conservative jury for an exhibition of contemporary American art at the Metropolitan Museum of Art.

Throughout the 1950s the popular press promoted Abstract Expressionism. The rebels of painting and sculpture were featured regularly in *Life*, *Time*, *Look*, and *Vogue*, often proving remarkably adept at self-promotion. Harold Rosenberg's December 1952 essay "The Action Painters" in *Art News* provided a way of talking about the style that helped to solidify its appeal to collectors. Clement Greenberg became its prophet.

Abstract Expressionism was a movement, not a specific style. The actual artistic productions of its proponents varied widely. Once he abandoned representational painting, Mark Rothko explored the possibilities of color, reducing his forms to luminous blurred oblongs. Philip Guston created lyrical, delicate compositions that one critic compared to "blown-up details from Claude Monet's water-lily impressions." Adolph Gottlieb constructed crude but powerful agglomerations of line and symbol. The abstract landscapes of

Doris Kreindler (1901–1974) were compounded of vigorous strokes of the brush or palette knife. Franz Kline painted largely in black and white with huge, slashing forms. **Helen Frankenthaler** introduced the technique of "staining" the canvas with paint so that the painting was no longer on the canvas but "in" or "of" it. Ad Reinhardt painted in an impersonal, geometric "hard-edge" style, as did Barnett Newman. Lee Krasner, the most highly trained of the New York School artists, used organic shapes and spectacular colors in paintings fueled by rage and sensuality.

American sculpture never fit as neatly into the Abstract Expressionist mode as painting did, nor as neatly as some critics could have hoped. There were a number of reasons for this, including the nature of the genre itself. One of the most significant, for our purposes, was the public, monumental nature of much sculptural work. The question arose, was abstract form capable of memorializing the causes of public grief, horror, or even pride? As Nathan Rapoport, the creator of the Warsaw Ghetto Monument of 1947, asked. "Could I have made a stone with a hole in it and said, 'Voila! The heroism of the Jews'?"

A striking catalyst for debate around this question was the 1953 competition for a Monument to the Unknown Political Prisoner, which became so hotly debated that the winner of the competition, submitted as a model, was never constructed. Indeed, it was destroyed by a young Hungarian artist who was angered by its "abstraction," although it was largely figurative and included three massive women at the bottom of a symbolic cross. Describing the abstract sculptures submitted for the competition, British critic John Berger called them "tolerant, uncommitted, remote, anesthetized, harmless and therefore, in the end, impertinent."

The American entries into the international contest, chosen in a competition arranged by the Museum of Modern Art, tended to the abstract and caused an outraged protest from traditional sculptors. Among these entries were works by Jewish artists Theodore Roszak, Seymour Lipton, Ibram Lassaw, and Herbert Ferber. Again, the criticism was somewhat confused. Roszak's entry, for example, was clearly figurative, celebrating freedom through the idea of flight. It was not, however, realistically representational. The same could be said of several of the other entries, as well as for a great deal of American sculpture in the second half of the twentieth century. Abstract and semi-abstract sculpture was widely accepted by the public as well, even by those who might have had some doubts about Jackson Pollock's drips. One evidence of this, at least in the Jewish community, was the widespread commissioning of such sculpture for synagogues. Ferber, Lassaw, and many other abstract sculptors created important works for congregations around the country.

Almost as eccentric in this context as Stettheimer was in the art world of the 1930s was **Louise Nevelson**. The daughter of Russian Jews who immigrated to the United States in 1905, when she was six years old, Nevelson grew up in a small town in Maine and studied at the Art Students League in New York City. Later, she went to Germany and studied with Hans Hoffman. Her early work was critically successful but did not sell. In the late 1950s, when she was nearing her sixties, she finally found popular and financial success with her sculptural environments in wood. Stacked cubes stuffed with found objects and dipped in black house paint, anthropomorphic totems, and monumental works of CorTen steel were all part of the Nevelson *oeuvre*.

Most of these sculptors seemed to find the freedom that abstraction offered exciting without being willing to abandon the figurative, the reference to reality, at least to the extent of allusion or overt inspiration. Painters, on the other hand, increasingly created paintings not about life but about painting, self-reflexive works that asked, "What is art?" and "What are the materials of art?" rather than "What is nature?" or "What is the human condition?" Ad Reinhardt's black canvases might be seen as the ultimate in this exploration. After the death of Jackson Pollock in an automobile accident in 1956, the tide in American art began to shift. The major Abstract Expressionist artists continued to work, exhibit, and sell, but a new generation of artists rose to challenge their intellectual lock on modern art.

It is possible to speculate that no one can keep artists from painting "things" for very long. In the entire history of Western art, there has been only one period, not quite two decades long, in which painters and sculptors abandoned the representation of trees and children and pigs and buildings to focus their attention on pure shape and color. This abandonment caused Ben Shahn to protest, "Is there nothing to weep about in this world any more? Is all our pity and anger to be reduced to a few tastefully arranged straight lines or petulant squirts from a tube held over a canvas?" Well, not for long, anyway.

In the late 1950s, artists began to react against non-representational painting. They did not flee back to Realism, for the most part, but they did begin to find acceptably modern ways to portray the world again. At first, the reaction came from a group who worked in mixed media and assemblage, who began to incorporate bits of real objects into the constructions. Among these was Jewish artist **Larry Rivers**. Then, a few artists began to paint the same sorts of objects in a hyperrealistic "Pop" style, including **Roy Lichtenstein** and **Jim Dine**. Lichtenstein became enormously famous and successful by using the techniques of illustration and popular culture in his representations. His oversized cartoon panels, with their iconic images and benday dots, became symbolic of the time.

Sculptor **George Segal** is sometimes considered a Pop artist, but his real artistic roots seem to be in the Social Realist tradition. His staggeringly realistic work bears more resemblance to George Bellows than to Lichtenstein or Warhol. Figures cast in plaster from life—and painted white or gray—are surrounded by environments made of real objects and, sometimes, painted backgrounds. They carry with them an unmistakable whiff of "the human condition."

Still, most artists were asking more questions about art than about humanity or beauty. That had not and would not change in the decades to come. Rather, the questions were rephrased. As philosopher/critic Arthur C. Danto put it, "As I saw it, the form of the question is: What makes the difference between a work of art and something not a work of art when there is no interesting perceptual difference between them?" It is a question that inevitably arises when looking at Warhol's Brillo Box or one of Lichtenstein's oversized cartoons, and the obvious answer is the idea behind it. Grasping the obvious with both hands, artists increasingly emphasized the conceptual in their art. Indeed, there was a short-lived style that called itself Conceptualism, but the influence of the conceptual goes far beyond that. It includes Pop Art, op art, post-painterly abstraction, Minimalism, happenings, earthworks, political art based on slogans, photorealism, assemblage, installations conceived by artists and executed by gallery staffs, performance art, and found art, all of which are or have been important styles in the modern art world.

In the Minimalist camp is Sol LeWitt, who actually sells "blueprints" for some of his works, with the exclusive right to implement them included in the sale. Not long ago, for example, he sold the right to draw ten thousand pencil lines on a wall, according to his instructions, for more than $26,000. **Eva Hesse**, who was born in Germany and fled the Holocaust as a child, was considered a post-Minimalist. She reduced her artistic expression to monochromatic repetitions of shapes, but critics seem to agree that hers was a more personal art, evoking at least some emotion.

Judy Chicago was a Minimalist artist until she rejected what she believed to be the male domination of the art world. She then turned to the creation of work that was redolent with imagery, politics, and sensuality, exploring both her womanhood and her Jewishness. Hannah Wilke (1940–1993) was one of the many artists of the late twentieth century who used a variety of media in their work. No longer classified as painters or sculptors or photographers, artists now combined video with paint and terra-cotta with lint and chewing gum. Wilke herself used her own nude body in photographs, chocolate sculptures, and videos. Like Chicago, she used art to explore a feminist perspective. Another important feminist artist who emerged in the 1970s was **Barbara Kruger**, who employed the techniques of the poster to create powerful political statements in her work.

It seems clear that the conceptual approach

brought to these shores by the horrors of World War II is still strong. The dominance of Abstract Expressionism has been broken, and a wide variety of styles is now tolerated by the art establishment. In the 1990s much of art is classified as Post-Modern. This term is used to cover art that employs a variety of media, as well as pastiche and appropriated images, in the service of irony. A number of young Jewish artists come under this rubric. A recent exhibit entitled "Too Jewish?" gave some sense of the diversity and the sensibility of these young artists. Ken Aptekar made and modified copies of old masters with titles such as *Goldfinch Used to be Goldfarb*. Neil Goldberg mounted photographs of Borsch-Belt comedians on matzoth. Deborah Kass made silkscreens with photographs of **Barbra Streisand**. Dennis Kardon sculpted forty-nine noses out of clay.

This new atmosphere has also enabled a reevaluation of a number of artists who were obscured by the shadow that was so long cast by Abstract Expressionism. Among these are Leonard Baskin, **Leon Golub**, and several others. As early as the 1950s, Golub was exhibiting his deeply disturbing, overtly political paintings to a less than welcoming reception. Always figurative, the works often depict acts of torture and other forms of violence in an explicit, graphic way. Golub, who has for the last forty years exhibited jointly with his wife Nancy Spero, has continued to be in direct and defiant opposition to any theory of "art for art's sake." A gentler artist and the son of a rabbi, Leonard Baskin also believes that art should serve humanity in a direct way. Beginning in 1949, he used the techniques of woodcut, etching, and lithography to create figurative works that deal with human problems and struggles. In the late 1960s, he also began doing bronze sculptures on themes of death and compassion. He has also been a prolific book illustrator.

The contributions of Jewish Americans to the artistic life of the United States in the twentieth century have been outstanding. It seems more than likely that they will be part of the continuing exploration of what art means to us as a people and where it will go from here.

PANOFSKY, ERWIN (1892–1968)

Art historian

One of the most important art historians of the twentieth century, Erwin Panofsky showed his brilliance early, being appointed professor at the University of Hamburg before he turned thirty. When the Nazis came to power in 1933 and banned Jews from teaching, he was forced to leave Germany for the United States. Panofsky was appointed visiting professor of fine arts at New York University and in 1935 was made a fellow at Princeton's famous Institute for Advanced Study (where his colleagues would include **Albert Einstein**). In 1947 he was named Charles Eliot Norton Professor of Poetry at Harvard, a position he would hold until his retirement.

Panofsky was a key figure in the study of the iconography of medieval, Renaissance, and baroque art. Among his major publications are *Studies in Iconology* (1939), *The Life and Art of Albrecht Dürer* (1955), and *Renaissance and Renascence in Western Art* (1960).

PENN, IRVING (1917–)

Photographer

Born in Plainfield, New Jersey, on June 16, 1917, Irving Penn initially wanted to be a painter. From 1934 through 1938 he attended the School of Industrial Art in Philadelphia. At age twenty-six he began designing covers for *Vogue* magazine and soon did the cover photography himself. His subtle and elegant style revolutionized fashion photography.

Penn began doing portrait photography after World War II. In addition to his photographs of celebrities, he is known for his evocative photographs of objects and "everyday people." His series *Small Trades* (1950–51) shows laborers posed in a formal manner, but wearing work clothes and holding their tools. Other books of Penn's photography include *Moments Preserved* (1960), *Worlds in a Small Room* (1974), and *Passage* (1991). Concentrating on composition and lighting, Penn's photographic style is noted for its simple and direct focus on the image. His work has been exhibited at the Museum of Modern Art and the Metropolitan Museum of Art in New York City.

PHOTOGRAPHY

Jewish Americans have played a significant role in the development of photography in the twentieth century from its technology to its aesthetics. The list includes some of the greatest innovators and artists in the field. Prior to the great Jewish immigration of the turn of the century, there were few notable Jewish American photographers. The best known—and earliest on record—is Solomon Nunes Carvalho. Carvalho is remembered for his visual documentation of the western United States as part of John C. Frémont's 1853–54 expedition.

Once the twentieth century gets under way, the number of Jews in every aspect of photography begins to grow. Among the great technical innovators, three of the most important are Leopold Godowsky (1900–), Leopold Manne (1899–1964), and Edwin Land (1909–1991). Godowsky and Manne—both also successful musicians—worked for fifteen years to develop an effective color film. In 1935 they invented Kodachrome film, which was the first to use a color-subtractive process. This process revolutionized color photography, giving it true color for the first time. Initially developed for use in animated films, the process was improved on and came to be one of the most popular color photographic films in the world. Edwin Land's immortality in photography came from inventing the world's first instant camera. A physicist, Land founded the Polaroid Corporation after he began experimenting with processes that used polarized light. Like Manne and Godowsky, many of Land's initial developments were for motion pictures. In 1947, as an outgrowth of his experiments with motion picture film, Land invented the Polaroid Land Camera.

Beyond the scientific inventors, many Jewish American artists have been vital to the development of photography. Two must be mentioned at the start: **Alfred Stieglitz** and Edward Steichen (1879–1973). Steichen and Stieglitz would have to top any list in the discussion of photography if for no other reason than they were the first to give American photography credence as a true art form. Through their group, Photo-Secession, founded in 1905, they promoted art photography. Through the Photo-Secession Gallery—located at 291 Fifth Avenue in New York City and called "291 Gallery" for short—Steichen and Stieglitz introduced American audiences to the world of art photography as well as European avant-garde artists such as Picasso, Rodin, and Matisse.

In addition to their promotion of photography, both Steichen and Steiglitz were influential artists in their own right. Steiglitz was the first photographer to capture falling snow on film and was the first to have his work exhibited in a museum in America. Concentrating on composition, lighting, and technique, as opposed to darkroom retouching, Steiglitz revolutionized the concept of what photography could do and how it could do it.

Steichen's early photography was Impressionistic, influenced by his background in painting. Later, after World War I, Steichen's style changed. He rejected his earlier work—going so far as to burn his paintings—and began to focus on Realism. In the 1920s and 1930s he ran his own commercial studio and was the chief photographer for both *Vogue* and *Vanity Fair*. His portraits of celebrities are among the most famous and evocative of the period.

In 1955 Steichen organized what is perhaps the most important photography exhibit in the history of the form, "The Family of Man," for the Museum of Modern Art in New York City. The exhibit of over 500 photographs by the major photographers of the day toured the world and was seen by 9,000,000 people.

Among the many photographers influenced by Steichen, Stieglitz, and the Photo-Secession Group was **Paul Strand**, the preeminent abstract photographer of the first half of the twentieth century. His work focussed on natural forms, patterns, and textures. His use of photography to capture the abstracted forms and shapes found in nature and architecture influenced an entire generation of photographers. He later became an important documentary filmmaker.

Another significant abstract photographer was Aaron Siskind (1903–1991). Starting out as a documentary photographer, his early series *Dead End: The Bowery* and *Harlem Document*, were noted for their focus on design as much as for their subject matter. After the late 1930s, he stopped photographing people and began to focus on capturing the textures and patterns of decay and ruin on two-dimensional surfaces.

While Strand and Siskind developed abstract photography, **Man Ray** (né Emmanuel Radenski) was truly an experimental photographer. He reintroduced earlier photographic techniques such as "cameraless" photographs and "solarized" photographs. His portraits of the Parisian cultural elite in the 1920s and 1930s are both amazing works of art and a vital historical record.

As portraiture and abstraction developed in the twentieth century, so, too, did documentary photography and photojournalism. One of the most notable photographers in this area was **Alfred Eisenstaedt**, already well respected by 1935 when he left Nazi Germany and came to the United States. A year later he was asked to join the staff of the newly created *Life* magazine—one of the first four photographers hired. He quickly became the magazine's foremost photographer, merging the documentary form with an artistic sensibility. Through his work for *Life* Eisenstaedt brought the art and power of photography to millions of people. The magazine published thousands of his photographs and his work graced the cover at least ninety times.

Another important freelance photographer to work for *Life* was **Robert Capa** (born Endre Friedmann), who photographed World War II battles. One of the finest photojournalists of the century, Capa initially gained renown for his photographs of the Spanish Civil War. After the war, he helped create Magnum Photos, the first cooperative agency for freelance photographers. Capa also photographed the confrontations in Palestine in 1948. In 1954 he was again working for *Life*, photographing the French-Indochina war, when he was killed by a land mine.

One of Capa's Magnum co-founders was another influential Jewish photographer, David "Chim" Seymour (1911–1956). Like Capa, Seymour came to international attention for his images during the Spanish Civil War and often photographed wars during his career. Unlike Capa, Seymour photographed war's effect on the civilian population, especially on children. Unfortunately, he shared one final and tragic fate with Capa: Seymour also died young, while on assignment. He was killed in 1956 while photographing the Arab-Israeli war.

While Capa and Seymour were documenting the Spanish Civil War, the photographers of the Farm Security Administration documented the life of the rural and urban poor of America. Two of the most important FSA photographers were Arthur Rothstein (1915–1985) and **Ben Shahn**—who is better known for his mosaics and public art murals. Their images, as varied as Southern sharecroppers and California factory workers, are still exhibited today and have come to form part of America's collective consciousness.

In another category entirely was Arthur Fellig—better known as Weegee (1899–1968). Sometimes considered an "ambulance chaser," he took harsh, shocking pictures of the "dark side" of New York City. Equipped with a police radio, he photographed murders, corpses, arrests, and fights. His most important work was from 1938 through 1947. After 1945, his photographs could be seen in *Vogue* magazine.

During the same period that Weegee was showing the world the stark reality of New York City nightlife, Arnold Newman (1918–) began changing the world of photographic portraiture by excelling at "environmental portraiture." Starting in 1940, Newman took a series of photographs of influential artists in their studios. He then began to photograph a wider range of famous people, including writers and political leaders, all in their own "environments." Many consider the pinnacle of his career to be his series, commissioned by the National Portrait Gallery in London, of celebrated Britons.

In the 1950s and 1960s many Jewish American photographers rose to prominence, including **Robert Frank**, Bruce Davidson (1933–), **Richard Avedon**, **Irving Penn**, and **Diane Arbus**. Influenced by photographers as diverse as Newman, Weegee, and Rothstein, this new generation built on their predecessors' innovations and successfully pushed the art of photography into new and exciting territory.

Robert Frank and Bruce Davidson both created amazing photographs of "everyday Americans." Frank started out as a fashion photographer in the 1940s. By the mid-1950s he had left the fashion world and was becoming increasingly well known for his photographs of working-class Americans. His work was noted for its social commentary, powerful composition, and irony. A *Life* magazine photographer before joining Magnum in 1958, Bruce Davidson created some of the most moving and evocative photo essays of the latter half of the twentieth century. One example is *East 100th Street* (1970), a series of 123 photographs that show life on a block in East Harlem, taken over a two-year period. Both photographers later became filmmakers as well.

During the 1950s and 1960s, Irving Penn and Richard Avedon became *the* giants of celebrity portraiture and fashion photography, revolutionizing both arts. Avedon's style is marked by stark contrasts that give his work a unique focus, clarity, and elegance. Penn—who is also known for his photographs of objects, most notably, cigarette butts—has a softer tonal quality in his work. Like Avedon, he revolutionized formal photography by simplifying it. His power is in his composition and directness.

The most dramatic of these photographers was Diane Arbus. Influenced by Weegee's work, Arbus exploded the boundaries of the form and charted new territory. Her photographs of the unusual and freakish side of life were exhibited at venues as important as the Museum of Modern Art. Whether she was photographing transvestites or midgets or was on a more traditional assignment shooting children's fashions or Mae West, her subjects were exposed, often disturbingly, by her style.

Today's most well-known Jewish American photographers are **Annie Leibovitz**, **Nan Goldin**, and **Cindy Sherman**. Known for her evocative photographs of celebrities, Leibovitz is the first woman and the second living photographer to have a one-person exhibition at the National Portrait Gallery. One of the best portraitists of her generation, she became famous as the chief photographer for *Rolling Stone* magazine. She has also been published in *Life, Vogue, Esquire,* and *Vanity Fair.* Goldin has become famous for her photographic diaries, especially her slide show *The Ballad of Sexual Dependency,* which chronicles her life of drugs and parties during the 1970s and 1980s. Cindy Sherman's best-known work is her self-portrait series entitled *Untitled Film Stills* (now owned by the Museum of Modern Art), in which she portrays archetypal film characters.

The artists mentioned here are only a small sampling of the many notable and groundbreaking American photographers of Jewish decent. There are many more who helped define modern photography in all its genres. For example, **Roman Vishniac** created an invaluable historical record when he photographed Jewish life in Eastern Europe prior to World War II. After his immigration to America, he became an important scientific photographer. Robert Capa's brother, Cornell (1918–), was an influential *Life* photographer and the founder and executive director of the International Center of Photography in New York. Photographer Joe Rosenthal (1911–) won the Pulitzer Prize in 1945 for his incredible Associated Press image of six marines raising the flag at Iwo Jima. The photograph became the basis for the World War II monument in Washington, D.C. Walter Rosenblum (1919–), the child of Romanian Jewish immigrants, was influenced by two close friends and teachers—Lewis Hine and Paul Strand. His photographic series range in content from the Lower East Side in 1938 to East Harlem in the 1950s to the South Bronx in 1980. A photographer with the United States Army during World War II, he recorded the landing in Normandy in 1944 and was the first Allied photographer to enter the concentration camp at Dachau. Philippe Halsman (1901–1979) had photographs on over 100 *Life* covers. Eliot Elisofon (1911–1973) photographed Africa for *Life* and *National Geographic.* Lisette Model (1901–1983), who worked for *Harper's Bazaar,* was an influential teacher and mentored Diane Arbus.

The list goes on and on. Jewish Americans have brought skill, innovation, and artistry to the world of photography. They have helped define and explode its boundaries. They have recorded the triumphs and tragedies of world history. They have given the world the power of the image and the image the power of the individual.

RAY, MAN (1890–1976)

Artist

The most prominent of the American branch of the surrealist movement, Man Ray brought a mordant wit and a sense of the mysterious to painting, sculpture, and film. Born Emmanuel Radenski to a Jewish family in Philadelphia, he was educated in Brooklyn at the Francisco Ferrer Center and later at the Art Students League in Manhattan. As a young man of eighteen, he was already meeting and exchanging ideas with prominent avant-gardists, but the shaping experience of his early artistic life was the 1913 Armory Show. With that famous aesthetic watershed as an inspiration, Ray (who had changed his name to something that would look better as a signature on a painting and instructed his family never to mention the name Radnitsky to the press or public) began working with the Dadaists, befriending Marcel Duchamp and imitating the latter's "readymades," ordinary objects given the status of *objets d'art* by the simple act of titling them.

In 1921 Ray moved to Paris, where he worked closely with Duchamp, Meret, Oppenheim, and others of a similar artistic bent. His first show there was a *succès de scandale* and made his reputation among the Dadaists and the Surrealists who succeeded them. He would be the only American artist to win acceptance in that largely French circle.

Ray earned a comfortable living as a photographer, becoming the chosen portraitist of the rich and famous in France as well as a highly regarded fashion photographer. The income from this "day job" made it possible for him to pursue his pun-laden, idea-filled serious art. In the 1920s he began working in another new medium, film, creating seminal avant-garde movies such as *Emak Bakia* (1926), *L'Etoile de Mer* (1929), and *Le Mystère du Château des Des* (1929).

Ray left Paris in 1940, one step ahead of the Nazis. He settled in Los Angeles, where he would live and work until 1951, when he returned to Paris again. He continued exploring the realms of the unconscious in his art for the rest of his career. In 1972 he was the subject of a major retrospective at the Musée de l'Art Moderne in his adopted home city; the eighty-one-year-old Ray wryly told the press, "If this had only happened forty years ago, I might well have been encouraged."

REINHARDT, AD (1913–1967)

Painter

Eminent abstract artist Ad Reinhardt was born in Buffalo, New York, in 1913. He studied art history at Columbia University and received further training in art at New York University's Institute of Fine Arts. During this time he was greatly interested in oriental art. In the 1930s he worked on the Works Project Administration's Federal Art Project. In the last years of the decade he became involved with the American Abstract Artists group. Together with such artists as Jackson Pollock, **Lee Krasner**, **Mark Rothko**, and Adolph Gottlieb, he challenged the art establishment and created the Abstract Expressionist movement. By the late 1940s, he was painting in a geometric style reminiscent of Piet Mondrian. His work became increasingly Minimalist until, in the last fifteen years of his life, he painted entirely in black. His canvases varied in shape and there were value variations in the black. Textural variations were also apparent. Reinhardt considered these works to be the "ultimate abstract painting." In addition to his painting, he contributed to the Abstract Expressionist movement through his writing and criticism. "Art is Art," he said. "Everything else is everything else. Art is Art. Art from Art. Art on Art. Art of Art, etc." He continued to be highly influential through the 1960s and is still considered an important painter today.

RIVERS, LARRY (1923–)

Painter, sculptor

Original artist Larry Rivers (née Larry Grossberg) was born in the Bronx, New York, and began a musical ca-

reer as a jazz saxophonist when he was seventeen. After five years working in various jazz bands in the New York area, he began studying music and composition at Juilliard. That same year he began painting. In 1947–48 he studied at the Hans Hofmann School, then went to New York University, where he studied under William Baziotes and met Willem de Kooning. He had his first one-man exhibition at the Jane Street Gallery, New York, in 1949. In 1951 he graduated from New York University and met Abstract Expressionist Jackson Pollock. During the early 1950s, he produced portraits, landscapes, and figure studies that combined highly realistic drawing with overlays of transparent color that fragmented and distorted them.

In 1953 Rivers completed *Washington Crossing the Delaware*, one of the first of a series of paintings on American history themes and began series of life-size outdoor sculptures. In 1954 he had his first exhibition of sculptures at the Stable Gallery, New York. For a time, he was loosely associated with the Pop Art movement because of some paintings of money and cigarette advertisements. In 1965 he had a comprehensive retrospective in five important American museums. In the next few years, he began to work using spray paints, the air brush, and later, video tapes. In 1978 he started revising his own earlier work, creating the *Golden Oldies Series*. In 1980–81 he was given his first European retrospective. Throughout his career, Rivers has created works in which there is a tension between abstraction and representation, often with a sketchy or half-finished quality. Never content to work entirely in the artistic mainstream, he has nevertheless been a successful and influential artist.

ROTHKO, MARK (1903–1970)

Painter

One of the most important of the Abstract Expressionist painters who ruled the New York art world in the 1950s, Rothko lived an American dream story of overcoming great poverty to achieve great fame. But his story had a most unhappy ending—suicide.

Born Marcus Rothkowitz (he changed his name in 1940) in Dvinsk,Latvia, on February 25, 1903, Rothko came to the United States with his mother and sister at age seven, joining his father and brothers in Portland, Oregon. When his father died shortly after their arrival, he began a daily routine that included delivering newspapers before school and working after classes. Even with that additional burden, he excelled in his studies, winning a scholarship to Yale. But he dropped out after two years, moving to New York.

While working at odd jobs in the city, young Rothkowitz began taking courses at the Art Students League in 1924. He had found his career. In the next few years, painting in an Expressionist style, he would exhibit at **Alfred Stieglitz**'s gallery among others, and work for the WPA. He also began teaching art to children in Hebrew school, which he would continue to do for two decades.

Rothko had a spiky, uncompromising personality, often difficult to deal with. He taught at Brooklyn College in the 1950s but was denied tenure because his fellow faculty members complained of his inflexibility. He was once commissioned to do murals for a restaurant but refused to deliver them when the architecture was altered, giving them to the Tate Gallery instead.

Although he painted in a representational style in his early years, Rothko's most important works were abstract, large canvasses of rectangular fields of color, seemingly suspended in space, with a soft, glowing quality. As he grew older the canvases, while becoming larger, also became darker as his palette increasingly consisted of dark browns and black. One hesitates to draw psychological conclusions, but it would be hard not to see in that evolution a sign of the depression of a man contemplating suicide.

Revered as a painter, Rothko achieved the highest goals to which an American artist can aspire. He was an invited guest at President Kennedy's inauguration. In 1968 he was elected to the National Institute of Arts and Letters and was given an honorary doctorate from Yale the following year. But his emotional downward spiral, exacerbated by poor health, led him to suicide in his New York City studio on February 25, 1970, his sixty-seventh birthday.

ROTHSTEIN, ARTHUR (1915–1985)

Photographer

Arthur Rothstein was born in New York City on July 17, 1915. He attended Columbia University, graduating with a B.A. in 1935. He then became a photographer for the famed Farm Security Administration. His photographs of the farmers, sharecroppers, and factory workers of Depression-era America are among the most powerful of the time. In 1940 he was hired by *Look* magazine. In 1946 he became the director of photography and associate editor for *Parade* magazine. He stayed at *Parade* until 1971. In 1972 he became a faculty member at the Columbia University Graduate School of Journalism, a position he held until his death. His books include *Photojournalism* (1956), *Creative Color Photography* (1963), *Look at Us* (1970), *The Depression Years* (1978), *Words and Pictures* (1979), and *American West* (1981). A founder of the American Society of Magazine Photographers, Rothstein won many awards for his work and was affiliated with several major photographic societies. He died on November 11, 1985.

SAFDIE, MOSHE (1938–)

Architect

Although Moshe Safdie came to international attention with his *Habitat '67* design for the Montreal World Expo, he was born in Haifa, Israel. Educated in Canada, he went to work in **Louis Kahn**'s Philadelphia office in 1962, opened a practice in Montreal in 1964, then became the Master Planner of the Expo. Following the principles of Modernism, he created the Habitat apartment complex, which was made up of factory-produced, concrete, trough-shaped units stacked together at different angles and in different combinations. It was an attempt to exploit the possibilities of technology to create the Modernist dream city. However flawed the vision was, Habitat was an exciting and inspiring event, bringing attention to both modern architecture in general and Safdie in particular.

A sudden celebrity, Sadie wrote *Beyond Habitat* (1970) and a number of others books while continuing his architectural practice. He opened offices in Boston, New York, and Jerusalem and served as Director of the Urban Design Program at Harvard from 1978 to 1984. He has designed many major cultural and civic projects in Canada, the Skirball Cultural Center and Museum in Los Angeles, and a number of buildings in Cambridge, Massachusetts, including the Cambridge Center, the Morgan Hall and Chapel at the Harvard Business School, and the Harvard Hillel Rosovsky Hall. Most recently, he has designed the Wichita Science Center and the Children's Museum in Wichita, Kansas, and several important buildings in Israel. His other books include *For Everyone a Garden* (1974), *Form and Purpose* (1980), *Jerusalem: The Future and the Past* (1989), and *The City after the Automobile: An Architect's Vision* (1998). After two decades of working in the Post-Modernist manner, he has lately returned to his early Modernist style.

SCHAPIRO, MEYER (1904–1996)

Art historian, critic

Outstanding art historian Meyer Schapiro was born in Shavly, Lithuania, in 1904 and came to the United States with his family when he was three years old. He grew up in the Brownsville section of Brooklyn, New York, and moved in young adulthood to Greenwich Village. He was trained as a medievalist, specializing in Romanesque art, but through his deep knowledge and understanding of modern art he became a guide and inspiration to some of the most important artists of the twentieth century. Although his 1931 dissertation on medieval scholarship had an immediate and important impact, he was not granted tenure at Columbia University, where he taught until 1948, presumably because of anti-Semitic prejudices. During the 1940s he began publishing criticism in the *Partisan Review* and **Commentary**. In the late 1960s, his use of semiotics placed him among the rebels of art history, despite his age.

Schapiro was known as a brilliant lecturer. In addition to Columbia, he taught at New York University, the New School, Cooper Union, and the New York Studio School at night. His influence on three generations of artists and art lovers cannot be overestimated. When he died, he was revising a series of lectures on Impressionism, which was published posthumously by his widow under the title *Impressionism: Reflections and Perceptions*. The *New York Times Book Review* began its review of the volume: "Few scholars of art history have written as insightfully on Impressionism as Meyer Schapiro, one of the most brilliant art historians of the twentieth century. . . ."

SCOTT BROWN, DENISE (1931–)

Urban planner, architect, teacher

A rebel and pioneer in the design of cities and urban architectures, Denise Scott Brown was born in Nkana, Zambia, and raised in a suburb of Johannesburg, South Africa. She attended the University of the Witwatersrand in Johannesburg and studied at the Architectural Association in London, England. She came to the United States in the late 1950s with her first husband, Robert Scott Brown, and continued her studies. She received both a master of city planning degree and a master of architecture degree from the University of Pennsylvania. After her husband's death, she married architect Robert Venturi and began teaching urban planning at a number of universities. She specialized in creating interdisciplinary courses for architects, social scientists, and urban designers.

Scott Brown was teaching with Venturi at Yale when she designed the Learning from Las Vegas and Learning from Levittown studio classes. Out of these classes came the revolutionary book *Learning from Las Vegas* (1972), co-written with Venturi and Steven Izenour. It suggested that architects look for design insight in places previously considered architectural eyesores— strip malls, parking lots, and casino advertising.

In 1967 Scott Brown became a partner in what would become Venturi Scott Brown and Associates. She directed the firm's planning, urban design, and architectural programming work. In the 1970s she led the firm's pioneer preservation planning for historic districts in Galveston, Texas, and Miami Beach, Florida. In the 1980s she and her team created a plan for downtown Memphis, Tennessee. In the 1990s she piloted the master planning and schematic design for the Denver Civic Center Cultural Complex and developed campus plans for Dartmouth College and the University of Pennsylvania. She and Venturi recently designed an addition to the National Gallery of Art in London.

SEGAL, GEORGE (1924–)

Sculptor

Modernist sculptor George Segal was born in New York City on November 26, 1924. He attended some of the city's most prestigious art schools. Starting with Cooper Union in 1941, he also attended Pratt Institute in 1947, and New York University, in 1949. Outside New York he spent four years at Rutgers University (1941–1946). By the 1950s he was studying painting with Hans Hofman.

The theme of Segal's most famous work is plaster-cast sculpture within an environment of found objects. He juxtaposes a rough, white plaster figure with the "realism" of its environment. *The Bus Driver* (1962) is a piece consisting of a male figure leaning over a steering wheel and change box. *The Bar* (1971) has a male figure sitting on a bar-stool facing a live television set. *Woman with Sunglasses on Park Bench* (1983) is self-explanatory.

In 1998 a major retrospective of Segal's work was mounted at the Jewish Museum in New York City. It included two pieces, *Depression Bread Line* and *Appalachian Farm Couple*, both of which were cast in bronze for the Franklin D. Roosevelt Memorial on the Mall in Washington, D.C.

George Segal plays a central role in contemporary art. He helped define Pop Art in the 1960s and he has transformed both sculpture and environmental art ever since.

SHAHN, BEN (1898–1969)

Artist

Painter, muralist, and printmaker, Ben Shahn was born on September 12, 1898, in Kovno, Lithuania, into a family of Jewish craftsmen and moved with his family to the United States when he was eight years old. After attending New York University and the City College of New York, he worked as an illustrator and lithographer's apprentice before deciding to concentrate on his painting. During the Depression Shahn was employed by the WPA and created several public art murals. He also designed mosaics for public buildings and created posters for both the Office of War Information and the CIO Political Action Committee. The first major retrospective of his paintings was held at the Museum of Modern Art in New York City in 1948 and was followed by many others all over the world. Much of Shahn's work contained Jewish themes, and his calligraphy frequently used the Hebrew alphabet. He died on March 14, 1969, in New York City.

SHERMAN, CINDY (1954–)

Photographer

Cindy Sherman grew up in Huntington Beach, Long Island, New York. She attended the State University of New York at Buffalo, where she began studying art before moving into photography. She received her B.A. in 1976. A year later, she moved to New York and began creating what would become her groundbreaking series, *Untitled Film Stills*. A series of sixty-nine photographs taken by Sherman, with Sherman as the subject, *Untitled Film Stills* took the art world by storm. The theme of the series is the female archetypes, loosely based on the Hollywood film still. Sherman's later explorations have included disturbing satires of soft porn and fashion photography. She has also created beautiful photographs that replicate the Old Masters. Using a timer-driven Nikon, Sherman is most often her own model—all of the above-mentioned photographs are self-portraits, which only add to their power. More recently she has begun photographing other people and objects, but she is still best known as "the photographer of a thousand faces."

In 1982 the Stedelijk Museum in Amsterdam held Sherman's first survey exhibition. In 1987 the Whitney Museum in New York presented a major retrospective of her work; she was only thirty-three. In 1995 she was awarded a MacArthur Foundation "genius" grant. Her work has been purchased by museums around the world. In 1996 New York's Museum of Modern Art purchased the entire *Untitled Film Stills* series.

SOYER BROTHERS

Artists

Three of America's important Realist painters were brothers born in Russia. Moses (1899–1974) and Raphael (1899–1987), twins, were exiled from Czarist Russia when they were fourteen years old. They immigrated to the United States and settled in New York. Their younger brother Isaac (1902–1981) came two years later. All three worked in factories and sold newspapers during the day while taking night classes at Cooper Union. The two elder brothers then attended the National Academy of Design, while Isaac went to the National Academy of Fine Arts.

Moses was strongly influenced by George Bellows and Robert Henri, members of the Ashcan School, and by Degas. Like Degas he often painted young working women—seamstresses, ballet dancers, and models. He also portrayed the harder side of life in the poor neighborhoods of New York.

Raphael went from the Academy of Design to the famous Art Students League and counts among his strongest influences Native Realists like Thomas Eakins and Winslow Homer. Indeed, one of his most famous paintings is *Homage to Eakins*, which pictures a group of New York Realist painters. He has also painted a great number of self portraits.

Isaac, like his brothers, falls at the gentle end of the continuum of Social Realist painters. After he left the Academy of Fine Arts, he went to the Educational Alliance Art School and then spent a year in Paris and Madrid.

All three of the brothers are widely collected and exhibited. They would, no doubt, have gained greater fame if the Abstract Expressionist movement had not become so dominant in the years after the Second World War. Still, their reputations are secure.

STEINBERG, SAUL (1914–1999)

Cartoonist, artist

Best known for his *New Yorker* cartoons, artist Saul Steinberg used the wit of the visual image to make his audience both laugh and ponder. Born in Ramnicul-Sarat, Romania, on June 15, 1914, Steinberg lived in Bucharest until 1933 then moved to Milan. While in Milan he studied architecture and began drawing cartoons for the magazine *Bertoldo*. While still in Italy, Steinberg's work began to be published in *The New Yorker* magazine and his style and humor became a hallmark of that publication. He escaped from Italy in 1941, spent a year in the Dominican Republic (an experience that was an important influence on his subsequent sketches), and came to the United States in 1942. He had his first one-man show in New York a year later. Steinberg's architectural background is clear in the precision of his lines, and much of his work has a visual clarity and simplicity that belies its internal commentary on the world and its eccentricities. Throughout his career he has had shows in galleries and museums all over the world. In 1978 the Whitney Museum of American Art in New York City presented a major retrospective of his work. His many books of published drawings include *All in Line* (1945), *The Passport* (1954), *The New World* (1965), *The Inspector* (1973), and *The Discovery of America* (1993). He died at his home in Manhattan on May 12, 1999.

Steinberg's front page obituary in *The New York Times* began: "Saul Steinberg, the metaphysically minded artist and cartoonist and brooding doodler whose drawings appeared in *The New Yorker* for more than half a century, elevating comic illustration to fine art, died yesterday.

"Mr. Steinberg was compared to Picasso, Miro, Duchamp, Daumier, Beckett, Pirandello, Ionesco, Chaplin, and Joyce. The art critic Harold Rosenberg called Mr. Steinberg 'a writer of pictures, an architect of speech and sounds, a draftsman of philosphical reflections.'" The *Times* headline sums up his fame: "Saul Steinberg, Epic Doodler, Dies at 84."

STERN, ROBERT A. M. (1939–)

Architect

Modern traditionalist architect Robert A. M. Stern grew up in Brooklyn, New York, and studied at Columbia and Yale Universities. He first made his mark in modern architecture in the early 1970s when he designed a series of houses in the Hamptons on Long Island, New York. Abandoning the tenets of Modernism, he created houses that drew their inspiration from the vernacular fisherman's shacks of the area, with pitched roofs, gables, and eyebrow windows. The houses fit into the existing landscape and provided comfort and grace. Their interiors also harked back to an era in which architects did not dictate the interior design of their clients' homes but created environments in which family heirlooms and belongings were aesthetically appropriate.

Stern continued to design buildings that elicited an emotional reaction and apparently satisfied certain basic cultural needs for his clients, an approach that was, in its way, as revolutionary as any in the Post-Modernist movement. He believes, for example, in porches. "You sit there while it's raining and listen to the crickets. It's magic." In 1982 he began teaching at Columbia University without abandoning his busy practice. In 1986 he hosted the Public Broadcasting Service program "Pride of Place," which presented an overview of American architecture in eight one-hour programs.

Stern's earliest moves away from Modernism were marked by irony and what he has referred to as a kind of self-conscious jokiness. In recent years he has be-come more serious about history and its impact on contemporary architecture. He now calls himself a modern traditionalist and is committed to overcoming a situation in which Americans have been forced to "buy the house we hate least." In 1994 he was commissioned by *Life* magazine to design an American dream house. More recently, he designed a new library for St. Paul's School in Concord, New Hampshire, where his son attended school, and a large addition to the Brooklyn Law School. In 1998 he was appointed dean of his alma mater, the Yale School of Architecture.

STETTHEIMER, FLORINE (1871–1944)

Painter

Florine Stettheimer's paintings have been called inspired, idiosyncratic, decorative, intensely original, and naive. All of those adjectives apply except the last. Born in Rochester, New York, to a wealthy Jewish family, Stettheimer received a remarkable education in art, even if most of it was not formal. Most of her childhood was spent in Europe. She began her formal training at the Art Students League in New York, where she studied with the great Robert Henri and Kenyon Cox. She then returned to Europe, traveling extensively with her family and gaining exposure to post-Impressionist trends. All this time, she was reading art history on her own and, from time to time, under the guidance of a teacher. When the family was forced home by World War I, she became a member of the social and artistic circle that included Marcel Duchamp, **Alfred Stieglitz**, Charles Demuth, Gaston Lachaise, and others with serious progressive ideas about art.

Stettheimer was now forty-three years old and had painted unremarkably for more than two decades. Her single one-woman show had been disappointing. Then, quite suddenly, she began to produce some of the most interesting, sophisticated work in New York. For fifteen years she created paintings that were, at one and the same time, portraits of her family and friends, commemorations of important events, and genre paintings. They reveal the influence of Persian miniatures, Watteau's *fêtes gallantes*, Japanese prints, and the *fin-de-siècle* rococo revival in France, not to mention Freud's new discoveries in psychiatry, the philosophy of Henri Bergson, Surrealism, and the sensibility of Marcel Proust. Astounding, sensuous, witty documents of Manhattan between the wars, they were anything but naive.

Stettheimer continued to work until she died at the age of seventy-three. Her 1934 decor for *Four Saints in Three Acts*, the opera with text by **Gertrude Stein** and music by Virgil Thomson, has been called a precipitating event in the American avant-garde theater. In the last decade, her work has been rediscovered by feminists and by gay culture, first, and finally by the art establishment. Her work received an important survey exhibit in 1995 at the Whitney Museum.

STIEGLITZ, ALFRED (1864–1946)

Photographer

Alfred Stieglitz fought throughout his life to have photography recognized as an art form and he succeeded. Born in Hoboken, New Jersey, on January 1, 1864, of German Jewish immigrants, Stieglitz moved back to Germany with his family when he was seventeen. While there he began to study photography and engineering. After graduating from the Berlin Polytechnic Institute in 1890, Stieglitz returned to the United States.

Living in New York, Stieglitz focused on his own photography and on promoting other artists. His own work, unlike most other exhibition photography at the time, was natural and not retouched. His only "tricks" were composition and camera technique. He was the first photographer to successfully capture snow on film and the first to be exhibited in a museum in the United States. In 1902, he co-founded, with Edward Steichen, Photo-Secession, an organization that promoted art photography. He directed the Photo-Secession Gallery from 1905 to 1917, introducing both photographers and avant-garde artists to American audiences. Among the artists who showed their work at the Photo-Secession Gallery were Pablo Picasso, Au-

guste Rodin, Henri Matisse, and Georges Braque. During the same period (1903–1917), Stieglitz created and edited the photo magazine *Camera Work*. Later, he continued to promote photography and art at New York City galleries such as the Intimate Gallery and An American Place. He married artist Georgia O'Keeffe in 1924 and died in New York on July 14, 1946.

STRAND, PAUL (1890–1976)

Photographer, documentary filmmaker

There were, in a manner of speaking, two Paul Strands, although they were united in one man by their commitment to documentary honesty and the dignity of humanity. The first Paul Strand was one of the world's great still photographers, a protégé of **Alfred Steiglitz**, and one of the founders of the Photo League. The second Paul Strand was one of the central figures in the group of innovative, politically committed artists who changed the way that documentary films were made in this country.

Paul Strand was born Paul Stransky, to Jewish immigrants in New York City. The son of a well-to-do enamelware manufacturer, Paul displayed an interest in the still-nascent art of photography at an early age, joining the Camera Club of New York and studying with the great photographers Charles H. Caffin and Lewis Hine. By the time he was twenty-two Strand had struck out on his own as a freelance photographer, his successful commercial photos showing the influence of the Surrealists whose work he had seen at the famous 1913 Armory Show. By 1917 Strand had become disenchanted with the common practice of manipulating and altering negatives and prints to achieve visual effects; he became deeply committed instead to "real respect for the thing in front of him," as one contemporary source put it. For the next two years, serving as an X-ray technician in the Army Medical Corps, he practiced that stricture at a different level, but it was an educational experience.

Returned to civilian life, Strand expanded his range of photographic interests to encompass architecture, machinery, and other urban subjects. He became one of the leading proponents of "straight" photography, eschewing the manipulations of the pictorialists with whom he had begun his career. He was gradually becoming a key figure in the Photo League, an organization of photojournalists committed to a social vision, most of them Jewish, coincidentally. With the coming of the Depression, this group, Strand prominent among them, served as a sort of elite troop of politically progressive photographers documenting the ravages of the economic disaster on the average American.

Strand had dabbled in motion pictures in the 1920s, but it was in the mid-1930s that he shifted his attention exclusively to film for the next dozen years with results that would transform the documentary film. In 1936 he produced, wrote, and shot a movie about Mexican fishermen, *Waves* (directed by Fred Zinneman), and followed it with work on Pare Lorentz's innovative *The Plow That Broke the Plains*. He met and offered to collaborate with the great Russian Jewish filmmaker Sergei Eisenstein, then co-produced and edited a stirring film about the Spanish Civil War, the 1937 *Heart of Spain*. Strand became president of Frontier Films, a leftist organization whose most important project, *Native Land*, he would co-direct, write, and shoot. A semi-documentary based on actual Congressional investigations, this controversial film revealed the illegal nature of union-busting tactics being used by industry.

Strand returned once again to Mexico, this time on a project commissioned by the Mexican government, to make a film about poor fishermen in a village near Vera Cruz, but the money ran out in mid-production and, for the first time in over a decade, he began shooting stills again. In a way, it was fortuitous that he had gone back to being the first Paul Strand; many of his friends and colleagues in the film industry would be savaged by the House Un-American Activities Committee, victims of the blacklist who would struggle to find work. In 1950 Strand and his wife, Hazel, relocated to France, where he lived for most of the rest of his life. Among his many projects was a book of photos of the small, poverty-stricken town of Luzzara,

Italy, with text by the great neo-realist screenwriter Cesare Zavattini, published in 1955. In the early 1960s he collaborated with the historian Basil Davidson on a photo-essay on Ghana's leader Kwame Nkrumah. Strand spent his last twenty-five years traveling beyond the purview of Congressional committees, photographing the world as he saw it, producing books of photographs set in Vermont, Italy, the New Hebrides, searching, as he put it, for the "perfect village," and teaching a new generation of photographers the value of photographic objectivity.

VISHNIAC, ROMAN (1897–1990)

Photographer, microbiologist

Roman Vishniac was born on August 19, 1897, near St. Petersburg, Russia. He grew up in Moscow—his family was one of the few Jewish families allowed to live there—and attended Moscow's Shanyavsky University. He earned an M.D. (1918) and a Ph.D. in zoology (1920). While still in his teens he became a member of Shanyavsky's faculty. In 1920 increasing anti-Semitism forced him to escape to Latvia, then Berlin. While in Berlin he supported his family by doing portrait photography. At the same time he pursued post-graduate work in endocrinology, optics, and oriental art. (He was barred from receiving a Ph.D. in oriental art because he was Jewish.)

In the mid-1930s Vishniac began a photographic project of enormous historical importance. He began to travel through Eastern Europe photographing Jewish community life. Many of his photographs from this period have been published in two books, *A Vanished World* (1983) and *To Give Them Light: The Legacy of Roman Vishniac* (1993). Prior to immigrating to the United States in 1940, he was arrested several times and twice sent to concentration camps.

Once he got to the States, Vishniac had a short and only moderately successful career as a portrait photographer. In 1950 he became a full-time freelance scientific photographer. Ultimately, he became one of the world's top photomicrographers. He is especially well known for photographing microorganisms as they appear in nature. He was the project director and cinematographer for the film series *Living Biology*. He also lectured at **Yeshiva University** and Pratt Institute. He died in early 1990, at the age of 92.

WEBER, MAX (1881–1961)

Artist

Born in Bialystock, Poland, in 1881 of Orthodox Jewish parents, Max Weber came to the United States with his family in 1891. He studied art theory and design at Pratt Institute in Brooklyn, New York, from 1898 to 1900 and spent the years 1905 through 1908 in Paris. While there he became close friends with Henri Rousseau and helped to organize a class taught by Henri Matisse. When he returned to the United States, he became a teacher at New York's famous Art Students League. In 1910 he arranged the first one-man show of Rousseau's work in America at **Alfred Stieglitz**'s 291 Gallery. Both in his teaching and his own work, Weber became an important influence on the development of modern art in America. One of the earliest Abstractionist painters, he later developed a kind of distorted naturalism that was highly effective and dramatic. The work of his final artistic period stressed Jewish themes and was the most representational of his styles. In 1948 he had a one-man retrospective exhibition at the Whitney Museum in New York City. In 1955 he was elected a member of the National Institute of Arts and Letters. He died in Great Neck, New York, on October 4, 1961.

For Further Reading

See Appendix 2 for a bibliography of general reference books about Jews and the Jewish experience in America. All of the volumes listed there include information about American Jews in art, architecture, and photography.

"From the Inside Out: Eight Contemporary Artists." Exhibition catalog. Jewish Museum, New York City, June 13–November 14, 1993.

"Jewish Experience in the Art of the Twentieth Century." Exhibition catalog. Jewish Museum, New York City, 1975.

"Jewish Themes/Contemporary American Artists." Exhibition catalog. Jewish Museum, New York City, June 2–September 12, 1982.

"Jewish Themes/Contemporary American Artists II." Exhibition catalogue. Jewish Museum, New York City, July 15–November 16, 1986.

Kampf, Avram. *Chagall to Kitaj: Jewish Experience in 20th Century Art*. London: Lund Humphries in association with Barbican Art Gallery, 1990.

Kleeblatt, Norman L. *Too Jewish? Challenging Traditional Identities*. New Brunswick, N.J.: Rutgers University Press, 1996.

Kleeblatt, Norman L., and Susan Chevlowe, eds. *Painting a Place in America: Jewish Artists in New York, 1900–1945*. New York: Indiana University Press and the Jewish Museum, 1991.

Landsberger, Franz. *A History of Jewish Art*. Revised edition. New York and London: Kennikat Press, 1973.

Rosenbloom, Naomi. *A History of Women Photographers*. New York: Abbeville Press, 1994.

———. *A World History of Photography*. Revised edition. New York: Abbeville Press, 1987.

Yochim, Louise Dunn. *The Harvest of Freedom: Jewish Artists in America, 1930–1980s*. Chicago, Ill.: American References, 1989.

Music, Dance, and Theater

OVERVIEW

The tremendous impact of Jewish Americans on this country's performing arts is almost impossible to comprehend unless you realize how profoundly Europe's loss in the late nineteenth century was America's gain. The population that immigrated to the United States from the continent included some of the best and most talented European artists in music and drama as well as in painting and sculpture. They came through Ellis Island, carrying with them talent, expertise, and enormously high standards. They spread this wealth around to other Americans and then passed it down to future generations.

Because of the language barrier many Jewish writers, directors, and performers remained isolated from the mainstream in Yiddish theaters. However, the Jewish impresario became the archetypal American theatrical producer. **David Belasco** almost single-handedly brought American theater out of the dark ages of hero-villain-distressed maiden melodrama. The Frohmans and the Shuberts transformed it into a thriving, prosperous industry. **Florenz Ziegfeld** made it a spectacle. **Lawrence Langner** and **Theresa Helburn**, of the Theatre Guild, taught the American theater to think of itself as an art.

Along the way there were great Jewish American performers such as **Fanny Brice** and playwrights such as **Clifford Odets**, but the greatest creative contributions probably came from the composers, lyricists, and librettists who molded the American musical theater. There were, of course, great classical composers like **Aaron Copland**, but even they worked with the more popular forms that were the backbone of the American musical. And the man who may be the greatest composer America has yet produced, **George Gershwin**, was a genius at bringing the classical tradition to Broadway and vice versa. With Gershwin's name in the popular music pantheon are other greats who wrote for Broadway and for Tin Pan Alley, such as **Irving Berlin**, Gus Kahn, **Harold Arlen**, **Jerome Kern**, Dorothy Fields, and Cy Coleman. These and other Jewish American songwriters gave us "Take Me Out to the Ball Game" (1908), "I Want a Girl Just Like the Girl" (1911), "I'll Be with You in Apple Blossom Time" (1920), "Yes Sir, That's My Baby" (1922), "I Can't Give You Anything But Love, Baby" (1928), "On the Sunny Side of the Street" (1930), "I've Got the World on a String" (1932), "Stormy Weather" (1933), "Blues in the Night" (1941), and Irving Berlin's quintessentially American songs "God Bless America" (1938) and "White Christmas" (1942).

It was two Jewish Americans, **Richard Rodgers** and **Oscar Hammerstein II**, who changed the American musical forever, introducing stories that made sense, characters that lived and breathed, and songs that were woven into the plot as though they belonged there. They were followed by Abe Burrows, **Comden** and **Green**, **Lerner** and Loewe, **Stephen Sondheim**, **Leonard Bernstein**, and a host of others. In the 1950s a new era began when a Jewish playwright made an indelible mark in non-musical theater, the first since **Lillian Hellman**. **Arthur Miller**'s dominance of the theater during that decade was a foretaste of what was to come—**Paddy Chayefsky**, **Neil Simon**, and **David Mamet**.

The Jewish influence on American dance has been strong as well. American ballet owes great debts to **Lincoln Kirstein** and **Jerome Robbins**, modern dance to **Pearl Lang** and **Meredith Monk**. Ballet great Jerome Robbins choreographed *The King and I* (1951) and *Gypsy* (1959) and adapted his classical choreographic debut, *Fancy Free*, into both a Broadway musical, *On the Town* (1944), and a film. He revolutionized Broadway dance with his work on *West Side Story* (1957) and brought Jewish folk dancing to Broadway with *Fiddler on the Roof* (1964).

In the second half of the century, there were far more American-born Jews than immigrants. Because language was no longer a barrier, performers, too, began to come to the forefront, from **Judy Holliday** to **Barbra Streisand** to **Mandy Patinkin**, from **Zero Mostel** to **Lauren Bacall** and Joel Grey. Today there is no part of the world of music, dance, and theater where Jews cannot be found. It is not just in the theater and popular music that Jewish Americans have made their mark. There have been the symphony orchestra conductors such as **Fritz Reiner**, **Arthur Fiedler**, Eugene

Ormandy, and, of course, **Leonard Bernstein**. Individual classical performers include pianists **Vladimir Horowitz**, Rudolf Serkin, and **Artur Rubinstein**; violinists **Jascha Heifetz**, **Yehudi Menuhin**, **Isaac Stern**, **Itzak Perlman**, and **Pinchas Zukerman**; and opera stars Regina Resnik, **Beverly Sills**, **Roberta Peters**, and Robert Merrill.

As for comedy, well, that would be too long a story to tell in an overview. You will have to read the entry in Part II, *Radio, Television, and Film*.

ADLER, JACOB (1855–1926)

Actor

The figure of Jacob Adler towers over the Yiddish theater in America. Born in Odessa, Russia, in 1855, he acted there until discriminatory laws made it almost impossible to continue. He then immigrated to London before coming to America in 1887. His first attempts to establish a theater in this country failed and he returned to London, but he was back in New York in 1889. Still, his first two performances were unsuccessful. His third, in *The Russian Soldier*, established his reputation. After touring for a time with **Boris Thomashefsky**, he founded the Independent Yiddish Art Company. His unofficial playwright-in-residence was Jacob Gordin, who wrote a number of plays for Adler including *The Yiddish King Lear* (1892) and *Elisha ben Avuya* (1909).

One of Adler's most impressive achievements was his interpretation of Shylock in a Yiddish translation of *The Merchant of Venice*. The production was so successful that in 1903 Adler performed the role of Shylock on Broadway in Yiddish while his fellow performers spoke in English. The actor's followers were almost fanatical in their devotion to him, and he performed regularly and with great success until a stroke ended his career in 1920. Adler's wife Sarah (1858–1953) was herself a popular actor and closely associated with her husband's work. Together they founded a notable theatrical family that included **Stella Adler** and Luther Adler (1903–1985), a noted stage and film actor.

"Ay, every inch a king." King Lear's description of himself could just as easily apply to Jacob Adler's position in Yiddish theater. He defined the art form as an actor and the founder of the Independent Yiddish Art, Company, and he and his wife, Sarah, led a notable theatrical family. He is seen here made up for the lead in The Yiddish King Lear. *(Courtesy of American Jewish Historical Society, Waltham, Massachusetts, and New York, New York*

ADLER, LARRY (1914–)

Musician

Virtuoso Larry Adler brought the harmonica into the classical music world. Born in Baltimore, Maryland on February 10, 1914, the child of Orthodox Jews, Adler was introduced to music through the synagogue. A pianist and singer as well as a harmonica player, at the age of ten he became Baltimore's youngest cantor. In the early 1920s, he enrolled in the renowned Peabody Conservatory of Music but was soon asked to leave for lack of ability. Undaunted, Adler continued to pursue a musical career. In 1927 he won the Maryland National Harmonica Championship with a performance of a Beethoven minuet.

In 1928 Adler moved to New York City, where he became a vaudeville performer and silent film accompanist. Later, he also performed in musicals and early sound films. He made his solo symphonic debut with the Sydney, Australia, symphony orchestra in 1939. All his life he had learned music by listening to it. In 1940 composer Jean Berger wrote a concerto for him and in order to perform the piece Adler finally learned to read music.

Other composers who wrote classical harmonica pieces for Adler include Darius Milhaud and Ralph Vaughan Williams. Blacklisted during the McCarthy era, Adler immigrated to England. He composed scores for both film and television and published several books including *How I Play* (1937) and *Larry Adler's Own Arrangements* (1960).

ADLER, STELLA (1902–1992)

Actor, director, teacher

Stella Adler was born in New York City on February 10, 1902, the youngest child of Sarah and **Jacob Adler**, two of the greatest actors of the Yiddish theater. A performer from childhood, and a star of the Yiddish theater in her teens, she became a student at the American Laboratory Theatre school in her twenties. There she was introduced to the new techniques of Konstantin Stanislavsky. In the early 1930s she became a member of the Stanislavsky-based Group Theatre. However, she disagreed strongly with the "Method" acting technique of founder **Lee Strasberg**. In 1935 she traveled to Europe where she met Stanislavsky. Legend has it that he gave her private instruction, which clarified the errors of Strasberg's "Method." Back in America, new technique in hand, she continued to develop her career: acting and directing for the Group, making films in Hollywood, and performing on Broadway. By the early 1940s, she was teaching acting. She soon opened her own school, the Stella Adler Theatre Studio (renamed the Stella Adler Conservatory of Acting in the 1960s). Among her most famous students are Marlon Brando and Robert De Niro. She died on December 22, 1992, in Los Angeles.

ARLEN, HAROLD (1905–1986)

Songwriter

Harold Arlen's music is a unique combination of Jewish and African American influences, an amalgam of jazz, blues, and Old World sounds that are a testimony to his own varied tastes and impeccable musical intelligence. A list of Arlen's compositions—particularly those written with his three favorite lyricists, E. Y. "Yip" Harburg, **Ira Gershwin**, and Johnny Mercer—includes dozens of standards that are a permanent part of the American musical repertoire.

Born Hyman Arluck, he was the son of a cantor, who grew up singing in his synagogue choir and studying classical piano. But Harold's greatest musical love was jazz, and he began playing that American music at the early age of twelve, graduating to the piano stool of local movie theaters at sixteen. He formed a series of local bands with names like the Snappy Trio and the Buffalodians, working as a singer, pianist, and arranger in the Buffalo area before deciding to try his luck in New York at the tender age of twenty-two. Within a year he was working in George White's *Scandals of 1928* and writing arrangements for Fletcher Henderson's band while playing the vaudeville circuit as a single.

In 1929 Arlen teamed with lyricist Ted Koehler to write his first hit song, "Get Happy." Arlen realized that vaudeville was dying and decided to concentrate on songwriting. Teamed with Koehler, he wrote songs for the famous Cotton Club revues including "Stormy Weather," "Between the Devil and the Deep Blue Sea," and "I've Got the World on a String." In 1934 he met and teamed up with Yip Harburg and Ira Gershwin for the score of *Life Begins at 8:40*, his last revue, this time for the Broadway stage. Arlen and Harburg followed the siren call of Hollywood (as Gershwin would, with his brother George, shortly after), and a third phase of Arlen's career began.

In 1939 Arlen and Harburg produced their most famous score, for MGM's *The Wizard of Oz*, winning the Best Song Oscar for "Over the Rainbow." The duo also collaborated on two Broadway shows, *Bloomer Girl*

(1944) and *Jamaica* (1957). It was in Hollywood that Arlen also teamed up with another singer-turned-songwriter, Johnny Mercer, turning out a string of memorable numbers including "Blues in the Night," "That Old Black Magic," and "One for My Baby." They also wrote the score for the Broadway show *St. Louis Woman* (1946). Arlen was reunited with Ira Gershwin for the 1954 remake of *A Star Is Born*, a collaboration that produced one of his most poignant songs, "The Man That Got Away." The same year saw one of Arlen's most unusual efforts, a collaboration with Truman Capote for the much-beloved (after the fact) *House of Flowers*. The following year, Arlen moved back to New York for good. He continued to write songs, turning out his last one, in collaboration with Harburg, in 1976.

ARONSON, BORIS (1900–1980)

Set designer

Groundbreaking set designer Boris Aronson was born in Russia and studied in Kiev, Moscow, and Berlin before he came to New York in 1923. He quickly began designing sets for the Yiddish Art Theatre and for the Unser Theatre. After a stint working with Eva LeGallienne's Civic Repertory Theatre, he began to design for the commercial theater. For the next fifty years Aronson's sets provided the backdrop for such shows as *Awake and Sing!* (1935), *Cabin in the Sky* (1935), *Bus Stop* (1955), *The Diary of Anne Frank* (1955), and *Pacific Overtures* (1976). Aronson's specialty was a stylized, almost abstract setting that reflected symbolically the themes and content of the play. However, he also provided the realistic sets required by most producers. He favored bright colors, when possible, and pioneered in the used of rear projections.

BELASCO, DAVID (1853–1931)

Producer, playwright

Legendary theater figure David Belasco was born to Portuguese Jewish parents in San Francisco and ran away from home when he was quite young. He seems to have made his debut as an actor when he was eleven, playing one of the young princes in Charles Kean's production of *Richard III*. He wrote his first play, *Jim Black; or, The Regulator's Revenge*, when he was twelve years old. At twenty, he was working backstage and on stage at the Metropolitan Theatre in San Francisco. For a time, he worked with and was mentored by prominent Irish American actor and playwright Dion Boucicault.

Belasco's earliest successes came as a playwright, sometimes in collaboration with Henry C. de Mille, for producer Daniel Frohman. His first real hit was *The Girl I Left Behind Me* (1893), a collaboration with Franklin Fytes, produced by Charles Frohman. After that he became his own producer, putting out a string of hits that included *The Heart of Maryland* (1895), *Madame Butterfly* (1900), and *The Girl of the Golden West* (1905), the last two turned into operas by Puccini. His only specifically Jewish play was *The Auctioneer* (1901), written in collaboration with Charles Klein and Lee Arthur and starring Jewish actor David Warfield, who also played Shylock in Belasco's 1922 production of *The Merchant of Venice*. Belasco began producing the work of other writers in the early years of the twentieth century. As with his own work, he focused strongly on realistic production. The Belasco Theater, which he opened in 1902, introduced important innovations in stage lighting.

BERLIN, IRVING (1888–1989)

Songwriter

Irving Berlin is the great American success story, the boy who came to the United States with his family seeking freedom from religious persecution, grew up in the streets of New York, graduated from singing waiter to songwriter, and eventually authored some of the greatest songs of love for his country of all time. From Israel Baline, the poor boy selling newspapers to Irving Berlin, American institution, author of "God Bless America" and "White Christmas," is a startling trajectory indeed.

Berlin was the youngest of eight children of Moses and Lena Baline. The family fled the oppressions of csarist Russia in 1892, settling on the Lower East Side of New York City. Moses, a cantor, died three years later, leaving the family virtually destitute. Israel worked as a newsboy and street singer, graduating to the role of singing waiter in Chinatown. There he co-authored the first of hundreds of songs, "Marie from Sunny Italy," which was published in 1907. Within two years, he was working as a song plugger and lyricist. In 1911 he changed his name legally to Irving Berlin (the name under which that first song had been published). That was also the year he authored his first major hit, "Alexander's Ragtime Band," and married Dorothy Goetz. When she died of typhoid six months after the wedding, Berlin wrote his first ballad, "When I Lost You" and threw himself into his work as therapy.

In 1914 Berlin authored his first complete score, *Watch Your Step*, for Vernon and Irene Castle. This was an era in which most shows had songs "interpolated," inserted into their score by other writers. Berlin contributed individual songs to dozens of shows as well as countless revues including the Ziegfeld Follies, the pinnacle of that form.

Drafted into the Army during World War I, Berlin convinced his superiors that his best contribution to the war effort would be to mount a show performed entirely by soldiers, *Yip Yip Yaphank* (named for the Long Island town where the training base was located). That show introduced "Oh, How I Hate to Get Up in the Morning," but another song, "God Bless America" didn't make it to the final version of the revue.

In 1919, a civilian again, Berlin formed his own music publishing firm and two years later built the Music Box Theater in conjunction with producer Sam H. Harris. The Music Box, which is still in use on West 45th Street, became the scene of numerous successful revues built around Berlin's music and lyrics. He also continued writing for the *Follies* and for shows like the Marx Brothers hit *The Coconuts* (1925).

The following year he married his second wife, Ellin Mackay. Her father was a prominent Catholic industrialist who, outraged by her choice of a Jewish husband, disinherited Ellin. No problem, though;

> "Irving Berlin has no place in American music; he *is* American music."   Jerome Kern
>
> A Russian Jewish immigrant born Israel Baline in Temun, Siberia, the composer wrote two of America's most beloved songs—"White Christmas" and "God Bless America."

Berlin's wedding present to his bride was the royalties to a new song, "Always." Between the Depression's disastrous effect on her father's fortune and the success of her wedding present, she ended up considerably wealthier than her progenitor.

A happy marriage may have been the cause of what is essentially the only prolonged dry spell in Berlin's output. The Depression, ironically, spurred him into a burst of new creativity. He wrote scores for several successful revues, most notably *As Thousands Cheer* (1933), the score for which included "Easter Parade," "Heat Wave," and "Suppertime," a stirring anti-lynching ballad. He also found himself in demand for the now-talking motion pictures. He authored original scores for Fred Astaire and Ginger Rogers, then for Bing Crosby and Astaire. It was for Crosby that he wrote another of his most beloved songs, "White Christmas," for the 1942 film *Holiday Inn*. With the coming of World War II, Berlin again organized an all-soldier revue for Broadway, *This Is the Army*; the score for that show finally included "God Bless America," which was a showstopper.

With the end of the war, Berlin authored his biggest hit and arguably his best show, *Annie Get Your Gun*. He followed the success of that Ethel Merman vehicle with another show for her, *Call Me Madam* (1950). His final Broadway shows, *Miss Liberty* and *Mr. President* (1962), represented a distinct falling off. After the lukewarm reception of *Miss Liberty*, Berlin essentially lapsed into silence, making occasional public appearances, receiving countless awards, medals, and honors. He died at the age of 101.

Berlin left behind an stunning legacy—over 1,200 songs, including some of the most performed offerings in American popular music.

BERNSTEIN, ALINE (1880–1955)

Set and costume designer, writer

One of the first and most important of American set designers, Aline Bernstein was born in New York City, daughter of the noted actor Joseph Frankau. She began her career as a designer at the Henry Street Settlement House, founded by Alice and Louise Lewisohn. In Henry Street's Neighborhood Playhouse, she began doing breakthrough work for such plays as *The Little Clay Cart* (1924) and *The Grand Street Follies* (1924). She went on to great success on Broadway with sets for a number of important plays, but her career was temporarily interrupted by a depression following the breakup of an affair with novelist Thomas Wolfe. He wrote about their love and her family in two of his novels and several short stories. She wrote from her own viewpoint in the novel *The Journey Down.*

When Bernstein recovered, she began designing again, doing costumes and/or sets for such shows as *Reunion in Vienna* (1931) and *The Children's Hour* (1934). In 1937, she co-founded the Museum of Costume Art, which later became a part of the Metropolitan Museum of Art. In 1949, when she was seventy years old, she received a Tony for her costume design for the opera *Regina* by **Marc Blitzstein** and in 1953 she designed the costumes for an off-Broadway production of *The World of Sholem Aleichem.*

BERNSTEIN, LEONARD (1918–1990)

Composer, conductor

Leonard Bernstein (pronounced BERN-stine) was a man of many parts, all of them extraordinary. He was that rare composer who could make the transition from the concert hall to the Broadway stage and back again, a mercurial conductor of great charisma, and a pedagogue who was equally comfortable in front of a seminar of Harvard graduate students, a recital hall full of schoolchildren, or a television camera. Handsome and dashing, he was the entry point into the world of classical music for an entire generation of young Americans.

Bernstein was the grandson of a Ukrainian rabbi and the son of immigrants who worked in the textile factories of Lawrence, Massachusetts. The oldest of three children, he was enchanted by the upright piano the family acquired when he was ten and began taking lessons. Bernstein was an apt pupil in both music and academic subjects, excelling at Boston Latin and then Harvard, where he studied music, finally going to the Curtis Institute to pursue his graduate music studies. At the Berkshire Music Festival (later known as Tanglewood) he came under the wing of **Serge Koussevitsky**, serving as the great conductor's assistant in 1942. In the fall, against his father's wishes, he began a career in music in earnest, working at the Harms-Resnick music publishing firm.

The following year Bernstein was named assistant conductor of the New York Philharmonic. In an incident that has taken on the aura of legend, he replaced an ailing Bruno Walter on the November 14, 1943, broadcast of the orchestra and received a glowing front-page review in the *New York Times*. Bernstein had already begun to make his mark as a composer, authoring a clarinet sonata and his first symphony (*Jeremiah*, the first of many Jewish-themed works), the latter of which won the New York Music Critics Circle Award. Now he was also in demand as a conductor. When his music for the ballet *Fancy Free* was expanded into the hit musical comedy *On the Town* (book and lyrics by Betty **Comden** and Adolph **Green**) in 1944, the third piece of the Bernstein puzzle fell into place.

Young and energetic, Bernstein was now unbelievably busy. Over the course of the 1950s he served as head of the orchestra and conducting departments of the Berkshire Music Center, and as a professor of music at Brandeis. He wrote and produced the opera *Trouble in Tahiti* (1952); wrote the Broadway musicals *Candide, Wonderful Town,* and *West Side Story*; composed music for the film *On the Waterfront*; and conducted at such famous venues as La Scala. In 1958 he became the first American-born conductor ever appointed music director of the New York Philharmonic. Utilizing that position as a "bully pulpit" he championed contemporary music and music education, bringing the joys of classical music to children through his Young People's Concerts, both live and through the relatively new medium of television. He continued in the post for twelve years, including a gala celebration on December 15, 1971, for his 1,000th concert with the orchestra.

In his later years Bernstein was a figure of some controversy, both for his unconventional lifestyle (he was gay, but married; a leftist whose most public political gesture was a fundraising party for the Black Panthers); and for his music, in which he dabbled in rock elements (in his *Mass*). But his reputation as one of the great conductors of this century was solidified by his tenure as the first American music director of the Vienna Philharmonic. With that distinguished orchestra, he produced a series of brilliant recordings that ranged over much of the history of classical music, serving as a valedictory and a powerful reminder of his brilliance.

BIKEL, THEODORE (1924–)

Actor, singer, activist

Cosmopolitan actor Theodore (Meir) Bikel was born in Vienna, Austria, from which he fled at fourteen after the Nazi occupation. He grew up in Palestine and began his acting career at the Hebrew national theater. When he was twenty-two he moved to London to study at the Royal Academy of Dramatic Art and remained there to perform in a number of theatrical productions. He made his film debut as a German soldier in *The African Queen* (1951). He immigrated to the United States in 1954 and became a citizen seven years later. He quickly became known as a powerful and versatile actor, appearing in many of the then-popular television anthology series, such as "The Du Pont Show of the Month" and "The Play of the Week." He also began performing character roles in American and British films, including *The Defiant Ones* (1958) and *The Russians Are Coming, The Russians Are Coming* (1966).

Bikel's second career was as a singer, performing in concerts around the country and in Canada and Europe. His highly popular albums ranged from *Israeli Folk Songs* (1955) to *Silent No More* (1972), which featured underground songs from the Soviet Union. His singing took him to Broadway in 1959 as Captain Georg Von Trapp in *The Sound of Music* and in 1969 as Tevye in *Fiddler on the Roof*, a role which was originated by **Zero Mostel**.

Theodore Bikel has also been active in political affairs, serving as a delegate to the Democratic National Convention in 1968 and as a leader of the **American Jewish Congress**. In that capacity, he was arrested at the South African Embassy in Washington, D.C., in 1984 while protesting apartheid.

BLITZSTEIN, MARC (1905–1964)

Playwright, composer

Playwright and composer Marc (Marcus) Blitzstein was born in Philadelphia, Pennsylvania, on March, 2, 1905. A child prodigy, he began performing when he was five years old. At age seven he began composing music. At fifteen he debuted as a soloist—on piano—with the Philadelphia Orchestra. In his early twenties, Blitzstein went to Berlin where he studied piano and composition with famed teachers Nadia Boulanger and **Arnold Schoenberg**.

After returning to the United States, Blitzstein began composing his own plays and operas. His first piece, *A Cradle Will Rock* (1937), was revolutionary in both subject matter and style. Transcending both the opera and the musical, *A Cradle Will Rock*, though not hugely popular, nonetheless changed modern American theater. Openly political in subject matter, the show had more in common with the work of Bertolt Brecht and Kurt Weill than with anything then being produced in America. His other work includes a musical/operatic version of **Lillian Hellman**'s *The Little Foxes* entitled *Regina* which premiered on Broadway (1949), and a translation/adaptation of Brecht and Weill's *The Threepenny Opera* (1954). He was composing an opera entitled *Sacco and Vanzetti* when he died on January 22, 1964 in Fort-de-France, Martinique.

BLOCH, ERNEST (1880–1959)

Composer

Composer Ernest Bloch was born on July 24, 1880, in Geneva, Switzerland. In 1916 he came to the United States as one of dancer Maud Allen's musicians. After living in New York for four years, he moved to Cleveland to become the director of the Cleveland Institute of Music. In 1925 he became the director of the San Francisco Conservatory. Five years later, he moved back to Switzerland. He returned to the United States in 1939 and settled in Oregon in 1943.

Bloch was influenced by both European post-Romanticism and Neoclassicism. He became famous as one of the few Jewish composers to incorporate both Jewish liturgical and cultural influences in his work. A leader in establishing what would later be called "Jewish national music," his Jewish-influenced work includes *Israel Symphony* (1916), *Trois poèmes juifs* (1913), *Schelomo* (1916), *Baal Shem* (1923), and *Avodath Hakodesh* (1933). Some of his non-Jewish compositions include *Concerto Grosso* (1925), *Quintet for Piano and Strings* (1923), *America (1926)*, and *Suite for Viola and Piano* (1919). He died in Portland, Oregon, on July 15, 1959.

BRAND, OSCAR (1920–)

Singer, songwriter, radio show host

Oscar Brand was born in 1920 in Winnipeg, Canada. He started playing music when he was only four. After serving in World War II, he headed for New York City, where tried to break into radio as a script writer. Instead, he landed a job (without pay) at WNYC radio. His famous Sunday evening radio broadcast, "Folksong Festival," debuted on December 9, 1945. Remaining on the air for over fifty years, it became the longest running program with a single host in the history of radio. Brand has never been paid and never had a contract for the radio show. He has, however, had every major folk personality as a guest including Woody Guthrie, the Weavers, Odetta, Harry Belafonte, and Peter Yarrow, not to mention Brand's own legendary performances.

As a songwriter, Brand has composed for voices as disparate as Doris Day, Ella Fitzgerald, and the Mormon Tabernacle Choir. He has had a hit Canadian television program, "Let's Sing Out," and has recorded close to 100 albums. He also co-wrote the music for the Broadway shows *A Joyful Noise* and *The Education of H*Y*M*A*N K*A*P*L*A*N* and produced many annual conventions for **Hadassah**.

CARLEBACH, SHLOMO (1925–1994)

Rabbi, vocalist

Rabbi Shlomo Carlebach was born in Berlin, Germany, in 1925 and was descended from a distinguished rabbinical family. He immigrated to the United States with his family in 1939. The son of a rabbi, he studied at Beth Medrash Govoha in Lakewood, New Jersey. From 1951 through 1959 he worked with Rabbi **Menachem Schneerson** in the Lubavitch community. In 1959 Rabbi Carlebach left the community and began what would become a highly successful recording and performing career.

Over the next thirty-five years he recorded over twenty-five albums of Jewish religious songs and stories, composing music to lyrics from prayer books and psalms. An important musician in the early 1960s folk scene as well as in more religious venues, Carlebach headlined the Berkeley Folk Festival in 1966. He invented and popularized a new neo-Hasidic style of Jewish folk song. He became the rabbi of his father's Manhattan synagogue, Kehillat Jacob, when his father died in 1967 and remained there for the rest of his life. In 1968, he opened the famed House of Love and Prayer in San Francisco

Rabbi Carlebach blended Orthodox observance with openness. This brought him many followers but also made him suspect in the eyes of more traditional Jewish leaders. He used his music and his stories to bring people closer to the joys of Judaism. He created a revolution and revitalization in Jewish folk music, paving the way for the today's successful bands and singers. Since his death in 1994 his fame has increased. In both the United States and Israel, there are now festivals honoring his contribution to Jewish spiritual and cultural life.

COMDEN AND GREEN

Lyricists, librettists

Betty Comden (1919–) and Adolf Green (1915–) were among the most successful songwriters and librettists of the 1950s and 1960s. Beginning their career in a cabaret act called The Revuers, with actor **Judy Holliday**, they split up the act to write songs for *On the Town* in 1944. The team went on to write lyrics and librettos for more than a dozen successful shows including *Wonderful Town* (1953), *Peter Pan* (1954), and *Applause* (1970). Usually, though not always, their subject was New York, which they treated with wit and affection. Both Comden and Green have also appeared on stage and in films as performers of charm and talent.

COPLAND, AARON (1900–1990)

Composer

Like **Leonard Bernstein**, Aaron Copland was a protean composer whose work bridged the worlds of classical and popular music. Although he didn't write hit Broadway shows like Bernstein, he did work in folk themes that were familiar to all Americans and, as a writer, tried to make new music accessible to non-specialist audiences. Like Bernstein, Copland was showered with every major award and medal the nation had to offer to an artist. And, like Bernstein, Copland was a gay man who lived with a personal silence.

Aaron Copland was the fifth child of Russian Jewish parents who had fled from anti-Semitic pogroms. As a boy Copland manifested a precocious musical talent, and after he graduated from Boys High in 1918 he studied counterpoint and sonata form with Rubin Goldmark. From there he went to Paris where he lived the life of the American artist abroad in the 1920s, studying with the great teacher-composer Nadia Boulanger. He met Stravinsky and the "Group of Six," avant-garde composers whose work was quite different from that of the conservative Goldmark. Boulanger encouraged experimentation with form and style and by the time he came home in 1925, Copland had a commission to write a symphony for organ and orchestra, to showcase Boulanger's considerable keyboard talents.

The America of the 1920s, the land of Babbitts and bromides, was far from ready for the jazz-inflected rhythms of Copland's early work. Conductor Walter Damrosch apologized to the audience at the premiere of the organ symphony and audiences stormed out of recitals that featured Copland's piano concerto. Gradually, Copland began to strip away the apparent complexities of his compositional style, moving toward a more austere sound, trying to find simpler ways of saying what he wanted. In the 1930s and 1940s, he turned increasingly to American folk idioms, drawing particularly from the American West for his music for the ballets *Billy the Kid* and *Rodeo* and the Southeast for *Appalachian Spring*, which won him a Pulitzer Prize. Like Bernstein, he tried his hand at opera and film music as well, winning an Oscar for his score for *The Heiress*.

If audiences were now entirely at home with the deceptive easiness of Copland, he would have none of it. In the 1950s and 1960s he reasserted his old iconoclasm, experimenting with serialism in works like *Connotations* (1962) and *Inscape* (1967). His *Lincoln Portrait* was banned from the Eisenhower inauguration because of the composer's alleged socialism (and some critics have speculated that this rebuff may have triggered his return to more radical forms). By the 1970s he was acknowledged as one of the "grand old men" of American music. He ceased composing at age seventy, embittered by negative criticism. He told interviewers that he never missed it, having said all he had to say.

Copland was as important as a champion of native-grown talent and new music as he was a composer. He wrote countless articles and several books in support of contemporary composers and taught at Harvard in 1935 and 1944.

DANCE

Dance has always been an intrinsic part of both secular and religious Jewish life. Miriam danced in victory after the parting of the Red Sea. The Talmud demands that wedding guests dance to insure the happiness of the bride and groom. In the Jewish tradition dance is an expression of joy, whether worldly or divine, and is part of the celebration of births and mitzvahs. Among the Hasidim, prayer is expressed not just through the mind but through the body. This historic connection is one reason for the influence of Jewish Americans on the development of dance, especially modern dance, in the United States.

Prior to the twentieth century most Jewish Americans kept their religious dances to themselves and, as part of the process of assimilation, their secular dancing was the mainstream dance of the day. Two exceptions were Imre and Bolossy Kiralfy, who in the 1870s staged huge ballet spectacles. Some of their ballets even had Jewish themes, including *The Fall of Babylon* and *The Destruction of Jerusalem*. The Kiralfys were the exception, though. The ascendancy of Jews in American dance began near the turn of the century, when the majority of Jews immigrated to the United States.

The early twentieth century saw a series of developments that led to the current Jewish influence in American dance. First, because the Eastern European Jewish influx during this period was significantly larger than any previous Jewish migration to America, the new immigrants were able to sustain their own cultural institutions. Second, the social reform movement led to the founding of scores of settlement houses that served as cultural centers. Finally, the entertainment industry in America was in a boom period. The turn of the century saw the rise of Broadway, vaudeville, and Yiddish theater. At the same time, both musical comedy and modern dance were developing into distinct artistic forms.

All these factors provided emerging dancers and choreographers with venues that were open to innovation, and, as in any artistically fertile period, there was a great deal of cross pollination going on. Modern dance and ballet found their way into Broadway musical comedies, the stylized steps of Hasidic dance were incorporated into art dance, and the settlement houses created schools and little theaters that brought together the old world and the new. As the twentieth century progressed, Jewish dancers had the training, the history, and the political and stylistic freedom to explore Jewish themes in their work.

BALLET

While classical ballet in America has not been influenced directly by Jewish dance forms, many European Jewish immigrants sought to train their children, especially their daughters, in the traditions of ballet. As classical ballet in America gained respect and recognition, many of its most influential artists have been Jewish.

Perhaps the most important Jewish American in the development of American ballet was **Lincoln Kirstein**. A writer, businessman, and impresario, Kirstein was the man responsible for bringing George Balanchine to the United States. Artistic and business partners for the rest of their lives, Balanchine and Kirstein virtually created American ballet. The two most important and long-lived contributions, among the many notable companies they founded, were the New York City Ballet (NYCB), which developed out of their company, Ballet Society, and the School of American Ballet. Kirstein directed the NYCB from 1948 through 1989. During this time, it became the most creative and inventive ballet company in the United States. He directed the School of American Ballet from 1940 through 1983. Under his leadership the school developed into the premier training ground for generations of dancers. Kirstein also wrote the librettos for several important ballets, including *Transcendence* and *Billy the Kid*.

Choreographer and dancer **Jerome Robbins** is second only to Kirstein and Balanchine in terms of his influence on American ballet. Also known for his work on Broadway, Robbins started his career in 1940 as a dancer with the American Ballet Theatre (ABT). Four years later, he began to choreograph. His first piece, *Fancy Free* (1944), was an enormous hit. In 1948 he left ABT and joined Kirstein and Balanchine at NYCB.

He became the company's ballet master in 1960 and co-ballet master-in-chief in 1983. Among his many pieces of classical choreography are *Interplay* (1945), *Afternoon of a Faun* (1953), *Dances at a Gathering* (1969), and the Jewish-themed *The Dybbuk Variations* (1974), with music by **Leonard Bernstein.**

Herbert Ross (1926–) is another influential choreographer. He started at ABT before forming his own company with his wife, ballerina Nora Kaye (1920–1987). He achieved huge success with *Serenade for Seven Dancers* to music by Bernstein, and with *The Dybbuk.* He later became a film director and popularized ballet with films such as *The Turning Point* (1977) and *Dancers* (1987).

Among the many other important choreographers and impresarios are Bruce Marks and Eliot Feld, who both started out as dancers with ABT. Bruce Marks (1937–) later became the director of the Boston Ballet. Eliot Feld moved into choreography and started his own company, the Eliot Feld Ballet Company. At least two of his pieces have Jewish themes: *Tzaddik* (1974), to music by **Aaron Copland,** and *Sephardic Song* (1974).

While American ballet was gaining international respect because of New York-based companies such as NYCB and ABT, it was also gaining national audiences because of the growth of impressive regional companies. Two of the most influential regional companies were founded by Jewish Americans: the Dayton Civic Ballet (later the Dayton Ballet), founded in 1958 by Hermene and Josephine Schwartz, and the Pennsylvania Ballet, founded in 1962 by Barbara Weisberger.

Among the dancers, Nora Kaye is still probably the most famous Jewish American ballerina. Called the "Duse of the Dance," she was the prima ballerina at ABT from its founding in 1939 when it was still called the Ballet Theatre through 1950. She then danced with Balanchine at NYCB from 1951 through 1954 and returned to ABT from 1954 through 1960. She went on to form a company with her husband Herbert Ross and later was the associate director of ABT (1977–1983).

There are many other notable American ballet dancers of Jewish descent. Melissa Hayden (1923–) was a Balanchine favorite and principal dancer with NYCB from 1949 through 1973. Allegra Kent (1938–) was another Balanchine dancer, performing leading roles with NYCB for thirty years. Ruthanna Boris was one of Balanchine's first pupils and danced with both NYCB and the famous Ballet Russe. Last but not least, Annabelle Lyon danced with almost every major American company including Balanchine and Kirstein's Ballet Caravan, ABT, NYCB, and the Boston Ballet.

MODERN AND CONTEMPORARY DANCE

While extremely influential in classical ballet, Jewish artists have been even more important in the development of modern dance in America. Jewish themes and movements have had an important effect on modern and contemporary dance.

Many of modern dance's greatest artists were introduced to their art at Jewish schools and organizations. The Henry Street Settlement House, on New York's Lower East Side, offered dance classes from its inception. In 1915 Irene and Alice Lewisohn, two workers at Henry Street, built their own theater and school, the Neighborhood Playhouse. Through the Neighborhood Playhouse Festival Dancers, Irene and later teacher Blanche Talmud, trained some of modern dance's most accomplished performers, including Lillian Shapero, **Helen Tamiris, Sophie Maslow,** and Anna Sokolow (1910–).

Many of the same dancers who trained at the Neighborhood Playhouse went on to dance with Martha Graham, who, though not Jewish herself, was an extremely important influence on Jews in modern dance. Not only were many of her principal dancers Jewish, but she also helped several of her dancers to develop their own companies and choreography. Three of Graham's earliest dancers, Anna Sokolow, Sophie Maslow, and Helen Tamiris moved on to produce their own work and became independent choreographers of note. All three used Jewish themes, rhythms, and steps in their work to a greater or lesser degree. Finally, all three were committed to using dance as an agent for social change.

Anna Sokolow worked for the WPA Dance Project

and founded La Paloma Azul Company of Mexico and the Players Project, among several other companies. She became quite well known for choreographing moving work based on Jewish themes and history. Still working at age eighty-five, she has created such classics of modern dance as *Lyric Suite* (1961) and *Opus '65* (1965). Among her most famous dances on Jewish themes are *Dreams* (1961) and *Song of Songs* (1976). She also choreographed important work for the theater.

Sophie Maslow co-founded the New Dance Group, a dance company dedicated to creating leftist, working-class-oriented work. She also helped found the New York City Center Dance Theatre and directed her own company, the Sophie Maslow Dance Company. Inspired by folk music and dance, Maslow's earliest successes were *Dustbowl Ballads* (1941) and *Folksay* (1942). Among her many works with Jewish themes, perhaps the most important is *The Village I Knew* (1950), a series of dances built on the stories of **Sholem Aleichem** and a precursor to *Fiddler on the Roof.*

Helen Tamiris went from dancing with Graham to founding the School of American Dance and her own company, Tamiris and Her Group. With Martha Graham and others she formed the cooperative venture the Dance Repertory Theatre. She also served as chief choreographer for the WPA Dance Project. Among her most famous works are *Negro Spirituals* (1927), *Trojan Incident* (1938), and the Jewish-themed *Memoir* (1959).

A later company member, **Pearl Lang**, was the first dancer to perform Graham's own roles. When Lang moved on to independent choreographic efforts, Graham helped finance Lang's company. Known for the predominance of Jewish themes in her independent work, she used such themes in what became her signature piece, *Shira* (Song). She has created works for many of the world's premier companies including the Boston Ballet, the Netherlands National Ballet, and the Batsheva Dance Company of Israel.

Another important Graham company member was Robert Cohan. In 1966 he was Graham's co-director. Later he became a director of the London School of Contemporary Dance, while at the same time choreographing for the London Contemporary Dance Theatre. In 1980 he became the artistic director of the Batsheva Dance Company.

In addition to the Neighborhood Playhouse, there was another major Jewish community center that influenced dance: the 92nd Street YMHA. Commonly known as the 92nd Street Y, it provided numerous modern dancers and choreographers with training and a venue for performance. The Y's earliest important dance influence was Russian dancer Benjamin Zemach (1902–1997) who came to the United States with the Habima Theatre's production of *The Dybbuk*. He began performing at the Y in 1928. Among the most important dances he created there were *Ruth* and *Farewell to the Queen Sabbath*. Later he moved to Hollywood, where he choreographed a number of dances with Jewish themes including *Fragments of Israel* (1933), which was the first Jewish-themed ballet to be performed at the Hollywood Bowl. A teacher as well as choreographer, Zemach had among his most famous Hollywood pupils the actors **Alan Arkin**, Herschel Bernardi, and **Lee J. Cobb**.

Among the many other Jewish dancers who created work at the 92nd Street Y are Katya Delakova and Fred Berk (1911–1980). The dance duo of Delakova and Berk, both trained in Europe, not only incorporated Jewish themes into their work, but also melded modern dance and Jewish folk dance. Among their most famous works are *Hora* and *Deathless Voices*. After the duo split up Delakova went on to become the artistic director of the Echobow Company, and Berk created the Y's Jewish Dance Division.

Berk's legacy lives on in **Meredith Monk**, who did her first Expressionist modern dance with him. Beyond her work with Berk, Monk also studied at the Martha Graham studio and at Sarah Lawrence College, where Bessie Schonberg was her teacher. Today, Monk and her company, The House, are considered the most innovative artists working in dance and performance art. She frequently returns to Jewish themes in her work.

Another 92nd Street Y alumna is Hadassah (1910–) who started at the Y performing with Zemach. She combined modern dance with traditional Jewish,

Middle Eastern, and Indian dance in her own work. In addition to giving performances in Israel, India, and throughout the United States, she performed her own work at the world-renowned Jacob's Pillow dance center and was the director of the Ethnic Dance Department of the New Dance Group.

Pauline Kroner (1912–), who studied at the 92nd Street Y and the Neighborhood Playhouse, became critically acclaimed as a soloist with Doris Humphrey and José Limon. She was also one of the first American modern dancers to tour the Middle East (1932). Known for choreographing modern dance pieces to the accompaniment of Jewish and Middle Eastern folk music, she gained fame for the dances *Yael* (1931) and *Yemenite Song* (1933), among many others.

At the close of the twentieth century there are hundreds of Jewish Americans at the top of the dance world. Choreographer Lar Lubovitch's company, for example, is now one of the most successful in contemporary dance. Prior to his death, Arnie Zane collaborated with world-renowned dancer/choreographer Bill T. Jones. Daniel Ezralow has worked with the Pilobolus company and has his own troupe, ISO. Irving Burton helped found the popular group "Paper Bag Players."

Outside New York, Anna Halprin (1920–) founded the San Francisco Dancers Workshop. Her explorations of personal experiences as subjects for dance pieces have revolutionized contemporary dance. Bella Lewitzky helped found the Dance Theatre of Los Angeles and her own dance school, Dance Associates. She then went on to start her own extremely influential company, the Lewitzky Dance Company. Also in Los Angeles, Margalit Oved (1934–), a Yemeni Jew, founded the Margalit Oved Dance Theatre Company. Incorporating modern and traditional dance and music, Oved is creating her own unique performance art. In Washington D.C., Liz Lerman's troupe, the Liz Lerman Dance Company, challenges preconceptions of the nature of dance as well as the nature of self-expression. Using a multi-racial, multi-generational company of professionals and amateurs, Lerman develops her dances out of a group improvisational process.

THEATRICAL DANCE

The world of theater, including Yiddish theater, Broadway, and vaudeville, have all been affected by innovations in dance. In turn, the theater has given many dancers and choreographers the opportunity to explore diverse dance forms. In the early years of the twentieth century, however, vaudeville and Broadway remained largely the venue for comedy, satire, and traditional chorus girl dances such as those in **Florenz Ziegfeld**'s famous Ziegfeld Follies. From the time they were first presented in 1907, it was primarily through the Follies that the chorus girl was brought out of the burlesque houses and into mainstream American entertainment.

In 1926, when the Russian Jewish Habima Theatre toured the United States, the dances in their production of *The Dybbuk* showed that modern interpretive dance had a place in theater. The Yiddish theater of New York responded to Habima's influence and Lillian Shapero became its most important choreographer. In 1933 the Yiddish Art Theatre presented *Yoshe Kalb*. In the production, Lillian Shapero interpreted traditional Hasidic dances through the eyes of modern dance, bringing her training from the Neighborhood Playhouse and Martha Graham's company into the theater. She continued to choreograph for the Yiddish Art Theatre with such productions as *The Wise Men of Chelm*, *The Water Carrier*, and the Art Theatre's production of *The Dybbuk*.

Jewish culture, and young Jewish girls especially, became so caught up in modern dance and ballet as the century progressed that comedienne **Fanny Brice**, a former Follies chorus girl, designed many of her skits for the Ziegfeld Follies as send-ups of the scores of girls on the Lower East Side who wanted to become dancers. Other skits included parodies of the classical ballet *Swan Lake*, of Martha Graham, and of strip-tease dancing.

There were also theater and film actors who got their start dancing in vaudeville, including **Danny Kaye**, **Sammy Davis, Jr.**, and Joel Grey (1932–), son of vaudeville performer Mickey Katz. It is in the Broadway musical that dancers and choreographers of Jewish descent have made their presence felt most. Among the dancers, Eliot Feld got his start dancing on Broadway in *West Side Story* (1957) and **Pearl Lang** made a living by appearing in musicals such as *Carousel* (1945) and *Finian's Rainbow* (1947). Benjamin Zemach choreographed the groundbreaking Broadway production *The Eternal Road* (1936) with Senia Gluck-Sandor. **Anna Sokolow** choreographed the dancing in *Street Scene* (1946) and *Hair* (1967). Helen Tamiris choreographed musicals *Annie Get Your Gun* (1946) and *Fanny* (1955) among many others. Choreographer **Michael Kidd**, who started his career at ABT, went on to win five Tony Awards. He has choreographed such musical theater classics as *Guys and Dolls* (1950), *Can-Can* (1953), *Finian's Rainbow* (1947), and *The Rothschilds* (1970).

Jerome Robbins revolutionized the world of classical ballet and was one of Broadway's most revered creative geniuses. In addition to the choreography for shows such as *The King and I* (1951) and *Gypsy* (1959), Robbins adapted his classical choreographic debut *Fancy Free* into a Broadway musical, *On the Town* (1944), and a film. The winner of numerous Tonys and Oscars, Robbins transformed Broadway dance with *West Side Story* (1957) and brought Jewish folk dancing to Broadway with *Fiddler on the Roof* (1964).

From Imre Kiralfy to Jerome Robbins, Jews have participated in the evolution of American dance and helped create it. From traditional ethnic dances to contemporary abstract work, dance continues to be a central expression of Jewish identity and storytelling. The innovations of Jewish Americans who sought to bring their ethnic heritage into their more mainstream work helped create the atmosphere for invention that is a hallmark of all American dance.

The one convert to Judaism included in this volume, Sammy Davis, Jr., was obviously sincere in his dedication to his new faith. He raised his children as Jews. His obituary in the Amer-ican Jewish Yearbook quotes him as having found "an affin-ity" between Jews and blacks as oppressed people. (Private Collection)

DAVIS, SAMMY, JR. (1925–1990)

Singer, dancer, actor

Sammy Davis Jr. wasn't quite born in a trunk but he was performing in black vaudeville by the time he was three. He joined his uncle Will Mastin's act as a child and throughout the Depression toured with them; the act gradually shrinking from an entire family of fourteen to a trio consisting of Uncle Will and Sammy Senior and Junior, billed as the Will Mastin Trio. The younger Davis quickly developed an impressive array of talents including song and dance, comedy, impressions, and playing a myriad of musical instruments, most memorably drums. After a stint in the Army in 1945, he came back to what was now billed as the Will Mastin Trio, Starring Sammy Davis, Jr.

Davis began working more as a single, putting out several successful records and making many television appearances. He became a fixture on the Las Vegas stage and was enjoying unprecedented success for an African American performer when a serious automobile accident nearly cost him his life in 1954. Davis lost his left eye and was hospitalized for months. During a chance visit from the hospital rabbi, Davis was moved by the simple truths the man told him about life, adversity, and courage. After a lifetime of no formal religion, Davis decided to convert to Judaism and embraced his course of study with the same passion as he had devoted to his career. He raised his children as Jews.

Only a few months after his accident, at a time when most ordinary men would still be in rehabilitation, Davis was back on stage in Las Vegas in an explosive one-man show that seemed designed for the express purpose of proving he was indestructible. Two years later he made his Broadway and Hollywood debuts. He became an integral part of the "Rat Pack," headed by Frank Sinatra and Dean Martin, appearing in movies and nightclubs with them. Davis was not a stranger to controversy; his second marriage, to a Swedish actress, May Britt, came at a time when racial intermarriage was still a powerful taboo in America. His conversion to Judaism and his support of Richard Nixon in the 1968 presidential election dismayed many of his fans. His repeated failure to crack series television was a major disappointment. In the 1980s he battled cocaine and alcohol problems, hip replacement surgery, and, finally, cancer. He made a successful comeback appearance in the 1989 film *Tap*, displaying the old Davis dancing form one last time before his death the following year.

DIAMOND, DAVID (1915–)

Composer

Composer David Diamond was born on July 9, 1915, in Rochester, New York. He attended the Cleveland Institute of Music from 1927 through 1929 and studied at the Eastman School of Music in Rochester from 1930 through 1934. Later he studied composition with both Roger Sessions and Nadia Boulanger. During the 1950s and early 1960s he lived in Italy, returning to the United States in 1965. He has taught at a large number of institutions, including the Manhattan School of Music, the University of Colorado, and the Juilliard School of Music.

Known for his expert blending of Neoclassical and Romantic elements, his first success was the orchestral work *Psalm* (1936). He also composed music for the ballet *Tom* (1936) and incidental music for Shakespeare's *Romeo and Juliet* (1947). Among his other orchestral work are the compositions *Cello Concerto* (1938) and *Rounds*, for string orchestra (1944). His many vocal arrangements include *Mizmor l'David* for tenor, chorus, and orchestra with text from the Bible (1951), which was commissioned by the Park Avenue Synagogue in New York City. Subsequently, he began to explore more modern musical forms using dodecaphonic techniques. His more recent work includes the piano piece *A Roust* (1980) and *Flute Concerto* (1986).

DYLAN, BOB (1941–)

Singer, songwriter

Bob Dylan was the defining voice of a generation. He replaced the movie anti-heroes of the 1950s, the James Deans and Marlon Brandos, with a similar but more sophisticated icon of disaffection, one that spoke defiantly against racism and the Bomb, complacency, and conformity. And just when the media thought it had him pigeonholed, he changed the rules on them—over and over again.

Dylan was born Robert Zimmerman in Duluth, Minnesota, but was raised in the nearby mining town of Hibbing. It was the kind of town in which his father, an avid golfer, was not able to join the local country club because he was Jewish, the kind of town calculated to nettle an already rebellious spirit. By 1959 Bob had left Hibbing on his motorcycle for Minneapolis, where he spent three rather desultory semesters at the University of Minnesota, pursuing a career as a folksinger (as Bob Dylan—he took this surname from the given name of Welsh poet Dylan Thomas, whose work he admired) with rather more interest than he did his studies. Within two years, he was on his way to New York where, in 1963, he met the folk singer Joan Baez, who helped advance his career.

In New York things began to gel rapidly for the young singer. He regularly visited his hospitalized hero, Woody Guthrie, who was in the final stages of a fatal illness. He performed regularly at Gerdes' Folk City, and he was discovered by John Hammond (whose other finds included Billie Holiday, **Benny Goodman**, and Bruce Springsteen), who signed him to a contract with Columbia Records. The result was a series of albums that showcased a fresh voice of protest in songs like "Blowin' in the Wind," "Masters of War," and "The Times They Are A-Changin'."

Dylan's rise coincided with the veritable rebirth of rock and roll spearheaded by a wave of British bands led by the Beatles and the Rolling Stones. No doubt inspired by them, Dylan began working with electric guitar and a band; folkies, feeling betrayed, booed him when he plugged his guitar into an amplifier at a concert in 1965. (Legend has it that his reaction was to turn to his backup group and snarl, "Play f***ing loud!") To add to their sense of betrayal, Dylan was moving away from the overtly political songs of his first albums into a more surrealistic lyrical style. He produced a series of recordings that must rank among the greatest creations in rock history: "Bringing It All Back Home," "Highway 61 Revisited," and "Blonde on Blonde."

The next phase of his career was triggered by a near-fatal motorcycle accident in July 1966. Dylan recuperated in Woodstock, New York, writing and recording songs with The Band (eventually released as *The Basement Tapes*), then released a new album, *John Wesley Harding*, which suggested another direction for his music to pursue, a country-influenced sound.

In the 1970s and 1980s, Dylan continued to perform, write, and record with mixed results. He also returned to political activism, working hard for the release of Rubin "Hurricane" Carter, a former boxer who was imprisoned for a murder he very likely didn't commit. In 1979, Dylan announced that he had become a born-again Christian and recorded two albums that bespoke that commitment. Shortly after that he was seen praying in a *tallit* at the Western Wall in Jerusalem and has subsequently embraced the Judaism of his father, albeit in a more private fashion. His son-in-law, Peter Himmelman, is an Orthodox Jew and a singer-songwriter very much in Dylan's own

> **"Bob Dylan has met the Establishment, and he is it."** The *New York Times*, 12/8/97
>
> The musician who wrote the lyrics sung by the countercultural revolution of the 1960s received Kennedy Center Honors for lifetime achievement in the performing arts in 1997. The awards evening ended with Dylan and the other 1997 recipients (including Lauren Bacall) standing on stage with President William Jefferson Clinton, another child of the 1960s, singing "America the Beautiful." The times have changed!

mold, and the influence back and forth between the two has been remarked on.

In the 1990s Dylan has undergone a rebirth of a different sort, emerging as an elder statesman of popular music, recording both old blues and folk songs and his own new compositions. His fiftieth birthday was an occasion for numerous retrospectives. When he does perform his older songs, it is always in new and usually startling arrangements. He received the Kennedy Center Honors for lifetime achievement in the arts in 1997. His album *Time out of Mind* won the 1998 Grammy for Best Album—the first of his over forty albums to win the award.

ELMAN, MISCHA (1891–1967)

Violinist

Violinist Mischa Elman was born in the Ukraine on January 20, 1891. A child prodigy, he studied at the St. Petersburg Conservatory under Leopold Auer. He made his professional debut at the age of thirteen in Berlin. After his debut, he began to tour extensively and quickly became known as one of Europe's greatest violinists.

Elman's first tour to the United States was in 1908. He became an American citizen in 1923. Throughout his career he toured in the United States, Europe, and Asia. Known for the resonant quality of his tone as well as for his command of a broad repertoire, Elman was a master of the Romantic tradition. Less well known are his compositions—short pieces for the violin. He also arranged works for violin and piano. The fiftieth anniversary of his debut in America was commemorated by a concert at Carnegie Hall. He died on April 5, 1967, in New York City.

FIEDLER, ARTHUR (1894–1979)

Conductor

Boston Pops maestro Arthur Fielder was born in Boston, Massachusetts, on December 17, 1894. In 1911 he went to Berlin, where he studied violin, piano, and conducting at the Royal Academy. Four years later he returned to Boston and became a member of the Boston Symphony. From 1918 through 1930, he was a member of the viola section. In 1924 he was unsuccessful in his bid to become conductor of the Boston Pops Orchestra (the Boston Symphony Orchestra without its principal musicians). Instead, he created his own chamber symphony, the Arthur Fiedler Sinfonietta. Five years later he started the Esplanade concerts, the first outdoor symphonic concerts in Boston's history. In 1930, Fielder was named the Pops conductor, a position he held for forty-nine years. During his tenure, the orchestra added more contemporary music to its repertoire, became popular throughout the United States, and sold over fifty million records. He died in Brookline, Massachusetts, on July 10, 1979.

FIERSTEIN, HARVEY (1954–)

Playwright, actor, activist

Flamboyant performer Harvey Fierstein was born in Brooklyn, New York. He made his acting debut in the Andy Warhol play *Pork* (1971) at La Mama E.T.C. and gained prominence in 1983 when his semiautobiographical play *Torch Song Trilogy* won him Tony Awards for both his script and his starring performance. The following year he won another Tony for the book of the musical *La Cage aux Folles*. While accepting that award, he thanked his male lover, thus winning fame of another sort. He then adapted *Torch Song* for the screen and starred in the 1988 film. Since

then he has appeared in a number of films, including *Mrs. Doubtfire* (1993), *Bullets over Broadway* (1994), and *Independence Day* (1996). He also narrated the Academy Award-winning documentary *The Life and Times of Harvey Milk*.

Fierstein's television appearances include a guest spot on "Cheers" that won him an Emmy nomination, a classic voice-over as Homer's executive secretary on an episode of "The Simpsons," many late night talk shows, and a regular role on the Dudley Moore series "Daddy's Girls" (1994). In the latter, he made television history as the first openly gay actor playing a gay principal character.

FLEISHER, LEON (1928–)

Pianist, conductor

Leon Fleisher was born on July 23, 1928, in San Francisco, California. A child prodigy, with very ambitious parents, he began studying the piano when he was four. At the age of seven he made his first public appearance; by age nine, he soloed with the San Francisco Federal Symphony Orchestra. He became a pupil of virtuoso Artur Schnabel, with whom he studied for the next ten years. In 1952, after winning the Queen Elisabeth International Piano Competition in Brussels, Belgium—the first American to earn highest honors in a significant European competition—Fleisher toured Europe, with enormous success. For the next thirteen years he was one of the most sought after pianists in the United States and Europe.

In 1965 Fleisher lost the use of his right hand to carpel-tunnel syndrome. He decided that the left-handed repertoire was too limited and turned to conducting. In addition to guest conducting all over the country, Fleisher co-founded the Theater Chamber Players of Washington, D.C. (1967), conducted the New York Chamber Orchestra's Mostly Mozart Festival (1970), and served as assistant conductor for the Baltimore Symphony (1973–1978). Since 1959 he has taught at the Peabody School of Music in Baltimore, Maryland. After undergoing surgery in 1981, he was able to resume his career as a pianist.

FRIEDMAN, DEBBIE (1951–)

Singer, songwriter, composer

Debbie Friedman is one of the most famous and successful writers and performers of modern Jewish liturgical and folk music. She is the first woman to add significantly to the canon of Jewish religious music.

Growing up in St. Paul, Minnesota, she began playing the guitar at age seventeen. By the time she was twenty she was composing. Her first piece of music was written to the words of the *V'ahaftah*. After she graduated from high school, she spent three months on an Israeli kibbutz where she learned Hebrew. She then returned to the United States and became a song leader in numerous Reform congregations and summer camps. In 1972 she released her first album, *Sing unto God*. Through the 1970s and early 1980s she served as a teacher and cantor in congregations all over the country. In 1984 she moved to Encino, California, to serve as the cantoral soloist at Shir Chadesh-New Reform Congregation, and in 1995 she moved to New York City. Her Carnegie Hall debut was on January 7, 1996.

Even though she has never had any formal musical training and doesn't read music, she has continually composed and written songs, many of which combine English and Hebrew. She has written renditions of the *Birchot Havdalah*, *Oseh Shalom*, and the *Kaddish D'Rabanan*. Her songs include "The Angel's Blessing," "Nasim Shalom," "L'chi Lach," "Thanksgiving Song," and "Mi Shebeirach." Her recent albums include *Live at Carnegie Hall* and *Shana Tova—Songs for the Jewish Holidays*.

GERSHWIN, GEORGE (1898–1937)

Composer

GERSHWIN, IRA (1896–1983)

Lyricist

George Gershwin was the man who put Tin Pan Alley in evening dress. Moving from the Broadway stage and the popular tune to the concert hall and *Rhapsody in Blue*, he gave a new respectability to pop hits and what he took to be the rhythms of the Jazz Age. His big brother, Ira, found scintillating ways of utilizing American vernacular in tandem with George's driving "fascinating rhythm," the perfect linguistic accompaniment to his brother's music.

Ira (born Israel) and George (born Jacob) were the oldest of four children of Moshe Gershovitz and Rose Bruskin, Russian Jewish immigrants struggling to work their way out of poverty in the New World of New York City. Moshe was a feckless dreamer who changed jobs regularly, as regularly as the family was forced to change apartments (according to one source, twenty-two times between 1895 and 1917).

Although neither parent had an aptitude for music, the family acquired a piano in 1910 with the idea of giving Ira lessons. But it was George who had music in his blood, and he very quickly replaced his brother at the keyboard (no doubt to the older boy's relief). George studied for two years with local teachers before being taken on as a pupil by Charles Hambitzer, who introduced the young Gershwin to the classics. George dropped out of high school to pursue a career in music, taking a job as a song plugger at a music publishing firm, a superb way for him to hone his keyboard skills while making exploratory stabs at songwriting. In 1917 he quit that job to take another one, this time as rehearsal pianist for the forthcoming **Jerome Kern** show, *Miss 1917*. Within a year the twenty-one-year-old George, already known in the New York theatrical world as a pianist, was offered a contract as a songwriter by Max Dreyfus, another music publisher. Between 1919 and 1925, Gershwin wrote scores for sixteen shows.

And during that phenomenal run of success, he was joined by his big brother. Ira had stayed in school, where he had made friends with another nice Jewish boy, E. Y. "Yip" Harburg. The two shared a love of words, wordplay, puns, and rhymes; that interest led each to a career as a lyricist. Ira wrote his first lyrics under the name Arthur Francis (taken from the two younger Gershwins, brother Arthur and the baby of the family, sister Frances), not wanting to cash in on his precocious kid brother. He was quickly able to drop that charade as the two Gershwins teamed up for a series of hugely successful shows.

But George's fertile musical mind and driving ambition were not sated. Through the 1920s, he studied with Rubin Goldmark, Wallington Riegger, and Henry Cowell, working toward the creation of "serious" music. On February 12, 1924, he realized some small part of that ambition when bandleader Paul Whiteman premiered Gershwin's *Rhapsody in Blue*. He followed that significant work with *An American in Paris*, inspired by a 1928 trip to Europe. With the coming of sound to motion pictures, he and Ira began to split their time between the coasts, writing songs for shows and movies, while George continuing churning out concert pieces as well. In 1931 the two brothers won a Pulitzer Prize for their Broadway satirical hit *Of Thee I Sing*. In 1935 they realized another of George's dreams, writing a full-length opera, *Porgy and Bess*.

They were back in Hollywood in mid-1937 working on a new musical film, *Goldwyn Follies*, when George began having headaches and dizzy spells. He had a brain tumor, which remained undiagnosed until it was too late. He died on July 11, two months short of his thirty-ninth birthday. The musical theater community was stunned, no one more so than his older brother. Ira became the keeper of the flame of George's memory, even creating a new Gershwin brothers musical film, *The Shocking Miss Pilgrim* in 1946 as a vehicle for Betty Grable, reworking material from George's "trunk."

For Ira life went on as before, albeit more somberly for a time. He was a brilliant lyricist and much in demand. In the years remaining—and he outlived his ill-fated brother by forty-six years—he worked with such great composers of stage and screen as Jerome Kern, Kurt Weill, and **Harold Arlen**, writing scores for memorable musicals like Weill's *Lady in the Dark* (1944) and films like *A Star Is Born* (1954).

George Gershwin received a posthumous Special Citation from the Pulitzer Prize Committee in 1998.

GETZ, STAN (1927–1991)

Jazz saxophonist

Born Stanley Gayetzby on February 2, 1927, in Philadelphia, Stan Getz popularized both Brazilian bossa nova and "cool" jazz, (a style of playing where there is no vibrato on the notes). A musician from early childhood, he played the tenor saxophone and debuted professionally when he was fifteen. He attended the Juilliard School of Music for a year but left to play with many of the jazz greats of the time, including **Benny Goodman** and Stan Kenton. In 1947, he became a member of Woody Herman's Herd and began to achieve national attention. After he left Herman's band, he led his own groups. He lived in Scandinavia during the mid-1950s, in the United States in the early 1960s, in Europe from 1969 through 1972, and moved back to this country to stay in 1972. Throughout his professional life he toured and recorded extensively. Among his most famous recordings are "Early Autumn" (soloist, the Woody Herman Herd), "The Girl from Ipanema" and "Anniversary." He died on June 6, 1991, in Malibu, California.

GLASS, PHILIP (1937–)

Composer

Composer Philip Glass was born in Baltimore, Maryland, on January 31, 1937. His initial introduction to music was through the flute, an instrument he still includes in many of his compositions. He studied mathematics and philosophy at the University of Chicago before moving on to study composition at the Juilliard School of Music, where he earned his M.S. degree in 1962. He later studied in Paris with Nadia Boulanger and traveled throughout Southeast Asia. His travels in India and his friendship with Indian sitarist Ravi Shankar led him to explore Eastern rhythms and tonalities, which became a hallmark of his compositional style.

After returning to New York, Glass developed a small ensemble comprised of electric keyboard and wind instruments. His distinct minimalist style uses repetition that contains minute changes taking place over an extended period of time. He is best known for the evocative sound track to the film *Koyaanisqatsi* (1982). He has also gained national renown for his operas, especially *Einstein on the Beach* (1976), which began to reincorporate certain Western harmonic traditions. His other operas include *Satyagraha* (1980) and *The Voyage* (1992).

GOLDFADEN, ABRAHAM (1840–1908)

Playwright, composer, theatrical producer

Considered the "father of Yiddish theater," Abraham Goldfaden was born in Russia on July 24, 1840. Already a published poet—in Hebrew and Yiddish—he graduated from rabbinical school in 1866, then taught for the next nine years. In 1875 he moved to Poland, where he founded two Yiddish-language newspapers, neither of which succeeded. The following year he moved to Romania and created what most consider to be the first Yiddish theater group—Iassi. Encouraged by its initial success, Goldfaden expanded the group and toured other cities, including Bucharest, and ultimately Odessa. By 1880 the performers were receiving an enthusiastic welcome throughout Russia. But in 1883, the government, fearing this new "mass entertainment," banned any performances in Yiddish. Many performers, writers, and producers chose to move to other countries and Yiddish theaters were established in Paris, London, and New York.

In 1887 Goldfaden moved to New York, but he found the Yiddish theater competition there overwhelming and soon returned to Europe. In 1903 he returned to New York City permanently and founded a drama school.

Over the course of his career Goldfaden wrote numerous plays, frequently composing the music for them as well. The great popularity of the plays and operettas is illustrated by the number of characters he created that became eponyms in Yiddish, such as *shmendrik*, a fool (from the play *Shmendrik*); *kuni leml*, a simpleton (from *Di Tsvey Kuni Lemls*); and *bobe yakhne*, a gossip or busybody. These characters became "real" to several generations of theatergoers. He also popularized many Yiddish folk songs, such as the now classic lullaby "Rozhinkes mit Mandlen" (literally "Raisins with Almonds"), which he included in his operetta *Shulamis* (1880). *Shmendrik* (1877) and *Der Fanatik oder de Tsvey Kuni Lemels* (1880), both satirical comedies, are among his most popular plays. They were both adapted for performance in Israel in the mid-1960s and *Tsvey Kuni Lemels* was made into a film there with an English title of *The Flying Matchmaker*. Goldfaden died on January 9, 1908, in New York City.

GOODMAN, BENNY (1909–1986)

Musician

Benny Goodman, "the King of Swing," was a major force in the development and popularization of big-band jazz in the 1930s and arguably the best clarinetist in the history of jazz. Goodman was an unrelenting perfectionist, often prickly and tight-fisted. But he was also a consummate musician and, in a small but significant way, a pioneer in the music as well.

Benjamin David Goodman was born in Chicago to poor Jewish immigrants, the ninth of twelve children of David and Dora Goodman. Although David was a tailor he saw music as a way for his children to escape poverty, so he put together a band utilizing several of his sons that played at local synagogues. Benny shone on clarinet almost immediately and began taking private lessons. This was the great era of jazz in Chicago, and the young Goodman fell in with the group of musicians who congregated around Austin High—Bix Beiderbecke, Frankie Teschemacher, Eddie Condon, and Jimmy McPartland. By his mid-teens, Goodman was playing professionally and signed with Ben Pollack's band in 1925. After his stint with Pollack he returned to freelancing with mixed success. Then came his first big breakthrough, discovery by John Hammond, the brilliant young producer who would help guide Goodman's career for many years to come.

Gradually, Goodman put together what would eventually become one of the most gifted of big bands, with Teddy Wilson, Lionel Hampton, Gene Krupa, Harry James, Ziggy Elman, and Bunny Berigan among its brilliant alumni, and Fletcher Henderson as one of its key arrangers. By adding Wilson and Hampton, Goodman became one of the first white leaders to breach the color barrier, which in the mid-1930s was a formidable achievement. After a rocky start, the band caught the public imagination in 1935 and began a string of hits that extended to the end of the decade. At the same time, Goodman put together a no-less-talented series of small groups, built around himself, Wilson, Hampton, Krupa and the brilliant young electric guitarist Charlie Christian. With the waning of the big-band era and the rise of bebop, Goodman, who certainly could have resisted the more radical new jazz, began an earnest experiment with a bop-oriented group. After he broke up that band in 1949, he dropped out of the jazz scene except for occasional engagements (most memorably a State Department tour of the Soviet Union in 1962).

Goodman's virtuosity on his instrument was such that he was equally at home playing classical music as well as jazz. This ambitious agenda expressed itself not only in Carnegie Hall concerts that Hammond put together for Goodman but also in Goodman's frequent performances of the clarinet repertoire with classical orchestras, and his commissioning of new pieces from contemporary composers. Even after he ceased to play in public regularly, Goodman's dedication to his instrument didn't wane; he played scales and exercises every morning before breakfast and when he died of a heart attack on June 13, 1986, it was while practicing Mozart.

GRANT, LEE (1931–)

Actor

A highly talented actor who battled and eventually overcame blacklisting, Lee Grant (Lyova Rosenthal) was born in New York City. Encouraged by her mother, an actor and model from Russia, she made her debut as a child with the Metropolitan Opera and later studied acting at Louise Lewisohn's Neighbor-

hood Playhouse. Her first professional role was as Celeste Holm's understudy in *Oklahoma!* Her Broadway debut was in *Joy to the World* (1948). The following year she joined the legendary Actors Studio and made her mark in the Broadway play *Detective Story* as a disturbed young woman caught shoplifting. She repeated the role in the film version in 1951 and a stellar career was predicted for the intense young actor when she was put on the Hollywood blacklist. Her "crime" was being married to Arnold Manoff, who was suspected of Communist connections by the House Un-American Activities Committee.

For the next decade, Grant made occasional stage appearances and reared a family. In the mid-1960s, she finally overcame the blacklisting and began working in both television and film. Among her important film appearances are *In the Heat of the Night* (1967), *Portnoy's Complaint* (1972), *Shampoo* (1975), for which she won an Academy Award, and *Voyage of the Damned* (1976). In that last film, she played one of a group of Jews that the Nazis sent by ship to Cuba in 1939. She has also made a number of television movies, including *Backstairs at the White House* (1979) and *Will There Really Be a Morning?* (1983), in which she played the mother of film star Frances Farmer. She has won two Emmy Awards for her television performances and is the mother of actor Dinah Manoff.

HAMMERSTEIN, OSCAR II (1895–1960)

Lyricist, librettist

The wordsmith half of the most important musical comedy-writing team in the history of American theater, Oscar (Greeley Glendenning) Hammerstein II was born in New York City on July 12, 1895, into a theatrical family. His grandfather, for whom he was named, was a theater owner and librettist, and his uncle was a producer. Hammerstein first worked with his future partner, **Richard Rodgers**, when they were in college together at Columbia. Then, while Rodgers collaborated with lyricist **Lorenz Hart**, Hammerstein found a mentor in writer Otto Harbach. They wrote lyrics and librettos for a number of musicals, including

Rose-Marie (1924) and *Sunny* (1925), working with several different composers, including **Jerome Kern**. Also with Kern, Hammerstein wrote *Show Boat* (1927), a landmark musical based on **Edna Ferber**'s novel, and *Sweet Adeline* (1929). He wrote the operetta *The New Moon* (1928) with composer **Sigmund Romberg**.

In 1943 Hammerstein teamed up with his old college friend, and the team of Rodgers and Hammerstein began writing some of the most famous and important musicals ever created. *Oklahoma!* was so innovative that it instantly made almost everything that had been produced to that time seem old fashioned. The team also wrote *Carousel* (1945), *South Pacific* (1949), *The King and I* (1951), and *The Sound of Music* (1959), along with four other successful, but less celebrated, shows. On his own, Hammerstein wrote *Carmen Jones* (1943), a re-telling of the Bizet opera in terms of Black America. He and Rodgers also produced many of their own and other's musicals. He died in Doylestown, Pennsylvania, on August 23, 1960.

HART, LORENZ (1895–1943)

Lyricist, librettist

Witty, sardonic lyricist Lorenz Hart was born in New York and attended Columbia University, where he met and worked with composer **Richard Rodgers**. After graduation the two continued to collaborate, selling a song to Lew Fields for his show *A Lonely Romeo* (1919) and following it up with interpolated songs for a number of other shows. For a time they worked with librettist Herbert Fields on such shows as *Dearest Enemy* (1925), *A Connecticut Yankee* (1927), and *Present Arms* (1928).

After a short time working in Hollywood, the two returned to Broadway, collaborating with a variety of librettists and co-librettists. Their string of hits included *I'd Rather Be Right* (1937), *The Boys from Syracuse* (1938), and *Pal Joey* (1940). Their hundreds of memorable songs include "The Lady is a Tramp," "My Funny Valentine," "This Can't Be Love," and "Bewitched." Personal problems, including alcoholism, cut short Hart's career and his life.

HART, MOSS (1904–1961)

Playwright

If not for his delightful memoir of growing up as a nice Jewish boy in poverty in the Bronx, *Act One* (1959), Moss Hart might have been remembered mainly as the junior partner in the playwrighting "firm" of Kaufman and Hart. Hart began his career in the theater as the social director for Jewish hotels in the Catskills. He was a nervy kid, though, and with the Depression just beginning, he took a draft of his first play, *Once in a Lifetime*, to **George S. Kaufman**, already a highly successful playwright and director, a member of the fabled Algonquin Round Table. Whether it was Hart's boyish brashness or something Kaufman sensed in the play, the older man was taken with him and the two set out to rewrite the script. The play opened on September 24, 1930, and the two playwrights had a hit, the first of many.

By the time they worked on their next play, Moss Hart was a self-assured young man willing to work on his own as well as with his famous partner. As a result, their collaboration became one of equals and close friends. *Merrily We Roll Along* (1934), their next offering, was a hit, too. It was followed by *You Can't Take It With You*, which won the Pulitzer Prize for Drama in 1936, and the musical *I'd Rather Be Right* (1937) (with a score by another pair of seemingly mismatched young Jewish men, **Richard Rodgers** and **Lorenz Hart** [no relation]). Hart also wrote on his own several musical comedies, including *Face the Music* (1932) and *As Thousands Cheer*, with music by **Irving Berlin**.

With storm clouds gathering over Europe, the two writers embarked on a series of somewhat more serious pieces: *Sing Out the New, The Fabulous Invalid* (1938), and *The American Way* (1939), about the immigrant experience in which they both must have drawn on family memories. Neither was a major success, but their next play, *The Man Who Came to Dinner* (1939), with its hilarious kidding of their good friend Alexander Woollcott, was a huge hit and is a perennial on the summer stock circuit. The pair would write one more play together, *George Washington Slept Here* (1940).

Hart continued to work on Broadway as a writer (he was responsible for the book for the innovative Weill-Gershwin musical *Lady in the Dark*) and director, guiding, among others, *My Fair Lady*, to theatrical success. Hart also wrote scripts for motion pictures, including Hollywood's landmark film on anti-Semitism, *Gentlemen's Agreement*, which won the 1947 Academy Award for best picture of the year. He and Kaufman were neighbors and close friends in Bucks County, Pennsylvania, and died within a few months of one another.

HEIFETZ, JASCHA (1901–1987)

Violinist

Jascha Heifetz was born on February 2, 1901, in Vilna, Lithuania, when it was still a part of the Russian Empire. He began playing the violin at the age of three, had his first public performance when he was only about six, and entered the St. Petersburg Conservatory when he was about nine. In 1912 he was asked to play with the Berlin Philharmonic Orchestra. A year later he was touring Europe. In 1917 he escaped the Russian Revolution, immigrated to America and debuted at Carnegie Hall. He became a citizen eight years later. A master of the violin, he was known for the restraint of his interpretations, his pure tone, and his technical ability. He toured frequently in Europe, Australia, Asia, and the Middle East. He played in Israel many times, the first in 1925, when he donated his fees to help further the development of music in Tel Aviv. In 1934, he returned to Russia to great acclaim. In 1962, he began teaching at the University of Southern California, Los Angeles. In 1975, the University created the Heifetz Chair in Music. He died on December 10, 1987, in Los Angeles.

HELBURN, THERESA (1887–1959)

Theatrical producer

It is difficult to estimate the tremendous impact made on American theater by the Theatre Guild, which *The Oxford Companion to American Theatre* calls: "The most exciting and responsible producing organization of the 1920s and 1930s." Its executive director, Theresa Helburn, was born in New York and developed an interest in theater while she was studying at Bryn Mawr. After continued studies at Radcliffe and the Sorbonne and a brief stint as an actor and a drama critic, she joined the Theatre Guild organization. She soon became its executive director and remained in that position for the rest of her career. In its early years, the Guild produced important British and European plays, such as Shaw's *Heartbreak House* and Čapek's *R.U.R.*. In 1923, however, with the production of Jewish playwright **Elmer Rice**'s *The Adding Machine*, the group began to support the presentation of important American plays. Under Helburn's management the Guild was responsible for much of the success of such playwrights as Eugene O'Neill, Philip Barry, and Maxwell Anderson. Helburn was primarily responsible for play selection, casting, and play doctoring. One of the few women in producing roles at that time, she was also in charge of Guild policy and decision making.

In the mid-1930s, there were problems within the organization that led to a split. Harold Clurman, Cheryl Crawford, and **Lee Strasberg** left to form the Group Theatre. Elmer Rice, Maxwell Anderson, and others founded The Playwrights Company. Theresa Helburn, however, remained at the Guild. For the next few years, although the company continued to produce important work, it struggled financially. Then, in 1943, Helburn produced *Oklahoma!*, revolutionizing musical comedy and saving the Guild. She remained active in the organization until 1953. Along with Cheryl Crawford and Eva Le Gallienne, she proved that women could be successful theatrical producers.

HERSCHMAN, MORDECHAI (1888–1940)

Cantor

Mordechai Herschman was born in Chernigov, Ukraine, in 1888. He started his singing career in synagogue choirs. In 1913 he secured his first post as a *haz-*

zan—for the synagogue of Zhitomir. Five months later he became the chief *hazzan* in Vilna, Lithuania. In 1920 he immigrated to the United States and became the *hazzan* of the Beth El Temple in Brooklyn. After ten years at Beth El he began to perform in concert. For the next ten years he toured Europe, Palestine, and the United States. A lyric tenor, he was known for the warmth of his interpretations. His recordings of both cantorial music and folk songs were extremely popular. Many consider his most famous recording to be "Ve-Hayyah be Aharit ha-Yamim" (And it shall come to pass at the End of Days), written by P. Jassinowsky.

HIRSCH, JUDD (1935–)

Actor

Actor Judd Hirsch has built a career on being able to communicate a sense of sanity and sympathy. Born in New York City, he began his career on the stage, but his first professional acting role did not come until he was in his late twenties and then it was in a stock company in Colorado. For another twelve years, he played largely minor roles until, in 1974, he was cast as a sane and sympathetic public defender in the television movie *The Law*. Two years later, he became Sergeant Dominick Delvecchio in the police drama "Delvecchio" (1976–77). In the next few years, he became one of the few contemporary American actors to warrant entries in references on television, film, and stage. In 1978, he starred in the **Neil Simon** play *Chapter Two*. He left his role in that hit to become Alex Rieger on "Taxi" (1978–83), a role for which he won popular and critical acclaim and two Emmy Awards. During breaks from filming that role, he scored a success on Broadway as the Jewish suitor of a Southern belle in *Talley's Folly* (1980), for which he won a Tony nomination He also played the psychiatrist in *Ordinary People* (1980), for which he received an Academy Award nomination.

Hirsch continued his work in all three media through the 1980s and early 1990s, starring in the television series "Dear John" (1988–92) and appearing in such films as *Teachers* (1984) and *Running on*

Empty (1988) and on stage in *I'm Not Rappaport* (1985) and *Conversations with My Father*, both of which won him Tony Awards for Best Actor. In 1996, he stole the show as a cranky Jewish father in the blockbuster film *Independence Day* and in 1997 returned to television for his third successful series, co-starring with Bob Newhart in "George and Leo."

HOROWITZ, VLADIMIR (1903–1989)

Pianist

Virtuoso pianist Vladimir Horowitz was born in Berdichev, Russia (now Ukraine) on October 1, 1903, and began attending the Kiev Conservatory at the age of twelve. Initially more interested in composing than in performing, he did not make his concert debut until he was nineteen. Already respected in the Soviet Union, in 1923 he became even more prominent when he played twenty-three recitals in a series without repeating a single piece of music. He then went on to successfully tour Europe and the United States. In 1940 he immigrated to the United States and became a citizen four years later. In 1953 Horowitz retired from the concert stage and did not reappear for twelve years, though he still made records. His rare live concerts became sought-after events. In 1982 he did a full tour of Europe; in 1986 he performed two concerts in the Soviet Union; and in 1987 (his final tour) he performed a series of recitals in Europe.

Respected for his technical brilliance and tonal quality, Horowitz was best known for his flawless interpretations of Romantic composers such as Liszt, Rachmaninoff, Chopin, and Prokofiev. He died In New York City on November 5, 1989. Married to Arturo Toscanini's daughter Wanda, he was buried in their family plot in Milan, Italy.

HOUDINI, HARRY (1874–1926)

Magician, escape artist

His stage name became synonymous with dazzling feats; he has been called the greatest showmen of all time. Harry Houdini enjoyed an unusual career for the son of an Orthodox rabbi.

Born Erich Weiss, he grew up in Appleton, Wisconsin, where his father led a small congregation. He began his performing career as a trapeze artist, but he turned to magic and took the name Houdini after Jean Eugène Robert-Houdin, a nineteenth-century French magician.

In 1899 Houdini hit upon the performance that would make him one of the most famous men of his time—his "challenge" act. He bragged that he could escape from any restraints imposed on him. He defied handcuffs and manacles of every sort, straitjackets, jail cells, sealed police vans, and (his most sensational performance) an airtight tank filled with water.

He honed his public performances for the remaining twenty-seven years of his life and also starred in silent films. The author of a number of books on magic and illusion, he also campaigned vigorously against fraudulent mediums, mind readers, and, indeed, any performers who claimed supernatural powers. In 1920 he published an expose on these "frauds" entitled *Miracle Mongers and Their Methods*. He also was active in charity work, particularly with an organization he helped found, the Rabbis' Sons Theatrical Benevolent Association. He died in Detroit, Michigan, on October 31, 1926, from peritonitis, which was the result of a ruptured appendix. He performed up to a few days before his death.

HOUSEMAN, JOHN (1902–1988)

Actor, director, producer

Born in Romania and educated in England, John Houseman (Jacques Haussman) began his theatrical career in the United States as director of **Gertrude Stein's** *Four Saints in Three Acts* (1934). After a number of other prestigious projects, including a production of *Hamlet* starring Jewish actor **Leslie Howard**, he was chosen as co-head of the Negro wing of the Federal Theatre Project with African American actor Rose McClendon. Beginning in 1937, he worked with Orson Welles at the Mercury Theatre, doing groundbreaking

theater, such as an African American version of *Macbeth* and a modern-dress version of *Hamlet*.

He continued to direct in New York, usually on Broadway, for the next two decades, except during World War II. In 1956 he became artistic director of the American Shakespeare Festival in Connecticut, where he remained for three years. He left to become artistic director of the Theatre Group at the University of California, continuing in that position until 1964, when he left to become drama director of Juilliard.

In 1972 Houseman and Margot Henley founded the Acting Company, a training ground for young performers, and then Houseman's career took an unexpected turn. He accepted the role of an ironically severe law professor in the film *The Paper Chase* (1974) and received an Academy Award for his performance. The movie launched Houseman on a highly successful film and TV career. He made over thirty appearances in the five years between 1975 and his death in 1988.

HUROK, SOL (1888–1974)

Impresario

When a young Jewish boy from a small Russian town arrived in New York City in 1906 with three rubles in his pocket, he probably never dreamed that he would become one of the most prominent promoters of classical music that New York would ever see. But Sol Hurok's humble beginnings as an organizer of concerts to benefit labor organizations led to a career that was much his own invention. Hurok's big breakthrough came when he booked Efrem Zimbalist, a world-famous violinist, to play a benefit for the Socialist Party.

Hurok became a United States citizen in 1914 and within two years he was booking major acts into the Hippodrome, one of the largest theaters in the city. Eventually, he expanded his purview to include not only classical musicians, but also theater companies and the ballet. He brought the Habimah Theater from Palestine to New York for their first American tour (1926), as well as the Bolshoi, Kirov, and

Sadlers' Wells ballet troupes, and the Moscow Art Players. The words "S. Hurok Presents" became synonymous with international stardom—over the years, Hurok "presented" Maria Callas, Isadora Duncan, **Isaac Stern**, and Pavlova. He is credited with discovering Marian Anderson. He also exported as many American acts abroad as he brought famous performers here. His autobiography, as told to Ruth Goode, *Impresario*, was published in 1946. He brought the account of his successes up to date in 1953 with *S. Hurok Presents: A Memoir of the Dance World*. He sponsored the Sadler's Wells Ballet on NBC-TV in December 1955 in *Sleeping Beauty*. The show was seen by 37 million people.

The *New York Times* once wrote that Hurok "...has done more for music in America than the invention of the phonograph." He remained active until his death in New York City on March 5, 1974.

KALICH, BERTHA (1874–1939)

Actress

Bertha Kalich was one of the rare stars of the American Yiddish theater to make the leap from Second Avenue to Broadway. She had enjoyed some success as an ingenue in operetta in Eastern Europe, but quickly realized that anti-Semitism created barriers to her career advancement. With her husband, producer Leonard Spachner, she immigrated to the United States in 1894. Within a year she was starring in Yiddish-language productions of operettas, then graduated quickly to dramatic roles. Her work attracted the attention of Harrison Grey Fiske and other Broadway producers, and she took her talents uptown to considerable acclaim, particularly as the female lead in a 1906 production of *The Kreutzer Sonata*, a role that was one of her most famous efforts. Kalich's career was cut short by an illness that left her almost completely blind. Although a series of operations restored her eyesight, she was severely weakened and limited her appearances over the last decade of her life to the occasional benefit performance.

Who could help but believe in a face like that? Bertha Kalich was called the "Jewish Bernhardt" by critics. Toward the end of her career, she estimated that she had played some 125 roles in seven languages. We do not know about the other five, but she was an enormous success in both Yiddish and English. (Courtesy of American Jewish Historical Society, Waltham, Massachusetts, and New York, New York)

KERN, JEROME (1885–1945)

Composer

Sometimes called the "father of the American musical," Jerome David Kern was encouraged in his early musical studies by his mother, a Jewish American of Bohemian descent. He sold his first "interpolated songs" to Lew Fields when he was only eighteen years old and began to develop a reputation a year later when he wrote half the score for the show *Mr. Wix of Wick-ham* (1904). For about a decade, Kern then wrote music in the American style for shows imported from England, traveling back and forth between the two countries and marrying a Englishwoman.

In 1914 Kern teamed with Guy Bolton to write *Ninety in the Shade*, an unsuccessful show that started a very successful collaboration. Kern and Bolton were joined in 1917 by P. G. Wodehouse and wrote a series of small musicals for the Princess Theatre. Light, liter-ate, and witty, these shows were critical and popular triumphs. Kern's specialty, during this time, was the dance song. He also, almost singlehandedly, shifted the emphasis in American popular music from the waltz to the ballad.

Kern participated in the creation of an American classic when he teamed with **Oscar Hammerstein II** to write *Show Boat* (1927), based on **Edna Ferber**'s novel. *The Oxford Companion to American Theatre* calls the show ". . . the first successful, totally American op-eretta." It featured such legendary songs as "Make Be-lieve," "Ol' Man River," and "Can't Help Lovin' Dat Man." The team followed up their achievement with *Sweet Adeline* (1929). After three more shows, with Otto Harbach and with Hammerstein, Kern went to Holly-wood for six years. A few years after he returned to New York, while he was getting ready to write the score for *Annie Get Your Gun*, Kern died at the age of sixty.

KIDD, MICHAEL (1917–)

Choreographer, director

Born Milton Gruenwald on August 12, 1917, Michael Kidd became one of Broadway's most important choreographers and a revolutionary film choreogra-pher. Initially a dancer, then a choreographer with the legendary American Ballet Theater, Kidd quickly moved into the world of musical theater where he choreographed some of Broadway's classic musicals. He has won five Tony Awards for choreography for his work on *Finian's Rainbow* (1947), *Guys and Dolls* (1950), *Can-Can* (1953), *Li'l Abner* (1956), and *Destry Rides Again* (1959).

Kidd's influence in Hollywood is even more far-reaching. Choreographing some of Hollywood's most striking dance sequences, Kidd brought a new and dif-ferent energy to movie dancing. Incorporating folk, ballet, and modern dance forms, his choreography had an exuberance and sophistication that was new to Hollywood. Two of his classic choreographic efforts are *The Band Wagon* (1953) and *Seven Brides for Seven Brothers* (1954).

Kidd brought professional dancers into some of his films. An example is Jacques d'Amboise, a dancer with George Balanchine's New York City Ballet, who ap-peared as one of the seven brothers in *Seven Brides*. Most recently, he choreographed Janet Jackson's music video "When I Think of You" and the Sixtieth Academy Awards. In 1997 he was given an honorary lifetime achievement Academy Award for his choreography.

KIRSTEIN, LINCOLN (1907–1996)

Ballet producer

Born into a wealthy family on May 4, 1907, in Rochester, New York, Lincoln Kirstein became one of the most important figures in American dance. Dur-ing the late twenties and early thirties he attended Harvard University. While there he created the literary magazine *Hound and Horn*. Among the magazine's most famous contributors were T. S. Eliot, Ezra Pound, and e. e. cummings. In 1933 he convinced choreographer George Balanchine to leave the Ballets Russes and come to the United States. They remained collaborators until Balanchine's death in 1983.

In 1934 Balanchine and Kirstein created the School of American Ballet. They also founded the Ballet Cara-van (1936) and Ballet Society (1946). These compa-nies, though short-lived, were the precursors to the duo's ultimate achievement, the New York City Ballet, founded in 1948. Kirstein was its general director until 1989.

In addition to founding and running ballet compa-nies, Kirstein wrote librettos for several ballets, includ-ing *Billy the Kid* and *Transcendence*. From 1942 through 1948 he edited *Dance Index*. His books include *Dance* (1935), *The Classic Ballet* (1952), *Movement and Metaphor* (1970), *Nijinsky Dancing* (1975), and *Thirty Years with the New York City Ballet* (1978). He died on January 5, 1996, in New York City.

KOUSSEVITSKY, SERGE (1874–1951)

Conductor

Conductor Serge Koussevitsky was born on July 26, 1874, in Vyshny Volochyok, Russia. He began his career by playing the double bass and gave concerts of his own compositions including *Double Bass Concerto* (1905). He made his conducting debut in 1908 in Berlin and a year later formed his own orchestra in Moscow. At the same time he founded his own music publishing firm. With the firm, he began the championing of new music that would become the hallmark of his career in the United States.

In 1920 Koussevitsky left Russia and his position as the director of the State Symphony Orchestra in Petrograd, a position he had held since the Revolution. In 1924, after several years in Paris, he came to America and took over the baton at the Boston Symphony Orchestra. He remained there until 1949. Among the many new composers he introduced were **Aaron Copland**, Maurice Ravel, **George Gershwin**, and Igor Stravinsky.

He was also an important mentor to a new generation of American conductors including **Leonard Bernstein** and Lukas Foss. In addition to his duties at the Boston Symphony, he directed the Berkshire Music Festival for many years. In 1940 he created the Berkshire Music Center and in 1942, the Koussevitsky Foundation, which commissioned and performed new music. He died on June 4, 1951, in Boston, Massachusetts.

KUSHNER, TONY (1956–)

Playwright

When Tony Kushner's *Angels in America* hit the stage in 1993, it reverberated through the theater commu-

nity. The first half, *Millennium Approaches*, won the Pulitzer Prize for Drama even before it reached New York. The second half, *Perestroika*, was one of the most anticipated plays in recent years.

Kushner was a born into an intellectual, politically active Jewish family. His theater career began slowly. When he began to write his magnum opus, he had seen only one of his plays produced, and it was not favorably received. Supported by a grant from the National Endowment for the Arts, he began working on what he thought would be a two-and-a-half hour play with songs. What he produced was what has been called ". . . a seven-hour gay fantasia on national motifs." The work is saturated with Jewish issues and motifs. Two of the characters are based on Jewish historical figures, Roy Cohn and Ethel Rosenberg. The main character is Jewish, Hebrew letters form part of the stage design, and the immigrant European experience is part of the backdrop for the action.

It remains to be seen whether Kushner will develop into a major American playwright, but there is no doubt that he and his play will remain a part of theatrical history.

LANG, PEARL (1921–)

Dancer, choreographer

Modern dancer and choreographer Pearl Lang (originally Lack) was born in Chicago, Illinois, on May 29, 1921. Her parents were both Russian Jewish immigrants who were active in Chicago's Jewish cultural societies. She attended both public school and the Workman's Circle, a Yiddish school.

In 1941 Lang moved to New York to study with Martha Graham, soon becoming a member of the company. She debuted in *Letter to the World* and performed in *Punch and Judy*, *Deaths and Entrances*, and *Appalachian Spring*. She later began to take over many of Graham's own roles in dances such as *Primitive Mysteries*, *Herodiade*, *Night Journey*, and *Clytemnestra*. She continued to dance with the company through 1978. In addition to dancing with Graham's company,

Lang also worked as a dancer and actress on Broadway, appearing in *Carousel*, *Finian's Rainbow*, and *Peer Gynt*, among many others. In 1958 Lang formed her own dance company. Most of her choreography explored Jewish stories and themes. She created over fifty works including *The Dybbuk*, *Tongues of Fire*, *Kaddish*, *Two Poems of the Holocaust*, and perhaps her most famous piece, *Shira*.

LANGNER, LAWRENCE (1890–1962)

Producer, playwright

One of the guiding lights of American theater, Lawrence Langner was born in Wales and worked in London before coming to the United States. Only twenty-four, he was one of the founders of the Washington Square Players in 1914. Langner and the other founders were all members of the Liberal Club, a gathering of intellectuals, and the theater they founded reflected the interests and tastes one would expect of such a group. They produced Maeterlinck, Shaw, and Chekhov, but they also did some of the first short works by Eugene O'Neill and **Elmer Rice**. The Players helped launch the careers of several fine actors, including Katharine Cornell.

Shortly after the group disbanded in 1918, Langner and some other members founded the Theater Guild. They were soon joined by **Theresa Helburn**, and together Helburn and Langner ran the Guild during its most successful years. Artistically the most important producing organization of the 1920s and 1930s, the Guild began doing primarily European plays, then helped to introduce several major American playwrights. Their work was so respected that Broadway stars often performed at a reduced salary in order to participate in their meaningful artistic endeavors.

Langner was also founder of the Westport Country Playhouse and the American Shakespeare Festival, both in Connecticut. He wrote several plays, some of which were co-written with his wife, Armina Marshall. The most notable of these was *The Pursuit of Happiness* (1933), which ran for more than 250 performances and inspired the 1950 musical *Arms and the Girl*.

LAVIN, LINDA (1937–)

Actor

Linda Lavin was born in Portland, Maine, on October 15, 1937, to parents who were active in their local Jewish community. She attended the College of William and Mary and then moved to New York. She made her name on Broadway in Charles Strouse's *It's a Bird, It's a Plane, It's Superman* (1966). However, she decided that perhaps musical theater was not for her. She turned to drama and found lasting success acting in plays such as *Little Murders* and *Last of the Red Hot Lovers*.

In 1976 she made the transition to television and began playing her best-known role, Alice in the television show of the same name. The show stayed on the air until 1985. She won Golden Globe Awards for Best Actress in 1979 and 1980 for the show. After the end of "Alice," Lavin returned to Broadway and has appeared in numerous productions including *Gypsy*, *Broadway Bound* (for which she won a Tony), *The Sisters Rosensweig*, *Death Defying Acts*, and *The Diary of Anne Frank*.

LERNER, ALAN JAY (1918–1986)

Lyricist, librettist

The man who wrote such classics as "Almost Like Being in Love" and "I've Grown Accustomed to Her Face" was born into a wealthy Jewish family in New York. After teaming with composer Frederick Loewe, Lerner participated in the creation of two interesting but not commercially successful shows before writing the book and lyrics to *Brigadoon* (1947). The romantic musical about a Scottish town that appears for only one day every century established the pair's reputation. Lerner and Loewe went on to write *Paint Your Wagon* (1951) and their two hugely successful shows, *My Fair Lady* (1956), based on George Bernard Shaw's *Pygmalion*, and *Camelot* (1960), a retelling of the legend of King Arthur and Queen Guinevere. In 1951 he won an Academy Award for his screenplay of *An*

American in Paris. Later, he and Loewe won an Oscar for the motion-picture musical *Gigi*, in 1958. After Frederick Loewe retired, Lerner wrote with composers Burton Lane, **André Previn**, **Leonard Bernstein**, and Charles Strouse.

LEVINE, JAMES (1943–)

Pianist, conductor

James Levine was born in Cincinnati, Ohio, on June 23, 1943. A child prodigy on the piano, he made his professional debut with the Cincinnati Orchestra when he was ten. He later studied piano and conducting at the Juilliard School of Music. When he was twenty-two, he became **George Szell**'s assistant conductor at the Cleveland Symphony Orchestra, staying there until 1970. In 1971 he made his debut at the Metropolitan Opera, conducting *Tosca.* Two years later, he became the Met's principal conductor, and in 1975, its musical director. In 1986, he rose to the position of artistic director. He is credited with raising the quality of operas at the Met during his tenure. He has also served as the musical director of the Chicago Symphony Orchestra's performances at the Ravinia Festival (summers, 1973–93) and has made numerous recordings of both operas and symphonies. He continues to give piano recitals.

MASLOW, SOPHIE (1910?–)

Dancer, choreographer, political activist

Dancer and choreographer Sophie Maslow was born to a Russian Jewish family and was exposed early to revolutionary politics and working class consciousness. She received her dance training at the legendary Neighborhood Playhouse and became a member of the Martha Graham Company, where she remained from 1931 to 1940. She appeared in a number of Graham's most memorable productions, including *Primitive Mysteries* (1931) and *Letter to the World* (1940). Although she insisted that her work was not politi-

cally motivated, she was always involved in the workers' movement, teaching dance classes for International Ladies Garment Union members and participating in Worker's Dance League concerts. Also, because her work was often based on Russian folk traditions, she received a great deal of attention from a leftist press that was passionately interested in all things Russian. *Folksay*, which is based on Carl Sandburg's *The People, Yes*, and contains ballads by Woody Guthrie, is usually considered Maslow's first masterpiece of choreography. Her second, a response to the destruction of so much that was Jewish in World War II, was based on the writings of **Sholem Aleichem** and entitled *The Village I Knew.* It premiered at the American Dance Festival in 1950 and has been restaged numerous times around the world. Maslow worked with Jane Dudley and Bill Bales in the New Dance Group (NDG) and later formed the Sophie Maslow Dance Company, choreographing around Jewish themes.

MENKEN, ADAH ISAACS (1835–1868)

Actress, poet

Adah Isaacs Menken was a figure of scandal and a subject of adoration. In an era in which women were supposed to be decorous and silent, she was boisterous and often underdressed. If her greatest stage triumph depended on the illusion of nudity, that did not discomfit her—it merely added to her allure.

Little is known of Menken's origins, a situation that was created in part by her own talents for myth-making. She claimed at various times to be an Irishwoman, an octoroon (a dangerous assertion in the era before the Civil War), or the daughter of a Portuguese rabbi. What is known, with a minimal degree of certainty, is that she was born around 1835 in the vicinity of New Orleans.

Whatever her roots, she was smart and undeniably attractive to men. By the time she was eighteen she had been squired to Havana as the mistress of a wealthy man (purportedly an Austrian nobleman). There, she asserted, she had earned a living as an actress and dancer. At twenty she was back in the States looking for stage work. In Texas she found, instead, a husband. Alexander Isaac Menken (she added the "s" to Isaac for reasons known only to herself) was a son of prosperous Jewish merchants from Cincinnati. The couple moved back to the family home, where Adah wrote and published poetry and essays, often for the *American Israelite*. It is not known whether Menken was born a Jew or converted when she married, but her fervor for Jewish causes was genuine and vocal. She studied Hebrew and Torah and often wrote on Jewish themes.

Restless and in pursuit of a renewed theatrical career, Menken went back to New Orleans, her husband in tow. She traveled in heady literary circles, numbering among her friends Walt Whitman, Algernon Swinburne, Charles Dickens, and George Sand. Wearied by her outrageous behavior, her husband returned to Cincinnati and secured a rabbinical divorce. Incorrectly believing herself to be single, Menken now married husband number two, the prizefighter John Heenan. The ensuing scandal, compounded by her pregnancy, made it nearly impossible for her to get work. She suffered a miscarriage, then divorced both her putative husbands. Luckily, a theater director who had seen her vaudeville act suggested she try her hand at the role of Mazeppa, drawn from the epic poem by Lord Byron.

As Mazeppa, Menken was clad only in a flesh-colored body stocking that made it look as if she were naked and tied to a horse that raced around the theater in a frenzy. Needless to say, she was a smashing success, and, for the four years beginning in 1861, she toured the United States in the role to packed houses (mostly male, one would presume). She then took the piece to England, where it was an even bigger hit. She spent her earnings freely and when she became pregnant—again in a marriage of doubtful provenance, this time to a fortune-hunter named Barkely—she went to Paris where she gave birth to her only child, a son. There, she enjoyed another great success, in *Les Pirates de la savane*, another adventure marked by its heroine's scanty clothing. Overwork took its toll on her;

she collapsed during a rehearsal for her next play and died shortly thereafter.

MENUHIN, YEHUDI (1916–1999)

Violinist

Violinist Yehudi Menuhin was born in New York City on April 22, 1916, but grew up in San Francisco. The son of Jewish immigrants from Palestine, he began playing the violin at age four. When he was only seven, he became well known in the San Francisco area for brilliantly performing Mendelssohn's *Violin Concerto*. He studied under George Enesco in Paris and by the time he was seventeen had toured much of Europe and the United States. He spent World War II playing for the Allied troops and was the first soloist to play in Paris after it was liberated. In 1959 he immigrated to England. Four years later, he founded a school for musically gifted children. He created and ran the Gstaad Music Festival in Switzerland in 1957 and the Bath Music Festival (England, 1959–1968).

Known as a virtuoso because of his technical ability and exquisite interpretations, Menuhin also played rarely performed work and new music. Sitarist and composer Ravi Shankar wrote the piece *Prabhati* for him. He also commissioned pieces such as *Sonata for Solo Violin* by Béla Bartók. He continued to tour all over the world, including to Israel, where he performed several times. In 1970 he received the Jawaharlal Nehru Prize for International Understanding. In 1985 Menuhin became a British citizen and was knighted. (He had been granted the knighthood in 1965, but had to wait until he became a citizen to receive it.) Menuhin often performed in concerts with his pianist younger sisters Hephzibah and Yalta. He died in Berlin on March 12, 1999.

MONK, MEREDITH (1942–)

Performance Artist

A performance artist before the term was coined, Meredith Monk was born in Lima, Peru, on November

20, 1942, to American parents. She grew up in Connecticut and attended Sarah Lawrence College, where she first studied music, then added modern dance. She graduated in 1964 and moved to New York. She created her first group in 1968, the House Foundation for the Arts. Their first piece was *Juice* (1969), performed in three sections, at three different sites. *Juice* incorporated dance, music, acting, and televised scenes. Her other work includes the operas *Vessel* (1971), *The Education of the Girlchild* (1972), and *Quarry* (1976), *Ellis Island* for piano (1983, performed on Ellis Island), a film, *Book of Days* (1989), and *American Archeology No. 1: Roosevelt Island* (1994, performed on Roosevelt Island). Self-described as "Inca Jewish," many of Monk's pieces use Jewish imagery and history. Choreographer, composer, librettist, and performer, she has used all her talents to broaden the concept of performance.

MUSIC

Jewish Americans have made enormous contributions to all types of music. They have been remarkable performers of classical European compositions and groundbreaking composers in the uniquely American musical styles.

American music itself can be defined as music in any of the genres—classical, jazz, rock 'n roll—that happens to be composed or performed by American citizens. On the other hand, it can be viewed as that which is uniquely American in style and form. Using the latter definition, American musical composition often reveals the best possibilities of American culture. In all its categories, American music often reflects the mix of cultures that is claimed, usually falsely, for other aspects of American life.

Among the reasons for the unusually large influence of Jews in the American music world are the twin threads of education and music that run through Jewish tradition. Judaism itself, whether looked at from a secular or a religious perspective, is steeped in music. The Jewish musicians who emigrated to the United States from Europe at the turn of the century and during the Nazi era were among the best and most talented artists the continent had to offer. They gave this country, for the first time, music on a par with any in Europe, bringing with them training, virtuosity, and high standards. They then educated future generations. All American musical styles benefited from this healthy injection of musical expertise.

CLASSICAL MUSIC

The earliest example of an American classical musician is also among the most unusual. Louis Moreau Gottschalk (1829–1869) was born in New Orleans, the child of a Creole mother and a Jewish father. The first American classical pianist to succeed internationally and a prodigy on many instruments, he was famous in Europe by the time he was thirteen. Like most classical musicians of the day, his fame was derived from his interpretations of the great European composers. His own musical compositions reflected his mixed ethnic background. While his style was similar to European composers such as Chopin or Berlioz, his melodies and rhythms reflected the vibrancy of American, Latin American, and Creole folk music. The first classical composer to incorporate this uniquely American mix of cultures into serious music, he predated Gershwin by fifty years. His compositions include *Grande Tarantelle* and *La Bamboula*.

Ernest Bloch can perhaps be called the first Jewish American classical composer who gained fame as a "Jewish composer." Born in Switzerland, he settled in New York in 1916. He blended the influences of European classical and Jewish liturgical and secular music and was a leader in the movement to create a Jewish national music. The melodic content of his compositions reveals Post-Romantic and Neoclassical influences, while the rhythmic patterns evoke Jewish music, both secular and religious. Many of his compositions, such as the tone poem *Schelomo* (1916), have openly Jewish themes. The pinnacle of his development in this area came with his composition for baritone, chorus, and orchestra *Avodah hakodesh* (Sacred Service) in 1933. A Sabbath morning service using the liturgy of the American Union prayer book,

Avodah hakodesh combines Ashkenazi and Gregorian religious musical elements with modern classical techniques.

Erich Wolfgang Korngold (1897–1957) is an example of a Jewish American immigrant who, rather than bringing American or Jewish influences to the European tradition, instead brought the romantic classical tradition to that most American of media, film. Born in Czechoslovakia, he made his reputation at an early age, causing a sensation when, at age thirteen, he premiered his ballet *Der Schneemann* (The Snowman) at the Vienna Opera. His scores for the films *Anthony Adverse* (1936) and *The Adventures of Robin Hood* (1938) brought him Academy Awards. His most famous work is *Die Tote Stadt* (The Dead City, 1920). It is considered by many to be one of the best operas composed in the twentieth century.

One of the greatest innovators and most influential teachers in modern classical music, **Arnold Schoenberg** (1874–1951) was born in Austria and spent much of his life in Austria and Germany. In the early 1900s he began to develop the compositional style called *atonality*, a form that avoids the traditional key structure. In the 1920s, frustrated with atonality, he began to experiment with a new compositional system called *dodecaphony*, which uses a twelve-tone chromatic structure. He immigrated to the United States in 1933, just after reconverting to Judaism (he had converted to Lutheranism in 1898), and his late work began to incorporate Jewish themes. An example of this is the twelve-tone work for narrator, men's chorus, and orchestra, *A Survivor from Warsaw* (1947).

By the 1920s the list of influential Jewish American classical composers had grown remarkably long. They had also become more difficult to classify as purely classical. Jewish classical composers of the twentieth century are known for their ability to meld musical traditions and jump between musical categories, bringing jazz and folk music into the classical tradition and the classical tradition to Broadway and film.

Two names can be said to define "American classical music": **George Gershwin** and **Aaron Copland**, both American-born children of Jewish immigrants. While best known for his theatrical compositions,

Gershwin deserves mention for *Rhapsody in Blue* (1924) and the opera *Porgy and Bess* (1935). These two works alone put him in the top rank of American composers. Copland, on the other hand, is more firmly rooted in the classical world and can be credited with making American concert music acceptable on the international scene. His early successes such as the *Piano Concerto* (1926) incorporated jazz idioms and rhythms into a classical score. In the 1930s, after exploring a more abstract style of composition—an example is the *Symphonic Ode* (1926)—and searching for a way to reach a broader audience, Copland began to write scores that incorporated folk music. It is the work of this period for which he is most famous. His triptych of three folk-inspired ballet scores—*Billy the Kid* (1938), *Rodeo* (1942), and *Appalachian Spring* (1944)—virtually defines what is considered American classical music. His work on film scores is another example of his efforts to reach a broad spectrum of the American public. It included scores for *Of Mice and Men* (1939), *Our Town* (1940), *The Red Pony* (1948), and *The Heiress* (1948), the last of which earned him an Academy Award.

Other American-born Jewish composers who rose to fame by incorporating American themes and musical idioms into their work include George Antheil, **William Schuman**, and Morton Gould. George Antheil (1900–1959), a student of Ernest Bloch, had his first major success with the jazz-influenced *First Symphony* (1922). His other work of this period was marked less by the jazz music of the day than by an ultramodern, violently percussive, dissonant quality. His *Le Ballet Méchanique*, written to be seen with a silent film of the same name, was the apex of his mechanical composition. His later work was more traditional, and his opera *Transatlantic* (1928) was among the first American operas to be produced in Europe. Composer, teacher, and administrator William Schuman (1910–1992) achieved great success with his work, which includes the *American Festival Overture* (1939) and the *New England Triptych* (1956). Morton Gould (1913–1996) conducted and composed for his own highly successful radio programs in addition to more traditional symphonies and orchestras. His work includes the *Latin American Symphonette* (1941), *Lincoln Legend* (1942), *Interplay* (1945), the Broadway musical *Billion Dollar Baby* (1945), and the ballet *Fall River Legend* (1948). His film and television scores include those for the film *Delightfully Dangerous* (1945) and the television miniseries "Holocaust" (1978).

Leonard Bernstein, perhaps the most famous name in American classical music, may have worked in more forms, styles, and categories than any other classical composer. Known for his brilliant conducting as well as his composing, he achieved immortality on Broadway, in film, and on the concert stage. His classical works show an enormous range of themes and musical influences. Jazz influenced his ballet score for *Fancy Free* (1944), which he later adapted for the Broadway musical *On the Town* (1944), and his *Second Symphony: The Age of Anxiety* (1949). The Jewish liturgy inspired the *Jeremiah Symphony* (1942) and the *Third Symphony: Kaddish* (1963).

Teacher/composer/conductor Gunther Schuller (1925–) not only uses jazz techniques in his classical work, but, unlike many of his colleagues, he also plays and composes directly for jazz. He helped to bring ragtime music back to national attention. In addition to the influence of jazz, his classical compositions are also sometimes more abstract and influenced by Schoenberg's twelve-tone chromatic scale. His work includes the *Fantasia Concertante* (1947), the *Double Bass Quartet* (1947), *12 by 11* (1955), which was written for chamber orchestra and jazz improvisation, and *Symphonic Tribute to Duke Ellington* (1955).

Among modern, more experimental composers, three names jump to the top of the list: Lukas Foss, Milton Feldman, and **Philip Glass**. All three have written in a variety of avant-garde styles. The latter two, however, are usually considered minimalists.

Born in Germany, Lukas Foss (1922–) came to the United States when he was ten. His compositions were initially neoclassical with a romantic bent. Some of his early work, including *The Prairie* (1944), mirrored Aaron Copland's populist American themes, while others, such as the *Symphony in G* (1945), were purely European influenced. Foss came into his own when he founded the Improvisation Chamber Ensem-

ble. With the ensemble, he began to experiment with aleatoric, or chance, and stochastic, or mathematical probability, music. Examples of his avant-garde experimentation include *Elytres* (1964) and *Concert for Cello and Orchestra* (1966). He has also explored minimalism and multimedia in his compositions. Morton Feldman (1926–1987) is often associated with the group of modern New York composers that includes John Cage. Among his best known pieces are *Durations I–V* (1960–62) and *Piano and Orchestra* (1975).

In a class by himself, Philip Glass left American musical idioms entirely. His composition, which retains Western elements, has more to do with Eastern musical ideology and rhythm. Marked by repetition and progression within a diatonic structure, his compositions often develop slowly, over the course of an extended time period. He has had critical success with his concert work, but his popular acclaim developed out of his film score for *Koyaanisqatsi* (1982) and his operas, which include *Einstein on the Beach* (1976).

In addition to composers, many of the men and women who conduct and play classical music are Jewish Americans. Among the conductors alone, the list of brilliant technicians, interpreters, and perhaps most importantly orchestra builders, is long. The careers of the leading Jewish American conductors have two major themes—the building of American orchestras into some of the best in the world and a commitment to new music.

Conductor **Serge Koussevitzky** tops the list on both scores. Born in Russia, he immigrated to the United States in 1924. As a composer and double bass player he gained fame in Europe. His *Double Bass Concerto* (1905) became his most popular composition. He is acknowledged as the leading proponent of new music in the twentieth century, not only commissioning and championing new works throughout his career, but while he lived in Europe and Russia, publishing it. When he came to the United States he became conductor of the troubled Boston Symphony Orchestra. During his tenure (1924–49), he turned it into the legendary ensemble it is to this day. Among the many modern American and European composers he championed are Aaron Copland, George Gershwin, and

William Schuman. He also directed the Berkshire Music Festival, created the Berkshire Music Center, and mentored both Leonard Bernstein and Lukas Foss. His conducting was known for its attention to detail and its emotional intensity.

Like Koussevitsky, **Fritz Reiner** taught Lukas Foss and Leonard Bernstein and raised all the orchestras he conducted from artistic decline, making them some of the best in the world. Born in Hungary, Reiner came to the United States in 1922 and became the principal conductor of the Cincinnati Symphony. In 1931 he became the head of the opera and orchestral departments at the Curtis Institute of Music. He was also the musical director of the Pittsburgh Symphony (1938–48) and New York's Metropolitan Opera (1948–53) before taking the job for which he is most famous, music director of the Chicago Symphony Orchestra (1953–62). He brought new compositions to all the symphonies where he worked. While known for his mastery of the great German Romantic and Classical composers, he had a restrained conducting style, with careful attention to rhythmic precision and textural quality, that was considered very effective with modern music.

Another conductor known for his ability to build orchestras was Artur Rodzinsky (1892–1958), who was born in what was then Dalmatia. He made his American conducting debut in 1925 with the Philadelphia Symphony Orchestra. The following year he obtained a permanent position as assistant to the symphony's conductor, Leopold Stokowski. From 1929 through 1933 he led the Los Angeles Philharmonic, then moved to the Cleveland Orchestra, where he spent the next ten years. In 1937 he created and trained the NBC Orchestra and in 1942 became the conductor of the New York Philharmonic. He resigned in 1947, moved to the Chicago Symphony Orchestra, and was dismissed the following year. Known for his jealousy and bad temper, he is particularly famous for once trying to strangle an assistant conductor, Leonard Bernstein. Despite his problems, he built every orchestra he led into a leading organization in the music world. His last appearance conducting was at the Chicago Lyric Opera in 1958.

Conductor Eugene Ormandy (1899–1985) was born in Hungary and came to the United States in 1921. He became the principal conductor of the Minneapolis Symphony Orchestra in 1931. Like many of his brethren, he turned the symphony around and added twentieth-century works to its repertoire. In 1936 he joined the Philadelphia Orchestra, where he had guest conducted six years before, sharing conductorship with music director Leopold Stokowski. In 1938 he took over the position of music director and became the orchestra's sole conductor. He stayed until 1980. During his tenure the Orchestra became known for a unique, string-oriented sound that came to be called the "Philadelphia Sound."

Like Eugene Ormandy, **George Szell** was born in Hungary and became known for his work with a single orchestra. He first came to the United States as a guest conductor at the St. Louis Symphony in 1930. In 1946 he became the principal conductor of the Cleveland Orchestra, staying until his death in 1970. He took over an orchestra that had been in decline since Rodzinsky's period and, during his tenure, not only rebuilt its reputation, but added a chorus and an apprenticeship program for young conductors. Szell was a reserved conductor who concentrated on faithfully rendering the composer's original intentions.

Then there are Bernstein and Fiedler, two of the most popular conductors of all time and the first American-born conductors to achieve international acclaim. Both brought classical music to American audiences who would not usually be exposed to it.

Leonard Bernstein was an incredibly popular figure for a classical musician. Wildly versatile, he was a classical composer, pianist, and conductor as well as a Broadway composer and a well-known television commentator. The first internationally renowned musician trained entirely in the United States, he studied conducting with Reiner and Koussevitsky. The latter became not only mentor and champion, but lifelong friend. Bernstein's conducting debut was at the New York Philharmonic in 1943, when he was asked at the last minute to replace conductor Bruno Walter. He so impressed critics and audiences with his technical efficiency and interpretive brilliance that his rise to fame was meteoric. He left his position as assistant conductor at the New York Philharmonic, became the conductor of the New York City Center orchestra (1945–47), then returned to the Philharmonic (1958–69) as musical director and principal conductor. He was the first native-born American in those positions. He also guest conducted all over the world and was the first American to conduct at La Scala (1953).

Known for his physicality at the podium, Bernstein quite literally threw himself into the music. He built the Philharmonic's Young People's Concerts and became a beloved national figure when he both conducted and commented on those concerts for television. He also commented on classical music for the "Omnibus" television show (1954–58), bringing an understanding and appreciation of classical music to millions of Americans. Like his mentor Koussevitsky and many other Jewish American conductors, Bernstein was a long-time champion of modern music and maintained close friendships with both Aaron Copland and **Marc Blitzstein.**

Arthur Fiedler's popularity, like Bernstein's, came largely from his dynamic television performances. While both men brought the classics to new audiences, Fiedler did it by bringing popular music, and popular music's audience, to the symphony orchestra. "Mr. Pops," as Fiedler was known, took the Boston Pops Orchestra and made it one of the most successful orchestras in the world. The first native-born American to conduct the Pops, he led the orchestra from 1930 through 1979.

Less well known, but still influential are conductors Alfred Wallenstein, William Steinberg, Anton Dorati, and Erich Leinsdorf. All had distinguished careers in traditional symphony orchestras and several helped to broaden the appeal of classical music in the media.

Chicago-born Alfred Wallenstein (1898–1983) was a pioneer in the development of classical music for the radio. Initially a successful cellist with a number of orchestras throughout the United States, he began conducting in 1931 when he led an orchestra in a radio broadcast. The following year he conducted at the Hollywood Bowl. In 1933 he created the Wallenstein Sinfonietta, which played serious music on radio station WOR in New York City. In 1943 he became the principal conductor of the Los Angeles Philharmonic, making him the first American-born artist to head such an important orchestra. After he left the Philharmonic in 1956, he continued to guest conduct and became an influential teacher of conducting at the Juilliard School of Music.

William Steinberg (1899–1978) was born in Germany. In 1936, after fleeing the Nazis, he founded, with Bronislaw Huberman, the Palestine Symphony, now the Israel Philharmonic. He settled in the United States in 1938, becoming Toscanini's assistant at the NBC Symphony. After conducting at the San Francisco Opera and serving as musical director at the Buffalo Philharmonic Orchestra, he accepted the position for which he is best known, music director of the Pittsburgh Symphony Orchestra (1952–76). He made the orchestra one of the most respected in the United States. He also served as music director of the London Philharmonic (1958–60) and of the Boston Symphony (1969–72).

Anton Dorati (1906–1988) was born in Hungary and came to the United States in 1937 to conduct at the National Symphony. Like Rodzinski, he is known as a builder of orchestras, starting with the new American Ballet Theatre Orchestra (1941–45). He both created and led the Dallas Symphony Orchestra (1945–49). He reorganized and improved the Minneapolis Symphony Orchestra (1949–60), among many others. He was also a great promoter of twentieth-century music, especially that of Béla Bartók, and was known for his attention to rhythm and his ear for orchestral tone.

Conductor Erich Leinsdorf (1912–1993) was born in Vienna and came to America in 1937. His positions in the United States included assistant conductor for the Metropolitan Opera Company (1937–39) and head of the company's German repertoire (1939–43). After World War II, in which he fought, he worked at the Rochester Philharmonic as principal conductor (1947–56), the New York City Opera as musical director and conductor (1956–57), the Metropolitan Opera as conductor and musical consultant (1957–62), and the Boston Symphony Orchestra as musical director

(1962–69). Sometimes criticized for being too controlled in his conducting, he was also praised for his detailed and precise interpretations.

Among the newer generation of conductors, **André Previn** (1929–) is the oldest and came to conducting relatively late in life. He first gained fame as a pianist and film score arranger and composer. Born in Germany, he came to this country when he was ten. He first conducted a major orchestra in 1963 at the age of thirty-four. Since then he has been principal conductor of the Houston Symphony Orchestra (1967–70), the London Symphony (1968–79), the Pittsburgh Symphony (1976–84), and the Royal Philharmonic (1987–). He has also served as musical director for the Los Angeles Philharmonic (1985–89) and the Royal Philharmonic (1985–86). Known for his interpretations of the French Impressionists and Russian and English music of the nineteenth and twentieth centuries, he usually avoids Baroque music and the avant-garde.

Conductor **James Levine** (1943–) is known for his work with the Metropolitan Opera. Taught by Alfred Wallenstein and coming out of George Szell's apprenticeship program at the Cleveland Symphony, he rose through the ranks at the Metropolitan Opera. He began as an assistant conductor and eventually became, in 1986, the company's artistic director.

Conductor Michael Tilson Thomas (1944–) is sometimes called "the new Leonard Bernstein" and is a winner of the Koussevitsky Conducting Prize from the Berkshire Music Center. After becoming an assistant conductor with the Boston Symphony Orchestra, Thomas, like Bernstein, achieved instant acclaim when he stepped in at an intermission to take over conducting from a seriously ill William Steinberg, then music director of the Boston Symphony. Also like Bernstein, he became the conductor and commentator of the televised New York Philharmonic Young People's Concerts (1970–71). He has been the musical director of the Buffalo Philharmonic Orchestra and headed the Los Angeles Philharmonic Institute and the Great Woods Center for the Performing Arts. A guest conductor, he is one of the few native-born American conductors with an international audience.

Among the hands and voices of the classical music world, some of the greatest virtuosos are Jewish Americans. The list of pianists includes such immortal names as Horowitz, Serkin, Lhevine, Bessie, and Rubinstein. The violin masters include Heifetz, Menuhin, Stern, Milstein, Perlman, and Zukerman. On the opera stage, the incomparable personalities include Alma Gluck, Regina Resnik, **Beverly Sills**, **Roberta Peters**, Robert Merrill, **Richard Tucker**, and Leonard Warren. These are only a few of the numerous Jewish American artists who have brought their skill and talent to the interpretation and performance of classical music.

Pianists Josef Lhevinne (1874–1944) and his wife Rosina Bessie (1880–1976) were two of the earliest Jewish American classical piano virtuosos in the United States. Originally from Russia, Lhevinne made his American debut in 1906. The couple immigrated in 1919. Though Lhevinne's career was far better known, Bessie appeared frequently with him at two-piano recitals. Lhevinne is remembered for his mastery of the great Romantic composers, especially Chopin, and his playing style was notable for its rich tone and technical control. Lhevinne and Bessie became respected teachers as well as performers, both privately and at the Juilliard School of Music.

Another pianist known for his interpretation of the Romantics, **Vladimir Horowitz** is often considered to have been the greatest technician on the piano in human history. He could play with unusual speed and power while maintaining an amazing control over a composition's articulation and dynamics. He immigrated to the United States at the outset of World War II, but frequent bouts of depression and exhaustion caused him to retire from performing frequently and sometimes for long periods of time. As a result, his concerts were treated as special events that "could not be missed."

Like Horowitz, pianist **Artur Rubinstein** excelled at playing the Romantics and came to the United States to escape the Nazis. He had toured in the United States in 1906 and 1937, but didn't immigrate until 1941. Unlike Horowitz, he was known later in life for his incredible energy and huge touring schedule. A child prodigy, he was a self-described lazy pianist for much of his youth. By the 1930s he found the discipline and energy for which he became famous. A champion of modern composers such as Prokofiev and Debussy, he was most famous for his interpretations of Chopin, which he played without sentimentality but with lyricism and genteel passion.

Another child prodigy who came to the United States just prior to World War II was Rudolf Serkin (1903–1991). Known both for his commitment to chamber music and for his interpretations of the great German composers, he was noted for his unusually clean and unsentimental renditions of Bach. An influential teacher, he was on the faculty of the Curtis Institute and later became its director. He also helped found both the Marlboro School of Music and the renowned Marlboro Music Festival in Vermont.

Internationally renowned virtuoso violinist **Jascha Heifetz** is often considered the best in the history of the instrument. A star in Russia as a child, he immigrated to the United States in 1917. He was known not only as an excellent performer of the standard repertoire of Classical and Romantic composers, but also as a proponent of new music. He frequently commissioned pieces from young composers such as Erich Wolfgang Korngold. Sometimes criticized for his lack of emotion, he possessed a mastery of and passion for the violin that were universally acknowledged. He also gained fame for his concerts with other virtuosos of his time. His 1949 concerts with pianist Artur Rubinstein and cellist Gregor Piatigorsky (1903–1976) were outstanding. In the early 1960s, he again played with Piatigorsky, for a long series of concerts in Los Angeles.

Another sometime ensemble player with Piatigorsky was Nathan Milstein (1903–1992). In the 1920s, while living in Europe, Piatigorsky played trio concerts with Horowitz on piano and Milstein on the violin. The latter two had toured together frequently when they both lived in Russia. Milstein immigrated to the United States at the outbreak of World War II and became known for his treatments of Bach's unaccompanied violin sonatas and of the works of the great Romantic composers.

Violinist **Yehudi Menuhin** was one of the first American-born violin virtuosos. He later became a British citizen. A child prodigy, he is best known for his skill in playing chamber music and for his broad repertoire. He was committed to playing rare and unusual works and frequently commissioned pieces from composers such as Ernest Bloch. A committed humanitarian, he was an influential teacher and founded the Yehudi Menuhin School of Music for educating young musicians. His playing style was known for its purity and depth.

Isaac Stern, though not born in America, came to the United States at a very young age. Like Menuhin, Stern was a child prodigy. Known for his enormous repertoire and his commitment to twentieth-century composers, he was among the first violinists to expand the solo-recital program and include chamber music in his programs. Perhaps the most loved violinist of the century, he focused on communicating the composition and its emotional intensity to the audience. Like Leonard Bernstein, whose work he has premiered, Stern used his outgoing personality, his love of music, and television and radio to bring classical music to a broad and varied audience.

Among the younger generation of virtuoso Jewish American musicians, two names stand out. **Itzhak Perlman** and **Pinchas Zukerman** are both violinists who were born in Israel and later immigrated to the United States. They have frequently played together, with Zukerman on the viola, and with Isaac Stern. Both men are brilliant technicians on their instruments. Perlman is known for his enormous repertoire, his openness to popular and folk music, such as klezmer and ragtime, and the directness and detail of his interpretations. Zukerman is admired for his versatility on the violin and viola, often playing both in one evening. His style is marked by its richness, expressive phrasing, and spiccato style of bowing. He is also a respected conductor.

In the world of opera and concert singing, Jewish Americans also made their mark. One of the earliest was Alma Gluck (1884–1938). Born in Rumania, she immigrated to the United States in 1890. She had her opera debut under Arturo Toscanini in 1909 but disliked performing in operas and soon gave it up to concentrate on her concert career. By 1914 she was the most popular concert singer in America, touring all over the country singing both classical music and American folk songs.

Among other leading Jewish American singers is tenor **Jan Peerce**, who was initially a great success singing popular music for "Radio City Music Hall of the Air." In 1938 Toscanini heard Peerce sing the role of Seigmund from Wagner's *Die Walküre* on the "Radio City Music Hall" and hired him to sing with the NBC Symphony Orchestra. They continued to work together for the next fifteen years. Peerce's Metropolitan Opera debut was in 1941 and he worked steadily and successfully with the company for the next twenty-five years. Another Met star, baritone Leonard Warren (1911–1960), sang with the Met from 1938 until his death onstage during a performance in 1960. He is best known for his interpretations of Puccini, Verdi, and Leoncavallo. **Richard Tucker**, a tenor, had his Met debut in 1945, but his career did not center there. Instead, he sang with major opera companies and orchestras throughout the United States. He also achieved great success in Europe, becoming one of the first American-born tenors to triumph there. An accomplished cantor, he received his early musical training in a synagogue choir. Baritone Robert Merrill (1919–) had his Met debut in 1945. For the next several years, concurrently with his position at the Met, he had his own popular music radio programs, "The Robert Merrill Show" and "Music America Loves Best." He stayed at the Met for close to thirty years with one short absence in 1951–52, becoming the first American to sing 500 performances with the company.

Regina Resnik (1922–) had her Met debut a year before Merrill and Tucker. For the next ten years she sang many of the company's leading soprano roles. By 1953 her voice had changed and she began singing mezzo-soprano and alto roles. Singing less at the Met—director Rudolf Bing offered her only minor roles after her voice changed—she began to perform extensively in Europe where she maintained a highly successful career. Known for her ability to act convincingly as well as sing beautifully, she is most famous for her portrayal of the title role in *Carmen*.

Soprano Roberta Peters (1930–) debuted at the Met in 1950 and went on to sing with the company longer than any other soprano in history. Initially a coloratura, she expanded her repertoire as she got older to include lyric roles. She also appeared on the "Ed Sullivan Show" a record sixty-five times and has maintained an extensive concert career.

All these artists made their names at the Met, but there is one fabulous exception to the rule. Coloratura soprano Beverly Sills made her debut with the New York City Opera in 1955 and sang with the company for the next twenty-five years. She then became the company's manager, a position she held for ten years. An amazingly popular figure, with a reputation for skillfully executing difficult and rarely performed roles, Sills is known as much for her acting ability as for her voice. When she finally had her Met debut in 1975, her name was already a household word. Through her work as a singer and as a manager, Sills brought opera to more people in America than any previous artist. She made numerous television appearances and has lobbied for the arts throughout her career.

As striking as the accomplishments of Jewish Americans in classical music have been, they are almost overshadowed by Jewish dominance in many areas of popular music. From "God Bless America" to "Hound Dog," Jewish performers and, especially songwriters, have helped to shape the sound of America.

POPULAR MUSIC

One of the first Jewish participants in American popular music was actually an Englishman, Henry Russell (1812–1900). Russell spent the 1830s and 1840s traveling throughout the United States, becoming the most popular singer and composer in the country. Among his most famous ballads are "Woodsman Spare That Tree" with lyrics by George P. Morris (1837) and "The Indian Hunter" with lyrics by Eliza Cook (1837). "The Indian Hunter" was the first American popular song to speak of the injustice being done to Native Americans.

For many years after Russell, there was little participation by Jewish Americans in music. Then, in the

Who Tells Aretha Franklin What to Sing?

Songwriter Carole King, a nice Jewish girl from Brooklyn that's who. She not only wrote the words for Franklin's hit "A Natural Woman," she inspired Little Eva to tell a generation about the latest dance craze in "The Loco-Motion," and let James Taylor warm our hearts with "You've Got a Friend." Inducted into the Rock and Roll Hall of Fame in 1990, she contributed to an album of Jewish liturgies, *Life's a Lesson* in 1994.

late nineteenth century, Eastern European Jews began to flood into New York City. At the same time, America's popular music industry began to take off. Nicknamed Tin Pan Alley, the industry was centered in the Flat Iron Building in New York City. The nickname is credited to lyricist and journalist Monroe Rosenfeld, who compared the sound of all the pianos in the building to the sound of coins hitting a tin pan. The Tin Pan Alley music industry developed because of immigration and industrialization. The urban population of middle and working classes was exploding, and for the first time in American history many people could now afford pianos in their homes. They did not have the money and leisure or, possibly, the inclination to study classical music. These new musicians needed something they could play at home. Tin Pan Alley and its composers produced a seemingly unending supply of sheet music to answer this need. Initially, Tin Pan Alley produced simple songs that could be easily learned and sung, but as the industry and the public became more sophisticated so, too, did the music.

There are several explanations of why Jewish immigrants excelled in composing popular music. First, they brought strong Jewish musical traditions to America. On the street, there was the custom of the "Jewish patter song," in which people in conversation responded to each other in rhyme. In the synagogue, there was the single cantoral voice. Both of these traditions certainly influenced early Tin Pan Alley music. Second, as we have seen, many Jewish people excelled in classical European music. As Tin Pan Alley developed and the music became more sophisticated, this European classical influence came into play.

The final piece of popular music's puzzle is the music of African Americans. Ironically, while African Americans were largely kept out of mainstream music until very recently, African American musical forms and styles came to define America to white audiences here and abroad. By the 1920s white American composers and lyricists were commonly incorporating traditionally African American music into their own work. Jewish musicians excelled at this. Perhaps this is because, as recent immigrants, Jewish composers did not have the historical prejudice that had relegated African American music to the minstrel show. Perhaps it is because, as a people who had suffered oppression, Jews found something in African American music they recognized. Or, perhaps, the Jewish composers of Tin Pan Alley simply knew a good thing when they heard it.

Of greatest importance though, is that the two musical traditions had something tonally in common. The traditional sound of Jewish music is the minor key, which is also used in the blues. Therefore, while some of Gershwin's music, for example, might sound African American to many audience members, it could easily sound Jewish to others. Of course, white musicians—Jewish and Christian—were also often guilty of homogenizing African American music. Luckily, there were notable exceptions. These exceptions helped to bring American popular music to new heights.

From 1890 to 1930 the Jewish Americans of Tin Pan Alley published literally thousands of classic songs. In fact, the first "million seller"—of sheet music—was "After the Ball Game" (1892) written by Jewish publisher/composer Charles K. Harris (1867–1930). Harry von Tilzer (1872–1946) was also a publisher/composer. Among his many hits were the classics "I Want a Girl Just Like the Girl" (1911) and "Wait Until the Sun Shines, Nellie" (1905). Harry's brother Albert von Tilzer (1878–1956) wrote "I'll Be with You in Apple Blossom Time" (1920) and the ever popular "Take Me Out to the Ball Game" (1908). Another early hit song was "Tammany" (1905), the official theme song of New York City's Democratic machine, written by Gus Edwards (1879–1945). Edwards also wrote "If a Girl Like You Loved a Boy Like Me" (1905) and "School Days" (1907).

A complete discussion of the predominance of Jews in Tin Pan Alley would take a book in itself. However, a short list of hit songs by Jews in Tin Pan Alley includes "Memories" (1915) and "Yes Sir, That's My Baby" (1922) by Gus Kahn, and "I Want to Be Loved by You" (1928) and "Who's Sorry Now" (1923) by Harry Ruby. Other examples are "Brother, Can You Spare a Dime" by E. Y. "Yip" Harburg (1932), who also wrote "April in Paris" (1932) with the Russian Jewish composer Vernon Duke. The list could continue with "Let a Smile Be Your Umbrella" (1927), by Sammy Fain, and "If You Knew Susie" (1925) and "California, Here I Come" (1921) by Joseph Meyer.

One of the earliest women lyricists was Dorothy Fields (1905–1974), who later wrote several successful Broadway shows with jazz pianist Cy Coleman. In the late 1920s Fields gained fame as a lyricist with songs such as "I Can't Give You Anything But Love, Baby" (1928) and "On the Sunny Side of the Street" (1930).

Many of the names above have faded into the mists of time, even if their songs have not. **Irving Berlin** still stands out. As the great Broadway composer **Jerome Kern** said, "[Berlin] *is* American music." Perhaps best known as the composer and lyricist of "God Bless America" (1938), Berlin mastered an enormous range of composition. The son of a cantor, he spent his entire life in the music business. He started out as a street singer and singing waiter before he moved into "song plugging" and composing for Tin Pan Alley. At first just a lyricist, he published his first song, "Marie from Sunny Italy," in 1907. He then began to write his own music to his lyrics. His first hit song as both lyricist and composer was "Alexander's Ragtime Band" (1911), which inaugurated the white ragtime era. He moved on to ballads with "When I Lost You" (1912). As he became more famous, he began to contribute songs to musical revues and Broadway shows, including many of **Florenz Ziegfeld**'s *Follies*. In 1919, he went out on his own and formed his own publishing company, the Irving Berlin Music Corporation. He wrote close to a thousand songs during his life-

time. They virtually define popular music for the first half of the twentieth century.

With less name recognition, but still of great importance, is **Harold Arlen**, who was also the son of a cantor. Starting out as a vaudeville musician, he began composing when he was in his early twenties and had his first major successes with lyricist Ted Koehler. They wrote many popular songs for the performers at Harlem's Cotton Club, early examples of the link between Jewish writers and African American performers that would continue through the Motown era of the 1960s. Examples of Arlen and Koehler's songs from this period include "Between the Devil and the Deep Blue Sea" (1931), "I Love a Parade" (1931), "I've Got the World on a String" (1932), and "Stormy Weather" (1933). Arlen also collaborated with other great Tin Pan Alley lyricists. Together with lyricist Yip Harburg, he wrote, "It's Only a Paper Moon" (1933) and "Lydia, the Tattooed Lady" (1939), for the **Marx Brothers** film *At the Circus*. **Billy Rose** contributed to the lyrics of the former. He wrote many songs with lyrics by Johnny Mercer, including "Blues in the Night" (1941).

Another great lyricist was Irving Caesar (1895–1996), who wrote the words to "Swanee." George Gershwin wrote the music. In 1918 **Al Jolson** popularized the song, and his recorded version sold over two million copies. Most other Caesar songs were written for Broadway shows or for films, as were many of Berlin's and Arlen's songs.

One of the early performers of popular music was Alma Gluck. In addition to her work in the classical repertoire, she was an enormously successful recording artist for the Victor Talking Machine Company.

Elvis's Jewish Hit

Presley's recording of "Hound Dog" in 1956 helped vault him to national prominence. The song was first recorded in 1953 by the African American vocalist "Big Momma" Thornton. It was written for her by the legendary Jewish songwriting team of Jerry Leiber and Mike Stoller, who also penned other hits for Presley, as well as for the Coasters, the Drifters, and many other groups.

Her recording of the classic "Carry Me Back to Old Virginny" sold close to two million copies.

From the 1920s on, Tin Pan Alley's greatest composers, lyricists, and librettists wrote largely for Broadway and Hollywood. Many, if not most, of the classic songs of that era were originally written for some form of performance in these venues, and most of the great singers of the era became famous through Broadway or vaudeville. An example is the blues classic "I Gotta Right to Sing the Blues " with lyrics by Koehler and music by Arlen, which was originally written for the stage show *The Earl Carroll Vanities of 1932.*

While many of the standards of the first half of the twentieth century came out of Tin Pan Alley, two other popular forms of music emerged from America's bars, nightclubs, and ballrooms: the blues and jazz. Jewish Americans were extremely significant in the development of both these forms. As we have already seen, Jewish composers brought elements of jazz and blues into both classical compositions and popular standards. In addition, Jews were at the forefront of the burgeoning musical movement as managers and producers. While somewhat less evident as performers of jazz and the blues, they truly led in the popular offshoot of jazz, swing music.

Benny Goodman, Jewish clarinetist and bandleader, is often credited with beginning the swing, or big band, era of jazz music. Swing music is characterized by more accessible melodies and less improvisation than traditional jazz. Goodman was the first major white bandleader to lead integrated groups. By asking for jazz arrangements of current popular songs, Goodman not only initiated the swing era, he also brought jazz music, through swing, to an enormous audience that had never heard it before.

One of Goodman's discoveries was the trumpeter Harry James (1916–1983). James excelled at both "hot jazz" and the more commercial "sweet style." Far more popular for his sweet style, James became a leader of the swing movement. Among his many popular hits are "You Made Me Love You," "Carnival in Venice," and "I've Heard That Song Before."

Another leader in swing was bandleader Artie Shaw (1910–) who, like Goodman, played the clar-

inet. Unlike Goodman, he also played the saxophone. After performing with several groups, he formed his own band. In 1938 Shaw hired Billie Holliday as a vocalist and had his first major success. In 1940 he composed one of his most famous pieces, the Clarinet Concerto, which combines elements of blues, boogie-woogie, and jazz. In the early 1940s Shaw created a huge ensemble that included an entire string section. In so doing, he brought together hot and sweet jazz and his band became one of the most successful of the swing era.

Saxophonist **Stan Getz** got his start performing with Benny Goodman. In 1947 he began playing with Woody Herman's jazz band and achieved international recognition for his solo on Herman's "Early Autumn" (1949). Later, with his own group, Getz popularized both Brazilian bossa nova and "cool jazz." Among his most famous recordings are "The Girl from Ipanema" and "Anniversary."

One of the most popular singers of the swing era, **Dinah Shore**, was turned down by all of the major big bands of the time, possibly because she was considered physically unattractive. She went on to become the only major singer of the era not connected with a major big band. Early in her career she was considered a blues singer and later a singer of popular standards. Some of her hits included "Yes, My Darling Daughter" (1940), "Memphis Blues" (1940), "Body and Soul" (1941), and "Blues in the Night" (1942). She sang on **Eddie Cantor**'s radio show "Time to Smile" and hosted several radio programs, including "The Dinah Shore Show." In the 1950s she moved to television, hosting one of the first successful musical variety shows before going on to become a talk show host.

Out of the blues developed "rhythm and blues." For many years, this was a traditionally African American form of music and was actively avoided by the white mainstream music industry. Jews were not in the forefront of composition or performance of early rhythm and blues, but they were important components on the publishing end of the industry.

Two of the most important were the Chess brothers, Phil and Leonard. Polish Jewish immigrants, they started out as nightclub owners. Their South Side

Chicago nightclub featured blues music and they began recording the acts who appeared there. By 1949 they had created their own record label, Chess Records. Hugely successful in the rhythm and blues market, Chess Records recorded such classic blues artists as Muddy Waters and Howlin' Wolf among many others.

Another important record label of this period was King Records in Cincinnati. Founded by Syd Nathan in 1945, King Records achieved success with both country and blues music. One of the only record labels of the period to market both African American and white artists, King Records was home to artists as diverse as country singer Moon Mullican and blues master Albert King.

During the 1950s, a new form of popular music began its takeover of America. This new music, rock 'n' roll, was an amalgamation of much of the popular music that had gone before. In one sense, early rock 'n' roll was simply rhythm and blues with white kids dancing to it. In another, rock 'n' roll was the coming together of several popular music genres, especially country and rhythm and blues.

Both Chess and King Records were important in rock's early development. In 1951, Chess records released what many consider the first rock 'n' roll record, "Rocket 88," by Jackie Brenson. By the mid-fifties, Chess forever changed popular music by recording Bo Diddley and Chuck Berry. King Records earned its place in rock 'n' roll history by introducing the world to the immortal James Brown.

Jewish influence has been significant in all areas of rock 'n' roll. In fact, the man who coined, or at least popularized, the term itself was Jewish. Alan Freed (1922–1965) was among the first radio men in the country to recognize the popularity and potential of electrified rhythm and blues music, rock 'n' roll's precursor. In 1951, at station WJW in Cleveland, he began to host "Moondog's Rock 'n' Roll Party." In 1954 he moved to WINS in New York City, where his popularity, and the music's, increased. Freed was unique among his contemporaries because he would not play white "cover" versions of African American songs. Sometimes considered rock 'n' roll's first martyr, he

was destroyed by the "payola" scandals in the early 1960s. Murray Kaufman, or "Murray the K," succeeded Freed as one of the most successful "deejays" of the rock era.

As in the Tin Pan Alley days, there were a number of Jewish songwriting teams in early rock 'n' roll. One of the first rock 'n' roll hits was written by a Jewish songwriting team. "Rock Around the Clock," which was a major hit for Bill Haley and the Comets, was written by Max C. Freedman (1893–1962) and James Myers (1919–) in 1953. The greatest single influence on rock 'n' roll songwriting teams was Don Kirshner (1924–). In 1958 he co-founded the Aldon Music publishing company. Located across the street from the Brill Building in New York, Aldon Music became rock 'n' roll's major "hit factory." The Brill Building itself became synonymous with music publishing because of the number of independent labels housed there.

One of the greatest teams that Kirshner brought together was the husband and wife team of Carole King (1942–) and Gerry Goffin (1939–). Together King and Goffin wrote such hits as "Will You Still Love Me Tomorrow" (1960), recorded by the Shirelles; "Up on the Roof" (1962), recorded by the Drifters; and "The Locomotion" (1962), recorded by Little Eva. Another great husband and wife teams working with Aldon Music was Barry Mann (1939–) and Cynthia Weil. Their hits include "Uptown" (1962), recorded by the Crystals; "Walking in the Rain" (1964), recorded by the Ronettes; and "You've Lost That Lovin' Feeling" (1964), recorded by the Righteous Brothers.

Three Aldon Music composers successfully recorded their own work. Lesley Gore (1946–) topped the charts with her songs "It's My Party" (1963) and "You Don't Own Me" (1963). Neil Sedaka (1939–) had hits with "Calendar Girl" (1960), "Stairway to Heaven" (1960), and "Love Will Keep Us Together" (1975). His songwriting partner was lyricist Howard Greenfield. Neil Diamond (1941–) is known for songs such as "Cherry, Cherry" (1966) and "Sweet Caroline" (1969). He also wrote songs for the Monkees, most notably "I'm a Believer" (1966).

Two non-Aldon Music songwriting teams of note

were Burt Bacharach (1928–) and Hal David (1921–), and Jeff Barry (1938–) and Ellie Greenwich (1940–). Bacharach and David had hits with "One Less Bell to Answer" (1967), "I'll Never Fall in Love Again" (1968), and "Raindrops Keep Falling on My Head" (1969), among many others. Barry and Greenwich's hits included "Be My Baby" (1963), recorded by the Ronettes; "Goin' to the Chapel" (1964), recorded by the Dixie Cups; and "Then He Kissed Me" (1963), recorded by the Crystals.

But at the very heart of early rock 'n' roll composition was the team of Jerry Leiber (1933–) and Mike Stoller (1933–). They wrote everything from novelty songs such as "Charlie Brown" (1959) to Elvis Presley classics such as "Hound Dog," which was written originally for blues star "Big Mama" Thornton, who had a hit with it in 1953. Their list of influential hits includes "Yakety Yak" (1958), recorded by the Coasters; "Lovin' You" (1957) and "Jail House Rock" (1957), recorded by Presley; "There Goes My Baby" (1959), recorded by the Drifters; "Kansas City" (1959), recorded by Wilbert Harrison; "What About Us?" (1959), recorded by the Coasters; and "Stand By Me" (1961), recorded by Ben E. King. Leiber and Stoller were also notable producers, producing most of their songs as well as those of others. They were also the first producers to be credited as such on a record label. Initially, Leiber and Stoller worked at the legendary record label Atlantic Records. Ultimately they formed their own company, Red Bird.

The importance of Atlantic Records cannot be overstated. Herb Abramson helped create the label in 1948 and, at least in part because of his influence and knowledge, Atlantic quickly became the preeminent blues labels in the country. In the early 1950s Jerry Wexler joined Atlantic. The man credited with coining the term "rhythm and blues" to replace the term "race music," Wexler is a legend in the music industry. After starting out as a producer, he later became a partner in the business. Recording at the legendary Stax studios in Memphis, he brought major artists such as Otis Redding and Sam and Dave to public attention. Later he convinced Aretha Franklin to leave Columbia Records, where she had never had a hit, and join his

---

Turning a Jewish Tombstone into a Hit Song

In his career as a record producer, Phil Spector (1940–) set the standards for the production of rock 'n' roll records that heavily influenced the Beatles, the Beach Boys, and, later, Bruce Springsteen. In 1958, he took the inscription on his father's tombstone in a Jewish cemetery on Long Island and used it as the title of his song "To Know Him Is to Love Him." It became a number one hit.

---

other artists at Atlantic. Once there, she had a string of hits that led to her reign as the Queen of Soul. Other Atlantic/Wexler stars included Wilson Pickett, the Drifters, Joe Turner, John Coltrane, and Ray Charles. As rhythm and blues became rock 'n' roll, Atlantic artists included Led Zeppelin, the Rolling Stones, Buffalo Springfield, and Sonny and Cher. In 1967 against Wexler's wishes, Atlantic was sold to Time Warner for $17 million.

The most famous producer of this era has to be Phil Spector (1940–). An apprentice with Leiber and Stoller, he had an early successes with "Spanish Harlem" (1961), which he co-wrote and that was recorded by Ben E. King. The following year he founded his record label, Philles. For the next four years he produced an enormous string of hits, all of which had the detail and energy that became known as "Phil Spector's Wall of Sound." His hits during this period included "Be My Baby" (1963), "Da Doo Ron Ron" (1963), and "You've Lost That Lovin' Feelin'" (1966). Later he produced the Beatles' album *Let It Be* (1970), as well as solo albums for John Lennon and George Harrison.

Less famous, but still important, was Florence Greenberg, one of the few women to own her own record company, Tiara Records. Greenberg gained her fame when she discovered the Shirelles and released the hit song "I Met Him On a Sunday" (1958), which she licensed to Decca Records for distribution. The song was written by King and Goffin and was their first major songwriting success. Greenberg then formed a new label, Sceptre Records, and had two number one hits with the Shirelles. The first, "Will You Still Love

Me Tomorrow" (1960), was written by King and Goffin, and the second, "Soldier Boy" (1962), Greenberg co-wrote with producer Luther Dixon.

Two giants of the contemporary popular music industry are Irving Azoff and David Geffen. Azoff served as the manager of the legendary rock group the Eagles. For many years he was also the chief of the industry giant, MCA Records. He left MCA to form his own record label, Revolution Records. Most recently, he has helped form the Entertainment Financial Group with Nomura Capitol.

The richest rock businessman is David Geffen. He started out his career managing songwriter and performer Laura Nyro. His first label was Tunafish Records, which he sold to CBS Records in 1969 for 4.5 million dollars. He was twenty-six. He then founded Asylum Records, which produced the work of artists such as Joni Mitchell, Jackson Browne, Linda Ronstadt, and the Eagles. He sold the label to Warner Brothers Records in 1972 for 7 million dollars. He then created Geffen Records, which produced groups such as Guns & Roses and Aerosmith. He sold the label to MCA for more than $500 million. Most recently Geffen was in the news when, along with Jeffrey Katzenburg and **Steven Spielberg**, he created Dream-Works SKG.

A leader in the folk and folk/rock world was manager Albert Grossman. He was instrumental in the huge folk revival of the 1960s. In 1959 he helped organize the Newport Folk Festival. His clients included stars such as Odetta, **Bob Dylan**, the Band, Paul Butterfield, Dr. John, Janis Joplin, and Peter, Paul and Mary. In the early 1970s he created both Bearsville Records and the Bearsville Recording Studios.

One of the fifties folk artists who helped create the foundation for the folk revival of the 1960s was Ramblin' Jack Elliot (1931–). Known for his commitment to the music of the legendary folk singer/songwriter Woody Guthrie, Elliot kept Guthrie's music before the public and helped to inspire an entire generation of folk musicians. These musicians brought the tradition of protest from Depression era folk music into the 1960s social protests. They also signaled a new type of musician, the singer/songwriter. The best of these

artists transcended any categorization and changed popular music forever. A large number of them were Jewish.

Among the earliest of 1960s folk musicians was Phil Ochs (1940–1976). Throughout his troubled career, he stayed closer to his folk roots than most of his contemporaries, although later in his career he was moving into rock 'n' roll. Perhaps his most famous song is "I Ain't Marchin' Anymore" (1965), which became an anthem of the antiwar movement. His albums included *All the News That's Fit to Sing* (1964) and *Pleasures of the Harbor* (1967).

Though not a songwriter, the singer who truly epitomizes the voice of folk rock is "Mama Cass" Eliot (1943–1974), of the Mamas and the Papas. The group was enormously influential in the early 1960s and had hits such as "Monday, Monday" and "California Dreaming." After the group broke up in 1968, Mama Cass released several successful solo albums and recorded a hit single, "Dream a Little Dream of Me" (1968).

However, *the* giant of 1960s music, both folk and rock, was Bob Dylan. In 1963 Dylan emerged as the greatest American folk musician of his generation when Peter, Paul, and Mary covered his classic song, "Blowin' in the Wind." His status solidified when he performed the song—with Peter, Paul, and Mary—at the Lincoln Memorial just before Dr. Martin Luther King, Jr.'s "I Have a Dream" speech. During the period from 1962 through 1964, Dylan wrote the most enduring protest songs of the era, including "A Hard Rain's Gonna Fall" (1962), "The Times They Are A-Changin'" (1964), and "Only a Pawn in Their Game" (1963). "With God on Our Side" (1964) is one of the few songs of the era to refer overtly to Jewish issues.

In 1965 Dylan took an enormous artistic risk and electrified. The response was overwhelming and very negative. Touring with the group The Band, Dylan suffered boycotts and abuse. He was literally booed off stage on several occasions. Slowly, both folk and rock audiences came to accept this "new" Dylan. The albums from this period are among his greatest: *Bringing It All Back Home* (1965), *Highway 61 Revisited* (1965), and *Blond on Blond* (1966). He largely disappeared from public view in the late 1960s, and his subsequent albums have been mixed successes both popularly and critically. Dylan remains one of the great legends of American popular music. His spirituality and religious quests are unusually public, and he is one of the few rock musicians who openly deals with religious issues—Christian and Jewish—in his music. Dylan's music, whether the early folk or his later rock and roll, is marked not only by its poetry but also its rhythm, its irony, and its challenge to authority and the status quo.

Paul Simon is perhaps a close second to Dylan in terms of his influence as a singer/songwriter. His first hit was with partner **Art Garfunkel** when, as teenagers, they got on the charts with the song "Hey, Schoolgirl" (1957). Their next big success came with the re-release of "The Sounds of Silence" (1965). A purely acoustic version of the song had been released already and hadn't done much. Producer Tom Wilson added strings and electric instruments to the background and re-released the song, which then shot to the top of the charts. Splitting with Garfunkel in 1970, Simon went on to have an extremely successful solo career marked by its exploration of various musical genres.

Among the other great folk/rock musicians from the 1960s and 1970s are Steve Goodman (1948–1984) and Arlo Guthrie (1947–). Guthrie, Woody Guthrie's son and whose mother, Marjorie Greenblatt, was Jewish, has stayed true to his father's tradition. He has also gained fame for his humorous monologues. His best-known monologue album, *Alice's Restaurant* (1967), stands out as the greatest counterculture satire of the 1960s establishment. His classic songs include "Chilling of the Evening" (1967), "Highway in the Wind" (1967), "Coming into Los Angeles" (1969), and "Washington County" (1970).

Steve Goodman rose to prominence in the 1970s when Arlo Guthrie covered his song "City of New Orleans" in 1972. Known as a songwriter's songwriter, Goodman wrote many songs that were performed by other artists. Apart from the beautiful and haunting "City of New Orleans," Goodman's most famous song is probably the country music parody "You Never Even Call Me by My Name." Country greats such as Waylon

---

It's True, the Beastie Boys Are Jewish

Part of the tradition of "bad boys" in popular music, these three performers from New York often seem to revel in their crude behavior. (They really must enjoy being every Jewish mother's worst nightmare.) They are a synthesis of different strands of contemporary music, which the band calls rap-metal. The "boys" are: Mike D. (Michael Diamond, b. 1967); MCA (Adam Yaunch, b. 1965); and King Ad-Rock (Adam Horovitz, b. 1967, whose father is the playwright Israel Horovitz).

Jennings, Merle Haggard, and Charlie Pride have all recorded it. Goodman's albums include *Steve Goodman* (1971) and *Artistic Hair* (1983).

Like Steve Goodman, Laura Nyro's (1947–1997) most successful compositions were recorded by other singers. Her compositional style is known for its blending of folk, jazz, and soul. Her composition "Wedding Bell Blues" (1969) became a hit for the Fifth Dimension and her "Stoney End" (1970) was a hit for **Barbra Streisand**. Her own albums include *Gonna Take a Miracle* (1971) and *Nested* (1978). She continued to record into the 1990s, before dying of cancer in 1997 at the age of forty-nine.

Perhaps influenced by the folk music's tradition of the singer/songwriter, but not a folk musician, is Lou Reed (1944–). Founder of the groundbreaking group Velvet Underground, in 1966, Reed is unusual in that, like Dylan, he refers to Judaism in some of his work. Unlike Dylan, Reed's reflections are generally on secular aspects of his heritage and are frequently negative. On the other hand, some critics have found elements of Yiddish humor in his sarcastic, self-referential compositions. Among his best and most popular songs are "Sweet Jane" (1970) and "Walk on the Wild Side" (1972). His albums include *Berlin* (1973) and *Songs for Drella* (1987).

A singer/songwriter in the pop/folk vein who came out of the "hit factories" of early rock 'n' roll was Carole King. After writing some of the greatest pop songs of the 1960s with Gerry Goffin, King went out on her own. Her second solo album, *Tapestry* (1971), stayed on the charts for three years and broke established

Barbra Streisand is one of the most successful vocalists ever. She first became famous as the lead in the Broadway musical Funny Girl *(1964), based on the life of Fanny Brice. She is shown here in a scene from the movie version of the play. Now a superstar, she has won more awards than anyone else in show business. And, she's affirmed her Jewishness while doing it! (Private Collection)*

records for album sales. Her other albums include *Thoroughbred* (1976) and *One to One* (1982).

Three other singer/songwriters, who write in the pop music vein are Carly Simon (1945–), Barry Manilow (1946–), and Billy Joel (1949–). Simon's most famous songs include "Anticipation" (1971) and "You're So Vain" (1972). Manilow is the ultimate pop music singer/songwriter. His hits include "Mandy" (1974), "Could It Be Magic?" (1975), "I Write the Songs" (1975), and "Copacabana" (1978). Manilow was also **Bette Midler**'s music director during her 1973 tour. Joel, who became popular in the late 1970s, is known for his powerful storytelling. His albums include *The Stranger* (1977), *Fifty-second Street* (1978), and *An Innocent Man* (1983).

Two satirists are worthy of note, Randy Newman (1943–) and Warren Zevon (1947–). Newman became infamous for his song "Short People" (1977). His albums include *Randy Newman* (1968) and *Trouble in Paradise* (1983). Ironically, considering the dark wit of his lyrics, many people think that Randy Newman helped to create the "soft rock" genre. Zevon's first major chart-topper was "Werewolves of London" (1978). His albums include *Warren Zevon* (1976) and *The Envoy* (1982).

Jews were also influential in many rock groups. Mark Volman (1944–) and Howard Kaylan (1945–) first gained fame as The Turtles. The Turtles had several top ten hits, including a cover version of Bob Dylan's "It Ain't Me Babe" (1965). Later, Volman and Kaylan became the lead singers of Frank Zappa's group, The Mothers of Invention, and renamed themselves Flo & Eddie. Mike Bloomfield (1944–1981), considered one of America's great blues guitarists, played with Bob Dylan, was a member of Paul Butterfield's Blues Band, and recorded several solo albums. Al Kooper (1941–), an organist with a blues background, helped found the Blues Project in 1965 and the jazz-rock-fusion group Blood, Sweat, and Tears in 1968.

After the heyday of rock 'n' roll in the 1960s, popular music developed an array of related idioms, from heavy metal and glitter rock to punk to rap. Among the heavy metal glitter rock bands of the 1970s, perhaps the most successful was Kiss, founded by Gene Simmons (1949–) and Paul Stanley (1952–). An early pioneer in the punk scene was the band the Ramones, with lead singer/songwriter Joey Ramone (1952–). More a cult band than a popular phenomenon, the Ramones influenced much of the later punk movement. The Beastie Boys came to national attention in the mid-1980s as one of the few white rap groups. They are also, at this writing, the only Jewish rap group. The members of the group are Mike Diamond, called "Mike D." (1967–); Adam Yaunch, called "MCA", (1965–); and Adam Horovitz, called "King Ad-Rock" (1967–). Their hit album *Licensed to Ill* (1986) was a notorious example of early rap crudity, much to their fans' delight.

THEATRICAL MUSIC

Dealt with in depth in the **Theater** entry, theatrical music can't be neglected here. For many years what was popular music in America came from what was performed on stage. Jewish influence was enormous, and the list of Jewish composers, lyricists, librettists and performers is huge.

If one thinks of these great musicians in terms of the classic American songs that are remembered independently from the shows where they originated, their significance is immediately apparent. Irving Berlin wrote thousands of classic songs for the stage, including "A Pretty Girl Is Like a Melody" for the *Ziegfeld Follies of 1919*, "Cheek to Cheek" for *Top Hat* (1935), and "There's No Business Like Show Business" for *Annie Get Your Gun* (1946).

Among the other great Jewish songsters of the era were **Jerome Kern**, **Sigmund Romberg**, Irving Caesar, and the **Gershwin** brothers, **George** and Ira. Kern wrote the music for the first musical to have a serious plot taken from a literary source (a novel by **Edna Ferber**), *Showboat* (1927), with lyrics by **Oscar Hammerstein II**. He also wrote the classic songs "Smoke Gets in Your Eyes" for *Roberta* (1933), with lyrics by Otto Harbach and "A Fine Romance" for *Swing Time* (1936), with lyrics by Dorothy Fields. **Sigmund Romberg** wrote "Deep in My Heart" for *The Student Prince* (1924), "One Alone" for *The Desert Song* (1926), and "Lover, Come Back to Me" for *The New Moon* (1928). Irving Caesar was an exceptional lyricist who wrote "Crazy Rhythm" for *Here's Howe* (1928), "Animal Crackers in My Soup" for *Curly Top* (1935), and "Tea for Two" for *No, No Nanette* (1925). George and Ira Gershwin contributed the classics "Summertime," "It Ain't Necessarily So," and "I Got Plenty o' Nuttin'" to the opera *Porgy and Bess* (1935). They also gave us "I Got Rhythm," written for *Girl Crazy* (1930), and "They Can't Take That Away From Me," written for *Shall We Dance* (1937).

Composer **Richard Rodgers** had two of the longest and most successful collaborations in the history of American music. With **Lorenz Hart** he wrote "Blue Moon" (1934), their only independently released song, and dozens of others, including "The Lady Is a Tramp" and "My Funny Valentine," both from *Babes in Arms* (1937) and "Bewitched, Bothered and Bewildered" from *Pal Joey* (1940). Rodgers and Oscar Hammerstein wrote a string of classic musicals that produced songs such as "Oh, What a Beautiful Mornin'" from *Oklahoma* (1943), "Some Enchanted Evening" from *South Pacific* (1949), and "My Favorite Things" from *The Sound of Music* (1959).

Frank Loesser wrote the words and music for most of his musicals. His contributions to the pantheon of American popular songs include "Once in Love with Amy" from *Where's Charlie* (1948), "Luck Be a Lady" from *Guys and Dolls* (1950), and "Baby It's Cold Outside" from the film *Neptune's Daughter* (1949). Lerner and Loewe gave us "They Call the Wind Mariah" from *Paint Your Wagon (1951)*, all of the songs from *My Fair Lady* (1956), and the incomparable "Thank Heaven for Little Girls" from the film *Gigi* (1959).

Composer Jules Styne and lyricist Sammy Cahn frequently wrote together, especially for films. They wrote the song scores for *Anchors Away* (1945) and *It Happened in Brooklyn* (1947), among many others. Styne's other tunes include "Diamonds Are a Girl's

---

Rocking All Night, in Hebrew

This headline from the August 9, 1998, *New York Times* sums up the special and powerful place that Yosi Piamenta occupies in contemporary Jewish music. Sometimes called the "Sephardic Santana" or the "Hasidic [Jimi] Hendrix" Mr. Piamenta is a forty-six-year-old Hasidic rock guitarist (with all-Hebrew lyrics), who has recently become more widely known after years of supporting himself by playing at weddings and bar mitzvahs. The *Times* article describes a late-night concert in the Aladdin Hotel in Woodbourne, New York (in the Catskill Mountains, where many Hasidim spend summer vacations), which "drove hundreds of . . . fans into a frenzy of whooping, stomping, Jewish rock-and-roll ecstasy." Make no mistake, there were no drugs and no alcohol among the largely Orthodox audience and no women dancing, although, in the words of the reporter, "[they] grooved quite expressively from their wooden chairs" off the dance floor. "In our culture," said one of the women, "we can't really go out there, but we love the music."

Best Friend" from *Gentlemen Prefer Blondes* (1949), "People" from *Funny Girl* (1964), and "Let Me Entertain You" from *Gypsy* (1959)

Steven Sondheim's influence on the modern American musical and modern American popular music cannot be understated. In addition to the lyrics for *Gypsy*, Sondheim wrote, with Leonard Bernstein contributing the music, what many consider the pivotal musical of the second half of the twentieth century, *West Side Story* (1957). The classic songs from other musicals, for which he wrote both the words and the lyrics, include "Side by Side by Side" from *Company* (1970), "Broadway Baby" from *Follies* (1971), and "Send in the Clowns" from *A Little Night Music* (1973).

Though less numerous than the theatrical composers and lyricists, there have been many significant Jewish theatrical singers, some of whom were also known as comedians. The man responsible for introducing most of the earliest of these singers to American audiences was **Florenz Ziegfeld**. From 1907 until his death, Ziegfeld presented the *Ziegfeld Follies* annually. In the process, he gave the world such great singer entertainers as **Sophie Tucker**, Nora Bayes (1880–1928), **Fanny Brice**, and **Eddie Cantor**.

Nora Bayes reached stardom in 1902, singing Harry von Tilzer's "Down Where the Wurzburger Flows." She began performing for Ziegfeld in the first presentation of the *Follies* (1907). Her most famous songs included "Has Anyone Here Seen Kelly?," "Take Me Out to the Ball Game," "Over There," and "Shine On, Harvest Moon." At her height she earned as much as $100,000 per year.

Follies star Sophie Tucker started out in 1909, appearing with Nora Bayes. She went on to become one of vaudeville's biggest performers. Her trademark song was "Some of These Days," and her early vaudeville billing was as the "Mary Garden of Ragtime." Later she became the "Queen of Jazz," and finally she was "The Last of the Red-hot Mamas." In addition to performing in the *Ziegfeld Follies*, Tucker appeared in many of the *Earl Carroll Vanities* revues and the Shubert *Gaieties* revues.

Ziegfeld star Fanny Brice is best known as a comedienne, but she was also a singer. Ziegfeld discovered her through her singing, at a burlesque house in 1910. Her most famous songs were the torch song "My Man" (1921) and the delightful "Second Hand Rose" (1921). She performed on Broadway and in almost every edition of the *Follies*.

Eddie Cantor also got his legs with the *Follies*, as well as with the Shubert revues. Master of the comic song, he had great success with "If You Knew Susie" (1925), "Makin' Whoopee" (1928), "Alexander's Ragtime Band" (1938), and "Yes, Sir, That's My Baby" (1941). His career included successes on Broadway, radio, and television.

Perhaps the most famous singer of the vaudeville era never performed for Ziegfeld. **Al Jolson**, noted for his black-face minstrel act, used the mask to bring a derivative of African American singing before the white American public. Among his most famous songs are "You Made Me Love You" (1913), "Toot, Toot, Tootsie" (1922), "California, Here I Come" (1924), "My Mammy" (1928), and, of course "Swanee" (1920). He played the lead role in *The Jazz Singer*, a film about a young Jewish man, trained to be a cantor, who turns his back on tradition to become a singer of jazz.

Danny Kaye is best known today as a comic film actor, but his skills were myriad. He started out as a singer, moved on to become a comedian dancer on the borscht circuit, then added singing back into his act. It was during this period that he truly developed his talent for comic "scat" singing. Here someone who is regularly ignored as a songwriter must be mentioned: Sylvia Fine, Danny Kaye's wife. Fine wrote most of Kaye's most successful songs, including "Anatole of Paris" and "Stanislavsky." Later, Fine and Kaye moved together into film, where the young actor was required to bleach his hair and assume a less Jewish identity. Kaye's most famous musical films include *Hans Christian Andersen* (1952) and *White Christmas* (1954).

Another star known for his comic film presence was **Sammy Davis, Jr.**, a convert to Judaism in 1958. Starting out as a vaudeville comedian and "hoofer" with the Will Mastin Trio, Davis ultimately became a successful nightclub headliner and recording artist. Among his most famous songs are "That Old Black

Magic" (1955), "What Kind of Fool Am I?" (1962), "The Candy Man" (1972), and, with Frank Sinatra, "Me and My Shadow" (1952).

The most successful and significant modern theatrical singer—often compared to Fanny Brice—is, of course, **Barbra Streisand**. Known for her vocal range, interpretive skill, and emotion, her first taste of fame began at the Bon Soir nightclub in Manhattan in 1960. Her first Broadway show was *I Can Get It for You Wholesale* (1962). The Broadway musical *Funny Girl* (1964) —based on the life of Fanny Brice—made her a star. Her first record album, *The Barbra Streisand Album*, came out in 1963, and in the next five years she recorded ten more albums, not including cast recordings for Broadway shows in which she appeared. In the 1970s, Streisand broadened her choice of songs and style of singing to include soft rock. She will always be best known, though, for her command of the theatrical and the torch song. Among her most famous songs are "People," "Second Hand Rose" (1966), "Where You Lead" (1971), "The Way We Were" (1973), and "You Don't Bring Me Flowers" (1978), with Neil Diamond.

Another versatile theatrical singer who has been frequently compared to Fanny Brice is **Bette Midler**. Midler's fame began to grow when she developed her famous cabaret act in the gay bathhouses of New York City. Just a few of her most famous songs are "Delta Dawn" (1972), "Boogie Woogie Bugle Boys" (1972), "Married Men" (1979), and "From a Distance" (1990). In addition to her singing, Midler, like Streisand, has gained respect for both her comic and dramatic acting, especially in films.

The artists discussed above are just a few of the significant Jewish American musicians. It would be easy to add names to any and all of the musical categories. In popular music and folk music there has not been room to detail the careers of such important performers as Eddie Fisher (1928–), **Theodore Bikel**, Janis Ian (1951–), Phoebe Snow (1952–), and the singing duo Steve Lawrence (1935–) and Eydie Gorme (1932–). Among notable instrumentalists, Jewish Americans have included trumpeter Herb Alpert (1935–), jazz saxophonist Al Cohn (1925–), and classical pianist Ruth

---

The Times They Did Change

When Bob Dylan released his earth-shaking albums *Highway 61 Revisited* and *Blonde on Blonde* in 1965 and 1966, the Grammy Awards for album of the year both went to Frank Sinatra. But at the 1998 awards, Mr. Dylan prevailed: *Time Out of Mind*, a haunting album of songs about lost love and intimations of death, was named album of the year. It was his forty-second album.

The *New York Times*, The Week in Review, 3/1/98

Laredo (1937–). There are hundreds more composers of importance, such as **Marc Blitzstein**, and Elizabeth Swados (1951–). And finally there are uncategorizables, like the oboist, record producer, and "sing-along king," Mitch Miller (1911–).

In every genre of music, American Jews have been prominent as creators, leaders, and interpreters. They have also been a significant part of the cross-pollination that made American music so rich. They brought to the mix a legacy of tradition, expertise, understanding, and joy.

OYSHER, MOISHE (1907–1958)

Composer, actor, cantor

Cantor, actor, and composer Moishe Oysher was born in Bessarabia on March 8, 1907. He was educated in Europe and became a cantor in his youth. After immigrating to the United States he expanded his repertoire and began a successful career as a secular singer. He acted both in Yiddish musical theater and in film. Throughout his career he also gave concerts, singing secular Jewish folk songs and liturgical music. His film performances include roles in *The Cantor's Son* (1937), *The Singing Blacksmith* (1938), and *Overture to Glory* (1940). A composer as well, Oysher wrote such popular songs as "Amar, Amar," "H'Aveley," "I Love This Land," and "Oh, My Mamma." He also wrote the score for the film *Singing in the Dark*. He died when he was only fifty on November 27, 1958, in New Rochelle, New York.

PAPP, JOSEPH (1921–1991)

Producer

Joseph Papp's first language was Yiddish, but he left an enduring legacy in the name of the greatest writer in the English language, William Shakespeare. As the director of the New York Shakespeare Festival and the Public Theater, Papp brought to the New York stage many of the most important innovators of the 1960s, 1970s, and 1980s.

Born Josef Papirosfky to Polish Jewish immigrants, he served in the Navy in World War II and studied at the Actors Laboratory in California. Returning to New York he took a job as a stage manager at CBS, changing his name because, he said, it was too long for the credits. In 1954 Papp began staging free performances of Shakespeare in a Lower East Side church. Two years later, with support from the Parks Department, he brought his productions to a nearby city park. In 1956 his company toured the city, performing in parks in all five boroughs. Eventually, they settled in Central Park, where the city built the Delacorte Theater as a permanent home for the Shakespeare Festival.

In 1966 Papp acquired a landmark building on Greenwich Village's Astor Place and christened it The New York Shakespeare Festival Public Theater. Within the large edifice he created six theatrical spaces and over the next thirty years they would be a home for the best of international theater, music, and film. One of the first plays produced at the Public was a groundbreaking musical, *Hair* (1967). It was the first of many plays Papp brought to the public that would move on to further success on Broadway. In later years, he could claim credit for Public-to-Broadway hits *No Place to Be Somebody*, *That Championship Season* and, most notably, *A Chorus Line*. Papp continued to produce free theater in the Park during the summers, too. Shortly before his death, he embarked on his most ambitious project, staging the complete works of Shakespeare over several seasons. The cycle was finally completed in 1997.

Papp insisted on the social power of theater. He was among the first to seek out multi-racial castings of

Mandy Patinkin is shown here as a Yeshiva student in Barbra Streisand's film Yentl. *His early singing in temple may have provided him with a grounding in music and in Hebrew, but he had to learn Yiddish for his one-man performance of all-Yiddish songs,* Mamaloshen *("mother tongue"), which opened on Broadway in 1998. (Private Collection)*

the classics. He also remained attached to his Jewish roots, even performing a cabaret evening of Yiddish theater songs.

PATINKIN, MANDY (1952–)

Actor, singer

The contemporary voice of Broadway, Mandy (Mandel) Patinkin was born on the South Side of Chicago and began singing in temple when he was eight or nine years old. He attended the University of Kansas and Juilliard before beginning his career on the off-Broadway stage. For several years he worked regularly on stage and in film. When he was twenty-seven, he astounded audiences and critics alike in the role of Che Guevara in *Evita* (1979) on Broadway, winning a Tony Award for that performance. During the next few years, he appeared on screen in *Ragtime* (1981), *Daniel* (1983), and *Yentl* (1983), in which he played opposite **Barbra Streisand**. He then went back to Broadway to star as Georges Seurat in the musical *Sunday in the Park with George* (1984). It was a huge success, running for 604 performances.

Great popular success came to Patinkin with his charming, passionate, and wildly funny performance as Inigo Montoya in **Rob Reiner**'s film *The Princess Bride* (1987). His many other films have included *Alien Nation* (1988), *Dick Tracy* (1990), and *The Doctor* (1991). The last, in which he played a brilliant, intense, and arrogant surgeon, led to his being cast in the television series "Chicago Hope" in a similar role. Debuting in 1996, the show was immediately successful, and Patinkin found himself a television star. After one season, however, he gave up his regular role on the show in order to spend more time with his children. The next year, he released a new album, *Experiment*, to considerable acclaim.

PEERCE, JAN (1904–1984)

Opera singer

Tenor Jan Peerce (Jacob Pincus Perelmuth) was born in New York City on June 3, 1904. A musician and singer throughout his life, he began his career by playing the violin. During the 1920s he played the violin and sang with popular dance bands. In 1933 he became a singer at Radio City Music Hall and performed popular tunes and operatic arias on the radio show "Radio City Music Hall of the Air." In 1938 Arturo Toscanini heard Peerce sing the role of Siegmund from Wagner's *Die Walküre* and hired him to sing with the NBC Symphony Orchestra. That same year, in Philadelphia, he had his live debut in *Rigoletto*. In 1941 he made his first appearance at the Metropolitan Opera, singing the part of Alfredo in *La Traviata*. Thereafter he became a mainstay at the Met, singing virtually the entire operatic canon.

PERAHIA, MURRAY (1947–)

Pianist

Pianist Murray Perahia was born in New York City on April 19, 1947. He began to play the piano at the age of three and a half. When he was seventeen, he entered the Mannes School of Music. At the same time, during the summers he performed at the renowned Marlboro Music Festival. This exposed him to many virtuoso musicians, including Pablo Casals and Mieczyslaw Horszowski. In 1972, he won the Leeds Festival Prize in England. After winning the prize, Perahia was much in demand throughout the world. In subsequent years, he developed into one of the major concert pianists of his generation. He is especially well known for his recordings of all of Mozart's piano concertos. His playing is admired for its lyric phrasing and subtle dynamics. In addition to both conducting and playing the Mozart concertos, he frequently performs the great Romantic composers.

PERLMAN, ITZHAK (1945–)

Violinist

Itzhak Perlman has been moving audiences with his violin since he was ten years old. Born in Tel Aviv, Israel, on August 31, 1945, he contracted polio when he was four, damaging his legs. When he was thirteen, already having performed publicly for three years, he moved to the United States to attend the Juilliard School of Music in New York City. In 1963 he debuted at Carnegie Hall and won the coveted Levintritt Competition the following year. He made his London debut in 1968 and has been on the faculty of Brooklyn College since 1975. He has performed for thirty-five years, touring the world as a solo recitalist, as guest soloist with symphony orchestras, and with chamber orchestras. His range is huge, from nineteenth-century Romantic to modern classical to ragtime to klezmer music. In chamber music concerts he has often appeared with fellow Israelis Daniel Barenboim and **Pinchas Zukerman**. Considered one of the best violinists of the century, he is admired for the richness of his tone, his technical abilities and the brilliance of his interpretations. Perhaps most importantly, Itzhak Perlman's love of music is beautifully evident whenever he plays.

PETERS, ROBERTA (1930–)

Opera singer

Soprano Roberta Peters (born Peterman) was born in New York City on May 4, 1930. She received no formal Jewish training but learned Yiddish at her grandmother's knee. An obvious talent from an early age, she made her debut at the Metropolitan Opera when she was nineteen, as Zerlina in *Don Giovanni*. She went on to sing opera's greatest roles and is famous for her large and varied repertoire. Some of her most famous roles are the Queen of the Night in *The Magic Flute*, Gilda in *Rigoletto*, Kitty in *The Last Savage*, and Rosina in *The Barber of Seville*. She also sings the works of Bach, the Strausses (Johann and Richard), and Handel. She performed longer with the Metropolitan Opera than any other soprano in history, appeared sixty-five times on the "Ed Sullivan Show," and has toured Europe and Asia. Committed to her Jewish heritage, Peters performs for synagogues and Jewish groups, including Yiddish folk songs in her repertoire. She is on the board of the **Anti-Defamation League** and performs benefit concerts for the Roberta Peters Scholarship Fund at Hebrew University.

PICON, MOLLY (1898–1992)

Actor

Molly Picon began performing at the age of five and was still working in her eighties. Born in New York, she became Baby Margaret to compete in amateur contests and perform in nickelodeons. She became a member of Michael Thomashefsky's Yiddish repertory company in Philadelphia when she was six and remained there for three years, before going on to performances at the Arch Street Theater from 1908 to

Jewish to the core in her devotion to Yiddish and her efforts on behalf of Jewish refugees and the State of Israel, it often seemed as if Molly Picon could do anything on the stage or screen. She is shown here in the role of Yente the Matchmaker in the 1971 film version of Fiddler on the Roof. *(Private Collection)*

1912. From 1912 until she was seventeen, she worked in cabarets.

This energetic youth and childhood was followed by an equally busy adult life. In 1919 she joined a Yiddish repertory company in Boston headed by Jacob Kalich, whom she soon married. She continued to performed with Kalich for the next two decades, becoming one of the biggest stars of the Yiddish theater. During World War II, she entertained in American military camps and in European displaced persons camps. After the war, Picon performed in the English-speaking theater, where her most successful role was in the musical *Milk and Honey* (1961). She also performed in a number of films, including *Come Blow Your Horn* (1963), *Cannonball Run II* (1984), and, as Yente the Matchmaker, in the film musical *Fiddler on the Roof*.

PREVIN, ANDRÉ (1929–)

Composer, conductor, pianist

One of America's best-known musicians, André Previn, was born in Berlin in 1929 and studied at the Berlin Conservatory while still a child. He moved with his family to Paris, studied at the Paris Conservatoire, then moved again, this time to California. At sixteen, he began working at the music department of the Metro-Goldwyn-Mayer film studios. He wrote many film scores and orchestrated others. Four of his original scores won Academy Awards. He also developed a reputation as a jazz pianist and performed as a concerto soloist with a number of American orchestras. At the same time, he studied conducting and composition.

In 1967 Previn was offered the post as chief conductor of the Houston Symphony Orchestra after an engagement as guest conductor. From that time on, he has conducted the world's great orchestras. He held the chief artistic posts at the London Symphony Orchestra from 1969 to 1979, the Royal Philharmonic from 1985 to 1988, and Los Angeles Philharmonic from 1985 to 1989, among others. He appears annually with the Vienna Philharmonic and regularly conducts other major orchestras, such as the Boston Symphony, the New York Philharmonic, and the San Francisco Symphony.

As a composer, Previn has written a works in a variety of forms. They include a piano concerto commissioned by Vladimir Ashkenzy, a cello sonata written for Yo-Yo Ma, a song cycle written for Dame Janet Baker, and a music drama, *Every Good Boy Deserves Favour*, written in collaboration with playwright Tom Stoppard. He also collaborated on the Broadway musical *Coco* with **Alan Jay Lerner**. An enormously versatile musician, Previn has recorded complete cycles of a number of important British and Russian composers, including Vaughan Williams, Shostakovich, and Prokofiev. In 1990 he wrote a memoir entitled *No Minor Chords: My Early Days in Hollywood*; in 1996, he was awarded a knighthood by Queen Elizabeth II; and in 1998 he received the Kennedy Center Honors for lifetime achievement in the performing arts.

RANDALL, TONY (1920–)

Actor

One of the few and the finest light-comedy actors of our time, Tony Randall (Leonard Rosenberg) was born in Tulsa, Oklahoma. He received his training as an actor at the Neighborhood Playhouse in New York, a part of the Henry Street Settlement. He made a few stage appearances before serving in the armed forces in World War II and upon his return worked in both radio and theater. He made his Broadway debut in *Anthony and Cleopatra* (1947) as Scarus. He continued on stage until 1952, when he scored a television success as a regular on the sitcom "Mr. Peepers" (1952–55). That television stint was followed by a succession of light, romantic film comedies, in which he usually played the second male lead. These included *Will Success Spoil Rock Hunter?* (1957), *The Mating Game* (1959), *Pillow Talk* (1959), and *Lover Come Back* (1961). He also did a number of comedy mysteries, playing Agatha Christie's Hercule Poirot in *The Alphabet Murders* (1966), among others.

Randall became familiar to a new generation of television watchers in "The Odd Couple" (1970–75), based on the **Neil Simon** play about two incompatible divorced men rooming together. Fussy Felix Unger became Randall's alter ego, one that has been difficult for the actor to shake. He had two other television series, "The Tony Randall Show" (1976–78) and "Love,

Sidney" (1981–82), where he played a recognizably Jewish character, and made several films in the 1980s. However, he increasingly turned his attention to supporting and being a commentator on classical music, as well as being active in support of Jewish causes. In 1992 he opened the National Actors Theater, attracting an impressive group of film and television actors to appear in classic drama.

REED, LOU (1944–)

Singer, songwriter

Lou Reed was born Louis Firbank on March 2, 1944, in Brooklyn, New York, and grew up on Long Island. In 1960 he attended Syracuse University, where he was introduced to one of his most important influences, the poet Delmore Schwartz.

In the mid-1960s Reed helped found The Velvet Underground, a band that reflected the dark side of the 1960s youth culture. With songs such as "Heroin," Reed and The Velvet Underground explored topics such as drug abuse, homosexuality, and sadomasochism. They initially rose to fame as members of Andy Warhol's circle of artists. In 1966, they performed for Warhol's Exploding Plastic Inevitable shows. The band went on to produce four albums that were important influences in the development of rock and roll.

When the band broke up in 1970, Reed went on to pursue a solo career. An erratic artist, Reed's solo career has had many ups and downs. Among his most famous songs are the classic "Walk on the Wild Side" (1972) and "Sally Can't Dance" (1974). In 1990 Reed and fellow Velvet Underground bandmate John Cale created the Warhol memorial album *Songs for Drella*. The Velvet Underground reunited to tour Europe in 1993/1994.

REINER, FRITZ (1888–1963)

Conductor

Conductor Fritz Reiner was born in Budapest, Hungary, on December 19, 1888. He attended the Bu-

dapest Royal Academy of Music and later went on to serve as the chief conductor of the Dresden Opera. In 1922 he immigrated to the United States, where he became the principal conductor of the Cincinnati Symphony. In 1931 he left Cincinnati to lead the opera and orchestral departments of the Curtis Institute of Music in Philadelphia. He stayed with the Curtis Institute until 1941. In 1938 he took on the additional position of director at the Pittsburgh Symphony, a position he held until 1948. From 1948 through 1953 he was the music director of the Metropolitan Opera in New York City. In 1953 he took on the job for which he is best known, director of the Chicago Symphony Orchestra, where he remained until 1962.

In both Chicago and Pittsburgh, Reiner rebuilt failing orchestras. Under his leadership, they became two of the best musical organizations in the country. Especially well known for his interpretations of Brahms, Strauss, and Bartók, Reiner was also a proponent of new music. He was considered a despotic conductor but was respected by both audience and performer for his technical mastery. He died in New York City on November 15, 1963.

REISENBERG, NADIA (1904–1983)

Pianist

Pianist Nadia Reisenberg was born in Vilna, Lithuania, on July 14, 1904. As a child she studied piano at the St. Petersburg Imperial Conservatory. She immigrated to the United States with her family in 1922. The same year she made her American debut, playing Paderewski's *Polish Fantasy* for an audience that included the composer. After eight years of successful recitals and guest soloist appearances with orchestras, Reisenberg returned to school, entering the Curtis School of Music. She earned her degree in 1935 and pursued post-graduate work until 1938. After her studies at Curtis, Reisenberg began to play a series of radio concerts. From 1938 until 1940 she performed weekly with the WOR Radio Orchestra, conducted by Alfred Wallenstein. During this two-year period she performed all of Mozart's piano concertos.

In addition to performing, Reisenberg was a respected teacher. She taught at the Curtis Institute while she was a graduate student and, later, at the Mannes School of Music, Juilliard, the Rubin Academy of Music in Jerusalem, and privately. In addition to her teaching, she was a lover of chamber music. Toward the end of her career she concentrated on teaching and playing with chamber ensembles all over the world. She died on June 10, 1983.

ROBBINS, JEROME (1918–1998)

Choreographer

Jerome Robbins changed the face of dance in both the classical world and the musical theater. Born Jerome Rabinowitz on October 11, 1918, in New York City, Robbins grew up in nearby Weehawken, New Jersey. He joined the American Ballet Theatre (ABT) in 1940, when it was still called the Ballet Theatre. Only four years later he had his choreographic debut with *Fancy Free*. It was a huge success and later that year was developed into a Broadway play, *On the Town*. In 1949 the play became the classic film of the same title. Robbins choreographed and directed *Peter Pan* (1952), *The Bells Are Ringing* (1956), *West Side Story* (1957), *Gypsy* (1959), and *Fiddler on the Roof* (1964). *Fiddler* was inspired by **Sholem Aleichem**'s short stories.

On the classical front, Robbins moved from ABT to the New York City Ballet (NYCB) in 1948, where he worked with George Balanchine. He became the ballet master in 1960 and was co-ballet master-in-chief, with Peter Martins, from 1983 through 1990. Among the many dances he created while at ABT and NYCB are *Interplay* (1945), *Afternoon of a Faun* (1953), *Dances at a Gathering* (1969), *Other Dances: The Goldberg Variations* (1971), and *West Side Story Suite* (1995), a re-staging of seven dances from the musical.

Robbins won four Tony Awards for his choreography; two Oscars—choreographer and director of the film version of *West Side Story* (1961); and an Emmy for a televised version of *Peter Pan*. He helped to create the Inbal Dance Company of Israel and founded the American Theatre Laboratory. In 1997 he completed a

Jerome Robbins and Judaism

"I grew up in the Jewish tradition that children must get all the culture possible," Mr. Robbins said in 1979. His professional debut was a two-word walk-on role in the Yiddish Art Theater's 1937 production of *The Brothers Ashkenazi*.

major work for the City Ballet, *Brandenburg*, set to the Bach concertos.

Jerome Robbins revitalized the world of classical dance and gave it a uniquely American flavor. He brought complexity and style to the Broadway musical theater, making it a more evocative art form. He died in New York City on July 29, 1998.

RODGERS, RICHARD (1902–1979)

Theatrical composer

With his two successive partners, Richard Rodgers wrote hundreds of the most memorable songs ever to come out of the musical theater and forever changed the American musical. Born in New York, he first worked with each of his two main collaborators—**Lorenz Hart** and **Oscar Hammerstein II**—during his college years at Columbia. After college he and Hart began selling "interpolated songs" to shows written by others. For a number of years they worked with librettist Herbert Fields to create such shows as *Dearest Enemy* (1925) and *Present Arms* (1928). Hart's lyrics were witty and slightly ironic, with clever multiple rhymes and word plays and Rodgers matched them with appropriately spritely music.

In 1943, after breaking with Hart, Rodgers joined with Oscar Hammerstein II and began to write both a different kind of music and a different kind of show. Hammerstein's lyrics were more sentimental than Hart's, but they were also simpler and more poetic. And when they were funny, they relied more on genuine humor than on wit. Rodgers' music was accordingly more substantial. Together, the two abandoned the modified revue style that had dominated American musicals. They turned to a more realistic form, with cohesive stories, fully drawn characters, and well integrated songs. These shows included *Oklahoma!* (1943), *Carousel* (1945), *South Pacific* (1949), *The King and I* (1951), and *The Sound of Music* (1959) as well as a number of others.

After Hammerstein's death in 1960, Rodgers continued to write lovely, melodic songs for a variety of shows, but he never again participated in creating a musical of the importance of those he did with his two partners.

ROMBERG, SIGMUND (1887–1951)

Composer

During the first half of the twentieth century, Sigmund Romberg composed the scores for more than seventy musicals. It was a long way from the engineering career he had planned.

Born on July 29, 1887, in Hungary, Romberg studied both engineering and music in Hungary and Vienna before immigrating to the United States in 1909. After working as a bandleader and pianist, Romberg began composing for Shubert revues. He composed his first successful song, "Memories," in 1911 and his first operetta, *Maytime*, in 1917. The show was an enormous success and Romberg never looked back. Some of his other scores include *The Student Prince* (1924), *Blossom Time* (1926), *The New Moon* (1928), *Up in Central Park* (1945), and the film *The Night Is Young* (1935). His operettas were frequently made into films. He died on November 9, 1951, in New York City.

ROSE, BILLY (1899–1966)

Nightclub owner

Billy Rose (born William Rosenberg) fought his way out of the poverty of the Lower East Side ghetto, using an unusual combination of skills and a lot of *chutzpah*. He began his career as a stenographer and quickly won numerous shorthand contests. His stenographic skills won him the attention of **Bernard Baruch**, who hired him as his personal secretary when the Wall Street genius became head of the War Industries Board during World War I.

After the war, Rose was looking for a career that would earn him lots of money. Having heard that successful songwriters grew rich, he settled on that métier. Typically, having made the decision, he studied song lyrics of the day for three intense months, seeking a success formula. He found it, too. He wrote over 400 songs, including such standards as "It's Only a Paper Moon" and "Me and My Shadow." By the age of twenty-four, the brash Rose had earned over $100,000 in royalties (a substantial amount of money in the 1920s) and with investment advice from Baruch, he earned considerably more. He plowed his earnings into speakeasies and nightclubs, enjoying even more success at the height of Prohibition.

In the 1930s and 1940s Rose turned his attention to producing shows, enjoying prestige, but losing money with the Rodgers and Hart classic *Jumbo*. He gained prestige and success with the money-making *Carmen Jones*. But he made his first million with his spectacular water show at the 1939 World's Fair, *Billy Rose's Aquacade*. He also went through five marriages, the first to **Fanny Brice**.

As a millionaire, Rose dabbled in real estate and art, wrote a newspaper column, and bought theaters. A staunch Zionist, he donated his valuable sculpture collection that included significant works by Rodin and Moore to Israel.

ROSENBLATT, JOSEF (YOSSELE) (1882–1933)

Cantor

The most famous Jewish cantor in modern history, Yossele Rosenblatt was born in Ukraine on May 9, 1882. He began to sing in his local synagogue when he was four. He never had any formal musical training, though he was profoundly influenced by the ecstatic music of Hasidism. He was a traveling cantor for much of his childhood. Immigrating to the United States in 1912, he became the cantor of the First Hungarian Congregation Ohab Zedek in New York City.

In the late 1910s he debuted at Carnegie Hall, where he publicly sang non-Jewish music for the first time as well as Jewish secular and religious music. After the success of this debut, Rosenblatt began went on tour throughout the United States and Europe. He also recorded Jewish folk songs and liturgical music. As the first artist to introduce a non-Jewish public to the music of the synagogue, he became known to many as the "King of Cantors" and was heralded as "the Jewish Caruso."

In 1918 the Chicago Opera Company offered to pay him the then enormous fee of $1,000 per performance if he would sing the role of Eléazar in Halévey's opera *La juive* (The Jewess). Rosenblatt refused because he felt that acting in opera would not be appropriate for a synagogue cantor.

Although he was one of the most successful recording and concert artists of the era, unwise business decisions forced him to declare bankruptcy in 1925. He left his position as cantor and began performing in vaudeville to pay off his debts. His encore piece was "When Irish Eyes Are Smiling." He also sang for the sound track of the first talkie, *The Jazz Singer* (1927). He was filming the movie *The Dream of My People* in Jerusalem, when he died on June 19, 1933.

RUBINSTEIN, ARTUR (1887–1982)

Pianist

Artur Rubinstein made his professional debut on the piano when he was only eleven years old and impressed audiences with his virtuosity for most of the twentieth century. He was born in Lodz, Poland, when it was still a part of Russia on January 28, 1887. When he was eight years old and already a prodigy on the piano, he moved to Berlin. His masters were Josef Joachim, a friend of Johannes Brahms, Max Bruch, who taught him theory, and Heinrich Barth, a former student of Franz Liszt. As might be expected considering his teachers, Rubinstein excelled in interpreting the late nineteen-century Romantic composers such as Chopin, Liszt, Schumann, and Brahms. He also played chamber music, notably with **Jascha Heifetz**.

Rubinstein came to the United States twice, in 1906 and 1937, before immigrating in 1941. His family perished in the Holocaust and after the war he refused to play in Germany. He became a citizen in 1946. Throughout his life he toured and recorded extensively. A supporter of Israel, Rubinstein never accepted payment for his concerts there. In 1963 the proceeds from his concerts were used to endow the Artur Rubinstein Chair of Musicology at the Hebrew University. He completed his memoirs, *My Young Years*, in 1973 and died on December 20, 1982, in Geneva, Switzerland.

SCHILDKRAUT, JOSEPH (1896–1964)

Actor

The first actor to play Otto Frank in *The Diary of Anne Frank* was born in Vienna, Austria, in 1896, the son of world-renowned actor Rudolf Schildkraut. He began his acting career in the United States, against his father's wishes, while Rudolf was performing in Yiddish plays in New York. He returned to Europe with his family, served in the Austrian army, and scored three consecutive triumphs on the Viennese stage before coming back to the United States to stay. He became a star with his performance of the carnival barker in *Liliom* (1921). This success was followed by many others on stage and in films. Among his best-known films are *The Shop around the Corner* (1940) and *The Life of Emile Zola* (1937), in which he played Captain Dreyfus to great critical acclaim.

During the 1950s, Schildkraut also worked a great deal in television, appearing in more than eighty live television programs. He hosted his own dramatic anthology, "Joseph Schildkraut Presents," during the 1953–54 season. In 1955 he created the role for which he is now most remembered, Otto Frank, the father of young Anne Frank. He played the role in the film version in 1959, as well. It was a powerful experience for an actor whose family had once thought of themselves proudly as German, but who had come to know that, in Schildkraut's words, their "soul and heartbeat were Jewish."

SCHOENBERG, ARNOLD (1874–1951)

Composer

Revolutionary composer Arnold Schoenberg was born in Vienna in 1874 and studied as a child at the Realschule. When his father died, sixteen-year-old Arnold got work arranging popular songs and orchestrating operettas. When he was twenty, he began taking counterpoint lessons from Alexander Zemlinsky, whose sister he married seven years later. In 1898 his *String Quartet No. 1* premiered in Vienna. That same year he converted to Christianity while under the influence of composer Gustav Mahler. The work considered his first masterpiece, *Verklärte Nacht* (1899), received its premiere in 1902.

Schoenberg's composing began to change after a three-year stay in Berlin, where he worked with an experimental artistic cabaret while he was teaching at a conservatory. On his return to Vienna, he worked exclusively on his compositions and, in 1905, premiered his symphonic poem *Pelleas und Melisande*, followed by the *Kammersymphonie*, Op. 9. His new harmonies were fiercely and bitterly opposed by both critics and audiences, but other composers with experimental interests sought him out. Soon he became a mentor to the great modern composers Alban Berg and Anton von Webern.

In the next decade, Schoenberg composed increasingly original and innovative works, meeting with shock and disbelief from all quarters. Not long after World War I, he created his twelve-tone system. Simply put, no one note of the chromatic scale may be repeated until the other eleven have been played. Ignoring all opposition, the composer continued to work within the strict limitations of this system. Berg and Webern adopted and modified the system in their own works. Other important composers used twelve-tone techniques to varying degrees, and the system became the hallmark of progressive composers until the 1970s.

In 1925 Schoenberg was appointed director of a master school for musical composition at the Prussian Academy of Arts in Berlin. In 1933 he was dismissed from the position because of his Jewish origins. He responded by returning to Judaism in a formal religious ceremony in Paris. He then immigrated to the United States. A year later, he began teaching at the University of Southern California and continued to teach at various American universities until his death. He also created some of his most important compositions, including *Kol Nidre* (1939) and *A Survivor from Warsaw* (1947). He also wrote several theoretical books, including *Models for Beginners in Composition* (1943) and *Fundamentals of Musical Composition* (1967). Schoneberg's influence on twentieth-century music is incalculable.

SCHUMAN, WILLIAM (1910–1992)

Composer, educator

William Schuman was born in New York City on August 4, 1910. He studied at the Malkin Conservatory at Columbia University and at the Juilliard School of Music. His earliest compositional successes include *American Festival Overture* (1939), Third String Quartet (1939), Symphony No. 3 (1941), and *A Free Song* (1942).

In addition to composing, Schuman became an important educator and administrator. From 1935 through 1945 he taught at Sarah Lawrence College and from 1945 through 1962 he served as president of Juilliard. He left Juilliard to become the president of Lincoln Center in New York City, where he remained until 1969. His presidency was marked by a significant increase in commissions for American composers.

Schuman's work is important in the history of American classical music not only for its overall artistic quality, but also because, like **Aaron Copland**, Schuman helped to develop a distinctly American classical style by taking traditional European forms and adapting them to American themes. He composed ten symphonies, several ballets, two operas, four string quartets, and many choral works. Perhaps his greatest symphonic achievement is Symphony No. 6. He died on February 5, 1992, in New York City.

SCHWARTZ, MAURICE (1890–1960)

Actor, producer

The "John Barrymore of the Yiddish theater," Maurice Schwartz was born Avrom Moishe Schwartz in Sedikor, Ukraine, and came to this country when he was eleven years old. He gave his first professional performance four years later in a Yiddish theater in Baltimore, Maryland. In 1912 he joined the Second Avenue Theater, home of noted Yiddish actor David Kessler. When a movement began to reform the Yiddish theater, replacing the low-brow emphasis on *shtick* and audience-pleasing claptrap with more serious work, Schwartz took over the Irving Place Theater in New York City's Bowery area and started the Yiddish Art Theater. For almost four decades, Schwartz appeared in that theater in more than 150 plays. He was greatly admired for his interpretation of Shylock in a Yiddish translation of *The Merchant of Venice* and for his aging Hasidic rabbi in *Yoshe Kalb*, a dramatization of Israel Joshua Singer's novel. Schwartz was striking in looks and flamboyant in action. He appeared in few English-language productions, but he did make one Hollywood film, *Salome* (1953). He died while on tour in Israel.

SECUNDA, SHOLOM (1894–1974)

Composer

Yiddish theater composer Sholom Secunda was born on August 23, 1894, in Aleksandriya, Ukraine. While still in Europe, he obtained his musical training from the *meshoyr'rim* and served as an assistant *hazzan*. He immigrated to the United States when he was fourteen. In 1913 he began working for the Oden Yiddish Theater. A year later *Yosher*, his first musical, was produced. He soon became one of Yiddish theater's most prolific and respected composers, working in New York, Philadelphia, and St. Louis. He studied music at the Juilliard School of Music, at Columbia University, and with composer **Ernest Bloch**. Three of Secunda's most successful songs were "Dos Yidishe Lid," "Dona, Dona," and "Bay Mir Bist Du Sheyn." In addition to his Yiddish operettas and operas, he composed orchestral and liturgical pieces. He served for eleven years as the music director of the Brooklyn Jewish Center (1950–1961) and as a lecturer on music at New York University and Hunter College. He died in New York City on June 13, 1974.

SHORE, DINAH (1917–1994)

Singer, talk show host

Dinah Shore (originally Frances Rose Stein) was born in Winchester, Tennessee, on March 1, 1917. She grew up in one of the few Jewish families in Nashville and attended Vanderbilt University, graduating in 1938. A year later she began singing on radio when she joined the Leo Reisman Orchestra. In 1940 she moved to the **Eddie Cantor** radio show, where she stayed for three years. At the same time, she began to host her own musical variety shows on the radio and recorded several major popular hits including "Yes, My Darling Daughter" and "I'll Walk Alone." During World War II she performed for the troops as one of the U.S.O.'s most popular performers. In the early 1950s, she made a few movies that were not particularly successful. She found her true home on the new medium of television. She hosted "The Dinah Shore Show" (1951–56) and "The Dinah Shore Chevrolet Show" (1956–63), she sang the famous song "See the U.S.A. in Your Chevrolet." Her next television show came in 1970 when she hosted the variety show "Dinah." Her talk show "Dinah's Place" ran from 1974 through 1979. She died on February 24, 1994.

SILLS, BEVERLY (1929–)

Opera singer, arts manager

A coloratura soprano, Beverly Sills (originally Belle Miriam Silverman) was born in the Sea Gate section of Brooklyn, New York, on May 25, 1929. Though she never received a formal Jewish education, she credits her success, at least in part, to the Jewish traditions of

After a distinguished career as a singer, Beverly Sills is having an equally distinguished one as an arts administrator. From 1979 to 1989 she managed the New York City Opera Company and, since 1994, she has chaired the board of Lincoln Center. She is shown here in 1998 receiving the Emma Lazarus Statue of Liberty Award of the American Jewish Historical Society. Presenting her with the award is the Society's president, Kenneth J. Bialkin. (Courtesy of American Jewish Historical Society, Waltham, Massachusetts, and New York, New York)

education and perseverance. Her career began when she was four and she appeared on "Uncle Bob's Rainbow Hour." By the time she was nine, she sang regularly on "Major Bowes' Amateur Hour." In 1945 she began touring with J. J. Shubert's Gilbert and Sullivan repertory company. Two years later she had her grand opera debut with the Philadelphia Civic Orchestra singing Frasquita in Bizet's *Carmen*.

In 1955, Sills joined the New York City Opera Company (NYCO). She became the company's prima donna, gaining fame for singing difficult and rarely performed roles such as Queen Elizabeth in *Roberto Devereux* (Donizetti). Finally, at the age of forty-five,

she had her Metropolitan Opera debut singing Pamira in *The Siege of Corinth*.

In 1979 Sills retired from singing and became the first woman and the first performer to manage the NYCO. (Her farewell concert took place on October 27, 1980.) During her tenure (1979–1989), she moved the company out of debt and introduced audiences to new composers and stars. At the same time, she frequently appeared on television and became an important spokesperson for the arts. In 1994 she became the first woman and the first performer to chair the board at Lincoln Center, where the NYCO has its home.

SIMON AND GARFUNKEL

Musicians, singers, actors

Paul Simon (born October 13, 1941 in Newark, New Jersey) and Art Garfunkel (born November 5, 1941 in Queens, New York) met when they were in sixth grade. In 1957 they had their first success as the duo Tom and Jerry with the song "Hey, Schoolgirl." In 1964 Simon and Garfunkel reunited under their own names. In 1966 their album *Sound of Silence* propelled them to the top of the charts. The 1967 soundtrack album for the film *The Graduate*, which included the song "Mrs. Robinson," made them worldwide successes. They remained at the top of the charts with albums such as *Bridge over Troubled Water* (1970) and songs such as "Old Friends," "Homeward Bound," and "The Boxer."

After the duo split up in 1970 they both made solo albums. Garfunkel's solo albums include *Angel Clare* (1973) and *Breakaway* (1975). Simon's solo career has been far more successful with albums such as *Still Crazy after All These Years* (1975), *Graceland* (1986), and *Rhythm of the Saints* (1990). Both have acted in films; Garfunkel appeared in *Catch 22* (1970) and *Carnal Knowledge* (1971). Simon appeared in *Annie Hall* (1977) and *One Trick Pony* (1981), which he also wrote. In 1981 they came together for a free reunion concert in New York City's Central Park. The concert was a huge success and resulted in the album *The Concert in Central Park* (1982). They were inducted into the Rock and Roll Hall of Fame in 1990. In 1998 Simon made his theatrical debut with a musical, *The Capeman*, which he and Derek Walcott wrote. Though widely publicized and anticipated, the show proved to be a critical failure and closed soon after its Broadway opening.

SMITH AND DALE

Vaudeville and screen comics

Joe Smith [Joseph Sultzer] (1884–1971) and Charlie Dale [Charles Marks] (1881–1981) were both born in New York City, meeting in 1898 when they ran into each other on bicycles. They began performing together shortly thereafter, acquiring the stage names "Smith and Dale" when they were offered a cut price on some unclaimed business cards. In the early years of the twentieth century, they joined with two singing waiters from a New York restaurant called the Avon Café. The four men called themselves the Avon Comedy Four, later the Smith and Dale Avon Comedy Four. Smith and Dale were the only members of the troupe who remained with it from beginning to end. By 1906 they were headliners, and their vaudeville success did not diminish. In 1929 they headlined at the London Palladium. They also made comedy recordings in the 1920s.

The team of Smith and Dale also appeared on the legitimate stage in such revues as *The Whirl of New York* (1921) and *The Sky's the Limit* (1934). Later they began to take roles in films including *Nob Hill* (1945) and *Two Tickets to Broadway* (1951). In the 1940s they often worked on radio and during the 1950s and 1960s were guests on a number of television variety shows. They retired in 1968. Smith and Dale were the models for **Neil Simon**'s play *The Sunshine Boys*.

SONDHEIM, STEPHEN (1930–)

Composer, lyricist

Stephen (Joshua) Sondheim changed the world of musical theater. Born in New York City on March 22, 1930, he began writing music when he was in his teens and later studied at Williams College, graduating in 1950. He worked under lyricist **Oscar Hammerstein II** and wrote the music for four of his shows.

At the age of twenty-five, Sondheim had his first major success when he wrote the lyrics for *West Side Story*, which had music by **Leonard Bernstein** and book by Arthur Laurents. Next he worked with Jule Styne on *Gypsy* (1959). For *A Funny Thing Happened on the Way to the Forum* (1962), he wrote both music and lyrics. Among his long list of credits are the music and lyrics for *Company* (1970), *Follies* (1971), *A Little Night Music* (1973), *Sweeney Todd* (1979), *Sunday in the*

Park with George (1984), and *Into the Woods* (1987). He won a Pulitzer Prize for drama in 1985 for *Sunday in the Park with George*.

In all of his musicals, Sondheim changes the rules. His music is sometimes experimental with intricate rhythms. His lyrics are character driven and often verbally complex. And his plots are frequently conceptual rather than narrative. Because of Stephen Sondheim, the Broadway musical is a more evocative, inventive, and entertaining art form.

STERN, ISAAC (1920–)

Violinist

Born on July 21, 1920, in Russia, virtuoso violinist Isaac Stern came to the United States when he was one year old. His family settled in San Francisco, where he attended the San Francisco Conservatory from 1928 through 1931. From 1932 until 1939 he studied with violinist Naoum Blinder. Making his professional debut at age eleven, Stern achieved national recognition after a New York concert in 1939. In 1948 he made his European debut and thereafter began to tour extensively. In addition to playing the standard classical violin repertoire, he introduced audiences to numerous new composers, among them George Rochberg and Paul Hindemith.

Musically, he is known for the emotional intensity of his interpretations as well as for his technical proficiency. A popular and outgoing performer, Isaac Stern has done more than almost any other classical performer to bring music to a large and varied audience. Active in arts promotion, Stern helped save Carnegie Hall when it was scheduled to be torn down. He also was instrumental in the formation of the National Endowment for the Arts.

STRASBERG, LEE (1901–1982)

Theatrical teacher, director, actor

Lee Strasberg was born on November 17, 1901, in Budzanow, Poland (now Ukraine). When he was seven, he immigrated to America, settling with his family on the Lower East Side of New York City. He began his theatrical career at age fifteen, acting in productions at the Christie Street Settlement House. He then moved on to study at the American Laboratory Theatre. There he studied under Richard Boleslavski and Maria Ouspenskaya, who introduced him to the acting techniques of famed Russian director and teacher Konstantin Stanislavsky.

In 1931, after a stint as an actor and stage manager with the Theatre Guild, Strasberg opened the Group Theatre. His co-founders were fellow American Laboratory classmates Cheryl Crawford and Harold Clurman. Designed to be a communal, democratic theater that used Stanislavsky's technique, the Group revolutionized American theater. For its ten-year existence, it introduced audiences to new playwrights including **Clifford Odets** and brilliant experimental productions such as *Men in White* (1934), which won a Pulitzer Prize. In 1941, after the Group closed, Strasberg went to Hollywood. He spent seven uneventful years there before returning to New York, where he became a member of the newly founded Actors Studio, Inc.

The Actors Studio was founded in 1947 by Elia Kazan, Cheryl Crawford, and Robert Lewis—all former members of the Group Theatre. When Strasberg joined them in 1948, he became the Studio's artistic director. He held that position for the next thirty-four years, becoming America's most famous acting teacher. Called "Method Acting," or simply "The Method," Strasberg's technique was an interpretation of Stanislavsky's teachings. It focused on developing an actor's ability to use personal emotional experience in bringing an immediacy and power to a performance. Among Strasberg's most famous students were stars such as Marlon Brando, Anne Bancroft, Marilyn Monroe, Sidney Poitier, **Dustin Hoffman**, and Robert DeNiro. Among the many important plays developed at the Actors Studio were *A Hatful of Rain*, *Any Wednesday*, and *The Night of the Iguana*. Toward the end of his life Strasberg began acting in films including *The Godfather, Part II* (1974) and *Boardwalk* (1979). He died on February 17, 1982, in New York City.

SZELL, GEORGE (1897–1970)

Pianist, conductor, composer

George Szell was born in Budapest, Hungary, on June 7, 1897. He began playing the piano and composing when he was quite young. By the time he was in his twenties and thirties he had conducted orchestras in many European cities including Strasbourg, Prague, and Düsseldorf. He spent six years conducting in Berlin (1924–1930), two years conducting in Glasgow, Scotland (1937–1938), and toured Australia. Between 1942 and 1956 he was frequently guest conductor with the New York Philharmonic Orchestra. In 1946 he became permanent conductor of the Cleveland Philharmonic Orchestra, a position he held for the rest of his life. Szell was known for his strong personality, cutting humor, and the power he exerted over the musicians he conducted. He died on July 30, 1970, in Cleveland, Ohio.

TAMIRIS, HELEN (1905–1966)

Choreographer

Pioneering choreographer Helen Tamiris (Becker) was born on April 24, 1905, in New York City. She first studied dance at the legendary Neighborhood Playhouse under Irene Lewisohn. She went on to study ballet with Michael Fokine and at the Metropolitan Opera Ballet School. She studied modern dance at the Isadora Duncan School and made her concert debut in 1927. In 1928 she successfully toured Europe and, in 1930, founded her own company and school, both of which she ran until 1945.

Tamiris, with Martha Graham, Doris Humphrey, and Charles Weidman, founded the Dance Repertory Theater, a cooperative of several of the most important modern dance companies of the day. During the Depression, Tamiris successfully lobbied to include dance in the WPA Federal Theater Project and then served as its principal choreographer (1937–1939). She also choreographed several Broadway musicals including *Annie Get Your Gun* (1946). Her choreography for *Touch and Go* (1949) won her a Tony Award.

One of the first choreographers to create dances to such American music as jazz and spirituals, Tamiris was also one of the few choreographers of her day to create dances with social and political themes. Among her best-known work is *How Long Brethren* (1937), which portrayed the desperation of unemployed Southern African Americans. The piece was danced to the music of a chorus singing Lawrence Gellert's "Negro Songs of Protest." After an exceptional career, Helen Tamiris died in New York City on August 4, 1966.

THEATER

The early American theater was limited by many factors. Established religious groups firmly opposed it and were able to get legislation passed against all forms of staged entertainment in various colonies and at various times until the end of the eighteenth century. Trained actors were few and far between, and few cities had populations large enough to support continuously producing theaters.

The beginning of professional theater in America is usually dated to the arrival of the Lewis Hallam company from England in 1752, fairly late in the colonial era. Among the company's first offerings was Shakespeare's *The Merchant of Venice* with its Jewish villain, Shylock. There is no indication, however, that its presentation was evidence that anti-Semitism was prevalent in the colonies. Indeed, the reverse seems to have been the case. Puritan America had a strong sense of identification with God's chosen people, and aside from the fact that profession of Christianity was sometimes a legal qualification in a highly church-oriented society, there seems to have been little prejudice against Jews.

Shortly after the American Revolution, drama and entertainment began to develop in earnest. Theaters sprang up in Charleston, Philadelphia, Newport, Boston, and, of course, New York. In the decades that followed, these and other theaters found their audience and thrived. Evidence of early American feelings about Jews may be found in the presentation of the sympathetic *The Jew* (1795), by Richard Cumberland, which had its American premiere less than a year after it opened in England.

In the early nineteenth century, the stereotypical male Jew, in the form of the greedy, scheming merchant, made its appearance more often. This may have been, in part, because American theater was still very much under the influence of England. At the same time, the image of the beautiful and virtuous—but tragic—Jewish woman was gaining currency in both countries, as in the Ivanhoe adaptation, *The Hebrew* (1823).

There were some very popular Jewish playwrights, but they did not feel any need to limit themselves to Jewish subjects. Mordecai Manuel Noah (1785–1851) wrote romantic comedies and melodramas including *She Would Be a Soldier* (1819). He is usually listed as one of the important American playwrights of the time. Isaac Harby (1788–1828) wrote revenge plays, including *Alberti* (1819). Jonas B. Phillips directed and wrote audience-pleasing melodramas.

During this period in the American theater no distinction was drawn between popular drama and "art." Playwrights worked hard to keep the uneducated working class happy and entertained while they also appealed to a more literate audience. That changed somewhat after a feud between the followers of the muscular American actor Edwin Forrest and those of the refined English actor William Macready erupted in violence. In 1849, in what came to be known as the Astor Place Riots, twenty-two people were killed in a conflict between supporters of popular entertainment and "serious theater." From approximately that time, the two forces developed separately. On the one hand there were the minstrel shows, saloon shows, and burlesques; on the other there was the "serious" theater, which mostly consisted of melodramas and bowdlerized classics.

During the same period, feelings about Jews began to change in this country. In the late 1840s there was an influx of immigrants from Europe, and the fear and resentment of some native-born Americans focused on anyone they perceived as "foreign," including Catholics and Jews. Stereotyping of ethnic and religious minorities, especially in the popular theater, became more common.

The first Jewish actor of significance is probably M. B. Curtis, who commissioned the play *Sam'l of Posen* (1861) to counteract some of this rising hostility. Written by Irish American George H. Jessop, the play featured a kind, sweet Jewish protagonist, whom Curtis played with considerable success. The next Jewish actor of note was **Adah Isaacs Menken** (1835–1869), a flamboyant figure known for her appearance in a dramatic adaptation of Byron's *Mazeppa* (1861). Particularly appealing to her audiences was her entrance strapped to the back of a live horse and wearing a body stocking. Her first run in San Francisco brought in $9,000, a figure as remarkable as her own. In England she was paid $500 per week for her performances, making her the highest-paid woman acting at the time.

Two other important actors emerged in the second half of the nineteenth century. One, Rose Eytinge (1853–1911), debuted and remained in the mainstream English-speaking theater. The other, **Jacob Adler** (1855–1926), became the pre-eminent Yiddish actor of the American theater.

Rose Eytinge spent ten seasons in a stock company before she made her New York debut, taking over the role of Nellie O'Donaghue in *Bantry Bay* (1863) when Laura Keene was ill. It would not be the last time she played a nice gentile girl. Although her ethnicity was well known, she played roles of every stripe, becoming Edwin Booth's leading lady in 1864 and going on to a long and highly successful career. Many considered her the most talented woman then acting in the American theater. There would not be another Jewish woman to rival her success in the English-speaking theater until Helen Menken (1901–1966) in the teens of the new century.

Jacob Adler, who came to the United States from Russia in 1887, was not immediately successful in the Yiddish theater. It was not until he performed in *The Russian Soldier* (1889) that his star ascended. Two years later, he founded the Independent Yiddish Art Company and began commissioning plays including *The Yiddish King Lear* (1892) and *The Wild Man* (1894), both by Jacob Gordin. Adler continued performing until 1920, retiring only when forced to by a stroke. He was the patriarch of what would become a Jewish acting dynasty to rival the non-Jewish Drew-Barrymore family. Both his daughter Celia, by his second wife, Dinah, and his sons and daughters by his third wife, Sarah—Luther, Jay, Frances, and **Stella**—became famous and respected actors.

Among the other important figures in the Yiddish theater were David Kessler (ca. 1859–1920), actor and theater manager; **Boris Thomashevsky** (1868–1939), actor and director; Keni Liptzin, whose nickname was the "Yiddish Eleonora Duse"; and **Bertha Kalich** (1875–1939), known as the "Jewish Bernhardt."

Until the last decades of the nineteenth century, American theater had produced little of lasting value. Then, in the two decades before and the two decades after the turn of the century, the theater bloomed. For these forty years, there were hundreds of companies touring the country—420 in 1904—to be greeted by audiences eager for all forms of theater. The prime movers behind this tremendous success were for the most part Jewish, with an able assist from the Irish.

The name that stands out in all histories of American drama for this period is **David Belasco** (1851–1940). A Sephardic Jew from London via Canada, he began his career as a playwright in 1881. He also worked as a stage manager and actor, learning everything there was to know about the theater. A collaboration with Franklin Fytes, *The Girl I Left Behind Me* (1893), was a solid success, and his next, solo effort, *The Heart of Maryland* (1895), consolidated his reputation. A string of hits followed, most of which he produced. He also produced the work of other playwrights. In 1901 he leased the Republic Theater and renamed it the Belasco. Four years later he built his own theater. Belasco produced work of higher quality than most of his predecessors and had an uncanny feeling for what the American public would respond to, including a higher degree of realism in sets, costumes, and acting. He continued to produce theater well into the 1920s.

Charles (1860–1915) and Daniel Frohman (1851–1940) did not have Belasco's personal flair or his interest in writing. They were producers, but they had a powerful impact on the theater. They began their careers in theater when, with their brother Gustav, they became managers of the Madison Square Theatre in New York City. While there, they inaugurated the practice of sending out a number of road companies for each successful show. Their companies brought theater to every part of the country, playing in school auditoriums and Masonic halls as well as the small regional theaters that sprang up to house them.

Charles Frohman had his first personal success with the play *Shenandoah* (1889), by Bronson Howard. Actor/playwright William Gillette then arranged for Frohman to produce his work. By 1890 Frohman had his own theater. In 1895 he formed the Theatrical Syndicate, or Trust, with Al Hayman, Abe Erlanger, Mark Klaw, and others. The Trust developed a virtual monopoly in theatrical bookings and extorted huge sums from independent producers and performers. Frohman used the power of the Trust to produce what seemed for some time to be an endless stream of successful plays and celebrity actors. Just as today, when many regional theaters take as their stock-in-trade plays that have had successful runs in New York, Charles Frohman tended to produce plays that had been successful in London. He did, however, develop many important acting careers and introduce the American audience to works by such playwrights as Oscar Wilde, James Barrie, and Somerset Maugham.

Daniel Frohman, Charles's older brother, also had a highly successful producing career. He set up a stock company at the old Lyceum Theatre in 1885, presenting some of Belasco's first plays and, later, many British plays. When he retired from producing, he stayed active in the theater community, serving as president of the Actors' Fund of America from 1904 until his death in 1940.

The Theatrical Trust met its match in another set of brothers, the **Shuberts**. Levy (?–1953), Samuel (1875–1905), and Jacob J. (1877–1963) Shubert came to the United States from Lithuania as children and began working in the theater before they were out of their teens. In 1900 Lee and Sam took on the Trust when they began producing in New York City. When J. J. joined them a few years later, they were able to break the monopoly and become the biggest theater-owners in the country.

Appearing in some of the plays written and/or produced by these towering figures was an actor named **David Warfield** (1866–1951), who specialized in comic roles as stereotyped, long-bearded Jewish men. In 1901 Belasco cast Warfield in his own play about the Lower East Side, *The Auctioneer*, a more serious look at Jewish life. After his performance in the play, Warfield was able to secure a number of more thoughtful roles.

Also active during this time were a great many Jewish vaudeville performers, some of whom made their way onto the legitimate stage. Foremost among these was Lew Fields [Lewis Maurice Schanfield] (1867–1941), a comedian who worked for many years with his boyhood friend Joe Weber (1867–1942). The team of **Weber and Fields** was highly successful. In 1896 the two opened their own theater, producing a number of short musicals with such names as *Hurly Burly* (1898), *Helter Skelter* (1899), and *Hoity Toity* (1901). Presented with each musical was a even shorter companion piece, a parody of a contemporary Broadway hit. The shows also had the most spectacular chorus lines around. It was a winning formula. In 1904, however, the team broke up and Fields began producing Broadway musicals, many of which he starred in. Late in his career he produced a series of musicals written by his son, Herbert, with **Richard Rodgers** (1902–1979) and **Lorenz Hart** (1895–1943), including *The Girl Friend* (1926).

Among the others who began in vaudeville and then made their way into Broadway musicals and revues were Al Shean (1868–1949) of the team Gallagher and Shean, **Sophie Tucker** (1884–1965), Nora Bayes (1880–1928), **Al Jolson** (1886–1950), Vivienne Segal (1897–1992), Lina Abarbanell (1880–1963), Louise Dresser (1882–1965), and **Ed Wynn**.

A different form of musical theater was developed during this time by **Florenz Ziegfeld** (1867–1932). His earliest productions were vehicles for his wife Anna Held (1873–1918), a tiny Polish-French Jewish singer and actor who specialized in mildly risqué songs. Ziegfeld surrounded Held with elaborate sets and cho-rus lines in gorgeous costumes. Held and Ziegfeld split up in 1906, and she went on to perform successfully in vaudeville, returning to Broadway only once in *Follow Me* (1916). Ziegfeld began his famous *Follies*, which ran from 1907 to 1925 and made him the most celebrated producer in America.

Singer/comedian **Fanny Brice** (1891–1951) started her career performing for customers in her parents' saloon, then joined a touring company performing a burlesque musical comedy called *College Girls*. It was there she was spotted by Ziegfeld and given a place in his *Follies of 1910*. She remained a star of the *Follies* and other Broadway productions for more than two decades. She is particularly significant because she grappled with, used, and overcame Jewish and female stereotyping to create funny, moving, and enormously popular entertainment.

A new wave of serious, nonmusical theater began to emerge during this period, and Jewish critic George Jean Nathan (1882–1958) did much to encourage it. The most influential and respected drama critic of his time, Nathan sharply denounced the superficiality of American drama. He recognized the genius of such playwrights as Eugene O'Neill, Sean O'Casey, and William Saroyan, and, as they began to appear, Jewish writers such as **Clifford Odets** (1906–1963) and **Elmer Rice** (1892–1967).

One of the most significant developments in serious theater at this time was the Theatre Guild, founded in 1919 by among others, director **Lawrence Langner** (1890–1962). The formidable **Theresa Helburn** (1887–1959) was managing director. The list of important plays that were first produced by the Theatre Guild is astounding. It includes major works by Jewish writers, such as Elmer Rice's *The Adding Machine* (1923) and **Richard Rodgers'** and **Oscar Hammerstein II**'s *Oklahoma!*, as well as O'Neill's *Strange Interlude* (1928) and *Ah, Wilderness!* (1933), Dorothy and Dubose Heyward's *Porgy* (1927), and Maxwell Anderson's *Mary of Scotland* (1933). The Guild was the primary producer in the United States of George Bernard Shaw. In the mid-1930s, the organization gave birth to two breakaway organizations that were also of tremendous importance, the Group Theatre and the Playwrights' Company.

A very different sort of theater also had an important impact on early twentieth-century drama. The Neighborhood Players was founded at the Henry Street Settlement House on the Lower East Side of New York by Alice and Irene (1892–1944) Lewisohn. In 1914 the group moved into its own building, the Neighborhood Playhouse, which was purchased by Irene. By 1920 the theater was professional and producing works by some of the most daring and experimental writers of the time. More important, perhaps, it was the creative home of a theater artist of great importance.

Aline Bernstein (1881–1955), daughter of actor Jacob Frankau, began her career as a scenic designer at the Neighborhood Playhouse, doing strikingly original work on very low budgets. She was soon noticed by Broadway, eventually becoming one of its most important designers and one of the few women at that time who were designing sets. Among her critically acclaimed designs were those for *The Children's Hour* (1934) and *The Male Animal* (1940). She continued to design award-winning sets and costumes into the 1950s and was the founder of the Costume Museum, which later became part of the Metropolitan Museum of Art. Other important designers include Jean Rosenthal (1912–1969), who designed lights for such productions as Orson Welles's *Julius Caesar* (1937) and later *West Side Story* (1957). **Boris Aronson** (1898–1980) designed sets for such productions as *Awake and Sing!* (1935) and *Fiddler on the Roof* (1964).

In the 1920s vaudeville was a training ground for musical and comedy performers. Some, such as singer Belle Baker (1895–1957), spent all or most of their careers on the vaudeville stage. Others, like the **Marx Brothers** and **Bert Lahr** (1895–1967), went on to Broadway and film, carving out permanent niches for themselves in the history of American entertainment. In non-musical theater, some important actors were performing exclusively or primarily in the Yiddish theater. These included **Maurice Schwartz** (1890–1960), Jacob Ben-Ami [Jacob Shtchirin] (1890–1977), and Jennie Goldstein (1897–1960). Others began in the Yiddish theater, then made the transition to Broadway. These included **Molly Picon** (1898–1992), Luther

(1903–1984) and **Stella Adler** (1902–1992), **Paul Muni** [Muni Weisenfreund] (1895–1967), and **Joseph Schildkraut** (1895–1964).

Another group of actors began their careers in the English-speaking theater. They were the first generation of Jewish actors in the mainstream theater and included **Gertrude Berg** (1900–1966), **Philip Loeb** (1894–1955), Sam Levene (1905–1980), **Edward G. Robinson** [Emanuel Goldberg] (1893–1973), **John Garfield** [Julius Garfinkle] (1913–1952), Melvyn Douglas [Melvyn Hesselberg] (1901–1981), Oscar Homolka (1898–1978), **Leslie Howard** [Steiner] (1893–1943), **Sam Jaffe** (1891–1984), and **Sylvia Sidney** (1910–1999). Many of these stage performers went on to long and distinguished careers in films.

The American theater in 1931 stepped into the future with the founding of the Group Theatre by director and critic Harold Clurman (1901–1980) and director **Lee Strasberg** (1901–1982), along with non-Jewish producer Cheryl Crawford. Formerly members of the Theatre Guild, all three founders were dedicated to creating a progressive, democratic, permanent acting company that would present seasons of distinguished theater. They soon gathered around them such important artists as actors Stella Adler and Luther Adler and Morris Carnovsky (1897–?), playwrights Clifford Odets and **Marc Blitzstein** (1905–1964), and a number of important directors and designers.

At the Group Theatre Lee Strasberg began teaching Konstantin Stanislavsky's method of acting. Eventually, he and Stella Adler disagreed about their interpretation of Stanislavsky, and Adler formed her own school. Between the two of them they trained or strongly influenced a new generation of actors for the theater including non-Jews Marlon Brando, Anne Bancroft, and Julie Harris, as well as Jewish actors **Shelley Winters**, **Lee J. Cobb**, **Eli Wallach**, and **John Garfield**.

There was a new generation of Jewish producers including Max Gordon (1892–1978), Jed Harris (1900–1979), Sam Harris (1872–1941), and **John Houseman** (1902–1988) as well as showman **Billy Rose** (1899–1966). Jed Harris was the original *enfant terrible* of the American theater. He produced his first

Born to dirt-poor German Jewish immigrants who moved all over New York City, often one step ahead of rent collectors, the Marx Brothers first came to national attention with three successive Broadway hits, I'll Say She Is (1924), The Coconuts (1925), and Animal Crackers (1928). The latter two were made into movies (on sound stages in Queens), and a legend was born. Pictured above are Zeppo, Groucho, Chico, and Harpo. (Private Collection)

play when he was twenty-five and quickly became one of the most successful producer/directors in the theater. His personal behavior was sometimes outrageous, perhaps deliberately so, as it did nothing to dim his reputation. Among his successes were *The Front Page* (1928) and *Our Town* (1938). John Houseman made many remarkable contributions to the theater. With African American actor Rose McClendon, he headed the Negro wing of the Federal Theatre Project during the Depression and, with Orson Welles,

founded the Mercury Theater. He continued to be an important figure in American theater into the 1980s.

Perhaps the most historically important aspect of American theater in the decades between 1920 and 1950 and was the musical comedy. Jewish writers, composers, and performers were at the forefront of this developing theatrical form. They came from the classical music schools, from Tin Pan alley, from the Yiddish art theater, and from vaudeville, and they reshaped the face of Broadway.

One of the first successful Jewish songwriters was **Irving Berlin** [Israel Baline] (1888–1989), a Russian Jewish immigrant whose first big hit was "Alexander's Ragtime Band" in 1911. His first complete score was written for *Watch Your Step* (1914). With producer Sam Harris, he opened the Music Box Theatre in 1921 and staged a number of *Music Box Revues*, out of which came some of his most famous songs, such as "What'll I Do?" and "All Alone." Perhaps his most important show was *As Thousands Cheer* (1933). His biggest success came in 1946, when he wrote the music for *Annie Get Your Gun*.

Possibly the most influential of the many Jewish artists involved in the creation of American musical theater was **Jerome Kern** (1885–1945). For the first decade of his career Kern wrote songs for other people's shows, many of which were very successful. He was particularly adept at writing "dance songs" during a time when ballroom dancing was a craze, immediately before the First World War. In 1914 he wrote the song that, in the words of the *Oxford Companion to American Theatre*, "changed the course of American musical comedy writing." Until that song, "They Didn't Believe Me," the waltz was the dominant form of popular music. Now it was the ballad.

Kern began writing musicals, alone and with a variety of collaborators, at about this time. His first major success was *Very Good Eddie* (1915) with Guy Bolton. This was followed by a number of small, successful musicals by the team of Kern, Bolton, and P. G. Wodehouse, and a number of large, successful musicals on his own. His most important work was done with Oscar Hammerstein on *Show Boat* (1927), based on the **Edna Ferber** novel. The show was a landmark in the development of the musical, dealing for the first time, with an American theme in a thoroughly American way. Because of his many innovations, Kern is usually considered the "father" of the American musical. Other influential Jewish artists were **Lorenz Hart**, Richard Rodgers, Oscar Hammerstein, **George** [Jacob] (1898–1937] and **Ira** [Israel] (1896–1983) **Gershwin**, and E. Y. Harburg [Isidore Hochberg] (1898–1981).

Probably the greatest, and certainly the most original, musical composer of the first half of the century was George Gershwin. Classically trained and strongly influenced by Jerome Kern, he first came to public notice when Al Jolson (1886–1950) sang his "Swanee" in the show *Sinbad* (1919). His first hit musical, written with his brother Ira, was *Lady, Be Good!* (1924). It was another musical landmark, introducing jazz to mainstream, white musicals and setting them apart from the more European-influenced operettas. Throughout his career, both his Jewish background and his interest in African American music were apparent in his songs.

During the twenties and thirties, Gershwin wrote hundreds of wonderful songs in more than a dozen successful musicals. The names of his songs, which continue to be performed all over the world, are instantly recognizable: "Fascinating Rhythm," "Someone to Watch Over Me," "'S Wonderful," "How Long Has This Been Going On?," "But Not for Me," "Embraceable You." The names of his shows—with the exception of Pulitzer Prize winner *Of Thee I Sing* (1931) and *Porgy and Bess* (1935), are not. They are seldom performed. This is no reflection on the quality of the shows themselves, but rather evidence of revolutionary change in American musicals by another team of Jewish writers.

Composer Richard Rodgers began working with his first lyricist, Lorenz Hart, when they were both in at Columbia. They began to enjoy success when they wrote songs for the 1925 and 1926 editions of the *Garrick Gaieties*. They created a string of successful shows and memorable songs until Hart's personal troubles overwhelmed him. He died in 1943 at the age of forty-eight. Hart was succeeded as Rodgers' partner by the brilliant Oscar Hammerstein II.

Before his association with Rodgers, Oscar Hammerstein co-authored lyrics and books with Otto Harbach, working with a variety of composers. After they began working together, Rodgers and Hammerstein dominated American musical theater. Their reign began when the curtain went up on *Oklahoma!* (1943) and revealed a scene on a quiet farm. There was no chorus line, no rousing first number. There was not even a single actor on the stage. From offstage, a voice began to sing, a cappella, "Oh, What a Beautiful Mornin'," and the revolution had begun. After that came *Carousel* (1945), *South Pacific* (1949), *The King and I* (1951), *The Sound of Music* (1959), and four other, less legendary, shows. Hammerstein wrote *Carmen Jones*, a retelling of the opera *Carmen* in an African American idiom. These musicals all have the strong story, fully drawn characters, and well-integrated songs that are a Rodgers and Hammerstein trademark and came to be de rigueur in American musicals.

The Rodgers and Hammerstein influence was seen in the important musicals of the next two decades. *Finian's Rainbow* (1947), with lyrics by E. Y. Harburg, who also co-authored the book, dealt in an oddly whimsical but effective way with racial discrimination in the South. Bella and Samuel Spewack adapted the story of Shakespeare's *Taming of the Shrew* for their musical *Kiss Me, Kate* (1948). Abe Burrows (1910–1985) wrote the book for *Guys and Dolls*, based on the stories of Damon Runyan, with music by composer Frank Loesser (1920–1969). Betty **Comden** (1919–) and **Adolph Green** (1915–) wrote the lyrics for *Wonderful Town* (1953) to music by **Leonard Bernstein** (1918–1990). The book was written by Jerome Chodorov (1911–), brother of playwright Edward Chodorov (1904–1988), and Joseph Fields (1895–1966), son of Lew Fields and brother of Dorothy Fields (1905–1974). Comden and Green teamed up again for *Bells Are Ringing* (1956), writing both book and lyrics, with music by Jule Styne. The show made a star of comic actor **Judy Holliday** (1922–1965).

A grittier musical premiered the next year. *West Side Story* (1957), with music by **Leonard Bernstein** and lyrics by **Stephen Sondheim** (1930–), set the *Romeo and Juliet* story in New York with rival gangs and a Puerto Rican heroine. It was hugely successful. *Gypsy* (1959) gave Ethel Merman an opportunity to prove herself as an actor in the role of stripper Gypsy Rose Lee's stage mother and paired composer Jule Styne with the up-and-coming lyricist Stephen Sondheim.

The most important musical team of the 1950s and 1960s was lyricist and librettist **Alan Jay Lerner** (1918–1986), and composer Frederick Loewe (1901–1988). Their first success came in the late forties with *Brigadoon* (1947), but it was in the next decade that they became theater legends with the spectacularly successful *My Fair Lady* (1956) and then with *Camelot* (1960), which almost equaled their earlier success. Lerner went on to work with other composers on such shows as *On a Clear Day You Can See Forever* (1965) and *Coco* (1969).

Jewish performers in the musical theater at this time who made or enhanced their reputations on Broadway included **Judy Holliday**, **Danny Kaye** (1913–1987), Hermione Gingold (1897–1987), **Jack Gilford** (1907–1990), **Sid Caesar** (1922–), **Phil Silvers** (1911–1985), Jessie White (1919–), **Theodore Bikel** (1924–), and **Bea Arthur** (1926–).

There was also another generation of Jewish dramatic actors. Unlike those who were active in the 1930s, most of these actors were able to keep their Jewish names and, often, play Jewish roles. They include Joseph Wiseman (1918–), **Zero Mostel** (1915–1977), Lou Jacobi (1913–), Howard da Silva (1909–1986), and Paul Lukas (1895–1971).

A new wave swept through dramatic theater in America in the late 1940s and early 1950s. Regional theaters began to appear all over the country and many of the most important of these were founded by Jewish theater artists. Margo Jones founded Theater 47 in Dallas, Texas, in 1947, and Nina Vance founded the Alley Theater in Houston in the same year. Zelda Fichandler founded the prestigious Arena Stage in Washington, D. C., in 1950. Herbert Blau (1926–) and Jules Irving (1925–) founded the Actor's Workshop in 1952.

In playwriting, the most important figure of the 1950s was **Arthur Miller** (1915–), whose significant works include *Death of a Salesman* (1949), *The Crucible* (1953), and *A View from the Bridge* (1955). More connected to his Jewish background was **Paddy Chayefsky** (1923–1981), who began his writing career in television but moved several of his works to Broadway, including his first, *Middle of the Night* (1956).

By the late 1950s most of the actors who came into prominence were again using Anglicized names, in part because many were also active in film. Hollywood had always shied away from overt ethnicity and investigations by the House Un-American Activities Committee intensified the fear. Some Jewish actors were blacklisted, including **Lee Grant** [Lyova Rosenthal] (1927–) and **Philip Loeb**, who subsequently committed suicide. Many others continued to work with great regularity, including **Shelley Winters** [Shirley Schrift] (1922–), **Walter Matthau** [Walter Matuschanskyasky] (1920–), **Ed Asner** (1929–), Martin Balsam (1919–1999), Susan Strasberg (1938–1999), Claire Bloom [Patricia Claire Blume] (1931–), **Kirk Douglas** [Issur Danielovich] (1918–), Peter Falk (1927–), Laurence Harvey [Larushka Mischa Skikne] (1928–1973), Hal Linden [Harold Lipshitz] (1931–), Nehemiah Persoff (1920–), and **Tony Randall** [Leonard Rosenberg] (1920–).

The 1960s brought an experimental theater movement, innovative in form and often highly political in content. Jewish playwrights who were among the vanguard of this movement included Israel Horovitz (1939–), Leon Katz and Murray Mednick, Susan Yankowitz, Rosalyn Drexler, and Karen Malpede.

Commercial theater in the 1960s witnessed the rise of the most successful playwright of our time, **Neil Simon** (1927–). His first big triumph was *Come Blow Your Horn* (1961), and he has been regularly selling out houses ever since. Other commercially prosperous Jewish playwrights who came to prominence in the 1960s and 1970s include Arthur Kopit (1937–) and **David Mamet** (1947–). The regional theater movement continued to grow, as Emily Mann became artistic director of McCarter Theater Center in Princeton, N.J., and Libby Appel assumed the same position at the Oregon Shakespeare Festival.

For most of the twentieth century, the Jewish presence in the theater was most powerfully felt in the person of producers, directors, and playwrights. But in the 1960s, even Neil Simon was overshadowed by a young Jewish actor and singer named **Barbra Streisand**. Beginning as a cabaret performer, she made her Broadway debut in *I Can Get It for You Wholesale* (1962). She stunned audiences and critics. An appearance on television with Judy Garland and a hugely suc-

> ## *West Side Story*'s Story
>
> *West Side Story*, the classic twentieth century musical drama of teenage love based on Shakespeare's *Romeo and Juliet*, was created by four Jewish men—Leonard Bernstein, Stephen Sondheim, Arthur Laurents, and Jerome Robbins.

cessful first album fueled what would quickly become a Streisand bonfire. In 1964 Streisand appeared on Broadway in *Funny Girl* as entertainer Fanny Brice, going on to re-create the role in the film in 1968. While most of her future performances would be on film, Streisand had forever changed the possibilities for Jewish actors, especially women, on stage. She was an overtly, even defiantly Jewish superstar, and the public not only accepted her; they adored her.

Indeed, it seemed as though Jewishness was becoming fashionable in an era that was beginning to recognize and honor the diversity of American society. In addition to *Funny Girl*, 1964 audiences saw the premiere of the musical *Fiddler on the Roof*, starring Zero Mostel (1915–1977), fresh from a triumph in *A Funny Thing Happened on the Way to the Forum* (1962). Based on stories by **Sholem Aleichem**, *Fiddler* was a warm, boisterous depiction of life in the Jewish shtetl in Russia. It was hugely popular.

Several older actors made their first appearances on the Broadway stage in the 1960s, including former Yiddish theater actor Herschel Bernardi (1924–1986), who replaced Mostel in *Fiddler*; comedian Shelley Berman (1926–), who started his stage career when he replaced Art Carney in *The Odd Couple* in 1966; and film actor **Lauren Bacall** (1924–). Bacall, who had last been seen on Broadway in a tiny role in 1942, scored a real triumph in *Cactus Flower* (1965) and has gone on to success after success in such plays as *Applause* (1970), *Woman of the Year* (1981) [she won the Tony Award for both], and *Sweet Bird of Youth* (1985).

During the 1960s and 1970s a large number of talented Jewish actors helped to illuminate the Great White Way. Joel Grey (1932–) stunned audiences in *Cabaret* (1972). **Dustin Hoffman** (1937–) began on

Broadway in the 1960s and returned in 1984 in *Death of a Salesman*. George Segal (1934–) first came to prominence in *Rattle of a Simple Man* (1963). **Madeline Kahn** (1942–) made a reputation in satirical revues in New York before going on to film. Stand-up comedian Robert Klein (1942–) began an acting career on stage with *The Apple Tree* (1966). **Judd Hirsch** (1935–) worked his way up slowly on the stage, became

In an American Jewish reference book, one can't run too many photographs of Molly Picon (this one has three). Just the list of her credits would make a small book by itself. On Broadway she played the role of the American widow Clara Weiss looking for a husband in Israel in the musical Milk and Honey, which required her to somersault with goats and sheep at age sixty-four. She is shown here in the role of one of her earlier characters in the Yiddish Theater. (American Jewish Archives)

a star on television's "Taxi" (1978–1983), and then returned to the stage in *Talley's Folly* (1980). Elliot Gould [Goldstein] (1938–) scored triumphs in *I Can Get It For You Wholesale* (1962) and *Little Murders* (1967), then left the stage to become one of America's favorite antiheroes in the late sixties and the seventies. **Alan Arkin** (1934–) also began his career on a stage, but it was the Second City stage in Chicago. From there he went to Broadway, establishing his reputation in such plays as *Enter Laughing* (1963) and *Lav* (1964). Other members of this new generation included Jill Clayburgh (1944–), Richard Dreyfuss (1947–), and **Gene Wilder** (1935–).

After the political and social upheavals of the sixties and seventies, it seemed that theater would go through a calmer phase, focusing more on pleasing than on provoking audiences. To some degree this was true of Jewish artists as well. **Wendy Wasserstein** (1950–) made her reputation, and even won a Pulitzer Prize, with funny, mildly stimulating plays about middle-class women, such as *Isn't It Romantic?* (1981) and *The Heidi Chronicles* (1989). Neil Simon continued to be the king of Broadway playwrights and began exploring his Jewish background and traditions.

AIDS changed all that. **Larry Kramer** (1935–), with *The Normal Heart* (1985) and *The Destiny of Me* (1992), was one of the first playwrights to treat the subject honestly and graphically on stage. **Tony Kushner** is one of the most spectacularly successful, with his *Angels in America* trilogy, the first part of which, *Millennium Approaches* (1993), won the Pulitzer Prize.

Typifying Jewish stage performers of the late eighties and the nineties are **Mandy Patinkin** (1952–) and former television star **Linda Lavin** (1937–). They have combined stage careers with lucrative work in films and on television.

Mandy Patinkin stunned Broadway with his brilliantly dramatic portrayal of Che Guevara in the musical *Evita* (1979), for which he won a Tony. In the next decade and a half, he consolidated his position in the theater while, at the same time, co-starring with Streisand in the film *Yentl* (1983) and captivating television audiences as the intense surgeon in the series "Chicago Hope." On stage, he starred in Sondheim's

Sunday in the Park with George (1984) and off-Broadway in the Public Theater productions of *The Winter's Tale* and *The Knife*.

Linda Lavin began her career on the stage, making her first mark in the musical *It's a Bird, It's a Plane, It's Superman* (1966). She became famous as the sardonic waitress in title role of television's "Alice," for which she won two Golden Globes. Since leaving the series, she has been extremely active in telefilms, many of which she produces herself, and in speaking appearances on behalf of a variety of women's issues. Nonetheless, she has appeared frequently on the New York stage. For her performance in Neil Simon's *Broadway Bound* (1986), she won a Tony Award and, for *Death-Defying Acts* (1995), she won an Obie. She also garnered critical acclaim in Wendy Wasserstein's play *The Sisters Rosensweig* (1992).

Other actors who began their careers on the stage or who return to it from time to time include Carol Kane (1952–), Estelle Getty (1923–), and actor/playwright **Harvey Fierstein** (1954–).

Jewish Americans have been involved in every aspect of American theater since the last decades of the nineteenth century. Both on stage and behind the scenes, they have been at the forefront of the artistic growth of American drama and expanded the possibilities of all forms of American entertainment.

THOMASHEFSKY, BORIS (1868–1939)

Actor, theater director

A key figure in the Yiddish theater in America, Boris Thomashefsky was at center stage for fifty years. The son of a prominent playwright and actor, Pincus Thomashefsky, he came to the United States as a boy of thirteen and worked on the Lower East Side rolling cigarettes. The cigarette workers sang as they worked, and Boris's ringing boy soprano attracted attention. He joined a synagogue choir and persuaded one of the synagogue's trustees to bankroll the New York appearance of a Yiddish theater troupe from London, possibly the first professional Yiddish theater performances in the New World.

The boy soprano was making career strides on the nascent American Yiddish stage. He sang with the visiting Londoners in a new play by the pioneering playwright **Abraham Goldfaden** and was cast regularly in women's roles, due to a shortage of actresses. By the turn of the century, he was a major star, playing male roles since his voice had changed.

Thomashefsky used his prestige to promote a new sophistication in the Yiddish theater. Besides the sentimental operettas of Goldfaden and his successors, the star appeared in and directed Yiddish productions of Shakespeare's *Richard the Third* and *Hamlet*, and Goethe's *Faust*. At a time when much American theater was meretricious trash, Thomashefsky's classical productions were a startling breath of fresh air.

He was also responsible for tours of the United States by outstanding Yiddish companies from Eastern Europe. He toured the United States and Europe frequently. In 1923 he even assayed an unsuccessful attempt to establish a Yiddish theater on Broadway. One of his descendants followed him into the performing arts: the conductor Michael Tilson Thomas is Thomashefsky's grandson.

TOUREL, JENNIE (1900–1973)

Singer

Coloratura mezzo-soprano Jennie Tourel was born Jennie Davidovich in Vitebsk, Russia, on June 22, 1900. After the Russian Revolution her family moved to Berlin, then to Paris. In Paris she studied with Anna El-Tour, whose name she assumed in anagram form. From the mid-twenties until the Nazi invasion, Tourel was the star of the Opéra Comique and especially well known for her interpretation of *Carmen*.

Tourel escaped the Nazis days before they entered her adopted city. After a long circuitous journey, she made her way to New York City, where she auditioned for Arturo Toscanini. Soon she was singing with the New York Philharmonic, the Boston Symphony, and the Philadelphia Orchestra. Her debut at the Metropolitan Opera was in the role of Adelgisa in *Norma*. However, her career in the United States focused on concert singing rather than full operatic performances. Her repertoire was very broad and she became a special muse for **Leonard Bernstein**. (He composed the *Jeremiah Symphony* for her voice.) Together Bernstein and Tourel toured throughout the world. She taught at the Juilliard School of Music and the Samuel Rubin Academy of Music in Jerusalem and continued to perform into her seventies. She died on November 23, 1973, in New York City.

TUCKER, RICHARD (1913–1975)

Cantor, opera singer

Tenor Richard Tucker (Reuben Ticker) was born in Brooklyn, New York, on August 28, 1913. He began his career in music as a member of a synagogue choir. As a child he sang on popular music radio shows. He studied voice with Paul Althouse. In 1945 he made his Metropolitan Opera debut as Enzo in *La Gioconda*. Two years later he made his European debut opposite Maria Callas, again as Enzo. Though he sang successfully all over Europe—in fact, becoming one of the first American tenors to succeed in Europe—Tucker's career centered in the United States. His American career included singing with most of the major American orchestras and opera companies as well as on radio and, later, television. Throughout his operatic career, Tucker remained a highly successful and respected cantor. He made many recording both of opera and of cantoral music. He died unexpectedly while on tour in Kalamazoo, Michigan, on January 8, 1975.

TUCKER, SOPHIE (1884–1966)

Singer and entertainer

The self-described "Last of the Red Hot Mamas," Sophie Tucker (Sophie Kalish) was a child of vaudeville and burlesque who made a totally unexpected but highly successful transition to the more sophisticated world of the night club and, later, to film and Broadway. An international star, she performed in both Yiddish and English for over fifty years.

Born of Russian Jewish parents as they were preparing to immigrate to the United States, she was three months old when her parents settled in Hartford, Connecticut. There they ran a highly successful kosher diner and boardinghouse, which catered to theater and vaudeville performers. A performer in amateur shows from childhood, Tucker ran away from an unhappy marriage at age twenty-two, leaving her infant son in the care of her parents as she pursued a career on the stage. Like many other Jewish vaudevillians of the period (**Al Jolson** and **Eddie Cantor**, for example), she began as a blackface act, singing ostensibly African-American material like her trademark song, "Some of These Days." A big plain woman, Tucker had a bluesy belting voice that won her a dedicated following and a major engagement at the Palace Theater in New York, the most prestigious vaudeville house in the country. She remained in the upper echelon of her chosen profession for the rest of her life, performing until she was seventy-eight, alternating rowdy songs with a clever line of tough, sexy gab reminiscent of Mae West.

Her recording of one of her trademark songs, "My Yiddishe Momme," became so famous that it was banned in Hitler's Europe. Audiences also loved the songs that flaunted traditional mores such as "I'm the 3-D Mama with the Big Wide Screen" and "I May Be Getting Older Every Day (But Younger Every Night)."

Tucker firmly believed in the principle of *tzedaka*—charity, justice, and righteousness. Over her lifetime, she contributed enormous sums of money to organizations such as the Jewish Theatrical Guild, the Negro Actors Guild, and the Catholic Actors Guild, as well as numerous hospitals and synagogues. In 1945 she established the Sophie Tucker Foundation specifically to distribute money to those individuals and institutions in need.

Her films included *Honky Tonk* (1929), *Broadway Melody of 1938* (1937), *Thoroughbreds Don't Cry* (1937), and *Follow the Boys* (1944). Her Broadway performances included Cole Porter's hit *Leave It to Me* (1938) and *High Kickers* (1941), which toured in London in 1948.

Tucker never retired, performing live until a few

The "Last of the Red Hot Mammas," Sophie Tucker, was funny, risqué, and full of life, but she could also bring tears with "My Yiddishe Momme." Her recordings of that song, which had the power to evoke a reverence for Jewish culture, were ordered smashed in Germany after Hitler gained power. (American Jewish Archives)

weeks before her death on February 9, 1966, in New York City. Three thousand mourners attended her funeral, and striking hearse drivers suspended their picket line in her honor.

VAUDEVILLE

Vaudeville emerged at the end of the nineteenth century in America out of the strange world of popular entertainment. For most of the century the most prevalent form of entertainment was the minstrel show, in which white men pretended to be African American men and women and performed music and comedy inspired by the African American culture. That was on the respectable stage. Less respectable were the saloon shows, in which performers were frequently also waitresses, and "museum" shows, in which low-brow entertainment masqueraded as high-brow education. Beginning respectably were the burlesque shows, which parodied classical plays and current hits. The largely female casts of the first burlesque shows, in order to take male roles, wore tights instead of skirts. The result was that audiences became more interested in their legs and less in their satire. Eventually, burlesque degenerated into sex shows with comic interludes. In 1881 a man named Tony Pastor decided that family audiences would pay for a clean show that gave them music, comedy, acrobats, magic acts, and whatever else might fit on the bill. This new "variety" show was called vaudeville, and it flourished for fifty years.

The first Jewish-dialect comedians in vaudeville were no more Jewish than the early minstrel performers were African Americans. Soon Jewish Americans such as Joe Welch [Joseph Wolinski] (1873–1918) began adopting the Jewish stereotype and performing it themselves. Welch's costume, which was copied by many other Jewish comedians, consisted of oversized clothes and a derby. His opening line was "Mebbe you t'ink I am a heppy man." He was followed by other Jewish dialect acts, including **Weber and Fields**, who went on to open their own, extremely successful, Broadway theater; **Smith and Dale**, who were the in-

---

Harry Stanley Dies at 100
Master of Erudite Nonsense

Harry Stanley, a vaudevillian turned lecturer who was such a subtle master of philolillogical orotundity and frammatical linguistation that when he got wound up it took a while before it became apparent that nobody had the foggiest idea of what he was talking about, died on February 15.

At countless conventions, panel discussions, business or professional gatherings he would appear with his signature pince-nez and conservative dress, looking very much like the expert in whatever relevant arcane field he would be introduced as being distinguished in.

After a bland but more or less intelligible opening in which he would use standard English without quite saying anything concrete, Professor Stanley would begin slipping in vaguely Latin-sounding words so naturally phrased and so convincingly delivered that in the context of his remarks they would strike his audience as plausible, if not immediately recognizable, words.

Once, for example, having been introduced as a Presidential adviser on foreign affairs, he made a series of vague statesmanlike generalities evoking the specter of war, then added: "But I for one feel that all the basic and sadum tortumise, all the professional getesimus and tortum kimafly will precipitously aggregate so that peace shall reign. I want to make that perfectly clear."

Indeed. As he gradually added more and more such gibberish until his speech was almost all gobbledy-gook, members of the audience would begin to tumble to his game and Mr. Stanley would give it—and his vaudeville background—away; "For those of you who might have missed my introduction, I'm Professor Harry Stanley, Harvard '39, Rutgers nothing."

Robert McG. Thomas, Jr. The *New York Times*, March 6, 1998

---

spiration for **Neil Simon**'s *The Sunshine Boys*; George Sidney, who later played Abe Postash in the classic film comedy *Potash and Perlmutter*; and Benny Rubin, who became one of Hollywood's most familiar comic character actors.

In about 1920 dialect comedy became less popular. This did not decrease the number of Jewish performers on the vaudeville stage; it simply changed the way they looked and sounded. Jewish comics were to be found in abundance, and they were changing the face of American comedy. There were still those who, like Will Rogers, followed in the tradition of the slow-talk-

Born Edward Israel Iskowitz in 1892 on New York's Lower East Side, Eddie Cantor discovered at an early age that he had a natural gift for making people laugh. He first made his name in vaudeville, where he starred in the Ziegfeld Follies *from 1916 to 1919. (Private Collection)*

ing country bumpkin who was able to see through the city folk, a tradition that went back to the 1700s. But more and more American audiences were seeing a faster, more physical, punchier comedy. There was wit, but it depended more on verbal and intellectual facility than on quiet insight into the foibles of humankind. This new generation of vaudeville comics included **Eddie Cantor**, the **Marx Brothers**, **Milton Berle**, **Ed Wynn**, the Ritz Brothers, Harry Stanley, **George Jessel**, Stubby Kaye, Pinky Lee, and **Jack Benny**. Their compatriots in the burlesque shows included **Fanny Brice**, **Bert Lahr**, and **Phil Silvers** (see **Comedy and Comedians**).

Not all of the Jewish performers in vaudeville were comics. One of the greatest was the singer **Sophie Tucker** (Sophie Kalish). Risqué, funny, and sometimes powerfully dramatic, she began her career as a blackface singer, against her own better judgment. Two years later, she emerged from behind her burnt cork and began drawing adoring audiences. Her popularity continued until the end of vaudeville and beyond. Another "red hot mama" was Belle Baker [Belle Becker] (1896–1957), who has been credited with introducing 163 songs, including "Blue Skies," "All of Me," and "Alexander's Ragtime Band." Louise Dresser [Louise Josephine Kerlin] (1882–1965) was a singer in vaudeville long before she played the wife of Will Rogers in a series of Hollywood films. Nora Bayes [Dora Goldberg] (1880–1928) was an enormously popular singer on the vaudeville circuit before becoming a musical comedy star. "Nan Halperin and her Suffragettes" toured the vaudeville circuit, then Halperin herself went on to become one of the highest paid musical performers in vaudeville. Ted Lewis [Theodore Leopold Friedman] (1891–1971) was a clarinetist, bandleader, and singer on vaudeville and burlesque stages, and famous for the song "Me and My Shadow" and the catch-phrase "Is everybody happy?" **Harry Houdini** (Erik Weisz), the magician, was one of the great stars of vaudeville. **Al Jolson** (Asa Yoelson) began as a comic but soon turned to music, becoming a highly popular blackface singer.

With the rise of motion pictures and radio, vaudeville's popularity began to decline. In 1932, when the Palace Theater in New York closed its doors, one of America's most successful entertainment venues was gone. Its Jewish American stars were not. They went on to conquer the very media that had destroyed vaudeville, as well as one not yet dreamed of. When television broadcast its first commercial season, its most popular shows starred old vaudevillians.

WALLACH, ELI (1915–)

Actor

Consummate actor Eli Wallach was born in New York City and grew up in Brooklyn. After graduating from college, he received his training as an actor at the

At Age 83 Eli Wallach Knocks 'Em Dead

For one of few times in his life, Eli Wallach had a Jewish role in the recent Broadway hit play by Jeff Baron, *Visiting Mr. Green.* The *New York Times* raved: "his portrayal of a bitter 86-year-old Jewish widower is lovely to behold, a tart slice of unsentimental acting in a role that easily could have congealed before our eyes like a puddle of maple syrup.

"But the robust Mr. Wallach is too proud a performer to allow such a familiar character as the irascible Mr. Green to recline on facile sugarcoated stereotypes. He works hard to make this small-minded old man as disagreeable as the author intended. And the real trick is he makes it look easy."

Neighborhood Playhouse School of the Theater, an offshoot of the Henry Street Settlement. After serving in the Army medical corps in World War II, he began working on stage. His Broadway debut was in *Skydrift* (1945); in 1947 he became a member of the Actors Studio, where he studied with **Lee Strasberg**. The following year he married Anne Jackson, another young actor.

Wallach's big break came when he was cast as a replacement in the hit show *Mister Roberts* and attracted the attention of directors and producers. Two years later, in 1951, he gave a widely acclaimed performance in *The Rose Tattoo*, by Tennessee Williams, and followed it with another critical success in Williams's *Camino Real* (1953). While continuing to perform on stage, often with his wife, he also began making films. His Hollywood debut came in *Baby Doll* (1956) in a role that set a pattern for him. He often played the villain but was able to engage the audience's sympathy in films such as *The Misfits* (1961), *The Tiger Makes Out* (1967), and *The Deep* (1977). In a television movie *The Wall* (1982), he played one of a group of Warsaw Jews trying to defend themselves against Nazis. He also guest-starred in a number of television dramatic series and starred in his own series, "Our Family Honor," in the 1985–86 season. In 1998 Wallach received rave reviews (from The *New York Times* among others) for his leading role in *Visiting Mr. Green* at the Union Square Theater in New York City. He played an eighty-six-year-old Jewish widower. "I'm in my Jewish phase," said Wallach, having gone through a full ethnic repertoire, playing everything from a Mexican bandit, an Okinawan, a Greek, and a Mafia don. He made over three dozen films, include the cult classic *The Good, the Bad and the Ugly;* and it is clear that acting was a way of life for him.

WEBER AND FIELDS

Comedians, producers

Boyhood friends Lew Fields [Lewis Maurice Shanfield] (1867–1941) and Joe Weber [Joseph Morris Weber] (1867–1942) began performing together when they were ten years old and went on to become one of the most popular comedy teams of their time. While they were still teenagers, they developed their basic "Dutch" routine, in which they spoke with German or Yiddish accents. Their comic formula was for Fields to tell Weber to do something, which Weber would then foul up, causing Fields to pummel him. Fields was the tall, skinny partner and Weber the shorter, stockier one, even using padding to exaggerate the difference.

In 1896, they opened their own theater, the Weber and Fields' Music Hall, and began producing short musicals, accompanied by short parodies of current Broadway productions. These shows were enormously successful, featuring a spectacular chorus line and popular supporting casts for Fields and Weber. In 1904 the team broke up. Fields began producing and starring in a series of hit musicals, including *The Girl behind the Counter* (1907). In the 1920s he produced musicals written by his son Herbert with **Richard Rodgers** and **Lorenz Hart**. Weber, too, became a producer, the most successful of his shows being *The Climax* (1909).

WEISGALL, HUGO (1912–1997)

Composer

Hugo Weisgall was born in Eibenschutz, Moravia (now Ivancice, Bohemia), on October 13, 1912. He immigrated to the United States in 1920. After studying at the Peabody Conservatory in Baltimore, he moved on to the Curtis Institute in Philadelphia, where he obtained degrees in conducting (1938) and composition (1939). In 1941 he received his doctorate from Johns Hopkins University. From 1949 through 1951 he was the director of the Baltimore Institute of Musical Arts. He later taught at Johns Hopkins and the Juilliard School of Music. In 1952 he founded the Hill Top Opera Company.

Weisgall composed ballets, song cycles, choral works, and liturgical and chamber music, but he is best known for his operas. Among his most famous are *The Stronger* (1952); *Six Characters in Search of an Author* (1959), based on Pirandello's play; *Nine Rivers from Jordan* (1968), libretto by Denis Johnston; and *Esther* (1993), taken from the Bible but reworked as an allegorical tale of the Holocaust. Known both for his socially relevant themes and for his commitment to English-language operas, he won Columbia University's William Schuman Award in 1955. He died on March 11, 1997, in New York City.

YIDDISH AND KLEZMER MUSIC

All of the various Jewish cultures of the Diaspora are rich with music, and the Eastern European tradition, which forms the roots of Jewish American traditional music, is especially so. However, because of the split between vocal and instrumental music in the Jewish tradition, it is sometimes difficult to trace the influences on Yiddish traditional music. The split followed the destruction of the Second Temple of Jerusalem, an important event in Jewish religious history. After this tragedy, instrumental music was banned, and the "official" Jewish musical tradition focused on the voice of the cantor and his apprentices.

The music of the cantors influences all Jewish folk music. Secular vocal music developed out of this tradition. Most Yiddish folk songs—the lullabies, work songs, love songs, and ballads—were sung unaccompanied by musical instruments and were passed down orally by the women of the community. In the late nineteenth century, the cantoral and folk song tradition gave birth to the early Yiddish musical theater, which was an important venue for the reuniting of vocal and instrumental music.

Klezmer music was also influenced by the vocal music of the Jewish religious tradition. An instrumental interpretation of the tradition, the term klezmer covers many styles and forms. It is Yiddish dance music and it is Yiddish wedding music. It can be wildly upbeat or heart-wrenchingly melancholic. To some it is only instrumental music, yet even in the most traditional klezmer setting, the wedding, the musicians were sometimes accompanied the chanting of the *badkhn*. This instrumental side of Eastern European Jewish folk music can be traced back to the thirteenth century, but what is now thought of as the classic klezmer probably didn't develop until the eighteenth and nineteenth centuries. The musical instruments were usually fiddle, flute, bass, drum, and hammer dulcimer. By the end of the nineteenth century, brass instruments such as trumpet, tuba, and clarinet were being added. By the 1920s the clarinet had become the predominant instrument in most bands.

"Klezmer music" is a new term. The word "klezmer" derives from the Hebrew words *klei zemer*, which mean "musical instrument" or literally "vessel of song." In Yiddish, the term *klezmer* originally meant, simply, "musician." It is only since the mid-1970s that klezmer music has become the defining term for the predominantly—but not solely—instrumental folk music of the Yiddish-speaking Jews.

Erroneously called "Jewish jazz" or "Yiddish Dixieland," klezmer shares qualities with the cantorial vocal tradition and European folk music, especially Romanian, Moldavian, Ukrainian, and Roman, or gypsy. Hasidic musical qualities and their more "Oriental" sounds were also important in the development of klezmer. This multi-ethnicity was not limited to the music's content. The music's early audiences and performers were multi-ethnic as well. Klezmer was popular with both Jewish and Gentile audiences and was performed by both Jewish and Gentile musicians, especially gypsies.

The traveling musicians, called *klezmorim*, became

Rescuing Yiddish Songs

Eleanor and Joseph Mlotek devote a substantial portion of their lives to preserving Yiddish songs and making them widely available. Their third anthology *Songs of Generations: New Pearls of Yiddish Songs*, was published by the Workman's Circle in 1997. It is based on "Pearls From Yiddish Poetry," a column they have published since 1970 in the *Forward*. They received the ultimate compliment on their efforts when Isaac Bashevis Singer described them as "the Sherlock Holmes of Yiddish song."

essential to Eastern European weddings as well as other religious and secular celebrations. In part because of the ancient ban, and because of the itinerant nature of their lives as trouping musicians, klezmorim were considered at best frivolous and at worst dangerous and morally suspect. For this reason, the term klezmer had negative connotations. Until the klezmer revival in the mid-1970s, many klezmer musicians would not have been pleased to be referred to as such.

All forms of Yiddish music were brought to the United States during the great Jewish immigration at the turn of the century and the Jewish music business thrived. From 1894 through 1942 there were more than 50,000 Jewish records made. For the first quarter of the twentieth century, the United States was the world center of klezmer recording. From klezmer to cantors to the stars of the musical theater, Jewish music was in demand, whatever its form. During this period, the great Yiddish theater composers included Joseph Rumshinsky (1881–1956), **Sholom Secunda**, and Alexander Olshanetsky, who later became a prominent booking agent. Among the noted Yiddish "art song" composers of the day were Leo Low (1878–1962) and Lazar Weiner (1897–1982). Both the musical theater composers and the "art song" composers influenced the development of American klezmer.

Klezmorim found work playing klezmer music and the new songs of the Yiddish theater in Yiddish theaters, in vaudeville houses, on Yiddish radio shows, and on Yiddish records. The new Borscht Belt hotels provided both a well-heeled audience and an important employment source that kept both klezmer music

and its musicians alive. Abe Katzman, Abe Schwartz (ca. 1880–1950), Harry Kandel (1890–1940), Naftule Brandwine (1884–1963), Abe Ellstein (1907–), and Dave Tarras (1897–1989) were among the great American klezmorim during these early days.

As the century progressed, American jazz idioms, especially swing, began to change the klezmer sound. Bandleader and clarinetist David Tarras started out playing traditional klezmer but, by the 1940s, he was heavily influenced by swing. Working with Tarras, clarinetist/saxophonist Sammy Musiker (1922–1963) was another influential jazz/klezmer musician. During the same period, the Bagelman Sisters—later the Barry Sisters—became the Yiddish version of the Andrews Sisters. Though some might argue that the Bagelman Sisters weren't klezmer, others consider that they continued the movement of klezmer from instrumental alone to instrumental and vocal.

Perhaps the most successful swing-klezmer impresario was clarinetist and bandleader Mickey Katz. Katz became prominent in the 1940s and 1950s with swing-style klezmer recordings. He later worked with comic musician Spike Jones and performed English-Yiddish parodies of well known songs such as "Haim afen Range." In 1948 he put together his highly successful touring company, *Borscht Capades*, in which his son Joel Grey got his show business start. Swing kings such as **Benny Goodman** and Artie Shaw (1910–) never played klezmer, but Goodman frequently played Jewish venues and would turn the stage over to his trumpeter Harry (Ziggy Elman) Finkelman (1914–1968) whenever a "Jewish sound" was needed. Both Goodman and Elman had successes adapting popular Yiddish songs to more American styles. Two examples are "Frailach in Swing" by Elman (1938) and "My Little Cousin" by Goodman (1942).

In the 1950s when the Eastern European immigrants of the Lower East Side of New York City began to disperse and assimilate into the broader American landscape, both klezmer and the more broadly defined Yiddish music began to disappear. The Holocaust decimated Eastern European Jewish culture, and the music had too many painful connotations for many American listeners. By the 1960s Jewish cultural focus centered on the State of Israel and its official language, Hebrew. Klezmer and Yiddish culture all but disappeared from Jewish American life.

The Hasidic community was an important support during this "dry period" for klezmer music, as were a few musicians who maintained an interest in the music. Both proved to be important bridges to the klezmer revival of the 1970s. The most important musician was Peter Sokolow, who began playing reeds and later switched to keyboards. In the late 1950s he played the Borscht Belt with Dave Tarras and the Epstein Brothers. By the time the klezmer revival was in full swing, in the mid-eighties, he had formed the Original Klezmer Jazz Band.

In the mid-1970s, Americans of all ethnicities began rediscovering their roots. Young Jewish musicians were among those who began to search for their ethnic heritage and modern klezmer was born. Many of these young musicians turned to the older, largely forgotten, generation of klezmer musicians. Andy Statman studied with the legendary Dave Tarras. Michael Alpert and his group, Brave Old World, recorded with Ben Bazyler. Frank London and Alicia Svigals and their

---

Mamaloshen on CD

Nonesuch has issued a CD of songs performed by Mandy Patinkin entitled *Mamaloshen* ("mother tongue" in Yiddish). The songs are all performed in Yiddish and include standards from the Lower East Side Yiddish theater and translations of classics by such American Jewish composers as Leonard Bernstein and Stephen Sondheim ("Maria" from *West Side Story*) and Irving Berlin ("God Bless America"). The *Forward* review quotes their interview with the singer:

> He argues that [their] Jewish roots are evident in the music of the Tin Pan Alley songs, if not in the lyrics. "I've corrected the error by translating them," he says.
>
> While he acknowledges its Jewish context, Mr. Patinkin believes that in the end Mamaloshen "isn't a Jewish album, it's an American album." He hopes it will inspire people to "go out and learn about your ancestors' history. It will fill your heart and open a world to you, and sing inside you. You won't understand why but it will, I promise you it will."

---

group, the Klezmatics, learned from Ray Musiker. Henry Sapoznick and his group, Kapelye, worked with both Sid Beckerman and Leon Schwartz.

The young individuals and groups mentioned above are among the most successful of the modern klezmorim. Other important members of today's klezmer community are Zev Feldman, Giora Feidman, and Hankus Netsky, founding member of the influential Klezmer Conservatory Band (KCB).

Today's klezmer is exciting, increasingly popular, and very hard to define. For many, klezmer music can now include both Yiddish folk songs as well as traditional wedding music. As open as it always was to outside influence, a klezmer tune can be one played almost exactly as it would have been one hundred years ago, or it can be tinged with Big Band influences, or it can be a mix of rock 'n' roll's drive and klezmer's wail.

Among the performers and audiences, as well as in the music itself, klezmer has maintained its historic multi-ethnicity. One example is Don Byron, a KCB alumni and an African American, who is considered to be one of jazz/klezmer's foremost clarinetists. At the same time, the music's Jewish roots are being proclaimed for all to see. Two examples are the Klezmatics' album *Rhythm and Jews* and the band Schreck's song "Yo! We Killed Your God!" Klezmer is also influencing the broader musical world around it. Frequently using Hebrew and klezmer melodies, avant-garde jazz musician John Zorn and his quartet Masada have created a space between klezmer and jazz.

Modern klezmer represents a new and diverse Jewish identity. However it is defined, one can be certain that klezmer music is alive and well and adding to the musical landscape of America.

YIDDISH THEATER

The Yiddish theater in America lasted for less than eighty years, but was a cultural phenomenon of great importance in Jewish America. It began only six years after the genre itself was born in Jassy, Romania, in 1876, and quickly became the most vital Yiddish theater in the world.

Professional entertainment of any kind did not become a part of Jewish life in Europe until the nineteenth century, when urbanization had begun to affect traditional village life. The earliest modern Jewish entertainers were traveling musicians. The first signs of what would become the Yiddish theater appeared in the form of bits of dialogue and other theatrical trappings used to add appeal to programs of music. Russian songwriter and intellectual **Abraham Goldfaden** created a dramatic structure for the music of singer Israel Grader, and the result was so successful that Goldfaden created a troupe and began to produce musical plays. When the Russian government outlawed Yiddish theater in one of its anti-Jewish laws in 1833, the performers and playwrights fled, mostly to London. London's West End was too small and too gentile to support the genre, which eventually moved to the United States.

The first Yiddish play presented in this country was a Goldfaden musical, produced in New York City by a Jewish American saloon owner named Frank Wolf. The cast was a troupe of Yiddish performers from London, some local people, and a young man named **Boris Thomashefsky**, who worked in a cigarette factory and would become one of the most famous actors of the Yiddish theater. The first performance, in August of 1882, was not particularly successful, but the English troupe, headed by Leon and Miron Golubok, remained, and by the end of the year Yiddish shows were being presented regularly in a beer hall called the Old Bowery Garden.

From these inauspicious beginnings grew a theater that, by the early 1900s, was drawing an audience of about two million people every year. In the early days actors played fast and loose with the scripts—they received a new one every several weeks—and often threw into the performance whatever song or dance they happened to be working on at the time. Their audiences were loud and loyal, almost fanatical.

There were those who wanted a more intellectual and dignified theater. The great actor Joseph Adler (1855–1926) was in the forefront of this new movement. He persuaded Russian immigrant writer Jacob Gordin (1853–1909) to write a play for him. The play,

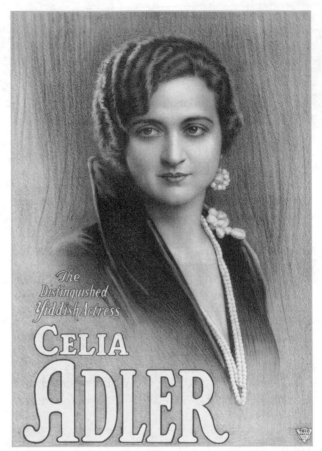

Celia Adler probably has the distinction of appearing on stage at a younger age than anyone else in this book. Her mother Sara used her as a prop in a performance when she was six months old. At the age of four she played a role especially written for her in Der Yidisher Kenig Lear (The Yiddish King Lear). *At age fifty-seven, she was called back to the stage (soon after she thought she had retired) by Ben Hecht, who cast her opposite Paul Muni (an old friend from the Yiddish theater) in his Zionist play* A Flag is Born. *(Courtesy of American Jewish Historical Society, Waltham, Massachusetts, and New York, New York)*

Siberia (1891), was a strong drama done in a realistic style and it revolutionized Yiddish theater. For eighteen years, Gordin's plays, often starring Adler, dominated the boards on the Lower East Side. This period is called, interchangeably, the Gordin Era and the Golden Epoch. The other actors most closely associated with Gordin were David Kessler (1859–1920), Keni Liptzin, and **Bertha Kalich**.

Because of the success of plays by Gordin and by his follower Leon Kobrin (1872–1946), Yiddish theater managers, many of whom were also the theater's stars, began to produce a different kind of theater. Plays by **Sholom Asch** and **Sholom Aleichem**, among others, ran in the four main Yiddish theaters: the Thalia, the Windsor, the People's, and the Grand. They were all in the Bowery area of New York City and all had between 2,000 and 3,500 seats. Plays were done in repertory. The current play ran on the weekends and older plays from the repertory were done during the week, often to benefit audiences. Ticket prices were from a quarter to a dollar and, at a time when many immigrants made no more than ten dollars a week, the houses were full.

As Yiddish theater prospered, it moved to Second Avenue, to what became known as "Yiddish Broadway." Theaters opened by Kessler and Thomashefsky occupied buildings that cost almost $1 million each. Yiddish Broadway had stars that were as well known in New York, and certainly as adored as those of the Great White Way. Among them were names that have become familiar to a broader audience. **Molly Picon** went on to fame in English-speaking theater and in films and television. **Jacob Adler** and his wife Sara (1858–1953) founded a dynasty that would dominate the Yiddish theater and powerfully influence the English-speaking theater. Among their children were Luther Adler (1903–1985), who became one of America's most distinguished character actors, and **Stella Adler**, who trained some of the most important actors of the modern theater including Marlon Brando and Robert DeNiro. There were other actors who remained in the Yiddish theater all their lives. They included Menasha Skulnik, Herman Yablokoff, and Jennie Goldstein.

There was another strain in the development of Yiddish theater. Among the immigrants of the first part of the century were many from Russia, who were accustomed to amateur dramatic societies. They created semi-professional troupes to perform more daring and experimental work. This movement was called the Yiddish art theater. A landmark production was that of *Green Fields*, by Peretz Hirshbein at the Fraye

At the beginning of the twentieth century Yiddish plays in New York City were drawing an audience of over two million people a year. The advertising posters for the productions were quite wonderful, as can be seen by the above example. (Courtesy of American Jewish Historical Society, Waltham, Massachusetts, and New York, New York)

Yiddishe Folksbine (the Free Yiddish People's Stage) in 1918. Part of its effect was to inspire a man named **Maurice Schwartz** to produce a more modern drama.

Schwartz has been credited with shaping the Yiddish art theater. He gave that name to his theater company. In the same year that the Folksbine produced *Green Fields*, the Yiddish Art Theater commercially produced another Hirshbein play at the Irving Place Theater. The play, *Forsaken Nook*, was presented with stunning simplicity and a new style of acting inspired by Russian theater great Konstantin Stanislavsky. In the years to come, Schwartz encouraged the careers of Jacob Ben-Ami (1890–1977), designer **Boris Aronson**, and a number of important playwrights. His theater's biggest success was a dramatization of **Isaac Bashevis Singer**'s novel *Yoshe Kalb* (1932).

Maurice Schwartz's Yiddish Art Theater lasted until 1950. During the 1930s, however, a number of other Yiddish theaters opened and quickly closed. Playwright David Pinski and actor Jacob Ben-Ami both attempted to create Yiddish theaters and failed. One survivor was the Artef Theater. Under the guidance of director Benno Schneider, the Artef specialized in avant-garde, stylized ensemble work and was quite successful for a number of years.

In the 1930s Jewish immigration slowed to a trickle, about 7,000 people a year. Most Jews born in America began to speak English and turned to English-speaking entertainments. The Yiddish theater audience became older and, smaller. The theaters became touring companies to find Yiddish speakers in other cities. Eventually, the last remnants of a great force in Jewish American culture disappeared.

YOUNGMAN, HENNY (1906–1998)

Comedian

The king of one-liners was born in White Chapel, England, on March 16, 1906. His family moved to New York six months later, settling in Brooklyn. He attended the Brooklyn Vocational Trade School and became a printer while, to please his father, he learned to play the violin. After becoming friends with legendary comic **Milton Berle**, he gave in to the draw of show business and started a band called Henny Youngman and the Swanee Syncopaters. While the band was performing at the Swan Lake Inn in the Catskills, he started telling jokes between songs. The owner of the resort fired the band and hired Youngman as a comedian. After several years on the comedy circuit, he was hired to appear on "The Kate Smith Show" in 1936. The engagement made his career as a comic, but he left after two years to try to make it in Hollywood. Not as successful in a film career, he returned to perform-

---

"Take my wife—please."

It may seem like a trite one-liner now, but the joke Henny Youngman told so frequently on the Borscht Belt circuit (and on national television) became so famous that it is now an entry in *Bartlett's Familiar Quotations*.

---

ing comedy in clubs, using the fiddle his father loved so much as a prop in his act and a rapid-fire delivery that promised "if you don't like this joke there's another one coming any second." He played all the great clubs. In the 1960s he became a household word among yet another generation when the popular television show "Laugh-In" adopted the line, "Oh, that Henny Youngman!" as one of its many catchphrases.

In 1974 New York Telephone established a service called Dial-A-Joke, and the man who could cram six jokes into one-minute did exactly that. During the 1990s Youngman appeared in the Martin Scorsese film *Goodfellas* and worked with **Steven Spielberg** on the "Tiny Toons" cartoon series. He ate lunch nearly every day at the Friar's Club in Manhattan where he was a member for forty-seven years (he always requested a table near a waiter). In 1996 a street corner in Manhattan was named after him. Youngman died on February 24, 1998, from pneumonia in New York City.

ZIEGFELD, FLORENZ (1867–1932)

Producer, showman

Legendary producer Florenz Ziegfeld was born in Chicago and began his career when he was sent to Europe by his father to sign distinguished musicians for the 1893 Columbian Exposition. Instead, he hired circus acts and music hall performers. Soon thereafter, he signed a contract to manage strongman Eugene Sandow and began to make a name for himself. His first Broadway productions were built around his wife Anna Held. He surrounded the petite singer with spectacular chorus lines and elaborate sets. After they divorced in 1906, he produced the *Follies of 1907*, forerunner of his *Ziegfeld Follies*, annual editions of which ran until 1925. He also produced a great many musical comedies including *Show Boat* (1927) and a number of dramatic plays.

It was the *Follies*, however, for which Ziegfeld was best known. Over two decades he introduced many Jewish stars including **Eddie Cantor**, **Fanny Brice**, and Nora Bayes, as well as African American stars such as Bert Williams, and numerous other performers. Among the songs that came out of these sensational productions are "By the Light of the Silvery Moon," "A Pretty Girl Is Like a Melody," and "My Man."

ZUKERMAN, PINCHAS (1948–)

Violinist, violist, conductor

Pinchas Zukerman was born in Tel Aviv, Israel, on July 16, 1948. A child prodigy, he began his musical training with his father, first on recorder, then clarinet, and then on violin. At the age of eight he began studying with Ilona Feher at the Israel Conservatory and the Tel Aviv Academy of Music. When he was fourteen, he came to the attention of violinist **Isaac Stern**. Stern was so impressed by the young musician that he sponsored Zukerman's attendance at the Juilliard School of Music in New York City, where he began studying in 1962. In 1967 he won First Prize in the twenty-fifth Leventritt International Competition. His solo career soon followed.

Zukerman has recorded prolifically, with over 100 releases. He has been nominated for a Grammy twenty-one times and won the award twice—as "Best Chamber Music Performance" in 1980 and "Best Classical Performance—Instrumental Soloist with Orchestra" in 1981. He has toured throughout the United States and Europe. Zukerman has played frequently with both Stern and violinist **Itzhak Perlman** (with Zukerman on viola) as well as for conductor Daniel Barenboim. Among his most famous recordings are the complete Beethoven violin sonatas, with Barenboim conducting. He is known for his versatility, skill, and expressiveness on both the violin and viola. He began conducting in 1970 with the English Chamber Orchestra and has led many of the world's leading orchestras, including the Chicago Symphony, the New York Philharmonic, the Boston Symphony, the Los Angeles Philharmonic, as well as European orchestras. He acts as Artistic Director of the Pinchas Zukerman Performance Program at the Manhattan School of Music and has established a summer violin study program in the name of Ilona Feher in Holon, Israel.

For Further Reading

See Appendix 2 for a bibliography of general reference books about Jews and the Jewish experience in America. All of these volumes include information about American Jews in music, dance, and theater.

Cohen, Sarah Blacher, ed. *From Hester Street to Hollywood: The Jewish-American Stage and Screen*. Bloomington, Ind.: Indiana University Press, 1983.

Kanter, Kenneth A. *The Jews on Tin Pan Alley: The Jewish Contribution to American Popular Music, 1830–1940*. New York: KTAV Publishing House, 1982.

Lyman, Darryl. *Great Jews on Stage and Screen*. Middle Village, N.Y.: Jonathan David Publishers, 1987.

———. *The Jewish Comedy Catalog*. Middle Village, N.Y.: Jonathan David Publishers, 1989.

Sandrow, Nahma. *Vagabond Stars: A World History of Yiddish Theater*. New York: Harper and Row, 1977.

Part 11

Radio, Television, and Film

OVERVIEW

Because of an accident of history, American Jews have played an enormously important role in the entertainment industry, especially the fields of radio, television, and film. That role began with the motion picture industry. At the time when film technology was coming to fruition, a great influx of Jewish immigrants was crowding into New York and other American cities. These immigrants were hungry, hard-working, and determined to carve out successful lives for themselves and their families. Undeterred by considerations that dampened the ardor of more secure and established businessmen, newly arrived Jews such as **Samuel Goldwyn**, the **Warner** brothers, and **Louis Mayer** threw themselves into the new industry with energy and intelligence. As producers, they dominated American film, but their own determination to assimilate prevented them from allowing Judaism and the Jewish culture to impact the content of their product. Indeed, they often rejected Jewish actors or forced them to hide their ethnicity.

By the time radio made its appearance on the commercial entertainment scene, that situation had changed somewhat. Jewish Americans such as **Robert Sarnoff** created and ran the major studios. Radio launched itself on the talents of vaudeville entertainers whose Jewishness, while not emphasized in most cases, was certainly not hidden. These performers went on to become the core of the new medium of television. **Milton Berle**, **Jack Benny**, **George Burns**, **Gertrude Berg**, **Groucho Marx**—these were the people who made Americans rush out to buy the box with the very small screen. However, television, with its emphasis on situation comedy and live drama, began again to emphasize assimilation. It was soon outdoing film in presenting a bland, de-ethnicized view of American life. As in film, Jewish producers and administrators were involved in decisions that put Dick Van Dyke in the role **Carl Reiner** had written for himself and kept Jewish women in comedy roles, usually as sidekicks. This situation would not change until the late 1980s and early 1990s, when **Roseanne**, **Jerry Seinfeld**, and Fran Drescher became staples of prime time.

The performers, directors, businesspeople, and decision-makers portrayed in this part shaped the way Americans viewed themselves, each other, and the world.

ALLEN, WOODY (1935–)

Filmmaker, author, comedian

Woody Allen was the first of the many brilliant stand-up comics to make the difficult transition from the club stage to the director's chair. He is still the most successful filmmaker to come out of the nightclub and TV comedy scene. But then, Allen was not your usual stand-up. Under the influence of the European art cinema and serious literature, his aspirations went far beyond merely making people laugh (although he did that supremely well).

Allan Stewart Konigsberg (who changed his name to Woody Allen in 1952) was born in the Flatbush section of Brooklyn, New York, on December 1, 1935. Allen began writing and performing his comedy while still a student. He dropped out of NYU to pursue a career as a stand-up comic in the early 1960s, quickly establishing himself as one of the best of the many talented purveyors of topical and personal humor in that period, a powerful departure from the old style of comedy, with its concentration on one-liners and prefab jokes on tired topics like mothers-in-law. From there it was no great leap for Allen to screenwriting and acting, with his first appearance in both roles coming in 1965 with *What's New Pussycat?* He followed that hit (in which he was paired for the first of several films with Louise Lasser, who would be his first wife) with a directorial debut of sorts, *What's Up Tiger Lily?* (1966), in which Allen took a Japanese James Bond rip-off and dubbed in new dialogue (much of it with a distinctly New York Jewish twist). Before he would return to the director's chair, Allen wrote two hit Broadway shows, *Don't Drink The Water* and *Play It Again Sam.*

In 1969 Allen began the career that has brought him the widest recognition, as actor, writer, and director of feature films. His first film, *Take the Money and*

Run (1969), was a mordant satire of documentaries and crime films. He followed with *Bananas* (1971), a send-up of political radicals and the FBI, the futuristic *Sleeper* (1973), and a *War and Peace* parody *Love and Death* (1975). His career in film soared and the films became more ambitious and self-conscious. With the success of *Annie Hall* (1977) and *Manhattan* (1979), he established himself as a genuine filmmaker rather than a mere manufacturer of spoofs. He essayed serious drama in the vein of his hero, Ingmar Bergman, with *Interiors* (1978).

Since the 1970s, Allen's films have become increasingly personal (and detractors might say, pretentious). In films as varied as *Zelig* (1983), *Broadway Danny Rose* (1984), *Hannah and Her Sisters* (1986), *Crimes and Misdemeanors* (1989), *Husbands and Wives* (1992), *Mighty Aphrodite* (1995), and *Deconstructing Harry* (1997), Allen explored the neuroses of the fashionably liberal Upper West Side Jew—himself. He remains the most consistent presence in his own work, occasionally to the film's detriment.

A reclusive and intensely private man, Allen has been involved in controversy from time to time. A strong supporter of the Israeli peace movement, he has contributed op-ed pieces to the *New York Times* and **Tikkun**. His most controversial public contretemps occurred when he split up with his long-term partner Mia Farrow and later married her nineteen-year-old adopted daughter, Soon-Yi Previn. Despite the negative publicity, Allen has continued working, turning out a film every ten months or so under a blanket of pre-release secrecy.

Allen has also distinguished himself as a writer. Between 1966 and 1980, he published over fifty humorous stories and essays, most of which appeared in *The*

New Yorker and later in his collections *Getting Even* (1971), *Without Feathers* (1976), and *Side Effects* (1980). An expert clarinetist specializing in New Orleans-style jazz, Allen has been playing at Monday-night sessions for many years with his own band at Michael's Pub in Manhattan.

AMSTERDAM, MOREY (1914–1996)

Comedian, actor, songwriter

The great wisecracking comedian Morey Amsterdam was born in Chicago to a concert violinist who expected his son to carry on the family tradition. Instead, the young man took his cello onto the vaudeville stage as a comic prop. With Will Rogers as a mentor, he also did nightclubs and radio, even writing a best-selling song "Rum and Coca-Cola." However, it was television that proved to be his gold mine. "The Morey Amsterdam Show" (1948–50) was a variety show with a fictional setting, a Times Square nightclub, and a cast of characters that included Art Carney as the waiter and Jacqueline Susann as the cigarette girl.

Amsterdam's next television job was as the host of "Broadway Open House" (1950), a late-night talk show that was the predecessor of "The Tonight Show." After a variety of guest appearances on situation comedies, he found the role that made him a television legend, that of Buddy Sorrell on "The Dick Van Dyke Show" (1961–66). With every wisecrack, he endeared himself to audiences on what has been called the best written situation comedy in television history. Although his character was Jewish, no reference was made to that fact until the final episode of the series, when Buddy had a long-postponed bar mitzvah. After the show closed, Amsterdam made mostly guest appearances.

ARKIN, ADAM (1956–)

Actor

Son of the great film actor **Alan Arkin**, Adam Arkin has received his father's legacy of talent and flexibility. He began acting in his father's films, such as *Chu Chu* *and the Philly Flash* (1981) when he was young but soon went on to make his own career. He acted on stage and in films but had his breakthrough to fame on television, as the surly but brilliant Adam on "Northern Exposure" (1990–95). In the film *The Doctor* (1991), he played surgeon Eli "The Rabbi" Blumfield in a cast that included actor **Mandy Patinkin** as another doctor. A few years later, the two were paired as doctors again, in the hit series "Chicago Hope." When Patinkin resigned as a regular on the series to spend time with his children, Arkin's character Aaron Shutt moved into first place on the show as subtly sexy and angst-ridden surgeon. In its second year, "Chicago Hope" won fifteen Emmys.

ARKIN, ALAN (1934–)

Actor

The exceptionally talented and versatile actor Alan Arkin was born in New York City and moved with his family to Los Angeles while he was in high school. He returned to New York after college and began a career as a singer/songwriter before turning to acting. Although he had several small roles in the New York theater, he found success in Chicago, as a member of legendary improvisational comedy troupe Second City. He made his Broadway debut in *From the Second City* (1961) and then became a star in the comedy *Enter Laughing* (1963). He scored another success in *Luv* (1964), then went on to films.

Arkin's film debut in *The Russians Are Coming! The Russians Are Coming!* (1966) foreshadowed many of his later roles. As a Russian sailor whose submarine has been grounded off New England, he was quirky, funny, and utterly brilliant. Later film portrayals included a variety of roles, such as a thug in *Wait until Dark* (1967), a deaf man in *The Heart is a Lonely Hunter* (1968), a Puerto Rican father in *Popi* (1969), and then, in an extraordinary performance, as Yossarian in *Catch-22* (1970). As the man who is too sane for war, Arkin established himself an the actor's actor. Dozens of other films have followed, including the hilarious *The In-Laws* (1980) with Peter Falk and *Slums*

of Beverly Hills (1998), in which he plays a sixty-something single father with teenage children. Films are not the limit of Arkin's creativity. He is also a children's songwriter and singer and has directed for both stage and film. He is the father of actor **Adam Arkin**.

ARTHUR, BEA (1926–)

Actor

Television's astringent and charismatic Maude, Beatrice Arthur (Bernice Frankel) was born in New York City and spent her adolescence in Baltimore, Maryland. After studying acting at the New School for Social Research in New York with fellow students such as Marlon Brando, she began to work in small theaters in the city. From 1947 to 1950 she performed important roles at the Cherry Lane Theater in Greenwich Village. From 1951 to 1953 she was part of the company at Atlantic City's Circle Theater. She then went on to Pennsylvania and the Tamiment Theater. She made her Broadway debut in 1957 in *Nature's Way*. During this time she helped to support herself singing in nightclubs such as New York's Blue Angel. She also appeared from time to time as a guest on television variety shows.

After a hiatus of several years in which she concentrated on the career of her then-husband, director Gene Saks, Arthur had her first big successes as Yente in *Fiddler on the Roof* (1964) and Vera Charles in *Mame* (1966). She gained national attention in 1971 when she guest-starred as Edith Bunker's liberal cousin on "All in the Family." She was so positively received that she and the character began their own series, "Maude" (1972–78), the next season. She then achieved a rarity in television, a second hit series, when she teamed with Estelle Getty, Betty White, and Rue McClanahan in "The Golden Girls" (1985–92).

ASNER, EDWARD (1929–)

Actor

Every generation seems to produce one actor who wins the hearts of his audience as the gruff, endearing man of integrity. Edward Asner has been that actor for the baby boomers. Born in Kansas City, Missouri, to Russian Jewish immigrants, he began his career on stage in Chicago. By 1955 he was performing regularly in off-Broadway productions, including *The Threepenny Opera* (1956) and a number of Shakespearean plays. In 1961 he turned his attention to television and began making guest appearances on a number of dramatic series. He was a regular on *Slattery's People* (1964–65). He found his niche in 1970 when he was cast as Lou Grant, boss of the WJM-TV newsroom on "The Mary Tyler Moore Show" (1970–77). It was one of the most popular shows on television for its entire run, and Lou Grant was the favored authority figure for a generation that was rejecting authority of all kinds.

During the run of the show, Asner was able to show his flexibility as an actor by performing in a number of television movies and mini-series including *Rich Man, Poor Man* (1976) and *Roots* (1977). When the show ended its long run, he took his character to a new series, "Lou Grant" (1977–82). Since that show went off the air, he has appeared largely in films, some of them made for television. Throughout his life, he has been politically active and a strong voice for human rights. He has supported a number of Jewish causes and, in 1985, received an award from the **Jewish Theological Seminary of America**.

BACALL, LAUREN (1924–)

Actor

Howard Hawks was looking for a new face to star opposite Humphrey Bogart in his film *To Have and Have Not* when his wife showed him the cover of an issue of *Harper's Bazaar* with the photograph of a striking model. She was a nice Jewish girl named Betty Joan Perske, working as Lauren Bacall. Hawks knew immediately that she was what he was looking for. Thus began one of the most fabled romances in Hollywood history, as the veteran director introduced Bogie and his "Baby," as the actor called her.

Hawks told Bogart that he was "the most insolent man in Hollywood films," but he was going to be paired with a woman "even more insolent." That was the role that Bacall made her own over the course of a film career that was still going strong in the late 1990s. In her films with Bogart—*To Have and Have Not* (1944), *The Big Sleep* (1946), *Dark Passage* (1947), *Key Largo* (1948)—Bacall projects a steamy sexuality, underpinned by a smart, tough independence. Although she was a quarter-century his junior, she held her own on screen and off with Bogart. They married in 1945 and remained deeply and happily in love until his painful and protracted death from cancer in 1957.

As an actor, Bacall seldom had as powerful roles as when she was opposite Bogart, although she offered memorable performances in Vincente Minnelli's *The Cobweb* (1955) and Douglas Sirk's *Written on the Wind* (1957). She won Tony awards for her roles in the Broadway musicals *Applause* (1970) and *Woman of the Year* (1981) and was nominated for an Academy Award for her role as **Barbra Streisand**'s sharp-tongued mother in *The Mirror Has Two Faces* (1996).

BARA, THEDA (1890–1955)

Actor

How a nice Jewish girl from Cincinnati, a tailor's daughter named Theodosia Goodman, became the most feared and lusted after of the "vamps" of the early silent cinema is one of those stories only Hollywood could have created. Bara began her career as a supporting player in stock companies at the turn of the century, finally reaching Broadway as Theodosia de Coppet in 1908. Like many other stage actors, she turned to film to make more money, despite a considerable drop in prestige. Her appearance in the 1915 mega-hit *A Fool There Was* brought her stardom almost instantly. It was also the role that typed her forever as the "vamp," the evil woman with sexual designs on any man who came under her spell.

The shrewd Bara was not above playing on her

A founder of the American-Israel Cultural Foundation, Jack Benny (right) actually began his career as a violinist, but Milton Berle was not renowned for his harmonica playing. Both became legends for their extended careers, ranging from vaudeville to television to films. Berle made a special appearance at the 1998 Emmy Awards ceremony, along with Bob Hope and Sid Caeser. (Private Collection)

screen persona. She allowed herself to pose with skulls, ravens, snakes, and other symbols of demonic destruction. She was interviewed while surrounded by "Nubian slaves" and burning incense. Although she essayed some non-vamp parts, the changing mood of audiences in the wake of World War I led to her persona's demise. She continued working in film and theater, returning to Broadway in 1919, but her career was essentially over.

BENNY, JACK (1894–1974)

Radio, television, film star

The perpetually thirty-nine-year-old, tightwad egomaniac that was Jack Benny's stage and screen persona was about as far removed from the real Benny (born Benny Kubelsky) as imaginable. But it was as that fictional "Jack Benny" that this ex-vaudevillian made himself a radio and television star of lasting popularity.

Born in Chicago, Benny began his career at seventeen as a vaudeville violinist (another subject of much self-deprecatory humor). While serving in the Navy during World War I he discovered his real talent was for comedy. He began working the vaudeville circuits as Ben K. Benny, gradually making it to the top of that field. Although he appeared in films as early as 1929, his real breakthrough came in radio, where he built up a stock company that included Phil Harris, Don Wilson, Dennis Day, Eddie "Rochester" Anderson, Mel Blanc, and his real-life wife, Mary Livingston (born Sadye Marks). Benny took much of his radio cast with him when his wireless stardom brought him back to Hollywood for a series of mostly undistinguished (but quite amusing) films.

The one exception was his 1942 appearance in Ernst Lubitsch's *To Be or Not to Be*; in this brilliant, mordant satirical attack on the Nazis, Benny worked without his familiar radio-film family. The result is one of the great film comedies, spurred in no small part by Benny's incredibly subtle work.

Benny was one of the most successful performers to make the transition from radio to television. "The Jack Benny Show" ran on television from 1950 through 1965 and is periodically revived in syndication and on cable.

BERG, GERTRUDE (1899–1966)

Actor, writer, producer

Creator of one of the most enduring fictional families in American entertainment history, Gertrude Berg began her career writing and producing shows for the guests of her family's resort hotel in the Catskills. After graduating from high school, she wrote and persuaded NBC to broadcast her series about Molly Goldberg and family. In addition to writing "The Rise of the Goldbergs," Berg played Molly on NBC Blue from 1929 to 1934 and on CBS from 1938 to 1945. In the interim, Molly took the show on the road, presenting it live around the country. In 1948, she took the family to Broadway in the play *Me and Molly*. In 1949 "The Goldbergs" became one of the first situation comedies on television airing first on CBS, then appearing on one network or another until 1954.

The success of the show was marred when the actor playing Molly Goldberg's husband, Jake, was blacklisted during the McCarthy era. Berg attempted to defend him but under threat of cancellation of the series, she finally replaced him. A few years later, unable to find work, the actor, **Philip Loeb**, committed suicide. After her series ended, Berg played characters similar to Molly in another series called "Mrs. G. Goes to College," which changed midseason to "The Gertrude Berg Show" (1961–62), and in the Broadway play *A Majority of One* (1959).

BERLE, MILTON (1908–)

Comedian

The man known as "Mr. Television" was born Milton Berlinger in New York City and began working in films while he was still a child. After a stint in kid acts in vaudeville in Philadelphia, he returned to New York. After appearing in the Broadway musical *Floradora* (1920), he shortened his name to Berle and entered big-time vaudeville. In 1931, at the age of twenty-three, he began doing nightclub work as well. During the 1930s he appeared regularly as a comedian on Broadway and, then, in the late thirties, began working in films.

Television, however, turned out to be Berle's medium. From 1948 to 1953, he hosted "The Texaco Star Theater," television's most popular variety show. "Mr. Television" or "Uncle Miltie" was the medium's

---

Milton Berle Had a Rival?

Even though Milton Berle was often referred to as "Mr. Television," he trailed in the ratings race in the mid-1950s to the show of an immensely popular Catholic priest—"The Bishop Fulton J. Sheen Hour." But Berle knew why—"he has better writers than I do."

first superstar. Later in the decade, he hosted two more variety shows. In the years that followed, he became a frequent guest on other shows, acted on Broadway, and appeared in a number of films, including *It's a Mad, Mad, Mad, Mad World* (1963) and *Broadway Danny Rose* (1984). When the Television Academy Hall of Fame was opened in 1984, Berle was one of the first seven people inducted.

BLANC, MEL (1892–1989)

Voice specialist, actor, musician

Mel Blanc began his show business career as a musician. He was a multi-talented performer with the NBC studio orchestra who doubled on violin, bass, and tuba. Someone discovered that he had an even more versatile speaking voice, and he began performing a wide range of voices, accents, and even sound effects on radio (most famously as the "voice" of Jack Benny's broken-down 1928 Maxwell). In 1937 Blanc went to Hollywood, where he became a key part of the Warner Brothers cartoon unit, the legendary "Termite Terrace." There he originated the voices of Bugs Bunny, Daffy Duck, Pepe Le Pew, Porky Pig, Elmer Fudd, Tweety Pie, Sylvester the Cat, and others. He was heard on over 3,000 cartoon soundtracks, countless TV shows, and commercials and often had cameo parts in films and television (particularly with his old friend **Jack Benny**). As his health began to fail, Blanc trained his son Noel to take over his many parts, and Noel Blanc has been carrying the family business for nearly a decade himself.

BRICE, FANNY (1891–1951)

Entertainer

Fanny Brice, born Fania Borach to Jewish immigrants on New York's Lower East Side, was an unlikely superstar. Ungainly and gawky, with an enormous nose and a New York Jewish accent, Brice was a brilliant mimic and a talented, energetic comedienne not averse to mocking herself. It was this last feature that propelled her directly to stardom. **Florenz Ziegfeld** heard Brice singing in a burlesque show and signed her for his famous *Follies of 1910*. Brice was an instant sensation. She performed some of her best comic material in the *Follies of 1921*, including spoofs of Ethel Barrymore and the memorable song "Second Hand Rose." In 1923, tired of being a sight gag, she decided to have a "nose job." **Dorothy Parker** quipped that Brice had "cut off her nose to spite her race." Eventually she would dabble in motion pictures as well as theater. But it was on the radio that she found the audience that fulfilled her dreams of success, capitalizing on one of her most popular comic creations, the bratty "Baby Snooks" presented in the *Ziegfeld Follies of 1934* and *1936*. The baby-talking little monster was the trademark that carried her into millions of American homes from 1938 until her death in 1951. Her earlier routines often involved Yiddish-accented characters, but with anti-Semitism rampant in both Europe and America, she realized that the unaccented Baby Snooks (combined with her incredible comic genius) would guarantee a national following. A brilliant clown, she delighted generations of Americans.

BROOKS, MEL (1926–)

Comedian, filmmaker, actor

The raucous, freewheeling comedy of Mel Brooks has its roots in his childhood, when the young Melvin Kaminsky was a mimic and classroom cutup. He was also a talented amateur pianist and drummer. After serving in the Army during World War II, he turned the latter skill into a profession, playing drums in the Borscht Belt hotels, eventually becoming social director and house comic at Grossinger's. In 1949 he left the Catskills to take a position as one of the writers on **Sid Caesar**'s successful television series "Your Show of Shows," joining a group of comic talents that included **Neil Simon** and **Carl Reiner**. It was partnering with Reiner as the 2,000-Year-Old Man that launched Brooks back into a career as a performer. Together they have done a seemingly endless series of records and books featuring Reiner as the straight man to

Brooks' character, who has literally "lived through it all" and somehow managed to pick up a Yiddish accent along the way. (Their book *The Two Thousand Year-Old-Man in the Year 2000* was published in 1998.)

But it is as a combination writer, director, and producer of wildly comic films that Brooks has made his mark on twentieth-century American culture. His first venture into film as a writer and a director, the 1968 hit *The Producers*, starring **Zero Mostel** and **Gene Wilder**, earned him an Oscar for best screenplay written directly for the screen. Since then he has written and directed a number of other feature films in the same manic, anything-for-a-laugh parodic style, often skirting the boundaries of bad taste (when not demolishing them outright), with a wild mix of Yiddishisms, bathroom jokes, and brutally on-target spoofs of popular conventions. Among the cult classics he has created are *Dracula: Dead and Loving It* (1995); *Robin Hood: Men in Tights* (1993); *Blazing Saddles* (1974); and *High Anxiety* (1977), a send-off of Alfred Hitchcock's films *Vertigo* and *The Birds*. He and **Gene Wilder** shared an Oscar nomination for best screenplay adapted from other material for *Young Frankenstein* (1974). He has also produced very different kinds of films, ranging from the serious *The Elephant Man* (1980) to a charming low-key vehicle for his wife, Anne Bancroft, *84 Charing Cross Road* (1986).

BRUCE, LENNY (1925–1966)

Comedian

The most controversial stand-up comic of his time, Lenny Bruce was lauded as a social satirist and denounced as a purveyor of obscenity. Born Leonard Schneider, he was raised largely by his divorced mother, a burlesque and nightclub comic. At age sixteen Lenny lied about his age and entered the Navy, participating in the landings at Anzio and Salerno. After his three-year hitch, he returned to the States determined to pursue a career in show business.

Bruce began as a conventional stand-up comic, doing impressions and one-liners. He was a voracious reader and fell in with the hip musicians who often backed him. His newfound milieu offered him two important things: more daring material and a drug problem. He began exploring riskier subjects (for the Eisenhower era), riffing on politics, sex, and religion, making fun of such seemingly off-limits targets as the Vatican, Billy Graham, Eleanor Roosevelt, and racism, frequently and famously using obscenities in his monologues. Now heralded as the master of "sick" humor, he played Carnegie Hall in 1960, his career at its peak.

But he was about to fall and he fell fast. In 1961 and 1962 he was arrested for narcotics possession and for obscenity. His irreverence and savagely satirical outlook made him a target for police and prosecutors. Bruce began to immerse himself in law books and even took to using his stand-up routines for serious discussions of the First Amendment, not what his audiences had bargained for. In 1964 he was banned from performing in New York. His finances were in disarray, sapped by legal fees. He declared bankruptcy in 1965 and was preparing his latest legal case when he died of a heroin overdose the following year.

BURNS, GEORGE (1896–1996)

Actor, comedian

George Burns's career falls into two neatly defined periods: with Gracie Allen and after Gracie Allen. Born Nathan Birnbaum in New York City, Burns was a minor-league vaudevillian, having begun as part of a boys' singing quartet and working his way up to comedy, when he met the charming young Allen in 1922. Pairing with her—as both her straight man and her husband—was the best thing he ever did, as he states in his biography of Gracie, *Gracie: A Love Story* (1988). Playing bewildered straight man to her blonde scatterbrain, he was catapulted along with Allen into the ranks of vaudeville, radio, then film and television success. Television's "Burns and Allen Show" ran from 1950 to 1958. When Gracie died in 1964, Burns went into a state of semi-retirement.

It could not last. He won an Oscar in 1975 for his role in *The Sunshine Boys*, in which he teamed up with

The 1938 edition of Who's Who in American Jewry *describes George Burns as the son of Louis Phillip and Hadassah (Bluth) Birnbaum and a member of the Reformed Temple in Los Angeles. He began his performing career in vaudeville, won an Academy Award for his role in the 1975 film* The Sunshine Boys, *and worked steadily in films up to his death at the age of 100 (playing, among other characters, God in the films* Oh, God! *(1977) and* Oh, God! Book II *(1980). He is shown here (right) in a "song and dance" number with Jack Benny and Gregory Peck. (Private Collection)*

Walter Matthau. His other notable films were *Oh, God!* (1977), *Going in Style* (1979), and *Oh God! Book II* (1980). Burns continued working steadily until his death at the age of 100.

BUTTONS, RED (1919–)

Actor, comedian

The brashly funny comic actor born Aaron Chwatt, Red Buttons began his career as a child, winning an amateur night contest at age twelve, then working as a combination bellhop-singer at a Bronx tavern and inn, where he won his new name as a tribute to his colorful uniform. He performed regularly in the Catskills and burlesque, eventually working his way up to Broadway in 1942 where he had a supporting role in the play *Vicki*. As part of his World War II army service he appeared in both the Broadway and film versions of *Winged Victory*. He had a short-lived TV series in the early 1950s but was out of work when Joshua Logan cast him in a supporting role in the 1957 *Sayonara*. He won an Oscar and the Golden Globe for best supporting actor for his performance as a GI who marries a Japanese girl, with tragic results. Since then he has been a fixture as a supporting performer in movies and television.

CAESAR, SID (1922–)

Comedian

Sid Caesar achieved his greatest fame as the inspired comic whirlwind behind the TV hit "Your Show of Shows." Working with a legendary crew of writers, including Neil and Danny **Simon**, **Carl Reiner**, and **Mel Brooks**, and a wonderful cast of equally clever improvisers and actors that featured Reiner, Imogene Coca, and Howie Morris, he was at the center of one of the most creative and witty programs in the history of the medium.

It was a far cry from his training as a classical musician, a saxophonist and clarinetist who had studied at Juilliard. Caesar switched to comedy while serving in World War II in the Coast Guard, becoming a featured

---

Sid Caesar's Writers

Sid Caesar's "Your Show of Shows" was one of the first major "hit" television productions. Many of his writers went on to enormous success, including Mel Brooks, Neil Simon, Carl Reiner, and Larry Gelbart. When asked why many of his fellow writers were "young and Jewish," Larry Gelbart (who went on to create "M*A*S*H," among other hits) replied: "[it] was probably because all of our parents were old and Jewish."

Sid Caesar spent the early part of his career as a comic on the Borscht Belt circuit in the Catskills, where he met and married Florence Levy, the niece of one of the lodge owners. His television shows were an integral part of the medium for an incredible fourteen years, from the premier of "Your Show of Shows" in 1950 to "The Sid Caesar Show," which ran in 1963 and 1964. (Private Collection)

comic performer in the service's stage show, *Tars and Stars*, and in the film version. From there he went on to the stage, then to television, where he enjoyed his greatest success. Caesar struggled with substance abuse problems, poignantly retold in his autobiography, *Where Have I Been?* (1982). He has continued performing sporadically on stage and occasionally in films.

CANTOR, EDDIE (1892–1964)

Comedian, actor, singer

Saucer-eyed Eddie Cantor is all but forgotten today except to historians of the musical stage and film. Yet he was a master of every medium he attempted and, in his variegated career, represents a microcosm of twentieth-century American show business, enjoying success in vaudeville, burlesque, musical comedy and revue, film, radio, and television. Cantor's success on radio was unprecedented and pivotal in the rise of that medium.

His origins were humble; born on the Lower East Side as Edward Israel Iskowitz, he was orphaned and raised by his doting grandma Esther in Dickensian poverty. As Iskowitz became Kantrowitz and Kantrowitz became Kantor and, eventually, Cantor, the boy learned that he had a natural gift for making people laugh—a gift that would win him approval and deflect potential beatings in the tough streets of turn-of-the-century Jewish New York. Cantor dropped out of school at the age of thirteen but didn't truly enter show business until he was sixteen, when he worked as a waiter and singer at a saloon, teamed with an equally young Jimmy Durante. Gradually, he drifted into a career in the entertainment business, slowly climbing the ladder of vaudeville success until he was starring in the *Ziegfeld Follies* (1916–1919). From there his stardom grew steadily, predicated on his boundless energy, boisterous comedy, and way with a song. He was discovered by **Samuel Goldwyn** and featured in a series of musical comedy films, including *The Kid from Spain* (1933), *Ali Baba Goes to Town* (1937), and *Banjo Eyes* (1941). Among the songs Cantor popularized are "If You Knew Susie," "Toot, Toot, Tootsie," and "Ain't She Sweet."

Cantor remained committed to the people he had left behind, a tireless worker for good causes (including the March of Dimes, which he founded) and a powerful advocate for the burgeoning unions in the entertainment industry.

COBB, LEE J. [LEO JACOBY] (1911–1976)

Actor

Powerful character actor Lee J. Cobb was born Leo Jacoby in New York City and spent the early years of his career moving back and forth between the New York stage and the Pasadena Playhouse. In 1935 he made his Broadway debut in *Crime and Punishment* and became a member of the Group Theater, where he performed for the next several years. His first movie appearance was in the film adaptation of *Golden Boy* (1939), and, until he went into the armed forces in World War II, he played character roles on film and on stage in New York. Resuming his career after the war, he achieved fame with his powerful performance as Willy Loman in **Arthur Miller**'s *Death of a Salesman* (1949) on Broadway. Although he continued to do stage work and made a number of guest appearances on television, Cobb's career was largely on film from that time on. Probably his most famous role was as gangster Johnny Friendly in *On the Waterfront* (1954).

During the House Un-American Activities hearings, Cobb testified that he had been a member of the **Communist Party** for a short time in the 1930s. He also, under pressure, provided the committee with the names of others. Shortly thereafter, he almost died from a massive heart attack. There were many who never forgave him for his testimony. He continued to offer powerful, sometimes brilliant, portrayals in such films as *Twelve Angry Men (1957)*, *The Brothers Karamozov* (1958), and *Exodus* (1960). He starred on television in "The Virginian" (1962–70) and "The Young Lawyers" (1970–71) and completed his last film in 1975, shortly before he died.

COHN, HARRY (1891–1958)

Movie mogul

The man who built Columbia Pictures began his career as a pool hustler and a trolley-car conductor. He moved on to nickelodeon performer and song plugger. Finally, he moved up to a producer of musical short pictures and traveling exhibitor of films. In 1924, reportedly after selling a film entitled *Traffic in Souls*, Harry Cohn and his brother Jack founded Columbia Pictures. Within a few years, Jack had been pushed out and Harry Cohn ruled Columbia alone.

For the next three decades, Cohn churned out a host of adequate movies, some real stinkers, and a few films of the highest quality. The positive part of his legacy includes *The Jolson Story*, *All the King's Men*, *Born Yesterday*, and *From Here to Eternity*. He produced the Frank Capra comedies *It Happened One Night* and *You Can't Take It With You*. He had a reputation for bullying, harassing, and sometimes destroying the people who worked for him. He apparently had a

---

Harry Cohn—To Know Him Is to . . .

Harry Cohn, the head of Columbia Pictures, reveled in cultivating an image as the "toughest" man in the motion picture industry. Needless to say, he didn't have many friends. When he died in 1958, his funeral was held at a Columbia sound stage with seating for over a thousand people. The comedian Red Skelton, noting that all the seats were taken, supposedly remarked "If you give the people what they want, they'll come."

---

need for power and control so great that he was unable to tolerate autonomy in anyone in his employ in any capacity. He detested the fine films *On the Waterfront* and *Bridge on the River Kwai*, produced by Columbia in his later years, because he had had no control over them. He was one of the most hated men in Hollywood. When large crowds turned out for his funeral, Red Skelton reportedly said, "It proves what they always say: give the public what they want and they'll come out for it."

COMEDY AND COMEDIANS

Imagining American comedy without Jews is more difficult than imagining Jewish Americans without comedy. For a variety of reasons, the two have grown up together in this country, and their kinship continues. While the participation of Jews in comedy has been constant, the visibility of Jewishness, as well as the manner in which it is treated, has undergone tremendous change.

The earliest Jewish American comedians of note were probably **Weber and Fields**. The team, made up of Joe Weber (Moisha Weber) and Lew Fields (Moisha Schanfield), was one of the most popular dialect acts in vaudeville. They performed with a German Yiddish accent and an exaggerated, slapstick violence that presaged such movie teams as Abbott and Costello and **The Three Stooges**. They went on to open their own Broadway theater, which became famous for its burlesques of current hits, then worked separately in a number of capacities in musical comedy.

Contemporary with Weber and Fields were Al

Shean [Adolf Schoenberg] (1868–1949), of the team of Gallagher and Shean, and Willie Howard [William Levkowitz] (1886–1949). These great comics also began in vaudeville and went on to Broadway. Shean went one step further, becoming a Hollywood regular in films such as *The Prisoner of Zenda* (1937) and *The Great Waltz* (1938). As with Weber and Fields, Jewishness was part of the substance of their comedy in a way that delighted their own audiences but would be politically incorrect today.

From vaudeville to Broadway to film, radio, and/or television was the pattern for Jewish comedians for the next several decades. **Smith and Dale**, a team made up of Joe Smith (Joseph Sultzer) and Charlie Dale (Charles Marks), went that route, as did **Ed Wynn** (Isaiah Edwin Leopold), **Bert Lahr**, **Fanny Brice** (Fannie Borach), and **Eddie Cantor** (Isidore Itzkowitz). This group shone brightest on Broadway, although all of them had some successes in the other media. Brice and Cantor, especially, were able to translate their Broadway stardom into radio fame.

The next important group of Jewish American comedians were successful on radio and later, television. **Jack Benny** (Benjamin Kubelsky), **Gertrude Berg** (Gertrude Edelstein), George Burns (Nathan Birnbaum) with his Irish American partner and wife Gracie Allen, George Jessel, and Groucho Marx (Julius Marx), of **Marx Brothers** fame were among the most important stars of radio. (See **Radio**.) Berg's comedy series "The Rise of the Goldbergs" (1929–34, 1937–45) began with a strong emphasis on ethnicity, including heavy accents and fractured English. It evolved into a gentler and more realistic depiction of Jewish American life. The other comedians in this group were unabashedly Jewish, regardless of name changes, but they seldom referred to their ethnicity in their humor. All except Jessel went on to highly successful careers in television when that medium gained popularity in the late 1940s.

Along with them in this brave new world was **Milton Berle** (Milton Berlinger), who was known as Mr. Television. Successful on stage and in films, Berle had been unable to translate his highly physical comedy to radio; but the television camera loved him, and so did audiences. His variety show "The Texaco Star Theater" (1948–53), also known as "The Milton Berle Show," was the most popular in television history. It was one of many shows hosted or starred in by Jewish comedians in the first decade of the medium, including Joey Bishop [Joseph Gottlieb] (1918–) **Red Buttons** (Aaron Chwatt), Soupy Sales (Milton Supman), **Molly Picon**, Jan Murray [Murray Janofsky] (1917–), **Phil Silvers** (Philip Silver), and the inimitable **Sid Caesar**. (See **Television**.)

There was another breed of comics who were most comfortable in the resorts of the Catskills and on the nightclub circuit. They were the stand-up comics, the joketellers. They told fast and funny gags or stories filled with the details and rhythms of Jewish life. They included Myron Cohen (1902–1986), Joey Adams [Joseph Abramowitz] (1911–), **Morey Amsterdam**, Mickey Katz, Jack E. Leonard [Leonard Lebitsky] (1911–), Joe E. Lewis (1902–1971), and **Henny Youngman**. Some of these comics, like Morey Amsterdam, spent a part of their careers on television. Others worked with great success in front of live audiences. All were Jewish comics in the classic mold.

Hollywood showcased comic actors and comedy teams including the Ritz Brothers, the Marx Brothers, the Three Stooges, **Danny Kaye** (David Daniel Kaminski), **Judy Holliday** (Judith Tuvim), **Jerry Lewis** (Joseph Levitch] and his Italian American partner Dean Martin. (See **Film**.) Most historians of comedy would choose the Marx Brothers as the most significant. Their wild, almost chaotic performances were comic genius and inspired both verbal and physical comedy imitators. Seldom were the two seen together as brilliantly as in the Marx Brothers films.

There were, beginning in about the 1940s, a number of Jewish comics who defy categorization. Victor Borge [Borge Rosenbaum] (1909–) and Oscar Levant (1906–1972) both began as musicians and built careers in comedy, but there the resemblance between them ends. Borge is silliness incarnate and has been charming audiences with sight gags and musical jokes on television and on the concert stage for more than sixty years. Levant was dour and melancholy, using his caustic wit in films in the forties and fifties. "Professor" Irwin Corey (1912–) was a master of inspired lunacy who enjoyed considerable popularity in nightclubs and on radio in the 1940s and early 1950s. He was equally successful on television until the political bent of his humor cut too close to the bone and, like the Smothers Brothers, he found himself off the air in the early 1960s. **Zero Mostel** (Samuel Joel Mostel) and **Jack Gilford** (Jacob Gellman) were close friends whose political convictions sometimes made life uncomfortable but found their niche on stage, scoring huge successes in the 1960s and beyond. (See **Theater**.)

The popularity of variety shows on television in the late 1950s and early 1960s produced a group of comedians whose work in nightclubs and on television were about equally important. They developed their routines in the clubs and then performed them on "The Ed Sullivan Show," "The Garry Moore Show," "The Perry Como Show," and others of the period. They also helped make "The Tonight Show" America's favorite late-night entertainment. The club and TV comedians included Jack Carter [Jack Chakrin] (1923–), **Alan King** [Irwin Alan Kinberg] (1927–), Don Rickles (1926–), Buddy Hackett [Leonard Hacker] (1924–), Shecky Greene [Sheldon Greenfield] (1926–), Marty Allen (1922–) of Allen and Rossi, Bill Dana [William Szathmary] (1924–), Norm Crosby (1927–), Totie Fields [Sophie Feldman] (1930–), and, later, Rodney Dangerfield [Jacob Cohen] (1921–). These comedians had a wide variety of styles, from the wistful confusion of Bill Dana to the sharp-edged sophistication of Alan King to the angry insults of Don Rickles. Together they dominated standup comedy on screen and off.

There was another group of comics working at the same time who foreshadowed the often painfully funny comedy of the seventies and eighties. The earliest of these was the hip, political, caustic **Mort Sahl**. The most influential may have been the angry and self-destructive **Lenny Bruce** (Leonard Schneider). The precursors of much "neurotic" comedy were Shelley Berman (1926–) and **Jackie Mason** [Yacov Moshe Maza] (1934–). In tracing the roots of the angry, incisive brilliance of comedians such as Richard Pryor and **Roseanne**, these men must be seen as major in-

fluences. Mason brought his Jewishness on stage with him in an entirely new way. His work was Jewish in content, in rhythm, and in sound. After an extremely difficult period in the late 1960s caused by a disagreement with Ed Sullivan, Mason's intensely personal ethnic and political humor has made him one of the most respected comedians in the business.

The 1960s brought a resurgence of sketch humor and comedy teams. The teams included Jerry Stiller (1927–) and his Irish American wife Meara, **Mike Nichols** (Michael Igor Peschkowsky) and **Elaine May** (Elaine Berlin), and Avery Schreiber (1935–) with his gentile partner Jack Burns. All addressed Jewish issues directly. Stiller and Meara dealt with their mixed marriage. Burns and Schreiber often enacted encounters between Jewish characters played by Schreiber and bigoted or ignorant gentiles played by Burns. Nichols and May touched on Jewishness in the course of their satires on everything from a mother's phone call to her son to quiz shows and political ghost writers. Elaine May had a hard, almost bitter edge that set the pair apart from other similar teams.

David Steinberg (1942–) dealt with Jewishness on the comedy stage in a different way. On the Smothers Brothers variety show in the late 1960s, he did comedy routines that directly satirized religion. One of his most memorable lines was "The Gentiles grabbed the Jews by the Old Testament." He shocked a great many people, but his obvious good humor disarmed most viewers. Other young comedians of this time included Robert Klein (1942–), Marilyn Michaels, David Frye [David Shapiro] (1934–), and **Joan Rivers** (Joan Alexandra Molinsky).

In Hollywood, the "Brooks Bunch" came into their ascendancy in the late 1960s. In wildly funny, eccentric films written, directed, and produced by **Mel Brooks** (Melvyn Kaminsky), an ensemble of talented actors created a new style of film comedy. The Jewish members of the ensemble included **Madeline Kahn**, Marty Feldman, and **Gene Wilder** (Jerome Silberman). At about the same time, **Woody Allen** (Alan Stewart Konigsberg) began his career as a professional neurotic in films that he wrote, directed, and usually starred in. **Goldie Hawn** went from dancing on television's "Laugh-In" to becoming a screen comedienne in the tradition of Carole Lombard and Judy Holliday.

The 1970s and early 1980s brought dozens of Jewish comic actors in regular roles in situation comedies. Sometimes these roles reflected no particular ethnicity. At other times Jewish actors played what has been called "crypto-Jewish" roles. That is, the actor is Jewish and the character reflects a "Jewish sensibility," even though the name of the character may be Italian or generically ethnic. A few played specifically Jewish characters. (See **Television**.) These actors included Larry Storch (1923–), **Bea Arthur** (Bernice Frankel), Gabe Kaplan (1945–), Carol Kane (1952–), Phil Foster [Fivel Feldman] (1914–), Estelle Getty [Estelle Scher] (1923–), Barbara Feldon (1939–), Julie Kavner (1951–), **Linda Lavin**, and **Rhea Perlman**. Also seen on both situation comedies and sketch comedy shows were the new generation of standup comedians.

The standup comedians of the seventies and eighties stood on the shoulders of all those vaudeville teams, Catskills joketellers, smoky nightclub veterans, and sketch artists who came before them. They tended to lean either toward the highly personal, self-denigrating, "neurotic" strain of humor epitomized by Shelley Berman and **Joan Rivers** or toward the wild and anarchic strain epitomized by the Marx Brothers and Irwin Corey. Some combined the two forms of comedy in a thoroughly modern way. These new comedians include David Brenner, Richard Belzer (1944–), Richard Lewis (1947–), **Billy Crystal**, Andy Kaufman, **Gilda Radner**, Yakov Smirnoff [Yakov Pokhis] (1951–), **Roseanne**, Sandra Bernhard (1955–), Paul Reiser (1956–), **Jerry Seinfeld**, Rita Rudner, Elayne Boosler (1952–), and Fran Drescher. Although they worked the clubs and "The Tonight Show," many of these comics were soon appearing in their own situation comedies on television, usually based on characters they had created for their standup routines. (See **Television**.)

In films, there was a new Brooks. Albert Brooks [Albert Einstein] (1947–), son of vaudeville comedian Harry Einstein, graduated from standup comic to writer, director, and star of the brilliantly funny films *Lost in America* (1985) and *Defending Your Life* (1991).

There was also a new **Bette Midler**. Midler had been creating herself as stage actor since 1966, a singer since 1970, and a film actor since 1974. In 1983 she found that comedy was her forte. After a successful comedy album, she began making her mark in films such as *Down and Out in Beverly Hills* (1986) with Richard Dreyfuss (1947–), and *The First Wives' Club* (1996), which also starred Goldie Hawn.

Jewishness in comedy has come full circle. It is no longer an aspect of life to be hidden or ignored. It contributes to the richness of the comic's view of life. However, the best Jewish comedians are able to transcend stereotypes and allow their Jewishness to be only one element in a fully rounded comic persona.

CORWIN, NORMAN (1910–)

Writer

Born in 1910, radio dramatist Norman Corwin is one of the most prolific, influential, and long-lived writers in that medium. In 1930, he began his radio career when, along with Orson Welles and others, he became a writer for CBS radio's "Columbia Workshop." To celebrate the Allied victory in World War II, he wrote the verse oratorio "On a Note of Triumph," which aired May 8, 1945. In 1950, as part of the McCarthy era's anti-Communist hysteria, Corwin was blacklisted. He survived this period and ultimately returned to radio. Among the great radio and literary figures he influenced were Edward R. Murrow, Walter Cronkite, Rod Serling, and Ray Bradbury. His radio drama "The Secretariat" was broadcast in 1997. He also wrote the screenplay for the film *Lust for Life* and is the author of the book *Norman Corwin's Letters*.

CRYSTAL, BILLY (1947–)

Comedian, actor

Versatile comic actor Billy Crystal was born in Long Beach, New York, into a family of music producers. Growing up around performers, he decided early that he wanted to be a comedian. He began doing standup work in clubs and on college campuses in the early 1970s, making some appearances on "The Tonight Show" and other television talk shows. He came to prominence when he was cast as the gay son in the quirky situation comedy "Soap" (1977–81). A few years later he solidified his reputation with a season on "Saturday Night Live."

A few years earlier, Crystal had appeared in a number of films including *Rabbit Test* (1978) and *This Is Spinal Tap* (1983). His biggest successes began in the late 1980s with *The Princess Bride* (1987) and *When Harry Met Sally* (1989). He quickly followed those up with *City Slickers* (1991) and was now considered a bankable star. He emceed the Academy Awards for several years, increasing his visibility to Hollywood audiences. One of Crystal's significant accomplishments was to establish himself as a leading man in romantic comedies without abandoning his ethnic identity and in spite of the fact that he did not fit the Hollywood mold.

CURTIS, TONY (1925–)

Actor

The son of a Hungarian actor turned American tailor, Tony Curtis was born Bernard Schwartz in New York City. Reared in a rough neighborhood, he became a gang member during adolescence and was introduced to acting at a settlement house where he was taken by a truant officer. After serving in the navy, he attended the Dramatic Workshop of the New School for Social Research, then began working on stage. By 1949 he had been spotted and signed by a Hollywood talent scout and started doing bit parts in films. In 1951 he made his first appearance in a leading role in *The Prince Who Was a Thief*. His popularity soared in the next few years as he played Jewish magician **Harry Houdini** in *Houdini* and a circus performer in *Trapeze* (1956), as well as at least other dozen characters in major films. The critics were unimpressed until he undertook more ambitious roles in the late 1950s and early 1960s.

Curtis began to build a reputation as a serious actor in *The Sweet Smell of Success* (1957). There followed a series of roles that played against his matinee idol image. In *The Defiant Ones* (1958) he played one of two desperate escaped convicts, one African American and one white, shackled together. In *Some Like It Hot* (1959) he spent most of the film disguised as a woman. He parodied himself as the daredevil hero in *The Great Race* (1965). He next played a homicidal maniac in *The Boston Strangler* (1968). He continued to make two or three, sometimes four pictures a year, until the early 1980s, when personal problems slowed his career. Then he made an impressive comeback as Salvatore "Sam" Giancana in the television film *Mafia Princess* (1986). He was married to the actor Janet Leigh (of *Psycho* fame) and is the father of Jamie Lee Curtis, who has a successful career in films.

DEREN, MAYA (1917–1961)

Filmmaker, writer

Maya Deren (born Derenkowsky) is one of the central figures of American avant-garde film. Working both with her husband Alexander Hammid and on her own, she brought a unique visual style to non-narrative experimental movies, a troubling combination of dream-like imagery and subtle choreography, seen as through a gauze and with a vivid sharpness.

Deren's parents were Russian Jewish intellectuals; her father was a doctor, later a psychiatrist, her mother an artist and teacher. Not long after the Revolution, they fled the Soviet Union, arriving in the United States in 1922 and settling in Syracuse, New York. Maya was sent to private school in Switzerland, then returned to the United States to complete her studies at Syracuse University, NYU, the New School for Social Research, and Smith College. While a student, she became a political activist, joining the socialist movement, as did many of her contemporaries during the Depression.

The turning point in Deren's life came in 1940, when she took a position as secretary to the brilliant African American choreographer and dancer Katherine Dunham. Dunham's work kindled in Deren what would become a lifelong fascination with Haitian dance and voodoo culture. Three years later she married Hammid and the two made their first film, *Meshes of the Afternoon*. This misty, dreamlike film was a breakthrough for experimental cinema in America. Although there had been some precedents for it in Europe, Americans had produced nothing quite like *Meshes*. Deren created several more films on her own between 1944 and 1959, including *At Land* (1944) and *Ritual in Transfigured Time* (1946). She also spent time in Haiti, producing her best-known book, *Divine Horsemen: The Living Gods of Haiti* (1953).

DIAMOND, SELMA (1921–1985)

Comedy writer, actor

The only woman in the men's club of early television comedy writers, Selma Diamond was born in London, Ontario, and grew up in Brooklyn, New York. She started her career writing radio comedy for Rudy Vallee and Jimmy Durante. With the advent of television, she became very busy. She wrote for **Groucho Marx**, **Milton Berle**, and Perry Como. She was one of the legendary team of writers for **Sid Caesar**'s "Your Show of Shows" (1950–54), a team that included **Carl Reiner**, **Neil Simon**, and **Mel Brooks**. Soon she was making guest appearances on talk shows, delighting audiences with her astonishingly raspy voice and her sharp wit. Her offbeat charm and stage presence gained her roles in film and on television. She was the voice of Spencer Tracy's wife in *It's a Mad, Mad, Mad, Mad World* (1963). She had a small, *homage* role in *My Favorite Year* (1982), which was inspired by the Caesar show. She also appeared in *Twilight Zone: The Movie* (1983) and *All of Me* (1984). She was best known to the general public as Selma Hacker, the sardonic bailiff on the situation comedy "Night Court," a role she played from 1984 until her death from lung cancer in 1985.

DOUGLAS, KIRK (1916–)

Actor

The title of Kirk Douglas's autobiography says it all— *The Ragpicker's Son*. Douglas, born Issur Danielovitch, grew up in squalor and poverty in upstate New York. He worked as a waiter to put himself through St. Lawrence University and parlayed a strong athletic body (he was a successful college wrestler), handsome face (with the famous cleft chin), and a powerful voice into an acting career that brought him fame and fortune far beyond his father's modest dreams of success. Douglas approached every role with an intensity that sometimes bordered on hysteria. At his best—as a corrupt newspaperman in Billy Wilder's *Ace in the Hole* (1951), an ambitious movie producer in Vincente Minnelli's *The Bad and the Beautiful* (1952), Van Gogh in Minnelli's *Lust for Life* (1955), a faded actor in Minnelli's *Two Weeks in Another Town* (1962)—he projects a driven quality that few actors can match. In other films, particularly westerns like Howard Hawks's *The Big Sky* (1952), King Vidor's *Man without a Star* (1955), and a rare pairing with John Wayne in the 1967 *The War Wagon*, Douglas is more easy-going and humorous, revealing a comic side that is seldom seen in his other work and even a pleasant way with a song and a banjo. Among his best-known works are the several films in which he was paired with Burt Lancaster, a close friend and fellow liberal Democrat—*I Walk Alone* (1948), *Gunfight at the O.K. Corral* (1957), *Seven Days in May* (1964), and *Tough Guys* (1986). A staunch supporter of Israel, Douglas had the rare opportunity, seldom given to Jewish actors, to play a Jewish hero, Colonel **Mickey Marcus**, in the 1966 film *Cast a Giant Shadow*.

Douglas has added writing to his list of achievements, publishing not only two volumes of memoirs but also several novels. He has extolled the virtues of his Jewish upbringing and talked of a return in recent years to his religious roots, including extensive study of the Torah and Talmud. His son, Michael Douglas, is also a successful producer and actor.

FILM

The history of Jewish Americans in the film industry is a complex and paradoxical one. Like African Americans and women, Jews have often been portrayed in stereotypical, derogatory ways. There are two factors that complicate the Jewish position. First, the vast majority of the people in positions of power in the American film industry were Jewish. Second, individual performers could, and did, conceal their Jewishness in a way that was impossible for women and most African American performers. As a result, there was a powerful Jewish presence in American films even when films with Jewish content were being suppressed.

EARLY FILMS

Despite the dominance of Jewish producers in **Hollywood** for most of its history, the earliest films were produced by non-Jews. The first Jewish producer was Gilbert Max "Bronco Billy" Anderson, who started producing his series of westerns in 1908. By the late 1920s, the eight major studios were owned and/or controlled by Jewish Americans. Their control seldom affected the Jewish content of films, at least not in a positive way.

The earliest Jewish films were produced by non-Jews. In 1903 Thomas Alva Edison produced two one-minute films, *Arabina Jewish Dance* and *A Jewish Dance at Jerusalem*, which featured a group of Hasidic men dancing the hora. The Edison company also produced *Cohen's Fire Sale*, a stereotyped comedy with a grasping, hook-nosed merchant in 1907. Another American film pioneer, D. W. Griffith, produced the film *The Romance of a Jewess* in 1908. Griffith, a non-Jew whose virulent racial prejudice is evident in the classic film *The Birth of a Nation*, sympathetically portrayed a young woman whose life turns to tragedy when she marries against her father's wishes.

Before the 1920s, films with Jewish content could be divided roughly into three genres, according to film historian Patricia Brett Erens. There were the ethnically stereotyped comedies; the ghetto films, which portrayed life on New York's Lower East Side; and the pogrom films, which depicted events in czarist Russia. There were also some Jewish roles in adaptations of classic dramas such as *The Merchant of Venice*.

The broad comedies of these early years dealt al-

The First Music Heard on American Film

The first vocal music heard in an American movie was in Hebrew in the movie *The Jazz Singer*, starring Al Jolson. It tells the story of the son of an Orthodox cantor who wants to go into show business, rather than succeed his father in the synagogue. The first music the audience hears is the *Kol Nidre*, sung by the famous cantor Yossele Rosenblatt. Rosenblatt does not actually appear in the film; he agreed to sing for the sound track on the condition that he would not be listed in the credits and that another cantor would take his place in the filming. He felt that movies were too much of a "commercial enterprise" for him to be publicly involved.

most exclusively with physical comedy and ethnic stereotypes, as did most vaudeville and music hall humor of the time. This was in the years before film became a middle-class, family-oriented entertainment form. The nickelodeons drew a poor, largely immigrant audience, and the short comedy films of the time played to that audience, whether it was Jewish, Italian, Irish, or Polish.

The Jewish stereotypes, at least for men, were the greedy merchant and the clever weakling. The merchants were often outwitted and therefore defeated in their schemes. The clever weaklings, on the other hand, belonged to a folkloric type that can be seen in many cultures, that of the powerless character who overcomes the powerful through the use of wit. Among African Americans, for example, Br'er Rabbit falls into this category. The type is generally considered to be a positive one among specialists in the folk literature. Among these early comedies were *Levitsky's Insurance Policy* (1908), *Foxy Izzy* (1911), *The Yiddisher Cowboy* (1909 and 1911), and *How Mosha Came Back*.

The ghetto films were more naturalistic than the comedies, but not significantly less limited in their portrayal of Jewish characters. The stock characters were the strongly Orthodox father, the maverick son, and the pure, sweet daughter. Again, these were not solely Jewish stereotypes. They existed in most Victorian popular literature and survived in the fiction, drama, and films of the early twentieth century.

In these films, however, there was an immigrant Jewish flavor that derived from the Lower East Side setting and the specifically Jewish religious and cultural traditions.

Among these early Jewish dramas were *Child of the Ghetto* (1910), *The Ghetto Seamstress* (1910), *Solomon's Son* (1912), *The Jew's Christmas* (1913), and *A Passover Miracle* (1914). Erens singles out two of these films as an instructive comparison. The Bureau of Education of the Jewish Community of New York helped to produce and distribute *A Passover Miracle*. *The Jew's Christmas*, on the other hand, was produced by non-Jews Lois Weber and Phillip Smalley. In *A Passover Miracle*, the maverick son returns to the traditions of his family. In *The Jew's Christmas*, an intermarriage ends with a rabbi celebrating Christmas in the interests of love and tolerance.

The other genre of Jewish dramatic films, the pogrom film, depicted oppression in Russia during the reign of the czars. In these highly dramatic short films, the main characters often faced death and were rescued by Christian characters, usually lovers. Among these dramas were *In the Czar's Name* (1910), *Russia, the Land of Oppression* (1910), *The Sorrows of Israel* (1913), *Escape from Siberia* (1914), and *Vengeance of the Oppressed*.

There were also some Jewish roles in films that were not primarily Jewish in content or perspective. One Jewish actor, a rabbi's daughter named Carmel Myers, appeared in Jewish roles in both *Intolerance* (1916) and *Ben-Hur* (1925).

Perhaps the most famous Jewish star of the silents was the exotic **Theda Bara**. Although the studio press releases declared that she was the daughter of an Eastern potentate, she was actually Theodosia Goodman, born in Cincinnati, Ohio. In films, she was a vamp, a seductive woman who lured men to their ruin. Among the thirty-eight films she made between 1915 and 1926 were *A Fool There Was* (1915) and *Cleopatra* (1917).

THE TALKIES AND ASSIMILATION

There were almost fifty films with Jewish content in the 1920s. Most of them followed the lead of *The Jew's Christmas*, emphasizing assimilation, success in the mainstream community, and intermarriage with gentiles, especially the Irish, who were of a similar social class. Indeed, assimilation and equality were frequently equated in such Irish-Jewish films as *Kosher Kitty Kelly* (1926) and *Clancy's Kosher Wedding* (1927).

The most significant of these films was the landmark "talkie" *The Jazz Singer*, starring **Al Jolson** as a young Jewish man who wants to forsake the family tradition of cantor for the world of jazz. The most influential was probably *Humoresque* (1920), which was based on a story by popular Jewish writer **Fannie Hurst**. Others included *Hungry Hearts* (1922)—with a screenplay by writer **Anzia Yezierska**—*His People* (1925), *We Americans* (1928), and *The Younger Generation* (1929), directed by Frank Capra and based on another Hurst story.

In comedies the stereotypes persisted, but they were gentler and more affectionate. They showed a genuine enjoyment of the working-class Jewish American culture and were widely popular. These included the Potash/Perlmutter series (1923–1926) and *The Cohens and the Kellys* (1926), which had six sequels.

One of the most popular "assimilation" films was based on the long-running theatrical production *Abie's Irish Rose*. The film, also entitled *Abie's Irish Rose* (1928), shows the fathers Levy and Murphy as traditionalists, trapped in the old world of religious and cultural differences. Their children Abie and Rosemary represent a new world of love and tolerance as they marry and bring a new little Irish-Jewish American into the world.

The Jewish presence in American film cannot be measured solely in terms of Jewish content in the films themselves. Both in front of the camera and behind it, Jewish Americans were extremely active in the film industry.

Some of Hollywood's finest performers and directors were Jews who came to the United States from Europe in the years between the wars. They included the great Ernst Lubitsch (1892–1947), whose sophisticated comedies were subtle, funny, and enormously successful. Erich von Stroheim (1885–1957) was outstanding both as the director of powerful films such as *Greed* and as an actor. Josef von Sternberg was Marlene Dietrich's director. William Wyler (1902–1981) came from Germany to direct some of Hollywood's most prestigious literary adaptations; and Billy Wilder (1906–), another German director, became Hollywood staples.

During the early thirties, Jewish performers from theater and vaudeville began to flood into Hollywood to perform in the newly verbal films. Many of them were comics such as **Jack Benny**, Ben Blue, **Fanny Brice**, **George Burns**, **Ed Wynn**, and the **Marx Brothers**.

The Marx Brothers exemplify Jewish American comedy, with their dazzling verbal displays and their broad physical humor. Groucho Marx was probably the first real smart-aleck in American films, and Harpo's leering innocence was unique. Chico transcended stereotypes by creating a non-specific "ethnic" wheeler dealer. Zeppo, who would later become a talent agent, was the straight man. Trained in the theater, they brought with them into films not only their fast-paced dialogue but their writer, playwright **George S. Kaufman**. The first two Marx Brothers films—*The Coconuts* and *Animal Crackers*—were based on theatrical productions scripted by Kaufman, their playwriting alter ego. It is said that Kaufman once stood at the back of the theater during one of the plays he had written for them, talking quietly with a friend. Suddenly he shushed the friend and listened intently, then turned back to him and said, "Sorry. I thought I heard one of my lines." Though an exaggeration, this anecdote reveals the extent to which Kaufman and the four comics were collaborators in creating their trademark humor.

After Zeppo's retirement, Groucho and his brothers Harpo and Chico went on to make *A Night at the Opera* (1935) and *A Day at the Races* (1937), usually considered their best films. With just a few films, they left a permanent mark on American film comedy.

One of the great Jewish stage comics, **Fanny Brice**, made significant forays into films, including *My Man* (1928), *The Great Ziegfeld* (1936), and *Ziegfeld Follies* (1946). Vaudeville star **Sophie Tucker** appeared in a number of films including *Honky Tonk* (1929) and *Follow the Boys* (1944).

Along with performers from the stage came directors such as George Cukor, Reuben Mamoulian, and Joseph Mankiewicz and writers such as **Dorothy Parker**, **S. J. Perelman**, and **Ben Hecht**. Many were attracted by the expanding artistic possibilities of the cinema. More, perhaps, had lost their money in the stock market crash of 1929 and were wooed by hugely remunerative contracts. This exodus to Hollywood had varying results. Some of these theater and literary figures fled tinsel town after a matter of weeks or months. Some remained and decayed. Others made great films.

In the early thirties there were a number of important films with Jewish content. They tended to reveal second thoughts about the virtues of assimilation and success in the American mainstream. In *Symphony of Six Million* (1932), a wealthy Park Avenue doctor gives up his prestigious practice and returns to his roots in the Lower East Side. In *Counsellor-at-Law* (1933), top criminal lawyer George Simon is forced to consider his values and the cost of his success. The comedy *The Heart of New York* (1932) dealt with the same issues.

1930–1950s

In the middle 1930s Jews began to disappear from films. *The Life of Emile Zola* (1937) even goes so far as to deal with the Dreyfus Affair without mentioning that Dreyfus was Jewish. The important Jewish performers of the 1930s and 1940s assumed Anglicized names and played primarily or exclusively non-Jewish roles. Some of the biggest stars of the era were **Edward G. Robinson** (Emanuel Goldberg), **Paul Muni** (Muni Weisenfreund), Paulette Goddard (Marion Levy), Melvyn Douglas (Melvyn Hesselberg), **Sylvia Sydney** (Sophia Koscow), Luise Rainer, **John Garfield** (Julius Garfinkle), Betty Hutton (Betty Thornberg), June Havoc (Ellen Evangeline Hovick), **Lauren Bacall** (Betty Joan Perske), and Joan Blondell.

Even as Hitler's power and his persecution of European Jews increased, so too did Hollywood's apparent determination to pretend that Jews were not a part of American society. In part this was probably a result of the increasing assimilation of the movie moguls, but it may also have been simply self-protection in an increasingly anti-Semitic world. As for exposing Nazism,

In more than eighty years of performing, Molly Picon *was successful in every venue she tried, from Yiddish theater to Hollywood. She is shown here opposite Frank Sinatra in the 1963 film version of Neil Simon's* Come Blow Your Horn. *She was nominated for an Academy Award as best supporting actress for her performance. (American Jewish Archives)*

the official policy of the federal government was to remain neutral, and that policy was reflected in American films. The sole exception to this was Charlie Chaplin's *The Great Dictator* (1940). Chaplin, a non-Jew, created a fiercely comic denunciation of Hitler

and his regime, starring himself and Jewish actor Paulette Goddard. Goddard played an openly Jewish role, a brave young waif who resists Nazi brutality.

After the war began in Europe, some anti-fascist films began to come out of Hollywood. They did not usually deal explicitly with Jews, possibly because the Jewish moguls believed that the United States would not enter a war to defend Jews. Finally, after Pearl Harbor, when America was committed to the war, Hollywood began to acknowledge the persecution of Jews in such films as *The Pied Piper* (1942), *None Shall Escape* (1944), and *Address Unknown* (1944).

When Hollywood started making war movies, Jewish characters made a comeback. In virtually every combat film there was one Jewish guy in the company, the Italian guy, the Irish guy, the hillbilly guy, and all the other guys required to make up a diverse, "All-American" group. More serious depiction of Jews and the war appeared in *The Purple Heart* (1944) and *Pride of the Marines* (1945).

Following World War II, some film writers and directors turned to exploring the causes of the Nazi horrors. Films denouncing anti-Semitism included RKO's *Crossfire* (1947) and 20th Century Fox's *A Gentleman's Agreement* (1947), which featured John Garfield and June Havoc, along with non-Jewish actor Gregory Peck as a man who assumes a Jewish identity to experience anti-Semitism firsthand.

In the early 1950s, the Motion Picture Project was created to encourage Jewish themes and positive images in Hollywood films. It received wide support from the Jewish community. The result was a very good decade. Some of the films that treated Jewish content positively and with sensitivity were *The Magnificent Yankee*, the life of **Louis Brandeis** (1951); *Ivanhoe* (1952) adapted by **Dore Schary**, with non-Jewish Elizabeth Taylor starring as the beautiful, virtuous Rebecca; *The Jazz Singer*, a remake with Lebanese Catholic Danny Thomas in the Al Jolson role; *Good Morning, Miss Dove* (1955); *Three Brave Men* (1957); *Home before Dark* (1958); *The Last Angry Man* (1959); and *Dark at the Top of the Stairs* (1960). Two films exposed anti-Semitism in the army: *The Naked and the Dead* (1958) and *The Young Lions* (1958). The first film

Laura Hobson's novel Gentleman's Agreement *was a spectacular critical, popular, and financial success. The screen adaptation by Moss Hart was also a hit. This scene shows Gregory Peck, the gentile journalist who "passes" for Jewish in order to write an article on anti-Semitism; Anne Revere, who plays his mother; and John Garfield (who actually was Jewish), who plays his Jewish friend. (Private Collection)*

to deal with Jewish domestic life since the 1920s was *Marjorie Morningstar* (1958), starring non-Jewish Natalie Wood in the title role.

Jewish performers were still in an ambiguous position. Most of the plum Jewish roles went to gentile actors. In *The Diary of Anne Frank* (1959), even the quintessentially Jewish role of the courageous young girl who lived for years with her family in an attic to escape Nazi persecution was played by non-Jewish actor Millie Perkins. At the same time, many Jewish actors were playing important non-Jewish roles. Lauren Bacall was Humphrey Bogart's intriguing, worldly co-star in *To Have and Have Not* (1944) and several other romantic suspense stories. **Judy Holliday** was one of Hollywood's great comic actors in *Born Yesterday* (1950)—written for the stage by Garson Kanin and Ruth Gordon—*The Solid Gold Cadillac* (1956) and *The Bells Are Ringing*. Betty Hutton was one of America's favorite tomboys in *Annie Get Your Gun* (1950) and *The Greatest Show on Earth* (1952). **Tony Curtis** and **Kirk Douglas** became matinee idols and Hollywood tried very hard to turn **Shelley Winters** into a sex symbol.

Behind the scenes of many of the popular films of the 1950s were a host of Jewish screenwriters, including a number of husband and wife teams. Frances Goodrich and her husband Albert Hackett adapted *Marjorie Morningstar* for the screen and wrote the *Thin Man* series, based on Dashiell Hammett's characters. They also wrote *It's a Wonderful Life* (1946) and *Father of the Bride* (1950). Poet and wit Dorothy Parker, with her husband Alan Campbell, wrote *A Star Is Born* (1937) and contributed dialogue to a number of other films, including the adaptation of **Lillian Hellman**'s *The Little Foxes*. Phoebe and Henry Ephron wrote the screenplays for *What Price Glory* (1952) and the remake of *Daddy Long Legs* (1955), as well as dialogue for *Carousel* (1956) and *Desk Set* (1957). Fay and Michael Kanin worked together on a number of films, including *Rhapsody* (1954). Fay Kanin later became the first woman to serve as president of the Academy of Motion Picture Arts and Sciences.

Other writing teams were not united by matrimony. Betty **Comden** and Adolph **Green** wrote some of Hollywood's finest and most popular musicals, including *Singin' in the Rain* (1952) and *The Band Wagon* (1953). Sonya Levien, alone or with collaborators such as **S. N. Behrman** and William Ludwig, wrote *Quo Vadis* (1951), *Oklahoma!*, and more than seventy other screenplays.

The Blacklist

There was an angry cloud on the 1950s horizon. During the infamous McCarthy era, the House Un-American Activities Committee launched an investigation that was riddled with anti-Semitism. Ten of the first nineteen witnesses the committee called were Jewish. Six of the "Hollywood Ten," who were indicted by the committee, were Jews: Alvah Bessie, Herbert Biberman, Lester Cole, John Howard Lawson, Albert Maltz, and Sam Ornitz. It seemed that any Jewish association was sufficient reason to call any Hollywood artist or producer before the committee. The response on the part of movie moguls was not to defend their people but to outdo the committee in "rooting out Communism." Their primary tool for this task was the Blacklist, onto which they put writers, directors, and actors who would not testify before the committee or who, in any other way, came under suspicion.

Lee Grant won an Academy Award nomination for her first film, *Detective Story* (1951), and acted in only two films in the next twelve years. Her crime was refusing to testify to the committee against her husband, playwright Arnold Manoff. Others who suffered from the blacklisting included Judy Holliday, Lillian Hellman, and **Gertrude Berg**.

1960 TO TODAY

The 1960s was a time of growing ethnic awareness. During this decade Jewish actors again began to play Jewish roles, and the positive value of assimilation was brought into question. The horrors of World War II and the Holocaust were brought to light in powerful, often graphic terms. Among the important dramatic films of the sixties were *Judgment at Nuremberg* (1961), *The Pawnbroker* (1965), *Cast a Giant Shadow* (1966), and *The Fixer* (1968). *The Pawnbroker*, starring Rod Steiger, was independently produced and distributed by Ely Landau and was the first American work of fiction to portray the concentration camp experience in such affecting detail.

Comedies, too, acknowledged the ethnicity of their

Would you allow your daughter to study Talmud with this "Yeshiva boy?" If he looks familiar it is because you saw him in the movie Funny Girl. *This still is from the film* Yentl. *Based on a story by Isaac Bashevis Singer, it tells how a girl (played by Barbra Streisand) who wants to study Talmud pretends to be a boy so she can attend Yeshiva. Her co-conspirator in this deception is played by Mandy Patinkin. (Private Collection)*

Jewish characters. *Bye, Bye Braverman* (1968), *The Producers* (1968), *Funny Girl* (1968), *Take the Money and Run* (1969), *Goodbye, Columbus* (1969), and *Fiddler on the Roof* (1969)—based on **Sholem Aleichem**'s stories about Tevya and his five daughters and their life in the Russian *shtetl*—were all successful at the box office.

In the 1970s however, Hollywood was struck by a rash of comedies dealing in new Jewish stereotypes. They were based on the idea of the suffocating Jewish mother and the neurotic son who spends his life trying to break away from her. In film after film, the finest women in the Jewish acting community, including Ruth Gordon, Shelley Winters, and Lee Grant, were trapped in this pernicious pigeonhole in films such as *Where's Poppa* (1970), *Portnoy's Complaint* (1972), *Move* (1970), *The Steagle* (1971), *Play It Again Sam* (1972), *Annie Hall* (1977), and *Manhattan* (1979). **Woody Allen**, Richard Benjamin, and George Segal played Jewish men whose differences were largely a matter of the degree of their neuroses. Their equally neurotic sisters appeared in *Such Good Friends* (1971), *Made for Each Other* (1971), *The Heartbreak Kid* (1972), and *Sheila Levine Is Dead and Living in New York* (1975).

Patricia Erens points out that only films made or strongly influenced by women managed to avoid these neurotic stereotypes. *The Way We Were* (1973), starring **Barbra Streisand**, explored the possibility that intermarriage might not work, a notion that would have horrified Abie's Irish Rose. In *Hester Street* (1975), which won Carol Kane an Oscar nomination, and was written and directed by Joan Micklin Silver, Orthodox Jewish life on the Lower East Side is presented realistically and affectionately. *Girlfriends* (1978), written and directed by Claudia Weill, presents an independent Jewish woman not looking for a husband.

Since the 1970s Jewish characters have gained considerably more acceptance. Jewish men and women are accepted easily as romantic leads, whether their Jewishness is explicit or implied. Settings in which Jewish customs and values are dominant are *Tell Me a Riddle* (1980), *My Favorite Year* (1982), *The Chosen* (1981), *Yentl* (1983), *Brighton Beach Memoirs* (1987), and *The Plot against Harry* (1989). For the most part, the "differentness" of Jewish life and culture is seen as positive, something to be explored rather than hidden.

Probably the most important Jewish performer of our time is Barbra Streisand, who has had such an enormous impact on the way Jewish women are portrayed and has broken so many other barriers in film as well. However, the list of prominent Jewish actors

---

The Long Way Home Wins an Academy Award

The Oscar for Best Documentary Feature of 1997 went to *The Long Way Home*, a film focusing on the agonizing plight of Europe's Jewish refugees immediately following the Holocaust, directed by Mark Jonathan Harris and produced by Rick Trank for the Simon Wiesenthal Center's Moriah Films unit. Rabbi Marvin Hier, founding dean of the Center, declared in accepting the award: "This is for the survivors of the Holocaust who walked away from the ashes, rebuilt their lives and helped create the State of Israel. God bless them."

Billy Crystal, host of the awards, quipped: "What a night when your rabbi *and* your best friend [Robin Williams, who won for best supporting actor in *Good Will Hunting*] win an Oscar."

would be almost endless. It would include **Dustin Hoffman**, **Bette Midler**, Richard Dreyfuss, **Goldie Hawn**, Dyan Cannon, **Mel Brooks**, Debra Winger, **Woody Allen**, Carrie Fisher, David Steinberg, Carol Kane, Jeff Goldblum, Steve Guttenberg, Melissa and Sarah Gilbert, Ron Silver, Barbara Hershey, Robert Klein, Amy Irving, Jill Clayburgh, and Michael Douglas. Jewish screenwriters, directors, and producers are equally numerous.

In the 1990s, **Stephen Spielberg** typifies Jewish participation in filmmaking. He has had tremendous success with films like *Star Wars* that do not focus on ethnicity or challenge traditional American values. He has confirmed the Jewish commitment to human rights with films such as *The Color Purple* (1985) and *Amistad* (1997), which explore the experience of people of other ethnic backgrounds. And he has made one of the most important Jewish films of all time, *Schindler's List* (1996), which portrays in horrible detail the suffering of Jews during the Holocaust. Hollywood has come full circle.

GARFIELD, JOHN (1913–1952)

Actor

In a tragically brief film career, John Garfield embodied an entire generation of immigrants and sons of immigrants, clawing their way up the spiky ladder of American success, often to find that the rewards were not worth the effort. Although Garfield almost never played an overtly Jewish character (with the notable exception of *Gentleman's Agreement*), it was always tacitly assumed that he was a Jew. After all, he had been born Julius Garfinkel.

Like the characters he played, Garfield was born and raised on the Lower East Side, growing up in the streets and just short of being a juvenile delinquent. But a victory in a debate contest sponsored by the *New York Times* gave him a ticket out, a scholarship that he applied to acting school. After a typical Depression-era post-grad course of hoboing cross-country, he returned to New York and became a member of the Group Theater. The handsome and intense Garfield

rose quickly to Broadway leads and in 1938 he signed a contract with Warner Brothers. His first film, *Four Daughters* (1938), won him an Oscar nomination. As was typical of that studio, he was rushed into a series of mostly undistinguished films that typecast him. He broke out of the mold by working as an independent, albeit with mixed results. His best work, *Body and Soul* (1947), *Force of Evil* (1948), and *He Ran All the Way* (1951), his last film, show Garfield as a mature actor no longer trading on his boyishness, but convincingly embodying the moral ambiguities of American life. Those very ambiguities were conspiring against him: long active in leftist circles, he was facing a subpoena from the House Un-American Activities Committee when he died of a heart attack.

GILFORD, JACK (1907–1990)

Actor, comic

The sweetly funny Jack Gilford (Jacob Gellman) was born in New York City and began performing at amateur nights in his late twenties. **Milton Berle** gave him his professional start in his vaudeville revue in 1935. For three years, Gilford appeared with Berle and on his own in vaudeville and as a solo act on the Borscht Belt circuit and in nightclubs. He made his Broadway acting debut in *Meet the People* (1940) and for the next several years went back and forth from his club work to the legitimate stage. In the early 1950s, he began to appear regularly on television but was blacklisted during the McCarthy era. He continued to find work on stage, and in 1955 he played the shy Dr. Dussel in *The Diary of Anne Frank* on Broadway. He was widely acclaimed for his roles as the finicky king in *Once upon a Mattress* (1959) and the timorous Hysterium in *A Funny Thing Happened on the Way to the Forum* (1962) with his long-time friend **Zero Mostel**.

As the power of the blacklist faded, Gilford found television work as a guest star on such shows as "All in the Family" and "Rhoda." He was also a regular on "The David Frost Revue" (1971) and "Apple Pie" (1978). At the same time, he appeared in a number of feature films including *Catch-22* (1970) and *Save the*

Tiger (1973). In 1982 he appeared on Broadway for the last time, playing in a revival of *The World of Sholem Aleichem*. In his last film, *Cocoon* (1985), he captivated a new generation of fans with his sweetness and gentle charm.

GOLDENSON, LEONARD (1907–)

Television pioneer

The grand old man of American television, Leonard Harry Goldenson, was born in Scottsdale, Pennsylvania. His career in television began when Paramount Pictures, which he then headed, took over ABC-TV in 1953. In the years that followed Goldenson produced the first adult television western, the dramatic medical series "Ben Casey," nighttime soap operas, primetime cartoons, and the "Wide World of Sports," not to mention "The Fugitive." He also made a deal with Walt Disney, providing significant financing for Disneyland in exchange for a percentage of the theme park and a Disney television show.

Goldenson went on to bring the American public "Roots," the first woman news anchor—**Barbara Walters**—and a host of other innovative programming. In 1990 he was given a Lifetime Achievement Award at the Emmy Awards ceremonies. Goldenson and his family also founded the United Cerebral Palsy Association.

GOLDWYN, SAMUEL (1882–1974)

Motion picture producer

Samuel Goldwyn's importance in American film history resides less in the films he actually produced, which ranged from the classic to the crass and the "Goldwynism" he allegedly spouted ("Include me out." "In two words, im possible," and so on), than in the fact that he survived as an independent producer outside the studio system for most of his career. This was a unique feat in an era during which his contemporaries, the other tough, streetwise Russian Jews who built the great studios, were the dominant force.

Goldwyn was born Shmuel Gelbfisz in Warsaw, the eldest son of poor Hasidic Jews. He received an Orthodox education and worked for his father in the family's antique store until he was fifteen, when the older Gelbfisz died. Shmuel knew that his only hope of escaping poverty (and military service under the Czar) lay in immigrating to America. He saved enough money to get to England, then worked his way across the Atlantic, arriving in America (by way of Canada) in 1895. There he established himself as a glove salesman, rising quickly to become a partner in the company.

In 1910, Gelbfisz, now Goldfish, married Blanche Lasky; her brother Jesse was a successful theatrical producer and the brothers-in-law formed a film company. Their first film was also the directorial debut of a young man named Cecil B. DeMille, *The Squaw Man* (1913). The film was a success and they merged their company with Adolph Zukor's Famous Players; that amalgamation, Famous Players-Lasky, eventually become Paramount Pictures. But Goldfish differed strongly with Zukor and, in what became a pattern for the next several years, he left the company (selling his shares for a million dollars, a formidable sum in 1917) to start again with new partners. He chose the Broadway producers Edgar and Archie Selwyn and, taking the last syllable of their family name, became Goldwyn.

Goldwyn tried his luck as an independent producer again in the 1920s, but the company went bankrupt and was absorbed into what became Metro-Goldwyn-Mayer. (It is a common misunderstanding that Goldwyn was involved in MGM; only his name was attached to the studio, he departed without ever producing there.) In 1926 he joined the cooperative effort known as United Artists, along with the more famous partners—Mary Pickford, Douglas Fairbanks, D. W. Griffith, and Charlie Chaplin. UA distributed Goldwyn's films until he sold his stock in the company in 1941; thereafter RKO handled his output.

As an independent producer at the beginning of the sound era, Goldwyn began to come into his own. He always believed that a strong story was the key to a successful film. He acquired literary properties promiscuously, meddling constantly in the work of the men who directed his films. As a result, some great directors did lesser work under the Goldwyn banner—John Ford's *Arrowsmith* (1931), King Vidor's *Street Scene* (1931), and *Stella Dallas* (1937). Howard Hawks worked for him repeatedly, but only with great reluctance. Perhaps the happiest artistic collaboration of Goldwyn's career was with the relentlessly stubborn Austrian Jew William Wyler. The two butted heads on several films, but the results, *Dodsworth* (1936), *Wuthering Heights* (1939), *The Little Foxes* (1941), and *The Best Years of Our Lives* (1946), are among the best work either did. Goldwyn also was responsible for launching several major stars in film: Will Rogers, **Eddie Cantor**, **Danny Kaye**, Gary Cooper, and Vilma Banky. Goldwyn's son, Samuel Jr., is a film producer as well. Of course, he is an independent.

HAWN, GOLDIE (1945–)

Actress, film producer

Goldie Hawn is one of those rare women who not only is an A-list star (someone whose presence in a project is enough to get it financed), but also an actress who has taken direct control over her own career, producing her films as well as acting in them.

Hawn grew up in an atmosphere of music and dance. Her father was a professional musician, her mother a Jewish dancer and owner of a dance school. She began her career while still a teenager, teaching dance to put herself through the drama program at American University. She dropped out at eighteen to try her luck in New York City. After a variety of bit parts, summer stock, and work as a go-go dancer, she made her big breakthrough as part of the stock company on TV's "Laugh-In."

Hawn won an Oscar for her supporting role in the 1969 film *Cactus Flower*, her first featured role. She received critical acclaim for her role in **Steven Spielberg**'s first film, *Sugarland Express*. But it was the role of Judy Benjamin in the 1980 film *Private Benjamin* that put her on the map. The movie shows Benjamin's metamorphosis from the stereotypical Jewish American Princess to a self-aware, self-possessed, and mature woman. She was nominated for an Academy Award for

Some of Goldie Hawn's first performances were as a tap dancer at the bar mitzvahs of friends. Bette Midler started performing as a way to build her self-esteem. She was, as she puts it, ". . . an ugly, fat little Jewish girl with problems." They are now two of the most powerful women in Hollywood. This scene is from their hugely successful 1996 film The First Wives Club *(co-staring Diane Keaton). (Private Collection)*

the part. *Private Benjamin* was also Hawn's debut as a producer. She has produced a number of films since and acted in over thirty. In 1996 she teamed with Diane Keaton and **Bette Midler** in the successful *The First Wives Club* and appeared in **Woody Allen**'s musical film *Everybody Says I Love You*. Goldie Hawn is one of the most successful women in Hollywood.

HOFFMAN, DUSTIN (1937–)

Actor

The unlikeliest of Hollywood stars, Dustin Hoffman's big breakthrough came when the thirty-year-old actor played a newly minted college grad. **Mike Nichols** saw

Hoffman in an off-Broadway play and chose the unknown actor to star in his 1967 film *The Graduate*. He was nominated for an Academy Award for the role. Before that, Hoffman, the son of a furniture designer, had struggled in dead-end jobs, slept on friends' floors, and made the rounds trying to forge a career as an actor. His first break came two years before *The Graduate*, when he won critical acclaim for a stage performance in *The Journey of the Fifth Horse*.

With the success of the Nichols film, Hoffman was a new and entirely unexpected star. As befits an unconventional leading man, he has made his reputation with a series of unconventional parts: the down-and-out Ratso Rizzo in *Midnight Cowboy* (1969); a prisoner on Devil's Island in *Papillon* (1973); a beleaguered single father in *Kramer vs. Kramer* (1979) (for which he won his first Oscar); and an autistic adult in *Rain Man* (1988). Perhaps his most outrageous role was as a failed actor who dresses as a woman to get a part in *Tootsie* (1982). He also has played several non-fictional characters, including reporter Carl Bernstein in *All the President's Men* (1988) and *Lenny Bruce* (1974). Hoffman returns periodically to the stage; he has played Willy Loman in *Death of a Salesman* (a performance subsequently captured on film) and Shylock in *The Merchant of Venice*.

In 1988 Hoffman won a Best Actor Oscar for his role in *Rain Man*. He was nominated for the seventh time for best actor for his part in the 1997 political drama *Wag the Dog*.

HOLLIDAY, JUDY (1921–1965)

Actor

Brilliantly funny "dumb blonde" Judy Holliday was born in New York to parents of Russian Jewish descent. Her father was a professional fund-raiser for Jewish and socialist groups and her mother a piano teacher. Holliday was strongly influenced by both. After graduating from high school, she got a job as switchboard operator at Orson Welles' and **John Houseman**'s Mercury Theater, then organized a cabaret act with lyricists Betty **Comden** and Adolph

Green. The act, called *The Revuers*, worked nightclubs, had a thirty-two week run on the radio, then went to Hollywood. There, Holliday played some bit parts. When the group returned to New York, it split up and Holliday had her first important role, in *Kiss Them for Me* (1945). She stole the show.

Later that year, Holliday stepped in for ailing Jean Arthur in a show headed for Broadway. When *Born Yesterday* opened in early 1946, it was hugely successful and Holliday was a star. She took a leave of absence to play a small role in the film *Adam's Rib* (1949) and, the next year, re-created her *Born Yesterday* role for the film version. In 1952 she was called to testify before the House Un-American Activities Committee and, by assuming her dumb blonde role while answering questions, was able to avoid naming names, to exonerate herself, and to show her contempt for the committee. Still, she was blacklisted from television for several years.

In films Holliday's career thrived. She starred in five films in five years, including *The Solid Gold Cadillac* (1956). In 1956, she returned to Broadway in *Bells Are Ringing*, a musical by her old friends Comden and Green. It was her first musical role, and she was again a huge success. While rehearsing for the play *Laurette*, based on the life of actor Laurette Taylor, Holliday was diagnosed with breast cancer. After treatment, she was able to appear in one last show, but she died of the cancer a few years later. Given the small number of plays and films in which she appeared, Judy Holliday had an amazing impact on audiences, becoming a legendary figure in American entertainment.

HOLLYWOOD

Jewish Americans did not invent the motion picture or any of its technology, but they certainly invented Hollywood.

EARLY FILMS

The first films were made by people who knew considerably more about science than about art, or even business, and few of them were Jews. First among these was inventor Thomas Alva Edison, who made primarily short films that we would probably call documentaries. The first "real" filmmaker was D. W. Griffith, also a gentile. However, within a matter of years, the American motion picture industry was dominated by Jewish immigrants from Germany, Hungary, Poland, and other Eastern European countries.

There are a number of explanations for this Jewish dominance, but the simplest is probably that motion pictures began to be produced at a time when an influx of Jewish immigrants were looking for an entree into American economic and cultural life. They were able to find their niche in Hollywood simply because no one was there before them.

In their early days, movies were a cheap, lower-class entertainment form. All you needed to open a theater was an empty room, chairs, and a sheet on which to project the film. You could rent a flickering silent film for very little and, if you were speedy on a bicycle, run it down the street for a showing in another empty storefront, getting two sets of box office receipts for one rental. The movies were enormously popular with immigrants, requiring no knowledge of English and depicting, or pretending to depict, life in America. In 1908 there were more than 400 small theaters in New York City. By 1910 there were about 20,000 of these "nickelodeons" in the northern United States between New York and Chicago. Running a nickelodeon was a logical business enterprise for an ambitious young immigrant, and it was from the ranks of these small theater owners that most of the Jewish movie producers rose.

The very first Jewish American producer took another route. "Bronco Billy" Anderson (Gilbert Max Aronson) was an actor, scriptwriter, and director. He played the lead in Edwin S. Porter's *The Great Train Robbery* in 1903. It was one of the first films to tell a coherent story of any length, in essence the first feature film, and it made Anderson a highly popular actor. Soon, he became a partner in the Essanay Company, where he was a writer and producer as well as an actor. In 1908 he made the first of the "Bronco Billy" films, which were so successful that

he starred in and produced 374 more of them in the next seven years.

The next important Jewish producer established a pattern that would quickly become common. Sigmund "Pop" Lubin, of Philadelphia, owned a chain of theaters. In order to fill them, he got into film distribution, then production. His first films came out in 1903–1904. William Selig, a theater owner from Chicago, also began producing at the same time.

In the next few years competition became fierce in the infant industry. In an attempt to strangle it, Edison formed the Motion Pictures Patent Company in 1909. Enlisting the cooperation of other large producers, he forced theater owners to rent projectors and films only from the company. Essanay, Lubin, and Selig went along with Edison. However, Carl Laemmle and William Fox opposed the inventor's power play. With the backing of **Marcus Loew**, owner of a large theater chain, they fought in the courts and the press. They also produced cheaper films, undercutting the more established producers. Laemmle, later founder of Universal Pictures, and William Fox, founder of the Fox Film Corporation, both fit the ambitious immigrant pattern. Laemmle was from Germany and Fox's parents were from Hungary. Fox began in the cloth business before moving on to moving pictures. They were the first to combine production, distribution, and exhibition in a single company, the model that would produce the huge studios of the 1920s and beyond.

In 1915 the court ruled against Edison's Motion Pictures Patent Company, ordering that it be liquidated. In the meantime, a new company had begun to command attention. Jewish Hungarian immigrant Adolph Zukor had decided, in 1912, to give the motion picture business a cultural boost by importing the French film *Queen Elizabeth*, starring Sarah Bernhard. Reviews in the legitimate press resulted in considerable prestige for Zukor, and he dedicated himself to the production of "Famous Players in Famous Plays," film adaptations of literary works with "star" actors. Zukor introduced the promotion of stars into the industry. The first star he promoted was Mary Pickford.

In 1917 Zukor joined with Jesse L. Lasky in the distribution of films. Two years later they merged the production wings of their companies. The result of these mergers was Paramount Pictures. Soon, Lasky brought into the company **Samuel** Goldfish **(Goldwyn)**, a Polish American Jew who had established himself as an independent producer, and Cecil B. De Mille. Paramount was the most powerful studio yet. The company owned its own worldwide theater chain. It insisted on block-booking, requiring that theater owners take a block of pictures in order to get the ones they really wanted. Its control was very nearly undisputed.

In order to compete with Paramount, smaller companies began to merge or go out of business. William Fox joined Twentieth Century and, as Twentieth Century-Fox, the company became one of the powers in Hollywood. Russian Jewish **Louis B. Mayer**, a New England theater owner, bought Metro Company and became Metro-Mayer. In 1919 Samuel Goldfish left Paramount and joined with the Selwyn Brothers to form the Goldwyn Company, which merged with Metro-Mayer in 1924. Goldwyn left the company to become one of Hollywood's most important independent producers. Carl Laemmle and his Universal Film Manufacturing Company, later Universal Studios, waged a battle to remain independent.

In the 1920s and 1930s the Jewish movie moguls, as they were soon called, really come into their own. Harry, Albert, Sam, and **Jack Warner**—Jewish American brothers whose father was from Russia—started with a small theater, managed a theater chain, then formed their own company. In 1923 they bought the Fitagraph Company, which manufactured the Vitaphone, a form of music recording that was played to accompany silent films. In 1926 Warner Brothers produced the first film with its own musical score, and in the studio 1927 produced *The Jazz Singer* with **Al Jolson**. The Warner Brothers had revolutionized motion pictures with a film about a young man who wants to be a popular entertainer rather than a cantor.

In 1929 **Harry Cohn** founded Columbia. Now, all the large Hollywood companies except United Artists were founded and controlled by Jewish Americans. Even United Artists, although it was founded by a group of film artists, was managed by Joseph Schenk. The first

bank to finance the film industry in 1919 was also Jewish—Kuhn, Loeb and Co. By the late 1920s Hollywood was ruled by the "Big Eight": Metro-Goldwyn-Mayer (MGM), under the control of Louis B. Mayer and his head of production, the brilliantly talented young Irving Thalberg; Warner Brothers; Universal Studios; Twentieth-Century-Fox; Paramount; Columbia; United Artists; and R. K. O., headed by **David Sarnoff**.

The moguls were powerful, wealthy men. They were also acutely aware of their Jewish immigrant backgrounds. They lived their Jewishness in private and attempted, in public, to present an "American" image. Through the first two decades of Hollywood film production, they often made films with Jewish themes. That would change in the 1930s. As motion pictures became more popular, and therefore more influential, they began to come under attack for promulgating the wrong values. What had been thoroughly acceptable in vaudeville, music halls, and saloons was not deemed appropriate for the increasingly family-oriented medium of film. People began to talk about the need to censor movies.

Apparently, the movie moguls experienced this criticism of their product as a rejection of themselves and their background. They grew increasingly eager to win the approval of mainstream Americans whom they saw as Christian and white. They created the Motion Picture Producers and Distributors Association and appointed former Republican National Chairman and Postmaster General William Hays as its head. In 1934 they chose Joseph Ignatius Breen to head the Production Code Administration. They saturated their films with "Americanism." During the 1930s, they eliminated almost all Jewish themes and overtly Jewish actors from motion pictures. Even when a film was made with a Jewish role, that role was usually taken by a non-Jew.

As Hitler's anti-Semitism took hold in Germany, Jewish characters were not seen on the screens of American theaters. When war threatened in Europe, the moguls made films attacking fascism but failed to mention the persecution of Jews. They feared that, while American might enter the war in defense of freedom, they would not fight in defense of Jews, and there was more than a little validity to their fear.

There was another group of Jewish Americans in Hollywood, and they directly opposed the moguls. This group was made up of émigré filmmakers who had experienced fascism firsthand in Europe and young, second-generation writers with strong leftist, even Communist, ties. Together they worked to unionize Hollywood, to get politically controversial films put into production, and to fight for social justice. They were a very serious thorn in the side of the Hollywood establishment.

Once World War II actually began the moguls and the intellectuals worked together to produce some of the most effective propaganda the world had ever seen. Jews were allowed back on the screen, to fight for freedom. When the war ended, a grateful country acknowledged Hollywood's contributions to winning the war. However, the federal government was casting a jaundiced eye on the power of the moguls. In 1938 the Big Eight companies had been slapped with an anti-trust suit, which was suspended during the hostilities. After the war, the suit was taken up again and, in 1948, the Supreme Court ruled that the studios had to give up their theater chains. The beleaguered moguls had little time to recover from this blow before they were struck by another, ultimately more damaging one—television. Between 1946 and 1957 movie production was cut in half.

It was in the panic caused by these threats to their profitability that the moguls faced one of their greatest challenges and failed. Under the influence of Senator Joseph McCarthy, the House Un-American Activities Committee launched an investigation into Communist activities in Hollywood, and the Jewish moguls threw the Jewish intellectuals to the wolves.

At this distance, it seems clear that much of what the HUAC did in Hollywood was motivated by anti-Semitism. Ten of the first nineteen witnesses called were Jewish. Seven of the "Hollywood Ten" who were indicted were Jewish. The response of the moguls was not to defend their colleagues and employees, but to denounce them and hundreds of others like them. Jews blacklisted Jews far more than any other group. The Jewish writers and intellectuals had their revenge, of course, by creating an image of the studio boss in fiction and on film that cruelly satirized the moguls. It is an image that persists today, one more anti-Semitic stereotype to be dismantled.

The big studio bosses were all dead by the late 1970s. In their place rose a new breed of moneymen and artists, a great many of them Jewish.

HOWARD, LESLIE (1893–1943)

Actor

Elegant, sensitive Leslie Howard (Leslie Howard Steiner) was born in London, England, and made his professional stage debut after returning from World War I in 1917. His American debut came in 1920 in *Just Suppose*. For the next several years, he traveled back and forth between New York and London, playing a variety of romantic juvenile leads. He made his mark opposite Jeanne Eagels in *Her Cardboard Lover* (1927) and consolidated his position in *Escape* (1927). Bored with acting, he turned to writing, producing, and directing, and all of his future acting work on stage involved his participation in some other aspect of the production.

In 1930 Howard began to make films. In his first film, *Outward Bound* (1930), he was enormously effective as one of a group of ship passengers who gradually come to the realization that they are dead. In the years to follow he made a number of light comedies but is most remembered for his powerful dramatic performances. These included roles in *Of Human Bondage* (1934), *The Petrified Forest* (1936), and *Gone With the Wind* (1939).

Howard returned to England in 1939 to participate in the war effort, making propaganda films and weekly radio broadcasts. In 1943, while he was returning from a series of goodwill lectures in Spain and Portugal, his plane was shot down by German aircraft and he was assumed dead.

JAFFE, SAM (1891–1984)

Actor

One of the finest character actors of his time, Sam Jaffe was born in New York City and grew up on the

Lower East Side. His earliest stage appearances were as a child, with his mother, Ada Steinberg Jaffe, an actor in the Yiddish theater. He did not begin acting professionally until he was in his middle twenties. His Broadway debut came in *The Idle Inn* (1921) and his first real recognition with his role as Yudelson in the film *The Jazz Singer* (1925).

Beginning in the 1930s Jaffe began to appear regularly in films. Often cast in ethnic roles, he soon gained a reputation as one of the great character actors in film. Among his most famous portrayals were the Grand Duke Peter of Russia in *The Scarlet Empress* (1934), the High Lama in *Lost Horizon* (1937), the title character of the noble and courageous water-carrier in *Gunga Din* (1939), and scientist Jacob Barnhardt in *The Day the Earth Stood Still* (1951). The 1950s brought a shift to television, first as a guest star in such series as "The Defenders" and "The Untouchables." Later he starred as Dr. David Zorba in the landmark medical drama series "Ben Casey" (1961–1965).

Jaffe went back to the stage and the silver screen after his television stint. His last Broadway appearance was in *A Meeting by the River* (1979). He continued to appear in films until 1983, the year before his death. Among the most notable of his later films were *The Great Bank Robbery* (1969) and the television film *QBVII* (1974).

JESSEL, GEORGE (1898–1981)

Entertainer, producer

The self-appointed "Toastmaster General," George Albert Jessel was a veritable encyclopedia of one-liners who would tell a joke at the drop of . . . anything. Jessel was born in New York City, the son of a playwright and producer. He grew up in the theater, singing professionally from the age of nine and teamed in vaudeville with a young **Eddie Cantor** at eleven. He starred in 1925 on Broadway in *The Jazz Singer*, but didn't get the part when Warner Brothers filmed it as the first "talkie" because he asked for too much money. Jessel ended up at Warner Brothers not long after, but his film career was minor. He became New York City's of-

ficial toastmaster and participated thereafter in countless fundraising and other events in the city's life. He was well known on radio and as an inveterate world-traveling fund-raiser for worthy causes, especially those involving Jewish charities and the State of Israel.

JOLSON, AL (1886–1950)

Singer, entertainer

The son of a cantor, Al Jolson (born Asa Yoelson) was born in Russia and grew up in Washington, D.C., singing in his father's synagogue. But he wanted a wider audience and went into show business (somewhat to his family's dismay). After brief stints as a circus performer, and blackface singing waiter, Jolson went on the vaudeville stage, where he was a nearly instant hit. A dynamic, relentless performer, he could milk a song and an audience like no one else. Within a few years he was starring on Broadway and making hit records that sold in unprecedented quantities. He was also enjoying a love affair with his audiences, often closing an evening's performance on Broadway with a post-curtain-call impromptu concert that could go on for over an hour.

But his greatest stardom was yet to come. It was heralded by one of his trademark lines, "You ain't heard nothin' yet." That line would be the first piece of dialogue ever spoken in a feature film, the 1927 Warner Brothers' *The Jazz Singer*, whose story is based on Jolson's own life. The combination of talking pictures and Jolson was like a lightning flash; he was now a star of unparalleled popularity, perhaps the first modern superstar. He made several more films for Warner Brothers, but his over-the-top style quickly wore thin in the intimacy of the camera.

Jolson continued working steadily, despite the slippage in his film career and the death of vaudeville, but his star had waned in the second half of the 1930s. With the coming of World War II, he began a comeback, entertaining tirelessly for the troops, most of whom were too young to know who he had been. Columbia Pictures decided to make a film of his life, *The Jolson Story* (1946), in which his singing voice was dubbed for actor Larry Parks, and once again Jolson's records topped the charts. The success of the film spurred a sequel, *Jolson Sings Again*, two years later. Jolson returned to the USO circuit with the Korean War and died of a heart attack after returning from one of his tours of the Korean front.

KAHN, MADELINE (1942–)

Comic actor

One of the great female clowns, Madeline Kahn was born in Boston and encouraged to train for show business by her mother. When she was still a child, she sang on New York radio on the show "Children's Hour." She began her professional career in musicals and light opera and made her Broadway debut at the age of twenty-six in *New Faces of 1968*. That same year she sang the female lead in the opera *Candide* at Lincoln Center. After several years in musical comedies and revues in New York, she made her first film, *What's Up Doc?* (1972). She was wildly funny as **Barbra Streisand**'s rival for the love of Ryan O'Neal. She made an even bigger impact in *Paper Moon* (1973), where she held her own comically against Tatum O'Neal's Academy Award-winning performance as a deadpan brat. She then appeared in a series of **Mel Brooks** films, including *Blazing Saddles* (1974), *Young Frankenstein* (1974), and *High Anxiety* (1977), as well as **Gene Wilder**'s *The Adventures of Sherlock Holmes' Smarter Brother* (1975).

In the 1980s Kahn's career was varied. It included a Muppet movie, Brooks's *History of the World, Part I* (1981), a short-lived situation comedy series, and several stage appearances, including the classic comedy

Born Yesterday (1988–89) with **Ed Asner**. In the 1990s she revealed a flair for more understated comedy as Phylicia Rashad's best friend and business partner in "Cosby."

KAYE, DANNY (1913–1987)

Actor, entertainer

The former David Daniel Kaminsky was a whirlwind of energy on screen and on stage, a high school dropout who became one of the world's most beloved entertainers, a spouter of musical tongue-twisters, and a gifted musician. As Danny Kaye, this son of a garment district tailor worked his way from the Borscht Belt hotels, where he was a comic singing busboy, to the Broadway stage and London's Palladium.

It was a slow, hard climb for Kaye, who worked as a soda jerk and insurance salesman while doing vaudeville and nightclubs. He made his Broadway debut in 1939 in *The Straw Hat Revue.* He had his first real success two years later in *Lady in the Dark*, nearly stealing the show from the legendary Gertrude Lawrence with "Tchaikowsky," an **Ira Gershwin** lyric that consisted essentially of fifty-four multi-syllabic names of Russian composers; Kaye reeled it off in thirty-eight seconds (according to one count) and stopped the show.

As a result of his Broadway success, Kaye was signed to a film contract by **Samuel Goldwyn** and made his feature film debut in 1943's *Up in Arms*. He made several more films for Goldwyn, playing sweet *schlemiels* who are inveigled into masquerades that involve unlikely derring-do and musical numbers (including a Kaye patter number, usually written by his wife, Sylvia Fine) before the happy ending. Kaye's most famous musical films include *Hans Christian Andersen* (1952) and *White Christmas* (1954). His other important films include *The Secret Life of Walter Mitty* (1947); *The Inspector General* (1949), based on Gogol's famous 1836 comedy of the same title; and *Me and the Colonel* (1958), based on Franz Werfel's 1944 play *Jacobowsky and the Colonel*. But by the late 1950s Kaye began devoting more time to world travel on behalf of UNICEF than to advancing his career.

Kaye's non-charitable professional work received a substantial boost when he became host of a weekly variety show on CBS, "The Danny Kaye Show," which ran from 1963 to 1967, winning both an Emmy and a Peabody. He returned to Broadway in 1970 in *Two by Two* (one of **Richard Rodgers**' last scores).

KING, ALAN (1927–)

Comedian, actor, producer

Born Irwin Alan Kniberg, Alan King began his career in show business as a musician at age fifteen, then became a stand-up comic working the Borscht Belt hotels. His acerbic take on the then burgeoning suburbia made him a comedy star on the nightclub and TV variety show circuit. He has made numerous film appearances, most memorably as the mordant Reform rabbi who hires Ron Silver to write for him in *Enemies, a Love Story* (1989). King is a tireless fund-raiser for Jewish causes and in recent years has branched out professionally to including producing among his many talents.

LAHR, BERT (1895–1967)

Actor

Best known as the Cowardly Lion in the film *The Wizard of Oz* (1939), Bert Lahr (born Irving Lahrheim) was one of the most versatile products of burlesque and two-a-day vaudeville. Like so many of his contemporaries, he began his career in vaudeville as a boy, but his greatest success was neither in vaudeville nor in films. Lahr was one of the great clowns of the Broadway musical theater—a rubber-faced comic with a wild series of vocal tricks in his repertoire—and a superb physical comic as well. Yet he was capable of moments of strange poignancy, as Samuel Beckett must have realized when he and director Alan Schneider cast Lahr as Vladimir in the American production of *Waiting for Godot*. His son, John Lahr, is a distinguished drama critic, as well as the author of a memorable biography of Bert, *Notes on a Cowardly Lion* (1969).

LEAR, NORMAN (1922–)

Writer, producer, civil liberties activist

Norman Lear might rightly be called the man who altered the face of television comedy forever. Before Lear's "All in the Family," "Maude," and "Mary Hartman, Mary Hartman," situation comedies focused on "wacky" antics of clowns like Lucille Ball or the rather predictable material of family sitcoms like "Father Knows Best" or "Leave it to Beaver." With "All in the Family," Lear introduced such unlikely subjects for comedy as racism, anti-Semitism, abortion, and homosexuality.

Lear returned to the United States after serving in the Army Air Force in World War II, determined to succeed as a comedy writer. His homecoming anticipated the rise of television, and his career trajectory coincides with the history of the medium. In 1959 he began a partnership with Bud Yorkin, with Lear writing and producing and Yorkin directing both for television and theatrical films. The real breakthrough came with "All in the Family"s' Archie Bunker. As played by Caroll O'Connor, Archie was the stereotypical working-class Queens bigot, a character that had never been seen on television before. Lear reversed field with "Maude," a series centering on a West Side liberal feminist. With "Mary Hartman, Mary Hartman," Lear took on the television medium itself with a dead-pan, dead-on parody of the daytime small-town soap opera.

In 1980, with the Reagan landslide powered by the Moral Majority, Lear decided to put his media savvy and power to practical political use, founding People for the American Way. The group quickly became one of the key civil liberties organizations in the country, focusing more on building grassroots support of the First Amendment than more law-oriented groups like the ACLU. It was an integral part of the coalition that blocked Robert Bork's confirmation as a Supreme Court Justice.

Lear has continued to produce, most recently filling executive producer duties on *The Princess Bride* (1987), *Fried Green Tomatoes* (1991), and *Way Past Cool* (1998).

LEWIS, JERRY (1926–)

Actor, comedian

Legendary comedian Jerry Lewis was born Joseph Levitch in Newark, New Jersey, into a show business family and began performing early in life. He quit school at sixteen and began working as a solo act. In 1946, at twenty, he met and teamed up with singer Dean Martin. Success followed quickly and grew when they began doing television appearances on Ed Sullivan's "Toast of the Town" and **Milton Berle**'s "The Texaco Star Theater." After hosting their own television and radio shows, the team became hugely successful in films such as *At War with the Army* (1951) and *Hollywood or Bust* (1956). After that film, Martin and Lewis split up the partnership.

Throughout the rest of the 1950s and the 1960s, Lewis appeared on his own in comedy films such as *The Bellboy* (1960) and *Which Way to the Front* (1970). On many of his films, he served as writer, director, and/or producer as well. Because of the demand for sex and violence during the seventies, Lewis took a break from making movies. More of his energies were devoted to the Muscular Dystrophy Association, for which he had been hosting telethons for some years and of which he became national chair.

When Lewis returned to films in the 1980s, he began to perform in dramatic as well as comic roles. His performance in *The King of Comedy* (1983), as an abrasive stand-up comedian, was highly praised. Lewis is an international star whose movies are even more popular abroad, in countries like France, than in the United States.

LEWIS, SHARI (1934–1998)

Ventriloquist, television performer, conductor

The world's most delightful sock handler, Shari Lewis (born Phyllis Hurwitz) began performing at the age of thirteen with the encouragement of her parents, Ann Ritz Hurwitz, a piano teacher and president of her **Hadassah** chapter, and her father Abraham B. Hur-

Shari Lewis' career started in 1948 when she appeared in a local NBC show in New York and pulled a rabbit out of a hat. Her magician father (also a professor at Yeshiva University) had taught her the trick only the day before. She said of her 1995 Chanukah special: "A Jew has to put the menorah in the window. I am very much putting my menorah in the window with this show." (Courtesy of Shari Lewis)

witz, a professor at **Yeshiva University** (and a noted magician). Her professional career began when, at eighteen, she and her puppets won first prize on Arthur Godfrey's "Talent Scouts" show on television. Four years later, she made an appearance on "Captain Kangaroo" and, by 1960, she had her own children's show. After three successful years, during which her puppet Lamb Chop was joined by Charlie Horse and Hush Puppy, the show became a casualty of the increasing popularity of animated cartoons.

Following the cancellation of the show and for the next twenty-seven years, Lewis did television specials and developed a second career as a conductor of symphony orchestras. She also performed in touring companies of Broadway shows and had her own television series in England. In 1990 Shari Lewis and Lamb Chop returned to American television in "Lamb Chop's Play-Along" on Public Broadcasting.

A Hand Puppet Testifies Before Congress

In 1993 Sheri Lewis testified before the House Telecommunications Subcommittee, strongly arguing that the Children's Television Act of 1990 should be strengthened. Let's let Lewis' *New York Times* obituary tell the rest of the story. ". . . [Lewis] then informed Representative Edward Markey, a Democrat from Massachusetts and chairman of the subcommittee, that Lamb Chop (her hand puppet) wanted to testify, too. Mr. Markey readily agreed.

"Lamb Chop turned to Ms. Lewis and said, 'O.K., you can go now.'

" 'If I go, you don't talk,' Ms. Lewis replied.

"So Ms. Lewis remained and Lamb Chop, who always rose to the occasion, gave an impassioned speech about the need for government to care about children and children's television and to protect young viewers from junk."

Lewis and the show won numerous awards for quality broadcasting, including twelve Emmys. Her holiday TV specials included "Lamb Chop's Special Chanukah" (1995, produced by Lewis' daughter, Mallory), which was released as a video in 1996 and won the Parent's Choice award, and "Shari's Passover Surprise." Her book *One-Minute Jewish Stories* was published in 1989. She died of uterine cancer in Los Angeles on August 2, 1998.

LOEB, PHILIP (1894–1955)

Actor, McCarthy era casualty

Actor Philip Loeb was born in 1894 in Philadelphia. After attending the University of Pennsylvania, he studied at the American Academy of Dramatic Arts and debuted on the New York stage in 1916. He had a long and distinguished career in the theater including a five-year stint with the historic Theatre Guild. In the 1930s he branched out into film and, later, television. At the height of his career, Loeb starred opposite **Gertrude Berg** in the play *Me and Molly*, as Jake Goldberg. When the play was adapted as the television situation comedy "The Goldbergs," Loeb again took on the role of Jake. At the time the show premiered, however, McCarthyism was rampant in the country, and Loeb was soon accused of being a Communist. He was fired from the show, which was then canceled, although it was the most popular sitcom on television at the time. Another network picked it up, without Loeb. Blacklisted and unable to find work, Loeb committed suicide in 1955.

LOEW, MARCUS (1870–1927)

Movie executive

Marcus Loew was born in New York City on May 7, 1870. At the age of nine he dropped out of school in order to support his family. His first business success was in the fur trade. With the profits from his fur business, he began buying nickelodeons. By 1905 he owned a chain. He then began purchasing combined vaudeville/movie theaters.

In 1920 he bought his first movie production house, Metro Pictures Corporation. Four years later he absorbed Goldwyn Pictures Corporation. In 1925 Louis B. Mayer Pictures joined with Loew and the company officially became Metro-Goldwyn-Mayer, Inc. Marcus Loew died in New York City on September 5, 1927. A pioneer in the early movie industry, he was an enormous financial success. In the years after his death, MGM became the largest movie production company in the world.

LUMET, SIDNEY (1924–)

Filmmaker

Sidney Lumet's career has spanned a wide range of popular American forms, from Yiddish theater to live television, radio drama to star-studded Hollywood spectaculars. His parents, Baruch Lumet and Eubgenia Wermus, were veterans of the Yiddish stage and put their boy on stage almost as soon as he could walk. At four Sidney was appearing on radio, at five on the boards of the Yiddish Art Theatre. He appeared in several Broadway plays, including *Dead End*. He went to

Columbia, the war came, and all that seemed to be over, a dream of childhood.

Lumet served four years in the Burma theater of operations as a radar repairman and came back to the States in 1946. He started an off-Broadway theater group and taught acting at the High School of Performing Arts. In 1950 a new medium beckoned; Lumet took a job with CBS in its nascent television drama department and quickly established himself as one of the top directors of live television.

In 1957 he became one of the first to make the leap from live television to feature films, directing a big-screen adaptation of a teleplay, *Twelve Angry Men*. Benefiting from the experience of working on a shoestring budget and slender schedule, Lumet was able to shoot the entire film in nineteen days. The result won the novice film director the Directors Guild Award and an Oscar nomination (one of the rare occasions on which the Academy did not give the Best Director award to the Guild honoree).

Lumet began working exclusively in film, albeit with mixed results. The next of his efforts to merit critical acclaim was a faithful adaptation of *Long Day's Journey into Night* with Katharine Hepburn, Ralph Richardson, and Jason Robards. Lumet, a staunch liberal, began to express himself more openly in his work. *Fail-Safe* (1964) and *The Pawnbroker* (1965) bespeak his commitment to a progressive vision of the world, with their heart-on-the-sleeve opposition to the nuclear arms race and the decay of the inner cities. Some critics have found fault with Lumet's use of the Holocaust survivor in the latter film as an exponent of a very Christian view of expiation of sin, and some have accused the film of trivializing the Shoah in order to preach about New York's ghettoes.

Lumet's career went into a sort of limbo of steady work with little substance. It was not until 1973 and *Serpico* that he found a subject and theme—police corruption in the multiracial stewpot of New York City—that led to some of his most memorable work. He returned to the subject in *Prince of the City* (1981), *Q and A* (1990), and *Night Falls on Manhattan* (1997). Lumet also won acclaim for his direction of *Network* (1976) and *The Verdict* (1982). He continues to work steadily, in no small part because he still shoots quickly, bringing films in ahead of schedule and under budget.

MARX BROTHERS, THE

Actors, musicians

The Marx Brothers Chico/Leonard (1891–1961); Harpo/Adolph (1893–1964); Groucho/Julius (1890–1977); Gummo/Milton (1894–1977); and Zeppo/Herbert (1901–1979) dispensed their blend of splendid anarchy in vaudeville, on Broadway, radio, in film, and television for over sixty years. That they were able to enjoy such success is largely attributable to the iron will of their mother, Minnie, who pushed their careers forward with implacable intensity.

The five brothers (a sixth, Manfred, died in 1888 at the age of three) were born to a poor couple, German Jewish immigrants who moved all over New York City, often one step ahead of rent collectors. Their father Samuel was a feckless soul, a well-meaning but untalented tailor (family legend has it that he was the inspiration for the vaudeville hit "Sam You Made the Pants Too Long"). Minnie had enough drive for the two of them and her brother was the highly successful vaudevillian Al Shean, a popular Jewish dialect comic. Uncle Al was always good for advice, material for the act, and the occasional dollar. Minnie's ambition was for each of her boys to follow Uncle Al's example of show business success and, by dint of her tremendous energy, they eventually did.

It was an era in which one bought an act ready-made or stole material mercilessly from more successful acts. The Marxes began with a combination of the two, a "school" act that was equal parts musical material (Julius was a gifted boy tenor, Leonard could play the piano) and feeble gags set in a one-room schoolhouse. The boys drifted in and out of the act; Milton hated being on stage and would quickly abandon show business, while his siblings would each try his hand at other vaudeville settings intermittently. Eventually, they discovered a talent and taste for ad-libbing, and the act began to attract attention, getting better bookings until it was working the top circuit. By 1919 they were playing the most famous venue in vaudeville, the Palace Theater in New York City. Somewhere along the way, supposedly in a poker game with comic Art Fisher in 1914, the boys picked up the nicknames under which they would become famous, and the characters that they would develop into much-beloved and often parodied icons: Groucho, the prowling con man with the quick quip and long cigar; Harpo, the angelic-looking mute with the car horn under his capacious raincoat; Chico, the Italian-dialectic wise guy in the porkpie hat; and Zeppo, poor bland Zeppo, playing straight man to his brothers until he could not stand it anymore and joined Gummo in business.

Success in vaudeville catapulted the Marx Brothers to Broadway. They had three successive hits: *I'll Say She Is* (1924), *The Coconuts* (1925), and *Animal Crackers* (1928). At a time when Paramount still had sound stages in Astoria, Queens, they were able to shoot their first two movies, *The Coconuts* (1929) and *Animal Crackers* (1930), while maintaining their comfortable lives in the city. But when Hollywood beckoned—the first two films were highly successful and Paramount wanted more—they surrendered to the inevitable and moved west.

The Marx Brothers' Paramount films are as close as we are likely to get to a glimpse of their stage act. The best of them, *Duck Soup* (1932), is the shortest (only seventy-two minutes) and most compact, and their only film with a first-rank director, Leo McCarey. But the sheer sustained lunacy of the Paramount films was too much for Depression-era audiences, who were flocking to the likes of Shirley Temple. Paramount dropped the boys' option; they were picked up by MGM and its "boy genius" Irving Thalberg.

Thalberg envisioned a different formula for the team; stronger plots, more musical numbers for romantic leads, the Marx Brothers as comic foils to serious romance between the likes of Allan Jones and Kitty Carlisle. In retrospect, this formula does not hold up well: one sits through Jones and Carlisle, waiting for the next outburst of Marxian mayhem. But it was a commercial success. *A Night at the Opera* (1935) and *A Day at the Races* (1937) rebuilt the Brothers' reputation

at the box office. They continued making films, with decreasing budgets and success, until 1949's dismal *Love Happy*. What kept them working was Chico's compulsive gambling. With their middle brother always in debt, Groucho and Harpo felt responsible for helping him make money.

Each of the three maintained artistic interests outside their films, too. Chico had a successful dance band. Groucho wrote humorous books and eventually tried his hand at television. Harpo gave occasional recitals on his harp but preferred to spend most of his free time either on the golf course or with his wife and children, gracefully easing into retirement while his older brothers kept working. Groucho enjoyed the greatest success after the brothers stopped working together, with his long-running TV game show, "You Bet Your Life," and frequent guest appearances on other television shows and in the occasional movie.

MASON, JACKIE (1934–)

Comedian

Jackie Mason (Yacov Moshe Maza), archetypal New York Jewish comedian, was born in Sheboygan, Wisconsin. Fortunately for American comedy, his family moved to New York City when he was five, and he grew up on the Lower East Side. He began his adult life as a rabbi and did not become a professional comic until after his father died in 1957. Beginning on the Borscht Belt circuit, he went on to New York City nightclubs. A course of psychoanalysis helped him personally and also influenced his comedy. He developed an intricate monologue style that seems to be stream of consciousness but is really more like a long Talmudic argument with life.

In 1960 appearances on Steve Allen's "Tonight Show" boosted Mason to the top nightclubs and other television shows. A misunderstanding with Ed Sullivan in 1964 badly damaged the young comic's career. For the next decade, everything that could go wrong for Mason did. In the early 1970s he found himself at the bottom again, working his way up. After another decade of club appearances and television guest shots and an occasional movie role, he opened his one-man show, *The World According to Me* in Hollywood and then Beverly Hills. In December of 1986, the show premiered on Broadway. It was a huge success, and his career was back, bigger and better than ever. He is now widely recognized as one of the most talented, intelligent, and important Jewish comedians.

MATTHAU, WALTER (1920–)

Actor

Hollywood's most beloved grouch, Walter Matthau, was born Walter Matuschanskayasky to a Russian Jewish father and a Lithuanian Jewish mother in New York. Reared by his mother on the Lower East Side, he began studying acting after serving in the army in World War II. His first Broadway job was understudying seven different roles in *Anne of a Thousand Days* (1948), but recognition came in *Will Success Spoil Rock Hunter?* (1955).

Matthau began appearing in films that same year and worked regularly throughout the fifties and early sixties in both Hollywood and New York. In 1965 he was cast in Neil Simon's *The Odd Couple* and made an outstanding success of the role of easygoing, sardonic Oscar Madison. After a heart attack during the filming of *The Fortune Cookie* (1966), he began to work almost exclusively in films. He re-created his Oscar Madison role in the film version of *The Odd Couple* (1968) and then went on to triumph in *Hello, Dolly!* (1969). A string of hit movies followed—sometimes two or three a year—in which he consolidated his position as a top box office draw. In recent years he has teamed up with his *Odd Couple* co-star, Jack Lemmon, in a series of septuagenarian buddy movies, beginning with *Grumpy Old Men* (1995).

MAY, ELAINE (1932–)

Comedian, screenwriter, director

Half of one of the most successful American comic teams of the 1950s and 1960s (the other was **Mike**

How did such a nice Jewish couple end up in show business? Walter Matthau's first performance was in a Yiddish play at the age of eleven. Elaine May's father was an actor in Yiddish theater and, as a child, she made several stage and radio appearances with him. They are shown here some years later in a scene from the film A New Leaf *(1971). It was written and directed by May. (Private Collection)*

Nichols—the two were described as "the world's fastest humans"), one of Hollywood's first important female directors in the 1970s and 1980s, Elaine May has come into the 1990s as a "superstar" screenwriter. Born Elaine Berlin in Philadelphia, May grew up in the theater; the daughter of Yiddish actor Jack Berlin, she appeared with her father on stage many times while still a child. It was not unexpected that when she went into a tailspin after a failed teenage marriage, she would study acting as a refuge. While a student at the University of Chicago, she met another Jewish student, Mike Nichols, and the two began working together as an improvisational comedy duo. The result was one of the legendary comic pairs in American theater history. They reached their peak with a hit Broadway performance in 1960, *An Evening with Mike Nichols and Elaine May.*

But centrifugal career forces were already coming into play as that apex was achieved. The pair split the following year, with each pursuing a career in writing and directing. May appeared in two films as an actress, *Enter Laughing* and *Luv*, then began directing theater. She made her film directing debut in 1971 with the critical success *A New Leaf*, in which she played the leading role and for which she wrote the screenplay.

Her next film, *The Heartbreak Kid* (1972), was both a critical and financial success. It also earned her daughter, Jeannie Berlin (who plays a stereotypical Jewish American Princess whose husband leaves her three days into their honeymoon for a non-Jewish society girl), an Oscar nomination. After some low-profile uncredited script doctoring work (on *Such Good Friends* and *Tootsie*), and a co-writing credit on *Heaven Can Wait* (for which she and Warren Beatty were nominated for the Writing Oscar), she established herself as a force in the film industry. She continued to act, appearing in *California Suite* (1978) and *In the Spirit* (1990). On the stage, she reunited with Mike Nichols in a production of *Who's Afraid of Virginia Woolf* (1980). During the 1990s she has concentrated on writing, including a collaboration with **Woody Allen** and **David Mamet** on *Death Defying Acts*, a trio of one-act plays that appeared off Broadway. She revised the screenplay for Nichols' 1994 film *Wolf* and they paired up as writer and director again for *The Birdcage* in 1996. Just as "zipper-gate" was sweeping the country, their version (again with May writing and Nichols directing) of Joe Klein's novel *Primary Colors* (staring John Travolta as the presidential candidate and Emma Thompson as his wife) hit the theaters.

MAYER, LOUIS B. (1885–1957)

Movie mogul

The archetypal movie mogul, Louis B. Mayer, began his working career as a scrap dealer. Later, when it became possible to be a movie theater manager by renting a storefront and hanging up a sheet for a screen, he went into the motion picture business. In 1924 he founded Metro-Goldwyn-Mayer with **Samuel Goldwyn**. When Goldwyn left a few years later, Mayer began to develop a reputation as one of the most colorful figures in an industry known for its color. He paid great attention to every detail of his movies, but his goal was not necessarily quality. He wanted to make the pictures Americans would want to watch—clean, sentimental, and supporting at every turn "American family values." He had great respect for talent and once said, "We are the only kind of company whose assets all walk out of the gate at night," but he was also tyrannical in his rule of MGM.

Mayer's astounding stable of stars included Greta Garbo, Wallace Beery, Joan Crawford, Clark Gable, Jean Harlow, John and Lionel Barrymore, William Powell, W. C. Fields, Errol Flynn, Rosalind Russell, Spencer Tracy, Ingrid Bergman, Greer Garson, Gene Kelly, Mickey Rooney, Judy Garland, **John Garfield**, Elizabeth Taylor, and literally hundreds of others whose names are legendary. He was responsible for many of the best and a few of the worst films to come out of Hollywood.

MAZURSKY, PAUL (1930–)

Director, writer, actor

One of Hollywood's most interesting directors, Paul Mazursky, began his career as an actor. After making his mark as a punk kid in *Blackboard Jungle* (1955), he found himself typecast and switched for a time to stand-up comedy. After about five years, he moved to California and got a job writing for **Danny Kaye**, which he continued to do for four years while he pursued his acting career. Then he co-wrote the screenplay for *I Love You Alice B. Toklas* (1968), which was a considerable success. This put him in the position to demand that he be allowed to direct his next screenplay, co-written with Larry Tucker. The resulting film, *Bob and Carol and Ted and Alice* (1970), was also very successful and garnered Academy Award nominations for screenplay, cinematography, and two of its acting performances.

Since then Mazursky has directed more than twenty films, ranging from the wildly funny *Moon over Parador* (1988) to the intensely dramatic *Enemies, A Love Story* (1989), based on **Isaac Bashevis Singer**'s Holocaust novel. His films have been commercially successful and include *Next Stop, Greenwich Village* (1976), *An Unmarried Woman* (1978), *Moscow on the Hudson* (1984), *Down and Out in Beverly Hills* (1986), and *Weapons of Mass Destruction* (1997). Most of them have also been critically acclaimed, and Mazursky has repeatedly been nominated for Oscars for his work as a director and writer.

MIDLER, BETTE (1945–)

Singer, actor

The Divine Miss M., Bette Midler, was born in Hawaii to the only Jewish family in a largely Asian community and began entertaining her peers as a key to acceptance. Her earliest professional performances were as an actor—she appeared in *Fiddler on the Roof* for three years—but fame came when she took a job singing at the Continental Baths. A Turkish bath in New York largely frequented by gay men, the Continental gave Midler an opportunity to develop her pull-out-all-the-stops style of performing. Billing herself as the Divine Miss M., she was soon appearing on the "Johnny Carson Show" and in a number of stage shows, including *Tommy* (1971) with the Seattle Opera Company and *Divine Madness* (1970) on Broadway. She also began recording and made her first important film, *The Rose* (1979).

Since her initial success in films, she has been active primarily in that medium. She has become a popular and critically acclaimed actor in such comedies as *Down and Out in Beverly Hills* and *Ruthless People*, both in 1986. In 1996 she co-starred with **Goldie Hawn** and Diane Keaton in the hugely successful *First Wives' Club.*

MOSTEL, ZERO (1915–1977)

Actor

The rotund comic actor Zero Mostel was born Samuel Joel Mostel in Brooklyn, New York. His poor grades at school earned him the nickname Zero. Yet he finished college and embarked on a career teaching art. He began performing in clubs in 1942 after his lectures on art became popular for their comic content. Within a few months he was on Broadway in the show *Keep 'Em Laughing* and in the film *Du Barry Was a Lady*. However, in the McCarthy era his left-leaning political activities led to an extended stint on the blacklist. His next success came in 1958 when he played Leopold Bloom in *Ulysses in Nighttown* off Broadway. The show that made him a star was Ionesco's *Rhinoceros* (1961), in which he played a clerk who turns into that animal. A year later, he was on Broadway in the musical comedy *A Funny Thing Happened on the Way to the Forum* (1962), performing with his close friend **Jack Gilford**.

Mostel went from success to success, starring next as Tevye in *Fiddler on the Roof* (1964), a role that would later be played by Herschel Bernardi and **Theodore Bikel**. For the next decade, until his death in 1977, he performed primarily in films, including the filmed versions of *A Funny Thing Happened on the Way to the Forum* (1966) and *Rhinoceros* (1974). One of his biggest triumphs was in the **Mel Brooks** comedy *The Producers* (1968) with **Gene Wilder**.

MUNI, PAUL (1895–1967)

Actor

Paul Muni enjoyed the greatest and most sustained success in mainstream American culture of the actors who made their start on the Yiddish stage. A versatile actor who was equally at home on the boards and in front of a movie camera, he was one of the great Jewish stars of the early sound era and, although much of his work looks dated and stiff today, his importance in opening doors for others cannot be underestimated.

Muni was the son of traveling Yiddish actors, born

Muni Weisenfreund in what is now Lvov, Russia. As is so often the case in such families, the child quickly went from "born in a trunk" to part of the act; young Weisenfreund joined his parents on stage while still a boy. When he was seven, the family immigrated to the United States, settling on the Lower East Side. Weisenfreund returned to the stage when he was twelve, never to leave it again. When his father died six years later, he became sole support of the family, a traveling player once more.

In 1918 the young Muni joined the Yiddish Art Theater, **Maurice Schwartz**'s prestigious troupe. For the next eight years, he worked—and learned—under the great Schwartz, playing the classics and serious contemporary drama. He also had honed his English skills and in 1926 he made his Broadway debut in *We Americans*. His next role, as an ex-convict in *Four Walls*, alerted Hollywood to his gifts and he signed a contract with Fox. But his two Fox films were not successful, although he was nominated for an Oscar for his debut in *The Valiant* (1929), and Muni returned to the stage.

By now he was a fixture on Broadway, and his next role, as the brilliant but beleaguered Jewish attorney in **Elmer Rice**'s *Counsellor-at-Law* (1931–1933), was his greatest success to date. Hollywood beckoned again. His next two film roles were his best, as the murderous Tony Camonte in Howard Hawks's classic *Scarface* (1932), and in the lead role in Mervyn LeRoy's *I Am a Fugitive from a Chain Gang* (1932). Now under contract to Warner Brothers, Muni played a series of wildly different roles, first working-class tough guys in typical social dramas like *Black Fury* (1935), then in historical roles like *The Story of Louis Pasteur* (1936), for which he won an Oscar, and *The Life of Emile Zola* (1937). It was the latter genre that appealed to Muni, with its didactic strain. Films like *Juarez* (1939) and *The Good Earth* (1939) haven't aged well, and Muni's make-up-heavy performances look stilted today, but in their time they were important for the progressive message they carried and respected for their good intentions.

By the 1940s Muni's brand of liberalism had worn out its box-office welcome and he returned once more to the theater, his first love (although he made films intermittently for the remainder of his career). He en-

joyed considerable success in *Key Largo* (1939) and *Inherit the Wind* (1955) on Broadway, before returning to the screen for one final role, as a benevolent Jewish doctor in *The Last Angry Man* (1959).

MYERSON, BESS (1924–)

Miss America, television personality, consumer advocate

The first Jewish Miss America was born in New York City to Russian immigrant parents and lived in the Sholom Aleichem Cooperative. She first encountered serious anti-Semitism after she was chosen Miss America of 1945, an experience that moved her to begin touring as a speaker for the **Anti-Defamation League**. In 1951, she began her television career as the "Lady in Mink" for a game show called "The Big Payoff" (1951–59). She also became a regular panelist on "I've Got a Secret" (1958–67). From 1954 until 1968, she was co-host of the Miss America Pageant. In 1969 New York City's mayor John Lindsay appointed her Commissioner of the Department of Consumer Affairs. In the four years she remained in that office, she created the most effective consumer protection agency in the country. A few years later, she wrote the book *The Complete Consumer* (1979).

In 1980 Myerson made a bid for the Democratic nomination for the United States Senate but was unsuccessful. Three years later she was appointed New York City's Commissioner of Cultural Affairs, a position she held for four years. She left that post when she was accused of misconduct in connection with her companion Andy Capasso. She was indicted on six counts and acquitted of them all. She then retired from public life. Throughout her career, she has been a powerful advocate for Jewish causes, serving at one time as the national commissioner of the ADL.

NICHOLS, MIKE (1931–)

Actor, director

Mike Nichols was born Michael Igor Peschkowsky, the son of an anti-Nazi Russian Jewish doctor in

Berlin. With the rise of the Nazis, life became difficult for the family and they fled to the United States in 1937. When Nichols was twelve, his father died suddenly, leaving the family in dire financial straits. But he was an unusually bright and gifted student and a hard worker. With a combination of odd jobs and scholarships, he was able to continue his education, going to the University of Chicago, where he joined forces with **Elaine May** and the two began working as an improvisational duo. They also teamed up with **Alan Arkin**, Paul Sills, and Barbara Harris to begin a cabaret comedy group, the Compass. Nichols and May went on the road as a team and enjoyed considerable success with their mordant satirical show, finally reaching Broadway in 1960 with a show entitled *An Evening with Mike Nichols and Elaine May*. They split up after the show closed and, after another play in which he was acting flopped out of town, Nichols reluctantly agreed to direct a Broadway-bound piece, *Barefoot in the Park*, written by a little-known ex-television writer, **Neil Simon**.

Needless to say, the show was a huge success and Nichols found himself a director in demand. He followed up that hit with two more, *Luv* and *The Odd Couple*. Hollywood came calling, and he made his film directing debut with *Who's Afraid of Virginia Woolf?* (1966), which won five Academy Awards. He followed it with *The Graduate* for which he won an Academy Award for best director, launching both himself and **Dustin Hoffman** to the "A" list. Subsequent films he directed and/or produced include *Catch-22* (1970), *Silkwood* (1983), *Working Girl* (1988), and *Postcards from the Edge* (1990).

In the 1980s Nichols successfully returned to the theater, with a production of *Waiting for Godot* starring Robin Williams and Steve Martin and a Tony-winning production of Tom Stoppard's *The Real Thing*. He also has begun performing again, winning plaudits for his acting in *The Designated Mourner* (1997). He worked again with Elaine May in the 1990s, most notably on *The Birdcage*, which he directed and produced and she wrote, and *Primary Colors*, which she wrote and he directed.

NIMOY, LEONARD (1931–)

Actor, director, writer

Until he won the role of Mr. Spock on the TV series "Star Trek," Leonard Nimoy's career was utterly forgettable, consisting of minor roles in such films as *Francis Goes to West Point* (1952) and the serial *Zombies of the Stratosphere* (1952). Nimoy was raised in a middle-class Jewish home in Boston, went to Boston College and Antioch, and trained at the well-regarded Pasadena Playhouse. He did not lack for serious ambition, even co-producing a film of Jean Genet's *Deathwatch* in 1966.

But it was "Star Trek" and the pointy-eared half-human rationalist Spock that made him a star and a cult figure. In addition to the three-year run of the show (1966–69), Nimoy returned to the role in six *Star Trek* movies, directing *Star Trek IV*. That launched one of several new careers for Nimoy, who subsequently directed several other films, including *Three Men and a Baby* (1987) and *The Good Mother* (1988). He also has published several volumes of poetry and two books of memoirs. More recently, Nimoy

The Vulcan Shalom

Actor Leonard Nimoy is best known as Mr. Spock, the pointy-eared half human/half alien in "Star Trek." The child of Russian Jewish immigrants, he reflected on "What Being Jewish Means to Me" in the nationally syndicated advertisement sponsored by The American Jewish Committee.

"When I was a boy, there was a particular blessing used in our local shul. The four fingers of each hand were split to create the Hebrew letter *shin*, representing Shad-dai, the name of the Almighty. When we were creating the television program 'Star Trek,' we needed a salute. I thought back to that hand symbol and proposed it. The rest, as they say, is history.

"Why did I think back to that hand gesture? Actors are always looking for something personal to bring to their professional lives. Maybe, then, it was the convergence of my spiritual and artistic lives. Maybe, in a way, I can call that salute my Vulcan shalom, my greeting of peace, my yearning for the blessing of peace—the age-old quest of the Jewish people, my people."

has also become actively involved in public radio, hosting and producing a series of programs of great Jewish short stories. At the same time, he has sought out other opportunities to reaffirm his Jewish identity in his work, most notably in a TV film based on the true story of an Auschwitz survivor who sued Holocaust deniers successfully in California. In 1997 he narrated the film *A Life Apart: Hasidism in America.*

PALEY, WILLIAM (1901–1990)

Television executive

The powerful and difficult CEO of the CBS media empire, William Paley was born in 1901, the son of a Ukrainian Jewish immigrant who built a small cigar shop into the successful Congress Cigar Company. In 1926 the family sold most of their shares in the company and William Paley started his business life with a nest egg of $1 million. In 1928 he used half the money to buy into a fledgling radio company, United Independent Broadcasters (UIB), which ran the Columbia Broadcasting System (CBS). The same year, Paley became the president of UIB.

In 1948 Paley expanded into the new medium of television, creating CBS TV, which soon became the shining star of the television world. Almost immediately ranked as the top television network, CBS stayed there for two decades. The network's most successful shows included "Gunsmoke," "I Love Lucy," and "All in the Family." Its roster of stars was filled with some of the legends of early television, including Edward R. Murrow, Walter Cronkite, **Jack Benny**, and Ed Sullivan. In the 1960s Paley began to branch out beyond television and radio. CBS acquired companies as diverse as the New York Yankees, Creative Playthings, and Fender Guitars. Paley also added new divisions within the company such as CBS Records.

In the 1970s CBS's position at the top ended. In 1976 the network dropped from first place in the ratings and Paley's acquisitions were not proving to be the success he had hoped. In 1985 Paley's position as CEO was taken over by mogul **Larry Tisch**. Paley is sometimes credited with founding CBS, but it was already in existence when he bought into UIB. He did, however, revolutionize the company, building it into one of the largest and most powerful media conglomerates in the world. Paley died in October 1990.

PERLMAN, RHEA (1948–)

Actor

The woman who made feisty Italian Carla Tortelli a television icon was born into a Jewish family in Coney Island, Brooklyn, and grew up in Bensonhurst. After Hunter College, she became active in off-off-Broadway theater, where she met her future husband Danny DeVito. When DeVito became a regular on television's "Taxi" (1978–83), Perlman snared the job of his girlfriend Zena. Her occasional appearances in that role led to her casting on "Cheers." During the course of the hit series, she won three Emmy Awards for Best Supporting Actress in a comedy (1984, 1985, and 1986) for the quirkily sexy waitress and mother with a sharp tongue. The role was a classic example of a Jewish actor's portrayal of an "acceptably ethnic" character, frequently, as in this case, Italian.

During and after "Cheers," Perlman began to appear in feature films, including *The Ratings Game* (1984), *Over Her Dead Body* (1989), *There Goes the Neighborhood* (1992), *Radio Flyer* (1992), and *Ted and Venus* (1996). She is often directed in her films by husband DeVito. In 1996 she returned to television in another situation comedy, "Pearl." This time she played the starring role of a woman with a grown son who returns to college.

POLLACK, SYDNEY (1934–)

Film director

Hollywood director Sydney Pollack was born in South Bend, Indiana, on July 1, 1934. His first career was as an actor. In the early 1950s he appeared on Broadway and in television classics such as "Ben Casey" and "Playhouse 90." In the late 1950s he turned to television directing. His credits include "Naked City" (1958,

1960–63), "The Defenders" (1961–65), "Ben Casey" (1961–66), and "Dr. Kildare" (1961–66).

In 1965 Pollack made his first feature film, *The Slender Thread*. The following year he made *This Property Is Condemned*. *They Shoot Horses, Don't They* (1969) proved to be his first significant box-office success and established him as a major Hollywood player. His subsequent films are Hollywood classics and include *Jeremiah Johnson* (1972), *The Way We Were* (1973), *Three Days of the Condor* (1975), *Absence of Malice* (1981), *Tootsie* (1982), and *The Firm* (1993). In 1985 he won an Academy Award as best director for *Out of Africa*, and the film won the Academy Award for best picture.

RADIO

American Jews were central participants in the radio industry from its inception. They were instrumental in the creation and marketing of the medium in its early years and Jewish actors, performers, and comedians were at center stage when radio reached its peak of popularity in the 1930s and 1940s. Jews also played pioneering roles as producers of news and public affairs programming, as advertising executives, and in top-level network positions.

Russian Jewish immigrant **David Sarnoff** was instrumental in developing and refining the technology necessary to send radio waves over the air. He used his entrepreneurial talents to become general manager in 1921 of the Radio Corporation of America (RCA), the first significant radio network in the United States, which became incorporated as the National Broadcasting Corporation (NBC) five years later. William Paley, a descendant of German Jews, became president of the Columbia Broadcasting System (CBS) after he purchased half of the new network in 1928. He was the first person to establish news reporting as a key component of radio programming. Under his leadership CBS radio gained a reputation for groundbreaking coverage of current events, with the hiring of William Shirer and Edward R. Murrow and the live broadcast of Hitler's takeover of Austria.

The Iceberg, the Radio, and David Sarnoff

As the *Titanic* sank on the night of April 14, 1912, twenty-one-year-old David Sarnoff was at his wireless telegraph listening post atop the Wanamaker department store in New York for seventy-two uninterrupted hours, relaying to newspapers and frantic family members news of the sinking. This action made his career—and assured the future of radio communication. Wireless communication had, up to that time, been regarded as a novelty. Sarnoff's career took off with the new medium, and he rose to become chairman of the board of the Radio Corporation of America (RCA).

The early Jewish stars of radio were former stars from vaudeville and the stage who combined comedy with cabaret-style musical selections. **Ed Wynn** became one of the most notable of these early radio performers with the "Texaco Fire Chief" show premiering in 1932. Wynn was so popular that one newspaper reported he had helped America forget the Depression. However, his style of humor often depended on sight gags and he could not sustain his radio popularity. His program went off the air in three years.

Eddie Cantor broadcast in front of a live audience and created a variety show featuring other Jewish character actors, including Bert Gordon and Harry Einstein. Cantor had worked his way up from an impoverished background to an enormous success in radio and vaudeville. He brought the previously unknown Southern singer **Dinah Shore** to prominence. Her popularity on his program led to Shore's hosting her own radio musical series and then going on to similar success on television.

Another Jewish woman who achieved great fame in radio was comic actress **Fanny Brice**, whose character Baby Snooks became a staple of evening radio for over almost two decades. Unlike most radio comedians of that era, Brice originally began as a burlesque performer, where she refined her act and developed the character of Snooks, a young, impish Jewish girl, based on Brice's own family background.

No single individual enjoyed more success in radio than **Jack Benny**, whose program premiered in 1932 at

For a generation of Americans, Gertrude Berg embodied Jewish motherhood in a series of radio, television, stage, and film performances. She is shown here in a scene from the film Molly *(1951), presumably giving out a taste of chicken soup. (Private Collection)*

the same time as Wynn and Cantor and continued for a phenomenal twenty-three years. Benny's characters, his sense of timing, and his ability to understand how to use radio for maximum comic effect, all contributed to his enormous success. **Mel Blanc**, who later became known for his cartoon voices, worked with Benny on some of his most famous sketches.

George Burns, from a poor Russian Jewish family on the Lower East Side of New York City (like Cantor), went from hosting a comedy show to developing one of the first situation comedies in radio, playing the straight man to the hilarious malaprop humor of his wife, Gracie Allen, an Irish Catholic from California. The team of Burns and Allen and Jack Benny made the successful transition to television in the 1950s.

Other lesser-known Jewish stars, Joe Penner and Arthur Tracey, enjoyed brief popularity in what became known as radio's golden age during the Depression decade. The first radio comedy writers, David Freedman and Harry Conn, also began their careers writing material for vaudeville performers.

Although none of these radio personalities hid their Jewish identity, neither did they generally make it a major focus of their acts. Those who did create dis-

tinctly Jewish characters (like Brice) used them purely for comic effect. One of the most popular radio dramas, "The Goldbergs," written by and starring **Gertrude Berg** in the lead role of Molly Goldberg, created a serious character whose Jewish ethnicity and dialect informed and animated the program. "The Goldbergs"'s first episode was broadcast in 1929 one month after the stock market crash, and Berg's portrayal of working class Jewish life in the Tremont section of the Bronx struck a chord with Depression-era audiences. The program was successful, running on NBC for its first five years and then on CBS for seven more. Berg also presented the show live on tour in 1934 and later produced a Broadway play *Molly and Me* based on the radio series, before making the transition to television in 1949.

Berg drew on her own family history to develop sketches for "The Goldbergs." She also sought to present a gentle maternal image of Jewish identity to counteract some of the earlier harsher attempts at dialect humor in popular culture. In addition, Berg framed Molly's Jewish ethnicity as in harmony with rather than opposed to her status as an acculturated American. For non-Jewish audiences, Molly appeared to be the keeper of the immigrant dream while Berg's Jewish listeners sent her a flood of letters thanking her for creating a "positive" image of Jews that the Christian majority could embrace. Ironically, although Berg continued to achieve success with the program well into the television era, her co-star **Phillip Loeb** was blacklisted during the McCarthy era, dropped from the show, and (unable to find other work) subsequently committed suicide.

Norman Corwin established himself as an innovator in creating radio drama. From the late 1930s to the end of the next decade, Corwin produced and directed a weekly series on CBS called "Words without Music," which dramatized his own scripts fused with classic theater and poetry. Corwin's greatest talent was his versatility—he could be satiric one week and deadly serious the next. His most famous scripts, "Descent of the Gods," a parable about Greek gods visiting twentieth-century America, "They Fly through the Air," an attack on fascism, and his masterwork, "Satan's Plot to

Overthrow Christmas," all garnered both popular and critical acclaim. His production "We Hold These Truths," written to commemorate the anniversary of the Bill of Rights and aired one week after the Japanese bombing of Pearl Harbor on all four networks, reached the largest audience in the history of radio. Corwin's greatest achievement, however, may have been "On a Note of Triumph," a program designed to celebrate V-E Day that was praised by a number of writers including poet Carl Sandburg.

In 1930s and 1940s among the most listened to and influential voices on radio was **Walter Winchell**, a commentator on politics, current affairs, and celebrity gossip. Winchell, famous for his opening lines, "Hello again Mr. and Mrs. America and all the ships at sea," expressed his opinions with ferocity, treating his friends with devotion and his enemies with an often mean-spirited vindictiveness. Winchell, a staunch supporter of FDR's New Deal and an early advocate of American intervention in World War II, became an ardent supporter of anti-Communist Senator Joseph McCarthy after the war.

Radio also brought baseball, the great American pastime, to the public in a whole new way and created memorable images for its fans. Mel Allen, a German Jew originally from the South, became well known for his colorful national broadcasts of baseball games. He later gained fame in New York as the voice of the Yankees for three decades. Ben Bernie and Gabriel Heatter were other notable voices in radio during its golden age.

Paley and Sarnoff also attempted to introduce high art to radio audiences. While Paley was unsuccessful in getting the Metropolitan Opera on CBS, Sarnoff convinced Arturo Toscanini, the director of the New York Philharmonic, to perform for NBC radio in 1938—a practice Toscanini repeated to great acclaim for many years afterwards.

The large Jewish community in New York City supported a local radio station, WEVD, founded in 1927 by the influential Yiddish-socialist newspaper the *Jewish Daily Forward*. The station combined programs in Yiddish and English and brought quality educational and cultural programs to its mostly Jewish audience. But from the beginning WEVD also sought to reach out to the wide variety of immigrant communities in New York City, airing programs in Italian and Polish. As the Jewish population became acculturated in the years following World War II, WEVD increasingly used the English language for its programs on topics of Jewish interest, although the station continues to broadcast public affairs and music programs in Yiddish.

Radio's golden age ended with the advent of television in the late 1940s, but new and innovative programming continued with significant Jewish participation. Henry Morgan's wild, anarchic comedy became a celebrated fixture of post-war radio. Louis Cowan, later to become known for creating "The $64,000 Question" for television, produced a gospel program for CBS starring Mahalia Jackson, and a highly regarded public affairs discussion show called "Conversation." Cowan was also influential in pushing the network to hire African American actors on several of its dramatic series.

Himan Brown produced radio dramas that were best known for their innovative and pioneering uses of sound. Examples include "Inner Sanctum Mysteries," with its opening of a creaking door, and the detective program "Bulldog Drummond," which used the sound of footsteps and the blast of a foghorn. Brown achieved his greatest success with the mystery "Grand Central Station" and also brought Dashiel Hammet's novel *The Thin Man* to the radio in 1941. Even though radio changed drastically in the 1950s and 1960s, Brown continued to advocate bringing drama back to the airwaves, and he made his comeback in 1974 with "The CBS Radio Mystery Theater."

A new generation of Jewish writers, producers, and performers successfully made the transition to the new world of radio in the contemporary era. When rock 'n' roll emerged on the scene in the late 1950s as the soundtrack for a new generation, disk jockey Alan Freed became the new music's most enthusiastic supporter. He was one of its most compelling personalities until his indictment in the payola scandals of the early 1960s, which effectively ended both his career and his life. Murray Kaufman, better known as "Mur-

Howard Stern—The Radio Personality You Love to Hate

For over a decade Howard Stern has had the number-one-rated radio show in New York City. He has succeeded by offending everyone, with his inimitable brand of locker-room humor and private sexual fantasies. If an attitude is "politically correct," he will make fun of it endlessly on the air. If you are a well-known personality, you can be certain that Stern will crack jokes about the most intimate parts of your life for all to hear.

And, wouldn't you know it? He's Jewish. His mother's parents came to the United States from Austria-Hungary and he was raised in Long Island. "My parents were fluent in Yiddish," he told *The Jewish Week* in 1997. "Whenever they wanted to hide something from me, they would speak in Yiddish." Stern went to Hebrew school three days a week and had his bar mitzvah at the Roosevelt Jewish Center, a Conservative temple. But, ever an equal opportunity offender, his anti-Semitic remarks were once described by the Chicago regional director of the Anti-Defamation League as "noxious tirades." We won't repeat them.

ray the K," took up where Freed left off as one of the best known rock 'n' roll personalities of the 1950s and 1960s.

Jews also continued to be an important presence in radio news divisions. Fred Friendly (born Ferdinand Wachenheimer) who, along with Edward R. Murrow, pioneered on-air investigative journalism, served as president of the news division at CBS, along with Richard Salant. Friendly then went on to achieve recognition for his role in the creation of public broadcasting in America. Daniel Schorr became one of the most respected radio commentators in the country. Sander Vanocur and Marvin Kalb also made names for themselves in radio as well as television news. Frank Mankiewicz served a long tenure as president of National Public Radio.

As talk radio became more and more a staple of the medium in the 1970s, 1980s, and 1990s, the Jewish presence could also be felt, whether it was the probing Larry King or the outrageous Howard Stern, both of whom commanded massive audiences. In addition, one of the most well-known voices on the radio in the

1980s belonged to Holocaust refugee and sex therapist **Dr. Ruth Westheimer**.

Although syndicated radio programs have dwindled in number, Jewish participation both behind the mike and in upper level management positions continues in both locally and nationally produced programming. Jews have taken on important positions in the radio broadcasting hierarchy which, while providing them with another taste of the American dream, has also been fodder for the anti-Semitic feelings of those who claim that the Jews "control" the media.

Radio as it evolved in the United States would be unimaginable without Jewish involvement. In providing information, entertainment, news, and music, Jewish men and women helped establish the medium during its golden age and contributed to its transformation in the television era.

RADNER, GILDA (1946–1989)

Comedienne, actor

In her short life Gilda Radner provided the American public first with laughter, then with tears. Born in a upper-class suburb of Detroit, she was introduced early to the stage when her realtor father received complimentary tickets to touring shows from tenants in a hotel he owned and managed. Young Gilda discovered her own talents for comedy as a defense against the social rejection she experienced as, in her own words, "a very fat little girl." After a degreeless stint at the University of Michigan, Radner moved to Toronto, where she appeared in a production of the musical *Godspell.* She then joined the Canadian branch of the Second City comedy improvisation troupe based in Chicago. It was here she first worked with her future "Saturday Night Live" colleagues Bill Murray and Dan Aykroyd.

Back in the United States, she worked in radio and cabaret until October 18, 1975, when NBC's outlaw comedy "Saturday Night Live" premiered. The Not Ready for Prime Time Players included, in addition to Murray, Ackroyd, and Radner, John Belushi, Chevy Chase, Jane Curtin, Garrett Morris, and Laraine Newman. Radner's absurd, off-beat characters included smart-aleck newscaster Roseanne Roseanadanna; confused commentator on "Soviet Jewelry" and "endangered feces" Emily Litella; and nerdy teenager Lisa Loopner. In 1978 she was awarded an Emmy for her work, and in 1979 she took her characters to Broadway in *Gilda Radner—Live from New York*. The following year she married rock guitarist G. E. Smith, whom she later divorced. In 1984 Radner appeared in the film *The Woman in Red*, which was written and directed by her co-star **Gene Wilder**, whom she later married. Not long after her marriage, she was diagnosed with ovarian cancer. During her battle with this disease, she wrote the book *It's Always Something* (1989) and became the focus of a crusade against this deadly form of cancer. After her death in 1989, Wilder continued the crusade, helping to create a chain of "Gilda's Clubs" to serve as oases of support and consolation to cancer patients.

REINER, CARL (1922–)

Actor, writer, director

Carl Reiner is one of the many talented actors, writers, and directors to emerge from **Sid Caesar**'s stable of writers for "Your Show of Shows." Reiner got his start as a performer in his teens in a WPA Dramatic Workshop, then was part of a troupe of touring GI performers during World War II. When he came back to civilian life, he continued working steadily as an actor, before achieving real celebrity playing straight man to Caesar.

With his experience as a writer (as well as performer) on "Your Show of Shows," Reiner embarked on a two-track career. As a performer, he worked with **Mel Brooks** on their 2,000-Year-Old Man routines on records; as a producer, writer, and director (and also as a performer) he created the "Dick Van Dyke Show," winning eight Emmys for his work in various capacities between 1956 and 1967. Reiner also wrote a gently comic autobiographical novel, *Enter Laughing*, which he adapted for the stage and later the screen. It was with this project that he made his film directing debut.

Since then, he has continued to work regularly as both performer and director, creating a series of memorably funny films starring Steve Martin, teaming up again with Brooks periodically, and siring two directors, Lucas and **Rob Reiner**.

REINER, ROB (1945–)

Actor, director

Rob Reiner grew up in show business. As **Carl Reiner**'s son, he was bi-coastal at an early age and, after completing his studies at UCLA, hit the road as an actor, working steadily in stock and touring companies. He made his big-screen debut in his father's *Enter Laughing* (1967), but his big break came in 1971 when he began appearing as Carroll O'Connor's feisty son-in-law, Mike "Meathead" Stivic, on "All in the Family." He continued in that role through 1978.

Reiner branched out into directing in 1984 with his mock-documentary *This is Spinal Tap*. He followed that cult hit with a series of successful films, rapidly establishing himself as a director with a sure hand for either comedy or drama. Among his most popular films are *Stand by Me* (1986), *The Princess Bride* (1987), *When Harry Met Sally* (1989), and *The American President* (1995). He also continues to appear as an actor, most memorably in *Sleepless in Seattle* (1993).

RIVERS, JOAN (1933–)

Comedian

For many years, the boys' club of comedy had only one member who wore a skirt without being in drag. Joan Rivers was born Joan Alexander Molinsky in New York City and, under pressure from her mother, suppressed her acting ambitions to go into business after college. In 1958 she turned back to acting and then went into comedy a couple of years later, performing for a time with Chicago's Second City troupe. In 1962, influenced by **Lenny Bruce**, she began to develop a comedy style based on exploring painful parts of her own life. She also created a casual, gossipy persona that appealed greatly to audiences and, when she made an appearance on "The Tonight Show," to Johnny Carson.

With Carson as mentor, Rivers rose quickly in the comedy world, working in the top clubs and frequently guest hosting "The Tonight Show." In the early 1980s she began using her acid wit against others as well as herself. She became notorious for attacking the physical appearance of other women, such as Elizabeth Taylor, whose weight problems she brutally ridiculed. She also developed a penchant for plastic surgery. From 1983 until 1986, she was the permanent guest host of "The Tonight Show." When Carson changed that arrangement, naming a number of guest hosts, Rivers left to star in her own show opposite her old mentor. The show failed and she had incurred Carson's apparently undying enmity. In the 1990s she was again hosting her own show, a daytime shopping show. She has written or co-written a number of books, a syndicated column, and several screenplays, including *The Muppets Take Manhattan* (1984) and *Serial Mom* (1994). She has long supported Jewish causes and was once **Hadassah** Woman of the Year.

ROBINSON, EDWARD G. (1893–1973)

Actor

Edward G. Robinson was the frog-faced tough guy who graduated from playing gangsters to portray a fascinating range of patriarchs and thoughtful losers. One of the most instantly recognizable and often imitated actors in Hollywood for most of his career, he was also a serious student of his craft and dedicated art collector.

Robinson was born Emanuel Goldenberg in Bucharest, Romania, and was brought by his family to America when he was ten. An excellent student, Emanuel dreamed of pursuing a career as a lawyer or rabbi until he got the acting bug while an undergraduate at City College of New York. He earned a scholarship to the American Academy of Dramatic Arts, changed his name to Edward G. (for Goldenberg)

Robinson and began working in stock in 1913. Within two years he was on Broadway, and he would never look back. Through the 1920s he worked steadily on stage, even co-authoring a play with (soon-to-be-screenwriter) Jo Swerling, *The Kibitzer* (1929). He also had a brief supporting role in a 1923 silent film *The Bright Shawl*. But it was the advent of talkies, with their insatiable thirst for stage-trained actors, that brought Robinson to Hollywood to stay.

In 1931 Robinson starred for Warner Brothers in *Little Caesar*, one of the prototypical gangster films. Almost immediately he became a fixture at the studio, churning out A and B films with equal facility, often paired with other studio stalwarts like Humphrey Bogart. Robinson's homely physiognomy made him an unlikely candidate for romantic leads, but his acting talent and the broadening range that came with maturity made him an essential part of the studio's galaxy of stars. He moved from playing ethnic types such as a Portuguese fisherman in *Tiger Shark* (1932), and an Italian American gambler in *Barbary Coast* (1935) for Howard Hawks to comedy in *A Slight Case of Murder* (1938), a deliciously broad send-up of the Robinson gangster persona. He also played in the historical dramas *A Dispatch from Reuters* (1940) and *Dr. Ehrlich's Magic Bullet* (1940).

Robinson and Warner Brothers parted company at the beginning of the 1940s. He became an independent, working memorably in the noir classics *Double Indemnity* (1944), *Scarlet Street* (1946), and *The Woman in the Window* (1944). Returning to his old studio, he starred in *Key Largo* with its gangster clichés in 1948. His career was about to take a sudden and unexpected downturn.

A proudly self-identified Jew and vocal anti-Nazi, Robinson found himself accused of Communist sympathies at the outset of the 1950s. Eventually he would be called by the House Un-American Activities Committee before he was "cleared." In 1956 he was forced to sell his prized art collection as part of a divorce settlement. His son, Edward Jr., was a troubled young man who spent much of the decade in brushes with the law and suicide attempts. Robinson's primary form of consolation and therapy was to continue working. He returned to Broadway successfully in the 1956 drama *Middle of the Night* and continued working in films until his death in 1973, shortly before he was scheduled to receive a special Academy Award for career achievement.

ROSEANNE (1952–)

Comedian, actor

Born in Salt Lake City, Utah, on November 3, 1952, Roseanne Barr cites the tradition of Jewish comedy and growing up Jewish in a Mormon city as among the major forces that influenced her choice of careers. She began her working life as a waitress in a Denver restaurant. She did stand-up routines at a local comedy club before moving to Los Angeles and the Comedy Store. Her first appearance on "The Tonight Show" was in 1985 and signaled her rise to national attention. Three years later she premiered her sitcom "Roseanne," which ran for nine seasons and was unlike anything else on television. The show explored family life from a feminist, working class perspective at a time when the working class did not exist on television and most TV moms were still vacuuming in high heels. In 1993 she won a Best Actress Emmy Award for her performance. With a personal life as well known and controversial as her television characters, Roseanne has been married three times, first to Bill Petland, second to Tom Arnold, and most recently to Ben Thomas. She has written two autobiographies, *My Life as a Woman* (1989) and *My Lives* (1994).

SAHL, MORT (1927–)

Comedian

Mort Sahl revolutionized standup comedy, but he began as anything but a rebel. Born in Montreal, Canada, he belonged to ROTC in high school, served in the Air Force, and earned a degree in city management and traffic engineering. In the years immediately after college, he began to do comedy. By 1953 he was at the famous hungry i in San Francisco, performing the caustic, iconoclastic material that would influence the development of comedy in America. Instead of puns, jokes, and one-liners, he did topical, political, and social satire with a vicious bite. Not as self-destructive as **Lenny Bruce**, he was more in control of his anger. The anger, however, was there. He often asked his audiences, "Is there any group I haven't offended?"

Sahl became preoccupied with the assassination of President John F. Kennedy and what he considered to be the inadequacy of the Warren Report in the mid-1960s. He managed to alienate enough people that his career suffered for a number of years. However, history caught up with him. By the time Watergate came around, most of his audiences were as cynical as he was. He has enjoyed a good deal of popularity ever since, especially in Las Vegas and on college campuses. He has also appeared in a several films including *In Love and War* (1958) and *Nothing Lasts Forever* (1984). In 1987, he appeared in a one-man show entitled *Mort Sahl on Broadway.*

SARNOFF, DAVID (1891–1971)

Businessman

A self-educated pioneer in both radio and television, David Sarnoff was born in Uzlian, Minsk, Russia, on February 27, 1891. Before immigrating to the United States in 1905, Sarnoff studied to be a Talmudic scholar. After his father died in 1906, the possibility of continuing his formal education, religious or otherwise, ended, as he became the family's main source of income. After a series of odd jobs, Sarnoff bought a telegraph, taught himself Morse code, and became a telegraph and radio operator. He first came to national attention when he used his telegraph to report on the *Titanic* disaster, staying at his post for seventy-two hours straight. After these reports, he was offered a job with the American Marconi Corporation, which was later bought by the Radio Corporation of America (RCA).

Sarnoff's "radio music box" (the forerunner to

modern radio) was tested for the first time in 1921 when he transmitted a ringside account of the Carpentier-Dempsey boxing match. Already the general manager of RCA, he became the vice-president. In 1926 he founded NBC, a subsidiary of RCA, and by 1930 he was president of RCA. By 1939 Sarnoff was introducing the world to the new technology of television, and in 1947 he became the chief executive officer and chairman of the board of RCA. He continued to pursue innovations in the industry through the advent and standardizing of color. He retired as president of RCA in 1966 but stayed on as board chairman until he died on December 12, 1971.

SARNOFF, ROBERT (1918–1997)

Television executive

Television executive Robert Sarnoff was the son of radio pioneer and RCA president **David Sarnoff**. Born in New York City in 1918, Robert Sarnoff graduated from Harvard University in 1939. He began his career in television in 1948 as an account executive with NBC Television. In 1951 he became a vice president of the company and in 1955, president. Sarnoff is most famous as the man who ushered in the era of color television. One year after he took the helm of NBC, an NBC-owned affiliate, WNBQ in Chicago, became the first "all color" television station in the world.

Sarnoff helped set up the first televised presidential debates between Nixon and Kennedy during the 1960 election. During his tenure NBC also took the lead in "integrating" television. It produced the first show hosted by an African American, Nat King Cole, and the first dramatic series with a black actor in a leading role—"I Spy," with Bill Cosby.

In 1965 Sarnoff left NBC and, in 1970, he succeeded his father as chief executive of RCA. Reportedly, RCA's board of directors was pushed by the elder Sarnoff to elect Robert to the position. Whatever the case, he only lasted five years before he was ousted by the board. Sarnoff also served as chairman of the New York Stock Exchange. He died in 1997.

SCHARY, DORE (1905–1980)

Movie producer, writer

A major player in Hollywood during its Golden Age, Dore Schary was born in Newark, New Jersey, and began his career in acting and journalism. He started writing for film in the middle 1930s, doing screenplays for *Fog* (1933), *Murder in the Clouds* (1934), *The Big City* (1937), and *Outcast* (1938). He won an Academy Award for his screenplay for *Boys' Town* (1938). He soon became a producer for MGM, in charge of B features, remaining there until 1945. That year he became head of production for RKO, a position he held until 1948, when he returned to MGM as the studio's head of production. Unable to stop the studio's decline in the face of competition from television, he left MGM for good in 1956. Thereafter, he wrote plays and independently produced several films.

Among Schary's film productions were *The Swan* (1956), *Designing Woman* (1957), *Lonelyhearts* (1958), and *Sunrise at Campobello* (1960).

SEINFELD, JERRY (1954–)

Comedian, actor

The man who made America laugh at nothing was born in New York City and grew up on Long Island. In 1976 he started performing in comedy clubs and, four years later, moved to Los Angeles. In 1981 he made his first appearance on "The Tonight Show," the young comic's dream. He was popular enough to be called back many times and later became a favorite on "Late Night with David Letterman." He then went on to several successful HBO specials. But he became a household word because of his situation comedy, "Seinfeld" (1989–98). The series started off slowly, was bounced around a bit from time slot, to time slot, and then took off. For the remainder of its nine years it dominated the ratings and made Thursday night on NBC "Must See TV." Then, at the beginning of his most successful season, Jerry Seinfeld decided it was time to leave gracefully. The network offered him an amazing $5 million per episode to continue the show, but he declined. He announced that he would be returning to standup comedy.

SHATNER, WILLIAM (1931–)

Actor

William Shatner was born in Montreal, Canada, on March 22, 1931. His Jewish parents wanted him to go into the family garment business, but he did not listen to them. Instead he wanted to go on the stage. He began working in regional Canadian theaters after completing his college degree at McGill University, his rugged good looks and stentorian voice standing him in good stead. When he moved to New York, he worked regularly in supporting parts on Broadway and in live television. Then he decided the time had come to tackle Hollywood.

Shatner made an immediate and strong impression in his first film role as Alexei in *The Brothers Karamazov* (1958). But that role didn't lead to the kind of steady work he had been getting in New York. It was not until 1966, when he was cast as the lead in a new science-fiction series on NBC, that Shatner would have the unlikely career breakthrough that made him a major star. The show, of course, was "Star Trek," and, after its brief three-year run, the series' cult status kept it in syndication.

In the meantime, an actor cannot live on the adulation of a cult. He has to work, which Shatner did. His next success came with the cop show "T. J. Hooker," which he followed by hosting "Rescue 911." Fans of "Star Trek" were myriad and vocal and, eventually, Paramount spun off a series of feature films from the show with most of the original cast in each of the first seven films. (Shatner even directed one of the films, *Star Trek VI: The Undiscovered Country*.) He made his final appearance (to date) as Captain Kirk in the 1995 *Star Trek Generations*. He has also dabbled in science-fiction writing, penning the *Trek War* series of novels.

SIDNEY, SYLVIA (1910–1999)

Actor

For more than seventy years, Sylvia Sidney (Sophia Kosow) entertained American audiences. From a sixteen-year-old to an eighty-year-old, she just seemed to be getting better. Born in the Bronx, she was the daughter of Jewish immigrants from Russia and Romania. Trained in acting at the Theatre Guild School, she made her debut on Broadway in the play *The Squall* (1926). She spent only a few years on the stage and had hardly become a leading lady when she was recruited by Hollywood. Her first film was *Thru Different Eyes* (1929), and throughout the 1930s she played a succession of sweet, waiflike young women who frequently had tears in their eyes. This typecasting did not please Sidney, but she was unable to break out of it. She had great success with *City Streets*, *An American Tragedy*, and *Street Scene*, all released in 1931. She then went on to do seventeen more films in that decade, sometimes filming three a year. She was active in films in the 1940s and into the 1950s, making such films as *The Searching Wind* (1946) and *Les Misérables* (1952).

In the late 1950s Sidney returned to the New York stage. In 1958 she took over the role Rosalind Russell had created in Auntie Mame, laying to rest forever her weepy waif image. In the next three decades, she performed in such successful plays as *Enter Laughing* (1963), *The Little Foxes* (1966), *Butterflies Are Free* (1972), and *Mornings at Seven* (1981). She also made more than a dozen television movies, including *F.D.R.: The Last Year* (1980) and *The Shadow Box* (1980). She also garnered an Academy Award nomination in *Summer Wishes, Winter Dreams* (1973) and delivered a wonderful performance in *I Never Promised You a Rose Garden* (1977).

Then, as if two careers were not enough for anyone, Sidney launched a third. At the age of seventy-eight she enchanted young and old in Tim Burton's *Beetlejuice* (1988) and then appeared in *Used People* (1992) and another Tim Burton film, *Mars Attacks* (1996). She died on July 1, 1999, in New York.

SILVERMAN, FRED (1937–)

Television executive

Television executive Fred Silverman was born in 1937 in the Bronx, New York. He became the head of CBS Television's daytime programming in 1963. In 1970 he was named chief programmer of CBS's entire television schedule. The following year his string of successes began with "All in the Family," which won the Emmy Award for best comedy only five months after it went on the air. Silverman's other successful shows on CBS include "MASH," "Kojak," "Maude," "The Waltons," and "Rhoda," among many others. Incredibly skilled at promotion, he was also known for his uncanny ability to schedule shows in the time slots where they would attract the biggest audiences.

In 1975 Silverman brought his talent to ABC Television, where he served as the president of the entertainment division. During his tenure at ABC he aimed for and got the younger audience that had been ignored by CBS. Though his critics charged that his ABC shows were sometimes vulgar and almost always unsophisticated, his reputation for choosing hits only increased. In the 1976–1977 season alone, ten of the top fourteen shows were from ABC. The ABC hits of this period include "Happy Days," "Laverne & Shirley," "Charlie's Angels," "The Six Million Dollar Man," and "The Bionic Woman." In 1977 ABC produced the ground breaking miniseries "Roots."

In 1978 Silverman moved over to NBC, where he was president of the entire network. However, his three years at NBC were not successful. The period was marked by low ratings, failed shows, and internal turmoil. Since leaving network programming, he has had considerable success as an independent producer. His post-network productions include "Matlock," "In the Heat of the Night," "Father Dowling Mysteries," "Jake and the Fatman," "Diagnosis Murder," and the Perry Mason movies.

SILVERS, PHIL (1912–1985)

Actor

Phil Silvers perfected the role of the fast-talking conman as the unflappable Sergeant Bilko on television, but his stardom was the result of a long, hard climb through the show business ranks. A boy singer in vaudeville, Silvers, then a comic in Minsky's burlesque in the 1930s, made the first of his film appearances in 1940. He invariably portrayed the hero's best friend, teaming notably with Gene Kelly in *Cover Girl* (1946) and *Summer Stock* (1950). Silvers also did a lounge act with fellow vaudeville veteran Rags Ragland.

Silvers's career took a turn for the better in 1951 when he was cast as the lead in the Broadway musical *Top Banana*, drawing on his experiences (and many of his routines) in burlesque. It was television that proved to be the medium best suited to his blustering style. From 1955 to 1959, "The Phil Silvers Show" showcased Silvers in digestible (and very funny) twenty-five-minute chunks. Silvers won an Emmy in 1955 for his work on the series. He plowed the same furrow with "The New Phil Silvers Show" in the mid-1960s. He continued to make films until 1980, perhaps most memorably as the "flesh peddler" in *A Funny Thing Happened on the Way to the Forum* (1966) opposite **Zero Mostel** and **Jack Gilford**.

SPIELBERG, STEVEN (1947–)

Filmmaker

Steven Spielberg has enjoyed one of the most meteoric careers in Hollywood history, rising from being a twenty-one-year-old contract TV director at Universal Studios to having directed or produced ten of the highest-grossing films of all time. More than that, with the success of *Schindler's List* (1993), he won the admiration of most of his detractors, shrugging off the reputation of being a lightweight maker of finely crafted thrill rides.

Spielberg grew up in an observant Jewish household. His parents were an ill-matched pair, his father an emotionally distant engineer working in computers, his mother a doting, overprotective former concert pianist. Spielberg grew up in a succession of suburbs, finally landing in Scottsdale, Arizona, while still very young. He was an introverted boy, fascinated with motion pictures. By age thirteen he had scripted and directed movies starring the kids in his neighborhood. By the time he had graduated from California State College, he had won several awards and made numerous short films, including the twenty-four-minute *Amblin'*, which led to a contract at Universal (and gave his production company its name). At Universal he directed series episodes and several made-for-TV movies, most notably *Duel* (1971), which was released theatrically in 1983.

Universal was more than happy to give the eager young man a chance to direct theatrical features. His first film, *The Sugarland Express* (1974), was a quirky comedy that received respectable reviews but didn't do much box office business. His next film more than made up for that. Spielberg was selected by the studio to direct *Jaws* (1975), which generated excellent reviews, grossed over $130 million in domestic rentals, and changed the face of the movie industry by spawning a blockbuster mentality that hasn't abated over twenty years later. Shifting gears, Spielberg chose a more personal project for his next film, *Close Encounters of the Third Kind* (1977), which was a more modest success but earned him his first Oscar nomination for best direction.

He chose to team up with another highly successful product of the college film programs, George Lucas, for the first of what would be three Indiana Jones films, *Raiders of the Lost Ark* (1981). A veritable paean to the thrill-a-minute serials of the 1940s, the film earned more than five times its initial cost in domestic rentals alone. But that success would be dwarfed by Spielberg's next film, *E.T. The Extra-Terrestrial* (1982). This charming child's-eye view of the suburban world probably owes more to Spielberg's own childhood than any of his other films, and its $228 million domestic earnings were unprecedented. In the meantime, he began producing films for other directors as

---

Steven Spielberg the Jew

Asked to describe the impact of *Schindler's List* and its phenomenal success on himself, as a man and a Jew, the filmmaker responds, "For one thing, I came out and stated for the first time in my life that I'm proud to be a Jew. That was something that Hollywood had never heard from my lips. It was a wonderful second bar mitzvah to have been able to do *Schindler's List* and start the two foundations. It's my second coming out. I was able to say, 'Today I am, yet again, a man.'"

The two foundations Spielberg is referring to are the Survivors of the Shoah Visual History Foundation, which uses cutting-edge video technology to preserve the testimonies of 100,000 survivors, and the Righteous Persons Foundation (RPF), which distributes all of Spielberg's personal profits from the film, an estimated thirty to forty million dollars, to Jewish causes.

From *Jewish Family and Life: Traditions, Holidays, and Values for Today's Parents and Children*, by Yosef I. Abramowitz and Rabbi Susan Silverman.

---

well, backing such hits as Tobe Hooper's *Poltergeist* (1982), *Gremlins* (1984), the *Back to the Future* trilogy, and *Who Framed Roger Rabbit?* (1988).

Once again Spielberg went for the unexpected in his next project, an adaptation of Alice Walker's novel *The Color Purple* (1985). Touted as his first "adult" film, the result was uneven, a bit saccharine and, due to the uneasy mix of white director and African American material and cast, even a little controversial. Spielberg was not nominated for a Best Director Oscar but received the Irving Thalberg Award for the body of his work. Seemingly bent on showing the Academy he could make a grown-up movie, Spielberg now went through the only extended fallow period of his career, with several honorable and ambitious failures: *Empire of the Sun* (1987), *Always* (1989), and the seemingly sure-fire *Peter Pan* take-off *Hook* (1991).

The drought ended in spectacular fashion in 1993, when the two sides of Spielberg's art and personality came to the fore in turn, first with *Jurassic Park*, then with *Schindler's List*. The former was a return to form in the kiddy matinee mode. The latter, perhaps totally unexpected by anyone except those closest to the filmmaker, was a somber, sober, and intelligent drama about the Holocaust, acclaimed by many scholars as well as most film critics and, surprisingly for a three-hour black-and-white drama with no humor and no star names, a modest hit. It also earned Spielberg his long-coveted Oscar for best direction.

Schindler's List launched Spielberg into another area of concern, related to but separate from filmmaking. Growing out of the research he did for the film, Spielberg began a massive project designed to interview and create a visual archive of survivor testimony of the Shoah. By comparison, his subsequent film, a *Jurassic Park* sequel, seems trivial. The film that followed was another drama of oppression and tragedy, *Amistad* (1997), based on an historical incident in which African slaves seized control of the ship transporting them to the Americas in 1839.

STREISAND, BARBRA (1942–)

Singer, actor, film director, producer

She kept her name and her nose, her sometimes abrasive Brooklyn Jewish personality and accent, but she became and remains one of the biggest stars in film and music. Barbra Streisand has struggled for her stardom, but she never struggled for acceptance; she has always presented her sometimes brassy but always powerful talents with an attitude that says "here I am, this is what I am, take it or leave it." And for over three decades audiences have been taking it and loving it.

Streisand always wanted to be in show business. The daughter of a hypercritical mother and a father who died when she was still a baby, she contrived to complete her high school education in two years so that she could turn her attention to her real love, the entertainment industry. Streisand worked as a switchboard operator and waitress to support herself as she plodded through the Greenwich Village cabaret scene. She eventually began to attract attention with her unconventional looks and explosive singing style. Nightclub appearances and an off-Broadway revue helped win her the attention of Broadway producers and a small but significant role in Harold Rome's *I Can Get*

> ### A Yeshiva "Girl" Breaks Through Hollywood's Glass Ceiling
>
> Barbra Streisand became the first woman to produce, direct, write, and star in a major Hollywood movie, *Yentl* (1983). Based on a story by Isaac Bashevis Singer, it tells how a girl who wants to study Talmud pretends to be a boy so she can attend Yeshiva. Streisand played the lead. She had the background for it. Born and raised an Orthodox Jew, she attended a Bais Yakov School in Brooklyn as a child.

It for You Wholesale in 1962. Although the show was not a hit, it launched Streisand

Within two years, she was bowling over audiences and critics with her magnetic performance as **Fanny Brice** in *Funny Girl*. Signed to expensive contracts by Columbia Records and the CBS network, she revealed a side that few had seen thus far, that of the obsessive perfectionist. She labored intensely over her TV specials and records to great effect. *My Name Is Barbra* (1965) won multiple Emmys; her recordings have netted her more gold records than any other entertainer in history, thirty-eight albums and thirty singles, not to mention seven Grammys.

The only world left to conquer was Hollywood. Streisand made her film debut in *Funny Girl* (1968) and shared the Best Actress Oscar award with Katharine Hepburn. The films she made throughout the 1970s and into the 1980s were generally lackluster, both critically and financially. She was a top box-office draw at first with a mega-hit in *The Way We Were* (1973), but movies like *Up the Sandbox* (1972), *The Main Event* (1979), and *All Night Long* (1981) dimmed her cinematic star.

Streisand responded in character. If her films were doing badly, she would take more control. The result of that decision was Streisand's directorial debut, *Yentl* (1983), adapted from an **Isaac Bashevis Singer** story. At forty, Streisand was too old for the part of the young girl who passes herself off as a yeshiva boy in order to study Torah, but it is hard to imagine any other Jewish film star who could even have gotten the film made. It was not a great success.

Since then, Streisand has continued to exercise her considerable clout in the industry, producing, starring, and directing herself in *The Prince of Tides* (1991) and *The Mirror Has Two Faces* (1996). She has thrown herself into political activity with great fervor. A protégé of **Bella Abzug** in her New York days, Streisand helped launch a Hollywood women's political group that raised large sums for Democratic candidates. She became close friends with President and Mrs. Clinton and even came out of self-imposed retirement from live performance (a product, she has maintained, of terrible stage fright) to do a series of fund raisers for Bill Clinton's presidential campaigns.

SUSSKIND, DAVID (1920–1987)

Television producer, talk show host

David Susskind was one of America's foremost television and film producers as well as a successful television talk show host. His two talk shows, "Open End" (1958–1967) and "The David Susskind Show" (1967–1986), were known for the variety of the guests as well as Susskind's own blunt questions. Two of his most influential guests were Nikita Khrushchev and Richard Nixon. He also interviewed comedy writers, and once, a professional killer, whose identity was hidden by a ski mask.

In addition to his talk shows, Susskind was also responsible for some of the most important television shows during the medium's Golden Age. Altogether his productions won forty-seven Emmy Awards and include "Ages of Man," "Death of a Salesman," and "Eleanor and Franklin." In 1956 he defied Hollywood's blacklist to hire Martin Ritt to direct the groundbreaking racial drama "Edge of the City." He also produced "Kraft Television Theater" and created "Play of the Week." He was the founder of Talent Associates, Inc. Among the many films he produced are *A Raisin in the Sun* (1961), *All the Way Home* (1963), *Alice Doesn't Live Here Anymore* (1975), and *Ft. Apache, The Bronx* (1981). He died on February 2, 1987.

TELEVISION

Jews have played a central part in the American television industry from its beginning. Regular television broadcasting in the United States began in 1939 at NBC's station W2XBS with a broadcast of President Roosevelt opening the New York World's Fair. Five months later RCA had still sold only 400 sets. In July of 1941 one NBC station and one CBS station received licenses as the first commercial stations in the United States. During World War II there was a virtual moratorium on commercial broadcasting, and during that time a great many technical problems were solved. When the war ended, there were 7,000 television sets in the country. By 1948 CBS and NBC had been joined by ABC and the short-lived Dumont Television Network, and manufacturers were making 140,000 sets a month.

The three major networks were all owned and/or operated by Jewish Americans from the 1950s until the 1990s. **David Sarnoff** was the first chairman of the board and CEO of RCA, and his son **Robert** became president of the company in 1955. **William Paley** had a controlling interest in CBS and ran it until the mid-1980s. **Leonard Goldenson** took control of ABC when his Paramount Pictures bought the network in 1955. The three men had different programming philosophies and the networks reflected those differences.

William Paley guided CBS to its status as the "Tiffany" network. In news it presented "CBS Reports" and newscasters Edward R. Murrow and Walter Cronkite. In entertainment CBS offered "I Love Lucy," "Gunsmoke," "All in the Family," and other classics of the medium. David, and later Robert, Sarnoff, were responsible for NBC's reputation for high quality of a slightly stodgier kind. Robert Sarnoff made NBC the first network to present an African American singer, Nat King Cole, as host of a show and an African American actor, Bill Cosby, as a lead in a prime-time dramatic series, "I Spy." Leonard Goldenson at ABC had a bit more of a struggle, but he introduced prime-time soaps with "Peyton Place," prime-time cartoons with "The Flintstones," and the "Wide World of Sports," making his network the most watched of the three by 1977. Later, Fred Silverman (in a job-hopping career) ran programming at each of the three networks.

EARLY TELEVISION

The year 1948 is usually considered the birth date of commercial television as we know it because, in that year, there were enough viewers to make it possible to sell time on the air to advertisers. At the top of the list of television entertainers in the years immediately following, were a great many Jewish performers, most of whom came to the small screen from radio and vaudeville.

First and foremost there was **Milton Berle**, whose broad comedy on "The Texaco Star Theater," also known as "The Milton Berle Show" (1948–53), was so popular that he is often credited with almost single-handedly popularizing the fledgling medium. For the next decade "Mr. Television," as Berle came to be known, hosted a string of variety shows, including "The Buick-Berle Show" (1953–55), "The Milton Berle Show" (1955–56), and "The Kraft Music Hall" (1958–59). In the 1960s his popularity waned and his hosting jobs diminished to "Jackpot Bowling" (1960–61) and one "comeback" season of "The Milton Berle Show" (1966–67). Still, Berle was a favorite guest on other shows, and he never lost his status as a television pioneer. He was in the first group of seven people inducted into the Television Academy Hall of Fame.

A number of the important members of Berle's creative team were also Jewish. Comedian Arnold Stang (1925–), for example, got his start in television on Milton Berle's variety shows. He was also a regular on "The Goldbergs" (1949–55) and "December Bride" (1954–59). Berle's writers included **Selma Diamond**, who went on to write for **Sid Caesar**, was the model for Sally Rogers on "The Dick Van Dyke Show," and scored an acting hit as the bailiff on "Night Court" in the course of her long career.

Sid Caesar was the second major Jewish comic on television and possibly the greatest sketch actor ever. His first appearance was on "The Admiral Broadway Revue" (1949), but he soon had his own show, the legendary "Your Show of Shows" (1950–54). This was followed by "Caesar's Hour" (1954–57) and "Sid Caesar Invites You" (1958). Besides Selma Diamond, the Caesar team included such great Jewish writers as **Mel Brooks** and **Neil Simon**. Among his Jewish comic sidekicks were Howard Morris (1919–), who later became a regular on "The Andy Griffith Show" (1960–68), and **Carl Reiner**, who went on to create "The Dick Van Dyke Show" (1961–66). Reiner became an important writer, producer, and director. Caesar was canceled by the network in 1958 and went into a deep depression from which he didn't recover until the 1980s, though he continued to perform in other venues and was even able to come back to television for one season in "The Sid Caesar Show" (1963–64).

There were also a number of Jewish radio stars who took their shows, with few changes, directly from the box to the tube. None was more beloved than **Gertrude Berg**, creator of "The Goldbergs" (1949–55). While still in her twenties, she had written and persuaded NBC to broadcast her series about Molly Goldberg and family. Berg played Molly in "The Rise of the Goldbergs" on the radio network NBC Blue from 1929 to 1934 and on CBS radio from 1938 to 1945. In 1948 the Goldbergs went to Broadway in the play *Me and Molly*. In 1949 "The Goldbergs" became one of the first situation comedies on television at a time when variety shows were the order of the day.

Jack Benny (Benjamin Kubelsky) brought to television a show that fell somewhere between variety and situation comedy. With a regular cast that included his wife, Mary Livingstone (Sadie Marks), as well as African American comedian Eddie Anderson, "The Jack Benny Show" ran from 1950 to 1965. Benny played himself and the comedian and his ensemble poked fun at his violin playing, his stinginess, and his vanity. Known for his "takes" and his timing, Benny was one of television's most loved stars.

When Groucho **Marx** (Julius Marx) brought his show "You Bet Your Life" (1950–61) from radio to the large screen, it was one of the first of a long line of television game shows. **George Burns** (Nathan Birnbaum) and his Irish Catholic wife, Gracie Allen, began in vaudeville, starred on radio, and then made a successful transition to television with "The George Burns and Gracie Allen Show" (1950–58), as did **Ed Wynn**. "The Ed Wynn Show" (1949–51) used the variety format, allowing Wynn to show off his wonderful physical comedy. A later show, also called "The Ed Wynn Show" (1958–59), was a situation comedy. The team of **Jerry Lewis** and Dean Martin spent five seasons doing "The Dean Martin, Jerry Lewis Show" (1950–55) before having even greater success in films. Lewis came back to television in "The Jerry Lewis Show" (1963, 1967–69). Yiddish actor **Molly Picon** had her own show for one season in 1949 and comedian **Red Buttons** (Aaron Chwatt) hosted "The Red Buttons Show" (1952–55). **Phil Silvers** appeared on "Welcome Aboard" (1948) and "The Arrow Show" (1948–49). He hit the big time with "You'll Never Get Rich" (1955–59), later called "The Phil Silvers Show," as Master Sergeant Ernie Bilko.

One of television's most enduring stars was **Dinah Shore**. Another transplant from radio, she successfully hosted "The Dinah Shore Chevy Show" (1951–56) and "The Dinah Shore Show" (1956–62), both in a variety format that depended on her wonderfully casual singing and her enormously likable persona. The latter secured her a talk-variety show, "Dinah's Place" (1970–74), almost twenty years later. That in turn led to her very successful daytime talk show, known variously as "Dinah!" (1974), "Dinah" (1975–79), and "Dinah and Friends" (1979).

Game shows began to replace variety shows in the hearts of the American public in the late 1950s. The most sensational of these was "The $64,000 Question" (1955–58), hosted by Hal March [Harold Mendelson] (1920–1970). Week after week, television audiences watched breathlessly as contestants answered increasingly difficult questions in their specialties, until one day it was revealed that answers were being supplied to some of those men in the glass booths, and the scandal destroyed the show. Still, tamer shows maintained their popularity for years, largely because of the wit and personalities of their panelists. Some of the Jewish celebrities who helped to give these shows their humor and appeal were Kitty Carlisle (1915–) on "To Tell the Truth" and **Bess Myerson** on "I've Got a Secret" (1958–68). Allen Funt hosted the unique and often hilarious "Candid Camera," which ran off and on from the late 1940s through 1978.

Two Jewish comics became hosts of children shows. Pinky Lee (1916–1993) began his television career on the variety show "Those Two" (1951–53), but made his mark on "The Pinky Lee Show" (1954–1956). Soupy Sales (1926–) charmed children and adults on "The Soupy Sales Show" (1959–62).

In these early years drama on television came largely in the form of the dramatic anthology series. The continuity on these shows was usually provided by the host, with each individual show a self-contained drama. Renowned Jewish actor **Joseph Schildkraut** hosted one of these series, "Joseph Schildkraut Presents" (1953–54). German Jewish actor Lilli Palmer (1914–1986) hosted "The Lilli Palmer Show" (1951) and "Lilli Palmer Theater" (1956). Many important or aspiring Jewish actors appeared regularly in the anthology dramas, including **Theodore Bikel**, Claire Bloom (1931–), **Lee J. Cobb**, Peter Falk (1927–), Jill St. John [Jill Oppenheim] (1940–), **William Shatner**, Rod Steiger (1925–), Susan Strasberg (1938–1999), Jesse White (1919–), and Joseph Wiseman (1918–).

Playwright **Paddy Chayefsky** began his career writing for a dramatic anthology series, gaining particular acclaim for *Marty* (1953), the story of a lonely man in the Bronx. Although Chayefsky originally wrote the character Marty as a young Jew, he was played as an Italian. This choice on the part of the producers was an indication of what was beginning to happen to Jewish characters on television. As policies began to replace seat-of-the-pants programming, television executives decided to appeal to the largest audience by making their shows reflect that audience. Overt ethnicity was largely eliminated from dramas and situation comedies. Even variety shows began to have more "American"—northern European Christian—hosts and performers.

A classic example of this turn away from ethnicity

was "The Dick Van Dyke Show." Carl Reiner created the show as a vehicle for himself, playing the role of a comedy writer. CBS saw the pilot and offered to buy the show if Reiner were replaced by another, less ethnic actor. The one character on the show who remained Jewish was Buddy, played by Jewish actor **Morey Amsterdam** (1914–), who had earlier been a panelist on "Stop If You've Heard This One" (1948–49) and host of "The Morey Amsterdam Show" (1948–50). However, nothing of his religious or ethnic identity was mentioned until the last episode, when he underwent a much-delayed **bar mitzvah**. The character of Sally Rogers, which Reiner had based on Selma Diamond, was played by non-Jewish actor Rose Marie.

Jewish actors, if not Jewish names, were still highly visible even in the late 1950s and early 1960s. They often didn't play Jewish characters. Gene Barry (1922–) was a huge success playing suave and debonair leads in "Bat Masterson" (1958–61), "Burke's Law" (1963–65), and "Amos Burke, Secret Agent" (1965–66). He continued into the seventies in "The Name of the Game" (1968–71) and "The Adventurer" (1972). Lorne Greene (1915–1987) began in "Sailor of Fortune" (1957) before being cast as the strong, compassionate and very American patriarch on "Bonanza" (1959–73). He continued in the seventies and eighties with "Griff" (1973–74), "Last of the Wild" (1974–79), "Battlestar Galactica" (1978–79), "Galactica 1980" (1980), and "Code Red" (1981–82). The other major patriarch of the time was **Lee J. Cobb** in "The Virginian" (1962–70), who also went on into the seventies in "The Young Lawyers" (1970–71). **Sam Jaffe** played the wise mentor on "Ben Casey" (1961–65).

Throughout the 1950s and into the 1960s there were certain Jewish actors who appeared as regulars on show after show. They were highly recognizable, even though they never played leads. Sidney Tomack (1907–1962) appeared on "The Life of Riley" (1949–50), "My Friend Irma" (1952–53), and "The Joe Palooka Story" (1954). Jesse White (1919–) was a regular on "Private Secretary" (1953–57), "Make Room for Daddy" (1954–57), and "The Ann Sothern Show" (1959–61). Herschel Bernardi (1923–1986), was Lieutenant Jacoby in "Peter Gunn" (1958–61) and later appeared on "Arnie" (1970–72). And Sheldon Leonard [Sheldon Bershad] (1907–1997) was a regular on "The Danny Thomas Show" (1957–64) before becoming a producer and director.

Other actors appeared repeatedly as guest stars. These included stars from vaudeville and Broadway, such as **Molly Picon**, **Bert Lahr**, Hermione Gingold (1897–1987), **Jack Gilford**, Howard da Silva (1909–1986), and Lou Jacobi (1913–). There were also younger actors who would later become well known, including **Eli Wallach**, Martin Balsam (1919–1996), **Judy Holliday**, Jack Klugman (1922–), Lloyd Bochner (1924–), Harvey Korman (1927–), and **William Shatner**.

Shari Lewis (Phyllis Hurwitz) began her television career in New York. By 1960, at the age of twenty-six, she had her own network children's show. Far more than a talented ventriloquist, Lewis was a songwriter, storyteller, singer, and comedian. Her puppet Lamb Chop was little more than a sock, but she had charm and a dry wit. "The Shari Lewis

---

Hunting the *Golem* in Brooklyn

The legend of the *golem* (a lifeless being) reaches as far back as the late fourth or early fifth century. There are several instances in the Talmud describing how the rabbis used Kabbalah—Jewish mysticism—to breathe life into lifeless beings fashioned from dirt or clay, usually in order to protect Jews.

In 1997 the legend was brought to life again in television's hit series "The X-Files." The plot revolves around the investigation of the death of Issac Luria, a young Hasidic man in Brooklyn whose killers are, in turn, murdered. The super-sleuth FBI agent stars, Gillian Anderson and David Duchovny, discover evidence from the second murders that points to the already dead Luria. The script was written by Howard Gordon, the show's executive producer, who came across the *golem* story during his Jewish upbringing in Long Island. We won't give away the ending, but in one of his "throw-away" lines Duchovny responds when asked by the anti-Semitic protagonist "What kind of Jew trick" is behind the seeming resurrection of the dead Luria: "A Jew pulled it off 2,000 years ago."

Show" (1960–63) was innovative, educational, and an enormous success. It is remarkable that one of the most memorable Jewish women on television in the early 1960s was talking to children and doing it with her mouth closed.

THE 1960s

The early 1960s brought a flock of silly sitcoms, and Jewish performers were not exempt from service to the muse of foolishness. Avery Schreiber (1935–) starred in "My Mother the Car" (1965–66) before going on in the next decade to somewhat more sophisticated comedy in "The Burns and Schreiber Comedy Hour" (1973). Barbara Feldon was delightful in "Get Smart" (1965–70), a spoof of spy dramas. "Hogan's Heroes" (1965–71), a bizarre comedy set in a German prison camp during World War II, featured two Jewish actors: John Banner (1910–1973) as Sergeant Hans Schultz and Robert Clary (1926–) as Corporal Louis LeBeau. Larry Storch (1923–) appeared in another war comedy, "F Troop" (1965–67). Tina Louise (Tina Blacker) played the movie star Ginger Grant on "Gilligan's Island" (1964–67).

One of the earliest daytime talk show hosts was **Joyce Brothers** (Joyce Bauer), who parlayed an winning stint on "The $64,000 Question" into an afternoon talk show called "The Dr. Joyce Brothers Show." Another early entrant into what would later become daytime television's entertaining staple was Virginia Graham, whose "Girl Talk" (1962–69) ran for seven years. Graham then enjoyed two more seasons on "The Virginia Graham Show" (1970–72). Selma Diamond was a regular guest on "The Jack Paar Show," an early nighttime talk show.

The variety show was making a last gasp in the middle sixties with **Danny Kaye** (David Daniel Kaminsky) in "The Danny Kaye Show" (1963–67), which also featured actor Harvey Korman (1927–). Korman went on to become part of the team that rejuvenated the genre on "The Carol Burnett Show" (1967–77). When that show ended, he starred in "The Harvey Korman Show" (1978) for one season.

Jewish dramatic actors on television in the late 1960s included Ross Martin [Martin Rosenblatt] (1920–1981) on "The Wild, Wild West" (1965–69) and Martin Landau (1934–) on "Mission: Impossible" (1966–69). The two men with the most lasting impact were **Leonard Nimoy** and **William Shatner** of "Star Trek" (1966– 69). Their characters, Mr. Spock and Captain Kirk, were certainly not Jewish. Spock was Vulcan and Kirk was the generic earthperson. It seemed as though television had taken the purging of ethnicity to its logical extreme. At the same time, the show portrayed what might be called "space ethnicities" co-existing in a model of multicultural diversity.

THE 1970s

The 1970s brought many changes to television. The militant political movements of the time began to have an impact on all parts of the culture, and ethnicity became more than respectable. Producer **Norman Lear** challenged the country's assumptions—and its sense of humor—with "All in the Family" (1971–83), "Maude" (1972–78), "The Jeffersons" (1975–85), and "Mary Hartman, Mary Hartman" (1976–78). Both "Maude" and "Mary Hartman" starred Jewish actors, **Bea Arthur** and Louise Lasser (1939–).

Still, the networks hedged their bets when introducing Jewish characters to the mainstream American audience. One of the first was Rhoda Morgenstern, the neighbor and best friend on "The Mary Tyler Moore Show" (1970–77). This thoroughly engaging and unabashedly Jewish young woman was part of an ensemble show and could have been reduced in importance or eliminated altogether if public reaction had not been favorable. She was played by a non-Jewish actor (Valerie Harper), as was her mother Ida (Nancy Walker). It was an important step and Harper was given her own spin-off series, "Rhoda" (1974–78), in which her sister was played by Jewish actor Julie Kavner, who went on to "The Tracy Ullman Show" (1987–90) and "The Simpsons" (1990–).

During the same season "The Odd Couple" (1970–75) debuted, written by Jewish writer **Neil**

Simon and starring Jewish actors Jack Klugman (1922–) and **Tony Randall** (Leonard Rosenberg). If Jewishness was irrelevant to the comedy about two divorced men in New York, there was nothing in the situation or dialogue to contradict the ethnicity of its creators. This was another way to hedge and was true of other shows of the time. Their characters were either "generically ethnic" or they were specifically non-Jewish—usually Italian or Polish—but played by Jewish actors with what some might call a Jewish sensibility. These shows included "Columbo" (1971–77) with Peter Falk (1927–); "Alice" (1976–85), with **Linda Lavin**; "Laverne and Shirley" (1976–83), with Phil Foster (Fivel Feldman) as Frank DeFazio; "Petrocelli" (1974–76), with Barry Newman (1938–); "All in the Family" (1971–78), with **Rob Reiner**; and later, "Cheers," with **Rhea Perlman**.

This kind of caution was relaxed as the decade continued. Gabe Kaplan (1945–) starred as a happily Jewish teacher in "Welcome Back, Kotter" (1975–79). **Judd Hirsch** was clearly Jewish in "Taxi" (1978–83), although Carol Kane (1952–) was of an imaginary eastern European ethnicity as Simka Gravas. Hal Linden's (1931–) "Barney Miller" (1975–82) was a good Jewish cop, if quietly so. In a spin-off series, "Fish," there was no attempt to conceal Abe Vigoda's (1921–) Jewishness. Toward the end of the decade, bigot Archie Bunker got a Jewish business partner, Martin Balsam (1919–), in "Archie Bunker's Place" (1979–81). In 1981 Tony Randall introduced "Love, Sidney" (1981–83), but Jewish and gay seemed to be one minority too many, and the show did not last long.

THE 1980s

During the 1980s there was a reaction against the political and social consciousness of the sixties and early seventies and ethnicity went out of fashion. For most of the decade, television viewers subsisted on a bland diet. African American shows like "Good Times" and "The Jeffersons" ended, as did shows with Jewish characters. From 1984 to 1987 there was not one iden-

tifiable, regularly appearing Jewish character in the Nielsen top twenty. Instead, prime-time soaps like "Dallas" showed the world of the modern American West with characters who might all have been named Smith. An exception to this trend was "The Golden Girls" (1985–92), with its generically ethnic mother and daughter, Estelle Getty [Estelle Scher] (1923–) and **Bea Arthur**.

Outside the realm of fiction, Jewish Americans were easier to find. Sally Jessy Raphael launched her long-running daytime talk show in 1985. News broadcasters included Andrea Mitchell, Lynn Sherr, Nina Totenberg, and the tragically fated Jessica Savitch. But the queen of television broadcasting was a woman who had been around for a quarter of a century.

Barbara Walters' rise began when, as a writer for NBC's "Today" show, she began to appear on the air in 1961. For more than a decade she built her role on the program, reporting and doing interviews. In 1974 she became co-host of the show with Hugh Downs and a year later acquired her own syndicated talk show. In 1976 she became the first woman anchor of a network news show when she moved to ABC's "Evening News." Her five million dollar, five-year contract made her the highest paid journalist in history. Unfortunately, co-anchor Harry Reasoner refused to cooperate and Walters left the show a year-and-a-half later. She began doing interview specials and her reputation as the world's best interviewer grew. Everyone from Princess Grace to Fidel Castro submitted to her gently probing technique. By 1984 she had her own show again with her old co-host Hugh Downs. One of the first investigative news shows, "20/20" has continued into the 1990s as one of the best.

The one group of Jewish entertainers that maintained a constant presence on the air was the comics. From classic standup comics like **Henny Youngman** and **Alan King** (Irwin Alan Kniberg) to young "Saturday Night Live" sketch artists like **Billy Crystal** and **Gilda Radner**, they were among television's funniest and often most trenchant voices. They are dealt with at length in the **Comedy and Comedians** entry earlier in this chapter. A number of the members of this group stepped out of the usual comedic mold to create the next wave of Jewish shows and characters on the small screen.

The first of these, and by far the most influential, was **Roseanne**, once known as Barr and then as Arnold. This latter-day, female **Lennie Bruce** is a Jew from the heartland and she created a situation comedy about family life in a small town in Illinois. It was not the usual context for Jewish television and is not usually recognized as part of the continuum. But "Roseanne" was clearly in the tradition of working-class comedy that occupied early Jewish writers and performers in theater and film. The show featured one of the first Chanukah episodes on television. At times Roseanne seemed more intent on excoriating than entertaining her audiences, but she presented the most realistic view of American working-class life ever seen on a situation comedy and revolutionized the way television depicted women. In addition to Roseanne, the show regularly featured Jewish actors such as Sandra Bernhard and **Shelley Winters**.

"Murphy Brown" (1988–98) brought a recognizably Jewish character into the comedy's newsroom in actor Grant Shaud's Miles Silverberg. Later, Murphy would become romantically involved with an abrasive right-winger played by Jay Thomas. In 1989 standup comedian Richard Lewis became the first Jewish male with his own show since Tony Randall in "Love, Sidney." In Lewis's "Anything But Love," Jamie Lee Curtis, daughter of Jewish actor **Tony Curtis**, co-starred as the *shiksa* (non-Jewish) girlfriend. The next summer Rob Morrow starred as young Jewish doctor Joel Fleischman in "Northern Exposure" (1990–95). Fleischman's Jewish heritage was repeatedly commented on and explored in the quirky comedy, which did not survive Morrow's departure in 1995. **Jerry Seinfeld** premiered the hugely successful "Seinfeld" (1990–98) the fall after "Northern Exposure"'s debut, and the next season Mayim Bialik became a hit in "Blossom," which was realistic and funny in its portrayal of the life of an intelligent teenager in the modern world.

THE 1990s AND BEYOND

These programs were followed by a flood of Jewish characters and Jewish actors. The 1992 season brought Jay Thomas in "Love and War" (1992–95), Paul Reiser in "Mad About You" (1992–), and Garry Shandling (1949–) in "The Larry Sanders Show" (1992–). Fran Drescher and Renee Taylor [Renee Wexler] (1945–) followed in "The Nanny" (1993–). **Adam Arkin** and **Mandy Patinkin** were next, in "Chicago Hope" (1994–). Subsequent seasons brought **Rhea Perlman** and Carol Kane in "Pearl" (1996), George Segal (1934–) in "Just Shoot Me" (1997), and a host of co-stars and regulars on other shows. These included Fyvus Finkel on "Picket Fences" (1992–96), Alan Rosenberg on "Cybill" (1995–), and Madeline Kahn (1942–) on "Cosby" (1996–).

Jewish executives, producers, writers, directors, and performers have played a large part in the development of television. However, as in the movie industry,

---

Fran Drescher—Performance Artist?

In an article in the *Forward* (February 14, 1997) reviewing Fran Drescher's movie *The Beautician and the Beast*, Robin Cembalest suggests that Drescher is a conceptual artist whose "career" is a complex performance piece in itself. Taking as her premise the statement from the catalogue of the Jewish Museum show "Too Jewish? Challenging Traditional Identities" that the works exhibited are "confrontational and often embarrassing" in their approach to ethnic identity and are "no longer an apologia for conspicuous Jewishness," Cembalest posits, "This is exactly what Ms. Drescher does. [She is] television's most ethnically Jewish character. She embodies several negative stereotypes: She is flashy, materialistic and a champion whiner.

"[Her critics] don't get Ms. Drescher's conceptual twist: she is not merely rehashing stereotypes, but questioning them. She subverts conventional assumptions: Who would have thought you could fashion a Hollywood starlet—who made *People's* 50 Most Beautiful list—out of real-life, bridge-and-tunnel *Yiddishkeit?*"

Fran Drescher: "Too Jewish?" *(Private collection)*

they often submerged their ethnic identity to reach or to please a mass audience. It is a measure of the change that has occurred in the medium that Jewish names, accents, and traditions are no longer taboo. It will be interesting to see whether the pendulum swings back, as it has before, or whether America is finally ready to reject permanently the domination of its entertainment media by an idealized white American image.

THALBERG, IRVING (1899–1936)

Film producer, executive

Irving Thalberg produced some of Hollywood's classic films at the pivotal period when the talkies were replacing silent movies. Born in New York City in 1899, Thalberg moved west while still in his teens. He first worked at Universal Pictures. While there he produced the silent classic *Hunchback of Notre Dame*. He became the company's general manager when he was only twenty-four. In 1924 he went to work for **Lewis B. Mayer**. Metro-Goldwyn-Mayer was formed that same year and he became the studio's production chief.

Among the classic films he produced for MGM were *Ben-Hur* (1926), *Broadway Melody* (1929), *Grand Hotel* (1932), *Mutiny on the Bounty* (1935), and *The Good Earth* (1936). His commitment to his Jewish identity can perhaps best be seen by the fact that his wife, Norma Shearer, converted to Judaism prior to their marriage in 1927. Thalberg died in 1936, when he was only thirty-seven, cutting short the career of one of Hollywood's giants.

THE THREE STOOGES

Comedy team

The Three Stooges, one of comedy's longest-running and most successful slapstick acts, was not just three people. There were six Stooges during the act's lifetime. The original Stooges were Moe Howard (Moses Horwitz) and Larry Fine (Feinberg)—Stooges throughout the group's history—and Moe's brother, Jerome (Curly). Starting out in the early 1930s as Howard, Fine, and Howard, they soon they renamed themselves The Three Stooges. They made ninety-seven shorts before Jerome succumbed, in 1947, to several strokes and the third Howard brother, Shemp (Samuel) joined the group. There is one Stooge film in which all three Howard brothers appear, *Hold That Lion* (1947). In 1952 Jerome died; Shemp died three years later. Many of today's fans consider Shemp's death to mark the end of the "real" Three Stooges.

Despite the fans—today's or yesterday's—the Stooges continued. Shemp was replaced by the second "Curly"—Joe Besser. Besser died in 1959 after only four years as a Stooge. The last "Curly," vaudeville veteran Joe De-Rita, then took over to act in the six feature films the Stooges made in the 1960s.

For over thirty years, the Stooges performed in vaudeville, in film shorts—for which they are most famous today—and in feature films. Their feature films include *Soup to Nuts* (1930), *Have Rocket Will Travel* (1959), *Snow White and the Three Stooges* (1961), and *The Three Stooges Meet Hercules* (1962). Larry Fine and Moe Howard both died in 1975 and the final Stooge, Joe DeRita, died in 1993.

WALTERS, BARBARA (1931–)

Television journalist

Barbara Walters had a leg up on becoming a celebrity journalist. Her father was Lou Walters, owner of the Latin Quarter and other nightclubs. Her childhood, split between New York City and Miami, was filled with the famous. She never had to make a difficult adjustment to interview the rich, powerful, and instantly recognizable—she had grown up with them. Naturally, after she received her B.A. from Sarah Lawrence in 1953, she went to New York to begin a career in television.

Walters started as a writer and public relations aide at RCA-TV, then the NBC affiliate in New York. With some production experience under her belt, she went to work for Dave Garroway, host of the "Today" show, in 1961, where she impressed network executives with her unerring head for news. Gradually she broke in with on-camera work, covering Jackie Kennedy's trip to India in 1962, revealing herself to be a skilled interviewer at a time when plum assignments invariably went to men. By 1963 her interviews had become a regular feature on "Today," and within nine years she rose to co-anchor.

In 1976 Walters became the subject of a bidding war, leaving NBC to take the job of co-anchor of ABC's ratings-poor "Nightly News with Harry Reasoner." Reasoner and other male staffers refused to take her seriously as a journalist, no doubt in part because she was a woman, and she was forced out shortly after Reasoner himself returned to CBS. But before she left she produced one of her greatest coups as a journalist, a joint interview with Anwar Sadat and Menachem Begin on the eve of the announcement of their meeting in Jerusalem.

ABC was not about to lose an interviewer of Walters's skill and reach. She became co-host of their magazine show "20/20" and was given a series of continuing specials dedicated to a wide range of celebrity interviews.

WARNER, HARRY (1881–1958)

Film executive

Harry Warner (Eichelbaum) was the eldest of the four Warner brothers. He founded and ran the famous movie studio of the same name. He was born in Poland on December 12, 1881. At the turn of the century, after the family immigrated to America, the four brothers began their careers by traveling through Ohio and Pennsylvania showing the new invention, motion pictures. In 1903 they began to buy movie theaters and to develop a film distribution business. In 1913 they added the final component to their future empire: they started producing their own films. In 1917 the production side of the company—run by brother Jack—moved to Hollywood, California. Harry, and the headquarters of the company, stayed in New York City. In 1923, the company—theaters, distribution and production—formally became Warner Brothers Pictures, Inc. with Harry as the president.

The first studio to make a "talkie" as well as the first color talkie, by the 1930s, Warner Brothers was among the top three motion picture studios. A frequently overlooked but equally as important aspect of the company's success was the fact that it controlled 360 theaters in the United States and over 400 overseas. Harry Warner died in Hollywood on July 25, 1958.

WARNER, JACK (1892–1978)

Movie producer

Jack Warner (Eichelbaum), the youngest of the four Warner brothers, was born on August 2, 1892, in London, Ontario. The four brothers started out traveling through Ohio and Pennsylvania showing films. They then moved into buying movie houses, then into distributing films, and finally, in 1913, into production. In 1917 Jack Warner and the production side of the business moved from New York City to Hollywood, California. In 1923 the company became Warner Brothers Pictures, Inc., and Jack was named the company's vice-president in charge of production.

In 1926, spurred by brother Sam, the treasurer, the company was saved from financial ruin by collaborating on the Vitaphone process. In 1927 Warner Brothers released the first "talkie," *The Jazz Singer*. The success of that film and subsequent ones insured that the company became one of the most important movie studios in Hollywood.

In the 1930s under the direction of Jack Warner, Warner Brothers became known for its gangster films as well as for musicals and adventure stories. Among the studios many stars were James Cagney, Bette Davis, Busby Berkeley, Errol Flynn, and Humphrey Bogart. From the 1940s through the 1970s, the studio produced such classic films as *Casablanca* (1942), *A Streetcar Named Desire* (1951), *My Fair Lady* (1964), and *The Exorcist* (1973).

In 1956, upon older brother Harry's retirement, Jack took over the position of president of the company. During his tenure the company diversified its interests and become involved in television programming, book publishing, and music recording. In 1969 it changed its name to Warner Bros. Inc., a subsidiary of Warner Communications Inc. Jack Warner retired from the company in 1972 and died on September 9, 1978, in Los Angeles, California.

WILDER, GENE (1935–)

Actor

High-strung comic actor Gene Wilder (Jerome Silberman) was born in Milwaukee, Wisconsin, and went to military school in Los Angeles. He was the only Jewish boy in the school and experienced daily anti-Semitic persecution. After training in college and in England, and two years in the army, he joined the Actors Studio to study with **Lee Strasberg**. That same year, 1961, he made his Broadway debut in *The Complaisant Lover*. For the next five years he performed on stage and in guest appearances on television. In 1967 he was cast in a small but significant role in the film *Bonnie and Clyde* His second film, **Mel Brooks'** *The Producers*, made him a star. He followed up with the hilarious *Start the Revolution without Me* (1970), which made use of his remarkable comic intensity, and *Willy Wonka and the Chocolate Factory* (1971), which didn't.

Wilder made two more films with Mel Brooks and the ensemble of actors that came to be identified with that director: *Blazing Saddles* (1974) and *Young Frankenstein* (1974). He seemed to be Brooks's perfect leading man and they shared a comic sensibility. In his first venture into writing and directing, *The Adventures of Sherlock Holmes' Smarter Brother* (1975), he used a number of Brooks actors, including **Madeline Kahn** and Marty Feldman, and went for the same kind of manic, smart-aleck humor, not quite as successfully. A similar attempt in *The World's Greatest Lover* (1977) was similarly disappointing.

However, Wilder had meantime starred in the romantic adventure film *Silver Streak* (1976), in which he toned down his manic persona and was quite appealing as a leading man. The film also paired him in a comic partnership with Richard Pryor, one that was followed up in the film *Stir Crazy* (1980). In *The Frisco Kid* (1979) he played Avram Belinsky, an Eastern European Yeshiva student at the absolute bottom of his class, who is shipped off to a be the rabbi of an 1850s San Francisco congregation. As might be expected, crossing the wide open spaces of America proves impossible for the failed Talmud scholar, until he is adopted by a friendly outlaw, played by Harrison Ford.

Wilder has continued to work regularly on screen, with one foray into television in the short-lived series "Something Wilder" (1994). He has also been very active in the fight against ovarian cancer following the death of his wife **Gilda Radner** from that disease in 1989.

Is this a scene from Raiders of the Lost Ark? *No, it is from the 1979 film* The Frisco Kid, *in which Avram Belinsky (Gene Wilder), a "bottom-of-the-class" Eastern European Yeshiva student, is packed off in the 1850s to lead a San Francisco congregation. Of course, he wouldn't be able to make it across the wide open spaces of America without the help of the kind-hearted outlaw Tommy (Harrison Ford), who befriends him. The movie may not have been the first Jewish western, but it is certainly the only one to have such top stars. (Private Collection)*

WINTERS, SHELLEY (1922–)

Actor

The meanest mama in Hollywood began as a sweet young thing on Broadway in 1942, in the operetta *Rosalinda*. After sharing the role of Ado Annie in the original run of *Oklahoma!* (1943), she left for Hollywood and a decade of innocent, vulnerable roles in such films as *A Double Life* (1948) and *A Place in the Sun* (1951). After a film hiatus, during which she returned to the stage and to study the Stanislavsky method of acting, she undertook a very different sort of role. Beginning with *The Diary of Anne Frank* (1959), she began to specialize in matronly women with a dark side. She developed the breadth of her acting ability, as well as its depth, in films such as *Lolita* (1962), *A Patch of Blue* (1965), and *Next Stop, Greenwich Village* (1976). She also became a staple of less artistically ambitious films such as *Bloody Mama* (1970).

In 1980 Winters published an autobiography entitled *Shelley: Also Known as Shirley*, the frankness of which shocked a great many people and embarrassed some. In the 1990s she played the role of **Roseanne**'s mother in the television series "Roseanne."

WYNN, ED (1886–1966)

Comedian, actor

The "Perfect Fool" was born Isaiah Edwin Leopold in Philadelphia and began his vaudeville career after running away from home while still in his teens. He first worked with a partner but soon went solo and, in the *Ziegfeld Follies of 1914*, became a star. During the 1920s and 1930s, he appeared in a great many Broadway shows, creating the character of the Perfect Fool. He was a charming clown who wore funny hats, giggled, fluttered, and generally developed a repertoire of sweet, silly, and very funny comic bits. He also performed on his own comedy show on radio from 1932 to 1935 and during the 1944–45 season.

In the early 1950s Wynn hosted a television variety show, but an entirely new career was about to open up for him. He began to play important dramatic roles, first in the film *The Great Man* (1957), then "Requiem for a Heavyweight" on "Playhouse Ninety" (1956). After one season on a television situation comedy, he spent the rest of his career as a respected actor in films. In 1959 he appeared in *The Diary of Anne Frank* and in 1961 was a delight as Mary Poppins' Uncle Al-bert, who floated to the ceiling every time he laughed. His son Keenan also became a fine actor, often appearing with his father.

For Further Reading

See Appendix 2 for a bibliography of general reference books about Jews and the Jewish experience in America. All of these volumes include information about American Jews in radio, television, and film.

Bedell Smith, Sally. *In All His Glory: The Life of William S. Paley.* New York: Simon and Schuster, 1990.

Bilby, Kenneth. *The General: David Sarnoff and the Rise of the Communications Industry.* New York: Harper and Row, 1985.

Cohen, Sarah Blacher, ed. *From Hester Street to Hollywood: The Jewish-American Stage and Screen.* Bloomington, Ind.: Indiana University Press, 1983.

Erens, Patricia. *The Jew in American Cinema.* Bloomington, Ind.: Indiana University Press, 1984.

Gabler, Neal. *An Empire of Their Own: How the Jews Invented Hollywood.* New York: Crown Publishers, 1988.

Lyman, Darryl. *Great Jews on Stage and Screen.* Middle Village, N.Y.: Jonathan David Publishers, 1987.

———. *The Jewish Comedy Catalog.* Middle Village, N.Y.: Jonathan David Publishers, 1989.

Part 12

Books, Newspapers, and Magazines

OVERVIEW

An informed public is crucial to a democracy, and Jewish Americans have played a significant role in disseminating information to the people of this country. In the late nineteenth century, their presence began to be felt in journalism in an important way when **Joseph Pulitzer**, who began his career in penny papers, bought two leading St. Louis papers in 1878. His new paper, the *St. Louis Post-Dispatch*, offered features never before seen in a major daily, including women's fashion, sports, comics, illustrations, and more advertising. The newspaper business would never be the same again. He purchased the *New York World* in 1883

and three years later it had the largest circulation of any newspaper in the country.

At the other end of the spectrum, stylistically, was **Adolph S. Ochs**. Reacting to the sensationalism of Pulitzer and other publishers, he managed *The New York Times* by the standards of objectivity, impartiality, and responsibility to the public. He was somewhat less responsible to his own people. His paper had no Jewish managing editor under the first three publishers—Ochs, his son-in-law Arthur Hays Sulzberger, and *his* son-in-law Orvil E. Dryfoos—and a number of staff members with "Jewish-sounding" first names were asked to use their initials on the masthead.

There have been many other important Jewish

names in American publishing. **Dorothy Schiff** was owner and publisher of the *New York Post*. **Samuel I. Newhouse** accumulated thirty-one newspapers, seven magazines, six television stations, five radio stations, twenty cable-television stations, and a wire service during his career. The list of influential American reporters and columnists includes names like Herbert Bayard Swope, **Walter Lippmann**, **Walter Winchell**, and **Art Buchwald**.

In the world of magazine publishing, Moses Annenberg and his descendants founded an empire on the *Daily Racing Form* and the *Philadelphia Inquirer* that would eventually include *Seventeen* magazine and *TV Guide*. **Harold Ross** founded *The New Yorker* and ran it as a forum for the best American fiction and reporting, fostering writers such as **Dorothy Parker**, E. B. White, and James Thurber. In 1938 *Commentary* began as one of the foremost journals of Jewish intellectual thought. In 1977 Leonard Fein and **Elie Wiesel** founded *Moment* to cover not only current events and politics, but also culture, family issues, and other subjects of interest to Jewish Americans. It is now the largest independent Jewish monthly in the country. More recently, Michael Lerner and Nan Fink founded *Tikkun* to counteract what they saw as a dangerous move toward conservatism by *Commentary*. **Mortimer Zuckerman** purchased the *Atlantic Monthly* in 1980 and became its chairman. Four years later he purchased *U.S. News and World Report* and became its editor-in-chief.

Three other magazines show the continuing interest of Jewish women in feminism and women's issues. In 1895, **Rosa Sonneschein**, supported by the **National Council of Jewish Women**, published the first edition of *American Jewess*. It was the first American magazine to be published in English for Jewish women. In 1971, **Gloria Steinem**, whose father was Jewish, co-founded *Ms* magazine. The magazine helped to lead and to publicize the women's movement that had been inspired by **Betty Friedan**'s book *The Feminine Mystique*. And, in 1976, the first issue of *Lilith*, The Independent Jewish Women's Magazine appeared.

There have been some important Jewish names in

book publishing as well. **Bennett Cerf** was co-founder of Random House, which published James Joyce's *Ulysses*, going to court to defend it against obscenity charges. Max Schuster was co-founder of Simon and Schuster. Benjamin Huebsch headed Viking Press for decades and Roger W. Straus, Jr., co-founded Farrar, Straus & Giroux.

Ironically, we owe today's highest honor in both journalism and literature to that sensationalist publisher of the late nineteenth century, Joseph Pulitzer. Pulitzer endowed a school of journalism at Columbia University which opened in 1912 and, before he died, created the prizes that are now such prestigious awards in the world of publishing.

BERNSTEIN, CARL (1944–)

Journalist

Carl Bernstein gained international fame for exposing the Watergate scandal. A graduate of the University of Maryland, Bernstein began his journalistic career with the *Washington Star* from 1960 to 1965, then spent ten years with the *Washington Post*. During that time, he and his colleague Robert Woodward uncovered the Watergate affair, resulting in a Pulitzer Prize for the *Post*. Their 1974 book about the Watergate exposé, *All the President's Men*, was made into a successful film two years later. They also co-authored *The Final Days*. Bernstein later left the *Post* to work for ABC News.

BUCHWALD, ART (1925–)

Humorist, newspaper columnist

Art Buchwald was born on October 20, 1925 in Mount Vernon, New York. He spent his childhood moving in and out of various foster homes and at age seventeen joined the Marines. Three and a half years later, he left the armed services and began to attend the University of Southern California in Los Angeles. In 1948 he obtained his first professional position as a journalist: the Paris reporter for *Variety*. A year later he joined the Paris office of the *New York Herald Tribune* where he began to write an off-beat column called "Paris After Dark." In 1951, he started a new column for the *Tribune* entitled "Mostly About People." The column featured interviews with the celebrities moving through the Paris "scene." A year later the two columns were combined under the title "Europe's Lighter Side" and began to be published in the United States.

Soon after this, Buchwald returned to the United States. He settled in Washington, D.C. and began to write humor columns about the American political scene. He has entertained the world with his insights ever since. Today, Buchwald's column is distributed by the Los Angeles Times Syndicate and is published in over 550 newspapers throughout the world. He is also the author of more than thirty books including *Son of the Great Society* (1966), *I Never Danced at the White House* (1973), *I Think I Don't Remember* (1987), *Leaving Home: A Memoir* (1994), and *I'll Always Have Paris* (1996). In 1982 he was awarded the Pulitzer Prize for Distinguished Commentary.

CAHAN, ABRAHAM (1860–1951)

Newspaper publisher

Abraham Cahan probably did more to ease the new Jewish immigrant into American society than almost any one else in the first half of the twentieth century. As the editor of the **Jewish Daily Forward**, the largest Yiddish-language newspaper in the United States, he reached almost a quarter of a million of these new Americans, offering them advice and guidance on integrating themselves into a radically different culture. It was a transition he had already made with surprising ease.

Cahan was born in a small village near Vilna, a Lithuanian city with a lively Jewish culture. His family was very poor, too poor to provide him with any education other than what could be found in the village Hebrew school, but he managed to get enough learning to become a teacher himself. While teaching in nearby Velizh he became involved in the anti-Czarist underground and eventually had to leave the country, immigrating to the United States in June 1882.

Abraham Cahan has been described as the most influential person in the lives of the Eastern European Jewish immigrants in New York City during the first half of the twentieth century. He served as editor of the Yiddish-language Jewish Daily Forward *from 1903 until 1946. The paper had a readership of a quarter of a million during its heyday and Cahan published such Yiddish writers as Isaac Bashevis Singer (under several pseudonyms). By far the most popular section of the paper was called "Bintl Brief" (Bundle of Letters), which dispensed advice to the new immigrants on how to adapt to their new country. (Courtesy of American Jewish Archives)*

Once he had arrived in the United States, Cahan immersed himself in the burgeoning Jewish-led labor movement, the lively Yiddish culture of the Lower East Side, and the English language. Within a few years, he read and wrote English well enough to contribute stories about life in the Jewish ghetto to the *New York World* and the *New York Sun*. He also worked as a union organizer and editor of a short-lived labor paper. In 1891 Cahan became editor of another Yiddish labor paper, *Arbeiter Zeitung*, a job he held for three years.

Over the next decade, Cahan began writing fiction, publishing his first novel, *Yekl*, in 1896 with the support of William Dean Howells. He continued to work as a journalist as well, first in a brief stint with newly founded *Forward* (a position he resigned after only six months), then as a reporter for Lincoln Steffens's progressive *New York Commercial Advertiser* from 1897 to 1901. He returned to the *Forward* twice more, the first time for only six months, then in 1903 for good. He remained editor of the *Jewish Daily Forward* for the remainder of his life, steering it through the shoals of the socialist movement; a strong anti-war stance in 1917 that brought him into conflict with U.S. postal authorities, support for the Russian revolution, and later denunciations of Stalin; and eventually to support of the New Deal. He continued to write fiction, including his best-known novel, *The Rise of David Levinsky* (1917). He suffered a stroke in 1946 and his involvement with the paper lessened progressively until his death on August 31, 1951.

CAPP, AL (1909–1979)

Cartoonist

The creator of "Li'l Abner," Al Capp (Alfred Gerald Caplin) was born in New Haven, Connecticut, on September 28, 1909. He attended the school at the Boston Museum of Fine Arts. Later, he studied at the Pennsylvania Academy of the Fine Arts in Philadelphia. At both institutions he studied landscape architecture, but upon graduation he quickly gravitated to cartooning. In 1933 he became an assistant to "Joe Palooka" creator Ham Fisher. A year later he began to draw his own strip, "L'il Abner." First published in the *New York Mirror*, "L'il Abner" was soon syndicated to most newspapers in the country and became extremely popular. The strip was even adapted into a successful Broadway musical. It centered on the humorous adventures of the hillbilly L'il Abner Yokum of Dogpatch, U.S.A. and his family and friends, including his wife Daisy Mae, his parents Mammy and Pappy Yokum, the sleuth (based on Dick Tracy) Fearless Fosdick, and Sadie Hawkins. Capp continued to

draw "L'il Abner" until his retirement in 1977. He died in New Haven two years later, on November 5, 1979.

CERF, BENNETT (1898–1971)

Publisher, television personality

Genial, witty publisher Bennett Cerf was born in New York City and studied at Columbia University where he edited the Columbia *Jester*. He began his career in publishing as a writer for the financial section of the *New York Tribune*. In 1923 he became vice president of the firm of Boni and Liveright and, in 1925, he and partner Donald S. Klopfer bought The Modern Library from that company for $215,000. An inexpensive line of classics that had been started seven years before, it formed the basis of what would grow to be a publishing empire. Two years later, the two men founded the publishing company of Random House in order, according to Cerf, "to publish a few books on the side at random." He turned out to be the perfect publisher for the time. Not only was he intelligent, well educated, and dedicated to quality, he also possessed a flair for publicity that helped make his company one of the most successful in publishing and himself a modest celebrity. Among the company's accomplishments were the United States publication of *Ulysses* (1934) by James Joyce and the *Random House Dictionary of the English Language* (1966).

As a publisher Cerf was often unconventional. On the one hand, he published the difficult, even obscurantist *Ulysses*, going to court to defend it against obscenity charges. On the other, he personally edited a number of anthologies of "bedside stories" and his personal specialty, jokes, including the *Encyclopedia of American Humor* (1954). He appeared widely on the lecture circuit, telling his favorite stories, and was a regular panelist on the television show "What's My Line?" which aired from 1950 until 1967. He also wrote a syndicated column with the highly dignified name of *Cerfboard*. His first wife was **Sylvia Sidney**, and his second, Phyllis, later married New York Mayor Robert Wagner. He lived in a world of wealth, literature, and glamour, and he knew and loved books, publishing, people, and puns.

COMMENTARY

In 1938 the **American Jewish Committee** began to publish a bimonthly periodical called the *Contemporary Jewish Record*. In 1945 the publication's name was changed to *Commentary* and was released on a monthly basis. Its first editor was Elliot E. Cohen. Under his leadership the magazine became a well-respected, post-war liberal intellectual forum. Though the magazine was designed to focus on issues of interest to a Jewish audience, its subject matter was quite comprehensive and the magazine appealed to a broader public. Its bias was anti-Soviet and in favor of a nuclear deterrent policy. Prior to 1948 the magazine held a "non-Zionist" stance—as opposed to anti-Zionist. After Israel was founded, however, both *Commentary* and Cohen became staunch supporters of the new state.

In 1960 **Norman Podhoretz** took over Cohen's position as editor-in-chief. For the next seven years the magazine's editorial slant was decidedly leftist and became closely tied with the radical movement growing throughout the United States. The magazine changed its position on Cold War nuclear policy and was among the earliest to question the wisdom of American involvement in the Vietnam War.

In 1967, however, Podhoretz began a political turnaround. By 1970 he had come to reject most of the radical views of the 1960s. This marked the beginning of *Commentary* magazine's transformation into one of the leading conservative forums in the country. Podhoretz himself applied the term **"neoconservatism"** to the magazine's new political philosophy.

In 1990, the American Jewish Committee announced that it would no longer be able to support its two magazines—*Commentary* and the more liberal *Present Tense*. The latter magazine was forced to cease publication, but *Commentary* turned to its supporters to raise sufficient funds to keep publishing. The AJC has also provided office space to the magazine, as well as other back office support, despite the committee's earlier decision to discontinue aid. Podhoretz became

editor-at-large in 1995 and the magazine's new editor-in-chief is Neal Kozodoy, who maintains the publication's conservative viewpoint.

FRIEDAN, BETTY (1921–)

Writer, feminist activist

Betty Friedan is one of the key figures in the feminist revolution of the 1960s and 1970s, both as co-founder of the National Organization for Women and as the author of a key text of the movement, *The Feminine Mystique*. It might be argued that all Friedan did was reflect on the barriers to happiness she had found in her own life and realize she was typical of women of her generation; but Friedan had the insight to make that recognition and to act on it.

Born Betty Naomi Goldstein, she was a psychology major at Smith College, editor of the college newspaper, and co-founder of its literary magazine. She was an excellent student and spent 1942 studying as a research fellow at Berkeley, but decided against pursuing a doctorate, preferring instead to follow her other interest, journalism. While working as a wire service reporter, she met and married Carl Friedan, an advertising executive. When her first child was born in 1949, she received maternity leave, returning to work afterward. When she tried to make the same arrangement for her second pregnancy five years later, she was fired. Years later, Friedan pointed to this incident as a major awakening for her feminist consciousness.

For the next eight years, Friedan struggled to play the role of the dutiful suburban wife and mother. In 1957 she was preparing a questionnaire for Smith alumni when she realized that she was not alone in her sense of alienation and intellectual deprivation. Expanding the purview of the questionnaire to include women from other colleges, she saw a larger trend. After publishing her findings in a seminal article in *Good Housekeeping* in September 1960, she began work on *The Feminine Mystique*.

It was on this foundation that a new generation of feminist activists was born, with Friedan at their forefront. She taught at New York University and the New

School and in 1966 co-founded the National Organization for Women. She eventually become disenchanted with the organization's increasingly radical politics and became a lightning rod for controversy within the movement in the 1970s and early 1980s by her insistence on moderating feminist goals and her willingness to work within electoral politics.

In recent years, while she has remained committed to feminism, Friedan has developed new interests. In 1988 she became a visiting faculty member at the journalism school of the University of Southern California and became affiliated with the university's Andrus Gerontology Center, part of her new concern with the treatment of America's aging population. She also began an in-depth course of personal study of Torah, as part of a serious re-examination of her Jewish roots.

JEWISH DAILY FORWARD

During the first two decades of the twentieth century, when Jewish immigrants from Eastern Europe arrived in the United States by the hundreds of thousands, the *Jewish Daily Forward* became the most widely read Yiddish newspaper in the world. In the major cities where Jews settled, and especially in the Jewish immigrant epicenter of New York City, the *Forward*, with a circulation of 200,000 and an influence that reached far beyond that readership, was as integral a component of working-class Jewish life as pushcarts, tenements, garment factories, and kosher food shops.

Founded in 1897 on New York City's Lower East Side by **Abraham Cahan** and Louis Miller, the *Forward* combined advocacy for democratic socialism and support for the Jewish labor movement with a desire to both encourage Yiddish creative writing and assist in the process of introducing Jewish immigrants to American mores and traditions. Cahan took over as full-time editor in 1903 and remained in that position until he suffered a stroke in 1946. Soon after he assumed editorial control, he molded the newspaper into a dominant voice for anti-clerical radicalism in the Jewish quarter and won a broad audience to whom its word was sacred. Although Cahan's belief in using "street" Yiddish rather than literary Yiddish in the

newspaper offended some intellectuals, it also helped make the *Forward* both eminently readable and a powerful progressive voice. Cahan also felt that only an enlightened socialist and secular morality would allow the Jewish immigrant to survive and thrive in the United States. Politically, the newspaper most resembled the viewpoint of socialist leader **Morris Hillquit** and the Social Democratic parties of Europe, who believed in working within established institutions, including labor unions, to build a successful movement.

Cahan used the pages of the *Forward* to publicize Yiddish writers and support Yiddish culture, especially in the areas of theater and performing arts. Besides publishing and publicizing the works of Yiddish writers and poets, some of whom, such as **Isaac Bashevis Singer**, gained considerable fame, the *Forward* elevated the status of such European social democratic thinkers as Karl Kautsky, Leon Blum, Raphael Abramowitch, and Eduard Bernstein. Cahan serialized his own classic novel, *The Rise of David Levinsky*, which chronicled in the first person the uneasy balance of cultural gain and loss for Jewish immigrants coming of age in New York City.

The *Forward*'s popularity was rooted in the close attention it paid to the everyday life of its own readers. Its reporters combed the streets to write about Jewish prostitutes on Allen Street, Jewish children starting to take piano lessons, or the increased attendance of Jews at New York City museums. Although sometimes accused of yellow journalism, the newspaper documented everything it printed and Cahan and his staff believed that all their stories told its readers something important about the lives of the immigrants.

Despite his desire to preserve Yiddish and to document the realities of working-class Jewish immigrant life, Cahan also believed strongly that Jewish newcomers needed to "Americanize" themselves rapidly, which sometimes put the newspaper at odds with many groups advocating Jewish cultural autonomy. Perhaps the most popular column in the *Forward* was its "Bintl Brief" (Bundle of Letters) in which Cahan and his contributing editors fielded letters and gave advice to immigrants struggling to cope with a new environment and culture. Although the "Bintl Brief" sought to offer comfort for a frequently desperate group of readers, it also reflected Cahan's own impatience with immigrants who held on to European *shtetl* values and refused to adapt to an American way of life. The *Forward* took on the role of folk preacher in encouraging and promoting upwardly mobility to its readership, and its words were taken to heart by thousands of Jewish newcomers to the United States.

Cahan and the *Forward* were pivotal in helping to mobilize Jewish trade union activism in the garment industry. The newspaper frequently used its pages to publicize the demands of the striking workers of the International Ladies Garment Workers Union and the Amalgamated Clothing Workers and to advocate improved working conditions, collective bargaining rights, and higher wages as the foundation of a new relationship between capital and labor based on democratic socialist principles. The *Forward* also provided tactical advice and material aid to the Jewish trade unions. In the 1911 New York tailors' strike, Cahan converted the offices of the newspaper into a strike headquarters and placed his staff at the service of the strikers.

Although the *Forward* initially supported and welcomed the Russian Revolution of 1917, from the 1920s on Cahan adopted a strong anti-Communist position and he used the newspaper to strongly and sometimes stridently advocate this point of view to the Jewish public. In the 1930s the *Forward* conducted its own war of words with Jewish members of the Communist Party of the United States. Cahan was bitterly denounced by the Yiddish Communist organ, the *Freiheit*, after he published a series of articles critical of the Soviet Union. Cahan was instrumental in founding the American Labor Party in 1936, which he hoped would be a socialist alternative to the Communist Party.

After World War II the *Forward* published a powerful pictorial memorial to Jewish communities destroyed in the Holocaust featuring photographs by **Roman Vishniac**, which later became highly influential in book form as *A Vanished World*. Nevertheless, the readership of the newspaper declined significantly as the former Yiddish-speaking immigrant community transformed into a second- and third-generation Jewish American population. In addition, Cahan's stroke and subsequent death in 1951 removed the most charismatic presence from the newspaper's masthead. The *Forward* persevered as a Yiddish daily through the 1960s and 1970s with Baruch Charney Vladeck as its managing editor. In 1983 it became a weekly with an English supplement. It now publishes three separate weekly editions, one in English, one in Yiddish, and one in Russian.

The importance of the *Jewish Daily Forward* to the immigrant-Jewish-socialist experience cannot be overestimated. Through its blend of labor union advocacy, community affairs reporting, advice columns, and contemporary fiction, the newspaper not only spoke directly to its immigrant audience, it also helped define a culture and a tradition. Without recognizing the importance of the *Forward*, one cannot adequately document or fully understand the history of Eastern European Jewry in early twentieth century America.

GOLDBERG, RUBE (1883–1970)

Cartoonist

Rube Goldberg may well be the only cartoonist whose name is part of the American lexicon. A "Rube Goldberg" refers to a complicated means of accomplishing a task that could be completed in more a simple manner—a tribute to Goldberg's cartooning theme of the fictitious "Professor Lucifer Gorgonzola Butts," who designs incredibly complex devices to perform elementary tasks.

Although trained as an engineer (University of California, 1904), Reuben Lucius Goldberg took up sportswriting and cartooning for the San Francisco press. He moved to New York in 1907 and spent fourteen years on the staff of the *New York Evening Mail*, for which he wrote and drew a series of successful ongoing cartoons, including "Mike and Ike," "Foolish Questions," and "Boob McNutt." He became the editorial cartoonist for the *New York Sun* in 1937 and later won a Pulitzer Prize for his work there. Goldberg helped found the National Cartoonists' Society and its annual award is called "The Reuben," in his honor.

JOURNALISM

Both enemies and friends of the Jewish people have often claimed that Jews have more than their fair share of influence on the American news media. The truth of this matter is difficult to determine, but certain facts can be elicited from the mass of unfounded assertions. Of the more than 1,700 daily newspapers published in the United States in the middle 1990s, about fifty were owned by Jewish Americans. That is under 3 percent, which is the percentage of Jews in the population. About 3.3 percent of editors and reporters are Jewish, certainly not an important disproportion. On the other hand, newspapers published in New York and Washington, D.C., have a large proportion of Jewish employees, in part because both cities have large Jewish populations.

Jewish Americans have been involved in some of this nation's most influential news media almost from the beginning of journalism in North America in the early eighteenth century. By the beginning of the nineteenth century, important names started to appear. Mordecai Noah, at about this time, became editor of the *City Gazette* of Charleston, South Carolina. He was later editor and publisher of the *New York Enquirer* and helped James Gordon Bennett to found the *New York Herald* in 1835.

Noah comes to our attention largely because of his early Zionist attitudes and beliefs. Most other Jewish journalists were simply journalists, integrated into their respective newspaper organizations. There are some names that stand out even in the middle of the nineteenth century, however. Edward Rosewater was a correspondent and owner of the *Omaha Bee* in Nebraska in 1871. A few years later, one of the most important names in American publishing came to prominence when **Joseph Pulitzer** bought the *New York World* in 1883.

PUBLISHERS

Pulitzer began his career in penny papers, which offered a highly sensational form of journalism, similar to today's supermarket tabloids. When he bought the *World*, he brought some of that attitude with him into the world of legitimate newspapers. Among his innovations were political cartoons, color pictures, and color comics. He was also fond of eye-catching illustrations and investigative reporting. Three years after he bought the *World*, it had the largest circulation of any newspaper in the country. Pulitzer endowed a school of journalism at Columbia University, which opened in 1912 and created the prizes that are now such prestigious awards in the world of publishing.

Adolph Ochs was philosophically far removed from Pulitzer. His management of *The New York Times*, dating from 1896, was a reaction against sensational journalism, emphasizing objectivity, impartiality, and responsibility to the public. This tradition was carried on by his son-in-law, Arthur Hays Sulzberger, and other members of the Sulzberger family.

Samuel I. Newhouse had still another approach to journalism. He was all business. His editors could do very much as they pleased so long has his papers sold. Beginning in 1912, when he was seventeen, Newhouse accumulated thirty-one newspapers, seven magazines, six television stations, five radio stations, twenty cable-television stations, and a wire service. His was the most profitable newspaper chain in the country.

Moses Annenberg, founder of Triangle Publications, began with the *Daily Racing Form*, but his publishing empire would one day own *Seventeen* magazine and *TV Guide*, which has the second largest circulation of any magazine in the country. **Dorothy Schiff**, daughter of banker Joseph Schiff, published the *New York Post* from 1939 to 1976 with more flair than philosophy.

These owners and publishers are important figures in the history of American journalism, but there are other Jewish Americans who have had more influence. They are the editors, reporters, and writers who shaped public opinion.

EDITORS, REPORTERS, AND WRITERS

Herbert Bayard Swope won the first Pulitzer Prize for reporting in 1917 and became executive editor of the

She Defined the Supreme Court for *New York Times* readers

When Linda Greenhouse won a Pulitzer Prize in 1998 for her *New York Times* reporting on the Supreme Court, it was not a surprise to her legion of fans. The only question was—why had it taken so long for her to get the "public" recognition she deserved?

In lucid, clear, straightforward, yet analytical prose (often in front page stories), she has explained the meaning and relevance of the Court's decisions in a way no other journalist has ever done. And, unlike academics who take years to write their thoughtful, theory-filled tomes, she did it on tight deadlines. As the *Times* itself quipped, she often wrote more opinions than the Court itself. In one remarkable ten day period during which the Court handed down a blizzard of opinions, she wrote *five* front page articles for the newspaper, which must be some kind of a record for an individual journalist.

And, sometimes the prose was so memorable that it will become as much a part of the literature of the Court as the opinions themselves.

Our own personal favorite was written in April of 1995 shortly after President Clinton (under attack on several different fronts) had felt compelled to hold a news conference defending the relevance and importance of the office of the Presidency. It is worth quoting.

"Unlike President Clinton, Chief Justice William H. Rehnquist does not hold news conferences. But if he did, it would not occur to anyone to ask him whether he was still relevant.

The Supreme Court's stunning decision of Wednesday that Congress lacked the authority to bar gun possession in or near schools was a forceful reminder not only of the Court's raw power—nine people, divided 5 to 4, invalidated a law that two houses of Congress and the President of the United States approved five years ago— but also of its inevitable role in shaping the country's ongoing political dialogue." (April 28, 1995)

Like the Chief Justice, Linda Greenhouse does not hold news conferences, but with her powerful prose ringing in the ears of Americans, she is a reminder of the ability of the printed word to inform, inspire, and, perhaps most importantly, to educate.

New York World. He was responsible for coining the terms "op ed" page and "Cold War," and for popularizing "new deal" as a label for Franklin Roosevelt's approach to government. A staunch supporter of civil rights, he worked to expose the Ku Klux Klan and began the practice of capitalizing the word Negro.

Working with Swope at the *World* was **Walter Lippman**, one of American journalism's most respected figures. It is difficult to communicate, in today's world of celebrity journalists, just how influential Lippman was in world politics and diplomacy. Stephen J. Whitfield explains that, in 1961, Nikita Kruschev asked Lippman to change a planned visit to the Soviet Union by a few days because of a political crisis in that country. Lippman refused, and Kruschev rearranged his plans to accommodate the American journalist.

Foreign correspondent Ruth Gruber was the first journalist, man or woman, to fly through Siberia into the Soviet arctic, where she lived among prisoners of the gulag and reported on their lives. During World War II she escorted a group of a thousand refugees of the Holocaust from Naples to Oswego, New York, at great personal risk. Her book about the experience became the basis for the permanent Holocaust exhibit in the State Museum of New York.

Less serious in their mission but still highly influential were many Jewish columnists. Franklin Pierce Adams wrote about New York night life and the Algonquin Round Table, several of whom were first published as humorists in his column. **Walter Winchell** reported on the lives of celebrities, from starlets to senators, as did Louis Sobol and Sidney Skolsky. Beginning in the early 1950s, twin sisters Esther and Pauline Lederer dominated the advice column business as Ann Landers and Abigail Van Buren.

A maverick in journalism was Harry Golden. During the 1950s his *Carolina Israelite*, published in Charlotte, North Carolina, became a voice for civil rights and sanity in the South. A bitingly funny writer, Golden was able to satirize Southern views and habits from both inside and out. He also wrote with affection of Jewish life on the Lower East Side and saw his columns turned into a Broadway hit titled *Only in America.*

In the latter half of the twentieth century, *The New York Times* was still owned by the Sulzberger family.

The *Washington Post*, its major rival, had been purchased by Eugene Meyer in the 1930s and was being run by his daughter, Katherine Graham, who was reared as a Lutheran. A 1979 survey indicated that 27 percent of the employees of *The Times* , the *Post*, and certain other influential periodicals—the *Wall Street Journal, Time, Newsweek, U. S. News and World Report*—as well as the three major networks and the Public Broadcasting System, were Jewish Americans. **William Paley** was chairman of the board at CBS. The Sarnoffs dominated NBC. **Leonard Goldenson** was president of ABC.

MODERN JOURNALISM

Perhaps the best known Jewish figure in modern American journalism is broadcaster **Barbara Walters**. In 1976 she became the highest-paid journalist in history when ABC offered her a five-year contract at 1 million dollars a year. Her interviewing technique is legendary, eliciting surprising reactions from leaders of state as well as movie stars. She has interviewed every president since Richard Nixon and every first lady since Lady Bird Johnson. She interviewed Cuban

---

Does Your Bubbe Bet on the Ponies? Maybe She Should.

When Rose Hamburger died at the age of 105 on August 6, 1996, she was certainly the oldest newspaper racing handicapper in the country. Her daily selections for the *New York Post* appeared with her photograph under a headline identifying her as "Gamblin' Rose." She had begun her "new" career only seven months before, after a lifetime of "firsts" and a lifelong interest in "the races." She was probably the last person alive to have seen all eleven Triple Crown winners, from Sir Barton in 1919 to Affirmed in 1978. But, she didn't spend all her time at the track. When she graduated from Normal College (the precursor of Hunter College), where she majored in both mathematics and music, in 1910 at age 19, she was the youngest graduate in the college's history (she was also to become the oldest living graduate). She became, at age forty-seven, the first woman in Baltimore licensed to sell real estate, and had an enormously successful career, which lasted well into her eighties.

Nice Jewish Boy From Krypton

No comic book hero embodies American ideals as does Superman. As everyone knows, the man with the "S" on his chest symbolizes "truth, justice and the American Way." What fewer people know is that the creators and definers of Superman's Americanism were Jerry Siegel (1914–1996) and Joe Shuster (1914–1992), two Jews from Cleveland. Superman obeys the talmudic injunction to do good for its own sake and heal the world where he can. His creators created a mythic character who reflected their own Jewish values.

President Fidel Castro. In 1977 she arranged the first joint interviews with President Anwar Sadat of Egypt and Prime Minister Menachem Begin of Israel. She also helped to create, and still co-hosts one of television's first investigative news shows, "20/20."

Walters, like most other contemporary Jewish journalists, has never made any attempt to hide her ethnicity. However, earlier journalists, such as Lippman and famed war correspondent A. J. Liebling, often played down or even denied their origins. Lippman insisted that Harvard, his alma mater, was right to limit Jewish admissions and at no time did he mention Nazi persecution of the Jews in his column. Even after the Holocaust, he never wrote about the death camps. At *The New York Times*, there was no Jewish managing editor under the first three publishers—Ochs, his son-in-law Sulzberger, and *his* son-in-law Orville Dryfoos—and many staff members with "Jewish-sounding" first names were asked to use their initials on the masthead.

The question of whether there has been a specifically Jewish contribution to American journalism, in terms of approach or philosophy, will have to remain open. As Whitfield points out, "*at most* only a segment of ethnic identity or religious heritage has ever been implicated in what journalists have done, and therefore the task of determining a distinctive Jewish contribution is complicated when so many Jews have blended so successfully into the structure of social organization." In other words, Jewish Americans can be proud of their achievements in journalism as individuals, rather than as a special interest group.

KRISTOL, IRVING (1920–)

One of America's most influential conservative intellectuals, Irving Kristol began his public life at the other end of the political spectrum. He was born into an Orthodox Jewish family in Brooklyn, but spurned religion for radical politics, joining a Trotskyist group at the City College of New York. He became part of a circle later known as "the New York Jewish intellectuals," who would emerge as some of the country's most prominent writers and scholars, including Daniel Bell, **Irving Howe**, and Nathan Glazer. As he gradually shifted from the far left to the center in the 1940s, Kristol joined the editorial staff of *Commentary* and helped shape its postwar philosophy of liberal anti-Communism. In 1953 he was named co-editor of a like-minded journal in England, *Encounter*. After returning to the United States in 1958, Kristol helped found the quarterly *The Public Interest* and became Professor of Urban Values at New York University, a post he retained until 1987.

By the late 1960s Kristol and his friends were popularly referred to as "**neoconservatives**," a term connoting a former liberal who has embraced conservatism. Within the Jewish community, Kristol stirred controversy by advocating increased public acceptance of traditional Judeo-Christian values, which he believes will benefit American society as well as encourage Jews to draw closer to their own heritage. He continues to serve as editor of *The Public Interest*, which offers a generally conservative perspective on domestic affairs, and is publisher of *The National Interest*, which focuses on foreign affairs. Kristol and his wife, the author and scholar Gertrude Himmelfarb, reside in Washington, D.C. Their son William, a leading conservative intellectual and activist, is editor-in-chief of *The Weekly Standard*.

LILITH

A magazine that concerns itself with feminism, Judaism, and relationships between the two, *Lilith* was founded in 1976 by a small group of women led by Susan Weidman Schneider, who continues to be

Founded in 1976 ". . . to foster discussion of Jewish women's issues and put them on the agenda of the Jewish community," Lilith *has succeeded. After over twenty years of publication it remains widely influential as "the independent Jewish women's magazine." This photo reproduces the cover of the first issue. (Courtesy of* Lilith)

editor-in-chief. Although it is not-for-profit, it is independent of any particular movement or organization but promotes the work of a number of campus and community organizations. It is named for the legendary predecessor of Eve who demanded equality with Adam. A national magazine that comes out quarterly, it features the work of Jewish women writers, artists, and educators and that of other writers who deal with subjects of particular interest to Jewish women. *Lilith* also focuses on the development of lifecyle rituals and holiday celebrations that are free of gender bias. Included in each issue are reviews of books, plays, films, music, and videos that are of particular interest to Jewish women and listings of resources.

LIPPMANN, WALTER (1889–1974)

Newspaper columnist, author

Walter Lippmann was born in New York City on September 23, 1889. He attended Harvard University, graduating with a B.A. in 1909. While at Harvard he was profoundly influenced by both William James and George Santayana. In 1914 he helped create *The New Republic* magazine and became its assistant editor. In the years following, he established a close relationship with President Woodrow Wilson. In 1917 Lippmann served as an assistant to the Secretary of War, and in 1919 he participated in the Treaty of Versailles negotiations.

From 1921 to 1929 Lippmann wrote editorials for the *New York World*. In 1929, he became its editor. In 1931, he moved to the New York *Herald Tribune*, inaugurating his historic column, "Today and Tomorrow." At the height of its popularity, the column was syndicated in over 250 newspapers—in twenty-five countries—and won two Pulitzer Prizes (1958 and 1962.) His many influential books include *A Preface to Politics* (1913), *Drift and Mastery* (1914), *Public Opinion* (1922), *In The Phantom Public* (1925), *The Good Society* (1937), and *Essays in the Public Philosophy* (1955). He died in New York City December 14, 1974, one of the most well-known and well-respected political columnists in the world.

MOMENT

Moment magazine is a not-for-profit magazine founded by Leonard Fein and **Elie Wiesel** in 1977. For ten years Fein served as both the magazine's editor and its publisher. While the magazine has always reported on a much wider variety of subjects than other Jewish magazines or journals, in its early years, *Moment* was also a venue for Fein's generally liberal political, social, and religious views.

In the early 1980s Wiesel separated from the magazine. In 1987 Herschel Shanks took over editorial control from Fein. With Shanks came a change in the editorial policy to a more diversified perspective. The magazine presently prides itself on welcoming all responsible opinions on issues of concern to Jews and appealing to a wide range of people, in every Jewish community.

Today, Shanks still serves as editor. In the early 1990s Suzanne Singer became the magazine's managing editor. Unlike other Jewish magazines and journals such as **Tikkun** and **Commentary**, *Moment* covers not only current events and politics but also culture, gossip, family issues, and other subjects. At a circulation of 150,000, it is the largest independent Jewish monthly in the country. It is funded by Jewish Educational Ventures, a not-for-profit organization, which exists to publish the magazine as well as to publish the journals *Biblical Archeology Review*, *Bible Review*, and *Archeological Odyssey*.

OCHS, ADOLPH S. (1858–1935)

Newspaper publisher

Adolph Simon Ochs was born on March 12, 1858 in Cincinnati, Ohio, and grew up in Knoxville, Tennessee. The child of Jewish immigrants, he began his newspaper career as a delivery boy. In 1872 he went to work at the *Knoxville Chronicle* as a printer's devil (a young worker below the level of apprentice). He then became a compositor for the *Louisville Courier-Journal*. When he was only nineteen he participated in the founding of the *Chattanooga Dispatch*. A year later he bought a controlling interest in the failing *Chattanooga Times*. He built it into one of the top newspapers in the South. In addition to being a co-founder of the Southern Associated Press, he also served as its chairman from 1891 though 1894.

In 1896 Ochs took over control of *The New York Times*. The newspaper was losing the battle with the more powerful and popular "yellow press." Ochs turned this trend around. He publicly announced his commitment to the quality and veracity of his new newspaper's reportage by adopting the slogan "All the News That's Fit to Print." Two years later he saved the newspaper from probable financial ruin by dropping the price from three cents to one cent. In doing so, Ochs provided readers an alternative to the more sensational papers at their same price.

In 1900 Ochs became the director of the Associated

Legendary publisher of The New York Times, *Adolph Ochs and his wife, Efie Wise Ochs, are shown here (on the left) in Madrid after an audience with the king. Among other philanthropic activities, he was a major fund-raiser for Hebrew Union College. (Courtesy of American Jewish Archives)*

Press, a position he held until his death. In addition to adding the Book Review and rotogravure pictures to *The Times*, in 1913 he inaugurated the *New York Times Index*, the most comprehensive U.S. newspaper index. Adolph Ochs died on April 8, 1935, in Chattanooga, Tennessee.

PODHORETZ, NORMAN (1930–)

Editor, essayist

Norman Podhoretz was born in Brooklyn, New York on January 16, 1930. He attended the **Jewish Theologi-** cal Seminary and Columbia University, graduating from both in 1950. At Columbia he came to know **Lionel Trilling**, who had a profound influence on Podhoretz's early political philosophy. Podhoretz then attended Cambridge University earning his B.A. in 1952 and his M.A. in 1957. In 1955 he became an assistant editor at **Commentary** magazine, known as one of the most notable Jewish intellectual journals in the country.

In 1960 Podhoretz became *Commentary*'s editor in chief, a position he held for thirty-five years. Initially, Podhoretz's—and therefore *Commentary*'s—political orientation was to the left. However, after 1967 he be-

Norman Podhoretz made his name as Editor-in-Chief of Commentary magazine, one of the leading Jewish intellectual journals in the country. Frequently outspoken, he is shown here at a 1962 symposium with Hannah Arendt, who was never shy about expressing her opinions. We imagine that it was a fascinating presentation. (Courtesy of American Jewish Historical Society, Waltham, Massachusetts, and New York, New York)

came increasingly conservative. Podhoretz points to the famed New York Teachers Union strike and the American liberal reaction to Israel's victory in the Six Day War as causes affecting this change.

Currently a self-described "neoconservative," Podhoretz has written many influential editorials for *Commentary*, and built the journal into one of the most provocative and spirited intellectual forums in America. He is also the author of several books, including *With the Present Danger* (1980), *Why We Were in Vietnam* (1982), and *The Bloody Crossroads: Where Literature and Politics Meet* (1986). His two volumes of autobiography, *Making It* (1968) and *Breaking Ranks* (1979), detail his rise to power in the world of New York's intellectuals and his crossover from left to right. In January 1995 Podhoretz announced his retirement as the editor of *Commentary*. However, he has continued his career as an influential neoconservative political thinker.

PULITZER, JOSEPH (1847–1911)

Newspaper publisher

The founder of the *St. Louis Post-Dispatch*, Joseph Pulitzer was born in Mako, Hungary, on April 10, 1847, and immigrated to the United States when he was seventeen. He served on the Union side in the Civil War before moving to St. Louis and turning to journalism. His first job was with the *Westliche Post*, a German-language newspaper. Becoming active in politics, Pulitzer won a seat in the Missouri legislature in 1869 and went on to participate in national politics, first with the liberal Republican movement and later with the Democratic Party.

In 1878 Pulitzer purchased both the *St Louis Dispatch* and *The Post*. He then merged them and added women's fashion, sports, comics, illustrations, and more advertising. His newspaper changed the industry. He purchased the *New York World* in 1883, and his publishing empire was established. At the time his only real competition was William Randolph Hearst and their battle over headlines during the Spanish Civil War led to a less-than-noble legacy—"yellow journalism." At his death, on October 29, 1911, Pulitzer left money to establish America's first journalism school, at Columbia University. His will also endowed prizes to be given for achievement in American journalism and letters.

ROSENBACH, A. S. W. (1876–1952)

Bibliographer, book collector and dealer, writer

Born on July 22, 1876, in Philadelphia, Pennsylvania, A. S. W. Rosenbach came from a religiously observant family. He attended the University of Pennsylvania, receiving his doctorate in 1900 and, in the process, fell in love with books. In 1903 he opened his first book shop. By 1904 he put out his first catalogue. He was known to pay enormous sums of money when a particularly valuable book was auctioned and frequently broke records at auction houses. Many famous and wealthy Americans of the period went to Rosenbach to build their book collections including J. Pierpont Morgan, Henry Folger, and Henry E. Huntington. Committed to Judaism, he was president for many years of the American Jewish Historical Society and compiled *The American Jewish Bibliography* (1926). He wrote many other books on his passion, including *The Unpublishable Memoirs* (1917), *Books and Bidders* (1927), and *A Book Hunters Holiday*. In 1930 Rosenbach created the Rosenbach Fellowship in Bibliography at the University of Pennsylvania. He died on July 1, 1952, in Philadelphia.

ROSS, HAROLD (1892–1951)

Magazine founder and editor

Harold Ross was born on November 6, 1892, in Aspen, Colorado. He never finished high school, instead dropping out to become a reporter. By World War I he was the editor of the U.S. Armed Services publication *Stars and Stripes*. In 1925 Ross obtained financial backing from his friend Raoul Fleischmann and founded *The New Yorker*. Intending the magazine to be a forum for the best American writers of fiction and reporting, Ross soon began to attract writers away from the magazine's well-established rival, *Vanity Fair*. Because of his commitment to quality, his innovative style, and his egalitarian approach to writers, Ross also developed an astounding array of talented new writers, including E. B. White and James Thurber. Among the many cartoonists who helped create *The New Yorker*'s style were Helen Hokinson, Peter Arno, Charles Addams, and Mary Petty. For twenty-five years, Harold Ross helped define America's cultural and intellectual landscape. He died in Boston, Massachusetts, on December 6, 1951.

SCHIFF, DOROTHY (1903–1989)

Newspaper publisher

Dorothy Schiff was born on March 11, 1903, the granddaughter of Kuhn, Loeb & Co. director **Jacob Schiff**. Educated largely at home, she later attended Brearley School and Bryn Mawr for a year each and was en-

rolled for a time at the New School's University in Exile. She was married four times. Prior to her first marriage, she converted to Christianity (Episcopalianism) and prior to her second, back to Judaism.

In 1939 on the suggestion of her second husband, George Backer, Schiff purchased the failing *New York Post*. Initially, Backer served as president and editor, and Schiff as vice-president and treasurer. In 1942, with the newspaper still deeply in debt, Schiff ended the marriage to Backer and took over leadership of the newspaper. Her third husband, Theodore Thackrey, previously the *Post*'s feature editor, became the paper's executive editor. During the Thackrey/Schiff era, the *New York Post* became a successful newspaper. It changed to the tabloid format, purchased the *Bronx Home News*, bought television and radio stations, started a Paris edition (1945–1948), created new popular features, established a foreign bureau, and began a syndication service. Personally and politically, however, Thackrey and Schiff didn't get along. They divorced in 1950.

Thereafter, Schiff ran the *Post* herself and increased its success by cutting costs, expanding advertising, and publishing a wider variety of political viewpoints. (Her final marriage, in 1953, to industrialist Rudolf Sonneborn, ended in divorce in 1965.) By 1976, however, the *Post* was again running into debt and Schiff was forced to sell the paper to Rupert Murdoch.

Throughout her career as a newspaper publisher, Schiff wrote outspoken columns and editorials. She was a friend to presidents and politicians—from Franklin D. Roosevelt to Nelson Rockefeller to Lyndon B. Johnson—and for a short time served as the anti-Tammany candidate for the Democratic State Committee from the Ninth Assembly District. She died in August 1989 at the age of 86.

SENDAK, MAURICE (1928–)

Book illustrator, author

Where the Wild Things Are (1963) won the American Library Association's Caldecott Medal and is a classic in children's literature. Maurice Sendak, the book's author, changed children's literature forever. Many credit Sendak as being the first American children's book author to acknowledge and explore the darker side of childhood and children's feelings.

Sendak was born in Brooklyn, New York, on June 10, 1928, and is a self-taught illustrator. He had his first major success in 1952 when he illustrated Ruth Krauss' book, *A Hole to Dig*. Four years later he began to publish children's books that he both wrote and illustrated. Starting with *Kenny's Window* (1956), his published works also include: *Very Far Away* (1957), *The Sign on Rosie's Door* (1960), *Higglety, Pigglety, Pop* (1967), *In the Night Kitchen* (1970), and *Outside Over There* (1981). In 1970 Maurice Sendak was given the Hans Christian Anderson Prize, the highest award for children's literature, in recognition of his body of work.

SONNESCHEIN, ROSA (1847–1932)

Journalist, publisher, clubwoman

Founder and editor of the *American Jewess* magazine, Rosa Sonneschein was born on March 12, 1847, in Morovia, Austria, and was brought up in Hungary. In 1864, she married Rabbi Solomon Sonneschein. They settled in St. Louis in 1869, where Rosa became a prominent clubwoman inside and outside the Jewish community. By the 1880s she was submitting stories to Jewish periodicals and reporting for German-language newspapers.

In 1893 the Sonnescheins divorced. The same year, the Jewish Women's Congress of the World's Columbian Exposition in Chicago founded the **National Council of Jewish Women** (NCJW), with Sonneschein one of the most vocal participants. Remaining in Chicago after the Exposition ended, she spent the next two years building support for her magazine. In 1895 she published the first edition of *American Jewess*. It was the first American magazine to be published, in English, for Jewish women. A few years later, she split with the Council and publicly chastised the organization because it wasn't committed to her two passions—**Zionism** and increased participation of women in Jewish religious life. In 1898

she sold the magazine while remaining its editor. In August 1899 the magazine closed and Sonneschein disappeared from public life. She died in St. Louis on March 5, 1932.

SPIEGELMAN, ART (1948–)

Cartoonist

Art Spiegelman was born in Stockholm, Sweden, on February 15, 1948, the son of a Holocaust survivor. He grew up in Rego Park, New York, and attended the High School of Art and Design. He later attended the State University of New York in Binghamton, but never graduated. In 1966 he went to work as an illustrator for the Topps Gum Company. The same year he began to produce underground comics. From 1971 through 1975, he lived in San Francisco where he co-founded *Arcade* ("a comix review"). In 1975 he returned to New York and began drawing for publications such as *The New York Times*, the *Village Voice*, and *Playboy*. Five years later, he co-founded the magazine *Raw* with his wife, Francoise Mouly.

Through *Raw*, Spiegelman came to national attention. The magazine serialized his most famous creation, "Maus," the story of the Holocaust in comic-book form with mice representing the Jews and cats representing the Nazis. (Spiegelman had been drawing the strip since 1973.) In 1986 he published his first Maus book, *Maus: A Survivor's Tale I: My Father Bleeds History*. The second book installment of Maus, *Maus: A Survivor's Tale II: And Here My Troubles Began* was published in 1991. In 1992, Spiegelman won a special Pulitzer Prize for the Maus stories. Currently, he is working as an illustrator for *The New Yorker*, and his cartoons are shown at galleries and museums throughout the world.

STEINEM, GLORIA (1934–)

Activist, journalist, magazine editor

Born on March 25, 1934, Gloria Steinem is one of modern feminism's most famous voices. Though she never formally converted to Judaism, she is thought to be Jewish by much of the public. (Her mother was Christian and her father was Jewish.) She says that while she has never thought of herself as Christian, when anti-Semitism arises, she identifies herself as Jewish.

After a difficult, unstable childhood, Steinem attended Smith College, graduating magna cum laude. She then spent two years in India, moving back to the United States in 1958. Pursuing a career in journalism, she moved to New York in 1960 and began to contribute articles to magazines including *Glamour*, *Ladies' Home Journal*, the satirical magazine *Help!*, and *Show*, which published her famous Playboy Bunny exposé. Throughout the 1960s, she developed her twin interests, journalism and progressive politics. In 1968 she was a founding editor of *New York* magazine and began publishing about the fledgling women's movement. A year later she had become a well-known feminist activist, and in 1971 she co-founded *Ms* magazine. She has published several books including *Outrageous Acts and Everyday Rebellions* (1983), *Revolution from Within: A Book of Self Esteem* (1992), and *Moving Beyond Words* (1994). She is a co-founder of the Women's Action Alliance and the National Women's Political Caucus. Since 1968, she has participated in, or reported on, most major political conventions and campaigns in the United States.

SULZBERGER, ARTHUR O. (1926–)

Newspaper publisher

Arthur Ochs Sulzberger was born in New York City on February 5, 1926, the grandson of Adolph Ochs and son of Arthur Hays Sulzberger both publishers of *The New York Times*. After serving in the Marines during World War II, he attended Columbia University, graduating with a B.A. in 1951. The following year he became a cub reporter for *The Times*. He then moved on to the *Milwaukee Journal* before returning to *The Times* as a foreign correspondent, working variously out of London, Paris, and Rome. In 1955 Sulzberger returned

---

July 1, 1971—A Date to Remember in Journalism History!

On this date *The New York Times* began publication of the *Pentagon Papers*, the classified history of the American policy decisions that led to military involvement in Vietnam. The decision to publish was made by Arthur Ochs Sulzberger. An injunction against publication was sought by the Department of Justice, but it was denied by the Supreme Court. Sulzberger was presented with a special award by the Committee to Protect Journalists' International Press Freedom in 1996, the twenty-fifth anniversary of the publication.

---

to New York to take the positions of assistant to the publisher and, later, assistant treasurer. When his brother-in-law, *Times* publisher Orvil E. Dryfoos, died in 1963, Sulzberger took over the position. He was only thirty-seven.

As publisher of *The New York Times*, Sulzberger strengthened the paper's reputation and modernized its organization. A year after he took the helm, he combined the previously separate management of the daily and Sunday editions. He also improved the newspaper's reporting on religion, science, and women's issues. He turned over the job of publisher to his son, Arthur Ochs Sulzberger, Jr., in 1992.

TIKKUN

In the fall of 1986 Michael Lerner and Nan Fink founded *Tikkun* magazine (the name in Hebrew means "to mend, repair and transform the world") to provide readers with a journal that would unify liberal-left political thought with Jewish religious and spiritual traditions. The magazine also provides a forum for Lerner's controversial philosophy of "Jewish Renewal," a movement he co-founded with Zalman Schachter-Shalomi. Lerner himself states that the magazine was created to serve as a liberal answer to the neoconservative Jewish periodical **Commentary**.

As *Tikkun*'s editor Lerner has remained the magazine's main editorial voice. He studied Judaism at the

Jewish Theological Seminary of America before moving on to post-graduate studies at the University of California, Berkeley. While at Berkeley, Lerner met his mentor, the philosopher and theologian **Abraham Joshua Heschel**. Among Lerner's most controversial stands was his support for a Palestinian state, put forth many years before the idea became acceptable to members of the American Jewish community. He has also been criticized for what many consider to be his questionable rabbinical ordination. (He never went through the traditional seminary, but was instead ordained by his Jewish Renewal co-founder Zalman Schachter-Shalomi.) He gained national attention when Hillary Clinton quoted his philosophy of "the Politics of Meaning." After heavy criticism, she soon dropped references to both Lerner and his philosophies.

In 1992 *Tikkun* moved its headquarters from Oakland, California, to New York City. In 1995 Lerner moved back to the Bay Area to open the first Jewish Renewal Synagogue and the *Tikkun* editorial offices are now located there.

TRILLIN, CALVIN (1935-)

Writer, humorist

Calvin Trillin was born on December 5, 1935, in Kansas City, Missouri. He attended public school in Kansas City and then Yale University, where he received his B.A. in 1957. He then worked for *Time* magazine reporting on the South. In 1967, he went to work for *The New Yorker,* contributing a column every three weeks entitled "U.S. Journal," until 1982. In 1978 he began writing another column, "Uncivil Liberties," which appeared every three weeks in *The Nation,* where it ran until 1985. The following year it became a syndicated column with King Features Syndicate.

Trillin also writes narrative columns under the title "American Chronicles" and a weekly comic verse for *The Nation.* He recently began a column for *Time* magazine. His many books include *An Education in Georgia: Charlayne Hunter, Hamilton Holmes and the Integration of the University of Georgia* (1964), *Barnet*

Frummer Is an Unbloomed Flower (1969), *U.S. Journal* (1971), *American Fried: Adventures of A Happy Eater* (1974), *Runestruck* (1977), *Alice, Let's Eat* (1978), *Third Helpings* (1983), and *Remembering Denny* (1993). In his 1996 memoir *Messages from My Father* he relates how Abe Trilinsky, a Russian immigrant who had been a part of the Galveston Plan, had a few concrete ambitions for his son Calvin—"he was to be a thoroughly American mensch, attend Yale, and become President. . . . Two out of three isn't bad." His most recent book, *Family Man* (1998), discusses the subjects of marriage and children. Pondering gay marriages, his only problem with them is, "At the end of a gay Jewish wedding ceremony, how would you decide who stomps on the glass?"

WEISS-ROSMARIN, TRUDE (1908–1989)

Writer, intellectual

Trude Weiss-Rosmarin was born on June 17, 1908, in Frankfurt-am-Main, Germany. As a child she participated in the German Zionist youth movement and attended a Hebrew Zionist school. Later, she attended the Frei Judische Lehrhaus before moving on to attend the Universities of Berlin, Leipzig, and Wurzburg. In 1931 she received her Ph.D. in Semitics, archeology, and philosophy. The same year she immigrated to the United States.

When Weiss-Rosmarin was only seventeen she founded a Hebrew language school in Duisburg. Two years after coming to the United States, she helped found the School of the Jewish Woman, initially under the authority of **Hadassah**. The school continued until 1939. In 1935 she created the newsletter *News from the School of the Jewish Woman.* A year later the name was changed to *Jewish Spectator.* In 1943 Weiss-Rosmarin took over sole editorship of the paper. For thirty-eight years, until 1974, the *Spectator* was published monthly. After 1974 it began to be published quarterly. She remained the paper's editor until her death in 1989.

Though the *Jewish Spectator* had a small circulation, the paper—and through it, Weiss-Rosmarin's editorials—was extremely influential within the Jewish community. Weiss-Rosmarin also gained fame and influence as a highly successful lecturer. She never gave up stressing the importance of Jewish education. This commitment led her, in 1940, to produce a series of books entitled *The Jewish People's Library*. A strong advocate for the rights of women, both inside and outside the synagogue, she sometimes split with feminists when she felt they were promoting "self-segregation."

An ardent Zionist throughout her life, Weiss-Rosmarin was nonetheless among the earliest to recognize and discuss the validity of Palestinian nationalism. In addition to her editorial and lecture work, she also wrote for other newspapers around the world, taught at New York University and at the Reconstructionist Rabbinical College, and served on the boards of many Jewish organizations. She died on June 26, 1989.

WHITE, THEODORE H. (1915–1986)

Journalist, author

Best known for his series of books, *The Making of the President*, Theodore White contributed to the modern American understanding of politics and the presidency. He was born in Boston, on May 6, 1915. Many of White's ancestors had been rabbis, though his father was an atheist socialist. Despite his father's split with orthodoxy, White attended Hebrew School. His experience there led him to his lifelong love of history and Judaism.

After graduating from Harvard in 1938, White became a correspondent for *Time* magazine, covering China, India, Europe, and the Japanese surrender at the end of World War II. Leaving *Time* in 1945, White went on to write for the *New Republic*, the *Saturday Review of Literature*, *The New York Times Magazine*, and *Harper's*. He also published several books including *Thunder Out of China* (1946); *Fire and Ashes* (1953); *The Mountain Road* (a novel, 1958); and his memoirs, *In Search of History* (1978). *The Making of the President 1960*, the first in his series about presidential elections, won a Pulitzer Prize in 1962. He followed that book with volumes covering the elections of 1964, 1968, and 1972. His book *Breach of Faith* (1975) focused on Watergate and Richard Nixon's resignation. He died in New York City on May 15, 1986 and was memorialized for his contributions to journalism and history at a service held at Temple Emanu-El.

WINCHELL, WALTER (1897–1972)

Journalist, gossip columnist, radio host

Often considered the father of the modern gossip column (and by one biographer, of celebrity journalism), Walter Winchell was a familiar voice in homes across America, first as a radio personality, later as the narrator of TV's "The Untouchables." Winchell began his career on the other side of the footlights, as a child performer in vaudeville, part of a singing act with a young **George Jessel**.

After a hitch with the Navy during World War I, Winchell looked on a return to small=time vaudeville with understandable distaste. He began contributing items to show business trade papers and finally became a columnist for *Vaudeville News* in 1922. From there he moved on to the *New York Daily Graphic* (a scurrilous sheet whose other alumni included Fulton Oursler and filmmaker Samuel Fuller) and then to the *Daily Mirror*. Eventually, Winchell's breathless style found a home in radio, where he held forth in a hammerlike staccato for over twenty years, his presence heralded by his oft-parodied signature line, "Good evening, Mr. and Mrs. America and all the ships at sea."

Winchell was one of the first entertainment reporters to parlay his large audience into political influence. He was a staunch defender of the New Deal and a Roosevelt adulator. But with Roosevelt's death, he began a fairly swift transition to vociferous Red baiter, becoming as ardent an adherent of Joseph McCarthy as he had been of FDR. Winchell proved unable to adjust to the decline of network radio, and after he repeatedly overreached himself as a purveyor of vicious anti-Communist slander, his star faded. When he died in California in 1972, he was all but forgotten.

ZUCKERMAN, MORTIMER (1937–)

Newspaper and magazine editor; publisher

Mortimer Benjamin Zuckerman was born in Montreal, Canada, on June 4, 1937. He attended McGill University where he graduated with degrees in economics and political theory (1957) and Law (1961). He also attended the University of Pennsylvania's Wharton School of Business where he received his M.B.A. (1961), and Harvard University, where he received his Master of Law (1962). He spent time as a student at the University of Paris Law School and the Harvard Graduate School of Business Administration.

In 1963 Zuckerman entered the world of real estate when he joined Cabot, Cabot & Forbes. Six years later he left the firm, and in 1970 he and partner Ed Linde opened Boston Properties, Inc., which soon built an impressive reputation for quality construction. Today, the company manages over ninety properties in New York, Boston, and Washington, D.C.

Zuckerman used the enormous profits from his real estate dealings to build his career as a publisher. In 1980 he purchased the *Atlantic Monthly* and became its chairman. Four years later he purchased *U.S. News and World Report* and became its editor-in-chief.

At the same time as he purchased *U.S. News*, he bought the company's subsidiary, Applied Graphics Technologies, the second largest pre-press company in the U.S. In 1992 he purchased the *New York Daily News* and became the newspaper's chairman and co-publisher.

In addition to his careers in real estate and publishing, Zuckerman has taught city planning at the Harvard Graduate School of Design and lectured on the same subject at Yale University. He is a trustee of New York University and of Memorial Sloan Kettering Cancer Institute and is a member of the Council on Foreign Relations and the International Institute for Strategic Studies.

For Further Reading

See Appendix 2 for a bibliography of general reference books about Jews and the Jewish experience in America. All of these volumes include information about American Jews in publishing.

Madison, Charles A. *Jewish Publishing in America*. New York: Sanhedrin Press, 1975.

Metzker, Isaac, ed. *A Bintel Brief*. New York: Schoken Press, 1990. (This is a collection of the "bundle of letters" column of the *Jewish Daily Forward*.)

National Museum of American Jewish History. *A People in Print: Jewish Journalism in America*. Philadelphia: National Museum of American Jewish History, 1987.

Part 13

Language and Literature

OVERVIEW

Four Jewish American writers have won the Nobel Prize. This is an extraordinary and revealing fact. Even more revealing are other facts about these four writers. None was born in the United States. Two did not write in English. One won the Nobel Prize for Peace, not for Literature. Jewish American writers have always come from a wide variety of backgrounds and have exhibited deep social and political concerns in their work.

There were significant Jewish American writers in this country early in the nineteenth century, but it was not until the massive immigration from Europe in the 1880s and 1890s that "Jewishness" became a distinct characteristic in literature. There had been little serious anti-Semitism and therefore little reason for Jewish writers to be self-conscious about their ethnicity. Playwright **David Belasco**, for example, wrote enormously popular, romantic plays about the American West, lost lovers, and high adventure. After the influx of immigrants at the end of the nineteenth century, the situation began to change. Now, many important writers chose to remain within the Yiddish language and culture. Others wrote in English, but addressed issues of religion, assimilation, and anti-Semitism. Poet **Emma Lazarus** reflected this shift. She came from an established, largely assimilated Sephardic family, and her earliest writings had little Jewish content. After the arrival of hundreds of thousands of Jews in this country, however, her consciousness changed and she began to write from a strongly Jewish perspective.

During the twentieth century these two strains in Jewish American writing have both been strong. Some writers, while not denying their background, have chosen not to focus on it in their work. They include poet **Gertrude Stein**, probably the most influential of the pre—World War II Jewish American writers, as well as poet and short-story writer **Dorothy Parker**, playwright **George S. Kaufman** and several of his collaborators, and novelist **Edna Ferber**, the first Jewish American to win the Pulitzer Prize. Playwrights **Lillian Hellman** and **Clifford Odets** brought a heightened social conscience to their work, as did, later in the century, **Arthur Miller**, **Paddy Chayefsky**, and many other Jewish writers. This may have been because of their Jewish experience and upbringing, but it was not necessarily expressed through Jewish characters or settings.

Poets **Muriel Rukeyser**, Karl Shapiro, and **Stanley Kunitz** treated their ethnicity as a central part of their life and work. The beginning of the really powerful influence of Jewish Americans and their particular experience, however, was probably the first novel by **Saul Bellow**, one of those four Nobel Prize winners. This tradition was continued by **Bernard Malamud**, **Philip Roth**, and **Tillie Olsen** in fiction and by **Adrienne Rich**, **Allen Ginsberg**, and others in poetry. Playwright Neil Simon has dominated Broadway with his comedies since the 1960s. Only since the 1980s, however, has he begun to write from his own experience as a Jewish American, winning a Pulitzer Prize in 1991 for *Lost in Yonkers*.

Novelist and essayist **Elie Weisel** came to this country after surviving the Holocaust and has spent his life writing about the Jewish experience, receiving the Nobel Prize for Peace in 1986. A survivor of another kind, **Joseph Brodsky** came to this country fleeing political persecution in the former Soviet Union in the early 1970s. In 1987 his poetry won him the Nobel Prize for Literature and in 1991 he served as poet laureate of the United States.

Paralleling the Jewish influence in American literature in English has been the rise and fall of the Yiddish language, literature, and culture. Yiddish speakers came to the United States as early as the eighteenth century, but the language was not a cultural force until the 1880s brought a wave of Yiddish-speaking immigrants. Although many families stopped speaking Yiddish in the second generation in this country, there were others who kept the language alive. American Yiddish writers began to emerge, and literature in the language flourished through the period before World War II and even, to some extent, after. **Isaac Bashevis Singer** won the Nobel Prize for Literature in 1978 for his Yiddish stories and novels. Although Yiddish has declined as a spoken language in the second half of the century, it remains an important part of Jewish culture.

ANTIN, MARY (1881–1949)

Writer

Mary Antin's experiences as a youthful immigrant in the New World were anything but typical. how many eighteen-year-old girls publish memoirs of their arrival in America? Yet her precocity made her an ideal spokesperson for a generation of new Americans at a time when immigrants were being demonized by political opportunists and bigots.

Antin's father, who had abandoned the rabbinate for a business career, left Russia for Boston in 1891. Three years later he sent for his family. Although her other siblings worked to supplement the family's meager income, Mary's academic success guaranteed that her parents would keep her in school somehow. At the age of fifteen, she had already published her first poems. Three years later she would write and publish her first book, *From Plotzk to Boston*, an epistolary memoir of her emigration, written in Yiddish and translated into English.

Two years later, Antin interrupted her education to marry a non-Jew, the geologist Amadeus William Grabau. The couple moved to New York when Grabau was offered a teaching position at Columbia University. Antin took classes at Columbia and began work on her second book, *The Promised Land*, which was published in 1912. A spirited recounting of her own experiences, the volume was clearly intended as a defense of her generation of immigrants, a defense she would continue two years later in her last book, *They Who Knock at Our Gates*. In 1920 her husband left her. She spent the rest of her life living with her family, pursuing a career in social work, having all but given up writing.

ASCH, SHOLEM (1880–1957)

Novelist, playwright

Sholem Asch was born in Kutno, Poland, on November 1, 1880. One of ten children, he attended the local Hebrew school before moving to Warsaw when he was nineteen. A year later he published his first story.

Written in Hebrew, it was an enormous critical success. Shortly after this, he was convinced by the great writer I. L. Peretz to continue his writing in Yiddish. His first story in Yiddish was *Dos Shtetl* (1904). This was followed by two novels, *Kidesh hashem* (1920) and *Motke ganef* (1916), and a play *Got fun nekome* (1907), which dealt with Eastern European Jewish village life.

Asch first visited the United States in 1910 and immigrated in 1914. His subsequent writing began to reflect the Jewish immigrant experience in America. His work during this "American period" includes *Onkl Mozes* (1918), *Khayim Lederers tsurikkumen* (1927), and *Toyt urteyl* (1926). During and after World War II, Asch entered his third—and most controversial—literary period. He began exploring the connections between Judaism and Christianity and published works such as *Der man fun Netseres* (1943), *The Apostle* (1943), *Mary* (1949), and *The Prophet* (1955).

Unlike many Yiddish authors, Asch was widely — and well—translated throughout his career. He became popular throughout Europe and the United States. Beyond any controversy surrounding his subject matter, Asch was widely respected for the energy and naturalism of his writing. He died in London on July 10, 1957.

ASIMOV, ISAAC (1920–1992)

Scientist, writer

One of the most significant and prolific popular science and science fiction writers of the century, Isaac Asimov was born in Petrovichi, Russia on January 2, 1920. He immigrated to Brooklyn, New York with his family when he was three. He attended Columbia University, where he received both his undergraduate degree (1939) and his doctorate in biochemistry (1948). After he obtained his Ph.D., he became a faculty member of Boston University where he taught until his death.

In his career as a writer, Asimov published over 500 works and had an enormous influence on the development of both popular science and science fiction writing. He began writing science fiction short stories in 1939. His story "Nightfall" (1941) is still considered one of the most exceptional science fiction short stories ever written. In 1950 he published his first full-length science fiction novel, *Pebble in the Sky*. From 1951 through 1953 he published *Foundation*, *Foundation and Empire*, and *Second Foundation*. The trilogy is a classic of the genre. His other science fiction novels include *The Stars, like Dust* (1951), *Foundation's Edge* (1982), and *The Robots of Dawn* (1983).

Asimov's many popular science books—though less well known—are both unusual and influential because they are written with clarity and humor, qualities for which science writing is not commonly noted. Among his many works on a wide variety of scientific subjects are *The Chemicals of Life* (1954), *The Human Brain* (1964), *Our World in Space* (1974), and *Views of the Universe* (1981). A true renaissance man, Asimov also wrote two volumes of his autobiography and a book of interpretations of Shakespeare's plays. He died in New York City on April 6, 1992.

BEHRMAN, S. N. (1893–1973)

Dramatist, biographer

Sophisticated comic playwright Samuel Nathaniel Behrman was born in Worcester, Massachusetts, and studied under the legendary drama teacher George P. Baker at Harvard University. The first of his highly successful comedies was *The Second Man* (1927), produced by the Theatre Guild. He continued to write witty commentaries on American life for the next four decades, including *Biography* (1932); *No Time for Comedy* (1939); and *Jacobowsky and the Colonel* (1943), an adaptation of a Franz Werfel story. *Rain from Heaven* (1934) was among the first American plays to take notice of the rise of Nazism and its threat to civilization. Behrman's writing, while it remained brilliantly comic, increasingly reflected his leftist political convictions and concern for social problems. His most specifically Jewish play was *The Cold Wind and the Warm* (1958), which was based on his experience of Jewish life in Worcester at the turn of the century. He also wrote several biographies, a memoir of Max Beerbohm entitled *Portrait of Max* (1960), and his own autobiography, *People in a Diary* (1972).

BELLOW, SAUL (1915–)

Writer

Saul Bellow was born on June 10, 1915, in Lachine, Canada, the son of Russian Jewish immigrants. His family was observant, and Bellow grew up speaking Yiddish. At the age of nine, he moved with his family to Chicago. He went to college at both the University of Chicago and Northwestern University, where he earned his B.S. degree in 1937.

Bellow is one of the most celebrated novelists of his generation. He received the Nobel Prize for Literature in 1976" for the human understanding and subtle analysis of contemporary culture that are combined in his works." The Nobel citation praises Bellow's "exu-

Saul Bellow was raised in an observant, Yiddish-speaking, family. His early novel, The Victim *(1947), is a penetrating analysis of anti-Semitism. The title character in* The Adventures of Augie March *(1953) has sometimes been called a "Jewish Huck Finn." (Courtesy of American Jewish Archives)*

berant ideas, flashing irony . . . and burning compassion." Modern man, in Bellow's fiction, "keeps trying to find a foothold during his wanderings in our tottering world, one who can never relinquish his faith that the value of life depends on his dignity not its success."

Bellow published his first novel, *Dangling Man*, in 1944. It was his third novel, *The Adventures of Augie March* (1953), however, which brought him to national attention. In addition to wide critical praise, the novel won the National Book Award. Bellow would go on to win two more National Book Awards—for *Herzog* in 1964 and *Mr. Sammler's Planet* in 1970. It was *Humbolt's Gift* (1975) that won him the Nobel, as well as the Pulitzer Prize. His other novels include *Henderson the Rain King* (1959), *The Dean's December* (1982), *More Die of Heartbreak* (1987), and *The Bellarosa Connection* (a novella, 1989). A collection of his non-fiction writing, *It All Adds Up: From the Dim Past to the Uncertain Future* was published in 1994. He served as Grunier Distinguished Services Professor and a member of the Committee on Social Thought at the University of Chicago from 1962 to 1993.

In his Nobel Prize acceptance speech he summed up his artistic convictions: "Only art penetrates what pride, passion, intelligence and habit erect on all sides—the seeming realities of this world. There is another reality, the genuine one, which we lose sight of. . . . art attempts to find in the universe, in matter as well as in the facts of life, what is fundamental, enduring, essential."

BRODSKY, JOSEPH (1940–1996)

Poet

Nobel Prize-winning poet Joseph Brodsky was born Iosif Alexandrovitch Brodski in the Soviet Union on May 24, 1940, to parents who experienced significant discrimination because of anti-semitism. Brodsky left school at fifteen and held a variety of jobs while beginning to write his witty but deeply moving poetry. In 1964, at the age of twenty-three, he was sentenced to five years' hard labor in the Arctic Circle for being a "social parasite" and writing poetry without academic qualifications. This sentence brought him to the attention of the Western literary world. After his release from prison, he continued to write, and his poetry had a wide underground circulation. By the time he was forced to leave the Soviet Union in 1972, he had been imprisoned three times and twice confined in mental institutions.

Befriended by poet W. H. Auden, Brodsky made a new home in the United States. In 1977 he published a book of poems, *A Part of Speech*. In 1980 he became a naturalized American citizen. A year later, he was given the MacArthur Award. In 1986 he received the National Book Critics Circle Award for his book *Less Than One: Selected Essays* and in 1987 he won the Nobel Prize for Literature. He was the second youngest person ever to be so honored. His second volume of poems, *To Urania: Selected Poems, 1965–1985* was published in 1988. In 1991 he served as Poet Laureate at the Library of Congress. A book of prose, *Watermark*, was published in 1992. He died of a heart condition at the age of fifty-five.

CALISHER, HORTENSE (1911–)

Novelist, memoirist

Prolific and highly acclaimed writer Hortense Calisher was born in New York City on December 20, 1911, to a Southern Jewish father and a German Jewish immigrant mother. After graduation from Barnard College, Calisher married a gentile and experienced the alienation of moving from one Christian suburb to another while secretly writing poems. When she turned to short stories, her success was rapid. In 1948 she won her first O. Henry Award, and in 1951 *In the Absence of Angels* was published. This first collection of stories established Calisher immediately, and during the 1950s she continued to publish short fiction. Her first novel, *False Entry* (1961), was also well received. Over the next several decades Calisher wrote more than a dozen novels and half a dozen collections of short stories. In 1994, at the age of eighty-two, she published her thirteenth novel, *In the Palace of the Movie King*. She has also written two autobiographies,

Herself (1972) and *Kissing Cousins* (1988). Recognized as a master stylist, she writes with lyricism and wit. She is most praised, however, for her remarkable intelligence and imagination.

CHAYEFSKY, PADDY (1923–1981)

Playwright, screenwriter

The best-known television playwright , Paddy (Sidney) Chayefsky was born in New York City, the site of several of his best works. He began his career when television was in its infancy, gaining wide acclaim for *Marty* (1953), the story of a lonely man in the Bronx and the love he almost finds. Originally conceived as a Jewish character, Marty became Italian for his television debut, in part because the protagonists of Chayefsky's first three dramas had been Jewish and in part because television was becoming aware of the political pressures of the 1950s. The play was made into a film with Ernest Borgnine.

Chayefsky's first Broadway play, *Middle of the Night* (1956), dealt with an older, middle-class Jewish man and his love for a younger woman. It, too, was performed on television as a non-Jewish story. In the 1960s, Chayefsky began writing screenplays, among which were *The Americanization of Emily* (1964), *The Hospital* (1971), and *Network* (1976). The latter was his most memorable work since *Marty*, a savage satire of television news. All three screenplays won Academy Awards, making Chayefsky the only person to date to win three Oscars as a screenwriter. A novel, *Altered States*, was filmed in 1980.

CHOMSKY, NOAM (1928–)

Linguist, political activist

As a linguist, Noam Chomsky is incontrovertibly among the key figures in Western thought in this century. His innovative thinking has changed the way we conceptualize language and its acquisition, and many have called him the creator of modern linguistics. As a political activist, Chomsky is controversial, inspiring admiration and rage in equal parts.

Chomsky was a child of the Depression, the older of two sons of William and Elsie Chomsky. His father, a Russian Jewish immigrant, was a distinguished linguist himself, an expert in Semitic languages, particularly Hebrew. Chomsky grew up in the era of the Spanish Civil War, and was shaped by the Zionist and socialist controversies of the era. From those debates, he derived the libertarian socialist political theories that he has espoused to this day. Even as a college student at the University of Pennsylvania in the late 1940s, Chomsky supported the idea of a binational socialist state in Palestine, a position that he adheres to today. At college he had thought of a career as a political activist, but then he discovered a love of linguistics. He completed his B.A. at the University of Pennsylvania and a master's in the field at the same school, with a thesis on Modern Hebrew. At Penn he studied linguistics under Zellig Harris, whose influence on the young Chomsky was seminal.

Chomsky entered his chosen field at a time when linguistics was dominated by the structuralists. Selected as a member of the Harvard Society of Fellows and working with such distinguished scholars as W. V. O. Quine, J. L. Austin, and Roman Jakobson, Chomsky began to develop a radical theory, approaching language not as a series of utterances but as a cognitive system. The result was a highly complex theory of "generative" grammar, in which speakers "generate" sentences, based on a series of tacitly understood rules. His work at Harvard was so revolutionary, so unlike the accepted paradigm in the field, that he was unable to find work. Eventually, he completed his doctorate at the University of Pennsylvania and, with some difficulty, secured a position at M.I.T, teaching undergraduate linguistics, logic, and the philosophy of language. He has remained at the school.

In the late 1950s, Chomsky began publishing his revolutionary ideas, unraveling the work of behaviorists like B. F. Skinner, and arguing that language is too complex and varied to be learned by simple imitation (as Skinner posited). Rather, he argued, the ability to acquire language is biologically present in human beings, activated in children by exposure to their native language. With this innate faculty, children are able to acquire language in a surprisingly brief time. Generative grammar became the keystone of the "cognitive revolution" of the 1950s, and has remained the model for modern linguistics ever since.

Chomsky playfully describes himself as a "part-time linguist." Since the Vietnam War he has been as involved with political activism as with his academic discipline. He denounced the war, and was among the first to attack the intellectuals who supported the war-making machinery of government. He became increasingly vocal in his attacks on Israeli policies in the Middle East, calling for a binational state. He also came under fire for his support of the right to publish in the case of Robert Faurisson, a French Holocaust denier. Chomsky has vehemently rejected Faurisson's ideas, stating that he has never even read the Frenchman's work and that the issue at stake is a free speech question, the right to espouse an unpopular position. Increasingly, Chomsky has found himself marginalized in the political realm, his political books seldom reviewed in the mainstream press; and even the sympathetic progressive press is out of tune with his often strident denunciations of the "consensus-making" machinery of public opinion.

But his domination of linguistics has continued, as he has labored to delineate a universal grammar that would represent the innate structures he believes underlie all human languages. He has repeatedly disavowed any connection between his political and linguistic work, but they do have one thing in common; whether it is in linguistics or politics, Noam Chomsky is a contrarian and an iconoclast.

His linguistic publications include *Syntactic Structures* (1957), *The Sound Patterns of English* (with Morris Halle, 1968), and *The Logical Structure of Linguistic Theory* (1975). His social and political works include *American Power and the New Mandarins* (1969) and *The Political Economy of Human Rights* (1979).

FALK, MARCIA (1946–)

Poet, liturgist

Feminist poet Marcia Falk has often shaken up the Jewish religious establishment during the past decade or so, but she was born and reared in a traditional Conservative family on Long Island, New York. After earning a doctorate in English and comparative literature at Stanford, she became a Fulbright scholar and postdoctoral fellow at Hebrew University, studying Bible and Hebrew literature. In the years that followed, she published two collections of poetry and translated the works of Yiddish poet Malka Heifetz Tussman. She also translated the biblical *Song of Songs*. In the 1980s, she began writing prayers that were used in Reconstructionist prayerbooks and feminist rituals.

Her fifth book broke many molds. A rewriting of traditional liturgy in both Hebrew and English, *The Book of Blessings: New Jewish Prayers for Daily Life, the Sabbath, and the New Moon Festival* is a 528-page prayerbook that makes no reference to God as king, father, lord, master, or any other male name. The book even omits the use of *yud-hay-vav-hay*, the ineffable name of God. Falk believes it cannot be separated from the "oppressive history" of uttering "Adonai" or "My Lord" in its place. However, she does not replace these references with feminine complements or even with gender-neutral terms. Instead, she avoids anthropomorphic terms entirely, making her work challenging in terms not only of language but of theology. She has been accused of being pantheistic but insists that her prayers are entirely consistent with monotheism. She has made it clear that women—and poets—can affect religious as well as cultural Judaism.

FERBER, EDNA (1887–1968)

Novelist, playwright

Edna Ferber made the jump from a miserable childhood in a small coal town in the Midwest to a storied career as a best-selling author by dint of sheer hard work. Her capacious multi-generational novels were the product of hard hours of research into faraway places, while giving voice to an entire generation of women struggling to find a place in a rigidly patriarchal America.

When her impoverished family was unable to send her to college after a successful high school career, Ferber became a newspaper reporter. A protracted illness forced her to return to her parents' home, where a used typewriter became her passport to fame. A highly successful series of short stories about a traveling saleswoman, Emma McChesney, enabled her to move to New York City. Thus launched, she began to write the novels that made her wealthy, *So Big* (which won the 1925 Pulitzer prize), *Showboat* (1926), *Cimarron* (1930), and *Giant* (1952) among them.

A member of the unofficial group of wits and pundits that congregated at the Algonquin Hotel, she also collaborated with fellow Algonquin Round Table member **George S. Kaufman** on three hit plays, *The Royal Family* (1927), *Dinner at Eight* (1932), and *Stage Door* (1936). Although her novels and plays seldom make direct mention of her Jewishness, two of her infrequent trips outside the United States were to Israel, and she was quite frank about her sense of estrangement from gentile Midwestern society in her memoirs.

FICTION

When the American colonies rebelled against their British governors, about 2,500 of the inhabitants were Jewish. This tiny minority made remarkable contributions in a number of fields, but they and their immediate descendants did not write anything that became part of American literature. At the beginning of the nineteenth century, when thousands of German Jews arrived on these shores, some fiction and poetry began to appear in Yiddish. At the same time, Jewish characters began to appear in fiction written by non-Jews. It was not until the immigration of more than two million Eastern European Jews in the late nineteenth century that the history of Jewish American fiction in English begins in earnest.

The experience of these immigrants was often one of poverty and alienation. Under tremendous pressure to assimilate, they were anguished by the loss of tradition, customs, and religion. The materialism of American society contradicted many of the tenets of Judaism and, even though many immigrants became enormously successful in material terms, this contradiction caused great tension in families, synagogues, and individual lives.

EARLY JEWISH AMERICAN NOVELS

The earliest Jewish American novels reflected these concerns. **Abraham Cahan**'s classic *The Rise of David Levinsky* (1917), although written in Yiddish, was the first important book in this thematic tradition. Often called America's greatest Yiddish novel, Cahan's work details the material and social successes of entrepreneur David Levinsky and their costs in personal and spiritual terms. *Haunch, Paunch, and Jowl* (1923), written by Samuel Ornitz but published anonymously, goes a step further. His protagonist, Meyer Hirsch, is gripped by a need to succeed that overpowers all other considerations. Russian Jewish immigrant **Anzia Yezierska** wrote novels about ghettos and sweatshops, including *Hungry Hearts* (1920) and *Salome of the Tenements* (1922), both of which were made into silent films, and *Breadgivers: A Struggle between a Father of the Old World and a Daughter of the New* (1925). Yezierska's protagonists were women struggling against poverty and the restrictions of Jewish patriarchy. Often these women found the understanding and equality they sought in relationships with intellectually sophisticated gentile men. Her work has been controversial because of its harsh depiction of certain aspects of Jewish family life.

A number of other Jewish American writers wrote about the Jewish immigrant experience in one or two of their works. Popular novelist **Fannie Hurst** wrote a collection of short stories, *Humoresque* (1919), dealing with Jewish life in New York. Ludwig Lewisohn dealt with the problems of Jews in America in *Up Stream* (1922) and *Mid-Channel* (1929), both of which are autobiographical. Most of his novels, however, do not concern Jewish issues. Konrad Bercovici, an immigrant from Rumania in 1916, wrote *Dust of New York* (1919) about the Jewish East Side. Many of his other novels depict gypsy life.

1920s–1930s

In the 1920s and 1930s a great many Jewish writers began to make their mark on American literature. Theatrical playwrights **George S. Kaufman** and **Moss Hart** were both critically acclaimed and popular, but they seldom wrote specifically about the Jewish experience. In fiction, the list of important Jewish writers was long and impressive, and, more frequently than playwrights or poets, they continued to take as their subject the life of the Jewish immigrant in America.

Edward Dahlberg wrote about growing up in slums and a Jewish orphanage in *Bottom Dogs* (1930) and about the lives of the poor in *From Flushing to Calvary* (1932). He also wrote one of the first books dealing with how Nazism was beginning to affect the American Jew in *Those Who Perish* (1934). Chicago writer Albert Halper wrote intensely proletarian novels such as *On the Shore* (1934) and *The Foundry* (1934). His *Sons of the Fathers* (1940) describes the anguish of a Jewish father who sees his country moving toward war and his sons preparing to fight.

Henry Roth wrote his most important book, *Call it Sleep* (1934), about a child's experience of ghetto poverty and despair. He and Charles Renikoff, author of *By the Waters of Manhattan* (1930), more clearly focus on literary and artistic values than do the authors of most of the earlier books, which were usually written in the service of some social or political ideology. Also in this new tradition was **Meyer Levin**, whose early books included *Yehuda* (1931), which dealt with a Zionist farm commune in Palestine; *The New Bridge* (1933), about a family's eviction from a tenement; and *The Old Bunch* (1937), about a family of Russian-Jewish immigrants. Social protest writer Nelson Algren began his career in the 1930s with *Somebody in Boots* (1935), about a poor young man in Texas who falls into a life of wandering and crime during the Depression. His next book, *Never Come Morning* (1942), concerned a Polish hoodlum who aspires to be a prizefighter.

Edna Ferber had a different perspective on being Jewish in America, having grown up in towns in the Midwest, rather than in one of the nation's large cities. Jewish religion and culture were less a part of her life than was anti-Semitism. Her Jewish identity, therefore, was largely a defiant pride. Like **Emma Lazarus**, Ferber had a great love for America and its people. She also liked to write about strong, independent women, and her earliest work comprised stories about business woman Emma McChesney, collected in *Roast Beef, Medium* (1913) and two other volumes. Most of her books have some recognizably Jewish characters, but only one focuses on Jewish issues—*Fanny Herself* (1917) was a semiautobiographical novel. She is best remembered for her regional novels, including *So Big* (1924)—for which she won a Pulitzer Prize—*Show Boat* (1926), and *Cimarron* (1930). In these books, women of various ethnicities are viewed as double outsiders in American society and are often involved in relationships with white, Christian men.

Also molded by anti-Semitism rather than the positive side of her Jewish heritage was **Dorothy Parker**. Child of a Jewish father and a Scottish mother, she was largely raised by a rigidly Christian stepmother and subjected to isolation and ridicule in Christian boarding schools. The resulting bitterness informed her ironic, satirical poetry, short stories, and reviews, collected in such books as *Sunset Gun* (1928), *Death and Taxes* (1931), *Laments for the Living* (1930), and *Here Lies* (1939).

Parker's rival in bitter irony was **Nathanael West**, born Nathan Wallenstein Weinstein. All four of his strange and savage novels were published in the 1930s and met with a deafening silence. After his death, however, critics recognized the brilliance of *The Dream Life of Balso Snell* (1931), *Miss Lonelyhearts* (1933), *A Cool Million* (1934), and especially his vicious attack on Hollywood, *The Day of the Locust* (1939). Although West's novels do not focus on Jewish life, they are significant as foreshadowing for the great importance of Jewish Americans in literature of the second half of the century.

In many ways, the most important Jewish American writer of the pre-World War II period was poet, playwright, and fiction writer **Gertrude Stein**. This daring innovator in style permanently influenced the writing of American prose. Although she was not reared a practicing Jew, Stein identified strongly and proudly with her Jewish heritage. One of the earliest generation of college-educated women, she studied with great American philosophers William James, George Santayana, and Josiah Royce. A brilliant student, she briefly attended medical school before moving to Paris, where her long life as an expatriate began. Even her earliest works are revolutionary in style and structure, including *Three Lives* (1909), *Tender Buttons* (1914), and *The Making of Americans* (1925). The publication of *The Autobiography of Alice B. Toklas* (1933), brought her credit by writers such as Sherwood Anderson and Ernest Hemingway for having revitalized American language.

1940–1960

In the 1940s Edna Ferber continued to be an important figure. Ferber's *Giant* (1950) and *Ice Palace* (1958) were both hugely successful, and *Giant* was made into a major film. Nelson Algren came into his own during this period. His *The Man with the Golden Arm* (1949) received acclaim as a book and in its film adaptation. *A Walk on the Wild Side* (1956), like its predecessor, explored the underside of urban life.

There were a number of Jewish popular novelists of significance in the forties. **Laura Z. Hobson** wrote, among many other novels and short stories, *Gentleman's Agreement* (1947), which concerned itself with what has been called "polite" anti-Semitism in American business and social life. The book was extremely popular and was made into an influential and award-winning motion picture, starring Gregory Peck as a journalist who adopts a false Jewish identity in order to experience anti-Semitism firsthand. Vera Caspary's best known novel, *Laura* (1943), was also made into a film, which has become a classic. The eight "Claudia" books of Rose Franken, published in the late thirties and early forties, formed the basis for her highly popular play, which she also directed. It ran for 722 performances. The decade also brought forward a generation of Jewish American writers who would, in the 1950s and 1960s, come to dominate American fiction. Over the years several themes virtually disappeared from Jewish literature. Jews in America were no longer primarily an immigrant group, with recent experience of Eastern Europe, exile, and grinding poverty. The setting of the ghetto or the sweatshop or the culturally diverse urban slum no longer had relevance for most Jewish Americans. Anti-Semitism, while it existed in America, did not usually carry with it the threat of violence or gross economic and political discrimination. The result was a kind of confidence, if not always a positive view of the world. Out of this confidence came the willingness to examine what it meant to be a Jew in America in psychological and emotional terms. The answer, for a generation of writers, seemed always to include the word *outsider*. In different ways, the three major writers of the post-war period all cast their protagonists in that role.

Saul Bellow's first novel, *Dangling Man* (1944), immediately established him as a writer to be reckoned with. In it, he told the story of a young man's conflicting feelings as he waits to enter the army. This and his second novel, *The Victim* (1947), are generally considered to have ended the WASP domination of American fiction and to have begun an era in which ethnicity was often at the base of creative exploration of the human condition. Bellow's third novel, *The Adventures of Augie March* (1953), won a National Book Award, and in 1976 he was awarded the Nobel Prize for Literature.

Another writer who explored many aspects of the human condition, including what it means to be a Jew in America, was Brooklyn-born **Bernard Malamud**. His first novel, *The Natural* (1952), is a mythic view of the American hero as baseball player, in which he symbolically compares America's pastime with the quest for the Holy Grail. Virtually all of his other novels, including his Pulitzer Prize–winning *The Fixer* (1967), view with compassion and humor Jewish characters struggling with the complexities of life. He ranks with Bellow as a major writer in the Jewish American tradition.

Jewish family dynamics became the focus of satirical, often bitter examination in the work of **Philip Roth**. Roth's first book, a collection of short stories entitled *Goodbye, Columbus* (1959), won the National Book Award and garnered no small amount of criticism for what many considered a negative view of American Jews bordering on anti-Semitism. After two more, reasonably successful novels, Roth became notorious with the publication of *Portnoy's Complaint* (1969). In this irreverent and often very funny book, a Jewish man tries to attain some personal identity while dealing with a repressive mother and a compulsive attraction to WASP women. Roth followed with a series of books about a Jewish writer named Nathan Zuckerman in which, again, his hero is nonheroic and his satirical view of Jewish American life is controversial.

There were a number of other highly significant figures in Jewish American fiction who began writing in the forties and fifties and continued into the last decades of the century. These writers have not been ranked as high as Bellow, Malamud, and Roth for a number of reasons, ranging from their popular orientation to their gender.

Herman Wouk wrote a number of important novels. His first, *Aurora Dawn* (1948), satirized the American advertising business. *The Caine Mutiny* (1951) won him a Pulitzer Prize and was made into a classic film starring Humphrey Bogart as the psychologically disintegrating Captain Queeg. Only one of Wouk's novels, *Marjorie Morningstar* (1955), deals specifically with a Jewish theme, and it has been criticized for perpetuating what some consider a negative stereotype of Jewish women.

Tillie Olsen, who wrote from a radical socialist point of view, captured the lives of Jewish women in *Tell Me a Riddle* (1962), a collection of short stories. Jo Sinclair explored the effects of anti-Semitism in *Wasteland* (1946) and discrimination against African Americans in *The Changelings* (1955).

Hortense Calisher entered the ranks of important American fiction writers with the publication of her first book of short stories, *In the Absence of Angels* (1951). She continued to publish largely autobiographical stories while working on her first novel, *False Entry* (1961). From that point on, she became quite prolific, writing eight novels in the next two decades, along with several collections of short stories and novellas and an autobiography. She was still extremely productive in the 1980s and 1990s.

Joseph Heller made a triumphant debut with *Catch-22* (1961), his outrageously funny satirical novel about life in the army. That book is still his best known, but later novels deal more with Jewish life and experiences. *Good as Gold* (1979) features a Jewish academic named Bruce Gold and his struggles with American society. *God Knows* (1984) is a very funny novel of serious import about the life of the biblical figure David.

Yiddish writer **Isaac Bashevis Singer** immigrated to the United States from Poland in 1935. His influence on other Jewish writers and, indeed, on American literature, is such that he must be included here, especially since most of his work was translated immediately into English. His stories and novellas, usually set in the past in Poland, are steeped in the Jewish tradition and alive with magic and mystery. He won the Nobel Prize for Literature in 1978.

Jewish American prose writers whose work deals only marginally with Jewish issues and concerns but who have had a major impact on contemporary literature and culture include **Norman Mailer**, **J. D. Salinger**, and **Ayn Rand**. From his first published novel, *The Naked and the Dead* (1948) through his Pulitzer Prize–winning nonfiction, *The Armies of the Night* (1968) and *The Executioner's Song* (1979), Mailer has been as successful as he has been controversial. The reclusive J. D. Salinger charmed a generation of readers with *The Catcher in the Rye* (1945), *Franny and Zooey* (1961), and *Raise High the Roof- Beam, Carpenters* (1963). Ayn Rand wrote two best-selling novels, *The Fountainhead* (1943) and *Atlas Shrugged* (1957), and became a cult figure representing the triumph of pure reason and selfishness.

HOLOCAUST FICTION

Beginning in the 1960s and 1970s, Jewish American writers made difficult and courageous attempts, almost two decades after the events, to deal with the Holocaust. Incited by the trial of Nazi Adolph Eichmann, the Six-Day War, and the general atmosphere of ethnic consciousness then current in the United States, both older and younger writers tackled the overwhelming task of making theological, ethical, and aesthetic sense of one of the most terrible human actions in the history of the world. The questions to be answered, or at any rate raised, involved the nature of God, the covenant supposed to have been made between Jehovah and the Chosen people, the nature of evil, and the implications of Jewish identity.

One of the first to undertake this task was Meyer Levin in his novel *Eva* (1959), which tells the story of a young woman who escapes from Auschwitz and finally makes her way to Israel to live. Levin wrote from the position of one who served as a foreign correspondent during World War II. Others, who had less immediate experience of the horrors, worked from the witness of survivors, as in Susan F. Schaeffer's *Anya* (1974) and Saul Bellow's *Mr. Sammler's Planet* (1970).

Literary critic Alan L. Berger divides Holocaust fiction into three groups: religious responses, secular responses, and symbolic responses. In the first group, Berger includes the novels and short stories of Arthur A. Cohen, Hugh Nissenson, **Cynthia Ozick**, **Chaim Potok**, Isaac Bashevis Singer, and **Elie Wiesel**. These writers emphasize the nature of the covenant between God and the Jews and how that covenant can be reconciled with the acts of Germany during the war. Among the works Berger puts into the second group are those of Saul Bellow, Mark Helprin, Robert Kotlowitz, Jay Neugeboren, and Susan F. Schaeffer, and certain Bernard Malamud stories. In the view of these writers, it is the Holocaust itself, not the covenant, that defines Jewish identity. The third group comprises Edward Lewis Wallant, Norma Rosen, Philip Roth, Leslie Epstein, and Hugh Nissenson, and Malamud in the novel *The Fixer* (1966).

RECENT FICTION

Among the Jewish American writers who have risen above the crowd in recent years are a number of women, including Cynthia Ozick, Norma Rosen, and **Grace Paley**. Ozick first came to prominence with her first novel, *Trust* (1966), but she has become better known for her short fiction, collected in a number of volumes, including *The Pagan Rabbi and Other Stories* (1971) and *Leviathan: Five Fictions*. In 1997 she published the "novel" *Puttermesser Papers*, actually a col-

---

Orthodox Mystery Novels? Who Would Care?

Faye Kellerman's mystery *The Ritual Bath* opens in a *mikvah* (ritual bath) in a yeshiva in Los Angeles, with Rina Lazarus discovering a friend murdered. LAPD detective Peter Decker ultimately solves the crime, but not before Rina and Peter find themselves attracted to each other. But Rina is Orthodox (recently widowed) and Peter is gentile . . . well . . . Peter turns out to be adopted. Don't guess how their personal relationship plays out, read the ten additional novels in the series to date and find out how the two cope with trying to live an Orthodox life in the modern world. Most of the novels don't have such explicitly Jewish settings, but Jewish issues are woven through them all.

Kellerman and her husband Jonathan are the only Orthodox novelists in America whose books routinely become best-sellers—over three million copies of her books have been sold to date. She describes herself as "a regular carpooling mom" (the couple have four children) who cooks and bakes every Friday for her family's Shabbat.

Here's a list of the Peter Decker/Rina Lazarus novels: *The Ritual Bath* (1986); *Sacred and Profane* (1987); *The Quality of Mercy* (1989); *Milk and Honey* (1990); *Day of Atonement* (1991); *False Prophet* (1992); *Grievous Sin* (1993); *Sanctuary* (1994); *Justice* (1995); *Prayers for the Dead* (1996); and *Serpent's Tooth* (1997).

---

lection of two stories and three novellas. She is also a perceptive essayist. Grace Paley also writes primarily short fiction, including *Enormous Changes at the Last Minute* (1974) and *Later the Same Day* (1985). She is also a gifted poet. Norma Rosen's most famous novel is *Touching Evil* (1969), in which two non-Jewish women witness the Holocaust through filmed and photographed records of the camps and the Eichmann war-crime trial. She also writes essays on Jewish issues.

In the last decade of the twentieth century, Jewish writers and Jewish subjects form a major current in American literature. Virtually every list of nominees for a prestigious literary award includes at least one Jewish name. In 1995, for example, *The Collected Stories of Grace Paley* was nominated for a Pulitzer Prize and in 1996, Philip Roth's *Sabbath's Theater* received a nomination. National Book Critics Circle Awards went to Roth in 1995 and Stanley Elkin in 1996. In the 1990s Jewish writers have also garnered an impressive number of nominations for the National Book Award, the PEN/Faulkner Award and others.

Jewishness is no longer an exotic ethnicity that is likely to appeal to readers looking for the colorful. As a result, some writers are going back to a deeper and more spiritual understanding of what it means to be Jewish, exploring the traditions and religious values that were for a time neglected. The result may very well be a renaissance in American Jewish literature.

GINSBERG, ALLEN (1926–1997)

Poet

Proclaimed by pundits the "poet laureate of the Beat Generation," Allen Ginsberg was a bundle of contradictions, a Jew turned Buddhist, the dutiful and loving son who signed the order for his mother's lobotomy, the ascetic who celebrated sexual liberation. That is only appropriate; after all, the poet whose work most resembles his, Walt Whitman, celebrated self-contradiction, and like Whitman, Ginsberg contained multitudes.

Ginsberg was born in Newark, New Jersey, to Louis and Naomi Ginsberg. Allen's father was a teacher and sometime poet, his mother a Russian émigré and devout Marxist. His brother, Eugene, also become a poet (writing as Eugene Brooks); but unlike his more famous brother, Eugene studied law and was a practicing lawyer as well.

Allen was a bright boy who attended Montclair State College for a year before a scholarship from the Paterson YMHA allowed him to transfer to Columbia University. There he became part of a circle that included Jack Kerouac and Neal Cassady (both of whom became Ginsberg's lovers). He realized that he was gay and began to act on that realization, and he began a lifelong experimentation with mind-altering drugs as part of the creative process. Out of his Columbia circle, which also included William Burroughs and Herbert Huncke, neither of them a student, grew the Beat movement. After a brush with the law that ended up with Ginsberg under observation in a psychiatric hos-

pital, he returned to Paterson, where his family now lived. It proved a fortuitous choice.

In Paterson, Ginsberg fell under the spell of William Carlos Williams, one of the central figures in twentieth-century American poetry and a neighbor of Ginsberg's. Williams's influence on Ginsberg can be seen in their shared use of colloquial American language and their focus on the concrete, objective physical world as the poet experiences it. Ginsberg also took a "day job" working for an ad agency. For five years he commuted to Manhattan and hated every minute of it. Finally, he left the firm and headed to San Francisco, where the Beat movement was gathering steam.

It was in San Francisco that he met fellow poet Lawrence Ferlinghetti, owner of City Lights Books, a bookstore and publishing house that issued most of Ginsberg's writings for the rest of his life. His first major effort, *Howl!* (1956), remains one of his most famous and controversial works, a spirited, incantatory ode to madness and sexual liberation, a slap in the face at the gray Eisenhower 1950s. Copies of the chapbook, published by Ferlinghetti, were seized by American customs official and Ginsberg was tried on obscenity charges but found not guilty.

Naomi Ginsberg had long suffered from undiagnosed mental illness; gradually she was sinking into an abyss of paranoiac despair and spent much of the last years of her life in and out of mental hospitals. With great anguish, Ginsberg signed the authorization for a lobotomy for his mother. She died in Pilgrim State Hospital on Long Island in 1956. Her suffering and death inspired what many believe to be his best poem, "Kaddish," an agonized rumination on her life and death.

Between the controversies surrounding *Howl!* and the brilliant pain of "Kaddish," Ginsberg was now being recognized as a major new voice in American poetry. For the remainder of his life, he was an apostle of Zen Buddhism, gay liberation (before it even had a label), and pacifism. His poetry took on increasingly incantatory tones, and he often performed it to music. His social conscience, a legacy from his mother, spurred him to protest the Vietnam War and the Russian invasion of Czechoslovakia. He continued to produce volumes of poetry up to his death from liver cancer in 1997, having outlived all the great figures of the Beat generation except Gary Snyder; William Burroughs (who died a few weeks after Ginsberg); and his lover, Peter Orlovsky.

GOLD, HERBERT (1924–)

Novelist, short-story writer

A writer of distinctly Jewish sensibility, Herbert Gold was born in 1924 into a Russian Jewish immigrant family. After serving in the U.S. Army during World War II, he traveled for a time and finally settled in San Francisco. His first novel, *Birth of a Hero* (1951), was published when he was only twenty-three years old and was received with considerable applause. His most successful novels are set in a Jewish milieu and are significantly autobiographical. These include *The Prospect Before Us* (1954); *The Man Who Was Not With It* (1956); *Therefore Be Bold* (1960, which was inspired by his childhood and youth in the 1930s); and, *Fathers* (1967), which was a fictionalized account of his own family's story. Gold also wrote short stories, collected in *Love and Like* (1960) and received favorable attention for his autobiography, *My Last Two Thousand Years* (1972). In 1996 Gold published *She Took My Arm as if She Loved Me*, the story of love and aging in the life of a middle-aged private investigator in San Francisco. Gold's novels are urbane, sardonic, and often concerned with distinguishing truth from falsehood in the world of values.

HECHT, BEN (1894–1964)

Journalist, novelist, screenwriter, playwright, Zionist activist

If there was a Chicago Literary Renaissance in the 1920s, Ben Hecht was its Renaissance man. He co-authored one of the great old chestnuts of the American theater, *The Front Page*, wrote brilliant feature articles for the city's newspapers, authored several novels that even today have a cult reputation, and for

forty years was one of America's most prolific and talented screenwriters. A list of films on which he worked without screen credit would be as lengthy (and as impressive) as most other writers' credited filmographies.

Although his name was most closely linked with Chicago, Hecht was born in New York City, the son of Russian Jewish immigrants Joseph and Sarah Hecht. Joseph, a tailor, moved the family to Racine, Wisconsin, where he successfully set up a small clothing factory. Ben grew up in Racine, graduated from high school there, and went off to the University of Wisconsin. He lasted all of three days.

Having discarded the idea of college, he went to Chicago, where he took a $12.50-a-week job on the *Chicago Journal* as a "picture chaser," assigned to find photos to accompany stories, usually about crime, by means fair or foul. From there he graduated to reporting, moving on to the *Daily News* in 1914, where he was fortunate to work for Henry Justin Smith. Smith helped shape the still raw young reporter and, by the time he left the paper in 1923, he had become a celebrated feature writer, a foreign correspondent in Germany and, finally, a columnist. But Hecht had greater ambitions. He published his first novel, *Erik Dorn*, in 1921 and a collection of his columns, *1001 Afternoons in Chicago*, the following year. That same year, his next novel, *Fantazius Mallare* (which was the basis for a motion-picture he co-produced, co-wrote, and co-directed with his longtime partner Charles MacArthur in 1935 under the title *The Scoundrel*), was charged with obscenity and unsuccessfully defended by Clarence Darrow.

Hecht spent most of 1923 and 1924 as founding editor of the *Chicago Literary Review*, a short-lived but wildly iconoclastic publication, When it folded, he left town; new literary challenges were beckoning him back to the city of his birth. For the rest of his life, Hecht divided his time between New York and Hollywood. With MacArthur he wrote the screenplays for *The Front Page* (1928) and *Twentieth Century* (1932). On his own he wrote *Underworld* (1927) for Josef von Sternberg, arguably the first true gangster movie; it won him an Oscar for best original story. He went on to write screenplays for some seventy more films for which he received credit on screen; as a script doctor, he worked on at least as many without credit, most notably *Gone With The Wind* (1939).

In 1940, Hecht returned to his first love, newspapers, contributing a column to *PM*, a liberal daily, writing about life in New York and, most tellingly, the extermination of Europe's Jews by Hitler. The following year, he returned to Hollywood once more. By now, though, Hecht was spurred to a new sense of his Jewish identity; throughout the 1940s he was a staunch supporter of the Revisionist wing of the Zionist movement, raising money and contributing his time and name to the cause of the establishment of a Jewish state in Palestine. In 1946 his play (a pageant really) *A Flag is Born* premiered, starring **Paul Muni** and Celia Adler. Its glorification of the Jewish homeland was intended to hasten the creation of the State of Israel. One result of his efforts was a five-year-long boycott of his films by British exhibitors. But, once the State of Israel came to be, he was not uncritical. He published a famously virulent attack on David Ben Gurion and the Israeli establishment entitled *Perfidy* in 1961.

Hecht's best-selling autobiography, *A Child of the Century*, was published in 1954. He continued to write screenplays and memoirs until his death of a heart attack in 1964. He died, appropriately, at his typewriter while working on a film script.

HELLER, JOSEPH (1923–)

Writer

Joseph Heller was born in Brooklyn, New York, on May 1, 1923. He served as a bombardier during World War II, flying on sixty combat missions in Europe. After the war ended, he returned to New York and attended Columbia University. He received his M.A. in 1949. He then moved on to Oxford University, where he spent a year as a Fulbright scholar.

From 1950 through 1952, Heller taught English at Pennsylvania State University. In 1952, he moved back to New York and entered the magazine business,

first as an advertising copywriter for *Time* magazine (1952–1956), then for *Look* magazine (1956–1958). He was the promotional manager at *McCall's* magazine from 1958 through 1961.

In 1961, Heller's masterpiece, the satirical novel *Catch-22*, was published. The title describes a fictitious Air Force regulation that deems a pilot insane if he continues to fly dangerous combat missions. Yet, if the pilot makes the necessary request to be pulled off those missions, he is considered sane. Hence the "catch." The book, and later the film—produced in 1970—were enormously successful, and the phrase "catch-22" entered the English vernacular. Heller's other work includes the novels *Something Happened* (1974); *Good as Gold* (1979); *God Knows* (1984); and the sequel to *Catch-22*, *Closing Time* (1994). He also wrote the play *We Bombed in New Haven* (1968).

HELLMAN, LILLIAN (1905–1984)

Playwright, memoirist

Stalinist or patriot? Woman of conscience or self-serving hack? Over a decade after her death, Lillian Hellman still inspires controversy and deep, bitter feelings among her supporters and detractors. Although she was a successful playwright, a viperish chronicler of small-town greed and backbiting, she is sometimes remembered as Dashiell Hammett's lover and an unrepentant leftist defying the House Un-American Activities Committee rather than for her writing.

Hellman was born in New Orleans to a well-to-do secular Jewish family. From the age of five, she divided her time between the city of her birth and New York. She attended New York University and Columbia University, but dropped out of the latter during her junior year. In 1924 she went to work in publishing, like so many other well-brought-up would-be literary young ladies of the period. She worked at Boni and Liverwright, then began writing book reviews for the *Herald Tribune* and serving as a script reader for several Broadway producers. In 1925 she married Arthur Kober and the two went to Hollywood. It was there, in 1930, that she met the dapper Hammett, an ex-private detective turned novelist. The two fell in love and remained together until his death in 1961. She divorced Kober amicably in 1932.

With Hammett prodding her, Hellman wrote her first play, *The Children's Hour*. Because it offered lesbianism as a sub-theme, the play was initially controversial; produced on Broadway in 1934, it was an instant hit and Hellman's writing career was launched in earnest. Her next play, an agitprop piece about a strike, was a failure, so she turned to a subject she knew—her own family background.

The result was *The Little Foxes* (1939), her best work in the theater and a huge success for Hellman and its star, Tallulah Bankhead. She followed it with another play about the rapacious Hubbard family, *Another Part of the Forest*, in 1946.

Hellman and Hammett were swept up in the political tides of the Depression and concerned about the fascism that raged across Europe and America. Hammett was an active member of the **Communist Party**; over the years, Hellman both avowed and disavowed membership in the Party, but her heart was clearly with the progressive movement. Her 1941 play, *Watch on the Rhine*, was a bitter anti-fascist work, and her next offering, *The Searching Wind*, explored the same theme.

When the political winds shifted in the post-war era and the anti-Communist hearings began, Hellman and Hammett were among the obvious targets. Hammett, who had served with distinction in the Aleutians during the war, despite being in his late forties, went to jail rather than provide the House Un-American Activities Committee with a list of contributors to the defense fund of an organization he chaired. Hellman, with the help of her lawyer, Joseph Rauh, offered the committee a now-famous statement that opened, "I cannot and will not cut my conscience to fit this year's fashions," and somehow managed to avoid appearing in person. Now unable to get film work because of the blacklist, she was forced to sell the farm she had bought with the proceeds from her theatrical successes.

She continued to work on Broadway, but did not have another hit until the 1960 *Toys in the Attic*. In the 1970s she turned her attentions inward, writing a series of autobiographical books of undeniable literary merit, if somewhat unreliable veracity. A series of talk show appearances by her, rebutted by an old nemesis from the 1930s, Mary McCarthy, led to a memorable lawsuit in which Hellman charged the novelist with libel. But if age had not mellowed the old antagonists, it robbed Hellman of her physical powers. She was blind and in failing health for much of the final two years of her life, passing away in 1984 in New York City.

HOBSON, LAURA Z. (1900–1986)

Writer

Laura Hobson (née Zametkin) was born on June 19, 1900, in New York City, the daughter of Russian Jewish political refugees. She attended Cornell University and spent her early career writing advertising copy. In 1947 her novel *Gentleman's Agreement* was published. An exploration of "civilized" anti-Semitism, the book was so successful that she could become a novelist full-time. She wrote two other books with Jewish themes, *The Trespassers* (1943), which depicts the story of refugees escaping Nazi Germany, and *Over and Above* (1979), which explores Jewish identity and the state of Israel.

In addition to her output as a novelist, Hobson wrote children's books, short stories, and articles. For twenty-seven years she was the editor of the *Saturday Review*'s "Double Crostics" puzzles. Her other novels include *The Other Father* (1950), *The Celebrity* (1951), *First Papers* (1964), *The Tenth Month* (1970), *Consenting Adult* (1975), and *Untold Millions* (1980). She also wrote two volumes of her autobiography, *Laura Z.: A Life* (1983) and *Laura Z.: A Life: Years of Fulfillment* (1986). She died on February 28, 1986.

HURST, FANNIE (1889–1968)

Writer

Writer Fanny Hurst was born in Hamilton, Ohio on October 18, 1889, and grew up in St. Louis, Mis-

Saturday Evening Post, and Cosmopolitan. Thirty of her works became films, some several times. Among the most famous are *Humoresque* (1920, 1946), *Back Street* (1932, 1941, 1961), and *Imitation of Life* (1934, 1959). Socially conscious while writing for a mass audience, Hurst included Jewish subjects in some of her stories, and eventually became an avid supporter of Israel.

JONG, ERICA (1942–)

Writer

Writer Erica Jong was the daughter of artists and the granddaughter of Russian Jewish immigrants. She attended New York's High School of Music and Art before moving on to Barnard College, where she received her B.A. in 1963. She then attended Columbia University, graduating with an M.A. in 1965. She began writing poetry while she was still in college, and by the time she dropped out of Columbia's Ph.D. program she had published two volumes, *Fruits & Vegetables* (1971) and *Halflives* (1973). Her other books of poetry include *Loveroot* (1975), *At the Edge of the Body* (1979), *Ordinary Miracles* (1983), and *Becoming Light* (1991). She has won numerous awards and is highly respected for her work in that medium.

Jong is best known for her first novel, *Fear of Flying* (1973), which—to date—has sold over 12.5 million copies worldwide. A groundbreaking book when it was published, *Fear of Flying* was among the first books to depict sex from a woman's point of view. Jong wrote two sequels: *How to Save Your Own Life* (1977) and *Parachutes & Kisses* (1984). Her other novels include *Fanny: Being the True History of the Adventures of Fanny Hackabout-Jones* (1980), *Any Woman's Blues* (1990), and *Inventing Memory: A Novel of Mothers and Daughters* (1997). Her non-fiction books include *The Devil at Large* (1993), a journal of her correspondence with the expatriate writer Henry Miller; *Fear of Fifty: A Midlife Memoir* (1994); and *What Do Women Want: Bread, Roses, Sex, Power* (1998), a collection of her essays.

Known as "the highest-paid short story writer in America," Fannie Hurst penned such works as Back Street, Imitation of Life, *and* Humoresque, *which became Hollywood films. Her family's ambivalence toward Judaism is reflected in her work, which nonetheless reveals her empathy for minorities and working people in general. This stunning photograph was taken on May 28, 1914. (Library of Congress)*

souri, the child of class-conscious, non-observant Jews who were ambivalent about their Jewish heritage. She attended Washington University, graduating in 1909. A writer throughout her life (much to her mother's dismay), in 1908 she published her first story, "Ain't Life Wonderful," in *Reedy's Mirror*. In 1912 the *Saturday Evening Post* published "Power and Horse Power," which was the start of her successful career.

Best known for the film adaptations of her stories, Hurst became one of the highest-paid writers of the era. Her stories appeared in *Century* magazine, the

KAUFMAN, GEORGE S. (1889–1961)

Playwright, director, journalist

Of all the wits associated with the Algonquin Round Table, George S. Kaufman left the most lasting literary and theatrical legacy, a sheaf of comedies that delighted Broadway audiences in their initial runs and are still playing in repertory around the world today.

Kaufman was born in Pittsburgh, the son of German Jewish émigrés. He began his career as a newspaperman, and over a fifteen-year career as a journalist, columnist, and critic, he developed a reputation as a scathing wit, particularly as a drama critic. (He once wrote in a review, "I saw the play at a disadvantage. The curtain was up.") Kaufman would remain one of *The New York Times*'s drama critics until 1930, long after he had established himself as a successful playwright.

As a dramatist, Kaufman invariably wrote in collaboration. His first successes were co-authored with other denizens of the Algonquin, Marc Connelly (notably *Dulcy*, 1921; *Merton of the Movies*, 1922; *Beggar on Horseback*, 1924) and **Edna Ferber** (*The Royal Family*, 1927; *Dinner at Eight*, 1932; *Stage Door*, 1936). He also had the exasperating and hilarious experience of working as both writer and director with the **Marx Brothers** on two of their three Broadway hits, *The Coconuts* (1925) and *Animal Crackers* (1928).

But Kaufman's greatest success came after he met a brash young man named **Moss Hart**. Fifteen years Kaufman's junior, Hart presented Kaufman with a draft of a comedy about Hollywood, *Once in a Lifetime*, and asked him for an opinion. Instead, he got a writing partner for much of the rest of his life. Kaufman and Hart (George invariably got top billing from his collaborators) authored witty comedies sparked by clever bantering dialogue and—quite often—thinly disguised versions of their famous friends, most notably Alexander Woollcott whom they caricatured in *The Man Who Came to Dinner*. Between 1930 and 1941, the duo wrote nine plays, most of them hits, including the Pulitzer Prize winner *You Can't Take It With You* in 1936.

Kaufman continued writing after he and Hart went their separate ways (although the two remained friends and Bucks County, Pennsylvania, neighbors). One of his next collaborators, the fetching Leueen McGrath, became Mrs. Kaufman as well. He also remained one of the most highly regarded directors on Broadway, with a particular triumph in his staging of *Guys and Dolls*. He also was one of the most sought-after "play doctors" in the American theater, and his unaccredited work undoubtedly saved many ailing theatrical endeavors.

KAZIN, ALFRED (1915–1998)

Educator, editor, critic

Distinguished literary critic Alfred Kazin was born in the Brownsville section of Brooklyn, New York, on June 5, 1915, the son of Russian Jewish immigrants—his father was a house painter and his mother a dressmaker. After attending the City College of New York, he became a book reviewer, freelancing for several different periodicals. He gained national recognition among the literary intelligentsia with the publication of *On Native Grounds* (1942), a study of the development of American literature. Only twenty-seven years old when the book came out, he proved himself an astute critic. His point of view, which he developed

---

A Boy from Brooklyn

Every time I go back to Brownsville it is as if I had never been away. From the moment I step off the train at Rockaway Avenue and smell the leak out of the men's room, then the pickles from the stand just below the subway steps, an instant rage comes over me, mixed with dread and some unexpected tenderness. It is over 10 years since I left to live in "the city"—everything just out of Brownsville was always "the city." Actually I did not go very far; it was enough that I could leave Brownsville, yet as I walk those familiarly choked streets at dusk and see the old women sitting in front of the tenements, past and present become each other's faces; I am back where I began.

From Alfred Kazin's *A Walker in the City* (1951).

throughout his career, was both political and critical. He felt that the development of technology was harming literature's force as a venue for both political and self-expression. An editor as well as a critic and writer, he edited *The Portable Blake* (1946), *The Stature of Theodore Dreiser* (1955), and *The Works of Anne Frank* (1959). His original work includes *Starting Out in the Thirties* (1965), *Bright Book of Life* (1973), *New York Jew* (1978), and *An American Procession* (1984). The author of thirteen books and the editor of ten collections, Kazin died in New York City on June 5, 1998, his eighty-third birthday.

KRAMER, LARRY (1935–)

Novelist, playwright, gay rights activist

Militant gay activist Larry Kramer was born in 1935 in Bridgeport, New York. He first came to public notice in 1977 with the publication of his novel *Faggots*, an attack on the widely held belief in the gay male community that promiscuity was a positive outgrowth of the sexual revolution and an important political statement. The following year he was again involved in controversy when, after a gay rights bill failed to pass in the New York City Council, he denounced the gay community as politically naive.

By 1981, the field of combat had changed and the stakes had gone up. Recognizing the signs of what would become the AIDS epidemic, Kramer founded the Gay Men's Health Crisis (GMHC), which became the largest AIDS service organization in the world, with an annual budget in the tens of millions. Kramer, however, withdrew from the group as it moved toward a methodology that he found too tame and too tactful. He dramatized his parting from the group in his play *The Normal Heart*, which had one of the longest runs ever at the Public Theater in New York and has been produced more than 600 times around the world. In 1987 Kramer founded another, more militant AIDS activist group, ACT UP. ACT UP went onto the streets to bring its message to the public, alienating many people in the process. "We're not here to make friends," Kramer stated. "We're here to raise the issues." In 1992, Kramer's sequel to *The Normal Heart*, *The Destiny of Me*, opened on Broadway to mixed reviews and controversy. *The Destiny of Me* expressed Kramer's concerns and his confusion about family, illness, death, and activism. Kramer has been vilified for his tactics and widely honored for his accomplishments.

KUNITZ, STANLEY (1905–)

Poet

Stanley Kunitz was born in Worcester, Massachusetts, on July 29, 1905. He graduated summa cum laude from Harvard University, where he also received the Garrison Medal for Poetry. He then took a job as a reporter on the *Worcester Sentinel* and began writing poetry. His first book, *Intellectual Things*, was published before he was twenty-five years old. In the years before World War II, he co-edited a number of anthologies; edited a magazine; and compiled a number of literary reference books, including *Twentieth Century Authors*. After serving in the military and spending a year in Santa Fe on a Guggenheim grant, he took his first teaching position in 1946 at Bennington College. Since then he has taught and lectured at various universities while continuing his distinguished career as a poet, winning such prestigious awards as the Brandeis University Medal of Achievement, the Levinson Prize, a Fellowship Award from the Academy of Poets, and the 1959 Pulitzer Prize for his *Selected Poems: 1928–1958*. Still active, he published a new collection of his work, entitled *Passing Through: The Later Poems, New and Selected*, to celebrate his ninetieth birthday. The book won the 1995 National Book Award in Poetry. He edited the Yale Series of Younger Poets from 1969 to 1977. At the same time he served as both consultant on poetry and honorary consultant in American letters to the Library of Congress.

Kunitz's poems have been translated into more than a dozen languages, including Russian, Dutch, Macedonian, French, Japanese, Hebrew, Arabic, and Swedish. He has translated into English the works of several Russian poets. He has lectured and read his work on a number of tours of the Soviet Union,

Poland, the West coast of Africa, Israel, and Egypt. Beyond his literary activities, he has been active in the civil liberties and peace movements.

LAZARUS, EMMA (1849–1887)

Poet

Although she wrote many volumes of poetry, including well-regarded translations of the great Hebrew poets Solomon Ibn Gabirol and Judah HaLevi, Emma Lazarus is one of those unfortunate poets who is remembered for only one work. But that poem, "The New Colossus," is inscribed on the base of the Statue

Although her family belonged to Congregation Shearith Israel in New York City, Emma Lazarus did not really feel committed to Judaism until she heard about the Russian pogroms in the early 1880s. She published Songs of A Semite: The Dance to Death and other Poems *in 1882, and many of the poems in this collection proclaim her self-identification as a Jewish poet. And it was in 1883 that she wrote "The New Colossus." (Library of Congress)*

The Poet Laureate of America's Immigrants

Not like the brazen giant of Greek fame,
With conquering limbs astride from land to land;
Here at our sea-washed, sunset gates shall stand
A mighty women with a torch, whose flame
Is the imprisoned lightening, and her name
Mother of Exiles. From her beacon-hand
Glows world-wide welcome; her mild eyes command
The air-bridged harbor that twin cities frame.
"Keep ancient lands, your storied pomp?" cries she
With silent lips. "Give me your tired, your poor,
Your huddled masses yearning to breathe free,
The wretched refuse of your teeming shore,
Send these, the homeless, tempest-tost to me:
I lift my lamp beside the golden door."

When Emma Lazarus wrote these words in her poem "The New Colossus" they attracted virtually no attention. She wrote the verses as part of a fund-rasing drive to build the Statue of Liberty. When the Statue was unveiled in 1886, the poem was not mentioned. In 1903 permission was finally obtained to place it on a plaque inside the statue, where it went virtually unnoticed. It was not until 1945 that the plaque was moved to its present place at the main entrance for all to see. Despite these precarious beginnings, it is now difficult to imagine the statue without the sonnet. Aside from the flag, the statue has become the most recognizable symbol of America. And Emma Lazarus is truly the poet laureate of America's immigrants.

---

of Liberty and is one of the most quoted works of American poetry. It speaks to the heart of the American Jewish experience, indeed the entire American immigrant experience.

Lazarus was born to a well-to-do Jewish family, equal parts prominent Sephardic and Ashkenazi. Privately educated, she had her first volume of poems published when she was only seventeen. At the time of its initial publication, it was enthusiastically received, particularly by Ralph Waldo Emerson. In her second collection, *Admetus and Other Poems* (1871), Lazarus authored her first verse work with a Jewish theme, "In the Jewish Synagogue at Newport." *The American Hebrew* reprinted this poem and asked the author for more contributions. Thus, Lazarus began writing extensively on the Jewish experience. She published many of her translations of Ibn Gabirol and HaLevi in the periodical. She also collaborated on verse for a new prayer book.

As a result of this newfound interest, Lazarus began working in the Jewish community, not only as a writer but as a social activist. She threw herself into relief work among the Eastern European Jewish immigrants of her native city, eventually writing a series of essays on their plight that was published in book form as *Songs of a Semite* (1882). Her finest moment came in 1883 when her sonnet "The New Colossus" was chosen to grace the base of the new statue to be raised on Bedloe's Island in New York Harbor.

MAILER, NORMAN (1923–)

Novelist, journalist, essayist

Whether writing non-fiction disguised as fiction or fiction disguised as non-fiction, directing and starring in films that seem like little more than vanity productions or running for mayor of New York City, Norman Mailer has been a lightning rod for controversy. Mailer has long been a roisterous figure, a hard drinker, and plain talker who expresses his ideas in brilliantly articulate prose that serves to hide the bluntness of his point of view. Even his greatest detractors would acknowledge the power of his densely layered prose. His adherents argue that he is one of the key American literary figures of the post–World War II era, if not the entire century.

Norman Mailer was born on the New Jersey shore, where his mother's family owned a resort hotel. When Mailer was four, the family moved to Brooklyn, where his father worked as an accountant and his mother ran a housekeeping service. Although Mailer has seldom written about growing up in Brooklyn, he must have retained some strong ties to the borough, for he has repeatedly returned there, and lives there today.

As a boy Mailer was fascinated by aviation and thought of following a career in flying; however, at Harvard he discovered the enchantments of literature, publishing his first story in the *Harvard Advocate*. In 1944 the twenty-one-year-old Harvard graduate enlisted in the Army. He saw combat in the invasion of the Philippines, an experience he would re-create in his first novel.

Published in 1948, *The Naked and the Dead*, instantly established Mailer as one of the preeminent voices of the post-war generation, along with his bright contemporaries Gore Vidal and Truman Capote. Mailer, whose delight in the sport of boxing is well documented, brought a competitive, club fighter's feistiness to the literary wars, looking on Vidal, Capote, and many of his other cohorts as competitors for a literary heavyweight crown. *The Naked and the Dead* was a near knockout blow, a brutal and convincing depiction of the strain that war puts on ordinary men.

However, his next two novels, *Barbary Shore* (1951) and *The Deer Park* (1955), were critical disappointments. Although the tide of opinion has subsequently turned, particularly regarding the latter, one of the best post-war Hollywood novels. Mailer, perhaps in reaction to that letdown, turned his attention to non-fiction. Co-founding the *Village Voice* in 1955, he quit the paper several years later in outrage over its plethora of typographical errors. He collected many of his *Voice* pieces in *Advertisements for Myself* (1959) and *The Presidential Papers* (1963).

Mailer made his next big splash with a now-infamous essay on hipsterism, "The White Negro" (1957). Mailer was also making a different kind of splash at this period of his life, getting into trouble with the police after several incidents involving heavy drinking and in one notorious instance, a violent fight with his then-wife Adele.

Whatever demons were pursuing Mailer, he brought them into sharper focus in his fiction. His next novel, *The American Dream* (1965), focused on a successful novelist and war hero who murders his wife and bests her father in a highly Oedipal duel of wills. Since the success of *The American Dream*, Mailer has alternated fiction and non-fiction with consummate skill and startling fluency, publishing more than a book a year. His best work—the "non-fiction novels" *Armies of the Night*; which won the 1968 Pulitzer Prize; *Miami and the Siege of Chicago* (1968); *Of a Fire on the Moon* (1970); and *The Executioner's Song* (1979), for which he won his second

Pulitzer Prize, bespeak an ongoing fascination with outcasts struggling against the nation's large institutions. In his fiction, the protagonists enjoy a more ambiguous relation with institutional power, whether it is the CIA of *Harlot's Ghost* (1992) or God himself in *The Gospel According to the Son* (1997). In 1998, on the fiftieth anniversary of the publication of *The Naked and the Dead*, Mailer published a 1200-page omnibus of his best work, *The Time of Our Time*.

Mailer has seldom treated Jewish issues directly, with the notable exception of one of the subplots of *The Naked and the Dead* in which the anti-Semitic sergeant taunts a Jewish GI into a suicidal mission. His consistent interest in alienated outsiders, whether they are killers like Lee Harvey Oswald or Gary Gilmore, or political and social rebels like the "Norman Mailer" of *Armies of the Night*, bespeak a very Jewish American sense of discomfort in the New World.

MALAMUD, BERNARD (1914–1986)

Novelist, short-story writer

In the aftermath of the Second World War and the Holocaust, a new generation of writers emerged with strong ethnic identities, forged from the strife of the Depression in the cities and the harsh realities of the war. At the forefront of these writers were two Jewish authors, **Saul Bellow** and Bernard Malamud (joined in the late 1950s by **Philip Roth**). Of the two, Malamud emerged later, schooled in the turmoil of Brooklyn's impoverished Jewish ghetto and the city's then superb public schools and universities. He left an indelible mark on American post-war fiction, the most authentically Jewish voice of the veritable army of Jewish writers of the era.

Malamud was born into the somewhat genteel poverty of the lower-middle class; his parents ran a small grocery in Brooklyn, perpetually perched on the uneasy edge of bankruptcy. Bernard began writing while still in school at Erasmus High, publishing his first story in the school literary magazine. In 1936 he earned his B.A. at City College of New York, following with a master's in literature from Columbia University. He took a teaching position at Erasmus (and later Harlem High School) shortly thereafter, and began publishing short stories while on the faculty there. In 1949 he was offered a teaching position at the University of Oregon, where he remained for twelve years. It was in this very un-Brooklyn-like environment that Malamud wrote his first four novels. In 1961 he joined the faculty at Bennington College (another markedly un-Jewish place) and spent the remainder of his teaching career there.

Malamud's first novel, *The Natural* (1952), is the only one of his books without significant Jewish content; rather, it turns the story of a superhumanly gifted baseball player into an exploration of the Grail myth. On the other hand, the book's title character, Roy Hobbs, achieves wisdom through suffering, a theme running through the remainder of Malamud's work and one that he gave an explicitly Jewish spin. His next novel, *The Assistant* (1957), returned Malamud to his boyhood, telling the story of a failing grocery owned by an elderly Jew and the vicissitudes of his life.

Malamud's next book was a collection of short fiction, a medium in which he excelled. *The Magic Barrel* (1958) won a National Book Award and established him as one of the best of contemporary short-story writers. His other collections, *Idiots First* (1963) and *Rembrandt's Hat* (1973), extended that mastery.

Malamud continued to work in the novel form as well. His biggest success came with 1966's *The Fixer*, a grim story based on the blood-libel trial of Mendel Beilis in turn-of-the-century Russia. Like the real-life Beilis, Malamud's protagonist is accused of the ritual murder of a gentile child and faced with torture and despair. Out of suffering he develops a greater sense of his Jewishness and a connectedness to his community. His next novel, *The Tenants* (1971), is a startling contrast, with two neighbors, both writers, one Jewish the other black, who engage in a demented struggle for ascendancy that ends in apocalyptic violence.

In the wake of a new edition of his complete stories published in 1997, Malamud is finally being acknowledged as one of the great short-story writers in the English language, a miniaturist who could layer meanings in a confined space with consummate craft.

MAMET, DAVID (1947–)

Playwright, screenwriter, filmmaker

David Mamet is a product of the generation of Jewish Americans that grew up in the suburbs and cities, born after World War II and spared the grim realities of Depression, war, and the Holocaust. Mamet's concerns, not untypical of that generation, are the death of the American Dream and the ugly underside of an American society driven by greed, comfort, and conformity. He expresses those concerns in brutally profane language that captures the currents of the American vernacular of his time.

Mamet was born in Chicago, a city he has been closely associated with ever since. He grew up on the South Side, a child of divorce. His father wanted him to become a lawyer, but Mamet had been exposed to the theater when he worked part-time as a busboy at the Second City cabaret, and he fancied a career as a writer. He went to Goddard College, where he studied literature and theater. He also began working under the legendary acting teacher Sanford Meisner at the Neighborhood Playhouse and dabbled in playwriting. After a series of dead-end jobs, he accepted a teaching position at Goddard, where he began writing in earnest and staging some of his plays. Eventually, his work found its way to several Chicago theaters.

His breakthrough in his home town came with 1974's *Sexual Perversity in Chicago*, which won that city's Joseph Jefferson Award as outstanding play of the year. Mamet was still unknown outside of Chicago until *Sexual Perversity* and *Duck Variations* received off-Broadway productions during the 1975–1976 season to great acclaim. His next play, *American Buffalo* (1977), a downbeat but darkly funny tale of three losers planning a penny-ante heist, won him an Obie and his first Broadway production; it was voted best play of 1977 by the New York Drama Critics Circle. His subsequent success peaked with a 1983 Pulitzer Prize awarded for *Glengarry Glen Ross*, a bleak examination of real estate small-timers.

Mamet has always been interested in film—his play *Speed-the-Plow* (1987) is set in Hollywood—and

his theatrical success enabled him to delve into that medium more fully. In addition to adapting several of his own plays for the screen, he has written and directed several motion pictures, including *Homicide* (1991), a film about a Jewish police detective who finds himself drawn into a case that may involve neo-Nazi violence against Jews, causing him to re-examine his own Jewish identity closely.

Mamet is also an outspoken essayist who has bragged that he is a lifetime member "of both the American Civil Liberties Union and the National Rifle Association." He also tried his hand at the short story, penning a novella about Passover that drew on his family memories of the holiday. In 1997 his play *The Old Neighborhood* opened on Broadway, and he published a novel, *The Old Religion*, which explored the interior world of Leo Frank, the Atlanta Jew who was lynched in 1915.

MILLER, ARTHUR (1915–)

Playwright

When the American theater came of age in the post–World War II era, it was largely through the efforts of Arthur Miller and Tennessee Williams. If Williams brought a highly refined sense of poetry and a dreamlike haze to the Broadway stage, Miller gave it a remorseless sense of the working out of social forces devouring ordinary men and women. When the anti-Communist witchhunts of the 1950s began, it was Miller who found the perfect metaphors for those who were doomed to defeat by their defiance but ennobled by their supposed loss.

Miller was born to Polish Jewish immigrant parents in Manhattan, but when the family's garment industry firm suffered financial setbacks, they moved to Brooklyn, where Arthur was raised. Miller was an indifferent student, more interested in sports than scholarly pursuits, but he was also captivated by vaudeville and theater. When he went to University of Michigan as an undergraduate, he began to try his hand at writing. He enjoyed some early successes there, including one play, *They Too Rise*, which won a 1938 Theater Guild award, and was encouraged to become a professional writer. Eventually, his first play on Broadway, *The Man Who Had All the Luck*, was produced in 1944; it was a failure and has been all but forgotten.

His next offering, *All My Sons*, premiered three years later to great acclaim. Like the earlier work, it centers on tortured father-son relationships and sibling rivalries, but filters them through a distinctly social consciousness, centered on war profiteering. Fresh from the success of *All My Sons*, which won the 1947 New York Drama Critics Circle Award, Miller enjoyed even greater success with the work that followed—*Death of a Salesman* (1949). Once more Miller turned to the interlocked themes of rival brothers and a weak father. Not only would this play, generally acknowledged to be his masterpiece, win a second Drama Critics Circle award, but it also received the Pulitzer Prize for drama.

With the rise of Senator McCarthy and the investigation of alleged Communist activity in the theater and film, Miller chose to speak out. First he adapted Ibsen's *An Enemy of the People*, a play about one honest man set against an entire community by circumstance. He then wrote his own rumination on—quite literally—witch-hunting, *The Crucible* (1953). In each of these works, the hero is eventually defeated by political and social forces larger than himself, but in his defeat his heroic stature is amplified. Miller had a chance to test this theme in his own life; he was called before the House Un-American Activities Committee in 1955. He readily acknowledged having attended events sponsored by the **Communist Party**, but denied having been a party member; he refused to "name names" and was found in contempt of Congress. Before he was sentenced, his conviction was overturned by the U.S. Court of Appeals.

Miller's personal life became more public thereafter, when he married his second wife, Marilyn Monroe. It was an ill-fated match, ending in divorce. The marriage and his political problems became the subject of Miller's first play in nine years, *After the Fall* (1964), which was not a success.

In the years since the mid-1960s, Miller and his third wife, photographer Ingeborg Morath (whom he met when the two worked on the 1961 Monroe film, *The Misfits*), have traveled extensively, producing several books that combine her images and his words. He has also continued to write plays, most notably, *Broken Glass*, which considers the Jewish experience of the Holocaust, and several lighter philosophical comedies, including *The Creation of the World and Other Business*, and the autobiographical *A Memory of Two Mondays*. In 1998 a revival of his early play, *A View from the Bridge* (1955), was produced on Broadway and met with critical and commercial success. In 1999 Miller received a special Tony Award for lifetime achievement. It was presented by Brian Dennehy, who was then playing Willy Loman (the father) in Miller's *Death of a Salesman* on Broadway. This production won a Tony for best revival of a play, and Dennehy won for best leading actor.

MÖISE, PENINA (1797–1880)

Poet, teacher

Born on April 23, 1797, in Charleston, South Carolina, Penina Möise was her era's most famous Jewish poet. She was published in both the Jewish and the mainstream press. In 1833 she published *Fancy's Sketch Book*, the first book of poetry by a Jewish American woman. In addition to her poetry, Möise wrote newspaper columns for papers all over the United States. A teacher throughout her life, in 1845 she became superintendent of the Sunday school at Congregation Beth Elohim in Charleston. She also wrote at least 190 hymns for Beth Elohim, making her the first Jewish American woman to have her work included in the worship service. After the Civil War, having become completely blind, she opened a school with her sister and niece and lived out her days in poverty. She died on September 13, 1880. The Reform movement's 1932 *Union Hymnal* still contained thirteen of her hymns.

NEMEROV, HOWARD (1920–1991)

Poet, novelist

Versatile writer Howard Nemerov was born into a wealthy Jewish family in New York City on March 1,

1920. Educated at Harvard University, he volunteered for service during World War II, as a pilot for the Canadian RAF and then for the U.S. Air Force. He taught at Hamilton and Bennington colleges, Brandeis University, and Washington University in St. Louis. Nemerov's first book of poetry, *The Image and The Law*, was published in 1947, introducing readers to an apparently simple, casual style that was full of wit and complexity. His books of poetry include *New and Selected Poems* (1960), *Collected Poems* (1978), for which he won a Pulitzer Prize, and *Inside the Onion* (1984). His fiction includes the novels *Federigo* (1954) and *Homecoming Game* (1957) and a collection of stories, *A Commodity of Dreams* (1959). His works of criticism include *Poetry and Fiction* (1963), *Reflections on Poetry and Poetics* (1972), and *New & Selected Essays* (1985). In 1988 Nemerov was named Poet Laureate of the United States. He died shortly after completing his term.

ODETS, CLIFFORD (1906–1963)

Playwright, screenwriter

Clifford Odets was a failed actor who became the poet laureate of the Depression-era Jewish working class. Born in Philadelphia to Austrian and Russian Jews, he grew up in the Bronx, where his father worked as the manager of a printing plant. Odets turned down an offer from his father to join the business and dropped out of high school to act. He worked intermittently in the field, supporting himself between theatrical engagements by working at odd jobs.

In 1933 he joined with other similarly minded progressive stage professionals to form the Group Theater. He acted in some of the Group's early productions, but was dissatisfied with the quality of writing. Believing he could do better, he began to write his own plays. The results were almost immediate and electrifying: *Waiting for Lefty* (1935) and *Awake and Sing* (1935). Here was a new voice in American theater, a committed leftist with a poetic bent and a distinctly Jewish accent. He also authored one of the very first anti-Nazi plays produced in the United States, the one-act *Till The Day I Die* (1935). When his next play, *Paradise Lost*, flopped, Odets took advantage of an offer from Hollywood to escape the pressure on him in New York.

In Hollywood, he wrote several unsuccessful films, met and married the actor Luise Rainer, then headed back to Broadway and the Group. Whatever Odets had intended to do in the film industry, the change had recharged his batteries. His next play was the biggest commercial success of his career, *Golden Boy* (1937) and the influx of cash saved the Group Theater from financial ruin. In his next several plays he turned his attention from the overtly political content of his earlier work to the problems of domestic relations, a reflection, no doubt, of his crumbling marriage. When the Group Theater disbanded in 1942, Odets returned to Hollywood.

Back in the film industry, Odets tried his hand at directing, filming his own script of Richard Llewelyn's novel *None But the Lonely Heart*, and authoring other screenplays. He was miserable in California and unhappy with his writing for the screen. His next play, *The Big Knife* (1949), was a scathing denunciation of the film industry; if the play that followed it, *The Country Girl* (1950), hadn't been a hit, it is hard to imagine that he would have been welcome in Hollywood again.

But Odets now faced a career crisis more serious than any he had encountered before. In the spring of 1952 he was called before the House Un-American Activities Committee to testify about alleged Communist influence in the film and theater industries. Reluctantly, Odets testified, admitted to his former membership in the Party, and named names. Filled with self-loathing, he found it increasingly difficult to write. He completed only one more play, *The Flowering Peach* (1954), a surprisingly sweet comedy about Noah, and a brilliant screenplay for a corrosive examination of corruption in the media, *Sweet Smell of Success* (1957). He died of cancer in 1963.

OLSEN, TILLIE (c. 1913–)

Writer, activist

Tillie Olsen (née Lerner) was born in Nebraska around 1912 or 1913. Both of her parents were Russian Jewish immigrants and socialists. It was the tradition of Jewish social consciousness rather than religious observance that pervaded her youth and influenced her adulthood. A high school dropout, Olsen struggled in her youth, holding a variety of low-paying jobs, including many in factories. In 1931 she became a member of the Young Communist League. Later, she was a member, on and off, of the **Communist Party**. Throughout her life she was politically active and was frequently jailed.

Though she started writing in her youth, both the struggle to survive and her political activity took up her time. It was not until the 1950s that Olsen was able to focus on her first love. Her published work includes *Tell Me a Riddle* (1961), a collection of short stories, *Yonnondio: From the Thirties* (1974), and *Silences* (1978). In 1961 the title story from *Tell Me a Riddle* won the O. Henry Short Story Award. In 1980 it was made into a film. Olsen was the recipient of a Stanford University writing fellowship (1956–1957), a Ford Foundation literature grant (1959), and a Guggenheim Fellowship, among many others. She has taught or been writer-in-residence at numerous universities and colleges including Stanford and Amherst.

OZICK, CYNTHIA (1928–)

Novelist, short-story writer, essayist

Cynthia Ozick was born New York City in 1928 and reared in a traditional Jewish family. Her work reflects both that tradition and the experience of anti-Semitism in her childhood. After receiving her master's degree from Ohio State University, she began writing seriously but did not publish her first novel until 1966, when she was thirty-eight years old. That novel, *Trust*, was experimental in style and highly allusive. It was followed by the short stories that have won Ozick her reputation as an important writer. Three of these stories have won O. Henry prizes. Ozick's stories have been regularly chosen for publication in the annual *Best American Short Stories* and are collected in a number of books, including *The Pagan Rabbi and Other Stories* (1971), *Bloodshed and Three Novellas* (1976),

Winner of numerous literary awards, writer Cynthia Ozick has created classic characters and stories of Jewish life. She was a successful essayist as well as novelist, short-story writer, and playwright. Her fictional works on the Holocaust are among her most moving. (Courtesy of American Jewish Archives)

Leviathan: Five Fictions (1982), and *The Puttermesser Papers* (1997). In 1996 her play *Blue Light*, which was based on one of her short stories, was produced off-Broadway to critical acclaim. Ozick's essays on a variety of subjects have been collected in several books, including *Art and Ardor* (1983) and *Fame and Folly* (1996). She is a highly respected and influential literary figure in contemporary America.

PALEY, GRACE (1922–)

Writer, activist

Writer and activist Grace Paley was born in the Bronx, New York on December 11, 1922. Her parents were both Ukrainian socialists who immigrated to the United States to escape czarist persecution. She grew up speaking Yiddish, Russian, and English, the rhythms of which resonate through her fiction. Paley is most famous for her short stories and poetry, her published work includes *The Little Disturbances of Man* (1959), *Enormous Changes at the Last Minute* (1974), *Later the Same Day* (1985), *Leaning Forward: Poems* (1985), and *Long Walks and Intimate Talks* (1991). Her writing focuses on the art of language, the importance of storytelling, and the voice of modern, often Jewish, women.

A committed political activist, Paley was an active participant in the 1960s peace movement and the anti-nuclear movement. She has traveled extensively and is an advocate for Palestinian rights. In 1987 she helped found the Jewish Women's Committee to End the Occupation of the West Bank and Gaza. She has taught at several universities, most notably Sarah Lawrence, where she spent twenty-two years (1966–1988). She has also received numerable fellowships and awards for her writing, including a Guggenheim Fellowship (1961), a PEN/Faulkner Prize for Fiction (1986), and a National Endowment for the Arts Senior Fellowship (1987).

PARKER, DOROTHY (1893–1967)

Writer

The linchpin of the Algonquin Round Table, Dorothy Parker is perhaps more famous for her quips and her drinking than for her writing, a regrettable state of affairs for one of America's better light verse authors. Parker was born Dorothy Rothschild, the daughter of a Jewish father and a Scottish mother. In 1917 she married Edwin Pond Parker II, a businessman, with whom she lived off and on until their divorce in 1928. She began her career as a writer reviewing theater for *Vogue* and *Vanity Fair*, but was fired by the latter after she gave a particularly savage notice to Billie Burke.

In 1924 Parker collaborated with **Elmer Rice** on a satirical play, *Close Harmony*, which failed. In 1926 Parker published her first volume of verse, *Enough*

Rope, which revealed her as a sharply witty crafter of light poetry. She followed it with two more books of poetry and several collections of short stories. In 1927 she began a long association with *The New Yorker*, writing the book column "The Constant Reader." In 1929 she received the O. Henry Prize for "Big Blond," a frequently anthologized story of an aging alcoholic prostitute.

Although the Algonquin circle prided itself on its devil-may-care attitudes, the Depression brought an end to their particular brand of insouciant humor. Parker developed a pronounced social conscience, eventually joining the **Communist Party**. She had already been arrested during the 1920s while demonstrating on behalf of Sacco and Vanzetti; now she would throw herself with surprising vigor into the battle for Spain, heading the Joint Anti-Fascist Refugee Committee. She also found herself in Hollywood with her then-husband, Alan Campbell, where the two worked on numerous screenplays, including Hitchcock's *Saboteur* (1942). Her last significant work was a play she wrote in collaboration with Arnaud d'Usseau, *Ladies of the Corridor* (1953). Eventually, Parker returned east where she sank into an alcohol-fueled spiral of depression and comparative silence as a writer.

PERELMAN, S. J. (1904–1979)

Humorist

When S. J. (Sidney Joseph) Perelman was in his heyday, he was one of the rare practitioners of a delicate craft, the writing of short humor pieces. Although he was often asked to write in longer forms—one always wonders what a Perelman novel would have been like—he steadfastly stuck to his sprinter's distance, anticipating (and inspiring) the flood of humor writers of the 1980s and 1990s.

Perelman was born in Brooklyn to a poor Jewish family and raised in Providence, Rhode Island. His father was a hapless sort, changing jobs as his fortunes fell repeatedly. Perelman was an excellent student, although he wanted to be a cartoonist when he arrived at Brown University. After graduating from Brown in

1925, he drew for *Judge*, a humor weekly, while living the bohemian life in Greenwich Village. He also found himself contributing humorous prose to that magazine and to *College Humor and Life*. Eventually he stopped providing drawings and limited himself to writing. In 1934 he found a writing home with his initial contributions to *The New Yorker*, a venue that he would enjoy for the rest of his life.

Perelman's first book, a compilation of much of his early writing, was published in 1929. In the early 1930s he was offered a contract as a screenwriter and contributed to several films, including the **Marx Brothers'** *Monkey Business* (1931) and *Horse Feathers* (1932). He dabbled in screenwriting and theater for his entire career, winning an Oscar for his script for *Around the World In 80 Days* (1956). He wrote a **Bert Lahr** vehicle, *The Beauty Part* (1962), which is legendary in theatrical circles as the great comedy that nobody saw because of the New York newspaper strike (a turn of events right out of an S. J. Perelman story).

His work includes the travel books *Westward Ha!* (1948) and *The Swiss Family Perelman* (1950). It also includes a series of humorous books mostly derived from his *New Yorker* pieces, including *Strictly from Hunger* (1937), *Look Who's Talking* (1940), *Crazy Like a Fox* (1944), *The Road to Miltown* (1957), and *Chicken Inspector No. 23* (1966).

PLAYWRIGHTS

In the early days of America's history, there was little evidence of the prejudice against Jews that developed after the influx of immigrants in the late nineteenth century. Indeed, Puritan religious attitudes were quite positive toward God's Chosen People. The earliest Jewish American playwrights, who emerged in the early nineteenth century, were usually not self-consciously Jewish. Like other playwrights of the time, they wrote about romantic characters of all sorts in plays designed to entertain the largest audiences possible.

The best known of these early playwrights was Mordecai Manuel Noah, who wrote everything from romantic melodrama to contemporary comedy, including *She Would Be a Soldier* (1819). Isaac Harby, a resident of Charleston, South Carolina, wrote romantic revenge melodramas that were popular with both critics and audiences. Among these were *The Gordian Knot* (1807) and *Alberti* (1819).

Significant dramatic writing began to emerge in the late nineteenth century, and Jewish playwrights were among those who broke through the melodrama, bowdlerism, and derivatism that had marked American theater to that point. The most popular and powerful of these was **David Belasco**, who was also one of the theater's most successful producers.

Belasco was born into a Portuguese Jewish family in San Francisco in 1853. He became involved in the theater as an actor when he was eleven years old and wrote his first play at twelve. From 1881 until the early 1920s, he wrote and produced dozens of hits saturated with romance, adventure, and entertainment value. One of these, *The Auctioneer* (1901), which he wrote with Charles Klein and Lee Arthur, told the story of a Lower East Side peddler. Most did not deal specifically with Jews or the Jewish experience.

1910–1920s

During the teens and early twenties, a number of Jewish American playwrights wrote comedies with strongly stereotyped characters. Underneath the stereotypical behavior, however, the message was that Jews were essentially the same as the rest of humanity. These plays had a genuinely positive impact as Russian and Polish Jews worked for success and acceptance in American society. Montague Glass was the author of *Potash and Perlmutter* (1913), which was so successful that it became a series on the stage and on film. A step beyond these stereotyped comedies was Aaron Hoffman's *Welcome Stranger* (1920), in which a kind and thoughtful Jewish merchant wins over the inhabitants of a small New England town.

At about the same time, the emergence of the musical theater brought a remarkable blossoming of Jewish American talent. Along with composers **Jerome Kern**, **Irving Berlin**, **George Gershwin**, and others, there were a number of Jewish songwriters and lyricists. There was, of course, George Gershwin's brother Ira, and Lew Fields' daughter Dorothy. They both wrote lyrics, and Dorothy Fields also wrote a number of books, including *Annie Get Your Gun* (1946).

1920s–1930s

In the 1920s and 1930s many Jewish writers began to make their mark on American literature. They were especially visible in the theater and, while little of their work was specifically concerned with Jewish issues, most of these playwrights were clear about their Jewish identity.

George S. Kaufman became America's leading comic playwright, beginning with *Dulcy* (1921), co-written with Marc Connelly, and continuing through his two Pulitzer Prize–winning plays: *Of Thee I Sing* (1932), written with Morrie Ryskind and **Ira Gershwin** and *You Can't Take It with You* (1930), written with Moss Hart. He also wrote *I'd Rather Be Right* (1937) and *The Man Who Came to Dinner* (1939) with Hart. Kaufman was a born collaborator, doing most of his best work with co-authors who were also Jewish. These included, in addition to Ryskind and Hart, **Edna Ferber** and Howard Teichmann.

Moss Hart wrote a number of plays and librettos on his own, including the powerful *Lady in the Dark* (1941). Ferber's plays were primarily collaborations and included the highly successful *Dinner at Eight* (1932) and *Stage Door* (1936), both with Kaufman.

Elmer Rice broke new ground with such plays as *The Adding Machine* (1923) and *Street Scene* (1929). His forty-year career as a playwright began with *On Trial* (1914), drawing on his earlier career as a lawyer. Presenting essentially an entire murder trial, the play used extensive flashbacks for the first time in the history of theater. It had a tremendous impact and was followed by two more law-inspired plays. In 1923 Rice again stunned the theater world with his impressionistic fantasy *The Adding Machine*. He was awarded the Pulitzer Prize for *Street Scene*, a highly realistic treatment of New York life. Rice had twenty-four Broadway productions and was a founder of the Playwrights' Company.

Clifford Odets became one of the theater's most respected playwrights for his trenchant socio-political plays, such as *Waiting for Lefty* (1935), *Awake and Sing!* (1935), and *Golden Boy* (1937). *Awake and Sing!* dealt with a poor, troubled Jewish family and, like Odets' other plays, reflected a strongly leftist point of view.

S. N. Behrman wrote high comedy that was unrivaled in the American theater, except for non-Jewish playwright Philip Barry. His first success came in 1927 with *The Second Man* and his last play was produced on Broadway in 1964. His best original plays were probably *Biography* (1932) and *No Time for Comedy* (1939). He also scored a triumph with an adaptation from Franz Werfel's *Jacobowsky and the Colonel* (1944), about a Jewish refugee and an anti-Semitic Polish colonel who flee together from the Nazis.

Lillian Hellman's first plays, *The Children's Hour* (1939)—about a child's allegation that two teachers were involved in a lesbian relationship—and *The Little Foxes* (1939)—about greed and family conflict in the South—were immediate critical and popular successes. Born and reared in the South, Hellman drew on both the region and her ethnic origins at one time or another in a long and notable career that also included *Watch on the Rhine* (1941) and *Toys in the Attic* (1960).

Sidney Kingsley won a Pulitzer Prize for his medical drama, *Men in White* (1933). It was his first play to be produced on Broadway. He also received great acclaim for *Dead End* (1935), a story of New York slum life that focused on youth gangs and for *Detective Story* (1949). Newspaper reporter **Ben Hecht** branched out into novels and short stories but made his mark with the play *The Front Page* (1928), written in collaboration with Charles MacArthur. Bella and Samuel Spewack also began as journalists before turning out a dozen successful Broadway plays, including *Boy Meets Girl* (1935) and *My Three Angels* (1953). The leading theater critic of the teens and twenties was George Jean Nathan, who also co-founded *The American Mercury* with H. L. Mencken. He continued to be influential in the American theater until his death in 1958.

1940s–1950s

Many Jewish playwrights drew their inspiration from Jewish life and tradition, although their characters were not necessarily, or recognizably, Jewish. Their work was marked by a profound social and political consciousness, usually leftist. In the 1940s, one of the most important of these playwrights appeared.

Arthur Miller's first Broadway production was not a success. *The Man Who Had All the Luck* (1944) only ran for one week. His next play, *All my Sons* (1947), won the New York Drama Critics Circle Award and established his reputation. *Death of a Salesman* (1949) consolidated that reputation and won him the Pulitzer Prize. During the 1950s, Miller was considered America's most important playwright. Two other plays, *The Crucible* (1953) and *A View from the Bridge* (1955) rank among the best American dramas, but his later work has been uneven.

Paddy Chayefsky, who began his writing career in television was more connected with his Jewish background. He drew with great success on Jewish tradition and his own experiences. His most successful theatrical work was *The Tenth Man* (1959), which concerned an exorcism in a synagogue. His best work was for film and television, ranging from the poignant *Marty* (1953) to the savagely satirical *Network* (1976).

1960s–PRESENT

The 1960s brought Jewish playwrights on both ends of the theatrical spectrum and a few in the middle. Experimental, avant garde drama was written by Israel Horovitz, Leon Katz and Murray Mednick, Susan Yankowitz, Rosalyn Drexler, and Karen Malpede. Commercial theater was exemplified by the work of the most successful playwright of our era, **Neil Simon**. Somewhere in the middle were Ronald Ribman, Arthur Kopit, and **David Mamet**.

The most lasting and influential of the experimental playwrights is Israel Horovitz. By the 1990s he had written fifty plays that were translated and performed in twenty-five languages. His works have been produced more often in France than any other American playwright in history. Among his most familiar plays are *The Indian Wants the Bronx* (1967), in which two young thugs torment an East Indian man who is searching for his son, and *The Primary English Class* (1975), about a teacher in an English-as-a-second-language class.

Neil Simon has been more successful in the second half of the twentieth century than George S. Kaufman was in the first. He began his career in radio and television, making his move to theater by writing sketches for *Catch a Star* (1955) and *New Faces of 1956*. His first full-length play was *Come Blow Your Horn* (1961), which was followed by a series of hits that no other American playwright has equaled. His successes include *Barefoot in the Park* (1963), *The Odd Couple* (1965), *The Sunshine Boys* (1972), and dozens of others. In the 1980s Simon began exploring his own experiences and his Jewish background in a semi-autobiographical trilogy that began with *Brighton Beach Memoirs* (1983).

Commercial success rewarded Arthur Kopit as well, though not on the level that Simon experienced it. He came into prominence with the darkly funny *Oh Dad, Poor Dad, Mamma's Hung You in the Closet and I'm Feelin' So Sad* (1962), which was made into a film starring Ruth Gordon and George Segal. His lyrical and moving study of a woman in recovery from a stroke, *Wings* (1979), was a triumph in regional theaters and on Broadway.

David Mamet began his writing career in Chicago, producing his early plays at his own theater. From the beginning, in such plays as *Sexual Perversity in Chicago* (1974) and *Duck Variations* (1975), it was clear that he had a remarkable ear for language, although his work was somewhat short on substance. When *American Buffalo* was produced in New York in 1977, it won the New York Drama Critics Circle Award. *Glengarry Glen Ross* (1984), which dealt with greed in the real estate business won a Pulitzer Prize. A later play, *Speed-the-Plow* (1987), examined greed in the film industry. Mamet also writes and directs films. He is enormously popular with actors and directors and is a major figure in contemporary American theater.

Rosalyn Drexler and Karen Malpede have continued to produce into the 1990s, as has Ronald Ribman. Other Jewish playwrights of significance in the contemporary theater include Donald Margulies, **Wendy Wasserstein**, and **Tony Kushner**. Margulies garnered critical and popular acclaim with *The Loman Family Picnic* (1989) and *Sight Unseen* (1992). *What's Wrong with This Picture?* (1994) was the first of his plays to reach Broadway. Wendy Wasserstein's first play, *Uncommon Women* (1975) received positive attention, in part because of its all-female cast, and was widely performed in regional theaters. Wassersteins's *The Heidi Chronicles* (1989) won a Pulitzer Prize, as did Kushner's *Angels in America, Part I: Millennium Approaches* (1993).

Angels in America stunned the national theatergoing audience. Kushner's two-part, seven-hour drama is very much informed by Judaism and the Jewish tradition, while dealing with the subject of AIDS. It was one of many AIDS plays written by Jewish men, including *The Normal Heart* (1985) by gay activist and dramatist **Larry Kramer**. Kramer followed that influential play several years later with *The Destiny of Me* (1992), which is more interesting for its revelation of Kramer's personality and history than for its dramatic merits.

In contemporary theater, "Jewish" has approximately the same weight as a label as that traditionally attached to "Southern" or "Irish." Jewishness provides a milieu audiences recognize and enjoy, as well as traditions that offer the playwright a context for discussion of ideas and values. At its worst, it slips into stereotype. At its best, it provides a structure for the meaningful exploration of the human condition.

POETRY

The earliest contributions of Jewish Americans to poetry date from the beginning of the nineteenth century. At this time the Sephardic Jews who came to colonial America were joined by an influx of German Jews. Many of these immigrants were highly cultured and educated, but most wrote in Yiddish and did not become part of the American literary mainstream. The primary writer whose work survives from this period is poet **Penina Moise**. Moise, a southern woman of Sephardic and German ancestry, wrote *Fancy's Sketchbook* (1833), the first book of poetry in English known to have been published by an American Jew. She also wrote the first Jewish hymnal. Later in the century, two other women poets would emerge. They were from strikingly different backgrounds and approached life and the writing of poetry in different ways.

Primarily known as a colorful, flamboyant actor, **Adah Isaacs Menken** published poetry that won her an entree into the literary salons of Europe. While it is not clear that Menken was actually born Jewish—she may have been a woman of color—she took her identity as a Jew seriously after her marriage to a Jewish husband when she was very young. A regular contributor to Rabbi **Isaac Mayer Wise**'s weekly newspaper, *The Israelite*, she studied classical Jewish texts, became fluent in Hebrew, and strongly supported a kind of pre-Zionism. Her greatest fame came from her appearance in the verse drama *Mazeppa*, in which she appeared in a flesh-colored body stocking, strapped to the back of a horse. Her poetry was collected and published posthumously in a the book *Infelicia* (1868).

Emma Lazarus was the daughter of an affluent and respectable Sephardic family. She was a serious poet and the first Jewish American poet to be accepted by the American literary establishment. Although her earliest work was not rooted in her Jewish heritage, the poetry beginning with her volume *Songs of a Semite* (1882) embraces and explores her identity as a Jew. She was also a very American poet, believing fiercely in the principles of freedom and democracy. Her most famous poem, "The New Colossus" (1883), combines these two powerful forces in her life as it speaks in the voice of the Statue of Liberty to welcome those in exile from their homelands, fleeing to America and freedom.

Among the exiles Lazarus welcomed were the more than two million Russian and Polish Jews who arrived in American between 1881 and 1914. These immigrants had few resources and were viewed with hostility by many of the German Jews who had already established themselves in this country, as well as by non-Jews who found them unpleasantly foreign. The newcomers were confused by demands that they assimilate in order to succeed and that success be measured in strictly material terms. These issues are apparent in the poetry of several Yiddish-language poets who came to America in this wave of immigration, and their work influenced later Jewish American poets writing in English.

One potentially important poet began and ended his brief career during this time. Having lived in pain and poverty, Samuel Greenberg died of tuberculosis in 1916. Allen Tate edited the *Selected Poems of Samuel Greenberg*, and critic Gerald Stern called his poem "The Tusks of Blood" one of the great poems of the century. Non-Jewish poet Hart Crane was profoundly influenced by Greenberg.

One important school, the Objectivist Group, was made up largely of Jewish members, including Charles Reznikoff, Louis Zukofsky, George Oppen, and Carl Rakosi. Reznikoff had the strongest sense of his Jewish identity and was probably the most powerful of these poets. Much of his work is overtly informed by the Jewish Bible; the Jewish experience in America; and, in later years, the experience of the Holocaust. Writing at the same time was Maxwell Bodenheim. Bodenheim, a close friend of writer **Ben Hecht**, lived most of his life in Chicago and New York but did not focus, as Hecht did, on the seamy world of city life. Strongly influenced by the Imagists, he wrote a mannered verse characterized by irony, cynicism, and the decadence of the jazz age.

It is difficult to underestimate the impact of **Gertrude Stein** on American poetry. Constantly working to revitalize the English language, she did with poetry, in many ways, what her contemporaries in the world of painting and sculpture were doing with our way of seeing. Discarding long-accepted conventions that were accepted as "realistic" or "natural" speech, she often worked in a stream-of-consciousness style that owed much to her studies with philosopher William James. *Tender Buttons* (1912) introduced her poetry to readers who were already unsure of what to make of her prose work. During World War I, she went further in her verbal explorations. Stein reached a large audience only with her prose work, especially *The Autobiography of Alice B. Toklas* (1937), but had a powerful impact on the writers and writing of her time.

The next few decades brought the work of literally dozens of important figures. Not as concerned with Jewish issues as some of the earlier poets, they nonetheless dealt with what it means to be a Jewish American.

Muriel Rukeyser has, until recently, been underestimated and overlooked by literary historians. Not until the feminist movement brought her to the fore in the 1970s did she receive the recognition she deserved as an important poet. She has, however, been recognized as a forerunner by such significant poets as Denise Levertov and **Adrienne Rich**.

When she was twenty-one Rukeyser won the Yale Younger Poets Award with the publication of her first book, *Theory of Flight* (1935). Over the next four decades, she wrote prolifically, publishing a new book of poetry every year or two. She also participated in the major political movements of her time, including the civil rights movement, the anti-war movement, and the new wave of feminism. Her Jewish identity was always an influence on her work, even though she was reared in a non-observant household. Passionately committed to social justice, she was an effective activist as well as a compassionate and moving poet. Rose Drachler and Eve Merriam were among the other female poets who explored the role of the Jewish American woman during this time.

Stanley Kunitz occupies a prominent position in American poetry. His first book, *Intellectual Things*, appeared in 1930, but it was in the 1950s that he began to make a lasting mark. In 1959 he won the Pulitzer Prize for *Selected Poems 1928–1958*. At the age of ninety, he was awarded the National Book Award for *Passing Through: The Later Poems New and Selected* (1995). Personal, sometimes spiritual, and informed by his sense of alienation, Kunitz's poetry has been widely acclaimed by the literary establishment. Delmore Schwartz's first book, *In Dreams Begin Responsibilities* (1937), was published when he was twenty-four to considerable critical acclaim. Often brilliant, Schwartz might have become a major figure if he had not been afflicted with alcoholism, which led to his death in 1966 at the age of fifty-three.

Karl Shapiro's first volume, *Person, Place, and Thing* (1942), appeared when he was twenty-nine. Three years later, he was awarded the Pulitzer Prize for his second book, *V-Letter and Other Poems* (1945). Since that time, he has been recognized as a significant poet whose work is marked by wit and candor and who is unafraid of ambiguity. In his poetry, he deals on a personal level with his Jewishness.

Denise Levertov is the only one of these Jewish American poets who was not born in this country. Immigrating from England in 1948 at the age of twenty-five, she published her first volume of poetry, *The Double Image* (1946), in England. Probably one of the greatest poets of our time, Levertov had a Welsh mother and a Russian Jewish father who believed himself to be a descendant of the founder of the Hassidic movement and who became an Anglican minister. Levertov has always declared herself to be Jewish and has dealt with Jewish issues and experiences directly from time to time.

The next "generation" of Jewish American poets includes Adrienne Rich, **Allen Ginsberg**, Anthony Hecht, Gerald Stern, Irving Feldman, John Hollander, Louis Simpson, Maxine Kumin, Philip Levine, Stanley Moss, Ruth Whitman, Shirley Kaufman, and others. Rich and Ginsberg are the best known of this group, for reasons that involve both the appeal of their work and the notoriety of their lives.

Allen Ginsberg came to prominence in the 1950s as the poet of the Beat generation. By the 1960s, when he participated in the rebellions of the time, he had become as much a political and social icon as a literary figure. His celebrity sometimes obscured the fact that he was a major American poet in the tradition of Walt Whitman, with a decidedly Jewish identification and consciousness.

When Adrienne Rich published her first book of poetry, *A Change of World* (1951), in the Yale Series of Younger Poets, she received immediate acclaim. Her book *The Diamond Cutters and Other Poems* (1955) secured her more positive critical attention. In the 1960s and 1970s, when the nation's consciousness was turned to issues of race and gender, Rich found a voice with dazzling intensity. *Diving into the Wreck: Poems 1971–1972* was militantly feminist and won her the National Book Award. In the years that followed, Rich explored her identity as a Jew and as a lesbian, with passion, anger, and insight.

There are strains of Jewish memories and attitudes in the work of Kumin, Simpson, Stern, and several of the other poets of this group. Jewish tradition was often a part of their upbringing and therefore a part of their work, consciously or not. The younger poets who began to emerge in the 1970s and 1980s have a somewhat different sense of Jewish identity. Less grounded in custom, tradition, and religious Judaism, it reflects rather a sense of pride in a heritage of endurance, humanity, and intellectual accomplishment. The styles and themes of these poets are enormously varied.

Marge Piercy, for example, began writing from a strongly feminist perspective in the late 1960s and maintained that position into the 1990s. She has, however, been able to extend both her poetic and her political empathy to people of both genders and all races and ages. C. K. Williams, too, writes from a political perspective, a very Jewish one. His tone is serious, even dark, and his outrage is mighty. A less political poet, Stephen Berg writes with great passion of grief, family, and the everyday events of life. Marvin Bell is a gentle ironist who writes of ideas and the world in which he lives with a quiet grace.

In the 1990s, it becomes increasingly difficult to talk about "Jewish" poets, in part because there are so many who could rightly claim this title. More important, there are simply so many ways to be Jewish in the contemporary world. At this distance from the immigrant experience, there is a heterogeneity of experience that reveals itself most acutely in the intensely individual act of writing a poem. For most contemporary Jewish American poets, the *American* is as crucial as the *Jewish*. Other qualifying terms enter into the equation as well, words such as *woman*, *urban*, *comic*, and *visionary*.

In 1997 Robert Pinsky became Poet Laureate of the United States. His latest collection of poetry. *The*

Figured Wheel: New and Collected Poems 1996–1996 was reviewed on page one of *The New York Times Book Review*. He chose the image used on the book's cover, a lovely Torah ark made in Jerusalem in 1923, explaining that it was Jewish but not in a conventional way. This typifies, if anything can, the attitude of Pinsky and his contemporaries, such as Marilyn Hacker, Jane Miller, Louis Glück, Philip Schultz, Susan Mitchell, Jorie Graham, Ira Sadoff, Mark Rudman, and dozens of others. They are Jewish, but not in a conventional way.

POTOK, CHAIM (1929–)

Writer

Chaim Potok was born February 17, 1929, in New York City, the son of an Hasidic rabbi. He attended the Talmudic Academy of Yeshiva College before moving on to **Yeshiva University**, where he earned his B.A. in English Literature in 1950. He then attended the **Jewish Theological Seminary of America**, becoming an ordained rabbi in 1954. In 1965 he received his Ph.D. in philosophy from the University of Pennsylvania. In addition to teaching at the University of Judaism and the Jewish Theological Seminary, he has also served as the managing editor of *Conservative Judaism* (1964–1975) and as editor-in-chief of the Jewish Publication Society of America (JPS). In 1974 he became the special projects editor for JPS, a position he still holds today.

Potok began writing fiction when he was sixteen and published his first novel, *The Chosen*, in 1967. His other novels include *The Promise* (1969), *My Name is Asher Lev* (1972), *In the Beginning* (1975), *The Book of Lights* (1981), *Davita's Harp* (1985), *The Gift of Asher Lev* (1990,) and *I am the Clay* (1992). He is also the author of two children's books, *The Tree of Here* (1993) and *The Sky of Now* (1995) and of several plays. His non-fiction work includes *Wanderings* (1978) and *The Gates of November* (1996). Throughout his career he has written many articles and short stories for periodicals and newspapers as diverse as **Commentary**, *Seventeen*, and *The New York Times Magazine*.

RAND, AYN (1905–1982)

Novelist, philosopher

Writer Ayn Rand was born Alissa Rosenbaum in St. Petersburg, Russia, on February 2, 1905. She attended Leningrad University, graduating in 1924 with a degree in history. In 1926 she immigrated to the United States and changed her name. In 1935, she had her first success, the play *Night of January 16th*. A year later, she published her first novel, *We the Living*, which received poor reviews. In 1943 her classic work *The Fountainhead* was published and the critics were again generally dismissive. Despite the critics, the book slowly gained in popularity and by 1949 was a best-seller. The film version, with Gary Cooper and Patricia Neal, has become a cult classic. Rand's next novel, *Atlas Shrugged*, was published in 1957. It, too, received mainly negative reviews and became a best-seller.

Through her novels, Rand developed "Objectivism," a philosophy that espoused the primacy of individual needs over societal, of human reason over religion, and of selfishness over altruism. From the 1940s through the 1960s, Objectivism's following grew, largely through the efforts of The Nathan Branden Institute, founded by Rand's confidante and lover Nathan Branden. The Institute offered lectures and published *The Objectivist*, a newsletter for which Rand wrote essays. In 1968 Rand forced Branden out of all Objectivist activities. At the same time, the philosophy was becoming less popular among the young, its traditional audience. Rand died on March 6, 1982, never having regained her following or her fame. However, her books are still in print and continue to sell steadily, demonstrating the continuing appeal of her ideas.

RIBALOW, MENAHEM (1895–1953)

Editor, anthologist, critic

Prominent critic and editor Menahem Ribalow was born and grew up in Chudnov, Volhynia, Russia.

When he was in his late teens, he moved to Odessa to study. There he also began writing and publishing his poems and essays, gaining a certain reputation. He came to the United States in 1921, when he was twenty-six years old. Ribalow was soon editor of the Hebrew weekly *Ha-Doar* and an active participant in the Jewish literary scene. Much of his fame came from his editing of a number of anthologies of American and Hebrew literature. He was also active in propagating Hebrew culture and language as a leader of the Histadrut Ivrit of America (founded in 1917) and as co-president with Itzhak Ben-Zvi, Israel's president, of the World Hebrew Union.

RICE, ELMER (1892–1967)

Playwright

Experimental playwright Elmer Rice was born Elmer Leopold Reizenstein, on September 28, 1892, in New York City. He started his professional life as a lawyer, having graduated from New York Law School in 1912. He soon dropped that career in favor of writing. His first play, *On Trial* (1914), was the first play to incorporate "flashbacks" as part of the narrative. The play reflected his past experience as a lawyer and his commitment to using experimental techniques in the theater.

Rice plays often, but not always, had themes that dealt with the poor and oppressed of society. Among his most successful productions were the expressionistic satire *The Adding Machine* (1923), *The Subway* (1929), *We, the People* (1933), *Dream Girl* (1935), *The Grand Tour* (1951), and *Love Among the Ruins* (1963). In 1929 he won a Pulitzer Prize for *Street Scene*, a play about life in a crowded urban apartment house. *Street Scene* was adapted into a musical by Kurt Weill and Langston Hughes in 1947. Rice served as the regional director for the Federal Theatre Project in New York City and was one of the founders of the Playwrights' Company. Long before most people, Rice spoke out against the rise of Nazism in Europe. He wrote two of the earliest anti-Nazi plays: *Judgement Day* (1934) and *Flight to the West* (1940). In 1963 Rice published his autobiography *Minority Report*. He died four years later, on May 8, 1967, in Southampton, England.

RICH, ADRIENNE (1929–)

Poet, essayist

Adrienne Rich began her career as a poet concerned with rigorous form, heavily influenced by the male teachers she studied under and the poets she was as-

In her 1994 collection What Is Found There: Notebooks on Poetry and Politics, *Adrienne Rich addresses the issue of Jewishness and "whiteness." Critic Peter Erickson says that Rich "does not find that her Jewishness cancels or mitigates her whiteness but instead explores both as valid aspects of her identity. Although Rich's Jewish affiliation is strongly in evidence here, she is also eloquent about the effects of her own whiteness." (Library of Congress)*

signed to read at Radcliffe. But as her own voice has evolved over the course of a lengthy writing career, her work has become more open, more confessional, and more overtly political. The result of that growth process has been her emergence as one of the most important American poets of the post–World War II era, a powerful feminist voice as well as a gifted writer.

Rich was born into a well-to-do Baltimore family, the daughter of a doctor who encouraged her writing ambitions. As a young poet in college, she fell under the spell of Wallace Stevens and T. S. Eliot. Her first book of poetry, *A Change of World* (1951), was published in her senior year of college and was selected for the Yale Series of Younger Poets by W. H. Auden. Two years after her graduation, she married Alfred Conrad, an economist. She gave birth to three sons over the next six years. The couple lived in Cambridge when Conrad was teaching at Harvard, then moved to New York when he took a position at CCNY in 1966. In short, a typical 1950s household, except that Rich continued writing and publishing her poetry.

By the end of a decade of marriage, the tensions in the household were being expressed in her poetry. In her 1963 volume, *Snapshots of a Daughter-in-Law*, Rich's mature voice began to emerge, more conversational, looser in its rhythms, more pointed in its confrontation with society's limiting expectations for women. Rich began to throw herself into civil rights activities, then the anti-war movement throughout the 1960s and her increasing political commitment, too, began to find a place in her writing. Her husband's death in 1970 contributed to her continuing transformation.

In 1973 Rich published *Diving Into the Wreck*, which won the National Book Award the following year. This breakthrough established her as one of the most important poets in the United States at a time when she was entering a period of tremendous fertility. Since then, she has published a new book every year or so, interspersing collections of essays and non-fiction books among the verse. Among her best works are *A Wild Patience Has Taken Me This Far* (1981), *Of*

Woman Born, her non-fiction book on the nature of motherhood (1976), and *What Is Found There*, a collection of brief ruminations on politics and poetry published in 1993. Rich came out as a lesbian and a radical feminist during the 1970s, and those concerns have animated her writing ever since. At the same time, she has been a vocally self-identified Jew for whom Jewish themes are an important element in her writing. She continues to be forthright and vocal in her political sentiments as well, most recently turning down a 1997 presidential medal for achievement in the arts as a protest against President Bill Clinton's welfare reform policies.

ROSTEN, LEO (1908–1997)

Writer

Leo Calvin Rosten was born in Lodz, Poland, on April 11, 1908. He immigrated to the United States with his family when he was three and grew up in Chicago. He attended the University of Chicago, where he received a Ph.D. in 1937. He also attended the London School of Economics and Political Science. In addition to teaching night school for immigrants—which provided material for some of his most famous stories—Rosten also held teaching positions at a number of institutions including the University of Chicago, Columbia University, Yale University, and the University of California, Berkeley. During World War II he held various positions in the U.S. government. From 1947 through 1949, he was employed by the RAND corporation. But it is as a writer of humorous works about Jewish immigrants that he is best known.

Rosten's first stories appeared in *The New Yorker* under the name Leonard Q. Ross. These stories were later compiled and published under his own name as *The Education of H*Y*M*A*N K*A*P*L*A*N* (1937). His wrote two sequels of Kaplan stories, *The Return of H*Y*M*A*N K*A*P*L*A*N* (1959) and *O K*A*P*L*A*N! My K*A*P*L*A*N!* (1976). His other work includes *Hollywood: The Movie Colony, the Movie Makers* (1941); six screenplay; and the clas-

Best known as the author of short stories based on his experience teaching night school to immigrants (collected as The Education of H*Y*M*A*N K*A*P*L*A*N*), Leo Rosten is also the author of the humorous reference book* The Joys of Yiddish. *The above is a publicity photograph for his book* The Power of Positive Nonsense. *(Courtesy of American Jewish Archives)*

sic humorous reference work, *The Joys of Yiddish* (1968). Rosten died in New York City on February 19, 1997.

ROTH, HENRY (1906–1995)

Novelist

Henry Roth authored one of the greatest novels ever written about the American Jewish immigrant experience—*Call it Sleep*. It was his first book, and when it was published in 1934, it augured well for the young writer. That promise would be fulfilled by the publication of his second novel—sixty years later. Roth was the victim of perhaps the most famous case of writer's block in the twentieth century. But he did finally come through.

Roth was born in what was the Austro-Hungarian Empire. A year after his birth, his family moved to New York City looking for economic opportunities. Roth was a bright boy and moved ahead in school while working part-time jobs to help out at home. Eventually he made his way to City College of New York, a haven for the city's brighter working poor. Although he had not intended to take up writing, he showed enough promise that he was taken under the wing of a left-wing writer, Eda Lou Walton. He became her lover and she helped him launch his career with *Call It Sleep*. The book is a searing, Joycean portrait of a timid young Jewish boy, madly in love with his mother, terrified of his father and almost everyone else around him in the strange streets of New York City. Although it was a financial failure when it was first published, it received respectful reviews, and in 1964 was rediscovered and re-released as the great work it clearly is.

Roth began work on a second book, an attempt at politically committed proletarian fiction that was, he later said, doomed to fail because he didn't know the milieu he was trying to depict. His inability to finish that book left him completely stuck, unable to write. He had broken with Walton and her circle of friends, met and married the composer Muriel Parker in 1939, and was trying to raise two children. Writing was the furthest thing from Roth's mind; he trained as a precision metal grinder and worked in wartime arms plants. Later he held jobs as a duck farmer and mathematics teacher. He was not writing, although the new edition of *Call It Sleep* brought him back into the public consciousness and, he later admitted, triggered in him a desire to return to his craft.

Ironically, the turning point in Roth's career came with the Six-Day War. He discovered within himself a fiercely held sense of Jewish identity, rejected the Stalinist position against Israel, and suddenly began jotting down his opinions with an eye toward publication. In 1968 he received a D. H. Lawrence fellowship from the University of New Mexico, and he and Muriel relocated to the southwest. There he began writing in earnest once more. Over a period of several years, he began and completed a vast four-volume autobiographical cycle, *The Mercy of a Rude Stream*. The first volume, *A Star Shines Over Mt. Morris Park* (1994), was published before his death. The other volumes of the opus—*A Diving Rock on the Hudson* (1995), *From Bondage* (1996), and *Requiem for Harlem* (1998)— were published posthumously.

ROTH, PHILIP (1933–)

Novelist

Philip Roth is the Jew Jews love to hate. A lightning rod for controversy, he is blunt, passionate, and obsessed with sex and Jewish identity. From *Goodbye Columbus* (1959), through *Portnoy's Complaint* (1969), to his most recent novel, *I Married a Communist* (1998), Roth has mined his own past and the mores of the suburban and urban American Jewish community for material. He ruffled feathers in the Jewish community in 1959 and has not stopped.

Philip Milton Roth was born in Newark, New Jersey, at a time when that city had a considerable Jewish population. After high school, he continued living at home, attending college for the next two years at the Newark campus of Rutgers University, before transferring to Bucknell, where he completed his degree in 1954. Roth earned a master's at the University of Chicago and was going to continue his post-graduate work there but dropped out to pursue a writing career, first as a film critic for *The Nation*, then as a short story writer and novelist. With his first published book, *Goodbye Columbus and Five Short Stories*, Roth hit paydirt, winning a National Book Award and infuriating his fellow Jews with a portrait of suburban life that was nothing less than scathing.

Roth's initial excursions into the novel were not nearly as successful. Neither *Letting Go* (1962), a Jamesian comedy of manners, nor *When She Was Good* (1967), Roth's only book with a female protagonist and his only book centered on a non-Jew, stirred as much interest as his first volume. But that situation was about to end.

In 1969 Roth published *Portnoy's Complaint*, a portrait of Alexander Portnoy, enslaved by his smothering Jewish mother, his libido, and his lust for gentile women. Whether by luck or design, Roth had caught the tenor of the times and raised the ire of the Jews once again. Perhaps no American novel since has stirred as much heated debate on the editorial pages of newspapers, from the pulpits of synagogues and churches, or on the airwaves. Roth has yet to create as great an uproar again, although many of his later books are more brilliantly written, more complex, and of greater literary merit.

Over the course of his next several books, Roth would offer a Swiftian assault on President Richard Nixon, a parody of Kafka, and a reworking of Greek myth in the form of a satirical baseball novel. But he would find his next great theme, one that has occupied him since 1974, with that year's *My Life as a Man*, a book about two novelists who appear to be sides of Roth's own personality and history. Nathan Zuckerman, one of the key figures in that book, has become a stand-in for Roth in numerous subsequent works, *The Ghost Writer* (1979), *Zuckerman Unbound* (1981), *The Anatomy Lesson* (1983), and *The Counterlife* (1987). Zuckerman even puts in an appearance in Roth's autobiography, *The Facts* (1988). Roth took this self-examination to its logical end in his 1993 book, *Operation Shylock: A Confession*, in which he narrates as himself, chasing his doppelganger, another Philip Roth who has traveled the world posing as the famous novelist and spouting bizarre theories of Jewish history. *Sabbath's Theater* followed in 1995. Not surprisingly, Roth's recent book, *American Pastoral* (1997), is a portrait of a middle-class Jewish family struggling to survive in Newark, New Jersey, during the Depression and World War II. The family name is not Roth, but it could have been. The book won the Pulitzer Prize for fiction.

RUKEYSER, MURIEL (1913–1980)

Poet

Muriel Rukeyser was born in New York City on December 15, 1913. Her family was neither literary nor particularly observant in its Judaism. Later, she rejected the assimilated lifestyle and embraced both Jewish culture and her own Jewish identity. She attended Vassar College and Columbia University, but had to end her education before graduation because her father went bankrupt. In 1935, when she was only twenty-one, she published her first book of poetry, *Theory of Flight*. The same year, she won the Yale Younger Poets Award. She continued to win awards throughout her career, including the first Harriet Monroe Poetry Award, the Levinson Prize, and the Copernicus Prize. She was also awarded a Guggenheim Fellowship. Among her other books of poetry are *U.S. 1* (1938), *Beast in View* (1944), *Selected Poems* (1951), *Bubbles* (1967), *29 Poems* (1972), and *The Collected Poems of Muriel Rukeyser* (1979).

A committed activist and world traveler, Rukeyser reported on the second Scottsboro trial. She was in Spain in 1936 and saw the beginning of that country's civil war. She protested the Vietnam War and was arrested for doing so. She also went an unofficial peace mission to Hanoi. In the 1970s she flew to Korea to protest the jailing of poet Kim Chi-Ha. Much of Rukeyser's life experience was translated into poetry. Though she was admired by many, she also had vehement detractors. Her poetry was marked not only by distinctive punctuation and spacing, but also by its sometimes radical themes. She openly explored feminist concerns as well as her Jewish identity long before it became popular to do so.

RUSKAY, ESTHER (1857–1910)

Writer, speaker, advocate of Jewish tradition

Influential writer and speaker Esther Ruskay was born in 1857 in New York City. A member of the first graduating class of Normal (Hunter) College, she was also the first woman to speak from the pulpit of Temple Emmanu-El in New York. In all of her work, she supported conservative Jewish values against the tendency, current around the turn of the century, to consider Jewish tradition lacking in relevance to the modern world. She was widely published in American periodicals and her writings were collected in *Hearth and Home Essays*, published in 1902 by the Jewish Publication Society.

SALINGER, J. D. (1919–)

Writer

J. D. (Jerome David) Salinger, the author of *The Catcher in the Rye* (1951), was born on January 1, 1919 in New York City. He attended the city's public schools, a military academy, and several colleges.

Though he published his first story in 1940, Salinger didn't achieve great acclaim until eleven years later when *The Catcher in the Rye* was published. The novel became an enormous success and an almost immediate classic. Thousands of high school and college age readers still identify with the novel's protagonist, Holden Caulfield, a prep-school dropout searching for the meaning of life in a series of comic misadventures.

Salinger's series of stories about the Glasses, an Irish-Jewish family, are best known from the book *Frannie and Zooey* (1963). Other stories in which the Glasses appear are *Nine Stories* (1953); *Raise High the Roof Beam, Carpenters*; and *Seymour: An Introduction* (1962). By 1965, Salinger ceased writing for publication and removed himself from public life. He has not been interviewed since then. His reticence seems to have only increased the public's fascination with him.

SAMUEL, MAURICE (1895–1972)

Writer, translator

Author and translator Maurice Samuel was born in Macin, Romania. His family soon moved to Manchester, England, where the young man was brought up. In 1914, at the age of nineteen, Samuel moved to the United States and began his long career as a writer. Most of his books had Jewish themes, including *Jews on Approval* (1931), *The Gentleman and the Jew,* (1950), and *The Second Crucifixion* (1960). Samuel also translated the works of writers in Yiddish and Hebrew, including **Sholem Aleichem**, **Sholem Asch**, and **Isaac**

Bashevis Singer. He wrote *In Praise of Yiddish* (1971) to encourage literature in that language.

SCHULBERG, BUDD (1914–)

Writer

Budd Schulberg is most famous for his Academy Award–winning screenplay, *On the Waterfront* (1954), although thirteen years earlier he attained fame as a novelist with his scathing satire of ruthless Hollywood opportunism in the classic *What Makes Sammy Run?* Budd Wilson Schulberg was born in New York City on March 27, 1914, but grew up in Hollywood where he was surrounded by the film industry elite. (His father, B. P. Schulberg, was the head of Paramount Studios.) He attended Dartmouth College, graduating in 1936. During World War II he documented Nazi atrocities and received a decoration for the photographic evidence he collected. The photographs were used at the Nuremberg Trials.

Many of Schulberg's novels and short stories have themes about the corruption and abuse of power in the film and television industries. He also wrote about corruption in labor unions and the boxing world. Some of his work includes *The Harder They Fall* (1947); *The Disenchanted* (1950); *Faces in the Crowd* (1953); *Loser and Still Champion: Muhammed Ali* (1972); and his memoir, *Moving Pictures* (1983). In 1965 he helped train a new generation of writers when he started a writing workshop for residents of the Watts neighborhood in Los Angeles.

SHAW, IRWIN (1913–1984)

Writer

Celebrated as the author of the novel *Rich Man, Poor Man* (1970), which became a popular television miniseries, Irwin Shaw attained early fame with the war novel *The Young Lions*, which appeared in 1948. Shaw was born in Brooklyn, New York, on February 27, 1913. He graduated from Brooklyn College in 1934 and worked for two years writing scripts for radio dra-

mas. His first play, *Bury the Dead*, was produced in New York City in 1936 and had a pacifist theme. His writing career was put on hold while he served in World War II, but out of the conflict came a book of short stories, *Act of Faith* (1946) and his first success, *The Young Lions*. One of the book's themes dealt with anti-Semitism in the army. His other novels include *The Troubled Air* (1951), *Two Weeks in Another Town* (1960), *Beggarman, Thief* (1977), the sequel to *Rich Man, Poor Man*, and *Short Stories: Five Decades* (1978). He died at the age of seventy-one on May 16, 1984, in Davos, Switzerland.

SHOLEM ALEICHEM (1859–1916)

Writer, humorist

The most widely read Yiddish writer of all time, Sholem Aleichem moved Yiddish from a disparaged vernacular to a respected literary language. He also created a cast of unforgettable characters drawn from his life in Russia, which led him to be referred to as "the Jewish Mark Twain." He captured this world with kind and forgiving humor and gave an international voice to the music and joy of the Yiddish language.

Born Sholem Rabinowitz in Pereyaslav, Russia (now Ukraine), on March 2, 1859, Sholem Aleichem came from a religious household and studied biblical Hebrew. He entered the gymnasium in Pereyaslav at

---

Sholem Aleichem Will Have Complete Works in English

The Sholem Aleichem Memorial Foundation announced in July of 1998 that they would be translating everything written by the great Yiddish writer into English for the first time. The project is expected to run to some twenty-five volumes and require at least ten years to complete. While some 40% of the writings have already been translated, they will have to be redone. David Roskies of the Jewish Theological Seminary, the director and editor-in-chief of the projects explains that norms of translation have changed over the years. "There's a greater sensitivity to cultural difference," he said, noting that today, "you don't have to soft-pedal the Jewishness."

the age of fourteen and graduated in 1876. For a time he served as a Russian tutor and also as a rabbi while he tried to earn a living from his writings. After marrying Olga Loyev in 1883, he succeeded in having a satirical essay of his published under the pseudonym Sholem Aleichem (a Yiddish/Hebrew greeting meaning literally "peace unto you"), which he adopted and used in all his subsequent work. He explained in his memoirs that the name was used to conceal his identity from his relatives, especially his father, who loved Hebrew and considered Yiddish a non-literary language.

Between 1884 and 1890 he published six novels as well as numerous stories, reviews, and poems. In 1888 he founded a Yiddish literary annual, *Di Yidishe Folksbibliotek* ("The Popular Jewish Library"), which he hoped would bring the language into the cultural mainstream. Unfortunately Sholem Aleichem went bankrupt in 1890, and the next ten years were the hardest of his life. However, he did publish the first monologue of *Tevye der Milkhiger* ("Tevye the Dairyman") in 1894. In 1899 his fortunes took a turn for the better when he became a regular contributor to *Der Yid*, the newly initiated Yiddish Zionist weekly. He also wrote for Yiddish daily papers that had begun to appear in Warsaw and in St. Petersburg. From 1900 to 1906 Sholem Aleichem supported himself almost exclusively with the income from his publications. He would continue to write constantly until his death.

In 1905 he left Russia, fleeing the pogroms and never settled in any one place again. He spent time in New York City, Italy, and Switzerland. He was diagnosed with advanced tuberculosis and had to be under constant medical supervision the rest of his life. His literary output continued unabated. He published the stories of *Motl Peyse dem Khazns* ("Motl, the Son of the Cantor Peyse") and (in serial form) his longest novel, *Blondzhende Shtern* ("Wandering Stars") between 1909 and 1911. He had become so famous that his fiftieth birthday in 1909 was celebrated throughout the Jewish world. In 1914 he moved to the United States for the second time. His illness became more serious, but he continued to write prolifically. He died in New York City on May 13, 1916, leaving behind him the most prodigious and accomplished body of work ever written

A goal early in Sholem Aleichem's career was to publish a Yiddish literary annual to show that great literature was being written in what was then considered a "common" language. With his own subsequent prolific output, he succeeded. He is shown here with his granddaughter, Bel Kaufman, who as an adult became the author of the best-selling novel Up the Down Staircase. *(Private Collection)*

in the Yiddish language. He was already recognized at his death as one of the major writers in world literature.

English translations of his principal works include *The Old Country* (1946), *Tevye's Daughters* (1949), *Wondering Star* (1952), *Adventures of Mottel, The Cantor's Son* (1953), *The Tevye Stories, and Others* (1959), and *The Adventures of Menahem-Mendl* (1969). The "Tevye the dairyman" stories were the basis for the ever-popular musical *Fiddler on the Roof*, which premiered on Broadway in 1964 and was an instant hit. *Fiddler* was made into a film in 1971.

Collections of his writings in English translation include *Collected Stories of Sholem Aleichem* (1965), *Old Country Tales* (1966), *Selected Stories* (1956), *Stories and Satires* (1959), and *Sholem Aleichem Panorama* (1948).

His daughter Lyala Kaufman wrote over two thousand sketches and short stories in Yiddish, and her daughter Bel Kaufman is the author of the best-selling novel *Up the Down Staircase* (1964).

SIMON, NEIL (1927–)

Playwright

Neil Simon is *the* comedy playwright of Broadway. No other writer, comedic or dramatic, has been more financially or popularly successful. Born in Washington Heights, New York City, on July 4, 1927, Neil Simon based many of his plays on his childhood and the Jewish characters who peopled it. He began his career writing sketches for various television shows in the 1950s, especially "The Sid Caesar Show" and "Your Show of Shows." His first play, *Come Blow your Horn*, opened in 1961. Among an incredibly long list, his most successful plays are *Barefoot in the Park* (1963), *The Odd Couple* (1965), *Prisoner of Second Avenue* (1971), *The Sunshine Boys* (1972), and *Chapter Two* (1977). He wrote the books for the musicals *Sweet Charity* (1966), *Promises, Promises* (1968), and *They're Playing Our Song* (1979). He has adapted his plays for the movies and written several original screenplays, including *The Out-of-Towners* (1970), *Murder by Death* (1976), and *The Goodbye Girl* (1977).

In the 1980s Simon wrote his autobiographical trilogy, *Brighton Beach Memoirs*, *Biloxi Blues*, and *Broadway Bound*. These plays gained him the critical respect to match his popular and financial success. In 1991 he achieved the ultimate cap to his career when he was awarded the Pulitzer Prize for *Lost in Yonkers*.

SINGER, ISAAC BASHEVIS (1904–1991)

Writer

Yiddish writer Isaac Bashevis Singer was born on July 14, 1904, in Radzymin, Poland, and came from a long line of rabbis. Brought up both in Warsaw and in small Hassidic Polish *shtetls*, Singer was educated in Jewish schools, and for a short period, he attended a rabbinical seminary. He finally rebelled against his parent's plans for him to continue the family tradition and become a rabbi. Instead, he moved to Warsaw and began his life as a writer. He was the younger brother of the famous Yiddish novelist and playwright, Israel Joshua Singer (1893–1944), who greatly influenced him to become a writer and whom he followed to New York two years after I.J. immigrated in 1933. The older brother wrote two classics: the monumental novel *The Brothers Ashkenazi* and the popular play *Yoshe Kalb*.

When he arrived in the United States, Isaac Bashevis Singer began work at the Yiddish newspaper **Jewish Daily Forward** in New York City. The *Forward* gave Singer his start as a novelist by printing his work in serialized form. An incredibly prolific writer, Singer wrote columns under three pseudonyms—Isaac Bashevis for fiction, Y. Varshvski for serious journalism, and D. Segal for more entertaining pieces.

His first opportunity to reach a broader audience came in 1950 when his novel, *The Family Moskat*, was translated from Yiddish into English. His stories were immediately popular and captured the attention of both the general public and the literary elite. Among his most famous works are the novels *Satan in Goray* (1955), *The Magician of Lublin* (1960), *Enemies, A Love Story* (1972), and *Shosha* (1978); the collection *Gimpel the Fool and Other Stories* (1964); and the story "Yentl, the Yeshiva Boy" (adapted as *Yentl* for the screen in 1983 by **Barbra Streisand**). In 1978, after many years of acclaim and literary awards from all over the world, he was awarded the Nobel Prize for literature. Isaac Bashevis Singer has given the world two precious legacies. First, by setting most of his stories in the *shtetls* of his youth, he reveals a bygone Jewish world and its traditions both secular and religious, everyday and mystical. And second, he acquaints his readers with the beauty of the Yiddish language.

Four of his novels have been published posthumously in English, the most recent being *Shadows on the Hudson* (1998). It was first serialized in Yiddish in *The Forward*, twice weekly, in 1957. All of Singer's other novels have been published in book form, although there are numerous *Forward* pieces that remain untranslated.

SONTAG, SUSAN (1933–)

Writer, critic

Controversial writer and cultural critic Susan Sontag was born in New York City on January 16, 1933. Growing up in a non-observant household, she lived first in New York; then in Tucson, Arizona; and finally in Los Angeles. She attended the University of California, Berkeley, before transferring to the University of Chicago. In 1952 she became a graduate student at Harvard, where she received masters' degrees in philosophy and English. She then attended both the Sorbonne and Oxford. In 1959 she moved to New York City and began to publish. Her essays have appeared in *Partisan Review*, *Playboy*, and *The New Yorker*, among many other publications. Her books include *Against Interpretation* (1966), *Styles of Radical Will* (1969), *On Photography* (1977), and *Under the Sign of Saturn* (1980).

In addition to her books of essays, Sontag has written several novels, a play, and a screenplay, and has directed both films and plays. Throughout her career, she has been the recipient of prestigious awards and grants, including Rockefeller Foundation grants (1964, 1974), Guggenheim fellowships (1966, 1975), and a MacArthur Fellowship (1990). An avid universalist, Sontag has been called everything from publicity hound to revolutionary for her views on modern culture and cultural criticism. At one time an advocate for the avant-garde, she is now considered a political and cultural conservative.

STEIN, GERTRUDE (1874–1946)

Writer

Writer Gertrude Stein was born in Allegheny, Pennsylvania, on February 3, 1874, to parents of German-Jewish descent. Though the Steins recognized their

Although Gertrude Stein's parents belonged to a synagogue, they did not raise their children to be practicing Jews. A startling innovator in her writing style, in both prose and poetry, she left a lasting mark on American literature. (Library of Congress)

cultural roots in Judaism and were members of a synagogue throughout Gertrude's childhood, they did not raise Gertrude and her four siblings to be practicing Jews. When Gertrude was an infant, the Stein family left Pennsylvania and moved back to Europe. She spent her early years in Austria and later in France. In 1879 the family returned to America, first settling in Baltimore and then in Oakland, California. Of Oakland Stein was later to utter the famous remark, "There is no there there."

She attended the Harvard Annex (later to become Radcliffe College) and graduated in 1897. Spurred on by her professor, the famous philosopher and psychologist William James, she moved on to Johns Hopkins Medical School but did not do well there and left before graduating. In 1903 she moved to Paris and began writing. Early examples of her work include *Things as They Are* (completed in 1903, but not published until after her death), *Three Lives* (published in 1909), and *The Making of Americans* (completed in 1911, but not published until 1966).

In 1907 Stein met the woman who became her life-long companion, Alice B. Toklas. With Toklas' support, Stein began to experiment more with her writing, doing on paper what her friends Picasso and Braque were doing on canvas. Her work was rarely published, however. Despite this, by the 1920s Stein was becoming a legend, and her salon was attracting young American expatriates including Ernest Hemingway. In 1933, she published her memoirs, *The Autobiography of Alice B. Toklas*. This brought her the literary fame she had long desired. Her other popular work includes *Four Saints in Three Acts* (1934), an opera with music by Virgil Thomson, *Everybody's Autobiography* (1937), *Paris, France* (1940), and *Brewsie and Willie* (1945). Her *Lectures in America* (1935) describes her unconventional philosophy of composition, based in part on the teachings of William James. Her writings deeply influenced the post–World War I generation of American writers, notably Hemingway and Sherwood Anderson. She died in Neuilly-sur-Seine on July 27, 1946.

TERKEL, STUDS (1912–)

Writer, radio show host, oral historian

Louis (Studs) Terkel was born on May 16, 1912, in New York City but grew up in Chicago. He went to the University of Chicago and the University of Chicago Law School. He began his interviewing career in the early 1950s on WFMT, a Chicago radio station. Initially a Sunday morning show, in 1958 the show became daily and hourly. Still on the air today, Terkel continues to amuse and enlighten five days a week. His show is now carried on stations across the country. In addition to his radio show, Terkel has also hosted a television show, "Studs Place," and has worked as a sports reporter, a stage actor, and a playwright.

However, Terkel is best known as the nation's fore-most interviewer and oral historian. His numerous books of American oral history include *Division Street: America* (1966), *Hard Times: An Oral History of the Great Depression* (1970), *Working* (1974), *Race: How Blacks and Whites Think and Feel about the American Obsession* (1992), and *Coming of Age: The Story of Our Century by Those Who've Lived It* (1995). In 1985 he was awarded the Pulitzer Prize for *The Good War: An Oral History of World War II* (1984). Among the many other honors that he has received are a Peabody Award and a Prix Italia. In 1997 he was awarded the National Book Foundation Medal for Distinguished Contribution to American Letters.

UNTERMEYER, LOUIS (1885–1977)

Poet, translator, anthologist

An important voice in modern American poetry, Louis Untermeyer was born in New York City and acquired little formal education. He was the son of a jewelry manufacturer and entered his father's firm when he was quite young. For almost two decades, he commuted every weekday to Newark, New Jersey, to work, and, in his spare time, he composed poetry. In 1911, his first book of poetry, *First Love*, was published. His own estimate of it was that "the influences of Heine and Housman were not only obvious but crippling." In his second book, *Challenge* (1914), his own voice made itself heard and in the next few years his work matured. After publishing *These Times* (1917), *The New Adam* (1920), and *Roast Leviathan* (1922), he retired from jewelry manufacturing and became a full-time writer. The last of these books brought him considerable acclaim from both American and English critics.

Untermeyer published several more well-received volumes of poetry, including *Burning Bush* (1928), *Food and Drink* (1932), and *Long Feud: Selected Poems* (1962). However, he was probably most influential as an editor and interpreter of modern poetry. His collections *Modern American Poetry* (1919) and *Modern British Poetry* (1920) were repeatedly revised and reissued. They became standard texts in college literature classes and had a significant impact on the reputations of early poets in the first half of the twentieth century. He also wrote a number of biographical works, including *Lives of the Poets* (1961) and the *Britannica Library of Great American Writing* (1960), as well as *Heinrich Heine: Paradox and Poet* (1937). Among Untermeyer's other works were poetic parodies, several important translations of other poets, including Heine, and two volumes of autobiography: *From Another World* (1939) and *Bygones* (1965).

Also of significance in American poetry was Jean Starr Untermeyer (1886–1970), who was married to Louis Untermeyer, on and off, from 1907 until 1951. Her poetry is traditional in form and has been described as "classically Hebraic." She also wrote a moving memoir, *Private Collection* (1965).

URIS, LEON (1924–)

Novelist, screenwriter

Historical novelist Leon Uris was born in Baltimore on August 3, 1924. As a marine in World War II he fought in the campaigns for Guadalcanal and Tarawa Islands. After returning to the United States after the war, he became a newspaperman before concentrating on writing novels. His experience in the war led to his first book *Battle Cry* (1953), considered an important war novel. His first major success came with a novel about the founding of the state of Israel, *Exodus* (1957). *Mila 18* (1960) deals with the Jewish community in the Warsaw Ghetto and its uprising against the Nazis. Other works include *Armageddon* (1964), *Topaz* (1967), *QB VII* (1970), and *Trinity* (1976). Several of his novels have been adapted for film or television, most notably *Exodus*, which Otto Preminger directed in 1960. *Gunfight at the OK Corral* (1957) is the most famous of his original screenplays.

WASSERSTEIN, WENDY (1950–)

Playwright

Wendy Wasserstein was born in New York City in 1950 and attended Mount Holyoke College, where she majored in history. After studying creative writing with **Joseph Heller** and Israel Horowitz, she moved on to the playwriting program at the Yale School of Drama. Her first play to receive a professional production was *Uncommon Women and Others*. It was her thesis production at Yale (1975), then was produced at the Phoenix Theater (1977) where it received high critical praise.

She won the Pulitzer Prize in 1989 for her play *The Heidi Chronicles*. The play also won a Tony Award, the New York Drama Critics Circle Award, the Drama Desk Award, and the Blackburn Prize. Her other plays include *Isn't It Romantic*, *The Sisters Rosensweig*, *An American Daughter*, and the musical *Miami*. Several of her plays have been adapted for television, most notably, *Uncommon Women and Others* for PBS's "Great Performances" series, and *The Heidi Chronicles* for TNT. She has also written numerous essays for publications such as *The New Yorker*, *Esquire*, and *Harper's Bazaar*. Her play *Isn't It Romantic* was criticized by some critics as "too Jewish." Wasserstein noted: ". . . when your name is Wendy Wasserstein and you're from New York, you are the walking embodiment of 'too Jewish.' "

WEST, NATHANAEL (1903–1940)

Writer

The son of Russian Jewish immigrants, Nathanael West was born on October 17, 1903, in New York City as Nathan Weinstein. He went through the city's public school system but never graduated. He did attend college, however. Tufts University admitted him, based on forged documents. He then forged a set of transcripts, and Brown University accepted him as a transfer student. After Brown, West went to Paris for a year and then returned to New York where he worked both as a hotel manager and on the magazine *Contact* with William Carlos Williams. In 1935 he moved to Hollywood, where he wrote screenplays. In 1940 he married Eileen McKenny. On December 22, 1940, both he and his wife were killed in a car crash.

Although he only wrote four short novels, they indicated that West had a unique and dark vision of America. His first novel was *The Dream Life of Balso Snell*, written in 1931. Two years later the book considered his masterpiece was published: *Miss Lonelyhearts*. His third novel, *A Cool Million* (1934), is often interpreted as an early exploration of fascism. His final novel, *A Day of the Locust* (1939), is one of the earliest books to reveal the dangerous superficiality of Hollywood.

WIESEL, ELIE (1928–)

Writer

A survivor of the Holocaust, Elie Wiesel has devoted his life to speaking out against man's inhumanity to man. Born in Sighet, Romania, on September 30, 1928, Wiesel was fifteen when he and all the other Jews of his town were herded into a train bound for Birkenau, the reception center for Auschwitz. He somehow survived his incarceration at Auschwitz and at Buchenwald, but his father, mother, and younger sister did not.

Elie Wiesel has been speaking and writing about the horrors of the Holocaust, the experience of being a survivor, and Judaism all his adult life. His writings (always in French) eloquently use elements from the Talmud, the Bible, Hassidism, and Jewish legend to explore and relate his experience. A few of the influen-

Elie Wiesel is probably the most well-known figure in American Judaism today. He continues to speak out against injustice wherever in occurs in the world, while, at the same time, never letting the world forget the genocide that was the Holocaust. He was instrumental in the creation of the United States Holocaust Memorial Museum in Washington, D.C. (Courtesy of American Jewish Archives)

Excerpts from Elie Wiesel's Nobel Prize Acceptance Speech (12/11/86)

"Have we failed? I often think we have. . . . If someone had told us in 1945 that in our lifetime religious wars would rage on virtually every continent, that thousands of children would once again be dying of starvation, we would not have believed it. Or that racism and fanaticism would flourish once again, we would not have believed it.

"Terrorism must be outlawed by all civilized nations—not explained or rationalized, but fought and eradicated. Nothing can, nothing will, justify the murder of innocent people and helpless children. . . .

"Mankind must remember that peace is not God's gift to his creatures, it is our gift to each."

tial works he has written include *Night* (1958); *The Gates of the Forest* (1964); *The Jews of Silence* (1966); *The Oath* (1973); *The Fifth Son* (1985); and his memoir, *All Rivers Run to the Sea* (1995).

Wiesel lived in Paris after the war and attended the Sorbonne from 1947 to 1951, then moved to New York City in 1956. He became a U.S. citizen in 1963. In the late forties he wrote for the Israeli newspaper *Yediot Aharonot* and in the late fifties for New York's **Jewish Daily Forward**. From 1972 through 1976, he taught Judaic studies at the City College of New York. Moving to Boston University, he was named the Andrew W. Mellon professor in the humanities. In 1983 Wiesel was awarded the International Literary Prize for Peace for the novels *The Testament* (1980) and *Words from Strangers* (1982). In 1985 he was awarded the Congressional Gold Medal of Achievement. The following year he won the Nobel Peace Prize. The Nobel citation read, in part: "Wiesel is a messenger to mankind. . . . His message is one of peace, atonement and human dignity. His belief that the forces fighting evil in the world can be victorious is a hard-won belief . . . repeated and deepened through the works of a great author."

Wiesel continues to speak out eloquently and passionately about injustice, wherever it occurs in the world.

WOUK, HERMAN (1915–)

Writer

A Pulitzer Prize–winning novelist, Herman Wouk was born in New York City on May 27, 1915, the son of Russian Jewish immigrants. His father's first job in the United States was as a laundry laborer at a salary of $3.00 per week. Wouk attended Columbia University and began his career as a joke writer for radio comedians. He was a scriptwriter for Fred Allen from 1936 to 1941. During World War II he wrote and produced radio plays to promote the sales of war bonds and also served on sea duty in the Pacific, where he began writing fiction.

His first novel, *Aurora Dawn*, was published in 1947 and was chosen as a Book-of-the-Month selection. It was the first of a series of best-sellers. Many of Wouk's novels have Jewish characters or themes and explore moral dilemmas facing modern men and women. He is a straight forward writer of engaging stories. His books are known for their accurate research and realistic details. His fame comes from the popularity of his novels, rather than from stylistic innovation.

The Caine Mutiny, his third novel, after *The City Boy* (1948), catapulted him to national attention when it won the Pulitzer Prize for fiction in 1952. Later, the book was made into a film with Humphrey Bogart playing Captain Queeg. Another early novel, *Marjorie Morningstar* (1955), was turned into a film starring Gene Kelly. The film *Marjorie Morningstar* was un-

usual in that it portrayed a non-stereotypical Jewish household at a time when Hollywood rarely, if ever, made films about the Jewish experience in America. (But things had not changed completely. Non-Jewish Natalie Wood was cast in the title role.) After *Marjorie Morningstar*, Wouk temporarily put aside his career as a novelist to write a compelling and very personal account of his Jewish faith—*This Is My God* (1959). The book is dedicated to the memory of his grandfather, Mendel Leib Levine, a rabbi from Minsk. Like his novels, it became a best-seller.

Two more highly successful novels followed in the 1960s, *Youngblood Hawke* (1962) and *Don't Stop the Carnival* (1965). After years of reading, interviewing, travel, and archival research, Wouk published a panoramic, global portrait of World War II in two novels: *The Winds of War* (1971) and *War and Remembrance* (1978). The books were the basis of two successful television miniseries, and it is sometimes said that more Americans learned about this war through Wouk's writing than any other single source.

Wouk has also written for the stage. His two-act play, *The Traitor*, was produced on Broadway in 1949 and his two-act comedy, *Nature's Way*, opened in 1957. He also wrote a play *The Caine Mutiny Court-Martial* (based on his novel), as well as the screenplays for the World War II TV miniseries.

Herman Wouk has been writing best-selling novels for almost half a century and they have earned him an enduring place in American popular culture.

YEZIERSKA, ANZIA (1885?–1970)

Novelist, short-story writer

When Anzia Yezierska died in a nursing home in 1970, just short of ninety, she was barely remembered as a writer. With the rise of feminist literary criticism in the following decade, her work was rediscovered and her pungent, poignant stories of self-willed young women seeking an escape from New York's ghettos have found an enthusiastic new audience.

Yezierska's family immigrated to the United States when she was about two. In New York the family name became Meyer and she was known as Hattie. After a series of menial jobs, she fought with her Orthodox father and left home, moving into the Clara de Hirsch Home for Working Girls. Her intelligence and industriousness impressed several of the institution's trustees, who helped her get a scholarship to Columbia University's Teachers College (which included an undergraduate component at the time). Although she performed well at school and received a teaching certificate, she never found a position in the field. Instead, she went through several short-lived and unhappy marriages, and began writing.

As a writer, Yezierska enjoyed almost instantaneous success. **Samuel Goldwyn** acquired the film rights to her first book, *Hungry Hearts*, in 1921, and she went west to work on the screenplay. It was a Cinderella story of epic proportions, with Yezierska down to her last pennies when Goldwyn wired her an offer of $10,000 and a salary of $200 a week. She published a series of successful books in the 1920s exploring the situation of young women not unlike herself, torn between the need to survive in a grim world of poverty and the pressures from Old World–educated parents. At the same time she also developed a close relationship with the philosopher John Dewey. As the decade waned, Yezierska's creativity faded with it. She would not publish another book until her autobiography, *Red Ribbon on a White Horse*, in 1950.

Initially heralded as an authentic voice of the tenements—Cinderella of the Sweatshops—Yezierskafell into relative obscurity for the last decades of her life. But the 1980s saw a renewed appreciation of her work. Her 1925 novel, *Breadgivers: A Struggle between a Father of the Old World and a Daughter of the New*, was reissued in 1975; Alice Kessler-Harris edited *The Open Cage: An Anzia Yezierska Collection* in 1979; and *How I Found America: Collected Stories of Anzia Yezierska* was published in 1991.

YIDDISH LANGUAGE AND CULTURE

Yiddish language and culture became a part of the American experience with the first influx of German-Jewish immigrants in the middle 1700s. Since then, it has undergone enormous changes in use and popularity. Today Yiddish is primarily a language of scholarship and nostalgia.

The Yiddish language developed around 1100 A.D. in Central Europe and started as a blend of medieval German dialects. It spread to Eastern Europe when German Jews fled their country in the 1300s to escape persecution. By the 1700s it was the almost universal language of European Jews. Basically Germanic, Yiddish is written as Hebrew is, from right to left, and uses a slightly modified Hebrew alphabet. The vocabulary includes words from Hebrew, Aramaic, and some of the Slavic and Romance languages, as well as English. Until the Holocaust, it was the first language of approximately eleven million people, mostly in Europe.

Today Yiddish is the first language of about four million people living mostly in the United States, Israel, Canada, France, Mexico, Argentina, Romania, and the former USSR. This change was the result of several forces, the most powerful and invidious, of course, being the Holocaust itself. Most of the six million Jews who died at the hands of the Nazis were Yiddish speakers. In addition, Jewish immigrants to the United States usually acculturated, abandoning in the process the language of the Diaspora. Finally, after an intense struggle, the State of Israel chose Hebrew as the one and only official language. As a result, the speaking of Yiddish went into a decline.

Although Yiddish arrived in the United States in the eighteenth century, its real influence began in the late nineteenth century. In the 1880s a wave of Yiddish-speaking immigrants entered the country, settling largely in New York City. With them came not just a language but a literature and a culture that powerfully influenced the larger culture of America. Among the Yiddish words and expressions that have become part of the American vernacular are *boo boo* (mistake), *klutz* (clumsy person), *maven* (expert), *schmaltz* (sentimentality), and *zaftig* (pleasingly plump). There are hundreds of others. Although a great many families stopped speaking Yiddish in the second generation in this country, there were others who kept the language alive. The first American Yiddish writers began to emerge, and the Yiddish theater became a powerful force in the Jewish community.

As early as 1877, a book of poems in Yiddish was published, written by Rabbi Jacob Sobel. However, the real beginning of Yiddish poetry in America is probably to be found among the leftist poets of the 1880s and 1890s, who concerned themselves with the plight of the working class. Among these are Morris Winchevsky, David Edelstadt, Joseph Bovshover, and Morris Rosenfield. The work of these men was often as sentimental as it was revolutionary, with titles such as "The Teardrop Millionaire" and "A Song of Struggle."

At about the same time the American Yiddish theater began its short, but illustrious history when a cigarette-factory worker named **Boris Tomashefsky** appeared in *The Witch*, produced in 1882 by a New York saloon owner named Frank Wolf. After that, Yiddish plays were presented on Friday nights and Saturday matinees at a Bowery beer hall. It was a small beginning for what would become a hugely popular entertainment. At the turn of the century, according to historian Moses Rischin, the four major Yiddish theaters in New York City presented more than a thousand performances each year to about two million patrons. The theaters were magnificent houses of two to three thousand seats. In 1902 ticket prices ranged from a quarter to a dollar, and, according to historian Hutchins Hopgood, people who earned ten dollars a week often spent half of it to go to the Yiddish theater. It remained a vital and thriving institution until the 1940s.

In the early part of the century, the first major American Yiddish literary movement developed. Called *Di Yunge*, it celebrated America and rejected the sentimentality of earlier Yiddish literature, especially in Eastern Europe. Among its members were H. Leivick, Isaac Raboy, and M. L. Halpern. Within the next decade other movements began to shape Yiddish literature in this country, especially the *Introspectionists*, who believed that the only true reality was what came from inside the person. However, the most important voice of the time was probably that of Leivick. In the years before World War II the *Young Vilna* movement began to be influential. Following in the tradition of Eastern European intellectual Judaism, it included such important writers as Isaac Meier Dick, Eliakhum Zinser, **Abraham Cahan**, and Abraham Reisin. Since the war, most Yiddish writers of fiction and poetry live, not in the United States, but in Israel.

Throughout the golden years of Yiddish in this country, there was the newspaper *Forverts*, or the **Jewish Daily Forward**. Founded in 1897 by Abraham Cahan and Louis Miller, it became the most popular Yiddish daily in the world. During World War I, it had 200,000 readers. With a strong unionist and socialist voice, the *Forward* attempted to represent the interests of its largely working class readership, providing information as well the best in Yiddish literature. Beginning in 1906, it ran a column called "*Bintl*

A "Yiddish" writer if there ever was one, Isaac Bashevis Singer had a universal concern with an understanding of human nature and human history that make him a "world" author. Certainly the Nobel Prize Committee thought so. (Courtesy of American Jewish Archives)

Brief " (Bundle of Letters) to help immigrants deal with their new culture. In 1935 the *Forward* hired **Isaac Bashevis Singer**, whose fiction was often serialized in the paper and who continued to publish there until well into the 1980s. (His novel *Shadows on the Hudson* was first published in the *Forward* and was not issued in English until 1997, six years after his death.) The newspaper became a weekly in 1983, with a supplement in English for those who did not read Yiddish. In 1990 an independent English edition began publication.

With the decline of the Yiddish-speaking population in the United States, the future of Yiddish as a language and a cultural base is in question. However, its importance to the Jewish community, though ill-defined, is being re-affirmed. In 1996 the $8 million, 10-acre National Yiddish Book Center opened in Amherst, Massachusetts. The center was originally founded in 1980 by Aaron Lansky to save and collect Yiddish books as their readers and owners died and left no Yiddish-speaking heirs. Under Lansky's leadership the center has collected more than 1.3 million volumes and a Yiddish linotype (typesetting) machine. It has helped to create core collections of Yiddish books at 225 universities and research libraries.

The National Yiddish Book Center also offers an eight-day summer camp in Yiddish culture for both children and adults. The camp, held at Mount Holyoke College, is so popular that the center has had to request that participants not sign up for two years in a row in order to give other people a chance. Generally, a growing desire to identify as Jewish, combined with a lack of interest in traditional religion, has led to a Yiddish revival in the United States. Some of its manifestations are the popularity of klezmer music, including that of the Klezmatics and the group Kapelye; academic Yiddish programs at universities in New York, Los Angeles, and even Austin, Texas; and the annual festivals that began to blossom in the 1990s. There is even an exercise video entitled *Shvitz! My Yiddishe Workout*, and **Mandy Patinkin** opened his all-Yiddish songfest *Mamaloshen* ("mother tongue" in Yiddish) on Broadway in 1998, after performing it in an arts center on the Lower East Side of New York City and releasing it as a CD. Debate rages, however, about the significance of these signs of interest in a language and culture often considered nearly extinct. Some find them encouraging. Others insist that they seal the fate of Yiddish as a living phenomenon, reflecting only nostalgia and not a genuine revitalization. What seems clear is that Yiddish culture and all that it represents will not be forgotten by the present generation.

For Further Reading

See Appendix 2 for a bibliography of general reference books about Jews and the Jewish experience in America. All of the volumes listed there include information about American Jewish writers.

Baskin, Judith R., ed. *Women of the Word: Jewish Women and*

Jewish Writing. Detroit, Mich.: Wayne State University Press, 1994.

Guttmann, Allen. *The Jewish Writer in America: Assimilation and the Crisis of Identity*. New York: Oxford University Press, 1971.

Harap, Louis. *Creative Awakening: The Jewish Presence in Twentieth-Century American Literature, 1900–1940s*. Westport, Conn.: Greenwood Press, 1987.

———. *Dramatic Encounters: The Jewish Presence in Twentieth-Century American Drama, Poetry, and Humor and the Black-Jewish Literary Relationship*. New York: Greenwood Press, 1987.

———. *The Image of the Jew in American Literature: From Early Republic to Mass Immigration*. Philadelphia: Jewish Publication Society of America, 1974.

———. *In the Mainstream: The Jewish Presence in Twentieth-Century American Literature, 1950s–1980s*. Westport, Conn.: Greenwood Press, 1987.

Lichtenstein, Diane. *Writing Their Nations: The Tradition of Nineteenth-Century American Jewish Women Writers*. Bloomington, Ind.: Indiana University Press, 1992.

Pinsker, Sanford. *The Schlemiel as Metaphor: Studies in Yiddish and American Fiction*. Carbondale, Ill.: Southern Illinois University Press, 1991.

Schwartz, Howard, and Anthony Rudolph, eds. *Voices within the Ark: The Modern Jewish Poets*. New York: Avon Books, 1980.

Shapiro, Ann, Sara Horowitz, Ellen Schiff, and Miriyam Glazer. *Jewish American Women Writers: A Bio-Bibliographical and Critical Sourcebook*. Westport, Conn.: Greenwood Press, 1994.

Walden, Daniel, ed. *On Being Jewish: American Jewish Writers from Cahan to Bellow*. Greenwich, Conn.: Fawcett Publications, 1974.

Wisse, Ruth R. *The Schlemiel as Modern Hero*. Chicago: University of Chicago Press, 1971.

Part 14

Science, Medicine, and Social Science

OVERVIEW

It would be idle to speculate about why the Jewish people have made so many contributions in the areas of science, medicine, and the social sciences. It is enough to say that these contributions have been as crucial in America as in the rest of the world.

The first Jewish doctors came to these shores with Columbus and they have been here, in our lives and our stand-up comedy routines, ever since. The ship's doctor and the ship's surgeon aboard Columbus's *Santa Maria* were both Jewish physicians. During the colonial period there were a number of Portuguese Jewish physicians, and Jewish names continue to appear in medical records throughout the pre-Civil War era. There was even a Jewish doctor, Moses Albert Levy, at the Alamo. By mid-nineteenth century, the immigration of thousands of German-speaking Jews from Western Europe had greatly increased the number of Jewish physicians in all major American cities, and many of them became quite prominent. Ophthalmic surgeon Isaac Hays, for example, served as editor of the highly influential *American Journal of Medical Sciences* and was one of the founders and the treasurer of the American Medical Association, and the author of its first Code of Ethics. Abraham Jacobi founded the American Pediatric Society, served as the first American chairman of pediatrics at New York University and Columbia University, and later became president of the American Medical Association.

The larger wave of Jewish immigration that came in the late nineteenth century also brought an increase in Jewish physicians in this country, and the number of native-born Jews in medicine increased as well. Indeed, from the turn of the twentieth century on, Jewish Americans have made tremendous contributions to all the sciences. Coming from a tradition of abstract reasoning in the study of the Talmud and perhaps taking refuge from prejudice in the objectivity of scientific processes, they began to make their mark as early as 1907, when a Jew, **Albert Michelson**, won the first Nobel Prize awarded to an American scientist.

The situation in medicine changed in the 1930s. In that decade another influx of Jewish immigrants coincided with the Great Depression and a time of increasing anti-Semitism and isolationism. Physicians in this wave of immigrants found tremendous resistance from the medical mainstream. At the same time, medical schools and other professional schools began to actively discriminate against Jews. They established quotas and either refused to accept or accepted in small numbers applications from undergraduate institutions known to have a large proportion of Jewish students. At Columbia University's College of Physicians and Surgeons, the percentage of Jews among matriculated students declined from 50 percent in 1920 to a low of 12 percent in 1938. The situation continued in some measure until the 1950s. In response, many Jewish hospitals and medical institutions went through a great expansion in order to create professional opportunities for Jewish physicians and medical scientists.

Refugee scientists found a different welcome. Among these refugees was the great **Albert Einstein**, who fled Nazi Germany in 1933 to accept a position at the Institute for Advanced Study in Princeton, New Jersey. The Manhattan Project, which resulted in the atomic bomb, employed the brilliance of Jewish émigré physicists such as German-born Hans Bethe, Danish Niels Bohr, and Hungarians Leo Szilard and Eugene Wigner. Its director was American-born **J. Robert Oppenheimer**. Other outstanding scientists whom America gained because of the horrors of Hitler's regime included physicist James Franck and biochemist Otto Meyerhoff, who had both received Nobel prizes as German citizens.

After World War II, anti-Semitism fell into disrepute, and opportunities for Jewish physicians and medical scientists began to expand. Along with these opportunities came achievements. **Jonas Salk** and **Albert Sabin** began their legendary battle to prevent poliomyelitis, with Salk developing the first effective polio vaccine in 1954 and Sabin completing an oral vaccine for the disease in 1960. By the 1960s and 1970s, Jewish physicians constituted almost 10 percent of the total physician population in the United States—three times the percentage of Jews in the population. Of the twelve Nobel Prizes awarded in medicine or physiology between 1975 and 1986, six were shared by American Jews who built their careers at institutions that had previously restricted the admission of Jews.

Jewish American physicians have long supported organizational innovations, prepaid group practice; and, most recently, national health insurance. They have also been more likely than the medical community at large to support education about sexuality, birth control, and abortion rights. In addition, Jews have played a crucial role in the fields of mental health and social work in the United States. Native-born and immigrant Jews have served as therapists and counselors as well as developers of new and important theoretical work. In major urban areas such as New York and Los Angeles, Jewish Americans may fill as many as half of all professional positions in the mental health field, and the accomplishments of social work pioneers such as **Lillian Wald** cannot be overestimated.

Jewish women have been enormously active in the field of social work in such areas as Jewish communal self-help organizations, national reform agencies, women's organizations, and community service associations. They have concerned themselves with Jewish social welfare, as well as that of Americans as a whole. In this, as in science and medicine, the United States has been greatly blessed in its Jewish citizens.

BETTELHEIM, BRUNO (1903–1990)

Psychologist

Child psychologist Bruno Bettelheim was born in Vienna, Austria, on August 28, 1903. In 1938, when the Nazis marched into Austria, he was sent to Dachau and later Buchenwald. He survived the camps for a year, and his harrowing experiences there informed many of his psychological theories. Released in 1939, he immigrated to America, where he became a research associate at the Progressive Education Association of the University of Chicago. In 1942 he was appointed an associate professor at Rockford College in Illinois. A year later he published his groundbreaking article, "Individual and Mass Behavior in Extreme Situations," based on his experiences in the concentration camps. It examined the Nazis' system of stripping individuals of their identity, and how and why this succeeded with some people but not with others.

In 1944 Bettelheim was selected to head the Sonia Shankman Orthogenic School at the University of Chicago, where he remained until 1972. Here he began his groundbreaking work on severely emotionally disturbed and autistic children. His writings include *Love Is Not Enough: The Treatment of Emotionally Disturbed Children* (1950), *Truants from Life: The Rehabilitation of Emotionally Disturbed Children* (1954), *The Informed Heart: Autonomy in a Mass Age* (1960), and *The Children of the Dream* (1967). His *The Uses of Enchantment: The Meaning and Importance of Fairy tales* (1976) won a National Book Critics Circle Award and a National Book Award. It was widely praised. Harold Bloom in the *New York Review of Books* called it "a splendid achievement, brimming with useful ideas, with insights into how young children read and understand, and most of all overflowing with a realistic optimism and with an experienced and therapeutic good will." Bettelheim's 1982 book, *Freud and Man's Soul*, argued that the standard English translations of Freud misrepresented Freud's ideas. It created a storm of controversy. In 1987 he published *A Good Enough Parent: A Book on Child Rearing*.

Bettelheim committed suicide on March 13, 1990, despondent over the death of his wife of almost fifty years and his own failing health.

BOAS, FRANZ (1858–1942)

Anthropologist

The German-born Franz Boas is widely regarded as the father of anthropology in the United States. Although his doctorate from the University of Kiel was in physics, Boas gradually became interested in anthropological studies, with a special focus on the culture of the Eskimos and the Kwakiutl Indians of the Pacific Northwest. After his initial explorations of British Columbia in 1886–1887, Boas settled in New York City, where, in 1899, he became Columbia University's first professor of anthropology. He also served on the editorial staff of *Science* and was appointed curator of ethnology at the American Museum of Natural History. Boas trained many of the best-known figures in American anthropology, such as Margaret Mead, Ruth Benedict, Alfred Kroeber, and Robert Lowie.

Boas's many books and hundreds of articles on anthropology, ethnology, linguistics, and archaeology included such influential works as *The Mind of Primitive Man* (1911), *Anthropology and Modern Life* (1932), and *Race, Language, and Culture* (1940). In contrast with other scientists of his era, who regarded race as a primary factor in shaping human development, Boas argued strongly against racism. He emphasized that culture, not race or geography, is the crucial factor in determining human behavior. During the 1930s Boas was active in assisting German intellectuals who sought haven from Nazi persecution.

BROTHERS, JOYCE (1929–)

Psychologist

Dr. Joyce Brothers—née Bauer—was born on October 29, 1929, in New York City. She attended Cornell University, graduating with a B.S. in psychology in 1947. She then moved on to Columbia University, receiving her M.A. in 1949 and her Ph.D. in psychology in 1953. In 1955 she came to national attention when she won the top prize on "The $64,000 Question"—as an expert on boxing! In 1957 she appeared on the show's successor, "The $64,000 Challenge" and again won. In 1958 Brothers hosted her first television show, "The Dr. Joyce Brothers Show." An afternoon talk show, it was soon augmented by a late-night show she also hosted. Both shows were devoted to providing personal advice to viewers on topics ranging from child-rearing to personal relationships to sex.

Brothers has since become a household name. She has had many successful radio shows; written a syndicated newspaper column; and, for over thirty years, written a monthly column for *Good Housekeeping* magazine. She has also written a number of books, including *What Every Woman Should Know about Men* (1982). Her 1990 best-seller, *Widow*, described in poignant detail how she survived the death of her husband with the support of her loving family.

EINSTEIN, ALBERT (1879–1955)

Physicist

One of the greatest scientific theorists in human history, Albert Einstein was born into a non-observant Jewish family in Ulm, Germany on March 14, 1879, and spent most of his early life in Munich. In 1894, having failed to obtain a diploma from any school, he moved with his family to Milan, Italy. Two years later, he was accepted at the Zurich Polytechnic, where he studied mathematics and physics. In 1902 he began work in a patent office in Bern, Switzerland, where he stayed until 1909.

In 1905 he wrote several papers for the German journal *Annalen Der Physik* that changed the course of modern science. One paper, entitled "A New Determination of Molecular Dimensions," gained him a Ph.D. from the University of Zürich. Another helped to explain the photoelectric effect and led to the development of quantum mechanics. A third introduced his special theory of relativity that postulated: (a) the laws of physics must be consistent within any frame of ref-

Perhaps the most famous of the German Jews who fled Nazism and immigrated to the United States was Albert Einstein. He came in 1932 and accepted a post at the Institute for Advanced Study in Princeton, New Jersey. He had received the Nobel Prize in physics in 1921. He became an American citizen in 1940. (Courtesy of American Jewish Archives)

erence, and (b) the speed of light is a universal constant. The final paper of that year was a mathematical expansion on the special theory of relativity and is the source of the famous $E = mc^2$.

After he left the patent office in 1909 Einstein held positions at several universities. In 1914 he joined both the prestigious Kaiser-Wilhelm Gesellschaft and the University of Berlin. In 1916 he published *The Foundation of the General Theory of Relativity*, which postulated that gravity was a curved field in space-time, formed by the presence of mass. His theory was proved by an English expedition studying the solar eclipse in 1919. In 1921 while he was in the United States raising money for the Palestine Foundation

Fund, he won the Nobel Prize for Physics (for photoelectrics, not relativity, which was still a controversial issue). He spent the rest of his life trying to formulate the unified field theory—a single equation that would convey the universal properties of energy and mass.

In 1933, in response to the rise of Nazism, Einstein immigrated to the United States, where he immediately became the preeminent scientist at the Institute for Advanced Study in Princeton, New Jersey. A longtime pacifist, Nazism led him to change his mind (at least temporarily) about the necessity of warfare. After his arrival in this country, he was convinced to write a letter to President Franklin Roosevelt urging him to fund the development of an atomic bomb.

One of the few scientists who became a popular figure, Einstein was known as much for his political stances as for his theories. In the 1950s he publicly disapproved of the House Committee on Un-American Activities. He was also a vocal proponent of nuclear disarmament and an ardent Zionist. He died in Princeton, on April 18, 1955.

ELION, GERTRUDE (1918–)

Biochemist

Nobel Prize winner Gertrude Belle Elion was born in New York City on January 23, 1918. Her father was a Lithuanian immigrant who came from a rabbinical family. Elion attended Hunter College, graduating with a B.A. in 1937. She moved on to New York University where she received her M.S. in 1941. She found work as a quality control chemist at Quaker Maid Company and then as a research chemist at Johnson & Johnson. In 1944 she became a research chemist for the pharmaceutical company Burroughs Wellcome, first as assistant to George L. Hitchings and, later, as the head of experimental therapy. She remained with the company until she retired in 1983.

Elion and Hitchings were the first researchers to examine the biochemistry of both healthy and pathogenic cells in order to develop possible treatments for disease. Their new approach was a huge breakthrough and revolutionized pharmaceutical research. Their work led to new treatments for leukemia, gout, lupus, rheumatoid arthritis, auto-immune disorders, and herpes. In 1988, Elion and Hitchings, along with Sir James Black, received the Nobel Prize for Physiology or Medicine. Elion has received numerous other awards and honorary doctorates, including the National Medal of Science (1991). She also became the first woman in the National Inventors Hall of Fame (1991).

ERIKSON, ERIK (1902–1994)

Psychoanalyst

Erik Erikson was born on June 15, 1902, in Frankfurt am Main, Germany. In 1927, after attending art school, he joined the faculty at Anna Freud's private school in Vienna where he taught art, history, and geography. While there he both entered psychoanalysis himself and began training to become a psychoanalyst. In 1933 he finished his training and entered the Vienna Psychoanalytic Institute. Later that year he immigrated to the United States, settling in Boston where he began to practice child psychoanalysis and to teach at Harvard University Medical School.

In 1936 Erikson left Harvard and joined the Institute of Human Relations at Yale. It was at the Institute that he began his groundbreaking work on cultural influences in psychological development. In 1939 he moved to San Francisco, and in 1942 he began teaching psychology at the University of California, Berkeley. In 1950, after refusing to take the university's loyalty oath, Erikson left Berkeley and became part of the Austen Riggs Center in Stockbridge, Massachusetts. Ten years later he returned to Harvard where he was a professor from 1960 until 1970. He then became professor emeritus, the position he held until his death.

Erikson's work in the areas of social psychology and individual identity, as well as his exploration of the connections between psychology and history, culture, and politics, was extremely influential. Among his many published works are *Childhood and Society* (1950), *Young Man Luther* (1958), *Gandhi's Truth on the Origins of Militant Nonviolence* (1969), *Life History and the Historical Moment* (1975), *The Life Cycle Completed: A Review* (1982), and *Vital Involvement in Old Age* (1986). He died on May 12, 1994, in Harwich, Massachusetts.

GENEALOGY

Jewish interest in genealogy has a long history and tradition that dates back to the Torah, where several "family trees" are listed. The *kohanim*, the priests of Israel, maintained a detailed genealogical list in the temple in Jerusalem. In the twentieth century, descendants of modern Jewish immigrants have explored their roots in an effort to discover and preserve their family history and cultural heritage.

Generally, genealogists begin by conducting interviews with older family members. They learn to chart the family tree and to focus on questions such as original family names and their origins, the location of the family's ancestral town or towns, and the existence of family documents and photographs. Family historians can then work back into history to develop a broader picture of the life and times of their ancestors. Frequently the surname will reveal an ancestral town, a trade or profession, the father's or mother's name, physical traits, or other characteristics.

Jewish genealogy has a variety of written sources at its disposal, including public records, archival material, and the records of individuals and organizations. Government offices, libraries, and archives supply genealogists with census records, voter registration applications, naturalization records, city directory listings, and birth, marriage, and death records.

The process of researching Jewish family history also includes studying rabbinic genealogy, since many rabbinic families can trace their origins as far back as twenty generations. Tombstone and cemetery records are also extremely valuable for researchers to examine. In the seventeenth, eighteenth, and nineteenth centuries, tombstones often described the person's life, occupation, and town, as well as other pertinent information. Mortuary records, obituaries, and governmental burials are all resources used by Jewish genealogists.

It has been difficult, however, for Eastern European Jews to trace their family roots. The continuing border changes in Europe make it frustratingly hard to determine which government maintains the relevant vital statistics and other records. When borders shifted, the language also frequently changed, along with the geographic names and sometimes the location of the records as well. Although previously inaccessible Russian archival records have become easier to make use of since the breakup of the Soviet Union, it is still difficult for most people with Russian roots to find the information they need.

For Holocaust survivors and historians attempting to learn about the roots of survivors, the best genealogical information can be found in books devoted to the history of an ancestral town. These books frequently provide a researcher with a deeper understanding of the period in which his or her ancestors lived, and sometimes they can also lead to direct information about family members. In addition, various towns in Poland, Germany, Russia, Hungary, Romania, and Czechoslovakia were memorialized in *yizker bikher*—memorial volumes written by survivors and immigrants. These first-person narratives document entire Jewish communities that no longer exist, and each memorial book includes Jewish institutions as well as stories about the residents; memoirs; and, in a number of cases, lists of people who perished and those who survived. Extensive collections of memorial books can be found at the YIVO Institute, New York Public

Library Jewish Division, **Yeshiva University**, and the **Jewish Theological Seminary**.

In addition to local historical societies and public libraries, there is an extraordinary number of organizations and repositories in the United States that assist researchers who are gathering genealogical information. There are also repositories that specialize in documenting Sephardic genealogical history.

Each year seems to bring about new and important material tracing genealogical patterns of specific Jewish families and communities. It is likely that the well for this material is endless and should continue to be an area of tremendous interest for American Jews.

LEVI-MONTALCINI, RITA (1909–)

Neurologist

Rita Levi-Montalcini was born in Turin, Italy, on April 22, 1909. Her family were non-observant but strictly patriarchal. Despite their lack of attention to her education, in 1936 she graduated from Turin School of Medicine. After graduation she began the concentration that would be the focus of her career: the cells of the nervous system. She continued to work in Turin until World War II. She survived the Nazis by hiding, first in the countryside and then with the anti-fascist urban underground.

In 1946 Levi-Montalcini immigrated to the United States, taking a position at Washington University in St. Louis. She would remain on the faculty until 1977. In the 1960s, she began to also work with the National Laboratory for Cell Biology in Rome, Italy. She ultimately became the laboratory's director.

Levi-Montalcini, together with biochemist Stanley Cohen, made her greatest contribution to modern science and medicine when she hypothesized and then proved the existence of nerve growth factor (NGF), a substance that stimulates and influences the growth of nerve cells. From 1953 to 1959 she and Cohen were able to develop a method of extracting NGF. Taking NGF from snake venom and from the salivary glands of mice, they were able to identify it as a protein. This information created a revolution in the understanding of diseases, especially cancer. In 1986 Levi-Montalcini and Cohen were jointly awarded the Nobel Prize in physiology or medicine for their discoveries.

MEDICINE

From the beginning of their history until modern times, Jews have had a significant influence on the development of medical science and have regarded it as one of the most honorable professions to pursue. In the United States Jewish physicians became prominent during the colonial era and have continued to gain in stature and importance throughout the nineteenth and twentieth centuries. Jews have contributed to the field of medicine both through the creation of new ideas and theories and by the transmission of medical knowledge.

Jewish involvement in the medical field can be traced to a number of origins. From a religious perspective, biblical and Talmudic law sanctified medical knowledge because it had an important bearing on spiritual matters. In addition, since it was considered unethical to gain financial reward for teaching or studying the word of God, the ancient Hebrews chose medicine as a means of livelihood. They created the position of rabbi-physician beginning in the Talmudic Era. Politically, the practice of medicine was one of the few honorable occupations in which Jews in the Middle Ages, excluded from almost all other occupations (including public office) could earn a living. The medieval Jewish physician-translators also helped preserve and transmit the medical knowledge of the East and much of Greek medical lore to the West.

THE FIRST JEWISH PHYSICIANS

Most accounts trace the beginning of Jewish participation in American medicine to the Jewish physicians who arrived with Columbus: Maestre Bernal, the ship's physician, and Marco, its surgeon. A number of Jewish physicians, mostly from Sephardic ancestry, established practices well before the founding of the republic, including Jacob Lumbroso in Maryland in 1656 and

John di Sequera in Virginia in 1745. Samuel Nunez Ribiero established a practice in Savannah in 1833.

By the early to mid-nineteenth century, the influx of German-speaking immigrants from Western Europe swelled the number of Jewish physicians in all major American cities, and four physicians in particular gained an exalted status in the medical field. Ophthalmic surgeon Isaac Hays served as editor of the highly influential *American Journal of Medical Sciences* and was one of the founders and the treasurer of the American Medical Association and the author of its first Code of Ethics. Jacob Mendes DaCosta wrote *Medical Diagnosis*, one of the first textbooks for medical students, which went through nine editions. Abraham Jacobi, a German refugee recognized as the "father of American pediatrics," founded the American Pediatric Society, served as the first American chairman of pediatrics at New York University and Columbia University, and later became president of the American Medical Association. Jacob da Silva Solis-Cohen performed the first laryngectomy for laryngeal cancer in 1867 and became a pioneer in this specialty. Jews in this era also made significant clinical and scientific advances in internal medicine, surgery, and neurology.

The idea of the Jewish hospital, which had its origins in medieval Europe, also emerged in nineteenth-century America, with the establishment of Jew's Hospital in New York in 1852 (later re-named Mt. Sinai) and Touro Infirmary in New Orleans in 1853. By 1868 there were hospitals under Jewish auspices in Philadelphia, Cincinnati, Baltimore, and Chicago.

Although the mid- to late nineteenth century witnessed a substantial increase in the overall number of Jews practicing medicine in the United States, it took the first few decades of the next century for medicine to became a popular career choice for first- and second-generation Jewish immigrants. The number of Jewish physicians increased more rapidly than did the percentage of Jews in the overall population. The early years of the century also continued the massive increase of Eastern European immigration that changed the ethnic and cultural pattern of American Jewry and greatly affected the composition of Jewish representation in the medical field. But whether émigré or native

born, Jews made their mark in the new century as some of the leading medical minds in the nation.

EARLY TWENTIETH CENTURY

Several doctors recognized as pioneers in the field of medicine during the first two decades of the twentieth century include: Paul Ehrlich, who developed the first effective drug for syphilis; Simon Flexner, who isolated a common strain of dysentery bacillus; Max Einhorn, who introduced new concepts and diagnostic devices that advanced the field of gastroenterology; and Joseph de Lee, who wrote and edited three classic books on obstetrics that made him an undisputed leader in the field. Milton Joseph Rosenau became the foremost teacher in the field of preventive medicine and, as professor of epidemiology at the Harvard, developed the standardization of tetanus antitoxin and published important studies on serum sickness, hyper-sensitivity, and dental caries prevention. His magnum opus, *Preventive Medicine and Hygiene*, has served as the standard text for generations of doctors. Joseph Goldberger served in the Public Health Service for several decades, made significant contributions to the diagnosis and prevention of infectious diseases, and spent considerable energy studying the influence of economic factors on individual and public health. **Abraham Flexner**, although not a physician, published the *Flexner Report* in 1906, which laid out the subsequent course of medical education in the United States and made the American medical school a world leader in education and research.

Jewish women entering the medical field also made important contributions to the health of the nation, despite considerable resistance and barriers placed on their full participation in the profession by elite physicians and the medical establishment. Frances Allen DeFord campaigned for better hygiene measures in the Kensington section of Philadelphia, an industrial and malaria-ridden neighborhood where she set up her practice. In the late 1920s, Rita Sapiro Finkler became one of the first female physicians to take an active role in understanding the new field of endocrinology. She went on to become one of the leading authorities in this and related areas focusing on women's reproductive health. Lena Kenin in Portland, Oregon and Bessie Moses in Baltimore both began careers in the field of obstetrics at this time with each conducting important work in family planning policy. Sophie Rabinoff gained a strong reputation as a New York City pediatrician, conducting important research on childhood diseases such as rickets, scurvy, and diphtheria. In 1930 Martha Wollstein became the first woman awarded membership in the American Pediatric Society.

1930s

The decade of the 1930s was a pivotal era on several different levels for Jews in the medical field. Refugees fleeing Nazi Germany included a considerable number of physicians who had made a name for themselves in Europe. This increased medical talent coincided with major advances in scientific medicine facilitated by the discoveries of antibiotics and cortisone, and the progress made in molecular biology and medical technology. At the same time, it was a period of severe economic hardship, increasing anti-Semitism, and isolationism in the United States, which created serious repercussions for Jews in American medicine.

Medical schools began to actively discriminate against Jews in their admissions policies, establishing quotas and either refusing to accept or accepting in small numbers applications from undergraduate institutions known for their large numbers of Jewish students. At Columbia University's College of Physicians and Surgeons, the percentage of Jews among matriculated students declined from 50 percent in 1920 to a low of 12 percent in 1938. This situation did not begin to completely reverse itself until the 1950s.

Those who were able to complete medical school often had great difficulties acquiring internships and residency positions. Those who did gain hospital positions were often subject to harassment and even driven out by gentile colleagues. Jewish medical school graduates had their opportunities circumscribed by the climate of the era and remained in general rather than specialty practice, unless they managed to luck into a staff position in one of the Jewish hospitals.

It also became difficult for émigré physicians and medical scientists to become established in the United States during the 1930s, with many American medical authorities and health organizations resisting the influx of refugee doctors for both economic and anti-Semitic reasons. In response to this problem Bernard Sachs, professor of neurology at Columbia and the discoverer of Tay-Sachs disease, formed the Emergency Committee in Aid of Displaced Physicians in 1933. The committee was able to grant scholarships to only 125 refugees and to find positions for 100 others at a time when more than 4,000 Jewish physicians immigrated to the United States. In most states the law prohibited immigrant physicians from taking licensing exams, and in some they were expected to re-graduate from American medical schools or to complete internships in local hospitals.

Although this backlash drastically reduced the number of refugee doctors entering practice, some of the most prominent Jewish émigré physicians did succeed in gaining academic appointments. Nobel Prize winner Otto Loewi secured a post at New York University, while fellow Nobel Laureate Otto Meyerhoff obtained a position at the University of Pennsylvania. Future Nobel winner Fritz Lipmann received posts at Cornell Medical School and then at Massachusetts General Hospital, while the eminent neuropsychiatrist Kurt Goldstein secured appointments at Columbia University and subsequently at Tufts Medical School. Other émigré clinicians of great accomplishments also acquired posts, as did a considerable number of psychoanalysts.

Nonetheless, most refugee Jewish physicians, along with quite a few American-born Jewish doctors, had great difficulty advancing in the United States mainstream medical world during these years. In response, many Jewish hospitals and medical institutions expanded drastically in order to create alternative professional opportunities for Jewish clinicians and investigators. This growth at Jewish hospitals usually developed in tandem with a dramatic increase in internship and residency positions, specialty training, and staff appointments.

POST-WAR OPPORTUNITIES

After World War II, the prejudices against Jews in the field of health and medicine lifted considerably, and Jewish physicians gained both expanded opportunities to develop professionally and increased recognition for their accomplishments. Perhaps the two most renowned Jewis associated with the profession of medicine, **Jonas Salk** and **Albert Sabin**, began their groundbreaking work to prevent poliomyelitis in the immediate post-war era. Salk developed the first effective polio vaccine in 1954 and Sabin completed an oral vaccine for the disease in 1960. Other Jewish physicians gaining recognition in this era included Nobel Laureates Herman Joseph Muller, Selman Waksman, and Fritz Lipmann. Muller gained recognition for his efforts in discovering the production of mutations and congenital defects by means of X-ray irradiation. Waksman won the Nobel Prize in 1952 for his work on the isolation of streptomycin, an antibiotic valuable in combating several diseases (especially tuberculosis). Fritz Lipmann received the honor in 1953 for his discovery of coenzyme and its importance for intermediary metabolism.

From the mid- to the late twentieth century, Jewish physicians contributed major breakthroughs in fields such as endocrinology, pathology, microbiology, pharmacology, biochemistry, immunology, and physiology. Two women, Frances Pascher and Naomi Kanof, achieved significant recognition for their work in dermatology—Pascher as a pioneer in describing the skin manifestations of lupus erythermatosis and the first to demonstrate the importance of skin absorption of drugs. Kanof was chair of the Department of Pediatric Dermatology at the Children's Hospital in Washington and editor of the *Journal of Investigative Dermatology* for twenty years.

CONTEMPORARY ERA

By the 1960s and 1970s Jewish physicians constituted almost 10 percent of the total physician population in the United States—three times the percentage of Jews in the population. In the state of New York alone, the number of practicing Jewish doctors had risen to surpass the entire country of Israel by 2,000. By the end of the 1970s, there were over sixty Jewish hospitals in

It is tempting to call this a group portrait of "My son, the doctor." It is a photograph of the senior staff of Mt. Sinai Hospital in New York City taken around 1914. (Courtesy of American Jewish Archives)

the country, many of which became important research and teaching institutions, including Albert Einstein Institute and the Mt. Sinai School of Medicine. In addition, two of the oldest hospitals for rehabilitation of the chronically ill, Montefiore in New York and the National Hospital for Consumptives in Denver, became important centers for research and teaching.

Jewish physicians gained prestige, recognition, and financial security in the American medical mainstream after World War II, holding high-level posts in medical societies, academic institutions, and the scientific establishment. But just as not all Jewish attorneys entered private law firms, many American Jews in the medical field chose to work in family practice, public health, and community-based clinics, providing health care for underserved and low-income populations in urban and rural communities both in the United States and in other countries.

Jewish physicians throughout the twentieth century have been notable for their support of organizational innovations; prepaid group practice; and, most recently, national health insurance. They have also been more likely than the medical community at large to support education about sexuality, birth control, and abortion rights. Jewish physicians such as Marie Pichel Warner devoted their lives to leadership in the area of family planning. Warner, an obstetrician by training, served as medical director of contraceptive clinics at New York City's Jewish Memorial Hospital and then spent the better part of her career publishing articles and books on birth control and infertility in addition to running a successful private practice.

By the same token, Jews have also been well represented among the more conservative health care establishments. For many years, the most vocal and effective representative of the American Medical Association was Morris Fishbein of Chicago, who served as the editor of the association's highly influential magazine. Toward the end of his career, especially, he fought against all attempts to challenge the "official line" of the medical establishment.

Jewish physicians continue to make important contributions to the field of health and medicine. Jewish doctors in all areas of practice have been more ac-

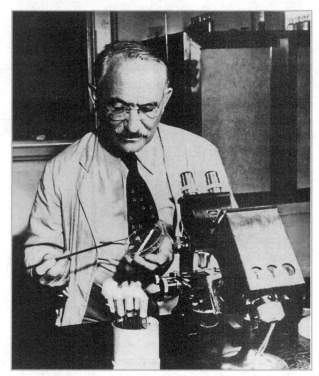

Selman Abraham Waksman was awarded the Nobel Prize in 1952 for his work on the isolation of streptomycin, an antibiotic valuable in combatting several diseases (especially tuberculosis). He was one of twenty-seven American Jews to receive the prize in Physiology and Medicine between 1922 and 1989. (Courtesy of Jewish Archives)

cepted in the last two decades at American medical institutions than at any time in history. Of the twelve Nobel Prizes awarded in medicine or physiology between 1975 and 1986, six were shared by American Jews who built their careers at mainstream institutions that had been inaccessible to many Jews in previous generations. A seventh, **Rita Levi-Montalcini**, who shared the award with Stanley Cohen, gained her professional recognition at Jewish institutions. Jewish students no longer have difficulty competing for medical school slots or earning postgraduate positions in a variety of specialties at prestigious institutions.

Although Jews may have entered the medical profession because it was one of the few occupations open to them, they have shown through their talents and perseverance a continued dedication to excel. The history of Jewish physicians in the United States has become a legacy of struggle, commitment, and achievement. The breadth and quality of Jewish participation in the advance of medical science is reflected by their outstanding contributions to research and education.

MENTAL HEALTH PROFESSIONS

Jews have played a seminal role in the fields of psychology, psychiatry, and psychoanalysis in the United States. As providers and theoreticians, native-born and immigrant Jews have a rich history of achievement and leadership and have arguably been the group most responsible for expanding the profession in twentieth-century America. In major urban areas such as New York and Los Angeles, Jewish mental health clinicians sometimes compose up to half of all professionals in the field.

Various theories have been advanced as to why so many Jews have gravitated to the field, including Jewish feelings of marginality, Jewish upward mobility, and the Jewish intellectual concern with the life of the mind. Some observers have surmised that Jews are more prone to identify with the suffering of others, while at the same time possessing a degree of detachment that provides them with an analytical perspective that helps enable them to understand human behavior. Others have cited the comfort that many Jews have in verbally expressing their emotions as a determining factor in their embrace of the profession.

PSYCHOANALYSIS

It is impossible to discuss the American Jewish contribution to psychoanalysis without beginning with Sigmund Freud and the series of lectures he gave at Clark University in 1909. These lectures presented the basic tenets of his early theories. Two years later, Abraham Brill, Freud's first American translator, founded the New York Psychoanalytic Society, the first such group in the country. Along with Brill, other early pioneers of the field included Alabama-born Clarence Oberndorf and Isador Coriat, who developed the Boston Psychoan-

alytic Association. Brill and Oberndorf, both major popularizers of Freud's theories, established a psychiatric outpatient clinic at New York's Mount Sinai Hospital that succeeded in promoting the importance of psychoanalysis among physicians.

In these early years, its adherents viewed psychoanalysis as part of an avant-garde movement rather than a clinical practice—as a cultural movement rather than a science. By the 1920s and 1930s this began to change as the field grew more established. Several American-born Jewish psychoanalysts such as Bertram Lewin, M. Ralph Kaufman, and Ruth Mack Brunswick began to popularize Freud's theories within a medical model. Brunswick served as one of Freud's key American colleagues, and she refined his theories so they paid more attention to the importance of the earliest relationship with the mother—what she referred to as the "pre-oedipal" phase of development. Freud also chose Brunswick to treat the "Wolfman"—the patient who was the subject of his most important published case.

For the next thirty years, Jewish psychoanalysts were more likely to affirm American ideals of adaptation and cultural pluralism than to challenge them. American psychoanalysis would, however, continue to be transformed in the next decade by the Jewish presence, this time from the influx of European refugees fleeing Nazi Germany. Men and women who would go on to become some of the most renowned members of the psychiatric profession entered the United States during and immediately after World War II. Among the notables who immigrated during this era were Theodore Reik, **Erik Erikson**, Ruth Jacobson, Hilde Bruch, Eric Fromm, Frieda Fromm-Reichmann, **Bruno Bettelheim**, David Rapaport, Helene Deutsch, and Therese Benedek.

A number of the female analysts who immigrated during these years were especially prominent in exploring specific mental health concerns of women in the post–World War II era. Helene Deutsch published a pioneering two-volume work, *The Psychology of Women*, in 1944–1945, which combined Freudian psychoanalysis with a special focus on women derived from her own personal experience and clinical observations. Therese Benedek's 1952 book, *Psychosexual Functions in Women*, focuses on the emotional response of women to the fluctuations of hormones during the menstrual cycle. Frieda Fromm-Reichman broke new ground in using art therapy to treat schizophrenic and manic-depressive clients, who had previously been considered unfit for psychoanalysis. Hilde Bruch, one of Fromm-Reichman's disciples, conducted important research on childhood obesity and later focused her efforts on understanding the causes of anorexia nervosa.

The field of psychoanalysis fit smoothly into the world of 1950s America, but not in the manner that Freud might have imagined. As the profession became more established and the Jews involved in it formed a significant bloc among the American Jewish elite, its focus shifted from the "id" and the instinctual drives to the "ego" and the need for the individual to exercise control over basic impulses. This direction fit well with the moralistic American ethos of the 1950s, which emphasized the need to help the individual adjust to society.

The 1960s represented a major shift from the psychoanalytic orientation toward adaptation and conformity as the counterculture embraced the ideas on repressed sexuality by the pariah of the psychoanalytic movement, Wilhelm Reich, and celebrated the Frankfort School's attempt to fuse Marxism with psychoanalytic theory through a biting critique of American consumer society. Jewish psychoanalysts who achieved prominence during the 1960s and 1970s included Otto Kernberg and Heinz Kohut, both of whom focused on exploring the theme of narcissism and its broader implications.

In the last two decades an increasing number of analytic institutes have successfully challenged the medicalization of the field, and, increasingly, clinical psychologists and social workers are trained to practice psychoanalysis. Not surprisingly, Jews compose a large percentage of these new practitioners as well.

PSYCHIATRY

While psychoanalysis was a twentieth-century phenomenon imported from Europe, psychiatry existed as a field in the United States well before the Civil War. The American Institution of Medical Superintendents (soon to become the American Psychiatric Association) had no Jews among its founding members. The first well-known Jewish psychiatrists in the United States, Sidney Kuh (1866–1934) and Bernard Sachs (1858–1954), held what is generally known as the neurological-organic model of the profession, which searches for the causes of mental illness in a dysfunctional brain. Kuh served as professor of nervous and mental diseases at Rush Medical College in Chicago. Sachs, who is best known for discovering Tay-Sachs disease, was professor of nervous and mental disease at Columbia University.

In the early twentieth century, however, Freud's focus on socialization problems and their role in contributing to emotional and behavioral difficulties began to gain favor among a number of Jewish psychiatrists, including Sidney Schwab, a former student of Freud in Vienna, Boris Sidis, Samuel Tannenbaum, and Meyer Solomon. At the same time as Jews became recognized within the profession of psychiatry, prominent leaders in the field also embraced eugenics and psychiatric explanations to support racist immigration restrictions, with many arguing that there existed a form of "Jewish psychopathology" and that Jews were more prone to insanity than other ethnic groups. This movement was so influential in the second and third decades of the century that many Jewish psychiatrists spent considerable energy refuting its basic premises.

By the 1930s the number of Jews in the world of psychiatry had expanded to such an extent that these theories became obsolete. It was the generation that came of age in the Depression and New Deal era that produced some of the most important names in the field, such as Harold Wolff, Roy Grinker, Lawrence Kolb, Manfred Guttmacher, Lauretta Bender, David Levy, William Malamud, and Nathan Ackerman. By the World War II and post-war era, Jews had risen to the forefront of the field, and, by the 1960s, they constituted nearly half of all members of the psychiatric profession—a remarkable proportion that continues today. In addition, Jews also took on leadership positions in university psychiatry departments, and many, including Milton Rosenbaum, Seymour Halleck, and Milton Greenbaum, headed major training centers for psychiatric research. During this time, German émigré Fritz Perls gained recognition in the psychiatric field for a highly emotive and interactive form of psychotherapy known as Gestalt Therapy.

Although women had a difficult time breaking through the male medical enclave that has generally characterized the psychiatric profession, Sadi Muriel Baron achieved considerable recognition as a pioneering neurologist and psychiatrist. In the 1920s she became the first female resident at Columbia Presbyterian Hospital's Neurological Institute, and, later served for several decades on the faculty of the hospital's Department of Psychiatry. In the 1960s Lena Kenin broke new ground in her combined practice of obstetrics and psychiatry, serving as associate professor of psychiatry at the University of Oregon Medical school and chief consultant for the school's health service.

A number of contemporary Jewish psychiatrists of note have also attempted to link the organic and psychological approaches to mental health. Robert J. Lifton has written and lectured extensively about individuals who have survived major traumas, and Aaron Beck has formulated a cognitive theory dealing with the problem of depression. Nathan Kline generated considerable controversy with his drug therapy research, and he was one of the first psychiatrists to introduce tranquilizers into the treatment of mental illness.

PSYCHOLOGY

The newer field of psychology began in the United States during the late nineteenth century as a discipline greatly influenced by German laboratory science methodology. It rapidly acquired a life of its own, however, as a broader field concerned with complex human actions and behavior embedded in everyday life. From its inception, psychology had many contributions from Jewish clinicians and scholars. The first doctorate ever awarded in psychology went to a Jewish man, Joseph Jastrow, who received his degree from Johns Hopkins University in 1886. He went on to develop the psychological laboratory at the University of Wisconsin. Jastrow wrote one of the earliest syndicated self-help columns, "Keeping Mentally Fit." Also making a name for himself in this era was Hugo Munsterberg, who di-

rected a laboratory founded by William James and developed the first analysis of the psychological components of early American film.

At the same time, the first generation of Jewish psychologists was limited in numbers because of the prejudice that developed against Jews in the university setting, where most psychological work took place. During the second generation, Jewish participation in the field grew significantly, assisted by the influx of European refugees, which began in the 1920s and 1930s and led to the evolution of groundbreaking work in the study of child development and social interaction. German émigré Kurt Lewin's pioneering research in this field at the Iowa Child Welfare Station paved with way for a new generation to study the world of childhood. Fellow refugees Charlotte Buhler, William Stern, and Heinz Werner were also pioneers in promoting the new specialty of developmental psychology. Hungarian-Jewish émigré Else Frenkel-Brunswick helped design and promote psychological studies of anti-Semitism. Together with Theodore Adorno, he published *The Authoritarian Personality* in 1950 and designed a measurement scale for analyzing prejudice in individuals and groups.

The next generation of thinkers in developmental psychology who followed in the footsteps of these thinkers included Jerome Bruner, Joseph Adelson, Uri Bronfenbenner, Jacob Gewirtz, William Goldfarb, Edward Ziegler, and Bernice Neugarten. Neugarten was one of the first female psychologists to focus exclusively on studies of adult development and aging. In the post–world War II era, Jews occupied a critical role in the rapidly new and evolving field of clinical psychology. Jewish psychologists gravitated to this arena because it represented a popularization of Freudian psychoanalytic concepts and provided a fusing of intellectual inquiry within an affective interpersonal and therapeutic foundation. Clinical psychology was not burdened by the history and tradition of the psychiatric model of mental health, while at the same time it offered Jews upward mobility and professional prestige.

David Shokow was perhaps the first prominent Jewish clinical psychologist. He served for many years as the chief psychologist at Worcester State Hospital in Massachusetts, where he conducted influential research on schizophrenia. Hans Strup and Leonard Luborsky also gained a reputation for their psychotherapy research. Joseph Zubin, Kurt Salzinger, and Sarnoff Mednick became known for their leadership in the specialty of experimental psychopathology. Emory Cowen and Seymour Sarasan made a name for themselves as specialists in community or public health psychology and the early prevention of psychological dysfunction. Dorothy Baruch was a renowned child psychologist who examined the expression of the child's fantasies and feelings and stressed the importance of their understanding by parents for the individual, the family, and the entire society. Perhaps the best known and most influential clinical psychologist of what became known as humanistic psychotherapy was Abraham Maslow.

Jewish clinicians have also taken on a significant role in conducting research that focuses specifically on the psychology of women. No scholar has been more important in this respect than Carol Gilligan, who argued that mainstream psychology operated from a male bias in its theoretical development and has generally ignored women's identity and experience. Gilligan contended that women frequently held a different moral voice from men. Her book, *In a Different Voice*, makes the case that prevailing standards of maturity and moral development generally used in psychological testing do not apply to women.

Another American-born Jewish psychologist, Florence Denmark, worked to establish the psychology of women as a recognized and legitimate scholarly field. She succeeded in getting funding from the National Science Foundation and the National Institute of Mental Health for the first research conference (held in Madison, Wisconsin, in 1975) that brought both senior and junior women scholars and practitioners together for a dialogue. The resulting book was entitled *The Psychology of Women*. In 1980 Denmark was elected the fifth woman president of the American Psychological Association (the first Jewish woman to hold this office).

Jewish psychologists have also made a name for themselves in the area of psychological testing and assessment. The two early leaders in the field, Bruno Klopfer and Samuel Beck, brought projective testing to public consciousness. Later, David Rappaport initiated groundbreaking research at the Menninger clinic and the Austin Riggs Foundation, where he served as a mentor to a number of younger psychologists. Sidney Blatt and Irving Weiner have taken on leadership roles in demonstrating the importance of clinical assessment and evaluation.

In the contemporary era, clinical service has become the primary focus among psychologists, and Jews continue to gain recognition in all aspects of the field. Arnold Lazarus and Marvin Gottfried stand out as experts in the behavioral therapies; Alan Gurman, Gerald Zuk, and Neil Jacobson are leaders in family therapy; and Nathan Farberow and Edward Schneidman have become authorities in the relatively new specialty of suicidology.

Jews played a significant role in defining the mental health professions in the United States, both as scholars and as practitioners. They have contributed pioneering ideas and theories to the fields of psychiatry, psychoanalysis, and psychology. They have also taken on leadership roles and initiated research and inquiry into new and previously understudied areas. The Jewish influence on the mental health professions must be measured not only by the sheer numbers of Jews who are practitioners, but also by their contribution to the expanded parameters of the profession itself and to the body of scholarly discourse that has been produced over the last century.

MICHELSON, ALBERT (1852–1931)

Physicist

Albert Michelson was born in Strelno, Prussia—now Poland—on December 19, 1852. He came to the United States when he was two and settled with his family in San Francisco. He attended the United States Naval Academy, graduating in 1873. In 1878, while a science teacher at the academy, he began to experiment at home with measuring the speed of light. In 1880, feeling he needed more education in order to continue his explorations, he went to Europe to study optics. While in Europe he resigned from the navy. In

1883, after returning to the States, he became a professor of physics at Case School of Applied Science in Cleveland, Ohio. Michelson left Case in 1889 and, after three years at Clark University in Worcester, Massachusetts, became the head of the physics department at the newly founded University of Chicago. He remained there until he retired in 1929. He also served as the president of the National Academy of Sciences from 1923 through 1927.

During his two years in Europe, Michelson made his earliest groundbreaking contribution to science: he invented the interferometer, a device that first split, then reconnected a single beam of light. In 1882, soon after he returned to the United States, Michelson used the interferometer to determine the speed of light to be 186,329 miles per second. In 1887, while at Case, he began to work with the chemist Edward Williams Morley. Together the two scientists discovered the great paradox of the day: that the speed of light plus any other velocity still equaled the speed of light. This came to be called the Michelson-Morley experiment. It forced a reexamination of the theoretical basis of physics that ultimately led to Einstein's theory of relativity. In 1907 Michelson was awarded the Nobel Prize for Physics, the first American to win a Nobel Prize in the sciences.

By the 1920s, Michelson was using the interferometer to find the first accurate measurement of the stars. In 1923 he reexamined his own measurement of the speed of light and, using more refined techniques, came up with 299,798 km/sec. Still not satisfied, he refined his experiment still further. On May 9, 1931, Michelson died in Pasadena, California, and he never learned the final results of this experiment. In 1933 the final figure was determined to be 299,774 km/sec. This figure was less than 2 km/sec higher than the figure arrived at in the 1970s.

NOETHER, EMMY (1882–1935)

Mathematician

Considered by many to be the most influential algebraist of the twentieth century, Emmy Noether was born on March 23, 1882, in Erlangen, Germany. She attended the university in Erlangen, and, in 1907, received her Ph.D. with a dissertation that included elements of what would later be called "computational" algebra. In 1915 she moved to Gottingen and became mathematician David Hilbert's assistant. By 1920 she was focusing on theories involving the algebraic theory of ideals and their application to number theory and algebraic geometry. In 1933, with the rise of Nazism, she lost her position at Gottingen and came to the United States, where she obtained a position at Bryn Mawr College. While teaching at Bryn Mawr, Noether also lectured at Princeton University and at the Institute for Advanced Study. She died on April 14, 1935, after a lifetime of both expanding mathematical theory and mentoring a future generation of mathematicians.

OPPENHEIMER, J. ROBERT (1904–1967)

Theoretical physicist

Known as the father of the atom bomb, J(ulius) Robert Oppenheimer was both its creator and its conscience. Born in New York City on April 22, 1904, he attended Harvard University, Cambridge, and Gottingen, where he received his doctorate in 1927.

Between 1929 and 1942 Oppenheimer taught at the University of California, Berkeley, and the California Institute of Technology, Pasadena, building well-respected theoretical physics departments at both schools. In 1942 he was asked to direct the development of the atom bomb at a laboratory in Los Alamos, New Mexico. By the time the bomb was dropped on Hiroshima and Nagasaki, Oppenheimer was deeply troubled by the potential power and destruction of the weapon he helped create. He resigned as director of the laboratory in 1945.

In the post-war years Oppenheimer became the director of the Institute of Advanced Study in Princeton, New Jersey, and the chairman of the board of scientific advisors for the Atomic Energy Commission (AEC). He served as the chairman of the AEC advisory board until 1952 and during his tenure the

The brilliant theoretical physicist J. Robert Oppenheimer was director of the "Manhattan Project," which developed the atomic bomb. He was a victim of the McCarthy-era witch-hunts, and his government security clearance was subsequently taken away from him. He was the long-time director of the famous Institute for Advanced Study in Princeton, New Jersey. (Courtesy of American Jewish Historical Society, Waltham, Massachusetts, and New York, New York)

RABI, ISIDOR ISAAC (1898–1988)

Physicist

The 1944 Nobel Prize winner for physics, Isidor Isaac Rabi was born in Rymanow, Poland, and was brought up in the United States. He attended Cornell and Columbia universities, obtaining his Ph.D. from the latter in 1927. He taught at Columbia from 1929 until 1967. He was the first Jewish member of the physics department there.

Raised in an Orthodox household, Rabi's entry into the world of science came out of an exploration of the alternatives to the traditional creation myth. His bar mitzvah speech was "How the Electric Light Bulb Works." From the light bulb through his studies at Cornell and Columbia, Rabi examined the world around him in smaller and smaller increments. He built Columbia's magnetic beam laboratory and discovered magnetic resonance measurement and theory. During World War II he worked for M.I.T.'s Radiation Laboratory and developed radar technology, which helped the Allies win World War II. He also served as an advisor to the Manhattan Project at Los Alamos. After the war he helped develop the Brookhaven National Laboratory (a nuclear research facility). He also pursued other avenues for the peaceful use of atomic energy. He was a member of the General Advisory Committee of the Atomic Energy Commission from 1946 to 1949 and the President's Scientific Advisory Committee from 1957 to 1961. He was against the development of thermo-nuclear bombs and later in life became a vocal proponent of arms control.

RESNIK, JUDITH (1949–1986)

Astronaut

One of the seven crew members who died in the tragic explosion of the space shuttle Challenger on January 28, 1986, Judith Resnik was the first Jew and the second American woman ever to travel in space. She had already logged over 144 hours on the space shuttle *Dis-*

board rejected a proposal to build hydrogen bombs. In 1953, due in large part to the McCarthy era hearings and his own opposition to the hydrogen bomb, his government security clearance was denied. In 1954, after Oppenheimer asked for, and received, a closed hearing, the committee determined that, though his loyalty to the United States was not in question, his security clearance would not be reinstated, thinking it unwise to trust him with government secrets. Nine years later the Atomic Energy Commission gave him its most prestigious award, the Fermi Award. He stayed on as the director of the Institute for Advanced Study until 1966 and died February 18 of the following year.

A gifted student, Judith Resnik not only made a perfect 800 on her math SAT test, but also excelled at Hebrew school and was an accomplished classical pianist. She was the second American woman to travel in space and, along with schoolteacher Christa McAuliffe, lost her life in the Challenger *disaster. (Courtesy of American Jewish Archives)*

covery when she and her fellow astronauts prepared for the ill-fated *Challenger* mission.

The granddaughter of a *shochet* (kosher slaughterer), she grew up in a family that was active in Akron's Jewish community. She had her bat mitzvah in 1962 and Rabbi Philip Salzman described her as "the best student I have ever had in Hebrew school." A brilliant student (she scored a perfect 800 on her math SAT tests), Resnik received her undergraduate degree in electrical engineering from Carnegie-Mellon and her Ph.D. with honors in the same subject from the University of Maryland. Highly regarded for both her dedication and her expertise, she was one of six women among the initial thirty-five members of the space shuttle program. Resnik served as a mission specialist on the 1984 *Discovery* flight, supervising the ship's solar power array.

On the *Challenger* flight she was to have assisted in photographing Halley's comet. Famous for its civilian crew member, schoolteacher Christa McAuliffe, the shuttle exploded in midair seventy-three seconds into the flight—the worst space disaster in history.

RICKOVER, HYMAN GEORGE (1900–1986)

Naval officer, father of the atomic submarine

United States Naval officer Hyman Rickover is regarded as the father of the atomic-powered submarine. Born in Russia and raised in Chicago, Rickover graduated from the U.S. Naval Academy in 1922. After a tour at sea, he studied electrical engineering at the U.S. Naval Academy and Columbia University. Rickover gradually assumed increasingly important staff and command positions in the Navy, and during World War II headed the Electrical Section of the Navy's Bureau of Ships. In 1947 he persuaded the Navy to undertake the construction of nuclear-powered submarines and was put in charge of the project. The first such submarine, the *U.S.S. Nautilus*, was launched in early 1954.

Rickover was promoted to rear admiral, then vice admiral. He also became active in the field of education, authoring two books critical of America's educational system, *Education and Freedom* (1959) and *American Education: A National Failure* (1963).

SABIN, ALBERT BRUCE (1906–1993)

Physician, virologist

Albert Sabin, the creator of the oral polio vaccine, was born in Bialystok, Russia (now Poland) on August 26, 1906. He and his family immigrated to the United States when he was fifteen. He got both his B.S. and his M.D. degrees from New York University, in 1928 and 1931, respectively. He became a faculty member of the Department of Pediatrics at the University of Cincinnati College of Medicine in 1939.

Albert Sabin began his research into the polio virus as soon as he received his M.D. degree. His vaccine was ready for widespread use by 1956 and was licensed for use in the United States in 1961. By that time, however, the virus had already been virtually eradicated in this country by **Jonas Salk**'s serum vaccine, in use since 1954.

During and after the race to develop the vaccines, Salk and Sabin conducted an angry public feud over both recognition and funding. While Salk based his vaccine on a killed form of the virus, Sabin used the live virus. Ultimately, Sabin's vaccine proved to be cheaper, more potent, and more easily administered. The World Health Organization confirmed the effectiveness of Sabin's vaccine shortly after it was introduced, and today it is the most common form of polio vaccination in the world.

Though best known for his groundbreaking re-

Albert Sabin, the creator of the oral polio vaccine, was subsequently president of the Weizmann Institute in Israel. He was fervently committed to the Arab-Israeli peace process. (Courtesy of American Jewish Historical Society, Waltham, Massachusetts, and New York, New York)

search into polio, Sabin also developed vaccines for dengue fever and Japanese encephalitis. He was a member of the Board of Governors of both Hebrew University and the Weizmann Institute (where he was later president), and he worked in Israel promoting issues of health, immigrant integration, and Arab-Israeli peace. He died on March 5, 1993, in Washington, D.C.

SAGAN, CARL (1934–1996)

Astronomer, writer

Most famous as the co-producer and narrator of the television series "Cosmos" (1980), Carl Sagan was born in Brooklyn, New York, on November 9, 1934. In 1960 he received his Ph.D. from the University of Chicago. He went on to become a professor at the University of California, Berkeley, and at Harvard. From 1962 through 1968 he worked on planetary astronomy at the Smithsonian Astrophysical Observatory. At the same time, he worked on the Smithsonian's Search for Extraterrestrial Intelligence (SETI) project. Later, he headed the Laboratory of Planetary Studies at Cornell University. In addition to his work in astrophysics, he also investigated the potential effects of nuclear war on the environment.

His success as a popular science writer began with *The Cosmic Connection: An Extraterrestrial Perspective* (1973). He won a Pulitzer Prize for *The Dragons of Eden: Speculations on the Evolution of Human Intelligence* (1977). Other books he wrote include *Broca's Brain: Reflections on the Romance of Science* (1979); *Contact*, a novel (1985); *Nuclear Winter* (1985); and *The Demon-Haunted World: Science as a Candle in the Dark* (1996). He died in Seattle, Washington, on December 20, 1996.

SALK, JONAS EDWARD (1914–1995)

Physician

Best known as the inventor of the "Salk vaccine" against polio, Jonas Salk was born in New York City on October 28, 1914. He attended New York City schools, including the City College of New York and New York University, where he received his medical degree.

Following NYU, he interned for two years at Mount Sinai Hospital in New York before moving on to a research fellowship at the University of Michigan. While there, he helped produce a successful vaccine against influenza.

In 1947 Salk became the director of the Virus Research Laboratory of the School of Medicine at the University of Pittsburgh. It was during the next seven years that he identified different strains of poliomyelitis and created a killed-virus serum vaccine against paralytic polio. It was tested on approximately one million children and found to be 60 to 90 percent effective. By 1955 the U.S. Public Health Service licensed the vaccine for manufacture. For his work on the polio vaccine, Salk received the Presidential Citation and was the first recipient (1955) of the Medal for Distinguished Civilian Achievement awarded by Congress. He received an honorary Ph.D. from Hebrew University in 1959 and an honorary Doctor of Humane Letters degree from **Yeshiva University** the same year. In 1977 he received the nation's highest civilian honor—the Presidential Medal of Freedom. Unfortunately, Salk's scientific work was clouded by his public feud with **Albert Sabin**, who discovered the live-virus vaccine against polio.

His many publications include: *Man Unfolding* (1972); *The Survival of the Wisest* (1973); *World Population and Human Values: A New Reality*, with Jonathan Salk (1981); *Anatomy of Reality: Merging of Intuition and Reason* (1982); and *How Like An Angel: Biology and the Nature of Man* (1975), planned and edited by Ruth Nanda Anshen.

In 1962 Salk established his own research center, the Salk Institute for Biological Studies, in La Jolla, California, where he did research on such diseases as multiple sclerosis and cancer. He devoted the last years of his life to attempting to find a way to prevent the HIV infection from developing into AIDS. He died on June 23, 1995.

SCHICK, BELA (1877–1967)

Pediatrician, allergist

Born on July 16, 1877, in Boglar, Hungary, Bela Schick helped develop modern-day pediatric medicine and was the co-discoverer of allergy medicine and the creator of the Schick test for diphtheria. Schick studied at Karl Franz University of Graz where he received his M.D. in 1900. Later he worked under Dr. Clemens von Pirquet at the university's Children's Clinic. Schick and von Pirquet coined the term "allergy" in a 1905 paper on serum sickness. In 1908, after moving to the University of Vienna, Schick proved that the diseases that affect people after scarlet fever are allergic diseases. In 1912 he became the *Privatdozent* of children's diseases at the University of Vienna, and the following year he developed his test for diphtheria.

In 1923 Schick became the director of the pediatric department at Mt. Sinai Hospital in New York City. He was a member of the New York Academy of Medicine and was a founder of the American Academy of Pediatrics. He received many awards for his work, including the Addingham Gold Medal and the John Howland Medal of the American Pediatric Society. He died on December 6, 1967, in New York City.

SCIENCE

Some of the most highly regarded scientists in twentieth-century America have been Jewish. In academia, government, and private enterprise they have distinguished themselves in a variety of scientific areas and have achieved extraordinary prominence as Nobel Prize winners. Science has been an important avenue of upward social mobility for Jewish Americans and has served as a natural steppingstone for European émigrés who brought a scientific background and research experience with them.

Jewish affinity for scientific knowledge and inquiry can be traced back to the Talmud, which places considerable focus on abstract reasoning and includes significant scientific information even though scientific knowledge did not figure as a primary objective of the Talmudic sages. The high literacy levels of Jews in the medieval era along with their cultural inclination toward intellectual endeavors also contributed to Jewish curiosity and interest in the study of science.

The entry of Jews into the modern scientific professions began in the mid-nineteenth century. Because science was a relatively new field without a history of anti-Jewish restriction, it was attractive for many Jews, especially in Germany, where science offered a refuge from the romantic nationalism that saturated German intellectual life in this period. In addition, the settlement of middle-class German Jewish families in urban centers in the United States, where education in the sciences was available, contributed to their children's entry into such fields as physics, chemistry, and biology.

THEORETICAL FIELDS

By the turn of the century, Jewish Americans had made inroads into the growing community of American scientists. In particular, they began to stake out their turf in the more theoretical fields such as physics, biochemistry, and the life sciences. Because these fields were relatively new, Jews generally did not face the same degree of anti-Semitic prejudice and entry quotas in science education that had worked against them in medical and law schools. There were fewer time-honored traditions that posed obstacles to them in the sciences than in other professions. American Jews entered the center of world science as the twentieth century evolved, which made the profession ripe for Jewish immigrants from both Central and Eastern Europe. Nevertheless, breaking into the scientific elite remained a struggle for Jews. Prior to World War II, only two Jewish American scientists had garnered Nobel prizes out of thirteen American Nobel laureates, even though the first American to win the award was Jewish physicist **Albert Michelson** in 1907.

In the 1930s City College became one of the first institutions to openly cultivate the development of Jewish scientists. In addition, the influx of Jewish refugees from Europe included an extraordinary collection of scientific thinkers. Although American residents as a whole were inhospitable to immigrants in this era of increased anti-Semitism, Jewish achievement and visibility in mainstream American scientific institutions contributed to their acceptance in the academy.

Included among these German Jewish refugees was the towering figure of **Albert Einstein**, the formulator of the Special and General Theories of Relativity and the winner of the 1921 Nobel prize for physics. Einstein fled Nazi Germany in 1933 to accept a position at the Institute for Theoretical Physics in Princeton, New Jersey. Although his scientific theories of relativity assisted the United States government in developing atomic weapons, Einstein later became a devoted pacifist and committed the last decade of his life to preventing the possibility of nuclear proliferation.

During World War II other Jewish refugee scientists particularly distinguished themselves in government-sponsored atomic research. Einstein wrote to President Theodore Roosevelt to warn him of Hitler's attempts to develop the atomic bomb, and Roosevelt responded by ordering the Manhattan Project. Jewish émigré physicists, including the German-born Hans Bethe, the Danish Niels Bohr, and the Hungarians Leo Szillard and Eugene Wigner, composed the bulk of brainpower involved with this secret program, which resulted in the development of the atomic bomb. After

Jews and the Creation of the Atomic Bomb

The first atomic bomb was built and tested at Los Alamos, New Mexico. The director of the effort (the Manhattan Project) was J. Robert Oppenheimer. Here is how Howard M. Sachar describes the research team in his splendid book *A History of the Jews in America*: "By 1943 [Oppenheimer] assembled at Los Alamos and elsewhere perhaps the most outstanding scientific talent in America. Refugees formed the core of that talent— [Leo] Szilard, [Eugene] Wigner, Emilio Segrè, John von Neumann, Edward Teller, Hans Bethe, Niels Bohr, Hans Staub, Victor Weisskopf, Stanislaw Ulam. At Los Alamos, so many European Jews overflowed the Mesa that 'bad English' was the prevalent language. Only three of the center's seven divisions were directed by American-born scientists (two of these also were Jews)."

the bombing of Japan in 1945, many of these same Jewish atomic scientists including American-born Jew **J. Robert Oppenheimer**, who directed the Manhattan Project at the Los Alamos lab in New Mexico, became outspoken critics of American nuclear policy.

Often referred to ironically as Hitler's gift to American science, the wave of Jewish émigré intellectuals moved west throughout the 1930s and 1940s and, in addition to the those already mentioned, included older distinguished figures such as physicist James Franck and biochemist Otto Meyerhoff, who had both received Noble prizes as German citizens. It also included Max Born, who would go on to conduct pioneering research in quantum mechanics, and Otto Stern, who discovered the molecular beam method of studying the atom. Although they have received less recognition, two Jewish émigré mathematicians, Polish-born Richard Courant and the Hungarian John Von Neumann, made significant breakthroughs in this era.

In the post–World War II era Jewish scientific talent moved increasingly to the fore in America and eleven universities in the New York City area which had significant Jewish representation ranked among the top fifty in science education and productivity in the years from 1950 to 1961. This period of Jewish scientific advancement coincided with the rapidly expanding role of science as a symbol of United States power and prowess at a time of heightened Cold War tensions. It was also a time of the emergence of a body

of scholarly writing about the scientific enterprise itself in which Jews played a prominent part.

The increasing military buildup by both superpowers, the ongoing threat of nuclear war, and mounting anxieties over the Communist threat and the specter of Soviet atom spies led to a climate of fear and distrust in the United States. In the late 1940s and 1950s, several Jewish atomic scientists working for the federal government had their careers derailed for alleged Communist leanings, while those who opposed them were rewarded. During the McCarthy era, Oppenheimer lost his security clearance both because of his left-wing associations and because of his vehement opposition to the American hydrogen bomb program. In contrast, one of his former atomic scientist colleagues, **Edward Teller**, became Oppenheimer's main antagonist. Teller's star continued to rise as the chief architect behind hydrogen weapons development as well as one of the strongest proponents of domestic nuclear energy production. Several other Jewish physicists, including Joseph Weinberg, Max Freedman, and Sidney Weinbaum, found themselves dismissed from government jobs.

Nevertheless, this era began an extraordinary period of opportunity and acknowledgment for Jewish scientists, with the institutional anti-Semitism of the 1920s and 1930s rapidly diminishing. This included Jewish women who began to make their marks and become recognized in what continued to be a male-dominated field. Biochemist Mildred Cohn, who had encountered significant obstacles in finding work in the late 1930s, gained a position in 1946 at Washington University and was appointed associate professor in 1958. German-émigré Tilly Edinger was a groundbreaking vertebrate paleontologist whose work at the Museum of Comparative Zoology at Harvard in the 1940s and 1950s proved the necessity of studying the brain's evolution based on fossil evidence, rather than by comparing modern species. This achievement is all the more remarkable considering that zoology, along with botany and agriculture, has been the scientific field in which Jews have had the smallest impact. Closer to the medical field, Judith Graham Pool earned recognition as a physiologist whose scientific

Jewish Science Education in Brooklyn, 1998

The Westinghouse Talent search looks each year for the best science projects in the country created by high school students. In 1998, out of a national total of 300 semi-finalists in the search, Midwood High School in Brooklyn (a part of the New York City public school system) had thirteen, the highest number for any school in the country. Of these thirteen, six were Jewish. And, they are Jews who epitomize what Brooklyn has always been about. They include two Russian émigrés, one student of Portuguese Sephardic descent, one with Trinidadian-Jewish roots, one of Israeli parentage, as well as a scion of a Satmar hasidic family.

discoveries at Stanford University in the 1950s and 1960s transformed the treatment of hemophilia.

LIFE SCIENCES

In the 1960s and 1970s American Jews gained important recognition in the life sciences, chemistry, and physics. Biochemist Melvin Calvin became the first Jewish Nobel Prize winner in the field in 1961. He was followed by William Howard Stein, who achieved Nobel Laureate status in 1972 for his contribution to the chemistry of enzymes. Over the next two decades, six more Jewish chemists would achieve similar honors.

In the early 1970s, a study of the religious origins of 60,000 American academics showed that Jews were most heavily represented in the fields of biology (especially molecular biology), virology, microbiology, and biochemistry. Several scholars speculated that the large representation of Jews in fields that were closely connected to the health sciences may have been a result of the barriers that Jews faced in entering medicine a generation earlier.

While this theory appears to have some validity, there were also several Jewish physicians, such as Joshua Lederberg and Arthur Kornberg, who finished medical school, then opted to become biological scientists instead. Both men eventually earned Nobel prizes in their new fields—Lederberg for his studies of genetics in bacteria and Kornberg for producing nucleic acids by artificial means. Thus, it is fair to say that for a number of Jewish scientists, research in biology was not a second hand substitute for life as a practicing physician but a deep calling and passion. Other nonphysicians who won Nobel prizes for physiology included **George Wald** in 1967 for his work on chemical and physiological processes in the eye and **Rosalyn Yalow** in 1977 for her work in applying nuclear physics to clinical medicine, becoming only the second American woman to win the Nobel prize in physiology or medicine and the first in thirty years.

Meanwhile Jews continued to excel in the physical sciences. Murray Gell-Mann, Nobel laureate in 1969, was best known for his theories highlighting the importance of new elementary particles in the atomic nucleus, which he dubbed "quarks," a discovery which led to the development of a new branch of physics known as quantum chromodynamics. Danish immigrant Benjamin Mottelson was honored in 1975 for his research on nonspherical atomic nuclei, and Burton Richter achieved similar recognition the following year for independently discovering the J or psi particle.

JUDAISM AND SCIENCE

As quickly as Jewish representation in academia increased overall after World War II, the movement of Jews into the ultra-elite of science proceeded at an even higher rate. The proportion of Jewish Nobel laureates relative to the Jewish population at large became even greater than the proportion of Jews in the professorate at large.

At the same time, certain Jewish spokespeople argued, based on some empirical evidence, that Jewish scientists in the academy tended to be considerably more indifferent or opposed to religion than their Catholic and Protestant colleagues. Researchers made the case that, despite the Jewish scientific tradition, American Jews had come to believe that science and religion represented opposed dichotomies and that the ethos of science in some ways served as a substitute for Judaism. In addition, Jewish scientists continued for many years to feel as if appointments to elite universities required that they shed their ethnic and religious identities.

This perception began to change slowly in the 1970s. Baruch Blumberg, Nobel laureate in physiology in 1976 went as far as to connect his scientific prowess to the traditional Jewish education he had received at Flatbush Yeshiva in Brooklyn. Arno Penzias, yet another Nobel Prize winner in physics, also prominently mentioned his Jewish background in contributing to his success. Rosalyn Yalow made a point of keeping a kosher home and inviting her lab assistants to Passover Seders.

Jewish scientists were in the forefront of the ecological and population control movements of the era as well. Chemist and biologist Paul Ehrlich published his influential book *The Population Bomb*, which gravely warned Americans about the dangers of unlimited reproduction, while biologist Barry Commoner in his classic volume *The Closing Circle* laid the blame for environmental degradation more squarely at the foot of resource depletion by industrial powers and transnational corporations. Another Jewish scientist who made his mark at this time was Richard Feynmann; who won a Nobel Prize in 1965 for developing the theory of quantum electrodynamics but gained even greater notoriety in the 1970s and 1980s for writing a number of best-selling popular books highlighting his theories for a non-scientific audience.

The 1980s and 1990s have witnessed a decline in Jewish entry into the scientific professions. In part this has to do with the increasing acceptance and prestige of Jews in business, medicine, and law, fields that were far less open to them in the past. No longer is science one of the few significant steppingstones to success and prestige. Yet the opportunities still exist, and Jewish scientists, including chemists Walter Gilbert, Roald Hoffman, Henry Taub, and Sidney Altman and physicists Leon Lederman, Melvin Schwartz, Jack Steinberger, and Jerome Friedman, have been recognized for their extraordinary achievements with the Nobel prize and other awards. From a historical perspective, science must be recognized as providing an important route to achievement and success for American Jews.

SOCIAL WORK/SOCIAL REFORM

Jews have taken significant leadership roles in America in promoting social welfare and in lobbying for social policy reforms on the legislative level. Jewish women, in particular, have been disproportionately represented in the evolving field of social work. Jewish participation has taken place in a variety of settings, including Jewish communal self-help organizations, national reform agencies, women's organizations, and community service associations. This involvement has focused on issues specifically related to Jewish social welfare and on causes and concerns that address the needs of a broad cross-section of Americans. Jews have been involved in organizing for public policy reforms, conducting research documenting social problems, providing one-on-one counseling services, and directing programs that offer an array of services for families and children.

Up through the mid-nineteenth century, Jewish social welfare work was generally limited to charitable giving through synagogue congregations. But several locally based voluntary organizations did emerge to address the needs of destitute members of the Jewish community. One of the most important Jewish reformers of this era, **Rebecca Gratz**, helped to establish several charitable institutions for Philadelphia's Jewish women and children. She founded the Female Hebrew Benevolent Society in 1819, which provided housing, food, travelers aid, and an employment bureau. In the 1850s she created the Jewish Foster Home.

By the time of the Civil War these organizations began to increase in number as the predominately German Jewish community in America established benevolent organizations geared to caring for the welfare of their needy brethren. The United Hebrew Charities in New York City, established in 1874, became one of the most important of these groups. None of these organizations, however, attempted to influence the political agenda of the nation when it came to public policy toward America's poor. The country's laissez-faire agenda in this era posited that government existed primarily to create an environment in which business could operate freely. Social Darwinism and the belief that society pre-ordained who would survive and flourish and who would fall by the wayside was at its zenith, providing little incentive to those who sought a public response to the plight of the country's neediest. Social welfare was limited almost exclusively to private charities.

The massive influx of largely poor and unskilled Jewish immigrants from Eastern Europe to urban neighborhoods, which began in the 1880s and 1890s, brought an immediacy to the concerns of a new breed of reformers who began to gain a voice in Progressive Era America. The social climate in the United States shifted dramatically in the turn of the century years toward an ethos emphasizing environmental and sociological rather than individual change as the key to alleviating the problems of immigrant ghetto dwellers. More than any other institution, the Settlement House exemplified the belief that material change through social reform combined with the "Americanization" of immigrants would help to alleviate the problems of urban poverty.

New York City's Educational Alliance, created by educator **Julia Richman**, exemplified the concept of the Settlement House as socialization tool. A German-Jewish institution, the Educational Alliance provided English classes, after-school activities, summer camp, and art and music classes with the goal of Americanizing the new Eastern European Jewish immigrants. At the same time, the Sisterhoods of Personal Service, originally devoted to offering assistance to the poor within synagogues, became devoted to philanthropic and educational work for the society at large. The Sisterhoods organized English classes and provided thousands of immigrants with financial, emotional, and spiritual aid. The **National Council of Jewish Women** combined social services and "Americanization" programs for the new immigrant population with a commitment to "saving Judaism" from the twin threats of assimilation and anti-Semitism.

The Henry Street Settlement under the leadership of **Lillian Wald**, a registered nurse of middle-class German Jewish heritage, was one of the first and most important of the settlements to embrace the belief that the two processes of Americanization and social reform had to be melded together. Influenced by the guiding philosophy, social thought, and patrician practices of the Christian gospel philosophy of the time, Wald advocated an agenda that called for initiatives in public health, education, recreation, housing, and employment. In particular she called for an end to child labor, the enactment of a new set of laws to upgrade housing and sanitation, and improved education and vocational training for immigrants. Henry Street was in the heart of New York City's Lower East Side, and Wald and her co-workers lived and worked directly with both Jewish and non-Jewish immigrants to create an environment where residents could learn to become more self suffi-

cient and better able to meet the health needs of their families and their community.

Closely tied to Wald and the Henry Street Settlement, Josephine Goldmark of the National Consumer's League gathered documentation to buttress the arguments for new laws regulating the working conditions of women and children. Goldmark successfully used the talents of her brother-in-law, future supreme court justice **Louis Brandeis**, to file a brief in 1908 that limited wage-earning women to ten hours of work each day. She later served on the committee that investigated the Triangle Shirtwaist Factory fire. Her sister Pauline, a Progressive era social worker, also worked for decades with the National Consumers League and served on the New York State Department of Labor's Industrial Board where she documented the negative impact of long hours and bad working conditions on women and their families. Both Goldmarks were important members of a community of New York City–based female social reformers that included Jewish women, such as Wald and Maud Nathan, and non-Jews, such as Florence Kelly, Frances Perkins, and Edith Abbot. Rose Gruening, another New Yorker from a middle-class German-Jewish family, followed in Wald's footsteps creating the Grand Street Settlement in 1916.

Florence Kahn, a Jewish social work leader in Chicago, Baltimore, and Philadelphia, was one of the leading proponents of the belief that the new field of social work should emphasize organizing for social justice and human rights rather than simply dispensing charity. During the Depression decade of the 1930s, she pioneered the importance of building a social welfare safety net. Other Jewish social reformers such as Boston's Golde Bamber and Milwaukee's Lizzie Kander adopted a more traditional focus, teaching immigrant girls and women a variety of technical, vocational, and domestic skills in voluntary and charitable organizations. Esther Loeb Kohn, also from Chicago, helped begin a trade school for girls forced to drop out of school to find work. She later became one of the vanguard members of the new field of medical social work. Minnie Low, sometimes called the "Jane Addams of the Jews" co-founded the Maxwell Street

The Henry Street Settlement was the most well-known of the institutions that worked to provide health care and education to immigrants. This "visiting nurse" from the Settlement is using rooftops to go from house to house to save climbing up and down stairs. (Courtesy of American Jewish Historical Society, Waltham, Massachusetts, and New York, New York)

Settlement House, an agency that served the needs of Eastern European Jewish immigrants in Chicago.

Not all Jewish reformers were supporters of settlement houses. Rose Pastor Stokes complained that altruistic settlement house workers patronized immigrant working women and that the settlements increased rather than alleviated the alienation between social classes. Other reformers argued that Americanization programs did not adequately address fundamental economic inequalities facing immigrants.

After World War I, Jewish unions instituted exten-sive social welfare programs that included medical care, housing, unemployment insurance, health insurance, and retirement benefits. These unions were also the first to develop educational programs and the first to consider philanthropic activity an important responsibility. The importance of these initiatives showed the extent to which the Jewish labor movement took on many of the social responsibilities formerly assumed in Eastern Europe by the Jewish community at large.

Between 1900 and 1930 the notion of public or social welfare began to challenge the older focus on private charity, and social work professional degree programs increased dramatically. As social work itself became professionalized in the 1920s, Jewish women entered the field in large numbers.

When the Depression ravaged the country in the 1930s, the world of social work and social reform went through a new set of changes. At no time in American history did it became more clear that the nation's minimal safety net failed to protect the vast majority of American citizens. The worsening condition of the American economy pushed many Jewish social workers and reformers to demand increased federal intervention to support its struggling citizenry.

Jews overwhelmingly supported the candidacy of Franklin Roosevelt and became important supporters of his administration. The ethos of his New Deal program with its concern for the nation's forgotten people and its welfare package meshed well with a Jewish political culture that believed that government had an important role in promoting social and economic justice. In fact, the term "New Deal" has frequently been thought to have been coined by Samuel Rosenman, Roosevelt's special counselor.

Jewish reformers served an important role as spokespeople and activists in the expansion of the welfare state during the New Deal era. Isaac Rubinow and Abraham Epstein, long-time advocates of a national program for social insurance, began to gain influence. Rubinow argued for increased government stimulation of the economy and redistribution of wealth and income. Although they were strong Roosevelt supporters, Rubinow and Epstein, along with Solomon Epstein, executive director of the New York Federation of Jewish Philanthropies, argued that the President's Social Security Act needed to go further to provide an adequate standard of living for the elderly Americans who depended on it.

The New Deal also raised the prestige of the social work profession in the United States. Many Jewish reformers shaped public policy, serving in high-level positions, and administered the programs designed to respond to the Depression. For example, prominent social workers like Alice Springer Liveright, who had worked with troubled youth in Philadelphia's Jewish community, served with the WPA in the 1930s and was particularly important for her role in shifting the responsibilities for providing relief from local private charities to the state and federal government. Radicalized by her political involvement, she also took on leadership roles with the Women's International League for Peace and Freedom and chaired the Bryn Mawr Summer School for Industrial Workers, which educated and trained working-class women. Other Jewish women social workers such as Celia Strakosch conducted pioneering studies of child poverty during this era.

The ascendancy of left-wing labor and other social movements in the 1930s created new alliances as well as new divisions. With the rise of state and federal relief agencies, many social workers began to perceive their interests as aligned with clients and agency clerical staffs. They formed rank-and-file union committees in predominantly Jewish unions such as the State, County, and Municipal Workers Association in New York City under the leadership of former relief worker, Abram Flaxer, which became affiliated with the CIO in 1937. Thus, the Depression era found unionized Jewish case workers striking against Jewish charitable institutions at a time when the Jewish community at large was becoming increasingly engaged in white-collar work. Pearl Willen went from child care case worker to organizer of the Southern School for Workers and chair of the Women's Division of the American Labor Party. At the same time, other social workers in private agencies sought to distance themselves as "professionals" having little in common with workers in large welfare bureaucracies.

Overall, the 1940s and 1950s saw most members of the profession make casework, rather than expanded public social services and improved living conditions, their priority. The prosperous economic climate and the increasing affluence of the American public at large coupled with the Cold War political environment contributed to an increased focus on the psychodynamics and psychological problems of conformity, adjustment, and identity formation in middle-class society rather than with economic inequalities or the conditions of the nation's poor. Jewish intellectuals and social theorists played leading roles in articulating the problems facing the autonomous individual in industrial society.

As a result, this era saw the increasing merging of social work with the fields of psychology, sociology, and the new "social science," and the ascendancy of highly influential works such as David Riesman and Nathan Glazer's *The Lonely Crowd*. The 1950s also witnessed the increasing concern of America with issues related to youth and adolescence. Social workers such as Eleanor Glueck and Sophia Moses Robison conducted extensive research and case studies documenting the causes and prevention of juvenile delinquency.

Throughout the 1950s questions regarding welfare reform and expansion of social programs, while generally ignored, did receive some attention. Chicago community organizer, Saul Alinsky challenged the nation to address the issues of poverty and inequality. In addition, the Committee on Social Issues and Policies of the National Social Welfare Assembly, an organization with heavy Jewish representation, began to mobilize a lobby in support of improved public welfare. With the publication of Michael Harrington's *The Other America* and the high-profile organizing of the southern civil rights movement drawing attention to institutional racism, the impetus for social reform increased dramatically as the nation entered the 1960s.

Beginning with the administration of John F. Kennedy and then especially under Lyndon B. Johnson's "Great Society" and "War on Poverty" programs, Jewish social workers began to regain important influence as policy makers, program developers, and activists. Many were deeply involved in the campaigns for Head Start, Food Stamps, and the Economic Opportunity Act. Idealists of the 1960s, influenced by the New Left, fought for improvements in the social safety net and joined movements to support the community-based demands of low-income families in rural and urban America. A growing number of younger social workers formed the radical, student-based Social Welfare Workers Movement, which argued that social workers should be advocates for the poor and not simply case workers or therapists.

From the 1970s to the present, Jewish social workers and social reformers have struggled to define their role and position in relation to economic and political changes in the Jewish community and society at large. As members of a privileged class, Jews in the field continue to experience major conflicts between their professional identity as service providers and a commitment to address institutional inequalities and promote system-wide reforms. At the same time, as a largely female workforce, Jewish social workers have suffered from low salaries, limited prestige, long hours, and sometimes difficult working conditions, especially with the cutbacks in social welfare programs in the 1980s and 1990s. Jews continue, however, to choose careers in social work and jobs as community organizers and reformers in the fields of education, health, and housing in large numbers, thus following a long tradition of Jewish activism and involvement in the civic life of America.

STEINMETZ, CHARLES PROTEUS (1865–1923)

Electrical engineer, inventor

Born in Breslau, Germany, on April 9, 1865, Charles Proteus Steinmetz was a committed socialist and genius when it came to understanding the new science of electricity. He attended the University of Breslau from 1882 to 1888, where he joined the Student Socialist Society and was editor of the radical weekly *The People's Voice* in 1884. In 1889 Steinmetz immigrated to the United States. Three years later he attended a meeting of the American Institute of Electrical Engineers and gave a talk that clarified the law of hysterisis. His understanding of the process of energy loss due to magnetization changed the design of transformers, generators, and alternating current motors. He discovered a mathematical method for calculating the alternating current theory, which was published in book form (with Ernest J. Berg as co-author) in 1897 as *Theory and Calculation of Alternating Current Phenomena*.

In 1893 Steinmetz was hired by the General Electric Company of Schenectady, New York, and his research enabled the company to obtain more than 200 patents, including an aluminum lightning arrester and the magnetic arc lamp. His designs also led to new patents for generators and motors and to a greater understanding of the theory of alternating current. He served as president of the American Institute of Electrical Engineers and as professor of engineering at Union College.

Steinmetz was concerned with the problems of society all his life. In his 1916 book *America and the New Epoch*, he argued that the ownership of property would eventually be transferred from private to government hands, although its management would remain private. He unsuccessfully ran for State Engineer of New York on the Socialist ticket in 1922. He was appointed president of the Schenectady board of education by the socialist mayor in 1911 and served until his death. One of the best-known scientists of his day, he died in Schenectady on October 26, 1923.

TELLER, EDWARD (1908–)

Physicist

One of the major contributors to the development of nuclear weapons, Edward Teller was born in Hungary but educated at the University of Leipzig in Germany, where he earned a doctorate in theoretical physics in 1930. Teller fled Germany after the rise of Hitler. He lectured for a time at the University of London, then emigrated to the United States in 1935 and accepted a teaching post at Washington University.

During World War II, Teller was a key member of the team of scientists working on the Manhattan Project, which developed the atomic bomb at the Los Alamos research facility in New Mexico. Teller's work on the project was particularly instrumental to the production of the hydrogen bomb. He disagreed with the decision of his colleague **J. Robert Oppenheimer** to give first priority to the atomic bomb, and the controversy between the two men continued for years.

Later, Teller became director of the Livermore Laboratory in California, and joined the faculty of the University of California at Berkeley. He was a prominent supporter of the Reagan administration's Strategic Defense Initiative.

WALD, GEORGE (1906–)

Biochemist

Biochemist George Wald was born in New York City in 1906. His discoveries about the mechanics of vision began in 1932, when he was a National Research Council fellow in Berlin. He discovered the presence and importance of Vitamin A in the retina. For the next two years, he continued his research in Heidelberg and at the universities of Zurich and Chicago. Most of his career, however, was spent at Harvard University. He became a faculty member in 1934 and a professor emeritus in 1977.

By the 1950s Wald had discovered the chemical process of the receptors on the retina. A few years later, while working with Paul K. Brown, Wald discovered the pigment in the retina that was sensitive to yellow-green light. Over the next few years Wald and Brown identified the pigments for red light and blue light and the importance of Vitamin A in creating these essential pigments in the eye. This led to an understanding of the causes of color blindness—an absence of one of these pigments in the retina. In 1967 George Wald won the Nobel Prize for Physiology or Medicine for his breakthroughs in the chemistry of sight (shared with Ragnar Granit of Sweden and Haldan K. Hartline of the United States).

WALD, LILLIAN D. (1867–1940)

Originator of public health nursing, Henry Street Settlement founder

A dedicated advocate of immigrant and working-class rights, Lillian D. Wald was born on March 1, 1867, in Cincinnati, Ohio. Her family moved to Rochester, New York, when she was eleven, and she attended Miss Cruttenden's English-French Boarding and Day School there. In 1889 she enrolled in the nursing program of the New York Hospital training school. Upon graduation two years later, she worked for a year as a nurse at the New York Juvenile Asylum, but eventually left institutional nursing to become a doctor. Shortly after she began taking classes at the Women's Medical College in New York City, she accepted an invitation to organize classes in home nursing for immigrant families on the Lower East Side. She experienced a "baptism of fire" into social reform work when a child led her into a dilapidated tenement. Shaken and profoundly moved by the deplorable living conditions she discovered, she left medical school and founded the Nurses' Settlement at 265 Henry Street.

Wald virtually invented the field of public health nursing. By 1905 Henry Street nurses were caring for more than 4,000 patients yearly at eighteen district centers, and Wald had begun the first public school nursing program in this country. In 1912 the National Organization for Public Health Nursing was founded, with Wald as its president.

The Nurses Settlement eventually became the Henry Street Settlement as it expanded its activities and services beyond nursing care into girls' and boys' clubs, classes in the arts, homemaking courses, the teaching of English, vocational guidance, and social events. Many activities were designed to help immigrants adjust to a new culture, but Wald and her colleagues were also dedicated to the idea of maintaining cultural traditions from other countries.

Wald's work with immigrants led her to publicly champion a number of causes, including safer working conditions, the abolition of child labor, women's suffrage, and pacifism. She offered the Henry Street

To the astonishment of many Americans, who tend to associate religion with sexual repression, therapist Dr. Ruth Westheimer declares that human sexuality is something to be joyful about and that her approach has its origin in Orthodox Judaism. She is shown here at the 1996 national convention of the National Council of Jewish Women, where she was a featured speaker. (Courtesy of National Council of Jewish Women)

Settlement quarters for the organizing conference of the National Association for the Advancement of Colored People.

Ill health forced her to retire from Henry Street in 1933. She moved to Westport, Connecticut, and published the second of her two books—the first was *The House on Henry Street* (1915)—*Windows on Henry Street*, in 1934. She died on September 1, 1940, after a long illness. In 1965 she was elected to the Hall of Fame of Great Americans at New York University, and in 1993 she was inducted into membership in the National Women's Hall of Fame. The Henry Street Settlement still serves its neighborhood,

which now has a largely Asian and African American population.

WESTHEIMER, RUTH (1928–)

Author, television personality, sexual advisor

A powerful communicator and sensible advisor on sexual matters, Karola Ruth Siegel Westheimer was born in Germany on June 4, 1928. When she was ten years old, shortly after *Kristallnacht*, her father was taken to a detention camp and her mother and grandmother sent her to an orphanage in Switzerland. Six years later, unable to find her family, the teenager went to Palestine. After a stint in the Haganah, the underground army, she married and went to Paris where she studied psychology at the Sorbonne. A few years later, divorced, she came to the United States, went to school on a scholarship for victims of the Holocaust, and remarried.

After a number of years working in the field of sex education, family planning, and sex therapy, Westheimer started hosting her own radio show, "Sexually Speaking." This was the beginning of her career as America's most famous advisor about sex. In books, on television, and even on the Internet, she spread the message of joyful, safe, guilt-free sex. Her advice—as she explains in *Heavenly Sex: Sexuality in the Jewish Tradition* (1995), which she co-authored with Jonathan Mark—is grounded in Orthodox Jewish teaching.

The diminutive (under five feet), vivacious, and irrepressible "Dr. Ruth" had published fifteen books at the end of 1998. She has three grandchildren (again, as of 1998) and two of her most recent books are based on this phase of her life—*Dr. Ruth Talks to Kids about Grandparents* and (with Steven Kaplan) *Grandparenthood.* She told a Reuters interviewer at the 1995 Frankfurt Book Fair, "I was kicked out in 1939 by being placed on a train right here in Frankfurt. . . . I never saw my parents again. Every time I am sad I just have to think about my five-year-old grandson. Hitler didn't want me to have that grandson. I put the picture of my grandson in my mind and say—You see, we did triumph. So I do therapy on myself."

Nobel Prize winning physicist Rosalyn Yalow makes a point of keeping a kosher home and inviting her lab assistants to Passover Seders. She was the first woman born and educated in the United States to win the Prize in a scientific field. (Courtesy of American Jewish Archives)

YALOW, ROSALYN (1921–)

Physicist

Rosalyn Yalow (née Sussman) was born in New York City on July 19, 1921. After graduating from high school, she attended Hunter College, where she graduated in 1941 with a B.A. in chemistry and physics. She then went on to graduate study at the University of Illinois in Urbana, where she received her doctorate in physics in 1945. In 1947 she became a consultant at the Bronx Veterans Administration Hospital. Three years later she became the hospital's physicist and assistant chief of radioisotope service. In 1968 she became its acting chief of radioisotope service.

With her research partner, Solomon Berson, Yalow discovered radioimmunoassay (RIA), which enables the measurement, with radioisotopes, of biological and pharmacological substances in the body, even if they exist only in trace amounts. Yalow and Bersen made their findings public in 1959. The medical and scientific influence of RIA has been enormous, and Yalow has won numerous awards, honors, and appointments in recognition of her work. In 1969 she became the chief of the RIA reference laboratory. A year later she was named chief of the nuclear medical service for the Veterans Administration. In 1972 she became the VA's senior medical investigator. The same year, Berson died and Yalow became the director of the laboratory named in his honor, the Solomon A. Berson Research Laboratory.

In 1976 Yalow was awarded the Albert Lasker Prize for basic medical research, the first woman to receive this honor. A year later she won the Nobel Prize for Physiology or Medicine. In 1988 she was awarded the National Medal of Science. As of 1996 she had written over 500 scientific papers. Throughout her career she remained committed to her home life, family, and Jewish identity. She has always maintained a kosher home.

For Further Reading

See Appendix 2 for a bibliography of general reference books about Jews and the Jewish experience in America. All of these volumes include information about American Jews in science, medicine, and the social sciences.

Berger, Natalia, ed. *Jews and Medicine: Religion, Culture, Science*. Philadelphia: Jewish Publication Society, 1997.

Kagan, Solomon R. *Jewish Contributions to Medicine in America from Colonial Times to the Present*. Second edition, revised and enlarged, Boston: Boston Medical Publishing Company, 1939.

Appendix 1

Finding Out about Jews Around the World

Books
World Jewish Congress

BOOKS

The definitive source for information about the history and culture of Jews around the world is the *Encyclopedia Judaica*, Cecil Roth, Editor-in-Chief; Geoffrey Wigoder, subsequent Editor. It was published in 1972 in sixteen volumes in Jerusalem. Eight *Yearbooks* followed as well as two *Decennial Books* (1982 and 1992). All twenty-six volumes are included on a CD-ROM published in 1997 in Jerusalem. It is available from several distributors in the United States.

The American Jewish Year Book: A Record of Events and Trends in American and World Jewish Life, (David Singer, Editor; Ruth R. Seldin, Executive Editor) is published annually by the **American Jewish Committee** in New York City. The first volume was published in 1899, and the 1998 *Year Book* is Volume 98 in the series.

It includes a wealth of information about Jews around the world. For example, the 1998 *Year Book* includes figures for the world Jewish population as of 1996, as well as essays on developments in Jewish life broken down by part of the world. The geographical sections are: United States, Canada, Latin America; Western Europe; Central and Eastern Europe, Australia, South Africa, and Israel. A section of the 1997 *Year Book* has an essay on Hong Kong.

It is in most libraries or can be ordered directly from the American Jewish Committee, The Jacob Blaustein Building, 165 East 56th Street, New York, New York 10022; Phone: (212) 751–4000; Fax: (212) 750–0326.

Another invaluable book for information about contemporary Jews is *Jewish Communities of the World*, edited by Dr. Avi Beker. It is published annually and the edition available as this is written is for 1998–1999. It includes figures on the Jewish population in countries throughout the world (Tahiti has 120 Jews, for example, while Ireland has 1,300), as well as useful information on individual countries, including addresses of organizations, Jewish population distribution, cultural information, and sites to visit. Put together by the Institute of the World Jewish Congress, it is available from the Institute at 21 Arlosoroff Street, P.O. Box 4293, Jerusalem 91042, Israel. The web site address is: www.virtual.co.il/orgs/orgs. In the United States it is published by Lerner Publications Company, 241 First Avenue North, Minneapolis, Minnesota, 55401. The web site address is: www.lernerbooks.com.

An enormous amount of information is available about world Jewry on the World Wide Web. Two books that will help you navigate the web are:

Lerner, Michael. *The Guide to the Jewish Internet.* San Francisco, CA: No Starch Press, 1996.

Romm, Diane. *The Jewish Guide to the Internet.* Northvale, NJ: Jason Aronson Publishers, 1997.

A few additional printed sources include:

Comay, Joan. *Who's Who in Jewish History: After the Period of the Old Testament,* 2d ed., revised by Lavinia Cohn-Sherbok. London and New York: Routledge, 1995.

Friesel, Evyatar. *Atlas of Modern Jewish History.* New York, 1990.

Gribetz, Judah, Edward L. Greenstein, and Regina Stein. *The Timetables of Jewish History: A Chronology of the Most Important People and Events in Jewish History.* New York: Simon & Schuster, 1993.

Holtz, Barry W. *The Schocken Guide to Jewish Books: Where to Start Reading about Jewish History, Literature, Culture and Religion.* New York: Schocken Books, 1992.

Hyman, Paula. *Gender and Assimilation in Modern Jewish History: Roles and Representations of Women.* Seattle: University of Washington Press, 1995.

Isaacs, Ronald H. *The Jewish Information Source Book: A Dictionary and Almanac.* Northvale, NJ: Jason Aronson Publishers, 1993.

Johnson, Paul. *A History of the Jews.* New York: Harper & Row, 1987.

Werblowsky, R., J. Zwi, and Geoffrey Wigoder, eds. *The Oxford Dictionary of the Jewish Religion.* New York: Oxford University Press, 1997.

Wigoder, Geoffrey, Editor-in-Chief. *The New Standard Jewish Encyclopedia,* 7th new rev. ed., New York: Facts on File, 1992.

WORLD JEWISH CONGRESS

Since 1936 the World Jewish Congress has been the representative body of Jewish communities across the globe. It continuously advocates Jewish concerns to governments and international organizations. Communities in over eighty countries are members of the Congress. Headquartered in New York City, the Congress has affiliate offices in Brussels, Budapest, Buenos Aires, Geneva, Jerusalem, Melbourne, Moscow, and Paris.

The New York headquarters are:

World Jewish Congress
501 Madison Avenue, 17th Floor
New York, New York 10022
Phone: (212) 755–5770
Fax: (212) 755–5883

Appendix 2

Organizations and Resources

Books
Organizations
Research Institutions
Museums
Libraries
Genealogy
Local Historical and Genealogical Societies
Newspapers and Magazines

BOOKS

Bibliographies

Cutler, Charles, and Micha Falk Oppenheim. *Judaica Reference Sources.* Juneau, Alaska: Denali Press, 1994.

Gurock, Jeffrey S. *American Jewish History: A Bibliographical Guide.* New York: Anti-Defamation League of B'nai B'rith, 1983.

Holtz, Barry W. *The Schocken Guide to Jewish Books: Where to Start Reading about Jewish History, Literature, Culture and Religion.* New York: Schocken Books, 1992.

Kaganoff, Nathan M. *Judaica Americana: An Annotated Bibliography of Publications from 1960 to 1990,* 2 vols. Brooklyn, NY: Carlson Publishing, 1995.

Singerman, Robert. *Judaica Americana: A Bibliography*

of Publications to 1900, 2 vols. NY: Greenwood Press, 1990.

Weisbard, Phyllis. "Annotated Bibliography and Guide to Archival Resources on the History of Jewish Women in America," pp. 1,553–1,586 in Hyman and Moore, *Jewish Women in America.* (See below.)

Reference Books

American Jewish Yearbook, annual. New York: American Jewish Committee.

Encyclopedia Judaica, 16 vols. *Decennial yearbook, 1973–1982. Yearbooks, 1983–1985, 1986–1989,* Jerusalem and New York: Keter Books, 1972.

Fischel, Jack, and Sanford Pinsker, Eds. *Jewish-American History and Culture: An Encyclopedia.* New York: Garland, 1992.

Hyman, Paula E., and Deborah Dash Moore, eds. *Jewish Women in America: An Historical Encyclopedia*. 2 vols. NY: Routledge, 1997

Marcus, Jacob Rader, and Judith M. Daniels, eds. *The Concise Dictionary of American Jewish Biography*. 2 vols. Brooklyn, NY: Carlson Publishing, 1994.

Slater, Elinor, and Robert Slater. *Great Jewish Women*. Middle Village, NY: Jonathan David Publishers, 1994.

ORGANIZATIONS (WITH ENTRIES IN THIS VOLUME)

American Jewish Committee
The Jacob Blaustein Building
165 East 56th Street
New York, NY 10022
Phone: (212) 751–4000
Fax: (212) 750–0326

American Jewish Congress
Stephen Wise Congress House
15 East 84th Street
New York, NY 10028
Phone: (212) 879–4500
Fax: (212) 249–3672
E-mail: pr@ajcongress.org

Anti-Defamation League (of B'nai B'rith)
823 United Nations Plaza
New York, NY 10017
Phone: (212) 885–7700
Fax: (212) 867–0779

B'nai B'rith
1640 Rhode Island Avenue, NW
Washington, DC 20036
Phone: (202) 857–6600
Fax: (202) 857–1099

Hadassah: The Women's Zionist Organization of America, Inc.
50 West 58th Street
New York, NY 10019
Phone: (212) 355–7900
Fax: (212) 303–8282

National Council of Jewish Women
53 West 23d Street
New York, NY 10010
Phone: (212) 645–4048
Fax: (212) 645–7466

Zionist Organization of America
ZOA House
4 East 34th Street
New York, NY 10016
Phone: (212) 481–1500
Fax: (212) 481–1515
E-mail: email@zoa.com

RESEARCH INSTITUTIONS

Center for Jewish History
15 West 16th Street
New York, NY 10011

The Center for Jewish History brings under one roof four major Jewish research institutions: the American Jewish Historical Society, the Leo Baeck Institute, the Yeshiva University Museum, and the YIVO Institute for Jewish Research. The American Sephardi Federation is headquartered at the Center. The 125,000-square-foot facility houses 100 million archival documents and tens of thousands of photographs, posters, paintings, and artifacts. The library includes over one-half million volumes. The center is the largest repository of documentation on Jewish cultural history outside Israel. See below for information about the individual institutions.

American Jewish Historical Society
Center for Jewish History
15 West 16th Street
New York, NY 10011

and

2 Thornton Road
Waltham, MA 02154
Phone:(617) 891–8110
E-mail: ajhs@ajhs.org
Web site: www.ajhs.org

American Jewish Archives
Jacob Rader Marcus Center
3101 Clifton Avenue
Cincinnati, OH 45220
(513) 221–1875

Leo Baeck Institute, Inc.
Center for Jewish History
15 West 16th Street
New York, NY 10011
Phone: (212) 744–6400
Fax: (212) 988–1305

National Yiddish Book Center
Harry and Jeanette Weinberg Building
1021 West Street
Amherst, MA 01002–3375
Phone: (413) 256–4900
Fax: (413) 256–4700
E-mail: yiddish@bikher.org

YIVO Institute for Jewish Research
Center for Jewish History
15 West 16th Street
New York, NY 10011
(212) 246–6860

MUSEUMS

An essential publication for getting information about Jewish museums is: Frazier, Nancy. *Jewish Museums of North America: A Guide to Collections, Artifacts, and Memorabilia.* New York: 1992.

Judah L. Magnes Museum-Jewish Museum of the West
2911 Russell Street
Berkeley, CA 94705
Phone: (510) 549–6950)
Fax: (510) 849–3673
E-mail: magnesadmin@eb.jfed.org

Museum of Jewish Heritage-A Living Memorial to
   the Holocaust
One Battery Park Plaza
New York, NY 10004–1484
Phone: (212) 968–1800
Fax: (212) 968–1366
Web site: www.mjhnyc.org

Museum of the Southern Jewish Experience
P.O. Box 16528
Jackson, MS 39236–0528

National Museum of American Jewish History
55 North Fifth Street
Independence Mall East
Philadelphia, PA 19106–2197
Phone: (215) 923–3811
Fax: (215) 923–0763

Spertus Museum, Spertus Institute of Jewish Studies
618 South Michigan Avenue
Chicago, IL 60605
Phone: (312) 922–9012
Fax: (312) 922–6406

United States Holocaust Memorial Museum
100 Raoul Wallenberg Place, SW
Washington, DC 20024
Phone: (202) 488–0400
Fax: (202) 488–2690
Web site: www.ushmm.org

Yeshiva University Museum
2520 Amsterdam Avenue
New York, NY 10033–3201
Phone: (212) 960–5390
Fax: (212) 960–5406
E-mail: glickber@aymail.yu.edu

LIBRARIES

A number of libraries around the country have strong collections in Jewish studies. Here are two of the largest.

The New York Public Library
Fifth Avenue & 42d Street
Jewish Division
New York, NY 10018
Phone: (212) 930–0601
Fax: (212) 642–0141

Harvard College Library
Judaica Collection
Cambridge, MA 02138
Phone: (617) 495–2401
Fax: (617) 496–4750

GENEALOGY

There are a number of local and regional Jewish genealogical societies listed in the local organizations section below. The place to start for information is:

Jewish Genealogical Society
P.O. Box 6398
New York, NY 10128
Phone (212) 330–8257
E-mail: jgsny@aol.com

LOCAL HISTORICAL AND GENEALOGICAL SOCIETIES

Arizona

Arizona Jewish Historical Society
Committee on Genealogy
Carlton Brooks
720 West Edgewood Avenue
Mesa, AZ 85210

Arizona Jewish Historical Society
4710 North Sixteenth Street, #201
Phoenix, AZ 85016

Jewish Historical Society of Southern Arizona
P.O. Box 57482
Tucson, AZ 85732–7482

Southern Arizona Jewish Historical Society
Committee on Genealogy
4181 East Pontatoc Canyon Drive
Tucson, AZ 85718

California

Western Jewish History Center
Judah L. Magnes Museum
2911 Russell Street
Berkeley, CA 94705

South Orange County
Jewish Genealogy Society
Dorothy Kohanski
2370 Via Mariposa West, #1D
Laguna Hills, CA 92653

Jewish Genealogical Society of Orange County
Michelle Sandler
11751 Cherry Street
Los Alamitos, CA 90720

Jewish Historical Society of Southern California
6505 Wilshire Boulevard, Suite 512
Los Angeles, CA 90048

Sacramento Jewish Genealogical Society
Iris Bachman
5631 Kiva Drive
Sacramento, CA 95841

San Diego Jewish Genealogical Society
Carol Davidson Baird
255 South Rios Avenue
Solana Beach, CA 92075–1903

San Diego Jewish Historical Society
1934 Pentuckett Avenue
San Diego, CA 92104–5732

San Francisco Bay Area Jewish Genealogical Society
Dana Kurtz, President
P.O. Box 471616
San Francisco, CA 94115–1404

Jewish Genealogical Society of Los Angeles
Geraldine Winerman
P.O. Box 55443
Sherman Oaks, CA 91343

Colorado

Rocky Mountain Jewish Historical Society
Center for Judaic Studies
University of Denver
Denver, CO 80208–0292

Connecticut

Jewish Historical Society of Greater Bridgeport
4200 Park Avenue
Bridgeport, CT 06604

Charter Oak Temple Restoration Association
21 Charter Oak Avenue
Hartford, CT 061006

Jewish Genealogical Society of Connecticut
Howard Siegel
17 Salem Walk
Milford, CT 06430

Jewish Historical Society of New Haven, Inc.
P.O. Box 3251
New Haven, CT 06515–0351

Jewish Historical Society of Greater Norwalk
163 East Rocks Road
Norwalk, CT 06851

Jewish Historical Society of Greater Stamford
1035 Newfield Avenue
Stamford, CT 06905

Jewish Historical Society of Waterbury
P.O. Box F
Waterbury, CT 06798

Jewish Historical Society of Greater Hartford
335 Bloomfield Avenue
West Hartford, CT 06117

Delaware

Jewish Historical Society of Delaware
505 Market Street Mall
Wilmington, DE 19801

District of Columbia

Jewish Historical Society of Greater Washington
701 Third Street, NW
Washington, DC 20001–2624

Florida

Jewish Genealogical Society of Palm Beach County, Inc.
P.O. Box 7796
Delray Beach, FL 33482–7796

Jewish Genealogical Society of Broward County
Gene Garlin
P.O. Box 17251
Fort Lauderdale, FL 33318

Central Florida Jewish Genealogical Society
Gene Starn
P.O. Box 520583
Longwood, FL 32752

Jewish Genealogical Society of Greater Miami
Arthur Chassman
8340 SW 151st Street
Miami, FL 33157

Jewish Historical Society of South Florida, Inc.
4200 Biscayne Boulevard
Miami, FL 33137

Georgia

Jewish Genealogical Society of Georgia
Peggy Freedman
345 Dalrymple Road
Atlanta, GA 30328

Southern Jewish Historical Society
1441 Mile Post Drive
Dunwoody, GA 30338

Illinois

Chicago Jewish Archives
Spertus College
618 South Michigan Avenue
Chicago, IL 60605

Chicago Jewish Historical Society
618 South Michigan Avenue
Chicago, IL 60605

Illinois Jewish Genealogical Society
Henry Landauer
404 Douglas
Park Forest, IL 60466

Iowa

Iowa Jewish Historical Society
910 Polk Boulevard
Des Moines, IA 50312

Kansas

Heart of America Jewish Historical Society
9648 Walmer Lane
Overland Park, KS 66212

Kentucky

Louisville Jewish Genealogical Society
Israel T. Naamani Library
3600 Dutchmans Lane
Louisville, KY 40205

Louisiana

Louisiana Jewish Historical Society
Temple Sinai
6227 St. Charles Avenue
New Orleans, LA 70118

Maryland

Jewish Historical Society of Annapolis Maryland, Inc.
Genealogy Department
5 Sampson Place
Annapolis, MD 21401

Jewish Historical Society of Maryland
Carol Rider
2707 Moores Valley Drive
Baltimore, MD 21209

Jewish Historical Society of Maryland
Jewish Heritage Center
15 Lloyd Street
Baltimore, MD 21202

Jewish Historical Society and Archives of
 Howard County Maryland
5403 Mad River Lane
Columbia, MD 21044

Massachusetts

North Shore Jewish Historical Society
31 Exchange Street
Lynn, MA 01901

Jewish Genealogical Society of Greater Boston
Attn: Fred Davis, President
Box 366
Newton Highlands, MA 02461

Berkshire Jewish Archives Council
75 Mountain Drive
Pittsfield, MA 01201

Michigan

Jewish Genealogy Society of Michigan
8050 Lincoln Drive
Huntington Woods, MI 48070–1328

Jewish Historical Society of Michigan
6600 West Maple Road
West Bloomfield, MI 48322

Minnesota

Jewish Historical Society of the Upper Midwest
Hamline University
St. Paul, MN 55104

Missouri

St. Louis Jewish Archives
Saul Brodsky
Jewish Com Library
12 Millstone Campus Drive
St. Louis, MO 63146

St. Louis Jewish Genealogical Society
10677 County View Drive
St. Louis, MO 63146
Nebraska
Nebraska Jewish Historical Society
333 South 132d Street
Omaha, NE 68154

Nevada

Southern Nevada Jewish Genealogical Society
2653 Topaz Square
Las Vegas, NV 89121

Las Vegas Jewish Genealogical Society
Carole Montello
P.O. Box 29342
Las Vegas, NV 89126

New Jersey

Association of Jewish Genealogy Society
155 North Washington Avenue
Bergenfield, NJ 07621

Trenton Jewish Historical Society
Ms. Selma Litowitz
282 Glenn Avenue
Lawrenceville, NJ 08648

Jewish Historical Society of Central Jersey
Edith Neimark
228 Livingston Avenue
New Brunswick, NJ 08901

North Jersey Jewish Genealogical Society
Evan Stolbach
1 Bedford Road
Pompton Lakes, NJ 07442

Jewish Historical Society of North Jersey
P.O. Box 708
West Paterson, NJ 07470–0708

Jewish Historical Society of MetroWest
901 Route 10 East
Whippany, NJ 07981–1156

New Mexico

New Mexico Jewish Historical Society
P.O. Box 23056
Santa Fe, NM 87502

New York

Albany Jewish Genealogical Society
Rabbi Don Cashman
420 Whitehall Road
Albany, NY 12208

Jewish Historical Society of Northeastern New York
P.O. Box 3193
Albany, NY 12203–0193

Buffalo Jewish Genealogical Society
Muriel Selling
174 Peppertree Drive, #7
Amherst, NY 14228

Long Island Jewish Genealogical Society
Linda Cantor
37 Westcliff Drive
Dix Hills, NY 11746

Westchester Jewish Historical Society
12 Clinton Lane
Harrison, NY 10528

Orthodox Jewish Archives of Agudath Israel
84 William Street, #1200
New York, NY 10038

Rochester Jewish Genealogical Society
Bruce Kahn
265 Viennawood Drive
Rochester, NY 14618

North Carolina

Charlotte Jewish Historical Society
P.O. Box 13574
Charlotte, NC 28270

Raleigh Jewish Genealogical Society
8701 Sleepy Creek Drive
Raleigh, NC 27612

Ohio

Jewish Genealogical Society of Greater Cincinnati
Bureau of Jewish Education
1580 Summit Road (JCC)
Cincinnati, OH 45237

Cleveland Jewish Archives of the Western Reserve Historical Society
10825 East Boulevard
Cleveland, OH 44106

Columbus Jewish Historical Society
Peggy H. Kaplan, Director
1175 College Avenue
Columbus, OH 43209

Dayton Jewish Genealogical Society
Dr. Leonard Spialter
P.O. Box 338
Dayton, OH 45406

Cleveland Jewish Genealogical Society
Arlene Blank Rich
996 Eastlawn Drive
Highland Heights, OH 44143

Oklahoma

Fenster Museum of Jewish Art
1223 East 17th Place
Tulsa, OK 74120

Oregon

Oregon Jewish Genealogical & Historical Society
Mittleman JCC
6651 SW Capitol Highway
Portland, OR 97219

Pennsylvania

Jewish Archives Librarian
Historical Society of Western Pennsylvania
1212 Smallman Street
Pittsburgh, PA 15222–4200

Pittsburgh Jewish Genealogical Society
Julian Falk
2131 Fifth Avenue
Pittsburgh, PA 15219

Jewish Museum of Eastern Pennsylvania
2300–B Mahantongo Street
Pottsville, PA 17901

Philadelphia Jewish Genealogical Society
Mr. Jon E. Stein
Cedarbrook Hill Apts, #A–1107
8460 Likekiln Pike
Wyncote, PA 19095–2612

Rhode Island

Society of Friends of Touro Synagogue
85 Touro Street
Newport, RI 02840

Rhode Island Jewish Historical Association
130 Sessions Street
Providence, RI 02906

Tennessee

Jewish Historical Society of Memphis and Mid-South
P.O. Box 17304
Memphis, TN 38187

Archives of Jewish Federation of Nashville &
*   Middle Tennessee*
801 Percy Warner Boulevard, #102
Nashville, TN 37205

Texas

Texas Jewish Historical Society
P.O. Box 10193
Austin, TX 78766

Dallas Jewish Historical Society
Jewish Community Center
7900 Northaven Road
Dallas, TX 75230

Jewish Genealogy Division
Dallas Jewish Historical Society
James R. Alexander
7900 Northaven Road
Dallas, TX 75230

Galveston County Jewish Historical Association
2613 Oak Street
Galveston, TX 77551

Jewish Genealogical Society of Houston
7603 Teal Run
Houston, TX 77071

Utah

Salt Lake City Jewish Genealogical Society
Thomas W. Noy
3510 Fleetwood Drive
Salt Lake City, UT 84109

Virginia

Peninsula Jewish Historical Society
25 Stratford Road
Newport News, VA 23601

Jewish Genealogical Club of Tidewater Virginia
c/o JCCT
300 Newport Avenue
Norfolk, VA 23505

Washington

Washington Jewish Genealogical Society
Jerome Becker
14222 NE First Lane
Bellevue, WA 98007–6941

Washington State Jewish Historical Society
2031 Third Avenue
Seattle, WA 98121

Wisconsin

Wisconsin Jewish Archives
State Historical Society
816 State Street
Madison, WI 53706

Wisconsin Jewish Genealogical Society
Penny Deshur
9280 North Fairway Drive
Milwaukee, WI 53217

Canada

British Columbia Jewish Historical Society
950 West 41st Avenue
Vancouver, British Columbia V5Z 2N7
Canada

Jewish Historical Society of South Alberta
1607 90th Avenue SW
Calgary AB T2V 4V7
Canada

NEWSPAPERS AND MAGAZINES

Commentary
165 E. 56th Street
New York, NY 10022
Phone: (212) 751–4000
Fax: (212) 751–1174
E-mail: 103115.2375@compuserve

Forward *(weekly national newspaper)*
45 East 33rd Street
New York, NY 10016
Phone: (212) 889–8200
Fax: (212) 447–6406
E-mail: newsdesk@forward.com
Web site: www.forward.com

The Jewish Week *(weekly New York newspaper)*
1501 Broadway
New York, NY 10036
Phone: (212) 921–7822
Fax: (212) 921–8420
E-mail: editor@jewishweek.org
Web site: www.thejewishweek.com

Lilith
250 West 57th Street, Suite 2432
New York, NY 10107
Phone: (212) 757–0818
Fax: (212 757–5705
E-mail: lilithmag@aol.com

Moment
4710 41st Street, NW
Washington, D.C. 20016
Phone: (202) 364–3300
Fax: (202) 364–2636

Tikkun: A Bimonthly Critique of Politics, Culture & Society
26 Fel Street
San Francisco, CA 94102
Phone: (415) 575–1200
Fax: (415) 575–1434

Index